TAX CONTROVERSIES: PRACTICE AND PROCEDURE

Second Edition

Leandra Lederman
Professor of Law
George Mason University
School of Law

Stephen W. Mazza
Associate Professor of Law
University of Kansas
School of Law

LexisNexis™
Matthew Bender®

ISBN#: 0-8205-539-56

Editorial Offices
744 Broad Street, Newark, NJ 07102 (973) 820-2000
201 Mission St., San Francisco, CA 94105-1831 (415) 908-3200
701 East Water Street, Charlottesville, VA 22902-7587 (804) 972-7600
www.lexis.com

(Pub.1160)

To my husband.
— LL

To my family.
— SWM

PREFACE

Unlike other areas of taxation you may have studied, tax procedure does not involve determining the tax consequences of particular transactions and events. Instead, a tax procedure course focuses on the process and procedure of the "voluntary compliance" system and federal tax disputes, including the chronology of a tax controversy from the filing of a return by the taxpayer through tax litigation. A thorough understanding of tax procedure is not only essential for a tax controversy expert, but is also extremely helpful for any tax practitioner. After all, tax planning involves, in part, an assessment of the risks of a transaction, contemplation of possible disputes with the Internal Revenue Service regarding the transaction, and judgment about the likely outcome of those disputes.

The law of tax controversy procedure is technical, but it can be illuminated by an understanding of its underlying theory. Throughout this book, we have tried both to explain the law and to raise important theoretical questions about tax controversies and current procedural rules. The book uses the problem method to promote application of the law to factual scenarios a tax lawyer might encounter. The problems also raise strategy considerations in resolving a tax dispute. Periodically, updates to the casebook will be posted on the Internet at www.taxtexts.com/controversies.htm.

The Internal Revenue Service Restructuring and Reform Act of 1998 (the IRS Reform Act) made major changes to many of the procedural rules applicable to tax controversies. The effects of those changes continue to unfold, making this a particularly exciting time to study tax procedure. We hope you enjoy the course.

LL
SWM

ACKNOWLEDGMENTS

We appreciate the help provided by many people as we wrote this book. In particular, we would like to thank Leslie Book of Villanova Law School; Terry Chorvat, Joanmarie Davoli, and Alison Price of George Mason Law School; and Anita Soucy of McKee Nelson for their valuable feedback as we prepared new Chapters 15 and 16; Robert Mead of Kansas Law School for his comments on Chapter 16; Michael O'Neill of George Mason Law School for his assistance on the criminal procedure materials for both the first and second editions of this book; Bryan Camp of Texas Tech Law School for his valuable contributions to the materials on summonses and erroneous refunds; Christopher Pietruszkiewicz of Louisiana State Law School for helpful suggestions and assistance with the summons material; and Kathryn Sedo of Minnesota Law School for helpful comments. In addition, we would like to express our appreciation to the individuals who read and commented on drafts of various chapters of the first edition: David Aughtry, Vivian Hoard, and Charles Hodges of Chamberlain, Hrdlicka, White, Williams & Martin; Leslie Book of Villanova Law School; and Bob Jacobs of Milbank, Tweed, Hadley & McCloy. We would also like to thank Erik Namee of Hinkle, Elkouri, who was an excellent resource for our questions while we were writing the first edition; Todd Zywicki of George Mason Law School for his assistance with bankruptcy procedure; and Donna Sneed of George Mason for her outstanding work on the tax controversy chart. We also thank Lisa Blodgett, Erin Moore and Sarah Robinson of George Mason Law School and Kari Coultis and Michael Roew of Kansas Law School for valuable research assistance on this edition.

SUMMARY TABLE OF CONTENTS

TABLE OF CONTENTS

Chapter 1

OVERVIEW OF FEDERAL TAX CONTROVERSIES

Reading Assignment: Code §§ 7525, 7602(a), 7701(a)(36), 7805(a); Treas. Reg. § 301.7701-15(b)(2).

§ 1.01 Introduction

Federal tax controversies generally involve disputes between private party "taxpayers,"[1] which may be individuals or entities such as corporations, and the Internal Revenue Service (IRS). The IRS is part of the Treasury Department, and is the administrative agency of the United States government responsible for administering the Internal Revenue Code (Code) and collecting federal taxes.

Other agencies in addition to the IRS are involved in the tax controversy process. Congress writes the tax law; the Joint Committee on Taxation must approve all refunds exceeding $2,000,000; the Treasury Department promulgates regulations to effectuate the laws; and the Department of Justice litigates civil tax cases, other than those in the Tax Court, as well as all criminal tax cases. In general, however, the IRS is the primary government player in a tax controversy. It is the IRS that issues the forms on which taxpayers file returns, selects returns for audit, attempts to resolve tax controversies administratively, collects taxes, and handles the high percentage of litigated tax cases that go to Tax Court. In addition, as discussed in Chapter 9, the IRS provides both public and private guidance to taxpayers to assist them in applying the Code.

Because of the importance of the IRS to tax procedure, this Chapter first provides information on the structure of the IRS and the types of rules the IRS promulgates. The Chapter goes on to outline the tax controversy process. Next, the Chapter describes the particular requirements for private practitioners to practice before the IRS or before the Tax Court, and the various ethical considerations that may arise in federal tax practice. Finally, the Chapter explores the tension between tax lawyers and accountants. Before covering those topics, a brief comment on the nature of the United States' federal tax system is in order.

§ 1.02 The Self-Assessment System

The United States' tax system is founded on the principle of "self assessment." The self-assessment (or "voluntary compliance") system does not mean

---

[1] Anyone subject to federal tax is termed a "taxpayer" by the Internal Revenue Code. *See* I.R.C. § 7701(a)(14).

1

that paying taxes is optional. Instead, it means that the IRS does not compute taxpayers' tax liabilities in the first instance. As discussed in further detail in Chapter 2, the Code requires taxpayers to determine their own tax liabilities, file returns reflecting those liabilities on proper forms, and pay the resulting liabilities by a specified date.

Although most taxpayers voluntarily attempt to carry out their obligations under the Code, the IRS's most recent estimates set the income "tax gap" — the amount of tax liability for a particular year that is not voluntarily and timely paid — at around $95 billion, just for individual taxpayers. This works out to an overall noncompliance rate for individual taxpayers of around 17 percent (the tax gap as a percentage of "true" tax liability).[2] Of course no one can realistically expect a 100 percent compliance rate. The goal, instead, is to achieve the highest level of compliance while expending the fewest resources.

Deciding upon the best way to achieve this goal raises some important questions. First, what type of noncompliance should the IRS be most concerned about: the failure of taxpayers to file returns in the first instance, or the failure of taxpayers to accurately report, intentionally or unintentionally, their income and deductions on returns that are submitted? Second, what causes taxpayers not to meet their filing and reporting obligations? Noncompliance results from a host of different causes: perceptions about the fairness of the tax system; frustrations with the complexity of the substantive tax law; uncertainty surrounding the application of particular Code provisions; and tendencies towards self-interest and dishonesty — just to name a few. Finally, what classes of taxpayers are most likely not to voluntarily comply — wage earners, small businesses, or multi-national corporations? Unfortunately, the IRS has made little effort in recent years to formulate empirical answers to these fundamental questions.

The two most effective techniques currently used by the IRS to stimulate compliant behavior are the withholding-at-source and information-reporting systems. The IRS has implemented an extensive withholding procedure through which a substantial portion of all collected tax is withheld by the payor and submitted directly to the government. In fact, when it comes to wages, the system is specifically designed to overwithhold, which in turn requires taxpayers to file returns in order to obtain a refund. Under the IRS's information-reporting program, payors submit information returns (such as Form W-2 for wages) to taxpayers and also send copies of these returns to the IRS. IRS computers match these information documents with taxpayers' tax returns in order to verify whether the correct amount of income was reported and to facilitate enforcement in the absence of such compliance. Do these techniques stimulate voluntary compliance or simply reduce the opportunity for noncompliance?

Beside withholding and information matching, the IRS has traditionally enforced the self-assessment system through audits (discussed in Chapter 2),

---

[2] Internal Revenue Service, "Federal Tax Compliance Research: Individual Income Tax Gap Estimates for 1985, 1988, and 1992," Publication 1415 (Rev. 4-96). These figures do not factor in unreported illegal income or noncompliance by corporate taxpayers.

civil tax penalties (discussed in Chapter 10), and criminal prosecution (discussed in Chapters 13 and 14). The IRS also has a number of collection enforcement tools at its disposal to help ensure that taxpayers meet their responsibilities. As discussed in Chapter 12, the IRS has the power to seize the taxpayer's assets and garnish his wages, among other remedies, to recoup unpaid taxes.

In the late 1990s, the IRS became the subject of intense Congressional scrutiny,[3] which eventually led to the enactment of the Internal Revenue Service Restructuring and Reform Act of 1998 (IRS Reform Act). With the mandate for a new IRS organizational structure (discussed below) came a call for a revised compliance effort focusing on improved taxpayer service, pre-filing assistance, and early intervention programs designed to resolve potentially contentious issues before the taxpayer files the return. At the same time, Congress placed new limitations on the power of the IRS to utilize its collection enforcement techniques. Budget constraints have also led to reductions in IRS staffing and, consequently, a decline in enforcement actions. Whether levels of compliance can be maintained or improved by changing taxpayer attitudes toward compliance through greater taxpayer rights and services — rather than through stiffer direct enforcement measures such as expanded audit and collection programs — remains to be seen. A widely held fear is that without strong and visible enforcement activities by the IRS, taxpayers may begin to take liberties with the Code because they may perceive that others are doing the same without adverse consequences. *See* Steven M. Sheffrin & Robert K. Triest, *Can Brute Deterrence Backfire? Perceptions and Attitudes in Taxpayer Compliance*, in WHY PEOPLE PAY TAXES 213 (Joel Slemrod ed., 1992) (empirical study suggesting that publicity concerning the lack of compliance in the system as a whole will lead to an increase in noncompliance by other taxpayers).

Controversy surrounding the issue of how best to encourage voluntary taxpayer compliance was sparked most recently when the IRS released figures showing that its audit and enforcement activities had dropped substantially when compared to 1995 levels. The figures reveal that the individual audit rate declined from 1.68% in 1995 to .49% in 2000, a drop of about 70%. Audits of small corporations (those with assets under $10 million) declined from 1.57% to .76%, while audits of large corporations declined from 25.77% to 16.3% over the same time period. *See* IRS Release (Examination Activity Numbers), Feb. 15, 2001. The IRS cited a combination of increased workload and fewer resources as the primary reasons for the decline. According to the Commissioner of Internal Revenue, who is the head of the IRS, the "IRS is deeply concerned about the continued drop in audit and collection activity. . . . [The declines] need to stop or the fairness and effectiveness of our tax system will be undermined." *Id. Compare* "An Open Letter to the New Commissioner of Internal Revenue from Donald C. Alexander," 59 Tax Notes 975 (1993) (warning that "the tax laws, like the traffic laws, must be enforced to be effective.") *with* Susan B. Long & David Burnham, "Solving the Nation's Budget Deficit with a Bigger, Tougher IRS: What Are the Realities," 48 Tax

---

[3] See National Commission on Restructuring the Internal Revenue Service, A Vision for a New IRS (1997).

Notes 741, 743 (1990) ("any hope that tougher enforcement of the *current* tax law can make a substantial dent in the national deficit is a pipe dream.") (emphasis in original), *see also* Income Tax Compliance: Report of the ABA Section of Taxation Invitational Conference on Income Tax Compliance (1983).

§ 1.03 The Internal Revenue Service

The IRS is an agency of the Treasury Department, one of the eleven bureaus of the federal government. As indicated above, the agency is headed by the Commissioner of Internal Revenue, who is appointed by the President and confirmed by the Senate. I.R.C. § 7802.[4] Until recently, the IRS had a three-tier structure. There were thirty-three district offices (each headed by a District Director) and ten service centers, organized geographically. These offices were responsible for applying the law to every taxpayer within the office's geographic boundaries. Four regional offices oversaw the district offices, and a national office in Washington, D.C. oversaw the regions. This structure has been largely dismantled because, as part of the IRS Reform Act, Congress required the IRS to reorganize its operations along functional lines, much like many private sector businesses. IRS Reform Act § 1001.

The new organizational structure was the brainchild of Commissioner Charles O. Rossotti, and was prompted by a series of highly publicized hearings before the Senate Finance Committee, during which taxpayers testified to poor quality service and alleged misconduct by IRS personnel.[5] The legislative history that accompanied the IRS Reform Act provides further insight into those factors leading up to the call for a new organizational framework.

> The Committee believes that a key reason for taxpayer frustration with the IRS is the lack of appropriate attention to taxpayer needs. At a minimum, taxpayers should be able to receive from the IRS the same level of service expected from the private sector. For example, taxpayer inquiries should be answered promptly and accurately; taxpayers should be able to obtain timely resolutions of problems and information regarding activity on their accounts; and taxpayers should be treated fairly and courteously at all times. The Commissioner of Internal Revenue has indicated his interest in improving customer service. The Committee should not only support the Commissioner's efforts, but also mandate that a key part of the IRS mission must be taxpayer service.
>
> The Commissioner has announced a broad outline of a plan to reorganize the structure of the IRS in order to help make the IRS more oriented toward assisting taxpayers and providing better taxpayer

[4] Although the Code provides that it is to be administered and enforced by the Secretary of the Treasury, the Secretary has delegated much of this power to the Commissioner. I.R.C. § 7801(a). In addition, the Code specifies certain duties and powers for which the Commissioner takes responsibility. *See* I.R.C. § 7803.

[5] An as-yet unreleased General Accounting Office report raises doubts about the truthfulness of charges of IRS abuse made during Senate Finance Committee hearings leading up to the IRS Reform Act. *See* Ryan J. Donmoyer, "Secret GOA Report is Latest to Discredit Roth's IRS Hearings," 87 Tax Notes 463 (2000).

service. Under this plan, the present regional structure would be replaced with a structure based on units that serve particular groups with similar needs. The Commissioner has currently identified four different groups of taxpayers with similar needs: individual taxpayers, small businesses, large businesses, and the tax-exempt sector (including employee plans, exempt organizations and State and local governments). . . . The proposed plan would enable IRS personnel to understand the needs and problems affecting particular groups of taxpayers, and better address those issues. The present-law structure also impedes continuity and accountability. For example, if a taxpayer moves, the responsibility for the taxpayer's account moves to another geographical area. Further, every taxpayer is serviced by both a service center and at least one district. Thus, many taxpayers have to deal with different IRS offices on the same issues. The proposed structure would eliminate many of these problems.

The Committee believes that the current IRS organizational structure is one of the factors contributing to the inability of the IRS to properly serve taxpayers and the proposed structure would help enable the IRS to better serve taxpayers and provide the necessary level of services and accountability to taxpayers. The Committee supports the Commissioner in his efforts to modernize and update the IRS and believes it appropriate to provide statutory direction for the reorganization of the IRS.

S. Rep. No. 105-174, 8–9 (1998). Is the comparison between the IRS and a private sector business a fair one to make? Should notions of customer service apply to the IRS?

The IRS has taken its cue from the legislative history, and is well into the process of dismantling the geographically based organizational structure and replacing it with four operating divisions, each with end-to-end responsibility for all tasks affecting a group of taxpayers with similar needs. This new, centralized focus is expected to result in greater responsiveness and reduce the likelihood of inconsistent treatment of taxpayers, another source of frustration under the old structure. The operating divisions are supported by four functional units focusing on law enforcement, appeals services, and taxpayer advocacy, and two agency-wide support services. The new organizational structure is illustrated in the chart below.

Internal Revenue Service

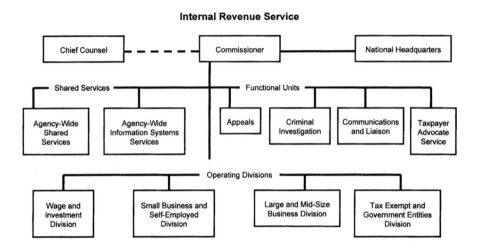

The IRS's national office in Washington, D.C. (now, officially, the National Headquarters) continues to exist and is responsible for setting general policy, reviewing the plans and goals of the operating divisions, and developing major improvement initiatives. As it did under the prior organizational structure, the Office of Chief Counsel represents the Commissioner in Tax Court cases and issues case-specific guidance and general legal advice to all components of the IRS. Although the Chief Counsel's efforts are concentrated in the national office, the IRS has established specialized groups of IRS field attorneys that are aligned with the four operating divisions. Each operating division has been assigned a "Division Counsel," and below the Division Counsel a number of "Area Counsel." Division Counsel is responsible for providing legal advice and other case resolution support for those IRS employees assigned to an operating division, while Area Counsel manages the field attorneys who carry out the IRS's Tax Court litigation function.[6]

The four operating divisions responsible for serving specific groups of taxpayers are the Wage and Investment Division (W & I); the Small Business and Self-Employed Division (SB/SE); the Large and Mid-Size Business Division (LMSB); and the Tax Exempt and Governmental Entities Division (TE/GE). The W & I division serves the approximately 88 million individual taxpayers who have only wage and investment income, almost all of which is reported to the IRS by third-party payors. W & I is organized into four segments: (1) Communication, Assistance, Research and Education (CARE), which focuses on providing pre-filing assistance, education, and filing support to taxpayers; (2) Customer Account Services (CAS), which is responsible for processing returns and payments; (3) Compliance, which concentrates on commonly encountered issues such as filing status, dependency exemptions, tax credits, and deductions; and (4) a W & I Headquarters, located in Atlanta, Georgia.

---

[6] The Division and Area Counsel structure replaces, for the most part, the Regional and District Counsel structure that existed under the prior IRS organizational form. Outside the national office, however, IRS field attorneys are still commonly referred to as District Counsel.

The SB/SE division is responsible for the 33 million taxpayers who are fully or partially self-employed, and the approximately 7 million small businesses (including C corporations, S corporations and partnerships) with assets of $10 million or less. In addition to serving these taxpayer groups, SB/SE will also handle estate and gift tax cases, employment tax matters, innocent spouse requests, and most collection cases. SB/SE is organized into three segments, similar in function to those of the W & I operating division, although tailored to the needs and filing patterns of small businesses, which tend to have more frequent contact with the IRS when compared to W & I taxpayers. Its headquarters is in New Carrollton, Maryland.

The LMSB division includes 210,000 of the largest filers (C corporations, S corporations, and partnerships), each with assets over $10 million. Almost 10 percent of LMSB filers are audited by the IRS each year and the largest of these taxpayers interact with the IRS on a continual basis through the IRS's Coordinated Examination Program (CEP). LMSB filers encounter the most complex issues relating to tax law interpretation, filing, and regulation. Many also have substantial international operations. Instead of being organized around function, LMSB is divided into five "industry segments": Retailers, Food and Pharmaceutical; Natural Resources; Financial Services; Heavy Manufacturing and Transportation; and Communications, Technology and Media. By focusing on specific industry groups, the IRS believes that it can develop a higher level of expertise and thereby be more responsive to these types of large taxpayers with common issues. LMSB headquarters is located in Washington, D.C.

The TE/GE division includes pension plans, exempt organizations, and governmental entities. These entities collectively remit to the government in excess of $198 billion in employment tax and income tax withholding. The TE/GE division includes a headquarters operation, located in Washington, D.C., and a Customer Account Service (CAS) division, responsible for customer service activities such as answering telephones and managing service center relations. The remaining three segments of the organization are aligned with three distinct "customer segments": Employee Plans (pension, profit-sharing, and individual retirement plans); Exempt Organizations (public charities, private foundations, and section 527 political organizations); and Governmental Entities (federal, state, and local government agencies, including tax-exempt bond financing, and Indian tribes). The function of these segments is to educate their respective taxpayer groups, issue determination letters and rulings, and conduct examinations and other compliance checks.

Although the four operating divisions will eventually replace the district and regional offices, each division will have operations in the field with a geographic structure that meets the specific needs of that division. Under the new structure, each division will have at least one "territory" in every state; an operating division's various multi-state geographic presences are called "areas."

As mentioned above, the restructured IRS also has four nationwide functional units that address specific issues. Those functional units are Appeals, Criminal Investigation, Communications and Liaison, and Taxpayer Advocate Service. The Appeals Division, discussed in Chapter 4, will remain an independent unit for dispute resolution with the authority to settle deficiency, refund, and collection cases. Similarly, the Criminal Investigation Division will continue its work on criminal enforcement of the tax laws. The Communication and Liaison Division, as the name suggests, is responsible for interacting with Congress and the general public, as well as confidentiality and disclosure issues.

The Taxpayer Advocate Service Division performs two functions. Its primary role is to ensure that, in those cases in which the IRS's standard procedures have broken down, taxpayer's problems are resolved quickly and fairly. In such instances, taxpayers may request a Taxpayer Assistance Order (TAO) in order to resolve pending issues with the IRS. In addition to taxpayer-specific casework, the Taxpayer Advocate Service Division coordinates with the operating divisions to identify potential administrative problems and implement solutions. Organizationally, the division consists of the National Taxpayer Advocate, headquartered in Washington, D.C., a number of Area Advocate offices aligned with the four operating divisions, and a series of local Taxpayer Advocate offices (at least one in each state) that handle most of the casework.

The IRS has also established two internal support organizations: Agency Wide Information Systems Services and Agency Wide Shared Services. Information Systems focuses on the delivery of forms and publications and updating IRS technology. Agency Wide Shared Services provides to the entire IRS such support services as facilities, procurement, and personnel processing.

Another new addition to the IRS's organizational structure is a nine-member Oversight Board. *See* I.R.C. § 7802. The Board is composed of the Treasury Secretary, the Commissioner, a federal employee representative, and six members from the private sector. One motivating influence behind its creation was to bring outside expertise in organizational development and management to the IRS and provide a fresh perspective on the administration of the tax laws from a group of "outsiders." Among its responsibilities, the Oversight Board (1) approves annual and long-range strategic plans for the IRS; (2) reviews the operational functions of the IRS, including training and education, and outsourcing of work; and (3) reviews IRS operations to ensure proper treatment of taxpayers. The Board is prohibited from participating in the development of tax policy, and may not intervene in specific taxpayer cases. After two years of political bickering, the Senate confirmed the private sector members of IRS Oversight Board in September of 2000. It is too soon to tell whether the Board, despite its expansive authority, will have a meaningful impact on the IRS.

Implementing the new organizational structure is an ongoing process. As of the end of 2001, the revised structure, including the four operating divisions, the four functional units, and the two support divisions, were officially in place. However, the IRS is still in the process of fine-tuning the organizational form, staffing new offices, transitioning employees and managers, and reassigning work. In fact, some of the terminology relating to the prior organizational form (such as "district offices" and "District Director") is still being used by the IRS in its procedural regulations. While the reorganization proceeds, taxpayers and their representatives continue to file returns and interact with the IRS as they have done in the past. Taxpayers within the W & I Operating Division, representing the largest percentage of all filers, will notice the least amount of change in the near term. These taxpayers might end up filing their annual returns at a different IRS office than they did in the past, but otherwise their reporting obligations will not change.

Three years after the restructuring process began, differences of opinion existed as to how much progress the IRS had made towards improving taxpayer service and implementing the new taxpayer-rights protections included in the IRS Reform Act. Consider the following statements of James White, Director of Tax Issues at the United States General Accounting Office, made before Congress in May of 2001.

> In October 2000, IRS largely completed its transaction to the new organizational structure. In a process that the Commissioner likened to putting together a giant jigsaw puzzle with literally thousands of pieces, IRS put the new organization in place without significant effect — positive or negative — on its processing of millions of returns this filing season. That the reorganization has not yet led to significant changes in filing season or other activities is not unexpected. The reorganization provides a focus on taxpayer segments that IRS expects will help it better understand taxpayers' needs and identify changes to its systems and procedures for meeting those needs. In the course of our work at IRS in the coming year, we will be monitoring how IRS' new operating divisions focus their efforts to address specific compliance and service problems associated with their particular taxpayer segments.

* * *

> Modernization of IRS' organizational structure, business processes, performance management system, and information technology is necessary if IRS is to achieve its goals of improving service to taxpayers and compliance with tax laws. While important progress has been made in laying the foundation for a new IRS, parts of the modernization effort have gone slower than expected. Clearly, this is disappointing. Unfortunately, it reflects the continuing need to build management capability. The goal of improving service to taxpayers quickly must be balanced with the need to prudently manage a massive, long-term effort like IRS modernization.

IRS Modernization: Continued Improvement in Management Capability Needed to Support Long-Term Transformation (GAO-01-700T).

§ 1.04 Rulemaking Authority of the Treasury Department and the IRS

The Treasury Department and the IRS have authority to promulgate various types of rules and pronouncements to assist taxpayers in interpreting and applying the Code. The precedential weight of these sources in tax practice is discussed in Chapter 9, while Chapter 16 examines these sources within the context of the tax research process. A brief discussion of these items at this point should assist your understanding of the material in later chapters.

Section 7805(a) grants the Secretary (of the Treasury) the authority to "prescribe all needful rules and regulations" for the enforcement of the Code. Accordingly, it is the Treasury Department that officially promulgates interpretative and procedural regulations, although the job of initially drafting most regulations is performed by the IRS Office of Chief Counsel. Taxpayers may rely on regulations to support a reporting position, and courts will generally uphold the government's interpretation if it is reasonable. Treasury regulations are numbered with a prefix, followed by the Code section number to which the regulation relates. The prefix indicates the regulation's basic subject matter: For example, income tax regulations carry the prefix "1," estate tax regulations the prefix "20," and procedural and administrative regulations the prefix "301." In addition, the IRS (without Treasury Department involvement) promulgates a separate set of procedural regulations applicable to its own internal processes. *See* Proc. Reg. § 601.101 *et seq.*

In addition to internal procedural regulations, the IRS releases published guidance in the form of Revenue Rulings, Revenue Procedures, and other announcements. Revenue Rulings provide guidance on substantive tax issues applicable to many taxpayers. The IRS uses a standard format. Each Revenue Ruling contains a generic set of facts, a statement of the issue, and the IRS's conclusion about the legal result. Revenue Procedures are similar, except that they provide guidance and instructions relating to procedural issues. For example, the first Revenue Procedure issued each year instructs taxpayers on how to apply for letter rulings. Revenue Rulings and Revenue Procedures are numbered by year and then by the order in which they were issued during the year. The first Revenue Procedure issued in 2002, for instance, was Revenue Procedure 2002-1. Revenue Rulings and Revenue Procedures are initially published in the Internal Revenue Bulletin, and are also collected in the Cumulative Bulletin, which is generally published twice each year.

The IRS also provides private guidance to taxpayers in the form of letter rulings and determination letters. Letter rulings and determination letters are responses written by the IRS to a particular taxpayer, and have no precedential value for other taxpayers. Letter rulings (often referred to as "private letter rulings" or PLRs) are numbered according to the year of issue, week of issue, and order within that week. For example, PLR 200123003 would have been the third letter ruling issued during the twenty-third week of 2001. Taxpayers may obtain a letter ruling concerning the tax consequences of a pending transaction by following the procedures set forth in the first Revenue Procedure of the year and by paying the applicable fee. The first Revenue Procedure of the year also sets forth matters on which the IRS will not rule. These issues are discussed in further detail in Chapter 9.

Determination letters are similar to letter rulings, except that they advise taxpayers on a narrower set of issues. Most determination letters relate to the qualification of an organization for tax-exempt status under section 501 of the Code or to the qualification of retirement plans under Code section 401. In some instances, the IRS will issue a determination letter relating to a completed transaction, if it involves applying clearly established precedent to particular facts.

The IRS also generates many different types of internal guidance, some of which only affect specific taxpayers, while other types impact broad categories of taxpayers. Technical Advice Memoranda (TAMs), for instance, are internal documents issued by the national office to the Appeals Division and other IRS offices for the purpose of clarifying technical and procedural issues arising during an audit, IRS appeal, or review of a refund claim. Issues commonly referred for technical advice are those for which there are inconsistent interpretations and those that are so unusual that they warrant the attention of the national office. A taxpayer involved in an IRS audit or appeal may also request that an issue be referred to the national office for technical advice. *See* Proc. Reg. § 601.105(b)(5); Rev. Proc. 2001-2, 2001-1 I.R.B. 79.

Until recently, the IRS issued "General Counsel Memoranda" (GCMs). GCMs typically contain the reasoning and legal analysis underlying a proposed PLR, TAM, or Revenue Ruling. GCMs have been largely replaced by another category of internal guidance known collectively as Chief Counsel Advice. *See* I.R.C. § 6110(i). Chief Counsel Advice includes Field Service Advice (FSA), which is prepared by attorneys in the Chief Counsel's office in response to requests from IRS field personnel concerning a broad array of substantive and procedural topics. Each FSA includes a statement of facts, a statement of issues, a conclusion, and legal analysis. Other forms of Chief Counsel Advice include Litigation Guideline Memoranda, Service Center Advice, and Litigation Bulletins. For an explanation of these sources, see Section 16.02[B] of Chapter 16.

The IRS also publishes in the Internal Revenue Bulletin its litigating position on adverse Tax Court opinions in the form of "acquiescence" (acq.) and "nonacquiescence" (nonacq). The IRS also prepares "action on decision" (AOD) recommendations when it loses on an issue in a Tax Court or district court case. The AOD contains a discussion of whether or not to appeal the decision, and the reasoning supporting that recommendation.

Another important source of internal guidance is the IRS's own Internal Revenue Manual (IRM). The IRM may be thought of as an agency-wide employee handbook. It includes material relating to the organization and operations of the IRS, policy statements, and detailed instructions to IRS personnel concerning audits, appeals, and collection activity. It is, therefore, particularly helpful to practitioners in determining the IRS's approach to a particular issue or type of transaction. The IRM, like most of the other forms of internal guidance, is released to the public under the Freedom of Information Act (FOIA). FOIA is discussed in Chapter 3.

§ 1.05   Overview of a Federal Tax Controversy

Under the federal income tax system, a taxpayer whose gross income exceeds a specified amount is required to file an income tax return each year. I.R.C. § 6012. In order for the IRS to use administrative procedures to collect the tax owed, it must first "assess" it, which merely requires a formal recording of the tax liability. The IRS generally has three years from the date the return was filed within which to assess tax. *See* I.R.C. § 6501.[7]

---

[7] Statutes of limitations on assessment of tax are discussed in further detail in Chapter 5.

The IRS can summarily (immediately) assess tax liability reported on a taxpayer's return. However, the IRS cannot assess a tax "deficiency" without first sending the taxpayer a written notice of deficiency. A deficiency can loosely be defined as an amount of tax the taxpayer allegedly owes the IRS in excess of any amounts reported on the taxpayer's return.[8]

Deficiencies generally arise out of IRS audits. As discussed in Chapter 2, each year the IRS audits a small percentage of all returns in order to encourage voluntary compliance with the tax laws and to enforce those laws.[9] If, on audit, a revenue agent determines that a deficiency exists, and the taxpayer does not agree, the revenue agent prepares a detailed report known as a "Revenue Agent's Report" or "RAR." The IRS generally sends the taxpayer the RAR with a cover letter and a settlement agreement (Form 870) for the taxpayer to sign if he wishes to waive restrictions on assessment. The cover letter is known as a "30-day letter" because it informs the taxpayer of the right to request a conference with the IRS Appeals Division within 30 days.

At this point, the taxpayer faces a strategic decision whether to request a conference with Appeals. The Appeals Division is highly successful at settling cases. Unlike revenue agents, Appeals Officers may consider the "hazards of litigation" in negotiating a settlement. Depending on the dollar amount in issue, the taxpayer may be required to file a written "Tax Protest" in order to obtain a conference with the Appeals Division. If a taxpayer requests an Appeals conference but the parties do not come to agreement, or if the taxpayer simply ignores the 30-day letter, the IRS ordinarily issues a notice of deficiency, which formalizes the amount in controversy. Cases that are not settled in Appeals may be settled later in the process. Chapter 4 explores settlements, including settlements at the Appeals level, in more detail.

A taxpayer who has received a notice of deficiency faces several choices. He may pay the asserted deficiency and follow the refund procedures, which are discussed in further detail below and in Chapter 8. A notice of deficiency also provides a taxpayer with the opportunity to petition the Tax Court to contest the deficiency assertion, generally within 90 days of the date on the notice. Because of this time restriction, the notice of deficiency is commonly referred to as a "90-day letter." If the taxpayer petitions the Tax Court and the case has less than $50,000 in issue for each tax year involved, the taxpayer has the additional option of filing the case as a "small tax case." Small tax cases are considered under more informal procedures, in return for which the taxpayer waives the right of appeal. Tax Court cases and small tax case procedures are discussed further in Chapter 7.

Regardless of whether a taxpayer files a regular petition or small tax case petition with the Tax Court, if the taxpayer petitions the Tax Court without having previously had a conference with the Appeals Division, the Tax Court will eventually send the case to Appeals where it will be considered on a "docketed" basis. "Docketed" appeals should be contrasted with "nondocketed" appeals, those appeals made on a "protest" basis in response to a 30-day letter. The availability of docketed and nondocketed appeals presents another

---

[8] *See* I.R.C. § 6211(a).

[9] *See also* Section 1.02., describing the recent decline in audit rates.

strategic choice; this choice is analyzed in Chapter 4. This entire tax controversy process is reflected in the chart below.

Overview of the Federal Tax Controversy Process

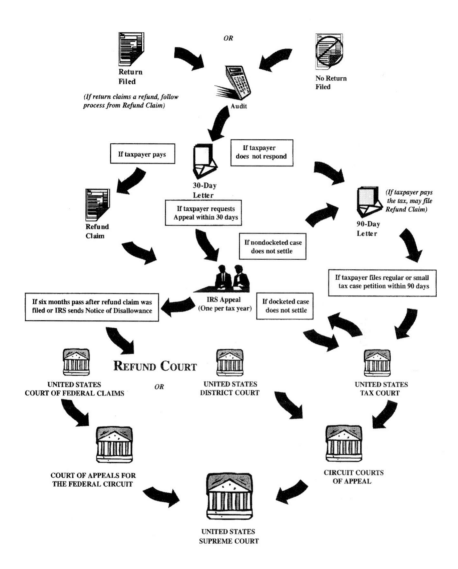

Because mailing a statutory notice of deficiency is a prerequisite to assessment of a deficiency, the IRS must mail the notice within the statute of
limitations on assessment. In addition, the IRS is prohibited from assessing
the tax during the 90-day period provided for the taxpayer to petition the Tax
Court ("the prohibited period"). If the taxpayer does petition the Tax Court,
the prohibited period lasts until the court's decision is final. The mailing of
the notice of deficiency also tolls the statute of limitations on assessment for
the length of the prohibited period, plus sixty days.

At any point in the controversy process, the taxpayer may pay the amount in issue and pursue the refund procedures alluded to above. Refund procedures require (as a prerequisite to bringing suit) that the taxpayer first claim a refund from the IRS. The taxpayer may not file suit until either six months have elapsed from the time he filed the refund claim or the IRS has sent a notice of disallowance of the claim. I.R.C. § 6532. Furthermore, the taxpayer may not file suit later than two years from the date the IRS mails a notice of disallowance of the claim to the taxpayer. *Id.* Suit may be filed in either the United States District Court or the Court of Federal Claims. Unlike deficiency litigation in Tax Court, which does not require any up front payment of the asserted deficiency, the refund procedures require "full payment" of the amounts disputed. *See Flora v. United States*, 362 U.S. 145 (1960). See Chapter 6 for a discussion of choice of forum issues.

If a taxpayer pursues the Tax Court option, the resulting decision may be appealed to the Court of Appeals for the Circuit within which the taxpayer resided at the time he filed the petition. *See* I.R.C. § 7482(b). District Court cases are similarly appealable to the Courts of Appeals. By contrast, Court of Federal Claims cases are appealable to the Court of Appeals for the Federal Circuit, resulting in the application of a different body of precedent in the Court of Federal Claims. Appeal from any of the Circuit Courts lies to the United States Supreme Court.

If a taxpayer does not respond to a notice of deficiency either by petitioning the Tax Court in the time provided by law or by paying the tax, the IRS can make an assessment. Once an amount is assessed, it becomes a debt of the taxpayer to the government. The IRS is required to give notice and demand for payment to the taxpayer as soon as practical and within 60 days of making an assessment. I.R.C. § 6303(a). Under Code section 6321, if a taxpayer refuses or neglects to pay the tax after demand for payment, the amount of the tax becomes a lien on all of the taxpayer's real and personal property until it is paid. If the taxpayer still refuses to pay the tax after receiving from the IRS the required pre-levy notices, the IRS can collect the tax by levying upon the taxpayer's property. I.R.C. § 6331(a). Collection procedures are explored further in Chapter 12.

§ 1.06   Ethical Restrictions on Tax Practice

Attorneys, certified public accountants, and enrolled agents may all practice before the IRS and the Tax Court. [10] Attorneys may also engage in other tax representation, such as representing clients in tax cases in the District Courts and Court of Federal Claims. Some ethical restrictions, such as the rules of Circular 230, applicable to practice before the IRS, apply to all tax practitioners. Others, such as the ABA Model Rules, apply only to attorneys. This part of the chapter provides a brief overview of ethical issues that arise in tax

---

[10] Attorneys may be admitted to practice before the Tax Court by filing a current certificate of good standing from a state bar along with the application form and the appropriate fee. By contrast, other applicants are required to pass a written examination and provide two letters of recommendation from persons admitted to practice before the Tax Court, in addition to completing the application and paying the appropriate fee. *See* Tax Court Rule 200.

practice.[11] Its focus is on rules applicable to attorneys, although it draws on examples involving other tax practitioners where appropriate.

Tax practitioners must be sensitive to statutory rules, such as the return preparer penalties in the Code; to generally applicable ethics rules, such as the ABA Model Rules;[12] and to specifically applicable rules such as Circular 230 and the Tax Court rules. Penalties for violating ethics rules include suspension and disbarment. Two of the cases reproduced in this chapter, *Harary* and *Thies*, consider the procedures for disbarring tax practitioners.

Tax attorneys in private practice confront the same conflict of interest, confidentiality, and duty of loyalty issues that any other practicing attorney encounters. Because of the unique interplay of statutory, judicial, and administrative law in the tax area, more precise ethical considerations have been developed in the context of advice given during tax planning (the pre-filing stage), preparation of the client's return (the filing stage), and the tax controversy process (the post-filing stage). Some of these considerations are discussed in more detail below. In addition, private practitioners who were previously government lawyers are prohibited from representing clients on matters in which they had substantial responsibility while working for the government. *See, e.g., United States v. Trafficante*, 328 F.2d 117 (5th Cir. 1964). Furthermore, all lawyers must be sensitive to rules regarding the unauthorized practice of law, such as restrictions on sharing fees with non-lawyers.

Government tax lawyers naturally are subject to the ethical rules of the state bar to which they are admitted, as well as to the restrictions of criminal law. However, government tax lawyers are in a somewhat different position than taxpayers' lawyers, in part because it is not immediately obvious who is the government lawyer's client. To address this type of concern, in 1973, the Federal Bar Association adopted ethical considerations and disciplinary rules applicable to government attorneys. *See* Bernard Wolfman et al., ETHICAL PROBLEMS IN FEDERAL TAX PRACTICE 294, 296 (3d ed. 1995).

[A] Tax Planning

Is a tax practitioner who provides tax planning advice to his client acting as an advocate, or is his role more that of a counselor or advisor? In other words, does the attorney's duty of loyalty to the client override any consideration of the government's need to maintain a fair system of tax collection and administration? Some taxpayer gambits are simply fraudulent and therefore do not present complicated ethical issues for the attorney. As any student of tax law knows, however, most tax questions do not lend themselves to precise answers: the facts underlying the client's transaction may be susceptible to more than one construction, the governing Code language may be unclear, or the applicable Treasury Regulations may reflect a doubtful interpretation of the statute. If the attorney harbors some doubt concerning an answer or

---

[11] For further reading, *see* Bernard Wolfman et al., ETHICAL PROBLEMS IN FEDERAL TAX PRACTICE (3d ed. 1995).

[12] Other practitioners are subject to generally applicable rules as well. For example, certified public accountants are subject to American Institute of Certified Public Accountants (AICPA) rules.

interpretation, may the attorney nonetheless advise his client to take a position on a return even if he believes that, if the IRS raised and litigated the position, the IRS would ultimately prevail?

Formal Opinion 314, issued by the American Bar Association's Committee on Professional Ethics and Responsibility in 1965, suggested the following guidelines at that time:

> In practice before the Internal Revenue Service, which is itself an adversary party rather than a judicial tribunal, the lawyer is under a duty not to mislead the Service, either by misstatement, silence, or through his client, but is under no duty to disclose the weaknesses of his client's case. He must be candid and fair, and his defense of his client must be exercised within the bounds of the law and without resort to any manner of fraud or chicane.

> * * *

> Similarly, a lawyer who is asked to advise his client in the course of the preparation of the client's tax returns may freely urge the statement of positions most favorable to the client just as long as there is reasonable basis for those positions. Thus where the lawyer believes there is a reasonable basis for a position that a particular transaction does not result in taxable income, or that certain expenditures are properly deductible as expenses, the lawyer has no duty to advise that riders be attached to the client's tax return explaining the circumstances surrounding the transaction or the expenditures.

Concerned that the "reasonable basis" standard in Formal Opinion 314 placed conscientious tax practitioners at a competitive disadvantage when compared to those willing to give more aggressive advice, the ABA revised its formulation in 1985:

> The Committee is informed that the standard of "reasonable basis" has been construed by many lawyers to support the use of any colorable claim on a tax return to justify exploitation of the lottery of the tax return audit selection process. This view is not universally held, and the Committee does not believe that the reasonable basis standard, properly interpreted and applied, permits this construction.

> * * *

> . . . [A] lawyer, in representing a client in the course of the preparation of the client's tax return, may advise the statement of positions most favorable to the client if the lawyer has a good faith belief that those positions are warranted in existing law or can be supported by a good faith argument for an extension, modification or reversal of existing law. A lawyer can have a good faith belief in this context even if the lawyer believes the client's position probably will not prevail. However, good faith requires that there be some realistic possibility of success if the matter is litigated.

ABA Formal Opinion 85-352.

A similar "realistic possibility" standard is used to determine whether the tax practitioner who advises a client with respect to a reporting position may be held liable for a return preparer penalty under section 6694 of the Code. The $250 penalty applies if the return preparer knows (or reasonably should know) that an understatement on the taxpayer's return is due to a position for which there is no "realistic possibility of being sustained on the merits." I.R.C. § 6694(a). The Treasury Regulations flesh out the standard as follows:

> A position is considered to have a realistic possibility of being sustained on the merits if a reasonable and well-informed analysis by a person knowledgeable in the tax law would lead such a person to conclude that the position has approximately a one in three, or greater, likelihood of being sustained on its merits (realistic possibility standard). In making this determination, the possibility that the position will not be challenged by the Internal Revenue Service (e.g., because the taxpayer's return may not be audited or because the issue may not be raised on audit) is not to be taken into account.

Treas. Reg. § 1.6694-2(b).[13] Should the application of the return preparer penalty guide the practitioner's behavior, or should the practitioner's ethical behavior conform to a higher standard?[14] Why not require at least a 50 percent likelihood of success as the appropriate standard for endorsing a return position?

The tax practitioner's role changes slightly when he is called upon by the client to issue a written opinion letter addressing the tax consequences of a proposed transaction. Opinions are common in tax planning, particularly in cases in which the client does not want to go through the delay or incur the expense of obtaining a letter ruling from the IRS. ABA Revised Formal Opinion 346, set out below, contains important guidance for the tax practitioner who renders an opinion letter relating to a tax shelter transaction. The ABA singled out tax shelter opinions for specialized guidance for a number of reasons. At the time Formal Opinion 346 was drafted, abusive tax shelter investments were becoming an increasing concern for the government as taxpayers sought to reap tax benefits (credits, losses, and deductions) from investments that were based on highly questionable factual assumptions and legal interpretations. Some of the blame for the proliferation of these abusive transactions was directed at the tax bar. Tax shelter promoters typically solicited opinion letters from tax attorneys, and then used the letters to market their investments to taxpayers who, often without reading the opinion letter in detail, viewed the attorney's opinion as a stamp of approval. In many cases, however, the tax shelter opinion contained inaccurate or hypothetical factual assumptions, or the opinion failed to draw any conclusion as to whether the expected tax benefits would be upheld if challenged by the IRS. Formal Opinion 346 sought to rectify some of these deficiencies.

---

[13] Return preparer penalties are discussed in Section 10.02[G] of Chapter 10.

[14] The Treasury Department also adopts the one-in-three realistic possibility standard as part of its Circular 230 regulations governing practice before the IRS. *See* 31 C.F.R. § 10.34.

FORMAL OPINION 346 (REVISED)*
TAX LAW OPINIONS IN TAX SHELTER INVESTMENT OFFERINGS
January 29, 1982

* This Opinion supersedes Formal Opinion 346 (June 1, 1981), which is withdrawn.

An opinion by a lawyer analyzing the tax effects of a tax shelter investment is frequently of substantial importance in a tax shelter Offering.[n.1] The promoter of the offering may depend upon the recommendations of the lawyer in structuring the venture and often publishes the opinion with the offering materials or uses the lawyer's name in connection with sales promotion efforts. The offerees may be expected to rely upon the tax shelter opinion in determining whether to invest in the venture. It is often uneconomic for the individual offeree to pay for a separate tax analysis of the offering because of the relatively small sum each offeree may invest.

Because the successful marketing of tax shelters frequently involves tax opinions issued by lawyers, concerns have been expressed by the organized bar, regulatory agencies and others over the need to articulate ethical standards applicable to a lawyer who issues an opinion which the lawyer knows will be included among the tax shelter offering materials and relied upon by offerees.

* * *

A "tax shelter opinion," as the term is used in this Opinion, is advice by a lawyer concerning the federal tax law applicable to a tax shelter if the advice is referred to either in offering materials or in connection with sales promotion efforts directed to persons other than the client who engages the lawyer to give the advice. The term includes the tax aspects or tax risks portion of the offering materials prepared by the lawyer whether or not a separate opinion letter is issued. The term does not, however, include rendering advice solely to the offeror or reviewing parts of the offering materials, so long as neither the name of the lawyer nor the fact that a lawyer has rendered advice concerning the tax aspects is referred to at all in the offering materials or in connection with sales promotion efforts. In this case the lawyer has the ethical responsibility of assuring that in the offering materials and in

---

[n.1] A "tax shelter," as the term is used in this Opinion, is an investment which has as a significant feature for federal income or excise tax purposes either or both of the following attributes: (1) deductions in excess of income from the investment being available in any year to reduce income from other sources in that year, and (2) credits in excess of the tax attributable to the income from the investment being available in any year to offset taxes on income from other sources in that year. Excluded from the term are investments such as, but not limited to, the following: municipal bonds; annuities; family trusts; qualified retirement plans; individual retirement accounts; stock option plans; securities issued in a corporate reorganization; mineral development ventures, if the only tax benefit would be percentage depletion; and real estate where it is anticipated that deductions are unlikely to exceed gross income from the investment in any year, and that any tax credits are unlikely to exceed the tax on the income from that source in any year.

connection with sales promotion efforts there is no reference to the lawyer's name or to the fact that a lawyer has rendered tax advice. The term also does not include the case where a small group of investors negotiate the terms of the arrangement directly with the offeror of securities and depend for tax advice concerning the investment entirely upon advisors other than the lawyer engaged to represent the offeror.

Disciplinary Standards

A false opinion is one which ignores or minimizes serious legal risks or misstates the facts or the law, knowingly or through gross incompetence. The lawyer who gives a false opinion, including one which is intentionally or recklessly misleading, violates the Disciplinary Rules of the Model Code of Professional Responsibility. Quite clearly, the lawyer exceeds the duty to represent the client zealously within the bounds of the law. *See* DR 7-101; EC 7-10. Knowingly misstating facts or law violates DR 7-102(A)(5) and is "conduct involving dishonesty, fraud, deceit, or misrepresentation," a violation of DR 1-102(A)(4). The lawyer also violates DR 7-102(A)(7) by counseling or assisting the offeror "in conduct that the lawyer knows to be illegal or fraudulent." In addition, the lawyer's conduct may involve the concealment or knowing nondisclosure of matters which the lawyer is required by law to reveal, a violation of DR 7-102(A)(3).

The lawyer who accepts as true the facts which the promoter tells him, when the lawyer should know that a further inquiry would disclose that these facts are untrue, also gives a false opinion. It has been said that lawyers cannot "escape criminal liability on a plea of ignorance when they have shut their eyes to what was plainly to be seen." United States v. Benjamin, 328 F.2d 854, 863 (2d Cir. 1964). Recklessly and consciously disregarding information strongly indicating that material facts expressed in the tax shelter opinion are false or misleading involves dishonesty as does assisting the offeror in conduct the lawyer knows to be fraudulent. Such conduct violates DR 1-102(A)(4) and DR 7-102(A). We equate the minimum extent of the knowledge required for the lawyer's conduct to have violated these Disciplinary Rules with the knowledge required to sustain a Rule 10b-5 recovery, *see* Ernst & Ernst v. Hochfelder, 425 U.S. 185 (1976), rather than the lesser negligence standard. * * *

But even if the lawyer lacks the knowledge required to sustain a recovery under the *Hochfelder* standard, the lawyer's conduct nevertheless may involve gross incompetence, or indifference, inadequate preparation under the circumstances and consistent failure to perform obligations to the client. If so, the lawyer will have violated DR 6-101(A). ABA Informal Opinion 1273 (1973).

Ethical Considerations

Beyond the requirements of the Disciplinary Rules, the lawyer who issues a tax shelter opinion should follow the Canons and the Ethical Considerations of the Model Code.[n.3] Although not constituting absolute requirements, the violation of which may result in sanctions, these Canons and Ethical Considerations constitute a body of principles which provide guidance in the application of the lawyer's professional responsibility to specific situations, such as the rendering of tax shelter opinions. The guidelines developed here are to be applied to each specific situation reasonably and in a practical fashion.

EC 7-22 says "a litigant or his lawyer may, in good faith and within the framework of the law, take steps to test the correctness of a ruling of a tribunal." *See also* EC 7-25. Principles similar to these are applied where the lawyer represents a client in adversarial proceedings before the Internal Revenue Service. In that case the lawyer has duties not to mislead the Service by any misstatement, not to further any misrepresentations made by the client, and to deal candidly and fairly. ABA Formal Opinion 314 (1965); * * *.

The lawyer rendering a tax shelter opinion which he knows will be relied upon by third persons, however, functions more as an advisor than as an advocate. *See* EC 7-3, distinguishing these roles. Since the Model Code was adopted in 1969, the differing functions of the advisor and advocate have become more widely recognized.

As advisor, a lawyer provides a client with an informed understanding of the client's legal rights and obligations and explains their practical implications. As advocate, a lawyer asserts the client's position under the rules of the adversary system.

The Proposed Model Rules specifically recognize the ethical considerations applicable where a lawyer undertakes an evaluation for the use of third persons other than a client. These third persons have an interest in the integrity of the evaluation. The legal duty of the lawyer therefore "goes beyond the obligations a lawyer normally has to third persons." Proposed Model Rules, *supra* note 3 at 117; *see also* ABA Formal Opinion 335 (1974).

* * *

Making Factual Inquiry

ABA Formal Opinion 335 (1974) establishes guidelines which a lawyer should follow when furnishing an assumed facts opinion in connection with the sale of unregistered securities. The same guidelines describe the extent to which a lawyer should verify the facts presented to him as the basis for a tax shelter opinion:

[T]he lawyer should, in the first instance, make inquiry of his client as to the relevant facts and receive answers. If any of the alleged facts, or the alleged facts taken as a whole, are incomplete in a material respect; or are suspect; or are inconsistent; or either on their face or on the basis of other

[n.3] Canon 1 says "[a] lawyer should assist in maintaining the integrity and competence of the legal profession." Canon 6 says "[a] lawyer should represent a client competently." The Ethical Considerations used to establish the guidelines in this Opinion are EC 1-5, EC6-1, EC6-4, EC6-5, EC7-1, EC7-3, EC7-5, EC7-6, EC7-8, EC7-10, EC7-22, EC7-25. *See also* Model Rules of Professional Conduct (ABA Commission on Evaluation of Professional Standards, Proposed Final Draft, May 30, 1981), Rule 2.3 at 116.

known facts are open to question, the lawyer should make further inquiry. The extent of this inquiry will depend in each case upon the circumstances; for example, it would be less where the lawyer's past relationship with the client is sufficient to give him a basis for trusting the client's probity than where the client has recently engaged the lawyer, and less where the lawyer's inquiries are answered fully than when there appears a reluctance to disclose information.

Where the lawyer concludes that further inquiry of a reasonable nature would not give him sufficient confidence as to all the relevant facts, or for any other reason he does not make the appropriate further inquiries, he should refuse to give an opinion. However, assuming that the alleged facts are not incomplete in a material respect, or suspect, or in any way inherently inconsistent, or on their face or on the basis of other known facts open to question, the lawyer may properly assume that the facts as related to him by his client, and checked by him by reviewing such appropriate documents as are available, are accurate.

The essence of this opinion * * * is that, while a lawyer should make adequate preparation including inquiry into the relevant facts that is consistent with the above guidelines, and while he should not accept as true that which he should not reasonably believe to be true, he does not have the responsibility to "audit" the affairs of his client or to assume, without reasonable cause, that a client's statement of the facts cannot be relied upon. ABA Formal Opinion 335 at 3, 5–6.

For instance, where essential underlying information, such as an appraisal or financial projection, makes little common sense, or where the reputation or expertise of the person who has prepared the appraisal or projection is dubious, further inquiry clearly is required. Indeed, failure to make further inquiry may result in a false opinion. See *supra*, Disciplinary Standards. If further inquiry reveals that the appraisal or projection is reasonably well supported and complete, the lawyer is justified in relying upon the material facts which the underlying information supports.

*   *   *

Opinion as to Outcome — Material Tax Issues

Since the term "opinion" connotes a lawyer's conclusion as to the likely outcome of an issue if challenged and litigated, the lawyer should, if possible, state the lawyer's opinion of the probable outcome on the merits of each material tax issue. However, if the lawyer determines in good faith that it is not possible to make a judgment as to the outcome of a material tax issue, the lawyer should so state and give the reasons for this conclusion.

A tax shelter opinion may question the validity of a Revenue Ruling or the reasoning in a lower court opinion which the lawyer believes is wrong. But there must also be a complete explanation to the offerees, including what position the Service is likely to take on the issue and a summary of why this position is considered to be wrong. The opinion also should set forth the risks of an adversarial proceeding if one is likely to occur.

Overall Evaluation of Realization of Tax Benefits

The clear disclosure of the tax risks in the offering materials should include an opinion by the lawyer or by another professional providing an overall evaluation of the extent to which the tax benefits, in the aggregate, which are a significant feature of the investment to the typical investor are likely to be realized as contemplated by the offering materials. In making this evaluation, the lawyer should state that the significant tax benefits, in the aggregate, probably will be realized or probably will not be realized, or that the probabilities of realization and nonrealization of the significant tax benefits are evenly divided.

In rare instances the lawyer may conclude in good faith that it is not possible to make a judgment of the extent to which the significant tax benefits are likely to be realized. This impossibility may occur where, for example, the most significant tax benefits are predicated upon a newly enacted Code provision when there are no regulations and the legislative history is obscure. In these circumstances, the lawyer should fully explain why the judgment cannot be made and assure full disclosure in the offering materials of the assumptions and risks which the investors must evaluate.

The Committee does not accept the view that it is always ethically improper to issue an opinion which concludes that the significant tax benefits in the aggregate probably will not be realized. However, full disclosure requires that the negative conclusion be clearly stated and prominently noted in the offering materials.

If another professional is providing the overall evaluation, the lawyer should nonetheless satisfy himself that the evaluation meets the standards set forth above.

* * *

The ABA is not alone in its concern about tax shelter opinions. Circular 230 has its own set of requirements for tax shelter opinions in 31 C.F.R. § 10.33(a), reproduced below, in part:

(1) *Factual matters.*

   (i)   The practitioner must make inquiry as to all relevant facts, be satisfied that the material facts are accurately and completely described in the offering materials, and assure that any representations as to future activities are clearly identified, reasonable and complete.

   (ii) A practitioner may not accept as true asserted facts pertaining to the tax shelter which he/she should not, based on his/her background and knowledge, reasonably believe to be true. However, a practitioner need not conduct an audit or independent verification of the asserted facts, or assume that a client's statement of the facts cannot be relied upon, unless he/she has reason to believe that any relevant facts asserted to him/her are untrue.

(iii) If the fair market value of property or the expected financial performance of an investment is relevant to the tax shelter, a practitioner may not accept an appraisal or financial projection as support for the matters claimed therein unless:

   (A) The appraisal or financial projection makes sense on its face;

   (B) The practitioner reasonably believes that the person making the appraisal or financial projection is competent to do so and is not of dubious reputation; and

   (C) The appraisal is based on the definition of fair market value prescribed under the relevant Federal tax provisions.

(iv) If the fair market value of purchased property is to be established by reference to its stated purchase price, the practitioner must examine the terms and conditions upon which the property was (or is to be) purchased to determine whether the stated purchase price reasonably may be considered to be its fair market value.

(2) *Relate law to facts.* The practitioner must relate the law to the actual facts and, when addressing issues based on future activities, clearly identify what facts are assumed.

(3) *Identification of material issues.* The practitioner must ascertain that all material Federal tax issues have been considered, and that all of those issues which involve the reasonable possibility of a challenge by the Internal Revenue Service have been fully and fairly addressed in the offering materials.

(4) *Opinion on each material issue.* Where possible, the practitioner must provide an opinion whether it is more likely than not that an investor will prevail on the merits of each material tax issue presented by the offering which involves a reasonable possibility of a challenge by the Internal Revenue Service. Where such an opinion cannot be given with respect to any material tax issue, the opinion should fully describe the reasons for the practitioner's inability to opine as to the likely outcome.

(5) *Overall evaluation.*

   (i) Where possible, the practitioner must provide an overall evaluation whether the material tax benefits in the aggregate more likely than not will be realized. Where such an overall evaluation cannot be given, the opinion should fully describe the reasons for the practitioner's inability to make an overall evaluation. Opinions concluding that an overall evaluation cannot be provided will be given special scrutiny to determine if the stated reasons are adequate.

(ii)   A favorable overall evaluation may not be rendered unless it is based on a conclusion that substantially more than half of the material tax benefits, in terms of their financial impact on a typical investor, more likely than not will be realized if challenged by the Internal Revenue Service.

(iii) If it is not possible to give an overall evaluation, or if the overall evaluation is that the material tax benefits in the aggregate will not be realized, the fact that the practitioner's opinion does not constitute a favorable overall evaluation, or that it is an unfavorable overall evaluation, must be clearly and prominently disclosed in the offering materials.

* * *

How much uncertainty about the expected tax benefits of a proposed transaction may the attorney harbor and still be permitted to issue, ethically and professionally, a favorable tax shelter opinion? Is the standard higher or lower than the "realistic possibility" standard applicable to return positions? Notice also that both ABA Revised Formal Opinion 346 and Circular 230 contemplate a tax shelter opinion letter that concludes that the expected tax benefits may not be realized. If the tax attorney comes to a negative overall evaluation of the transaction, what use would the opinion letter be to the client?

ABA Formal Opinion 346 and the excerpt from Circular 230 both respond primarily to the "old" variety of abusive tax shelter transactions marketed to individual taxpayers, which were popular in the 1970s and 1980s. A more sophisticated variety of *corporate* tax shelters has developed, many of which involve international transactions. During the past three years, a heated debate has developed among practitioners and policymakers over how best to eradicate these tax avoidance transactions. The IRS, for its part, issued temporary and proposed regulations that require certain corporate taxpayers to attach tax shelter disclosure statements to their federal income tax returns, and require tax shelter promoters to register their corporate tax shelters and maintain a list of investors. *See* Prop. Reg. § 1.6011-4T (disclosure statement); Prop. Reg. § 301.6111-2T (confidential shelter registration); Prop. Reg. § 301.6112-1T (investor lists). The ABA Section of Taxation's Standards of Practice Committee is working to revise the standards for tax opinions, and the Treasury Department has proposed revisions to Circular 230 governing tax shelter advice. *See* 66 Fed. Reg. 3275 (Jan. 12, 2001). Proposed changes to Circular 230 would strengthen the existing standards regarding factual due diligence and require the tax attorney drafting the opinion to consider all potentially relevant judicial doctrines in the analysis section.

[B] Return Preparation

As discussed in Chapter 13, the criminal provisions of the Code sanction a variety of conduct, including certain conduct in connection with preparing tax returns. Section 7206(2) provides that it is a felony for any person to "willfully aid[ ] or assist[ ] in, or procure[ ], counsel[ ], or advise[ ] the preparation or presentation under, or in connection with any matter arising under, the internal revenue laws, of a return, affidavit, claim, or other document, which is fraudulent or false as to any material matter, whether or not the falsity or fraud is with the knowledge or consent of the person authorized or required to present such return, affidavit, claim, or document . . . " The Code also provides penalties specifically to sanction income tax return preparers for proscribed conduct. An "income tax return preparer" is a person who prepares, for compensation, all or a substantial part of an income tax return or refund claim. I.R.C. § 7701(a)(36).[15] Code section 6694(b) imposes a $1,000 penalty on a preparer who understates a client's tax liability willfully or with intentional disregard of rules or regulations. A preparer penalty of $250 also applies where the preparer knew that there was no realistic possibility that the reported position would be sustained. I.R.C. § 6694(a). Other penalties are discussed in the Revenue Ruling reproduced below.

Is a person in a business other than tax preparation, who prepares returns for free as a service to customers an "income tax return preparer?" What about a person who buys income tax refunds at a discount, and prepares returns as part of the service? Consider the following Revenue Ruling:

REVENUE RULING 86-55
1986-1 C.B. 373

* * *

ISSUE 1

In the situations described below, if a person in a business other than tax return preparation fills out or reviews income tax returns for the person's customers without charging a separate fee, is the person an income tax return preparer under section 7701(a)(36) of the Internal Revenue Code?

ISSUE 2

If such person is an income tax preparer, then what requirements and potential penalties apply to that person under the Internal Revenue Code?

* * *

FACTS

Situation 1. X, a used car dealer, advertises that it will fill out and review income tax returns and that any resulting refund will be applied as a down payment on a used car. These services are available to those who purchase a vehicle. X or X's employee then either fills out a complete return or reviews a return prepared by the customer for both substantive correctness and mechanical accuracy. X does not charge its customers a separate fee for these services. The customer executes a power of attorney authorizing X to receive

---

[15] *See* Treas. Reg. § 301.7701-15(b)(2) for what constitutes a "substantial" part.

and endorse or negotiate the refund check. The address of X is substituted for that of the customer on the return. When X receives the customer's refund check, X endorses it and applies it as a down payment.

Situation 2. Y is a firm that offers discounted cash payments for tax refunds. Y or Y's employee either fills out a complete return or reviews a return prepared by the customer for both substantive correctness and mechanical accuracy. After the return is filled out or reviewed, Y pays the customer the amount of the refund requested on the return, less a discount typically equal to 20 to 40 percent of the refund amount requested. As in situation 1, the customer executes a power of attorney, and Y's address is substituted on the return for that of the taxpayer. Y does not charge a separate fee for its services in filling out or reviewing the return. Upon receipt of the customer's refund check, Y endorses the customer's name on the back of the check and deposits it in Y's account.

LAW AND ANALYSIS

ISSUE 1

Section 7701(a)(36)(A) of the Code defines an income tax return preparer as any person who prepares any return of tax, or any claim for refund of tax, imposed by subtitle A, for compensation, or any person who employs one or more persons to prepare such returns or claims for refund for compensation.

Section 301.7701-15(a) of the Regulations on Procedure and Administration provides the general rule that an income tax return preparer is any person who prepares for compensation, or who employs (or engages) one or more persons to prepare for compensation, other than for the person, all or a substantial portion of any return of tax under subtitle A of the Code or any claim for refund of tax under subtitle A.

Section 301.7701-15(a)(4) of the regulations provides that a person must prepare a return or claim for refund for compensation to be an income tax return preparer. A person who prepares a return or claim for refund for a taxpayer with no explicit or implicit statement for compensation is not a preparer.

In *Papermaster v. United States*, No. 79-C-710 (E.D. Wis., Apr. 21, 1980), aff'd by unpublished order, No. 80-1612 (7th Cir., June 25, 1982), an individual who was both an attorney and an accountant prepared a taxpayer's individual income tax return. He also prepared a return for a corporation in which the taxpayer was a shareholder. The attorney/accountant received compensation for preparing the corporation return, but was not separately compensated for preparing the taxpayer's individual return. The court held that he was an income tax return preparer under section 7701(a)(36) of the Code with respect to taxpayer's individual return. The court reasoned that he was offering the businessman a "package deal" for preparing the individual return; his compensation was included in the compensation for the corporate return.

In both situations 1 and 2, X and Y either fill out the entire return or review information on returns prepared by others. That action is preparation of the return for purposes of section 7701(a)(36) of the Code. *See* Rev. Rul. 84-3, 1984-1 C.B. 264.

In situation 1, although X does not charge the customers a separate fee for the preparation of their returns, X is offering its customers a "package deal." X's compensation is included in the price of the cars required to be purchased by the customers. Similarly, in situation 2, Y's compensation for filling out or reviewing the return is a part of, or is incident to, the various discount charges (ranging from 20 to 40 percent) that Y charges its customers for their refund checks.

ISSUE 2

Sections 6694(a) and 6694(b) of the Code provide that any person who is an income tax return preparer with respect to a return or claim for refund may be subject to a penalty if any part of an understatement of liability with respect to that return or claim is due to a negligent or intentional disregard of rules or regulations by that preparer, or if the understatement is due to a willful attempt by that preparer to understate the liability.[16]

Under section 6107(a) of the Code, an income tax return preparer has an obligation to furnish a completed copy of the return to the taxpayer and may be penalized under section 6695(a) for failure to do so. Under section 6107(b), an income tax return preparer has an obligation to retain a copy of the return or a list of taxpayers for whom returns have been prepared and may be penalized under section 6695(d) for failure to do so. When one preparer employs or engages another, the responsibility for these acts falls on the employer. See section 1.6107-1(c)(1) of the Income Tax Regulations.

Section 6695(b) of the Code imposes an obligation to sign the return and imposes a penalty for failure to do so. Under section 1.6695-1(b)(2) of the regulations, this obligation falls on the individual preparer with primary responsibility for the overall substantive accuracy of the return.

Section 6109(a)(4) of the Code provides that any return or claim for refund prepared by an income tax return preparer shall bear such identifying number for securing proper identification of such preparer, such preparer's employer, or both, as may be prescribed.

Section 1.6109-2(a) of the regulations requires that a return prepared by an income tax return preparer shall bear the identifying number of the preparer required to sign the return or claim for refund. In addition, if there is a partnership or employment arrangement between two or more preparers the identifying number of the partnership or the person who employs (or engages) one or more other persons to prepare for compensation the return or claim for refund shall also appear on the return or claim for refund. In general, if the preparer is an individual, the preparer's social security number shall be affixed, but if the preparer is a person (whether an individual, corporation, or partnership) that employs (or engages) one or more persons to prepare the return or claim for refund, the preparer's employer identification number shall generally be used. Special rules apply to preparers that are not citizens or residents of the United States.

---

[16] [In 1989, Congress changed the standard of conduct that triggers a penalty under section 6694. As discussed in Chapter 10, under current law, the return preparer may be subject to a penalty if any part of an understatement is due to a position for which there was not a realistic possibility of being sustained on the merits. Eds.]

Under sections 6060 of the Code and 1.6060-1 of the regulations, any person who employs an income tax return preparer to prepare a return or claim for refund other than for that employer must retain a record concerning each preparer so employed and may be penalized under section 6695(e) for failure to do so.

Section 6695(f) of the Code imposes a penalty of $500 on income tax return preparers who endorse or otherwise negotiate refund checks that are issued to taxpayers. There is no reasonable cause exception.

Section 7216 of the Code imposes a criminal penalty for unlawful disclosure or use of return information by persons who prepare or provide services in connection with the preparation of returns.

*   *   *

HOLDINGS

ISSUE 1

X and Y are income tax return preparers with respect to their customers' income tax returns.

ISSUE 2

As income tax return preparers, X and Y are subject to the various requirements and potential penalties applicable to preparers, as previously set forth in this ruling. X and Y are potentially subject to penalties under sections 6694(a) or 6695(b) of the Code if any part of an understatement of liability on a customer's return is due to a negligent or intentional disregard of rules or regulations by the preparer, or if the understatement is due to the preparer's attempt to willfully understate the liability.

X and Y are required to furnish copies of the returns to the customers and retain a list of taxpayers for whom returns have been prepared. They may be subject to penalties under sections 6695(a) or 6695(d) of the Code for failure to do so.

The individual preparer with primary responsibility for the overall substantive accuracy of the customer's return is required to sign the return as preparer and is subject to the penalty under section 6695(b) of the Code for failure to do so. X and Y are required to furnish their identifying numbers on the customers' returns and they may be subject to the penalty under section 6695(c) for failure to do so.

Under section 6060 of the Code, X and Y must keep records of all persons in their employ that meet the definition of income tax return preparer, and X and Y are subject to the penalty under section 6695(e) of the Code for failure to do so.

X and Y are subject to the penalty under section 6695(f) of the Code when they endorse or otherwise negotiate a customer's refund check.

X and Y may be subject to the criminal penalty under section 7216 of the Code if they make unlawful disclosure or use of return information.

Consider *Tiddy v. United States*, 1992 U.S. App. LEXIS 3979 (4th Cir. 1992) (unpublished op.). In that case, the Court of Appeals for the Fourth Circuit held that Tiddy, an individual who purchased tax refunds at a discount, and prepared returns as part of the service, was *not* an "income tax return preparer." However, the court noted a factual dispute over whether any part of Tiddy's compensation was for preparing tax returns, and that the IRS did not present evidence on whether Tiddy's return preparation was even part of a "package deal." In addition, there was evidence that Tiddy had prepared some returns without charge, which tended to corroborate his assertion.

[C] Tax Controversies

Practitioners representing clients in tax controversies may at times practice before the IRS, the Tax Court, the District Courts, the Court of Federal Claims, the Bankruptcy Courts, the Courts of Appeals, and even the United States Supreme Court. Each of these fora has its own governing rules. Because the rules applicable to tax attorneys practicing before federal courts other than the Tax Court are the same as the rules applicable to attorneys practicing in those courts who do not specialize in tax, this section focuses on rules applicable to practice before the IRS and before the Tax Court.

[1] Representing a Taxpayer Before the IRS

Any person engaged in "practice before the IRS" is subject to the rules of Circular 230, which is published by the Treasury Department under the authority of 31 U.S.C. § 330(a) and (b). *See* 31 C.F.R. Part 10.

> Practice before the Internal Revenue Service comprehends all matters connected with a presentation to the Internal Revenue Service or any of its officers or employees relating to a client's rights, privileges, or liabilities under laws or regulations administered by the Internal Revenue Service. Such presentations include preparing and filing necessary documents, corresponding and communicating with the Internal Revenue Service, and representing a client at conferences, hearings, and meetings.

31 C.F.R. § 10.2(e).

Any attorney or certified public accountant who is not currently under suspension or disbarment from practice before the Internal Revenue Service may practice before the IRS upon filing with the IRS a written declaration that he or she is currently qualified as an attorney or CPA, as the case may be, and is authorized to represent the particular party on whose behalf he or she acts. 31 C.F.R. § 10.3(a), (b).

Enrolled agents may also practice before the IRS. Enrolled agents are individuals who have been certified by the IRS after passing an examination or based on prior IRS service. An individual who is enrolled in the Joint Board for the Enrollment of Actuaries may also practice before the IRS upon filing with the IRS a written declaration that he is currently qualified as an enrolled actuary and is authorized to represent the particular party on whose behalf he acts. Practice as an enrolled actuary is limited to representation with respect to issues involving certain statutory provisions. 31 C.F.R. § 10.4.

Subpart B of Circular 230, 31 C.F.R. §§ 10.20–10.34, provides duties and prohibitions applicable to representatives practicing before the IRS. In general, these duties include:

(1) submitting records or information upon a proper request by a duly authorized IRS officer or employee;

(2) advising a client promptly of any noncompliance, error, or omission in any tax return, affidavit or other legally required document, if the representative is aware of the noncompliance, error, or omission; and

(3) exercising due diligence in preparing or assisting in the preparation of, any documents, in determining the correctness of oral or written representations made by him to the Treasury Department, and in determining the correctness of oral or written representations made by him to clients.

The prohibitions generally include:

(1) unreasonably delaying the prompt disposition of any matter before the IRS;

(2) employing or accepting assistance from any person who is under disbarment or suspension from practice before the IRS, accepting employment from, or sharing fees with, any such person, or accepting assistance from any former government employee where any Federal law would be violated;

(3) representation by any partner of an officer or employee of the executive branch of the U.S. Government, of any independent agency of the United States, or of the District of Columbia in any matter administered by the IRS in which the officer or employee of the Government participates or has participated personally and substantially as a Government employee or which is the subject of his official responsibility;

(4) representation or knowing assistance by any former Government employee who participated in a transaction to any person who is or was a specific party to that transaction.

(5) administration of oaths or certification of papers or performance of other official acts in connection with matters in which the representative is employed as counsel, attorney, or agent, or in which he may be in any way interested before the Internal Revenue Service;

(6) charging an unconscionable fee for representing a client in a matter before the IRS, or charging a contingent fee for preparing an original return;

(7) representing conflicting interests in practice before the IRS, except by express consent of all directly interested parties after full disclosure has been made;

(8) with respect to any IRS matter, using or participating in the use of any form of public communication containing (i) a false, fraudulent, unduly

influencing, coercive, or unfair statement or claim, or (ii) a misleading or deceptive statement or claim; and

(9) endorsing or negotiating any check made in respect of income taxes which is issued to a taxpayer other than the representative.

Subpart C of Circular 230 provides the rules applicable to disciplinary proceedings. Under Subpart C, the Secretary of the Treasury, after notice and an opportunity for a proceeding, may suspend or disbar any practitioner from practice before the Internal Revenue Service. *See* 31 C.F.R. § 10.50.[17]

> Disreputable conduct for which an attorney, certified public accountant, enrolled agent, or enrolled actuary may be disbarred or suspended from practice before the Internal Revenue Service includes, but is not limited to:
>
> (a) Conviction of any criminal offense under the revenue laws of the United States, or of any offense involving dishonesty, or breach of trust.
>
> (b) Giving false or misleading information, or participating in any way in the giving of false or misleading information to the Department of the Treasury or any officer or employee thereof, or to any tribunal authorized to pass upon Federal tax matters, in connection with any matter pending or likely to be pending before them, knowing such information to be false or misleading. Facts or other matters contained in testimony, Federal tax returns, financial statements, applications for enrollment, affidavits, declarations, or any other document or statement, written or oral, are included in the term "information."
>
> (c) Solicitation of employment as prohibited under § 10.30, the use of false or misleading representations with intent to deceive a client or prospective client in order to procure employment, or intimating that the practitioner is able improperly to obtain special consideration or action from the Internal Revenue Service or officer or employee thereof.
>
> (d) Willfully failing to make Federal tax return [sic] in violation of the revenue laws of the United States, or evading, attempting to evade, or participating in any way in evading or attempting to evade any Federal tax or payment thereof, knowingly counseling or suggesting to a client or prospective client an illegal plan to evade Federal taxes or payment thereof, or concealing assets of himself or another to evade Federal taxes or payment thereof.
>
> (e) Misappropriation of, or failure properly and promptly to remit funds received from a client for the purpose of payment of taxes or other obligations due the United States.
>
> (f) Directly or indirectly attempting to influence, or offering or agreeing to attempt to influence, the official action of any officer

[17] Proposed revisions to section 10.50 would create an additional sanction for violation of the Circular 230 standards of conduct. As an intermediate sanction, short of suspension or disbarment, the Secretary could censure the offending practitioner.

or employee of the Internal Revenue Service by the use of threats, false accusations, duress or coercion, by the offer of any special inducement or promise of advantage or by the bestowing of any gift, favor or thing of value.

(g) Disbarment or suspension from practice as an attorney, certified public accountant, public accountant, or actuary by any duly constituted authority of any State, possession, territory, Commonwealth, the District of Columbia, any Federal court of record or any Federal agency, body or board.

(h) Knowingly aiding and abetting another person to practice before the Internal Revenue Service during a period of suspension, disbarment, or ineligibility of such other person. Maintaining a partnership for the practice of law, accountancy, or other related professional service with a person who is under disbarment from practice before the Service shall be presumed to be a violation of this provision.

(i) Contemptuous conduct in connection with practice before the Internal Revenue Service, including the use of abusive language, making false accusations and statements knowing them to be false, or circulating or publishing malicious or libelous matter.

(j) Giving a false opinion, knowingly, recklessly, or through gross incompetence, including an opinion which is intentionally or recklessly misleading, or a pattern of providing incompetent opinions on questions arising under the Federal tax laws. False opinions described in this paragraph include those which reflect or result from a knowing misstatement of fact or law; from an assertion of a position known to be unwarranted under existing law; from counseling or assisting in conduct known to be illegal or fraudulent; from concealment of matters required by law to be revealed; or from conscious disregard of information indicating that material facts expressed in the tax opinion or offering material are false or misleading. For purposes of this paragraph, reckless conduct is a highly unreasonable omission or misrepresentation involving an extreme departure from the standards of ordinary care that a practitioner should observe under the circumstances. A pattern of conduct is a factor that will be taken into account in determining whether a practitioner acted knowingly, recklessly, or through gross incompetence. Gross incompetence includes conduct that reflects gross indifference, preparation which is grossly inadequate under the circumstances, and a consistent failure to perform obligations to the client.

31 C.F.R. § 10.51.

Subpart C also provides for a suspension or disbarment hearing and the procedures applicable to such hearings.[18] See 31 C.F.R. §§ 10.54-10.76. In

---

[18] Subpart D of Circular 230 contains rules applicable to disqualification of appraisers. See 31 C.F.R. §§ 10.77-10.97. Subpart E contains general provisions. See 31 C.F.R. §§ 10.98–10.101.

general, these procedures are as follows:[19]

(1) The Director of Practice may reprimand or institute a proceeding for disbarment or suspension of any practitioner that he has reason to believe has violated any provision of the laws or regulations governing practice before the IRS. 31 C.F.R. § 10.54.

(2) The Director of Practice institutes the proceeding by filing a complaint with his office. *Id.*

(3) Before filing a complaint, the facts or conduct are brought to the attention of the practitioner in writing, except in cases of willfulness, or where time, the nature of the proceeding, or the public interest does not permit, and he is accorded an opportunity to demonstrate or achieve compliance with all lawful requirements. *Id.*

The complaint filed by the Director of Practice provides a description of the allegations constituting the basis for the proceeding. 31 C.F.R. § 10.56. The complaint or a separate document attached to the complaint notifies the practitioner of the place and time within which to file his answer and that a decision by default may be entered if the practitioner fails to file his answer as required. The deadline for filing the answer must be at least 15 days from the date of service of the complaint. 31 C.F.R. § 10.56(b). The answer must contain a statement of facts constituting the grounds of defense, and it must specifically admit or deny each allegation set forth in the complaint. Every allegation in the complaint that is not denied in the answer shall be deemed to be admitted and may be considered as proved. The answer may also include affirmative defenses. 31 C.F.R. § 10.58. The Director of Practice has discretion whether to file a reply. 31 C.F.R. § 10.60.

An Administrative Law Judge presides over IRS suspension and disbarment hearings. 31 C.F.R. § 10.65(a). Except in cases where the practitioner has failed to answer the complaint or where a party has failed to appear at the hearing, the Administrative Law Judge provides the parties, prior to making a decision, with a reasonable opportunity to submit proposed findings and conclusions. 31 C.F.R. § 10.69. As soon as practicable thereafter, the Administrative Law Judge renders his decision. 31 C.F.R. § 10.70. Either party may appeal the decision to the Secretary of the Treasury within 30 days from the date of the decision. 31 C.F.R. § 10.71. The Secretary of the Treasury makes the final decision for the IRS. 31 C.F.R. § 10.72. If the final order against the respondent is for suspension, the practitioner respondent is not permitted to practice before the IRS during the suspension period. 31 C.F.R. § 10.73. If the final order is for disbarment, the practitioner is not be permitted to practice before the IRS unless and until he is authorized to do so by the Director of Practice. *Id.* Once five years elapse following the disbarment, the Director of Practice can entertain a petition for reinstatement. The Director of Practice cannot grant reinstatement to practice unless he is satisfied that the practitioner is not likely to conduct himself contrary to the regulations

---

[19] There are special, expedited, suspension procedures provided for situations in which a practitioner has lost his license to practice as an attorney, certified public accountant, or actuary; has his license suspended or revoked for cause; or has been convicted of any crime under Title 26 of the United States Code or of a felony under Title 18 of the United States Code involving dishonesty or breach of trust. *See* 31 C.F.R. § 10.76.

in Circular 230, and that reinstatement would not be contrary to the public interest. 31 C.F.R. § 10.75.

Consider this case on disbarment from practice before the IRS. Would the case have been different if Harary were an attorney rather than a certified public accountant?

HARARY v. BLUMENTHAL
United States Court of Appeals, Second Circuit
555 F.2d 1113 (1977)

OAKES, CIRCUIT JUDGE:

Appellant, a certified public accountant, seeks by this appeal to avoid "disbarment" from practice before the Internal Revenue Service (IRS). He was disbarred in an administrative disciplinary proceeding before the Secretary of the Treasury, pursuant to 31 U.S.C. § 1026 and regulations thereunder, and sought review of the administrative decision in the United States District Court for the Southern District of New York, Thomas P. Griesa, Judge. * * * We affirm.

I.

Appellant's disbarment arose out of a prior criminal proceeding in which he was charged with bribing and conspiring to bribe a special agent of the IRS in violation of 18 U.S.C. §§ 201(b), 371, and with paying the agent a gratuity in violation of 18 U.S.C. § 201(f). He admitted that he had paid the agent the sum of $1,250 on behalf of his client, that he had told the client that the agent wanted $2,000 and that he (appellant) had kept the $750 difference.

Appellant was tried before a jury and was acquitted of the conspiracy and bribery charges, but was convicted of the gratuity charge. On appeal this court reversed the conviction on the gratuity charge and ordered that count of the indictment dismissed. United States v. Harary, 457 F.2d 471 (2d Cir. 1972). The court held that the district court had erred in submitting the lesser included gratuity offense to the jury, because there was no disputed factual element that would have allowed the jury rationally to conclude that appellant was guilty of the lesser offense but not of the greater offense of bribery. Id. at 477–78.

Subsequently, Treasury Department officials filed an administrative complaint, pursuant to 31 C.F.R. § 10.54, seeking appellant's disbarment from practice before the IRS. The grounds alleged included appellant's attempt to influence an agent in the conduct of an audit of appellant's client and appellant's overstating to his client the amount of the payment that the agent had agreed to accept. Following a hearing, at which the parties jointly offered in evidence the transcript from appellant's criminal trial, an administrative law judge (ALJ) found that appellant had committed the acts charged and ordered appellant disbarred. Appellant's appeal to the Secretary of the Treasury resulted in an opinion by the Department's General Counsel, acting on behalf of the Secretary, affirming the ALJ's decision in all respects.

Appellant then sought relief in the district court and from that court's order took the instant appeal.

II.

In support of appellant's contention that the disbarment decision should be overturned, the principal argument is that collateral estoppel prevents his being disbarred for bribery and conspiracy to bribe, since he was acquitted of those charges at his prior criminal trial. This acquittal, appellant reasons, "definitively" establishes that he was entrapped by the IRS into paying the bribe, because at his trial appellant admitted the payment and relied wholly on an entrapment defense. Appellant's legal premise, however, is clearly wrong. The standard of proof in a criminal trial is guilt beyond a reasonable doubt. In re Winship, 397 U.S. 358, 364, 25 L. Ed. 2d 368, 90 S. Ct. 1068 (1970). An acquittal in such a trial, under such a standard, cannot control a subsequent disbarment proceeding, in which a lower standard of proof is required, *see* In re Echeles, 430 F.2d 347, 352–53 (7th Cir. 1970); In re Doe, 95 F.2d 386, 387 (2d Cir. 1938) (per curiam). *See generally* One Lot Emerald Cut Stones and One Ring v. United States, 409 U.S. 232, 235, 34 L. Ed. 2d 438, 93 S. Ct. 489 (1972) (per curiam); United States v. National Association of Real Estate Boards, 339 U.S. 485, 492–94, 94 L. Ed. 1007, 70 S. Ct. 711 (1950); Helvering v. Mitchell, 303 U.S. 391, 397–98, 82 L. Ed. 917, 58 S. Ct. 630 (1938); Neaderland v. Commissioner, 424 F.2d 639, 642–43 (2d Cir.), *cert. denied*, 400 U.S. 827, 27 L. Ed. 2d 56, 91 S. Ct. 53 (1970). Moreover, the issue in a disbarment proceeding is essentially fitness to practice, rather than the criminality of the acts involved. *See* Bar Association v. Anonymous Attorneys, 41 N.Y.2d 506, 362 N.E.2d 592, 393 N.Y.S.2d 961, 45 U.S.L.W. 2478 (1977) (per curiam).

Even were appellant's legal premise correct, however, his factual premise that the jury's verdict constituted a finding of entrapment is clearly incorrect in the circumstances of this case. As noted above, the jury at appellant's trial, while acquitting him of the bribery charges, found him guilty of giving the IRS agent a gratuity. This court later stated that the jury's verdict amounted to "a compromise." United States v. Harary, *supra*, 457 F.2d at 479. The jury, in the court's view, could not rationally have concluded that appellant had been entrapped by the IRS into giving a bribe but not entrapped into giving a gratuity. *Id.* at 478. From such a compromise verdict it cannot be said that the question of entrapment was "necessarily determined" against the Government, as is required to support a later holding of collateral estoppel, *see* United States v. Kramer, 289 F.2d 909, 916 (2d Cir. 1961); 2 C. Wright, Federal Practice and Procedure § 468, at 263 (1969), nor can it be said that a finding of entrapment was the only one consistent with the evidence and the verdict, *compare* Sealfon v. United States, 332 U.S. 575, 579–80, 92 L. Ed. 180, 68 S. Ct. 237 (1948); United States v. Kramer, *supra*, 289 F.2d at 914–15. Under these circumstances, when it is uncertain exactly what the jury decided on a particular issue in a prior criminal action, the issue may be relitigated in a later, noncriminal action. *See* United States v. Davis, 460 F.2d 792, 799 (4th Cir. 1972)[n.2]

III.

As a separate ground for disbarring appellant, a ground unrelated to his prior criminal trial, the Secretary held that appellant had willfully deceived his client. As stated above, appellant told his client that the IRS agent had to be paid $2,000, but appellant in fact paid the agent $1,250, pocketing the $750 difference for himself. The Secretary held that this conduct violated 31 C.F.R. § 10.22(c), which requires that each attorney, certified public accountant or enrolled agent "exercise due diligence . . . in determining the correctness of oral or written representations made by him to clients with reference to any matter administered by the Internal Revenue Service." Appellant argues that this regulation has not been violated or, in the alternative, that the regulation is unconstitutionally vague.

With regard to the first point, appellant's position is that 31 C.F.R. § 10.22(c) was not meant to apply to conduct of the type here involved. A requirement that practitioners before the IRS make correct representations to clients with regard to illegal courses of conduct, appellant reasons, would encourage illegality by practitioners in situations in which it could otherwise be avoided. He cites the hypothetical example of an IRS agent soliciting a bribe from an accountant and argues that, under the Secretary's interpretation of the regulation, the accountant could be disbarred for failing truthfully to communicate the criminal overture to his client. We need not determine the correctness of appellant's resolution of the hypothetical, for, even if he were correct that the overture had to be reported to the client, the accountant would also have an obligation to advise his client against participation and to report the entire matter to the proper officials of the IRS. *See* 31 C.F.R. § 10.51(d), (f). Hence there would be no fostering of illegality unless the accountant were already so disposed.

The regulation at issue, 31 C.F.R. § 10.22(c), requires, quite simply, that a representative be honest with his clients in connection with all IRS-related matters. While the phrasing of the regulation ("due diligence in determining correctness") suggests a principal concern with making representatives accountable for negligence, nothing in the regulation limits it to cases of negligence. The term "diligence" carries connotations of loyalty and devotion as well as care and prudence. A deliberate conveying of misinformation is certainly more opprobrious conduct than a careless misrepresentation. Appellant does not dispute the fact that he was deliberately dishonest with his client

---

[n.2] Appellant argues that this court should not consider the inconsistency in the jury's verdict at his trial, but rather should look only at the acquittal, because it was the Government's "misguided trial tactics," United States v. Harary, 457 F.2d 471, 477 (2d Cir. 1972), pursued over appellant's objections, *see id.* at 479, that led to submitting the gratuity count to the jury, which in turn led to the compromise verdict. The collateral estoppel requirement that an issue actually be determined in the prior proceeding, however, cannot be overlooked simply because the trial strategy used in good faith by the party against whom estoppel is sought is held on appeal (here by a 2-1 panel majority) to have been erroneous. It is not certain here, moreover, that the jurors would have acquitted appellant of bribery if they had not had the gratuity alternative available to them. * * *

and, since the dishonesty related to an IRS agent's audit, it was plainly a representation "with reference to [a] matter administered by the [IRS]." Appellant accordingly violated 31 C.F.R. § 10.22(c).

In view of our construction of the regulation, appellant's vagueness argument is rejected. He contends that the words of the regulation did not give notice that a misrepresentation to a client in connection with an audit could lead to disbarment. Apart from the fact that every professional knows or should know that cheating a client can lead to disbarment, the regulation here gave quite specific notice that representations to clients must be correct with regard to a wide but clearly defined range of matters.

Judgment affirmed.

————————————

Do you agree that disbarment was an appropriate sanction for the misconduct in *Harary*?

Would a special agent of the IRS who accepted a bribe be in violation of applicable law? *See* 18 U.S.C. § 201.

[2] Practice Before the Tax Court

In Tax Court, unlike in District Court and the Court of Federal Claims, taxpayers may be represented not only by attorneys admitted to practice before the Tax Court, but also by other individuals, including accountants, who have passed an examination. *See* Tax Court Rule 200. Under Tax Court Rule 202, the court "may deny admission to its Bar to, or suspend, or disbar, any person who in its judgment does not possess the requisite qualifications to represent others, or who is lacking in character, integrity, or proper professional conduct." Tax Court Rule 201(a) provides, "Practitioners before the Court shall carry on their practice in accordance with the letter and spirit of the Model Rules of Professional Conduct of the American Bar Association."

As reflected above, Circular 230 prohibits a practitioner from representing conflicting interests in practice before the IRS without full disclosure and consent of the interested parties. *See* 31 C.F.R. 10.29. Similarly, ethical rules applicable to attorneys, such as the Model Rules of Professional Conduct, reflect concern for conflicting loyalties that may arise out of multiple representation. Conflict of interest issues that may arise out of multiple representation are discussed in the following case. Note who requested the disqualification of the attorney, Mr. Izen, and the Tax Court's response to that fact.

PARA TECHNOLOGIES TRUST v. COMMISSIONER
United States Tax Court
T.C. Memo. 1992-575

COHEN, JUDGE:

Each of these [consolidated] cases is before the Court for ruling on respondent's Motion to Compel Withdrawal of Petitioners' Counsel of Record for Conflict of Interest. The issue for decision is whether a conflict of interest exists that requires the disqualification of petitioners' counsel of record. * * *

BACKGROUND

Nassau Life Insurance Company, Ltd. (Nassau Life), promoted the use of domestic and foreign entities to shelter United States business and investment income from United States Federal income taxation. Nassau Life engaged in this activity through representatives known as "information officers" and through the dissemination of printed materials. From 1982 through 1988, Joe Alfred Izen, Jr. (Izen), was counsel to Nassau Life. In the course of that representation, among other services, he prepared and issued two opinion letters that related to the multiple-entity tax shelter promoted by Nassau Life. In a legal opinion letter dated September 26, 1983, Izen discussed the legal status of "contractual trust companies" that were being promoted by Nassau Life (the 1983 opinion letter).

[Petitioner] Ferber is a songwriter with a high school education. [Petitioner] Anderson completed the eighth grade. At the time of hearing on the pending motions, Ferber was 36 years old and Anderson was 30 years old.

Ferber and Anderson met in India in 1977 and became friends. In late 1984, Anderson began to engage in an electronics business, VideoLab, as a sole proprietor. Because of his limited education, Anderson wanted to adopt a structure for VideoLab that would minimize the amount of paperwork that was necessary to carry on the business. He discussed his plans with Ferber, who was then employed as an information officer for Nassau Life. Ferber, relying at least partially on the 1983 opinion letter, advised Anderson, who also had access to the 1983 opinion letter, to structure his business as a trust such as those promoted by Nassau Life.

In January 1985, Anderson formed Para Technologies (Para Tech) as a common-law business trust. From its creation and thereafter, Para Tech conducted the business in which VideoLab had previously been engaged. Ferber was the trustee of Para Tech. The beneficial owner of Para Tech was another trust, Atram Investment Group (Atram), formed under the laws of the Turks and Caicos Islands, British West Indies. Anderson was one of the beneficiaries of Atram.

In a legal opinion letter prepared for Nassau Life dated June 20, 1985, Izen discussed the tax aspects of contractual trust companies (the 1985 opinion letter). Among other things, the letter concluded that the grantor trust provisions of the Internal Revenue Code did not apply to "contractual trust companies." Izen's letter failed to discuss decided cases contrary to the positions he was espousing. Anderson and Ferber gained access to the 1985 opinion letter.

Respondent determined deficiencies in petitioners' Federal income taxes for 1987 and 1988. Respondent determined that Para Tech was an association taxable as a corporation for Federal income tax purposes and disallowed its claimed distribution deductions. Respondent determined that Anderson and Ferber were each taxable on an amount equal to the taxable income of Para Tech. Respondent asserted three alternative theories in support of this determination. First, because Para Tech should be taxed as a corporation and because of their control over Para Tech and Atram, Anderson and Ferber were in constructive receipt of dividend income equal to the amounts transferred from Para Tech to Atram. Second, if Para Tech was a trust, it was a grantor trust owned by Anderson and Ferber, who were therefore taxable on Para Tech's income. Third, because both Para Tech and Atram were sham entities that should be disregarded for Federal income tax purposes, Anderson and Ferber are taxable on the income from Para Tech's business. Respondent also determined that all three petitioners are liable for additions to tax for fraud.

Para Tech, Anderson, and Ferber filed petitions for redetermination with this Court. Izen is counsel of record for petitioners in these cases. Nassau Life is bankrupt. All legal fees are being paid by Para Tech. No discovery and no settlement negotiations have taken place, and none of the cases has been set for trial.

Respondent's counsel in these cases wrote letters to Izen dated September 19, 1991, and November 15, 1991, questioning Izen regarding possible conflicts of interest in his representation of petitioners. Izen did not respond to these letters. Respondent, therefore, moved the Court to compel withdrawal of Izen as petitioners' counsel.

DISCUSSION

Petitioners contend, based on *Appeal of Infotechnology, Inc.*, 582 A.2d 215 (Del. Super. 1990), that respondent lacks standing to make this motion because a nonclient litigant does not have the power to enforce a technical violation of the Model Rules of Professional Conduct (Model Rules). These cases, however, are distinguishable from *Appeal of Infotechnology, Inc., supra*, in which the court held that it had "become apparent that * * * [the opposing party] was seeking to use disqualification as a litigation tactic." *Id.* at 221. The Court is generally reluctant to disqualify counsel of a taxpayer's choice on motion of the adversary. *See* Alexander v. Superior Court, 685 P.2d 1309, 1317 (Ariz. 1984). In these cases, however, respondent promptly moved for disqualification prior to conducting discovery or engaging in settlement negotiations and before these cases were set for trial. *See* Duffey v. Commissioner, 91 T.C. 81, 84 (1988).

Rule 201(a) provides that "Practitioners before the Court shall carry on their practice in accordance with the letter and spirit of the Model Rules." This Court, therefore, has the power to compel withdrawal of petitioners' counsel if such representation would violate the Model Rules. Specifically, Rule 24(f) provides:

> If any counsel of record (1) was involved in planning or promoting a transaction or operating an entity that is connected to any issue in a case, [or] (2) represents more than one person with differing interests with respect to any issue in a case, * * * then such counsel must either secure the informed consent of the client * * *; withdraw from the case; or take whatever other steps are necessary to obviate a conflict of interest or other violation of the ABA Model Rules of Professional Conduct, and particularly [Rule] 1.7 * * *

Rule 24(f), which became effective July 1, 1990, emphasizes the provisions of the Model Rules to which practitioners before this Court were already subject. Rule 24(f) was added "to insure that the bar of this Court disclose or rectify any conflict of interest." Rules of Practice and Procedure of the United States Tax Court, 93 T.C. 821, 858 Note.

Model Rule 1.7(b) provides:

> A lawyer shall not represent a client if the representation of that client may be materially limited by the lawyer's responsibilities to another client or to a third person, or by the lawyer's own interests, unless:
>
> (1) the lawyer reasonably believes the representation will not be adversely affected; and
>
> (2) the client consents after consultation. When representation of multiple clients in a single matter is undertaken, the consultation shall include explanation of the implications of the common representation and the advantages and risks involved.

Petitioners contend that Izen's representation of them does not violate Model Rule 1.7(b) because no potential conflict of interest exists among petitioners. Petitioners contend that each petitioner is contesting the deficiency and will argue that Para Tech should be recognized as a trust and that Para Tech's Federal income tax returns for 1987 and 1988 were correct.

Respondent contends that Izen's representation of each petitioner may be materially limited by his responsibilities to the other petitioners and by his own interests. Respondent states:

> There are positions which can be advanced on behalf of each Petitioner which, if established, would enable that Petitioner to avoid liability for all or part of the deficiencies and additions to tax determined against that Petitioner, but which cannot be established without irreparably damaging some other Petitioner's case.

As set forth above, respondent determined that Anderson and Ferber were each taxable on an amount equal to the taxable income of Para Tech. One of respondent's alternative theories is that Para Tech is a grantor trust. Generally, the grantor trust rules apply to a person, such as Anderson, who created the trust. *See* secs. 671 through 678. Anderson formed the trust and transferred his business to it and is a beneficiary of the trust. Ferber, although serving as a trustee, is less likely to be a grantor. Ferber, and, hypothetically, Para Tech, would avoid taxation if respondent successfully established that the income was taxable to Anderson as the grantor.

Further, respondent has determined that each petitioner is liable for the additions to tax for fraud. In support of that determination, respondent's answer alleges that books and records made available to respondent during the examination of petitioners' returns were false and fraudulent, that petitioners "individually and in concert, refused to cooperate with Respondent's agents and attempted to obstruct Respondent's examination by various means," and that each petitioner understated or failed to report taxable income and tax due from them. In this regard, Anderson and Ferber can each argue that the other was responsible for maintaining the books and records of Para Tech and for preparing its tax returns and that each relied on the other. Each may also claim that he relied on Izen's opinion letters. In addition, Ferber, as trustee of Para Tech, is putatively making decisions for Para Tech, including using its funds to pay for litigation of these cases, while Anderson, not Ferber, has a beneficial interest in Para Tech.

Although it is too early in this litigation to anticipate all of the arguments that will be made, and the foregoing possibilities may not be the positions that petitioners should or will adopt at trial, there is a serious possibility that petitioners' positions may become adverse to each other. *See* Figueroa-Olmo v. Westinghouse Elec. Corp., 616 F. Supp. 1445, 1451–1454 (D. Puerto Rico 1985); Shadid v. Jackson, 521 F. Supp. 87, 89 (E.D. Tex. 1981).

* * *

We are not persuaded that Izen made a full and fair disclosure or that petitioners understood the inherent potential conflicts between them. The backgrounds of the individuals suggest a lack of sophistication in assessing matters such as these, and they relied solely on the advice of Izen in deciding to waive the conflicts of interest. Compare Adams v. Commissioner, 85 T.C. at 372–374 (holding that taxpayers could not be relieved of a settlement agreement based on their attorney's conflict of interest because taxpayers were sophisticated, knew all of the relevant facts, and had been advised by independent counsel before employing the author of an opinion letter). It appears to us that the waiver is not based on informed consent but on the cost of employing independent and separate counsel and having such counsel become familiar with the underlying facts of the cases.

Izen admitted during the hearing on respondent's motion that he had not secured written consents or waivers from petitioners and that he had not contacted Nassau Life or other beneficiaries of the Para Tech trust. Under these circumstances, we conclude that it is "more important that unethical conduct be prevented than * * * [that petitioners] have an unfettered right to counsel of * * * [their] choice." Kevlik v. Goldstein, 724 F.2d 844, 849 (1st Cir. 1984). The potential for unfairness to petitioners and damage to the integrity of the judicial process is too serious to permit Izen's representation of petitioners to continue, even in the face of an apparent waiver. Figueroa-Olmo v. Westinghouse Elec. Corp., *supra* at 1451; Shadid v. Jackson, *supra* at 90; and Model Rules Rule 1.7 comment (1983) (stating that, "when a disinterested lawyer would conclude that the client should not agree to representation under the circumstances, the lawyer involved cannot * * * provide representation on the basis of the client's consent.")

Therefore, Izen must be disqualified from representing petitioners in these cases.

Respondent's motions will be granted.

Multiple representation is not the only ethical issue that may arise in practice and that is addressed by *Para Technologies Trust.* As the case indicates, Mr. Izen was not only representing Mr. Anderson and Mr. Farber in Tax

Court; he had also drafted the opinion letters on which they may have relied in creating the trust. What conflict of interest issues might that create? The court addresses those issues as follows:

> Izen's personal interests in this case may also conflict with the interests of petitioners. Anderson and Ferber relied, at least partially, on opinion letters that Izen had written. Therefore, Izen has an interest in vindicating the positions he took in the opinion letters in order to maintain his professional reputation and to protect himself from any potential future liability to petitioners. *See, e.g.,* Eisenberg v. Gagnon, 766 F.2d 770, 779–780 (3d Cir. 1985) (holding that investors in a tax shelter could recover from an attorney who had misrepresented facts relating to the tax shelter). He would therefore be less likely to advise petitioners disinterestedly with regard to such matters as accepting a settlement offer. *See* Model Rules Rule 1.7(a) and 1.7 comment (1983) (stating that, "If the probity of a lawyer's own conduct in a transaction is in serious question, it may be difficult or impossible for the lawyer to give a client detached advice."). *See also* Adams v. Commissioner, 85 T.C. 359, 372–373 (1985). Izen's failure to advise petitioners of the potential adverse defenses or affirmative claims available to them would constitute a breach of his duty of loyalty to them. Figueroa-Olmo v. Westinghouse Elec. Corp., *supra* at 1453–1454; Eriks v. Denver, 824 P.2d 1207, 1211–1212 (Wash. 1992) (citing Model Rules Rule 1.7 comment (1984) and holding that as a matter of law there was a conflict of interest between promoters of and investors in a tax shelter). Finally, Izen is potentially a witness with respect to matters set forth in his tax opinion, and testimony on that subject could appropriately be obtained without violation of the attorney-client privilege. *See* In re Grand Jury Proceedings, 727 F.2d 1352 (4th Cir. 1984); and United States v. Jones, 696 F.2d 1069 (4th Cir. 1982).

> Izen and petitioners contend that petitioners have been informed of and waive Izen's conflict of interest. We are not persuaded, however, that the apparent consent of petitioners is informed and voluntary. * * *

Id.

Tax Court Rule 202, quoted at the beginning of this section, reflects the Tax Court's power to disbar members lacking in the requisite qualifications or character. Should an attorney be disbarred from the Tax Court automatically upon disbarment from a State bar? Consider the following case:

IN RE **WINTHROP DRAKE THIES**
United States Court of Appeals, District of Columbia Circuit
662 F.2d 771 (1980)

Per Curiam:

Appellant was disbarred by the United States Tax Court on August 9, 1979. The court relied exclusively on appellant's 1978 automatic disbarment from the New York State courts, which followed his 1976 felony conviction for assaulting a federal officer. The sole issue on this appeal is whether the Tax Court's exclusive reliance on the state disbarment was error.

In *Selling v. Radford*, 243 U.S. 46 (1971), the Supreme Court considered the effect of disbarment from state court in a federal disbarment action. The Court found that although admission to a state bar may be a predicate to admission to a federal bar, a state disbarment order does not automatically bind a federal court. The Court reconciled the interest in judicial economy with the "quasi-criminal nature" of a disbarment proceeding, and concluded that a state disbarment gives rise to a rebuttable presumption that an attorney lacks the "private and professional character" to remain a member of the federal bar.

The federal court should give conclusive effect to this presumption of unfitness

> unless, from an intrinsic consideration of the state record, one or all of the following conditions should appear: 1. That the state procedure from want of notice or opportunity to be heard was wanting in due process; 2. that there was such an infirmity of proof as to facts found . . . that we could not . . . accept as final the conclusion on [the attorney's lack of character]; 3. that some other grave reason existed [which would make disbarment inconsistent with] principles of right and justice . . . [*Selling*, 243 U.S. at 51.]

The relevant facts are undisputed. On November 22, 1976, Thies was convicted of assaulting a federal officer in violation of 18 U.S.C. § 111 (1978).[5] This conviction was affirmed on December 5, 1977. Thies was subsequently convicted of selling stolen securities, but this conviction was overturned on appeal. On March 13, 1978, the New York State Appellate Division disbarred Thies without a hearing on the ground that § 90(4) of the New York Judiciary Law mandated automatic disbarment upon any felony conviction. The State court initially relied on both convictions, but later amended its judgment when the second conviction was reversed.

The Tax Court, without prior notice, suspended Thies from practice on April 24, 1978, and directed him to show cause why he should not be disbarred. Both the suspension and the show cause order cited only the state disbarment. The appellant requested a hearing, which was held in January 1979.[11]

---

[5] The sentencing judge characterized the incident underlying this conviction as a "kindergarten shouting and pushing match," and concluded that "a five hundred dollar fine would be sufficient punishment for Mr. Thies's fit of pique and temper. . . ." *See* Memorandum in Support of Petitioner's Application for Reinstatement (Jan. 10, 1979), p. 6–7 (Record Document No. 10).

[11] A letter to the appellant from the Chairman of the Tax Court's Committee on Admission and Discipline accompanied the notice of the January hearing. The letter advised appellant, in pertinent part, that

> since you were admitted to practice before this Court because of being an attorney in good standing of the New York bar, it would appear that regardless of the evidence you might be able to produce at a hearing before this Court, your suspension could not be lifted and you should be disbarred because of not now possessing the qualifications required for your admission. The Committee considered it appropriate to call the matter stated to your attention so that you could, if you chose, in lieu of

Appellant contends that if the Tax Court made and relied on independent factual findings, he was denied due process because he received inadequate notice of the hearing.[12] Counsel for the appellee acknowledged that the Tax Court relied exclusively on the state disbarment. The court's order cites only the state disbarment, and contains no findings other than a bare statement that the *Selling v. Radford* criteria were satisfied.

We find that, in these circumstances, the Tax Court erred in its exclusive reliance on the state disbarment. The state court did not offer appellant the procedural guarantees specified by *Selling v. Radford*.[14] No hearing was held. Instead, the disbarment followed automatically upon Thies' felony conviction. Nor was the state's "conclusion on [Thies'] character" supported by recorded findings; the state made no factual findings whatsoever. Accordingly, we need not consider the third factor listed in *Selling*: whether under all of the circumstances,[16] Thies' disbarment from federal court would violate principles of "right and justice."

The order of the Tax Court is vacated.

Tax Court Rule 202(a) provides, in part:

> Upon the conviction of any practitioner admitted to practice before this Court for a criminal violation of any provision of the Internal Revenue Code or for any crime involving moral turpitude, or where any practitioner has been suspended or disbarred from the practice of his or her profession in any State or the District of Columbia, or

---

appearing at the hearing . . . submit your written resignation from the bar of the United States Tax Court. . . .

Letter from Judge Irene F. Scott to Winthrop D. Thies (Dec. 18, 1978). J.A. at 25–26.

[12] A lawyer facing disbarment is "entitled to procedural due process, which includes fair notice of the charge." In Re Ruffalo, 390 U.S. 544, 550 (1968). The transcript of the appellant's hearing before the Tax Court suggests that some members of the court considered the appellant's second conviction relevant to his federal disbarment. *See* J.A. at 51, 94. Appellant contends, however, that due process barred reliance on the second conviction because neither the original suspension nor the show cause order referred to the second conviction in the "charge" of unfitness.

The suspension notice and show cause order did refer to the first conviction, but the appellant contends that Judge Scott's letter, *see* note 11 *supra*, hardly provided fair notice that the court would make independent factual findings. The appellee notes that Judge Scott sought to clarify her position when the hearing began, *see* J.A. at 32. *But cf.* In Re Ruffalo, 390 U.S. 544, 551–52 (1968).

[14] "It is not for this [court] . . . to sit in judgment on [New York] disbarments. . . ." Theard v. United States, 354 U.S. 278, 281 (1957); *see* In Re Ruffalo, 390 U.S. 544, 552 (Harlan, J., concurring). All we decide is that the process which was afforded the appellant by the state court "should not be accepted as adequate for the purposes of disbarment from a federal court." *Id.* *Cf.* Restatement (Second) of Judgments § 68.1(c) (Tent. Draft No. 4, 1977) ("New determination of issue . . . warranted by differences in quality or extensiveness of the procedures followed in the two courts. . . .").

[16] Appellant contends that because his conviction for selling stolen securities was vacated, it has no probative value in a disbarment action, *cf.* Restatement (Second) of Judgments § 68.1(a) (Tent. Draft No. 1, 1973). We find no evidence that the Tax Court relied on anything other than the state disbarment, *see* p. 773 *supra*, and express no view regarding what the court may consider in any future action.

any commonwealth, territory, or possession of the United States, the Court may, in the exercise of its discretion, forthwith suspend such practitioner from the Bar of this Court until further order of Court; but otherwise no person shall be suspended for more than 60 days or disbarred until such person has been afforded an opportunity to be heard. A Judge of the Court may immediately suspend any person for not more than 60 days for contempt or misconduct during the course of any trial or hearing.

Does this rule comport with the *Selling v. Radford* criteria discussed in *Thies*?

Tax Court disciplinary and disbarment proceedings function as follows: When misconduct or allegations of misconduct come to the attention of the Tax Court, the court has the discretion to refer the matter to counsel for the Tax Court for investigation and a formal disciplinary proceeding. To initiate disciplinary proceedings, the court enters an order requiring the practitioner to show cause within 30 days why the practitioner should not be disciplined. If the practitioner's answer to the order to show cause raises any issue of fact, or if the practitioner wishes to be heard in mitigation, then the court sets the matter for hearing before a Tax Court judge or judges. *See* Tax Court Rule 202(b). A practitioner suspended for 60 or fewer days is automatically reinstated to the Tax Court bar after the suspension period elapses. A practitioner suspended for more than 60 days or disbarred from the Tax Court may not resume practice before the Tax Court until he is reinstated by a Tax Court order. Tax Court Rule 202(c)(1).

§ 1.07 Tension Between Tax Lawyers and Accountants

As noted above, nonlawyers are authorized to practice tax law by representing taxpayers in certain administrative and judicial proceedings. For example, the United States Code authorizes accountants to practice before the IRS, *see* 5 U.S.C. § 500, and Circular 230 allows other individuals to become enrolled agents. *See* 31 C.F.R. § 10.4. Similarly, Tax Court Rule 200 allows nonlawyers who pass an exam to practice before the Tax Court. Because these rules are relatively clear, there are few direct disputes between lawyers and nonlawyers over the practice of tax law before the IRS or the Tax Court. Nonetheless, there is a longstanding turf war between lawyers and accountants. Consider this short article:

WHY DO LAWYERS AND ACCOUNTANTS FIGHT?*
24 Tax Notes 823 (1984)
By Lee A. Sheppard

I vividly remember how, in a very impressionable period in my life, I told a very old and respected tax lawyer that I wanted to practice tax law. It was one of those quasi-social situations where you had to make the right conversation. "Are you a CPA?" was his only comment. "No" was the wrong answer. That should have told me something.

---

* Copyright 1984 Tax Analysts. Used with permission.

Since the late forties, there has existed a group called the National Conference of Lawyers and Certified Public Accountants (NCLCPA), in which equal numbers of ABA and AICPA members are represented. Their purpose is to discuss the same issue that doctors and dentists fought about at the beginning of this century — that one group is practicing the other's profession. Like dentists, CPAs believe that they can practice tax law, and are able to represent clients before Treasury, and some are permitted to practice before the Tax Court. CPAs are, it seems, so complacent about their right to do so that Albert B. Ellentuck, Chairman of the AICPA Federal Tax Division, declined to appear at an August 4 ABA Tax Section panel discussion of the issue at the ABA annual convention in Chicago. Ellentuck's reason for not appearing was that the discussion would be "inappropriate" at that time and place. Bernard Barnett, AICPA liaison to the ABA Tax Section, was in the audience. (Ellentuck and Barnett were on vacation when this article was being written.)

What Ellentuck might have said is contained in two columns in the AICPA Federal Tax Division Newsletter written by him and his predecessor, William L. Raby. CPAs fervently believe that, in the tax area, they are advocates for their clients rather than independent public watchdogs, as they are in the area of financial audits. Hence it is no wonder that the Supreme Court's perception of the proper role of CPAs in its *Arthur Young*[20] opinion distresses them. * * * Ellentuck's column talks about CPAs resisting the IRS attempts to get them to discourage their clients from aggressive return positions pursuant to the penalty provisions of [the Code]. Raby goes even further, seeing the world of professional tax advice in terms of a battle for business among CPAs, lawyers, financial planners and tax preparers.

Everybody in His Place

K. Martin Worthy of Hamel & Park in Washington, D.C., began the discussion with a history of the NCLCPA, noting that many of the problems that lawyers have with accountants practicing law is due to the failure of accountants themselves to distinguish between CPAs (certified public accountants, who must adhere to higher standards) and mere accountants. The NCLCPA has produced a plethora of non-binding (for antitrust reasons) platitudes about how, in tax and estate planning matters, lawyers and CPAs must advise a client that the presence of the other professional is necessary at the outset of a project. Lawyers, says the NCLCPA, are supposed to prepare legal documents, and CPAs are supposed to prepare financial statements. All well and good; everybody in his place.

The situation gets sticky before Treasury and the Tax Court, where non-lawyers are admitted to represent clients. Raby refers to this as the "authorized" practice of law. The Tax Court * * * would prefer that only lawyers come before it, now that it is an Article I court. The effort to allow CPAs to practice before it recently failed. (Note, however, that taxpayers may also represent themselves before the Tax Court, and many of them do.)

Raby and the ABA panel both point out another item of concern to lawyers, the fact that many CPAs, and all of the Big Eight,[21] write tax opinions for

---

[20] [*United States v. Arthur Young & Co.*, 465 U.S. 805 (1984), is discussed further below and in Chapter 14. Eds.]

[21] [Now the Big Five. Eds.]

use by third parties in tax shelter deals. Treasury Circular 230 does not, according to panelist Steven C. Salch, of Houston, contemplate this because it invokes local law, but holds any opinion writer to the same standard. "We are not about to abandon the tax practice field to anyone," Raby wrote, by which he meant third-party tax opinions and planning. Citing *Arthur Young*, Worthy openly disagreed with Raby's statement about the established right of CPAs to render third-party tax opinions, saying that investors should not see CPAs as advocates for management. Maybe Worthy was not at the *Arthur Young* argument when Justice John Paul Stevens casually observed that CPAs practice more tax law than do lawyers.

———————————

The *Arthur Young* opinion referred to in Lee Sheppard's article, set out above, involved the question of whether tax accrual workpapers prepared by accountants were subject to a privilege similar to the work product privilege that applies to attorneys. In holding that accrual workpapers had to be turned over to the IRS, the Court refused to recognize a work product privilege for accountants. The Supreme Court's statements in *Arthur Young* that have generated so much conflict relate to the proper role of attorneys and accountants in the self-assessment system:

> [The W]ork-product doctrine was founded upon the private attorney's role as the client's confidential advisor and advocate, a loyal representative whose duty it is to present the client's case in the most favorable possible light. An independent certified public accountant performs a different role. By certifying the public reports that collectively depict a corporation's financial status, the independent auditor assumes a *public* responsibility transcending any employment relationship with the client. The independent public accountant performing this special function owes ultimate allegiance to the corporation's creditors and stockholders, as well as to the investing public. This "public watchdog" function demands that the accountant maintain total independence from the client at all times and requires complete fidelity to the public trust. To insulate from disclosure a certified public accountant's interpretations of the client's financial statements would be to ignore the significance of the accountant's role as a disinterested analyst charged with public obligations.

United States v. Arthur Young & Co., 465 U.S. 805, 817–18 (1984).

Although courts do not recognize an accountant work product privilege, they have recognized that accountant-client communications could, in certain circumstances, fall within the protection of the attorney-client privilege, as explained in the following excerpt:

> It is well established that no accountant-client privilege existed at common law. *See* United States v. Arthur Young & Co., 465 U.S. 805 (1984); United States v. Mullen & Co., 776 F. Supp. 620, 621 (D. Mass. 1991). * * * However, while no privilege "attaches specifically to an accountant/client communication, such matters may be withheld if

they meet the traditional requirements of the attorney/client privilege." *Mullen & Co.*, 776 F. Supp. at 621 (*quoting* Summit Ltd. v. Levy, 111 F.R.D. 40, 41 (S.D.N.Y. 1986)).

To determine whether the attorney-client privilege exists, the First Circuit applies the elements set forth in *United States v. Massachusetts Inst. of Tech*, 129 F.3d 681 (1st Cir. 1997):

> (1) Where legal advice of any kind is sought (2) from a professional legal adviser in his capacity as such, (3) the communications relating to that purpose, (4) made in confidence (5) by the client, (6) are at his instance permanently protected (7) from disclosure by himself or by the legal adviser, (8) except the protection may be waived.

Id. at 684 (*quoting* 8 J. Wigmore, EVIDENCE § 2292, at 554 (McNaughton rev. 1961)). The rationale behind the attorney-client privilege is straightforward: "by safeguarding communications between lawyer and client, [the privilege] encourages disclosures by client to lawyer that better enable the client to conform his conduct to the requirements of the law and to present legitimate claims or defenses when litigation arises." *Id.* (*citing* Upjohn Co. v. United States, 449 U.S. 383 (1981)). Although the attorney-client privilege is well established, it is narrowly construed because any expansion of the privilege hinders the Court in its search for truth. *See id.* at 684–85.

Some courts have been willing to extend this privilege to certain accountant communications, recognizing that "the complexities of modern existence prevent attorneys from effectively handling clients' affairs without the help of others." United States v. Kovel, 296 F.2d 918, 921 (2d Cir. 1961). In *Kovel*, which both parties recognize as the leading case, an accountant who was employed by a law firm refused to answer questions before a grand jury investigating federal income tax violations by the law firm's client. *See id.* at 919. Analogizing the accountant's role to that of an interpreter who performs "a menial or ministerial responsibility" to translate communications for an attorney, the Second Circuit held that the attorney-client privilege was not destroyed by the presence of an accountant who is "necessary, or at least highly useful, for the effective consultation between the client and the lawyer." *Id.* at 921–22. "[T]he presence of an accountant, whether hired by the lawyer or by the client, while the client is relating a complicated tax story to the lawyer, ought not destroy the privilege, any more than would that of the linguist . . . ." *Id.* at 922. *Kovel* limits the privilege to situations where "the communication [is] made in confidence *for the purpose of obtaining legal advice from the lawyer.*" *Id.* (emphasis added). "If what is sought is not legal advice but only accounting service . . . , or if the advice sought is the accountant's rather than the lawyer's, no privilege exists." *Id.*

Cavallaro v. United States, 153 F. Supp. 2d 52, 56–57 (2001). To help ensure that the accountant's advice came within the scope of the attorney-client privilege, the attorney would often use an agreement under which the attorney retained the accountant to assist the attorney in providing legal advice to the client. These agreements are known as *Kovel* agreements. *See* John A.

Townsend, "Audits and Appeals: Developments," 54 N.Y.U. Ann. Inst. Fed. Tax'n § 26.03, at 26–27 (1996).

Non-attorneys have continued to seek greater rights in the practice of tax law. In what some attorneys consider a disturbing move, Congress passed, as part of IRS reform, a tax practitioner-client privilege applicable to individuals authorized to practice before the IRS. Code section 7525 provides that, in certain contexts, "With respect to tax advice, the same common law protections of confidentiality which apply to a communication between a taxpayer and an attorney shall also apply to a communication between a taxpayer and any federally authorized tax practitioner to the extent the communication would be considered a privileged communication if it were between a taxpayer and an attorney." Lee Sheppard believes that Code section 7525 has not accomplished much for non-lawyers, as reflected in the following excerpt. Do you agree?

WHAT TAX ADVICE PRIVILEGE?[*]
80 Tax Notes 9 (1998)
By Lee A. Sheppard

The Supreme Court has just told us that the attorney-client privilege survives the death of the client.[22] The privilege does not, however, survive the filing of the client's tax return.

That is, accountants and others licensed to practice before the IRS got a lot less than they bargained for when Congress granted them a privilege co-extensive with the attorney-client privilege in tax cases. New code section 7525 states: "With respect to tax advice, the same common law protections of confidentiality which apply to a communication between a taxpayer and an attorney shall also apply to a communication between a taxpayer and any federally authorized tax practitioner to the extent that the communication would be considered a privileged communication if it were between a taxpayer and an attorney."

Congress briefly considered the very sensible alternative of denying all tax advisers, including lawyers, the privilege for tax shelter advice. The lawyers, through the American Bar Association, threw a fit about that alternative, and have opposed new code section 7525. They need not have bothered. The federal case law that interprets the privilege shows that it is far narrower in tax cases than is widely assumed. The operative words in code section 7525 are "to the extent that the communication would be considered a privileged communication if it were between a taxpayer and an attorney." That extent is not very great in tax cases, as this article will show.

The functions that tax advisers perform can be seen as a continuum between tax return preparation and litigation. Return preparation is not privileged; litigation is protected by the attorney-client privilege and the work product doctrine. In between those two extremes is a gray area called tax planning, which lawyers seem to believe is protected by the privilege, and accountants

---

[*] Copyright 1998 Tax Analysts. Used with permission.

[22] [See Swidler & Berlin and James Hamilton v. United States, 524 U.S. 399 (1998). Eds.]

hope to have protected by their own new privilege. In this gray area are tax shelter opinions, which accountants hoped to have protected by their new privilege, but were excluded at the last minute. * * *

Return Preparation

The history of the application of the attorney-client privilege in tax matters is fascinating. For years, judges assumed, and held, that tax return preparation was a mere clerical function that was not deserving of the privilege because it did not rise to the level of legal advice. Then, as the tax law got more complicated — and taxpayers became more sophisticated and lawyers were engaged to prepare tax returns — judges began to recognize the tax law and tax return preparation as a fit subject of legal advice. (Colton v. U.S., 306 F.2d 633 (2nd Cir. 1962), *cert. denied*, 371 U.S. 951 (1963).) Judges still did not afford return preparation the attorney-client privilege, however.

To understand what the courts have said, the questions that need to be answered in determining whether the privilege applies should be understood. The first question is whether the communication was made to a lawyer acting in the capacity as such for the purpose of securing legal advice. The second question is whether there was an expectation that the communication be kept confidential. The third question is whether confidentiality has been waived.

The federal courts have a number of different grounds, representing different points in the privilege inquiry, for refusing to grant the attorney-client privilege to tax return preparation. In *U.S. v. Gurtner*, 474 F.2d 297 (9th Cir. 1973), the court held that the preparation of tax returns is not the rendering of legal advice. (*See also* U.S. v. Davis, 636 F.2d 1028 (5th Cir.1981), *cert. denied*, 454 U.S. 862 (1981).) The Eighth Circuit was even more contemptuous in *Canaday v. U.S.*, 354 F.2d 849 (8th Cir. 1966), using the word "scrivener" to describe a process that the court apparently believed involves little more than the transcribing of numbers into spaces on a form. (For discussion of the cases, see Graves, "Attorney Client Privilege in Preparation of Income Tax Returns: What Every Attorney-Preparer Should Know," 42 Tax Lawyer 577 (Spring 1989).)

* * *

Some courts have acknowledged that return preparation has an element of legal advice but that there was either no expectation of confidentiality or there has been a waiver. In *U.S. v. Lawless*, 709 F.2d 485 (7th Cir. 1983), the court held that there is no expectation of confidentiality in information transmitted for use on a tax return, regardless of whether the information was actually disclosed on the return. (*See also* Dorokee Co. v. U.S., 697 F.2d 277 (10th Cir. 1983).) In *U.S. v. Cote*, 456 F.2d 142 (8th Cir. 1972), the Eighth Circuit changed its rationale to hold that disclosure of information in a tax return waives the privilege not only to the disclosed data but also as to the details underlying that information. Other circuit courts eventually adopted the waiver theory. (U.S. v. El Paso Co., 682 F.2d 530 (5th Cir. 1982), *cert. denied*, 466 U.S. 944 (1984).)

Some lawyers hold out the hope that courts will hold that return preparation is privileged. This is a vain hope. A tax return is an attested document. It is signed by the taxpayer and the preparer under penalties of perjury. However much tax advisers may want to perpetuate gamesmanship in tax return positions, a tax return is not an opening offer. It is not a legal brief. Moreover, an IRS examination is not litigation. (U.S. v. Baggot, 463 U.S. 476 (1983).) Indeed, courts have refused to consider IRS Appeals, which is administrative arbitration, to be litigation for purposes of the work product doctrine. Yet new section 7525, and the IRS restructuring bill as a whole, send the harmful message that all tax discussions with the government are adversarial.

Indeed, Treasury, which licenses all these non-lawyer tax advisers to practice before it, takes a narrow view of the attorney-client privilege that is consistent with the code's recordkeeping requirements. In section 10.20 of Circular 230, as revised in 1994, Treasury commands that no practitioner "shall neglect or refuse promptly to submit records or information in any matter before the Internal Revenue Service, upon proper and lawful request . . . unless he believes in good faith and on reasonable grounds that such record or information is privileged or that the request for, or effort to obtain, such record or information is of doubtful legality." That is, Treasury sees the privilege as an exception to a general obligation to turn over all requested records.

Litigation

Given the extensive protections, both under the attorney-client privilege and the attorney work product doctrine, for materials generated in litigation, it is not surprising that some taxpayers have tried to shoehorn their tax advice into the definition of litigation preparation. These taxpayers take the view that any aggressive tax return position is likely to generate a fight with the tax administrator, and some courts agree.

In *U.S. v. Adlman*, 68 F.3d 1495 (2d Cir. 1995), the Second Circuit held that the attorney-client privilege did not apply to a legal memorandum prepared by an outside accounting firm for an in-house corporate legal officer. The subject of the memo was the application of the tax rules governing corporate reorganizations to a combination of subsidiaries aggressively recast to enable the corporation to recognize a large capital loss. Because the corporation, Sequa Corp., was under continuous audit, it was reasonably foreseeable that the IRS would challenge the desired result. Adlman, the in-house lawyer, argued that under *U.S. v. Kovel*, 296 F.2d 918 (2d Cir. 1961), the outside accounting firm was just helping him render legal advice, so that the firm's advice would be covered by his privilege. Circuit Judge Leval rejected this argument, holding that the accounting firm communicated directly with the corporation in the normal course of providing accounting services.

Adlman's principal practical failure was his failure, under *Kovel*, to make sure that the outside accountants communicated only with him and segregated their work on the acquisition from their other work. To fit within *Kovel*, routing of advice through lawyers to protect it is common. Would this still be necessary after the enactment of section 7525? Arguably not, but there is the question of waiver when multidisciplinary advice is involved. Section 7525 only covers tax advice.

Adlman got a second bite at the apple, however. On his second appeal, he succeeded in keeping the memo out of the government's hands under the attorney work product doctrine.[23] In *Adlman v. U.S.*, 134 F.3d 1194 (2d Cir. 1998), a divided three-judge panel led by Judge Leval concluded that the phrase "in anticipation of litigation" as used in Fed. Rul. Civ. P. 26(b)(3) could be read broadly enough to encompass a memo prepared to assess the desirability of a business transaction, which, if undertaken, would give rise to litigation. Circuit Judge Kearse, dissenting, would not stretch the work product rule so far, and noted that the court had only done so because Adlman had failed to prevail in his assertion of attorney-client privilege.

In remanding, Judge Leval emphasized that he would not extend the work product doctrine to documents that are prepared in the ordinary course of business or that would have been created in essentially similar form irrespective of the litigation. Five circuits apply this test, which is called the "because of" test, but none has stretched it as far as Judge Leval did in *Adlman. * * ** Only the Fifth Circuit, in *Davis* and *El Paso*, (cited earlier above) takes the position that the primary purpose for which a document was prepared must be litigation for it to enjoy work product protection.

Judge Leval apparently found a likelihood of litigation in Adlman's correct prediction that it would occur, Sequa's continuous audit, and the necessity of Joint Committee approval of Sequa's giant refund claim. The latter two are not properly considered litigation indicators, but Judge Leval would not be the first to mistake them as such. Courts, like the present Congress, routinely mistake IRS examinations as the commencement of litigation in work product doctrine cases. In *Bernardo v. Commissioner*, 104 T.C. 677 (1995), the Tax Court, a specialized court that should know better, took as the commencement of litigation the IRS's informing the taxpayer that its Art Advisory Panel disagreed with the taxpayer's valuation of a donation of a sculpture. At that point, Judge Wells said, it was reasonable for the taxpayer to conclude that litigation was in the offing.

So, under *Adlman*, a taxpayer who is about to undertake a transaction that the IRS may well question can take the position that documents created in analyzing that transaction are litigation work product. Section 7525 notwithstanding, *Adlman* itself creates a problem of inappropriate extension of litigation privileges. As Judge Wells noted in *Bernardo*, "the scope of the protection provided by the work product doctrine is broader than the protection afforded by the attorney-client privilege." Given that the Fifth Circuit disagrees with the other circuits, and the Second Circuit takes the "because of" test too far, the IRS is reportedly looking for a work product case to take to the Supreme Court.

---

[23] [The work product doctrine protects from compelled disclosure documents that are prepared by an attorney in anticipation of litigation, including opinions, strategies, and records of mental impressions. *See* Fed. Rul. Civ. P. 26(b)(3). Eds.]

That Gray Area

New section 7525(a)(3)(B) defines "tax advice" as "advice given by an individual with respect to a matter which is within the scope of the individual's authority to practice" as a federally authorized tax practitioner; that is, one admitted to practice before the IRS under Circular 230. But Circular 230 only authorizes representation of a client before the IRS and the Tax Court. Literally, writing an opinion or giving advice may not constitute representation before the IRS or the Tax Court. Circular 230 defines the class of practitioners Congress wanted to benefit, but does not adequately define what they do. So the new statute may not, by its terms, fulfill congressional intent to create a practice privilege.

The attorney-client privilege only applies to communications between clients and lawyers when the lawyers are acting as legal advisers, rather than as business advisers. A lot of legal advice has a business component and business ramifications. * * * And as in *Adlman*, it is the memorandums and opinions created in the ordinary course of giving tax advice, which should not be eligible for work product protection, that the accountants wanted to protect with their new privilege.

Few courts have addressed the fuzzy line between legal advice and business advice. It is not that the question does not arise, but that taxpayers tend to settle with the IRS. * * *

Of course, in arguing for the new privilege, accountants hoped to obtain confidentiality for corporate tax shelter opinions. Because of the tax shelter exception of new section 7525(b), their tax shelter opinions will enjoy no more protection than investment bankers' tax shelter opinions. This is a big loss, and not just because corporate tax shelters can be billed at a premium. (Indeed, any plan for which a premium can be demanded probably constitutes a tax shelter.) It is a big loss because just what constitutes a corporate tax shelter has not been fully defined.

Section 7525(b) refers to section 6662(d)(2)(C)(iii) for its definition of tax shelter. The latter section defines a "tax shelter" as "a partnership or other entity, any investment plan or arrangement, or any other plan or arrangement, if a significant purpose of such partnership, entity, plan, or arrangement is the avoidance or evasion of federal income tax." Regulations interpreting this definition have not been updated since the words "a significant purpose" replaced the words "the principal purpose" in the Taxpayer Relief Act of 1997. (Reg. section 1.6662-4(g)(2)(i), (g)(3).)

Section 7525(b) says that the new privilege for accountants does not apply to any written communication with corporate representatives "in connection with the promotion of the direct or indirect participation of such corporation in any tax shelter." The words "promotion of" were added at the last minute. But those who think "promotion of" narrows the scope of the broad phrase "in connection with" may be mistaken. Case law interpreting the tax shelter promotion penalties of the limited partnership era interpreted the idea of promotion loosely to encompass assistance in getting the investor into the shelter. * * *

It is reasonably foreseeable that the IRS will take a broad view of what constitutes a corporate tax shelter under section 7525(b). The IRS can add tax shelter to an array of anti-privilege arguments that include return preparation, business advice, and, as discussed below, waiver. The IRS already has numerous privilege disputes with taxpayers under continuous audit, who use assertion of the privilege to prevent on-site agents from looking at documents. Usually these disputes are not pursued unless the underlying substantive dispute goes to litigation. With more practitioners poised to assert the new privilege, it is safe to say that there will be more and messier disputes.

* * *

Waiver

The attorney-client privilege is easily waived, and the new section 7525 privilege can be waived the same way. In *Bernardo*, the Tax Court, relying on *Lawless* and *Cote*, stated that materials provided by a taxpayer for use in return preparation — here an art appraisal — are intended to be disclosed on the return and are not privileged. The *Bernardo* court further held that voluntary disclosure to a third party — here an accountant who was not participating in legal advice — implies a waiver of all communications *on the same subject*. This holding, called subject matter waiver, is very broad. The IRS can be expected to assert subject matter waiver in forthcoming privilege disputes with taxpayers.

Those who take a broad reading of new section 7525 would argue that *Bernardo* is obsolete, since the accountant to whom the documents were disclosed was representing the taxpayer before the IRS, which is now a privileged activity. However, *Bernardo* is still relevant, and waiver is still an important question, as long as there are people who are not lawyers or tax practitioners hanging around. This decision means, for example, that if persons who are not lawyers, tax practitioners, or contributors to a client's transfer pricing study were permitted to look at it, the privilege would be waived as to the study, its backup material, and all communications on the subject of transfer pricing.

Disclosure of privileged information to another federal agency constitutes a waiver. * * *

Posting tax information on accounting firm intranets may constitute waiver. It is the too many fingers in the pie problem again. The in-house counsel's failure in *Adlman* to obtain the attorney-client privilege was due in part to his and the accounting firm's failure to segregate the memorandum at issue from all the other advice, legal and not legal, tax and not tax, rendered by the accounting firm to the corporation. Accounting firms could find it difficult to make the Chinese walls necessary to separate tax advice from other advice, when practitioners of various disciplines are sharing client information and sharing an intranet.

There is not much case law interpreting the scope of the federally authorized tax practitioner privilege. The first Court of Appeals opinion discussing it was written by Judge Posner. *See United States v. Frederick*, 182 F.3d 496 (7th Cir. 1999). Frederick was both a lawyer and an accountant, and he had both provided legal advice to the client and prepared the client's tax returns. *See id.* at 496. The section 7525 privilege did not apply to the case because of its effective date. *See id.* at 502. Nonetheless, Judge Posner discussed the privilege, stating in part that "[i]t does not protect work product." *Id.* (dictum). In addition, with respect to the attorney-client privilege, Judge Posner stated: "a dual-purpose document—a document prepared for use in preparing tax returns and for use in litigation—is not privileged; otherwise, people in or contemplating litigation would be able to invoke, in effect, an accountant's privilege, provided that they used their lawyer to fill out their tax returns." *Id.* at 501.

Frederick has been criticized by commentators. *See, e.g.,* Robin L. Greenhouse & James L. Malone III, "Privilege in the IRS Audit Process—How and When Does It Apply?," 91 J. Tax'n 133 (1999) ("The *Frederick* opinion, even as amended, is troubling."); Steven M. Harris, "Nominee for Worst Tax Decision," 83 Tax Notes 1812 (1999) (calling *Frederick* "a blunderous foray into the world of attorney-client privilege in tax practice and the new section 7525."); Burgess J.W. Raby & William L. Raby, "Illusions, Delusions, and Tax Practice Privilege," 83 Tax Notes 697 (1999) (calling *Frederick* "a mild bombshell tossed into the discussion of section 7525.").

Do you agree with Judge Posner that section 7525 does not extend the work product privilege to non-attorneys? Consider the legislative history of section 7525, which states, in part:

> The House bill extends the present law attorney-client privilege of confidentiality to tax advice that is furnished by any individual who is authorized to practice before the Internal Revenue Service, acting in a manner consistent with State law for such individuals' profession, to a client-taxpayer (or potential client-taxpayer) in any noncriminal proceeding before the Internal Revenue Service.

> The House bill does not modify the attorney-client privilege. Accordingly, except for criminal proceedings, the privilege of confidentiality under this provision applies in the same manner and with the same limitations as the attorney-client privilege of present law.

> * * *

> The Senate amendment extends the present law attorney-client privilege of confidentiality to tax advice that is furnished to a client-taxpayer (or potential client-taxpayer) by any individual who is authorized under Federal law to practice before the IRS if such practice is subject to regulation under section 330 of Title 31, United States Code.

> * * *

> The conference agreement follows the Senate amendment with a modification. The privilege of confidentiality created by this

provision will not apply to any written communication between a federally authorized tax practitioner and any director, shareholder, officer, employee, agent, or representative of a corporation in connection with the promotion of the direct or indirect participation of such corporation in any tax shelter. * * *

The privilege created by this provision may be waived in the same manner as the attorney-client privilege. * * *

This provision relates only to matters of privileged communications. No inference is intended as to whether aspects of federal tax practice covered by the new privilege constitute the authorized or unauthorized practice of law under various State laws.

H.R. Rep. No. 105–599, at 268–69 (1998).

Another aspect of the turf war between lawyers and accountants is being played out in the context of the ethical restrictions surrounding Multi–Disciplinary Practice (MDP). In July 2000, the ABA House of Delegates voted by a three to one margin against loosening ethical restrictions that would have permitted lawyers to share fees and join with nonlawyers in a partnership that delivers both legal and nonlegal professional services. Model Rule of Professional Conduct 5.4 currently prohibits such fee-sharing between lawyers and nonlawyers. By voting to oppose amendments to the ethical rules, the House of Delegates rejected the recommendation of an ABA-appointed MDP Commission that issued a study concluding that the best interests of the public are served by permitting one-stop shopping for legal and nonlegal services. The two main players in the dispute are the Big Five accounting firms (in favor of MDPs) and ABA members concerned about preserving core values of the legal profession. *See* Laurie Hatten-Boyd, "Ebbs and Tides and Water Rise — What's the *Real* Concern with MDPs?," 53 Tax Law. 489 (Winter 2000).

PROBLEMS

1. The self-assessment system is sometimes referred to as a "voluntary compliance" system. What does that term mean? Is compliance with federal tax laws "voluntary" in the sense in which that word is generally used in everyday speech?

2. Terry has received a "30-day letter" from the IRS. Attached to the letter is a Revenue Agent's Report explaining adjustments to income that result in a $20,000 underpayment of tax. What are Terry's options in response to the 30-day letter?

3. Gina, who is single, has received a notice of deficiency in the amount of $4,000 from the IRS. What are Gina's possible responses to the notice?

4. Gene is a sole proprietor of an electronics store. The store generally sells its merchandise at regular retail price, but occasionally has "25% off" promotions. A new customer, Barbara, is interested in buying an expensive stereo. When Gene discovers that Barbara is a tax attorney, he offers her

a 40% discount on the price of the stereo if she will prepare his individual tax return (which will include a Schedule C for the electronics business). There is no sale at the store at that time. Barbara agrees to Gene's proposal and prepares the return. Is Barbara an "income tax return preparer" of Gene's return within the meaning of the Code?

5. Is an attorney who prepares an initial tax return for a client and files it on behalf of the client engaged in "practice before the IRS?"

6. Shirley willfully failed to file tax returns for the years 1998-2001.

    A. After receiving notices of deficiency for those years, Shirley paid the amounts due, including interest and penalties. She seeks to become an enrolled agent and obtain admission to practice before the IRS. Will she be entitled to obtain admission to practice?

    B. If Shirley had already been admitted to practice before the IRS prior to 1998, could she have been disbarred from practicing before the IRS based on her willful failure to file tax returns?

7. Walter, a tax attorney admitted to the Tax Court bar, was disbarred by the IRS for filing fraudulent tax returns. Can the Tax Court automatically disbar him based on the IRS disbarment?

8. What policy rationale(s) might justify allowing non-attorneys to practice before the IRS and the Tax Court? Do those rationales counsel allowing the same individuals to practice before the District Courts and Court of Federal Claims in tax refund cases?

9. Frances received a luxury car from her grateful longtime business contact, Seth. On his tax return, Seth treated the car as a business expense and deducted it. When preparing her return, Frances treated the car as a gift and therefore did not include it in her gross income. The IRS has audited both taxpayers. An IRS agent has informed Frances that the IRS's position is that the car constitutes gross income for her. However, as a protective matter, the agent plans to assert that Seth is not entitled to a business expense deduction for the car. Both Frances and Seth are eager to settle the matter at the least possible expense. Can one attorney represent both taxpayers before the IRS?

10. Carmen is a certified public accountant who was retained by Bill Billionaire. Would the "federally authorized tax practitioner privilege" of Code section 7525 apply to protect from disclosure to the IRS the following documents created by Carmen for Bill?

A. A worksheet used to prepare Bill's complicated tax federal income tax return.

B. A memorandum providing tax advice on state income tax law to Bill to assist him in deciding where to locate the headquarters of his next business venture.

C. An investment plan for Bill's billions.

D. A letter to Bill encouraging him to invest in a tax shelter that Carmen has developed.

E. A memorandum advising Bill of a possible strategy in a pending tax controversy with the IRS with respect to which Bill has received a notice of deficiency.

F. Oral advice to Bill in the presence of his girlfriend of a possible litigation strategy if Bill should decide to take the pending tax controversy to Tax Court.

G. Oral advice to Bill on how to handle various aspects of a criminal tax investigation of Bill by special agents of the IRS.

Chapter 2

TAX RETURNS AND THE
EXAMINATION PROCESS

Reading Assignment: Code §§ 6001, 6011(a), 6012, 6013(a), 6015, 6061–6065, 6072, 6081, 6151(a), 6161(a)(1), 6201, 6702, 7502, 7503, 7601, 7602, 7609, 7612; Treas. Reg. § 1.6011-1; 1.6013-4(d); Prop. Reg. 1.6015-1(a)(2), (g)(3), -2(a)(4)(C), (c), -3; Proc. Reg. § 601.105(a), (b)(1)–(4), (c).

§ 2.01 Introduction

As noted in Chapter 1, the federal income tax is a "voluntary compliance" or "self-assessment" system. Instead of the IRS billing taxpayers, the law requires taxpayers to timely file tax returns reflecting their tax liabilities and to timely pay the tax due.[1] *See* I.R.C. §§ 6001, 6011; Treas. Reg. § 1.6011-1. The IRS enforces the self-assessment process in part by collecting information from payors to verify the amounts shown on taxpayers' returns; collecting tax throughout the year through withholding and estimated tax payments; and auditing a percentage of returns each year to ensure that taxpayers are reporting their tax liabilities correctly.

§ 2.02 Tax Returns and Tax Payments

[A] Formal Requirements of a Return

It is important that the document a taxpayer files constitute a "return" because only a sufficient return starts the running of the statute of limitations on assessment against the IRS. *See Blount v. Commissioner*, 86 T.C. 383 (1986).[2] In order to constitute a "return," a document filed with the IRS must be on a proper form;[3] supply enough information to permit the IRS to calculate

---

[1] The privilege against self-incrimination does not relieve a taxpayer from the obligation to file a tax return. *See* United States v. Sullivan, 274 U.S. 259 (1927). Instead, the taxpayer may elect the privilege on the return in response to specific questions, the answers to which might incriminate the taxpayer. *See id*. However, a claim of privilege with respect to filing the return may properly be made where the particular return requirement is directed at a class "inherently suspect of criminal activities" and where there is a "real and appreciable" hazard of self-incrimination in filing the return. Marchetti v. United States, 390 U.S. 39, 47, 48 (1968). These issues are discussed further in Chapter 14.

[2] The statute of limitations on assessment is discussed in detail in Chapter 5.

[3] If the taxpayer fails to use the proper form, a statement describing gross income and deductions is a "tentative return" that, if timely filed, avoids delinquency penalties as long as the taxpayer thereafter files a proper form "without unnecessary delay." Treas. Reg. § 1.6011-1(b).

the tax; contain the taxpayer's name, address and identifying number; and be properly signed under penalties of perjury,[4] see I.R.C. §§ 6001, 6011, 6065. A document does not constitute a return if it does not make reference to income, deductions, and credits. The taxpayer must also compute the tax unless he makes a special election under section 6014 to have the IRS perform the computation. *See* Treas. Reg. § 1.6014-2. Failure to make computations can result in the imposition of a delinquency penalty, absent reasonable cause. *See* I.R.C. § 6651.

In Service Center Advice (SCA) 200010046, 2000 SCA LEXIS 1, the IRS stated that a return that is complete except for a required form or schedule constitutes a valid return for purposes of the statute of limitations on assessment. Such a return that also makes a refund claim generally will also constitute a sufficient claim for refund;[5] for that purpose, it must set forth the amount of the overpayment and specify whether such amount shall be refunded to the taxpayer or applied as a credit against the taxpayer's estimated income tax for the succeeding taxable year. However, an individual income tax return that lacks a form or schedule needed to corroborate the mathematics and data reported by the taxpayer is not a "processible" return within the meaning of section 6611(g) of the Code.

In addition to any other applicable penalties, a $500 "frivolous return penalty" may be imposed where a document purporting to be a return reflects conduct that (1) omits information on which the substantive correctness of the self-assessment may be judged or (2) contains information that on its face indicates that self-assessment is substantially incorrect, if the conduct is due to a frivolous position or a desire to impede the administration of the tax laws. I.R.C. § 6702.

Consider whether the document filed in the following case constituted a "return" for purposes of section 6011:

BEARD v. COMMISSIONER
United States Tax Court
82 T.C. 766 (1984)

WHITAKER, JUDGE: This case is before us on respondent's motion for summary judgment.* * *

In the notice of deficiency issued to petitioner, respondent determined a deficiency in petitioner's 1981 Federal income tax in the amount of $6,535. In the answer, respondent alleged that additions to tax were due under section 6651(a)(1) for failure to file a return, and section 6653(a) [currently I.R.C.

---

[4] Under Code section 6064, a signature is presumed authentic. An agent with an appropriate power of attorney form may sign a return for an individual if the taxpayer is unable to do so because of disease or injury; is continuously absent from the United States for at least 60 days before the return is due; or the taxpayer requests permission in writing from the IRS, which then determines that good cause exists. Treas. Reg. § 1.6012-1(a)(5). Joint returns require both spouses' signatures. However, there are special procedures for one spouse to sign the other's name where the other spouse is incapacitated and that spouse gives oral permission. *Id. See* Code sections 6062 and 6063 for the authorized signatories for corporate returns and partnership returns.

[5] Refund claims are discussed in Chapter 8.

§ 6662. Eds.] for negligence or intentional disregard of the rules and regulations. Additionally, damages pursuant to section 6673 for instituting proceedings before the Tax Court merely for delay were requested.

* * * Petitioner denies he was required to file a 1981 income tax return on or before April 15, 1982, in that he owed no tax liability for that year. He admits that the document in question in this case is the only submission he made to the Internal Revenue Service for the 1981 year, claiming that it is a return under section 6012 because it contains figures and numbers from which to compute a tax. * * *

FINDINGS OF FACT

Petitioner resided in Carleton, Mich., when the petition was filed in this case. During the 1981 taxable year, petitioner was employed by, and received wages from, Guardian Industries totaling $24,401.89. Such amounts were actually received by petitioner during that year.

He submitted to the Internal Revenue Service the below-described form and an accompanying memorandum dated February 22, 1982, as his 1981 return, thus indicating his protest to the Federal income tax laws. No other document alleged to be a return for the 1981 year was submitted. This document (the tampered form) was prepared by, or for, petitioner by making changes to an official Treasury Form 1040 in such fashion (by printing or typing) that the changes may not be readily apparent to a casual reader.

In that part of the first page of the official form intended to reflect income, petitioner deleted the word "income" from the item captions in lines 8a, 11, 18, and 20, and inserted in those spaces the word "gain." On line 21 of the form, he obliterated the word "income" from the item caption. In addition, in the margin caption to this section, petitioner deleted the word "Income" and inserted the word "Receipts."

In that part of the first page of the form intended to reflect deductions from income, he deleted the words "Employee business expense (attach Form 2106)" from line 23 of the form and inserted "Non-taxable receipts." In addition, in the marginal caption to this section, petitioner deleted the word "Income" and inserted the word "Receipts," so that the caption reads "Adjustments to Receipts" instead of "Adjustments to Income."

Petitioner filled in his name, address, Social Security number, occupation, and filing status in addition to the name, occupation, and Social Security number of his spouse. He claimed one exemption on the tampered form. The relevant information entries are as follows: On line 7 entitled "Wages, salaries, tips, etc.," taxpayer inserted the amount of $24,401.89. On line 23, under the category of "Non-taxable receipts," petitioner claimed an adjustment to "Receipts" of $24,401.89. He therefore showed a tax liability of zero. On line 55, entitled "Total Federal income tax withheld," he showed an amount of $1,770.75. The total $1,770.75 that had been withheld from his wages was claimed as a refund. This tampered form was signed by petitioner and dated February 22, 1982. Petitioner's Form W-2 issued by Guardian Industries was attached.

Petitioner's scheme in submitting this tampered form apparently was to conceal from the IRS Center operators the fact that his inclusion of his wages on the tampered form was negated by his fabrication of "Non-taxable receipts" on line 23, thus simultaneously excluding the wages theoretically reported. The net effect of the two steps was to create a zero tax liability. Since his employer had withheld against the amounts paid to him for the 1981 year, this scheme allowed him to claim a refund for that year.

*   *   *

The instant case is one of 23 cases that were on the March 5, 1984, trial calendar for Detroit, Mich., in which tampered forms are at issue. Many other similar cases are pending before this Court. All of these 23 cases contain a fabricated adjustment for "Non-taxable receipts." All were submitted to the Internal Revenue Service in the year 1980 or 1981. All but 2 of the 23 were submitted with two- or three-page memorandums advocating that wages are not taxable income. Twenty-two of the petitions in these cases contained identical language except for entries relevant to the petitioners' personal data. The remaining case contained a handwritten, individually composed petition. In cases in which replies or responses to respondent's motion for summary judgment were filed, all but one were the same format and language, with minor deviations to suit the petitioners in each case. It is abundantly clear that these docketed cases and documents represent a coordinated protest effort — an attempt to obtain refunds where employers had withheld against amounts paid, as well as to drain further the limited resources of this Court with these frivolous contentions.

The Internal Revenue Service has been forced to develop special procedures to handle tampered forms like those in the group referred to above. The tampered forms are also referred to as *"Eisner v. Macomber* returns" because *Eisner v. Macomber*, 252 U.S. 189 (1920), is usually cited either in the form or in the literature attached. From a cursory look, they appear to be official Forms 1040, but upon closer inspection, definitively are not. Internal Revenue Service employees must identify and then withdraw these from the normal processing channels, and gather and deliver them to a special team for review. After such review, the person who submitted such a tampered return is often, but not always, informed that it is not acceptable as a return because it does not comply with the Internal Revenue Code. Petitioner was so informed by a letter dated July 16, 1982, stating that the tampered form was "not acceptable as an income tax return because it does not contain information required by law, and it does not comply with Internal Revenue Code requirements."

ULTIMATE FINDINGS OF FACT

Petitioner actually received $24,401.89 from his employer as wages during the 1981 taxable year. The only documents he submitted for the 1981 taxable year were the tampered form and its accompanying memorandum. Petitioner has extensively studied the rules and regulations regarding the income tax laws in addition to income tax cases and, thus, his actions were the product of informed deliberation.

OPINION

Summary Judgment Issue

The threshold issue is whether a motion for summary judgment is appropriate in this case. We conclude that it is. * * *

Failure To File

Respondent alleges an addition to tax under section 6651(a)(1) for failure to file a Federal income tax return for taxable year 1981. * * * Respondent maintains that the tampered form submitted by petitioner was not a return within the meaning of sections 6012, 6072, and 6651(a)(1), that it will not be accepted as such (and was not accepted in this case), and thus petitioner is liable for an addition under section 6651(a)(1). We agree.

The general requirements of a Federal income tax return are set forth in section 6011(a), in relevant part as follows:

> When required by regulations prescribed by the Secretary any person made liable for any tax * * * shall make a return or statement *according to the forms* and *regulations* prescribed by the Secretary. [Emphasis added.]

Regulations implementing this legislative mandate provide:

> (a) *General rule.* Every person subject to any tax, or required to collect any tax, under subtitle A of the Code, shall make such returns or statements as are required by the regulations in this chapter. The return or statement shall include therein the information required by the applicable regulations or forms.

> (b) *Use of prescribed forms.* Copies of the prescribed return forms will so far as possible be furnished taxpayers by district directors. A taxpayer will not be excused from making a return, however, by the fact that no return form has been furnished to him. Taxpayers not supplied with the proper forms should make application therefor to the district director in ample time to have their returns prepared, verified, and filed on or before the due date with the internal revenue office where such returns are required to be filed. Each taxpayer should carefully prepare his return and set forth fully and clearly the information required to be included therein. Returns which have not been so prepared will not be accepted as meeting the requirements of the code. * * *

[Treas. Reg. § 1.6011-1. Eds.].

The statutory grant of authority to the Treasury requires that taxpayers make a return or statement according to the forms and regulations prescribed by the Secretary of the Treasury. These regulations mandate the use of the proper official form, except as noted below. The U.S. Supreme Court in the case of *Commissioner v. Lane-Wells Co.*, 321 U.S. 219 (1944), has recognized this mandate in stating:

Congress has given discretion to the Commissioner to prescribe by regulation forms of returns and has made it the duty of the taxpayer to comply. It thus implements the system of self assessment which is so largely the basis of our American scheme of income taxation. The purpose is not alone to get tax information in some form but also to get it with such *uniformity*, *completeness,* and *arrangement* that the physical task of handling and verifying returns may be readily accomplished. [321 U.S. at 223; emphasis added.]

This discretionary authority outlined in the regulations at section 1.6011-1, Income Tax Regs., has also been recognized in the case of *Parker v. Commissioner*, 365 F.2d 792 (8th Cir. 1966). Although the facts of that case are distinguishable from the instant case, the court did note that —

Taxpayers are required to file timely returns on forms established by the Commissioner. * * * The Commissioner is certainly not required to accept any facsimile the taxpayer sees fit to submit. If the Commissioner were obligated to do so, the business of tax collecting would result in insurmountable confusion. * * * [365 F.2d at 800.]

For years, the only permissible exception to the use of the official form has been the permission, granted from time to time to tax return preparers by the Internal Revenue Service, to reproduce and vary very slightly the official form pursuant to the Commissioner's revenue procedures. These revenue procedures require advance approval of a specially designed form prior to use as well as following the guidelines for acceptable changes in the form. The philosophy of the revenue procedure is and has been required forms to conform in material respects to the official form for the obvious reasons of convenience and processing facilitation but also to be clearly distinguishable from the official form, thereby removing the opportunity for deceit. * * *

On the tampered form, various margin and item captions, in whole or in part, have been deleted and most replaced with language fabricated by the petitioner. These changes were not in conformity with the Revenue Procedure[20] rules at section 5.01(2)(a)(1) requiring each substitute or privately designed form to follow the design of the official form as to *format, arrangement, item caption,* line numbers, line references, and sequence. Also, Revenue Procedure section 3.04(1) and (2) prohibits any change of any Internal Revenue Service tax form, graphic or otherwise, or the use of a taxpayer's own (nonapproved) version without prior approval from the Internal Revenue Service. Petitioner made no attempt to obtain such approval. Additionally, petitioner was required by Revenue Procedure section 6.01 to remove the Government Printing Office symbol and jacket numbers, and in such space (using the same type size), print the employer identifying number of the printer or the Social Security number of the form designer. Petitioner did not remove the symbol and numbers and did not insert in their place his appropriate number. The tampered form deceptively bore the markings of an official

[20] Rev. Proc. 80-47, 1980-2 C.B. 782. The current version of this revenue procedure is Rev. Proc. 84-9, I.R.B. 1984-7, 14. [The most current version to date is Revenue Procedure 2001-45, 2001-37 I.R.B. 227. Eds.]

form. Section 8.01, Revenue Procedure rules, prohibits the filing of reproductions of official forms and substitute forms that do not meet the requirements of the procedure. The only filing made by petitioner for the 1981 taxable year was the nonconforming tampered form.

Petitioner's prohibited tampering with the official form, the net effect of which is the creation of a zero tax liability, adversely affects the form's useability by respondent. The tampered form, because of these numerous irregularities, must be handled by special procedures and must be withdrawn from normal processing channels. There can be no doubt that due to its lack of conformity to the official form, it substantially impedes the Commissioner's physical task of handling and verifying tax returns. Under the facts of this case, taxpayer has not made a return *according to the forms and regulations* prescribed by the Secretary as required by section 6011(a). The rejection of the tampered form was authorized by the regulations for failure to conform to the revenue procedure. But whether or not rejected in this case, the question remains — Is the Internal Revenue Service nevertheless required to accept and treat as a tax return this tampered form? We conclude that it is not.

There have been factual circumstances in which the courts have treated as returns, for statute of limitations purposes, documents which did not conform to the regulations as prescribed by section 6011(a). Since the instant case is one of first impression, we will consider these cases that were decided on the statute of limitations issue because a return that is sufficient to trigger the running of the statute of limitation must also be sufficient for the purpose of section 6651(a)(1).

The Supreme Court test to determine whether a document is sufficient for statute of limitations purposes has several elements: First, there must be sufficient data to calculate tax liability; second, the document must purport to be a return; third, there must be an honest and reasonable attempt to satisfy the requirements of the tax law; and fourth, the taxpayer must execute the return under penalties of perjury.

It is important to consider the factual circumstances under which this test has been applied. In *Florsheim Bros. Drygoods Co. v. United States*, 280 U.S. 453 (1930), at issue was whether the filing of a "tentative return" or the later filing of a "completed return" triggered the statute of limitations. * * *

The Court recognized that the filing of a return that is defective or incomplete may under some circumstances be sufficient to start the running of the period of limitation. However, such a return must purport to be a specific statement of the items of income, deductions, and credits in compliance with the statutory duty to report information and *"to have that effect it must honestly and reasonably be intended as such."* (Emphasis added.) Thus, the filing of the tentative return was not a return to start the period of limitation running.

This issue of whether the document was a return for the statute of limitation purposes was again before the Court in *Zellerbach Paper Co. v. Helvering*, 293 U.S. 172 (1934). Justice Cardozo, speaking for the Court, said:

> Perfect accuracy or completeness is not necessary to rescue a return from nullity, if it purports to be a return, is sworn to as such

* * * and evinces an honest and genuine endeavor to satisfy the law. This is so even though at the time of filing the omissions or inaccuracies are such as to make amendment necessary. [*Zellerbach Paper Co. v. Helvering, supra* at 180. Citations omitted.]

* * *

The tampered form before us may purport to be a return in that it may "convey, imply or profess outwardly" to be a return. Black's Law Dictionary 1112 (rev. 5th ed. 1979). It was also sworn to. But it does not reflect an endeavor to satisfy the law. It in fact makes a mockery of the requirements for a tax return, both as to form and content. Whether or not the form contains sufficient information to permit a tax to be calculated is not altogether clear. We have held that the attachment of a Form W-2 does not substitute for the disclosure on the return, itself, of information as to income, deductions, credits, and tax liability. Reiff v. Commissioner, 77 T.C. 1169 (1981). Ignoring the Form W-2, the tampered form does show an amount of "Wages, salaries, tips, etc.," but with the margin description altered from "Income" to "Receipts." Similarly, in place of a deduction, the form has an amount for "Non-taxable receipts." Thus, to compute a tax from this tampered form, one must effectively ignore the margin and line descriptions, imagining instead the correct ones from an official Form 1040, or one must simply select from the form, including the Form W-2, that information which appears to be applicable and correct, and from the information so selected, irrespective of its label, compute the tax. We do not believe such an exercise is what the U.S. Supreme Court had in mind in *Commissioner v. Lane-Wells Co., supra* at 222-223, and *Germantown Trust Co. v. Commissioner*, 309 U.S. 304, 309 (1940).

The tampered form here is a conspicuous protest against the payment of tax, intended to deceive respondent's return-processing personnel into refunding the withheld tax. Since such intentional tampering could go undetected in computer processing, respondent was forced to develop and institute special procedures for handling such submissions. The critical requirement that there must be an honest and reasonable attempt to satisfy the requirements of the Federal income tax law clearly is not met. * * *

The tampered form is not in conformity with the requirements in section 6011(a) or section 1.6011-1(a) and (b), Income Tax Regs., and it is not a return under the judicial line of authority set forth above.

* * * Respondent has met his burden of proving that petitioner did not file a return for sections 6011, 6012, 6072, and 6651(a)(1) purposes, and thus an addition to tax is due.

* * *

Accordingly, we grant the motion for summary judgment.

* * *

NIMS, J., concurring:

I write this concurring opinion only to expressly dissociate myself from the views expressed in a concurring and dissenting opinion in support of petitioner's travesty tax return. I find it impossible to suppose that the Supreme Court intended its reasoning in *Badaracco*[6] to be applied so totally out of context as to give intellectual aid and comfort to petitioner and others like him, whose so-called returns on their face make clear a concerted effort to disrupt the tax system.

I fully agree with the reasoning and the result reached in the majority opinion.

CHABOT, J., concurring in part and dissenting in part:

* * *

From the majority's determination to grant summary judgment that the Form 1040 filed by petitioner was not a tax return, I respectfully dissent.

In *Badaracco v. Commissioner*, 464 U.S. [386] (1984), the Supreme Court confronted the contention of the taxpayers therein that the first documents they had filed "were 'nullities' for the statute of limitations purposes." In the course of its analysis, the Supreme Court stated as follows:

> a document which on its face plausibly purports to be in compliance, and which is signed by the taxpayer, is a return despite its inaccuracies. * * *
>
> *Zellerbach Paper Co. v. Helvering*, 293 U.S. 172 (1934), which petitioners cite, affords no support for their argument. The Court in *Zellerbach* held that an original return, despite its inaccuracy, was a "return" for limitations purposes, so that the filing of an amended return did not start a new period of limitations running. In the instant cases, the original returns similarly purported to be returns, were sworn to as such, and appeared on their faces to constitute endeavors to satisfy the law. Although those returns, in fact, were not honest, the holding in *Zellerbach* does not render them nullities. [464 U.S. at 396–97.]

An examination of the Form 1040 in question * * * shows the following: (1) It is a document which on its face plausibly purports to be in compliance with the law; (2) it is signed by the taxpayer (under penalties of perjury); (3) it does not make believe that only gold and silver coins need be reported; (4) it is not chock-full of refusals to provide information (indeed, it provides all the information requested as to petitioner's "Wages, salaries, tips, etc.", and respondent does not contend that petitioner had any other reportable income); (5) the income is reported on the correct line of the return; (6) an unwarranted deduction is reported on a line reserved for deductions; and (7) apparently

---

6 [*Badaracco v. Commissioner*, 464 U.S. 386 (1984), is reproduced in Chapter 5. In *Badaracco*, the United States Supreme Court considered the question of whether a nonfraudulent amended return filed subsequent to a fraudulent original return was sufficient to start the statute of limitations running, or whether the unlimited statute of limitations for fraud applied instead. Eds.]

the Form 1040 includes everything respondent needed in order to determine petitioner's income tax liability. Compare the instant case with *Reiff v. Commissioner*, 77 T.C. 1169, 1177–1179 (1981), and the cases cited therein. Nothing in the majority's opinion or on the face of the Form 1040 shows that respondent is led into error *because of the change in the text of any line on the Form 1040.*

I would hold that the document filed by petitioner constitutes a tax return under the standards adopted by the Supreme Court, as most recently articulated in *Badaracco v. Commissioner, supra.*

* * *

The majority's opinion * * * states that petitioner's alteration of the Form 1040 had "the net effect of * * * the creation of a zero tax liability" and that "because of these numerous irregularities, [it had to] be handled by special procedures and must be withdrawn from normal processing channels." This misdescribes the situation. Both the zero tax liability, and the requirement of special procedures, result from the unwarranted deduction. These problems would exist — because of the deduction — even if there were no alterations to the Form 1040.

* * *

The Form 1040 in question shows the necessary income information, and does so on the correct line, and that line has not been altered. This information is in accord with the Form W-2 (and not in conflict with it, as was the case in *Reiff v. Commissioner, supra*, relied on by the majority). There is no need to imagine the correct margin and line descriptions from an official Form 1040 because respondent's problems are no different, with the altered Form 1040, than they would be with an official Form 1040.

* * *

I understand and share the majority's frustration at having to deal with frivolous arguments. * * * However, this Court should not confuse the law as to what is a tax return, just to punish a particular individual or even a class of individuals. The Congress has given the courts more effective tools. We have used these tools to impose damages of up to $5,000 for frivolous or groundless actions. (Sec. 6673.) The District Courts have used these tools to uphold penalties of $500 for frivolous filings. (Sec. 6702.) As the majority note * * *, the injunction has been used to prevent conduct which interferes with proper administration of the Internal Revenue laws. (Secs. 7402(a), 7407.) When civil fraud is found, the sanction therefor now includes an additional amount under section 6653(b)(2).[7] The criminal fraud fine has been increased from a maximum of $10,000 to a maximum of $100,000 ($500,000 in the case of a corporation). (Sec. 7201.)

---

[7] [This is now section 6663. Eds.]

I would hold that petitioner's Form 1040 is a tax return. Since there is no finding that it was filed late, I would not impose an addition to tax under section 6651(a)(1). From the majority's contrary holding, I respectfully dissent.

Who do you think has the better argument, the majority or the dissent?

[B] Filing Tax Returns

Individual calendar year returns are due on April 15 of the subsequent year. I.R.C. § 6072(a). Individual fiscal year returns are due by the 15th day of the fourth month following the close of the fiscal tax year. *Id.* Corporate calendar year returns are due March 15, I.R.C. § 6072(b), and corporate fiscal year returns are due the 15th day of the third month following the close of the fiscal year, *id.* However, under section 7503, if the last day for filing falls on a Saturday, Sunday or legal holiday, filing is timely if made on the next day that is not a Saturday, Sunday or legal holiday.[8] For example, in years when April 15 falls on a Saturday, the last day for filing is Monday, April 17.

Returns are generally considered filed when received by the IRS. However, timely mailing is considered timely filing if the requirements of section 7502 are met: (1) the postmark falls within the date for filing (including extensions), (2) the return or other document is deposited in the mails in an envelope or wrapper properly addressed to the appropriate IRS office with postage prepaid, and (3) the return or other document is delivered to the IRS after it is due. Under section 7502(f), a taxpayer can use a designated private delivery service (such as Federal Express, UPS, or Airborne Express) instead of the United States mail and benefit from the "timely mailed is timely filed" rule. *See* Notice 97-50, 1997-2 C.B. 305 (providing a list of designated private delivery services).

The taxpayer bears the risk that a document deposited in the mail will be postmarked after the due date, and when arriving after the due date, will be deemed untimely. Treas. Reg. § 301.7502-1(c)(iii). Consider the following excerpt from *Cardinal Textile Sales Inc. v. United States*, 88 A.F.T.R. 2d 5850 (N.D. Ga. 2001):

> On September 15, 1995, Jerome Maurer, a staff accountant with the Russe Firm, mailed the envelope containing plaintiff's Form 1120X refund claims[9] for the 1988, 1989, and 1990 tax years from the United States Post Office in downtown Chattanooga, Tennessee. * * * Although the post office itself closed at 5:30 p.m. on September 15, 1995,

[8] If the return is filed before the due date, the statute of limitations begins to run on the actual due date (even if it was a Saturday, Sunday or legal holiday). Rev. Rul. 81-269, 1981-2 C.B. 243. If the return is filed on the extended due date (such as April 16 in a year that April 15 falls on a Sunday), then the statute of limitations starts to run only on the date the return is filed. If the statute of limitations runs on a Saturday, Sunday or legal holiday, assessment on the next business day is timely. *Id. See* Chapter 5 for further discussion of statutes of limitations on assessment of tax.

[9] [A Form 1120X is an amended corporate income tax return. Here, the amended returns were used to claim refunds. Refund claims are discussed in Chapter 8. Eds.]

the last mail pickup from the mail receptacle outside the post office was scheduled to occur at 7:00 p.m. * * * Mr. Maurer deposited the envelope containing plaintiff's Form 1120X refund claims for the 1988, 1989, and 1990 tax years into the mail receptacle outside the post office after 5:30 p.m., but prior to 7:00 p.m., on September 15, 1995. * * *

The IRS has no record of receiving Plaintiff's Form 1120X refund claims for the 1988, 1989, and 1990 tax years. * * * The claims were never returned to the Russe Firm. * * *

Plaintiff argues that a genuine dispute exists whether Plaintiff filed its 1120X claims for refund for the 1988, 1989, and 1990 tax years. For the following reasons, the Court rejects Plaintiff's argument.

First, Plaintiff did not send its claims for refund by certified or registered mail. Plaintiff therefore cannot rely upon § 7502(c) to show that its claims for refund were filed with the IRS.

Second, the majority of courts interpreting § 7502(a) have concluded that § 7502(a) applies only if IRS actually receives the claims for refund. * * * It is not sufficient merely to place the claims for refund in a mail receptacle. * * * Because the undisputed evidence in the case shows that the IRS never received Plaintiff's claims for refund, § 7502(a) does not apply. * * *

Mail stamped by private meter, to be timely, must be postmarked within the filing period and arrive within the time it would normally take a letter to arrive. If the arrival time is not reasonable, the taxpayer bears the burden of proving that it was deposited in the mails and delay was caused by transmission of the post. Sending a return by registered or certified mail avoids the risk of a dispute over timeliness of a return by providing evidence to establish the date the return was sent. I.R.C. § 7502(c).

> *Example*: Marsha, an individual, mails her tax return by registered mail to the IRS on April 15. The IRS receives the return on April 20. So long as Marsha's return is postmarked April 15, her return is timely. The registration constitutes *prima facie* evidence that the return was mailed to the IRS on the registration (postmark) date.

Under current law, taxpayers may mail or hand carry returns to specified IRS offices. *See* I.R.C. § 6091(b); Treas. Reg. § 31.6091-1. In addition, in the past fifteen years or so, the IRS has embraced electronic filing. "Electronic filing" refers to transmission of tax returns to the IRS by modem. It was introduced in 1986, and by the 1994 tax year, 13.5 million returns were filed electronically. In 1996, the electronic filing program was expanded so that taxpayers could file using their own personal computers. *See* IR 96-4. The IRS Reform Act calls for an expansion of the electronic filing program so that only 20 percent of all returns in 2007 would be filed on paper. The IRS has also instituted a program called Telefile, allowing certain taxpayers to file by phone. The IRS Reform Act mandates that the IRS expand Telefile and provide a comparable program on the Internet.

As discussed in Chapter 1, representation of taxpayers before the IRS requires a completed Form 2848, Power of Attorney and Declaration of

Representative. In order to facilitate return preparer resolution of certain basic return-processing issues, in April 2001, the IRS announced a simple "checkbox initiative." *See* IR-2000-23. Beginning with the 2001 filing season, all 1040 forms, except for Telefile, contain a box that taxpayers may use to designate a preparer to resolve matters involving math error notices, processing of tax refunds, and processing of tax payments. The goal is a reduction in paperwork for taxpayers. In 2001, over 20 million taxpayers checked the box on their tax returns. *See* IR-2001-71.

[C] Filing Extensions

An extension of time for filing a return is permitted only if the request is made on or before the due date for filing the return, the extension is granted by the IRS and the extension requested is a reasonable one, not longer than six months. I.R.C. § 6081(a). A corporation may obtain an automatic three-month extension for filing its income tax return if it files Form 7004 before the return due date and pays the full amount of the estimated tax due for the year. I.R.C. § 6081(b).

An individual taxpayer may obtain an automatic four-month extension by filing Form 4868, Application for Automatic Extension of Time to File U.S. Individual Income Tax Return, before the return due date. In addition, in March 2001, the IRS announced that taxpayers may now obtain the automatic extension of time to file by calling a 1-800 number or by e-filing by computer, as well as by filing Form 4868. A taxpayer using either system must provide two figures from his prior tax year's return in order to verify his identity.

Although Form 4868 requires the taxpayer to make a good faith estimate of the net tax amount due for the year, technically he need not pay any tax at the time of the extension request. However, the extension of time to file does not extend the time to pay tax. Therefore, it is advisable for the taxpayer to submit the estimated tax due with the extension request in order to reduce, to the greatest extent possible, accrual of interest and penalties. A duplicate of the extension form should be attached to the return when it is filed.

If an individual needs even more time to file the return, he can complete Form 2688, Application for Additional Extension of Time to File. The taxpayer must explain on the form why he or she needs more time and the extension must be approved by the IRS; approval is not automatic. An illness or natural disaster is normally an acceptable excuse. When an extension is denied, the taxpayer must file by the later of the original due date of the return or 10 days from the date the extension is denied. *See* Treas. Reg. § 1.6081-4(c).

[D] Amended Returns

A taxpayer has the option of amending his return if he discovers a mistake on the original return. An amended return filed on or before the due date is considered the taxpayer's return for that year. By contrast, the IRS has the discretion to accept or reject an amended return filed after the due date. Rev. Rul. 83-86, 1983-1 C.B. 358. Even if the IRS accepts the amended return, the original return is the relevant one for statute of limitations purposes. *See Badaracco v. Commissioner*, 464 U.S. 386 (1984). However, note that, in general, an amended return must be filed to claim a refund or credit of most tax overpayments. *See* Chapter 8. In addition, regulations provide that a taxpayer should file an amended return and pay additional tax due if he discovers that an item of income should have been included in a prior tax year and the statute of limitations is open. *See* Treas. Regs. §§ 1.451-1(a); 1.461-1(a)(3).

[E] Tax Payments

An extension of time to file does not extend the time to pay tax. Tax is due with the return, without assessment or notice and demand. I.R.C. § 6151. The date fixed for payment is the last day the return is due, determined without regard to extensions for filing. *Id.* However, an extension of time to file may allow the taxpayer to avoid penalties for late filing, provided that the tax is paid on or before the extended due date of the return. *See* Treas. Reg. § 301.6651-1(c)(3). Payments must be made in check or money order payable to the U.S. Treasury and collectible in United States currency.[10] In addition, the IRS accepts payment on the taxpayer's debit or credit card. Procedures and restrictions on the use of credit and debit cards are found in Treasury Regulation 301.6311-2.

In unusual circumstances, the IRS may grant an extension of time for payment of tax, generally for up to a six-month period. I.R.C. § 6161. Interest will, nevertheless, run from the due date of the return.[11] I.R.C. § 6601(b)(1). Extensions on payment are not freely given, and no extension is permitted if nonpayment was due to negligence, intentional disregard of rules or regulations, or fraud. The regulations require a showing of "undue hardship" to get the extension. Treas. Reg. § 1.6161-1. The application must be filed before the due date for payment and include supporting financial data (a balance sheet and income statement for three months). In addition, a taxpayer who states that he cannot pay a tax liability in full when due may be eligible to enter into an installment agreement with the IRS, which is discussed in Chapter 12.

In some cases, tax may actually be due earlier than the due date of the return. The Code provides for withholding from employees' wages so that the government receives tax on behalf of employees regularly throughout the year.[12] *See* I.R.C. § 3402. In addition, taxpayers whose withholding is inadequate to cover their tax liabilities may be required to file "estimated tax" forms quarterly. In general, the amount due with each estimated tax form is twenty-five percent of the amount of tax due for the year.[13] I.R.C. § 6654(d). This is enforced through an "estimated tax penalty" if the taxpayer owes too

---

[10] There is a penalty under section 6657 for tendering a bad check.

[11] Interest on tax liabilities is discussed in Chapter 11.

[12] Withheld taxes are known as "trust fund taxes," *see* I.R.C. 7512(b), and there is a 100 percent penalty for willful failure to pay over such tax. I.R.C. § 6672. Other penalties may also apply. *See, e.g.*, I.R.C. § 7215.

[13] Each installment must be 25 percent of the "required annual payment." The "required annual payment" is generally the lesser of 90 percent of the tax liability for the current year or 100 percent of the tax liability for the prior year.

much tax with the annual return. *See* I.R.C. § 6654. The estimated tax penalty is discussed in more detail in Chapter 10.

§ 2.03 Examinations

[A] IRS Investigatory Authority

As a backstop to the self-assessment system, the IRS examines taxpayers' returns in order to verify whether the return filed reflects the correct tax liability. To carry out this examination function, Congress has granted the IRS very broad authority to "examine any books, papers, records, or other data which may be relevant" to determining the correctness of any tax return. I.R.C. § 7602(a)(1). Under section 6201, the IRS also is authorized to make inquiries, determinations, and assessments of all taxes under the internal revenue laws. This authority, along with that granted in sections 7601 and 7602, forms the basic underpinning of the IRS examination function.

> The Service gathers information for use in an examination from the following primary sources:
>
> (1) The taxpayer's tax and information returns;
>
> (2) Information returns filed by third parties;
>
> (3) The taxpayer's books and records;
>
> (4) The workpapers of the taxpayer's accountant;
>
> (5) Informal information provided to the Service by the taxpayer, the taxpayer's employees or other third parties; and
>
> (6) Information provided from summonses issued to third parties.

* * *

Barbara T. Kaplan, "Leveling the Playing Field in Federal Income Tax Controversies," 56 N.Y.U. Ann. Inst. Fed. Tax'n § 32.01, at 32-7 (1999). Note that, once the examination is complete, Code section 7605(b) prohibits more than one inspection of the taxpayer's books for each taxable year unless the taxpayer requests an additional inspection or the IRS notifies the taxpayer in writing that another inspection is necessary.[14]

Among other functions, the IRS's summons power backs up its investigatory authority.[15] Section 7602(a)(2) provides the IRS with summons power, which

---

[14] *See* Revenue Procedure 94-68, 1994-2 C.B. 803, for examples of IRS contacts that do not constitute an examination, inspection, or reopening of an examination and instances in which reconsideration of a case does not constitute reopening of it.

[15] The authority under Code section 7602 may also be used with respect to tax collection (discussed in Chapter 12) and criminal tax cases (discussed in Chapters 13 and 14). Summonses in the criminal tax context are discussed in Section 14.04[A] of Chapter 14. In addition, the IRS will sometimes use a summons to obtain documents for the tax investigation of a foreign country, under an applicable tax treaty. *See, e.g.*, United States v. Stuart, 489 U.S. 353 (1989) (at the request of Canadian Department of National Revenue, under the U.S.-Canada Tax Treaty, IRS issued summons to United States bank for records to be used to determine Canadian income tax liability of certain Canadian citizens and residents); Mazurek v. United States, 271 F.3d 226 (5th Cir. 2001) (under U.S.-France tax treaty, IRS issued summons to United States bank to obtain financial records of French resident, at the request of French Tax Authority).

enables the IRS to compel a taxpayer or third party to produce records or to testify under oath. IRS examination personnel (who consist of revenue agents and tax auditors, as well as special agents who handle criminal tax matters) are all authorized to issue a summons. T.D. 6421; Delegation Order No. 4 (as revised). The summons must be left at the taxpayer's last and usual place of residence. I.R.C. § 7603.

> To be enforceable, a summons must contain the following information:
>
> (1) The name and address of the person whose taxes are being inquired into along with the periods under consideration. . . .
>
> (2) The identity of the person summoned. A summons directed at a corporation must be served on a corporate official, director, management agent or other person authorized to accept service of process. . . .
>
> (3) A description of the items summoned, which must be described with reasonable certainty. I.R.C. § 7603. The summoned party must know what is required of him with "sufficient specificity to permit him to respond adequately to the summons." *United States v. Medlin*, 986 F.2d 463 (11th Cir. 1993); *United States v. Wyatt*, 637 F.2d 293, 302 n.16 (5th Cir. 1981).
>
> (4) The date, place and time for compliance. . . . The summons must provide at least 10 days for the party to respond. I.R.C. § 7605(a).

Kaplan, *supra* at 32-11.

Code section 7602, which covers examination of books and witnesses, provides, in part, that the Secretary of the Treasury must provide to a taxpayer periodically, and also when requested, a record of "person[s] other than the taxpayer" contacted with respect to the determination or collection of tax of that taxpayer. I.R.C. § 7602(c)(2). On January 2, 2001, the IRS issued proposed regulations under that section. *See* RIN 1545-AX04, 66 F.R. 77–84. The proposed regulations touch on six general categories. First, the proposed regulations clarify who constitutes a "person other than the taxpayer" with respect to business entities. In general, a taxpayer's employee is generally not a "person other than the taxpayer" with respect to employees acting within the scope of their employment.

Second, the regulations define the phrase "with respect to a determination or collection" of tax. In general, the proposed regulations generally provide that only contacts directly connected to the purpose of determining or collecting an identified taxpayer's liability are governed by the statute. Third, the regulations clarify the "reprisal" exception. They provide that "reprisal" includes not only physical harm, but also emotional and economic harm. They also provide that a statement by the person contacted that harm may occur is good cause to believe that there is a possibility of reprisal.

Fourth, the regulations provide that the required periodic report should be produced once each year. However, taxpayers may request the report more frequently, subject to any reasonable restrictions that the IRS may impose. Fifth, with respect to records of persons contacted, the regulations provide, in part, that naming the person contacted will always satisfy the standard of reasonable identification. Finally, the proposed regulations provide that contacts with government entities generally need not be reported.

What happens if a party summoned does not appear?

> If the IRS has issued a summons to appear and produce documents, and the taxpayer then does not appear, the IRS has three options. It can seek an order of contempt from the district court, I.R.C. § 7604(b) * * *; it can criminally prosecute the witness, I.R.C. § 7210 (nonappearing witness subject to fine of up to $1,000 and one year in prison); or it can ask the district court to enforce the summons, [I.R.C.] § 7604. If * * * the IRS asks the district court to enforce the summons, the court will order the taxpayer to show cause why the summons should not be enforced. * * * At the enforcement hearing the taxpayer may challenge enforcement of the summons on any appropriate ground, * * * and the district court will determine whether the taxpayer's objections have merit. * * * If the district court orders the summons enforced, the taxpayer may appeal. If the taxpayer has not appealed or the appellate court has upheld enforcement, and the taxpayer still refuses to comply, then the court may issue an order to show cause why the taxpayer should not be held in contempt for failing to comply with the summons. A taxpayer's failure to show cause at that stage will justify the entry of a civil contempt order.

United States v. Riewe, 676 F.2d 418, 420-421 (10th Cir. 1982).

What are the limits on what the IRS may review? In *United States v. Euge,* 444 U.S. 707 (1980), an IRS agent who was investigating Euge's income tax liability for years in which Euge had not filed any tax returns used the "bank deposits method" of reconstructing Euge's income.[16] The agent found only two bank accounts in Euge's name. However, he also found twenty additional bank accounts that appeared to be maintained by Euge under aliases. Accordingly, the agent issued a summons requiring Euge to appear and execute handwriting exemplars of the signatures appearing on the bank signature cards. In *Euge,* the Supreme Court enforced the summons, thus requiring Euge's production of the handwriting samples.

The following case also considers the limits of the IRS's access to taxpayer information under the summons power:

UNITED STATES v. NORWEST CORPORATION
United States Court of Appeals, Eighth Circuit
116 F.3d 1227 (1997)

BEAM, Circuit Judge.

In the course of an audit of Norwest Corporation, the Internal Revenue Service sought to enforce a designated summons directing Norwest to produce tax preparation software licensed to it by Arthur Andersen & Co., as well as related documents and data. Norwest and Andersen objected to the summons,

---

[16] The "bank deposits method" of reconstructing income involves analyzing bank deposits to determine if they reflect unreported income. It is discussed in *Cooper v. Commissioner, T.C. Memo. 1987-431,* reproduced later in this chapter.

claiming that the material was not within the scope of the IRS's authority, and that in any event it was not relevant to the audit. After a hearing, the magistrate judge issued an order enforcing the summons. The district court, adopting most of the findings and conclusions of the magistrate judge, affirmed the order. Norwest and Andersen appeal, and we affirm.

I. BACKGROUND

Norwest is a large bank holding corporation that has more than 300 subsidiaries in the financial services industry. Norwest files consolidated corporate federal income tax returns for all of its subsidiaries. Since at least 1983, Norwest has used tax preparation software in preparing its tax returns. In 1990, Norwest entered into a three-year licensing agreement with Andersen for use of Andersen's copyrighted "Tax Director" tax preparation software. Norwest first used Tax Director in preparing its 1990 returns, and used the program again for its 1991 returns.

A. The Tax Director Program

Tax Director is a group of related programs developed by Andersen that a corporation can use to calculate federal and state tax liability and prepare and print tax returns. Andersen has licensed Tax Director to approximately 700 corporate customers, including Norwest. The agreement between Norwest and Andersen states that Tax Director contains trade secrets and prohibits Norwest from transferring Tax Director to others or allowing others to use it. According to Norwest and Andersen, Tax Director operates in the following way. First, the company inputs year-end account balances from its books to be used in calculating the tax, either by manually entering the applicable figures or exporting this data from a previously compiled database. Next, the entered figures are assigned certain codes that instruct the program how they are to be classified for tax purposes. "Tax destination codes" (TDC codes) assign figures to particular lines on the return; for example, figures to be identified as gross rents are assigned the number "052.0." Similarly, "ALT codes" are used to identify figures with their proper destination on schedules to be attached to the return. All TDC and ALT codes to be assigned to particular entries are determined before the year-end balances are entered into Tax Director. In other words, how certain figures are classified for tax purposes is determined by the program's operator; Tax Director itself does not perform such classifications.

The operator must also enter any adjustments needed to reconcile the difference between the company's book income and its tax income. These adjustments between a corporation's book income and the taxable income it reports on the return are reflected by the IRS's Schedule M. These Schedule M adjustments are determined before they are entered into Tax Director; the program itself does not determine Schedule M adjustments. Finally, the operator enters certain background information required by the return, such as the name and address of the taxpayer.

After the company's financial data is entered and the applicable codes and adjustments assigned, Tax Director generates the return and appropriate schedules. This process apparently involves simple arithmetical processes: Tax Director identifies all the information with a particular code, adds it up, and enters it on the appropriate line of the return. The program does, however, perform certain automatic adjustments to the information it receives. For example, Tax Director caps the figure calculated for reporting on the return as charitable deductions * * * as the Tax Code requires. The program also automatically reports taxable income as zero on the return if the data it receives would indicate a negative taxable income. Tax Director stores all of the entered data, including the account balances, codes, and adjustments, into data files which are segregated from the actual program. Tax Director thus does not itself retain any direct information about the company's finances or tax liability.

Tax Director can also generate and print certain "audit trail reports" based on the financial data it is given. These include the "Detail Spreadsheet Report" (R2 report) and the "Adjusting Entry Edit Report" (E3 report). The R2 report organizes and tabulates the year-end summary information for book balances and indicates for each account the TDC and ALT codes assigned, the Schedule M adjustments made, and the resulting adjusted tax balance. The E3 report likewise indicates the classifications and Schedule M adjustments assigned to each account. According to Norwest and Andersen, when Tax Director creates audit trail reports, it is not designed to save the data so that it may be viewed or manipulated by other commercially available software such as a spreadsheet program, nor is Tax Director itself designed to further view or edit this data. The program does, however, save this information as "print files." According to Norwest and Andersen, skilled computer technicians can convert these print files to spreadsheet-accessible files, and Norwest did in fact create such files for use in preparing its state income tax returns.

B. The Audit of Norwest

In April of 1992, the IRS began an audit of Norwest for the 1990 tax year. This audit later was expanded to included Norwest's 1991 tax liability. In the course of the audit, the IRS issued to Norwest numerous "Information Document Requests" (IDRs) requesting production of certain documents and records deemed relevant to the audit. On September 11, 1992, the agency issued IDR 26, requesting "a copy of the 'mapping' that takes place to translate the account totals on the [general ledger] report into line items on the tax return [including] Schedule M adjustments." Appellants' App. at 410. IDR 26 also indicated that "we anticipate that this process includes the use of Personal Computer based software of either an 'in-house' nature or a commercial package. Please provide a copy of these files in computer readable form." *Id.* In response to IDR 26, Norwest provided the IRS with a copy of an R2 report from the 1991 return.

In October of 1993, John Kuchera, the IRS computer audit specialist assigned to the Norwest project, orally requested that Norwest provide a copy of Tax Director. Norwest refused to produce Tax Director, but did provide the agency with two sets of computer diskettes. One set contained the unadjusted book balances entered into the program in completing the returns. The agency was able to easily access these files. The second set of diskettes were the adjusted tax balance files created by a Norwest employee from Tax Director's audit trail print files. These files presented the agency with some difficulty. Kuchera was eventually able to access the files, but testified that he was unable to verify whether they were accurate or complete.

The agency made no further requests for Tax Director until May 19, 1994, when it issued the designated summons at issue in this appeal. The summons directed Norwest to produce, among other things, the complete Tax Director program and all manuals and similar documents relating to the program. Norwest again refused to produce the software and its documentation. Instead, Norwest and Andersen met with agency auditors for several hours to demonstrate the program and its operation. This demonstration used generic data, and did not involve any Norwest-specific information.

Paragraph 2 of the summons requested "all data files, in machine sensible form, used by Tax Director to prepare the tax returns, or supporting computations, or upon which the Tax Director programs performed their functions." Appellants' App. at 16. In response to Paragraph 2, Norwest produced the original data files created by the program in creating the 1990 and 1991 returns. When the agency was initially unable to view these files, an Andersen employee explained that Tax Director itself had no capacity to manage the files, but instructed the agency computer specialists on how to convert these files into a readable format. When the agency was still unsatisfied with its access to the Paragraph 2 files, Andersen offered to construct a "bridge program" that would allow the agency to download and view the files. Andersen created such a program, but the agency refused to accept the program when Andersen and Norwest offered the bridge program on the condition that the agency accept it in lieu of Tax Director and that the agency agree not to pursue the summons.

With the statute of limitations for the 1990 audit on the verge of expiration, the agency initiated this enforcement action, which suspended the statute. Andersen intervened in the proceedings. Following a hearing, the magistrate judge concluded that the summons should be enforced, with certain limitations intended to protect Andersen's proprietary interest in Tax Director. The district court modified certain aspects of the magistrate judge's order, but affirmed enforcement. On appeal, Norwest and Andersen reiterate their position that this kind of software is not within the IRS's summons authority, that it is not material to the audit, and that the agency has acted in bad faith. Norwest and Andersen also argue that production of Tax Director will require that Norwest violate Andersen's copyright, and that this vitiates the agency's summons authority.

II. DISCUSSION

Under section 7602 of the Internal Revenue Code, the IRS has the authority to issue summonses requiring taxpayers to produce records, documents, or other material relevant to an audit or to give testimony. As it has done in this case, the agency may also issue a "designated summons" under IRC § 6503(j). During the enforcement period of a designated summons, the statute of limitations for issuing a notice of deficiency is suspended. IRC

§ 6503(j)(1). The IRS is entitled to summon material if it satisfies a deferential standard for relevancy. *United States v. Powell*, 379 U.S. 48, 57-58, 13 L. Ed. 2d 112, 85 S. Ct. 248 (1964).

No court has addressed whether the agency's summons authority encompasses tax preparation software that itself contains no direct information about a particular taxpayer. Therefore, we face two important questions of first impression: whether the section 7602 summons power applies to this situation, and, if so, whether the agency has shown that its summons for this material is enforceable under *Powell*.

A. The Applicability of Section 7602

Section 7602 authorizes the IRS to summon "any books, papers, records, or other data which may be relevant or material" to an IRS investigation. Given the agency's "broad mandate to investigate and audit 'persons who may be liable' for taxes," courts should be wary of "restricting that authority so as to undermine the efficacy of the federal tax system." *United States v. Bisceglia*, 420 U.S. 141, 145–46, 43 L. Ed. 2d 88, 95 S. Ct. 915 (1975). The Supreme Court has stated that " 'the administration of the statute may well be taken to embrace all appropriate measures for its enforcement, [unless] there is . . . substantial reason for assigning to the phrases . . . a narrower interpretation.' " *United States v. Euge*, 444 U.S. 707, 715, 63 L. Ed. 2d 141, 100 S. Ct. 874 (1980) (*quoting United States v. Chamberlin*, 219 U.S. 250, 269, 55 L. Ed. 204, 31 S. Ct. 155 (1911)). With these principles in mind, we must determine whether "books, papers, records, or other data" includes Tax Director.[n.6]

Norwest and Andersen argue that Tax Director is not a "record" or "other data" because the program itself does not contain or save any financial information particular to Norwest. Like any other computer program, it is a series of coded instructions that enable a computer to perform certain operations on data entered into it. The financial information that Tax Director used to generate Norwest's tax returns is not stored within the program, but is saved into completely segregated data files which have been provided to the agency. The copy of Tax Director the agency would receive from Norwest is no different from the software that Anderson licenses to hundreds of other corporate clients. Norwest and Andersen liken Tax Director to a calculator an individual taxpayer might use to complete a return, and argue that this kind of tool or asset is not within the agency's summons power.

Perhaps because it will usually be apparent whether a particular item is a "record" or "other data" under section 7602, there is a dearth of relevant case law.[n.7] *Euge*, however, suggests that "books, records, papers, or other

---

[n.6] The manuals, documents, and other written information related to Tax Director demanded in Paragraph 1 of the summons are obviously "books" or "papers." Thus, the only issue with regard to that material is whether it is relevant to the IRS's audit.

[n.7] We agree with Norwest and Andersen that two cases the IRS relies on are not entirely apposite. *See* United States v. Arthur Young & Co., 465 U.S. 805, 813–17, 79 L. Ed. 2d 826, 104 S. Ct. 1495 (1984) (upholding a summons for tax accrual workpapers retained by the taxpayer's accountant); United States v. Davey, 543 F.2d 996, 999–1000 (2d Cir. 1976) (enforcing a summons for magnetic tapes containing taxpayer-specific data). *Arthur Young* and *Davey* do, however, indicate the broad summons authority section 7602 gives the agency.

data" under section 7602 cannot be defined as narrowly as Norwest and Andersen urge. In *Euge*, the Court considered "whether [the] power to compel a witness to 'appear,' to produce 'other data,' and to 'give testimony,' [pursuant to a section 7602 summons] includes the power to compel the execution of handwriting exemplars." 444 U.S. at 711. The Court held that this exercise of the summons power was "necessary for the effective exercise of the Service's enforcement responsibilities [and] entirely consistent with the statutory language." *Id*.

Norwest's and Andersen's arguments are reasonable, but they basically urge us to adopt a narrow interpretation of the types of information section 7602 encompasses. This is inconsistent with the approach in *Euge* and with our obligation "to liberally construe the powers given" the agency under the statute. *United States v. Giordano*, 419 F.2d 564, 569-70 (8th Cir. 1969). As Norwest itself states in its brief, "Tax Director consists of a set of instructions to the computer (i.e., algorithms) on how to sort and arrange financial data entered by a licensee, how to do simple arithmetic, and how to cause the data entered by the licensee to be printed on the lines of a federal income tax return." Appellant's Br. at 22. In light of the broad effect we are to give section 7602, a coded set of algorithms that sorts and arranges a taxpayer's financial information and then uses that information to generate the audited return can certainly be considered a "record" or "other data."

Norwest's and Andersen's argument that Tax Director is merely a "tool" such as a calculator is unpersuasive. First, simply labeling Tax Director a "tool" and pointing out that, in the end, numbers on the return are generated by arithmetical processes does not mean that the program is not also a "record" or "other data." Second, as the magistrate judge found, Tax Director is clearly much more sophisticated than a mere adding machine. It recognizes significant codes assigned to certain information based upon its intended tax treatment, organizes information based on those assignments, contains built-in limitations on the assignments a taxpayer can make, generates a return, creates files containing taxpayer financial data, and can generate detailed reports. We hold that the magistrate judge and district court correctly concluded that Tax Director was a "record" or "other data" under section 7602.

B. *Powell* Test

Under *United States v. Powell*, 379 U.S. 48, 57–58, 13 L. Ed. 2d 112, 85 S. Ct. 248 (1964), a court must enforce a section 7602 summons if the IRS shows: (1) that the investigation is for a legitimate purpose; (2) that the requested material is relevant to the investigation; (3) that the material is not already in the agency's possession; and (4) that the proper administrative steps have been followed.[8] Norwest and Andersen argue on appeal that the agency has not shown that the summoned material may be relevant, and that the summons was issued for an improper purpose.

---

[8] Norwest and Andersen argue that because Tax Director contains trade secrets of Andersen, we should apply a stricter test, and require the agency to show a "clear nexus" between the summoned material and Norwest's tax liability or that the material is necessary to complete the audit. Neither the statute nor the case law provides any basis for a higher standard of relevancy in this case, and we therefore reject this argument.

1. Relevance

The agency points to a number of ways Tax Director may be relevant to the audit. For the returns at issue, Tax Director was the final step in translating the company's summary book income into the information reported on the returns. The agency thus contends that Tax Director is a critical link in the "audit trail," that is, the steps and processes that Norwest took in preparing its tax returns based on particular financial information. According to the agency, access to Tax Director may assist the audit team in gaining a "big picture" view of Norwest's returns and in identifying areas for more detailed investigation.

The agency also points out that Norwest's consolidated returns represent financial information from more than 300 subsidiaries and affiliates, and that the company's use of Tax Director was the most important step in organizing this vast amount of information. Tax Director itself contains algorithms that generate return information based upon interpretations of the Tax Code and that affect how the return is generated. While some of these functions, such as the automatic cap on charitable deductions, are clearly reflected on the return, others may not be; an Andersen employee testified that Tax Director contains other such automatic functions, but could not recall what they were. Finally, while Norwest did produce data files and audit trail reports created by Tax Director, the agency maintains that without Tax Director it is unable to verify whether this information is complete or accurate.

Norwest and Andersen offer a number of arguments for why they believe the agency's access to Tax Director will be unfruitful. "Relevance" under the *Powell* test does not depend, however, on whether the information sought would be relevant in an evidentiary sense, but merely whether that information might shed some light on the tax return. *Arthur Young*, 465 U.S. at 813–14 & n.11. The IRS need not state with certainty how useful, if at all, the summoned material will in fact turn out to be. *Id.* at 814. Furthermore, it is for the agency, and not the taxpayer, to determine the course and conduct of an audit, and "the judiciary should not go beyond the requirements of the statute and force IRS to litigate the reasonableness of its investigative procedures." *United States v. Clement*, 668 F.2d 1010, 1013 (8th Cir. 1982).

Norwest and Andersen also contend that the agency has never before felt a need to examine Norwest's tax preparation software in prior audits, and that the IRS can adequately "tie up" Norwest's returns to the book financial data by way of the data files and audit trail reports already provided. The issue, however, is not whether the IRS needs the software and supporting material in order to tie the final entries on the return to the detailed or summary financial data. There is, indeed, little question that it would be possible for the agency to tie the return information back to the input (that is, reconcile Norwest's tax income with its book income) without the software. But the agency's summons authority does not depend on whether the lack of certain information would make such reconciliation impossible, but whether the summoned material might "illuminate any aspect of the return." *Arthur Young*, 465 U.S. at 815. Under this broad standard, the agency has sufficiently shown that the material it seeks may assist the audit team in understanding the return and in focusing the investigation.

2. Legitimate Purpose

Norwest and Andersen contend that the agency's actual purpose in issuing the designated summons was to suspend the statute of limitations, which otherwise would likely have expired before the audit was completed. This, they maintain, was not a legitimate tax collection or determination purpose under the *Powell* test.

The appellants' arguments, however, basically boil down to repeating their position that the agency's stated purposes for seeking Tax Director are inadequate, and concluding from this that the IRS's real purpose could only be to extend the statute of limitations. Because we conclude that the agency's explanations for how Tax Director may be relevant to the audit are legitimate, we cannot accept appellants' premise. Because the audit was conducted in order to verify Norwest's tax liability for 1990 and 1991 and the IRS has demonstrated how Tax Director may be relevant to the audit, we hold that the summons was issued for a legitimate purpose. The IRS has therefore met its minimal burden under *Powell*, and is entitled to enforcement of the designated summons.

C. Summons of Copyrighted Material

Norwest and Andersen argue that because the summons forces Norwest to copy and produce to the IRS Andersen's copyrighted products, the summons will require Norwest to violate Andersen's copyright. Appellants maintain that this puts section 7602 in conflict with the Copyright Act, and that the district court thus should not have enforced the summons. The district court noted that appellants' argument is "essentially . . . that, when in conflict, the Copyright Act trumps the IRS's statutory authority to issue summonses." *United States v. Norwest Corp.*, 1995 U.S. Dist. LEXIS 21360, No. 4-94-MC-36, slip op. at 2-3 (D. Minn. Dec. 12, 1995). We agree with the district court that there is no authority for this proposition. Section 7602 does not indicate that a properly issued summons for relevant material is limited to uncopyrighted material. Nor does the Copyright Act indicate that copyright protection insulates either the copyright owner or the possessor of the particular item from producing that item in response to an IRS summons. To the extent that Andersen's proprietary interest in Tax Director may be threatened by enforcement of the summons, the restrictions imposed by the district court on the IRS's use of Tax Director adequately protect that interest.

Finally, Norwest and Andersen maintain that the agency waived any right to issue a summons for Tax Director when it entered into a records retention Letter Agreement with Norwest shortly after the audit began. Appellants also argue that the summons was not a "designated summons" because it was not issued to determine Norwest's tax liability. We have considered these and other arguments and find them without merit.

III. CONCLUSION

For the reasons discussed above, we affirm the order of the district court in all respects.

Norwest discussed the four-factor test of *United States v. Powell*, 379 U.S. 48 (1964). Was it difficult for the IRS to demonstrate to the court its compliance with these factors? Congress responded to the *Norwest* decision with Code section 7612, enacted as part of IRS Reform. How does that section address the issue that faced the *Norwest* court?

What happens once the IRS demonstrates its compliance with *Powell*? At an enforcement hearing in district court,

> Appropriate defenses include (1) the summons was issued after the IRS had recommended criminal prosecution to the Department of Justice * * *;[17] (2) the summons was issued in bad faith * * *; (3) the materials sought are already in the possession of the IRS, * * *; and (4) the materials sought by the IRS are protected either by the attorney-client privilege, * * * the work-product doctrine, . . . or other traditional privileges or limitations * * *. Although no blanket Fourth or Fifth Amendment privileges against testifying or producing documents are recognized * * * the taxpayer may assert those rights in response to specific questions asked or specific documents sought by the IRS.[18]

Riewe, 676 F.2d at 420 n.1 (citations omitted).

A party who claims that a summons seeks documents that are protected from disclosure (typically because of a claimed privilege) will compile for the court and the government an index identifying each document and the protection claimed. The index is sometimes called a "privilege log." Information identifying a document might include the document's date, subject matter, nature (such as letter or memorandum), and recipient(s). *See, e.g.*, *United States v. United Technologies Corp.*, 979 F. Supp. 108, 113 (D. Conn. 1997) ("Document 16: A June 1982 memo from the head of UTC's tax department to the company's in-house counsel requesting legal advice on the significance and application of a tax ruling."); *United States v. Derr*, 1991 U.S. Dist. LEXIS 17987 *3 (N.D. Cal. 1991) ("The privilege log for each box shall describe for each document the privilege claimed and shall list the date, title, description, subject and purpose of each document and the name, position and

---

[17] [Under Code section 7602(d), the IRS's authority to use a summons terminates in a case that has been referred to the Justice Department for criminal prosecution or a grand jury investigation. If the Attorney General notifies the IRS in writing that the taxpayer will not be prosecuted or subject to a grand jury investigation, the prohibition on the use of the summons power terminates. Similarly, once the criminal proceedings against the taxpayer reach a final disposition, the IRS can once again avail itself of the summons power. Tax procedure in criminal cases is discussed in Chapters 13 and 14. Eds.]

[18] [Privileges are discussed in Section 1.07 of Chapter 1. The Fourth and Fifth amendments to the Constitution are discussed in Section 14.06 of Chapter 14, in the context of criminal tax cases. Eds.]

last known addresses of the author(s) and recipient(s) of each document.").
Generally, the party seeking to shield the documents from view will provide
as little information as possible.

It is possible that a court will conduct an *in camera* review of documents
alleged to be protected. *See United States v. Zolin*, 491 U.S. 554, 565 (1989);
see also United States v. Frederick, 182 F.3d 496 (7th Cir. 1999) (documents
the subject of summonses issued to attorney/accountant were not protected
by attorney-client privilege or work-product privilege; there is no protection
for documents prepared for use in preparing tax returns), *reh'g en banc denied*,
84 A.F.T.R.2d 5760 (7th Cir. 1999), *cert. denied*, 528 U.S. 1154 (2000). In *Derr*,
cited above, the court ordered Chevron Corporation to submit each privilege
log to the court and to submit for *in camera* review copies of the documents
listed in the first privilege log so that the court could "inform the parties after
reviewing the documents listed on the first privilege log whether Chevron
shall lodge with the Court the documents from subsequently produced
privilege logs." *Derr, supra*, at *3.

In a litigated tax case, another method the IRS can use to compel a taxpayer
to produce documents is the discovery process. As discussed in Chapter 6, the
Tax Court does not allow open-ended discovery by either the taxpayer or the
IRS when preparing for Tax Court trial. The use by the IRS of its summons
power could undermine Tax Court discovery by providing a one-sided tool
broader than that generally available. In certain circumstances, the Tax Court
will issue a protective order to prevent the IRS from using information
obtained through a summons in a pending case. The Tax Court set forth
guidelines in the following case:

ASH v. COMMISSIONER
United States Tax Court
96 T.C. 459 (1991)

OPINION

WRIGHT, JUDGE:

This matter is before the Court on petitioner's motion for protective order
filed on July 6, 1990. Petitioner [Mary Kay Ash] seeks a protective order under
Rule 103 to restrict respondent's use of information obtained through administrative summonses.

*   *   *

THE SUMMONSES

On September 20, 1989, respondent issued an administrative summons
pursuant to section 7602 to Lawrence Cox, treasurer of Mary Kay Corp.,
seeking certain information, testimony, and documents (the MKC summons).
The MKC summons relates to the 1985 and 1986 taxable years of Mary Kay
Corp. and its subsidiaries. The return date of the summons was October 18,
1989.

On October 3, 1989, respondent issued a third-party recordkeeper summons (see section 7609(a)) to Jack Morris, a partner with the accounting firm of Ernst & Young, seeking certain information, testimony, and documents (the petitioner/Morris summons). The petitioner/Morris summons relates to petitioner's 1985 and 1986 taxable years. The return date of the summons was November 3, 1989.

Also on October 3, 1989, respondent issued another third-party recordkeeper summons to Jack Morris (the Rogers/Morris summons). * * *

During May and June 1990, respondent issued third-party recordkeeper summonses to officials of Morgan, Stanley & Co., Inc., Merrill Lynch Capital Markets, and Rothchild, Inc. (the adviser summonses), seeking certain testimony, information, and documents relating to Mary Kay Corp.'s 1985 and 1986 taxable years.

On October 18, 1989, the return date of the MKC summons, the treasurer of MKC provided certain documents to respondent, but withheld other documents that MKC concluded are subject to the attorney-client privilege. On November 3, 1989, the return date of both the petitioner/Morris summons and the Rogers/Morris summons, Jack Morris provided to respondent the information requested in the summonses and some of the requested documents. Morris withheld other documents on advice of counsel that such documents are subject to the attorney-client privilege.

On April 12, 1990, respondent commenced an action in the U.S. District Court for the Northern District of Texas to enforce the petitioner/Morris summons and the MKC summons. As of the date of petitioner's motion, no action had been taken to enforce the Rogers/Morris summons or the adviser summonses.

In her motion for protective order petitioner seeks an order prohibiting respondent's attorneys, agents, and employees engaged in representing him before this Court from obtaining access to, reviewing, or using any testimony, documents, or other information obtained pursuant to the MKC summons, the petitioner/Morris summons, the Rogers/Morris summons, and the adviser summonses after December 29, 1989, the date her petition was filed.

DISCUSSION

As a preliminary matter we note that the enforceability of the summonses is not at issue. The parties agree that the District Court, not this Court, has jurisdiction to decide such issue. Sec. 7604. We therefore do not address the issue of whether the summonses are enforceable.

I. Tax Court Rules of Practice and Procedure

Section 7453 provides that proceedings of the Tax Court shall be conducted in accordance with such rules of practice and procedure as the Court may prescribe. Petitioner argues that respondent's use of administrative summonses to obtain information related to the case pending before this Court allows respondent to undermine the discovery rules contained in title VII of our Rules of Practice and Procedure (Rules 70 through 76) and gives him an unfair advantage. Title VII provides rules addressing interrogatories, production of documents and things, examination by transferees, depositions upon consent of the parties, depositions without the consent of the parties, and deposition of expert witnesses.

The purpose of discovery in the Tax Court is to ascertain facts which have a direct bearing on the issues before the Court. *Penn-Field Industries, Inc. v. Commissioner*, 74 T.C. 720, 722 (1980). Discovery is not as broad in the Tax Court as it is in the Federal District Courts. *Estate of Woodard v. Commissioner*, 64 T.C. 457, 459 (1975). The discovery procedures established by our Rules in essence follow the Federal Rules of Civil Procedure (Federal Rules), but are not identical. *See* 60 T.C. 1097 (1973) (note accompanying Rule 70(a) (1974), which, for the first time, permitted interrogatories and requests for production and inspection of papers and other things). * * *

II. Authorization to Issue Summonses

Respondent is authorized by sections 7602 and 7609 to issue summonses and to utilize the information obtained through them. In relevant part section 7602(a) provides that for the purpose of determining the liability of any person for any internal revenue tax the Secretary is authorized: (1) To examine any books, papers, records, or other data which may be relevant or material to such inquiry; (2) to summon the person liable for tax, any officer or employee of such person, or the person having possession, custody, or care of books of account containing entries relating to the business of the person liable for tax, or any other person the Secretary may deem proper, to appear before the Secretary and to produce such books, papers, records, or other data, and to give such testimony, under oath, as may be relevant or material to such inquiry; and (3) to take such testimony of the person concerned, under oath, as may be relevant or material to such inquiry. Section 7609(a) provides for special procedures when a summons is served on any person who is a third-party recordkeeper.

III. Prior Opinions of This Court

A. *Universal Manufacturing Co. v. Commissioner*

* * *

In *Universal Manufacturing Co.* [*v. Commissioner*, 93 T.C. 589 (1989),] an agent of the Commissioner's Criminal Investigation Division served summonses on or about January 10, 1989, on two employees of WNC and third-party recordkeeper summonses upon two accountants for WNC. The testimony and documents sought by the Commissioner under those summonses were directly related to the matters at issue in the pending civil cases. The taxpayers moved for a protective order under Rule 103, asserting that the Commissioner's use of administrative summonses to obtain information directly related to the issues of civil cases pending before this Court allowed him to circumvent the discovery rules contained in title VII of our Rules of Practice and Procedure and gave him an unfair advantage in the prosecution of litigation before this

Court. The taxpayers urged the Court to exercise its inherent authority over the proceedings to prevent the Commissioner from utilizing in the Tax Court proceedings any information obtained pursuant to those administrative summonses.

In *Universal Manufacturing Co.*, respondent argued that he was entitled to free and unfettered use of information developed through the administrative summonses in question. We noted that respondent chose to issue the notices of deficiency at issue and, in effect, chose to give the taxpayers the opportunity to come to this Court and invoke our Rules before his criminal investigation was completed, even though his internal administrative guidelines seemed to provide that a notice of deficiency normally would not be issued in such a situation. *Universal Manufacturing Co. v. Commissioner, supra* at 594. We went on to reason that the subject motion required us to reconcile two competing considerations. First, this Court has no desire to interfere in any way with respondent's investigations into violations of the internal revenue laws. We noted that respondent has the obligation to initiate such investigations and to pursue them to completion. Second, respondent's use of administrative summonses in a criminal case to interview third-party witnesses and obtain relevant documents concerning the issues in civil cases pending before the Court circumvents our discovery rules. *Universal Manufacturing Co. v. Commissioner, supra* at 594.

After balancing both considerations, the Court found that the Commissioner's use of administrative summonses to interview third-party witnesses and obtain relevant documents concerning the issues in cases pending before the Court impermissibly undermined the Court's discovery rules. The Court held that this was so even if the Commissioner's motives were fully proper. The Court stated its objective in so holding was to "require respondent to present his position in the civil cases pending before us without utilizing any information obtained pursuant to an administrative summons served after the cases were docketed in this Court." 93 T.C. at 595. The Court issued an order providing that the Commissioner was not to "obtain or use any testimony, documents or other information obtained pursuant to an administrative summons served after September 2, 1988," the date the petition to this Court was filed. *Universal Manufacturing Co. v. Commissioner, supra* at 595.

* * *

IV. Summonses Issued Prior to Filing of Petition

With regard to the summonses issued in the instant case before petitioner filed her petition with this Court (MKC summons, petitioner/Morris summons, and Rogers/Morris summons), we find that *Universal Manufacturing Co. v. Commissioner, supra*, is inapplicable. That case involved a summons issued after the filing of the petition.

Petitioner argues that we should extend our holding in *Universal Manufacturing Co.* to information obtained after the filing of her petition through the MKC summons, petitioner/Morris summons, and Rogers/Morris summons, which were issued before her petition was filed, because respondent's purpose in issuing them was to undermine this Court's discovery rules. First, we note that relatively few notices of deficiency result in the filing of a petition in this Court. Respondent had no way of knowing whether petitioner would file a petition. In addition, until a petition is filed, we have no basis on which to impose the rules provided for in title VII of our Rules of Practice and Procedure, and any administrative summonses issued by respondent prior thereto do not pose a threat to the integrity of our Rules. Nor will the summonses pose a threat to the administration or effectiveness of our Rules of Practice and Procedure. When the petition was filed, the parties on whom summonses were served were already under an obligation to provide the information called for pursuant to sections 7602 and 7609. Therefore, the competing considerations addressed in *Universal Manufacturing Co.* are not present here. If the summonses are for any reason invalid, petitioner's remedy lies with the U.S. District Court, not here.

We deny petitioner's motion for protective order with respect to the MKC summons, petitioner/Morris summons, and Rogers/Morris summons, which were all served prior to the filing of the petition in this case.

V. Summonses Issued After Filing of Petition

With respect to the adviser summonses, petitioner asks that we grant her motion pursuant to Rule 103. Rule 103 authorizes this Court to restrict the use of discovery procedures or information obtained through discovery when required to protect a party or other person against "annoyance, embarrassment, oppression, or undue burden or expense." As an initial matter, we must address the issue of whether this Rule may be used to restrict a party's use of information which is obtained through means *other than* our discovery rules.

Rule 103 is derived from, and for all practical purposes is identical to, Rule 26(c) of the Federal Rules. 60 T.C. 1057, 1122 (1973). Accordingly, we look to cases construing Rule 26(c) of the Federal Rules for guidance on the breadth of application of Rule 103. *Willie Nelson Music Co. v. Commissioner*, 85 T.C. 914, 917 (1985). Those cases uniformly hold that Rule 26(c) provides no authority for the issuance of protective orders to regulate the use of information or documents obtained through means other than discovery in the proceedings before the Court. * * * Thus, based on these cases we could conclude that this Court does not have the authority to issue protective orders under such Rule restricting the use of information *which was not obtained through the use of the Court's discovery procedures*, but was obtained through other legal procedures. To the extent that *Universal Manufacturing Co. v. Commissioner*, 93 T.C. 589 (1989), may be read as applying Rule 103 more broadly, we reject such a reading. Because a ruling under Rule 103 would not be definitive here, we do not express a conclusion as to the application of that Rule to the question before us.

That is not to say, however, that this Court is powerless to regulate the processes of this Court, viz, the use in this Court of information obtained by administrative summons. It is undisputed that courts have inherent powers vested in the courts upon their creation and not derived from any statute. *Eash* *v. Riggins Trucking, Inc.*, 757 F.2d 557, 561 (3d Cir. 1985) (and cases cited thereat). * * *

Moreover, our own rules contemplate questions of practice and procedure for which there is no applicable rule of procedure and direct the Judge before whom the matter is pending to prescribe an appropriate procedure. Rule 1(a).

As we have already stated, *supra*, our Rules of discovery in essence follow the Federal Rules but are not identical. Rule 26(a) of the Federal Rules (Rule 26(a)) allows, generally, nonconsensual discovery by deposition; our Rules do not. To give respondent carte blanche with regard to the admission of evidence obtained by administrative summons would, in effect, give him the full advantage of Rule 26(a), an advantage that we have withheld. We need not do so; we have the power to uphold the integrity of the Court's process by enforcing the limited discovery that, by rule, we have adopted. Where litigation in this Court has commenced, and an administrative summons is issued with regard to the same taxpayer and taxable year, we will exercise our inherent power to enforce the limited discovery contained in our Rules. We will do so unless respondent can show that the summons has been issued for a sufficient reason, independent of that litigation. Where litigation in this Court has commenced, and an administrative summons is issued not with regard both to the same taxpayer and taxable year (for instance where the summons concerns another taxpayer or a different taxable year), *normally* we will not exercise our inherent power. We will exercise that power, however, when petitioner can show lack of an independent and sufficient reason for the summons. In the instant case, only the adviser summonses were issued after litigation commenced. Those summonses fall within that situation where normally we will not exercise our inherent power. Since petitioner has not shown a lack of independent and sufficient reason for the adviser summonses, we need not exercise our inherent power nor detail how that power could be exercised. Rule 1 authorizes the Judge before whom a matter is pending to prescribe an appropriate procedure. What would be appropriate would depend on how best to maintain control "over [our] own process, to prevent abuse, oppression and injustice." *Gumbul v. Pitkin*, [124 U.S. 131, 146 (1888).]

Universal Manufacturing Co. presents the first situation (post-petition summons, same taxpayer, same year), and, we believe, the Court there may have concluded that there was no real prospect of a criminal investigation, although the Court did not make such a finding. *Westreco, Inc.* [*v. Commissioner,* T.C. Memo. 1990-501] presents a different situation. The Court there stated that it found compelling facts that justified its protective order but cautioned that no implication was to be drawn that all activities of respondent's trial counsel in an audit would justify a similar order. * * *

We next consider petitioner's argument that this Court's power to exclude the evidence in question is inherent in its obligation as a judicial body to protect the integrity of its processes and to regulate the proceedings and parties that appear before it. We already have discussed the circumstances that would allow us to regulate the proceedings as requested by petitioner and, based on the record before us, we find that the summonses *in issue* are not a threat to the integrity of this Court's processes. The development of additional evidence through the summonses *in issue* will in fact benefit this

Court's processes because it will result in a more fully developed factual background in which to consider petitioner's case. The additional evidence may also lead to the settlement of the case.

We also find that we are not compelled to grant petitioner's motion in order to regulate the proceedings and parties that appear before us. Our holding in this case that a protective order is not appropriate involves legitimate and good faith summonses with respect to other years, to related taxpayers, and to related tax liabilities, and involves the absence of any other underlying facts or circumstances that would justify the issuance of a protective order in this case. Petitioner has failed to show respondent's lack of an independent and sufficient reason for the summonses. The rule we announce herein in no way limits this Court's exercise of its power to issue protective orders or to impose other appropriate sanctions where the underlying facts and circumstances of a particular case establish an abusive or prejudicial situation that warrants relief. If, as we proceed, an abusive or prejudicial situation becomes apparent (which petitioner has so far not shown), we will be able to regulate the proceedings regardless of the rule we announce herein.

* * *

In conclusion, we deny petitioner's motion for protective order. With regard to each of the summonses other than the adviser summonses, we do so since all were issued prior to commencement of the litigation herein. With regard to the adviser summonses, we do so since petitioner has not shown a lack of a sufficient, independent reason for their issuance.

Compare *Ash* with *United States v. Admin. Enters., Inc.*, 46 F.3d 670 (7th Cir. 1995). In that case, the IRS issued a summons to a tax preparer in 1990 with respect to Mr. and Mrs. Kanter. The IRS did not request an order from the District Court to enforce the summons until three and a half years later, at which time a Tax Court case to determine the Kanters' tax liability was pending. In an opinion focusing primarily on the delay between the issuance of the summons and the request for an order enforcing it, Judge Posner found the summons enforceable. Is this decision consistent with *Ash*?

With respect to the delay, the court stated, in part:

> When there is no statute of limitations in the picture, the law, including federal common law, relies upon the doctrine of laches to protect the recipient of the summons from unreasonable delay in enforcement. This versatile, flexible, and serviceable doctrine, originally equity's counterpart to statutes of limitations (which were not applicable to suits in equity), is a ground for dismissing a suit if the defendant can show that the plaintiff delayed unjustifiably in filing and that as a result the defendant was harmed, either by being hampered in his ability to defend or by incurring some other detriment. * * * There is no defense of "staleness," despite a dictum in *United States v. Gimbel*, 782 F.2d 89, 93 (7th Cir. 1986), on which the

appellants rely. Laches is a legal doctrine; it has structure; "staleness" is an epithet.

* * *

We need not pursue the question of the existence and scope of a defense of laches in government suits to resolve this case. * * * The appellants assert that they were lulled into thinking the summons had been abandoned. The plausibility of the assertion may be questioned. The summons had no time limit, was never withdrawn, and, as we are about to see, required the recipient to retain — indefinitely — the documents within its scope. Even if this point is ignored, being lulled and then rudely awakened is not the kind of harm, if it is a harm at all rather than merely another metaphor, that allows laches to be used to deprive a plaintiff of his rights. A more concrete harm must be shown.

Can summonses be conditionally enforced? That is, can a court require compliance with a condition as a prerequisite to enforcement? In *United States v. Jose*, 131 F.3d 1325 (9th Cir. 1997) (*en banc*), the District Court had enforced certain summonses subject to the condition that the IRS notify the party summoned five days before circulating, transferring, or copying the summoned documents outside the Examination Division. The Ninth Circuit reversed, holding that the lower court was limited to enforcing or denying summonses. *See also United States v. Barrett*, 837 F.2d 1341, 1350-51 (5th Cir. 1988) (*en banc*), *cert. denied*, 492 U.S. 926 (1989) (regarding summons enforcement conditioned on compliance with Code section 6103).[19] In *Barrett*, the Fifth Circuit stated:

> In a summons enforcement proceeding, the district court's only task is to determine whether the summons should or should not be enforced. This inquiry is limited to ensuring that the government has complied with the four *Powell* criteria, and that its process is not being abused. * * * There is no statutory authority, nor Congressional indication that existing statutes supply the authority, nor Supreme Court authority, to allow the district court to make any consideration except whether to enforce or not enforce the summons. * * * There is no middle ground because to create that remedy would unduly hamper the investigative efforts of the IRS.

Id. at 1350 (citation omitted).

Note that summonses may be served on third parties. Under Code section 7609, if a summons is served on a third party, requiring that party to give testimony or produce records relating to a taxpayer identified in the summons, then notice of the summons must be given to that taxpayer within three days of the date on which the summons was served, and no later than the 23rd day before the date fixed in the summons as the day on which the records

---

[19] An earlier decision in *Barrett*, 795 F.2d 446 (5th Cir. 1986), a suit under Code section 7431 alleging that the IRS sent to Dr. Barrett's patients letters disclosing tax return information (the fact that he was under criminal investigation), is cited in *DiAndre v. United States*, 968 F.2d 1049 (1992), reproduced in Chapter 3.

are to be examined.[20] The notice to the taxpayer must be accompanied by a copy of the summons and must contain an explanation of the right to bring a proceeding to quash the summons. The taxpayer then has twenty days to bring a proceeding in district court to quash the summons. I.R.C. § 7609(b). The third party summoned can intervene in this proceeding, and is bound by the proceeding whether or not he intervenes. I.R.C. § 7609(b)(2)(C). Note also that in addition to the right to bring a proceeding to quash the summons, the taxpayer identified in the third-party summons has the option of intervening in any proceeding to enforce the summons. I.R.C. § 7609(b)(1).

A taxpayer cannot avoid the intent of a summons for production of records held by a third party simply by having the third party transfer to his attorney records that were the subject of the summons. *See Couch v. United States,* 409 U.S. 322, 329 n.9 (1973). In addition, the person transferring the records in that context may be subject to criminal prosecution under 18 U.S.C. § 1503 for obstructing justice. *See United States v. Curcio,* 279 F.2d 681 (2d Cir.), *cert. denied,* 364 U.S. 824 (1960).

Code section 7609(f) contemplates summonses that do not identify the taxpayer whose liability is in issue, so-called "John Doe summonses." Under that section, issuance of a John Doe summons requires a prior court hearing in which the IRS establishes that:

(1)   the summons relates to the investigation of a particular person or ascertainable group or class of persons,

(2)   there is a reasonable basis for believing that such person or group or class of persons may fail or may have failed to comply with any provision of any internal revenue law, and

(3)   the information sought to be obtained from the examination of the records or testimony (and the identity of the person or persons with respect to whose liability the summons is issued) is not readily available from other sources.

I.R.C. § 7609(f). The IRS has used John Doe summonses to obtain documents relating to offshore transactions as well as domestic transactions. For example, in 2000, a District Court judge authorized the IRS to serve summonses on MasterCard International and American Express Services Co. in order to obtain customer records of unnamed United States taxpayers with accounts in the Bahamas, the Cayman Islands, Antigua and Barbuda that they may have been using to evade federal taxes. *See* "Judge Enforces IRS Summons to Obtain Credit Card Records," Daily Tax Rep. (BNA), November 1, 2000, at G-4.

Does the IRS need to comply with the requirements of section 7609(f) if a summons serves the dual purposes of investigating both a named taxpayer and unnamed persons? In *Tiffany Fine Arts, Inc. v. United States,* 469 U.S. 310 (1985), the Supreme Court ruled in a unanimous opinion that dual purpose summonses issued under section 7602 are not subject to section 7609(f) so long as the information sought is relevant to a legitimate investigation of the summoned taxpayer. The Court stated:

---

[20] Section 7609 is discussed further in Section 14.04[A] of Chapter 14.

The [Congressional] Reports [with respect to the enactment of section 7609(f)] discuss only one specific congressional worry: that the party receiving a summons would not have a sufficient interest in protecting the privacy of the records if that party was not itself a target of the summons. S. Rep. No. 94-938, at 368-369; H. R. Rep. No. 94-658, at 307. Such a taxpayer might have little incentive to oppose enforcement vigorously. Then, with no real adversary, the IRS could use its summons power to engage in "fishing expeditions" that might unnecessarily trample upon taxpayer privacy.

* * *

When, as in this case, the summoned party is itself under investigation, the interests at stake are very different. First, by definition, the IRS is not engaged in a "fishing expedition" when it seeks information relevant to a legitimate investigation of a particular taxpayer. In such cases, any incidental effect on the privacy rights of unnamed taxpayers is justified by the IRS's interest in enforcing the tax laws. More importantly, the summoned party will have a direct incentive to oppose enforcement. In such circumstances, the vigilance and self-interest of the summoned party — complemented by its right to resist enforcement — will provide some assurance that the IRS will not strike out arbitrarily or seek irrelevant materials.

Id. at 320-21. Why do you think Congress was concerned that John Doe summonses might be used for "fishing expeditions"?

[B] Audits

[1] Overview of Audits

The IRS audits tax returns for a number of reasons. According to the IRS, its primary objective in auditing returns is to promote voluntary compliance. I.R.M. 1.4.10. Because every taxpayer bears some risk of audit, the so-called "audit lottery," the theory is that taxpayers are encouraged to report their income and expense items correctly. Another reason the IRS audits returns is to generate additional revenue. Therefore, those returns selected for audit are generally ones that the IRS expects will reflect an understatement of tax.

Audit coverage has declined over the years. The percentage of individual taxpayers audited is now less than one percent, and the percentage of corporation income tax returns audited is slightly over two percent. That latter figure is somewhat misleading, however. Each year, close to 90 percent of all corporations with revenue of $50 million or more are audited in some manner.[21] The IRS also conducts what it terms the Coordinated Examination Program (CEP). Under the CEP, an IRS agent is essentially permanently assigned to a corporation. The agent is given an office at the corporation and continually checks to make sure that the corporation is complying with federal tax law.

---

[21] Internal Revenue Service Data Book, Publication 55-B (Rev. 11-1998) Table 11.

The IRS uses various methods of selecting returns for audit. The most common method the IRS uses is the Discriminate Function (DIF). The DIF is a mathematical technique used by the IRS to classify income tax returns as to their error potential. The DIF formula divides returns into various audit classes. For example, individual income tax returns are classed based on their total positive income figure shown on the return. The computer formula then assigns weights to certain return characteristics. Those weights are then added together to obtain a DIF score. Generally the higher the DIF score, the greater the potential is that the return will be selected for audit. *See* Treasury Release IR 1669, September 14, 1976; IR 1906, November 16, 1977. Those returns with very high DIF scores are then examined manually to determine whether the return should be audited and the type of audit that is necessary. The DIF formula is cloaked in secrecy. *See* I.R.C. § 6103(b)(2). Under the current IRS structure, IRS Service Centers, where tax returns are sent for initial processing, assign each return a DIF score.

The DIF formula was developed from data that the IRS gathered through its Taxpayer Compliance Measurement Program (TCMP). Tax returns were selected purely randomly for the TCMP program. Those returns were then subjected to a very detailed, line-by-line audit. The purpose of the TCMP program was to discover what items on a return predict the greatest potential of error. The TCMP program was suspended in 1995 because it became too expensive. The TCMP may be replaced with a new, less-invasive program called the National Research Program.

There are other methods of targeting returns for audit. If a taxpayer files a claim for refund, the IRS normally will screen the original return to determine whether an examination should be made to substantiate the claim for refund. The IRS's information return matching program (discussed in Chapter 1) may also trigger an audit if the receipt reported on the taxpayer's return differs in amount from that reported on the information return. *See Portillo v. Commissioner*, 932 F.2d 1128 (1991). Audits may also arise from the process of "infection." If a corporation's tax return is being audited and there are discrepancies or other suspicious circumstances, this might lead the IRS to audit the shareholders of the corporation as well. Newspaper reports can also lead to audits. In addition, the IRS has an informant program, which provides for rewards for individuals who provide information leading to the collection of tax.[22] *See* I.R.C. § 7623.

---

[22] *Jarvis v. United States*, a breach of contract action brought by an informant, is interesting because it lays out the terms of the informant's agreement with the IRS:

> The IRS will pay to the Informant amounts per the below-outlined schedule of the net taxes, fines, and penalties (but not interest) collected from the Taxpayers as a direct result of information provided by the Informant that caused the investigation and resulted in the recovery:
>
> 10% of first $10,000,000.00
> 15% of next $10,000,000.00
> 20% of next $10,000,000.00
> 25% of amount over $ 30,000,000.00
>
> With a maximum reward not to exceed $ 25 million.

Jarvis v. United States, 43 Fed. Cl. 529, 530 (1999). The court ruled that Jarvis was entitled to $1,769,099.18, the amount that the Office of Chief Counsel had calculated that Jarvis would be entitled to if he met all contractual conditions. *Id.* at 530–531.

Once a return is selected for audit, there are various ways in which the audit may be carried out. There are three main types of audits, correspondence audits, office audits, and field audits. Correspondence audits are normally conducted by mail; as a result, they are limited to issues that lend themselves to verification from records that can be forwarded to the IRS. Under the current structure of the IRS, Service Centers carry out correspondence audits.[23] The Service Center sends the taxpayer an initial contact letter requesting information, or explaining why the return had to be corrected. If the taxpayer agrees with the correction, then the taxpayer generally pays the additional tax liability and the case is closed. Alternatively, if the taxpayer can explain the item in question and provide the necessary information the IRS needs to verify the item, then the issue is resolved. Another possible response to a correspondence audit would be to request an interview. However, if the taxpayer requests an interview, the audit is transferred to an examining agent, which may lead to a more in-depth review of the return.

Whether the IRS conducts a field audit or an office audit of a particular taxpayer will depend primarily on the complexity of the issues involved. Office audits are conducted at the IRS by a tax auditor. The initial contact letter usually contains a request to meet with the auditor at the IRS office. Normally the contact letter will request the taxpayer to bring specified pieces of information or documentation to support the treatment of a particular item. Returns selected for office audits generally involve issues that are too complex to be resolved by mail but not complex enough to warrant a field audit. Office audits are used to handle such issues as unusual or large itemized deductions, dependency exemptions, travel and entertainment expenses, and the like.

Field audits are reserved for more complex business and individual returns. They are conducted by revenue agents at the taxpayer's place of business. A revenue agent, as opposed to a tax auditor, is generally more experienced and has more education. A taxpayer must be more sensitive when it comes to a field audit. Generally, the potential issues involved in a field audit are not as clear as in a correspondence audit or an office audit. Thus, the taxpayer should cooperate with the agent and provide the requested information, but the taxpayer should not be overly generous, given that the scope of the audit may expand later on.

The IRS also conducts an Industry Specialization Program (ISP) designed to provide better identification and development of issues and to obtain consistent treatment of issues nationwide. "An industry specialist is a case manager who serves as a nationwide specialist for an industry selected for specialization as a designated industry. The industry specialist also coordinates audit programs when local agents are assigned to audit a member of the industry." I.R.M. (35)641. Industry specialists provide examining agents with ISP Coordinated Issue Papers, as well as other information to help them carry out the audit.

Examples of information that the Industry Specialist can furnish, which would be helpful in setting the scope and depth of the examination, include:

---

[23] As discussed in Chapter 1, the IRS Reform Act has reorganized the IRS around functional lines. Service Centers (campuses) responsible for processing returns and payments remain. The nature of the three types of audits discussed above will likely be unaffected by the reorganization.

(a)   identification of unique, industry-specific issues and the Service's position on those issues;

(b)   economic conditions of the industry;

(c)   descriptions of accounting and business practices in the industry;

(d)   suggested audit procedures; and

(e)   computer programs that may have potential application.

I.R.M. 4.12 Exhibit 4.4.1-1. To date, the ISP covers 24 nationwide industries, including Health Care, Constuction and Real Estate, Food, Petroleum, and Motor Vehicles. A similar IRS program, the Market Segment Specialization Program, also gathers industry-specific information and prepares "Audit Technique Guides" for use by agents examining businesses ranging from Alaskan commercial fishing to mortuaries.

[2]   Partnership Audit Procedures Under TEFRA

Partnerships are not taxable entities, so, prior to 1982, the IRS was required to audit the return of each partner in order to adjust a partnership item. In 1982, Congress decided to enact the Tax Equity and Fiscal Responsibility Act (TEFRA),[24] to improve the audit procedures applicable to partnerships. In general, TEFRA applies to partnerships with more than ten partners. *See* I.R.C. § 6231(a)(1)(B). It provides auditing and litigation procedures at the partnership level for partnership items, thereby enabling the IRS to audit a partnership without auditing each partner. The TEFRA rules also provide a procedure for judicial review of adjustments to partnership items.

After making an adjustment determination, the IRS must send a notice of Final Partnership Administrative Adjustment (FPAA) to the "tax matters partner" (TMP). I.R.C. §§ 6223(a)(1), 6223(d)(2). In general, the TMP is either the general partner designated to the IRS as such, or the general partner having the largest profits interest in the partnership at the close of the taxable year involved. *See* I.R.C. § 6231(a)(7); *see also* Rev. Proc. 88-16, 1988-1 C.B. 691. The TMP is required to keep the other partners informed of the progress of administrative and judicial proceedings. I.R.C. § 6223(g).

Within 60 days after the FPAA is sent to the TMP, the IRS must send copies to each notice partner. I.R.C. § 6223(d)(2). A notice partner is any partner whose name, address, and profit interest appears on the partnership return, and any partner that has furnished its name and address to the IRS at least 30 days prior to mailing of the FPAA to the TMP. I.R.C. §§ 6223(a), 6231(a)(8). The TMP has 90 days from the date the FPAA was mailed to petition the Tax Court, the Court of Federal Claims, or an appropriate federal district court. I.R.C. § 6226(a). Once the 90-day period expires, any notice partner can file a petition within the next 60 days. I.R.C. § 6226(b).

Any partner may file a request for administrative adjustment with the IRS within three years of the time the partnership return was filed, so long as the IRS has not already sent the TMP an FPAA. I.R.C. § 6227(a). The request for administrative adjustment is analogous to a refund claim. If the IRS does

---

[24] Pub. L. No. 97-248, 96 Stat. 324.

not grant the request in full, the partner can sue in Tax Court, district court, or the Court of Federal Claims. I.R.C. § 6228. The time limitations are similar to those discussed in Chapter 8 with respect to refund suits, *see* I.R.C. § 6228(a)(2)(A), except that no court petition may be filed after the IRS mails the partnership a notice of the beginning of an administrative proceeding, I.R.C. § 6228(a)(2)(B).

Many partnerships with over 100 partners may elect to be governed by simplified procedures. *See* I.R.C. §§ 775, 6240. The IRS is not required to notify the partners in an electing partnership that it has commenced an audit. I.R.C. § 6245(b). Unless the partnership designates a representative, the IRS can select any partner to represent the partnership. I.R.C. § 6255(b)(1). The representative can bind the partnership and all its partners, including past partners. I.R.C. § 6255(b)(2). Only the partnership can obtain judicial review of the IRS's adjustments. I.R.C. § 6247.

Adjustments to an electing large partnership will generally affect only the persons who are partners in the year the adjustment becomes final, rather than those who were partners in the year the item arose. I.R.C. § 6241(c)(1). Except for adjustments to partners distributive shares, *see* I.R.C. § 6241(c)(2), an electing partnership has the option of paying the deficiency, interest, and penalties directly, rather than passing it through to the partners. I.R.C. § 6242(b). The partnership must provide each partner with an information return by March 15 of the year after the close of the partnership's taxable year, regardless of when its own return is due. I.R.C. § 6031(b). A partner in an electing large partnership must report all partnership items in a manner consistent with the partnership's reporting or it will be subject to penalties. I.R.C. § 6241(a).

[3] Audit Strategy

Ideally, taxpayers should begin preparing for a possible audit on the first day of the taxable year, by retaining documents and receipts, and documenting transactions. Of course most taxpayers are generally neither that farsighted nor that diligent. Consideration of how to minimize the risk of audit should also occur at the return preparation stage. For example, assume that the taxpayer has an unusually large deduction for the year. Because of that large deduction, a likelihood exists that the return will be selected for examination. One strategy would be simply to file the return without any explanation of the deduction. An alternative strategy might be to attach a statement to the return explaining why the deduction amount is so great or attach a copy of the receipt confirming the amount expended. The theory behind the latter approach is that if the return receives a high DIF score, the examiner will look at the explanation and conclude that the matter is not worth pursuing. Which approach do you think is better?

Once the taxpayer's return is selected for examination, many taxpayers allow their accountants to handle audits; a taxpayer may call in an attorney only after receiving a notice of deficiency, or even after filing a Tax Court petition. Before an initial interview with the taxpayer, the IRS is required to provide the taxpayer with information about the audit process and the taxpayer's rights under that process. I.R.C. § 7521(b)(1). Unless the taxpayer is summoned, the taxpayer need not be present at the interview, and the taxpayer can be represented by a tax practitioner with a written power of attorney. I.R.C. § 7521(c). Either the taxpayer or the IRS can record an audit conference, if that party notifies the other party in advance. *See* I.R.C. § 7521(a). Moreover, during the audit process, under Code section 7525, any "federally authorized tax practitioner" may assert a privilege regarding confidential communications.

One of the best sources of information on how an examination is conducted is the Internal Revenue Manual (IRM). The IRM is a manual that is intended primarily for internal use at the IRS, but has been made available to the public under the Freedom of Information Act, discussed in Chapter 3. The IRM is divided into several different parts. Of special interest to taxpayers and to attorneys are the various handbooks that are included in the IRM. For example, IRM ¶ 4231 contains Audit Guidelines for IRS examiners. These guidelines set forth audit procedures, along with exhibits and instructions to examining agents about commonly encountered taxpayer errors. The IRM can be very helpful to a tax practitioner in planning a taxpayer's response to an audit. If, for example, an office audit involves travel and entertainment expenses, the attorney can consult the section in the audit handbook that tells an auditor what questions to ask, what information to request, and the like. By knowing the approach of the auditor before the meeting, the attorney can prepare the client to answer the questions correctly and honestly, but without providing any additional information.

Audit strategy varies depending on the type of audit. For correspondence audits, the best course generally is to respond to the requests for information and documentation quickly and concisely, in order to prevent the audit from being expanded to cover other issues. Resolving the matter with the Service Center means it is unlikely that a tax auditor or revenue agent will be assigned to the case. As a general rule, an office audit is limited to the issues that are listed in the initial contact letter. A tax auditor generally must get permission from a superior to expand the scope of the audit. In contrast, a revenue agent conducting a field audit may use his own discretion to expand the audit. In either case, it normally does not pay to antagonize the examiner.

With respect to strategy in dealing with an audit, one article suggests:

§ 32.04 AUDIT PLANNING TECHNIQUES

[1] — Pre-audit

For each actual or planned commercial transaction, the taxpayer should identify all potential litigation risks and, to the extent possible, structure the transaction such that it is supported by existing authority. For example, when transacting commercially with unrelated parties, taxpayers should allocate by contract each party's rights and obligations under a tax allocation provision. For significant transactions, taxpayers should consider obtaining a private letter ruling. * * *

The taxpayer should establish procedures for collecting and maintaining pertinent records. For corporate taxpayers, the taxpayer's tax or legal department should maintain files containing all relevant documents and identifying all knowledgeable witnesses.

[2] — During the Audit

[a] — Audits of Individuals and Smaller Companies

It is useful for the taxpayer or his representative to establish a good working relationship with the revenue agent conducting the examination. From the very first contact with the revenue agent, whether on the telephone or in person, a respectful (non-condescending) demeanor will set the right tone. It is preferable to have an initial telephone discussion with the agent to establish the ground rules for the audit. These include:

(1)   submission of the representative's power of attorney if it has not previously been provided;

(2)   determination of whether an extension of the statute of limitations is being solicited and, if so, the terms of the requested waiver;

(3)   discussion of the issues that will be examined;

(4)   determination of what material will be requested; and

(5)   scheduling a meeting and learning the revenue agent's expected time frame for completing the examination.

Contact with the revenue agent also provides the opportunity to assess the agent's intelligence and level of experience. One also should be able to discern a number of other insights into the revenue agent, such as his or her attitude toward the job, any prejudices or preconceived notions that may cloud the agent's judgment about the particular case or issue, how aggressive or demanding he or she may be in requesting information or meeting deadlines, etc. The representative should be able to take cues from these perceptions that will help in steering the revenue agent through the audit and yielding a better resolution for the taxpayer in the end. Establishing rapport with the revenue agent can go a long way to making the audit less painful for the taxpayer and to achieving an agreed case.

Despite the taxpayer's or representative's best efforts to be cooperative and cordial, there are times when a revenue agent steps out of bounds or behaves irrationally. The taxpayer or representative cannot let these impulses go unchecked or let the revenue agent run amok. Thus, even at the risk of offending the revenue agent, it will be necessary to let the agent know that you wish to speak with his or her manager, and to do so. Managers will often support their agents but also know their agents' weaknesses and strengths. If the taxpayer's complaint is legitimate, the manager will usually intervene to fix the problem. Managers are also helpful in resolving issues over which the revenue agent may have little or no authority or experience.

When the audit has moved beyond the information-gathering stage, it is often helpful to meet with the manager to discuss the revenue agent's findings, particularly where the revenue agent appears not to understand the facts or the taxpayer's business, or the law. Contact with the manager or other personnel advising the agent can eliminate factual misimpressions that were conveyed by the revenue agent to his or her superiors and can provide an opportunity to address the substantive issues. The purpose for all of these efforts during the examination phase is to keep the audit as narrow as possible and to produce an agreed case at the end of the process.

[b] — The Large Case Audit

At the beginning of a large case audit, the Service's audit team, the Service's case manager, and the taxpayer typically meet. During the meeting, the taxpayer should attempt to establish an overall framework for the audit. Topics for discussion include:

(1)   Identifying formal communication channels between the audit team and the taxpayer's tax or legal personnel.

(2)   Reviewing with the Service's audit team, the team's proposed audit plan.

(3)   Determining whether the taxpayer is subject to the Service's Industry Specialization Program.[25]

* * *

(5)   Advising the Service of the taxpayer's position regarding the Service's requests for extending the I.R.C. § 6501(a) statute of limitations.

(6)   Probing the degree to which the audit team intends to utilize District Counsel and specialists (e.g., economists).

* * *

Taxpayers should provide the audit team with a comfortable working space (e.g., a private office), to avoid charges of hardship. The space should not be so comfortable, however, that the Service would prefer to spend time at the taxpayers' office over other offices. Taxpayers should control access to all documents and files, and should establish a system to funnel all information requests through the taxpayers' tax department. Each department should supervise the copying process and maintain a log of all information that the taxpayer turns over.

Kaplan, *supra*, at 32-45–32-48.

Another article adds the following:

One of the most important factors for success by the taxpayer at the audit level will be the quality of his or her documentation. Given that most audits occur a few years after completion of the transactions, the taxpayer should be instructed to be diligent in preserving potentially pertinent records and documents. If a taxpayer is notified of an audit and the records are not in the best condition, an attempt should be made to organize any supporting information which might exist.

---

[25] [The IRS's Industry Specialization Program is discussed in Section 2.03[B][1] of Chapter 2. Eds.]

If the requested documents do not exist, the representative should attempt to obtain corroborating evidence from outside parties. If there was absolutely no basis for the original tax position, the representative should simply concede the issue in the reply to the IRS. Although there is a risk that the IRS will then expand the scope of the audit in the belief that other areas of the taxpayer's return might also lack documentation, there is no viable alternative. Attempts to mislead the IRS may constitute professional misconduct for the representative, destroy his or her reputation with the IRS, and seriously damage the taxpayer's status with the IRS. * * *

The ability to present facts in a clear, concise, and convincing presentation is a factor that increases the chances for the taxpayer's success during an audit. This skill requires that the representative display a full understanding of all of the facts during the interview and be ready to rely upon an exhaustive research of the applicable law. In constructing the argument for each issue, the representative should outline legal authority. If the representative is able to direct the interview, usually the simple issues and those which present the strongest arguments in favor of the taxpayer should be discussed first. * * *

There are two common negotiating techniques that often help the taxpayer. First, if the IRS has not taken a position on the issue in question and the examiner is not conceding the point, then the representative should consider requesting the examiner to seek technical advice from the National Office.[26] The examiner may be hesitant to delay the audit on the issue and might concede to the representative. Second, the representative should bring attention to any deductions which were not claimed. If a more beneficial method of tax computation is available to the taxpayer, the IRM directs the examiner to secure any information necessary to make the computation. This strategy might also help the taxpayer on other issues if the examiner believes this evidence shows the taxpayer is cautious in taking advantage of deductions and credits.

Thomas C. Pearson & Dennis R. Schmidt, "Successful Preparation and Negotiation May Reduce the Time and Breadth of an IRS Audit," 40 Tax'n for Acct. 234, 235–236, 238 (1988).

If an IRS examiner requests to see books and records, it is wise to have the examiner issue an Information Document Request (IDR), which is Form 4564. An IDR serves two purposes. It allows the attorney to evaluate the request and negotiate its scope. It also may reveal a particular issue the examiner is considering, which helps in preparing an appropriate response. An IDR also provides the opportunity to respond with a cover letter that makes a favorable impression. *See generally* A. Steve Hidalgo & Percy P. Woodward, IRS EXAMINATIONS AND APPEALS: DOMESTIC AND INTERNATIONAL PROCEDURES (1993).

---

[26] [Requests for technical advice are discussed in Chapter 9. Eds.]

If the requested documents do not exist, the representative should attempt to obtain corroborating evidence from outside parties. If there was absolutely no basis for the original tax position, the representative should simply concede the issue in the reply to the IRS. Although there is a risk that the IRS will then expand the scope of the audit in the belief that other areas of the taxpayer's return might also lack documentation, there is no viable alternative. Attempts to mislead the IRS may constitute professional misconduct for the representative, destroy his or her reputation with the IRS, and seriously damage the taxpayer's status with the IRS. * * *

The ability to present facts in a clear, concise, and convincing presentation is a factor that increases the chances for the taxpayer's success during an audit. This skill requires that the representative display a full understanding of all of the facts during the interview and be ready to rely upon an exhaustive research of the applicable law. In constructing the argument for each issue, the representative should outline legal authority. If the representative is able to direct the interview, usually the simple issues and those which present the strongest arguments in favor of the taxpayer should be discussed first. * * *

There are two common negotiating techniques that often help the taxpayer. First, if the IRS has not taken a position on the issue in question and the examiner is not conceding the point, then the representative should consider requesting the examiner to seek technical advice from the National Office.[26] The examiner may be hesitant to delay the audit on the issue and might concede to the representative. Second, the representative should bring attention to any deductions which were not claimed. If a more beneficial method of tax computation is available to the taxpayer, the IRM directs the examiner to secure any information necessary to make the computation. This strategy might also help the taxpayer on other issues if the examiner believes this evidence shows the taxpayer is cautious in taking advantage of deductions and credits.

Thomas C. Pearson & Dennis R. Schmidt, "Successful Preparation and Negotiation May Reduce the Time and Breadth of an IRS Audit," 40 Tax'n for Acct. 234, 235–236, 238 (1988).

If an IRS examiner requests to see books and records, it is wise to have the examiner issue an Information Document Request (IDR), which is Form 4564. An IDR serves two purposes. It allows the attorney to evaluate the request and negotiate its scope. It also may reveal a particular issue the examiner is considering, which helps in preparing an appropriate response. An IDR also provides the opportunity to respond with a cover letter that makes a favorable impression. *See generally* A. Steve Hidalgo & Percy P. Woodward, IRS EXAMINATIONS AND APPEALS: DOMESTIC AND INTERNATIONAL PROCEDURES (1993).

---

[26] [Requests for technical advice are discussed in Chapter 9. Eds.]

[C]   Reconstructing a Taxpayer's Income

If a taxpayer has failed to keep books and records, the records allegedly are inadequate or false, or if the taxpayer allegedly has unreported income, the IRS may "reconstruct" the taxpayer's income using any of a variety of techniques. Common techniques include the net worth method, cash transactions method, the bank deposits method, the specific items method, the source and application of funds method, and the T-account method. Each method seeks to establish the amount of taxable income earned by the taxpayer and to compare it to the return to determine the amount of unreported income. The most commonly used methods are the specific items method, which focuses on a specific receipt or receipts that were not included on the taxpayer's return, and the net worth method. I.R.M. 9.5.

The net worth method compares the taxpayer's net worth at the beginning of the taxable year with his net worth at the close of the taxable year. By adding all expenditures made during the year, this computation reflects the amount by which the taxpayer's wealth increased. *See, e.g., United States v. Scott*, 660 F.2d 1145, 1147 (7th Cir. 1981) (criminal case). The increase in wealth is then examined to determine the extent to which it came from nontaxable sources such as gifts, loans, or savings from prior years. Any excess is putative unreported income. *See Estate of Beck v. Commissioner*, 56 T.C. 297, 339 (1971), *acq.*, 1972-2 C.B. 1, and *acq.* 1972-2 C.B. 3 ("By a showing of a substantial increase in net worth in excess of reported income without reasonable explanation of such discrepancy as being attributable to loans, gifts, or other nontaxable receipts, the net worth method furnishes persuasive evidence of unreported income and reflects on the overall accuracy of income reported on the books and on the returns.").

The application of the net worth method in a criminal case is described in *United States v. Smith*, 890 F.2d 711 (5th Cir. 1989), which is reproduced in Chapter 14. In general, the net worth method functions the same way in both civil and criminal cases. However, the burden of proof differs; in criminal cases, the government bears the burden of proving the taxpayer's guilt beyond a reasonable doubt. In civil cases, the "preponderance of the evidence" standard applies in cases other than fraud cases, and, as discussed in Chapter 6, either the IRS or the taxpayer may bear the burden of persuasion.

Note that the specific items method, discussed both in this chapter in *Cooper*, and in Chapter 14 in *Smith*, may be used in conjunction with the net worth method. *Smith, supra*, at 717; *Estate of Beck, supra*, at 353; *see also United States v. Lewis*, 759 F.2d 1316, 1328 (8th Cir. 1985); *Scott, supra,* at 1147, 1148. The following case illustrates the application of the net worth method in the civil context:

SCHWARZKOPF v. COMMISSIONER
United States Court of Appeals, Third Circuit
246 F.2d 731 (1957)

STALEY, CIRCUIT JUDGE:

A challenge to the Commissioner's use of the net worth method of determining income is presented by this petition seeking review of a decision of the Tax Court of the United States.

Petitioner George Schwarzkopf, an oculist and eye surgeon, was a resident of Atlantic City, New Jersey, during 1947 through 1951, the taxable years under review. His residence contained not only his living quarters but also his office, operating room, and hospital rooms. Taxpayer kept his own receipts book from which he reported his yearly income. He admitted that many of the sums entered on his receipts book represented not gross but net fees, after deducting certain hospitalization expenses. Taxpayer did not show any of the receipts from these expenses to the investigating agents, and most of the receipts from earlier years were admittedly destroyed.

Finding a substantial discrepancy between bank deposits and reported income, the Commissioner reconstructed the income of Schwarzkopf by resort to the net worth method, with the following comparative results:

Year	Net income report	Net income as determined by respondent	Unreported taxable income determined by respondent
1946	$14,688.25	$49,140.24	$34,451.99
1947	14,244.31	31,908.91	17,664.60
1948	14,200.00	50,744.70	37,544.30
1949	16,040.59	34,376.53	19,335.94
1950	17,000.79	48,125.46	31,124.67
1951	21,721.06	175,466.96	153,745.90

The Commissioner then determined the taxpayer's deficiencies for the respective years and additions to tax under sections 293(b) [currently I.R.C. § 6663(a). Eds.] and 294(d)(2) [currently I.R.C. § 6654(a). Eds.] of the Internal Revenue Code of 1939. * * *

Most of the amounts utilized in the Commissioner's net worth analysis were stipulated. Only undeposited cash on hand was disputed, and the Commissioner determined that there was none as of January 1, 1946 and $32,000 undeposited cash as of December 31, 1951; these amounts were prorated over the years in question. The Tax Court, however, found that taxpayer had $101,000 in undeposited cash as of January 1, 1946, and the following amounts thereafter:

December 31, 1946	$62,000
December 31, 1947	52,000
December 31, 1948	32,000
December 31, 1949	32,000
December 31, 1950	32,000
December 31, 1951	32,000

The Tax Court determination, of course, completely eliminated the 1946 deficiency and made certain changes in the deficiencies of the other years involved. Finally, the Tax Court found that petitioner's income tax returns for 1947 through 1951 were false and fraudulent and were made with intent to evade tax, and that part of the deficiency for each of the years 1947 through 1951 was due to fraud with intent to evade tax.

The salient thrust of petitioner's principal argument is that the Commissioner's use of the net worth method of income reconstruction was unwarranted as his books of account were correct and adequate.

Holland v. United States, 1954, 348 U.S. 121, 75 S.Ct. 127, 99 L.Ed. 150, has become the *fons et origo* of the law concerning the use of the net worth method of income reconstruction. In giving its approval to the net worth method, the Supreme Court said, 348 U.S. at page 132, 75 S.Ct. at page 134:

> " * * * To protect the revenue from those who do not 'render true accounts,' the Government must be free to use all legal evidence available to it in determining whether the story told by the taxpayer's books accurately reflects his financial history."

This quoted portion of the *Holland* case is recognized by petitioner as sanctioning the use of the net worth method to test the accuracy and completeness of the books of account. Thus, the net worth method serves two purposes: first, it may be used to test the correctness of the books; secondly, it is cogent evidence of the amount of income which went unreported. The fact that the books on their face appear to be adequate does not preclude the use of the net worth method. *Holland v. United States, supra,* 348 U.S. at pages 131–132, 75 S.Ct. at page 133. In any event, the books involved here contained items of net income with hospital expenses already deducted. The disposal by the taxpayer of bills evidencing these expenses made the computation of their amount impossible, and thus left vague and unreported some unknown amount of income. The taxpayer's practice of cashing checks representing his patients' fees and receiving the money in large denominations rather than depositing the checks themselves made it impossible to test the accuracy of the books from that source. If taxpayer's contention is correct, everyone could keep a set of apparently accurate books, carefully destroy other evidences of the source and amount of income, and defend by an alien rule that the net worth method may not be used in those circumstances — and thus the government could be defrauded with impunity. However, it is when other methods of disclosing income fail that the net worth computation becomes especially important in the collection of revenue.

A favorite defense in net worth cases is that taxpayer had a large amount of undeposited cash on hand at the beginning of the investigation period. This may explain the disproportionate increase in net worth over the increase of taxable income. Petitioner here likewise contends that he had on hand a sizeable amount of undeposited cash at the beginning of the investigation period. Evidence as to the amount and source of this cash is questionable at best. Petitioner contends that the Tax Court committed clear error in refusing to find that a certain large sum came to him by way of an inheritance from an uncle who died in a land now occupied by Russia. Documentary proof of death and of the inheritance were not available because the records there were destroyed, and the only evidence of the inheritance were self-serving notations on the taxpayer's passports of the amounts he allegedly brought back from Europe. The fact that the Commissioner did not directly contradict this evidence would not compel the Tax Court to accept it in the circumstances of this case. The Tax Court, evaluating witness credibility, simply did not believe the story. We think it was eminently proper to use the net worth method here.

*   *   *

The cause will be remanded to the Tax Court for an adjustment of the penalties under Section 294(d)(2) and, as adjusted in accordance with this opinion, the decision will be affirmed.

———————————

The source and application of funds method is very similar to the net worth method, which was applied in *Schwarzkopf*:

> The source and application of funds method is a variation of the net worth method. Comparing the two methods reveals that they differ only in format. The source and application of funds method entails the use of only those assets and liabilities which change during the year, whereas the net worth method requires the use of all assets and liabilities. The adjustments for nondeductible and nontaxable items are the same for both methods. The same result will be obtained under either method. However, the net worth method is preferable when the examination covers several years and the balances of assets and liabilities at the end of each year can be determined more readily than changes during the year.

I.R.M. 4.10.4.6.5.10.

What do you think of the taxpayer's "cash hoard" defense in *Schwarzkopf*? The defense is very common, particularly in net worth cases. The Internal Revenue Manual instructs IRS Special Agents to prepare for this defense in criminal cases:

(2)   In all cases where the net worth method is the primary method of proving income, the special agent should anticipate this defense and attempt to get evidence to negate it.

(3)   Admissions of the taxpayer are most effective to pin down the cash amount, and should be obtained at the initial interview or early in the investigation. The line of questioning should be directed toward developing:

    a.   The amount of cash on hand (undeposited currency and coin) at the starting point and at the end of each prosecution year.

    b.   The amount of cash on hand at the date of the interview. (This data is sometimes useful in computing cash on hand for earlier years.)

    c.   The source of cash * * *

    d.   Where the cash was kept.

    e.   Who knew about the cash.

    f.   Whether anyone ever counted it.

    g.   When and on what was any cash spent.

    h.   Whether any record is available with respect to the alleged cash on hand.

      i.   The denominations of the cash on hand.

(4)   In most cases the spouse should also be questioned about cash on hand as well as other matters. In order to avoid any misunderstanding by the taxpayer, it is suggested that the meaning of cash on hand be explained prior to discussing the matter.

(5)   The taxpayer (and spouse) also should be questioned regarding financial history from the time he or she was first gainfully employed, employers, salary, etc. This information will serve in many cases to check the accuracy of the taxpayer's statements about cash on hand.

(6)   In addition to admissions, evidence used to establish the starting point will most often be sufficient to refute the defense of cash on hand.

I.R.M. 9.5.8.2.

The cash hoard defense appears in *Cooper* as well, which applies the specific items method and the bank deposits methods to reconstruct the taxpayers' income.

COOPER v. COMMISSIONER
United States Tax Court
T.C. Memo. 1987-431

WRIGHT, JUDGE:

By notice of deficiency dated June 3, 1983, respondent determined deficiencies in petitioners' Federal income tax and additions to tax * * *. After concessions by both parties, the issues remaining for our consideration are: (1) whether petitioners had unreported income for the taxable years 1972, 1974, 1975 and 1976 as determined by respondent; (2) whether petitioner Milton B. Cooper is liable for the additions to tax under section 6653(b) [currently I.R.C. § 6663. Eds.]; and (3) whether petitioners are liable for the additions to tax under section 6654(c) for the taxable years in issue.

FINDINGS OF FACT

Some of the facts have been stipulated and are so found. The stipulation of facts, together with the exhibits attached thereto, are incorporated herein by this reference.

*   *   *

Petitioner was a shareholder, officer and manager of William Cooper and Sons, Inc., an appliance store located in Mount Vernon, New York. Petitioner reported his salary from this appliance store as income on the returns for each of the years at issue. On the joint returns petitioner reported adjusted gross income in the amounts of $6,998, $3,838, $16,505 and $38,533 for the taxable years, 1972, 1974, 1975 and 1976, respectively. Petitioner is a high school graduate and has completed two years of liberal arts study at New York

University. During the taxable years in issue, Bernice Cooper was a full-time homemaker.

During each of the taxable years at issue, petitioner had winnings and losses from wagering which were not reported on the joint tax returns. With the exception of some losing tickets for 1974 and 1975, petitioner kept no records of his wins and losses. Petitioner, however, maintained an account at an Offtrack Betting Parlor (OTB). Annual activity in that account is reflected below:

Year	Deposits	Withdrawals	Net Winnings or Losses
1974	$ 3,500	$ (6,500)	$ (3,098.70)
1975	6,495	-0-	6,716.10
1976	7,239	-0-	7,178.10
	$ 17,234	$ (6,500)	$ 10,795.50

Gambling expenditures, other than those shown above, were incurred in 1974, 1975 and 1976 in the amounts of $18,433, $791 and $13,055, respectively. In addition, petitioner made several payments to "touters," individuals or companies that provide tips or information regarding horse races and who are generally paid ten percent of the proceeds from a successful bet. Petitioner did not report any income or losses from gambling activities.

Petitioner employed an accountant, Ms. Barbara Kaufman, to prepare the joint income tax returns for the taxable years at issue. Petitioner did not disclose his gambling activities to Ms. Kaufman when the returns were prepared but after he received notice of the investigation of his 1972 return, petitioner informed Ms. Kaufman that he had unreported income from gambling.

On or about March of 1977, respondent began investigating petitioner's income tax returns. For the tax year 1972, respondent recomputed petitioner's income for that year using the specific item method. These computations are the basis for the statutory notice of deficiency and are summarized as follows:

	1972
Adjusted Gross Income (as reported)	$ 6,998.00
Add: Income from Forms 1099	
Off Track Betting	3,006.90
Off Track Betting	2,262.30
Off Track Betting	1,203.30
Yonkers Raceway	1,957.50
Roosevelt Raceway	2,824.20
Roosevelt Raceway	890.00
Total Adjusted Gross Income	$ 19,142.20

Respondent recomputed petitioner's income for the years 1974, 1975 and 1976 using the bank deposits plus cash expenditures method. The computations are the basis of the statutory notice of deficiency at issue in this case and are summarized as follows:

	1974	1975	1976
Total Deposits	$ 55,991.30	$ 64,036.69	$ 67,499.92
Total cash Expenditures	21,233.00	9,000.00	15,855.00
Total Deposits & Cash Expenditures	$ 77,224.30	$ 73,036.69	$ 83,304.92
Less: Non-Income Items[n.3]	(18,009.66)	(16,841.39)	(8,237.85)
Net Deposits	$ 59,214.64	$ 56,195.30	$ 75,067.07
Add: Net OTB Telephone Account Winnings	3,098.70	–0–	–0–
Total Gross Income	$ 62,313.34	$ 56,195.30	$ 75,067.07
Less: Sources of Income per Return	(16,691.80)	(20,265.35)	(41,396.15)
Revised Unreported Income	$ 45,621.54	$ 35,929.95	$ 33,670.92

OPINION

Unreported Income

The first issue for our consideration is whether petitioner had unreported income in the amounts as determined by respondent for the taxable years 1972, 1974, 1975 and 1976.

Petitioner has the burden of proving that respondent's determination of his tax liability in the statutory notice of deficiency is not correct. *Welch v. Helvering*, 290 U.S. 111, 115 (1933); *Rockwell v. Commissioner*, 512 F.2d 882 (9th Cir. 1975), *affg.* a Memorandum Opinion of this Court; Rule 142(a).[27]

A taxpayer is required to maintain records sufficient to show whether or not he is liable for Federal income taxes. Sec. 6001. It is well established that where the taxpayer fails to maintain adequate records, the Commissioner may prove the existence and amount of unreported income by any method that will, in his opinion, clearly reflect the taxpayer's income. Sec. 446(b); *Holland v. United States*, 348 U.S. 121, 130-132 (1954); *Harper v. Commissioner*, 54 T.C. 1121 (1970).

In the notice of deficiency respondent did not allow any deductions for wagering losses.

---

n.3.

Non-Income Items:	1974	1975	1976
Loans	$ 5,116.66	$ 9,565.02	$ 4,300.00
Credit memos	168.00	237.37	-0-
Federal tax refund	1,708.00	1,846.00	211.00
Refund of gambling losses	1,397.00	1,048.00	1,030.00
Cash withdrawals savings	2,120.00	285.00	375.00
Checks payable to cash	-0-	1,000.00	180.00
O.T.B. check withdrawals	6,500.00	-0-	-0-
Cash on hand	1,000.00	1,000.00	1,000.00
Repayment of personal loans	-0-	-0-	100.00
Madison Sq. Garden reimbursement	-0-	860.00	860.00
Proceeds — death of horse	-0-	1,000.00	-0-
Travel agency refund	-0-	-0-	154.00
Payment from Gellers	-0-	-0-	27.85
Total	$ 18,009.66	$ 16,841.39	$ 8,237.85

[27] [As discussed in Chapter 6, current law on burden of proof no longer automatically places the burden on the taxpayer. Eds.]

Two methods of reconstruction of income which have received judicial approval are the specific item method, *Schooler v. Commissioner*, 68 T.C. 867 (1977), and the bank deposits plus cash expenditure method, *Estate of Granat v. Commissioner*, 298 F.2d 397 (2d Cir. 1962). *See also Nicholas v. Commissioner*, 70 T.C. 1057, 1065 (1978); *Estate of Mason v. Commissioner*, 64 T.C. 651, 656 (1975), *affd.* 566 F.2d 2 (6th Cir. 1977); *Gromacki v. Commissioner*, 361 F.2d 727, 728-729 (7th Cir. 1966).

For the taxable year 1972, respondent used the specific item method. The income as reported on the 1972 joint income tax return was adjusted by adding gambling winnings which were reported on Forms 1099 from Off Track Betting, Yonkers Raceway and Roosevelt Raceway to petitioner but not shown on the return.

For 1974, 1975 and 1976, respondent used the bank deposits plus cash expenditures reconstruction method. The premise underlying this method of income reconstruction is that, absent some explanation, a taxpayer's bank deposits represent taxable income. The total of all deposits is determined by the Commissioner to arrive at the taxpayer's income. An adjustment is then made to eliminate deposits that reflect non-income items such as gifts, loans and transfers between various bank accounts. Cash expenditures are then added to bank deposits to determine gross income. The Commissioner will also make a further adjustment for the taxpayer's ascertainable business expenses, deductions, and exemptions. *See Percifield v. United States*, 241 F.2d 225 (9th Cir. 1957); *Gromacki v. Commissioner*, *supra*; *Harper v. Commissioner*, *supra* at 1129.

* * *

During the taxable years in issue, petitioner was a manager and shareholder of a family-run appliance business. As indicated by the activity in his OTB account he gambled frequently, with mixed results.

Petitioner, throughout the course of this proceeding, had various inconsistent explanations for the source of the additional income as determined by respondent.[n.4] While admitting that he had additional income from gambling, petitioner claimed at trial that his winnings were always exceeded by his losses. Moreover, petitioner maintained at trial that the source of the bank deposits resulted from cash gifts given to him by his in-laws, Benjamin and Rose Geller (the Gellers). These gifts were allegedly taken from a safety deposit box maintained by the Gellers.[n.5] Petitioner testified initially that he

[n.4] According to Internal Revenue Service Special Agents Alvin Goldberg and William Sembler, who testified at trial, petitioner vacillated between claiming that the deposits were from checks written by his father-in-law, Benjamin Geller, withdrawals from the Gellers' savings accounts, and cash from a safety deposit box maintained by his mother-in-law, Rose Geller. However, extensive analysis of the eight savings and two checking accounts by the special agents showed that all savings withdrawals were deposited in the checking accounts of the Gellers and checks were written only for their personal expenditures. With the exception of checks made out to cash totaling approximately $100 and a check for $27.85 written to Bernice Cooper, the Gellers made no checks out to petitioner or Bernice Cooper.

[n.5] The Gellers operated a retail liquor store from 1940 to 1968 in Yonkers, New York. In 1968, due to a condemnation for road construction, Mr. Geller sold the property for $56,000 and retired. Petitioner asserted that the proceeds from the sale and accumulated income formed the cash horde which generated the gifts.

drove his wife to the bank 7 to 10 times a year over a period of years to make the withdrawals. On cross-examination, petitioner increased the frequency of the alleged trips to once a week. Yet despite the alleged frequency of these trips, he was unable to remember the name or exact location of the bank.

Petitioner's explanation as to the source of the unreported income was vague, rambling, inherently improbable and lacks credibility. This Court need not accept uncorroborated, self-serving testimony. *Geiger v. Commissioner*, 440 F.2d 688 (9th Cir. 1971). It is inconceivable that he could have participated in retrieving money from a safety deposit box so frequently over a long period of time and be unable to remember the name or location of the bank. Because petitioner has not provided any credible explanation nor has he presented any records or testimony which would establish that the amounts were nontaxable gifts, we conclude that petitioner had unreported income from his gambling activities.

Because we have determined that petitioner had wagering income and because he asserted at trial that his losses exceeded winnings, we now must address the issue of whether petitioner is entitled to any deductions for these alleged losses. Section 165(d) permits the deduction of "Losses from wagering transactions * * * only to the extent of the gains from such transactions." Petitioner has the burden of proving that his alleged losses in fact occurred. *Stein v. Commissioner*, 322 F.2d 78 (5th Cir. 1963), *affg.* a Memorandum Opinion of this Court. Because there are unreported winnings, petitioner must establish that his losses exceeded the unreported winnings in order to be entitled to deduct any such losses. *Schooler v. Commissioner*, 68 T.C. 867, 869 (1977).

The issue is a factual one, to be decided on the basis of all the evidence. *Schooler v. Commissioner, supra*; *Fogel v. Commissioner*, 237 F.2d 917 (6th Cir. 1956), *affg. per curiam* a Memorandum Opinion of this Court; *Green v. Commissioner*, 66 T.C. 538, 545 (1976). However, in this case, petitioner has presented no evidence concerning the extent of his losses for the years at issue. Petitioner kept no records as required by section 6001 and the regulations thereunder.[n.6] Although his OTB account shows losses, however, it is only a partial record of his gambling activities.

We recognize that this Court has applied the rule of *Cohan v. Commissioner*, 39 F.2d 540, 543–544 (2d Cir. 1930), to estimate the amount of losses incurred despite the absence of adequate records. *See Green v. Commissioner, supra* at 548; *Drews v. Commissioner*, 25 T.C. 1354 (1956). Before we will apply the *Cohan* rule, however, there must be sufficient evidence in the record to show some losses were in fact sustained. *Schooler v. Commissioner, supra* at 871. *Stein v. Commissioner, supra* at 83. The record in this case, however, leaves us with no satisfactory basis for estimating the amount of total losses nor does it convince us that losses exceeded petitioner's unreported gains. We therefore decline to apply the *Cohan* rule in this case.

[n.6] *See* sec. 1.6001-1(a), Income Tax Regs. The Commissioner has suggested that gamblers regularly maintain diaries of winnings and losses to comply with sec. 6001. *See* Rev. Proc. 77-29, 1977-2 C.B. 538.

Accordingly, we conclude that petitioner has not met his burden of proof in regard to this issue and that he is taxable on the unreported gambling winnings in the amounts determined by respondent.

Prior to the IRS Reform Act, the IRS sometimes used indirect methods of reconstructing income — such as the bank deposits method discussed in *Cooper* — for "financial status audits." Section 7602(e), which was added by the IRS Reform Act, limits the use of these audits. A financial status audit is actually an audit *technique* used by the IRS for returns reflecting gross income that is less than indicated by the lifestyle enjoyed by the taxpayer. Section 7602(e) prevents the IRS from employing this examination technique unless it has a reasonable indication that there is a likelihood of unreported income.

§ 2.04 Joint Returns and Joint and Several Liability

[A] Background

Code section 6013(a) authorizes a joint return for husband and wife. In general, husband and wife are jointly and severally liable for any tax for a tax year in which they filed a joint return. I.R.C. § 6013(d)(3). Note that, under recently proposed regulations, if one spouse signed the return under duress, the return does not constitute a "joint return." Treas. Reg. § 1.6013-4(d). In addition, in order to alleviate the burden on a spouse who did not engage in the activity giving rise to an understatement of tax, and who was unaware of the understatement, Congress enacted an "innocent spouse" exception to joint and several liability. Code section 6013(e) provided the innocent spouse exception until 1998, when it was amended and recodified as section 6015.

Section 6013(e) had four main requirements: (1) the spouses filed a joint return for the taxable year, (2) on the return there was a substantial understatement of tax attributable to grossly erroneous items of one spouse, (3) the other spouse established that in signing the return he or she did not know, and had no reason to know, that there was such substantial understatement, and (4) taking into account all the facts and circumstances, it was inequitable to hold the other spouse liable. I.R.C. § 6013(e)(1) (1998). In addition, in erroneous deduction cases, the understatement had to exceed a certain percentage of the purported innocent spouse's adjusted gross income for the "preadjustment year," a requirement that was overlooked all too often.

"Grossly erroneous items" meant any unreported item of gross income and any claim of a deduction, credit, or basis in an amount for which there was "no basis in fact or law." I.R.C. § 6013(e)(2) (1998). Taxpayers had a difficult time proving the presence of "grossly erroneous items" in erroneous deduction cases. *Crowley and Cockrell v. Commissioner*, T.C. Memo. 1993-503, provides an example. In that case, the Tax Court stated:

Petitioner [Elizabeth Cockrell] contends that the fact that the parties entered into a compromise settlement is proof that the deductions in question are grossly erroneous items. Under the terms of the stipulated settlement, petitioner and Mr. Crowley were allowed to deduct 20 percent of the losses attributable to the commodities straddle transactions for the years in issue. The stipulations of settled issues filed in the instant case do not disclose the basis for the allowance of 20 percent of the deductions claimed by petitioner and Mr. Crowley. Consequently, we do not think that such compromise shows that the deductions in question were grossly erroneous items. To the contrary, the fact that respondent agreed to a compromise settlement suggests that the deductions in question were less than grossly erroneous. Anthony v. Commissioner, T.C. Memo. 1992-133; Neary v. Commissioner, T.C. Memo. 1985-261. * * *

Id. Do you agree with the court's reasoning?

In addition to the difficult hurdle posed by the "grossly erroneous items" standard, because the innocent spouse issue usually was litigated in Tax Court as part of the underlying substantive proceeding, the spouse seeking innocent spouse relief would often be forced to argue both that the deduction was valid and that it had no basis in fact or law. Similarly, if one attorney represented both husband and wife, the attorney would be faced with the conflict inherent in making those contradictory arguments. Moreover, a substantive ruling that the deduction was invalid did not necessarily establish that it had no basis in fact or law.

Elizabeth Cockrell filed a petition for rehearing, in which she pointed out that two of the principals of John Crowley's company, TSM Holding Company, had been convicted on tax fraud and conspiracy charges, which might indicate that the tax straddle deductions were grossly erroneous. The two attorneys representing the IRS in Cockrell's case were the same ones who had represented the IRS in the Tax Court case involving the two TSM Holding Company principals. *Id.* The Tax Court granted the rehearing petition. On rehearing, the court decided the case on the "no reason to know" prong of the innocent spouse statute. As indicated by the excerpt below, taxpayers have had trouble proving that they did not know and had no reason to know about the understatement. In the second *Cockrell* opinion, the court states, in part:

The Court of Appeals for the Second Circuit, the court to which an appeal in the instant case would lie, interprets subsection 6013(e)(1)(C) as requiring a taxpayer to establish that " 'she [or he] did not know and did not have reason to know that the deduction would give rise to a substantial understatement.' " Hayman v. Commissioner, 992 F.2d 1256, 1261 (2d Cir. 1993), (*quoting* Price v. Commissioner, 887 F.2d 959, 963 (9th Cir. 1989), *revg.* an Oral Opinion of this Court), *affg.* T.C. Memo. 1992-228.

In the instant case, respondent contends that petitioner knew that the deductions in issue would give rise to substantial understatements when she signed the returns for the taxable years in issue. Respondent relies primarily on the testimony of Robert Kraft to support such contention. During the trial of the instant case, Mr. Kraft testified that he had received a law degree from Georgetown University Law Center. At a subsequent hearing, Mr. Kraft admitted that he has never received a law degree. In light of Mr. Kraft's admission, we regard his testimony as inherently untrustworthy and, therefore, do not accept his testimony. Respondent also argues that, because petitioner was a stockbroker who had passed the "series seven" stockbroker examination prior to the time she signed the returns in issue, she must have been exposed to the mechanics of commodities straddle transactions. Respondent, therefore, contends that petitioner knew that the deductions claimed on the returns for the taxable years in issue would give rise to substantial understatements. Nothing in the record, however, establishes that petitioner's studies or her work as a stockbroker exposed her to the intricacies of commodities straddle transactions. Accordingly, we find that petitioner, when she signed the returns for the taxable years in issue, did not have actual knowledge that the deductions would give rise to the substantial understatements.

Even if a taxpayer does not have actual knowledge that deductions claimed on a return would give rise to a substantial understatement, a taxpayer who has reason to know of such an understatement is not entitled to innocent spouse relief. Sec. 6013(e)(1)(C). At the trial of the instant case, petitioner admitted that she signed the returns for the taxable years in issue without reviewing them. Nevertheless, she is charged with constructive knowledge of their contents. *Hayman v. Commissioner, supra* at 1262. Petitioner was educated and should have realized her responsibility for reviewing the returns she signed. Consequently, petitioner's failure to review returns that she signed under penalties of perjury cannot be excused. Terzian v. Commissioner, 72 T.C. 1164, 1170–1171 (1979).

The Court of Appeals for the Second Circuit has held that the magnitude of the deductions claimed on a return may give rise to a duty to inquire as to the propriety of the deductions. Friedman v. Commissioner, 53 F.3d 523, 531 (2d Cir. 1995), (*citing Hayman v. Commissioner, supra, affg. in part and revg. in part and remanding* T.C. Memo. 1993-549.) The duty of inquiry generally arises with respect to "tax returns setting forth large deductions, such as tax shelter losses offsetting income from other sources and substantially reducing or eliminating the couple's tax liability." *Hayman v. Commissioner, supra*, at 1262.

In the instant case, we believe that even a cursory review of the returns for the taxable years in issue would have alerted petitioner to the high probability that such returns contained substantial understatements. The 1980 return reported a gain of $408,097 on Schedule D that was offset by a loss of $407,884 reported on Schedule E, which included a loss of $508,045 from TSM Associates. That return reported adjusted gross income of only $8,055 for the taxable year 1980, and tax due of $240. The 1981 return, which was filed untimely on January 31, 1983, reported a gain of $697,896 on Schedule D that was offset by a loss of $679,327 reported on Schedule E, which included a loss of $413,765 from TSM Associates and a loss of $399,489 from APEX Associates. That return reported adjusted gross income of $90,658, and tax due of $13,980. Both the income and deductions with respect to Mr. Crowley's commodities straddle transactions reported on the 1980 and 1981 returns were larger than the other income and deductions reported by Mr. Crowley and petitioner. Under such circumstances, petitioner had a duty to look into the propriety of the deductions taken on the returns in issue, a duty she has failed to satisfy in the instant case. *Id.* Petitioner cannot obtain the benefits of section 6013(e) by simply turning a blind eye to facts that would reasonably put her on notice that further inquiry would need to be made. Bokum v. Commissioner, 94 T.C. 126, 148 (1990), *affd.* 992 F.2d 1132 (11th Cir. 1993). As we have previously noted, section 6013(e) is designed to protect the innocent, not the intentionally ignorant. Shannon v. Commissioner, T.C. Memo. 1991-207.

In deciding whether petitioner "had reason to know" of the substantial understatements when she signed the returns, we also take into account the factors that the Court of Appeals for the Second Circuit has held are to be considered in making such a decision: (1) The spouse's level of education; (2) the spouse's involvement in the family's business and financial affairs; (3) the presence of expenditures that appear lavish or unusual when compared with the family's past levels of income, standard of living, and spending patterns; and (4) the culpable spouse's evasiveness and deceit concerning their finances. *Friedman v. Commissioner, supra* at 531–532 (*citing Hayman v. Commissioner, supra* at 1261). The foregoing factors are considered "because, ordinarily, they predict what a prudent person would realize regardless of the other spouse's evasiveness or deceit." Bliss v. Commissioner, 59 F.3d 374, 379 (2d Cir. 1995), *affg.* T.C. Memo. 1993-390.

Applying such factors to the facts of the instant case, we conclude that petitioner had reason to know of the substantial understatements when she signed the returns for the taxable years in issue. Petitioner was a college-educated stockbroker who had passed the "series seven" examination. She was a former life insurance agent. Petitioner's involvement in the couple's business and financial affairs was also significant. Petitioner knew that Mr. Crowley was a "commodities trader." She traveled with him to several commodities seminars, where she attempted to attract clients for her husband at the hospitality suites provided by his employer after those seminars. They routinely entertained Mr. Crowley's clients at their apartment. Petitioner and Mr. Crowley lived lavishly during 1980 and 1981, the years for which petitioner seeks relief as an innocent spouse. They frequently dined at expensive restaurants during those years. During 1980, they vacationed in Canada, Vermont, and Florida. Mr. Crowley's American Express bill for that year was approximately $90,000, and a substantial portion of that amount was charged by petitioner. During 1981, petitioner and Mr. Crowley rented a two-bedroom apartment in Manhattan for approximately $1,400 or $1,500 per month and garaged

Mr. Crowley's BMW automobile for approximately $250 to $300 per month. Finally, there is no evidence in the record that shows that Mr. Crowley was evasive or deceitful about their finances or that he attempted to conceal the fact that he had engaged in commodities straddle transactions. Based on the record in the instant case, we conclude that, at the time she signed the returns for the taxable years in issue, petitioner had reason to know of the substantial understatements in issue.

Petitioner contends that the Court of Appeals' decision in *Friedman v. Commissioner, supra,* "limits" *Hayman v. Commissioner, supra,* with respect to the "reason to know" requirement of subsection 6013(e)(1)(C). * * *

We disagree with petitioner's interpretation of *Friedman v. Commissioner, supra,* as well as her characterization of herself as unsophisticated with respect to financial matters. * * *

Petitioner, unlike the taxpayer in *Friedman v. Commissioner, supra,* was a college-educated stockbroker when she signed the returns in issue, who admits that she failed to review those returns prior to signing them. Petitioner's failure to review the returns before signing them was apparently deliberate because nothing in the record indicates that she could not have reviewed them had she wished to do so. Petitioner claims that she signed the returns because she trusted Mr. Crowley. That trust alone, however, does not eliminate a spouse's duty to inquire when a perusal of the return would indicate that further inquiry is necessary. *Hayman v. Commissioner, supra* at 1262; Stevens v. Commissioner, 872 F.2d 1499, 1507 (11th Cir. 1989), *affg.* T.C. Memo. 1988-63. Consequently, we hold that petitioner has failed to prove that she did not know and had no reason to know that the deductions claimed on the returns for the taxable years in issue would give rise to substantial understatements.

Crowley v. Commissioner, T.C. Memo. 1995-551.

The case went to the Second Circuit, which affirmed without a published opinion. *See Cockrell v. Commissioner,* 116 F.3d 1472 (2d Cir. 1997) (reported in table case format); *Cockrell v. Commissioner,* 97-2 U.S.T.C. ¶ 50,549 (2d Cir. 1997) (unpublished op.). The United States Supreme Court denied certiorari. *Cockrell v. Commissioner,* 522 U.S. 1147 (1998).

Elizabeth Cockrell's situation received considerable publicity. The notice of deficiency she had received was in the amount of $650,000, and related to tax liability resulting from her brief marriage to John Crowley, during which time she had earned only $9,000 per year. "You Think *You've* Got Problems," New York Magazine 16 (April 10, 1995). Mr. Crowley had sent Ms. Cockrell a statement exculpating her, *id.,* but private agreements do not bind the IRS. In addition, in the initial *Cockrell* case cited above, the IRS's only two witnesses were John Crowley and Robert Kraft. Kraft was caught lying to the court, as described above.

[B]   Section 6015

Elizabeth Cockrell testified before Congress about the problems caused to women in her position. In response to the testimony and the testimony of others, Congress repealed subsection 6013(e) and enacted Code section 6015. Section 6015 reflects a major overhaul of both the eligibility for and the procedures for obtaining innocent spouse relief. As discussed below, it provides three forms of relief from joint and several liability for taxes: "innocent spouse" relief under Code section 6015(b), which largely reenacts prior Code section 6013(e); elective proportionate liability under section 6015(c); and discretionary equitable relief under section 6015(f).

[1]   Procedures

Under the new procedures for claiming innocent spouse relief, a taxpayer may elect innocent spouse status on IRS Form 8857, Request for Innocent Spouse Relief (And Separation of Liability and Equitable Relief). The Community Renewal Tax Relief Act of 2000 provided that an innocent spouse election may be made at any point after the IRS has asserted a deficiency; the taxpayer need not wait for a formal notice of deficiency. *See* I.R.C. § 6015(c)(3)(B). Note that a taxpayer may raise an innocent spouse claim with the IRS as late as the collections phase of the controversy.[28] I.R.C. § 6015(b)(1)(E). If a claim under section 6015(b) or (c) is rejected by the IRS, the taxpayer may obtain judicial review in the Tax Court in a separate proceeding from the proceeding on the underlying liability. *See* I.R.C. § 6015(b)(1)(E), (e). Proposed regulations issued in January 2001 provide that if a spouse requests relief under section 6015(b) or (c), the IRS will automatically consider whether that spouse qualifies under other relief provisions of section 6015. However, if a spouse elects relief under section 6015(f), relief will only be considered under that section. *See* Prop. Reg. 1.6015-1(a)(2). Note that there is no statutory deadline to apply for equitable relief under section 6015(f), though Form 8857 uses the same deadline as under (b) and (c).

The Tax Court has jurisdiction over most denials of innocent spouse relief. *See* I.R.C. § 6015(e). The Community Renewal Tax Relief Act of 2000 clarified that the 90-day period for filing a Tax Court petition with respect to denial of innocent spouse relief begins on the day *after* the IRS mails its denial, rather than the day of the denial. This makes the 90-day period parallel to the period for petitioning the Tax Court in response to a notice of deficiency.

The Tax Court has held that it has jurisdiction to review denials of equitable innocent spouse relief under section 6015(f) although the jurisdiction-granting provision of section 6015(e) arguably does not provide that jurisdiction. *See Butler v. Commissioner*, 114 T.C. 276 (2000); *Fernandez v. Commissioner*, 114 T.C. 324 (2000); *Charlton v. Commissioner*, 114 T.C. 333 (2000). *Butler* was a tax deficiency case coupled with an innocent spouse claim. *Fernandez* involved a "stand-alone" innocent spouse claim. In AOD 2000-6, the IRS acquiesced in *Fernandez*. Shortly thereafter, in Chief Counsel Notice N(35)000-338, the IRS announced that it would no longer contest court jurisdiction over claims for equitable innocent spouse relief. In fact, it found that

---

[28] Collections are discussed in detail in Chapter 12.

the Tax Court has jurisdiction over section 6015(f) claims regardless of whether the taxpayer has also claimed relief under subsections (b) or (c).

In innocent spouse litigation, the non-electing spouse also has rights. In particular, the nonelecting spouse is given an opportunity to become a party to the Tax Court proceeding. I.R.C. § 6015(e)(4). In *King v. Commissioner*, 115 T.C. 118 (2000), the Tax Court held that in any case in which an individual taxpayer seeks innocent spouse relief, the other spouse is entitled to notice and, if not already a party in the case, an opportunity to intervene to challenge the propriety of relieving the taxpayer from liability. In *Corson v. Commissioner*, 114 T.C. 354 (2000), the Tax Court held that a non-electing spouse must be afforded an opportunity to litigate a decision by the IRS to afford the electing spouse innocent spouse relief. In *Hale Exemption Trust v. Commissioner*, T.C. Memo. 2001-89, the Tax Court held, citing *Corson*, that, under section 6015(e), the successor in interest of a deceased taxpayer could contest the IRS's grant of innocent spouse relief to the electing spouse. In Notice N(35)000-173, the IRS updated the procedures that should be followed in proceedings in which a taxpayer raises a section 6015 claim and the other spouse (or former spouse) is not a party to the case.

Intervention may raise safety issues in cases involving allegations of abuse by the non-electing spouse. The proposed regulations issued in January 2001 provide that the non-requesting spouse must be given notice that the requesting spouse has filed a claim for relief and be given an opportunity to participate in the proceedings. At the request of one spouse, the IRS will omit from documents shared with the other spouse information about that spouse's location. Intervention may also not necessarily include a right to appear at a hearing with the electing spouse. In February 2001, in IR-2001-23, the IRS announced a procedure to protect victims of domestic violence who claim innocent spouse relief. A taxpayer who has been the victim of domestic violence and fears retaliation for filing a claim should write "Potential Domestic Abuse Case" on the top of the form claiming innocent spouse relief. In addition, the taxpayer must explain his or her concerns in a statement attached to the claim. The statement must also explain the reasons the taxpayer believes that he or she qualifies for relief.

As the discussion above reveals, the new procedures under section 6015 differ in important ways from the old innocent spouse procedures. What problems of the old system might the new procedures alleviate? Are the new procedures efficient?

[2] Substance

As indicated above, Code section 6015 provides three avenues of relief. Section 6015(b) is very similar to prior section 6013(e). For example, section 6015(b), like section 6013(e), includes an element that "taking into account all the facts and circumstances, it is inequitable to hold the other individual liable for the deficiency in tax for such taxable year attributable to such understatement." I.R.C. § 6015(b)(1)(D). This provision focuses, in part, on whether the "innocent" spouse had received a benefit beyond normal support from the tax savings occasioned by the item or items in question. *See* Prop. Reg. § 1.6015-2(d). Proposed regulations clarify that case law interpreting former Code section 6013(e) will be used to interpret language that is identical in section 6015.

Of course, section 6015(b) does vary from the old language in certain respects. Compare its language to the requirements of old Section 6013(e), listed at the beginning of Section 2.04[A]. Notice, among other things, that "grossly erroneous items" was changed to "erroneous items."

Section 6015(b) also requires for relief that the electing spouse "establish[] that in signing the return he or she did not know, and had no reason to know, that there was . . . [an] understatement" of tax. Does that mean that the electing spouse had no knowledge, actual or constructive, of the understatement itself, or the underlying *item* in question? Among other things, the proposed regulations mentioned above provide that "[a] requesting spouse has knowledge or reason to know of an erroneous item if he or she either actually knew of the item giving rise to the understatement, or if a reasonable person in similar circumstances would have known of the item giving rise to the understatement." Prop. Reg. § 1.6015-2(a)(4)(C). An "item" is generally defined as something required to be separately reported on an individual income tax return or its attachments; knowledge of an item does *not* require knowledge of the tax consequences of the item. Prop. Reg. § 1.6015-1(g)(3).

> All of the facts and circumstances are considered in determining whether a requesting spouse had reason to know of an erroneous item. The facts and circumstances that are considered include, but are not limited to, the nature of the item and the amount of the item relative to other items; the couple's financial situation; the requesting spouse's educational background and business experience; the extent of the requesting spouse's participation in the activity that resulted in the erroneous item; whether the requesting spouse failed to inquire, at or before the time the return was signed, about items on the return or omitted from the return that a reasonable person would question; and whether the erroneous item represented a departure from a recurring pattern reflected in prior years' returns (*e.g.*, omitted income from an investment regularly reported on prior years' returns).

Prop. Reg. § 1.6015-2(c).

In *Von Kalinowski v. Commissioner*, T.C. Memo. 2001-21, the Tax Court found that Mrs. Kalinowski had "reason to know" of understatements on returns prepared by an accountant that she had signed without reviewing. *Van Kalinowski* was decided January 30, 2001, before the effective date of the regulations. Consider also *Cheshire v. Commissioner*, 115 T.C. 183 (2000), decided before the proposed regulations were promulgated. Does it take the same approach as the regulations on the knowledge element of section 6015(b)?

CHESHIRE v. COMMISSIONER
United States Tax Court
115 T.C. 183 (2000)

JACOBS, JUDGE: Respondent determined a $66,069 deficiency in Kathryn and David Cheshire's 1992 Federal income tax * * *. Only Kathryn Cheshire has contested this determination; she does so claiming innocent spouse relief under section 6015(b), (c), and/or (f).

After concessions by respondent, * * * the issue to be resolved is whether Mrs. Cheshire is entitled to innocent spouse relief with respect to * * * The taxation of an omitted portion of the distributions Mr. Cheshire received upon his retirement from Southwestern Bell Telephone Co., and omitted interest income from a joint bank account * * *.

* * *

BACKGROUND

Petitioner resided in Cedar Creek, Texas, at the time she filed her petition.

Petitioner and Mr. Cheshire were married on June 20, 1970; they permanently separated on July 13, 1993, and were divorced on December 5, 1994. For 1992, petitioner and Mr. Cheshire (collectively, the Cheshires) filed a joint Federal income tax return.

Petitioner received a bachelor of science degree in secondary education. Upon graduating from college in 1970, she worked approximately 3 years as an elementary school teacher, then stayed home for approximately 10 years (1974-84) in order to raise her 2 children. She returned to teaching in 1984.

In September 1985, the Cheshires purchased property located at 24A Simpson Avenue, Cedar Creek, Texas, for use as the family residence. The Cheshires borrowed $99,000 to purchase the property.

DAVID CHESHIRE'S RETIREMENT AND COMPENSATION PACKAGE

Mr. Cheshire took early retirement from Southwestern Bell Telephone Co. (Southwestern Bell), effective January 1, 1992. * * *

On January 31, 1992, Mr. Cheshire deposited $184,377 of the retirement distributions into an account (account No. 9633-09) in the name of "David D. Cheshire and Kathy Cheshire" at the Austin Telco Federal Credit Union (the Austin Telco account). In 1992, the funds in this account earned $1,168 in interest.

Petitioner was aware of Mr. Cheshire's receipt of the retirement distributions and the amount thereof, as well as the interest earned on the Austin Telco account.

THE CHESHIRES' USE OF THE RETIREMENT DISTRIBUTIONS

The Cheshires made several large disbursements out of the Austin Telco account in 1992. Specifically, $99,425 was withdrawn to pay off the mortgage on the family residence, and $20,189 was withdrawn to purchase a 1992 Ford Explorer.

The retirement distributions were also used to pay family expenses, provide startup capital for Mr. Cheshire's newly formed sole proprietorship, Academic

Resources Management Systems (ARMS), and for investments. In addition, the retirement distributions were used to satisfy loans taken out to acquire a family truck and a car for one of their children as well as to open a college bank account for their daughter. The Cheshires retained joint ownership of this account.

On September 22, 1992, Mr. Cheshire opened a second account (account No. 25239-87) at the Austin Telco Federal Credit Union and transferred the remaining proceeds of the retirement distributions from account No. 9633-09 into this account. On November 12, 1992, Mr. Cheshire wrote a check from this second account in the amount of $6,300 payable to "A.R.M.S."; this amount was subsequently deposited into ARMS' bank account. In 1992, the funds in account No. 25239-87 earned $26 in interest.

PETITIONER'S SEPARATION AND DIVORCE

Mr. Cheshire was arrested several times for driving while intoxicated (DWI). In June 1993, he was involved in an alcohol-related automobile accident. Approximately a month later, petitioner and Mr. Cheshire permanently separated; they divorced 17 months after their separation.

Pursuant to a divorce decree, Mr. Cheshire transferred to petitioner his interest in the property constituting the family residence and title to the 1992 Ford Explorer. At the time of transfer, the family residence and the Ford Explorer were unencumbered.

THE CHESHIRES' 1992 FEDERAL INCOME TAX RETURN

Mr. Cheshire prepared and filed his and Mrs. Cheshire's joint income tax returns. Mr. Cheshire prepared the Cheshires' 1992 joint Federal income tax return (the 1992 return) in March 1993, prior to beginning a jail sentence for a DWI conviction. Before signing the return, petitioner questioned her husband about the potential tax ramifications of the retirement distributions. Mr. Cheshire falsely told petitioner he had consulted with a local certified public accountant, J.D. Mican (Mr. Mican), and had been advised that proceeds used to pay off the mortgage on their home would reduce the taxable amount of the retirement distributions. Accepting her husband's answer, petitioner did not inquire further and signed the 1992 return on March 14, 1993. Petitioner assumed that the 1992 return would be timely filed. On the 1992 return, the Cheshires reported that they had received a $199,771 retirement distribution and that $56,150 of that amount constituted taxable income. In addition, they reported $477 in interest income, as well as a $12,349 loss on their Schedule C, Profit or Loss From Business.

In August 1994, petitioner received a letter from the Internal Revenue Service (IRS) stating that it had not received the Cheshires' 1992 return. In searching for a copy of the 1992 return, petitioner discovered in a desk drawer the original 1992 return as well as a check for the amount of tax shown to be owing ($23.86). Petitioner immediately contacted Mr. Mican; he advised her to file the 1992 return and enclose payment for the tax liability reflected on the return as soon as possible. Petitioner filed the 1992 return along with the remittance on August 15, 1994.

In early October 1994, petitioner received notification from the IRS that $8,502 in estimated tax payments claimed on the Cheshires' 1992 return had not been paid. Despite Mr. Cheshire's reassurance that he had made the estimated tax payments, petitioner discovered that the payments in fact had not been made. Upon the advice of Mr. Mican, petitioner paid the estimated tax using borrowed funds.

NOTICE OF DEFICIENCY

Respondent determined that $187,741 of the retirement distributions ($229,924 total distributions less the $42,183 rollover) constituted taxable income, and thus the Cheshires understated the taxable amount of the retirement distributions by $131,591 ($187,741 − $56,150). Respondent further determined that the Cheshires understated (1) their interest income by $717, (2) their dividend income and capital gains by $132 and $1,889, respectively, and (3) their self-employment tax by $353. In addition, respondent disallowed $14,843 in Schedule C expenses. As a result of these determinations, as well as the late filing of the 1992 return, respondent determined that a section 6651(a)(1) addition to tax and a section 6662(a) accuracy-related penalty should be imposed.

* * *

OPINION

As a general proposition, if a joint return is filed by a husband and wife, liability with respect to any tax shown on the return or found to be owing is joint and several. See sec. 6013(d)(3). * * *

AVAILABILITY OF RELIEF TO PETITIONER

For the reasons that follow, we conclude that petitioner is not entitled to innocent spouse relief except to the extent provided below.[29]

A. RELIEF UNDER SECTION 6015(b)

Neither party disputes that in this case the requirements of subparagraphs (A), (B), and (E) of section 6015(b)(1) have been satisfied. Their dispute involves whether the requirements of subparagraphs (C) and (D) of section 6015(b)(1) have been met.

Section 6015(b)(1)(C) contains a no "knowledge of the understatement" requirement. Petitioner maintains that the standard of inquiry to be used in determining whether the putative innocent spouse knew, or had reason to know of, an understatement of tax is whether, at the time the return was signed, a reasonably prudent taxpayer in the spouse's position could be expected to know that the stated tax liability was erroneous or that further investigation was warranted. Based on this standard, petitioner posits that

---

[29] [Under section 6015(f), the court awarded Mrs. Cheshire equitable relief from liability for an accuracy-related penalty. Eds.]

even though she knew of the retirement distributions and the interest income, she did not know that there was an understatement of tax on the 1992 return.

We do not agree with petitioner's standard of inquiry. The no knowledge of the understatement requirement of section 6015(b)(1)(C) is similar to that found in former section 6013(e)(1)(C). Where relief was requested under section 6013(e) with respect to the omission of income (the situation involved herein), both this Court and the Court of Appeals for the Fifth Circuit, the court to which an appeal in this case would lie, have concluded that where a spouse seeking relief has actual knowledge of the underlying transaction that produced the omitted income, innocent spouse relief is denied. *See* Reser v. Commissioner, 112 F.3d 1258, 1265 (5th Cir. 1997), *affg. in part and revg. in part* T.C. Memo 1995-572; Bokum v. Commissioner, 94 T.C. 126, 148 (1990), *affd.* 992 F.2d 1132 (11th Cir. 1993). We believe this standard applies for section 6015(b)(1) relief as well.

Here, petitioner possessed actual knowledge of the underlying transactions (the distribution of retirement proceeds and the interest earned on the Austin Telco account) that gave rise to the Cheshires' understatement of tax. Petitioner had been informed by Mr. Cheshire that he was contemplating retirement and was eligible to receive a substantial sum of money from his retirement plan. By the end of January 1992, petitioner was aware of both the retirement distribution proceeds and the existence of the Austin Telco account. In fact, Mr. Cheshire showed petitioner the deposit slip and discussed with her the purposes for which the retirement distribution proceeds would be used.

Petitioner also had actual knowledge that interest was earned on the Austin Telco account. At all times, petitioner was aware of the balance in this account and frequently wrote checks drawn on its funds. Moreover, bank statements and a Form 1099, Interest Income, setting forth the amount of interest earned on the account were sent to petitioner's home. Thus, petitioner does not satisfy the no knowledge of the understatement requirement of section 6015(b)(1)(C). Moreover, because petitioner knew, or had reason to know, of the entire amount of the retirement distributions and the interest earned on the Austin Telco account, she is not entitled to proportionate relief under section 6015(b)(2).

* * *

To reflect the foregoing and respondent's concessions,

Decision will be entered under Rule 155.

Reviewed by the Court.

* * *

What does *Cheshire* suggest about whether Elizabeth Cockrell would have qualified for innocent spouse relief under section 6015(b)? *Should* she qualify for innocent spouse relief?

Section 6015(c) provides a form of relief from joint liability for taxpayers who are no longer married, legally separated, or not living together. Under that section, a spouse or ex-spouse may elect to allocate the deficiency between the spouses. The election will not apply to any item of the other spouse with respect to which the electing spouse had *actual knowledge*. Again, the knowledge referred to is knowledge of the item, not its tax consequences. *See* Prop. Reg. § 1.6015-3(c)(4) Ex. 2. Section 6015(c) also provides that the "actual knowledge" prohibition on relief does not apply if the spouse with that knowledge establishes that he or she signed the tax return under duress. I.R.C. § 6015(c)(3)(C). Proposed regulations that provide that a return signed by one spouse under duress does not constitute a joint return may limit the importance of this duress exception. *See* Prop. Reg. § 1.6013-4(d).

Note that, unlike section 6015(b), 6015(c) does not have a constructive knowledge provision. *See* Prop. Reg. § 1.6015-2(c). "Actual knowledge cannot be inferred from the requesting spouse's reason to know of the erroneous item." Prop. Reg. § 1.6015-3(c)(2). Section 6015(d) contains allocation provisions. The proposed regulations provide methods for allocating a deficiency between spouses under subsections (c) and (d) of section 6015. *See* Prop. Reg. § 1.6015-3.

Section 6015(f) provides a last-resort equitable relief provision. In Revenue Procedure 2000-15, 2000-1 C.B. 447, the IRS provided guidance for taxpayers seeking equitable innocent spouse relief under Code section 6015(f). The Revenue Procedure provides various threshold conditions for relief, and also provides various factors that weigh in favor of or against granting relief. Abuse that does not rise to the level of duress is a factor that weighs in favor of relief. *See* Rev. Proc. 2000-15, 2000-1 C.B. 447. A significant benefit (beyond normal support) from the item in question is a factor that weighs against relief. *See id.*

PROBLEMS

1. Having put off for months filing her 2001 income tax return, Beth finally decided on the evening of April 15, 2002, to make an effort to file. With no IRS forms at her disposal, she wrote on a sheet of paper her name, address, social security number, and an estimate of her gross income and deductions for 2001. She signed and dated the letter, included a personal check for the estimated tax due, and rushed to the post office to mail the letter before midnight. Beth mailed the letter by regular mail, properly addressed, with a postmark of April 15. The letter arrived at the IRS Service Center on April 19.

    A. Has Beth satisfied her filing requirements for 2001?

    B. Assume instead that Beth decided to submit an extension of time to file her 2001 return. She properly completed Form 4868, Application for Automatic Extension, and mailed the form to the IRS on April 16, 2002, with payment of the correct estimated amount. The IRS received the extension form on April 18. When is Beth's 2001 income tax return due?

2.   Marc is the sole proprietor of a local bicycle repair shop in Los Angeles that has been in business for three years. During the previous year, Marc incurred a loss from the operation of the shop resulting primarily from a currently deductible repair expense he was forced to make on the building in which the shop is located. Marc also deducted other business-related expenses for the previous year, some of which he retained receipts for and some of which he did not.

   A.   Marc is concerned that the large repair expense will "red flag" his return and cause the IRS to select the return for audit. He asks you whether he might reduce his audit chances by attaching copies of receipts documenting the repair expense directly to his return. How would you advise Marc?

   B.   Assume that Marc has received a letter from the IRS questioning the deductibility of the repair expense. What are Marc's options for responding to the letter? What advice can you provide him in order to limit the scope of the IRS's examination?

3.   Ned and Stacey were married in 1996 and divorced in 1999. In 2002, Stacey received a notice of deficiency with respect to the joint return Ned and Stacey had filed for 1998. The notice asserts a deficiency of $5,000 based on expenses from Ned's business that the couple deducted on the return. Stacey had reviewed and signed the return without any pressure from Ned. She has since remarried.

   A.   Can the IRS pursue Stacey for the deficiency? Does it matter whether the IRS pursues Ned as well?

   B.   If the IRS does pursue Stacey, does she have a procedural defense? When can she raise it?

4.   Sid, a financial consultant with a large firm, has been married for 5 years to Jeanne. Jeanne has a two-year Associates degree in bookkeeping from a local junior college. The couple has two young children, and Jeanne stays home with them. Sid is highly successful, but he is known for his violent temper.

   During 1998, Sid received several fees, amounting to $50,000, "under the table." As in each year of their marriage, Sid prepared the couple's joint return. The 1998 return reported $220,000 of gross income attributable to Sid's salary plus $5,000 of interest and dividend income. Thus, the return reported $225,000 of gross income. On April 15, 1999, Sid handed Jeanne the return and told her that she had better sign it right away so he could send it in to the IRS on time. She questioned him about what was on the return, but he yelled at her to hurry up and sign it or she would be very sorry. Jeanne feared Sid's temper because of previous occasions during which he had assaulted and injured her, so she signed the return without asking any more questions. Sid mailed the return in from the U.S. Post Office later that day. A week later, Sid gave Jeanne a diamond bracelet and apologized to her for his behavior.

The IRS recently sent the couple a notice of deficiency based on unreported income. Assume that the notice is timely. The deficiency amount is $30,000, which includes penalties. Sid and Jeanne divorced in 2000, and Sid fled the country. The IRS is thus seeking to collect the entire $30,000 from Jeanne. How might she defend against payment of the $30,000 deficiency? Will she likely be successful?

5.   Bubba Ellis operates the Texas Flight Training Academy (the "Academy"), a flight instruction school in Boline, Texas. Since its opening 10 years ago, the Academy's faculty has consisted solely of retired airline pilots. At all times, Bubba has treated the faculty members as independent contractors rather than employees, with the result that Bubba has not withheld on behalf of the faculty members federal income taxes, FICA (federal social security taxes) or FUTA (federal unemployment taxes). Instead, he has relied on the faculty members to comply with their tax law obligations. Bubba recently received a letter from the IRS contesting the classification of the faculty as independent contractors and requesting a meeting to discuss the issue. Contrary to your advice, Bubba has agreed to meet with the examining agent personally. How might you prepare Bubba for the meeting? Specifically, what types of questions should he be prepared to answer concerning the appropriate classification of the Academy's faculty? See Form SS-8.

6.   Rayanne owns a restaurant named *Chez Ray* in Coral Gables, Florida. The tax return she filed two years ago was recently audited, and the examining agent seemed concerned about the Schedule C she filed for the restaurant business.

   A.   Rayanne has not kept very good books and records for the business. Given that fact, how might the IRS set about proving that Rayanne has unreported income from the restaurant?

   B.   Rayanne suspects that the examining agent's concern about her Schedule C is actually a reflection of the high profile Rayanne has in the community. In order to promote her restaurant, Rayanne attends all the major local events, dressed in the latest designer fashions. She also routinely hosts large parties at her mansion.

If Rayanne's suspicion is correct, does this provide a possible defense to an assertion by the IRS of unreported income from the restaurant?

Chapter 3

ACCESS TO IRS INFORMATION VERSUS CONFIDENTIALITY OF TAXPAYER INFORMATION

Reading Assignment: Code §§ 6103, 6110, 7213, 7431; 5 U.S.C. §§ 552, 552a; Treas. Reg. § 601.702(c).

§ 3.01 Introduction: The Tension Between Confidentiality and Disclosure

As part of its effort to achieve the highest level of taxpayer compliance possible, the IRS collects and assembles millions of pages of information each year pertaining to virtually every citizen of the United States. While the IRS obtains the vast majority of this information from voluntarily submitted tax and information returns, it also obtains a considerable amount of information from its audit and collection efforts. Moreover, the IRS prepares internal memoranda and other materials intended primarily for use by the IRS's own personnel.

Efforts by taxpayers to obtain or control the release of IRS information have taken place on many fronts, and involve a tangle of statutory provisions. As you will see, some of these provisions favor taxpayers' privacy interests, while other provisions support full disclosure by the IRS to the public. In part, this chapter raises the issue of how the current statutory scheme affecting confidentiality and disclosure of information operates to reconcile these competing interests. The chapter also considers remedies for violations of the various non-disclosure statutes.

As you read the remainder of the chapter, consider these fundamental questions: Under what circumstances should information be disclosed, to whom, and for what purposes? More specifically, should the nature of the information sought or the identity of the requesting party play a role in determining whether the IRS should release the information? In addition, how might a policy of full disclosure by the IRS affect a taxpayer's willingness to provide complete and accurate financial information to the IRS?

§ 3.02 Access to IRS Information

Taxpayers may obtain information from the IRS pursuant to a combination of Internal Revenue Code provisions and other statutes. This section describes these statutory provisions and highlights the connections among them.

[A] Disclosure Under the Freedom of Information Act

[1] Categories of Information Subject to Disclosure

Congress enacted the Freedom of Information Act ("FOIA"), 5 U.S.C. § 552, to provide the general public with ready access to information held by government agencies, including the IRS, relating to the organization, procedures, and policies of the agencies. FOIA describes the broad categories of information and records subject to disclosure and the methods by which the information must be made available by the government agency. *Id.* § 552(a). The statute also expresses Congress' intent not to authorize withholding of information or to limit the public's access to government records, except as specifically stated in the statute. *Id.* § 552(d). This "spirit of disclosure" has been reinforced through judicial interpretations of FOIA, resulting in more and more information being released by the IRS.[1] As a result, FOIA remains a taxpayer's primary means of compelling the IRS to disclose information.[2]

Three categories of agency information must be made available. The first category includes descriptions of the agency's organizational structure and operations, procedural rules, available forms, and statements of general policy and interpretations. *Id.* § 552(a)(1). Because of its broad appeal, this type of information must be published on a current basis in the Federal Register. Pursuant to this mandate, for example, the IRS publishes proposed, temporary, and final Treasury regulations in the Federal Register the day after they are issued. The second category of information, described in section 552(a)(2), need only be made available by an agency for public inspection and copying, or for sale. This category includes final opinions and orders made during the processing of a case, administrative staff manuals and instructions to employees that might affect a member of the public.[3]

The final category of information consists of "records" of the agency. Unlike the documents that fall into the first two categories, the types of agency records contemplated in section 552(a)(3) need not be automatically disclosed. In order to obtain access to these types of records from the IRS, a taxpayer must request the information in accordance with the published rules described below. Agency records encompass a wide array of information, from statistical studies derived from data submitted by thousands of taxpayers to a revenue agent's report prepared in connection with the audit of a single individual. As the following case confirms, agency records are not limited to items or information prepared by officials or employees of the agency from which the information is being requested.

---

[1] In the tax area, Tax Analysts, a publisher of several tax magazines, has been at the forefront of FOIA litigation. *DOJ v. Tax Analysts*, which is reproduced in this chapter, describes Tax Analysts' interest in bringing these lawsuits.

[2] FOIA has generated considerable litigation involving government agencies other than the IRS. Cases involving these other administrative agencies establish principles that necessarily influence the IRS's obligations under the statute. However, this chapter is confined, for the most part, to those cases specifically bearing upon the IRS's duties under the statute.

[3] Much of the information within the second FOIA category is published commercially by private firms such as Commerce Clearing House and Tax Analysts. Chapter 16 describes in greater detail the sources of this information.

UNITED STATES DEPARTMENT OF JUSTICE
v. TAX ANALYSTS
United States Supreme Court
492 U.S. 136 (1989)

JUSTICE MARSHALL delivered the opinion of the Court.

The question presented is whether the Freedom of Information Act (FOIA or Act), 5 U.S.C. § 552 (1982 ed. and Supp. V), requires the United States Department of Justice (Department) to make available copies of district court decisions that it receives in the course of litigating tax cases on behalf of the Federal Government. We hold that it does.

I.

The Department's Tax Division represents the Federal Government in nearly all civil tax cases in the district courts, the courts of appeals, and the Claims Court. Because it represents a party in litigation, the Tax Division receives copies of all opinions and orders issued by these courts in such cases. Copies of these decisions are made for the Tax Division's staff attorneys. The original documents are sent to the official files kept by the Department.

* * *

Respondent Tax Analysts publishes a weekly magazine, Tax Notes, which reports on legislative, judicial, and regulatory developments in the field of federal taxation to a readership largely composed of tax attorneys, accountants, and economists. As one of its regular features, Tax Notes provides summaries of recent federal-court decisions on tax issues. To supplement the magazine, Tax Analysts provides full texts of these decisions in microfiche form. Tax Analysts also publishes Tax Notes Today, a daily electronic data base that includes summaries and full texts of recent federal-court tax decisions.

In late July 1979, Tax Analysts filed a FOIA request in which it asked the Department to make available all district court tax opinions and final orders received by the Tax Division earlier that month. The Department denied the request on the ground that these decisions were not Tax Division records. Tax Analysts then appealed this denial administratively. While the appeal was pending, Tax Analysts agreed to withdraw its request in return for access to the Tax Division's weekly log of tax cases decided by the federal courts. These logs list the name and date of a case, the docket number, the names of counsel, the nature of the case, and its disposition.

Since gaining access to the weekly logs, Tax Analysts' practice has been to examine the logs and to request copies of the decisions noted therein from the clerks of the 90 or so district courts around the country and from participating attorneys. In most instances, Tax Analysts procures copies reasonably promptly, but this method of acquisition has proven unsatisfactory approximately 25% of the time. Some court clerks ignore Tax Analysts' requests for copies of decisions, and others respond slowly, sometimes only after Tax Analysts has forwarded postage and copying fees. Because the

Federal Government is required to appeal tax cases within 60 days, Tax Analysts frequently fails to obtain copies of district court decisions before appeals are taken.

Frustrated with this process, Tax Analysts initiated a series of new FOIA requests in 1984. Beginning in November 1984, and continuing approximately once a week until May 1985, Tax Analysts asked the Department to make available copies of all district court tax opinions and final orders identified in the Tax Division's weekly logs. The Department denied these requests and Tax Analysts appealed administratively. When the Department sustained the denial, Tax Analysts filed the instant suit in the United States District Court for the District of Columbia, seeking to compel the Department to provide it with access to district court decisions received by the Tax Division.

The District Court granted the Department's motion to dismiss the complaint, holding that 5 U.S.C. § 552(a)(4)(B), which confers jurisdiction in the district courts when "agency records" have been "improperly withheld,"[n.2] had not been satisfied. 643 F. Supp. 740, 742 (1986). The court reasoned that the district court decisions at issue had not been "improperly withheld" because they "already are available from their primary sources, the District Courts," *id.*, at 743, and thus were "on the public record." *Id.*, at 744. The court did not address whether the district court decisions are "agency records." *Id.*, at 742.

The Court of Appeals for the District of Columbia Circuit reversed. 269 U.S. App. D.C. 315, 845 F.2d 1060 (1988). It first held that the district court decisions were "improperly withheld." An agency ordinarily may refuse to make available documents in its control only if it proves that the documents fall within one of the nine disclosure exemptions set forth in § 552(b), the court noted, and in this instance, "[n]o exemption applies to the district court opinions." *Id.*, at 319, 845 F.2d, at 1064. As for the Department's contention that the district court decisions are publicly available at their source, the court observed that "no court . . . has denied access to . . . documents on the ground that they are available elsewhere, and several have assumed that such documents must still be produced by the agency unless expressly exempted by the Act." *Id.*, at 321, 845 F.2d, at 1066.

The Court of Appeals next held that the district court decisions sought by Tax Analysts are "agency records" for purposes of the FOIA. The court acknowledged that the district court decisions had originated in a part of the Government not covered by the FOIA, but concluded that the documents nonetheless constituted "agency records" because the Department has the discretion to use the decisions as it sees fit, because the Department routinely

---

[n.2] Section 552(a)(4)(B) provides:

"On complaint, the district court of the United States in the district in which the complainant resides, or has his principal place of business, or in which the agency records are situated, or in the District of Columbia, has jurisdiction to enjoin the agency from withholding agency records and to order the production of any agency records improperly withheld from the complainant. In such a case the court shall determine the matter de novo, and may examine the contents of such agency records in camera to determine whether such records or any part thereof shall be withheld under any of the exemptions set forth in subsection (b) of this section, and the burden is on the agency to sustain its action."

uses the decisions in performing its official duties, and because the decisions are integrated into the Department's official case files. *Id.,* at 323–324, 845 F.2d, at 1068–1069. The court therefore remanded the case to the District Court with instructions to enter an order directing the Department "to provide some reasonable form of access" to the decisions sought by Tax Analysts. *Id.,* at 317, 845 F.2d, at 1062.

We granted certiorari, 488 U.S. 1003 (1989), and now affirm.

II.

In enacting the FOIA 23 years ago, Congress sought " 'to open agency action to the light of public scrutiny.' " Department of Justice v. Reporters Committee for Freedom of Press, 489 U.S. 749, 772 (1989), quoting Department of Air Force v. Rose, 425 U.S. 352, 372 (1976). Congress did so by requiring agencies to adhere to " 'a general philosophy of full agency disclosure.' " *Id.,* at 360, quoting S. Rep. No. 813, 89th Cong., 1st Sess., 3 (1965). Congress believed that this philosophy, put into practice, would help "ensure an informed citizenry, vital to the functioning of a democratic society." NLRB v. Robbins Tire & Rubber Co., 437 U.S. 214, 242 (1978).

The FOIA confers jurisdiction on the district courts "to enjoin the agency from withholding agency records and to order the production of any agency records improperly withheld." § 552(a)(4)(B). Under this provision, "federal jurisdiction is dependent on a showing that an agency has (1) 'improperly' (2) 'withheld' (3) 'agency records.' " Kissinger v. Reporters Committee for Freedom of Press, 445 U.S. 136, 150 (1980). Unless each of these criteria is met, a district court lacks jurisdiction to devise remedies to force an agency to comply with the FOIA's disclosure requirements.[n.3]

In this case, all three jurisdictional terms are at issue. Although these terms are defined neither in the Act nor in its legislative history, we do not write on a clean slate. Nine Terms ago we decided three cases that explicated the meanings of these partially overlapping terms. Kissinger v. Reporters Committee for Freedom of Press, *supra;* Forsham v. Harris, 445 U.S. 169 (1980); GTE Sylvania, Inc. v. Consumers Union of United States, Inc., 445 U.S. 375 (1980). These decisions form the basis of our analysis of Tax Analysts' requests.

A

We consider first whether the district court decisions at issue are "agency records," a term elaborated upon both in *Kissinger* and in *Forsham. Kissinger* involved three separate FOIA requests for written summaries of telephone conversations in which Henry Kissinger had participated when he served as Assistant to the President for National Security Affairs from 1969 to 1975, and as Secretary of State from 1973 to 1977. Only one of these requests —

[n.3] The burden is on the agency to demonstrate, not the requester to disprove, that the materials sought are not "agency records" or have not been "improperly" "withheld." *See* S. Rep. No. 813, 89th Cong., 1st Sess., 8 (1965) ("Placing the burden of proof upon the agency puts the task of justifying the withholding on the only party able to explain it"); H.R. Rep. No. 1497, 89th Cong., 2d Sess., 9 (1966) (same); *cf.* Federal Open Market Committee v. Merrill, 443 U.S. 340, 352 (1979).

for summaries of specific conversations that Kissinger had had during his tenure as National Security Adviser — raised the "agency records" issue. At the time of this request, these summaries were stored in Kissinger's office at the State Department in his personal files. We first concluded that the summaries were not "agency records" at the time they were made because the FOIA does not include the Office of the President in its definition of "agency." 445 U.S., at 156. We further held that these documents did not acquire the status of "agency records" when they were removed from the White House and transported to Kissinger's office at the State Department, a FOIA-covered agency:

> "We simply decline to hold that the physical location of the notes of telephone conversations renders them 'agency records.' The papers were not in the control of the State Department at any time. They were not generated in the State Department. They never entered the State Department's files, and they were not used by the Department for any purpose. If mere physical location of papers and materials could confer status as an 'agency record' Kissinger's personal books, speeches, and all other memorabilia stored in his office would have been agency records subject to disclosure under the FOIA." *Id.*, at 157.

Forsham, in turn, involved a request for raw data that formed the basis of a study conducted by a private medical research organization. Although the study had been funded through federal agency grants, the data never passed into the hands of the agencies that provided the funding, but instead was produced and possessed at all times by the private organization. We recognized that "[r]ecords of a nonagency certainly could become records of an agency as well," 445 U.S., at 181, but the fact that the study was financially supported by a FOIA-covered agency did not transform the source material into "agency records." Nor did the agencies' right of access to the materials under federal regulations change this result. As we explained, "the FOIA applies to records which have been in fact obtained, and not to records which merely could have been obtained." *Id.*, at 186 (emphasis in original; footnote omitted).

Two requirements emerge from *Kissinger* and *Forsham*, each of which must be satisfied for requested materials to qualify as "agency records." First, an agency must "either create or obtain" the requested materials "as a prerequisite to its becoming an 'agency record' within the meaning of the FOIA." *Id.*, at 182. In performing their official duties, agencies routinely avail themselves of studies, trade journal reports, and other materials produced outside the agencies both by private and governmental organizations. *See* Chrysler Corp. v. Brown, 441 U.S. 281, 292 (1979). To restrict the term "agency records" to materials generated internally would frustrate Congress' desire to put within public reach the information available to an agency in its decision-making processes. *See id.*, at 290, n.10. As we noted in *Forsham*, "The legislative history of the FOIA abounds with . . . references to records *acquired* by an agency." 445 U.S., at 184 (emphasis added).

Second, the agency must be in control of the requested materials at the time the FOIA request is made. By control we mean that the materials have come into the agency's possession in the legitimate conduct of its official duties. This requirement accords with *Kissinger's* teaching that the term "agency records" is not so broad as to include personal materials in an employee's possession, even though the materials may be physically located at the agency. *See* 445 U.S., at 157. This requirement is suggested by *Forsham* as well, 445 U.S., at 183, where we looked to the definition of agency records in the Records Disposal Act, 44 U.S.C. § 3301. Under that definition, agency records include "all books, papers, maps, photographs, machine readable materials, or other documentary materials, regardless of physical form or characteristics, made or received by an agency of the United States Government *under Federal law or in connection with the transaction of public business . . . .*" *Ibid.* (emphasis added).[n.5] Furthermore, the requirement that the materials be in the agency's control at the time the request is made accords with our statement in *Forsham* that the FOIA does not cover "information in the abstract." 445 U.S., at 185.

Applying these requirements here, we conclude that the requested district court decisions constitute "agency records." First, it is undisputed that the Department has obtained these documents from the district courts. This is not a case like *Forsham*, where the materials never in fact had been received by the agency. The Department contends that a district court is not an "agency" under the FOIA, but this truism is beside the point. The relevant issue is whether an agency covered by the FOIA has "create[d] or obtaine[d]" the materials sought, *Forsham*, 445 U.S., at 182, not whether the organization from which the documents originated is itself covered by the FOIA.

Second, the Department clearly controls the district court decisions that Tax Analysts seeks. Each of Tax Analysts' FOIA requests referred to district court decisions in the agency's possession at the time the requests were made. This is evident from the fact that Tax Analysts based its weekly requests on the Tax Division's logs, which compile information on decisions the Tax Division recently had received and placed in official case files. Furthermore, the court decisions at issue are obviously not personal papers of agency employees. The Department counters that it does not control these decisions because the district courts retain authority to modify the decisions even after they are released, but this argument, too, is beside the point. The control inquiry focuses on an agency's possession of the requested materials, not on its power to alter the content of the materials it receives. Agencies generally are not at liberty to alter the content of the materials that they receive from outside parties. An authorship-control requirement thus would sharply limit "agency records" essentially to documents generated by the agencies themselves. This

---

[n.5] In *GTE Sylvania, Inc. v. Consumers Union of United States, Inc.*, 445 U.S. 375, 385 (1980), we noted that Congress intended the FOIA to prevent agencies from refusing to disclose, among other things, agency telephone directories and the names of agency employees. We are confident, however, that requests for documents of this type will be relatively infrequent. Common sense suggests that a person seeking such documents or materials housed in an agency library typically will find it easier to repair to the Library of Congress, or to the nearest public library, rather than to invoke the FOIA's disclosure mechanisms. *Cf.* Department of Justice v. Reporters Committee for Freedom of Press, 489 U.S. 749, 764 (1989) ("[I]f the [requested materials] were 'freely available,' there would be no reason to invoke the FOIA to obtain access"). To the extent such requests are made, the fact that the FOIA allows agencies to recoup the costs of processing requests from the requester may discourage recourse to the FOIA where materials are readily available elsewhere. *See* 5 U.S.C. § 552(a)(4)(A).

result is incompatible with the FOIA's goal of giving the public access to all nonexempted information received by an agency as it carries out its mandate.

The Department also urges us to limit "agency records," at least where materials originating outside the agency are concerned, "to those documents 'prepared substantially to be relied upon in agency decisionmaking.' " Brief for Petitioner 21, quoting Berry v. Department of Justice, 733 F.2d 1343, 1349 (CA9 1984). This limitation disposes of Tax Analysts' requests, the Department argues, because district court judges do not write their decisions primarily with an eye toward agency decisionmaking. This argument, however, makes the determination of "agency records" turn on the intent of the creator of a document relied upon by an agency. Such a *mens rea* requirement is nowhere to be found in the Act. Moreover, discerning the intent of the drafters of a document may often prove an elusive endeavor, particularly if the document was created years earlier or by a large number of people for whom it is difficult to divine a common intent.

B

We turn next to the term "withheld," which we discussed in *Kissinger*. Two of the requests in that case — for summaries of all the telephone conversations in which Kissinger had engaged while serving as National Security Adviser and as Secretary of State — implicated that term. These summaries were initially stored in Kissinger's personal files at the State Department. Near the end of his tenure as Secretary of State, Kissinger transferred the summaries first to a private residence and then to the Library of Congress. Significantly, the two requests for these summaries were made only after the summaries had been physically delivered to the Library. We found this fact dispositive, concluding that Congress did not believe that an agency "withholds a document which has been removed from the possession of the agency prior to the filing of the FOIA request. In such a case, the agency has neither the custody nor control necessary to enable it to withhold." 445 U.S., at 150–151.[n.9] We accordingly refused to order the State Department to institute a retrieval action against the Library. As we explained, such a course "would have us read the 'hold' out of 'withhold . . . . A refusal to resort to legal remedies to obtain possession is simply not conduct subsumed by the verb withhold.' " *Id.,* at 151.[n.10]

[n.9] Although a control inquiry for "withheld" replicates part of the test for "agency records," the FOIA's structure and legislative history make clear that agency control over requested materials is a "prerequisite to triggering any duties under the FOIA." *Kissinger,* 445 U.S., at 151 (emphasis added); *see also id.,* at 152–153; Forsham v. Harris, 445 U.S. 169, 185 (1980).

[n.10] *Kissinger's* focus on the agency's present control of a requested document was based in part on the Act's purposes and structure. With respect to the former, we noted that because Congress had not intended to "obligate agencies to create or retain documents," an agency should not be "required to retrieve documents which have escaped its possession, but which it has not endeavored to recover." 445 U.S., at 152 (citations omitted). As for the Act's structure, we noted that, among other provisions, § 552(a)(6)(B) gives agencies a 10-day extension of the normal 10-day period for responding to FOIA requests if there is a need to search and collect the requested materials from facilities separate from the office processing the request. The brevity of this extension period indicates that Congress did not expect agencies to resort to lawsuits to retrieve documents within that period. *See id.,* at 153.

The construction of "withholding" adopted in *Kissinger* readily encompasses Tax Analysts' requests. There is no claim here that Tax Analysts filed its requests for copies of recent district court tax decisions received by the Tax Division after these decisions had been transferred out of the Department. On the contrary, the decisions were on the Department's premises and otherwise in the Department's control, *supra*, at 146–147, when the requests were made. * * * Thus, when the Department refused to comply with Tax Analysts' requests, it "withheld" the district court decisions for purposes of § 552(a)(4)(B).

The Department's counterargument is that, because the district court decisions sought by Tax Analysts are publicly available as soon as they are issued and thus may be inspected and copied by the public at any time, the Department cannot be said to have "withheld" them. The Department notes that the weekly logs it provides to Tax Analysts contain sufficient information to direct Tax Analysts to the "original source of the requested documents." Brief for Petitioner 23. It is not clear from the Department's brief whether this argument is based on the term "withheld" or the term "improperly."[n.11] But, to the extent the Department relies on the former term, its argument is without merit. Congress used the word "withheld" only "in its usual sense." *Kissinger*, 445 U.S., at 151. When the Department refused to grant Tax Analysts' requests for the district court decisions in its files, it undoubtedly "withheld" these decisions in any reasonable sense of that term. Nothing in the history or purposes of the FOIA counsels contorting this word beyond its usual meaning. We therefore reject the Department's argument that an agency has not "withheld" a document under its control when, in denying an otherwise valid request, it directs the requester to a place outside of the agency where the document may be publicly available.

C

The Department is left to argue, finally, that the district court decisions were not "improperly" withheld because of their public availability. The term "improperly," like "agency records" and "withheld," is not defined by the Act. We explained in *GTE Sylvania*, however, that Congress' use of the word "improperly" reflected its dissatisfaction with § 3 of the Administrative Procedure Act, 5 U.S.C. § 1002 (1964 ed.), which "had failed to provide the desired access to information relied upon in Government decisionmaking, and in fact had become 'the major statutory excuse for withholding Government records from public view.' " 445 U.S., at 384, quoting H.R. Rep. No. 1497, 89th Cong., 2d Sess., 3 (1966). Under § 3, we explained, agencies had "broad discretion . . . in deciding what information to disclose, and that discretion was often abused." 445 U.S., at 385.

In enacting the FOIA, Congress intended "to curb this apparently unbridled discretion" by "clos[ing] the 'loopholes which allow agencies to deny legitimate information to the public.' " *Ibid.* (citation omitted); *see also* EPA v. Mink, 410

---

n.11 The Court of Appeals believed that the Department was arguing "that it need not affirmatively make [the district court decisions] available to Tax Analysts because the documents have not been *withheld* to begin with." 269 U.S. App. D. C. 315, 319–320, 845 F.2d 1060, 1064–1065 (1988) (emphasis in original).

U.S. 73, 79 (1973). Toward this end, Congress formulated a system of clearly defined exemptions to the FOIA's otherwise mandatory disclosure requirements. An agency must disclose agency records to any person under § 552(a), "unless they may be withheld pursuant to one of the nine enumerated exemptions listed in § 552(b)." *Department of Justice v. Julian,* 486 U.S. 1, 8 (1988). Consistent with the Act's goal of broad disclosure, these exemptions have been consistently given a narrow compass. *See, e.g., Ibid.;* FBI v. Abramson, 456 U.S. 615, 630 (1982). More important for present purposes, the exemptions are "explicitly exclusive." *FAA Administrator v. Robertson,* 422 U.S. 255, 262 (1975); *see also Rose,* 425 U.S., at 361; *Robbins Tire & Rubber Co.,* 437 U.S., at 221; *Mink, supra,* at 79. As Justice O'Connor has explained, Congress sought "to insulate its product from judicial tampering and to preserve the emphasis on disclosure by admonishing that the 'availability of records to the public' is not limited, 'except as specifically stated.' " *Abramson, supra,* at 642 (dissenting opinion) (emphasis in original), quoting § 552(c) (now codified at § 552(d)); *see also* 456 U.S., at 637, n. 5; H.R. Rep. No. 1497, *supra,* at 1. It follows from the exclusive nature of the § 552(b) exemption scheme that agency records which do not fall within one of the exemptions are "improperly" withheld.[n.12]

The Department does not contend here that any exemption enumerated in § 552(b) protects the district court decisions sought by Tax Analysts. The Department claims nonetheless that there is nothing "improper" in directing a requester "to the principal, public source of records." Brief for Petitioner 26. The Department advances three somewhat related arguments in support of this proposition. * * *

First, the Department contends that the structure of the Act evinces Congress' desire to avoid redundant disclosures. An understanding of this argument requires a brief survey of the disclosure provisions of § 552(a). Under subsection (a)(1), an agency must "currently publish in the Federal Register" specific materials, such as descriptions of the agency, statements of its general functions, and the agency's rules of procedure. Under subsection (a)(2), an agency must "make available for public inspection and copying" its final opinions, policy statements, and administrative staff manuals, "unless the materials are promptly published and copies offered for sale." Under subsection (a)(3), the general provision covering the disclosure of agency records, an agency need not make available those materials that have already been disclosed under subsections (a)(1) and (a)(2). Taken together, the Department argues, these provisions demonstrate the inapplicability of the FOIA's disclosure requirements to previously disclosed, publicly available materials. "A fortiori, a judicial record that is a public document should not be subject to a FOIA request." *Id.,* at 29.

[n.12] Even when an agency does not deny a FOIA request outright, the requesting party may still be able to claim "improper" withholding by alleging that the agency has responded in an inadequate manner. *Cf.* § 552(a)(6)(C); *Kissinger v. Reporters Committee for Freedom of Press,* 445 U.S., at 166 (Stevens, J., concurring in part and dissenting in part). No such claim is made in this case. Indeed, Tax Analysts does not dispute the Court of Appeals' conclusion that the Department could satisfy its duty of disclosure simply by making the relevant district court opinions available for copying in the public reference facility that it maintains. *See* 269 U.S. App. D.C., at 321–322, and n.15, 845 F.2d, at 1066–1067, and n.15.

The Department's argument proves too much. The disclosure requirements set out in subsections (a)(1) and (a)(2) are carefully limited to situations in which the requested materials have been previously published or made available by the agency itself. It is one thing to say that an agency need not disclose materials that it has previously released; it is quite another to say that an agency need not disclose materials that some other person or group may have previously released. Congress undoubtedly was aware of the redundancies that might exist when requested materials have been previously made available. It chose to deal with that problem by crafting only narrow categories of materials which need not be, in effect, disclosed twice by the agency. If Congress had wished to codify an exemption for all publicly available materials, it knew perfectly well how to do so. It is not for us to add or detract from Congress' comprehensive scheme, which already "balances, and protects all interests" implicated by Executive Branch disclosure. *Mink, supra*, at 80, quoting S. Rep. No. 813, 89th Congress, 1st Sess., 3 (1965).

It is not surprising, moreover, that Congress declined to exempt all publicly available materials from the FOIA's disclosure requirements. In the first place, such an exemption would engender intractable fights over precisely what constitutes public availability, unless the term were defined with precision. In some sense, nearly all of the information that comes within an agency's control can be characterized as publicly available. Although the form in which this material comes to an agency — *i.e.*, a report or testimony — may not be generally available, the information included in that report or testimony may very well be. Even if there were some agreement over what constitutes publicly available materials, Congress surely did not envision agencies satisfying their disclosure obligations under the FOIA simply by handing requesters a map and sending them on scavenger expeditions throughout the Nation. Without some express indication in the Act's text or legislative history that Congress intended such a result, we decline to adopt this reading of the statute. * * *

III.

For the reasons stated, the Department improperly withheld agency records when it refused Tax Analysts' request for copies of the district court tax decisions in its files. Accordingly, the judgment of the Court of Appeals is

Affirmed.

JUSTICE BLACKMUN, dissenting.

The Court in this case has examined once again the Freedom of Information Act (FOIA), 5 U.S.C. § 552. It now determines that under the Act the Department of Justice on request must make available copies of federal district court orders and opinions it receives in the course of its litigation of tax cases on behalf of the Federal Government. The majority holds that these qualify as agency records, within the meaning of § 552(a)(4)(B), and that they were improperly withheld by the Department when respondent asked for their production. The Court's analysis, I suppose, could be regarded as a fairly routine one.

I do not join the Court's opinion, however, because it seems to me that the language of the statute is not that clear or conclusive on the issue and, more important, because the result the Court reaches cannot be one that was within the intent of Congress when the FOIA was enacted.

Respondent Tax Analysts, although apparently a nonprofit organization for federal income tax purposes, is in business and in that sense is a commercial enterprise. It sells summaries of these opinions and supplies full texts to major electronic data bases. The result of its now-successful effort in this litigation is to impose the cost of obtaining the court orders and opinions upon the Government and thus upon taxpayers generally. There is no question that this material is available elsewhere. But it is quicker and more convenient, and less "frustrat[ing]," * * * for respondent to have the Department do the work and search its files and produce the items than it is to apply to the respective court clerks.

This, I feel, is almost a gross misuse of the FOIA. What respondent demands, and what the Court permits, adds nothing whatsoever to public knowledge of Government operations. That, I had thought, and the majority acknowledges, * * * was the real purpose of the FOIA and the spirit in which the statute has been interpreted thus far. *See, e.g.,* Forsham v. Harris, 445 U.S. 169, 178 (1980); NLRB v. Robbins Tire & Rubber Co., 437 U.S. 214, 242–243 (1978). I also sense, I believe not unwarrantedly, a distinct lack of enthusiasm on the part of the majority for the result it reaches in this case.

If, as I surmise, the Court's decision today is outside the intent of Congress in enacting the statute, Congress perhaps will rectify the decision forthwith and will give everyone concerned needed guidelines for the administration and interpretation of this somewhat opaque statute.

Notice that the majority's analysis of whether the district court decisions were improperly withheld by the Justice Department did not take into account Tax Analyst's motivation for requesting the information (a point that seemed to concern Justice Blackmun). As a general matter, a taxpayer who requests information under FOIA need not specify a reason for doing so or otherwise explain how the materials requested may be relevant to the taxpayer. *See EPA v. Mink*, 410 U.S. 73, 79, 92 (1973); *NLRB v. Sears Roebuck & Co.*, 421 U.S. 132 (1975). Instead, the burden of proof falls on the government agency to specify the reason for withholding all or a portion of the requested documents. What other procedural safeguards has Congress included in FOIA to help ensure full disclosure of government information?

[2] FOIA Exemptions Most Relevant to Tax Practice

The IRS's burden of justifying its failure to make requested agency records available for inspection normally plays out in the context of the nine exemptions from disclosure listed in section 552(b).[4] These exemptions specify

---

[4] FOIA also contains a series of exclusions permitting the IRS to respond to a request by claiming that the requested records do not exist. *See* 5 U.S.C. § 552(c). This exclusion may be used by the IRS where disclosure would reveal the identity of an informant participating in a criminal investigation or identify the subject of the investigation.

circumstances under which the IRS may deny access to records. Many of these exemptions are either relatively uncontroversial or are not particularly relevant to the field of tax practice.[5] Those exemptions of principal importance to tax administration are Exemption 3 (relating to information specifically exempted from disclosure by other statutes), Exemption 5 (relating to agency memoranda) and Exemption 7 (relating to documents gathered for law enforcement purposes).

Courts have consistently ruled that each of the FOIA exemptions must be narrowly construed in favor of disclosure. *See, e.g., Vaughn v. Rosen*, 523 F.2d 1136 (D.C. Cir. 1975). Moreover, if a requested document contains information that is exempt from disclosure under the statute, the IRS is required to segregate the portion that is exempt and disclose the remaining material. 5 U.S.C. § 552(b); *see also King v. United States Department of Justice*, 830 F.2d 210, 224 (D.C. Cir. 1987) ("[T]he withholding agency must supply 'a relatively detailed' justification, specifically identifying the reasons why a particular exemption is relevant and correlating those claims with the particular part of a withheld document to which they apply."). Only when the nonexempt material is "inextricably intertwined" with the exempt material may the IRS properly withhold the entire document. *Schiller v. NLRB*, 964 F.2d 1205, 1209 (D.C. Cir. 1992).

Under Exemption 3, the IRS may withhold information if that information is specifically exempted from disclosure by another statute. With respect to FOIA requests made to the IRS, the principal statute implicated by Exemption 3 is section 6103 of the Code. *See Chamberlain v. Kurtz*, 589 F.2d 827 (5th Cir. 1979), *cert. denied*, 444 U.S. 842 (1980). Section 6103 seeks to ensure that a taxpayer's return and tax return information remain confidential and not subject to disclosure except where disclosure is specifically permitted by the statute. Accordingly, FOIA does not require disclosure of information that may not be lawfully disclosed by the IRS under section 6103. The operation of section 6103 as a confidentiality statute and the scope of its many exceptions are discussed in more detail in Section 3.03 below.

Does Exemption 3 protect material governed by the federally authorized tax practitioner privilege of section 7525? What about Exemption 5?

Pursuant to Exemption 5, the IRS may refuse to disclose inter-agency or intra-agency memoranda that would not be available by law to a private party in litigation with the IRS. 5 U.S.C. § 552(b)(5). The Supreme Court interprets this provision to exempt from disclosure those documents that would otherwise be privileged and not discoverable by a party requesting the information as part of a hypothetical civil case. *NLRB v. Sears Roebuck & Co.*, 421 U.S. 132 (1975). The privileges incorporated into Exemption 5 include the (1) attorney-client privilege, (2) the attorney work product privilege, and (3) to a limited extent, the deliberative process privilege.

The attorney-client privilege encourages communication between client and attorney by assuring that a client's confidences to his attorney will not be

---

[5] These include the exemption for documents relating to national defense and foreign policy, trade secrets, and information that would result in an unwarranted violation of personal privacy. 5 U.S.C. § 552(b)(1), (4), (6).

disclosed without his consent. *Coastal States Gas Corp. v. Department of Energy*, 617 F.2d 854, 862 (D.C. Cir. 1980). The privilege extends to situations in which a client seeks an attorney's counsel on a legal matter. *Id.* The federal courts also extend the privilege to an attorney's written communications to a client, to ensure against disclosure of information that the client has previously confided to the attorney. *Mead Data Central, Inc. v. United States Dept. of Air Force*, 566 F.2d 242, 254 n.25 (1977). However, the privilege is narrowly construed and is limited to those situations in which its purposes will be served; it "protects only those disclosures necessary to obtain informed legal advice which might not have been made absent the privilege." *Fisher v. United States*, 425 U.S. 391, 403 (1976).

The attorney work product privilege was established by the Supreme Court in *Hickman v. Taylor*, 329 U.S. 495 (1947). The privilege protects documents prepared in contemplation of litigation, providing an attorney with privacy within which to prepare the case and plan litigation strategies. *Coastal States Gas Corp.*, 617 F.2d at 863. "Whatever the outer boundaries of the attorney's work-product rule are, the rule clearly applies to memoranda prepared by an attorney in contemplation of litigation which set forth the attorney's theory of the case and his litigation strategy." *NLRB v. Sears Roebuck & Co.*, 421 U.S. at 154. These types of documents are therefore protected from disclosure under Exemption 5.

The deliberative process privilege covers " 'all papers which reflect the agency's group thinking in the process of working out its policy and determining what its law shall be.' " *Arthur Andersen & Co. v. Internal Revenue Service*, 679 F.2d 254 (D.C. Cir. 1982), citing *NLRB v. Sears, supra*. Courts have limited the privilege to materials that are both "predecisional" and "deliberative." *See Tax Analysts v. Internal Revenue Service*, 117 F.3d 607, 616 (D.C. Cir. 1997). The issue of whether requested information is pre- or post-decisional, or deliberative or non-deliberative, is illustrated in *Tax Analysts v. Internal Revenue Service*, 97 F. Supp. 2d 13 (2000). In that case, the District Court for the D.C. District granted the IRS's motion for summary judgment on the issue of whether FOIA compelled the IRS to disclose "legal memoranda" (LMs). LMs are prepared by attorneys in the Office of Chief Counsel (referred to by the court as "docket attorneys") to assist in the preparation of a proposed Revenue Ruling. The memorandum contains the drafter's legal research as well as the drafter's evaluation of the strengths and weaknesses of the proposed ruling. The memorandum ultimately serves as briefing material for IRS reviewers before the Revenue Ruling is finalized.

> The IRS contends that LMs are shielded from disclosure by the executive or governmental deliberative process privilege, which is one of three privileges incorporated by FOIA's Exemption 5. * * * The deliberative process privilege protects only those "government 'materials which are both predecisional and deliberative.' " Tax Analysts v. Internal Revenue Svc., 117 F.3d 607, 616 (D.C. Cir. 1997) (*quoting* Wolfe v. Department of Health & Human Svcs., 839 F.2d 768, 774 (D.C. Cir. 1988)). As a general rule, a document is predecisional if it was "generated before the adoption of agency policy" and deliberative if it "reflects the give-and-take of the consultative process." *Coastal*

States, 617 F.2d at 866; *Tax Analysts*, 117 F.3d at 616 (same). Thus, the IRS must establish that the withheld LMs "contain 'the ideas and theories which go into the making of the law' and not 'the law itself.'" Arthur Andersen & Co. v. Internal Revenue Svc., 679 F.2d 254, 258 (D.C. Cir. 1982) (*quoting* Sterling Drug, Inc. v. FTC, 450 F.2d 698, 708 (D.C. Cir. 1971)). "An agency will not be permitted to develop a body of 'secret law' used by it in the discharge of its regulatory duties and in its dealings with the public, but hidden behind a veil of privilege . . . ." *Coastal States*, 617 F.2d at 867. Accordingly, this "exemption is to be applied 'as narrowly as consistent with efficient Government operation.'" *Id.*, 617 F.2d at 868 (*quoting* S. Rep. 89–813 at 9 (1965).

*   *   *

Applying this Circuit's law to these undisputed facts, the Court finds that the deliberative process privilege protects from disclosure those portions of LMs that do not reflect the official position of the Office of Chief Counsel. In this regard, the Court finds that LMs function like the Background Information Notes ("BINs") at issue in *Arthur Andersen*, 679 F.2d 254, 258 (D.C. Cir. 1982).[6] Like LMs, BINs are part of a proposed revenue ruling's publication package. After conducting an *in camera* review of the contested draft Revenue Rulings and their accompanying BINs, the D.C. Circuit noted that "the flow of the documents was from subordinate to superior. Because approval was required at each higher level, all the participants up to the Commissioner were without authority to make a final determination." *Arthur Andersen*, 679 F.2d at 259; *see also* Pies v. Internal Revenue Svc., 668 F.2d 1350, 1353 (D.C. Cir. 1981) (protecting draft proposed regulations and a draft transmittal memorandum that were "never subjected to final review, never approved by the officials having authority to do so, and never approved within the Legislation and Regulations Division"). Because the drafters lack ultimate authority, their views are necessarily pre-decisional. Similarly, LMs are directed upward from docket attorneys to reviewers and, ultimately, to the Office of the Assistant Secretary (Tax Policy) at the Department of Treasury. Although LMs are sometimes returned to their drafters for revisions, they are not officially approved, nor do they emanate from the Office of Chief Counsel with any appearance of authority. Instead, the Court finds that LMs "reflect the agency 'give-and-take' leading up to a decision that is characteristic of the deliberative process." 679 F.2d at 257; *see also Coastal States*, 617 F.2d at 868 (emphasizing that documents are predecisional is they are produced in the process of formulating policy).

Contrary to Plaintiff's characterization, the Court finds that LMs are distinguishable from the General Counsel Memoranda ("GCMs")

---

[6] [The Background Information Notes at issue in *Arthur Andersen* were described by the court as follows: "On their face there appear the number, identities and titles of the various persons in successively higher positions to whom the drafts were submitted for 'approval' and the alterations these persons made in the text of the background note and revenue ruling." 679 F.2d at 259. Eds.]

at issue in *Taxation with Representation Fund v. Internal Revenue Service*, 646 F.2d 666 (D.C. Cir. 1981) ("TWRF") and the Field Service Advices ("FSAs") at issue in *Tax Analysts v Internal Revenue Service*, 117 F.3d 607 (D.C. Cir. 1997). Whereas GCMs and FSAs are used to promote uniformity in IRS policy, *see, e.g., Tax Analysts*, 117 F.3d at 617, LMs are tools for formulating policy. Unlike GCMs, which are "revised to reflect the final position of the Assistant Commissioner (Technical)"; "widely distributed throughout the agency," and "constantly updated to reflect the current status of an issue within the Office of Chief Counsel," *TWRF*, 646 F.2d at 681–82, LMs are not updated, officially reconciled, or widely distributed. Furthermore, LMs do not necessarily reflect the official position of the Office Chief Counsel on a given issue. This treatment stands in sharp contrast to the procedures utilized with GCMs, which "are retained by the Office of Chief Counsel, and extensively cross-indexed and digested, as well as 'updated,' much like the service provided by Shepard's." *Id.* at 682. Whereas LMs flow "upward" from staffers to reviewers, FSAs flow "outward" from the Office of Chief Counsel to personnel in the field. *See Tax Analysts*, 117 F.3d at 617. The FSA case is also distinguishable because LMs are not used to guide personnel in the field or elsewhere. Admittedly, IRS attorneys sometimes retain LMs for future reference, but such use does not automatically convert LMs to "agency law." *See Pies*, 668 F.2d at 1353–54 (noting that use as a research tool, without more, does not convert unfinalized or unapproved materials into agency working law).

In keeping with these general principles, the IRS has redacted portions of LMs that reflect the opinions and analysis of the author and did not ultimately form the basis of the final revenue ruling. Because the Court finds that this approach to segregability is consistent with the D.C. Circuit's mandate that the deliberative process privilege be applied as narrowly as possible, the Court shall grant IRS's motion for summary judgment as to LMs.

Tax Analysts, 97 F. Supp. 2d at 15–18.[7]

Documents protected from disclosure by Exemption 5 typically include some type of legal or policy analysis. Factual information gathered by the IRS, on the other hand, is generally considered to be outside the scope of Exemption 5 because it is non-deliberative. Consider, however, whether a summary of third party testimony prepared by an IRS agent, which contains the agent's opinion concerning the witness's credibility and the usefulness of the testimony at trial, would be protected by the deliberative process privilege.

The remaining exemption from FOIA's disclosure requirements that is of significance to tax practice is the exemption in § 552(b)(7). Exemption 7

---

[7] As part of the same suit, Tax Analysts sought disclosure of litigation guidance memoranda (LGMs), technical assistance bulletins, and tax litigation bulletins. Because those documents fell within the definition of chief counsel advice under Code section 6110, which trumps FOIA for documents covered by that section, the court held that it did not have subject matter jurisdiction over those FOIA requests. Tax Analysts v. Internal Revenue Service, 2000-1 U.S.T.C. (CCH) ¶ 50,370 (March 31, 2000).

applies to "records or information compiled for law enforcement purposes." The phrase "law enforcement purposes" encompasses both civil and criminal proceedings, including civil audits and criminal tax investigations. Prior to 1974, the IRS successfully used the exemption for investigatory files as an excuse for refusing to disclose broad categories of information, including most of the records compiled by the IRS in connection with an audit of a taxpayer's return. *See, e.g., Williams v. Internal Revenue Service*, 479 F.2d 317 (3d Cir.), *cert. denied sub nom., Donlon v. Internal Revenue Service*, 414 U.S. 1024 (1973). Fearing that FOIA was being used more often as a withholding statute rather than a disclosure statute, Congress enacted amendments in 1974 designed to narrow the exemption. *See* Pub. L. No. 93-502, § 2(b), 88 Stat. 1561, 1563–64 (1974) (codified at 5 U.S.C. § 552(b)(7) (1976)).

Under current law, the IRS may withhold investigatory records under Exemption 7 only when it can establish that disclosure of such records could result in, among other effects, interference with law enforcement proceedings. 5 U.S.C. § 552(b)(7)(A). This exemption most commonly applies where a party subject to an ongoing criminal investigation seeks documents compiled by the IRS in order to defend against a future enforcement proceeding.[8] Based on the argument that disclosure during a pending investigation could hamper the agency's inquiry, the IRS has successfully asserted this exemption to deny access to documentary evidence collected during the inquiry. Witness statements, as well as internal memoranda that would reveal investigative techniques and procedures pertaining to the case, have also been protected from disclosure. *See generally Kanter v. Internal Revenue Service*, 478 F. Supp. 552 (N.D. Ill. 1979); *Barney v. Internal Revenue Service*, 618 F.2d 1268 (8th Cir. 1980).

[3] Using FOIA During the Tax Controversy Process

[a] Access to the IRS's "Secret Law"

Over the years, FOIA has been used by taxpayers to compel the IRS to disclose letters, memoranda, and other materials that provide important insights into the agency's internal operations and procedures. During the 1970s, for example, FOIA lawsuits resulted in the release of extensive portions of the Internal Revenue Manual, which provides instructions to IRS agents and employees for handling such things as audits, appeals, and collection actions. As discussed below, FOIA suits also led to the enactment of Code Section 6110, which requires the IRS to release letter rulings and technical advice memoranda. As explained in more detail in Chapter 9, these types of sources (sometimes referred to as the IRS's "secret law") contain a wealth of useful information for the taxpayer and his representative. Audit guidelines contained in the Internal Revenue Manual, for instance, tip the taxpayer off to issues likely to be raised during examination and allow the taxpayer to

---

[8] The exemption in 5 U.S.C. § 552(b)(7)(A) generally applies only to pending enforcement proceedings, rather than closed investigations. Once the investigation of the taxpayer is closed or abandoned, the exemption no longer applies. Moreover, should the IRS institute legal proceedings against the taxpayer, much of the information otherwise protected by (b)(7)(A) may be obtained through pre-trial discovery.

prepare for the examination in advance. Similarly, the materials covered by section 6110 contain the IRS's legal analysis of important issues, which may prove helpful to taxpayers when structuring transactions and, if the transaction is consummated, when preparing tax returns.

[b]   Access to Administrative Files Prepared by the IRS

The types of information discussed immediately above are disclosed by the IRS on a continuing basis and are widely available from commercial publishers without the need for a formal request to the IRS. However, if a taxpayer wishes to obtain materials that were prepared by the IRS during an investigation of the taxpayer's own return, the taxpayer may have to make an individual FOIA request. Restrictions in section 6103 and FOIA Exemption 7 limit a taxpayer's access to information about his own case while the examination is still in progress. *See* I.R.C. § 6013(e)(7) (disclosure authorized if it will not seriously impair tax administration); 5 U.S.C. § 552(b)(7)(A). Once the examination has concluded and the IRS issues a 30-day letter, the taxpayer may submit a FOIA request seeking access to all materials contained in the taxpayer's administrative file prepared by the examining agent. It is common practice for the IRS to make this information available, but only after deleting otherwise confidential third party information and any material relating to a potential criminal investigation of the taxpayer. *See* I.R.M. Disclosure 13.5.

A taxpayer's administrative file becomes an important source of information during the settlement process. The administrative file will normally contain a copy of the agent's working file, which may include workpapers, notes, intraagency memoranda, affidavits, and interview transcripts. The file also contains all records compiled by the agent during the audit, including records obtained from third parties. Although much of this information will appear or be reflected in the revenue agent's report issued to the taxpayer at the conclusion of the audit, significant facts and alternate legal theories may be buried in the administrative file. A taxpayer who hopes to settle the case with the IRS Appeals Division, rather than litigate the matter, can use this information to decide what to include (or not include) in the protest letter submitted to the Appeals Division. The taxpayer's negotiating position during the settlement process is also greatly improved if the taxpayer is aware of all of the facts known by the IRS.

[4]   Requesting Information Under FOIA

The IRS has issued detailed regulations specifying the procedures a taxpayer should follow when requesting information under FOIA. These regulations also describe the required contents of a FOIA request. Proc. Reg. § 601.702(c); *see also* I.R.M. 13.5(4). Among other requirements, a FOIA request must be submitted in writing, signed by the requesting taxpayer, and addressed to the appropriate IRS disclosure officer. The requesting party must also "reasonably describe" the records sought. A reasonable description is one that would "enable the Internal Revenue Service employees who are familiar with the subject area of the request to locate the records without placing an unreasonable burden upon the Internal Revenue Service." Proc. Reg.

§ 601.702(c)(4)(i)(A). The IRS has indicated that a request for "all records concerning me" would be rejected as overly broad. I.R.M. 13.5.1.

Where the potential exists that the IRS may deny access to the requested records because the records fall within one of the FOIA exemptions, the requesting party should include with the initial request sufficient identification or authorization to confirm the requesting party's right of disclosure. As an example, a partner seeking to obtain access to information returns filed by the partnership under an exception to section 6103 must submit a notarized statement confirming that he is, in fact, a member of the partnership. I.R.C. § 6103; Proc. Reg. § 601.702(c)(4)(ii). Similarly, a request made by a representative on behalf of a taxpayer should include a copy of the representative's Power of Attorney (Form 2848). If a FOIA request does not conform to the requirements set forth in the regulations, it will be returned to the requesting party with a statement notifying the party of any defects. Proc. Reg. § 601.702(c)(3).

A sample FOIA request is reproduced below:[9]

SAMPLE FOIA REQUEST

Internal Revenue Service
FOIA Request
Att'n: Disclosure Officer
[address]

    [Date]
    Re: [Taxpayer's name,
    Social Security number,
    Tax years]

Dear ⸻⸻⸻:

    I, ⸻⸻⸻, am the attorney for the taxpayer named above; I have attached a power of attorney and declaration of representative. Under the authority of the Freedom of Information Act, 5 U.S.C. § 552, I request a copy of each of the following records:

    (1) All workpapers, correspondence, and other documents relating to the examination and investigation of the federal income tax liability of the taxpayer named above, for the taxable years ⸻⸻⸻, including but not limited to [detailed description of records].

    (2) All statements given by the taxpayer named above to the Internal Revenue Service (IRS) during the course of its examination, including all written statements; all oral statements reduced to writing by any employee of the IRS, whether or not verbatim, and whether or not signed by the taxpayer; and all oral statements of the taxpayer that were recorded by any mechanical device.

---

[9] The regulations in section 601.702 also include a schedule of fees imposed by the IRS for search and duplication of the requesting materials. Proc. Reg. § 601.702(g)(5). As part of the FOIA request, the requesting party must state his willingness to pay the resulting fees. *Id.* at § 601.702(c)(3).

My return address is:

_____

_____

_____

I am authorized and I agree to pay the hourly search fee and the current fee per copy obtained pursuant to this request. I attest under penalty of perjury that I am not in any of the following categories: (a) commercial use requester, (b) media requester, (c) educational institutions requester, or (d) noncommercial scientific institutions requester, but instead that I am a category (e) other requester.

Very truly yours,

_____

[name of representative]

_____

Once the FOIA request is received by the IRS, the agency normally has 10 days in which to notify the requesting party of its initial determination to grant or deny the request. 5 U.S.C. § 552(a)(6); Proc. Reg. § 601.702(c)(7). Requests by the IRS for additional time are common. If the IRS denies the request, in whole or in part, a notification letter is sent to the requesting party informing him of the denial. The notification letter includes a brief statement of the grounds for denial (normally based on a FOIA exemption) and informs the party of his right to appeal the matter administratively. Proc. Reg. § 601.702(c)(7)(iii).

In order to trigger the administrative appeals process, the taxpayer must submit a letter to the IRS within 35 days after receipt of the denial letter. This appeals letter should describe the records requested, identify the office to which the initial request was submitted and include copies of both the initial FOIA request and the letter denying the request. Proc. Reg. § 601.702(c)(8). The appeals letter should also include any arguments the requesting party may have in support of his right of access. These arguments normally take the form of a statement rebutting the disclosure officer's use of a FOIA exemption to deny the request.

The IRS has 20 days in which to grant or deny the appeal. If the IRS denies the appeal or fails to respond within the specified time periods, the requesting party may file an action in a United States District Court seeking an order requiring the IRS to release any document improperly withheld. 5 U.S.C. § 552(a)(4)(B). In the disclosure proceedings, the District Court reviews the matter *de novo* and may examine the contents of the requested records *in camera* in order to determine whether the IRS has sustained its burden of proving that the records are exempt from disclosure.

Where the volume of records at issue is great, rather than requiring the IRS to produce copies of each disputed record at trial, the court normally allows the IRS to submit an itemized index of the documents withheld, along with a corresponding explanation of the IRS's justification for withholding the documents. This *"Vaughn* Index," named for the *Vaughn v. Rosen* case in which the technique was first applied, 484 F.2d 820 (D.C. Cir. 1973), can also prove very useful for the party seeking disclosure. The index not only specifies the IRS's claimed exemptions with respect to each item or category of items requested, but also describes the specific nature of the documents being withheld. With this information, the requesting party should be able to rebut the IRS's arguments more effectively. A requesting party who prevails in the FOIA suit may be entitled to recover attorney's fees and other costs. 5 U.S.C. § 522(a)(4)(E).

[5] Relationship of FOIA to Discovery Rules

As discussed above, under FOIA, a taxpayer is entitled to obtain agency records that do not fall within one of FOIA's nine exemptions. In litigation, a taxpayer may obtain access to relevant government documents that are not privileged. Therefore, FOIA and discovery each provide a separate method for obtaining government documents, raising the question of whether a taxpayer should be able to use FOIA as a discovery tool in litigation. Courts have pointed out that FOIA was not intended to serve as a mechanism for private litigation discovery, *see, e.g., Renegotiation Board v. Bannercraft Clothing Co.*, 415 U.S. 1, 24 (1974), but rather to make agency information available to the public. In fact, a litigant may have access to some documents through discovery that would not be released to him under FOIA. *Jones v. FBI*, 41 F.3d 238, 250 (1994). On the other hand, FOIA's Exemption 7 (discussed above) incorporates the privileges of civil discovery, generally precluding a taxpayer-litigant access under FOIA to material the taxpayer cannot obtain through discovery procedures.

[B] Access to Information Under the Privacy Act of 1974

In addition to FOIA, there is a second, although less commonly employed, avenue that an individual taxpayer may use to obtain disclosure of information from the IRS. This is the Privacy Act of 1974, 5 U.S.C. § 552a. The Privacy Act leads, in effect, a double life. To protect against unwarranted invasions of personal privacy, the legislation imposes restrictions on federal government agencies, including the IRS, relating to the use and dissemination of personal information. *Id.* § 552a(b). The Privacy Act also grants an individual the right, upon request, to gain access to records or information compiled with respect to him. This right of access applies only to individuals and only with respect to the individual's own records. The Privacy Act does not permit a taxpayer to gain access to third party records or to internal agency documents. *Id.* § 552a(d).

Exemptions in section 552a severely limit the usefulness of the Privacy Act as a means of obtaining information from the IRS. Section 552a(d)(5), for example, denies access to "any information compiled in reasonable anticipation of a civil action or proceeding." Furthermore, the Act permits the IRS to promulgate rules exempting from disclosure a wide variety of information, including investigatory materials compiled for law enforcement purposes. *Id.* § 552a(k)(2). The IRS has used this grant of authority to exempt from disclosure under the Privacy Act most records compiled by the agency during the audit and appeals stage of a tax controversy. I.R.M. Ex. 1.3.15.12-2.[10] And while the Privacy Act also permits an individual to request that the agency correct any records that the individual believes are not accurate or complete, section 7852(e) of the Code specifically prohibits the individual from using this correction provision to seek a redetermination of the taxpayer's liability for taxes or penalties. As a practical matter, therefore, the Privacy Act rarely provides an individual access to information from the IRS greater than that otherwise available under FOIA. *See Gardner v. United States*, 213 F.3d 735 (D.C. Cir. 2000), *cert. denied*, 121 S. Ct. 1099 (2001) (Section 6103 preempts Privacy Act regarding claims that the IRS made unauthorized disclosures of taxpayer's return information to a third party); *Lake v. Rubin*, 162 F.3d 113 (D.C. Cir. 1998) (taxpayers cannot rely on Privacy Act to gain access to tax return information but must instead rely on the more specific provisions in Code section 6103).

[C] Access to Written Determinations Under Section 6110

In addition to the statements and pronouncements voluntarily disclosed by the IRS under the first two prongs of FOIA, another important source of information about the IRS's positions is the material subject to inspection under section 6110 of the Code. As a general matter, section 6110 requires the IRS to make available for inspection copies of letter rulings, Technical Advice Memoranda, determination letters, and Chief Counsel Advice (referred to collectively in the statute as "written determinations"). Most of these written determinations are published in complete form by commercial services and are most easily accessed via an on-line research service. The statute also makes available "background file documents," which include written information submitted in support of the requested letter ruling or determination letter, as well as other material compiled by IRS personnel to support the IRS's ultimate conclusion. I.R.C. § 6110(b)(2); Treas. Reg. § 301.6110-2(g). Background file documents are available only upon specific written request by the taxpayer. Chapter 9 contains a detailed discussion of the administrative and judicial rules regarding the precedential value of written determinations and their usefulness when planning transactions.

Section 6110, enacted as part of the Tax Reform Act of 1976, is the result of a series of court decisions brought by taxpayers under FOIA. *See, e.g., Fruehauf Corp. v. Internal Revenue Service*, 566 F.2d 574 (6th Cir. 1977) (seeking disclosure of letter rulings); *Taxation With Representation Fund v. Internal Revenue Service*, 646 F.2d 666 (D.C. Cir. 1981) (seeking disclosure of technical advice memoranda and other unpublished IRS documents). More recently, the D.C. Circuit Court of Appeals, reviewing a FOIA action brought against the IRS, ordered the agency to disclose "Field Service Advice memoranda" (FSAs), after redacting all material protected by the attorney work product privilege or other privileges or exemptions. *Tax Analysts v. Internal Revenue Service*, 117 F.3d 607, 620 (D.C. Cir. 1997). FSAs reflect case-specific legal advice from the IRS's Chief Counsel's Office to IRS personnel. Concerned about the IRS's continued resistance to releasing this type of information,

---

[10] As discussed above, this type of information is routinely available under FOIA.

Congress amended section 6110 in 1998 to include within its disclosure requirements "chief counsel advice," a term encompassing not only FSAs but also other written advice issued by the Office of Chief Counsel to IRS personnel if it contains a legal interpretation or IRS position. *See* I.R.C. § 6110(i).

Section 6110 sets forth a detailed procedure by which the IRS must make written determinations available to the public. The statute also contains a series of exemptions from disclosure, many of which closely follow the exemptions listed in FOIA. Most notably, section 6110(c)(1) requires that, before any material is made available for public inspection, the IRS must delete "the names, addresses and other identifying details of the person to whom the written determination pertains and of any other person, . . . identified in the written determination or any background file document." As further protection against disclosure of otherwise confidential information, the IRS must notify the person to whom the written determination pertains and allow this person an opportunity to discuss with the IRS, prior to disclosure, what information should be deleted. I.R.C. § 6110(f); Treas. Reg. § 301.6110-5. These confidentiality protections are backed up by section 6110(j), which permits a taxpayer to file an action against the United States in the Court of Federal Claims if the IRS publicizes a written determination without first making the required deletions.[11]

Does forcing the IRS to release written determinations to the public impair its ability to effectively administer the federal tax law? How so? Does the fact that these documents generally may not be used or cited as precedent affect your view?

§ 3.03   Preserving Taxpayer Confidentiality: Code Section 6103

[A]   Disclosure Prohibitions Under Section 6103

As discussed above, a primary function of section 6103 is to implement Exemption 3 of FOIA. In this role, the statute limits a taxpayer's access to information held by the IRS. Section 6103 also operates independently of FOIA as a confidentiality provision, limiting the circumstances under which, and to whom the IRS may disclose information about the taxpayer. The statute mandates that tax "returns and return information" remain confidential and, except as authorized by the statute, can not be disclosed. For these purposes, a taxpayer's return is broadly defined to include any tax or information return, amended return, declaration of estimated tax, claim for refund, as well as any supporting schedules or attachments. I.R.C. § 6103(b)(1). As a fine example of inclusive statutory drafting, section 6103(b)(2) defines the term "return information" to mean:

> [A] taxpayer's identity, the nature, source, or amount of his income, payments, receipts, deductions, exemptions, credits, assets,

---

[11] These protections apply more restrictively in the case of Chief Counsel Advice. *See* I.R.C. § 6110(i)(4).

liabilities, net worth, tax liability, tax withheld, deficiencies, overas-sessments, or tax payments, whether the taxpayer's return was, is being, or will be examined or subject to other investigation or processing, or any other data, received by, recorded by, prepared by, furnished to, or collected by the Secretary with respect to a return or with respect to the determination of the existence, or possible existence of liabilities (or the amount thereof) of any person under this title for any tax, penalty, interest, fine, forfeiture, or other imposition, or offense.

This formulation would encompass virtually all information collected by the IRS as part of an audit of the taxpayer's return.

As part of the Community Renewal Tax Relief Act of 2000, Congress expanded the definition of "return information" in section 6103(b) to include "any agreement under section 7121, and any similar agreement, and any background information related to such an agreement or request for such an agreement." Pub. L. No. 106-554 § 304(a) (adding I.R.C. § 6103(b)(2)(D)). As a result, closing agreements between taxpayers and the IRS entered into under section 7121 are protected from disclosure. Tax Analysts, involved in FOIA litigation with the IRS over the release of closing agreements at the time section 6103(b)(2)(D) was added, along with some accounting firms, maintain that fundamental fairness requires disclosure of these agreements in order to ensure that unequal treatment of taxpayers by the IRS does not go undetected. *Compare* Letter from Thomas Field, "Houghton Bill Would Create Information Monopolies," 88 Tax Notes 1397 (September 11, 2000), *with* Betty M. Wilson, "TEI Throws Support Behind Closing Agreement Confidentiality Bill," 88 Tax Notes 1399 (September 11, 2000).[12]

The one limitation on the definition of return information appears in section 6103(b)(2). This exception, commonly known as the Haskell Amendment, excludes from the definition of return information any data in a form that cannot be associated with, or otherwise identify a particular taxpayer. The following case considers the scope of this limitation on the definition of return information. Notice, in particular, the interaction of the section 6103(b)(2) limitation and FOIA.

CHURCH OF SCIENTOLOGY OF CALIFORNIA
v. INTERNAL REVENUE SERVICE
United States Supreme Court
484 U.S. 9 (1987)

CHIEF JUSTICE REHNQUIST delivered the opinion of the Court.

Section 6103 of the Internal Revenue Code, 26 U.S.C. § 6103, lays down a general rule that "returns" and "return information" as defined therein shall be confidential. "Return information" is elaborately defined in § 6103(b)(2); immediately after that definition appears the following proviso, known as the Haskell amendment:

---

[12] At the same time, Congress amended section 6110 to confirm that closing agreements are not considered "written determinations" subject to disclosure under section 6110. Community Renewal Tax Relief Act of 2000, Pub. L. No. 106-554 § 304(c) (adding I.R.C. § 6110(b)(1)).

> "[B]ut such term does not include data in a form which cannot be associated with, or otherwise identify, directly or indirectly, a particular taxpayer."

Petitioner Church of Scientology of California, seeking disclosure under the Freedom of Information Act, contends that the Haskell amendment excepts from the definition of "return information" all material in the files of the Internal Revenue Service (IRS) which can be redacted to delete those parts which would identify a particular taxpayer. Respondent IRS in opposition argues that the mere redaction of identifying data will not, by virtue of the Haskell amendment, take the material out of the definition of "return information." We agree with the IRS.

Petitioner filed a request with respondent under the Freedom of Information Act (FOIA), 5 U.S.C. § 552, for the production of numerous documents. Among the materials sought by petitioner were "[c]opies of all information relating to or containing the names of, Scientology, Church of Scientology, any specific Scientology church or entity identified by containing the words Scientology, Hubbard and/or Dianetics in their names, L. Ron Hubbard or Mary Sue Hubbard in the form of written record, correspondence, document, memorandum, form, computor [sic] tape, computor [sic] program or microfilm, which is contained in" an extensive list of respondent's case files and data systems. FOIA Request Dated May 16, 1980, App. 20a-27a. Petitioner also requested similar information from the offices and personal areas of a number of respondent's officials.

Dissatisfied by the slow response to its request, petitioner filed suit in the United States District Court for the District of Columbia to compel release of the materials. In the District Court the parties agreed — as they continue to agree here — that § 6103 of the Internal Revenue Code is the sort of statute referred to by the FOIA in 5 U.S.C. § 552(b)(3) relating to matters that are "specifically exempted from disclosure by statute . . . "; thus, if § 6103 forbids the disclosure of material, it may not be produced in response to a request under the FOIA. Respondent argued that many of the records were protected as "returns" or "return information" under § 6103.

* * *

The District Court, after an *in camera* review of representative documents, held that respondent had correctly limited its search for and disclosure of materials requested by petitioner. *See* 569 F. Supp. 1165 (DC 1983). Petitioner appealed that decision to the United States Court of Appeals for the District of Columbia Circuit. Following briefing and argument before a three-judge panel, the Court of Appeals *sua sponte* undertook en banc review of the meaning of the Haskell amendment and the modification it works upon § 6103(b)(2). The Court of Appeals concluded that, by using the words "in a form," Congress contemplated "not merely the deletion of an identifying name or symbol on a document that contains return information, but agency *reformulation* of the return information into a statistical study or some other composite product . . . ." 253 U.S. App. D.C. 85, 92, 792 F.2d 153, 160 (196) (emphasis in original). Thus, the court held, before respondent may produce documents otherwise protected, the Haskell amendment requires that some modification have occurred in the form of the data contained in the documents. "[M]ere deletion of the taxpayer's name or other identifying data is not enough, since that would render the reformulation requirement entirely duplicative of the nonidentification requirement."[n.1] *Id.*, at 95, 792 F.2d, at 163.

We granted certiorari, 479 U.S. 1063 (1987), to consider the scope of the Haskell amendment and its relation to the confidentiality provisions of §§ 6103(a) and (b). Petitioner believes that the Haskell amendment makes significantly greater inroads on the definition of "return information" than did the Court of Appeals. It makes two interrelated contentions: first, that the Haskell amendment removes from the classification of "return information" all data which do not identify a particular taxpayer, and, second, that 5 U.S.C. § 552(b) — requiring that "[a]ny reasonably segregable portion" of a record be provided to a requestor after deletion of the portions which are exempt — compels respondent to redact "return information" in its files where possible so as to bring that material within the terms of the Haskell amendment. We reject both of these arguments.

We are told by the IRS that, as a practical matter, "return information" might include the report of an audit examination, internal IRS correspondence concerning a taxpayer's claim, or a notice of deficiency issued by the IRS proposing an increase in the taxpayer's assessment. Tr. of Oral Arg. 24–25. Petitioner asserts that the segregation requirement of the FOIA, § 552(b), directs respondent to remove the identifiers from such documents as these and that, once the materials are purged of such identifiers, they must be disclosed because they no longer constitute return information described in § 6103(b)(2).

We find no support for petitioner's arguments in either the language of § 6103 or in its legislative history. In addition to the returns themselves, which are protected from disclosure by § 6103(b)(1), § 6103(b)(2) contains an elaborate description of the sorts of information related to returns that respondent is compelled to keep confidential. If the mere removal of identifying details from return information sufficed to put the information "in a form" envisioned by the Haskell amendment, the remainder of the categories included in § 6103(b)(2) would often be irrelevant. The entire section could have been prefaced by the simple instruction to respondent that the elimination of identifiers would shift related tax data outside the realm of protected

---

[n.1] The decision of the District of Columbia Circuit was thus in substantial agreement with the Seventh Circuit's opinion in *King v. IRS*, 688 F.2d 488 (1982), and the Eleventh Circuit's determination in *Currie v. IRS*, 704 F.2d 523 (1983). The Seventh Circuit concluded in *King* that § 6103 "protects from disclosure all nonamalgamated items listed in subsection (b)(2)(A), and that the Haskell Amendment provides only for the disclosure of statistical tabulations which are not associated with or do not identify particular taxpayers." 688 F.2d, at 493. Similarly, in *Currie* the Eleventh Circuit held that the Haskell amendment does not obligate the IRS, in a suit under the FOIA, to delete identifying material from documents and release what would otherwise be return information. 704 F.2d, at 531–532.

The Ninth Circuit, however, reached a different result in *Long v. IRS*, 596 F.2d 362 (1979), *cert. denied*, 446 U.S. 917 (1980). In *Long*, the court found that the Haskell amendment removes from the category of protected return information any documents that do not identify a particular taxpayer once names, addresses, and similar details are deleted. *See* 596 F.2d, at 367–369.

return information. Respondent would then first determine whether the information could be redacted so as not to identify a taxpayer; only if it could not would the extensive list of materials that constitute "return information" become pertinent. And if petitioner correctly interprets the intent of the Haskell amendment, Congress' drafting was awkward in the extreme. The amendment exempts "data in a form" that cannot be associated with or otherwise identify a particular taxpayer. A much more natural phrasing would omit the confusing and unnecessary words "in a form" and refer simply to data.

*   *   *

The legislative history of the Tax Reform Act of 1976, Pub. L. 94-455, 90 Stat. 1520, of which the amendments to § 6103 are a part, also indicates that Congress did not intend the statute to allow the disclosure of otherwise confidential return information merely by the redaction of identifying details. One of the major purposes in revising § 6103 was to tighten the restrictions on the use of return information by entities other than respondent. *See* S. Rep. No. 94-938, p. 318 (1976) ("[R]eturns and return information should generally be treated as confidential and not subject to disclosure except in those limited situations delineated in the newly amended section 6103"). Petitioner's suggestion that the Haskell amendment was intended to modify the restrictions of § 6103 by making all nonidentifying return information eligible for disclosure would mean that the amendment was designed to undercut the legislation's primary purpose of limiting access to tax filings.

The circumstances under which the Haskell amendment was adopted make us reluctant to credit it with this expansive purpose. During debate on the Senate floor, Senator Haskell proposed that § 6103(b)(2) be amended to make clear that return information "does not include data in a form which cannot be associated with, or otherwise identify, directly or indirectly, a particular taxpayer." He then added this explanation of his proposal:

> "[T]he purpose of this amendment is to insure that statistical studies and other compilations of data now prepared by the Internal Revenue Service and disclosed by it to outside parties will continue to be subject to disclosure to the extent allowed under present law. Thus the Internal Revenue Service can continue to release for research purposes statistical studies and compilations of data, such as the tax model, which do not identify individual taxpayers.

> "The definition of 'return information' was intended to neither enhance nor diminish access now obtainable under the Freedom of Information Act to statistical studies and compilations of data by the Internal Revenue Service. Thus, the addition by the Internal Revenue Service of easily deletable identifying information to the type of statistical study or compilation of data which, under its current practice, has [sic] been subject to disclosure, will not prevent disclosure of such study or compilation under the newly amended § 6103. In such an instance, the identifying information would be deleted and disclosure of the statistical study or compilation of data be made." 122 Cong. Rec. 24012 (1976).

After these remarks, the floor manager of the legislation, Senator Long, added that he would "be happy to take this amendment to conference. It might not be entirely necessary, but it might serve a good purpose." The Haskell amendment was then passed by voice vote in the Senate and became part of the conference bill.

We find it difficult to believe that Congress in this manner adopted an amendment which would work such an alteration to the basic thrust of the draft bill amending § 6103. The Senate's purpose in revising § 6103 was, as we have noted, to impose greater restrictions on the disclosure of tax data; a change in the proposed draft permitting disclosure of all return information after deletion of material identifying a particular taxpayer would have, it seems to us, at a minimum engendered some debate in the Senate and resulted in a rollcall vote. More importantly, Senator Haskell's remarks clearly indicate that he did not mean to revise § 6103(b)(2) in this fashion. He refers only to statistical studies and compilations, and gives no intimation that his amendment would require respondent to remove identifying details from material as it exists in its files in order to comply with its requirement. All in all, we think this is a case where common sense suggests, by analogy to Sir Arthur Conan Doyle's "dog that didn't bark," that an amendment having the effect petitioner ascribes to it would have been differently described by its sponsor, and not nearly as readily accepted by the floor manager of the bill.

We thus hold that, as with a return itself, removal of identification from return information would not deprive it of protection under § 6103(b). Since such deletion would not make otherwise protected return information discloseable, respondent has no duty under the FOIA to undertake such redaction. The judgment of the Court of Appeals is accordingly affirmed.

Should the source of the information released by the IRS play a role in the decision of whether the information constitutes, in the first instance, return information? Consider the following excerpt.

RICE v. UNITED STATES
United States Court of Appeals, Tenth Circuit
166 F.3d 1088 (1999)[13]

BALDOCK, CIRCUIT JUDGE:

In March 1994, a jury convicted Plaintiff Jerry V. Rice on two counts of filing a false tax refund claim and three counts of making and subscribing a false tax return in respective violation of 18 U.S.C. § 287 and 26 U.S.C. § 7206(1). The district court imposed a thirty-month term of imprisonment on Rice, ordered him to pay restitution, and fined him $20,000. Consistent with its policy of publicizing successful tax prosecutions, the Internal Revenue Service (IRS) issued two press releases regarding the criminal proceedings against Rice. The first release, issued March 2, 1994, reported Rice's convic-

---

[13] *Cert. denied,* 528 U.S. 933 (1999).

tion. * * * The second release, issued June 13, 1994, reported Rice's sentence. * * *

Rice, a certified public accountant and lawyer, subsequently filed a *pro se* civil action against the United States, the IRS, and those officials responsible for issuing the press releases, alleging that Defendants wrongfully disclosed confidential tax information about him. The district court dismissed all but three of Rice's claims pursuant to Fed. R. Civ. P. 12. Remaining were (1) a claim against the United States arising under the Internal Revenue Code, 26 U.S.C. §§ 6103 & 7431; (2) a claim against the United States arising under the Federal Tort Claims Act, 28 U.S.C. §§ 2671–80; and (3) a claim against the IRS arising under the Federal Privacy Act, 5 U.S.C. § 552a.

Following discovery, the United States and IRS moved for summary judgment pursuant to Fed. R. Civ. P. 56 on the remainder of Rice's claims. In a thorough memorandum opinion, the district court concluded that no genuine issue of material fact existed as to whether the two press releases disclosed confidential tax information about Rice. The court found that all the information contained in the press releases came from public documents and proceedings. Specifically, the court found that to prepare the releases, an IRS public affairs officer had reviewed the indictment against Rice, attended his trial and sentencing, and researched the possible criminal penalties for his crimes. These the court found were the only sources for the information contained in the press releases. Accordingly, the district court held that Rice had no claim against the United States or the IRS for violating the confidentiality provisions of the Internal Revenue Code. The court further determined that because the IRS had not released confidential taxpayer information about Rice from its records, but obtained the information for the releases from public sources, he similarly had no claim against Defendants under the Federal Torts Claim Act or the Federal Privacy Act.

On appeal, Rice raises two issues worthy of review. First, Rice contends that because the information contained in the press releases was, as a matter of law, confidential tax return information, Defendants necessarily violated the confidentiality provisions of the code by issuing the releases. In the alternative, Rice contends that genuine issues of material fact precluding summary judgment exist as to the source of the information contained in the press releases. Our jurisdiction arises under 28 U.S.C. § 1291. We review a grant of summary judgment de novo employing the same legal principles as the district court. Kane v. Capital Guardian Trust Co., 145 F.3d 1218, 1221 (10th Cir. 1998). Applying these principles, we affirm.

I.

Section 6103(a) of the Internal Revenue Code prohibits disclosure of tax return information unless expressly authorized by an exception. *See generally* Baskin v. United States, 135 F.3d 338, 340–42 (5th Cir. 1998) (discussing history of disclosure prohibition). * * * One of the numerous exceptions to § 6103's general prohibition allows disclosure of "return information" in federal court where "the taxpayer is a party to the proceedings." *Id.* § 6103(h)(4)(A).

Section 7431(a) of the code in turn provides a cause of action to an aggrieved taxpayer for a violation of § 6103: "If any officer or employee of the United States knowingly, or by reason of negligence, . . . discloses any return or return information with respect to a taxpayer in violation of any provision of section 6103, such taxpayer may bring a civil action for damages against the United States . . . ." 26 U.S.C. § 7431(a)(1). Subsection (b) of § 7431 provides an exception to liability where the officer's or employee's disclosure "results from a good faith, but erroneous interpretation of section 6103." *Id.* § 7431(b)(1).

II.

Rice complains that the press releases contain "return information" as defined in § 6103(b) because they identify him, his accounting firm, and the fact that he unlawfully claimed tax refunds for the years 1988 and 1989, based on false withholdings. Regardless of the source of the information contained in the releases, Rice claims that the government's dissemination of such information without his authorization violated § 6103(a). In other words, Rice asks us to hold that an IRS press release which contains information about a taxpayer's criminal tax liability necessarily constitutes an unauthorized disclosure of tax return information, exposing the government to liability under § 7431. We decline to do so.

The Seventh Circuit rejected an identical argument in *Thomas v. United States*, 890 F.2d 18 (7th Cir. 1989). In that case, the taxpayer claimed a violation of § 6103, although he admitted that the immediate source of the information contained in an IRS press release about him was a tax court opinion. The court acknowledged that the disclosed information may have come *indirectly* from the taxpayer's tax return. Notwithstanding, the court stated:

> Nothing in the background of the statute suggests so broad a scope as Thomas is urging and so direct a collision with the policies that animate the free-speech clause of the First Amendment . . . . [W]e believe that the definition of return information comes into play only when the immediate source of the information is a return, or some internal document based on a return, as these terms are defined in § 6103(b)(2), and not when the immediate source is a public document lawfully prepared by an agency that is separate from the Internal Revenue Service and has lawful access to tax returns.

Thomas, 890 F.2d at 21. We adopt this reasoning. If, as the government claims, the two press releases about which Rice complains were based solely on public documents and proceedings, *i.e.* the IRS public affairs officer's review of the indictment, her attendance at trial and sentencing, and her research into the possible criminal penalties, then Rice's assertion that the government violated § 6103 by issuing the press releases must fail.

Despite Rice's assertion, our decision in *Rodgers v. Hyatt*, 697 F.2d 899 (10th Cir. 1983), is not to the contrary. In *Rodgers*, we rejected the government's argument that the disclosure of return information in a public record bars a taxpayer from complaining about any subsequent disclosure of such information. *Accord* Chandler v. United States, 887 F.2d 1397, 1398 (10th Cir. 1989);

* * *. Instead, we held that an IRS agent's prior "in court" testimony at a hearing to enforce an IRS summons did not alone justify the agent's subsequent out of court statement to a third party regarding an ongoing investigation of the taxpayer. *Rodgers*, 697 F.2d at 904–06. We upheld the jury's verdict in favor of the taxpayer and its implicit finding that the agent had not obtained his information from the court hearing — a public proceeding, but rather had obtained it from internal documents based on the taxpayer's tax return. Thus, under both *Thomas* and *Rodgers*, whether information about a taxpayer may be classified as "return information" invoking application of § 6103 turns on the immediate source of the information.

*   *   *

The judgment of the district court as to both Rice and JVR Accounting, Inc., is affirmed.

———————

Not every court agrees with the conclusion drawn in *Rice*. *Mallas v. United States*, 993 F.2d 1111 (4th Cir. 1993), also involved dissemination by the IRS of information relating to a taxpayer's prior criminal conviction for tax fraud (which was subsequently reversed on appeal). According to the Fourth Circuit there is no "exception . . . permitting the disclosure of 'return information' simply because it is otherwise available to the public." *Id.* at 1120. Consider also *Johnson v. Sawyer*.

In *Johnson v. Sawyer*, 760 F. Supp. 1216 (S.D. Tex. 1991), Elvis Johnson obtained a $10 million judgment under the Federal Tort Claims Act for press releases publicizing his plea of guilty to a one-count criminal information that he had underpaid his 1975 federal income tax by approximately $3,500.[14] Johnson was a key executive of an insurance company, and the executive committee of the company assured Johnson that he could retain his position, even if he pled guilty to a crime, so long as there was no publicity that would embarrass the company. The Assistant U.S. Attorney prosecuting Johnson agreed not to publicize the plea, but neglected to inform the IRS of that agreement. The IRS released the following press release to 21 media outlets:

> "GALVESTON, TEXAS—In U.S. District Court here, Apr. 10, Elvis E. Johnson, 59, plead [sic] guilty to a charge of federal tax evasion. Judge Hugh Gibson sentenced Johnson, of 25 Adler Circle, to a six-month suspended prison term and one year supervised probation. Johnson, an executive vice-president for the American National Insurance Corporation, was charged in a criminal information with claiming false business deductions and altering documents involving his 1974 and 1975 income tax returns. In addition to the sentence, Johnson will be required to pay back taxes, plus penalties and interest."

---

[14] The following facts of this case are summarized in the Fifth Circuit's decision, *Johnson v. Sawyer*, 120 F.3d 1307, 1310 (5th Cir. 1997).

The release was incorrect in that Johnson had been charged only for 1975, and the criminal information did not charge him with claiming false business deductions or altering documents. Upon learning that, the IRS notified the media outlets that the release might contain errors, and should not be publicized. The IRS then released a revised release. Following the second release, the insurance company asked Johnson to resign from his position with the company.

In his complaint and first two amended complaints, Johnson sued various IRS employees under Code sections 6103 and 7217, claiming wrongful disclosure of five items of tax return information: his age; his home address; that he was charged with false business deductions and altering documents on his 1974 and 1975 returns; that he would be required to pay back taxes, plus penalties and interest; and that he was executive vice-president of the insurance company in question. He also made a claim against the United States under the Federal Tort Claims Act, 28 U.S.C. §§ 2671-80, for negligent supervision. The District Court severed the claims against the individual defendants, and the jury awarded Johnson $10 million on the Federal Tort Claims Act claim. *Johnson v. Sawyer*, 760 F. Supp. 1216 (S.D. Tex. 1991). On appeal, the Fifth Circuit affirmed, then reversed in an *en banc* decision, remanding for dismissal of the Federal Tort Claims Act claim. *See Johnson v. Sawyer*, 980 F.2d 1490 (5th Cir. 1992); *Johnson v. Sawyer*, 47 F.3d 716, 737–38 (5th Cir. 1995) (*en banc*).

On remand, Johnson filed a third amended complaint, adding a claim that "identifying" him constituted a sixth item of wrongful disclosure. The jury awarded Johnson a $9 million judgment. 1996 U.S. Dist. LEXIS 7702, 96-2 U.S.T.C. ¶ 50,337 (S.D. Tex 1996). On appeal, because of an erroneous jury instruction, the Fifth Circuit vacated the District Court's opinion and remanded for consideration of liability under section 7217 and damages. *Johnson v. Sawyer*, 120 F.3d 1307, 1338 (5th Cir. 1997). On the issue of whether tax information that was already public is subject to section 6103, the Circuit Court stated:

> Congress considered a taxpayer's privacy interest in tax return information when enumerating the exceptions to § 6103. In evaluating the areas in which tax return information was formerly subject to disclosure and deciding whether to maintain such disclosure provision, the committee "balanced the particular office or agency's need for the information involved with the citizen's right to privacy and the related impact of the disclosure upon the continuation of compliance with our country's voluntary assessment system." [S. Rep. No. 94-938,] at 318 [(1976), reprinted in] 1976 U.S.C.C.A.N. at 3747. In spite of this consideration, however, Congress chose not to create an exception for "public record" tax return information.

> In judicially creating that exception, the Sixth Circuit explained: "The approach we adopt today strikes the proper balance between a taxpayer's reasonable expectation of privacy and the government's legitimate interest in disclosing tax return information to the extent necessary for tax administration functions." *Rowley* [*v. United States*, 76 F.3d 796, 802 (6th Cir. 1996)] * * *. We, however, agree

with the Fourth Circuit: "It is for Congress . . . to 'strike a balance' between these interests [and it] has done so in section 6103, without articulating [this] exception." *Mallas* [*v. United States*, 993 F.2d 1111, 1121 (4th Cir. 1993)] * * *. We are a federal appellate court, not a super-legislature; we are not vested with plenary authority to re-evaluate the policy choices made by our elected representatives. *See* The Federalist No. 78 (Alexander Hamilton) ("The courts must declare the sense of the law; and if they should be disposed to exercise WILL instead of JUDGMENT, the consequence would equally be the substitution of their pleasure for that of the legislative body.")

Section 6103 provides blanket protection to tax return information. If we recognized an exception for "public record" tax return information, as the Ninth and Sixth Circuits have, we would be concluding that § 6103 distinguishes between confidential (private) and non-confidential (public) tax return information. *See Lampert* [*v. United States*, 854 F.2d 335, 338 (9th Cir. 1988)] * * * ("Once tax return information is made a part of the public domain, the taxpayer may no longer claim a right of privacy in that information."); *see also Rowley*, 76 F.3d at 801–02 (information in public domain loses confidentiality and protection of § 6103). Appellants ask us to hold that § 6103 makes that distinction. But, again, this flies in the face of § 6103. It states that "[r]eturns and return information *shall be confidential*, and except as authorized by this title . . . shall [not be] disclosed"; not that "[confidential] [r]eturns and return information . . . shall [not be] disclosed." (Emphasis added.) This is a critical, indeed dispositive, difference.

* * *

Thus, § 6103's protection does not disappear simply because tax return information has been disclosed in the public record and has therefore arguably lost its confidentiality. In enacting § 6103 as a prophylactic ban, Congress was determining that a taxpayer has a statutorily created "privacy" interest in all his tax return information, despite the fact that some of it is not entirely "secret".

* * *

Johnson v. Sawyer, 120 F.3d at 1321–1323.

To what extent can disclosure improve voluntary compliance by taxpayers? The Illinois Department of Revenue (IDOR) initiated in 2000 an internet "Taxpayer Hall of Shame" in an effort to collect delinquent taxes. The IDOR electronically posts the names of taxpayers who have owed more than $10,000 for more than 6 months. Illinois is one of a handful of states that use this type of disclosure as an enforcement tool. In response to a Joint Committee on Taxation request for a study of whether disclosure of delinquent taxpayers increases compliance, the General Accounting Office concluded that, despite evidence from state officials that disclosure improves compliance levels, "such statistics were not good indicators of program impact because they do not isolate the effect of public disclosure on accounts receivable and collections." *See* GAO, Tax Administration: Few State and Local Governments Publicly Disclosure Delinquent Taxpayers (GAO/GGD-99-165).

[B]   Exceptions Under Section 6103 Permitting Disclosure

Having established the general rule that taxpayer information should remain confidential, section 6103 then proceeds to list circumstances under which information may be made available without subjecting the IRS to liability for wrongful disclosure. For example, returns and return information may be disclosed by the IRS to a third party designated by the taxpayer to receive the information and to a person having a material interest in the return or return information. I.R.C. § 6103(c), (e).[15] This latter authorization permits the taxpayer to obtain a copy of his own return, each spouse to obtain a copy of a jointly filed return, and a partner to obtain a copy of the partnership's return. Section 6103 also authorizes the IRS to exchange taxpayer information (including names, social security numbers, addresses, and wage information) with various federal, state, and local agencies. These agencies are entitled to use this information for several specified purposes, such as administering state tax programs, enforcing child support payments, and conducting criminal investigations. *See, e.g.*, I.R.C. § 6103(i), (j), (k), (l).

On a broader level, these exemptions under section 6103 highlight the tension between the need for other government agencies and third parties to use tax return information and the taxpayer's need for some assurance that the information he submits to the IRS will remain private. As you read the statutory language, notice the limitations surrounding the release of return information and the elaborate procedures employed by the IRS to ensure that the information, once in the hands of the recipient, remains confidential. The regulations under section 6103 and the Internal Revenue Manual provide more specific examples of when and for what purpose information may be disclosed. *See, e.g.*, Treas. Reg. § 301.6103; I.R.M. Disclosure Handbook. Consider also the following case.

DIANDRE v. UNITED STATES
United States Court of Appeals, Tenth Circuit
968 F.2d 1049 (1992)[16]

EBEL, CIRCUIT JUDGE:

In this appeal, we consider whether, and to what extent, section 6103 of the Internal Revenue Code ("I.R.C.") (26 U.S.C. § 6103) limits the scope of an Internal Revenue Service ("IRS") investigation. We hold that IRS circular

---

[15] Recently issued Temporary Regulations provide procedures for an oral request by a taxpayer for disclosure of his return information to a person he designates. *See* Temp. Reg. § 301.6103(c)-1T(c)(2).

[16] *Cert. denied sub. nom.* Metro Denver Maintenance Cleaning v. United States, 507 U.S. 1029 (1993).

letters sent to the taxpayer's customers requesting information on all payments made to the taxpayer did not violate section 6103. Accordingly, we reverse the district court's judgment awarding damages to the taxpayer under I.R.C. § 7431 (26 U.S.C. § 7431) based upon an alleged violation of I.R.C. § 6103.

I.

This suit arises out of an IRS criminal investigation of a corporation, plaintiff-appellee Metro Denver Maintenance Cleaning, Inc. ("MDMCI"), and its owner, plaintiff Anthony F. DiAndrea, concerning possible tax fraud. MDMCI provided janitorial services primarily to corporate customers.

In July 1985, the IRS began auditing DiAndrea and MDMCI. The investigation apparently remained dormant for some time, but resumed in early 1986. The agent assigned to the audit was unable to reconcile the corporation's records with its tax returns. In addition, he observed evidence of potential fraud: DiAndrea appeared to be intentionally uncooperative with the audit; there appeared to be two sets of profit and loss statements containing different figures for the same time period; DiAndrea allegedly admitted that he habitually inflated his travel and entertainment expense deductions; and DiAndrea appeared to be living beyond his means based on the income he declared on his tax returns. However, the agent did not suspect that MDMCI or DiAndrea was receiving unreported cash payments from customers. Appellant's App. at 178. On the basis of the other badges of fraud, the agent referred the case to the IRS's Criminal Investigation Division ("CID").

In September 1986, Shirley Kish Thomas, a CID Special Agent, undertook the criminal investigation of MDMCI and of DiAndrea. Agent Thomas issued a summons to DiAndrea and MDMCI for all of MDMCI's books and records, bank statements, deposit slips and cancelled checks, information on all bank accounts, and all financial statements for the period under investigation.

As part of her investigation, Agent Thomas prepared a "circular letter," a type of form letter, to obtain information from MDMCI customers. This letter, which appeared on CID letterhead, provided in relevant part:

> The Internal Revenue Service is conducting an investigation of Metro Denver Maintenance, Inc., Lakewood, Colorado, for the years 1983 through 1985. Mr. DiAndrea is an officer of Metro Denver Maintenance whose address is 6800 West 6th Avenue, Lakewood, Colorado, 80215.

> During the course of our investigation, we noted transactions between you and Metro Denver Maintenance, Inc. and/or Mr. DiAndrea for [the] previously mentioned period. As part of our investigation, we need to verify the purpose of these transactions. Your assistance is needed in determining all payments made to or on behalf of Metro Denver Maintenance and/or Mr. DiAndrea for the previously mentioned period. We would appreciate you furnishing the information indicated on Attachment 1, for use in a Federal tax matter.

Appellant's App. at 91. Attachment 1 requested the following information: "the date, check number, amount and form of all payment(s). By form of payment, it is meant if the payment(s) was made in cash, check, money order, etc." *Id.* at 94. Attachment 2, which was a form upon which the required information was to be entered, specified that the response should include "any payments made in the form of cash." *Id.* at 95.

Agent Thomas mailed this letter to all MDMCI customers. She subsequently issued a summons to all of DiAndrea's and MDMCI's banks for all records pertaining to either of them.

Using the bank records together with the MDMCI records, Agent Thomas and an accountant were substantially able to reconcile the records with MDMCI's and DiAndrea's tax returns. In addition, the bank records revealed that DiAndrea had several money market accounts, which explained his apparent ability to live beyond his means. The responses to the circular letters failed to reveal any further pertinent information. Agent Thomas ultimately concluded that the amount of potential underreporting of income did not meet the IRS's guidelines for criminal prosecution. The criminal investigation was then terminated.

DiAndrea and MDMCI filed suit against the United States pursuant to I.R.C. § 7431. The plaintiffs alleged that by mailing the circular letters, Agent Thomas had wrongfully disclosed confidential tax return information in violation of I.R.C. § 6103. The district court conducted a bench trial, at the end of which it orally entered its findings of fact and conclusions of law.

In its ruling, the district court found that the circular letters did not disclose any of DiAndrea's personal return information. The court found, however, that the circular letters did disclose a number of items of MDMCI's return information: the name of the taxpayer (MDMCI), the taxpayer's address, that DiAndrea was an officer of the taxpayer, that the IRS was investigating the taxpayer, that it was a criminal investigation, and that IRS records revealed transactions between the taxpayer and the recipient of the circular letter. The court further found that certain information sought via the circular letters— the payments cleared through DiAndrea's and MDMCI's banks— was reasonably available using bank and corporate records. The court rejected the government's argument that the circular letters were necessary to obtain information on unrecorded cash payments that may have been received by DiAndrea or MDMCI for undocumented "side jobs." The court specifically noted the absence of any evidence indicating that customers were making undocumented cash payments, except for statements by a former employee that DiAndrea had large amounts of cash available to him. Moreover, the court found that normal IRS procedure required that its agents first attempt to account for discrepancies in a tax return using bank records prior to sending out circular letters. Because Agent Thomas was not focusing specifically on cash payments at the time she sent out the circular letters, the court concluded that the government's argument that cash payments could not be discovered through examination of the bank records was "a belated attempt to justify what the special agent was doing at the time." Appellant's App. at 225.

The district court concluded that, in revealing MDMCI's return information, the disclosures violated section 6103 and that at least some of the information disclosed did not result from a good faith, but erroneous, interpretation of the section. The court accordingly awarded damages and entered judgment in favor of MDMCI. Because the circular letters had revealed none of DiAndrea's personal return information, the court dismissed DiAndrea's complaint.

The United States filed a timely notice of appeal. We have jurisdiction pursuant to 28 U.S.C. § 1291.

II.

The statute under which DiAndrea and MDMCI brought suit, section 7431 of the Internal Revenue Code, permits a taxpayer to bring a civil action against the United States if a federal employee or official violates that taxpayer's rights under section 6103. I.R.C. § 7431(a)(1). However, section 7431 provides that the United States is not liable if the violation occurred because of "a good faith, but erroneous, interpretation of section 6103." I.R.C. § 7431(b). The government argues that no violation of section 6103 occurred. Alternatively, it argues that if a violation did occur, it resulted from a good faith, but erroneous, interpretation of the statute, and that therefore the government has no liability.

Congress enacted section 6103 of the Internal Revenue Code to protect taxpayers' privacy and to prevent the misuse of the confidential information obtained in the course of collecting taxes. *See* S. Rep. No. 938, 94th Cong., 2d Sess. 19, 317–18 (1976), *reprinted in* 1976 U.S.C.C.A.N. 3439, 3455, 3746–47. * * *

Section 6103 provides a safe harbor for IRS agents that is relevant here:

> An internal revenue officer or employee may, in connection with his official duties relating to any audit, collection activity, or civil or criminal tax investigation or any other offense under the internal revenue laws, disclose return information to the extent that such disclosure is necessary in obtaining information, which is not otherwise reasonably available, with respect to the correct determination of tax, liability for tax, or the amount to be collected or with respect to the enforcement of any other provision of [the Internal Revenue Code].

I.R.C. § 6103(k)(6). Thus, an IRS agent may disclose return information during an investigation in order to obtain information, provided three requirements are met: (1) The information sought is "with respect to the correct determination of tax, liability for tax, or the amount to be collected or with respect to the enforcement of any other provision of [the Internal Revenue Code]." (2) The information sought is "not otherwise reasonably available." (3) It is necessary to make disclosures of return information in order to obtain the additional information sought.

The parties do not dispute that Agent Thomas disclosed return information by sending out the circular letters. Whether, in doing so, she violated section 6103 depends on whether her actions fell within the safe harbor of section 6103(k)(6). Accordingly, we must determine whether the three requirements of section 6103(k)(6) were met.

It should be self-evident that the first requirement — that the information sought related to determining tax liability — was met in this case. Information regarding all payments made to a taxpayer clearly relates to a determination of tax liability.

The parties dispute whether the second of these requirements was met: that the information sought must not be otherwise reasonably available. The circular letter requests information on "all payments," including those "made in cash." *See* Appellant's App. at 91, 94, 95. Cash payments do not appear to be the primary focus of the circular letter, but the letter clearly does request information on this subject. Information on receipt of undocumented cash payments was not available from any source other than from the payor, thereby meeting the second requirement. Although the circular letter also requested information that was potentially available from other sources, section 6103 does not prohibit requesting additional information beyond that not otherwise reasonably available if the additional request requires no further disclosure.

The final requirement — that the disclosures were necessary to obtain the information sought — was also met. There is no dispute that obtaining the information sought from MDMCI's customers required disclosure of all the return information contained in the circular letter, with the possible exceptions of the taxpayer's address and the fact that the tax investigation underway was criminal in nature. With regard to the former disclosure, given the necessity of revealing the taxpayer's identity, we hold that, under the circumstances of this case, disclosure of nonsensitive public information such as a business address to aid in identification was appropriate and necessary and therefore not a violation of section 6103. *Cf.* I.R.C. § 6103(b)(6) (taxpayer identity includes name, mailing address, and taxpayer's identifying number). With regard to the latter disclosure, the district court concluded that the government was protected by the good faith exception of section 7431(b). *Accord* Diamond v. United States, 944 F.2d 431, 435–37 (8th Cir. 1991). MDMCI does not appeal that ruling, so we do not review it here.

The district court strayed beyond the parameters of section 6103 when it sought to determine Agent Thomas' subjective intent and when it concluded that insufficient justification was shown to warrant delving into whether cash payments were made. That inquiry misperceives the function of section 6103(k)(6), which is to limit disclosures to those necessary to obtain the information sought. The section does not require the IRS to justify the appropriateness or need for the information sought so long as such information relates to the determination of tax liability and is not otherwise reasonably available. In other words, section 6103 does not provide a vehicle to test the probable cause or any other level of justification to investigate. *See* Barrett v. United States, 795 F.2d 446, 451 (5th Cir. 1986) ("in a section 7431 action, the court does not inquire whether the information sought is necessary"); *cf.* United States v. Powell, 379 U.S. 48, 57, 13 L. Ed. 2d 112, 85 S. Ct. 248 (1964) (IRS does not require probable cause to issue summons); United States v. MacKay, 608 F.2d 830, 832 (10th Cir. 1979) (same). The plain language of section 6103 does not limit in any way what information the IRS may seek in the course of an investigation. Section 6103 merely imposes certain restrictions on the IRS's ability to make disclosures in seeking that information. *See Barrett*, 795 F.2d at 451 ("We do not question the right, wisdom, or necessity of a particular IRS investigation. We do question, however, the means of investigation, but only to the limited extent consistent with section 7431."). The three requirements that section 6103(k)(6) imposes to permit an IRS agent to disclose return information were all met here. Thus, we hold that section 6103 did not prevent Agent Thomas from seeking information regarding cash payments even if she did not suspect cash payments and even if the badges of fraud could be legitimately explained.

We do not hold — indeed, we do not mean even to imply — that the IRS may investigate any subject and seek any information it wishes based on mere whim, caprice, or malice. Section 6103(k)(6) permits disclosures of return information only to obtain information relating to tax liability. Whatever other limits there may be on the scope of an IRS investigation, *cf., e.g.,* United States v. LaSalle Nat'l Bank, 437 U.S. 298, 313, 57 L.Ed.2d 221, 98 S.Ct. 2357 (1978) ("the IRS must use its summons authority in good faith"); *Powell*, 379 U.S. at 58 (court may refuse to enforce summons if issued for an improper purpose such as to harass or to apply pressure in a collateral matter); United States v. Malnik, 489 F.2d 682, 686 n.4 (5th Cir.) ("enforcement of an unclear and overly broad summons would violate the Fourth Amendment's proscription of unreasonable searches and seizures"), *cert. denied*, 419 U.S. 826, 42 L. Ed. 2d 50, 95 S. Ct. 44 (1974), it is not section 6103 that imposes those limits.

Because we conclude that no violation of section 6103 occurred, we need not and do not address the government's arguments regarding a good faith, but erroneous, interpretation of section 6103.

Accordingly, we reverse the judgment of the district court and remand with instructions to enter judgment for the United States.

In the context of a pass-through entity such as a partnership or S corporation, does return information pertaining to the entity's operations belong the entity itself or to the equity holder? Resolving this issue is important for purposes of applying the exception in section 6103(e). The following case illustrates the dilemma.

MARTIN v. INTERNAL REVENUE SERVICE
United States Court of Appeals, Tenth Circuit
857 F.2d 722 (1988)

Seymour, Circuit Judge:

Robert J. Martin filed suit under the Freedom of Information Act (FOIA), 5 U.S.C. § 552 (1982), to compel the Internal Revenue Service (IRS) to disclose to him tax protests filed by three other individuals. The protests concerned proposed adjustments to those individuals' tax returns based on proposed adjustments to the returns of certain pass-through corporate and partnership entities in which Martin and the other individuals had interests. The district court ordered the IRS to disclose the protests to Martin. Because we conclude that the protests are not "return information" of the corporate entities within the meaning of 26 U.S.C. § 6103 (1982 & Supp. IV 1986), we reverse.[n.1]

I.

From 1980 to 1983, Robert J. Martin, Robert L. Mehl, Patrick D. Maher, and Jordan R. Smith were shareholders in Western Oil Marketing (WOM), a subchapter S corporation. They were also partners in a limited partnership, Industrial Energy Partners (IEP). WOM and IEP were the sole partners in a general partnership, Western Operating Joint Venture (WOJV). All of these entities are pass-through entities. They file information returns with the IRS but pay little or no tax. Their partners/shareholders are primarily responsible for the tax consequences of the entities' income and expenses. 26 U.S.C. §§ 701, 1372 (1982). Any adjustments to the entities' returns thus affect the liabilities of their partners/shareholders. Martin severed his relationship with the entities in 1983.

The IRS audited the returns of the three entities and proposed adjustments to the income and expenses reported by each from 1980 through 1983. A copy of the revenue agent's report proposing the adjustments was sent to each of the partners/shareholders. The IRS then audited and sought adjustments to the returns of these individuals.[n.2] Martin alleges, and the IRS has not denied, that Mehl, Maher, and Smith filed protests with the IRS contesting these proposed adjustments.[n.4] The IRS agent auditing Martin's returns has stated that she will adopt the same position as that taken by the IRS in response to Mehl, Maher and Smith's protests in her audit of Martin's returns. Rec., doc. 5, at 10, para. 7. Martin therefore seeks disclosure of the protests, to the extent they relate to the entities' returns, in order to prepare his own response to the IRS.

After exhausting his administrative remedies, Martin filed this FOIA suit seeking disclosure of such parts of the protests as relate to the entities. A magistrate recommended that his request be granted with respect to WOM

[n.1] It is undisputed in this case that if section 6103 prohibits disclosure of this information, it is exempt from disclosure under FOIA. *See* 5 U.S.C. § 552(b)(3) (FOIA does not apply to matters that are "specifically exempted from disclosure by statute").

[n.2] After an audit, a revenue agent's report is sent to those under audit along with a letter explaining the taxpayers' alternatives. IRS regulations provide that if audited taxpayers disagree with the revenue agent's proposed adjustments to their tax returns, they may file a response to the IRS letter. This response must be sent within 30 days; thus, the letter is known as a 30-day letter. One form of response is to file a protest and appeal to an IRS appeals officer. 26 C.F.R. § 601.105 (1988). Mehl, Maher and Smith have responded by filing protests.

[n.4] The parties' statements of facts are not entirely clear as to whether the protests were filed in response to the proposed adjustments to the entities' information returns in themselves, or whether they contest the resulting proposed adjustments to Mehl, Maher and Smith's own returns. While the distinction between these is technical, it is significant. Protests that were filed in direct response to proposed adjustments to the entities' information returns would be return information of the entities. * * * Finally and most significantly, although Martin asserts in his brief that the protests were furnished to the IRS with respect to the entities' returns, he does not contest the IRS's argument that the protests are return information of Mehl, Maher and Smith. We thus assume that the protests were submitted by Mehl, Maher and Smith to contest adjustments to their own tax liability.

and IEP and denied as to WOJV, because Martin is not a partner or share-holder of WOJV. The district court granted the request as to all three entities and ordered the IRS to redact information identifying the taxpayers who filed the protests. After the court denied the IRS's motion to suspend the injunction pending appeal, the IRS made an emergency motion to this court for stay pending appeal. We granted the stay, conditioned on an IRS extension of time for Martin to respond to his 30-day letter, and expedited the appeal.

II.

Section 6103 of the Internal Revenue Code, 26 U.S.C. § 6103, governs the confidentiality and disclosure of tax returns and return information. It provides that returns and return information may not be disclosed except as authorized by title 26. *Id.* § 6103(a). * * * Partners and shareholders may obtain access to returns and return information of their partnerships and corporations pursuant to section 6103(e), which governs disclosure to persons having a material interest. That section authorizes a partner to examine the return of his partnership, *id.* § 6103(e)(1)(C), and a shareholder of a subchapter S corporation to examine the return of that corporation, *id.* § 6103(e)(1)(D)(v), upon written request. They may examine the return information of such partnerships or corporations if the Secretary determines that such disclosure would not seriously impair Federal tax administration. *Id.* § 6103(e)(7).

The parties agree that the same item of information may be the return information of more than one taxpayer. They also agree that the source of that information is not controlling. Therefore, data supplied to the IRS by A that may affect B's tax return may in theory be return information of A alone, of A and B, of B alone, or of no one. The parties disagree on how to determine whose return information such data would be in any given case. Martin argues that the key factor is whose tax liability may be affected by the data. The IRS argues that the key factor is whose tax liability is under investigation by the IRS. Specifically, the IRS defines "any person," as the term is used in the definition of return information, as "the person or persons whose liabilities are under investigation and as to whom information collected by the IRS is germane to a determination of their tax liabilities." Brief for the Appellant at 11–12.

The facts of this case make Martin's argument very appealing. Pass-through entities are to a large extent legal fictions in the tax context and that is particularly evident here. One could say with some justification that Martin is in fact contesting his tax liability with his former co-partners/shareholders. The IRS agent auditing his returns has stated that she will adopt the same approach to his returns as the IRS adopts with respect to Mehl, Maher and Smith's returns. While Martin may appeal this approach if it does not favor him, both with the IRS and in court, the IRS may already have considered and rejected the arguments he is likely to make before he gets that opportunity. It may seem both unjust and contrary to common sense to read the statute to allow Mehl, Maher and Smith to attempt to affect Martin's tax liabilities without permitting him to know their arguments and to reply to them.

To counter this argument, the IRS stresses the privacy rights that section 6103 is designed to protect. The Government points out that information supplied by one taxpayer with respect to his own tax liability often affects the liability of another taxpayer, and that such information does not thereby become disclosable to the second taxpayer merely because of its possible effect. At oral argument, counsel for the IRS drew a mental picture that illustrates the IRS' position. Suppose the IRS has a basket for each taxpayer and corporate entity. When the IRS makes a determination about an entity's return, the report is placed in the entity's basket. Under the authority of section 6103(e), it is also placed in the baskets of the entity's partners/shareholders. Individual reactions to the report are placed only in the basket of that taxpayer. If the IRS then reacts to the protests and changes the entity's return, that information is again placed both in the entity's basket and in those of its partners/shareholders.

We have found only two circuit cases, one of them ours, that have considered whether a specific item of information is the return information of a corporate entity. See Mid-South Music Corp. v. United States, 818 F.2d 536 (6th Cir. 1987); First Western Gov't Securities v. United States, 796 F.2d 356 (10th Cir. 1986). Mid-South and First Western do not provide us with much guidance, however, because of significant differences between their facts and the facts of this case. Those cases concern information released by the IRS; the communications did not reveal that the information supplier was under investigation or the substance of the legal basis for the IRS determination; and the information was arguably corporate information released to investors. Here, on the other hand, a third party is seeking information the IRS has determined to be nondisclosable; the information would necessarily reveal that Mehl, Maher and Smith are under investigation, and the substance of their legal arguments;[n.5] and the information is that of individual taxpayers and would be released to a corporate entity.[n.6] Furthermore, Mid-South and First Western concluded that the information in question was not the return information of the supplier. Here there can be no doubt that the protests are the return information of Mehl, Maher and Smith.

Two cases with facts more similar to those of this case are Church of Scientology v. Internal Revenue Service, 484 U.S. 9, 108 S. Ct. 271, 98 L. Ed. 2d 228 (1987) (rejecting attempt by Church to require IRS to disclose information relating to Church in IRS case files and data systems) and Ryan v. Bureau

---

[n.5] The IRS describes tax protests as follows:

"A taxpayer's written protest may . . . be argumentative and adversarial in nature. The taxpayer . . . may cite and argue from precedent, may argue that the agent has misconstrued or misunderstood facts and transactions, and may attempt to cast the facts relied upon by the agent in a light more favorable to his own position. Even if a taxpayer used the return information of an entity in formulating his protest, that information may have been recast, reformulated or reorganized by an advocate . . . Thus, a protest, although based upon the [revenue agent's report] issued by the agent, consists primarily of the analyses, interpretations and conclusion of the taxpayer or his attorney."

Brief for the Appellant at 27–28.

[n.6] Martin argues that the protests are return information of the entities. Martin's right to the protests, if any, derives from his status as a partner/shareholder; if the entities are entitled to the information, he is as well, to the extent permitted by section 6103(e)(7).

of Alcohol, Tobacco and Firearms, 230 U.S. App. D.C. 170, 715 F.2d 644 (D.C. Cir. 1983) (rejecting attempt to require IRS to disclose information supplied by liquor bottle manufacturers in aid of determination of tax liabilities of liquor manufacturers). In those cases, however, the issue was whether the information was return information at all. It is not disputed here that the protests are the return information of Mehr, Maher and Smith. The question we address is whether they are also the return information of the entities; that is, our question is whose return information it is, not whether it is return information. We note that *Ryan* explicitly rejected the argument made by the IRS in this case, although with respect to an arguably different term, and held that information supplied to the IRS is the return information of "any person with respect to whom information is received." *Ryan*, 715 F.2d at 647.

Ultimately, we are convinced by two arguments. First, we agree with the IRS that the mere fact that information supplied by one person may affect the tax liability of another is insufficient to give the second a right to see that information. If one considers tax returns rather than return information, that principle is not difficult to accept. It is frequently the case that one transaction is reflected in many tax returns. If two taxpayers' returns were based on different allocations of resulting tax liability from a transaction, that difference in itself would not give one taxpayer a right to see the other's return. The right to see return information is no greater than the right to see tax returns. *See* 26 U.S.C. § 6103(e)(7).

Second, given the structure of section 6103, acceptance of the argument made by Martin would render section 6103(e) superfluous. Pass-through entities are to a large extent legal fictions for tax purposes. They pay little or no tax themselves. The information they submit is useful to the IRS primarily insofar as it affects the tax liabilities of their partners/shareholders. They present perhaps the quintessential case for Martin's argument that the key factor in determining access to return information should be whose liability is at stake. Were that argument the basis on which section 6103 is constructed, however, the returns submitted by pass-through entities to the IRS would automatically be the return information of their investors, the taxpayers. No statutory provision other than section 6103(c), which provides for the disclosure of a taxpayer's return and return information to that taxpayer or his designee, would be needed.

In fact, however, entity returns and return information are disclosable to partners/shareholders only because of section 6103(e), which provides for the access of *third parties* to the return information of *others*. Congress recognized that persons with a material interest, as defined by statute, in another's tax return or return information, have a legitimate basis for disclosure. Partners and shareholders in subchapter S corporations are included in the class of such persons. Since we must give meaning to this statutory provision, and since Martin's argument would make section 6103(e) unnecessary in this context, we must reject it. If Congress thinks it necessary to specify that partners are persons with a material interest in a partnership, it cannot be the case that partners can automatically obtain access to partnership returns or return information on the ground that it is their own return information. The reverse must also be true. In short, the returns and return information of pass-through entities are disclosable to the taxpayers whose liability is actually at stake only because Congress so provided in explicit terms. We do not think that we can read the statute to permit such information to flow in the other direction — from partners shareholders to entities — without a corresponding explicit statutory provision.[n.8]

III.

The parties raise additional arguments which we do not address given our disposition of this case. In particular, Martin argues that disclosure is warranted under section 6103(h)(4)(C).[n.9] *See First Western*, 796 F.2d at 360–61. After reviewing the record, we conclude that this argument was not raised below, and we do not address it.

As directed in our order staying the judgment below, Martin has two weeks from the date of this judgment to respond to his 30-day letter.

Reversed.

The IRS Reform Act requires the Treasury's Inspector General for Tax Administration (TIGTA) to periodically audit FOIA requests that the IRS denies on the basis of section 6103. The first such study, issued in 2000, and covering a five-month period from July to December 1998, concludes that the IRS improperly withheld information requested under FOIA in 12.1 percent of a statistically valid sample of cases. TIGTA, Semi-Annual Report to Congress (March 31, 2000). The procedures for appealing the denial of a FOIA request are discussed in Section 3.02[A][4], above. The material that follows explains the taxpayer's remedies if the IRS discloses confidential return information in violation of section 6103.

[C] Remedies for Unlawful Disclosure Under Section 6103

In order to give teeth to the prohibition in section 6103, Congress established both civil and criminal liability for wrongful disclosure of return and return information. Section 7431 affords an aggrieved taxpayer a cause of action against the United States for damages resulting from any disclosure

---

[n.8] This statutory construction cannot be evaded by asserting that Martin has a material interest in Mehl, Maher and Smith's tax protests insofar as they contain information relating to the entities. The meaning of the term "material interest" is defined by statute. A partner has a material interest in his partnerships' return and return information under 26 U.S.C. § 6103(e)(1)(C) & (e)(7); he does not have a material interest in the return information of a co-partner because no provision so provides.

[n.9] Section 6103(h)(4)(C) provides:

> "(4) Disclosure in judicial and administrative tax proceedings.—A return or return information may be disclosed in a Federal or State judicial or administrative proceeding pertaining to tax administration, but only— . . .
>
> (C) if such return or return information directly relates to a transactional relationship between a person who is a party to the proceeding and the taxpayer which directly affects the resolution of an issue in the proceeding . . ."

26 U.S.C. § 6103(h)(4)(C).

of return or return information knowingly or negligently made by an employee or officer of the United States. I.R.C. § 7431(a)(1).[17] Concerned about reports that IRS employees were browsing through files containing taxpayer information, Congress expanded Code section 7431 to impose liability not only for unauthorized disclosure, but also for unauthorized inspection of return information. Liability on the part of the government does not arise, however, where the IRS can prove that the unauthorized disclosure or inspection resulted from a good faith, but erroneous, interpretation of section 6103. I.R.C. § 7431(b).

The cause of action under section 7431, arising in a U.S. District Court, must be brought within two years after the taxpayer discovers that an unauthorized disclosure has been made. I.R.C. § 7431(d). The measure of damages available includes actual damages sustained by the taxpayer, court costs, and possibly reasonable attorney's fees. At a minimum, the statute specifies a damage award of not less than $1,000 for each act of unauthorized disclosure. Punitive damages are also available in situations where the unlawful disclosure is willful or where disclosure results from gross negligence. *Ward v. United States*, a portion of which is reproduced below, provides an entertaining example of how a district court determines the government's liability under section 7431.

WARD v. UNITED STATES
United States District Court, District of Colorado
973 F. Supp. 996 (1997)

DOWNES, DISTRICT JUDGE:

[The plaintiff apparently owned a chain of stores known as Kid's Avenue. She alleged that IRS agents told various employees and customers that she had not paid her taxes, was using several different Social Security Numbers and aliases, that she had been on a number of trips to South America, and that she was suspected of money laundering and/or involvement with drugs. *See Ward*, 973 F. Supp. at 998–999. She also alleged that the IRS posted similar information in the windows of some Kid's Avenue stores. The court did not give credence to this testimony, but focused on the IRS' admitted disclosures of return information on a live radio talk show, to Inside Edition, and in a letter to the editor of a newspaper. The court rejected the Government's argument that a consent executed by the plaintiff to a reporter for the radio station served to authorize disclosure under section 6103(c). Eds.]

* * *

The Court will briefly outline the issues. Plaintiff, Carol Ward, has filed suit against the United States Internal Revenue Department, asserting that the IRS and its employees and agents made unauthorized disclosures of her "return information" in violation of 26 U.S.C. § 6103(a) and seeks damages pursuant to 26 U.S.C. § 7431. Plaintiff alleges five instances of unauthorized

---

[17] Liability also extends to a narrowly defined group of private individuals (specified in section 6103(a)) if such individuals violate section 6103. I.R.C. § 7431(a)(2).

disclosure of "return information" by Defendant: (1) verbal disclosures by IRS employees to Plaintiff's customers and to Citadel Mall management; (2) the alleged posting of "return information" in the windows of three "Kid's Avenue" stores operated by Plaintiff's son; (3) disclosure of "return information" on August 3, 1993, during a live radio talk show on KVOR radio in Colorado Springs by the IRS District Director, Gerald Swanson and IRS employee Patricia Callahan; (4) disclosure of Plaintiff's "return information" in an IRS "fact sheet" provided to Inside Edition/American Journal (*See* Pltf.'s Exhibit No. 19); and (5) disclosure of "return information" in a published letter to the editor of the Colorado Springs Gazette Telegraph by James Scholan, a revenue officer in the Colorado Springs office of the IRS (*See* Pltf.'s Exhibit No. 21.).

* * *

FINDINGS OF FACT

* * *

Radio Talk Show

4. Defendant has conceded and this Court finds that Defendant, through IRS employees Gerald Swanson and Patricia Callahan, disclosed Plaintiff's "return information" during their August 3, 1993, appearance on a live talk show broadcast on KVOR radio. The Court further finds that Mr. Swanson and Ms. Callahan's disclosures were negligently made. As this Court previously found, Defendant's reliance upon the written consent by Plaintiff was mistaken and, in light of the IRS's own regulations, 26 C.F.R. § 301.6103(c)-1, it cannot be found to be a "good faith, but erroneous, interpretation of section 6103" exempt from liability under 26 U.S.C. § 7431(b). *See* Barrett v. United States of America, 51 F.3d 475 (5th Cir. 1995) *citing with approval* Huckaby v. United States Department of the Treasury, 794 F.2d 1041, 1048–49 (5th Cir. 1986). Furthermore, pursuant to *Rodgers v. Hyatt*, 697 F.2d 899, 906 (10th Cir. 1983), the Court finds that Plaintiff's prior disclosure of return information, including debating the merits of the jeopardy assessment with Swanson and Callahan while on the radio talk show, did not waive the confidentiality of Plaintiff's return information. Nonetheless, the Court finds that Mr. Swanson and Ms. Callahan's disclosures were not willful or the result of gross negligence supporting an award of punitive damages. *See* Barrett v. United States, 100 F.3d 35, 40 (5th Cir. 1996) (defining willful conduct as that which is done without ground for believing that it was lawful or conduct marked by careless disregard of whether one has a right to act in such manner and grossly negligent as conduct which is willful or marked by wanton and reckless disregard of the rights of another). The Court finds that, prior to the radio broadcast, Defendant sought and received advice (although incorrect), as to whether disclosure of Plaintiff's return information was authorized in light of the prior consent executed by Plaintiff. (*See* Pltf.'s Exhibit No. 71, Declaration of Michael S. Perkins.)

5. Over the objection of Defendant the Court accepted the testimony of Mr. Greg Sher. Mr. Sher is the director of sales for the Citadel Group which owns

and operates KVOR and other radio stations. Mr. Sher testified that, based upon his review of Arbitron Company ratings, there were approximately 3,200 to 3,300 listeners tuned into the KVOR radio talk show on which Mr. Swanson and Ms.Callahan appeared and discussed Plaintiff's return information. (See Pltf.'s Exhibits No. 25 and 74.) The Court finds that Mr. Sher's estimate is too speculative to support a finding by this Court that 3,200 to 3,300 listeners were tuned into the radio talk show. Nonetheless, based upon the evidence and a review of the taped radio show, the Court finds that Mr. Swanson and Ms. Callahan each committed an act of disclosure in violation of 26 U.S.C. § 6103. (See Pltf.'s Exhibit 16).

Fact Sheet

6. Based on Defendant's concessions, this Court finds that a disclosure of Plaintiff's return information was made when Defendant provided Inside Edition with a "fact sheet" concerning Plaintiff's dispute with the IRS. (See Pltf.'s Exhibit No. 19.) As with the disclosure made on KVOR radio, the Court finds that Defendant's disclosure was negligent, but not willful or grossly negligent, supporting an award of punitive damages. Ms. Callahan, who had provided the "fact sheet" to Inside Edition, testified that prior to release she had checked with the IRS disclosure officer, Mike Perkins, who incorrectly advised her that Plaintiff's prior consent authorized the disclosure of Plaintiff's return information. The Court rejects Plaintiff's suggestion that the material contained in the fact sheet made intentional misstatements of the "facts" surrounding Plaintiff's case. Accordingly, the Court finds that one act of unauthorized disclosure was made as a result of the "fact sheet" being provided to Inside Edition.

Letter to the Editor

7. This Court finds that the letter written to the editor of the Colorado Springs Gazette Telegraph by the Colorado Springs IRS Revenue Officer, James Scholan, which was published in the October 12, 1993 edition of that paper contained "return information." (See Pltf.'s Exhibit No. 21.) Based upon the testimony of Tom Miller and James Scholan, this Court also finds that this return information was obtained by Mr. Scholan in his capacity as a revenue officer for the IRS.

Mr. Miller testified that Mr. Scholan would have had to have been "in a coma" not to have known that there was a collection action going on involving Plaintiff. In addition, contrary to his declaration, which was filed with this Court, Mr. Scholan was forced to acknowledge that he did serve a levy for Mr. Miller, making ¶ 2 of his declaration inaccurate. (See Pltf.'s Exhibit No. 68.) Mr. Scholan also acknowledged that ¶ 3 was inaccurate in that he did become aware of Plaintiff's tax information, partly based upon his official duties. In fact, Mr. Scholan testified that he knew from his job as a revenue officer that there had been a seizure against Plaintiff because of her outstanding tax liability. Finally, Mr. Scholan testified that ¶ 6 of his declaration was inaccurate, in that he did have access to Plaintiff's return information gathered by the IRS.

Mr. Scholan testified that, despite his prior IRS training concerning the disclosure of return information, he thought that he was not disclosing return information because of Plaintiff's prior letter to the editor and her appearance on the radio. Mr. Scholan testified that he learned only recently that a tax payer's disclosure does not allow a subsequent disclosure by an IRS official. However, Defendant offered no evidence to show that Mr. Scholan, unlike Mr. Swanson and Ms. Callahan, sought a determination as to whether his writing of the letter would be a violation of pertinent tax laws or IRS regulations. Moreover, it is not suggested that Mr. Scholan knew or even relied upon Plaintiff's prior execution of a release.

The Court finds that Mr. Scholan's conduct constituted a blatant violation of 26 U.S.C. § 6103. In addition, the Court finds Mr. Scholan's conduct was grossly negligent, meriting an award of punitive damages. Mr. Scholan's conduct, in light of his prior training and IRS regulations, was in reckless disregard of the law and the rights of Plaintiff. *See* Barrett v. United States, 100 F.3d at 40.

Damages

8. Plaintiff seeks to recover the greater of her statutory or actual damages. Based upon the findings set forth above, the Court finds that Plaintiff is entitled to recover $4,000.00 in statutory damages for four acts of wrongful disclosure made by Swanson, Callahan and Scholan. Plaintiff is also entitled to punitive damages.

Plaintiff claims actual damages as a result of Defendant's wrongful disclosures in the form of mental distress and emotional damages, humiliation, loss of the Citidel Mall lease and loss of peripheral vision in Plaintiff's right eye as a result of a grand mal seizure.

The Court finds that Plaintiff has failed to prove that the injury to her eye was caused by Defendant's conduct. Plaintiff testified that she had previously suffered grand mal seizures (five in the last eighteen years) and has suffered from epilepsy since she was twenty-eight. The evidence offered is insufficient to show that Plaintiff's seizure and resulting vision loss were caused by Defendant's wrongful conduct. * * *

The Court finds that Plaintiff's claims for mental distress, emotional damages and humiliation have merit. *See* Hrubec v. National Railroad Passenger Corporation, 829 F. Supp. 1502, 1504–06 (N.D. Ill. 1993) (analyzing the issue of whether emotional distress damages are available under 26 U.S.C. § 7431(c)(B)). The evidence offered by Plaintiff establishes that Defendant's wrongful conduct caused Plaintiff's personality to change. She became bitter and consumed by a battle with the IRS in an effort to establish that what Defendant's agents and employees had said and done was incorrect. As stated by Plaintiff's mother, Ms. Altavilla, Plaintiff was so enraged and obsessed by Defendant's conduct that "we all began to hate her." Similar testimony was offered by Plaintiff's son, Tristan Ward and her daughter, Kelly Gilmour. Plaintiff's daughter testified that as a result of Defendant's actions, her mother became irritable and she frequently cried. Plaintiff also testified that the information released by Defendant caused a number of her friends and family members to question whether Plaintiff really was a drug dealer and/or tax protestor. The Court finds that, as a result of Defendant's wrongful disclosures, Plaintiff suffered actual damages in the form of emotional distress. The Court further finds that $75,000 will fairly compensate Plaintiff for the damages she suffered as a result of Defendant's wrongful conduct over a three month period.

9. Based upon this Court's finding, that Mr. Scholan's conduct was grossly negligent, Plaintiff is also entitled to recover punitive damages pursuant to 26 U.S.C. § 7431(c)(1)(R). Considering the conduct of Mr. Scholan, the harm inflicted upon Plaintiff; the deterrent aspect of a punitive damage award and the public medium through which Plaintiff's return information was disclosed, this Court finds that Plaintiff is entitled to recover $250,000 in punitive damages. *See* Continental Trend Resources, Inc. v. OXY USA, Inc., 101 F.3d 634 (discussing factors to be considered in an award for punitive damages).

As a public employee and a revenue officer for the IRS Mr. Scholan holds a position of trust and power. Along with that trust and power comes a high degree of responsibility. Part of that responsibility requires that you accept criticism, however inaccurate and/or unjustified, in silence and that you act in accordance with the law. While admittedly equipped with 20/20 vision, every other revenue officer, when asked, acknowledged that Mr. Scholan's conduct was clearly inappropriate in light of the disclosure laws. In addition, the Court notes that the medium which Mr. Scholan used was expected to and did reach a public audience, resulting in a wide dissemination of Plaintiff's return information. *See* Miller v. United States, 66 F.3d 220, 224 (9th Cir, 1995).

The conduct of our Nation's affairs always demands that public servants discharge their duties under the Constitution and laws of this Republic with fairness and a proper spirit of subservience to the people whom they are sworn to serve. Public servants cannot be arbitrarily selective in their treatment of citizens, dispensing equity to those who please them and withholding it from those who do not. Respect for the law can only be fostered if citizens believe that those responsible for implementing and enforcing the law are themselves acting in conformity with the law. By this award, this Court gives notice to the IRS that reprehensible abuse of authority by one of its employees cannot and will not be tolerated.

CONCLUSIONS OF LAW

In addition to those findings of law which are included in the Court's findings of fact set forth above the Court makes these additional findings of law:

1. Plaintiff contends that she is entitled to recover the $1,000 statutory damage for each listener to the KVOR radio talk show on which Mr. Swanson and Ms. Callahan appeared. Plaintiff takes the position that there was an act of disclosure for each listener. The Court disagrees. Pursuant to 26 U.S.C. § 7431(c)(1)(A), Plaintiff is only entitled to recover $1,000 "for each act of unauthorized disclosure." (emphasis added). Under 26 U.S.C. § 6103(b)(8) "[t]he term 'disclosure' means the making known to any person in any manner whatever a return or return information."

* * *

In *Mallas [v. United States*, 993 F.2d 1111 (4th Cir. 1993)], the district court found and the Fourth Circuit Court of Appeals affirmed that an act of disclosure occurred for each named person to which the IRS mailed return information. *Mallas*, 993 F.2d at 1124–25. In making this finding the district court found that two acts of disclosure were committed where only one envelope was sent, but the envelope was addressed to two named persons. In its affirmance, the Court of Appeals, after reviewing § 7431(c)(1)(A) and § 6103(b)(8), concluded:

> that the "act" to be counted for computing damages is the "making known to any person in any manner whatever" the return information. Each time the Government "makes known" return information to a person in violation of 6103, it has committed an "act of unauthorized disclosure." If the IRS addresses and mails a single RAR to two people, it makes the information in the RAR known to each of them no differently than if it had decided to use two copies of the RAR, two envelopes, and two stamps . . . .

Id. at 1125. Liability is triggered under § 7431(c)(1)(A) by the "act" of "making known to any person in any manner whatever a return or return information." In *Mallas*, Defendant committed 73 different "acts" by addressing and placing in the mail envelopes that were addressed and directed to seventy-three different individuals. Thus, Defendant committed 73 separate "acts" of disclosure. In the case at bar Swanson and Callahan each committed an act of disclosure when they discussed Plaintiff's return information on the radio. Nevertheless, to the extent that *Mallas* could be interpreted as holding that an act of disclosure is committed for every person who learned about Plaintiff's return information, as a consequence of Swanson and Callahan's act of appearing on the radio, this Court disagrees with such an analysis. It is the "act" of disclosure, not the receipt of information which triggers liability. Moreover, taken literally, the analysis applied in *Mallas* is inconsistent with the implicit finding made in *Rodgers v. Hyatt*, 697 F.2d 899 [10th Cir. 1983], where plaintiff was found to be entitled to only $1,000 for a single disclosure made by an IRS official in a meeting at which two Amax officials were present. *Id.* at 905–06. It is for these reasons that the Court further rejects Plaintiff's argument that she is entitled $1,000 for every listener to the KVOR radio talk show.

* * *

Therefore, it is ordered that, based upon the foregoing findings of facts and conclusions of law, Plaintiff is entitled to a Judgment in her favor and against the Defendant in the amount of $325,000 and the Clerk of Court is hereby directed to enter the Judgment. * * *

In addition to civil liability under section 7431, the statute makes unauthorized disclosure of a return or return information by an IRS employee a felony and imposes a fine of up to $5,000 or a jail term or up to five years, or both. I.R.C. § 7213. It is also a felony, subject to the same penalties, for other persons who obtain return information under section 6103 (for example, state employees, one percent shareholders of a corporation) to disclose that information to unauthorized parties. I.R.C. § 7213(a)(2)–(5). Somewhat reduced criminal penalties (a $1,000 fine/one year of imprisonment) may apply in the case of unauthorized inspection by IRS employees of return information. I.R.C. § 7213A.

§ 3.04 The Tension Between FOIA and Section 6103

Section 6103, as it applies to FOIA requests made by taxpayers for tax return information, has been used by the IRS as a shield against disclosure. This interrelationship between the FOIA disclosure statute and the section 6103 confidentiality statute has led to disagreement over which statutory provision should take precedence over the other and, more broadly, whether privacy concerns or the public's right of access to information should control the analysis. From a policy standpoint, should section 6103 preempt FOIA when it comes to releasing a taxpayer's return or return information or should section 6103 merely implement FOIA Exemption 3?

The preemption question raises a number of issues, including the standard of review a court should apply when reviewing the IRS's refusal to release information that otherwise falls within the auspices of section 6103. As noted above, a district court reviewing a denial of a FOIA request does so on a *de novo* basis. Conversely, if section 6103 takes priority over FOIA with regard to disclosure of tax return information, the district court would be limited to a determination of whether the IRS's decision to withhold documents was arbitrary or an abuse of discretion. *Compare Zale Corp. v. Internal Revenue Service*, 481 F. Supp. 486 (D.D.C. 1979) (section 6103 is the sole standard governing the release of returns and return information) *with Grasso v. Internal Revenue Service*, 785 F.2d 70 (3rd Cir. 1986) ("It is thus evident that section 6103 was not designed to displace FOIA."); *see also White v. Internal Revenue Service*, 707 F.2d 897 (6th Cir. 1983).

Because of the abuse of discretion standard of review, the IRS would generally prefer that section 6103 take precedence over FOIA. The Joint Committee on Taxation made such a recommendation to Congress as part of a study into the confidentiality and disclosure provisions relating to tax administration. *See* Volume I, Joint Committee on Taxation, Study of Present-Law Taxpayer Confidentiality and Disclosure Provisions as Required by Section 3802 of the Internal Revenue Service Restructuring and Reform Act of 1998 (2000). The recommendation suggests that section 6103 would be the sole means by which returns and return information could be requested. The Joint Committee explained the recommendation as follows:

> While the courts have tried to harmonize section 6103 and the FOIA through FOIA exemption 3, it is an imperfect fit. The purpose of the FOIA is to provide information about agency operations. In contrast, the purpose of section 6103 is to maintain the confidentiality of returns and return information of a taxpayer. The FOIA provides information

to the general public without a showing of need. The intended use of the information or the requester's identity generally has no bearing on who has access to agency records under the FOIA. On the other hand, section 6103 only permits disclosure of returns and return information if the person seeking the information meets certain criteria. Thus under section 6103, examining the identity of the person requesting returns or return information is a prerequisite to disclosure.

The core purpose of the FOIA is to contribute significantly to public understanding of the operations or activities of the government. Taxpayer representatives often use the FOIA as an alternate means to obtain information the IRS has collected in building its case against their clients. Very little, if any, information about IRS operations, however, is gleaned from the release of a specific taxpayer's return or return information in response to a FOIA request. The disclosure of returns and return information of specific taxpayers is not consistent with the main purpose of FOIA.

*   *   *

The staff of the Joint Committee recognizes that the FOIA has several important administrative provisions that are not contained in section 6103. These include response time limitations and administrative appeal of the IRS decision to withhold documents. The FOIA also affords a requester the opportunity for *de novo* judicial review by a U.S. District Court. The staff of the Joint Committee recommends that these provisions should be incorporated into section 6103. This will provide persons seeking disclosure of returns and return information with the same administrative protections and remedies currently available to them under FOIA.

Do you agree with the Joint Committee's statement that little information about the IRS's operations has been gleaned from the release of a specific taxpayer's return information in response to a FOIA request? What about the FOIA litigation in *Tax Analysts & Advocates v. Internal Revenue Service*, 362 F. Supp. 1298 (D.C. D. Ct. 1973), *modified*, 505 F.2d 350 (D.C. Cir. 1974), and *Fruehauf Corp. v. Internal Revenue Service*, 522 F.2d 284 (6th Cir. 1975), *vacated on other grounds* 429 U.S. 1085 (1977), which led to the release of private letter rulings and technical advice memoranda? Would these actions have been heard by the court if the preemption recommended had actually been in place?

A few months after the release of the Joint Committee study, the House of Representatives unanimously passed the Taxpayer Bill of Rights 2000, H.R. 4163, which incorporated the Joint Committee's recommendation concerning section 6103's preemption over FOIA. The bill was not introduced in the Senate. The House drafters described the bill as simply a clarification of existing law and not a substantive change.[18] Some Circuit Courts of Appeal

---

[18] The bill did not incorporate the procedural protections and remedies that are now available to the requesting party only through a FOIA request.

(including the First, Third, Fifth, Ninth, Tenth, and Eleventh) might be surprised to hear of this "clarification," having held that section 6103 is an Exemption 3 statute under FOIA. *See, e.g., Aronson v. Internal Revenue Service*, 973 F.2d 962 (1st Cir. 1992); *Grasso, supra; Chamberlain v. Kurtz*, 589 F.2d 827 (5th Cir. 1979); *Williamette Indus. v. United States*, 689 F.2d 865 (9th Cir. 1982); *DeSalvo v. Internal Revenue Service*, 861 F.2d 1217 (10th Cir. 1988); *Currie v. Internal Revenue Service*, 704 F.2d 523 (11th Cir. 1983).

PROBLEMS

1. Jared is representing a client who did not keep copies of his tax returns, and who is being audited by the IRS. Jared would like copies from the IRS of his client's returns and any financial information about his client that the IRS is using for the audit. Can Jared get this information, and, if so, how?

2. Sally is considering filing a Tax Court petition on behalf of a client. She would like to see files of prior Tax Court cases on the relevant issues. Can she use FOIA to obtain access to those files from the Tax Court? Why or why not?

3. Vincent is structuring a corporate transaction for a client, and is considering taking an aggressive tax position. He is concerned about the possibility that his client's return will get audited, so he would like to obtain a copy of the DIF formula that the IRS uses to score returns for audit. Can he obtain this under FOIA? Why or why not?

4. Clara is requesting a letter ruling on behalf of a corporate client. Her client is concerned that the letter ruling will be made public under FOIA and that competitors will find out that the company is engaging in the transaction in question. How can Clara reassure her client?

5. Patrick represents a celebrity client who is concerned that IRS employees might look through her tax returns out of curiosity about her private life. Can Patrick assure his client that this will not happen?

6. Janine was convicted of tax fraud, and the IRS issued a press release publicizing the conviction. All of the information in the press release was correct, including Janine's full name, her address, the name of her employer, and the counts on which she was convicted. However, Janine was embarrassed because not only did her local newspaper publish the information, but, in addition, a local radio personality read the news report aloud on his show and made scathing comments about her. Does she have a viable cause of action against the federal government or the IRS agents involved?

7. Earlier this year, Blake Wright, who is single, sold a rental property he had owned and leased out for the past six

years. Throughout the six-year period, he took depreciation deductions with respect to the property. Unfortunately, a fire destroyed all of his records relating to the property as well as his copies of his prior years' tax returns. Blake cannot remember exactly what he paid for the property, and without any records, he is not certain of his current basis in it. In order to properly report his gain from the sale, Blake would like to obtain copies from the IRS of his tax returns for the past six years. He has retained you to make the request on his behalf. Blake's social security number is 215-55-0955. He resides at 507 Oakwood Boulevard, Falls Church, Virginia 22043. Draft a FOIA request letter for him.

Chapter 4

SETTLEMENT OF TAX DISPUTES

Reading Assignment: Code §§ 6673, 7121, 7122, 7123, 7430, 7491; Proc. Reg. § 601.106; IRS Publication 5.

§ 4.01 Introduction

Most disputes between a taxpayer and the IRS are settled or compromised in some way. In fact, tax controversies are no exception to the general policy favoring settlement of disputes. The IRS provides a taxpayer numerous opportunities after an examination has been completed to come to some agreement on the extent of the taxpayer's liability. In addition, there are formal processes that encourage and facilitate negotiation and settlement prior to trial, including the IRS Appeals process and a recently enacted statutory provision for "qualified" settlement offers by taxpayers. In order to obtain the most favorable settlement possible, the taxpayer and his representative must understand these processes.

Probably the most important avenue for settlement with the IRS is its administrative dispute resolution process through its Appeals Division.[1] The chapter analyzes this appeals procedure from a strategic and planning standpoint. The chapter explores the alternative routes within the IRS Appeals Division for contesting a proposed increase in the taxpayer's liability, and identifies factors that might make one route more favorable than another. In this regard, the chapter provides an introduction to Tax Court litigation, which is taken up in detail in Chapters 6 and 7. The chapter also considers how the Appeals Division views its role in the dispute resolution process and why an understanding of that view is helpful for obtaining a favorable settlement.

Although, as discussed in this chapter, the IRS Appeals Division is very successful at settling tax controversies, cases that are not settled at Appeals may nonetheless be settled prior to entry of a decision by a court. In fact, courts themselves may encourage settlement of docketed cases. The final section of this chapter considers the special issues that arise regarding settlement of tax cases that have been docketed in court, such as what constitutes a "settlement" in such a case.

---

[1] As part of IRS Reform, the IRS Appeals Division has been reorganized into a headquarters unit and three operating units. The headquarters unit will focus on strategic planning and resolution alternatives, while the three operating units will service the IRS Operating Divisions. The new appeals units are: the Appeals Large and Mid-Size Operating Unit; the Appeals General Business Unit (handling cases arising out of the Small Business/Self Employed and the Wage and Investment Operating Divisions); and the Appeals Tax Exempt and Governmental Entities Unit.

§ 4.02 Settlement Opportunities After IRS Examination of the Taxpayer's Return

[A] Strategy in Timing of Settlement

According to many tax practitioners, the earlier a case is settled, the better. Whether this is true depends, of course, on the terms of the settlement that can be obtained at the earlier juncture. Certain variables, however, are time-sensitive. Representation fees normally increase the longer a controversy remains unresolved, and eventually the taxpayer will encounter filing fees and other litigation costs. The taxpayer must also factor into this mix of variables interest charges that are imposed should the IRS's determination of a tax deficiency ultimately prevail. Unless the taxpayer takes steps to limit interest accrual by submitting a deposit, or the charges are otherwise tolled, interest continues to build, compounded on a daily basis, until the additional tax liability is paid.[2] As explained below, extending the duration of the dispute resolution process also increases the risk that additional deficiencies will be asserted against the taxpayer.

In 1998, Congress added to Code section 7430 a provision designed to encourage settlement that is similar to Federal Rule of Civil Procedure 68's "Offer of Judgment."[3] The new provision, section 7430(c)(4)(E), provides a "qualified offer" rule that will treat the taxpayer as the "prevailing party" in a court case for purposes of section 7430 if (1) the taxpayer made a "qualified" settlement offer to the government, which was rejected by the government and (2) the taxpayer's liability subsequently determined by a court is less than or equal to the amount that was offered. By being treated as the prevailing party, a taxpayer who meets the other requirements of section 7430 is eligible for reimbursement of reasonable administrative costs and reasonable litigation costs, as discussed in Chapter 6.[4] Making a qualified offer thereby renders irrelevant an IRS claim that it was "substantially justified" in its position.

A "qualified offer" is an offer designated as a qualified offer and made in writing to the United States at some time during the period beginning on the date the 30-day letter was sent and ending "30 days before the date the case is first set for trial." I.R.C. § 7430(g). The offer must also remain open until the earliest of the following: (1) the government rejects the offer, (2) the trial begins, or (3) the 90th day after the offer was made. I.R.C. § 7430(g)(1)(D).

---

[2] Interest on underpayments is discussed in detail in Chapter 11.

[3] Under Federal Rule of Civil Procedure 68:

> At any time more than 10 days before the trial begins, a party defending against a claim may serve upon the adverse party an offer to allow judgment to be taken against the defending party for the money or property or to the effect specified in the offer, with costs then accrued . . . . If the judgment finally obtained by the offeree is not more favorable than the offer, the offeree must pay the costs incurred after the making of the offer.

[4] Because the qualified offer rules are part of section 7430, which provides for awards of reasonable administrative and litigation costs to the "prevailing party" in a court case, the statute specifies that a party who is a prevailing party under a provision of section 7430 other than the qualified offer rules is not subject to the application of the qualified offer rules. *See* I.R.C. § 7430(c)(4)(E)(iv).

In addition, the relevant qualified offer is the final qualified offer made by the taxpayer, and only costs and fees incurred by the taxpayer after that date are subject to reimbursement. I.R.C. § 7430(c)(4)(E)(iii).

Note that although the qualified offer rules apply only when there is a court determination of liability, a qualified offer may be made before litigation is instituted. Therefore, as early as the date the 30-day letter was mailed, a taxpayer may make a written settlement offer to the IRS that may result in an eventual award to the taxpayer of administrative costs and litigation fees if the IRS rejects the offer and subsequently fails to obtain a higher amount in court. Before or after making a qualified offer, the taxpayer must still exhaust any available administrative remedies in order to recover his costs, I.R.C. § 7430(b)(1), which generally means that the taxpayer must participate in an Appeals conference before filing a Tax Court petition. *Haas & Associates Accountancy Corp. v. Commissioner*, 117 T.C. 48 (2001). The new provision is intended to encourage settlement of tax cases. Do you think it will succeed in increasing the frequency of settlement?[5]

[B]   Options at the Conclusion of the Examination

The procedures employed by the IRS following an examination of the taxpayer's return depend in part upon how the examination was conducted. At the conclusion of most office and field audits, the revenue agent who conducted the examination will discuss his findings with the taxpayer or his representative before submitting a formal report. If the revenue agent concludes that no changes should be made to the taxpayer's liability, the agent will prepare a "no change" report and the case is closed. I.R.M. Ex. 4.4.1-16. More commonly, the revenue agent will propose an adjustment to the taxpayer's liability. Although the revenue agent does not have formal settlement authority, the taxpayer normally is given an opportunity at the conclusion of the examination to reach a compromise with the agent or his supervisor. This compromise must be based on the IRS's published positions with respect to legal issues (such as regulations or Revenue Rulings) and the examiner's determination of the facts involved. According to one experienced tax practitioner:

> This is a very important stage in the processing of a tax case; many settlements are reached that might not be possible if discussions were deferred until after formal reports have been written or issued. Speculative and debatable questions of fact, which have no precise answer, may frequently be compromised on a fair basis, and quite often one doubtful legal question may be traded off against another.

Hugh C. Bickford, SUCCESSFUL TAX PRACTICE 206 (4th ed. 1967). Even where the likelihood of a compromise with the revenue agent seems remote, the taxpayer can use the informal conference as an opportunity to reiterate his arguments and to ensure that the agent correctly understands the surrounding facts.

---

[5] For further discussion of the qualified offer rules and how they might encourage settlement, *see* Robert B. Nadler, "Treating Qualified Offerers as Prevailing Parties Encourages Settlement," 81 Tax Notes 1657 (1998). *See also* Temp. Reg. § 301.7430-7T (effective for qualified offers made after January 3, 2001).

If settlement negotiations at the examination level have stalled because of disagreement over a single issue, the taxpayer might consider availing himself of the IRS's Early Referral Program. The Early Referral Program allows the taxpayer to request during the examination phase that a specific issue be transferred directly to the Appeals Division for resolution, while any remaining issues continue to be developed by the revenue agent. *See* I.R.C. § 7123. This procedure is designed to encourage quick resolution of key issues in the hope that such resolution might facilitate agreement on other outstanding issues. Revenue Procedure 99-28, 1999-2 C.B. 109, describes the procedures for initiating an early referral request and lists issues that will and will not be considered for early referral. A related program currently being tested by the IRS allows the taxpayer (or the examining agent) to request "fast track" mediation. Under this procedure, if a taxpayer disagrees with the examining agent's findings, he may request that a mediator from within the Appeals Division be assigned to meet with the taxpayer and the examining agent's manager. The goal is to create an impartial forum for the taxpayer and the IRS in which to resolve the dispute. The role of the mediator is to encourage communication between the parties and to elicit information necessary to understand the nature of the issues. The mediator has no authority to require either party to accept a result. If unagreed issues remain, the taxpayer retains all of his appeals rights (discussed below).

[1] Agreed Cases

If the taxpayer and the revenue agent can reach a mutually acceptable agreement at the conclusion of the examination, the taxpayer normally will be asked to evidence this agreement by signing Form 870, Waiver of Restrictions on Assessment and Collection of Deficiency in Tax.[6] Review the Form 870 waiver agreement, reproduced below. If the taxpayer is willing to agree to some of the revenue agent's proposed adjustments but not others, the taxpayer may file a waiver agreement covering only those agreed-upon issues. I.R.M. 14.4.2. As the language of the waiver makes clear, the IRS may subsequently assert an additional deficiency with respect to the same taxable year.

An executed Form 870 allows the IRS to summarily assess the agreed-upon liability without complying with statutory restrictions that otherwise apply to tax deficiencies. *See* I.R.C. § 6213(d). In particular, the taxpayer waives his right to receive a statutory notice of deficiency, which, as explained in more detail below, will prevent the taxpayer from later contesting the liability in the Tax Court. This is not to say, however, that the taxpayer has no recourse should he decide to challenge the adjustment. In order to do so, the taxpayer will have to pay the liability, make a claim for refund, and assert such claim in either the Court of Federal Claims or a United States District Court.[7]

---

[6] Signing Form 870 also stops the accrual of interest on the underlying liability, such that no interest is charged from a date 30 days after the taxpayer files the form. I.R.C. § 6601(c).

[7] Refund procedures are discussed in detail in Chapter 8.

Form **870** (Rev. March 1992)	Department of the Treasury — Internal Revenue Service **Waiver of Restrictions on Assessment and Collection of Deficiency in Tax and Acceptance of Overassessment**	Date received by Internal Revenue Service

Names and address of taxpayers *(Number, street, city or town, State, ZIP code)*	Social security or employer identification number

Increase (Decrease) in Tax and Penalties

Tax year ended	Tax	Penalties			
	$	$	$	$	$
	$	$	$	$	$
	$	$	$	$	$
	$	$	$	$	$
	$	$	$	$	$
	$	$	$	$	$
	$	$	$	$	$

(For instructions, see back of form)

Consent to Assessment and Collection

I consent to the immediate assessment and collection of any deficiencies *(increase in tax and penalties)* and accept any overassessment *(decrease in tax and penalties)* shown above, plus any interest provided by law. I understand that by signing this waiver, I will not be able to contest these years in the United States Tax Court, unless additional deficiencies are determined for these years.

YOUR SIGNATURE➤ HERE		Date
SPOUSE'S SIGNATURE➤		Date
TAXPAYER'S REPRESENTATIVE HERE ➤		Date
CORPORATE NAME ➤		
CORPORATE OFFICER(S) SIGN HERE		Title	Date
		Title	Date

Catalog Number 16894U   Form **870** (Rev. 3-92)

Instructions

General Information

If you consent to the assessment of the deficiencies shown in this waiver, please sign and return the form in order to limit any interest charge and expedite the adjustment to your account. Your consent will not prevent you from filing a claim for refund *(after you have paid the tax)* if you later believe you are so entitled. It will not prevent us from later determining, if necessary, that you owe additional tax; nor extend the time provided by law for either action.

We have agreements with State tax agencies under which information about Federal tax, including increases or decreases, is exchanged with the States. If this change affects the amount of your State income tax, you should file the required State form.

If you later file a claim and the Service disallows it, you may file suit for refund in a district court or in the United States Claims Court, but you may not file a petition with the United States Tax Court.

We will consider this waiver a valid claim for refund or credit of any overpayment due you resulting from any decrease in tax and penalties shown above, provided you sign and file it within the period established by law for making such a claim.

Who Must Sign

If you filed jointly, both you and your spouse must sign. If this waiver is for a corporation, it should be signed with the corporation name, followed by the signatures and titles of the corporate officers authorized to sign. An attorney or agent may sign this waiver provided such action is specifically authorized by a power of attorney which, if not previously filed, must accompany this form.

If this waiver is signed by a person acting in a fiduciary capacity *(for example, an executor, administrator, or a trustee)* Form 56, Notice Concerning Fiduciary Relationship, should, unless previously filed, accompany this form.

---

[2] Unagreed Cases

If the taxpayer and the revenue agent cannot come to an agreement, the agent normally will prepare and submit to the taxpayer a preliminary notice of deficiency, commonly called a "30-day letter." A sample is reproduced below. The 30-day letter is a form letter that sets forth the amount of the proposed adjustment to the taxpayer's liability. Included with the letter will be a copy of the revenue agent's report (RAR), which explains in detail the agent's findings and the basis for the proposed liability. I.R.M. 14.3.7. The RAR may also include separate reports from IRS economists and appraisers addressing valuation and other technical calculations. The IRS will also include with the 30-day letter an explanation of the taxpayer's appeal rights within the IRS (Publication 5) and an explanation of the collection process (Publication 594).

After receiving the 30-day letter, the taxpayer faces a number of important options. The taxpayer may decide, having analyzed the revenue agent's report, to reconsider his potential exposure and agree to the agent's proposed adjustments. If so, the 30-day letter instructs the taxpayer to sign a Form 870 waiver. As noted above, agreeing to the agent's proposed adjustments and paying the resulting liability is also a viable option for a taxpayer who intends to pursue the matter as a refund action.

A second possible response to the 30-day letter is to contest the revenue agent's findings with the IRS Appeals Division. The taxpayer is granted 30 days (hence the preliminary notice's commonly used name) in which to request a conference with the Appeals staff. The procedures surrounding the administrative appeals process are discussed below.

If the taxpayer elects not to pursue an appeal or otherwise fails to respond to the 30-day letter, he will receive from the IRS a statutory notice of deficiency (also referred to as a 90-day letter). Like the 30-day letter, the 90-day letter sets forth the additional amount that the IRS believes the taxpayer owes. The notice of deficiency also authorizes the taxpayer, within 90 days after the notice of deficiency is sent, to file a petition with the Tax Court to redetermine the amount of the proposed liability. In fact, if, at the conclusion of the examination, the taxpayer decides that litigation in the Tax Court is the best option, he may consider foregoing the preliminary notice of deficiency and requesting that the IRS issue a 90-day letter without additional delay. The advantages and disadvantages of pursuing Tax Court litigation without a prior administrative appeal are discussed below.

A 30-day letter typically looks something like this:

SAMPLE 30-DAY LETTER

Internal Revenue Service   Department of the Treasury

Date: Taxpayer Identifying Number:
                                         Form:
                                         Tax Period(s) Ended and
                                             Deficiency Amounts:
                                         Person to Contact:
                                         Telephone Number:
                                         Employee Indentification
                                             Number:
                                         Last Date to Respond to This
                                             Letter:

Dear Taxpayer:

We have enclosed an examination report showing proposed changes to your tax for the period(s) shown above. Please read the report, and tell us whether you agree or disagree with the changes by the date shown above. (This report may not reflect the results of later examinations of partnerships, "S" Corporations, trusts, etc., in which you may have an interest. Changes to those accounts could also affect your tax.)

If you agree with the proposed changes . . .

1. Sign and date the enclosed agreement form. If you filed a joint return, both taxpayers must sign the form.

2. Return the signed agreement form to us.

3. Enclose payment of the tax, interest and any penalties due. Make your check or money order payable to the **United States Treasury**. You can call the person identified above to determine the total amount due as of the date you intend to make payment.

4. After we receive your signed agreement form, we will close your case.

If you pay the full amount due now, you will limit the amount of interest and penalties charged to your account. If you agree with our findings, but can only pay part of the bill, please call the person identified above to discuss different payment options. We may ask you to complete a collection information statement to determine your payment options, such as paying in installments. You can also write to us or visit your nearest IRS office to explain your circumstances. If you don't enclose payment for the additional tax, interest, and any penalties, we will bill you for the unpaid amounts.

If you are a "C" Corporation, Section 6621(c) of the Internal Revenue Code provides that an interest rate 2% higher than the standard rate of interest will be charged on deficiencies of $100,000 or more.

If you don't agree with the proposed changes . . .

1. You may request a meeting or telephone conference with the supervisor of the person identified in the heading of this letter. If you still don't agree after the meeting or telephone conference, you can:

2. Request a conference with our Appeals Office. If the total proposed change to your tax is:

   - $25,000 or less for *each* referenced tax period, send us a letter requesting consideration by Appeals. Indicate the issues you don't agree with and the reasons why you don't agree. If you don't want to write a separate letter, you can complete the Statement of Disputed Issues at the end of this letter and return it to us.

   - More than $25,000 for *any* referenced tax period, you must submit a formal protest.

The requirements for filing a formal protest are explained in the enclosed Publication 5, *Your Appeal Rights and How to Prepare a Protest If You Don't Agree*. We've also enclosed Publication 1, *Your Rights as a Taxpayer* and Publication 594, *The IRS Collection Process*.

If you request a conference with our Appeals Office, an Appeals Officer will call you (if necessary) for an appointment to take a fresh look at your case. The Appeals Office is an independent office and most disputes considered by the Appeals Office are resolved informally and promptly. By requesting a conference with our Appeals Office you may avoid court costs (such as the Tax Court $60 filing fee), resolve the matter sooner, and/or prevent interest and any penalties from increasing your account.

If you decide to bypass the Appeals Office and petition the Tax Court directly, your case will usually be sent to an Appeals Office first to try to resolve the issue. Certain procedures and rights in court (for example, the burden of proof and potential recovery of litigation costs) depend on you fully participating in the administrative consideration of your case, including consideration by the IRS Appeals Office.

If you don't reach an agreement with our Appeals Office or if you don't respond to this letter, we will send you another letter that will tell you how to obtain Tax Court review of your case.

You must mail your signed agreement form, completed Statement of Disputed Issues, or a formal protest to us by the response date shown in the heading of this letter. If you decide to request a conference with the examiner's supervisor, your request should also be made by the response date indicated.

MAIL RESPONSES TO: **Internal Revenue Service**
                               Attn: J. Smith
                               200 Granby Mall Rm 539
                               Norfolk Federal Building Norfolk, VA 23510

If you have any questions, please contact the person identified in the heading of this letter. We will be glad to discuss your options with you.

Sincerely yours,

for Joel A. Goverman

Director, Compliance Area 4-SBSE

Enclosures:
Copy of this letter
Examination Report
Agreement Form
Publications 5, 1, 594
Envelope

Letter 950 (DO) (Rev. 9-2000)

[C]   Settlement at the IRS Appeals Division

[1]   Background on the IRS Appeals Division

The appeals process involves an administrative review by an officer from the IRS Appeals Division, who negotiates with the taxpayer or his representative over the appropriate tax treatment of items on the return. The stated mission of the Appeals Division is to resolve tax controversies on a basis that is fair and impartial to both the government and the taxpayer, without litigation. I.R.M. 8.1.3.2. Statistics confirm the Appeals Division's apparent success in carrying out its mission. The latest statistics available from the General Accounting Office reveal that over 85 percent of large cases handled by the Appeals Division are settled (representing 88 percent of the tax dollars in dispute). General Accounting Office, Report on IRS Initiatives to Resolve Disputes Over Tax Liabilities, GAO/GGD-97-71 (May 9, 1997). If the taxpayer is unable to come to a compromise with the Appeals Division, the taxpayer's only recourse is to pursue the matter either through Tax Court litigation or as a refund action.[8]

Under the IRS's new organizational structure, the Appeals Division is integrated into the four operating divisions, but continues to function as an independent organization reporting directly to the Commissioner. To ensure

---

[8] The Appeals Division has jurisdiction to hear a variety of issues, not all of which stem from an assessment made after examination. A taxpayer may also appeal a case to the Appeals Division after the taxpayer's refund claim is rejected. As a result of the IRS Reform Act, the Appeals Division took on added responsibility in collection cases. Appeals procedures relating to these matters are discussed in Chapters 8 and 12, respectively.

its independence from other units, Congress mandated as part of the IRS Reform Act that the IRS implement procedures specifically prohibiting an Appeals Officer and another IRS employee from conferring on a taxpayer's case outside the presence of the taxpayer or his representative. IRS Reform Act § 1001(a)(4). This prohibition primarily impacts discussions between the Appeals Officer and the revenue agent who conducted the audit. It is not uncommon, in fact, for the Appeals Officer to remain in contact with the revenue agent during the appeals process. The prohibition against *ex parte* communications applies only to the extent such communications appear to compromise the independence of the Appeals Division. As you become more familiar with the settlement techniques and procedures utilized at the Appeals Division, consider why Congress emphasized the need for independence and the appearance of independence of Appeals Officers.

Revenue Procedure 2000-43, 2000-43 I.R.B. 404, sets forth the IRS's current view on what constitutes a permissible or prohibited *ex parte* communication between an Appeals Officer and another IRS employee. As a general rule, the taxpayer or his representative must be given the opportunity to participate in communications between Appeals Officers and other IRS employees *unless* those communications relate to matters that are entirely "ministerial, administrative, or procedural" in nature. Communications addressing the "substance of the issues in the case" are prohibited unless the taxpayer is given an opportunity to participate. Examples of prohibited communications include: (1) "Discussions about the accuracy of the facts presented by the taxpayer and the relative importance of the facts to the determination"; (2) "Discussions of the relative merits or alternative legal interpretations of authorities cited in a protest or in a report prepared by the originating function"; and (3) "Discussions of the originating function's perception of the demeanor or credibility of the taxpayer or taxpayer's representative."

Revenue Procedure 2000-43 also limits *ex parte* communications between Appeals Officers and the Office of Chief Counsel in nondocketed cases.[9] Appeals Officers commonly rely on attorneys in the Chief Counsel's Office to supply legal advice concerning specific issues and settlement guidelines.

> Appeals employees should not communicate ex parte regarding an issue in a case pending before them with Counsel field attorneys who have previously provided advice on that issue [during the examination process]. * * * Counsel will assign a different attorney to provide assistance to Appeals. If an Appeals employee believes it is necessary to seek advice from any Counsel field attorney who previously provided advice to the originating function regarding that issue in the case, the taxpayer/representative will be provided an opportunity to participate in any such communications.

> Appeals' requests for legal advice that raise questions that cannot be answered with a high degree of certainty by application of established principles of law to particular facts will be referred to the Chief Counsel National Office and will be handled as requests for field

---

[9] According to Revenue Procedure 2000-43, the prohibitions against *ex parte* communications do not apply in docketed cases.

service advice or technical advice, as appropriate, in accordance with applicable procedures. The response of the National Office to Appeals will be disclosed to the taxpayer in accordance with section 6110.

Appeals employees are cautioned that, while they may obtain legal advice from the Office of Chief Counsel, they remain responsible for independently evaluating the strengths and weaknesses of the specific issues presented by the cases assigned to them, and for making independent judgments concerning the overall strengths and weaknesses of the cases and the hazards of litigation. Consistent with this assignment of responsibility, Counsel attorneys will not provide advice that includes recommendations of settlement ranges for an issue in a case pending before Appeals or for the case as a whole.

Id.

Revenue Procedure 2000-43 also confirms that taxpayers or their representatives may waive the prohibitions on *ex parte* communications by following specified procedures. Under what circumstances might the taxpayer waive his right to participate in communications involving Appeals employees? Do you expect the prohibition against communications between Appeals Officers and other IRS employees outside the presence of the taxpayer to facilitate or delay the settlement process?

[2] The Protest Letter

As a prerequisite to Appeals jurisdiction, the taxpayer generally must request Appeals consideration. As the sample 30-day letter makes clear, the manner in which this is done primarily depends upon the amount of tax liability in controversy. The taxpayer normally is *required* to file a written protest in order to obtain Appeals consideration only if the amount of the proposed adjustment exceeds $25,000 for any taxable period. If the total amount at issue is $2,500 or less, a telephone request for an Appeals conference is normally sufficient. I.R.M. 8.6.1.1.4.

Where a formal written protest is required, it must be filed within 30 days from the date appearing on the 30-day letter. However, the IRS readily grants extensions of time to file. I.R.M. Ex. 8.1.1.10-9. Although there is no official form for filing a written protest, the protest must include the following information:

- The taxpayer's name, address, and telephone number;
- A statement that the taxpayer wants to appeal the examination findings to the Appeals Division;
- A copy of the 30-day letter (or the date and symbols appearing on the 30-day letter);
- The taxable years involved;
- An itemized schedule of the adjustments with which the taxpayer disagrees;
- A statement of facts supporting the taxpayer's position on any contested factual issue;

- A statement setting forth the law and other authorities on which the taxpayer relies; and

- A specifically provided declaration under penalties of perjury that the factual representations are true and correct.

See Publication 5, Your Appeal Rights and How to Prepare a Protest if You Don't Agree.

If the written protest is prepared by the taxpayer's attorney or agent, it must include a declaration indicating that the representative prepared the protest and a statement of whether the representative personally knows that the factual assertions included in the protest are true and correct. *See id.* If the protest is prepared by a representative who has not previously filed a power of attorney with the IRS on behalf of this taxpayer, the protest should also be accompanied by a power of attorney, Form 2848, executed by the taxpayer. A sample form for a protest letter is printed below.

SAMPLE PROTEST

Internal Revenue Service
[Address]

[Date]
Re: Taxpayer's Name
Address
T.I.N. or E.I.N.

Dear Sir or Madam:

In response to your correspondence dated _____, asserting an income tax deficiency for the taxable year(s) _____, this letter protests certain findings in your letter and its attached examination report (copies of which are attached).

The following information is submitted in support of this protest:

1.   Appeals Conference Request

An appeals conference with an officer of the IRS Appeals Division is requested for a time convenient to both parties.

2.   Taxpayer's Name, Address and Telephone Number

[Name

Address

Telephone Number]

3.   Date and Symbols of the Transmittal Letter

[Date

Symbols]

4.   Taxable Years Involved

[Calendar (or Fiscal) Year(s) _____]

5.   Schedule of Contested Adjustments

[Set forth in separately itemized paragraphs the adjustments included by the examining agent in the 30-day letter (including penalty assertions) with which the Taxpayer disagrees].

6. Statement of Facts

[Set forth an organized description of the relevant facts surrounding each of the protested adjustments. Where appropriate, reference and attach affidavits and other supporting documents.]

7. Statement of Law

[Set forth the law applicable to each of the protested adjustments and apply the law to the facts of the case.]

The undersigned prepared this protest on behalf of the taxpayer but does not know personally whether the statement of facts contained in this protest is true and correct.

A Form 2848, Power of Attorney, authorizing the undersigned to represent the taxpayer in this matter, is also enclosed.

Respectfully yours,

[Representative]

Enclosures

Ideally, the protest letter should convey to the Appeals Officer the merits of the taxpayer's position and highlight the weaknesses in the revenue agent's analysis. From a more practical standpoint, the content of the letter will depend, to a large degree, on the amount in controversy and the drafter's familiarity with the taxpayer's case. (Frequently, a taxpayer does not consult a representative, particularly an attorney, until after the 30-day letter has been issued.) The amount of detail to be included in the protest letter also represents a strategic decision. Consider the following suggestions.

IRS EXAMINATIONS AND APPEALS: DOMESTIC AND INTERNATIONAL PROCEDURES*
By A. Steve Hidalgo & Percy P. Woodward

¶ 514 CONSIDERATIONS WHEN PREPARING A PROTEST

* * *

(2) The taxpayer has three options for filing a protest, which are:

(a) a "skeletal" protest;

(b) an agent's report responsive protest; and

    (c)   a comprehensive protest.

(3)   The taxpayer should consider filing a skeletal protest that meets the minimum requirements for filing a protest when there is a concern for continued involvement of the agent at the examination level.

If the taxpayer includes challenges to the agent's facts, introduces new facts, challenges the agent's technical determinations, or introduces new technical arguments, the agent can, at his or her discretion, continue the examination process. A skeletal protest eliminates this possibility but places the taxpayer in somewhat of a dilemma. An appeals officer can return a case to the examination division to continue the examination process if the taxpayer introduces significantly new facts and introduces new technical concepts not previously considered by the agent (less likely). There are strategies and techniques for accomplishing the introduction of new facts or technical arguments which can be successful in avoiding the case being returned to the agent. These involve a judgment as to the types of facts or arguments being added, the timing of their introduction, and the method for introducing them. These decisions are totally dependent on the facts and circumstances in each case and are therefore not being discussed here.

An additional benefit to filing a skeletal protest is that it is often difficult to have all of the facts and arguments analyzed by the time a protest is required to be filed. A skeletal protest allows the taxpayer to proceed to Appeals by meeting the minimum protest requirements. Also, certain types of factual issues or legal positions are better reserved for the actual Appeals conference meeting rather than being discussed in the protest. * * *

(4)   An agent's report responsive protest is one that addresses all of the facts and legal arguments presented in the agent's report, but does not interject additional facts or arguments. This protest is more complete than a skeletal protest but may not contain the taxpayer's complete facts and arguments. An agent's report responsive protest is often utilized when a taxpayer's facts or laws are weak and the strategy is to attack the error or misrepresentations in the agent's report thereby limiting the focus to those items.

(5)   A comprehensive protest is one where the taxpayer develops fully all of the factual and legal arguments to be presented at the appeals conference. This concept is generally used when a taxpayer believes he has a strong probability of prevailing on the issues and is not concerned with the agent or appeals officer having time to fully analyze the taxpayer's position.

* * *

¶ 517 GENERAL CONSIDERATIONS

The taxpayer should consider the following general matters when preparing a protest:

(1)   The protest should concentrate on the facts of each issue. Settlements are often not accomplished because the appeals officer did not agree to the facts asserted by the taxpayer, but the taxpayer did not realize that this was the case. Appeals officers vary as to their communication ability, and what is believed to be a disagreement as to the application of the law as applied to the facts may in reality be a disagreement as to the effect of the facts. Consequently, care should be given to a full development and explanation of the facts.

(2)   When development of the facts is difficult or impossible because they do not exist in recorded form or involve an element of intent or business purpose, a taxpayer should give consideration to the use of affidavits. Care should be given when making the decision to use affidavits and when determining the contents of an affidavit. Although affidavits should be used with caution, they are frequently the last piece of fact or evidence necessary to accomplish the desired settlement.

(3)   When developing the technical aspects of an argument, the taxpayer should cite supporting cases and, as importantly, distinguish unfavorable cases. Although citing unfavorable cases brings their existence to the attention of the appeals officer, avoiding such cases runs the risk of not rebutting cases on which the appeals officer has placed significant weight, even though they were not discussed at the appeals conference. Additionally, the taxpayer should know that cases decided in the circuit where the taxpayer resides carry more weight than other cases. * * *

Although practitioners disagree over how a protest letter should be drafted, the general consensus seems to be that the taxpayer will start from a better negotiating position by preparing a comprehensive protest that details the taxpayer's factual and legal arguments. At the very least, a strong protest letter lets the Appeals Officer know that the taxpayer has considered the issues seriously and is intent on pursuing the case aggressively. For further explanation of the advantages of a comprehensive protest, see the excerpt from Junghans & Becker, FEDERAL TAX LITIGATION: CIVIL PRACTICE AND PROCEDURE, reproduced below.

As noted above, however, there are risks associated with a comprehensive protest. Detailed factual assertions not previously considered during the audit might cause the Appeals Officer to return the case to the revenue agent for further investigation, I.R.M. 8.2.1.2.2, while detailed legal arguments run the risk of tipping off the Appeals Officer to legal theories he might not otherwise have considered.[10] These risks are reduced somewhat by the IRS's own procedural rules that discourage an Appeals Officer from reopening issues previously resolved at the examination level, and from raising new issues or theories unless there are substantial grounds underlying the new issues and the potential effect on the taxpayer's liability is material. *See* Proc. Reg. § 601.106(d).

[3] Docketed Versus Nondocketed Appeals

If the taxpayer chooses to file a protest letter, it is forwarded by the examining agent, along with the administrative file he prepared, to the Appeals Officer who will participate in the negotiations. If the taxpayer chooses not to protest the 30-day letter, the IRS will ultimately issue a statutory notice of deficiency, which permits the taxpayer to file a petition in the Tax Court. If the taxpayer follows this course of action, initially bypassing the Appeals process and filing directly in the Tax Court, he will still be provided an opportunity to settle the case administratively. Under IRS procedures designed to encourage case resolution before trial, the IRS attorney handling the Tax Court case must refer it back to the Appeals Division for possible settlement before the case is scheduled for trial. *See* Rev. Proc. 87-24, 1987-1 C.B. 720. Cases that are protested directly to Appeals in response to the 30-day letter are referred to as nondocketed cases. Cases that reach Appeals after a Tax Court petition has been filed and the case has been entered on the Tax Court's calendar (the docket) are referred to as docketed cases.[11]

The settlement guidelines and policies that the Appeals Officer is instructed to follow generally do not vary based on whether the case is presented as a docketed or nondocketed case. I.R.M. 8.2.1.1. On a general level, the Internal Revenue Manual instructs the Appeals Officer to maintain impartiality with respect to the taxpayer and the government. Unlike a revenue agent negotiating at the examination level, an Appeals Officer may compromise issues based on the "hazards of litigation," that is, the possibility that the IRS's stated position may not be sustained if litigated. Proc. Reg. § 601.106(f).[12] As a result, even if the taxpayer's position is contrary to a published ruling or regulation, it is not uncommon for an Appeals Officer to concede the issue if the applicable case law supports the taxpayer's position. Determining the hazards of litigation, of course, requires a careful analysis of IRS rulings and

---

[10] The threat of new issues being raised may also have an impact on the taxpayer's decision to skip the Appeals process initially and instead file a petition in the Tax Court. This decision is discussed in the next section.

[11] The IRS requires that the limitations period during which the IRS can assess additional liability (generally three years) remain open during the Appeals process. If, at the time the Appeals Division considers the case, the statute of limitations will expire in 60 days or fewer, the taxpayer will be asked to extend the limitations period to permit a full consideration of the case. If the taxpayer refuses to extend the limitations period, he will automatically be sent a 90-day letter and may lose the ability to negotiate the issues as a nondocketed case. I.R.M. 8.2.1.3.3.

[12] While most Appeals Officers are not attorneys, they are generally capable of understanding the relative risks of taking a case to trial.

pronouncements, court decisions, as well as pending court cases addressing similar fact situations. Another policy of the Appeals Division is that it will not consider a settlement based on the nuisance value of a case. I.R.M. 8.6.1.3.3.

With respect to nondocketed cases, the Appeals Officer retains exclusive settlement authority. For docketed cases, settlement authority is divided between the Appeals Division and the IRS attorney handling the case. Once a docketed case has been referred to the Appeals Division for settlement, Appeals has sole settlement authority until such time as the case is returned to IRS counsel. The Appeals Division generally must return a case to the IRS attorney when it becomes clear that no progress is being made toward settlement or when the case is placed on the Tax Court trial calendar. When returned, IRS counsel takes up authority to dispose of the case by trial or settlement. *See* Rev. Proc. 87-24, *supra.*

Given that a taxpayer's case will be routed through the Appeals Division eventually, why might the taxpayer decide to defer Appeals consideration until after a petition has been filed in the Tax Court? This approach, like many of those in this chapter, represents an important strategic decision based upon a broad range of factors; there are no clear answers. The following excerpt highlights a few of the considerations involved.

FEDERAL TAX LITIGATION:
CIVIL PRACTICE AND PROCEDURE, (SECOND EDITION) *
By Paula M. Junghans & Joyce K. Becker

¶ 1.14[5] Timing of Appeals Office Review

> The practitioner is always faced with the decision of whether to negotiate with the Appeals Office before his case is docketed, or afterwards. There are two main advantages to negotiating a case at the nondocketed stage. First, evidence that may not be admissible in the Tax Court or in one of the refund forums may well be considered by an Appeals Officer during settlement negotiations. An Appeals Officer, unlike a litigation attorney, probably is not familiar with the intricacies of the rules of evidence. With regard to a docketed case, an attorney from District Counsel or from the Department of Justice may already have read the Service's report, detected the possibility of inadmissible evidence, and alerted the Appeals Officer. Second, there is almost always more time to settle a case when it is in the nondocketed stage, and District Counsel may be loath to relinquish jurisdiction to the Appeals Office where, sometime prior, the taxpayer refused a conference with Appeals Office and the Appeals Office subsequently issued a statutory notice of deficiency. Therefore, if a case appears to be susceptible to settlement, there is much less pressure during the settlement negotiations if the case is nondocketed.

On the negative side, there are a number of risks to consider in trying to settle a nondocketed case with Appeals Office. An Appeals Officer is not permitted to reopen an issue about which taxpayer and the Office of the District Director agree, nor may he raise any new issues unless the grounds for such action are substantial and the potential effect upon tax liability is material.[n.112] Unfortunately, there are no clear guidelines about what constitutes substantial grounds or a material tax liability, and there is serious doubt about whether this procedural rule is binding upon the Service. An Appeals Officer, on balance, is a more sophisticated tax practitioner than a revenue agent. If a revenue agent has developed weak legal theories to support his adjustments, the Appeals Officer may detect and correct this by asserting new and stronger legal theories in the statutory notice of deficiency. In comparison, when a case is docketed, the government must amend its pleadings to assert any new issues, and, in so doing, it acquires the burden of proof regarding all new issues. Similarly, if a nondocketed case is not factually well developed, the Appeals Officer can return the case to the Examination Division for further development and the Examination Division can direct revenue agents to confirm certain facts and, if necessary, invoke the summons power to obtain additional information.[n.114] Once a case is docketed, new factual information that the taxpayer chooses not to disclose is available only through the exercise of appropriate discovered techniques in accordance with the rules of the tribunal in which the case is docketed. In a docketed case, the Service bears the burden of proving any new theory raised as a result of the discovery of new factual information. In summary, if the practitioner is concerned about new theories being asserted, or if he feels that his case may be referred back to the Examination Division for further factual development, it is safer to negotiate settlement after the case has been docketed.

As the excerpt above points out, once an IRS attorney becomes involved in a docketed case, he may emphasize litigation-related issues such as discovery procedures, admissibility of evidence, and burden of proof more heavily than the Appeals Officer. Whether this slightly different perspective will facilitate or impede a settlement depends on the particular facts of the case. As noted in Chapter 6, the burden of proof in a litigated tax case generally falls on the taxpayer unless he can establish the statutory criteria necessary to shift that burden to the IRS. I.R.C. § 7491(a). However, even if the taxpayer does not succeed in shifting the burden of proof to the IRS under Code section 7491, in a Tax Court case, the IRS bears the burden of proof with respect to issues that are not included in the statutory notice of deficiency (commonly called "new matter"). Interim Tax Court Rule 142(a)(1).[13] Procedurally, new matters

---

[n.112] Proc. R. § 601.106(d)(1).

[n.114] Proc. R. § 601.106(b).

[13] One of the statutory conditions necessary to cause the burden of proof to shift to the IRS

generally are presented by the IRS in its answer to the taxpayer's Tax Court petition or in an amended answer.[14] How might this procedural rule affect the decision to approach Appeals through docketed versus nondocketed status?

Time delays and expense are also important factors to consider in determining whether to pursue a nondocketed appeal. While litigation is expensive, if the taxpayer can predict that the case will ultimately be brought to trial, he may not wish to waste time and resources protesting a potential adjustment, but instead should devote his efforts to drafting the Tax Court petition and preparing for trial. Docketing the case in Tax Court will also result in an earlier trial date. Conversely, if the taxpayer foresees settlement possibilities, prior docketing in Tax Court can delay Appeals consideration until after the IRS files an answer to the taxpayer's Tax Court petition. Once at Appeals, however, docketed cases generally take priority over nondocketed cases in order to ensure sufficient time to explore settlement possibilities before the scheduled trial date arrives. This priority may also result in additional pressure on both the taxpayer and the IRS to achieve a prompt settlement.

Keep in mind that if a case is not settled, the taxpayer is not precluded from litigating the case after the conclusion of the Appeals process. By docketing his case in Tax Court without requesting prior Appeals consideration, the taxpayer locks in his forum choice. By comparison, filing a protest in response to the 30-day letter allows the taxpayer additional time to consider whether the Tax Court or one of the refund fora is more advantageous should settlement negotiations break down. Choice of forum issues are discussed in Chapter 6.

[4] Statutory Provisions Affecting the Timing of Appeals Consideration

The IRS Appeals process presents an opportunity to resolve disputes more quickly and with less cost than through litigation. Concerned particularly about the size of the Tax Court's "inventory" of cases, Congress has taken legislative steps to encourage taxpayers to negotiate with the Appeals Division before filing a Tax Court petition. Section 7430, for example, which is discussed in more detail in Chapter 6, allows a taxpayer to recover from the IRS reasonable litigation costs, including attorney's fees, if the taxpayer was the "prevailing party" and the position maintained by the IRS during administrative and court proceedings was not "substantially justified." *See* I.R.C. § 7430(a), (b). The award is conditioned upon a number of requirements, including the taxpayer's exhaustion of his administrative remedies with the IRS. If the IRS issues a 30-day letter and invites Appeals consideration, regulations

---

is that the taxpayer fully cooperate with reasonable requests by the IRS for documents and information within the taxpayer's control. The legislative history to section 7491 specifies that a necessary element of full cooperation with the IRS is that the taxpayer must exhaust his administrative remedies, including any appeal rights provided by the IRS. S. Rep. No. 105-174 (1998). The legislative history does not specify whether the taxpayer must pursue the appeal as a nondocketed case, or whether engaging in negotiations with the Appeals Division after the case is docketed with the Tax Court fulfills this condition. *See id.*

[14] These issues are discussed in more detail in Chapter 7.

require that the taxpayer participate in an Appeals conference prior to filing a petition in the Tax Court in order to establish that this condition was met. Treas. Reg. § 1.7430-1(b). Therefore, the possibility of recovering litigation costs hinges upon pursuit of Appeals consideration on a nondocketed basis.

Code section 6673 grants the Tax Court authority to award up to $25,000 in damages against a taxpayer where it appears to the Tax Court that the taxpayer unreasonably failed to pursue administrative remedies. I.R.C. § 6673(1)(c). The underlying purpose of the statute, according to the Tax Court, is "to penalize taxpayers who needlessly involve the Tax Court in a dispute that should have been resolved in the Appeals Division of the IRS." *Birth v. Commissioner*, 92 T.C. 769 (1989). The Tax Court normally imposes the section 6673 penalty in tax protestor-type cases. The IRS has not sought to impose this penalty merely because a taxpayer pursues an appeal as a docketed rather than a nondocketed case.

[5] Negotiating a Settlement with Appeals

An Appeals Officer is afforded a great deal of flexibility in determining whether to accept a final settlement offer from the taxpayer. He may resolve each issue individually based on an assessment of the hazards of litigation, or may reach a overall settlement on the basis of concessions by both parties. A general discussion of offer and concession techniques is included in Section 15.04 of Chapter 15.

The Internal Revenue Manual recognizes two broad categories of settlements at the Appeals level: mutual concession and split issue. I.R.M. 8632, 8633. A mutual concession settlement, as the name implies, results when neither party is willing to concede an issue in full but the parties are willing to negotiate a compromise. The amount compromised on each side will depend upon the relative level of uncertainty surrounding how a court would interpret and apply the law to the facts of the case. Valuation issues, for instance, lend themselves to mutual concession settlements because the parties may agree to a final valuation somewhere between their initial valuation numbers. A split issue settlement, on the other hand, is normally used when an issue involved, if litigated, would result in a complete victory for one of the parties, such as whether the taxpayer's incorporation transaction qualifies under the nonrecognition rule of section 351. A split issue settlement is reached based on a percentage or stipulated amount of the asserted deficiency.

These two broad categories of settlements allow for creativity and old fashioned horse-trading. As the following excerpt makes clear, the negotiating techniques and procedures used during the Appeals conference will vary. Tips on preparing for an Appeals conference are also included in the excerpt.

HOW TO HANDLE AND WIN A FEDERAL TAX APPEAL: A COMPLETE GUIDE FOR A TAX PROFESSIONAL[*]
By Robert C. Carlson

¶ 2.05 BETWEEN THE PROTEST AND THE CONFERENCE

* * *

[b]   Taxpayer Strategies

Several times in this chapter the importance of carefully drafting the protest and preparing for the appeals conference have been emphasized. This section describes in more detail the preparation that is recommended for the conference.

Many taxpayer representatives appear at conferences unprepared because several features of the conference mislead representatives. The conference is a fairly informal meeting between the appeals officer, the representative, and perhaps the taxpayer. Rules of evidence do not apply, and there is no formal structure to the conference. In addition, while the appeals officer serves in effect as judge during the conference, representatives frequently forget that the officer also will be serving as an adversary during the proceeding. The officer's judgelike role occurs mainly after the conference when the hazards of litigation are balanced to determine an acceptable settlement. During the conference the appeals officer will be a staunch advocate of the IRS's position.

The representative can best protect the taxpayer's interests by preparing for the conference as though it were a trial. The steps described in this section should be familiar to representatives experienced in litigation.

The taxpayer should be interviewed thoroughly. This means asking questions that will elicit all unfavorable information from the client and ensure that the facts are not being hidden or distorted. After the interview, all records and documents should be reviewed to check the accuracy of the taxpayer's statements. Frequently even taxpayers with strong cases will color their statements to strengthen their cases. Such actions can damage the credibility of both the representative and the taxpayer and must be avoided. Any witness other than the taxpayer also should be interviewed, and their statements should be checked against any other evidence available. An intensive investigation of the facts can give the taxpayer's representative a substantial edge over the appeals officer, because the officer will not conduct a separate investigation of the facts. The facts known to the officer will be those uncovered and reported by the audit agent. These agents are frequently the least experienced and knowledgeable of the IRS employees who deal with substantive

---

[*] How to Handle and Win a Federal Tax Appeal by Carlson, Copyright 1989. Reprinted by permission of Prentice-Hall, Inc., Upper Saddle River, NJ.

tax matters, so a skilled practitioner can expect to prepare a superior case.

Investigation of the facts should be followed by legal research. Then, once the facts and the law have been collected, an outline of the points to be made at the conference can be prepared. This outline should be a checklist of the points that must be proved according to the law and the evidence that supports each point. The points that will be made by the appeals officer also must be anticipated and counterarguments should be prepared. Unlike the protest, the conference should focus on the taxpayer's strongest arguments. A weak argument that is made in writing is less damaging to credibility than one that is made in person.

Whenever possible, third-party evidence such as affidavits and reports should be used. This will add to the credibility of taxpayer-generated evidence. Exhibits and documents should be used at the conference whenever possible so that the appeals officer will have more to rely on than the oral statements of the taxpayer and counsel. Any independent support for the taxpayer's positions will enhance the credibility of all the taxpayer's statements and should be used.

After preparing the case, settlement proposals should be prepared. The proposals should be structured issue-by-issue because the appeals officer is not permitted to trade concessions on one issue for concessions on another. On each issue there should be an initial proposal that reflects the doubt created by the taxpayer's presentation and that shows a good faith intention to settle the case based on the hazards of litigation. Several proposals should be prepared on each issue, because the best proposal should not be offered first. The taxpayer should determine in advance the maximum amount on each issue that will be conceded in order to avoid the time and expense of litigation. Each settlement proposal should compute the exact amount of additional tax that would be due under the proposal. It is critically important that all settlement offers be stated in terms of the likelihood of the taxpayer's winning the issue in litigation or the uncertainty of the outcome.

One caveat in preparing for conference is that new evidence cannot be presented for the first time at the appeals conference. When faced with new evidence at the conference, the appeal officer has the option of returning the entire case or the new evidence back to the district to be investigated. This is another reason for preparing a detailed protest that includes all possible arguments.

¶ 2.06 THE APPEALS CONFERENCE

Procedure at a conference varies between appeals officers but is always informal. Generally the parties begin discussing the issues, gradually find their areas of agreement and disagreement, and work their way towards discussing specific settlement possibilities. In most cases all this is done in one conference, though sometimes the officer will refer the case back to the district for additional fact finding. Cases involving complicated legal issues or fact situations can be expected to take more than one conference. Whether the taxpayer or the appeals officer makes the first presentation and the exact format of the presentations depend entirely on the individuals involved. The taxpayer or representative might want to discuss such procedural matters with the officer when scheduling the conference.

The IRS issued updated guidelines on appeals conference procedures in 1986. The guidelines say that the conferences are to be informal "to promote frank discussion and mutual understanding." Appeals officers "must handle cases objectively" with the goal of reaching a decision based on the "merits of the issues in dispute and not with the attitude that settlements must be made." The new procedures also state that "ideological kinds of arguments" have no place in a conference. The guidelines emphasize two additional points. First, the conference is to be an informal procedure. Second, the appeals officer is not to be an advocate or a rubber stamp for the auditor's positions. While the appeals officer's objective posture might not be clear during the conference, the officer will try to settle a case that the government is not likely to win at trial.

All physical evidence that supports the taxpayer's position should be brought to the conference. Evidence should be brought even when the taxpayer believes that it would not be admissible in court, because the rules of evidence do not prevail at an appeals conference. It is important that copies of the evidence be presented to the officer because any settlement proposal must be sent to a reviewing officer, who must be convinced that the settlement conforms to the IRS's standards. Further, a graphic presentation of the taxpayer's evidence should make the appeals officer more amenable to a favorable settlement. A carefully prepared conference presentation also can convince the officer that the taxpayer is willing to litigate the issues if a favorable settlement is not reached. An inadequate presentation at the conference, however, will give the officer little reason to believe that there are hazards in litigating the case.

After the issues and evidence have been discussed, the appeals officer will either state that the parties are too far apart for a settlement to be possible or will ask the taxpayer for a settlement offer. Usually the taxpayer makes the first offer. If that offer is rejected, the officer should state a proposal that would be acceptable. If not, the taxpayer should ask what the officer would consider acceptable. Through this exchange of offers the parties can gradually move toward a mutually acceptable settlement or conclude that a settlement is not possible.

Even if the taxpayer and the Appeals Officer are unable to resolve all issues, efforts should be made to resolve as many as possible. Before agreeing to a full or partial settlement, however, the taxpayer should carefully consider how the settled issue might affect the taxpayer's exposure for past and future taxable years. If the settlement involves issues that have a continuing effect, such as the taxpayer's basis in property, the impact of these issues on other years should be included in the settlement agreement.

[6] Alternative Dispute Resolution

In recent years, the IRS has established a series of programs designed to encourage settlement through the use of alternative dispute resolution techniques. For example, if the Appeals Officer and the taxpayer have been unable to negotiate a settlement between themselves, the parties may request binding arbitration to resolve unsettled factual disputes. *See* I.R.C. § 7123(b)(2). Because arbitration is optional, both parties must agree to be bound by the process. The type of factual issue appropriate for arbitration is one that is susceptible to resolution based upon a combination of (1) a finding of fact and (2) an agreement between the parties as to any applicable interpretation of law, regulation, ruling, or other legal authority. Examples of the type of issue appropriate for arbitration include valuation and reasonable compensation. Because binding arbitration is final, neither side can appeal or contest the arbitrator's factual findings in court. *See* Announcement 2000-4, 2000-1 C.B. 317 (containing language for a model arbitration agreement).

The IRS Appeals Division also offers a post-Appeals mediation program for nondocketed cases. *See* I.R.C. § 7123(b)(1); Announcement 2001-9, 2001-3 I.R.B. 357 (limiting mediation to factual issues involving adjustments of $1 million or more). Unlike arbitration, mediation is nonbinding: The mediator has no authority to impose a decision on the parties. Instead, the mediator functions as a neutral party to promote settlement by helping the parties define the issues.[15] Unlike under the "fast track" mediation procedure discussed above, the mediator chosen by agreement between the taxpayer and the Appeals Division may be either from within the Appeals Division or from outside the IRS. If the parties choose an outside mediator, they share the costs equally. A mediator from within the Appeals Division is provided at no charge. If a final settlement agreement between the parties still cannot be reached, the IRS will issue a notice of deficiency and the case will proceed as any other case would.

In addition to arbitration and mediation, the IRS has established a series of more specialized programs designed to expedite case resolution.[16] A pilot initiative called the Comprehensive Case Resolution program, established under the auspices of the Large and Mid-Sized Business (LMSB) Operating Division, involves revenue agents, Appeals Officers, and IRS Counsel working in teams to resolve disagreements with large business taxpayers. Notice 2001-13, 2001-6 I.R.B. 514, provides the criteria for participation and other details. According to the Notice:

---

[15] For insight into the mediation process involving tax cases, *see* Amy S. Wei, Note, "Can Mediation Be the Answer to Taxpayers' Woes?: An Examination of the Internal Revenue Service's Mediation Program," 15 Ohio St. J. on Disp. Resol. 549 (2000).

[16] Because of fairly stringent eligibility requirements and high dollar thresholds, none of these specialized techniques is currently available to resolve typical individual income tax disputes.

The goal of the Comprehensive Case Resolution program is to help taxpayers that have tax years under examination by LMSB and in Appeals (including docketed cases under Appeals jurisdiction) resolve all open issues in all such years through an IRS Comprehensive Case Resolution process (CCR process). In some situations it may also be appropriate to include tax years which are docketed before the Tax Court and not under Appeals' jurisdiction. The effect of this program will be to expedite the taxpayer's LMSB years, where the audit is substantially complete, into a resolution process. This CCR process will constitute the taxpayer's formal administrative appeal for the LMSB years. . . . The CCR process will plan aggressive timelines for completion, with a target of closing all years within six to twelve months. If agreement cannot be reached using this process, Appeals will not again consider the unagreed issues from the years under examination by LMSB.

The Appeals Division also plans to implement a new case resolution process called the "Mutually Accelerated Appeals Program." The program will require taxpayers to agree on an audit schedule and to a commitment of specified resources that will be devoted to reaching a settlement. If an agreement can be reached, the IRS will create special appeals teams to handle the case on an accelerated basis. *See* IR-2000-42. The MAAP program is available only in cases involving $10 million or more in disputed tax liability.

In an attempt to resolve a potential issue before an affected tax return is even filed, the LSMB Operating Division has established a pilot pre-filing agreement program. Details relating to the program are spelled out in Revenue Procedure 2001-22, 2001-9 I.R.B. 745.[17] Factual issues potentially suitable for pre-filing resolution include asset valuation, capitalization issues, inventory issues, and issues relating to start-up costs under section 195. Questions regarding whether a transaction lacks a business purpose, the applicability of penalties, and transfer pricing disputes are not subject to resolution through a pre-filing agreement. Moreover, disagreements between a taxpayer and the IRS over legal interpretations of the Code are generally not subject to the program. According to the Revenue Procedure, questions regarding the interpretation of legal issues are more properly resolved by requests for letter rulings (discussed in Chapter 9).

[7] Disposing of a Case at Appeals

If the taxpayer and the Appeals Division can reach a mutually acceptable settlement, the parties normally memorialize that settlement by signing Form 870-AD, Offer to Waive Restrictions on Assessment and Collection of Tax Deficiency (a copy of which is reproduced below). Form 870-AD contains substantially the same terms as Form 870, discussed above, with the addition of a statement to the effect that if the agreement is accepted by the IRS, the IRS agrees not to reopen the case for the taxable years involved except in

---

[17] Revenue Procedure 2001-22 treats pre-filing agreements (PFAs) as closing agreements under Code section 7121. Following the enactment of section 6103(b)(2)(D), discussed in Section 3.03 of Chapter 3, the IRS treats PFAs as confidential return information under Code section 6103, and accordingly exempt from disclosure under the Freedom of Information Act.

certain specified circumstances. In return, the taxpayer agrees to the assessment of any settled liability and commits himself not to file a claim for refund for the taxable year in issue.[18]

Form **870-AD** (Rev. April 1992)	Department of the Treasury – Internal Revenue Service **Offer to Waive Restrictions on Assessment and Collection of Tax Deficiency and to Accept Overassessment**	
Symbols	Name of Taxpayer	SSN or EIN

Under the provisions of section 6213(d) of the Internal Revenue Code of 1986 (the Code), or corresponding provisions of prior internal revenue laws, the undersigned offers to waive the restrictions provided in section 6213(a) of the Code or corresponding provisions of prior internal revenue laws, and to consent to the assessment and collection of the following deficiencies and additions to tax, if any, with interest as provided by law. The undersigned offers also to accept the following overassessments, if any, as correct. Any waiver or acceptance of an overassessment is subject to any terms and conditions stated below and on the reverse side of this form.

		Deficiencies (Overassessments) and Additions to Tax			
Year Ended	Kind of Tax	Tax			
		$	$	$	
		$	$	$	
		$	$	$	
		$	$	$	
		$	$	$	
		$	$	$	

Signature of Taxpayer	Date
Signature of Taxpayer	Date
Signature of Taxpayer's Representative	Date
Corporate Name	Date
By Corporate Officer Title	Date

For Internal Revenue Use Only	Date Accepted for Commissioner	Signature
	Office	Title

Cat. No. 16896Q   (See Reverse Side)   Form **870-AD** (Rev. 4-92)

---

[18] Form 870 may be used to conclude a case with Appeals where the settlement does not involve mutual concessions or where the amount of tax liability in issue is not large. I.R.M. 8.8.1.1.4.

This offer must be accepted for the Commissioner of Internal Revenue and will take effect on the date it is accepted. Unless and until it is accepted, it will have no force or effect.

If this offer is accepted, the case will not be reopened by the Commissioner unless there was:

* fraud, malfeasance, concealment or misrepresentation of a material fact
* an important mistake in mathematical calculation
* a deficiency or overassessment resulting from adjustments made under Subchapters C and D of Chapter 63 concerning the tax treatment of partnership and subchapter S items determined at the partnership and corporate level
* an excessive tentative allowance of a carryback provided by law

No claim for refund or credit will be filed or prosecuted by the taxpayer for the years stated on this form, other than for amounts attributed to carrybacks provided by law.

The proper filing of this offer, when accepted, will expedite assessment and billing (or overassessment, credit or refund) by adjusting the tax liability. This offer, when executed and timely submitted, will be considered a claim for refund for the above overassessment(s), if any.

This offer may be executed by the taxpayer's attorney, certified public accountant, or agent provided this is specifically authorized by a power of attorney which, if not previously filed, must accompany this form. If this offer is signed by a person acting in a fiduciary capacity (for example: an executor, administrator, or a trustee) Form 56, Notice Concerning Fiduciary Relationship, must accompany this form, unless previously filed.

If this offer is executed for a year for which a joint return was filed, it must be signed by both spouses unless one spouse, acting under a power of attorney, signs as agent for the other.

If this offer is executed by a corporation, it must be signed with the corporate name followed by the signature and title of the officer(s) authorized to sign. If the offer is accepted, as a condition of acceptance, any signature by or for a corporate officer will be considered a representation by that person and the corporation, to induce reliance, that such signature is binding under law for the corporation to be assessed the deficiencies or receive credit or refund under this agreement. If the corporation later contests the signature as being unauthorized on its behalf, the person who signed may be subject to criminal penalties for representing that he or she had authority to sign this agreement on behalf of the corporation.

Notwithstanding the agreement in Form 870-AD, taxpayers have on occasion sought to reopen a case by filing a refund claim arising from issues covered by the agreement. As discussed in *Kretchmar*, reproduced below, courts have reached differing conclusions over whether and under what circumstances the taxpayer's commitment not to seek a refund is binding.

KRETCHMAR v. UNITED STATES
United States Claims Court
9 Cl. Ct. 191 (1985)

REGINALD W. GIBSON, JUDGE:

In this tax refund action, plaintiffs, Frank R. and Bertha M. Kretchmar, jointly seek a refund of federal income taxes, interest, and penalties in the amounts of $19,006.05, $27,404.64, and $24,250.02 for the taxable years 1976, 1977, and 1978, respectively. * * *

Without addressing the merits of these claims as to any of the foregoing years, defendant, in moving for summary judgment, avers that (1) plaintiffs' previous execution of IRS Form 870-AD, Offer of Waiver of Restrictions on Assessment and Collection of Deficiency in Tax and of Acceptance of Overassessment, now estops plaintiffs from seeking a refund for each of said taxable years; * * *. Because we find that plaintiffs failed to pay the amount (tax and penalty) fully assessed for the taxable year 1978, this court is without jurisdiction to entertain a claim for such year. As for the taxable years 1976 and 1977, we find that the plaintiffs are also barred from litigating the merits of their refund suit on the grounds that the doctrine of equitable estoppel, stemming from their previous execution of IRS Form 870-AD, is a complete impediment.

FACTS

Plaintiffs, husband and wife residing in West Brookfield, Massachusetts, filed timely federal income tax returns for the taxable years in question, 1976, 1977, and 1978. Schedule C of each of said returns described plaintiffs' business, euphemistically, as "novelty sales," and reported gross receipts and net income in the identical amounts of $11,700, $19,140, and $30,000, for the taxable years 1976, 1977, and 1978, respectively.[n.4] No deductible expenses were claimed as having been incurred in connection with earning these amounts of income.

During the calendar year 1980, Internal Revenue Agent (IRA) Robert B. Puzzo conducted an audit of the plaintiffs' 1976, 1977, and 1978 returns. That audit report (December 12, 1980) resulted in plaintiffs being assessed income tax deficiencies of $12,156.76, $13,867.49, and $24,180.99, for the taxable years 1976, 1977, and 1978, respectively. In addition, plaintiffs were also assessed civil fraud penalties at the rate of 50% of the assessed tax deficiency plus deficiency interest ($6,078.39, $6,933.75, and $12,090.49 as to each respective tax year, pursuant to 26 U.S.C. § 6653(b)). * * *

Plaintiffs rejected, *i.e.*, refused to execute, the Form 870 settlement offer and appealed the foregoing proposed deficiencies to the Appeals Office of the Internal Revenue Service (IRS). Upon further settlement negotiation, the IRS agreed in 1982 to *decrease* plaintiffs' assessed gross income by the amount of $6,000 for 1976, and $20,000 for 1978. No adjustment, however, was made for 1977 given the agreed diminution in 1976 and 1978. As a result of said readjustments by the Appeals Office, plaintiffs' reassessed taxes and penalties were reduced to $14,063.52, $20,801.24, and $20,104.15, for the three taxable years in question or an aggregate amount of $54,968.91. As evidence of the results of the compromise/settlement negotiations, and in order to preclude future assessments against such taxable years, plaintiffs executed Form 870-AD on January 29, 1982, which was accepted for the Commissioner of Internal Revenue on February 9, 1982. * * *

In spite of plaintiffs' promise in the Form 870-AD that "no [future] claim for refund or credit shall be filed . . . . other than for amounts attributed to carrybacks" for the years in issue after the execution of the Form 870-AD, they nevertheless filed a timely claim for refund (Form 1040X), for each of the years in question, "other than for amounts attributed to carrybacks" with the Boston Appeals Office of the IRS on or about May 23, 1983. At that date, despite plaintiffs' previous execution of several forms extending the general three-year limitations period for deficiency assessment for 1976 and 1977 to December 31, 1982, defendant's right to assess any further deficiency as to all years under *the general three-year period* of limitations (§§ 6501(a) and

---

[n.4] "Euphemistically" is the appropriate adjective given subsequent revelations as to the real source of the understated income. From the documentation reflected in defendant's exhibits, it appears that on January 18, 1978, the Massachusetts State Police conducted a raid on plaintiffs' residence at which time $50,000 in cash was confiscated. A five-count indictment relating to illegal gambling activity followed therefrom, and plaintiff, Frank Kretchmar, pleaded guilty to each count. The Service, therefore, contends that given the fact that no income from the admitted gambling activities was listed on either of the 1976, 1977 or 1978 returns, the subsequently discovered unreported cash must have emanated from said illegal activity. * * *

(c)(4)) had then expired. On each such Forms 1040X, plaintiffs claimed, *inter alia*, that the originally reported income amounts on their returns for each year were correct; that the Form 870-AD was executed by a representative of plaintiffs who was acting outside the scope of his authority; that the Form 870-AD was itself illegal as it was executed beyond the three year statute of limitations contained in 26 U.S.C. § 6501; and that no grounds existed to assess civil fraud penalties pursuant to 26 U.S.C. § 6653(b). The IRS rejected plaintiffs' contentions and disallowed all of plaintiffs' refund claims on December 12, 1983.

Plaintiffs, thereafter, commenced a refund action in this court on February 3, 1984. The petition here did not seek refunds "for amounts attributed to carrybacks," but rather requested refunds of the same amounts for each year which were sought in plaintiffs' earlier appeal to the Appeals Office dated May 23, 1983. In opposition, on January 22, 1985, defendant moved for summary judgment in which it invoked the doctrine of equitable estoppel for all years as a result of plaintiffs' execution of Form 870-AD, and also averred that this court lacks jurisdiction with regard to the claim respecting the taxable year 1978.

For reasons hereinafter delineated, we find that judgment should be granted in favor of defendant on its motion for summary judgment as to all taxable years in issue.

DISCUSSION

* * *

B. Equitable Estoppel

1. Background

Defendant has * * * moved for summary judgment on plaintiffs' refund claims (the taxable years 1976-1977) on the ground that their previous execution of IRS Form 870-AD equitably estops plaintiffs from litigating these now compromised and settled claims. In short, defendant avers that it would be most inequitable and unjust, in the face of the bargained-for-concessions implicit in Form 870-AD signed by plaintiffs on January 29, 1982, and approved by defendant on February 9, 1982, to permit plaintiffs to file an efficacious claim for refund (May 23, 1983) long after the running of the general three-year statute of limitations (26 U.S.C. § 6501(a)) on additional assessments. Conversely, and in opposition, plaintiffs argue that (1) any estoppel of their claims would be "inequitable" given the fact that no compromise of their claims was made through the execution of Form 870-AD; (2) no prejudice would be visited on defendant should the agreement be revoked inasmuch as the statute had not run on additional assessments at the time plaintiffs filed their claims to the extent the defendant can prove either fraud or an omission in excess of 25 percent of the amount of gross income originally reported; (3) in fact the Form 870-AD was executed by an unauthorized person; and (4) the Form 870-AD is not valid because the statute of limitations (§ 6501(a)) expired prior to January 29, 1982.

Research discloses that the application of the doctrine of equitable estoppel, to bar the prosecution of tax refund claims settled and concluded by the execution of a Form 870-AD, has provoked not only controversy but outright inconsistency among various federal circuits. On the one hand, there are those courts which strictly hold, according to the Supreme Court in *Botany Worsted Mills v. United States*, 278 U.S. 282, 73 L. Ed. 379, 49 S. Ct. 129 (1929), that the only binding form of tax settlement is one which conforms to the finality prescribed through a settlement agreement pursuant to 26 U.S.C. § 7121 (1982). The justification for this conclusion is apparently premised on the fact that Form 870-AD specifically states that it is not such an agreement. Absent strict adherence to the formality envisioned in § 7121, these courts, therefore, reject the application of the doctrine of equitable estoppel relying instead on the Supreme Court's admonishment that "when a statute limits a thing to be done in a particular mode, it includes the negative of any other mode." *Botany*, 278 U.S. at 289. *Cf.* Uinta Livestock Corp. v. United States, 355 F.2d 761 (10th Cir. 1966); Associated Mutuals, Inc. v. Delaney, 176 F.2d 179, 181 n. 1 (1st Cir. 1949); and Bank of New York v. United States, 170 F.2d 20 (3d Cir. 1948).

On the other hand, there are also those courts which have a tradition of affirmatively applying the doctrine of equitable estoppel to bar the litigation of claims previously concluded through the taxpayer's execution of a settlement Form 870-AD. These courts, *infra*, in essence, acknowledge the continued vitality of Botany, but they persuasively distinguish its holding by arguing that that case did not present the estoppel issue squarely to the Court. In support of this position, they refer to the following often cited *dicta* in *Botany*, to wit:

> It is plain that no compromise is authorized by this statute which is not assented to by the Secretary of the Treasury. For this reason, if for no other, the informal agreement made in this case did not constitute a settlement which in itself was binding upon the Government or the Mills. *And, without determining whether such an agreement, though not binding in itself, may when executed become, under some circumstances, binding on the parties by estoppel, it suffices to say that here the findings disclose no adequate ground for any claim of estoppel by the United States.*

Botany, 278 U.S. at 289 (emphasis added, citations omitted). Since the Supreme Court has expressly reserved the issue of what circumstances might ultimately raise the execution of a Form 870-AD to a binding settlement, certain courts have consequently held that *Botany* does not estop the courts from developing their own law on the subject. Thus, it is on the foregoing premises that a properly executed Form 870-AD has become a recognized impediment, in certain circuits, to estop taxpayers from litigating the merits of tax refund claims settled therein. *Cf.* Stair v. United States, 516 F.2d 560 (2d Cir. 1975); * * * Elbo Coals, Inc., v. United States, 763 F.2d 818 (6th Cir. 1985).

2. Equitable Estoppel in the Predecessor Court of Claims

Research further discloses that the predecessor Court of Claims saw fit on a number of occasions to apply the doctrine of equitable estoppel on facts arising out of a taxpayer's previous execution of a Form 870-AD. *See* Guggenheim v. United States, 111 Ct. Cl. 165, 77 F. Supp. 186 (1948); H.W. Nelson Co., Inc. v. United States, 158 Ct. Cl. 629, 308 F.2d 950 (1962); D.D.I., Inc. v. United States, 199 Ct. Cl. 380, 467 F.2d 497 (1972); McGraw-Hill, Inc. v. United States, 224 Ct. Cl. 324, 623 F.2d 700 (1980) (doctrine affirmed but not applied on the specific facts of the case). In so doing, said Court of Claims made particular mention of the language cited from *Botany, supra*. For example, in the seminal case adopting the doctrine in the predecessor Court of Claims, *Guggenheim v. United States*, all of the formalities required for executing an efficacious Form 870-AD were present. *Guggenheim*, 77 F. Supp. at 196. Both parties had signed, and the form was properly accepted by the Commissioner on the same day. *Id.* at 194. There, the court noted in contradistinction to *Botany* that:

> Many of the elements in the formal agreement involved in this case [*Guggenheim*] were lacking in that case [*Botany*]. Moreover, we do not understand that case to hold, as plaintiff contends, that under no circumstances will a closing agreement be held binding unless executed in accordance with Section [7121] . . . .

Guggenheim, 77 F. Supp. at 196. Having effectively distinguished *Botany*, the Court of Claims in *Guggenheim* went on to dismiss the tax refund action therein holding that cause of action to be equitably barred due solely to the plaintiff's previous execution of Form 870. *Id.* at 197.

* * *

3. Application of the Doctrine — Equitable Estoppel

As outlined above, we apply the doctrine of equitable estoppel to preclude the litigation of plaintiffs' claims as to the taxable years 1976 and 1977. * * * The discussion which follows demonstrates that in accordance with Court of Claims precedent, plaintiffs did, by executing the Form 870-AD, waive their right to further litigate the 1976 and 1977 claims, so that to reopen them at this juncture would significantly prejudice the defendant. On such facts, we find that equity favors the enforcement of plaintiffs' agreement.

In general terms, binding precedent teaches that the doctrine of equitable estoppel, arising out of the execution of a Form 870-AD, may be applied to hold a taxpayer to his bargain if the following three criteria are established: (1) the execution of the Form 870-AD was the result of mutual concession or compromise; (2) there was a meeting of the minds that the claims be extinguished; and (3) that to allow the plaintiff to reopen the case would be prejudicial given the defendant's reliance on the extinguishment thereof. *Guggenheim*, 77 F. Supp. at 196; *H.W. Nelson Co.*, 308 F.2d at 956–59; *D.D.I., Inc.*, 467 F.2d at 500–01; *McGraw-Hill, Inc.*, 623 F.2d at 706. As the pleading of the doctrine raises an affirmative defense, the burden is on the defendant to establish these criteria by the requisite quantum of proof.

a. Mutual Concession and Compromise

With respect to the first criterion, mutual concession or compromise, the defendant's documentary evidence clearly establishes this fact for all taxable years with striking similarity to the facts in *Guggenheim*. In *Guggenheim*, the court stated in that connection that:

> Plaintiff protested the proposed disallowance and thereafter confer- ences were held with plaintiff's representatives. A further investiga- tion was made by a revenue agent. As a result of these discussions, the representatives of the Commissioner agreed to recommend for allowance a deduction . . . . claimed by plaintiff. Plaintiff abandoned his contention that the other deductions claimed were allowable. The Commissioner's representative also agreed to make an adjustment in plaintiff's favor on account of certain dividends.

Guggenheim, 77 F. Supp. at 194. In the case at bar, plaintiffs similarly protested the audit report which initially assessed them some $75,307 in deficiencies (taxes and penalties) in December 1980 for all of the years in issue. Likewise, as in *Guggenheim*, a further investigation was held in which an IRS report was issued containing the following revelations:

> *Taxpayers, in an effort to close this case, propose that the Government accept in the year 1976 a reduction of $6,000* as representing a repayment of the loan to Ray Heck as outlined above. *Taxpayers concede all adjustments in 1977. In 1978, it is proposed that the Government concede the inclusion of $13,661* deemed to have been for the purchase of JTC stock. *In the year 1978, taxpayers also pro- pose that an amount of $6,339 be considered as cash on hand. It is recommended that this proposal of settlement be accepted as a reasonable conclusion to this case.*

Appeals Transmittal Memorandum and Supporting Statement, Feb. 12, 1982 (emphasis added). This paraphrase of the ongoing dialogue between plaintiffs and defendant as contained in the referenced IRS report, evidencing the negotiations leading to the final adjustments which were then recorded on Form 870-AD, persuasively belies plaintiffs' assertion that "the numbers placed on the Form 870-AD were not a compromise at all." Indeed, as in *Guggenheim*, it is clear beyond cavil, and we so find, that plaintiffs' settlement, manifested by the execution of Form 870-AD in this case, was a bilateral process driven by mutual concession and compromise.

* * *

b. Meeting of the Minds

The second criterion cited above requires that, concomitantly, there must also be a meeting of the minds to the effect that the right to raise any prospective claims or to otherwise reopen the case, for such years, be extin- guished (save exceptions not here relevant). In *Guggenheim*, the court added substance to the evaluation of this concept by examining two additional factors: (1) the parties' course of conduct; and (2) the express language adopted by the parties on the Form 870-AD. *Guggenheim*, 77 F. Supp. at 195. As to course of conduct, the court stated:

> The conclusion is inescapable from the evidence that there was a meeting of minds as to the final disposition of the case. When that

occurred, the Commissioner recomputed plaintiff's tax liability and transmitted to plaintiff the settlement document wherein was set out a deficiency for each of the years. In transmitting that document to plaintiff at that time, the Commissioner stated that he was accepting plaintiff's "proposal for settlement," and also referred to the document as an "agreement" when executed by plaintiff and approved on his behalf. In returning the document after execution, plaintiff likewise referred to it as an "agreement."

Id. at 195. In *Guggenheim*, at no time did either party objectively manifest a belief that what was being negotiated was anything less than a complete settlement for the taxable years in issue. While no correspondence similar to that in *Guggenheim* has been presented to the court in the case at bar, neither has any demonstrative evidence been submitted supporting plaintiffs' contention that a definitive settlement was not intended for all taxable years. In fact, on this issue the documentary evidence is thoroughly supportive of defendant's position, particularly when we examine defendant's Form 5278, Statement-Income Tax Changes, prepared by the Appeals Office of the IRS which contains a box plainly checked "settlement computation." Similarly, in the Appeals Transmittal Memorandum and Supporting Statement, *supra*, the words "Proposal of Settlement" are used consistently throughout to characterize the nature of the procedural posture of plaintiffs' appeal. While plaintiffs may, as an afterthought, *now* contend otherwise, the evidence is wanting and it strains credulity to contend that the lengthy and detailed negotiations, which led to the preparation and execution of Form 870-AD, were conducted with any purpose other than that they were aimed at a definitive settlement.

Moreover, in reviewing the undeniable language contained in the Form 870-AD together with other referenced evidence, *supra*, the ultimate intentions of the parties leave no room for doubt. This conclusion is compelled when one carefully reviews the Form 870-AD, wherein the following unambiguous statement appears directly above the plaintiffs' signatures:

> *If this offer is accepted for the Commissioner, the case shall not be reopened* in the absence of fraud, malfeasance, concealment or misrepresentation of material fact, an important mistake in mathematical calculation, or excessive tentative allowances of carrybacks provided by law; *and no claim for refund or credit shall be filed or prosecuted for the year(s) stated above other than for amounts attributed to carrybacks provided by law.*

Appendix B to the Memorandum for the United States in Support of Its Motion for Summary Judgment, January 22, 1985, Exhibit C (emphasis added). Thus, by signing the Form 870-AD containing the referenced language, plaintiffs, in essence, waived all further rights to contest the assessment for the stated taxable years, save for the specific exception not present in this case. While the Form 870-AD was drafted by the defendant, no ambiguity exists as to the clear import of the intendment of the parties, *i.e.*, each side *expressly* waived its right (with exceptions not pertinent here) to subsequently litigate the settlement contained therein. For this court to find otherwise, at this posture, would contravene and directly ignore the clearly exhibited objective manifestations of the signatories.

* * *

c. Detrimental Reliance

The third, and final, criterion defendant must establish to effect the application of the doctrine of equitable estoppel is that of detrimental reliance. In the precise context of this case, to meet this burden, the proof must show that defendant detrimentally relied upon plaintiffs' execution of the Form 870-AD in question. The degree of detrimental reliance sufficient to support the application of the doctrine of equitable estoppel has been characterized by the courts in various ways. In *McGraw-Hill,* for example, the court stated that "equitable estoppel [is to be applied] whenever the IRS cannot be placed in the same position it was when the agreement was executed." *McGraw-Hill,* 623 F.2d at 706. More specifically, perhaps, is the definition given in *D.D.I.* wherein the court states that detrimental reliance is the result which obtains "where the statute of limitations has run on the collection of further deficiencies between the time an informal compromise agreement was executed and the time the refund claim was filed . . . ." *D.D.I.,* 467 F.2d at 500.

Quite logically, the predecessor Court of Claims has also, by implication, suggested the necessity for the defendant's reliance to have been reasonable under the circumstances. In this regard, the key variable is the timing of the defendant's knowledge regarding the plaintiff's decision to change its position, *i.e.,* whether the repudiation of the Form 870-AD occurs at a time when the statute of limitations on assessment has expired. Or, on the other hand, the question is whether such knowledge preceded the running of the statute of limitations to the extent that the Service could be restored to the "same position," *i.e.,* by expeditiously effecting an additional assessment within the general three-year period of limitations (§ 6501(a)). The case of *Erickson v. United States,* 159 Ct. Cl. 202, 309 F.2d 760 (1962), is particularly instructive on this issue. In *Erickson,* the Court of Claims estopped the plaintiff from seeking a refund of deficiency interest made payable under a compromise agreement proposed by the taxpayer as a settlement of a claim being litigated in the Tax Court. The settlement agreement contained an award of interest, yet the Tax Court in ratifying the agreement, omitted the award of interest. In accordance with the written settlement agreement itself, the Commissioner collected the interest. In estopping plaintiff from suing for a refund of the interest, the Court of Claims commented on the reasonableness of the defendant's reliance as follows:

> Taxpayer tells us that his counsel orally indicated to representatives of the defendant in October 1958, before the Tax Court orders had become final, that he intended to sue for most of the interest assessed and not refunded. This, he says, was sufficient warning to the Government that his position had changed. *But such informal oral statements, even if strongly asserted, would not change the reliance which the Government had already placed on the prior*

> *written agreement and could rightfully continue to place, at least*
> *until the agreement was formally repudiated in writing.*

Id. at 764–65 (emphasis added). Consistent with the foregoing statement by the court in *Erickson,* we construe the quoted language of *D.D.I.*, cited *supra,* to mean that the cut-off date for the defendant to claim detrimental reliance is certainly the date the Form 870-AD is "formally repudiated in writing." Thus, the prejudice to defendant emanating from detrimental reliance because of the running of the three-year limitations period, must have accrued at the date just prior to the time the claim for refund was filed with the IRS, or just prior to the date when any other written notice of repudiation was served on defendant, whichever occurs first. For defendant to proceed in allowing the three-year statute to run, after having received such written notice of repudiation, would clearly not be reasonable, nor indicative of the requisite prejudice required to be caused by the plaintiff. In other words, equity will only estop a plaintiff based on that prejudice which is traceable to its own action or inaction, not for that which is self-imposed by the defendant.

Plaintiffs insist that at the time they repudiated the Form 870-AD and filed their refund claims with the Service on May 23, 1983 (as well as at the date plaintiffs' petition was filed here (February 3, 1984)), the defendant was in no worse position to assess further deficiencies than it was in at the date the Form 870-AD became effective (February 9, 1982). That is to say plaintiffs argue that defendant was then "in the same position it was when the agreement was executed," as contemplated in *D.D.I.*, *supra,* and it is, therefore, not barred from effecting additional assessments for taxable years 1976 and 1977 upon the proof of fraud (26 U.S.C. § 6501(c)(1)); nor would it be so barred upon proof of an omission of income in excess of 25 percent of reported gross income (26 U.S.C. § 6501(e)). Defendant, on the other hand, has strenuously insisted that due to the running of the general three-year statute of limitations on assessment on December 31, 1982 (26 U.S.C. § 6501(a)), and a concomitant shift in the burden of proof relative to the necessity of proving fraud as a basis for assessing a *deficiency* for the taxable years 1976 and 1977, defendant was *not* in the *same* position on May 23, 1983, as it was in at the time the Form 870-AD was executed (*i.e.*, January 29, 1982 and February 9, 1982). As discussed below, we find that at the date on which defendant received notice of plaintiffs' repudiation of the Form 870-AD (May 23, 1983), defendant had previously sufficiently relied to its detriment on the Form 870-AD so as to support the application of equitable estoppel to plaintiffs' refund claims. Therefore, regarding the existence of this final element — detrimental reliance, we agree with defendant as to both taxable years 1976 and 1977.

The detriment which we find sufficient to support defendant's claim of estoppel is both traditional, as contemplated under the standards articulated by *Guggenheim* and *D.D.I.,* and unique to the peculiar facts of this case. Starting with an examination of the facts as of the critical date of notice, May 23, 1983, we note that at that date, the three-year statutory period (inclusive of plaintiffs' extensions) had clearly run for both taxable years 1976 and 1977. For each of these two years, plaintiffs' consent to an extension of the three-year statutory period on assessment was effective up to December 31, 1982. The three-year period of limitations on assessments as extended for each year, therefore, expired approximately five months *before* plaintiffs filed their May 23, 1983 claims with the IRS. Consequently, on these facts, we find the precise prejudice which is cited to by the court in both *D.D.I.* and *McGraw-Hill*. Defendant cannot be put back in the "same position" today (or at any time after December 31, 1982) as it held before the Form 870-AD was signed simply because the *general statute* of limitations on additional assessments (§ 6501(a)), extended by § 6501(c)(4), which had *not* then run on February 9, 1982, had in fact expired at the date plaintiffs' claims for refund were filed.

On the foregoing, we are convinced that the *Guggenheim* case is, therefore, dispositive of this issue because substantially the same facts present here gave rise to a finding of prejudice there by the Court of Claims. Citing *cf.* to the case of *R.H. Stearns Co. v. United States*, 291 U.S. 54, 78 L. Ed. 647, 54 S. Ct. 325 (1934), the predecessor court stated:

> At the time the agreement in this case was executed the statute had not run on the collection of further deficiencies, but when the claims for refund were filed the statute had run. It would obviously be inequitable to allow the plaintiff to renounce the agreement when the Commissioner cannot be placed in the same position he was when the agreement was executed. A clear case for the application of the doctrine of equitable estoppel exists and should be applied.

Guggenheim, 77 F. Supp. at 196. For the reasons discussed *infra*, and contrary to plaintiffs' assertions in the case at bar, it is to the running of the *general three-year statute of limitations* (where extended, of course, by § 6501(c)(4)), and *only* to that statute, that we must look to determine the existence of the necessary prejudice to the defendant.

* * *

CONCLUSION

The foregoing outlines the various forms of prejudice inuring to defendant which we have found based upon the detailed facts as presented in this case. Since we have also found the requisite concession or compromise, and a meeting of the minds with regard to extinguishing of the claim, we see no legal basis for denying defendant's motion for summary judgment. In short, the following language in *Guggenheim* thoroughly summarizes our position:

> A reasonable interpretation of the entire document is that what the parties sought to do was to close the case in such a manner that it could not be reopened either for a refund or for the assessment of deficiencies except in the case of fraud, malfeasance, etc. We see no reason for interpreting the document otherwise. * * *

Guggenheim, 111 Ct. Cl. at 181. * * *

It is so ordered.

What if the Kretchmars had offered, just prior to the Claims Court trial, to waive the statute of limitations on assessment so that the IRS could have timely asserted additional deficiencies against the Kretchmars to offset their claimed refund? Would the waiver have prevented the IRS from using the estoppel defense? *Cf. Ihnen v. United States*, 272 F.3d 577 (2001) (taxpayer's offer to waive an expired statute of limitations on assessment made for the first time during oral arguments at the appellate level held untimely).

The *Kretchmar* case highlights the danger of relying on the possibility of litigating an issue once a Form 870-AD has been signed. Why do you think that Form 870-AD contains an agreement that the taxpayer will not seek a refund but Form 870 does not?

From an ethical perspective, should an attorney counsel a client to enter into a settlement agreement with the intention of later repudiating that agreement?

§ 4.03   Closing Agreements

A statutory closing agreement under Code section 7121 is intended to provide the taxpayer with absolute finality with respect to a particular issue or item. Once executed, the formal closing agreement prevents either party from reopening the case absent a showing of fraud, malfeasance, or the misrepresentation of a material fact. "A closing agreement determining tax liability may be entered into at any time before such liability determination becomes a matter within the province of a court of competent jurisdiction and may thereafter be entered into in appropriate circumstances when authorized by the court (*e.g.*, in certain bankruptcy situations)." Rev. Proc. 68-16, 1968-1 C.B. 770. Closing agreements under section 7121 of the Code are ordinarily reflected on Form 866 (for final determination of tax liability) or Form 906 (for final determination of specific matters).

"A closing agreement may be entered into in any case in which there appears to be an advantage in having the case permanently and conclusively closed. . . ." Treas. Reg. § 301.7121-1(a). The regulations provide the following example of when a closing agreement might be appropriate:

> A owns 500 shares of stock in the XYZ Corporation which he purchased prior to March 1, 1913. A is considering selling 200 shares of such stock but is uncertain as to the basis of the stock for the purpose of computing gain. Either prior or subsequent to the sale, a closing agreement may be entered into determining the market value of such stock as of March 1, 1913, which represents the basis for determining gain if it exceeds the adjusted basis otherwise determined as of such date. Not only may the closing agreement determine the basis for computing gain on the sale of the 200 shares of stock, but such an agreement may also determine the basis

(unless or until the law is changed to require the use of some other factor to determine basis) of the remaining 300 shares of stock upon which gain will be computed in a subsequent sale.

Treas. Reg. § 301.7121-1(b)(4).

Revenue Procedure 68-16, 1968-1 C.B. 770, provides further discussion of appropriate uses of closing agreements:

.01 A determination of tax liability by closing agreement may be entered into for good reasons shown by the taxpayer where there is no disadvantage to the Government or where desired by the Government. Representative of acceptable reasons for entering into such agreements are the following circumstances:

1. The taxpayer wishes to definitely establish its tax liability in order that a transaction may be facilitated, such as the sale of its stock.

2. The fiduciary of an estate desires a closing agreement in order that he may be discharged by the court.

3. The fiduciary of a trust or receivership desires a final determination before distribution is made.

4. A corporation in the process of liquidation or dissolution desires a closing agreement in order to wind up its affairs.

5. A taxpayer wishes to fulfill creditors' demands for authentic evidence of the status of its tax liability.

6. Where proposed assessments are contested on the theory that the years are barred and the parties wish to agree, with finality, to some portion or all of the assessments.

7. A taxpayer wishes to assure itself that a controversy between it and the Service is conclusively disposed of.

8. To determine personal holding company tax in order to permit deficiency dividends under section 547 of the Code.

.02 A determination of one or more specific matters may be accomplished by closing agreement for good reasons shown by the taxpayer where there is no disadvantage to the Government or where desired by the Government. A few examples of circumstances that may merit entering into such closing agreements are as follows:

1. To determine cost, fair market value, or adjusted basis as at a given past date. It may be desirable to have both an estate and its legatees or devisees (or both donors and donees) sign such agreements.

* * *

5. To determine the amount of a net operating loss.

6. To provide determinations for disposition of cases involving sections 1311 to 1315 of the Code.

7. To determine an alternative method of adjusting basis under section 1.1017-2 of the Income Tax Regulations as a result of receipt of income from cancellation of indebtedness under section 108(a) of the Code.

* * *

8. To prevent inconsistencies in "whipsaw" situations such as those that could result where a related taxpayer concedes an issue (with the result that the other related party obtains a benefit) and then subsequently, after the statutory period of limitations has expired against the other related party, contests the issue by filing a claim. * * *

9. To determine the consequences of deferred intercompany transactions of domestic public utilities (see section 1.1502-13(j) of the regulations).

10. To determine the amount of income from a transaction, the amounts of deductions or the year of includibility or deductibility.

* * *

As you can see from the Revenue Procedure excerpted above, closing agreements are limited to specific situations that are much narrower than the situations in which a Form 870 or 870-AD might be used to settle a case.

§ 4.04 Settlement of Court Cases

Many cases settle after being docketed in court. As discussed in Chapter 1, the Tax Court, District Courts, and Court of Federal Claims all conduct trials in federal tax cases, with the Tax Court hearing the vast majority of those cases. Post-docketing settlements raise additional issues, such as when a case actually is settled, and what obligations, if any, the IRS has to offer consistent settlements to litigants in related cases. This part of the chapter addresses those issues, focusing primarily on settlement in Tax Court cases.

In an Article III court such as a United States District Court, a mutually agreed upon settlement moots a case, requiring its dismissal. That is because the United States Supreme Court has interpreted the "cases or controversies" clause of Article III of the United States Constitution as prohibiting decision in any "non-justiciable" case. *See, e.g., Honig v. Doe,* 484 U.S. 305, 317 (1988). Article I courts (such as the Tax Court and the Court of Federal Claims) are subject to no such Constitutional restriction.

A Tax Court case that is settled by agreement of the parties is entered by the judge as a "stipulated decision." In Tax Court, however, a concession by one party is not the same as a settlement. If one party offers a full concession and the other party rejects the offer, the Tax Court has the option whether to treat the unilateral concession as a settlement and enter a stipulated decision. In making that determination, the court considers not only the interests of the parties but also the interests of non-parties in the potential precedential value of the case. *See* Leandra Lederman, "Precedent Lost: Why Encourage Settlement, and Why Allow Non-Party Involvement in Settlement?" 75 Notre Dame L. Rev. 221 (1999). Similarly, if one party accepts the other's offer of full concession but reneges prior to executing a decision document, the Tax Court treats the situation like a rejected offer of full concession with the additional factor of the reneging party's prior acceptance of the concession. *See, e.g., Greenlee v. Commissioner*, T.C. Memo. 1985-218; *Smith v. Commissioner*, T.C. Memo. 1965-224.

The Tax Court's jurisprudence on full concessions should be contrasted with its jurisprudence on repudiation of settlement agreements. If one party seeks to be relieved of a settlement made in a case docketed in Tax Court, the Tax Court sets a high threshold for relief from that agreement. *See Dorchester Indus., Inc. v. Commissioner*, 108 T.C. 320, 337 (1997) (reviewed by the court). Under current law,

> The party seeking modification . . . must show that the failure to allow the modification might prejudice him . . . . Discretion should be exercised to allow modification where no substantial injury will be occasioned to the opposing party; refusal to allow modification might result in injustice to the moving party; and the inconvenience to the Court is slight . . . .

Adams v. Commissioner, 85 T.C. 359, 375 (1985) (citations omitted).[19]

If the Tax Court has cancelled the trial date in reliance on a purported settlement agreement, and a party makes a motion to be relieved of that agreement on the eve of trial, the Tax Court will hold the parties to their agreement absent fraud, mistake, or some other factor that vitiates the consent on which the settlement agreement was based. *See Dorchester Indus., supra.; see also Mearkle v. Commissioner*, 87 T.C. 527, 528 (1986), *rev'd and remanded,* 838 F.2d 880 (6th Cir. 1988). Why might the Tax Court, which exercises discretion to enter a settlement in the context of a unilateral offer of full concession, be so strict in its refusal to relieve a party of a settlement agreement in this context? Does a unilateral offer of full concession differ from a bilateral settlement agreement in such a way that the Tax Court should engage in different tests in deciding whether to enter a stipulated decision in each of these situations?

---

[19] However, note that three Tax Court judges joined in a 1997 dissent by Judge Parr that expressed the view that the Tax Court has a right to reject a bilateral settlement agreement:

> I write separately . . . to emphasize that nothing in the majority opinion should be understood to limit the sound discretion of the Court to reject an agreement between the parties, where good cause is shown and the interests of justice require it.
>
> It is easy to imagine a situation, not here present, where an agreement between the parties may not be in the interests of justice. For instance, agreements that would abuse the process of this Court, would usurp the Court's control over its calendar, or that would be contrary to sound public policy should not be enforced.

Dorchester Indus., Inc. v. Commissioner, 108 T.C. 320, 343 (1997) (reviewed by the court) (Parr, J., concurring).

Issues about the finality of settlement also arise when a taxpayer seeks to repudiate a settlement with the IRS and to force the IRS to settle the taxpayer's case on terms the IRS has offered others. In *Slovacek v. United States*, 40 Fed. Cl. 828 (1998), the taxpayers executed a Form 870-L(AD), Settlement Agreement for Partnership Adjustment and Affected Items, that disallowed all losses flowing through from a partnership, and imposed penalties on them. The taxpayers then filed a refund suit on the basis that the statute of limitations had expired before their settlement was executed. As you might expect after reading *Kretchmar*, the court ruled against the taxpayers on that issue, finding, in part, that the taxpayers had waived their right to a refund by signing the Form 870-L(AD). *Slovacek v. United States*, 36 Fed. Cl. 250, 256 (1996). Subsequently, the IRS offered to the partners in the partnership who had not pursued refund claims a more favorable settlement agreement, allowing the deduction of seventeen percent of the partnership losses, and abating the penalties. The Slovaceks formally requested settlement of their case on the same terms the IRS extended to the other partners, but the Department of Justice, handling the case because it had been filed as a refund suit, rejected the offer and refused to settle. The Court of Federal Claims agreed with the government, stating that settlement discretion includes discretion to treat similarly situated cases differently. *Slovacek,* 40 Fed. Cl. at 832 (*citing Bunce v. United States*, 28 Fed. Cl. 500, 509–510 (1993), *aff'd*, 26 F.3d 138 (Fed. Cir. 1994)).

PROBLEMS

1.   Sylvester, who is single, is a highly successful labor attorney with a large Washington, D.C. law firm. During 1999, Sylvester received numerous "business gifts" from one of his clients, including a new BMW roadster and the use of the client's beach house during the month of July. Sylvester consulted with the firm's tax department about the tax consequences of the "gifts" and was told that, under the circumstances, the rental value of the beach house probably did not constitute gross income, but the fair market value of the BMW should be reported. Nevertheless, Sylvester decided not to report either "gift" on his 1999 tax return. Excluding the gifts, Sylvester reported on his 1999 return $220,000 of gross income, $5,000 of which represented interest and dividend income and the remainder of which was salary income.

Sylvester also deducted on his 1999 return various charitable contributions, including weekly contributions of $20 in cash to his church (for which Sylvester did not receive a receipt from the church acknowledging the gifts) and a one-time contribution of 100 shares of stock in a closely held corporation to his alma mater. The book value of the stock was $25 per share. Although Sylvester's ownership in the closely held corporation represented a minority interest, he deducted the value of the stock at its book value, without reducing the valuation for a minority discount. Sylvester's tax return preparer explained to him the risk of reporting the cash contributions without supporting documentation and the potential controversy over the appropriate valuation of the gifted stock.

Sylvester was audited by the IRS during 2002. At the conclusion of the audit late in 2002, he received a 30-day letter asserting that the value of the BMW was reportable as gross income and that the appropriate value for the contributed stock was $15 per share. The 30-day letter contained a recalculation of his 1999 tax liability (with interest) resulting from the failure to report the BMW and the stock revaluation. No penalties were asserted. The examining agent did not ask Sylvester about the use of the beach house, nor did the agent mention the charitable contributions to Sylvester's church. Moreover, neither of these issues was mentioned in the Revenue Agent's Report attached to the 30-day letter. Sylvester believes he has a possibility of establishing that the BMW did not constitute gross income. He also believes that, under applicable law, the minority discount imposed by the IRS was excessive and should not have exceeded 10 percent.

A.   Should Sylvester pay the asserted deficiency in the 30-day letter and settle on that basis? How would you advise him?

   i.   If he decides to settle, should he execute Form 870 or 870-AD?

   ii.   How does the potential shift of the burden of proof in a litigated tax case from Sylvester to the IRS under Code section 7491 impact on Sylvester's decision to settle based on the asserted deficiency in the 30-day letter? If Sylvester decides to take the case to the IRS Appeals Office, how would the possible burden of proof shift affect his settlement negotiations?

B.   Regardless of your advice in part A, Sylvester would like to continue settlement negotiations with the IRS. If a settlement is not reached, he would prefer to contest the deficiency in Tax Court, rather than pay the asserted amount and sue for a refund. Having received the 30-day letter, would Sylvester be better off procedurally (a) requesting an Appeals hearing in response to the 30-day letter or (b) ignoring the 30-day letter and waiting for (or even requesting) a notice of deficiency and filing suit in Tax Court? What factors should he consider?

2.   Clara is negotiating a closing agreement with the IRS to reflect an agreed valuation of certain rare books that Clara donated to a charitable organization. Does the closing agreement need to reflect the IRS's determination of Clara's entire tax liability for the taxable year in question in order to be valid under section 7121?

3.   Trina invested in a partnership that was marketed to her as a tax shelter. She and many other investors have been audited

by the IRS. After Trina received a 30-day letter and filed a tax protest, the IRS offered Trina a settlement. The settlement, which would be recorded on Form 870-AD, would allow 10 percent of Trina's deductions. Trina has heard that other investors in the partnership have filed Tax Court petitions, and she thinks a Tax Court judge might be sympathetic to allowing a larger share of the deductions. She asks you the following questions.

    A.   If she signs the 870-AD, can she preserve her right to petition the Tax Court?

    B.   If she signs the 870-AD, can she preserve her right to pursue a refund claim for the amounts she will pay over to the IRS with the 870-AD?

    C.   If she signs the 870-AD and does not petition the Tax Court or file a refund claim, and the Tax Court issues favorable decisions to other investors, will the IRS be required to modify the 870-AD to reflect the favorable Tax Court decisions?

4.   Brad has filed a tax protest on behalf of one of his clients, and he is preparing to negotiate with the IRS Appeals Division for a settlement. Brad recently realized that access to the IRS's file on his client might help his settlement efforts. He is considering sending a FOIA request to the IRS.

    A.   Do you advise that he follow this approach?

    B.   Would your answer to A. differ if Brad were pursuing the IRS Appeal on a docketed basis?

5.   Marina's tax deficiency case has been docketed in Tax Court for several months. A month before the scheduled trial date, the IRS offers Marina a settlement.

    A.   Does Marina need Tax Court permission to accept the settlement?

    B.   If Marina refuses the settlement, can the Tax Court require her to accept it?

    C.   Assume that Marina accepts the settlement.

        i.   What result will the settlement agreement have on the Tax Court case?

        ii.   If Marina reneges on the settlement shortly after accepting it, can the Tax Court require her to adhere to her acceptance of the settlement?

6.   Until 2000, Laura Black worked in a high school cafeteria, earning approximately $15,000 per year. In 2000, the school experienced budget problems and let her go. After looking for a similar job for months, Laura decided to devote herself full-time to the activity she had previously pursued only in the summer months, deep sea fishing. Since 1990, Laura had fished

for two months every summer, reporting approximately $5,000 per year as earnings from fishing.

Laura had never owned a boat but had always rented a small boat for the months she needed one. In 2000, she decided to try to purchase a boat. Her savings were minimal, so she decided to try to buy a new boat with financing from the seller. However, she soon discovered that the payments would be more than she could comfortably manage. She began looking to buy a used boat and soon found an appropriate one for a reasonable price, $100,000. She looked into obtaining a bank loan but discovered that interest rates were more than she could afford.

After the summer of 2000, during which Laura again rented a boat, Laura called her relatives and asked to borrow some money. Several of her relatives were surprisingly generous, particularly her extended family living overseas. In addition, one of her former co-workers, Dan, took up a collection at the high school and gave Laura a check totaling $2,000, representing the funds he had collected. Laura discovered that the used boat was still available and agreed to buy it. With the $2,000 check, a little of her own money, and the approximately $96,000 her relatives had furnished, some of which was in cash, Laura purchased in 2000 a cashier's check from her bank, made payable to the owner of the boat.

In 2002, Laura was audited and the IRS sent Laura a revenue agent's report and a 30-day letter asserting that the $100,000 used to purchase the cashier's check was unreported income from her fishing activity. Laura tells you that most of the $96,000 was loans, although she does not have documentation in all instances and has not paid any interest. She tells you that her extended family is very close and generally does not require documentation of loans to family members. She also tells you it is their custom not to pay interest but to repay the loan as soon as possible, and perhaps pay a "bonus" at the end to the lender, if that is financially feasible. Laura thinks some of her relatives may not expect repayment at all, but she intends to repay them when she can. Laura said she knows that Dan and her former co-workers at the high school intended to give her a gift, and she does not plan to pay them back. She tells you that although it is possible to make $100,000 in a summer of deep sea fishing, her operation is too small to earn that much. According to Laura, she has tried to be honest in reporting her earnings on her tax return, but she cannot be sure she was completely accurate because she was often paid in cash and did not always keep good records.

Draft a protest for Laura and prepare a power of attorney (Form 2848) for her to sign. Laura's address and telephone number are 1478 Hickory Drive, Macon, GA 38746; 912-752-5555. Her Social security number is 878-46-4827. The 30-day letter is dated August 3, 2002, and the symbols of the letter of transmittal are "Letter 951(DO)."

Chapter 5

RESTRICTIONS ON ASSESSMENT OF TAX

Reading Assignment: Code §§ 1311–1314, 6201, 6203, 6211, 6212, 6213(a)–(d), 6303(a), 6401(a), 6501(a), (b), (c)(1)–(4), (d), (e)(1), 6502(a), 6503(a), 7421(a), 7502, 7503.

§ 5.01 Introduction

"Assessment" is merely the IRS's formal recording of a tax liability. *See* I.R.C. § 6203. In essence, it is nothing more than a bookkeeping entry. However, assessment is a key act; the IRS cannot legally collect tax through its administrative collection powers without first assessing it.[1] As discussed in Chapter 12, the IRS's lien and levy powers depend on a notice and demand for payment, *see* I.R.C. §§ 6321, 6331(a), the issuance of which, in turn, cannot be made prior to assessment. *See* I.R.C. § 6303(a). This chapter discusses the various types of assessments, the statutes of limitations on assessment of tax, and the statutory mitigation provisions, which, in certain circumstances, can allow reopening of a year closed by the statute of limitations.

§ 5.02 Types of Assessments

There are four main types of assessments: summary assessments, deficiency assessments, jeopardy assessments, and termination assessments. The IRS can summarily assess an admitted tax liability, such as the amount a taxpayer reflects in his tax return for the year. Deficiency assessments require that the IRS first send the taxpayer a timely notice of deficiency, *see, e.g., Philadelphia & Reading Corp. v. United States*, 944 F.2d 1063, 1072 (3d Cir. 1991), and give the taxpayer the period required by statute, generally 90 days, to petition the Tax Court, *see* I.R.C. §§ 6212, 6213. For reasons discussed more fully below, the procedures leading to assessment and collection of a deficiency may take months or even years to complete. While these procedures are designed to give taxpayers a means of contesting the IRS's proposed assessment before collection proceedings begin, taxpayers may be tempted to utilize these delays to avoid paying tax that is properly owed. The interest provisions, discussed in Chapter 11, reduce this incentive but may not eliminate it. Therefore, Code sections 6851 and 6861 allow for immediate assessment where the IRS believes that assessment or collection of the tax will be jeopardized by delay. Section 6851 further allows the IRS to terminate the taxpayer's tax year mid-year. Procedures for summary, deficiency, jeopardy and termination assessments are discussed in further detail below.

---

[1] Chapter 8 considers the question of whether the IRS is legally obligated to refund to the taxpayer a voluntary remittance of tax made while the statute of limitations was open but never formally assessed before the statute expired.

[A] Summary Assessments

Most tax receipts are assessed based on a taxpayer's "voluntarily" submitted tax return. Code section 6201(a) authorizes the IRS to summarily (immediately) assess and collect any tax computed and shown to be due on a taxpayer's original tax return, as well as any additional taxes computed and shown to be due on a subsequently filed amended return. *See also* Treas. Reg. § 301.6211-1(a). The IRS is not required to send the taxpayer a notice of deficiency. Assessment takes place once an IRS officer signs a summary record of assessment (Form 23C) containing identifying information about the taxpayer and the character and amount of the tax liability. Treas. Reg. § 301.6203-1.

The IRS may also use its summary assessment authority in other instances. If the taxpayer waives the statutory restrictions on deficiency assessment or otherwise fails to take advantage of the deficiency procedures within the time period specified in the Code, the IRS may immediately assess the tax and proceed with collection activities. I.R.C. § 6213(c), (d). In addition, the Code authorizes the IRS to summarily assess any additional tax due as a result of a mathematical or clerical error made by the taxpayer on the return. However, before so doing, the IRS must notify the taxpayer of the alleged error and include an explanation of the basis for recomputation. The taxpayer is given 60 days from the date the notice of assessment is sent to contest the error by filing a request for an abatement of the assessment. Whether or not the IRS agrees with the taxpayer's position, it must abate the proposed summary assessment upon receipt of the request. At that point, any attempt by the IRS to reassess the tax must be made pursuant to the deficiency procedures. I.R.C. § 6213(b). The statute defines a "mathematical or clerical error" to include arithmetic errors, inconsistent entries on the return, omissions of information necessary to properly substantiate a return item, and deductions or credits that exceed limits provided in the Code. I.R.C. § 6213(g)(2).

[B] General Restrictions on Deficiency Assessments

Before assessing a deficiency in income, estate and gift taxes, and before assessing most penalties, the IRS must first send the taxpayer a "notice of deficiency" or "statutory notice," provided for in Code section 6212.[2] The formal requirements of a notice of deficiency (also called a 90-day letter) are discussed in more detail in Chapter 7. Once the IRS sends the notice of deficiency, it cannot assess the tax during the 90-day period (or 150-day period, if applicable) following issuance of the notice (commonly called the "prohibited period"). I.R.C. § 6213(a). This assessment delay gives the taxpayer an opportunity to contest the deficiency by petitioning the Tax Court,

---

[2] A fundamental element of the deficiency procedures is the right afforded the taxpayer to seek judicial review (in the Tax Court) prior to assessment. In other cases–most commonly employment taxes imposed under Subtitle C of the Code–the IRS can immediately assess tax without a notice of deficiency and without granting the taxpayer the opportunity for pre-assessment judicial review. Once employment taxes have been assessed, the taxpayer's sole remedy is to follow the refund procedures in order to recoup the previously paid tax. Certain types of civil tax penalties, including the preparer and information reporting penalties, also may be assessed by the IRS without regard to the deficiency procedures.

the only court that grants taxpayers pre-assessment review. If the taxpayer petitions the Tax Court, the "prohibited period" lasts until the Tax Court's decision becomes final.[3] *Id.* If the IRS violates this prohibition, the taxpayer can obtain an injunction and a refund of any tax collected, as this is a stated exception to the Anti-Injunction Act, section 7421. *See* I.R.C. §§ 6213(a); 7421.

> *Example*: The IRS mails Andrew a notice of deficiency on December 1, 2003. It is sent to his last known address in Arlington, Virginia. Andrew receives the notice on December 5. Unless Andrew signs a Form 870 permitting immediate assessment of the deficiency, the IRS is prohibited from assessing the deficiency until March 1, 2004, because Andrew has until February 29 to petition the Tax Court. If Andrew petitions the Tax Court, the IRS cannot assess any deficiency determined by the Tax Court until after the Tax Court's decision becomes final.

[C] Jeopardy and Termination Assessments

Section 6861 allows for immediate assessment where the IRS believes that assessment or collection of the tax will be jeopardized by delay. The IRS will then send notice and demand for payment, I.R.C. § 6861(a), and if it has not already sent a notice of deficiency, the IRS must mail one to the taxpayer within 60 days of the assessment. I.R.C. § 6861(b). Treasury regulations set forth the most commonly encountered conditions under which a jeopardy assessment may be made: (1) the IRS believes the taxpayer is designing to depart quickly from the United States or to conceal himself; (2) the IRS believes the taxpayer is planning to quickly place his property beyond the reach of the Government by concealing the property, dissipating it, transferring it to other persons, or removing it from the country; or (3) the IRS believes the taxpayer's financial solvency is imperiled. *See* Treas. Reg. § 301.6861-1 (referring to the conditions described in Treas. Reg. § 1.6851-1).

For these same reasons, the IRS may make a termination assessment against the taxpayer pursuant to section 6851. For the most part, the procedures relating to jeopardy and termination assessments are the same. A jeopardy assessment is employed when a deficiency is determined by the IRS after the end of the taxable year to which the assessment relates. A termination assessment, in contrast, is utilized when collection is put in jeopardy before the taxpayer's taxable year has ended. As its name implies, a termination assessment terminates the taxable year for the purpose of computing the amount of tax to be assessed and collected. Section 6851(b) requires the IRS to mail the taxpayer a notice of deficiency for the full taxable year within 60 days of the later of the due date of the taxpayer's return or the date the return is filed.

Under the Code, the Chief Counsel of the IRS or his delegate must approve, in writing, any jeopardy or termination assessment. I.R.C. § 7429(a)(1)(A). Because of the drastic consequences resulting from these types of assessments, Congress enacted an expedited administrative and judicial review process. *See*

---

[3] In general, a Tax Court decision becomes final when the time for all appeals has run. *See* I.R.C. § 7481. However, assessment and collection are not stayed during a taxpayer's appeal unless the taxpayer files a bond. *See* I.R.C. § 7485.

I.R.C. § 7429. Section 7429 requires the IRS, within five days of making such an assessment, to provide the taxpayer with a written statement of the information on which the IRS relied in making the assessment or levy. I.R.C. § 7429(a)(1)(B). The taxpayer then has 30 days to request administrative review. I.R.C. § 7429(a)(2). Section 7429(b) provides for expedited follow-up judicial review in the United States District Courts. In these proceedings, the IRS bears the burden of establishing that it acted reasonably. I.R.C. § 7429(g). The taxpayer also has the option of filing a bond to stay collection. *See* I.R.C. § 6863.

§ 5.03   The Statutes of Limitations on Assessment of Tax

[A]   General Rules

Section 6501 contains the statutory periods for assessing tax. The general rule is that the IRS must assess tax within three years of when the return was filed.[4] I.R.C. § 6501(a). What constitutes a "return" for this purpose is discussed in Chapter 2 in connection with the *Beard* case, and in this chapter in the *Badaracco* case, reproduced below. The date of assessment is the date that the assessment officer signs the summary record of assessment. Treas. Reg. § 301.6203-1. To confirm that date, the taxpayer may request a copy of the summary record, which section 6203 requires the IRS to furnish.

For purposes of section 6501, an early return is deemed filed on its due date. I.R.C. § 6501(b)(1). For example, the statute of limitations on a 1998 return, which was due April 15, 1999, and was actually filed on April 2, 1999, would expire April 15, 2002. An amended return filed after the due date, although it modifies or adds to the original return, generally has no effect on the period of limitations.[5] Thus, when an original return is subsequently amended, the statute of limitations normally begins to run from the date the original return was filed, not from the date the amended return was filed. *Zellerbach Paper Co. v. Helvering*, 293 U.S. 172 (1934).

The filing date of a return is generally the date on which the return is delivered to the IRS. Code section 7502, which allows a taxpayer who properly mails his return to rely on the postmark date as the date of delivery, applies to determine the date of filing if the return arrives after the due date.[6] *Hotel*

---

[4] If a partnership or S corporation is audited pursuant to the TEFRA procedures specified in section 6229, the statute of limitations for assessing tax against a partner or S corporation shareholder with respect to an item of income or deduction generated at the entity level is calculated based on the time the entity files its information return. I.R.C. § 6229(a)(1). If the unified audit procedures do not apply, the statute of limitations is based on the time the individual equity holder files his own return. *See* I.R.C. § 6501. For example, assume that a calendar year partnership files its 1998 information return on March 1, 1999. An individual partner in the partnership does not file his individual return reporting his share of the partnership's income for 1998 until April 15, 1999. The limitations period with respect to that individual's share of partnership items begins to run on April 16, not March 2.

[5] However, when a taxpayer files an amended return reflecting additional income tax liability within 60 days before the last date for assessment, the IRS is granted an additional 60 days beyond the applicable limitations period in which to assess tax. I.R.C. § 6501(c)(7).

[6] On January 10, 2001, the IRS issued final regulations under section 7502. *See* T.D. 8932. Because the regulations, which replace temporary regulations, address the treatment of a claim for refund made on a late-filed return, they are discussed in Chapter 8.

Equities Corp. v. Commissioner, 65 T.C. 528 (1975), *aff'd,* 546 F.2d 725 (1976). If the return is mailed late, section 7502 cannot operate, so the return is not considered filed until it is actually received by the IRS.

> *Example*: Tara mails her return to the IRS on Friday, April 15, and it arrives on Monday, April 17. Because Tara mailed her return on time but it arrived late, her return is deemed filed on April 15, if she complied with the mailing requirements of section 7502. If, instead, Tara had mailed her return on Monday, April 17, and it arrived on Thursday, April 20, her return would be deemed filed April 20.

In addition to section 7502, section 7503, relating to due dates falling on a Saturday, Sunday, or legal holiday, may also apply to determine the date on which the return was filed. Assume, for example, that April 15, the required filing date for individual calendar-year taxpayers, falls on a Saturday. The taxpayer mails his return from the Post Office that Saturday, April 15, and it arrives on April 18, so it is deemed filed on April 15 under section 7502. Pursuant to section 7503, the taxpayer's return would still be considered timely if filed on Monday, April 17. In the latter case, for purposes of calculating the statute of limitations under section 6501, does the three-year period begin to run on April 15 or April 17? The following Revenue Ruling addresses that question.

REVENUE RULING 81-269
1981-2 C.B. 243

ISSUE

When will the period of limitation for assessment of tax expire in the following situations?

FACTS

Situation 1. A, an individual taxpayer, files his or her federal income tax return on a calendar year basis. A filed the return for 1978 with the Internal Revenue Service on March 1, 1979.

Situation 2. B, an individual taxpayer, also files on a calendar year basis. B filed the return for 1978 on Monday, April 16, 1979.

LAW AND ANALYSIS

Section 6072(a) of the Internal Revenue Code provides that individual income tax returns made on the basis of the calendar year must be filed on or before April 15 of the following year.

Section 6501(a) of the Code provides the general rule that tax must be assessed within 3 years after the return was filed.

Section 6501(b)(1) of the Code provides that, for purposes of section 6501, a return filed before the last day prescribed by the Code or regulations is considered as filed on the last day.

Section 7503 of the Code provides that when the last day for performing any act falls on a Saturday, Sunday, or legal holiday, performance of the act is considered timely if it is performed on the next day that is not a Saturday, Sunday, or legal holiday.

The purpose of section 7503 of the Code is to extend the time for filing a document when the last day for filing is a Saturday, Sunday, or legal holiday. Section 7503 does not change the date prescribed for performing an act, nor does it provide that an act performed on the day following a Saturday, Sunday, or legal holiday will be deemed to have been performed on the actual due date. Rev. Rul. 75-344, 1975-2 C.B. 487.

In *Situation 1*, section 7503 of the Code does not operate to change the "date prescribed for filing" to April 16. Accordingly, because an early return is deemed filed on the date prescribed for filing the return, which remains April 15, 1979, the period of limitations under section 6501(a) starts running from April 15.

In *Situation 2*, while the return filed on April 16 is considered timely filed under section 7503 of the Code, it is not deemed to have been filed on April 15. In this case, the period of limitations under section 6501(a) starts running from the actual date of filing, or April 16. See Brown v. United States, 391 F.2d 653 (Ct. Cl. 1968).

HOLDINGS

Situation 1. The period of limitation for assessment of tax (or mailing of the notice of deficiency) will expire April 15, 1982.

Situation 2. The period of limitation for assessment of tax (or mailing of the notice of deficiency) will expire April 16, 1982.

Note that section 7503 may apply to the *expiration* of the statute of limitations, as well. That is, if the last day of the statute of limitations on assessment were to fall on a Saturday, Sunday, or legal holiday, section 7503 of the Code would operate to extend that period to the next day that is not a Saturday, Sunday, or legal holiday.

In *Estate of Mitchell v. Commissioner*, 250 F.3d 696 (9th Cir. 2001),[7] a case involving the valuation of stock held by the estate of the famous hairdresser Paul Mitchell, the Estate had received a six month extension of time to file its estate tax return, postponing the filing deadline from January 21, 1990 to July 21, 1990. July 21, 1990 fell on a Saturday. The Estate actually mailed the return on Friday, July 20, 1990, and it arrived at the IRS on Monday, July 23, 1990.

Both the Tax Court and the Court of Appeals for the Ninth Circuit held section 7502 inapplicable because the fact that the filing deadline would otherwise end on a Saturday rendered section 7503 applicable to extend the

---

[7] Much of *Estate of Mitchell* is reproduced in Chapter 7 in connection with its discussion of arbitrary notices of deficiency.

deadline to Monday, July 23, 1990. As discussed above, section 7502 only applies when a timely mailed document arrives *late*. Under the courts' analysis, the return arrived on time, and therefore was deemed filed on the date it was *received*, Monday, July 23, 1990. Under Revenue Ruling 81-269, when did the statute of limitations on assessment start running? The IRS mailed its notice of deficiency to the Estate on July 21, 1993. Was it timely? What if the Estate's return, mailed on Friday, July 20, 1990, had arrived at the IRS on Tuesday, July 24, 1990—would a notice of deficiency mailed to the Estate on July 21, 1993 have been timely?

[B] Exceptions to the Three-Year Statutory Period

[1] Request for Prompt Assessment

Although the general limitations period on assessment of tax is three years, there are several exceptions.[8] Under section 6501(d), the executor of an estate or a liquidating corporation may make a "request for prompt assessment" that will shorten the limitations period to 18 months. In the case of an estate, the prompt assessment procedures apply to any tax (other than estate tax) for which a return is required and for which the decedent or the estate may be liable. An executor might request prompt assessment in order to close the estate before making distributions to the beneficiaries. A corporation that has dissolved or is being dissolved will request prompt assessment for the benefit of its shareholders or, if it has been the target of an acquisition, the acquiring corporation. The procedural prerequisites surrounding a request for prompt assessment are in section 6501(d).

[2] Substantial Omission of Items

Statutory limitations periods longer than three years apply in certain cases. Under section 6501(e), if the return reflects a "substantial omission of items," a six-year period applies. A "substantial omission of items" includes an omission "from gross income [of] an amount properly includible therein which is in excess of 25 percent of the amount of gross income stated in the return," I.R.C. § 6501(e)(1)(A). The six-year statute does not apply unless an *entire item* is omitted. *See The Colony, Inc. v. Commissioner*, 357 U.S. 28 (1958).

The deficiencies in *The Colony, Inc.* arose out of a determination that the taxpayer had understated the amount of its realized gain resulting from the sale of certain lots. The understatement resulted from the taxpayer's over-statement of its adjusted basis in the lots by including unallowable develop-ment costs in the basis. The Tax Court held that the extended statute of limitations under section 6501(e) applied, taking the view that the statutory language, " 'omits from gross income an amount properly includible therein,' embraced not merely the omission from a return of an item of income received by or accruing to a taxpayer, but also an understatement of gross income resulting from a taxpayer's miscalculation of profits through the erroneous

---

[8] Section 6501 also contains subsections relating to various specialized limitations periods that are not further discussed in this chapter, such as limitations periods applicable to holding companies and foreign tax credits.

inclusion of an excessive item of cost." The Supreme Court took a different view:

> The Commissioner also suggests that in enacting § 275(c) [currently I.R.C. § 6501(e), Eds.] Congress was primarily concerned with providing for a longer period of limitations where returns contained relatively large errors adversely affecting the Treasury, and that effect can be given this purpose only by adopting the Government's broad construction of the statute. But this theory does not persuade us. For if the mere size of the error had been the principal concern of Congress, one might have expected to find the statute cast in terms of errors in the total tax due or in total taxable net income. We have been unable to find any solid support for the Government's theory in the legislative history. Instead, * * * this history shows to our satisfaction that the Congress intended an exception to the usual three-year statute of limitations only in the restricted type of situation already described.
>
> We think that in enacting § 275(c) Congress manifested no broader purpose than to give the Commissioner an additional two [now three, Eds.] years to investigate tax returns in cases where, because of a taxpayer's omission to report some taxable item, the Commissioner is at a special disadvantage in detecting errors. In such instances the return on its face provides no clue to the existence of the omitted item. On the other hand, when, as here, the understatement of a tax arises from an error in reporting an item disclosed on the face of the return the Commissioner is at no such disadvantage. And this would seem to be so whether the error be one affecting "gross income" or one, such as overstated deductions, affecting other parts of the return. To accept the Commissioner's interpretation and to impose a five-year [now six-year, Eds.] limitation when such errors affect "gross income," but a three-year limitation when they do not, not only would be to read § 275(c) more broadly than is justified by the evident reason for its enactment, but also to create a patent incongruity in the tax law. * * *

The Colony, Inc. at 36–37.

What if, instead, the taxpayer reports a receipt as gross income, but understates the amount of that receipt? Does/should the extended period apply under these circumstances? Notice also section 6501(e)(1)(A)(ii), which provides that "[i]n determining the amount omitted from gross income, there shall not be taken into account any amount which is omitted from gross income stated in the return if such amount is disclosed in the return, or in a statement attached to the return, in a manner adequate to apprise the Secretary of the nature and amount of such item."

If the six-year period does apply, does it apply only to the omitted item, or to the entire tax year? The Tax Court answered that question in *Colestock*:

COLESTOCK v. COMMISSIONER
United States Tax Court
102 T.C. 380 (1994)

PANUTHOS, CHIEF SPECIAL TRIAL JUDGE:

This matter is before the Court on a motion for partial summary judgment filed by Stephen G. Colestock and Susan F. Colestock (petitioners). Petitioners seek partial summary judgment that an increased deficiency and related additions to tax asserted by respondent in an amendment to answer are time barred by virtue of the general 3-year period of limitations prescribed in section 6501(a).

The issue for decision concerns the scope of the 6-year period of limitations prescribed in section 6501(e)(1)(A). Specifically, we must decide whether section 6501(e)(1)(A) extends the assessment period with respect to a taxpayer's entire tax liability for a particular taxable year or whether the provision simply extends the period for assessment with respect to those items constituting a substantial omission of gross income.

* * *

BACKGROUND

On or about April 22, 1985, petitioners filed a joint Federal income tax return for the 1984 taxable year. Petitioners filed an amended return for 1984 on or about October 28, 1985.

By statutory notice of deficiency dated April 15, 1991, respondent determined deficiencies in and additions to petitioners' Federal income tax. * * * The deficiency in tax is attributable to respondent's determination that petitioners failed to report taxable income arising from transactions involving a corporation known as Hunter Industries, Inc.

Petitioners filed a timely petition for redetermination with this Court. The petition includes an affirmative allegation that respondent erred in issuing a deficiency notice to petitioners more than 3 years after the filing of petitioners' tax return for the 1984 taxable year. Respondent filed a timely answer to the petition, including therein an allegation that the 6-year period of limitations set forth in section 6501(e)(1)(A) is applicable in this case. Petitioners filed a reply to respondent's answer in which they allege that the 6-year period of limitations does not apply.

Respondent subsequently filed a motion for leave to file an amendment to answer out of time and lodged an amendment to answer with the Court. We granted respondent's motion for leave to file an amendment to answer out of time over petitioners' objection, and respondent's amendment to answer was filed. Respondent's amendment to answer includes allegations that petitioners are liable for an increased deficiency and additions to tax as the result of the disallowance of a portion of a depreciation deduction claimed on petitioners' 1984 return. Petitioners filed a reply to respondent's amendment to answer in which they deny the allegations set forth in the amendment to answer and allege that respondent is barred by the applicable period of limitations from claiming the increased deficiency.

In their motion for partial summary judgment, petitioners argue that the general 3-year period of limitations prescribed in section 6501(a) bars respondent from seeking the increased deficiency and additions to tax set forth in respondent's amendment to answer. In conjunction with this argument, petitioners maintain that respondent cannot rely on the 6-year period of limitations prescribed in section 6501(e)(1)(A) because that provision only applies to items of omitted gross income in excess of 25 percent of the amount of gross income reported in the particular return. Respondent objects to petitioners' motion for partial summary judgment asserting that the 6-year period of limitations does apply to the increased deficiency, notwithstanding that it is attributable to a disallowed depreciation deduction, so long as respondent can otherwise establish a substantial omission of gross income on petitioners' 1984 return.

DISCUSSION

* * *

In sum, respondent generally may claim an increased deficiency any time at or before trial in the Tax Court if such deficiency could have been included in the original notice of deficiency mailed to the taxpayer. Smith v. Commissioner, 925 F.2d 250, 254 (8th Cir. 1991), *affg.* T.C. Memo. 1989-432; Teitelbaum v. Commissioner, 346 F.2d 266, 267 (7th Cir. 1965), *affg.* T.C. Memo. 1964-141.

As indicated, petitioners assert that the increased deficiency and additions to tax set forth in respondent's amendment to answer could not have been included in the original deficiency notice that was mailed to petitioners almost 6 years after the filing of their 1984 return. In petitioners' view, a deficiency notice issued under the 6-year period of limitations prescribed in section 6501(e)(1)(A) may only include deficiencies in tax directly attributable to items constituting a substantial omission of gross income. Because the increased deficiency and related additions to tax that respondent asserts in her amendment to answer are attributable to the disallowance of a depreciation deduction (as opposed to an item of omitted gross income), petitioners contend that the 6-year period of limitations under section 6501(e)(1)(A) is not applicable and that respondent's determination with respect to the depreciation item is otherwise barred under section 6501(a). Respondent reads section 6501(e)(1)(A) more broadly.

* * *

Neither party cites a case involving the specific question presented.

As a preliminary matter, we observe that the parties' comparisons of the various provisions set forth in section 6501 result in conflicting, yet fairly plausible, interpretations of section 6501(e)(1)(A). Nonetheless, an analysis of the provision in conjunction with a review of its legislative history compels the conclusion that petitioners' interpretation must fail.

It has been said that limitations statutes barring the collection of taxes otherwise due and unpaid are strictly construed in favor of respondent. *See* Badaracco v. Commissioner, 464 U.S. 386, 391–392 (1984); *see also* Bufferd v. Commissioner, 506 U.S. [927], 113 S. Ct. 927, 930 n.6 (1993); Northern Ind. Pub. Serv. Co. v. Commissioner, 101 T.C. 294, 300 (1993); Estate of Smith v. Commissioner, 94 T.C. 872, 874 (1990). Further, it is a well-established rule of statutory construction that statutes are to be construed so as to give effect to their plain and ordinary meaning unless to do so would produce absurd or futile results. United States v. American Trucking Associations, 310 U.S. 534, 543–544 (1940).

* * *

Notably, the prefatory language of subsection (e)(1) provides that the provision covers "any tax imposed by subtitle A" — a reference to the Federal income tax. In this regard, we interpret the phrase "the tax may be assessed * * * at any time within 6 years after the return was filed" as referring to any tax imposed by subtitle A for the particular taxable year. Sec. 6501(e)(1)(A). In other words, if the taxpayer omits the requisite amount of gross income from his return, the taxpayer's entire tax liability for the particular taxable year is subject to the 6-year limitations period.

* * *

We reject petitioners' interpretation of section 6501(e)(1)(A) under which the phrase "the tax may be assessed" is read as referring solely to a deficiency in tax resulting from an omission of gross income from the return. In our view, Congress would have used more exacting language if petitioners' interpretation were intended. *Cf.* sec. 6501(h). In the absence of such exacting terms, we decline to otherwise limit the scope of section 6501(e)(1)(A).

Our interpretation of section 6501(e)(1)(A) finds support in the legislative history of the provision. Section 6501(e)(1)(A) was originally codified as section 275(c) under the Revenue Act of 1934, ch. 277, tit. I, 48 Stat. 680. As originally introduced in a preliminary report of a subcommittee of the House Committee on Ways and Means, however, a proposal was made to add the provision to then-existing section 276 of the Revenue Act of 1934. The preliminary report states in pertinent part:

> Section 276 provides for the assessment of the tax without regard to the statute of limitations in case of a failure to file a return or in case of a false or fraudulent return with intent to evade tax.

> Your subcommittee is of the opinion that the limitation period on assessments should also not apply to certain cases where the taxpayer has understated his gross income on his return by a large amount, even though fraud with intent to evade tax cannot be established. It is, therefore, recommended that the statute of limitations shall not apply where the taxpayer has failed to disclose in

his return an amount of gross income in excess of 25 percent of the amount of the gross income stated in the return. The Government should not be penalized when a taxpayer is so negligent as to leave out items of such magnitude from his return. [Preliminary Report to the House Comm. on Ways and Means, 73d Cong., 2d Sess. 21 (Comm. Print 1933).]

* * *

The subcommittee's proposal was adopted by the House Committee on Ways and Means as reflected in H. Rept. 704, 73d Cong., 2d Sess. 35 (1934), which states:

> Section 276(a). No return or false return: The present law permits the Government to assess the tax without regard to the statute of limitations in case of failure to file a return or in case of a fraudulent return. The change in this section continues this policy, but enlarges the scope of this provision to include cases wherein the taxpayer understates gross income on his return by an amount which is in excess of 25 percent of the gross income stated in the return. It is not believed that taxpayers who are so negligent as to leave out of their returns items of such magnitude should be accorded the privilege of pleading the bar of the statute.

The Senate Committee on Finance took a slightly different approach to the issue as reflected in S. Rept. 558, 73d Cong., 2d Sess. 43–44 (1934), which states in pertinent part:

> Your committee is in general accord with the policy expressed in this section of the House bill. However, it is believed that in the case of a taxpayer who makes an honest mistake, it would be unfair to keep the statute open indefinitely. * * * Accordingly, your committee has provided for a 5-year statute in such cases.

In sum, the Committee on Finance resolved that, in fairness to the taxpayer, the period of limitations should be held to 5 years as opposed to allowing the assessment period to stay open indefinitely. H. Conf. Rept. 1385, 73d Cong., 2d Sess. 25 (1939), 1939-2 C.B. (Part 2) 627, 634, reveals that the Committee on Ways and Means accepted the change proposed by the Senate.

Viewed in its entirety, the legislative history indicates that Congress intended for the extended period of limitations under former section 275(c) to apply broadly in the same general manner as in the case of a fraudulent return. * * * Neither [the statute's] text nor legislative history limits the scope of the statute as petitioners contend.

Based on the preceding discussion, we conclude that, if the 6-year period of limitations is otherwise applicable, respondent was not barred at the time of the issuance of the deficiency notice in this case from determining a deficiency attributable to the disallowed depreciation deduction. It follows that respondent is not precluded from claiming an increased deficiency with respect to that item in her amendment to answer. *See* Teitelbaum v. Commissioner, 346 F.2d 266, 267 (7th Cir. 1965), *affg.* T.C. Memo. 1964-141. Of course, should respondent fail to prove that there was an omission of more than 25 percent of the amount of gross income stated in petitioners' return, then respondent would be barred from assessing both the deficiency determined in the notice of deficiency and the additional deficiency asserted in the amendment to answer.

To reflect the foregoing, an order denying petitioners' motion for partial summary judgment will be issued.

---

[3]   False or Fraudulent Return

If the taxpayer files no return, a false return, or a fraudulent return, the statute of limitations is unlimited. I.R.C. § 6501(c)(1)–(3). How can the taxpayer cure the filing of "no return" in order to start the statute of limitations running? Will the statute then be deemed to run from the date that the return was due?

What if the taxpayer intentionally files a fraudulent return and then files an amended, nonfraudulent return—which limitations period applies?[9] The United States Supreme Court resolved that issue in the following case:

BADARACCO v. COMMISSIONER
United States Supreme Court
464 U.S. 386 (1984)

JUSTICE BLACKMUN delivered the opinion of the Court.

These cases focus upon § 6501 of the Internal Revenue Code of 1954, 26 U.S.C. § 6501. Subsection (a) of that statute establishes a general 3-year period of limitations "after the return was filed" for the assessment of income and certain other federal taxes. Subsection (c)(1) of § 6501, however, provides an exception to the 3-year period when there is "a false or fraudulent return with the intent to evade tax." The tax then may be assessed "at any time."

The issue before us is the proper application of §§ 6501(a) and (c)(1) to the situation where a taxpayer files a false or fraudulent return but later files a nonfraudulent amended return. May a tax then be assessed more than three years after the filing of the amended return?

I.

No. 82-1453. Petitioners Ernest Badaracco, Sr., and Ernest Badaracco, Jr., were partners in an electrical contracting business. They filed federal partnership and individual income tax returns for the calendar years 1965-1969, inclusive. "[For] purposes of this case," these petitioners concede the "fraudulent nature of the original returns." App. 37a.

In 1970 and 1971, federal grand juries in New Jersey subpoenaed books and records of the partnership. On August 17, 1971, petitioners filed

---

[9] In FSA 200104006, the IRS determined that fraud committed by a tax return preparer could not be used to hold open the statute of limitations on assessment without showing that the taxpayer himself had intended to evade tax.

nonfraudulent amended returns for the tax years in question and paid the additional basic taxes shown thereon. Three months later, petitioners were indicted for filing false and fraudulent returns, in violation of § 7206(1) of the Code, 26 U.S.C. § 7206(1). Each pleaded guilty to the charge with respect to the 1967 returns, and judgments of conviction were entered. United States v. Badaracco, Crim. No. 766-71 (NJ). The remaining counts of the indictment were dismissed.

On November 21, 1977, the Commissioner of Internal Revenue mailed to petitioners notices of deficiency for each of the tax years in question. He asserted, however, only the liability under § 6653(b) of the Code, 26 U.S.C. § 6653(b) [currently I.R.C. § 6663. Eds.], for the addition to tax on account of fraud (the so-called fraud "penalty") of 50% of the underpayment in the basic tax. *See* App. 5a.

Petitioners sought redetermination in the United States Tax Court of the asserted deficiencies, contending that the Commissioner's action was barred by § 6501(a). They claimed that § 6501(c)(1) did not apply because the 1971 filing of nonfraudulent amended returns caused the general 3-year period of limitations specified in § 6501(a) to operate; the deficiency notices, having issued in November 1977, obviously were forthcoming only long after the expiration of three years from the date of filing of the nonfraudulent amended returns.

* * *

II.

Our task here is to determine the proper construction of the statute of limitations Congress has written for tax assessments. This Court long ago pronounced the standard: "Statutes of limitation sought to be applied to bar rights of the Government, must receive a strict construction in favor of the Government." E.I. du Pont de Nemours & Co. v. Davis, 264 U.S. 456, 462 (1924). *See also* Lucas v. Pilliod Lumber Co., 281 U.S. 245, 249 (1930). More recently, Judge Roney, in speaking for the former Fifth Circuit, has observed that "limitations statutes barring the collection of taxes otherwise due and unpaid are strictly construed in favor of the Government." Lucia v. United States, 474 F.2d 565, 570 (1973).

We naturally turn first to the language of the statute. Section 6501(a) sets forth the general rule: a 3-year period of limitations on the assessment of tax. Section 6501(e)(1)(A) (first introduced as § 275(c) of the Revenue Act of 1934, 48 Stat. 745) provides an extended limitations period for the situation where the taxpayer's return nonfraudulently omits more than 25% of his gross income; in a situation of that kind, assessment now is permitted "at any time within 6 years after the return was filed."

Both the 3-year rule and the 6-year rule, however, explicitly are made inapplicable in circumstances covered by § 6501(c). This subsection identifies three situations in which the Commissioner is allowed an unlimited period within which to assess tax. Subsection (c)(1) relates to "a false or fraudulent return with the intent to evade tax" and provides that the tax then may be assessed "at any time." Subsection (c)(3) covers the case of a failure to file a return at all (whether or not due to fraud) and provides that an assessment then also may be made "at any time." Subsection (c)(2) sets forth a similar rule for the case of a "willful attempt in any manner to defeat or evade tax" other than income, estate, and gift taxes.

All these provisions appear to be unambiguous on their face, and it therefore would seem to follow that the present cases are squarely controlled by the clear language of § 6501(c)(1). Petitioners Badaracco concede that they filed initial returns that were "false or fraudulent with the intent to evade tax." * * * Section 6501(c)(1), with its unqualified language, then allows the tax to be assessed "at any time." Nothing is present in the statute that can be construed to suspend its operation in the light of a fraudulent filer's subsequent repentant conduct. Neither is there anything in the wording of § 6501(a) that itself enables a taxpayer to reinstate the section's general 3-year limitations period by filing an amended return. Indeed, as this Court recently has noted, Hillsboro National Bank v. Commissioner, 460 U.S. 370, 378–380, n. 10 (1983), the Internal Revenue Code does not explicitly provide either for a taxpayer's filing, or for the Commissioner's acceptance, of an amended return; instead, an amended return is a creature of administrative origin and grace. Thus, when Congress provided for assessment at any time in the case of a false or fraudulent "return," it plainly included by this language a false or fraudulent *original* return. In this connection, we note that until the decision of the Tenth Circuit in *Dowell v. Commissioner*, 614 F.2d 1263 (1980), *cert. pending*, No. 82-1873, courts consistently had held that the operation of § 6501 and its predecessors turned on the nature of the taxpayer's original, and not his amended, return.[8]

The substantive operation of the fraud provisions of the Code itself confirms the conclusion that § 6501(c)(1) permits assessment at any time in fraud cases regardless of a taxpayer's later repentance. It is established that a taxpayer who submits a fraudulent return does not purge the fraud by subsequent voluntary disclosure; the fraud was committed, and the offense completed, when the original return was prepared and filed. *See, e.g.,* United States v. Habig, 390 U.S. 222 (1968); Plunkett v. Commissioner, 465 F.2d 299, 302–303 (CA7 1972). "Any other result would make sport of the so-called fraud penalty. A taxpayer who had filed a fraudulent return would merely take his chances that the fraud would not be investigated or discovered, and then, if an investigation were made, would simply pay the tax which he owed anyhow

---

[8] The significance of the original, and not the amended, return has been stressed in other, but related, contexts. It thus has been held consistently that the filing of an amended return in a nonfraudulent situation does not serve to extend the period within which the Commissioner may assess a deficiency. *See, e.g.,* Zellerbach Paper Co. v. Helvering, 293 U.S. 172 (1934); National Paper Products Co. v. Helvering, 293 U.S. 183 (1934); National Refining Co. v. Commissioner, 1 B.T.A. 236 (1924). It also has been held that the filing of an amended return does not serve to reduce the period within which the Commissioner may assess taxes where the original return omitted enough income to trigger the operation of the extended limitations period provided by § 6501(e) or its predecessors. *See, e.g.,* Houston v. Commissioner, 38 T.C. 486 (1962); Goldring v. Commissioner, 20 T.C. 79 (1953). And the period of limitations for filing a refund claim under the predecessor of § 6501(a) begins to run on the filing of the original, not the amended, return. Kaltreider Construction, Inc. v. United States, 303 F.2d 366, 368 (CA3), *cert. denied*, 371 U.S. 877 (1962).

and thereby nullify the fraud penalty." George M. Still, Inc. v. Commissioner, 19 T. C. 1072, 1077 (1953), *aff'd*, 218 F.2d 639 (CA2 1955). In short, once a fraudulent return has been filed, the case remains one "of a false or fraudulent return," regardless of the taxpayer's later revised conduct, for purposes of criminal prosecution and civil fraud liability under § 6653(b). It likewise should remain such a case for purposes of the unlimited assessment period specified by § 6501(c)(1).

We are not persuaded by [Petitioners' suggestion] that § 6501(c)(1) should be read merely to suspend the commencement of the limitations period while the fraud remains uncorrected. The Tenth Circuit in *Dowell v. Commissioner*, *supra*, made an observation to that effect, stating that the 3-year limitations period was "put in limbo" pending further taxpayer action. 614 F.2d, at 1266. The language of the statute, however, is contrary to this suggestion. Section 6501(c)(1) does not "suspend" the operation of § 6501(a) until a fraudulent filer makes a voluntary disclosure. Section 6501(c)(1) makes no reference at all to § 6501(a); it simply provides that the tax may be assessed "at any time." And § 6501(a) itself contains no mechanism for its operation when a fraudulent filer repents. By its very terms, it does not apply to a case, such as one of "a false or fraudulent return," that is "otherwise provided" for in § 6501. When Congress intends only a temporary suspension of the running of a limitations period, it knows how unambiguously to accomplish that result. *See, e.g.*, §§ 6503(a)(1), (a)(2), (b), (c), and (d).

The weakness of petitioners' proposed statutory construction is demonstrated further by its impact on § 6501(e)(1)(A), which provides an extended limitations period whenever a taxpayer's return nonfraudulently omits more than 25% of his gross income.

Under petitioners' reasoning, a taxpayer who *fraudulently* omits 25% of his gross income gains the benefit of the 3-year limitations period by filing an amended return. Yet a taxpayer who *nonfraudulently* omits 25% of his gross income cannot gain that benefit by filing an amended return; instead, he must live with the 6-year period specified in § 6501(e)(1)(A). We agree with the conclusion of the Court of Appeals in the instant cases that Congress could not have intended to "create a situation in which persons who committed willful, deliberate fraud would be in a better position" than those who understated their income inadvertently and without fraud. 693 F.2d, at 302.

We therefore conclude that the plain and unambiguous language of § 6501(c)(1) would permit the Commissioner to assess "at any time" the tax for a year in which the taxpayer has filed "a false or fraudulent return," despite any subsequent disclosure the taxpayer might make. Petitioners attempt to evade the consequences of this language by arguing that their original returns were "nullities." Alternatively, they urge a nonliteral construction of the statute based on considerations of policy and practicality. We now turn successively to those proposals.

III.

Petitioners argue that their original returns, to the extent they were fraudulent, were "nullities" for statute of limitations purposes. *See* Brief for

Petitioners in No. 82-1453, pp. 22–27; Brief for Petitioner in No. 82-1509, pp. 32–34. Inasmuch as the original return is a nullity, it is said, the amended return is necessarily "the return" referred to in § 6501(a). And if that return is nonfraudulent, § 6501(c)(1) is inoperative and the normal 3-year limitations period applies. This nullity notion does not persuade us, for it is plain that "the return" referred to in § 6501(a) is the original, not the amended, return.

Petitioners do not contend that their fraudulent original returns were nullities for purposes of the Code generally. There are numerous provisions in the Code that relate to civil and criminal penalties for submitting or assisting in the preparation of false or fraudulent returns; their presence makes clear that a document which on its face plausibly purports to be in compliance, and which is signed by the taxpayer, is a return despite its inaccuracies. * * * Neither do petitioners contend that their original returns were nullities for all purposes of § 6501. They contend, instead, that a fraudulent return is a nullity only for the limited purpose of applying § 6501(a). *See* Brief for Petitioners in No. 82-1453, p. 24; Brief for Petitioner in No. 82-1509, pp. 33–34. The word "return," however, appears no less than 64 times in § 6501. Surely, Congress cannot rationally be thought to have given that word one meaning in § 6501(a), and a totally different meaning in §§ 6501(b) through (q).

Zellerbach Paper Co. v. Helvering, 293 U.S. 1972 (1934), which petitioners cite, affords no support for their argument. The Court in *Zellerbach* held that an original return, despite its inaccuracy, was a "return" for limitations purposes, so that the filing of an amended return did not start a new period of limitations running. In the instant cases, the original returns similarly purported to be returns, were sworn to as such, and appeared on their faces to constitute endeavors to satisfy the law. Although those returns, in fact, were not honest, the holding in *Zellerbach* does not render them nullities. To be sure, current Regulations, in several places, *e.g.*, Treas. Reg. §§ 301.6211-1(a), 301.6402-3(a), 1.451-1(a), and 1.461-1(a)(3)(i) (1983), do refer to an amended return, as does § 6213(g)(1) of the Code itself, 26 U. S. C. § 6213(g)(1) (1976 ed., Supp. V). None of these provisions, however, requires the filing of such a return. It does not follow from all this that an amended return becomes "the return" for purposes of § 6501(a).

We conclude, therefore, that nothing in the statutory language, the structure of the Code, or the decided cases supports the contention that a fraudulent return is a nullity for statute of limitations purposes.

IV.

Petitioners contend that a nonliteral reading should be accorded the statute on grounds of equity to the repentant taxpayer and tax policy. "Once a taxpayer has provided the information upon which the Government may make a knowledgeable assessment, the justification for suspending the limitations period is no longer viable and must yield to the favored policy of limiting the Government's time to proceed against the taxpayer." Brief for Petitioner in No. 82-509, p. 12. *See also* Brief for Petitioners in No. 82-1453, p. 17.

The cases before us, however, concern the construction of existing statutes. The relevant question is not whether, as an abstract matter, the rule advocated by petitioners accords with good policy. The question we must consider is whether the policy petitioners favor is that which Congress effectuated by its enactment of § 6501. Courts are not authorized to rewrite a statute because they might deem its effects susceptible of improvement. *See* TVA v. Hill, 437 U.S. 153, 194–195 (1978). This is especially so when courts construe a statute of limitations, which "must receive a strict construction in favor of the Government." *E.I. du Pont de Nemours & Co. v. Davis*, 264 U.S., at 462.

We conclude that, even were we free to do so, there is no need to twist § 6501(c)(1) beyond the contours of its plain and unambiguous language in order to comport with good policy, for substantial policy considerations support its literal language. First, fraud cases ordinarily are more difficult to investigate than cases marked for routine tax audits. Where fraud has been practiced, there is a distinct possibility that the taxpayer's underlying records will have been falsified or even destroyed. The filing of an amended return, then, may not diminish the amount of effort required to verify the correct tax liability. Even though the amended return proves to be an honest one, its filing does not necessarily "remov[e] the Commissioner from the disadvantageous position in which he was originally placed." Brief for Petitioners in No. 82-1453, p. 12.

Second, the filing of a document styled "amended return" does not fundamentally change the nature of a tax fraud investigation. An amended return, however accurate it ultimately may prove to be, comes with no greater guarantee of trustworthiness than any other submission. It comes carrying no special or significant imprimatur; instead, it comes from a taxpayer who already has made false statements under penalty of perjury. A responsible examiner cannot accept the information furnished on an amended return as a substitute for a thorough investigation into the existence of fraud. We see no "tax policy" justification for holding that an amended return has the singular effect of shortening the unlimited assessment period specified in §§ 6501(c)(1) to the usual three years. Fraud cases differ from other civil tax cases in that it is the Commissioner who has the burden of proof on the issue of fraud. *See* § 7454(a) of the Code, 26 U.S.C. § 7454(a). An amended return, of course, may constitute an admission of substantial underpayment, but it will not ordinarily constitute an admission of fraud. And the three years may not be enough time for the Commissioner to prove fraudulent intent.

Third, the difficulties that attend a civil fraud investigation are compounded where, as in No. 82-1453, the Commissioner's initial findings lead him to conclude that the case should be referred to the Department of Justice for criminal prosecution. The period of limitations for prosecuting criminal tax fraud is generally six years. *See* § 6531. Once a criminal referral has been made, the Commissioner is under well-known restraints on the civil side and often will find it difficult to complete his civil investigation within the normal 3-year period; the taxpayer's filing of an amended return will not make any difference in this respect. *See* United States v. LaSalle National Bank, 437 U.S. 298, 311–313 (1978); *see also* Tax Equity and Fiscal Responsibility Act of 1982, Pub. L. 97-248, § 333(a), 96 Stat. 622. As a practical matter, therefore, the Commissioner frequently is forced to place a civil audit in abeyance when a criminal prosecution is recommended.

We do not find petitioners' complaint of "unfair treatment" persuasive. Petitioners claim that it is unfair "to forever suspend a Sword of Damocles over a taxpayer who at one time may have filed a fraudulent return, but who has subsequently recanted and filed an amended return providing the Government with all the information necessary to properly assess the tax." Brief for Petitioner in No. 82-1509, p. 26. *See* Brief for Petitioners in No. 82-1453, p. 16. But it seems to us that a taxpayer who has filed a fraudulent return with intent to evade tax hardly is in a position to complain of the fairness of a rule that facilitates the Commissioner's collection of the tax due. A taxpayer who has been the subject of a tax fraud investigation is not likely to be surprised when a notice of deficiency arrives, even if it does not arrive promptly after he files an amended return.

Neither are we persuaded by [the taxpayer's] argument that a literal reading of the statute "punishes" the taxpayer who repentantly files an amended return. *See* Brief for Petitioner in No. 82-1509, p. 44. The amended return does not change the status of the taxpayer; he is left in precisely the same position he was in before. It might be argued that Congress should provide incentives to taxpayers to disclose their fraud voluntarily. Congress, however, has not done so in § 6501. That legislative judgment is controlling here.

V.

Petitioners contend, finally, that a literal reading of § 6501(c) produces a disparity in treatment between a taxpayer who in the first instance files a fraudulent return and one who fraudulently fails to file any return at all. This, it is said, would elevate one form of tax fraud over another.

The argument centers in § 6501(c)(3), which provides that in a case of failure to file a return, the tax may be assessed "at any time." It is settled that this section ceases to apply once a return has been filed for a particular year, regardless of whether that return is filed late and even though the failure to file a timely return in the first instance was due to fraud. *See* Bennett v. Commissioner, 30 T. C. 114 (1958), *acq.*, 1958-2 Cum. Bull. 3. *See also* Rev. Rul. 79-178, 1979-1 Cum. Bull. 435. This, however, does not mean that § 6501 should be read to produce the same result in each of the two situations. From the language employed in the respective subsections of § 6501, we conclude that Congress intended different limitations results. Section 6501(c)(3) applies to a "failure to file a return." It makes no reference to a failure to file a timely return (*cf.* §§ 6651(a)(1) and 7203), nor does it speak of a fraudulent failure to file. The section literally becomes inapplicable once a return has been filed. Section 6501(c)(1), in contrast, applies in the case of "a false or fraudulent return." The fact that a fraudulent filer subsequently submits an amended return does not make the case any less one of a false or fraudulent return. Thus, although there may be some initial superficial plausibility to this argument on the part of petitioners, we conclude that the argument cannot prevail. If the result contended for by petitioners is to be the rule, Congress must make it so in clear and unmistakable language.

* * *

Justice STEVENS, dissenting.

The plain language of § 6501(c)(1) of the Internal Revenue Code conveys a different message to me than it does to the Court. That language is clear enough: "In the case of a false or fraudulent return with the intent to evade tax, the tax may be assessed, or a proceeding in court for collection of such tax may be begun without assessment, at any time." 26 U.S.C. § 6501(c)(1). What is not clear to me is why this is a case of "a false or fraudulent return."

In both cases before the Court, the Commissioner assessed deficiencies based on concededly nonfraudulent returns. The taxpayers' alleged prior fraud was not the basis for the Commissioner's action. Indeed, whether or not the Commissioner was obligated to accept petitioners' amended returns, he in fact elected to do so and to use them as the basis for his assessment. When the Commissioner initiates a deficiency proceeding on the basis of a nonfraudulent return, I do not believe that the resulting case is one "of a false or fraudulent return."

* * *

In light of the purposes and common-law background of the statute, as well as this Court's previous treatment of what a "return" sufficient to commence the running of the limitations period is, it seems apparent that an assessment based on a nonfraudulent amended return does not fall within § 6501(c)(1). Once the amended return is filed the rationale for disregarding the limitations period is absent. The period of concealment is over, and under general common-law principles the limitations period should begin to run. The filing of the return means that the Commissioner is no longer under any disadvantage; full disclosure has been made and there is no reason why he cannot assess a deficiency within the statutory period.

* * *

Whatever the correct standard for construing a statute of limitations when it operates against the Government, *see ante*, at 391–392, surely the presumption ought to be that some limitations period is applicable.

> "It probably would be all but intolerable, at least Congress has regarded it as ill-advised, to have an income tax system under which there never would come a day of final settlement and which required both the taxpayer and the Government to stand ready forever and a day to produce vouchers, prove events, establish values and recall details of all that goes into an income tax contest. Hence, a statute of limitation is an almost indispensable element of fairness as well as of practical administration of an income tax policy." Rothensies v. Electric Storage Battery Co., 329 U.S. 296, 301 (1946).

However, under the Commissioner's position, adopted by the Court today, no limitations period will ever apply to the Commissioner's actions, despite petitioners' attempts to provide him with all the information necessary to make a timely assessment.

*   *   *

If anything, considerations of tax policy argue against the result reached by the Court today. In a system based on voluntary compliance, it is crucial that some incentive be given to persons to reveal and correct past fraud. Yet the rule announced by the Court today creates no such incentive; a taxpayer gets no advantage at all by filing an honest return. Not only does the taxpayer fail to gain the benefit of a limitations period, but at the same time he gives the Commissioner additional information which can be used against him at any time. Since the amended return will not give the taxpayer a defense in a criminal or civil fraud action, *see ante*, at 394, there is no reason at all for a taxpayer to correct a fraudulent return. Apparently the Court believes that taxpayers should be advised to remain silent, hoping the fraud will go undetected, rather than to make full disclosure in a proper return. I cannot believe that Congress intended such a result.

I respectfully dissent.

Does the position of the majority with respect to a fraudulently filed return discourage a taxpayer from making an effort to meet his reporting obligations by filing an amended return? On the other hand, what might a rule that allowed subsequent honesty after filing a fraudulent return to trigger the three-year statute of limitations encourage taxpayers to do?

In *The Colony, Inc. v. Commissioner*, 357 U.S. 28 (1958), discussed above, the court held that the six-year statute under section 6501(e) does not apply unless an entire item is omitted, presumably because partial reporting of the item by the taxpayer discloses that item to the IRS, which then requires less investigatory time. Compare the majority's opinion in *Badaracco* with this principle of *The Colony*. If the policy behind the unlimited assessment period for false or fraudulent returns is similarly to grant the IRS additional time in which to discover the taxpayer's fraudulent behavior, should an amended return that provides the IRS enough information to make an accurate assessment trigger some sort of limitations period? How does the *Badaracco* majority respond to this potential inconsistency?

Also consider *Badaracco* in light of the holding of *Bennett v. Commissioner*, 30 T.C. 114 (1958), which is cited approvingly by the Court. In *Bennett,* the Tax Court ruled that where a taxpayer fraudulently fails to file a return at all, a subsequently filed nonfraudulent return is sufficient to trigger the three-year statute of limitations. Under *Bennett,* if the IRS discovers a taxpayer's failure to file and begins an investigation, the taxpayer need only file a nonfraudulent return in order to start the limitations period. Which of these two scenarios—a fraudulently filed return or a fraudulent failure to file— seems more egregious in terms of preserving the system of voluntary compliance? Do these cases mean that a taxpayer intent on perpetrating a fraud is better off filing no return at all rather than filing a fraudulent return?

[C] Tolling of the Statute of Limitations on Assessment

The IRS must assess tax before the statute of limitations on assessment expires, or any amount assessed must be refunded to the taxpayer. I.R.C. § 6401. Because the notice of deficiency is a prerequisite to assessment of a deficiency, the notice must be sent before the expiration of the statute of limitations on assessment. As discussed above, the notice triggers a "prohibited period," and the statute of limitations is tolled during the period that the IRS is prohibited from assessing tax, plus 60 days. *See* I.R.C. §§ 6213(a), 6503(a). Determining the timeliness of an assessment therefore can require counting days fairly precisely.

> *Example:* Larry filed his 1997 return on April 1, 1998. On February 1, 2000, the IRS mailed a notice of deficiency with respect to Larry's 1997 tax year to Larry's last known address in Chappaqua, New York. Larry receives the notice on February 7, but does not respond to it. On these facts, the notice of deficiency was mailed within the three-year period under section 6501. That period started to run on the due date of the 1997 return, which was April 15, 1998. The *first* day the IRS can assess tax is when the prohibited period expires, May 1, 2000. The *last* day the IRS can assess tax, assuming the three-year period applies, is September 12, 2001. That is, the statute of limitations was tolled for 150 days (the 90-day prohibited period plus the 60-day grace period). Therefore, instead of expiring on April 15, 2001, the statute is extended 150 days until September 12, 2001.

If the taxpayer signs Form 870, permitting immediate assessment of tax, that cuts short the prohibited period. That, in turn, will shorten the time period during which the statute is tolled.

> *Example*: On January 4, 2001, the IRS mails a notice of deficiency to Caitlin's last known address in Winston-Salem, North Carolina. Caitlin receives the notice on January 8. On February 1, she signs a Form 870, waiving restrictions on assessment of the deficiency. The statute of limitations on assessment is tolled 88 days (the 28 days from January 4 through February 1, plus 60 days).

What is the rationale for tolling the statute during the prohibited period?

[D] Extensions of Time to Assess Tax

It is often the case that the IRS is unable to complete an examination of the taxpayer's return during the prescribed assessment period. Even when the case has progressed to the Appeals stage, an expiring limitations period may give the Appeals Officer very little time in which to consider the taxpayer's protest letter and attempt to settle. If the statutory period is about to expire before an assessment has been made, the IRS commonly requests that the taxpayer sign a consent extending the general statute of limitations. It is not uncommon, in fact, for the IRS to request seriatim extensions of the statute of limitations as each extension nears expiration. Section 6501(c)(4) provides that where, before the expiration of the limitations period, both the taxpayer and the IRS agree in writing to its extension, the tax may be assessed at any time prior to the expiration of the agreed-upon period. Note that an extension is only valid if executed prior to the expiration of the statute of limitations. *See* I.R.C. § 6501(c)(4). Why might the taxpayer agree to extend the statutory period?[10]

Extensions can be made on Form 872, Consent to Extend the Time to Assess Tax, or Form 872-A, Special Consent to Extend the Time to Assess Tax. Form 872 (the "fixed-date" consent) provides for an extension for a finite period of time stated in the agreement, typically one year or less. Form 872-A (the "open-ended" consent) is an unlimited extension of time, which is terminated 90 days after (1) the IRS receives a Form 872-T from the taxpayer, (2) the IRS mails the taxpayer a Form 872-T, or (3) the IRS mails the taxpayer a notice of deficiency. In the latter case, the extension period will not expire until 60 days after the prohibited 90-day period specified in section 6213. Form 872-A is discussed further below.

The fundamental question of whether a taxpayer should agree to sign a consent does not lend itself to an easy answer. If the taxpayer refuses to extend an expiring limitations period, the IRS will very likely issue the taxpayer a notice of deficiency. As discussed in later chapters, the notice of deficiency sets into motion the litigation phase of the tax controversy process and forces the taxpayer to consider within a relatively short period of time whether to pursue the case in Tax Court or one of the refund fora. A taxpayer's failure to consent to an extension may also place pressure on the IRS to prepare the notice of deficiency based on an investigation that may be ill-developed or incomplete. In such a case, the examining agent's response may be to include in his report all items that the agent believes are questionable, even if the items have a weak legal or factual basis.

Houlberg discusses one circumstance in which the IRS might seek an extension of the statute, and also illustrates the kinds of questions that taxpayers may raise after the fact about the validity of consents to extend the statutory period. What does the case indicate about whether a taxpayer has a "right" to a conference with the IRS's Appeals Division?

HOULBERG v. COMMISSIONER
United States Tax Court
T.C. Memo. 1985-497

GERBER, JUDGE:

By statutory notice, respondent determined the following deficiencies in petitioners' Federal income tax:

Year	Deficiency
1976	$ 7,443
1977	5,553
1978	3,276

---

[10] Concerned that taxpayers were unaware of their right to refuse to extend the statute of limitations, the IRS Reform Act requires the IRS, on each occasion when the taxpayer is asked to sign an extension consent, to notify the taxpayer of the taxpayer's right to refuse to extend the statutory period, and to notify the taxpayer of his right to limit the extension to a particular issue or period of time. *See* I.R.C. § 6501(c)(4)(B).

1979   9,895

The issues for decision are (1) whether the period of limitations on assessment for 1976 and 1977 was extended by valid consents or had expired prior to issuance of the notice of deficiency, and (2) whether the notice of deficiency was issued by a person lacking proper authority and, therefore, was invalid.

FINDINGS OF FACT

Some of the facts have been stipulated. The stipulation of facts and accompanying exhibits are so found and incorporated by this reference.

Petitioners are husband and wife and resided in Los Angeles, California, when they filed their petition. They timely filed joint Federal income tax returns for 1976, 1977, 1978, and 1979.

In November 1979, petitioners received a Form 872 (Consent to Extend the Time to Assess Tax) to extend the period of limitations on assessment for 1976 until September 30, 1981. The form provided in part: "MAKING THIS CONSENT WILL NOT DEPRIVE THE TAXPAYER(S) OF ANY APPEAL RIGHTS TO WHICH THEY WOULD OTHERWISE BE ENTITLED." The form was accompanied by a cover letter from the Internal Revenue Service (IRS) notifying petitioners that the return of K. T. Associates, a partnership with which they were involved, was under examination. The letter in part stated:

> We do not expect to receive the results of the entity(s) audit before the expiration of the normal statute of limitations. Generally, a delay in time is the result of the taxpayers exercising their right to appeal the IRS decision. In order to allow time for adequate consideration of your case in conjunction with the audit of the entity(s), we request that you sign the enclosed consent * * *.

After consulting with their accountant, Michael J. Ravin, petitioners signed the form and returned it to the IRS which accepted the consent.

In May 1981, petitioners received a Form 872A (Special Consent to Extend the Time to Assess Tax), which in part provided that any tax due for 1976 could be assessed on or before the 90th day after the IRS mailed a notice of deficiency. The form and its accompanying cover letter contained the same language regarding appeal rights as cited above. After consulting with Ravin, petitioners signed the form and returned it to the IRS which accepted the consent.

In October 1980, a Form 872A was sent to petitioners for 1977. Ravin advised petitioners to sign the consent and prepared a letter to be used by them in forwarding the consent to the IRS. The letter, dated December 5, 1980, provided in part:

> Our signing this extension of time is expressly contingent upon the fact that we are not waiving any of our rights to the normal administrative procedures afforded to us by the Internal Revenue Service in connection with audit of our 1977 income tax return.

The following language was added to the bottom of the last page of the Form 872A: "SUBJECT TO THE ATTACHED LETTER DATED Dec. 5, 1980."

On receipt of the letter and conditional extension, an IRS representative called Ravin and advised him that the IRS would accept only an unmodified consent. Ravin then suggested to petitioners that they sign an unaltered consent, which they did. The signed Form 872A and the cover letter sent with respect to 1977 contained the language regarding appeal rights previously cited.

In October 1981, a Form 872A was sent to petitioners with respect to 1978. Petitioners refused to sign it.

On April 15, 1982, petitioners were sent a notice of deficiency covering 1976, 1977, 1978, and 1979. The notice bore the District Director's name, and was initialed by Jerold M. Ching, a Quality Review Section Chief, Grade GS-13.

Petitioners did not have a conference with the IRS prior to issuance of the notice of deficiency. Subsequent to issuance of the notice, an administrative hearing was held between counsel for petitioners and a representative of respondent's appeals division, at which time the parties agreed that the deficiencies for the taxable years at issue were as follows:

Year	Deficiency
1976	$ 474
1977	5,553
1978	3,276
1979	0
TOTAL:	$ 9,303

The parties agree that, if this Court rules for respondent with respect to the validity of the consents and the notice of deficiency, the deficiencies are as above.

OPINION

Validity of Consents

Petitioners argue that the period of limitations on assessment for 1976 and 1977 expired prior to issuance of the notice of deficiency. They assert that they consented to extend the period of limitations in return for administrative review and the opportunity to present their views before issuance of a statutory notice, and that the consents are invalid because this condition was not met. Respondent maintains that the period of limitations was extended by valid consents. We agree with respondent.

Section 6501 states the general rule that a tax must be assessed within three years of the filing of a return. Section 6501(c)(4) permits the IRS and taxpayers to extend the period of limitations on assessment by written agreement. Since petitioners timely filed their tax returns for 1976 and 1977, the notice of deficiency, issued April 15, 1982, was barred unless the assessment period had been validly extended.

Petitioners maintain that they received both oral and written assurances that they would receive a hearing prior to issuance of a deficiency notice. At trial, petitioner Jens Houlberg (Houlberg) testified that towards the end of

1979, he was notified by mail that the IRS was conducting an audit of calendar years 1976 through 1979. Houlberg stated that he called Ravin, who told him that he would be afforded an opportunity to be heard before a notice of deficiency was issued. Houlberg further testified that other than his wife, Ravin, and counsel, he had not discussed the extensions with anyone. When asked the basis of his understanding, other than from his discussions with Ravin, that he would receive a pre-notice hearing, Houlberg described his experience with past audits. At no time did Houlberg testify that the IRS promised him a pre-notice hearing for the taxable years at issue.

Ravin, petitioner's accountant, also testified at the hearing. He stated that after receiving a copy of the first extension request, he called the IRS representative whose name appeared on the accompanying cover letter. Ravin related:

> I asked him at that point in time * * * [if] signing of the consent would preclude the Service from sending a notice of deficiency prior to Mr. Houlberg or myself * * * expressing our position before and during the normal administrative review procedure.

> And he told me that this would in no way preclude that.

Ravin further related that he had spoken with another IRS representative regarding the requested extension for 1978. Ravin stated:

> [I] reiterated the taxpayers' position with appeal rights being confirmed, that this is no way would jeopardize their ability to go through the normal administrative appeals prior to the notice of deficiency being issued.

Ravin continued that he had contacted still another IRS representative regarding the extension requested for 1977. He stated:

> [I] again reiterated the same position, with respect to the administrative appeal rights. She agreed with me.

Ravin further testified that he was contacted by an IRS representative regarding the modified Form 872A petitioners had sent to the IRS. According to Ravin, the IRS representative—

> said that they could not accept a conditional extension, and that they would be sending out a normal extension of time requesting Mr. Houlberg to sign it. And at that point in time, I asked, well, did they understand that they were not waiving their appeal rights. And they said they certainly did, and it was very evident in the letter that I had sent — or Mr. Houlberg had sent.

At no time did Ravin testify that an IRS representative promised petitioners a hearing prior to issuance of a notice of deficiency. He essentially related that he was told that by signing the consents petitioners would not harm their appeal rights.

The final witness at the hearing was Glenn Marker. During 1981, Marker was chief of a unit involved with solicitation of consents to extend the period of limitations on assessments. Marker testified that he did not recall having had any conversations with petitioners or Ravin. He stated that he had never indicated to a taxpayer or a taxpayer's representative that by extending the statute of limitations they would be guaranteed an appeals conference prior to issuance of a deficiency notice. Marker further testified as to what taxpayers were told would occur if a taxpayer chose to extend the statute:

> We would go on further to explain that if they chose to extend the statute, the case would then be retained in the Suspense Unit, awaiting the resolution of partnership adjustments, depend [sic] upon the outcome of the adjustments. If it was in the government's favor, we would try to solicit an agreement from the taxpayer, based upon the results of the partnership audit. And if the taxpayers then chose not to, the case would be moved forward for issuance of the 30-day letter.

> The 30-day letter would then be issued, and they would have 30 days to file a protest to the government's position. And then, if they had not filed that letter, then it would go default to the 90-day section for against [sic] the issuance of the statutory notice of deficiency.

Marker was subsequently asked if —

> the process is the consent is signed, you finish up your audit, you then contact the taxpayer, the taxpayer is given an opportunity to settle it at that level, if he can't, then he is allowed to protest?

He responded affirmatively. He stated that he knew of no cases in which a consent was signed and a notice issued before an appeals conference was allowed. Later, however, he stated that although it was normal procedure to issue a 30-day letter, there were instances where statutory notices went out without such letters being sent. He described these instances as—

> cases where we have determined them [the cases] to be litigating vehicles, that they cannot be resolved at the appellate level * * *. The manager looks at the case and makes a determination, and can actually recommend the issuance of a 90-day letter, because he doesn't feel that anything could be resolved at that level, the 30-day level.

Marker's testimony does not demonstrate that respondent promised petitioners pre-notice of deficiency appeal rights in return for petitioners' consent to extend the period of limitations, as petitioners assert. On the contrary, Marker stated that no such promises are made to taxpayers. Marker indicated that although pre-notice conferences are commonly held, taxpayers are not always afforded such meetings.

The waiver forms and accompanying cover letters similarly contain no explicit promise for a pre-notice conference. Like the oral communications with IRS representatives that petitioners note, these written communications merely did not rule out the possibility of such a meeting.

The same contention petitioners make regarding the conditional nature of their consents was made previously by their accountant, Ravin, in his own case which was decided by this Court. Ravin v. Commissioner, T.C. Memo 1981-107, *affd. without published opinion* 755 F.2d 936 (9th Cir. 1985). In *Ravin v. Commissioner, supra,* we held that consents signed by Ravin were valid, even though an IRS agent had made, and a letter from the IRS contained, inaccurate statements concerning his appeal rights. With respect to the effect to be given statements of IRS agents to taxpayers, we stated:

> [t]he often stated general rule is that a revenue agent does not have the authority to bind the Commissioner. *See* United States v. Stewart, 311 U.S. 60 (1940); Bornstein v. United States, 170 Ct. Cl. 576, 345 F.2d 558 (1965); Wilkinson v. United States, 157 Ct. Cl. 847, 304 F.2d 469 (1962). A claim of estoppel is usually rejected, although the taxpayer contends that he followed the erroneous advice of an agent and acted in reliance upon it. *Cf.* Montgomery v. Commissioner, 65 T.C. 511, 522 (1975); Boulez v. Commissioner, 76 T.C. 209 (1981). [41 T.C.M. at 1064, 1066, 50 P-H Memo T.C. par. 81, 107 at 81-381]

We further observed, with respect to the same language on the Forms 872 and 872A regarding appeal rights that we quote in this case, that—

> [this language] does not state that any conferences will be automatically provided, but it merely states that by signing the Form 872 the taxpayer retains the same rights to an appellate conference prior to the issuance of the notice of deficiency as all other taxpayers. Put differently, it is nowhere indicated on the Form 872 that by signing it a taxpayer will improve his appeal rights. [41 T.C.M. at 1066, 50 P-H Memo T.C. at 382-81]

In *Ravin v. Commissioner, supra,* we additionally pointed out that procedural rules with respect to administrative appeals are merely directory, and compliance with them is not essential to the validity of a notice of deficiency. *See also* Luhring v. Glotzbach, 304 F.2d 560, 563 (4th Cir. 1962); Rosenberg v. Commissioner, 450 F.2d 529, 532 (10th Cir. 1971), *affg.* a Memorandum Opinion of this Court; Collins v. Commissioner, 61 T.C. 693, 701 (1974); Flynn v. Commissioner, 40 T.C. 770, 773 (1963). Accordingly, we find that the IRS did not violate its procedural rules by not conferring with petitioners prior to issuing a deficiency notice and, consequently, the requirements of section 6501(c)(4) have been met.

Petitioners further suggest that the consents are ineffective because petitioners signed them under the mistaken belief that a pre-notice hearing would be held.[n.3] As is implicit in our opinion in *Ravin v. Commissioner, supra,* a consent is valid where no hearing is held, even though a taxpayer expects such review. We know of no authority holding that a valid waiver of the period of limitations on assessment requires knowledge that a pre-notice administrative hearing may not be held. Petitioners note that they are not accountants. Petitioners were represented by an accountant (Ravin) and we are not persuaded that petitioners' backgrounds should dictate a different result than that reached in *Ravin v. Commissioner, supra,* with respect to the effectiveness of the waivers.

[n.3] Petitioners were under no duress to sign the waivers. *Compare* Robertson v. Commissioner, T.C. Memo. 1973-205 (taxpayers, who had never previously dealt with the IRS, signed consents under threat of seizure of their property and without the opportunity to consult with their attorney).

The Code imposes no general requirement on the IRS to confer with a taxpayer who has signed a waiver prior to issuing a notice of deficiency. For the reasons we have stated, we do not find that pre-notice administrative review was required in the specific circumstances of this case. Accordingly, we hold that the period for assessment for 1976 and 1977 was extended by valid consents.

Authority to Issue Deficiency Notice

Petitioners argue that Jerold M. Ching, the Quality Review Section Chief (Grade GS-13), who issued the deficiency notice, lacked properly delegated authority to do so, and that the notice therefore is invalid. Respondent maintains that Jerold M. Ching had the delegated authority to issue the notice. We agree with respondent.

In *Ravin v. Commissioner, supra,* the taxpayers also argued that the IRS representative who issued the statutory notice did so without authority. The circumstances in which the statutory notice was issued are very similar in the two cases and, accordingly, *Ravin v. Commissioner, supra,* provides appropriate precedent for this case.

In *Ravin v. Commissioner, supra,* we pointed out the authority by which certain IRS representatives could issue deficiency notices:

> Section 6212(a) provides that if the Secretary determines that there is an income tax deficiency, he is authorized to send a notice of deficiency to the taxpayer by certified mail or registered mail. The term "Secretary" is defined in section 7701(a)(11)(B) as the "Secretary of the Treasury or his delegate." The phrase "or his delegate" is defined in section 7701(a)(12)(A)(i) as "any officer, employee, or agency of the Treasury Department duly authorized by the Secretary of the Treasury directly, or indirectly by one or more redelegations of authority, to perform the function mentioned or described in the context." Under the provisions of section 301.7701-9(b), Proced. & Admin. Regs., when a function is vested by statute in the Secretary of the Treasury or his delegate, and the Treasury regulations provide that such function may be performed by a district director, then the provision in the regulations constitutes a delegation by the Secretary to the district director of the authority to perform such function. Section 301.6212-1(a) [Proced. & Admin. Regs.] provides that if a district director determines that there is an income tax deficiency, he is authorized to notify the taxpayer of the deficiency. Thus, the authority to issue notices of deficiency has been delegated by the Secretary to district directors. Under section 301.7701-9(c) [Proced. & Admin. Regs.] an officer authorized by regulations to perform a function has the authority to redelegate the performance of such function except to the extent that "such power to do so redelegate is prohibited or restricted by proper order or directive."

* * * Since the authority of a District Director to delegate his authority to issue notices of deficiency is derived from sections 301.6212-1(a) and

301.7701-9, Proced. & Admin. Regs., the fact that Delegation Order LA-41 (Rev. 9) referred to Delegation Order 77 (Rev. 14), which had been superseded by Delegation Order 77 (Rev. 15) at the time the notice of deficiency was issued, is irrelevant to the validity of the notice. *See Estate of Brimm v. Commissioner*, 70 T.C. 15, 19–22 (1978), and *Ravin v. Commissioner, supra.* In both *Estate of Brimm v. Commissioner, supra,* and *Ravin v. Commissioner, supra,* although the District Director's delegation order in effect at the time the deficiency notice was issued cited as authority a superseded revision of Delegation Order No. 77, we found no jurisdictional defect. * * *

Accordingly, we hold that the delegation to Jerold M. Ching was proper, and that he had authority to issue the notice of deficiency.

To reflect the foregoing, decision will be entered for respondent.

Because Form 872-A extends the statute of limitations on assessment indefinitely, taxpayers should be cautious about signing a Form 872-A. If a Form 872-A leaves the statute open, the equitable doctrine of laches does not bar an assessment even years later. *See Stenclik v. Commissioner*, 907 F.2d 25, 28 (2d Cir.), *cert. denied,* 498 U.S. 984 (1990); *Mecom v. Commissioner*, 101 T.C. 374, 391 (1993), *aff'd without op.,* 40 F.3d 385 (5th Cir. 1994); *see also St. John v. United States*, 951 F.2d 232 (9th Cir. 1991) (extension does not terminate by operation of law even if IRS does not assess any tax within reasonable time period). However, consider the equitable doctrine applied on the unusual facts of the following case:

FREDERICKS v. COMMISSIONER
United States Court of Appeals, Third Circuit
126 F.3d 433 (1997)

OPINION OF THE COURT

ALDISERT, CIRCUIT JUDGE.

We must decide whether this is an appropriate case to apply the doctrine of estoppel against the Internal Revenue Service (IRS). Barry I. Fredericks appeals a decision of the United States Tax Court that approved a deficiency assessed by the Commissioner of Internal Revenue in July 1992 for Fredericks' 1977 income tax return. The IRS action requires the taxpayer to pay an additional tax of $28,361 and approximately $158,000 in interest on the basis of a disallowed tax-shelter deduction. The taxpayer filed a timely 1977 tax return, but the IRS took 14 years to decide if the tax-shelter deduction taken by the taxpayer was appropriate.

The IRS' assessment was filed long after the three-year statute of limitations had expired. However, at the request of the IRS Fredericks signed various consent agreements extending the time for the government to assess his 1977 tax return. The taxpayer's estoppel contention is based on alleged misrepresentations and misconduct by the IRS regarding its possession, solicitation and use of these consent forms. The appeal requires us to determine whether the IRS was estopped from making the assessment in 1992 because of its conduct regarding these consent agreements.

The taxpayer alleges the IRS committed the following misconduct in connection with the forms he and the IRS executed to extend the statute of limitations. First, the IRS misrepresented in 1981 that it never received a Form 872-A (Special Consent to Extend the Time to Assess Taxes), which Fredericks had signed to authorize an indefinite extension of the statute of limitations. Second, the IRS confirmed this misrepresentation in 1981, 1982 and 1983, by soliciting and executing three separate Forms 872, which extend the statute of limitations for one year. Third, the IRS discovered that it possessed the Form 872-A sometime before June 30, 1984, the date the last one-year extension expired, decided to rely on that form in continuing its investigation of Fredericks' tax return and failed to notify the taxpayer of its changed course of action. Fourth, the IRS used the Form 872-A to assess a deficiency in 1992, 11 years after informing the taxpayer that the Form 872-A did not exist, and eight years after the final one-year extension expired. Finally, the IRS imposed interest penalties totaling over five times the amount of the tax and covering the entire duration of its protracted investigation of the tax shelter.

The IRS rejected the taxpayer's statute-of-limitations defense, which was based on the third Form 872 executed by Fredericks and the government. The Commissioner argued that the Form 872-A remained in effect, even though the IRS had represented for the previous 11 years that no such form existed. The taxpayer contended that he relied on the IRS' affirmative misrepresentations over the years to his detriment and, thus, the Commissioner is estopped from using that Form 872-A.

We conclude that this taxpayer has met his burden of proving the traditional elements of equitable estoppel, and has mounted the high hurdle of establishing other special factors applicable to estoppel claims against the government. Accordingly, we will reverse the Tax Court's decision approving the assessment.

*   *   *

I.

In 1978, Fredericks and his former wife filed a timely joint federal income tax return for 1977. In October 1980, the IRS sent Fredericks a Form 872-A, Special Consent to Extend the Time to Assess Taxes, requesting him to extend for the 1977 tax year the three-year statute of limitations within which the government must assess deficiencies. J.A 22a. See 26 U.S.C. § 6501(a). On October 17, 1980, Fredericks signed and returned the Form 872-A, authorizing the government to assess deficiencies within 90 days of:

(a)   the IRS' receipt of a Form 872-T, Notice of Termination of Special Consent to Extend the Time to Assess Tax, from the taxpayer; or

(b)   the IRS' mailing of a Form 872-T to the taxpayer; or

(c)   the IRS' mailing of a notice of deficiency for the relevant year.

None of these events occurred. According to the government's "received" date stamp on the Form 872-A, it was received by the Audit Division of the Manhattan District Director's Office on November 3, 1980, and signed and dated by the IRS on November 4, 1980.

In January 1981, an IRS agent telephoned Fredericks and requested him to sign a Form 872, Consent to Extend the Time to Assess Tax, for the 1977 tax year. According to Fredericks' trial testimony:

> [The] IRS agent . . . indicated that he was reviewing my tax return involved in the audit of my 1977 tax return, and . . . the statute of limitations was about to run and that the Government needed an extension of that statute . . . . I told the . . . agent that I had already executed and returned . . . an extension . . . . He told me he was in charge; he had my file and there was no extension in the file. He asked me did I receive . . . a copy of the extension back from the IRS signed. I said I did not. He indicated . . . that therefore the Government did not have it, it was probably lost in the mail, and that he needed me to execute another extension, otherwise the Government was going to assess the tax. But they didn't want to do that. They wanted time to review, and would I send them an 87 — a new form. We did not mention numbers.

J.A. 81a-82a. The IRS did not contradict this testimony.

Consistent with Fredericks' testimony, the government sent a Form 872, which he signed and returned to the IRS. The Form 872 expressly extends the statute of limitations for only one year, whereas the Form 872-A authorizes an indefinite, although revocable, extension of the statute of limitations. This first Form 872 executed by the IRS and Fredericks extended the statute of limitations until December 31, 1982.

The agents telephoned Fredericks on two additional occasions and requested him to sign and return two additional Forms 872. On June 13, 1982, Fredericks signed and returned a consent to extend the statute of limitations to December 31, 1983; and on February 3, 1983, Fredericks signed and returned a Form 872 agreeing to extend the statute of limitations until June 30, 1984. Each of these Forms 872 was received and signed by an agent of the IRS Newark District Director's Office, and copies of these signed forms were subsequently forwarded to, and received by, Fredericks.

Throughout oral argument, counsel for the IRS made abundantly clear why the government requested these extensions of the statute of limitations:

> IRS COUNSEL: What really took so long in this case was the fact that it took a very long time for the IRS and the tax shelter which the IRS was investigating in which Mr. Fredericks had invested, to reach an agreement . . . . [A] number of years went by, ... I believe that a couple of organizations were involved. It was a complicated settlement.

* * *

> IRS COUNSEL: [I]t's very common when you have complicated tax shelters like this to ask for very long . . . extensions.
>
> THE COURT: But you didn't ask for any additional extensions after the . . . expiration in 1984 did you?
>
> IRS COUNSEL: No, we did not . . . .

Counsel for the IRS also made clear that the consent agreements extending the statute of limitations were repeatedly obtained for both the IRS' and the taxpayers' benefit:

> IRS COUNSEL: Mr. Fredericks didn't want that tax assessed any more than the IRS agent did. And why was that? Because they were still in negotiation on the underlying tax shelter which was not resolved until 1988. That's why he didn't want the tax assessed and that's why the IRS agent didn't want the tax assessed . . . .

After February 1983, the IRS made no attempt to extend the statute of limitations, which pursuant to the third Form 872 expired on June 30, 1984. In light of the IRS' representations that it neither signed nor possessed a Form 872-A indefinite extension of the statute of limitations, the taxpayer concluded that the government lacked authority to assess a deficiency on his 1977 income tax return after that date.

On July 9, 1992—eight years and nine days after the June 30, 1984 expiration date—the IRS mailed a notice of deficiency to Fredericks and his former wife alleging they were liable for $28,361 in income tax, plus interest for the 1977 tax year. Fredericks filed a petition in the Tax Court challenging the deficiency assessment on grounds that it was barred by the June 30, 1984 statute of limitations agreed to in the third Form 872. Thus, Fredericks claimed the Commissioner was estopped from relying on the Form 872-A to avoid the statute-of-limitations defense, which completely bars the assessment of any deficiency.

The Tax Court held a trial at which Fredericks testified and the Commissioner presented no witnesses. Significantly, the IRS presented no evidence as to the date it discovered its possession of the Form 872-A which it invoked to assess Fredericks' 1977 return in 1992. This is the same form the IRS affirmatively represented to the taxpayer as non-existent. Moreover, the IRS does not dispute that it waited until 1992 to notify the taxpayer that it had the Form 872-A and intended to rely on that form instead of the third Form 872 signed by the parties. At oral argument, counsel for the IRS stated that she did not know when the IRS discovered the Form 872-A or when it decided to rely on that form.

The Tax Court concluded that the government's action did not constitute an affirmative misrepresentation about any fact concerning the Form 872-A, and that Fredericks failed to prove the elements of estoppel. The court found that Fredericks did not establish that he relied to his detriment on the government's acts regarding the Forms 872 (one-year extensions) because he could have at any time filed a Form 872-T to terminate the previously executed

Form 872-A (unlimited extension). The court decided that a deficiency of $28,361 was due. Fredericks now appeals that decision.

II.

The question is whether Fredericks sufficiently established the elements of an estoppel claim against the government such that it should be prevented from relying on the Form 872-A indefinite extension of the statute of limitations to pursue an otherwise time-barred assessment on Fredericks' 1977 tax return. Fredericks contends the government's July 9, 1992 assessment on his 1977 tax return was barred as of June 30, 1984, the date on which his and the IRS' agreement to extend the statute of limitations expired pursuant to the third Form 872 sought by the government. The Commissioner contends the Tax Court correctly concluded that estoppel is inappropriate here because Fredericks failed to demonstrate that the government's conduct constituted affirmative misconduct.

"Estoppel is an equitable doctrine invoked to avoid injustice in particular cases." Heckler v. Community Health Servs. of Crawford County, Inc., 467 U.S. 51, 59, 81 L. Ed. 2d 42, 104 S. Ct. 2218 (1984). Parties attempting to estop another private party must establish that they relied to their detriment on their adversary's misrepresentation and that such reliance was reasonable because they neither knew nor should have known the adversary's conduct was misleading. Id.; U.S. v. Asmar, 827 F.2d 907, 912 (3d Cir. 1987).

The Tax Court has set forth the essential elements of estoppel:

> 1) a false representation or wrongful misleading silence; 2) an error in a statement of fact and not in an opinion or statement of law; 3) person claiming the benefits of estoppel must be ignorant of the true facts; and 4) person claiming estoppel must be adversely affected by the acts or statements of the person against whom estoppel is claimed.

Estate of Emerson v. Commissioner, 67 T.C. 612, 617–618 (1977).

This court is among the majority of circuits recognizing estoppel as an equitable defense against government claims, but in such a context we impose an additional burden on claimants to establish some "affirmative misconduct on the part of the government officials." Asmar, 827 F.2d at 911 n.4, 912; see also Kurz v. Philadelphia Elec. Co., 96 F.3d 1544 (3d Cir. 1996). The additional element reflects the need to balance both the public interest in ensuring government can enforce the law without fearing estoppel and citizens' interests "in some minimum standard of decency, honor, and reliability in their relations with their Government." Asmar, 827 F.2d at 912 (citing Community Health Servs. of Crawford County v. Califano, 698 F.2d 615 (3d Cir. 1983), rev'd on other grounds sub nom. Heckler v. Community Health Servs. of Crawford County, 467 U.S. 51, 81 L. Ed. 2d 42, 104 S. Ct. 2218 (1984)). See also United States v. St. John's Gen. Hosp., 875 F.2d 1064, 1069 (3d Cir. 1989).

* * *

As the foregoing cases instruct, we must determine whether Fredericks sufficiently met his burden of establishing the traditional elements of estoppel.

This requires us to consider the elements of misrepresentation, reliance and detriment. We will discuss the affirmative-misconduct element in conjunction with our consideration of the IRS' misrepresentations, and then proceed to the reliance and detriment elements. Subsequently, we will address the special factors that must be present in an estoppel claim against the government.

III.

Misrepresentations

Fredericks argues that the oral representations the IRS made to him that the Form 872-A indefinite extension was lost in the mail, coupled with its three successful attempts to obtain Form 872 limited extensions of the statute of limitations, misrepresented the fact that the IRS had in its possession the Form 872-A. He contends the government affirmatively maintained that misrepresentation for over 11 years, even after it found and decided to rely on the Form 872-A. Thus, Fredericks argues the government's misrepresentations and his detrimental reliance thereon should estop the IRS from invoking the Form 872-A in 1992 and from denying the effectiveness of the third Form 872, which extended the statute only to June 30, 1984. He contends estoppel is appropriate in this case because the government failed to correct its misrepresentations when it finally learned the Form 872-A was on file and decided to rely on that form.

The government argues that any purported misrepresentations were the result of a lack of communication between its district offices. It claims that the Newark office that obtained Fredericks' three Form 872 limited extensions of the statute of limitations was unaware of the Manhattan office's possession of his previously executed Form 872-A indefinite extension. Such conduct, the government contends, does not constitute the "affirmative misconduct" required to equitably estop the IRS from now relying on the Form 872-A. The government also argues that its reliance on the Form 872-A is valid because, as the Tax Court correctly concluded, that form may be terminated only in the manner set forth in the form; and neither Fredericks nor the IRS filed the requisite 872-T termination form.

* * *

We believe that the misrepresentations here were more egregious than those in *Community Health Servs. of Crawford County v. Califano,* 698 F.2d 615 (3d Cir. 1983), and that they rise to affirmative misconduct. At least in *Califano,* the government immediately notified the health provider upon realizing the erroneous nature of its prior representations. *See also* United States v. Pepperman, 976 F.2d 123, 131 (3d Cir. 1992) (finding no estoppel where government's representations were at most ambiguous and where further explanation was immediately sent upon discovery that an earlier representation was erroneous).

Here, the IRS did not refute evidence that it told Fredericks the Form 872-A "was probably lost in the mail." On three occasions over a period of two years the IRS induced Fredericks to sign Forms 872, establishing an agreement to three consecutive specific dates on which the statute of limitations would expire. The government's misrepresentation went beyond mere erroneous oral advice from an IRS agent; it consisted of affirmative, authorized acts inducing Fredericks to sign and rely on the terms of the Form 872 on three different occasions in three different years. Moreover, the IRS' misleading silence after finding and deciding to rely on the Form 872-A, coupled with its failure to notify Fredericks of its decision and its effective revocation of the third Form 872, constitute affirmative misconduct.

* * *

As in *Dana Corp.* [*v. United States*, 200 Ct. Cl. 200, 470 F.2d 1032 (Ct. Cl. 1972)], because of the government's silence after its discovery of, and decision to rely on, the Form 872-A, the IRS agents induced Fredericks to continue to rely on the Forms 872. Had the taxpayer been informed of the IRS' discovery and its decision to adopt an alternative plan of action, he could have—and testified that he would have—exercised his right to terminate the Form 872-A.

When the IRS discovered its mistake in denying the existence of a previously executed Form 872-A, any number of agents presumably had authority to alert Fredericks to the prior misrepresentation that the form did not exist. * * *

The IRS confirmed its earlier misrepresentations by failing to notify the taxpayer that it possessed the Form 872-A and that the Commissioner intended to rely upon that form. The government's misleading silence was a perpetuation of its misrepresentation that the Form 872-A was never signed or received by the IRS. It was an affirmative decision to usurp the Form 872 agreement entered by the IRS setting June 30, 1984 as the expiration of the statute of limitations. The IRS' decision to lie doggo, and induce the taxpayer into thinking all was well, coupled with its additional eight-year delay in producing a document it previously represented as non-existent, compels us to conclude that the IRS was guilty of affirmative misconduct at least as of June 30, 1984. Fredericks has met his burden of establishing the misrepresentation and affirmative-misconduct elements of an estoppel claim against the government. We, therefore, proceed to an examination of the reliance and detriment elements of this doctrine.

IV.

Reliance

Parties claiming equitable estoppel must demonstrate not only that they relied on the alleged misrepresentations, but also that such reliance was reasonable "in that the party claiming the estoppel did not know nor should it have known that its adversary's conduct was misleading." *Crawford County,* 467 U.S. at 59. Fredericks argues that if he had known the IRS was in possession of the Form 872-A, he would have filed the necessary document (Form 872-T) to terminate the indefinite consent. Relying on the IRS' misrepresentation that the Form 872-A was not in his file, followed by the IRS' repeated requests for Form 872 agreements, Fredericks concluded that it was unnecessary to terminate a consent agreement which the IRS maintained that it never received. He concluded that the subsequent Forms 872 were the only agreements relevant to his 1977 return. On June 30, 1984, when the last one-year Form 872 extension expired, Fredericks believed that the statute of limitations prevented the IRS from assessing any deficiencies.

We conclude that Fredericks acted reasonably in relying on the IRS' misrepresentation that the Form 872-A was not in his file, and in relying on the subsequent Forms 872 executed by him and the IRS. Fredericks' reliance would have been unreasonable had it been based solely on the initial oral misrepresentation that the Form 872-A was "probably lost in the mail." But in this case, the IRS repeatedly confirmed its stated position for three years by requesting on three separate occasions the one-year Form 872 extensions. The language of the Form 872 agreements is clear and unequivocal. The third Form 872 executed by the taxpayer stated:

> [Fredericks] and the District director of Internal Revenue consent and agree to the following: (1) that the amount of any Federal [Income] tax due on any return(s) made or for the above taxpayer(s) for the period(s) ended [December 31, 1977 . . .] may be assessed at any time on or before [June 30, 1984].

J.A. 61a.

We believe that Fredericks' reliance on the text of this written IRS form was reasonable. Reading this form in conjunction with the IRS' earlier statements, Fredericks reasonably concluded that June 30, 1984 was the last date for the IRS to assess a deficiency on his 1977 tax return. The IRS itself has characterized a similar Form 872-B as "a contract," and urged us to read its terms literally. *See* Walsonavich v. United States, 335 F.2d 96, 99 (3d Cir. 1964). The taxpayers' reliance on the terms of such contracts is reasonable. *See, e.g.,* Woodworth v. Kales, 26 F.2d 178 (6th Cir. 1928).

The IRS now suggests that Fredericks is attempting to circumvent the requirement that taxpayers can terminate a Form 872-A only by filing a Form 872-T. However, Fredericks is not arguing, as the Tax Court suggested, that mere execution of a Form 872 negates the terms of a valid Form 872-A. Tax Ct. Op. at 7; *see* Kernen v. Commissioner, 902 F.2d 17, 18 (9th Cir. 1990). He concedes he read Form 872-A and understood the procedures set forth therein for terminating that form. He argues that the IRS misled him to believe there was no Form 872-A on file; and that he reasonably relied on the IRS' misrepresentations and concluded there was no need to terminate the non-existent form. We believe this was not only a reasonable conclusion, but *the only* reasonable conclusion that a taxpayer could draw from the IRS' conduct.

As indicated above, courts examining claims of estoppel against the government have looked beyond mere reasonableness to determine whether the alleged reliance was sufficient to invoke estoppel. Courts are more likely to find the reliance reasonable in governmental-estoppel claims if three additional factors exist: (1) if the government agents had authority to engage in the acts or omissions at issue; (2) if the agents' misrepresentation was one of fact, not law; and (3) if the government benefitted from its misrepresentation. We will address each of these in turn to illuminate the appropriateness of estoppel in this instance.

A.

Courts have held that a private party's reliance on governmental actions or omissions is not reasonable if such acts or omissions are contrary to the law or beyond the agents' authority. We stated the rule in *Ritter v. United States*:

> The acts or omissions of the officers of the government, if they be authorized to bind the United States in a particular transaction, will work estoppel against the government, if the officers have acted within the scope of their authority.

28 F.2d 265, 267 (3d Cir. 1928). * * *

Here, the government does not dispute that the IRS had the authority to inform Fredericks that it did not have the Form 872-A, nor does the government dispute that the IRS had the authority to solicit or terminate agreements extending the statute of limitations. To the contrary, the government's counsel at oral argument suggested that IRS agents routinely enter such agreements. Moreover, the government has conceded that the IRS had an obligation—not merely the authority—to notify Fredericks that it had the Form 872-A when it realized its error and that Fredericks had been misled. The agents here acted within the scope of the law and their authority. Therefore, we conclude Fredericks' reliance on their acts and misleading silence was reasonable.

B.

Courts are more likely to apply estoppel when the government's conduct involves a misrepresentation of fact, rather than a misrepresentation of law. *See, e.g.*, Miller v. United States, 500 F.2d 1007 (2d Cir. 1974); Estate of Emerson v. Commissioner, 67 T.C. 612 (1977); Exchange & Sav. Bank of Berlin v. United States, 226 F. Supp. 56, 58 (D. Md. 1964). However, some courts have gone further and invoked estoppel against the IRS even where the misrepresentation involved a question of law. *See* Schuster v. Commissioner, 312 F.2d 311 (9th Cir. 1962) (IRS estopped from correcting prior mistake of law on which bank reasonably relied); Stockstrom v. Commissioner, 88 U.S. App. D.C. 286, 190 F.2d 283 (D.C. Cir. 1951); Joseph Eichelberger & Co. v. Commissioner, 88 F.2d 874 (5th Cir. 1937). We need not go that far because in this case the IRS misrepresented its possession of a Form 872-A consent agreement. This was a misrepresentation of fact, not of law; and we find Fredericks' reliance thereon to be reasonable.

C.

Courts are more willing to estop the government when the government itself benefited from the acts or omissions relied upon by the private party. *See, e.g.,* Walsonavich v. United States, 335 F.2d 96 (3d Cir. 1964) (IRS benefited from agreement to extend the statute of limitations for assessing deficiencies, and taxpayer was justified in relying on the same agreement to extend the period for filing a refund); Joseph Eichelberger & Co. v. Commissioner, 88 F.2d 874, 875 (5th Cir. 1937) ("The United States got the benefit of [the Commissioner's] decision then and ought to abide by it now."); Staten Island Hygeia Ice & Cold Storage Co. v. United States, 85 F.2d 68 (2d Cir. 1936) (IRS is bound by the burdens as well as the benefits of taxpayer's agreement to waive future claims).

One case focussing on the benefits obtained by the government has facts strikingly similar to those in the case at bar. In *Stockstrom v. Commissioner*, 88 U.S. App. D.C. 286, 190 F.2d 283 (D.C. Cir. 1951), the taxpayer made gifts of less than $5,000 to several trusts in 1938. The IRS had ruled in 1937 that no gift tax was due on such transfers. An IRS officer affirmed this position in 1941, telling the taxpayer that no tax was due on his 1938 gifts. The taxpayer relied on the IRS' representations and, because no tax was due, did not file a gift tax return covering the 1938 transfers. In 1948, the IRS attempted to assess a deficiency based on the 1938 gifts, arguing that there was no statute of limitations on the assessment because the taxpayer never filed a return. The D.C. Circuit estopped the Commissioner from assessing the deficiency, finding that the taxpayer's failure to file a return was due entirely to the actions of the IRS. The court held: "[The Commissioner] induced the omission which he now relies upon as giving him unlimited time to assess a tax. The law as to such a situation has long since been established . . . . He who prevents a thing from being done may not avail himself of the non-performance which he has himself occasioned . . . ." *Id.* 190 F.2d at 288.

As in *Stockstrom,* the IRS induced the omission which it relies upon in assessing a deficiency against Fredericks. The IRS misrepresented that it did not have the Form 872-A, induced Fredericks to rely on three subsequently executed Forms 872 to aid the government in its investigation, and induced him to reasonably believe there was no Form 872-A to terminate. The government now attempts to benefit from Fredericks' failure to terminate this form many years after its initial misrepresentation and many years after its realization of—and silence regarding—its own error. As the D.C. Circuit stated in *Stockstrom,* "we regard as unconscionable the Commissioner's claim of authority to assess a tax . . . when the Commissioner himself was responsible for that failure." *Id.* 190 F.2d at 289.

V.

Detriment

"To analyze the nature of a private party's detrimental change in position, we must identify the manner in which reliance on the Government's misconduct has caused the private citizen to change his position for the worse." *Crawford County,* 467 U.S. at 61. Fredericks argues that he suffered a substantial economic detriment by relying on the IRS' misrepresentations. He reasonably relied on the third Form 872 and reasonably believed that the statute of limitations expired on June 30, 1984. He relied on the IRS' misrepresentations that there was no Form 872-A indefinite extension of the statute of limitations and, to his detriment, did not terminate that form. Fredericks permanently lost his right to terminate the Form 872-A and he lost the benefit of the statute of limitations in the third Form 872. Moreover, he was penalized by the IRS' application of an enhanced rate of interest that continues to be compounded daily. This interest accrued while the IRS waited eight years after the June 30, 1984 statute of limitations expired to assess a deficiency.

* * *

The detriment Fredericks suffered becomes readily apparent by comparing the penalty-enhanced rates to those he could have earned in savings accounts, certificates of deposit, treasury securities or top-rated corporate bonds. * * * Concededly, Fredericks retained and could have earned interest on $28,361 that he owed to the IRS, but even in a best-case scenario he could not have earned the amount of interest the government now seeks to collect. This fact is dramatically illustrated by comparing the penalty-enhanced interest charged by the government, as set forth in Appendix B, with the market interest rates shown in Appendix C. This penalty—this economic detriment—is more than a mere technicality because the amount of interest involved here greatly exceeds the underlying liability.

At oral argument, Fredericks stated: "from direct numbers that the government has given me . . . the interest is about $158,000." This figure is more than five times the underlying tax deficiency of $28,361. Counsel for the IRS responded to a question about the amount of interest the government charged Fredericks by stating:

> I don't dispute Mr. Fredericks' estimate that it might be a hundred and fifty thousand dollars in his case. I don't know for certain, but I would not dispute that.

The government relies on the reasoning in *Crawford County* and argues that Fredericks obtained a benefit, rather than a detriment, by the IRS' delay. The government contends that he was allowed to retain money to which he was not entitled, money owed to the IRS in 1978. In our view, the case at bar stands in stark contrast with *Crawford County*.

In *Crawford County*, the Court found no detriment because the private party had suffered only "the inability to retain money that it never should have [kept] in the first place." 467 U.S. at 61. Fredericks' detriment arises not from his inability to retain the $28,361, which he admittedly should have paid the government in 1978. His detriment results from the loss of his right to terminate the Form 872-A and the high rate of interest he is being charged, interest that accrued while Fredericks reasonably believed assessments were barred by the statute of limitations. Fredericks was not "merely . . . induced to do something which could be corrected later." *Id.* at 62, 104 S. Ct. at 2225. He was induced to forfeit his right to terminate the Form 872-A consent agreement. The IRS' subsequent action was not simply a correction of prior misrepresentations, It was a penalty compounded daily as the IRS continued its 12-year investigation well beyond the statute of limitations for any assessments. We conclude these are sufficient detriments to establish an estoppel defense.

As we have observed, courts must consider additional factors when estoppel is asserted against the government and one such factor is whether the government's action permanently deprived the party claiming estoppel of a benefit or right to which it was entitled. For example, in *Payne v. Block*, 714 F.2d 1510, 1517–1518 (11th Cir. 1983), the court effectively estopped the government from closing a loan application period because government agents failed to advertise the loans. Estoppel was appropriate in part because the loan applicants would forever lose their opportunity to apply unless the government was estopped from closing the application period. *Id.* at 1518; *accord* Vestal v. Commissioner, 80 U.S. App. D.C. 264, 152 F.2d 132, 135 (D.C. Cir. 1945) (estopping IRS from changing its characterization of taxable entity in part because the statute of limitations had expired; "restoration to the taxpayers of the taxes originally collected being impossible," estoppel was appropriate).

*   *   *

Like the loan applicants in *Payne*, * * * Fredericks suffered a permanent loss of a legal right. He forever lost his right to terminate the Form 872-A, the only means through which the government could in 1992 assess his 1977 tax return. He was irreversibly deprived of the benefit of the three-year statute of limitations enacted by Congress, the benefit of the terms of the contracts he entered with the IRS to extend that period, and of any opportunity to terminate the revocable 872-A that the IRS misrepresented as lost. The loss of this right created a tangible economic detriment in the form of penalty-enhanced interest rates. Accordingly, we find that Fredericks has satisfied the detriment element of an equitable estoppel claim against the government.

VI.

Estoppel And The Government

The Supreme Court has not directly met the issue whether estoppel against the IRS may be appropriate in certain circumstances. However, contrary to counsel for the Commissioner's emphatic statement at oral argument that in no case has estoppel been asserted successfully against the IRS, this court and others have applied the doctrine of estoppel to the IRS under various circumstances. In *Walsonavich v. United States*, 335 F.2d 96 (3d Cir. 1964), we held that the IRS was estopped from asserting the statute of limitations as a defense to a taxpayer's claim for a refund where the government and taxpayer had entered a written agreement extending the statute of limitations. *See also* Miller v. United States, 500 F.2d 1007 (2d Cir. 1974) (IRS estopped from relying on a statute of limitations contained in a previously signed waiver-of-notice form as a bar to taxpayer's refund claim, where the IRS had erroneously disregarded the waiver, unnecessarily issued the notice to taxpayer and, pursuant to the notice, the statute of limitations had not run); Staten Island Hygeia Ice & Cold Storage Co. v. United States, 85 F.2d 68 (2d

Cir. 1936) (equitable relief available against IRS where erroneous advice induced taxpayer to enter agreement with IRS waiving future claims for refund); * * *.

The IRS is not the only federal agency against which courts have applied the doctrine of estoppel. Case law demonstrates that courts have invoked estoppel against the Post Office Department, the Department of Housing and Urban Development, the Land Management Office, the Postal Service, the Parole Commission, the Farmer's Home Administration, the War Department, the Department of Interior, the Department of Commerce and Labor and the General Land Office. This plethora of precedent suggests that "it is well settled that the doctrine of equitable estoppel, in proper circumstances, and with appropriate caution, may be invoked against the United States in cases involving internal revenue taxation," and in a variety of other contexts. Simmons v. United States, 308 F.2d 938, 945 (5th Cir. 1962).

Although the Supreme Court has neither rejected outright nor articulated a specific test for estoppel claims against the government, the foregoing case law illuminates certain factors beyond the traditional elements of estoppel that we should consider before estopping the IRS. Those factors are: 1) the impact of the estoppel on the public fisc; 2) whether the government agent or agents who made the misrepresentation or error were authorized to act as they did; 3) whether the governmental misconduct involved a question of law or fact; 4) whether the government benefitted from its misrepresentation; and 5) the existence of irreversible detrimental reliance by the party claiming estoppel. We have addressed all but the first factor in conjunction with the traditional elements of estoppel, and we conclude that each of those factors cuts in favor of Fredericks. We now proceed to consider the impact on the public fisc in this case.

Impact on the Public Fisc

Courts are more likely to estop the government when the public fisc—in particular, Congress' power to control public expenditures—is only minimally impacted, if at all. This consideration derives from *Schweiker v. Hansen*, 450 U.S. 785, 790–793, 67 L. Ed. 2d 685, 101 S. Ct. 1468 (1981). The Court in *Schweiker* observed that future cases could be distinguished if the government entered written agreements that supported estoppel or if estoppel did not threaten the public fisc.

* * *

The public-fisc consideration cuts in favor of estopping the government in the case at bar. By enacting a three-year statute of limitations on the time within which the IRS must assess tax deficiencies, Congress clearly contemplated that in some instances taxpayers would retain funds—because the statute of limitations had run—to which they were not initially entitled. Therefore, invoking the statute of limitations to bar an IRS assessment cannot be deemed an intrusion into Congress' power to expend and allocate public funds. Neither Congress' power to control public expenditures nor its authority to enact statutes of limitations is impacted when a taxpayer invokes such a statute, either at the end of its original life or 11 years later pursuant to written agreements between the taxpayer and IRS.

*   *   *

Estoppel here affects the public fisc by approximately $28,361, plus any interest that would have accrued before June 30, 1984—the day the statute of limitations in the last Form 872 signed by the IRS and Fredericks expired. We are satisfied that in the scope of the IRS' operations, this impact on the public fisc is not only minimal, but also a necessary result of Congress' enactment of enforceable statutes of limitations.

We conclude that Fredericks has met his burden of establishing the traditional elements of estoppel. The IRS misrepresented its possession of a Form 872-A indefinite extension of the statute of limitations and confirmed that misrepresentation by obtaining three Forms 872. The IRS' conduct constituted affirmative misconduct when it remained silent upon realizing its mistake and upon deciding to change its course of action to rely on the previously lost Form 872-A without notifying the taxpayer. Its decision to effectively revoke the third Form 872 without notice to the taxpayer also adds to the affirmative misconduct here. Fredericks relied upon the IRS' oral and written representations as to the relevant statute of limitations and lost his right to terminate the Form 872-A. His detriment is compounded by the IRS' assessment of an increased penalty rate of interest covering the entire duration of its protracted investigation.

*   *   *

Having concluded that the IRS is estopped from relying on the Form 872-A to extend the statute of limitations, we hold that the Commissioner was time-barred from making any assessment, in full or in part, in 1992. The original three-year statute of limitations had run, as had the three one-year extensions agreed to by the parties. Any assessment by the IRS on Fredericks' 1977 tax return was time-barred by 1984. The taxpayer asserted the statute of limitations as a defense to a 1992 assessment, and the Commissioner is thus estopped from refusing to recognize that defense and from denying the effectiveness of the 1984 statute of limitations.

The dissent agrees that the IRS should be estopped, but argues that we should allow the government to assess a deficiency for the period before September 30, 1984—90 days after the last Form 872 one-year extension expired. This contention fails to recognize the precise nature of the estoppel here. The Commissioner is estopped from using the Form 872-A to deny that the statute of limitations had run in 1984. Thus, the entire 1992 assessment was time-barred. By operation of the estoppel doctrine, the Commissioner was stripped of authority to make any assessment whatsoever. The effect of the estoppel here does not raise a question of "equities"; it presents one of pure law—the operation of a statute that bars the Commissioner's action beyond a date certain.

270   RESTRICTIONS ON ASSESSMENT OF TAX   CH. 5

Because we rule the Commissioner is estopped from asserting a deficiency in the 1977 tax return of Barry I. Fredericks, the decision of the Tax Court will be reversed.

* * *

Whether a taxpayer agrees to a fixed-date or open-ended consent, the taxpayer can seek to limit the extension agreement to specific items or issues on the return. I.R.C. § 6501(c)(4)(B). Revenue Procedure 68-31, 1968-2 C.B. 917, lists the circumstances under which the IRS will allow the taxpayer to restrict an extension agreement. The practical effect of a restrictive consent is to allow the statute of limitations on assessment to expire except with respect to those issues specified in the agreement. A restrictive consent is best accomplished by typing on the form itself a contractual limitation. Because courts interpret these types of limitations based solely upon the language in the consent, the restriction should be drafted in a clear and unambiguous manner and should be signed by both the taxpayer and the appropriate IRS official.[11] The Internal Revenue Manual offers the following suggested language: "The amount of any deficiency assessment is to be limited to that resulting from any adjustment to (description of the area(s) of consideration), including any consequential changes to other items based on such adjustment."[12] I.R.M. 25.6.22.8.12. From a procedural standpoint, a restrictive consent not only limits the taxpayer's overall exposure to adjustments by the IRS, but affords the taxpayer an opportunity to negotiate further with the IRS over the scope of continued examination or appeal activity.[13]

§ 5.04   Exceptions to the Statutes of Limitations

[A]   The Statutory Mitigation Provisions

By their nature, statutes of limitations cut off otherwise valid claims. To prevent a double benefit to either the taxpayer or the government, Code sections 1311 through 1314, the statutory mitigation provisions, allow reopening of a barred year in specified circumstances. In general, if the taxpayer has received the double benefit, the mitigation provisions may allow a year barred by the statute of limitations on assessment to be reopened to allow assessment. On the other hand, if the government received the double benefit, the

[11] Although a consent to extend the period of limitations results in a unilateral waiver of a defense by the taxpayer, contract principles are significant because section 6501(c)(4) requires that the IRS and taxpayer reach a mutual agreement over the terms of the extension. Piarulle v. Commissioner, 80 T.C. 1035 (1931).

[12] This language is not necessarily unambiguous. Compare the differing interpretations of the term "adjustment" in *Mecom v. Commissioner*, 101 T.C. 374, 391 (1993), *aff'd without op.*, 40 F.3d 385 (5th Cir. 1994) and *Powell v. Commissioner*, T.C. Memo. 1990-329. The differing interpretations resulted in opposite holdings in those cases.

[13] Unless otherwise suspended, interest continues to accrue during the period the extension was granted. Interest is discussed in further detail in Chapter 11.

mitigation provisions may allow reopening of a year barred by the statute of limitations on refund claims. The statute of limitations on refund claims is discussed in detail in Chapter 8.

The mitigation provisions are technical and complex. The Tax Court explains:

> In the aggregate, sections 1311 through 1314 set forth a highly complicated and confusingly interrelated set of provisions authorizing the correction of error which is otherwise prevented by operation of law, *e.g.*, the expiration of the statutory period of limitations for assessment. Considerably oversimplified but nevertheless sufficiently accurate for present purposes, sections 1311–1314 were designed to prevent a windfall, in specified circumstances, either to the taxpayer or to the Government arising out of the treatment of the same item in a manner inconsistent with its erroneous treatment in a closed year. Thus, provision is made to correct an error in the closed year where, for example, the same item was erroneously included or excluded from income or where the same item was allowed or disallowed as a deduction in a barred year. The authorized mechanism for correction is an "adjustment," a term of art the meaning and scope of which emerges from the mitigation provisions of sections 1311–1314.

Bolten v. Commissioner, 95 T.C. 397, 402-403 (1990).

The following example provides a more detailed illustration of the application of the statutory mitigation provisions:

> *Example:* Jeanne and Peter entered into a contract under which Peter paid Jeanne for architectural services. In 1995, they had a dispute over whether Jeanne had earned $10,000 of her fee for the year. Peter paid Jeanne but sued her in state court for return of the $10,000. Although Jeanne filed her 1995 return on time, she did not include the $10,000 in her 1995 gross income because she was uncertain of the outcome of the lawsuit. In 1997, Jeanne won the suit, which Peter did not appeal. Jeanne filed her 1997 return on April 5, 1998, but did not include the payment in her gross income for 1997, having decided that it really should have been included in her gross income for 1995.
>
> On January 10, 2000, the IRS sent Jeanne a notice of deficiency for the 1997 tax year. Its deficiency is based on the $10,000 fee, which the IRS asserts should have been included in Jeanne's 1997 gross income. Jeanne petitions the Tax Court. Assume that Jeanne wins the litigation, based on her argument that 1995 was the proper year for her to include the amount in gross income. Also assume that because the statute of limitations on assessment applicable to Jeanne's 1995 return is three years, it has expired by the time the Tax Court renders its decision.
>
> The Tax Court decision constitutes a "determination" for purposes of section 1311(a). I.R.C. § 1313(a)(1). The double exclusion of the amount from gross income is the situation described in section

1312(3)(B). Therefore, section 1311 applies to permit an "adjustment" under section 1314. Under section 1314(a), the adjustment is to Jeanne's 1995 tax, in the amount of the increase in tax determined by adding $10,000 to her 1995 gross income. The resulting tax liability can be assessed and collected in the same manner as a deficiency. I.R.C. § 1314(b).

The following case further demonstrates the application of the mitigation provisions to reopen a year barred by the statute of limitations on assessment:

GILL v. COMMISSIONER
United States Court of Appeals, Fifth Circuit
306 F.2d 902 (1962)

JONES, CIRCUIT JUDGE.

The two proceedings here before us for decision involve federal income tax liability of Robert S. Gill and his wife, Sara Louise Gill who is now deceased. All of the transactions from which the asserted tax liability arose were those of Robert S. Gill and he will herein be referred to as the taxpayer. Mrs. Gill was, and her executor is, a party because of the filing of joint husband and wife returns. The original controversy was before this Court in 1958. Gill v. United States, 5 Cir., 258 F.2d 553. The taxpayer had been a partner in Gill Printing and Stationery Company. It reported income on a fiscal-year basis, closing its books as of April 30 of each year. In July of 1945 the taxpayer became the sole proprietor of the business. He continued to file his income tax returns, as before, on a calendar-year basis but continued to report the earnings of the printing business on the basis of the accounting periods previously employed. Thus his return for a particular calendar year would include the net earnings of the business for the fiscal year beginning on May 1st of the prior year through April 30 of the current year. He filed claims for refund for the years 1949, 1950, 1952, and for a period of 1951 ending April 30 of that year. In support of his claim for refund of tax paid for 1949, and it is with the 1949 tax that we are concerned, the taxpayer made a recomputation of his income by excluding two-thirds of the income of the business for its accounting year ending April 30, 1949, and adding two-thirds of the business income for the fiscal year ending April 30, 1950. These adjustments put the Gills' tax computation for the 1949-1952 period on a calendar-year basis except for the two-thirds of the business income for annual period ending April 30, 1949.

The claim for refund was disallowed, suit was brought and judgment was for the Government in the district court. This Court reversed, and by its decision, *supra*, determined that the taxpayer's income should be computed on a calendar-year basis. As a result, a judgment of the district court was entered, following the remand of this Court, which eliminated from the taxpayer's 1949 computation the business income for the May 1 to December 31, 1948, period. No amended return for 1948 was filed, no waiver of limitations has been made for the year 1948, and no charge of fraud has been asserted. On September 28, 1958,[14] a notice of deficiency was sent to the taxpayer

---

[14] [This date apparently should read September 28, 1959 instead of 1958. Eds.]

proposing an increase in the tax for 1948 by the inclusion in that year the business income which had been excluded from the 1949 determination. In so doing the Commissioner invoked the provisions of Sections 1311–1314 of the Internal Revenue Code of 1954 usually referred to as the mitigation provisions. We first consider whether the assessment was made within a year after the "determination" of the error in computing the 1949 tax. To be collectible the assessment must have been made, under the provisions of Section 1314(b), within a year.

The taxpayer contends that the "determination" was made by the opinion of this Court, issued on July 18, 1958, in which it was held that the tax on all of the income of the taxpayer should be computed on an annual basis. The taxpayer takes the position that a determination was made on July 18, 1958, the date of the opinion, and the deficiency notice mailed on September 28, 1959, was sent too late. The Tax Court was of the opinion that there was no "determination" until the expiration of the time for applying to the Supreme Court for certiorari. It held the notice was timely. An opinion of a Court of Appeals permits a losing litigant to seek a rehearing or to apply to the Supreme Court for a writ of certiorari, or both. In the absence of any action by the Supreme Court, a Court of Appeals retains jurisdiction, and none is relinquished to the district court, until a mandate or judgment is issued. 36 C.J.S. Federal Courts § 301(32), p. 1370 et seq.; 5B C.J.S. Appeal & Error § 1959, p. 530 et seq. The mandate of this Court was issued on September 29, 1958, and this is the earliest date at which it could be said there was a "determination." Louis Pizitz Dry Goods Company v. United States, D.C.N.D. Ala. 1950, 185 F. Supp. 186, *aff. sub. nom.* Louis Pizitz Dry Goods Co., Inc. v. Deal, 5th Cir., 1953, 208 F.2d 724, *cert. den.* 347 U.S. 952, 74 S.Ct. 676, 98 L.Ed. 1097; Bishop v. Reichel, D.C.N.D. N.Y. 1954, 127 F. Supp. 750, 54 A.L.R.2d 532, *aff.* 2 Cir., 221 F.2d 806, *cert. den.* 350 U.S. 833, 76 S.Ct. 68, 100 L.Ed. 743, 2 Mertens Law of Federal Income Taxation, ch. 14, p. 48 *et seq.* § 14.12. The notice of deficiency was given on September 28, 1959, and so was within the year prescribed by the statute. It is not necessary to consider whether the time of the determination might have been postponed until the right to apply for certiorari had expired. Since our 1958 review was of a district court judgment, we do not express any view with respect to the statutes which relate to the time when decisions of the Tax Court become final. 26 U.S.C.A. (I.R.C. 1939) § 1140; 26 U.S.C.A. (I.R.C. 1954) § 7481. It was suggested that, in view of the provisions of the remand of this Court as set out in the opinion of July 18, 1958, the determination was made by the district court's judgment after the remand. The disposition we have made of the "determination" issue makes it unnecessary to pass upon this question.

The taxpayer makes a contention that the mitigation provisions of the statute are specific and limited, that they cannot be extended or enlarged, and that they do not cover the situation. He asserts, in connection with this contention, that the adjustment made by the exclusion from 1949 taxable income of the amount which should have been included in 1948 income was not an "item" within the meaning of the statute. It was, though, a stated sum specified by the taxpayer. "Item" as used in the statute, has been construed "to include any item or amount which affects gross income in more than one year, and produces, as a result, double taxation, double deduction or inequitable avoidance of the tax." Gooch Milling & Elevator Co. v. United States, 111 Ct. Cl. 576, 78 F. Supp. 94. *See* H.T. Hackney Co. v. United States, 111 Ct. Cl. 664, 78 F. Supp. 101; Dubuque Packing Co. v. United States, D.C.N.C. Iowa 1954, 126 F. Supp. 796, *aff.* 8 Cir., 233 F.2d 453. Under this principle the mitigation provisions of the Internal Revenue Code were properly invoked.

The taxpayer finally argues that, if unsuccessful on his other contentions and the Government is permitted, under the mitigation statute to adjust his 1948 tax by the inclusion for the year of the income excluded from 1949 income by this Court's determination, there should be a complete reopening of the 1948 tax computation so as to permit the exclusion of the May 1 to December 31, 1947, business income. The difficulty with the taxpayer's position is that the statute does not permit the doing of that which he would have done. The statute authorizes adjustments only with respect to the items involved in the determination. The statute of limitations precludes reopening as to any item which was not involved in the determination. First National Bank of Philadelphia v. Commissioner, 18 T.C. 899, *aff.* 3 Cir., 205 F.2d 82; Central Hanover Bank 3 Trust Co. v. United States, 2 Cir., 163 F.2d 60.

We find no basis for disturbing the decision of the Tax Court in the one case or the decision of the District Court in the other. Each is

Affirmed.

Why does this case involve both a District Court decision and a Tax Court decision? Where in the mitigation provisions does it require the IRS to send a notice of deficiency within one year of the determination that triggers the applicability of the provisions? More specifically, what is the taxpayer's argument about that one-year limitation period and how does the Court of Appeals resolve it?

[B] Equitable Recoupment

Another doctrine that alleviates the harshness of an expired limitations period is called "equitable recoupment." In general, it allows a party, the IRS or the taxpayer, to defend against a claim of the other by offsetting a time-barred amount owed to the first party, arising out of the same transaction. For example, assume that the IRS has issued a notice of deficiency in estate tax based on an increased valuation of certain property included in the estate, the estate had sold some of that property using the valuation as its basis, and the statute of limitations has run on the refund claim. The estate might be able to use the defense of equitable recoupment to offset any deficiency in estate tax with the time-barred overpayment of income tax. *See Estate of Branson v. Commissioner*, 113 T.C. 6 (1999), *aff'd*, 264 F.3d 904 (9th Cir. 2001), *cert. denied*, No. 01-928 (2002); *Estate of Mueller v. Commissioner*, 101 T.C. 551 (1993). However, there is some dispute as to whether the Tax Court has the power to apply equitable recoupment. That issue is discussed further in Chapter 6. Equitable recoupment may arise in refund cases, as well. In that regard, it is discussed further in Chapter 8.

PROBLEMS

1.   During 1996, Margaret received from her employer, in addition to her annual salary of $50,000, an antique work of art as additional compensation.

   A.   Assume that Margaret properly reported the artwork as gross income on her 1996 return, which she filed on April 15, 1997. Her return reflected her valuation of $10,000. The IRS audited Margaret's return. On February 1, 2000, the IRS mailed to her a notice of deficiency reflecting its determination that the correct value of the artwork, includible in her gross income, was $20,000. Margaret has not responded to the notice of deficiency.

   i.   When is the last day that the IRS can assess additional tax with respect to Margaret's 1996 return?

   ii.   What would be the last day for the IRS to assess additional tax with respect to Margaret's 1996 return if Margaret had filed her return on March 1, 1997 instead of April 15?

   iii.   What would be the last day for the IRS to assess additional tax with respect to Margaret's 1996 return if Margaret had filed her return on June 2, 1997 instead? Does it matter whether Margaret had obtained an extension of time to file her 1996 return?

   iv.   What would be the last day for the IRS to assess additional tax with respect to Margaret's 1996 return if Margaret's annual salary were $25,000 instead of $50,000?

   B.   Assume instead that Margaret did not report the receipt of the artwork on her 1996 return, which she filed on April 15, 1997. On February 1, 2000, the IRS mailed to her a notice of deficiency reflecting its determination that Margaret has $20,000 of additional gross income, attributable to the artwork.

   i.   Assume Margaret was unaware that the artwork constitutes gross income to her, and that is why she did not report it on her return.

   a.   If Margaret does not respond to the notice of deficiency, when is the last day the IRS may assess additional tax with respect to Margaret's 1996 return?

   b.   If Margaret responds to the notice of deficiency on March 10, 2000 by signing a Form 870 waiving restrictions on assessment of tax, when is the last day the IRS may assess additional tax with respect to Margaret's 1996 return?

    c. Assume that Margaret responds to the notice of deficiency by filing a Tax Court petition on April 3, 2000. The Tax Court hears the case on May 4, 2001, and its decision, which is adverse to Margaret, becomes final on June 3, 2002. When is the last day the IRS may assess additional tax with respect to Margaret's 1996 return?

    ii. If Margaret had instead intentionally failed to report the value of the artwork as gross income, and she does not respond to the notice of deficiency, when is the last day the IRS may assess additional tax with respect to Margaret's 1996 return? How would your answer change if Margaret had filed an amended return on June 16, 1997, reporting $20,000 of gross income from the receipt of the artwork?

  C. Assume that Margaret fraudulently failed to file a return for 1996. She subsequently filed the return on June 1, 2000. When is the last day the IRS may assess tax with respect to Margaret's 1996 tax year?

2. Assume that the statute of limitations on José's return will expire in three months. José is currently negotiating a settlement with the IRS Appeals Division. The Appeals Officer has requested that José extend the statute of limitations on assessment for an additional six-month period.

  A. What factors should José consider in deciding whether to agree to extend the statute of limitations?

  B. If José does agree to extend the statute, should the extension be made on Form 872 or Form 872-A?

3. Although she left her job in November of 1996, Patrice was entitled to a year-end bonus. On December 30, her former boss called her to let her know the check was available. Patrice did not pick it up until January 3, 1997. Her W-2 for 1996 did not include the bonus, so Patrice did not include it in gross income for her 1996 tax year when she filed the return on April 15, 1997. In 1997, she received a W-2 in the amount of the bonus, but Patrice decided that she should have included it in her 1996 gross income because she "constructively received" it in 1996. Therefore she did not include it in her 1997 return, which she filed on April 15, 1998. On May 1, 2000, the IRS mailed Patrice a notice of deficiency for her 1997 tax year based on the unreported bonus. Patrice petitioned the Tax Court, and on June 1, 2002, the Tax Court's decision in Patrice's favor became final. The decision was made on the ground that the bonus should have been income for Patrice's 1996 tax year. The statute of limitations on assessment for 1996 has expired.

  A. What recourse does the IRS have?

    B.   In order to avail itself of its options under A., what action must the IRS take, and by what deadline?

4.   Maya filed her 1993 return on April 15, 1994. On March 3, 1997, the IRS asked Maya to agree to extend the statute of limitations on assessment. On March 5, 1997 Maya signed a Form 872, specifying an extension of the statute until April 15, 1998. Subsequently, Maya signed additional Forms 872, on April 1, 1998 and March 1, 1999, each providing an additional 1-year extension. When is the last day that the IRS can send Maya a notice of deficiency as a prerequisite to assessing tax with respect to Maya's 1993 tax year?

5.   The IRS has asked Drake to extend the statute of limitations on a tax year that is under audit. In deciding whether to agree to extend the statute, Drake would be interested in ascertaining whether taxpayers who agree to extend the statute of limitations obtain better settlements or better results in court than those who do not. Would Drake likely be able to obtain this information under FOIA?

Chapter 6

OVERVIEW OF TAX LITIGATION

Reading Assignment: Code §§ 6212, 6213, 6512(b)(1), 7422(a), (e), 7430, 7441–7446, 7452, 7453, 7458–7463, 7481, 7482, 7491.

§ 6.01 Introduction to the Federal Tax Fora

Three courts have trial-level jurisdiction over most federal tax cases, the United States Tax Court, the United States District Courts, and the United States Court of Federal Claims. *See* I.R.C. § 6213; 28 U.S.C. § 1346(a)(1); 28 U.S.C. § 1491(a)(1). The Tax Court has jurisdiction over both tax "deficiencies" and overpayment claims that arise out of the same tax year for which the taxpayer received a notice of deficiency. I.R.C. §§ 6213(a); 6512(b)(1). The District Court and Court of Federal Claims share jurisdiction over "refund" actions. 28 U.S.C. § 1346(a)(1). In addition, the United States Bankruptcy Courts can consider tax claims that arise in the context of a bankruptcy proceeding.

Although this chapter provides only an overview of tax litigation concerning deficiencies and refunds, it is important to note that the Tax Court, Court of Federal Claims, and District Courts also have jurisdiction over certain other types of tax claims. The Tax Court and the District Court for the District of Columbia have jurisdiction over disclosure actions under section 6110 of the Code, discussed in Chapter 3. *See* I.R.C. § 6110(f)(4)(A). The Tax Court, Court of Federal Claims, and the District Court for the District of Columbia have declaratory judgment jurisdiction over cases involving a determination by the IRS with respect to the tax-exempt status of various types of organizations.[1] *See* I.R.C. § 7428(a). Various courts have jurisdiction over petitions for innocent spouse status, which are discussed in Chapter 2, depending on whether or not the tax years are the subject of a refund suit. *See* I.R.C. § 6015(e).

Appeals from the Tax Court and the District Courts lie to the United States Courts of Appeals. *See* I.R.C. § 7482 (Tax Court cases); 28 U.S.C. § 1291

---

[1] The Tax Court also has jurisdiction to redetermine an IRS determination that one or more individuals performing services for the taxpayer are employees rather than independent contractors. *See* I.R.C. § 7436. Code section 7436 was enacted as part of the Taxpayer Relief Act of 1997. *See* Pub. L. No. 105-34, 111 Stat. 788, 1055 § 1454(a). These cases may be conducted as small tax cases if the amount of employment taxes placed in dispute is $50,000 or less for each calendar quarter involved. I.R.C. § 7436(c). In addition, the Community Renewal Tax Relief Act of 2000 provides that the Tax Court has jurisdiction over the amount of employment tax due so long as part of the controversy with the IRS is the employment tax status of workers (employee or independent contractor). *See* I.R.C. § 7436(a). The provision is effective as of August 5, 1997. It overrules the contrary jurisdictional holding of *Henry Randolph Consulting v. Commissioner*, 112 T.C. 1 (1999).

(District Court cases). For the Tax Court, appeals go to the Court of Appeals for the circuit in which the taxpayer resided at the time he filed the petition.[2] I.R.C. § 7482(b)(1). Appeals from the Court of Federal Claims go to the United States Court of Appeals for the Federal Circuit. 28 U.S.C. § 1295(a)(3). Appeals from all of the circuit courts lie to the United States Supreme Court. 28 U.S.C. § 1254.

This chapter provides an overview of the three trial-level fora generally available in civil federal tax litigation. It also discusses bankruptcy jurisdiction over federal tax issues. In addition, the chapter considers various procedural issues that may arise in a tax case litigated in any of the three fora, such as burden of proof rules, awards to taxpayers of administrative and litigations costs, and litigation sanctions against taxpayers.

§ 6.02   The United States Tax Court

[A]   Overview

The Tax Court was created by Congress under its Article I power.[3] The statute creating the Tax Court is section 7441 of the Internal Revenue Code. By statute, the Tax Court has 19 judges. I.R.C. § 7443(a). These judges are appointed by the President with the advice and consent of the Senate, *id.,* each for a 15-year term, I.R.C. § 7443(e). The Code also allows the Chief Judge of the Tax Court to appoint "special trial judges." I.R.C. § 7443A(a). Special trial judges hear "small tax cases" as well as other cases, I.R.C. § 7443A(b); the small tax case procedure is discussed below.

The Tax Court is based in Washington, D.C., but its judges travel to hear cases on regular calendars in various cities around the country, and also may travel additional times or to additional locations for "special sessions" of the court if warranted. *See* I.R.C. § 7446. The taxpayer may be represented by anyone admitted to practice before the Tax Court, which includes non-attorneys who have passed an examination. *See* I.R.C. § 7452. The IRS is represented in Tax Court by attorneys from the IRS Chief Counsel's Office.

The Tax Court issues three types of decisions: Division Opinions, which have precedential value and are officially published; Memorandum Opinions, which have no official precedential value, but are privately published; and Summary Opinions in small tax cases, which have no precedential value but, beginning

---

[2] The rules governing tax cases in District Court in general, and appeals from tax cases in District Court in particular, are the same as the rules governing any other District Court case. Because that material is covered in other courses, this book does not focus on District Court litigation except to the extent it differs in tax cases or contrasts with other types of tax litigation.

[3] Congress established the Board of Tax Appeals in 1924. See Revenue Act of 1924, ch. 234, sec. 900, 43 Stat. 253, 336–338. Previously, it was an administrative agency of the executive branch, though it carried out judicial functions. Steve R. Johnson, "The Phoenix and the Perils of the Second Best: Why Heightened Appellate Deference to Tax Court Decisions Is Undesirable," 77 Or. L. Rev. 235, 280 (1998). In 1942, the Board of Tax Appeals was renamed the Tax Court of the United States. Revenue Act of 1942, ch. 619, sec. 504, 56 Stat. 957. In 1969, Congress made the court an Article I court and renamed it the United States Tax Court. Tax Reform Act of 1969, Pub. L. No. 91-172, 83 Stat. 487, 730–736.

in 2001, are privately published. Small tax cases are discussed below, in Section 6.02[E].

It is up to the Chief Judge to determine whether to issue a decision as a Division Opinion or Memorandum Opinion. *See* I.R.C. § 7460. Division Opinions are generally the Tax Court's first pronouncement on a question of law, while Memorandum Opinions generally apply clear law to new facts. The Chief Judge can also refer a Division Opinion for review by the entire court.[4] *Id.* A reviewed case is not retried *en banc*, but rather the conference of 19 judges reconsiders the case from the written record. Such opinions are labeled "reviewed by the Court." Court-reviewed cases are generally ones that (1) decide legal issues not previously considered by the Tax Court; (2) invalidate a Treasury Regulation; (3) would conflict with existing Tax Court case law; (4) involve a legal issue not previously considered by the Tax Court, and, as written, would conflict with the decision of a Court of Appeals other than the one to which appeal would lie; or (5) involve an issue on which the Tax Court was previously reversed by a circuit other than the one to which appeal would lie.[5]

As indicated above, Special Trial Judges have the authority to decide regular cases assigned to them by the Chief Judge. *See* I.R.C. § 7443A. When a Special Trial Judge decides a case other than one involving $50,000 or less per tax year, he must submit a "report" on it to a regular judge of the Tax Court. *See* Interim Tax Court Rule 183(b). The Tax Court rules do not provide an opportunity for the parties to the case to see the Special Trial Judge's report. Does shielding the Special Trial Judge's report from the parties' view raise due process concerns? *Compare* Gerald A. Kafka & Jonathan Z. Ackerman, "Fact-Finding in the Tax Court: Access to Special Trial Judge Reports," 91 Tax Notes 639, 640 (2001) (arguing that it does) *with* Allen Madison, "Access to the Tax Court's Deliberative Processes," 91 Tax Notes 2247 (2001) (arguing that it does not).

The Tax Court follows its own procedural rules, which are based on the Federal Rules of Civil Procedure. *See* Tax Court Rule 1. Tax Court judges generally provide to the parties a Standing Pretrial Order accompanying the notice of the date and location of the trial. *See* Tax Court Rule 131(b). The order contains instructions for preparation for trial. *See id.* Unexcused failure to comply with that order can subject the noncomplying party to sanctions. *Id.*

[B] Pleading Requirements

Tax Court jurisdiction over federal tax deficiencies is based on a notice of deficiency mailed by the IRS to the taxpayer and a timely responsive petition. *See* IRC § 6213(a); *see also* Tax Court Rules 20, 34. To initiate litigation, the taxpayer must file a petition with the Tax Court, generally within 90 days of the date of the notice of deficiency, and attach the notice to the petition.[6]

---

[4] In 1996, for example, the Tax Court produced 564 memorandum opinions and 46 division opinions, four of which were reviewed by the court. Johnson, *supra* note 3, at 268 n.139.

[5] Nina Crimm, TAX COURT LITIGATION: PRACTICE AND PROCEDURE, at ¶ 10.2[2][c][iv] (1999).

[6] The fee for filing a Tax Court petition is $60. *See* I.R.C. § 7451.

The taxpayer can also claim in the petition a refund of an overpayment. I.R.C. § 6512(b).[7] Tax Court rules provide for calculation of the amount of the deficiency or overpayment, which is necessary in any case in which the judgment (including any concession) is not entirely for one party, petitioner or respondent. (In Tax Court, the taxpayer is the "petitioner" and the IRS is the "respondent.") The calculation is referred to as a "Rule 155" calculation, and the resulting decision is entered under Tax Court Rule 155.

The taxpayer's petition must include the taxpayer's legal name and residence (or, for a corporation, its principal place of business); the taxpayer's mailing address and taxpayer identification number; the office of the IRS with which the return in question was filed; the date of the notice of deficiency; the amount of the alleged deficiency; the type of tax involved; the tax years or periods in issue; clear and concise assignments of the IRS's errors; clear and concise lettered statements of the facts on which the taxpayer bases the errors; a prayer for relief; the signature, mailing address, and telephone number of each taxpayer or each taxpayer's counsel, and counsel's Tax Court bar number; and a copy of the notice of deficiency. Tax Court Rule 34(b). A Tax Court petition generally looks something like this one, which was filed in an actual case.

SAMPLE TAX COURT PETITION

JANE PARKER,
Petitioner,
v.
COMMISSIONER OF INTERNAL REVENUE,
Respondent.

PETITION

The Petitioner hereby petitions for a redetermination of the deficiency set forth by the Commissioner of Internal Revenue in his Notice of Deficiency (bearing symbols "SS:ESP MD:STP") dated December 14, 1998, and as a basis for the petitioner's case alleges as follows:

1. The Petitioner has a legal residence at 125 Oak Street, Jordan, Minnesota, 55352-9307. Petitioner Jane Parker's taxpayer identification number is [TIN OMITTED]. The return for the period ending December 31, 1996 was filed with the Office of Internal Revenue Service at Kansas City, Missouri.

2. The Notice of Deficiency for the tax year ending December 31, 1996 (a copy of which is attached hereto and marked as Exhibit "A") was mailed to the Petitioner on or after December 14, 1998, and was issued by the office of the Internal Revenue Service at St. Paul, Minnesota.

3. The deficiency as determined by the Commissioner is in income tax and additions to tax pursuant to the Internal Revenue Code Section 6662 as follows:

---

[7] Overpayment claims are discussed in detail in Chapter 8, which covers the various methods of pursuing a refund of overpaid taxes.

Tax Year Ended	Deficiency	Additions to Tax IRC Section 6662(a)
12/31/96	$30,825	$6,165

all of which is in dispute.

4. The determination of addition to tax set forth in the Notice of Deficiency is based upon the following errors:

A. The Commissioner erred in determining that Petitioner received funds from the Estate of Robert Bennett as compensation or income from services.

B. The Commissioner erred in determining that the addition to tax provided by Section 6662 is applicable.

5. The facts upon which the Petitioner relies as the basis for her case are as follows:

A. The Petitioner's first husband, John Parker, died from malignant brain cancer in 1964. Petitioner and her first husband operated a restaurant "Parker Cafe" in Plato, Minnesota for many years which Petitioner continued to operate after the death of her first husband.

B. Petitioner met Mr. Robert Bennett in 1966. In 1977, Mr. Bennett persuaded Petitioner to retire from active business, sell the restaurant, move to Jordan, Minnesota and establish a common household with him in a house that he was building in Jordan, Minnesota.

C. Petitioner helped Mr. Bennett complete the construction of the house by contributing funds, materials and her time and efforts to completing the construction of the house.

E. Petitioner provided most of the furnishings, appliances and utensils used in the house by this couple in an amount greater than $50,000.00.

F. During the years during which they maintained their common household, Petitioner met her own personal living expenses and also contributed significantly more to the couple's joint living expenses than Mr. Bennett did. For example, for the period from August 23, 1989 through early 1996, Petitioner contributed in excess of $50,000.00 to the couple's joint living expenses.

G. Mr. Bennett was aware of Petitioner's large and disproportionate contributions to their joint living expenses. Also, Mr. Bennett wished to express his love for Petitioner and gratitude for the life they shared. Therefore, he verbally promised Petitioner that upon his death, in his will, he would give her the house that they had built, furnished and lived in from its construction.

H. Mr. Bennett died on February 7, 1996. No will for Mr. Bennett was ever found.

I. Mr. Bennett's brother, a Mr. Richard Bennett, became the administrator of Mr. Bennett's estate.

J. Mr. Richard Bennett refused to honor Mr. Robert Bennett's promise to bequeath the house to Petitioner.

K. As a result, Petitioner filed a claim against the estate in the probate proceeding for Mr. Robert Bennett.

L. Petitioner and the estate of Robert Bennett settled this claim by transferring the house to Petitioner. The parties agreed the house had a fair market value of $138,000 as per an appraisal. Petitioner paid $35,000 in cash to the estate and the estate agreed to credit $103,000 against the value of the house.

M. Petitioner paid more towards the construction and furnishing of the house and their joint living expenses than the $103,000 credited towards the purchase price of the house.

N. Therefore, the $103,000 represented a reimbursement of expenses incurred and funds advanced by Petitioner and an expression by the decedent of love and gratitude toward Petitioner for the life they had shared.

O. Therefore, none of the $103,000 credited to the value of the house in the settlement agreement is attributable to compensation for service.

P. Petitioner informed her return preparer about the bequest that she had received from the estate of Robert Bennett in the form of a credit against the purchase price of the house at the time the 1996 Federal Income Tax Return was prepared. Therefore, in not reporting this amount as income, she relied upon the advice of her return preparer and accountant.

Q. The accountant's treatment of this transaction as a bequest rather than as compensation for services was correct as a matter of fact and law.

WHEREFORE, it is prayed that the Court hear this case and determine that there is no deficiency and no addition to tax due from Petitioner for the taxable year of 1996.

Dated: January 21st, 1999

>By:
>Attorney for Petitioner
>Address
>Telephone Number
>Attorney No.

[Attachments omitted.]

Because a petition is required for Tax Court subject matter jurisdiction, a Tax Court case will be dismissed if the taxpayer was sent a valid notice of deficiency but filed his petition late.[8] In addition, although the Tax Court may allow the taxpayer to file an amended petition, an effort should be made to assure that the proper party files the petition in the first instance so that obtaining permission to amend the petition is not necessary. *See* Tax Court Rule 60(a)(1); *see also Fletcher Plastics, Inc. v. Commissioner*, 64 T.C. 35 (1975) (amendment to reflect proper petitioner allowed); *Great Falls Bonding Agency, Inc. v. Commissioner*, 63 T.C. 304 (1974) (case dismissed for lack of jurisdiction because petitioning corporation had legally ceased to exist two years prior to petitioning Tax Court); *Starvest U.S., Inc. v. Commissioner*, T.C. Memo. 1999-314 (appropriate parties ratified filing of petition).

---

[8] Issues of Tax Court subject matter jurisdiction are discussed in more detail in Chapter 7.

Other cases that raise an issue of whether parties properly petitioned the Tax Court involve married taxpayers who filed a joint return and received a notice of deficiency in both names but filed a petition in one name only. *See, e.g., Holt v. Commissioner*, 67 T.C. 829 (1977) (court found that husband was acting as his wife's agent as well as on his own behalf); *Beaumont v. Commissioner*, T.C. Memo. 1986-373 (court found that letter from husband was imperfect petition with respect to both spouses). In *Martin v. Commissioner*, T.C. Memo. 2000-187, the Tax Court upheld Alfred Martin's argument that because he had not authorized his name to be included on a Tax Court petition for tax year 1980, the Tax Court lacked jurisdiction over him. The court therefore dismissed him from the case. Mr. Martin's accountant had received a notice of deficiency, and sent a copy of it to a law firm that included his name on the petition, along with the name of his ex-wife.

If only one spouse becomes a party to the Tax Court proceeding, such as in *Martin v. Commissioner* and *Williams v. Commissioner*, T.C. Memo. 1999-105 n.3, could the IRS assess the tax liability (for which the spouses are jointly liable) and seek to collect from the non-petitioning spouse? If so, could the non-petitioning spouse then pay the deficiency and pursue a refund action for the same tax year over which the Tax Court had jurisdiction and entered a decision?[9]

The IRS's responsive pleading is called an answer. The petition and answer are generally the only two pleadings in Tax Court; in most cases, the taxpayer does not have to file a reply. *See* Tax Court Rules 30, 37, 38. At times, the IRS may file an amended answer. For instance, *Scar v. Commissioner*, 14 F.2d 1363 (9th Cir. 1987), reproduced in Chapter 7, involves a dispute over an amended answer.

[C] Discovery Procedures

While the Federal Rules of Evidence apply in Tax Court, the Tax Court has established its own rules of Practice and Procedure, which, as indicated above, are based on the Federal Rules of Civil Procedure. I.R.C. § 7453; Tax Court Rule 1. Discovery is somewhat more limited in Tax Court than in the District Courts. A key difference between Tax Court discovery and discovery in other courts is that the Tax Court relies heavily on stipulations of facts. The parties to a Tax Court case are required to stipulate to the facts to the fullest extent possible. *See* Tax Court Rule 91. This includes stipulations of the evidence, so that key documents such as tax returns are attached to the stipulation of facts as exhibits. It is therefore unnecessary for the Tax Court to take the time for the taxpayer to testify in order to lay a foundation for the taxpayer's return to be admitted as evidence. The Tax Court also encourages the use of informal discovery as much as possible. Consider the following case:

---

[9] In a different context, that of whether one spouse who signed a joint return is collaterally estopped from litigating fraud where the other spouse is estopped because of a criminal conviction, courts have held that the noncriminal spouse may litigate the issue because that spouse was not a party to the criminal proceeding. *See, e.g.,* Moore v. United States, 360 F.2d 353, 357 (4th Cir. 1965), *cert. denied*, 385 U.S. 1001 (1967); Surber v. United States, 285 F. Supp. 775, 779 (S.D. Ohio 1968).

THE BRANERTON CORPORATION v. COMMISSIONER
United States Tax Court
61 T.C. 691 (1974)

DAWSON, JUDGE:

This matter is before the Court on respondent's motion for a protective order, pursuant to Rule 103(a)(2), Tax Court Rules of Practice and Procedure, that respondent at this time need not answer written interrogatories served upon him by petitioners in these cases. Oral arguments on the motion were heard on February 20, 1974, and, in addition, a written statement in opposition to respondent's motion was filed by the petitioners.

The sequence of events in these cases may be highlighted as follows: The statutory notices of deficiencies were mailed to the respective petitioners on April 20, 1973. * * * Petitions in both cases were filed on July 2, 1973, and, after an extension of time for answering, respondent filed his answers on September 26, 1973. This Court's new Rules of Practice and Procedure became effective January 1, 1974. The next day petitioners' counsel served on respondent rather detailed and extensive written interrogatories pursuant to Rule 71. On January 11, 1974, respondent filed his motion for a protective order. The cases have not yet been scheduled for trial.

Petitioners' counsel has never requested an informal conference with respondent's counsel in these cases, although respondent's counsel states that he is willing to have such discussions at any mutually convenient time. Consequently, in seeking a protective order, respondent specifically cites the second sentence of Rule 70(a)(1) which provides: "However, the Court expects the parties to attempt to attain the objectives of discovery through informal consultation or communication before utilizing the discovery procedures provided in these Rules."

It is plain that this provision in Rule 70(a)(1) means exactly what it says. The discovery procedures should be used only after the parties have made reasonable informal efforts to obtain needed information voluntarily. For many years the bedrock of Tax Court practice has been the stipulation process, now embodied in Rule 91. Essential to that process is the voluntary exchange of necessary facts, documents, and other data between the parties as an aid to the more expeditious trial of cases as well as for settlement purposes.[n.1] The recently adopted discovery procedures were not intended in any way to weaken the stipulation process. See Rule 91(a)(2).

Contrary to petitioners' assertion that there is no "practical and substantial reason" for granting a protective order in these circumstances, we find good cause for doing so. Petitioners have failed to comply with the letter and spirit of the discovery rules. The attempted use of written interrogatories at this stage of the proceedings sharply conflicts with the intent and purpose of Rule 70(a)(1) and constitutes an abuse of the Court's procedures.

[n.1] Part of the explanatory note to Rule 91 (60 T.C. 1118) states that —

"The stipulation process is more flexible, based on conference and negotiation between parties, adaptable to statements on matters in varying degrees of dispute, susceptible of defining and narrowing areas of dispute, and offering an active medium for settlement."

Accordingly, we conclude that respondent's motion for a protective order should be granted and he is relieved from taking any action with respect to these written interrogatories. The parties will be directed to have informal conferences during the next 90 days for the purpose of making good faith efforts to exchange facts, documents, and other information. Since the cases have not been scheduled for trial, there is sufficient time for the parties to confer and try informally to secure the evidence before resorting to formal discovery procedures. If such process does not meet the needs of the parties, they may then proceed with discovery to the extent permitted by the rules.

An appropriate order will be entered.

As *Branerton* points out, interrogatories and other discovery procedures, such as requests for admissions and depositions, are available in Tax Court. *See* Tax Court Rules 70–76, 90. However, they are available only if necessary after the parties have conducted discovery through informal means. *Branerton* is a leading case on Tax Court discovery. Letters making an informal request for information or for a conference to communicate informally have become known as *Branerton* letters. *See, e.g., DeLucia v. Commissioner*, 87 T.C. 804, 807 (1986); *Williams v. Commissioner*, T.C. Memo. 1997-541, *aff'd*, 176 F.3d 486 (9th Cir. 1999); *Raquet v. Commissioner*, T.C. Memo. 1996-279.

[D] Precedent Applicable to Tax Court Cases

The Tax Court is a national court yet its appeals lie to the various Courts of Appeals. What precedent should apply in Tax Court cases — Tax Court precedent or Court of Appeals precedent? The Tax Court answered this question in the following case.

GOLSEN v. COMMISSIONER
United States Tax Court
54 T.C. 742 (1970)[10]

The Commissioner determined a deficiency of $2,918.15 in petitioners' income tax for 1962. The only issue is whether a $12,441.40 payment made by petitioner Jack E. Golsen to the Western Security Life Insurance Co. is deductible as an interest payment pursuant to section 163, I.R.C. 1954.

* * *

OPINION

RAUM, JUDGE:

This case involves an ingenious device which, if successful, would result in petitioner's purchase of a substantial amount of life insurance for the protection of his family at little or no aftertax cost to himself, or possibly even with

---

[10] *Aff'd*, 445 F.2d 985 (10th Cir.), *cert. denied*, 404 U.S. 940 (1971).

a net profit in some years. The device is based on an unusual type of insurance policy that appears to have been specially designed for this purpose in which the rates were set at an artificially high level with correspondingly high cash surrender and loan values to begin immediately during the very first year of the life of the policy. The plan contemplated the purchase of a large amount of such insurance, the "payment" of the first year's premium, the simultaneous "prepayment" of the next 4 years' premiums discounted at the annual rate of 3 percent, the immediate "borrowing" of the first year's cash value at 4 percent "interest," and the immediate "borrowing" back of the full reserve value generated by the "prepayment," also at 4-percent "interest." Each year thereafter, the plan called for the "borrowing" of the annual increase in the loan or cash value of the policy at 4-percent "interest"; such increase, as a result of the artificially high premium, was more than sufficient to "prepay" the discounted amount of the premium which would become due 4 years thereafter. The net result of these complicated maneuvers would be that the insured's net out-of-pocket (pretax) expenditures each year would be equal to the true actuarial cost of the insurance benefits that he was purchasing (*i.e.*, net death benefits in substantial amounts even after the policies had been stripped of their cash surrender values) — although, in form, he appeared to be paying large amounts of "interest." At the heart of the device is the deduction allowed in section 163(a) of the 1954 Code with respect to "interest paid * * * on indebtedness." * * *

The precise question relating to the deductibility of "interest" like that involved herein has been adjudicated by two Courts of Appeals. In one case, *Campbell v. Cen-Tex., Inc.*, 377 F.2d 688 (C.A. 5), decision went for the taxpayer; in the other, *Goldman v. United States*, 403 F.2d 776 (C.A. 10), *affirming* 273 F. Supp. 137 (W.D. Okla.), the Government prevailed. *Goldman* involved the same insurance company, the same type of policies, and the same financial arrangements as are before us in the present case. *Cen-Tex* involved a different insurance company but dealt with comparable financing arrangements. Despite some rather feeble attempts on the part of each side herein to distinguish the case adverse to it, we think that both cases are in point. It is our view that the Government's position is correct.

Moreover, we think that we are in any event bound by *Goldman* since it was decided by the Court of Appeals for the same circuit within which the present case arises. In thus concluding that we must follow *Goldman*, we recognize the contrary thrust of the oft-criticized[n.13] case of *Arthur L. Lawrence*, 27 T.C. 713. Notwithstanding a number of the considerations which originally led us to that decision, it is our best judgment that better judicial administration[n.14] requires us to follow a Court of Appeals decision which is

---

[n.13] *Norvel Jeff McLellan,* 51 T.C. 462, 465–467 (concurring opinion); *Automobile Club of New York, Inc.,* 32 T.C. 906, 923–926 (dissenting opinion), *affirmed* 304 F. 2d 781 (C.A. 2); *Robert M. Dann,* 30 T.C. 499, 510 (dissenting opinion); Del Cotto, "The Need for a Court of Tax Appeals: An Argument and a Study," 12 Buffalo L. Rev. 5, 8–10 (1962); Vom Baur & Coburn, "Tax Court Wrong in Denying Taxpayer the Rule Laid Down in His Circuit," 8 J. Taxation 228 (1958); Orkin, "The Finality of the Court of Appeals Decisions in the Tax Court: A Dichotomy of Opinion," 43 A.B.A. J. 945 (1957); * * *.

[n.14] The importance of the *Lawrence* doctrine in respect of the functioning of this Court has been grossly exaggerated by some of the critics of that decision. That case was decided Jan. 25,

squarely in point where appeal from our decision lies to that Court of Appeals and to that court alone.

Section 7482(a), I.R.C. 1954,[16] charges the Courts of Appeals with the primary responsibility for review of our decisions, and we think that where the Court of Appeals to which appeal lies has already passed upon the issue before us, efficient and harmonious judicial administration calls for us to follow the decision of that court. Moreover, the practice we are adopting does not jeopardize the Federal interest in uniform application of the internal revenue laws which we emphasized in *Lawrence*. We shall remain able to foster uniformity by giving effect to our own views in cases appealable to courts whose views have not yet been expressed, and, even where the relevant Court of Appeals has already made its views known, by explaining why we agree or disagree with the precedent that we feel constrained to follow. * * *

To the extent that *Lawrence* is inconsistent with the views expressed herein it is hereby overruled. We note, however, that some of our decisions, because they involve two or more taxpayers, may be appealable to more than one circuit. This case presents no such problem, and accordingly we need not decide now what course to take in the event that we are faced with it.

* * *

Decision will be entered for the respondent.

WITHEY, J., dissenting: While I agree with the conclusion of the Court on the merits of this case, I dissent on the reversal of this Court's position on *Arthur L. Lawrence*, 27 T.C. 713, by the majority.

Note that if two similar cases are governed by conflicting Court of Appeals precedent, the *Golsen* decision allows the possibility of inconsistent Tax Court decisions, even if the two cases are decided by the same Tax Court judge. Therefore, when analyzing any Tax Court case, it is important to determine whether a Tax Court case reflects the Tax Court's application of its own rule or of binding circuit precedent. *See, e.g., Perryman v. Commissioner*, T.C. Memo. 1988-378 ("Despite our holding in [a prior Tax Court case], we will follow the precedent established in the court to which appeal would lie.").

1957, and this is the first time during the intervening period of somewhat in excess of 13 years that the Court has ever deemed it appropriate to face the question whether or not to apply the *Lawrence* doctrine.

[16] SEC. 7482. COURTS OF REVIEW.

(a) Jurisdiction. — The United States Courts of Appeals shall have exclusive jurisdiction to review the decisions of the Tax Court, except as provided in section 1254 of Title 28 of the United States Code, in the same manner and to the same extent as decisions of the district courts in civil actions tried without a jury; and the judgment of any such court shall be final, except that it shall be subject to review by the Supreme Court of the United States upon certiorari, in the manner provided in section 1254 of Title 28 of the United States Code.

[E] The Tax Court's Small Tax Case Procedure

Section 7463 of the Code provides for an elective, informal procedure for cases in which neither the deficiency placed in dispute nor any claimed overpayment exceeds $50,000 for any one taxable year.[11] To obtain eligibility to elect the small tax case procedure, the taxpayer can concede amounts that exceed the jurisdictional cap. *Kallich v. Commissioner*, 89 T.C. 676 (1987), *acq.* 1988-2 C.B. 1. The S case jurisdiction was clarified by the Community Renewal Tax Relief Act of 2000 to specify that it also includes innocent spouse relief determinations and collection due process cases. *See* I.R.C. § 7463. The taxpayer has the option to elect the small tax case procedure, so long as the Tax Court agrees. I.R.C. § 7463(a). In general, the Tax Court will agree to the designation as a small tax case unless there is a recurring issue in the case for which precedent is needed — as indicated below, small tax case opinions have no precedential value.

In deciding whether to elect the small tax case procedure, taxpayers and their representatives should consider the several ways in which small tax cases differ from regular cases. First, small tax cases are conducted more informally than regular cases, *see* I.R.C. § 7463(a). In addition, the Tax Court travels on a regular basis to more cities to hear small tax cases than it does to hear regular cases. *See* Tax Court Rules Appendix IV. Special Trial Judges hear small tax cases, I.R.C. § 7443A(b)(2), and write Summary Opinions in those cases, *see* I.R.C. § 7463(a). Also very important is that (1) there is no appeal from a small tax case, and (2) the decision has no precedential value. I.R.C. § 7463(b).

In January 2001, the Tax Court began posting Summary Opinions in S cases on its web site. The S case opinions are available at the same site as other Tax Court opinions, www.ustaxcourt.gov/ustcweb.htm. Division and Memorandum Opinions are available from January 1, 1999, and Summary Opinions are available from January 1, 2001. The Tax Court site has limited search features, but Tax Analysts publishes the S opinions online in a searchable format. *See, e.g., Helmich v. Commissioner*, Summary Op. 2001-3, 2001 TNT 11-22, Tax Anal. Doc. 2001-1654.

Beside the amount in issue, what factors might a taxpayer consider in deciding whether to elect the small tax case procedure?

[F] Equity in the Tax Court

As indicated above, the Tax Court is an Article I court. The boundaries of its jurisdiction are strictly determined by statute. The Code does not contain a provision authorizing the court to use equitable principles to mitigate otherwise harsh results in deficiency cases. In 1987, the Supreme Court stated, "the Tax Court is a court of limited jurisdiction and lacks general equitable powers." *Commissioner v. McCoy*, 484 U.S. 3, 7 (1987). Nonetheless, the Tax Court has applied a number of equitable doctrines since then, most

---

[11] When the small tax case procedure was first enacted, it was limited to disputes involving no more than $1,000. Tax Reform Act of 1969, Pub. L. No. 91-172, § 957, 83 Stat. 487, 730–36. Congress has increased that over the years, most recently in 1998 from $10,000 to its present level of $50,000, as part of the IRS Reform Act.

notably equitable recoupment,[12] the substance of which is discussed in Chapter 8.

The Supreme Court stated in 1943, with respect to the Tax Court's predecessor, an executive agency called the Board of Tax Appeals:

> The Internal Revenue Code, not general equitable principles, is the mainspring of the Board's jurisdiction. Until Congress deems it advisable to allow the Board to determine the overpayment or underpayment in any taxable year other than the one for which a deficiency has been assessed, the Board must remain impotent when the plea of equitable recoupment is based upon an overpayment or underpayment in such other year.

Commissioner v. Gooch Milling & Elevator Co., 320 U.S. 418, 422 (1943). For years after *Gooch Milling* was decided, the Board (and then the Tax Court) expressed the view that it lacked jurisdiction over equitable recoupment claims. *See, e.g., Estate of Schneider v. Commissioner*, 93 T.C. 568, 570 (1989); *Poinier v. Commissioner*, 86 T.C. 478, 490–491 (1986), *aff'd in part and rev'd in part*, 898 F.2d 917 (3d Cir.), *cert. denied*, 490 U.S. 1019 (1988); *Estate of Van Winkle v. Commissioner*, 51 T.C. 994, 999–1000 (1969); *Vandenberge v. Commissioner*, 3 T.C. 321, 327–328 (1944), *aff'd*, 147 F.2d 167 (5th Cir.), *cert. denied*, 325 U.S. 875 (1945). The IRS shared that view. *See* Rev. Rul. 71-56, 1971-1 C.B. 404, 405 ("the Tax Court lacks jurisdiction to consider a plea of equitable recoupment").

In 1990, in *United States v. Dalm*, 494 U.S. 596, 611 n.8 (1990), a refund case, the Supreme Court stated that because Dalm had not raised the issue in her prior deficiency litigation, the Court had "no occasion to pass upon the question whether Dalm could have raised a recoupment claim in the Tax Court." In dissent, Justice Stevens also raised the possibility that the Tax Court might have equitable recoupment jurisdiction. *See id.* at 615 n.3 (Stevens, J., dissenting). *Dalm* thus provided an opening for the Tax Court to reconsider its equitable recoupment jurisdiction.

The Tax Court took that opportunity in 1993, in *Estate of Mueller v. Commissioner*, 101 T.C. 551 (1993). In that case, the taxpayer-estate raised "the partial affirmative defense of equitable recoupment" with respect to a time-barred overpayment of income tax by the estate's residuary legatee, the Bessie I. Mueller Trust. Both the deficiency and overpayment were based on the estate's valuation of stock in the Mueller Company, which the IRS had contested. The IRS moved to dismiss the defense for lack of jurisdiction. The court held that it had jurisdiction to consider the affirmative defense of equitable recoupment when raised in tax deficiency cases over which it had jurisdiction, stating, "in deciding this case, we may take into account all facts that bear on petitioner's deficiency and may apply equitable principles in so doing." *Id.* at 561. Judge Chabot dissented, stating in part, "The majority do not reveal to us where in subtitle B, or anywhere else in the Internal Revenue

---

[12] For a discussion of other equitable doctrines applied by the Tax Court and an argument that the Tax Court's use of equity is improper, *see* Leandra Lederman, "Equity and the Article I Court: Is the Tax Court's Exercise of Equitable Powers Constitutional?", 5 Fla. Tax Rev. 357 (2001). The discussion here about the Tax Court's equitable powers is adapted from that article and is used, as adapted, with permission.

Code, is the element of petitioner's tax that might be affected by possible application of equitable recoupment. Obviously, equitable recoupment does not affect the amount shown as the tax on the taxpayer's tax return." *Id.* at 566 (Chabot, J., dissenting).

Subsequently, in a follow-up decision, the Tax Court considered the application of equitable recoupment principles to the case, and held that because equitable recoupment can only be used as a defense, and because, based on its valuation of the shares of the Mueller Company, the taxpayer-estate was entitled to an overpayment of estate tax regardless of whether equitable recoupment applied, the doctrine did not apply to the case. *Estate of Mueller v. Commissioner*, 107 T.C. 189, 199 (1996). On appeal, the Court of Appeals for the Sixth Circuit held that the Tax Court lacked jurisdiction to apply equitable recoupment. *Estate of Mueller v. Commissioner*, 153 F.3d 302 (6th Cir. 1998), *cert. denied*, 525 U.S. 1140 (1999).

Subsequent to the Sixth Circuit's adverse holding in *Mueller*, the Tax Court nonetheless applied equitable recoupment in three cases, *Estate of Bartels v. Commissioner*, 106 T.C. 430 (1996), appealable to the Seventh Circuit, *Estate of Branson v. Commissioner*, 113 T.C. 6 (1999), *aff'd*, 264 F.3d 904 (9th Cir. 2001), *cert. denied*, 122 S. Ct. 1296 (2002), which was affirmed by the Ninth Circuit, and *Estate of Orenstein v. Commissioner*, T.C. Memo. 2000-150, appealable to the Eleventh Circuit.

The Court of Appeals for the Ninth Circuit, in affirming *Estate of Branson*, held that the Tax Court had the power to apply equitable recoupment. It found that within the sphere of cases over which the Tax Court has jurisdiction, the Tax Court has "the authority to apply the full range of equitable principles generally granted to courts that possess judicial powers." *Estate of Branson*, 264 F.3d at 908. In part, it relied on cases holding that the Tax Court has the power to apply the equitable doctrine of reformation of an agreement. *See Kelley v. Commissioner*, 45 F.3d 348, 351 (9th Cir. 1995); *Buchine v. Commissioner*, 20 F.3d 173, 178 (5th Cir. 1994).

The Ninth Circuit's decision in *Branson* created a split in the circuits, but the Supreme Court denied certiorari. The *Branson* opinion both disagrees with and distinguishes *Mueller*. The *Branson* court stated that its reading of relevant statutes disagreed with that of the *Mueller* court, but it also found that the income tax and estate tax in *Mueller* were for two different tax years, unlike in *Branson*. It stated, "We have no occasion to pass upon the question whether the Tax Court would have jurisdiction to consider an equitable recoupment claim where the tax sought to be recouped was from a previous tax year." *Estate of Branson*, 264 F.3d at 913 n.5. However, this analysis is flawed because the estate tax is not an annual tax, so it is not assessed for a particular "tax year."

One reason some courts have given for allowing the Tax Court to apply equitable doctrines is that the federal district courts, which also have jurisdiction over tax cases, have that power. For example, Judge Posner used this approach to uphold the Tax Court's power to apply equitable estoppel, stating, "[w]e are given no reason to suppose that statutes of limitations are intended to be administered differently in the Tax Court than in the federal district courts, which share jurisdiction in federal tax cases with the Tax Court."

Flight Attendants Against UAL Offset, 165 F.3d 572, 578 (7th Cir. 1999). Part of the Ninth Circuit's reasoning in *Branson* was similar. However, in *Lundy*, a statute of limitations case reproduced in Chapter 8, the Supreme Court noted numerous procedural ways in which the Tax Court and refund fora differ. It stated, in part:

> We assume without deciding that . . . a different limitations period would apply in district court, but nonetheless find in this disparity no excuse to change the limitations scheme that Congress has crafted. The rules governing litigation in Tax Court differ in many ways from the rules governing litigation in the district court and the Court of Federal Claims. Some of these differences might make the Tax Court a more favorable forum, while others may not.

Commissioner v. Lundy, 516 U.S. 235, 252 (1996).

§ 6.03   Refund Litigation

[A]   Overview of Refund Litigation in the United States District Courts

As discussed in detail in Chapter 8, the jurisdictional prerequisites in the "refund courts" include filing a timely refund claim with the IRS and following up with a timely complaint. Tax litigation in a District Court is much like other litigation in that court. Because District Courts are Article III courts, either party is entitled to demand a trial by jury. Applicable Court of Appeals precedent governs the case and both the Federal Rules of Civil Procedure and the Federal Rules of Evidence apply. Fed. R. Evid. 101, 1101. Litigation in a District Court begins when the taxpayer files a complaint. Fed. R. Civ. P. 3. The fee for filing a complaint is $150. 28 U.S.C. § 1914(a). The IRS's responsive pleading is termed an answer. Fed. R. Civ. P. 7. If the answer contains a counterclaim, the taxpayer must file a reply. *See id.* The following is a complaint filed in an actual case. (The taxpayer's complaint might instead be divided into various counts.)

SAMPLE COMPLAINT

FREDERICK STEVENS AND ELIZABETH JAMES,
Plaintiffs,
v.
UNITED STATES OF AMERICA,
Defendant.

COMPLAINT

NOW COME Plaintiffs, Frederick Stevens and Elizabeth James, appearing pro se, and for their Complaint state:

1. The Plaintiffs seek a refund herein of federal income taxes paid for calendar year 1995, and therefore the court has jurisdiction over this matter pursuant to 28 U.S.C. 1346.

2. At all pertinent times, Plaintiffs were husband and wife, and resided in Cook County, Illinois.

3. In 1996, Plaintiffs timely filed Form 1040 for calendar year in 1995 and paid a total of $49,677 in federal taxes plus an estimated tax penalty of $2,181.

4. On or about April 1, 1998, Plaintiffs timely filed with the United States Internal Revenue Service Form 1040X Amended U.S. Individual Income Tax Return for calendar year 1995, properly executed under penalty of perjury, requesting a refund ("Request for Refund") of $17,529 in federal income taxes paid for calendar year 1995 and $744 in estimated tax penalty paid for calendar year 1995.

5. The Request for Refund was made by reason of an overpayment of federal income taxes by Plaintiff for year 1995. Specifically Plaintiffs erroneously paid and recorded on their 1995 return $17,529 pursuant to Section 72 of the Internal Revenue Code of [1986], as amended, constituting an "increase in tax" ("Penalty") equal to ten percent (10%) of the amount of an annuity distribution received by Plaintiff Frederick Stevens in 1995.

6. This Penalty was not applicable to the annuity distribution received by Plaintiff Frederick Stevens in 1995 because he was "disabled" within the meaning of Section 72(m)(7) of the Internal Revenue Code of [1986], as amended, and Regulation 1.72-17(f)(1)–(2) promulgated by the Internal Revenue Service.

7. Thereafter on or about November 19, 1998, the Internal Revenue Service directed a letter to Plaintiffs denying the Request for Refund. The denial was based upon the Internal Revenue Service's assertion that Plaintiff Frederick Stevens was not disabled within the meaning of Section 72(m)(7) although Plaintiff had submitted a doctor's statement as to the impairment. Specifically Defendant's letter stated that in the Internal Revenue Service's opinion Plaintiff Frederick Stevens was "able to engage in some form of occupation" and the fact that "you cannot engage in your usual occupation is not criteria sufficient to abate the . . . penalty".

8. The Internal Revenue Service's denial of the Request for Refund is contrary to the Internal Revenue Code of [1986], as amended, and to the Regulations thereunder promulgated by the Internal Revenue Service itself.

9. Plaintiffs have fully paid all Federal taxes for tax year 1995.

10. This lawsuit is timely filed, six months have elapsed since the request for refund was filed with the Internal Revenue Service and three months having elapsed since the denial of such request.

WHEREFORE, Plaintiffs pray for entry of judgment in their favor and against Defendant as follows:

1. In the principal amount of $18,379.

2. Interest on the principal amount, commencing April 15, 1996, at the rate in the Internal Revenue Code of [1986], as amended, and the Regulations thereunder, for which the Defendant is to pay respecting refunds.

3. Costs, and such other relief as is just.

Respectfully submitted,

Frederick Stevens

Elizabeth James
[Address and
telephone number omitted.]

[Attachments omitted.]

[B] Overview of Refund Litigation in the Court of Federal Claims

Tax litigation in the United States Court of Federal Claims begins when the taxpayer files a complaint. U.S. Ct. Fed. Claims Rule 3. The complaint will resemble the District Court complaint reproduced above. The IRS then files an answer. U.S. Ct. Fed. Claims Rule 7. "[I]f the answer contains a counterclaim or offset or a plea of fraud, there shall be a reply thereto." *Id.* Like the Tax Court, the Court of Federal Claims is an Article I court. *See* 28 U.S.C. § 171. The court has sixteen judges, who are appointed by the President with the advice and consent of the Senate. *Id.* The judges each have a 15-year term. 28 U.S.C. § 172. Each trial is heard by a single judge. U.S. Ct. Fed. Claims Rule 77(e).

The Court of Federal Claims is based in Washington, D.C. but the judges travel to hear cases in other cities. 28 U.S.C. § 173. The Court of Federal Claims' rules are particularly flexible about the place of trial, so that some trials consist of sessions in various parts of the country, for the convenience of witnesses. The Federal Rules of Evidence apply. Fed. R. Evid. 101, 1101. Decisions are appealable to the Court of Appeals for the Federal Circuit, and its precedent applies.[13] 28 U.S.C. § 1295(a)(3).

§ 6.04 Choice of Forum

As indicated above, the current structure of civil federal tax litigation provides the taxpayer with a forum choice. If the taxpayer receives a notice of deficiency and wishes to litigate, he can either choose to timely petition the Tax Court, or to pay the deficiency, claim a refund, and follow up the claim with a timely suit in a refund court. Approximately 95 percent of litigated federal tax cases are heard by the Tax Court. What factors might influence this choice?

If the taxpayer did not receive a notice of deficiency but wishes to litigate a refund claim, the taxpayer can choose between the District Court and the Court of Federal Claims. What factors might influence that decision?

---

[13] Decisions of the United States Court of Claims, the predecessor to the Court of Federal Claims, entered prior to September 30, 1982, also apply as precedent. South Corp. v. United States, 690 F.2d 1368, 1370–71 (Fed. Cir. 1982).

Commentators have argued that the choice of fora in federal tax cases is inappropriate. According to some, the multiplicity of trial-level fora in federal tax cases breeds inconsistency. In addition, the review of federal tax cases by thirteen different Courts of Appeals only exacerbates this problem. Does the *Golsen* rule eliminate inconsistency in the precedent that applies to cases in each of the three courts? Consider the following arguments in favor of a single trial-level court and a single appellate court for all federal tax cases. Do you agree?

SHOULD THE FEDERAL CIVIL TAX LITIGATION SYSTEM BE RESTRUCTURED?*
40 Tax Notes 1427 (1988)
By Judge Howard A. Dawson, Jr.

In 1986, when most people were saying it would never happen, the most significant substantive tax reform legislation in many years was passed by Congress and signed into law by the President. In these times of major economic, social, and international problems, our leaders should not simply look at things as they are and say why; they should consider things that never were and say why not. I want to address just one of those "why nots." Hasn't the time come for us to make a careful and critical examination of our trial and appellate systems for litigating Federal civil tax controversies? Now that some degree of *substantive* tax reform has been achieved, why not turn our attention to *procedural* tax reform in the judicial system? The present litigation system for civil tax cases is severely flawed at both the trial level and the appellate level. To put it bluntly — I think it is an unsatisfactory system — one that promotes unfairness, inefficiency, and uncertainty. As Roswell Magill, a Columbia University law professor and a former Treasury Department official, said 45 years ago: "If we were seeking to secure a state of complete uncertainty in tax jurisprudence, we could hardly do better than the system now in place." Generally the difficulty with any system lies not in formulating new ideas but in escaping from the old ones. It seems to me, as Justice Cardozo once commented, that there comes a time in the course of substantive and procedural law when it becomes necessary to pick up the driftwood and leave the waters pure.

Our system for resolving tax disputes is structured to allow three trial courts — the Tax Court, the Claims Court, and the Federal district courts — 12 circuit courts of appeals, and the court of appeals for the Federal Circuit to express their disparate views freely on tax issues. Inevitably, conflicts arise at the trial and appellate levels and, sooner or later — usually years later — the Supreme Court must resolve the conflicts. In the interim there is uncertainty; there is inconsistency; and there is unpredictability. It is very costly to taxpayers and the Federal government alike. Even when the Supreme Court speaks, while there is a "final" answer, we cannot always be sure we have been blessed with the "right" answer.

The greatest oddity of our Federal system for adjudicating tax disputes lies in the area of forum selection. Trial court jurisdiction is trifurcated. Which

---

of the three courts will you choose? Each court has different rules and procedures; each court has judges of different backgrounds and expertise; and each
court is governed by a different body of precedents. If you choose not to pay
the asserted tax, you are in a deficiency posture and off to the Tax Court.
Alternatively, if you choose to pay the asserted tax, assuming you can afford
to pay *all* of it, and are not given a refund after you claim it, then you have
two choices. You can go to the Federal district court in your home area and
get a jury trial if you want one. Or you can take your case to the Claims Court
in Washington. This is delightful if you see any merit in forum shopping, and
I guess a lot of tax lawyers do. My own view is that it is better to promote
the development of a coherent body of case law and that can be done by
restructuring the civil tax litigation system in a way that will eliminate forum
shopping. It is very unfortunate and unfair that a taxpayer's financial
condition is an important aspect of forum selection. It is obviously inequitable
to have a procedure where the doors of certain courts are open to those with
the financial resources to pay their putative tax liability in advance and closed
to those who cannot raise the money required. This is an aberration in the
system that is indefensible. It clearly favors rich individuals and wealthy
corporations over low-and middle-income persons and small corporations. I
am too much of a populist to believe that this is good for the tax litigation
system. Why should a select group of taxpayers be able to utilize differences
in court procedures to gain a significant advantage? Why should some
taxpayers be able to select a forum where the trend of prior decisions seems
more conducive to success while others for financial reasons do not have that
choice? Perhaps the major objection to forum shopping is the undue delay in
obtaining certainty in tax results — a plague on all taxpayers and the
government.

As I see it, the present litigation system at the trial level cannot be improved
simply by some tinkering or minor modifications. I think consideration should
be given to its replacement or restructure. I speak only for myself and not
for the Chief Judge or any judges of the Tax Court. * * *

In short, the tax litigation system at the trial level would be improved by
removing Federal tax refund jurisdiction from the Federal district courts and
the Claims Court and placing it entirely in the Tax Court — the premier court
of tax specialists. It is capable of handling all tax refund litigation. At the
present time there are only about 3,000 tax refund suits pending in all the
Federal district courts and the Claims Court. During the last fiscal year about
150 non-jury cases were tried in the district courts and there were only 34
jury trials. I also think it would be advisable to eliminate jury trials in civil
tax cases, particularly if jurisdiction over all tax refund suits is given to the
Tax Court. These suggestions would eradicate forum shopping and provide
consistency and uniformity of treatment for all taxpayers at the trial level
by a single court of tax specialists. It is also possible that with all deficiency
and refund jurisdiction in the Tax Court, the present IRS system of acquiescence and nonacquiescence in Tax Court opinions could be modified or
eliminated if an appeal could be taken to a single National Court of Tax
Appeals rather than to 12 different courts of appeals.

That brings me to the second prong of my suggestions for restructuring the
Federal civil tax litigation system. Would it improve the system to have a

single court of tax appeals? The concept is not new and it has generated different views. In 1944, Dean Erwin Griswold of Harvard first advocated a National Court of Tax Appeals and in 1973, Judge Henry Friendly of the Second Circuit Court of Appeals also proposed it. In 1978, in hearings before a Senate Judiciary Subcommittee, Dean Griswold, three former Commissioners of Internal Revenue — Mortimer Caplin, Sheldon Cohen, and Donald Alexander — as well as officials of the Treasury Department and some members of the tax bar testified in favor of creating a National Court of Tax Appeals. At that time, most Tax Court judges opposed the idea and almost all of them still oppose it. I disagreed with the Tax Court's view in 1978 and I disagree with it now. In these times when our Federal tax laws are so complicated that they often defy comprehension, we continue to operate under a cumbersome and complex litigation system for resolving civil tax disputes. A major criticism of the present system is that, absent a controlling Supreme Court decision, it lacks a practical and reliable method for permanently resolving tax disputes.

The Tax Court has done an incredibly effective job of attempting to provide uniformity and consistency at the trial level. But that effort alone does not solve the problems of conflicting decisions by the courts of appeals, which review its decisions. There is no doubt that appeals from Tax Court decisions leave it in an awkward position — should it apply uniform rules at the risk of reversal by a particular court of appeals or should it sacrifice uniformity for practicality and better judicial administration? Initially in *Lawrence v. Commissioner*, 27 T.C. 713 (1957), the Tax Court chose uniformity, but in *Golsen v. Commissioner*, 54 T.C. 742 (1970), it opted in favor of following the particular circuit to which an appeal would lie. Since the Supreme Court seldom grants *certiorari* in tax cases, we have 13 courts of appeals engaged in deciding tax issues. The system creates substantial problems for taxpayers and for the government. Delay and uncertainty in the resolution of tax issues, in defining judicial interpretation of ambiguous statutory terms, and in the application of the law exacerbate difficulties faced by taxpayers who want to meet their responsibilities and also by the Internal Revenue Service, which must inform taxpayers of their rights and duties and how to comply with the law.

It has been argued that the present system results in a better final product — a more ideal set of ultimate tax decisions — than a system in which a single court of appeals would resolve issues at an earlier stage and without extended debate and ferment. In reply to this argument, former Commissioner Donald Alexander said:

> I think this suggestion has more validity in theory than in reality. If it were correct, then one would think the government should reject any two-Circuit or three-Circuit rule and litigate to the bitter end. Moreover, this theory apparently assumes that the final decision must be better than and differs in material respects from the first decision, and I doubt that this is so. And even if the final product of 10 years or more judicial consideration of a tax issue of broad application were different and were better, is such benefit worth the cost? As a former tax administrator and as a long-time tax practitioner, I think not.

The real defect in today's system of Federal tax litigation is the long period of uncertainty engendered by the delay in getting a final decision on a particular issue. We should be able to find a way to achieve finality in tax litigation in a more rapid fashion.

Because decisions of no court, except the Supreme Court, are final, both the Internal Revenue Service and taxpayers continue to assert positions contrary to existing precedents. For example, just look at *Commissioner v. Kowalski*, 434 U.S. 77 (1977), which involved cash meal allowances for state highway police. That issue was in litigation for more than 20 years.

The fundamental goal of the Federal tax litigation process should be the development of authoritative rules to guide the administrative disposition of tax controversies.

The creation of a National Court of Tax Appeals would make our tax system fairer and more efficient. It would eliminate situations in which different Federal tax obligations are imposed on taxpayers located in different parts of the country. It would eliminate repetitious litigation that is burdensome to the judicial system and requires an inordinate amount of judicial resources. It would place a less heavy burden on the administrative process through which the vast majority of tax disputes are settled. And it surely would make it less difficult and less expensive for lawyers to give advice. Advice in grey areas of the tax law often does not provide the clear guidance a client seeks.

After many years of proposals and criticisms of the present system, isn't it in the public interest to adopt a workable solution to the horrendous tax litigation problems that now exist? I certainly think so.

In summary, I advocate a single trial court — the Tax Court — for all deficiency and refund actions and a single appellate court — a United States Court of Tax Appeals. It would be a giant step forward. I call for the resurrection and serious consideration of these suggestions for the improvement of our Federal civil tax litigation system. It should be given its long-needed overall revision. Let us join together — tax academicians, tax lawyers, and accountants, the Treasury and Justice Departments, the Judiciary and Congress — to create a better system for all of our people.

In 1997, Congress established the Commission on Structural Alternatives for the Federal Courts of Appeals, chaired by retired Supreme Court Justice Byron White, to study the circuit courts and make recommendations for change. The Commission's final report, released on December 18, 1998, noted the possibility of centralizing appellate tax jurisdiction in the Court of Appeals for the Federal Circuit, but did not make a recommendation on this point. *See* David Lupi-Sher, "National Court of Tax Appeals: An Idea That Never Quite Goes Away," 81 Tax Notes 1159 (1998). What objections do you see to the proposal to have all appellate tax cases heard by the Court of Appeals for the Federal Circuit?

§ 6.05 The Burden of Proof in Tax Cases

The "burden of proof" in a court case has two components: The burden of going forward (or "burden of production") and the burden of persuasion. The burden of going forward requires the party who bears the burden to produce sufficient evidence to make a *prima facie* case, or that party loses the case. Once one party makes a *prima facie* case, the case goes forward. The party who bears the burden of persuasion must persuade the court that its version of the relevant facts is the correct version.

Prior to the IRS Reform Act, the general burden of proof rules in tax cases were established by judicial decision, and in the Tax Court, by Tax Court Rule 142(a). In 1998, the IRS Reform Act created the first generally applicable statutory burden of proof rule for tax cases, effective for court proceedings arising in connection with examinations begun after July 22, 1998. *See* I.R.C. § 7491. Section 7491(a) has several threshold requirements, discussed below, that make eligibility quite difficult. If the taxpayer fails to meet these requirements or chooses not to present evidence on these requirements, the default rule is that the burden of proof remains on the taxpayer. Jurisprudence developed under prior law still applies when the burden does not shift.

Although analysis of the burden of proof in refund suits and deficiency suits raises similar questions, the questions are not identical. In Tax Court cases, the notice of deficiency plays an important role in allocating the burden of proof, as discussed in Chapter 7. In a refund suit, the taxpayer may not have ever received a notice of deficiency. Instead, the refund suit is premised on the refund claim the taxpayer must first have made with the IRS. In refund suits, unlike in Tax Court cases, the taxpayer traditionally has borne the additional burden of establishing the correct amount of the tax. *See Helvering v. Taylor*, 293 U.S. 507, 513 (1935) ("Obviously the burden was on the plaintiff, in order to establish a basis for judgment in his favor, specifically to show not merely that the assessment was erroneous but also the amount to which he was entitled.") (dictum); *see also Lewis v. Reynolds*, 284 U.S. 281, *modified*, 284 U.S. 599 (1932).

Section 7491 generally provides that the burden of proof with respect to a factual issue shifts from the taxpayer to the IRS where the taxpayer meets five requirements: (1) the taxpayer produces "credible evidence" on the factual issue; (2) the taxpayer has complied with all substantiation requirements; (3) the taxpayer has maintained all required records; (4) the taxpayer has cooperated with the IRS's reasonable requests for witnesses, information, documents, meetings, and interviews; and (5) if the taxpayer is a partnership, corporation or trust, it meets a net worth limitation.

What is "credible evidence"? The Senate Finance Committee stated, "Credible evidence is the quality of evidence which, after critical analysis, the court would find sufficient upon which to base a decision on the issue if no contrary evidence were submitted (without regard to the judicial presumption of IRS correctness)." S. Rep. 105-174, at 45–46 (1998), 1998-3 C.B. 537, 581–582. What does that mean? In *Sykes v. Commissioner*, T.C. Memo. 2001-169, the IRS determined that $149,200 seized from the Sykes' home constituted gross income in 1997. The Sykes argued that it was not gross income because they already had a "cash hoard" in that amount. The Tax Court considered whether the taxpayers had presented credible evidence under section 7491 of the cash hoard:

> Petitioners contend that petitioner had a $ 149,200 cash hoard on December 31, 1996. Thus, we first decide whether petitioners introduced evidence of petitioner's cash hoard which, after critical analysis, we would find sufficient upon which to base a decision on the issue if no contrary evidence were submitted (without regard to the judicial presumption of IRS correctness). *See id.* at 46, 1998-3 C.B. at 582.

2. PETITIONERS' EVIDENCE

Petitioner testified that he accumulated a cash hoard over a 30-year period from his various jobs and from selling two houses he owned. He introduced bank records showing that he had a safe deposit box which he entered 53 times from December 1987 to March 1998. Danney Sykes and Gary Sykes each testified that they saw petitioner with a large amount of cash on several occasions.

Petitioner testified that, by 1970, he had saved $ 4,000 from working at a store and doing odd jobs, and that, by 1971, he had saved another $ 3,000 from working at a pallet mill and as a tree trimmer. He said that he saved about half of his income from International Paper from 1973 to 1981 and that he had saved $ 54,000 from International Paper by 1981. He testified that he saved $ 6,000 from a settlement he received from International Paper for an injury on the job. He said that he saved $ 17,000 from the sale of a house in Kansas City in 1981, and $ 23,000 from the sale of a house in Yellville in 1985. He stated that he saved $ 6,000 from selling personal possessions when he sold the house in Yellville in 1985. He stated that his grandmother gave him $ 20,000 in 1986 to replace personal items he had kept in her house and that were lost when the house burned down. He said that he saved about $ 22,000 from 1987 to 1997 from his buying and selling activity.

Petitioners' son, Gary, testified that he once "took a bunch of money" from petitioner when he was about 6 or 7 years old and got in a lot of trouble.

Petitioner's brother, Danney, testified that petitioner told him he had saved money for many years. Danney said: "Every time I'd turn around he [petitioner] had a roll of bills." "I've seen him with * * * [what] appeared to be large sums of money." Danney also testified that petitioner sold his personal items from the Yellville house at auction.

Petitioner's uncle, Ireland, testified that he did not know how much money, if any, his mother (petitioner's grandmother) gave petitioner for items he lost when her house burned down. Ireland said that petitioner's grandparents lived through the Depression and taught petitioner and him how to save money. He testified that he saw petitioner with "a lot of U.S. savings bonds in his car" when petitioner visited him in the early 1980's. He also saw petitioner with "hands full of money" and "a considerable sum" of money.

3. WHETHER PETITIONERS INTRODUCED CREDIBLE EVIDENCE OF THE EXISTENCE AND AMOUNT OF PETITIONER'S CASH HOARD

Petitioners introduced credible evidence that petitioner had a cash hoard, such as the fact that he entered his safe deposit box 53 times from December 1987 to March 1998 and that his family saw him with large amounts of cash over the years. However, petitioners did not introduce credible evidence that petitioner had accumulated $ 149,200 before 1997. Petitioner testified that he received a $ 6,000 settlement from International Paper because he cut his finger while on the job. However, he did not state when the injury occurred or when he received the money. He did not mention the alleged payment in the jeopardy assessment proceeding or to respondent before the trial in this case. Petitioner's explanation of his grandmother's alleged $ 20,000 gift to him changed over time. He told Fridley that he received $ 20,000 from his grandmother's estate in 1992. He stated in his December 1999 affidavit prepared for the jeopardy assessment proceeding that his grandmother gave him $ 20,000 in 1986 to replace valuable items he had kept in her house and then lost in a house fire. At trial, he testified that his grandmother gave him $ 20,000 shortly before she went into the nursing home; i.e., around 1990.

Petitioners bought the houses in Kansas City and Yellville for $ 16,000 and $ 20,000, respectively, and sold them for $ 17,000 and $ 23,000, respectively. Petitioner's claim that he made a profit of $ 40,000 from the sale of those houses is not credible. Petitioner testified that he paid $ 6,000 towards the purchase price of the Kansas City house from a settlement he received from International Paper for an injury he sustained on the job, and that he paid the remainder owed on the house ($ 10,000) with wages he received from International Paper. Petitioner's claim that he paid the remainder owed on the house from his wages from International Paper is implausible in light of the fact that he also claims that he saved $ 54,000 from his $ 96,825 wages from 1973 to 1981; that would leave less than $ 33,000 for petitioners to live on for 9 years. Petitioners' claim that they made a $ 23,000 profit in selling the Yellville house is also implausible. Petitioner and his uncle made an $ 8,000 downpayment for the Yellville house, and petitioner later traded his pickup truck for his uncle's share of the house. There is nothing in the record to show that petitioner had the means to pay the $ 12,000 balance on the house and pay petitioners' living expenses while working various odd jobs from 1981 to 1985.

Petitioners contend that petitioner saved half of what he earned. This claim conflicts with their claim that he saved $ 54,000 from his work for International Paper from 1973 to 1981 and $ 22,000 from his buying and selling activity from 1987 to 1997 because his total earnings from International Paper were $ 96,825 (half of this would be $ 48,413), and his tax returns from 1989 to 1997 show that his adjusted gross income totaled $ 25,602 (half of this would be $ 12,801).

Petitioner's claim that he saved half of his wages from International Paper is also implausible because that would leave only $ 48,413 to support himself and his family for 9 years.

Petitioner's claim that he accumulated $ 149,200 of cash by his frugal lifestyle, e.g., petitioners did not have long distance telephone service, and because Mrs. Sykes received disability payments, lacks credibility. Petitioner stated that Mrs. Sykes received disability payments of about $ 494/month, i.e., about $ 5,928/year; however, he did not indicate for what years she received those amounts.

Petitioner's claim that he received $ 6,000 from International Paper for a work-related injury is suspicious because he had not previously made that claim.

Danney, Gary, and Ireland testified that they saw petitioner with a large amount of cash on several occasions in the early 1980's, but they did not testify about the amount of the cash hoard.

Petitioner admitted that he incorrectly told Fridley that the source of the cash seized from petitioners' house on March 19, 1998, was loans. He incorrectly certified to the Missouri Division of Family Services that he did not have property in a safe deposit box. He told Pierce that he had put about $ 25,000-$ 30,000 in the safe deposit box between January 1 and March 18, 1998. However, the last time petitioner entered the safe deposit box before March 18, 1998, was December 10, 1997.

* * *

Petitioners introduced evidence relating to the amount of petitioner's cash hoard, but a substantial amount of that evidence was not credible. Section 7491(a)(1) refers to credible evidence relating to "any factual issue." We do not place the burden on respondent to prove one part of that issue and on petitioner to prove the rest. Thus, petitioners bear the burden of proving the amount of the cash hoard.

Consider also *Higbee v. Commissioner*, reproduced below, one of the first decisions interpreting section 7491(a) and (c).[14]

HIGBEE v. COMMISSIONER
United States Tax Court
116 T.C. 438 (2001)

VASQUEZ, JUDGE: * * *

After concessions, we must decide whether petitioners are entitled to the following deductions: (1) $1,328 for a casualty loss, (2) $6,937.20 for charitable contributions, (3) $6,468.09 for unreimbursed employee expenses, (4) certain amounts paid on account of a failed business as part of a chapter 13 bankruptcy proceeding, and (5) various expenses related to two rental properties.

---

[14] An excerpt from Part II of *Higbee* is reproduced in Chapter 10.

Finally, we must decide whether petitioners are liable for an addition to tax under section 6651(a)(1) and an accuracy-related penalty under section 6662(a).

BACKGROUND

* * *

At trial, the only issue remaining with regard to the notice of deficiency was whether petitioners were entitled to the $1,920 in Schedule C deductions reported on petitioners' 1996 tax return and disallowed by respondent. Petitioners, however, raised new issues at trial by claiming additional deductions for a casualty loss, charitable contributions, unreimbursed employee expenses, and Schedule C and E expenses that were neither claimed on their returns nor raised in the notice of deficiency.

* * *

DISCUSSION

I. DISALLOWED DEDUCTIONS

Deductions are a matter of legislative grace, and a taxpayer bears the burden of proving that he is entitled to the deductions claimed. *See* Rule 142(a); INDOPCO, Inc. v. Commissioner, 503 U.S. 79, 117 L. Ed. 2d 226, 112 S. Ct. 1039 (1992); New Colonial Ice Co. v. Helvering, 292 U.S. 435, 78 L. Ed. 1348, 54 S. Ct. 788 (1934). The taxpayer is required to maintain records that are sufficient to enable the Commissioner to determine his correct tax liability. *See* sec. 6001; sec. 1.6001-1(a), Income Tax Regs. In addition, the taxpayer bears the burden of substantiating the amount and purpose of the claimed deduction. *See* Hradesky v. Commissioner, 65 T.C. 87, 90 (1975), *affd. per curiam* 540 F.2d 821 (5th Cir. 1976).

Section 7491(a), a new provision created by Internal Revenue Service Restructuring and Reform Act of 1998 (RRA 1998), Pub. L. 105-206, sec. 3001, 112 Stat. 685, 726, places the burden of proof on respondent with regard to certain factual issues. Section 7491 applies to examinations commenced after July 22, 1998. * * * The examination in the instant case commenced after July 22, 1998; accordingly, we evaluate whether respondent bears the burden of proof pursuant to section 7491(a).

Section 7491(a)(1) provides that if, in any court proceeding, the taxpayer introduces credible evidence with respect to factual issues relevant to ascertaining the taxpayer's liability for a tax (under subtitle A or B), the burden of proof with respect to such factual issues will be placed on the Commissioner. For the burden to be placed on the Commissioner, however, the taxpayer must comply with the substantiation and record-keeping requirements of the Internal Revenue Code. *See* sec. 7491(a)(2)(A) and (B). In addition, section 7491(a) requires that the taxpayer cooperate with reasonable requests by the Commissioner for "witnesses, information, documents, meetings, and interviews". Sec. 7491(a)(2)(B). Finally, the benefits of section 7491(a) are unavailable in the cases of partnerships, corporations, and trusts unless the taxpayer meets the net worth requirements of section 7430(c)(4)(A)(ii). *See* sec. 7491(a)(2)(C).

Respondent argues that because petitioners have failed to meet the requirements of section 7491(a)(1) and (2), the burden of proof should remain with petitioners as to the remaining issue associated with respondent's determination of petitioners' 1996 tax liability. We therefore examine the evidence to establish whether petitioners have presented credible evidence and have met the other requirements of section 7491(a)(1) and (2) so as to place the burden of proof on respondent.

A. CASUALTY LOSSES

Pursuant to section 165(a) and (c)(3), a taxpayer is allowed a deduction for an uncompensated loss that arises from fire, storm, shipwreck, or other casualty. Section 165(h), however, states that any "loss * * * shall be allowed only to the extent that the amount of the loss to such individual arising from each casualty * * * exceeds $100" and only to the extent that the net casualty loss "exceeds 10 percent of the adjusted gross income".

When property is damaged rather than totally destroyed by casualty, the proper measure of the amount of the loss sustained is the difference between the fair market value of the property immediately before and after the casualty, not to exceed the property's adjusted basis. *See* sec. 1.165-7(b)(1), Income Tax Regs. * * *

Petitioners claim a casualty loss deduction in the amount of $1,328 on account of alleged damage to their home and personal property which was not deducted on their tax return. Mr. Higbee testified that the $1,328 represents the damage to petitioners' property which was not reimbursed by their insurance company but awarded by a small claims court. In support, petitioners provided a form document entitled "Small Claims Complaint/ Summons/Answer" which appears to be issued by the Glendale Justice Court in Glendale, Arizona, but which does not bear any type of notation or certification by a governmental official.

In order for section 7491(a) to place the burden of proof on respondent, the taxpayer must first provide credible evidence. The statute itself does not state what constitutes credible evidence. The conference committee's report states as follows:

> Credible evidence is the quality of evidence which, after critical analysis, the court would find sufficient upon which to base a decision on the issue if no contrary evidence were submitted (without regard to the judicial presumption of IRS correctness). A taxpayer has not produced credible evidence for these purposes if the taxpayer merely makes implausible factual assertions, frivolous claims, or tax protestor-type arguments. The introduction of evidence will not meet this standard if the court is not convinced that it is worthy of belief. If after evidence from both sides, the court believes that the evidence is equally balanced, the court shall find that the Secretary has not

sustained his burden of proof. [H. Conf. Rept. 105-599, at 240–241 (1998), 1998-3 C.B. 747, 994–995.]

Further, the conference report explains the purpose of the limitations set forth in section 7491(a)(2):

> Nothing in the provision shall be construed to override any require-ment under the Code or regulations to substantiate any item. Accord-ingly, taxpayers must meet applicable substantiation requirements, whether generally imposed or imposed with respect to specific items, such as charitable contributions or meals, entertainment, travel, and certain other expenses. Substantiation requirements include any requirement of the Code or regulations that the taxpayer establish an item to the satisfaction of the Secretary. Taxpayers who fail to substantiate any item in accordance with the legal requirement of substantiation will not have satisfied the legal conditions that are prerequisite to claiming the item on the taxpayer's tax return and will accordingly be unable to avail themselves of this provision regarding the burden of proof. Thus, if a taxpayer required to substantiate an item fails to do so in the manner required (or destroys the substantia-tion), this burden of proof provision is inapplicable.

Petitioners' evidence does not meet the requirements of section 7491(a). Besides the fact that the form document entitled "Small Claims Complaint/ Summons/Answer" does not actually indicate whether litigation in small claims court was commenced or completed, the document itself does not qualify as a competent appraisal or reliable estimate of the cost of any repairs. Because petitioners have failed to provide credible evidence of a casualty loss, the burden of proof as to this issue is not placed on respondent. Further, for similar reasons regarding our discussion of petitioners' evidence for purposes of section 7491, we conclude that petitioners have not met their burden of proof. *See* Rule 142(a). Consequently, we reject petitioners' claimed casualty loss deduction.

B. CHARITABLE CONTRIBUTIONS

Section 170(a)(1) provides that a taxpayer may deduct "any charitable contribution * * * payment of which is made within the taxable year. A charita-ble contribution shall be allowable as a deduction only if verified under regulations prescribed by the Secretary." Pursuant to the Treasury regula-tions, contributions of money are required to be substantiated by canceled checks, receipts from the donee organizations showing the date and amount of the contributions, or other reliable written records showing the name of the donee, date, and amount of the contributions. *See* sec. 1.170A-13(a)(1), Income Tax Regs. Similarly, contributions of property other than money must be substantiated, at a minimum, by a receipt from the donee showing the name and address of the donee, the date and location of the contribution, and a description of the property in detail reasonably sufficient under the circum-stances. *See* sec. 1.170A-13(b)(1), Income Tax Regs. Where it is unrealistic to obtain a receipt, taxpayers must maintain reliable written records of their contributions. *See id.*

To substantiate additional charitable contributions of $6,937.20 for 1996 not previously claimed on their return for that year, petitioners offered several documents to the Court. Some of the documents do not have any indication of being provided by a donee organization but instead appear to have been generated by petitioners. Other documents consist of preprinted forms issued by alleged charitable organizations which petitioners filled in with the type and number of items donated and the estimated value of the donation. In addition, petitioners submitted checks and receipts which appear to be for the purchase of goods and services. Lastly, at trial, petitioners attempted to buttress their claims by describing the types of goods allegedly donated.

While the preprinted forms appear authentic, we nevertheless conclude that petitioners' self-generated receipts and other documents are not credible evidence of the order necessary to substantiate the deductions claimed in the instant case. *See* Tokh v. Commissioner, T.C. Memo 2001-45. Further, we do not find petitioners' testimony credible. We hold that petitioners have failed to introduce credible evidence to substantiate the actual items contributed and their fair market values.[n.4] *See* sec. 7491(a)(1) and (2)(A). Consequently, the burden of proof is not placed on respondent. Because petitioners have failed to present us with any credible evidence, they have not met their burden of proof pursuant to Rule 142(a) to support their claimed deductions. We therefore hold that petitioners are not entitled to a deduction for charitable contributions in excess of the $1,500 that respondent has already allowed.

* * *

In reaching our holdings herein, we have considered all arguments made, and to the extent not mentioned above, we find them to be moot, irrelevant, or without merit.

To reflect the foregoing,

Decision will be entered under Rule 155.

Does the Tax Court's opinion in *Higbee* provide any insight into the differences, if any, in the proof required to meet the "credible evidence" standard of Code section 7491(a) and the burden of persuasion under Tax Court Rule 142(a)?

Many questions regarding the application and effect of section 7491 remain unanswered. Having read section 7491 and the brief discussion above about the law that applies if the taxpayer does not meet the section 7491 requirements, consider how you might advise a client in a dispute with the IRS. The IRS, one presumes, will need to prepare for the possibility that it will bear the burden of persuasion.[15] How might the IRS obtain the evidence necessary

---

[n.4] For instance, on one of the preprinted forms, petitioners listed a charitable contribution of $700 for "cribs" and $200 for "baby clothes". Because petitioners have failed to establish how they arrived at those fair market values, we are unable to allow such deductions. Further, petitioners have not produced any other independent and credible evidence indicating that those donations were actually made.

[15] The IRS will not know during the audit or Appeals stage which cases will go to trial, and in which of those trials the taxpayer will meet the requirements of section 7491.

to meet that burden? Which party controls that evidence? How should a taxpayer prepare for litigation if he hopes to shift the burden of proof to the IRS? Who bears the burden of going forward under section 7491? At the audit stage, what might you advise your client to consider in planning a strategy that contemplates possible litigation of the controversy later?

Consider also whether the application of section 7491 in some cases, shifting to the IRS the burden of proof, is likely to affect who wins those cases.[16] Keep in mind that burden of proof applies only to factual questions. If the only situations in which burden of proof affects the outcome of a case are those where either no proof is presented by either side or exactly equal proof is presented, the shift might have little significance as a practical matter.

§ 6.06   Awards of Administrative and Litigation Costs and Fees to Taxpayers

The Code provides a mechanism for taxpayers prevailing in tax controversies to obtain reimbursement of administrative and/or legal expenses if the government's position was not "substantially justified." Specifically, Code section 7430 allows an award to a "prevailing party" for "reasonable administrative costs" in connection with an administrative proceeding involving the IRS and "reasonable litigation costs" in connection with a civil action in a federal court (which includes both Tax Court and refund court actions). *See* I.R.C. § 7430(a), (c)(6). To qualify as a prevailing party, the taxpayer must "substantially prevail" with respect to either the amount in controversy or with respect to the most significant issue or set of issues litigated, and must meet a net worth requirement. *See* I.R.C. § 7430(c)(4)(A). The taxpayer will not be treated as the prevailing party if the United States establishes that its position was "substantially justified." *See* I.R.C. § 7430(c)(4)(B). In determining whether the government's position was substantially justified, courts take into account whether the government has lost substantially similar issues in courts of appeal in other circuits. *See id.*

If section 7430 otherwise applies, the award allowed to a prevailing party is for "reasonable administrative costs" and "reasonable litigation costs." The definitions of these terms were amended in 1998. Under current law, reasonable administrative costs means administrative fees or charges imposed by the IRS; reasonable expenses of expert witnesses (not to exceed the highest rate paid to expert witnesses by the United States); reasonable costs of studies, tests, and engineering reports determined by the IRS to be necessary to the taxpayer's case; and reasonable attorney's fees (generally not to exceed $125 per hour, except as adjusted for inflation). *See* I.R.C. § 7430(c)(2). The award, however, can only include such costs incurred after the earliest of the date the taxpayer receives the notice of the Appeals decision in his case, the date

---

[16] Section 7491 may have effects outside of who wins tax cases. Tax Court Judge Tannenwald pointed out that the threshold requirements for the burden of proof shift may delay proceedings, a particular problem in small tax cases, which are meant to follow a streamlined procedure. In addition, he has noted the difficulty for the taxpayer to substantiate nonreceipt of income. There will also likely be continuing litigation with respect to, the threshold requirements of section 7491. *See* The Hon. Theodore Tannenwald, Jr., "The United States Tax Court: Yesterday, Today, and Tomorrow," 15 Am. J. Tax Policy 1, 13–15 (1998).

of the notice of deficiency, or the date of the 30-day letter. Similarly, under current law, reasonable litigation costs includes reasonable court costs; reasonable expenses of expert witnesses; reasonable costs of studies, tests, and engineering reports; and reasonable attorney's fees. *See* I.R.C. § 7430(c)(1). Attorney's fees also include fees paid to a non-attorney authorized to practice before the IRS or the Tax Court. I.R.C. § 7430(c)(3)(A).

A Tax Court case has held that the costs of having an accountant file the taxpayer's delinquent returns and having an attorney correct the returns were not recoverable as "administrative costs" under Code section 7430. *See Corkrey v. Commissioner*, 115 T.C. 366 (2000). The court stated, in part:

> In the instant case, most of the expenses petitioner seeks to recover are associated with preparing or correcting petitioner's 1987 and 1988 tax returns. Those costs were incurred to provide respondent with the information necessary to make adjustments to petitioner's accounts and to fulfill petitioner's basic obligations as a taxpayer. Petitioner was required to file a tax return and until he properly filed that return, respondent was not in a position to abate the assessments and penalties and make the proper adjustments to his account. Indeed, until petitioner provided such information, the Service was substantially justified in relying upon wage information received from the school, the Minneapolis Postal Data Center, and the Veterans Administration. . . . Accordingly, we hold that petitioner's costs incurred in preparing and correcting petitioner's tax returns are not recoverable pursuant to section 7430. The Service, moreover, took no more than a reasonable amount of time to process petitioner's refunds after he filed his return. Consequently, we hold that any costs associated with procuring a refund after petitioner provided the information necessary to process the refund are not recoverable by petitioners.

Id. at 375-376.

Note that, unless the parties agree on who was the prevailing party, it is the IRS that makes the determination of whether a taxpayer was the prevailing party at the administrative level. I.R.C. § 7430(c)(4)(C). The IRS also makes the determination of the amount of the award. *See* I.R.C. § 7430(c)(2). On January 3, 2001, the IRS released proposed and temporary regulations on the definition of prevailing party in cases concluded with a qualified offer by the taxpayer. *See* T.D. 8922, 66 FR 725. In general, the taxpayer must meet the requirements of section 7430, including the net worth requirements and, for an award of litigation costs, exhaustion of administrative remedies. The regulations contain twelve illustrative examples.

The IRS's decision on these matters is subject to appeal to the Tax Court. *See* I.R.C. § 7430(f)(2). The Tax Court's disposition of the petition is then subject to appeal in the same manner as any other Tax Court decision. I.R.C. § 7430(f)(3). In litigated cases in which a court has ruled on costs and fees, that determination may be made part of the court's decision or judgment, and subject to appeal accordingly. *See* I.R.C. § 7430(f)(1).

§ 6.07 Sanctions

Taxpayers and others who abuse the litigation process may be subject to sanctions. Code section 6673(a) specifies:

(a) Tax court proceedings.

(1) Procedures instituted primarily for delay, etc. — Whenever it appears to the Tax Court that —

(A) proceedings before it have been instituted or maintained by the taxpayer primarily for delay,

(B) the taxpayer's position in such proceeding is frivolous or groundless, or

(C) the taxpayer unreasonably failed to pursue available administrative remedies,

the Tax Court, in its decision, may require the taxpayer to pay to the United States a penalty not in excess of $ 25,000.

A position is frivolous "if it is contrary to established law and unsupported by a reasoned, colorable argument for change in the law." *Coleman v. Commissioner*, 791 F.2d 68, 71 (7th Cir. 1986). Furthermore, if the Tax Court finds that someone admitted to practice before it has "multiplied the proceedings in any case unreasonably and vexatiously," the court can require that person, or, if an IRS representative, the United States, to pay "the excess costs, expenses, and attorneys' fees reasonably incurred because of such conduct. . . ." I.R.C. § 6673(a)(2).

> The courts' determination to use their sanctions authority to discourage the filing of frivolous tax suits is evident in the case discussions that follow, which are taken from the public court records from the court proceedings:
>
> This month [June 2001], the Tax Court penalized two California residents in separate cases for trying to avoid taxes through the use of trusts. On June 21, the Court . . . fined [Charles and Francesca Sigerseth of El Macero] $ 15,000. The Court pointed out that the case was "a waste of limited judicial and administrative resources that could have been devoted to resolving bona fide claims of other taxpayers." (*Sigerseth v. Commissioner*)
>
> On June 7, the Court found that Andy Hromiko of Roseville, Calif., not his trust, was the true earner of income. It noted that he had made "shopworn arguments characteristic of the tax-protester rhetoric that has been universally rejected by this and other courts," and fined him $ 12,500. (*Matrixinfosys Trust v. Commissioner*)
>
> Last Dec. 4, the Tax Court imposed a $ 25,000 penalty against Hae-Rong and Lucy Ni, of San Jose, Calif. Contesting the IRS rejection of various deductions on their tax returns, the Nis were not responsive to orders for supporting records. Instead, they challenged the authority of the IRS to audit their returns and of the government to impose taxes. The Court concluded that the Nis had chosen "to pursue a strategy of noncooperation and delay, undertaken behind a smokescreen of frivolous tax-protester arguments." The Court also imposed

sanctions of more than $ 10,600 against the Nis' attorney, Crystal Sluyter, for arguing frivolous positions in bad faith. (*The Nis Family Trust v. Commissioner*)

While at the Federal Prison Camp in Duluth, Minn., for tax evasion, Darlow Madge contended that he wasn't a taxpayer, that his income from selling hospital supplies wasn't taxable, and that only foreign income is taxable. On Dec. 7, the Tax Court imposed the maximum $ 25,000 fine after having warned Madge that continuing with his frivolous arguments would likely result in a penalty. (*Madge v. Commissioner*)

Regina Davis of Cincinnati, Ohio received a $ 4,000 penalty from the Tax Court on April 10 for frivolous and groundless arguments, including that the IRS is not an agency of the United States and that it is a function of the Puerto Rican Bureau of Alcohol, Tobacco and Firearms. Davis persisted in her contentions even after the Court warned her that she could be fined for doing so. (*Davis v. Commissioner*)

IR-2001-59.

Note that in *The Nis Family Trust v. Commissioner*, 115 T.C. 523 (2000), the Tax Court imposed penalties not only on the taxpayers, but also on their attorney. In that case, when the taxpayers brought in an attorney, she echoed their tax-protestor type arguments and added similar ones of her own. Neither the taxpayers nor their attorney, whom the court found acted in bad faith, responded to orders to show cause why they should not pay costs or sanctions. As these cases reflect, the Tax Court is quite unsympathetic to "tax protestors" who allege, for example, that the income tax is unconstitutional or that they are not subject to tax. Consider the following case:

PHILIPS v. COMMISSIONER
United States Tax Court
T.C. Memo. 1995-540[17]

FOLEY, JUDGE: * * *

This case presents the following issues:

1. Whether petitioner is liable for the deficiencies determined by respondent. We hold that petitioner is liable.

* * *

4. Whether petitioner has asserted frivolous and groundless arguments that warrant the imposition of a penalty pursuant to section 6673. We hold that petitioner has asserted frivolous and groundless arguments, and the Court shall impose a penalty.

---

[17] *Aff'd*, 99 F.3d 1146 (9th Cir. 1996).

FINDINGS OF FACT

The parties have stipulated all relevant facts, and these facts are so found.

Petitioner resided in San Clemente, California, at the time he filed his petition. Petitioner has acknowledged that he received income from several sources in taxable years 1987 through 1991 yet did not file individual income tax returns for those years. In 1987, petitioner received $70,500 from Ronco Plastics, Inc., and $809 from Buckhorn, Inc. In 1988, petitioner received $60,000 from Ronco Plastics, Inc. In 1989, petitioner received $76,100 from Ronco Plastics, Inc., $10,250 from American Telephone & Telegraph Co., $160 from ADAC Laboratories, and $10 from American Transtech. In 1990, petitioner received $100,738 from Ronco Plastics, Inc., $40 from ADAC Laboratories, and $14 from U.S. Clearing Corp. In 1991, petitioner received $93,600 from Ronco Plastics, Inc. The amounts received from Ronco Plastics, Inc., were compensation; the other amounts were dividends and returns on stock and bond investments.

In answering respondent's notice of deficiency, petitioner on June 9, 1994, filed a defective petition with this Court. The petition submitted did not comply with the form and content rules set forth in Rule 34(b). Petitioner presented typical tax protester arguments and claimed that he is not subject to the income tax. He also challenged respondent's "SUBJECT MATTER JURISDICTION", questioned whether he could "BE LIABLE FOR AN INCOME TAX" on his wages, and asserted that wages "ARE NOT A REVENUE TAXABLE EVENT WITHIN THE PURVIEW OF THE INTERNAL REVENUE CODE."

On June 14, 1994, the Court ordered petitioner to file an amended petition by August 15, 1994. In response, petitioner submitted on August 11, 1994, the same defective petition that had been rejected by the Court on June 14, 1994 (except that it bore a new date). On October 13, 1994, respondent filed a Motion to Dismiss for Failure to State a Claim upon Which Relief Can Be Granted. In her motion, respondent also asked the Court to impose a penalty pursuant to section 6673.

On October 14, 1994, the Court issued an order directing petitioner to file a written objection setting forth clear and concise reasons why respondent's motion to dismiss should not be granted or, in the alternative, setting forth clear and concise allegations of error and facts concerning the merits of the specific adjustments contained in the notices of deficiency. In its order, the Court also advised petitioner that penalties have been imposed under section 6673 in similar cases.

On November 14, 1994, petitioner filed a second amended petition that complied with the Court's form and content requirements. Accordingly, the Court denied respondent's motion to dismiss on November 21, 1994.

On September 11, 1995, respondent filed a Motion for Sanctions Pursuant to I.R.C. § 6673. A trial was held in Los Angeles, California, on September 12, 1995.

OPINION

The Internal Revenue Code provides that gross income means all income from whatever source derived. Sec. 61(a). The Supreme Court has held that income includes "gain derived from capital, from labor, or from both combined." Eisner v. Macomber, 252 U.S. 189, 207 (1920). The Court of Appeals for the Ninth Circuit, to which any appeal in this case would lie, has expressly held that wages are income and are subject to taxation. United States v. Romero, 640 F.2d 1014, 1016 (9th Cir. 1981).

In affirming this Court's decision in a tax protester case, the Court of Appeals for the Seventh Circuit aptly noted: "Some people believe with great fervor preposterous things that just happen to coincide with their self-interest. 'Tax protesters' have convinced themselves that wages are not income, that only gold is money, that the Sixteenth Amendment is unconstitutional, and so on." Coleman v. Commissioner, 791 F.2d 68, 69 (7th Cir. 1986).

In this case, petitioner advanced a variety of constitutional arguments that the courts have uniformly rejected. Generally, he argued that: (1) He is not a "taxpayer" as defined in the Internal Revenue Code; (2) the Tax Court lacks jurisdiction to decide this case; and (3) an income tax violates the Sixteenth Amendment because it is an impermissible "direct tax". We see no need to fully describe each of petitioner's constitutional arguments or to address them individually. To do so might imply that the arguments have some colorable merit when in fact they are groundless.

It is sufficient to note that petitioner readily acknowledges that he received income yet refuses to pay tax on it. Accordingly, we hold that petitioner is liable for the deficiencies determined by respondent.

* * *

Finally, we consider whether a penalty should be imposed under section 6673. Section 6673(a)(1) provides that, whenever it appears to the Tax Court that the taxpayer's position in a proceeding is frivolous or groundless, the Court may impose a penalty not in excess of $25,000. This Court has often imposed such penalties on taxpayers who make frivolous tax protester arguments. See, e.g., Coulter v. Commissioner, 82 T.C. 580, 584–586 (1984); Abrams v. Commissioner, 82 T.C. 403, 408–413 (1984); Wilkinson v. Commissioner, 71 T.C. 633, 639–643 (1979); Santangelo v. Commissioner, T.C. Memo. 1995-468; McNeel v. Commissioner, T.C. Memo. 1995-211; Devon v. Commissioner, T.C. Memo. 1995-206; Carr v. Commissioner, T.C. Memo. 1995-138; cf. Connor v. Commissioner, 770 F.2d 17, 20 (2d Cir. 1985) (noting that the argument that wages are not income "has been rejected so frequently that the very raising of it justifies the imposition of sanctions").

In this case, petitioner knew that courts have repeatedly rejected his constitutional arguments and repeatedly imposed the section 6673 penalty on taxpayers who have made such arguments. Indeed, the Court so advised petitioner in its October 14, 1994, order.

In his trial memorandum, however, petitioner continued to assert the same groundless claims. Petitioner stated, for example, that "the free exercise and enjoyment of the God-given and *constitutionally secured right* to lawfully acquire property or compensatory income, by lawfully contracting one's own labor in innocent and harmless activities, for lawful compensation, cannot be (and therefore has not been) taxed for *revenue purposes.*" Petitioner made similar assertions in his request for admissions, in his proposed joint stipulation of facts, and in a list of 21 "Special Questions for the Tax Court" that served no function but to restate petitioner's antitax views.

At the beginning of the trial, the Court warned petitioner that it would impose a penalty, up to $25,000, if it found his position to be frivolous and groundless. During the trial, the Court admonished petitioner several times to set forth a legitimate argument for not paying the taxes due. Ignoring these admonitions, petitioner consumed all of his trial time asserting that his income is not subject to taxation, contending that this Court did not have jurisdiction, and asking extraneous questions. Among his inquiries, he asked: "Am I here under common law?", "Is this a Court of Admiralty?", and "Does this Court have anything to do with the Uniform Commercial Code?" He also stated that he did not "see a corpus delicti" in this case.

In sum, petitioner has advanced trite constitutional arguments in his submissions to this Court and at trial. Petitioner has received $412,221 during the tax years in issue yet has steadfastly refused to honor his obligation to pay taxes. Indeed, his actions have wasted the time and resources of the Internal Revenue Service and this Court. Accordingly, we hold that petitioner's position in these proceedings is frivolous and groundless, and the Court shall impose a penalty of $10,000.

Respondent's motion for sanctions will be granted, and decision will be entered for respondent.

The District Courts can impose sanctions for filing a frivolous complaint under Rule 11 of the Federal Rules of Civil Procedure; courts have applied this sanction in some tax protestor cases. *See, e.g., Cheek v. Doe*, 828 F.2d 395 (7th Cir.), *cert. denied*, 484 U.S. 955 (1987); *In re Busby*, 1998 U.S. Dist. LEXIS 16674 (M.D. Fla. 1988); *LaRue v. United States*, 959 F. Supp. 959 (C.D. Ill. 1997); *see also Shrock v. United States*, 907 F. Supp. 1241 (N.D. Ind. 1995), *aff'd*, 92 F.3d 1187 (7th Cir.), *cert. denied*, 519 U.S. 994 (1996). The Court of Federal Claims can similarly impose sanctions under its Rule 11, as well as its Rule 16(f).[18] *See Lonsberry v. United States*, 97-2 U.S.T.C. ¶ 50,888 (Ct.

---

[18] Court of Federal Claims Rule 16(f) provides:

> If a party or party's attorney fails to obey a scheduling or pretrial order, or if no appearance is made on behalf of a party at a scheduling or pretrial conference, or if a party or party's attorney is substantially unprepared to participate in the conference, or if a party or party's attorney fails to participate in good faith, the court, upon motion or its own initiative, may make such orders with regard thereto as are just, and among others any of the orders provided in Rule 37(b)(2)(B), (C), (D). In lieu of or in addition to any other sanction, the court shall require the party or the attorney representing the party or both to pay the reasonable expenses incurred because of any noncompliance with this rule, including attorneys' fees, unless the court finds that the noncompliance was substantially justified or that other circumstances make an award of expenses unjust.

Fed. Cl. 1997). The Courts of Appeals can impose sanctions such as costs, attorney's fees, and double costs for the filing of frivolous appeals. *See* Fed. R. App. P. 38; *Van Sickle v. Holloway*, 791 F.2d 1431,1437 (10th Cir. 1986).[19] Consider the following cases, which were publicized by the IRS:

> On Feb. 2[, 2001], the Tenth Circuit Court of Appeals imposed an $ 8,000 penalty on Larry and Sandee Gass of Capulin, Col., for appealing district court decisions which rejected their contentions that taxes on income from real property are unconstitutional. The Appeals Court had earlier fined them $ 2,000 for using the same arguments in another case. (*Gass v. U.S.*)

> Michele Brashier and Richard Hembree, of Tulsa, Okla., each drew $ 1,000 penalties on April 13 for arguing that requiring them to file sworn income tax returns violated their Fifth Amendment right against self-incrimination. The Tenth Circuit Court of Appeals noted that sanctions were warranted because the Tax Court had warned them that their argument — rejected consistently for more than seventy years — was frivolous. (*Brashier v. Commissioner*)

> After losing the argument that his wages were not income and receiving a $ 500 penalty, Garnell McAfee, Jr., of Flowery Branch. Ga., returned to U.S. District Court in Northern Georgia to try to stop the government from collecting the penalty by garnishing his wages. On April 4, the judge stated that "bringing this ill-considered, nonsensical litigation before this court for yet a second time is nothing but contumacious foolishness which wastes the time and energy of the court system." He then imposed a $ 1,000 penalty, added 10 percent to the original penalty, and ordered McAfee to pay the U.S. Marshal's costs of serving the writ of garnishment on his employer. (*McAfee v. U.S.*)

IR-2001-59. Consider the following case, as well:

CHRISTENSEN v. WARD
United States Court of Appeals, Tenth Circuit
916 F.2d 1462 (1990)[20]

STEPHEN H. ANDERSON, CIRCUIT JUDGE.

These cases are another chapter in Mr. Christensen's quarrel with the government over federal taxes, including his conviction and imprisonment for failure to file returns beginning in 1972, the subsequent assessment of taxes against him, and the collection of his liabilities through the seizure and sale of property. Having had or, in some instances, having waived his day in court on the merits of both civil and criminal proceedings against him, all without

---

[19] Monetary sanctions, penalties, and court costs awarded to the United States with respect to a tax case in District Court, the Court of Federal Claims, or the Courts of Appeals may be assessed by the IRS and collected in the same manner as a tax following notice and demand for payment. I.R.C. § 6673(b)(2), (3).

[20] Later proceeding, 916 F.2d 1485 (10th Cir.), *cert. denied*, 498 U.S. 999 (1990), *reh'g denied*, 498 U.S. 1075 (1991), *appeal dismissed sub nom.* United States v. Christensen, 1992 U.S. App. LEXIS 7250 (10th Cir. 1992).

success, Mr. Christensen has now sued almost everyone in the government who has disagreed with him, from the Supreme Court to IRS agents. One suit was filed in state court and removed to federal court. The other suit was filed in federal court. The district court opinions filed on May 8 and June 2, 1989, copies of which are attached hereto, identify the parties sued and describe and address Mr. Christensen's contentions in detail. For the reasons set forth in the district court's opinion of June 2, 1989, the court granted the respective defendants' motions to dismiss pursuant to Fed. R. Civ. P. 12(b) and 56.

* * *

Mr. Christensen believes that he has no obligation to file income tax returns, that federal employees have no authority to pursue collection of the tax, and that federal courts have no constitutional grant of jurisdiction relating to such matters. Examples of his arguments in the cases before us are illustrative:

> A law requiring individuals to file returns of their income, private financial information, with public employees would be in conflict with both the Fourth and Thirteenth Amendments of the U.S. Constitution.

Reply Brief of Appellant at 6.

> Those who would cite the Sixteenth Amendment are destitute of mentality because the power to lay and collect Taxes, as provided in the Sixteenth Amendment, is totally different from the power to require individuals to report their private financial information to government employees.

Id. at 5.

* * *

> Defendant Sam violated the liberty provision of the Constitution . . . by finding a liability without citing a law making Plaintiff liable for the income Tax, which there is none.

Memorandum in Support of Motion to Vacate Memorandum Opinion, Order and Judgment, R. Vol. II, Tab 26 at 6–7.

> The power to require Edward D. Christensen to make income Tax returns is not delegated to the United States by the Constitution, nor is it reasonably to be implied from the power to lay and collect Taxes, an entirely different subject.

Memorandum and Conclusions of Law in Support of Motion to Vacate Sentence, January 9, 1986, R. Vol. I, Tab 12 at 13.

* * *

> Further, this Court must have jurisdiction over the persons. Neither the Plaintiff nor any of the Defendants live on a federal enclave in the State of Utah where the United States has exclusive

territorial jurisdiction, therefore this Court lacks jurisdiction over all persons.

Id. at 3.

* * *

As indicated above, Mr. Christensen had an opportunity to test those or similar arguments on the merits in his criminal case, Tax Court case and collection cases. The problem is that he refuses to accept the finality of the decisions against him in those cases. The history of his litigiousness on the point includes the following.

With respect to his criminal conviction, Mr. Christensen knowingly waived his right to a direct appeal. Transcript of Proceedings in No. CR77-276S, R. Vol. I, Tab 12, at pp. 2, 4. Thereafter, he pursued collateral challenges to that conviction on three separate occasions. * * *

The Tax Court filed its decision upholding taxes and penalties against Mr. Christensen on November 22, 1982. Christensen appealed to this court which dismissed the appeal for failure to prosecute. Christensen v. Commissioner, No. 83-1227, slip. op. (10th Cir. Aug. 17, 1983). Christensen then petitioned for a writ of certiorari to the United States Supreme Court which denied the petition. 465 U.S. 1037, 104 S. Ct. 1313, 79 L. Ed. 2d 710 (1984). Thus, the Tax Court decision became final and unreviewable. Yet, almost four years after the judgment was entered, Christensen filed a motion [with] the Tax Court to vacate the judgment. In his motion he reasserted his original claims. The Tax Court denied the petition. Christensen then appealed once again to this court which affirmed the Tax Court and imposed sanctions against Christensen in the amount of $3,383.79 for filing a legally frivolous appeal. Christensen v. Commissioner, No. 86-2788, slip. op. (10th Cir. Dec. 23, 1987). To date those sanctions remain unpaid.

In addition to the appeals just listed, Mr. Christensen has filed five other appeals in this court, and one in the Ninth Circuit, all relating to his federal income tax controversy: United States v. Christensen, No. 87-2158, slip op. (10th Cir. Feb. 24, 1988) (appeal dismissed for lack of jurisdiction); United States v. Christensen, No. 84-2459, slip op. (10th Cir. March 4, 1985) (affirming judgment of the district court directing the sale of 1,293 silver dollars in partial satisfaction of Christensen's tax liabilities), *cert. denied*, 475 U.S. 1018, 106 S. Ct. 1203, 89 L. Ed. 2d 316 (1986); Christensen v. United States, No. 84-2503, slip op. (10th Cir. March 4, 1985) (affirming judgment of the district court denying Christensen's motion to vacate two writs of entry pursuant to which IRS Agents seized personal property in partial satisfaction of Christensen's tax liability), *cert. denied*, 475 U.S. 1018, 106 S. Ct. 1203, 89 L. Ed. 2d 316 (1986); Christensen v. Commissioner, No. 80-2302, slip op. (10th Cir. May 7, 1981) (denying Christensen's Petition for a Writ of Mandamus against the Commissioner of Internal Revenue and the Chief Judge of the Tax Court); Christensen v. Commissioner, No. 80-1065, slip op. (10th Cir. Jan. 26, 1981) (dismissing an appeal from the Tax Court); and United States v. Christensen, 831 F.2d 303 (9th Cir. 1987), *cert. denied*, 485 U.S. 1035, 108 S. Ct. 1595, 99 L. Ed. 2d 910 (1988).

Now we have before us yet again Mr. Christensen's persistent attack on these final judgments, using the same arguments he lost on originally to support a claim that judges and employees in the executive branch were wrong on the law. * * *

It is apparent from the history of this litigation that Mr. Christensen will not accept the judgment of the courts. The cases before us are not only another example of that fact, they yield insight into Mr. Christensen's thinking. The district court patiently explained its reasoning, with supporting authority, in two opinions running thirty pages in length. In response, Mr. Christensen characterizes the cases cited against him as "garbage decisions" and with respect to the laws in question he states: "Such laws, for lack of a better term, are 'garbage laws' which corrupt the law books and undermine those laws which are pursuant to the Constitution. The same is true of Rules and court decisions which are not pursuant to the Constitution." Brief of Appellant at 15, 17.

The district court did not impose sanctions against Mr. Christensen, but warned him that he is "edging toward the line where sanctions are warranted for frivolous, insupportable suits." R. Vol. II, Tab 24 at 23. We think Mr. Christensen has crossed that line, especially since he is reurging positions which we have previously determined to be frivolous, and for which we imposed sanctions. He is clearly determined to continue to litigate the same arguments which have been repeatedly rejected, by simply repackaging those arguments and adding new defendants. This court has the power to impose sanctions such as costs, attorneys fees and double costs for the filing of frivolous appeals, Fed. R. App. P. 38, and the inherent power to impose sanctions that are necessary to regulate the docket, promote judicial efficiency, and most importantly in this case, to deter frivolous filings. *Van Sickle v. Holloway*, 791 F.2d 1431, 1437 (10th Cir. 1986). *See also Tripati v. Beaman*, 878 F.2d 351, 353 (10th Cir. 1989). As in *Van Sickle v. Holloway*, we think that the following sanctions are appropriate: (1) Double costs are imposed against Mr. Christensen; (2) Mr. Christensen is prohibited from filing any further complaints in the United States District Court for the District of Utah, or any appeals in this court, that contain the same or similar allegations as those set forth in his complaints and other pleadings in the cases at bar (including any direct or indirect challenge to the previous court proceedings or judgments referred to herein), and the clerks of those courts are directed to return any such complaints or appeals to Mr. Christensen without filing; and (3) Mr. Christensen shall pay to the Clerk of the United States Court of Appeals for the Tenth Circuit $500.00 as a limited contribution to the United States for the cost and expenses of this action.

Although Mr. Christensen has already had an opportunity to respond to a request for sanctions, he has not been able to address the specific sanctions proposed herein. *See Braley v. Campbell*, 832 F.2d 1504 (10th Cir. 1987).

Accordingly, the clerk is directed to issue an order requiring Mr. Christensen to show cause why the above sanctions should not be imposed. Mr. Christensen's response will be limited to five pages. If the response is not received by the clerk within ten days from the filing of this opinion, the sanctions will be imposed. *See Van Sickle v. Holloway*, 791 F.2d at 1437.

* * *

What do you think of the sanction the court applied in this case? Do you think it was likely to effectively deter the sanctioned behavior?

§ 6.08   Bankruptcy Court Jurisdiction over Federal Tax Claims

Under the Bankruptcy Code, the filing of a bankruptcy petition by a debtor creates an "estate" of the debtor's property. 11 U.S.C. § 541(a). The bankruptcy petition also triggers an automatic stay prohibiting a wide variety of acts, including collection of taxes, 11 U.S.C. § 362(a)(6), and "the commencement or continuation of a proceeding before the United States Tax Court concerning the debtor," 11 U.S.C. § 362(a)(8). The automatic stay remains in effect until the earliest of three events: (1) the case is closed; (2) the case is dismissed; or (3) if the case concerns an individual and is under Chapter 7 of the Bankruptcy Code, or is under Chapters 11 or 13 of the Bankruptcy Code, the time a discharge is granted or denied. 11 U.S.C. § 362(c)(2).

Once the taxpayer files a bankruptcy petition, the bankruptcy court has jurisdiction to "determine the amount or legality of any tax, any fine or penalty relating to a tax, or any addition to tax, whether or not previously assessed, whether or not paid, and whether or not contested before and adjudicated by a judicial or administrative tribunal of competent jurisdiction." 11 U.S.C. § 505(a)(1). However, the bankruptcy court may not determine a tax which was "contested before and adjudicated by a judicial or administrative tribunal of competent jurisdiction before the commencement of the case under this title," 11 U.S.C. § 505(a)(2)(A).[21]

Although the IRS may issue a notice of deficiency during the automatic stay,[22] a taxpayer cannot file a Tax Court petition during the pendency of the stay. *See Moody v. Commissioner*, 95 T.C. 655 (1990); *McClamma v. Commissioner*, 76 T.C. 754, 757 (1981). However, a party in interest can file a motion in the bankruptcy court to lift the stay to allow litigation in another court to go forward. 11 U.S.C. § 362(d). On such a petition by the taxpayer-debtor or the IRS, the bankruptcy court determines whether to decide the tax issues itself or to release the stay to allow the taxpayer to petition the Tax

---

[21] The bankruptcy court also may not determine entitlement to a tax refund until 120 days after the bankruptcy trustee properly requests the refund or the governmental unit makes a determination on the request. 11 U.S.C. § 505(a)(2)(B).

[22] The IRS uses a slightly different form for a notice of deficiency issued in bankruptcy than the sample notice included in Chapter 7.

Court. "While both a bankruptcy court and a tax court may have jurisdiction to determine tax matters, the bankruptcy court acts as 'traffic cop,' determining which of the courts with jurisdiction ultimately will decide the claim." Stephen W. Sather, "Tax Issues in Bankruptcy," 25 St. Mary's L.J. 1364, 1400 (1994). As a result, the bankruptcy court has decided many complex federal tax issues.[23] Therefore, in a sense, the bankruptcy courts provide a fourth trial-level forum for federal tax cases, albeit not a forum a taxpayer chooses for that purpose.

§ 6.09 Unpublished Opinions

The precedential value of "unpublished" or "nonprecedential" court opinions may become more of an issue following the Eight Circuit's decision in *Anastasoff v. United States*, 223 F.3d 898 (8th Cir. 2000). In *Anastasoff*, the Eighth Circuit not only followed its prior unpublished decision in *Christie v. United States*, No. 91-2375MN (8th Cir. 1992) (unpublished), but also stated that it considered *Christie* binding precedent. The court held that "the portion of [the Eighth Circuit's] Rule 28A(i) that declares that unpublished opinions are not precedent is unconstitutional under Article III, because it purports to confer on the federal courts a power that goes beyond the 'judicial.'" *Id.* at 899. Although the Tax Court is an Article I court, and its opinions therefore do not raise the same constitutional issues, *Anastasoff* raises some interesting questions about the status of Tax Court Memorandum Opinions, which the Tax Court considers to have no precedential value. *See Nico v. Commissioner*, 67 T.C. 647, 654, *aff'd in part and rev'd in part*, 565 F.2d 1234 (2d Cir. 1977); *McGah v. Commissioner*, 17 T.C. 1458 (1952), *rev'd on other grounds*, 210 F.2d 769 (9th Cir. 1954).

PROBLEMS

1. An IRS agent has been in touch with Janice regarding her 2001 return, but she has not received a notice of deficiency from the IRS. After looking over the return, she believes she is entitled to a refund. Must she wait for a notice of deficiency to pursue refund litigation? What must Janice do to pursue her refund claim?

2. Phillipe has received a notice of deficiency from the IRS.

   A. May he pursue refund litigation over the issues in the notice? What must he do to pursue a refund suit?

   B. Assume that Phillipe believes that the notice is incorrect, and that he is in fact entitled to a refund. May he litigate in Tax Court both the issues in the notice and the issues he believes entitle him to a refund?

3. Doris mailed her 1995 return to the IRS on May 1, 1996, without having obtained an extension of time to file. The return reflected her $30,000 wages, a tax liability of $4,000 for the

---

[23] *See* Johnson, *supra* note 3, at 241 & n.22, 23.

1995 year, and her wage withholding credits of $3,000. Accordingly, she mailed a $1,000 payment in with the return, which the IRS received with the return on May 7, 1996. On April 20, 1999, the IRS mailed Doris a notice of deficiency in the amount of $2,000 based on lottery winnings Doris allegedly received but did not report. Doris responded to the notice by paying in full the $2,000 deficiency on May 10, 1999 and by filing a refund claim on June 21, 1999 for the $2,000. The IRS denied the refund claim, sending Doris a notice of disallowance on June 1, 2000, which she received on June 5. Doris filed suit in the District Court on June 10. The IRS counterclaimed for an additional deficiency of $1,000 based on deductions claimed on Doris's return that the IRS alleges are erroneous.

A.   Does Doris have any procedural defense to the counterclaim?

B.   Assuming the IRS is entitled to pursue the counterclaim, who will bear the burden of persuasion on it?

4. If tax litigation were to be reformed, would you advocate a single trial-level court for all federal tax cases, a single appellate court, or both? Why?

5. Alice and Alan Andrews own and operate as a sole proprietorship a small soda distributing company called Mom and Pop's One Stop Pop Shoppe. They report the tax events in the life of the business on their Form 1040, Schedule C. Last month, the Andrews received a timely notice of deficiency reflecting a deficiency of $20,000 for their 1999 tax year and $35,000 for their 2000 tax year. The notice of deficiency contained an adjustment for a business deduction they took on the advice of their daughter, an accountant. Their daughter has advised the Andrews to file a petition in the United States Tax Court, contesting the deficiencies. The Andrews do not plan to hire an attorney, but instead represent themselves, with the informal assistance of their daughter.

A.   Are the Andrews eligible to file a petition to have their case heard as a small tax case? Would your answer change if the Andrews planned to include an overpayment claim for the earlier tax year, claiming a refund of $25,000?

B.   Assume that the Andrews are eligible to file a small tax case petition in the Tax Court, and they consult you informally on how to proceed. The only issue they plan to raise is the deduction questioned in the notice of deficiency. Would you advise the Andrews to file a small tax case petition or a regular petition with the Tax Court?

   i.   Would your answer to B. change if the amounts in issue were instead only $3,000 for each tax year?

   ii. Would your answer to B. change if the Andrews were to tell you that they take the business deduction in question every year, and that they hope to take it again each year going forward?

    iii.   Would your answer to B. change if the Andrews told you that their daughter believes that the deduction in issue is taken by all similar businesses, including some very large ones, and that the IRS may be using the Andrews' case to establish a precedent?

    iv.   Would your answer to B. change, if, after speaking with you, the Andrews decide to hire an attorney to represent them in the Tax Court?

6.   Dawn has received a preliminary notice (30-day letter) from the IRS reflecting adjustments to her 2002 tax return that would increase her tax liability for 2002 by $25,000. The adjustments relate to a large deduction Dawn took on her return. Dawn feels that the IRS's position is completely wrong, and although she will consider settling, she is willing to litigate the issue if necessary. Dawn's attorney has informed her that there is a possibility that Dawn might obtain a shift to the IRS of the burden of proof under Code section 7491 if the matter is litigated.

    A.   Will the potential for a shift in the burden of proof likely affect negotiations with the Appeals Division if Dawn's attorney files a tax protest on her behalf in response to the 30-day letter?

    B.   Would you advise that Dawn and her attorney make an effort to shift the burden of proof to the IRS under section 7491? Does your answer depend at all on whether the dispute between Dawn and the IRS is primarily factual or primarily legal?

    C.   Assume that Dawn is interested in preparing for the possibility of shifting the burden of proof to the IRS in eventual litigation.

        i.   What should Dawn and her attorney do to prepare for a request to shift the burden of proof to the IRS under section 7491?

        ii.   If Dawn were Dawn, Inc., a Subchapter C corporation (instead of an individual), what additional requirement(s) would it have to meet in order to be eligible for a burden of proof shift under section 7491?

7.   On April 15, 1996, Paul, who is single and has no dependents, filed a 1995 tax return reflecting zero tax liability. He reported wages of $35,000, in accordance with the W-2 he attached, and took a deduction for $35,000 which he labelled "value of labor expended." On the bottom of the return, below his signature, he wrote "It is unconstitutional to tax wages without allowing a deduction for labor." Paul claimed a refund of all of the

withholding tax reflected in his W-2 (a small amount because Paul had claimed nine personal exemptions on his W-4 form). On September 1, 1998, the IRS mailed Paul a notice of deficiency reflecting gross income of $35,000, the standard deduction, and one personal exemption. Paul timely petitioned the Tax Court. In his petition, he asserted the alternative arguments that (1) wages are not income within the meaning of the Sixteenth Amendment to the Constitution; and (2) if wages are income, the Sixteenth Amendment requires that the value of labor be allowed as a deduction. The IRS denied the allegations in the petition and made a motion for sanctions under section 6673. Are sanctions available? If so, what is the maximum amount that may be imposed against Paul?

8. Judy and Donald Smith were legally divorced on May 3, 1992. Their property settlement, which was incorporated into their divorce decree, awarded to Mr. Smith Mrs. Smith's half-interest in the Smiths' personal residence. Pursuant to the property settlement, Mr. Smith was required to pay Mrs. Smith $50,000 per year plus 10 percent interest for 10 years. He issued a promissory note to her, and also conveyed to her a mortgage deed on the residence as security for the debt. The deed was subordinate to a preexisting mortgage on the property from First State Bank.

   Mr. Smith deducted the interest of $5,000 per year on the promissory note on his federal income tax return as an itemized deduction for qualified residence interest under section 163. On the first day of last month, the Atlanta, Georgia IRS office sent Donald Smith a notice of deficiency for the years 1995 through 1999 in which it denied the $5,000 interest deduction for each year, arriving at a deficiency of $1,500 for each of the five years in question. (Assume that the statute of limitations was open for each of those years.) The notice of deficiency contained the symbols "SP:END MP:SLD." The explanation attached to the notice of deficiency stated that the interest deduction was disallowed because the interest was not qualified residence interest under section 163(h) of the Code. Mr. Smith still resides in the residence in question, which is located at 765 Peach Street in Atlanta, GA 30319. His social security number is 999-88-7777.

   A. Assume that the IRS mailed a valid notice of deficiency to Mr. Smith's last known address. Mr. Smith wishes to litigate the issue but does not want to pay the deficiency in advance. Draft a Tax Court petition for him.

   B. Assume that the IRS did not mail the notice of deficiency last month, but instead that the IRS mailed a valid notice of deficiency to Mr. Smith's last known address one year ago, and that Mr. Smith paid the deficiencies in full. Six months ago, he filed refund claims with the IRS for each of the years in question, claiming that the $5,000 interest paid each year was deductible as qualified residence interest. He received notices of disallowance of his claims two months ago. He asks for your help litigating the case. Draft a District Court Complaint for him.

Chapter 7

REQUIREMENTS OF THE NOTICE OF DEFICIENCY AND ITS FUNCTIONS IN TAX COURT

Reading Assignment: Code §§ 6212, 6213, 7454, 7455, 7458, 7491, 7522; Tax Court Rule 142(a).

§ 7.01 Introduction

Most tax litigation begins with the letter from the IRS known as a "notice of deficiency." Code section 6212 governs notices of deficiency. Section 6212(a) provides:

> If the Secretary determines that there is deficiency in respect of any tax imposed by subtitle A or B or chapter 41, 42, 43 or 44, he is authorized to send notice of such deficiency to the taxpayer by certified mail or registered mail. Such notice shall include a notice to the taxpayer of the taxpayer's right to contact a local office of the taxpayer advocate and the location and phone number of the appropriate office.

Although it may sound from this statutory language as if a notice of deficiency is optional, the IRS cannot assess a deficiency without first sending the taxpayer a notice. I.R.C. § 6213(a); *see also, e.g., Philadelphia & Reading Corp. v. United States*, 944 F.2d 1063, 1072 (3d Cir. 1991). In fact, the "authorization" language refers only to the method of delivery.

A notice of deficiency (also commonly called a 90-day letter) typically resembles this one:

SAMPLE NOTICE OF DEFICIENCY

Department of the Treasury
Internal Revenue Service
P.O. Box 8120
CHAMBLEE, GA 39901

Date: August 24, 2001

Taxpayer Identification
Number: 123-456-7890
Contact Person: A. Jones
Contact Telephone Number:
   (800) 829-3009 Toll Free

Hours to Call:
   7:00 AM to 8:00 PM
Last Date to Petition Tax
Court:
   November 23, 2001

John A. Doe and
Jane B. Doe   CERTIFIED MAIL
123 Main Street
Duluth, GA 30026

Tax Year Ended: December 31, 1999

Deficiency: See attached statement

Dear Taxpayer:

   We have determined that there is a deficiency (increase) in your income tax as shown above. This letter is a NOTICE OF DEFICIENCY sent to you as required by law. The enclosed statement shows how we figured the deficiency.

   If you want to contest this deficiency in court before making any payment, you have until the Last Date to Petition Tax Court (90 days from the above mailing date of this letter or 150 days if addressed to you outside the United States) to file a petition with the United States Tax Court for redetermination of the amount of your tax. You can get a petition form and the rules for filing a petition from the Tax Court. You should file the petition with the United States Tax Court, 400 Second Street, NW, Washington, D.C. 20217. Attach a copy of this letter to the petition.

   The time in which you must file a petition with the Court (90 or 150 days as the case may be) is fixed by law and the Court cannot consider your case if the petition is filed late. As required by law, separate notices are sent to spouses. If this letter is addressed to both a husband and wife, and both want to petition the Tax Court, both must sign the petition or each must file a separate, signed petition.

The Tax Court has a simplified procedure for small tax cases when the amount in dispute is $50,000 or less for any one tax year. You can get information about this procedure, as well as a petition form you can use, by writing to the Clerk of the United States Tax Court at 400 Second Street, NW, Washington, DC 20217. You should write promptly if you intend to file a petition with the Tax Court.

If you decide *not* to file a petition with the Tax Court, please sign and return the enclosed waiver form to us. This will permit us to assess the deficiency quickly and will limit the accumulation of interest. We've enclosed an envelope you can use. If you decide not to sign and return the statement and you do not timely petition the Tax Court, the law requires us to assess and bill you for the deficiency after 90 days from the above mailing date of this letter (150 days if this letter is addressed to you outside the United States).

When you send information we requested or if you write to us about this letter, please provide a telephone number and the best time to call you if we need more information. Please attach this letter to your correspondence to help us identify your case. Keep the copy for your records.

The person whose name and telephone number are shown in the heading of this letter can access your tax information and help you get answers. You also have the right to contact the Taxpayer Advocate. You can call 1-877-777-4778 and ask for Taxpayer Advocate Assistance. Or you can contact the Taxpayer Advocate for the IRS Office that issued this Notice of Deficiency by calling (770) 936-4500 or writing to:

> ATLANTA IRS CENTER
> TAXPAYER ADVOCATE
> PO BOX 48-549
> STOP 29A
> DORAVILLE, GA 30362

Taxpayer Advocate assistance is not a substitute for established IRS procedures such as the formal appeals process. The Taxpayer Advocate is not able to reverse legally correct tax determinations, nor extend the time fixed by law that you have to file a petition in the United States Tax Court. The Taxpayer Advocate can, however, see that a tax matter that may not have been resolved through normal channels gets prompt and proper handling.

Thank you for your cooperation.

> Sincerely yours,
>
> Commissioner
> By
> /s/ Gwen A. Green
> Gwen A. Green
> Field Director, Compliance
> Services

Enclosures:
Copy of this Letter
Waiver
Envelope

Attached schedules typically explain the calculation of the deficiency and penalties.[1]

§ 7.02 The Notice of Deficiency

The notice of deficiency is probably the single most important document in tax procedure. As explained in more detail below, the IRS's assessment authority typically hinges on its timely mailing a legally valid notice of deficiency. In addition, because assessment is generally a legal prerequisite for collection of tax, a notice of deficiency is also a prerequisite for collection of any tax deficiency.[2]

[A] The Multiple Functions of the Notice

The notice of deficiency serves multiple functions in the tax controversy process. First, it is an indispensable prerequisite to Tax Court subject matter jurisdiction, the Tax Court's authority over the case. I.R.C. § 6213(a); *see also* Tax Court Rules 20, 34. The notice is well known as the taxpayer's "ticket to the Tax Court." *See, e.g., Commissioner v. Shapiro*, 424 U.S. 614, 630 (1976); *Corbett v. Frank*, 293 F.2d 501, 503 (9th Cir. 1961); *Bourekis v. Commissioner*, 110 T.C. 20 (1998). Second, and equally important, the notice of deficiency informs the taxpayer of the IRS's claim, analogous to legal process. In an ordinary civil suit, legal process is the notice to the defendant of a pending action. *See R. Griggs Group, Ltd. v. Filanto Spa*, 920 F. Supp. 1100, 1103 (D. Nev. 1996).

Once a case is docketed in Tax Court, the notice serves yet a third function—it becomes part of the Tax Court pleadings. "Issuing a statutory notice is in many ways analogous to filing a civil complaint." *Clapp v. Commissioner*, 875 F.2d 1396, 1403 (9th Cir. 1989). "Like a complaint, the statutory notice generally identifies the amount in issue and helps frame the issues in dispute in any subsequent Tax Court proceeding." Leandra Lederman, " 'Civil'izing Tax Procedure: Applying General Federal Learning to Statutory Notices of Deficiency," 30 U.C. Davis L. Rev. 183, 198–199 (1996) (footnotes omitted).

In addition to these three primary functions, the notice of deficiency has other effects on the tax controversy process. Once the IRS sends the notice,

---

[1] "(1) An explanatory paragraph in a notice of deficiency should reflect a twofold purpose: (a) to inform the taxpayer in clear and concise language of the adjustment; and (b) to state the position or positions of the Service with respect to the adjustments being made." I.R.M. 8.17.4.5.5.

[2] Notice and demand for payment cannot be made prior to assessment. *See* I.R.C. § 6303(a). The IRS's lien and levy powers follow the notice and demand for payment. *See* I.R.C. §§ 6321, 6331(a). These issues are discussed in Chapter 12.

the IRS is prohibited from assessing tax during the time period the taxpayer has to file a Tax Court petition (generally 90 days), and if the taxpayer does file a petition, until the Tax Court decision becomes final. I.R.C. § 6213(a). Not surprisingly, the notice tolls the statute of limitations on assessment during the period the IRS is prohibited from assessing tax (plus an additional 60 days). I.R.C. § 6503. A notice of deficiency also terminates an indefinite waiver of the statute of limitations made on Form 872A. *See Roszkos v. Commissioner*, 850 F.2d 514 (9th Cir. 1988), *cert. denied*, 489 U.S. 1012 (1989). Furthermore, as discussed below, the notice of deficiency historically has played an important role in the allocation of the burden of proof.[3]

[B] General Requirements of the Notice

Case law establishes that a valid notice of deficiency must identify the taxpayer and the taxable year involved, indicate that a deficiency has been determined, and specify the amount of the deficiency. *See, e.g., Estate of Yaeger*, 889 F.2d 29 (2d Cir. 1989), *cert. denied,* 495 U.S. 946 (1990); *Scar v. Commissioner*, 814 F.2d 1363, 1367 (9th Cir. 1987); *Abrams v. Commissioner*, 787 F.2d 939, 941 (4th Cir.), *cert. denied*, 479 U.S. 882 (1986). Effective July 22, 1998, the notice must also notify the taxpayer of his "right to contact a local office of the taxpayer advocate and the location and phone number of the appropriate office." I.R.C. § 6212(a). In addition, the notice must specify the deadline date for filing a Tax Court petition. IRS Reform Act § 3463(a).

Because a deficiency assessment is a nullity if the IRS failed previously to send a valid notice of deficiency, many taxpayers have challenged the validity of the notices they received[4] by petitioning the Tax Court and moving to dismiss the case for lack of subject matter jurisdiction.[5] If the Tax Court finds the notice invalid, it must dismiss the case for lack of jurisdiction. *See, e.g., Pietanza v. Commissioner*, 92 T.C. 729, 735 (1989), *aff'd*, 935 F.2d 1282 (3d

---

[3] As discussed in Chapter 6, prior law on the burden of proof in tax cases still governs the many cases in which section 7491 does not apply.

[4] Of course, the IRS theoretically can send a new notice if one is invalidated, but by then the statute of limitations on assessment often has expired. *See* I.R.C. § 6501.

[5] This is the most common approach for challenging defective notices, but it is not the only one. Taxpayers have sometimes sought injunctive relief to restrain assessment or collection of the tax, particularly for violations of the last known address rule of section 6212. *See, e.g.,* Cool Fuel v. Connett, 685 F.2d 309 (9th Cir. 1982); Williams v. United States, 264 F.2d 227 (6th Cir.), *cert. denied*, 361 U.S. 862 (1959); Ponchik v. Commissioner, 1986 U.S. Dist. LEXIS 16870 (D. Minn. 1987); Garmany v. Baptist, 1979 U.S. Dist. LEXIS 8072 (N.D. Ala. 1979). Code section 7421(a), which is known as the Anti-Injunction Act, provides that "no suit for the purpose of restraining the assessment or collection of any tax shall be maintained in any court by any person." However, it includes exceptions for the provisions of Code sections 6212(a) and 6213(a). Section 6213(a) expressly provides that collection or assessment during the "prohibited period" may be enjoined.

The United States Supreme Court has held that in order to obtain injunctive relief in a tax case, the taxpayer must show that (1) "under the most liberal view of the law and the facts . . . under no circumstances could the Government ultimately prevail," (2) the taxpayer "would suffer irreparable injury if collection were effected" and (3) "equity jurisdiction otherwise exists." Enochs v. Williams Packing & Navigation Co., 370 U.S. 1, 7 (1962). Taxpayers have therefore not generally been successful in injunction actions based on invalid notices of deficiency. *See, e.g., Cool Fuel, supra*, at 314 (Cool Fuel's admitted ability to pay the deficiency precluded equitable relief).

Cir. 1991); *Keeton v. Commissioner*, 74 T.C. 377, 379 (1980). If the Tax Court finds that it does not have jurisdiction over the subject matter in the first instance, how can it make a determination that the notice was not valid? For purposes of ruling on the status of the notice, the Tax Court has "jurisdiction to determine jurisdiction."

If the taxpayer files a petition after the applicable 90-day or 150-day filing period has expired, the *IRS* may move to dismiss for lack of jurisdiction on that ground. If, as part of the same proceeding, the taxpayer alleges that the notice is invalid, whose claim should be considered first? In such a case, the parties will each be arguing that the Tax Court should dismiss the case for lack of subject matter jurisdiction. The Tax Court considers the taxpayer's motion first, and does not consider dismissal based on a late-filed petition unless it finds that the IRS's notice of deficiency was valid. *See Dubin v. Commissioner*, 99 T.C. 325, 326 (1992); *Heaberlin v. Commissioner*, 34 T.C. 58, (1960), *acq.* 1960-2 C.B. 5. How do the consequences of dismissal differ if the Tax Court dismisses based on an invalid notice of deficiency rather than based on an untimely petition?

Judge Learned Hand has stated that the purpose of the notice of deficiency "is only to advise the person who is to pay the deficiency that the Commissioner means to assess him; anything that does this unequivocally is good enough." *Olsen v. Helvering*, 88 F.2d 650, 651 (2nd Cir. 1937). In fact, when Congress added what is now section 7522, which requires that notices of deficiency and other notices include a description of the basis for and the amounts of any tax due, interest, penalties and the like, it stated, "An inadequate description under the preceding sentence shall not invalidate such notice." Why might Congress have included this provision in section 7522?

Many taxpayer challenges to notices of deficiency have been unsuccessful. Courts have refused to invalidate a notice that was not signed by an IRS official, *Urban v. Commissioner*, 964 F.2d 888, 889 (9th Cir. 1992); *Commissioner v. Oswego Falls Corp.*, 71 F.2d 673, 677 (2d Cir. 1934); or that related to a full tax year despite its reference to only part of the tax year, *Estate of Scofield v. Commissioner*, 266 F.2d 154 (6th Cir. 1959). Similarly, a notice was valid where it covered a period longer than the one asserted by the taxpayer to be the proper period, and the notice included the taxable event in question. *Sanderling v. Commissioner*, 571 F.2d 174 (3d Cir. 1978).

More recently, in *Smith v. Commissioner*, 114 T.C. 489 (2000), *aff'd*, 275 F.3d 912 (10th Cir. 2001), the IRS failed to include in the notice of deficiency the deadline for filing a Tax Court petition. The taxpayers timely filed anyway. In fact, the taxpayers' counsel were aware of the issue; they telephoned IRS counsel to advise them of the omission. Judge Foley found that the notice of deficiency was valid, noting that IRS Reform Act section 3463(a), which required inclusion of the deadline date, failed to specify a remedy for failure to do so.

In *Rochelle v. Commissioner*, 116 T.C. 356 (2001), a court-reviewed opinion, Rochelle, an attorney, received a notice of deficiency on July 23, 1999 that was dated July 20, 1999. The IRS also mailed the notice to a certified public accountant listed as Rochelle's representative under a power of attorney. The notice failed to specify the last day for filing a Tax Court petition but did contain the standard language setting forth the 90-day period for filing a petition. Rochelle mailed his petition to the Tax Court 143 days after the mailing of the deficiency notice, and it was received 3 days later.

Citing *Smith*, Judge Vasquez, joined by Judges Wells, Cohen, Gerber, Ruwe, Whalen, Halpern, Beghe, Laro, and Thornton, rejected Rochelle's argument that the notice was invalid, noting that Rochelle had received it in time to meet the deadline. The majority also rejected Rochelle's argument that failure to include the deadline date rendered Rochelle's petition timely. Judge Beghe also filed a separate concurring opinion. Judge Chabot, joined by Judges Gale and Marvel, filed a dissent. Judge Swift and Judge Foley each filed separate dissents, as well. Judge Colvin joined in Judge Foley's dissent. This issue may gain more attention now that the Tax Court has split on how to approach it.

[C]   The Notice of Deficiency and the Burden of Proof

As discussed in Chapter 6, the "burden of proof " " has two components: The burden of going forward and the burden of persuasion. In a Tax Court case, the notice of deficiency plays a role in allocating each of these burdens. The details of this role are discussed below.

[1]   The "Presumption of Correctness"

The notice of deficiency traditionally has benefitted from a "presumption of correctness." *Welch v. Helvering*, 290 U.S. 111, 115 (1933). Effectively that means that the taxpayer bears the burden of going forward with evidence to rebut the IRS's determination. *See* Leandra Lederman Gassenheimer, "The Dilemma of Deficient Deficiency Notices," 73 Taxes 83, 85 (1995).

In line with the presumption of correctness afforded the notice, case law has established that courts generally will not "look behind" the notice of deficiency to examine the motives or methods of the IRS in determining the deficiency. The following case lays out the rationale:

GREENBERG'S EXPRESS, INC. v. COMMISSIONER
United States Tax Court
62 T.C. 324 (1974)

TANNENWALD, JUDGE.

These cases are before us on petitioners' motion for a protective order under Rule 103(a)(10), Tax Court Rules of Practice and Procedure. We deny the motion for the reasons stated below and append some additional comments which we hope will facilitate the further proceedings in these cases.

The substantive gravamen of petitioners' complaint is that the deficiency notices involved herein stem from second examinations of the books and records of the corporate petitioners under section 7605; that such second examinations, although ultimately made in compliance with the formal requirements of section 7605(b), were not instituted or conducted in good faith and for a legitimate purpose; and that such second examinations and the deficiency notices which issued as a result thereof were based upon discriminatory selection of petitioners because two of their number are the sons of one Carlo Gambino, a purported target of a governmental investigation into organized crime. In support of this claim, petitioners allege that the revenue agent in charge of the second examinations, and a member of the Strike Force, stated, "Your trouble is that 'The Godfather' got so much publicity, everybody was breathing down everybody's neck and we were told that we had to do something to take the heat off, so we went out to get a Gambino." Petitioners further allege that the deficiency determinations in themselves were arbitrary, unreasonable, and capricious because of respondent's failure to follow his established audit procedures and, in the case of certain of the corporate petitioners, his blanket disallowance of claimed business expense deductions and/or increases of round dollar amounts of taxable income.

On the basis of the foregoing, petitioners seek an order directing respondent to produce and deliver into the custody of the Court, and thereby make available for inspection by the petitioners prior to trial, all documents (whether in the custody of the Commissioner of Internal Revenue, the Secretary of the Treasury, the Attorney General of the United States, or any of their agents or designees) relating to the audit of petitioners' Federal income tax returns for 1966 through 1968 and any investigation of petitioners Thomas Gambino and Joseph Gambino by the Department of Justice, the Internal Revenue Service, or the Federal Strike Force Against Organized Crime operating in New York City. Petitioners assert that such an order is necessary to prevent the possible destruction or concealment of the documents involved and to enable the petitioners to prove, by such documents, the allegations of their amended petitions that respondent's determination of deficiencies in each of their Federal income tax liabilities for 1968 arose from official actions violating their constitutional rights.

Petitioners also ask us, in the event that their allegations are established, to declare respondent's determinations null and void and therefore decide that there is no deficiency due from any of them for 1968; alternatively, petitioners ask that we shift to respondent the burden of proof or the burden of going forward with the evidence.

In terms of petitioners' primary request herein — to wit, an impounding order under Rule 103(a)(10) — we are satisfied that they are not entitled to such relief. * * *

We come now to what we consider the crux of the matter before us: if petitioners were able to establish their allegations of discrimination in their selection as objects of an otherwise legitimate tax audit, would they be entitled to the benefit of any of the requested forms of relief? If not, such allegations would be immaterial to the resolution of the instant cases and petitioners would, therefore, not be warranted in their attempts to compel the production of any documents sought to establish those allegations. *Cf.* William O'Dwyer, 28 T.C. 698, 702–704 (1957), *affd.* 266 F.2d 575, 581 (C.A. 4, 1959).

As a general rule, this Court will not look behind a deficiency notice to examine the evidence used or the propriety of respondent's motives or of the administrative policy or procedure involved in making his determinations. Human Engineering Institute, 61 T.C. 61, 66 (1973), on appeal (C.A. 6, Jan. 2, 1974); Efrain T. Suarez, 58 T.C. 792, 813 (1972). Thus, we will not look into respondent's alleged failure to issue a 30-day letter to the petitioners or to afford them a conference before the Appellate Division. Cleveland Trust Co. v. United States, 421 F.2d 475, 480–482 (C.A. 6, 1970); Luhring v. Glotzbach, 304 F.2d 560 (C.A. 4, 1962); Crowther v. Commissioner, 269 F.2d 292, 293 (C.A. 9, 1959), *affirming* 28 T.C. 1293 (1957). The underlying rationale for the foregoing is the fact that a trial before the Tax Court is a proceeding de novo; our determination as to a petitioner's tax liability must be based on the merits of the case and not any previous record developed at the administrative level. *William O'Dwyer, supra.*

This Court has on occasion recognized an exception to the rule of not looking behind the deficiency notice when there is substantial evidence of unconstitutional conduct on respondent's part and the integrity of our judicial process would be impugned if we were to let respondent benefit from such conduct. *Efrain T. Suarez, supra.* But even in such limited situations, we have refused to declare the deficiency notice null and void, as petitioners would have us do. *See Efrain T. Suarez*, 58 T.C. at 814. *See also* Marx v. Commissioner, 179 F.2d 938, 942 (C.A. 1, 1950), *affirming* a Memorandum Opinion of this Court dated Jan. 24, 1949.

In the area of the criminal law, "mere selectivity in prosecution creates no constitutional problem." *See* United States v. Steele, 461 F.2d 1148, 1151 (C.A.9, 1972). On the other hand, "While the Fifth Amendment contains no equal protection clause, it does forbid discrimination that is 'so unjustifiable as to be violative of due process.' " (Citations omitted.) *See* Shapiro v. Thompson, 394 U.S. 618, 642 (1969). Even the conscious exercise of some selectivity is not in and of itself a Federal constitutional violation. *See* Oyler v. Boles, 368 U.S. 448, 456 (1962). Within these boundaries, the Federal courts have developed the test that before the complainant is entitled to relief, it must appear that the law has been "applied and administered by public authority with an evil eye and an unequal hand" (*see* Yick Wo v. Hopkins, 118 U.S. 356, 373–374 (1886), or with "questionable emphasis" (*see* United States v. Steele, 461 F.2d at 1152), through the use of an unjustifiable criterion such as race, religion, or expression of unpopular views. *See also* Two Guys v. McGinley, 366 U.S. 582, 588 (1961); United States v. Falk, 479 F.2d 616 (C.A. 7, 1973).

Assuming without deciding that a similar standard should be applied to civil tax litigation (*cf.* Hugo Romanelli, 54 T.C. 1448 (1970), *reversed in part* 466 F.2d 872 (C.A. 7, 1972), and John Harper, 54 T.C. 1121 (1970)), it is conceivable that there may be situations where a taxpayer should be accorded some relief, if he were able to prove that he was selected for audit on a clearly unjustifiable criterion. But we think that such situations will be extremely rare and we are satisfied that petitioners' allegations, even if true, would not be sufficient. Petitioners do not deny — indeed, they assume for the purposes of their motions — that the audits involved herein stemmed from the Government's attempts to deal with organized crime. Nor do they at any point assert that the deficiency notices are without foundation, i.e., that they owe no tax. *Cf.* Enochs v. Williams Packing Co., 370 U.S. 1, 7 (1962); Miller v. Nut Margarine Co., 284 U.S. 498, 510 (1932). *Compare* Bob Jones University v. Simon, 416 U.S. 725 (1974).

* * *

We are also satisfied that the circumstances alleged herein do not constitute unconstitutional action on the part of the respondent which would justify, at least at this stage of the proceeding, shifting to respondent the burden of proof or of going forward with the evidence as we did in *Efrain T. Suarez, supra.* Nor do the allegations of blanket disallowances of deductions and/or increases of round dollar amounts of taxable income, in the case of the corporate petitioners, dictate any such action. To be sure, the evidence presented at the trial may be such that the Court will be required to determine the extent of petitioners' tax liabilities, if any, on the basis of the record before it and not merely on the basis that petitioners have failed to sustain their burden of proof. Helvering v. Taylor, 293 U.S. 507 (1935); *Marx v. Commissioner, supra*; Durkee v. Commissioner, 162 F.2d 184, 187 (C.A. 6, 1947), remanding 6 T.C. 773 (1946). *Compare Human Engineering Institute*, 61 T.C. at 66. But whether this situation will obtain will have to abide the event.

We conclude that petitioners' motion should be denied and that these cases should proceed to trial in due course.

An appropriate order will be entered.

Other than those mentioned in the case, for what reasons might it be inappropriate for the court to look behind the notice of deficiency?

Although section 7491 does not provide whether the presumption of correctness applies in cases in which the taxpayer succeeds in shifting the burden of proof under section 7491, application of the presumption would seem inconsistent with shifting the burden to the IRS. The presumption of correctness therefore probably will play its main role in the many cases in which the taxpayer opts not to attempt, or is unsuccessful in obtaining, a shift in the burden of proof. Issues surrounding section 7491 are discussed in more detail in Chapter 6.

[2] "Arbitrary and Erroneous" Notices of Deficiency

The "presumption of correctness" afforded a notice of deficiency has been a powerful tool for the IRS because it places the burden on the taxpayer to produce evidence rebutting the IRS's determination of a deficiency. What if the IRS's determination lacks any factual basis — should the notice still be presumed correct? In *United States v. Janis*, 428 U.S. 433, 440-443 (1976), the United States Supreme Court considered how the taxpayer would meet its burden of proof if all of the government's evidence were suppressed because it was obtained illegally. The court stated, in part:

> The policy behind the presumption of correctness and the burden of proof, *see Bull v. United States*, 295 U.S. 247, 259–260 (1935), * * * accords * * * with the burden-of-proof rule which prevails in the usual preassessment proceeding in the United States Tax Court. Lucas v. Structural Steel Co., 281 U.S. 264, 271 (1930); Welch v. Helvering, 290 U.S. 111, 115 (1933); Rule 142(a) of the Rules of Practice and

Procedure of the United States Tax Court (1973). In any event, for purposes of this case, we assume that this is so and that the burden of proof may be said technically to rest with respondent Janis.

Respondent, however, submitted no evidence tending either to demonstrate that the assessment was incorrect or to show the correct amount of wagering tax liability, if any, on his part. In the usual situation one might well argue, as the Government does, that the District Court then could not properly grant judgment for the respondent on either aspect of the suit. But the present case may well not be the usual situation. What we have is a "naked" assessment without *any* foundation whatsoever if what was seized by the Los Angeles police cannot be used in the formulation of the assessment. The determination of tax due then may be one "without rational foundation and excessive," and not properly subject to the usual rule with respect to the burden of proof in tax cases. Helvering v. Taylor, 293 U.S. 507, 514–515 (1935).[n.8] *See* 9 J. Mertens, LAW OF FEDERAL INCOME TAXATION § 50.65 (1971).

* * *

Certainly, proof that an assessment is utterly without foundation is proof that it is arbitrary and erroneous. For purposes of this case, we need not go so far as to accept the Government's argument that the exclusion of the evidence in issue here is insufficient to require judgment for the respondent or even to shift the burden to the Government. We are willing to assume that if the District Court was correct in ruling that the evidence seized by the Los Angeles police may not be used in formulating the assessment (on which both the levy and the counterclaim were based), then the District Court was also correct in granting judgment for Janis in both aspects of the present suit. * * * [n.11]

Janis involved a refund suit, but its "naked assessment" reasoning has been applied in many deficiency suits in the Tax Court. If a notice's determination of a deficiency is based on alleged unreported income, the taxpayer's situation is analogous to a "naked assessment;" he would have to prove a negative (nonreceipt of the income). Consider the court's approach to that problem in the following case:

[n.8] *Taylor*, although decided more than 40 years ago, has never been cited by this Court on the burden-of-proof issue. The Courts of Appeals, the Court of Claims, the Tax Court, and the Federal District Courts, however, frequently have referred to that aspect of the case.

[n.11] Although the present case presents only the issue whether such evidence may be used in the formulation of the assessment, there appears to be no difference between that question and the issue whether the evidence is to be excluded in the refund or collection suit itself. We perceive no principled distinction to be made between the use of the evidence as the basis of an assessment and its use in the case in chief.

ANASTASATO v. COMMISSIONER
United States Court of Appeals, Third Circuit
794 F.2d 884 (1986)

HUNTER, CIRCUIT JUDGE:

Pano Anastasato, the taxpayer, has been involved in the travel business since 1954. In 1960, he established his own travel agency, Panmarc, Inc. ("Panmarc"), and a tour operation business, Wholesale Tours International ("WTI"). During the years 1974 through 1976, both companies were wholly owned by the taxpayer.

Panmarc purchased tickets for WTI's customers. Panmarc was licensed by the International Air Transport Association ("IATA"), a trade association of international carriers, to purchase tickets directly from the airlines. Under IATA regulations, the maximum commission that airlines could pay travel agents was ten percent of the ticket price. Compliance with these regulations was not required by law. Despite the regulations, it was common for airlines to pay excess commissions known as overrides or override commissions. Payment of overrides had to be made with strict confidentiality because IATA imposed severe sanctions for the violation of its regulations.

Panmarc did a large volume of business with KLM Royal Dutch Airlines ("KLM"). On April 15, 1981, the Commissioner issued statutory notices of deficiency to Anastasato totaling $633,468.00 for the years 1974, 1975, and 1976. The deficiency notice included additions to tax for fraud pursuant to I.R.C. § 6653(b) (1982). The Commissioner alleged that KLM had paid override commissions to the taxpayer by making payments into a Swiss bank account identified by the code name "GIGE." This account contains over one million dollars.

The Tax Court heard the testimony of revenue agents, employees of Panmarc, and employees of KLM. * * * In 1973, * * * Andre Luber was promoted to the position of Assistant Manager for Passenger Sales in the United States and given the responsibility for negotiating overrides.

In 1973, the taxpayer approached Luber seeking additional override commissions. From 1973 to 1975, the taxpayer and Luber engaged in negotiations. * * * From April 1974 to December 1974, override commissions were set at fifteen percent. From January 1975 to March 1975, they were set at twenty-one percent. The taxpayer often complained to his employees that KLM was not making its payments. The agreement was renegotiated and the override commissions set at eighteen percent for April 1975 through October 1975. Four million dollars worth of tickets were sold in 1974 and 1975 and were subject to the override commissions. For the period February 1976 to October 1976, override commissions were again set at eighteen percent.

* * *

In late 1979, Bohdan Huzar, a special agent with the Internal Revenue Service, began the investigation of the taxpayer. Huzar met with Paul Mifsud, general counsel to KLM in the United States, both in the United States and at the KLM headquarters in The Netherlands. Huzar also met with a Mr.

Westpladt, an employee in the KLM accounting department in The Nether-lands. Huzar did not take copies of any documents with him, but he recorded the contents of several in a notebook and prepared a report describing the documents. He described debit slips showing payments of approximately one million dollars from KLM to a Swiss bank account with the code name GIGE. He also saw KLM cash paid out slips totaling $26,000 signed by the taxpayer. Huzar's report stated that Westpladt had said that KLM made the payments to the Swiss bank account on behalf of the taxpayer. As hearsay, Huzar's report was admitted at trial only for the limited purpose of describing the methodology used by the Commissioner in issuing the notice of deficiency.

At trial, the taxpayer denied that he had ever received the override commissions. He admitted that he had discussed overrides with KLM officials, but he maintained that he never accepted overrides because he was worried about the IATA penalties. He seemed to imply that [an employee of KLM] was pocketing the overrides and that he merely went along with the scheme to maintain his business relationship with KLM.

On the basis of this evidence, the Tax Court upheld the Commissioner's determination of deficiencies and additions to tax in the amount of $641,288 for income tax liability for the years 1974, 1975, and 1976. However, the court held that the Commissioner had not proven fraud by the taxpayer.

The taxpayer claims that the Commissioner's deficiency determination was arbitrary and unreasonable. In addressing this contention, we first note that the government's deficiency assessment is generally afforded a presumption of correctness. *See* United States v. Janis, 428 U.S. 433, 441, 49 L. Ed. 2d 1046, 96 S. Ct. 3021 (1976); Helvering v. Taylor, 293 U.S. 507, 515, 79 L. Ed. 623, 55 S. Ct. 287 (1935); Welch v. Helvering, 290 U.S. 111, 115, 78 L. Ed. 212, 54 S. Ct. 8 (1933); Baird v. Commissioner, 438 F.2d 490, 492 (3d Cir. 1970). This presumption is a procedural device that places the burden of producing evidence to rebut the presumption on the taxpayer. *See Janis*, 428 U.S. at 441. A court usually will not look behind the Commissioner's determi-nation, even though it may be based on hearsay or other evidence inadmissible at trial. *See* Dellacroce v. Commissioner, 83 T.C. 269, 280 (1984).

Several courts, including this one, have noted an exception to the general rule that they will not examine the basis of the deficiency determination before recognizing the Commissioner's presumption of correctness. Under this exception, a court must not give effect to the presumption of correctness in a case involving unreported income if the Commissioner cannot present "some predicate evidence connecting the taxpayer to the charged activity." Gerardo v. Commissioner, 552 F.2d 549, 554 (3d Cir. 1977). Most of the cases stating that the Commissioner is not entitled to the presumption based on a naked assessment without factual foundation have involved illegal income. *See* Weimerskirch v. Commissioner, 596 F.2d 358 (9th Cir. 1979) (drugs); Gerardo v. Commissioner, 552 F.2d 549 (3d Cir. 1977) (gambling); Pizzarello v. United States, 408 F.2d 579 (2d Cir.), *cert. denied,* 396 U.S. 986, 24 L. Ed. 2d 450, 90 S. Ct. 481 (1969) (gambling); Dellacroce v. Commissioner, 83 T.C. 269 (1984) (racketeering payoff); Llorente v. Commissioner, 74 T.C. 260 (1980), *aff'd in part and rev'd. in part*, 649 F.2d 152 (2d Cir. 1981) (drugs). Given the obvious difficulties in proving the nonreceipt of income, we believe the

Commissioner should have to provide evidence linking the taxpayer to the tax-generating activity in cases involving unreported income, whether legal or illegal.

Along with other courts, we have recognized that the Commissioner's deficiency determination is entitled to a presumption of correctness and that the burden of production as well as the ultimate burden of persuasion is placed on the taxpayer. *See* Sullivan v. United States, 618 F.2d 1001, 1008 (3d Cir. 1980). The government meets its initial burden of proof in an action to collect tax merely by introducing its deficiency determination. *See* United States v. Stonehill, 702 F.2d 1288, 1293 (9th Cir. 1983), *cert. denied*, 465 U.S. 1079, 79 L. Ed. 2d 761, 104 S. Ct. 1440 (1984). The presumption of correctness establishes a prima facie case, but it arises only if supported by foundational evidence connecting the taxpayer with the tax-generating activity. *See Gerardo*, 552 F.2d at 554. The presumption shifts the burden of proof to the taxpayer. *See* DiMauro v. United States, 706 F.2d 882, 884 (8th Cir. 1983).

If the taxpayer rebuts the presumption by showing that it is arbitrary and erroneous, *see* Helvering v. Taylor, 293 U.S. at 515, the presumption disappears. Courts differ on whether the burdens of production and persuasion can be shifted to the Commissioner. Most agree that if the presumption drops out the burden of going forward shifts to the Commissioner. However, some courts have stated that at this point the ultimate burden of persuasion, or risk of nonpersuasion, remains on the taxpayer. *See* Higginbotham v. United States, 556 F.2d 1173, 1176 (4th Cir. 1977); United States v. Rexach, 482 F.2d 10 (1st Cir.), *cert. denied*, 414 U.S. 1039, 94 S. Ct. 540, 38 L. Ed. 2d 330 (1973); *Sullivan,* 618 F.2d at 1008. Other courts, however, have indicated that in unreported income cases the ultimate burden shifts to the Commissioner. *See* Keogh v. Commissioner, 713 F.2d 496, 501 (9th Cir. 1983); *United States v. Stonehill*, 702 F.2d at 1294; Stout v. Commissioner, 273 F.2d 345, 350 (4th Cir. 1959). In 1976, the Supreme Court noted, but did not reconcile, this conflict in the circuits. *See United States v. Janis*, 428 U.S. at 442.

In *Sullivan*, we stated that if the taxpayer rebuts the presumption with credible and relevant evidence sufficient to establish that the determination was erroneous, the procedural burden of going forward with the evidence shifts to the Commissioner, 618 F.2d at 1008. We further held, however, that the ultimate burden of proof or persuasion remains with the taxpayer. If the taxpayer offers evidence that the determination was incorrect and the Commissioner offers no evidence to support the assessment, the taxpayer will have met his ultimate burden "unless such evidence is specifically rejected as improbable, unreasonable, or questionable." *Id.* at 1009. *See also* Demkowicz v. Commissioner, 551 F.2d 929, 931 (3d Cir. 1977). The court can reject the taxpayer's evidence if it is contradicted by the Commissioner.

In the case before us, the Commissioner was entitled to the presumption of correctness because he introduced evidence linking the taxpayer to the tax-generating activity. The taxpayer was involved in the travel business and purchased a large volume of tickets from KLM. The taxpayer and KLM engaged in extensive negotiations regarding override commissions and the taxpayer was entitled to receive these commissions. The taxpayer has not shown that the deficiency determination was arbitrary and without factual foundation and he therefore cannot rely on *Gerardo* to dispel the presumption.

After discussing the relevant law and the facts of the case, the Tax Court properly concluded that the deficiency determination was entitled to its usual presumption of correctness. The court then should have determined whether the taxpayer had at trial, nevertheless, met his burden of ultimate persuasion and shown that the determination was incorrect. The court noted only that "petitioners herein (the taxpayer) presented no affirmative evidence to demonstrate any error in respondent's said determinations, having contented themselves throughout this trial with attacking only the basis for respondent's determinations, rather than the accuracy thereof." This statement indicates that the court believed that, once the Commissioner was granted the usual presumption of correctness, the question whether the taxpayer received the allegedly unreported income no longer remained at issue and only the amount of the assessment could be considered.

Even if the Commissioner is entitled to the initial presumption of correctness, the taxpayer must be given the opportunity to prove that the determination was incorrect. In this case, the taxpayer's evidence consisted of denials that he ever received the income in question. A general denial of liability is insufficient to meet the taxpayer's burden of nonpersuasion. *See* Avco Delta Corp. v. United States, 540 F.2d 258 (7th Cir. 1976), *cert. denied*, 429 U.S. 1040, 97 S. Ct. 739, 50 L. Ed. 2d 752 (1977). We are "not bound to accept taxpayer's testimony at face value even when it is uncontradicted if it is improbable, unreasonable, or questionable." *Baird*, 438 F.2d at 493. The Tax Court apparently rejected the taxpayer's testimony on nonreceipt of income not as "improbable, questionable, or unreasonable," *Baird*, 438 F.2d at 493, but as irrelevant once the Commissioner provided a factual foundation for the assessment and the presumption of correctness arose. The court erred since it was possible that the taxpayer could ultimately prevail by proving that while he engaged in the activity in question he never received the income in question.

It is possible that the Tax Court, on proper consideration of the taxpayer's denial of receipt of the income, will find such denials improbable. Nevertheless, because the court did not explicitly or implicitly reject the taxpayer's testimony, we will remand the case for consideration of this point.

* * *

The principle applied in *Anastasato* was developed in cases where the alleged unreported income was income from illegal activities. Why might it matter if the alleged unreported income was from legal or illegal activities? Was the *Anastasato* court correct in applying the same principle in that case?

[3]   The Role of the Notice of Deficiency in the Burden of Persuasion

Disputes over whether the notice of deficiency retains the "presumption of correctness" are really disputes over which party bears the burden of going forward.[6] Historically, the notice of deficiency has also played an important role in the allocation of the burden of persuasion in Tax Court cases, which is explored below. As discussed in Chapter 6, the taxpayer may have the burden of proof shifted to the IRS if the taxpayer meets certain threshold requirements. *See* I.R.C. § 7491; Interim Tax Court Rule 142(a)(2). If the taxpayer does not meet the requirements of Code section 7491, Rule 142(a)(1) applies. *See* Interim Tax Court Rule 142(a)(2). Interim Tax Court Rule 142(a)(1) provides:

> The burden of proof shall be upon the petitioner, except as otherwise provided by statute or determined by the Court; and except that, in respect of any new matter, increases in deficiency, and affirmative defenses, pleaded in the answer, it shall be upon the respondent
>
> . . . .

Note that Rule 142(a)(1) places the burden of persuasion on the IRS (the respondent) "in respect of any new matter."[7] The following case explains what constitutes "new matter." It may help your understanding of the case to review briefly Code section 482, which allows the IRS to reallocate income and deductions among two or more commonly controlled entities, if the reallocation is necessary to clearly reflect income.

ACHIRO v. COMMISSIONER
United States Tax Court
77 T.C. 881 (1981)

Achiro and Rossi each owned 50 percent of the stock of Tahoe City Disposal, and each owned 25 percent of the stock of Kings Beach Disposal. In 1974, Achiro and Rossi incorporated A & R for the purpose of rendering management services to Tahoe City Disposal and Kings Beach Disposal. Achiro and Rossi each owned 24 percent of A & R's stock, and Renato Achiro (Achiro's brother and Rossi's brother-in-law) owned the remaining 52 percent. A & R entered into management service agreements with Tahoe City Disposal and Kings Beach Disposal pursuant to which A & R provided those corporations with management services and, in exchange, received management fees. Achiro and Rossi entered into exclusive employment contracts with A & R, and, acting in their capacities as A & R's employees, rendered management services to Tahoe City Disposal and Kings Beach Disposal.

* * *

---

[6] *See* Chapter 6 for explanations of the burden of going forward and the burden of persuasion. *See also* Leandra Lederman, "'Civil'izing Tax Procedure: Applying General Federal Learning to Statutory Notices of Deficiency," 30 U.C. Davis L. Rev. 183, 194 (1996).

[7] Is the burden of persuasion placed on the respondent only for "new matter . . . pleaded in the answer" or for all "new matter" wherever raised?

HALL, JUDGE.

* * *

In his notice of deficiency, respondent adjusted the income of Tahoe City Disposal by disallowing as deductions the management fees paid to A & R totaling $ 65,000 and $ 170,286 for the fiscal years ending March 31, 1975, and 1976, respectively. Respondent determined that these amounts were not expended for the purpose designated or were not ordinary and necessary business expenses. Respondent further adjusted Tahoe City Disposal's income by allowing it to take all the deductions for compensation, interest, depreciation, etc., originally taken by A & R, totaling $ 47,316 and $ 133,754 for the fiscal years ending March 31, 1975, and 1976, respectively. In so doing, respondent stated: "These allocations are made to you [Tahoe City Disposal] from A & R Enterprises, Inc., in order to clearly reflect your income and A & R Enterprises, Inc. income."

At trial, respondent amended his answer and asserted that all of the income and deductions of A & R should be allocated to Tahoe City Disposal and Kings Beach Disposal pursuant to section 482, section 269, or section 61 (the assignment of income doctrine or the sham corporation theory). In the alternative, respondent asserted in his amended answer that the employees of Tahoe City Disposal should be aggregated with the employees of A & R pursuant to section 414(b) for purposes of applying the antidiscrimination provisions of section 401 to A & R's pension and profit-sharing plans.

OPINION

A. Burden of Proof

As a preliminary matter it is necessary to decide which party bears the burden of proof with respect to the various issues.

At trial, respondent requested leave to file an amended answer, which this Court granted. In that amended answer, respondent alleged for the first time that section 482, section 269, or section 61 (assignment of income doctrine or the sham corporation theory) also justified the deficiency. The amended answer also contains the alternative argument that section 414(b) requires petitioners to include in their gross incomes their aliquot portions of the contributions made by A & R to its pension and profit-sharing plans.

In response to this amended answer, petitioners filed a motion to shift burden of proof with respect to the matters pleaded therein. Generally, the burden of proof is on the taxpayer. Welch v. Helvering, 290 U.S. 111 (1933); Rule 142(a), Tax Court Rules of Practice and Procedure. Rule 142(a) provides:[8]

> The burden of proof shall be upon the petitioner, except as otherwise provided by statute or determined by the Court; and except that, *in respect of any new matter*, increases in deficiency, and affirmative

---

[8] [Notice that Interim Rule 142(a)(1), set forth above, contains the same langugage as Rule 142(a) before Congress enacted section 7491. Eds.]

defenses, pleaded in his answer, *it shall be upon the respondent.* [Emphasis added.] * * *

At trial, this Court agreed with petitioners that respondent's amended answer presented new matters under Rule 142(a) and, accordingly, we shifted the burden of proof to respondent. On brief, respondent argues that the Court improperly shifted the burden of proof because his amended answer presented new theories, not new matters. He asserts that the statutory notice is sufficiently broad to encompass these theories and that petitioners knew at least as early as 5 weeks prior to trial that these theories would be relied upon by respondent and, thus, petitioners were neither surprised nor disadvantaged thereby. We are still of the view that respondent's amended answer raised new matters and that, therefore, respondent bears the burden of proof.

The assertion of a new theory which merely clarifies or develops the original determination without being inconsistent or increasing the amount of the deficiency is not a new matter requiring the shifting of the burden of proof. Estate of Jayne v. Commissioner, 61 T.C. 744, 748–749 (1974); McSpadden v. Commissioner, 50 T.C. 478, 492–493 (1968); Estate of Sharf v. Commissioner, 38 T.C. 15, 27–28 (1962). However, if the assertion in the amended answer either alters the original deficiency or requires the presentation of different evidence, then respondent has introduced a new matter. Estate of Falese v. Commissioner, 58 T.C. 895, 898–899 (1972); *McSpadden v. Commissioner, supra;* Papineau v. Commissioner, 28 T.C. 54, 57 (1957); Tauber v. Commissioner, 24 T.C. 179, 185 (1955). The factual bases and rationale required to establish that the amounts paid by Tahoe City Disposal as management fees were expended for that purpose and were ordinary and necessary business expenses are entirely different from the factual bases and rationale necessary to establish that sections 482, 269, 61, and 414(b) do not apply to the present situation. Sanderling, Inc. v. Commissioner, 66 T.C. 743, 757–758 (1976), *affd.* 571 F.2d 174 (3d Cir. 1978). Respondent's new positions raised in his amended answer require the presentation of new evidence and do not simply clarify or develop his original position.

Although we believe the general rules governing the burden of proof require the transfer of that burden to respondent with regard to his determination under section 482, we feel compelled to further comment on the specific burden of proof problems under section 482. Cases dealing with the burden of proof under section 482 have set up a three-tier approach in determining whether respondent may assert section 482, and, if so, whether respondent or petitioner bears the burden of proof thereunder.

First, if the notice of deficiency is clear that respondent is relying on section 482 in support of his deficiency, then the burden is upon the taxpayer to establish that respondent's allocation was unreasonable, arbitrary, or capricious. Brittingham v. Commissioner, 66 T.C. 373, 395 (1976), *affd.* 598 F.2d 1375 (5th Cir. 1979) (*quoting* Ach v. Commissioner, 42 T.C. 114, 125–126 (1964), *affd.* 358 F.2d 342 (6th Cir. 1966)).

Second, if respondent does not indicate in the notice of deficiency that he is relying on section 482, but alerts the taxpayer of his reliance on section 482 formally in pleadings far enough in advance of trial so as not to prejudice the taxpayer or take him by surprise at trial, then the burden of proof shifts to respondent to establish all the elements necessary to support his allocation under section 482. *See* Rubin v. Commissioner, 56 T.C. 1155, 1162–1 164 (1971), *affd.* 460 F.2d 1216 (2d Cir. 1972); Rule 142(a), Tax Court Rules of Practice and Procedure. *But see* Abatti v. Commissioner, 644 F.2d 1385 (9th Cir. 1981), *revg.* a Memorandum Opinion of this Court.

Third, if respondent raises section 482 at such a late date that the principles of fair play and justice would be abrogated by permitting him to rely on section 482, then he will not be allowed to rely on section 482 at all. United States v. First Security Bank, 334 F.2d 120, 122 n. 4 (9th Cir. 1964); Commissioner v. Chelsea Products, 197 F.2d 620, 624 (3d Cir. 1952), *affg.* 16 T.C. 840 (1951). *See Abatti v. Commissioner, supra.*

In the present case, petitioners' counsel admits that petitioners had notice of respondent's reliance on section 482 at least 5 weeks prior to the scheduled trial. Petitioners do not contend that such notice brings them within the limited circumstances which call for denying respondent the right to raise section 482, but, rather, petitioners contend they fall within the second category requiring the burden of proof to shift to respondent. We agreed at trial with petitioners, and we still agree. We note, however, that even if petitioners were to bear the burden of proof, we would find that they have met their burden of showing that respondent's section 482 allocation was arbitrary, capricious, or unreasonable.

* * *

Decisions will be entered under Rule 155.

In *Achiro*, the court stated that "if respondent raises section 482 at such a late date that the principles of fair play and justice would be abrogated by permitting him to rely on section 482, then he will not be allowed to rely on section 482 at all." This reflects the doctrine of "surprise and prejudice," which if applied, precludes the IRS from raising a new issue so late in the litigation as to surprise and prejudice the taxpayer.

Unlike in other courts, Tax Court briefs are generally filed after trial, *see* Tax Court Rule 151(a). The Tax Court will not consider issues raised for the first time in the parties' post-trial briefs if it finds surprise and prejudice. *See, e.g., Robertson v. Commissioner*, 55 T.C. 862, 865 (1971), *acq.* 1972-2 C.B. 3 (1972); *Philbrick v. Commissioner*, 27 T.C. 346, 353 (1956), *acq.* 1958-2 C.B. 7 (1958); *Hettler v. Commissioner*, 16 T.C. 528, 535 (1951), *acq. sub nom. Commissioner v. Crilly*, 1951-2 C.B. 2 (1951). However, the court is unlikely to find surprise and prejudice if the matter is raised at or any time before trial, and even as to some issues raised in the IRS's post-trial briefs. *See, e.g., Levy v. Commissioner*, 91 T.C. 838, 865 (1988) ("at trial we allowed respondent to amend his answer to raise the at-risk argument under section 465(b)(3) . . . . In post trial briefs, respondent also raised the at-risk argument that arises under section 465(b)(4) . . . . In our opinion and on the facts of this case, petitioners are not prejudiced by our allowing respondent to rely on section 465(b)(4) in making his at-risk arguments."); *Grow v. Commissioner*, 80 T.C. 314, 329 (1983) ("With respect to the specific point involved here, petitioners complain that respondent first called attention to the second sentence of section 48(c)(1) in his reply brief; that this constituted the raising of a new issue by respondent in his reply brief . . . ; that this new issue caught petitioners completely by surprise and should not, therefore, be considered by the Court. We find petitioners' objections without merit.").

How does the application of the "new matter" provision of Interim Tax Court Rule 142(a)(1) affect the IRS's likelihood of including more matters up front in the notice of deficiency? Will section 7491, which allows a shift in the burden of proof to the IRS in certain circumstances, likely affect the way the IRS drafts notices of deficiency? If Rule 142(a)(1) applies, and the IRS has failed to include an issue in the notice of deficiency, can the IRS circumvent the Tax Court's "new matter" rule simply by sending the taxpayer a second notice of deficiency for the same tax year, raising the new issue? *See* I.R.C. § 6212(c). What other technique might the IRS use to try to avoid having late-raised issues characterized as "new matter"? Consider this excerpt from a Tax Court case:

NICHOLSON v. COMMISSIONER
United States Tax Court
T.C. Memo. 1993-183

HALPERN, JUDGE:

* * *

Normally, in this Court, a taxpayer bears the burden of proving respondent's determination to be incorrect. Rule 142(a). That burden placed upon the taxpayer is sometimes described as giving a "presumption of correctness" to respondent. In certain circumstances, however, the burden of going forward with the evidence will be placed upon respondent (depriving her of what is termed the presumption of correctness). Petitioners make two arguments for stripping respondent of her presumption of correctness and, instead, placing upon her the burden of going forward with the evidence.

* * *

1. New Matter

In the notice of deficiency, respondent determined that petitioners received unreported income of $387,055 with respect to 1980. The notice of deficiency does not state the specific basis of that determination.[n.5] Respondent's

---

[n.5] The "explanation" contained in the notice of deficiency is as follows: "It is determined that you received income in the amount of $387,055.00 which was not reported on your income tax return for the taxable year ended Dec. 31, 1980. This amount is determined to be taxable to you because you have failed to establish that this amount is excludable from gross income under the provisions of the Internal Revenue Code."

amendment to answer and brief, however, demonstrate that her determination was based on a source and application of funds analysis. Subsequent to the trial, on brief, respondent formally abandoned that theory, relying instead on other theories first raised by respondent in her amendment to answer. Specifically, respondent's new theories and arguments concern: (1) Unreported income, actually or constructively received (individually), as an associate of CSN; (2) unreported income, actually or constructively received, as a dental practice owner; (3) unreported rent income, actually or constructively received, (individually) as the lessor of the dental clinics; (4) unreported income from pension plan withdrawals; and (5) unreported interest income. On account of respondent's new theories, petitioners contend that respondent has raised a "new matter", within the meaning of Rule 142(a), and therefore ought to bear the burden of proof.

We disagree. None of respondent's new theories are inconsistent with respondent's notice of deficiency, which says nothing more than that petitioners had unreported income of $387,055 in 1980, which is taxable to them inasmuch as they have failed to establish the applicability of any exclusion. We have repeatedly stated that a theory will not constitute a new matter, within the meaning of Rule 142(a), if it is consistent with the theory (or theories) advanced by respondent in the notice of deficiency. *E.g.,* Achiro v. Commissioner, 77 T.C. 881, 890 (1981) ("The assertion of a new theory which merely clarifies or develops the original determination without being inconsistent or increasing the amount of the deficiency is not a new matter requiring the shifting of the burden of proof."). Accordingly, where, as here, the theory advanced by respondent in her notice of deficiency is broadly worded, respondent is at liberty to advance in her answer (or amended answer) any argument consistent with that broad theory, without assuming the burden of proof under the new matter doctrine. Spangler v. Commissioner, 32 T.C. 782, 793 (1959), *affd.* 278 F.2d 665 (4th Cir. 1960). All of respondent's new theories deal with unreported income and therefore are consistent with respondent's extremely broad notice of deficiency, which, as discussed, does no more than charge petitioners with unreported income to which no exclusion applies. Accordingly, we find that respondent's new arguments do not constitute new matters under Rule 142(a).

* * *

What kind of problems might the court's holding in this part of the case pose for the taxpayer? Recall that the notice of deficiency forms part of the Tax Court pleadings. Under Tax Court Rule 34(b)(4), the taxpayer has to make "clear and concise assignments of each and every error which the petitioner alleges to have been committed by the Commissioner in the determination of the deficiency or liability." Look again at Code section 7522. Does it ameliorate the problem the taxpayer in *Nicholson* faced? Also recall that section 7522 states that noncompliance by the IRS will not invalidate the notice. What possible remedies might be available to enforce section 7522?[9]

---

[9] *See* Leandra Lederman Gassenheimer, "The Dilemma of Deficient Deficiency Notices," 73 Taxes 83 (1995).

In *Shea v. Commissioner*, 112 T.C. 183 (1999), *nonacq.*, 2000-44 I.R.B. 430, the Tax Court used as its section 7522 analysis the standards under Tax Court Rule 142(a) for determining whether the IRS has raised "new matter" — the court considered whether new issues required evidence different from the issues raised in the notice of deficiency. Specifically, the court stated, in part, "In the final analysis, we think that section 7522 makes the question of whether reliance on . . . [a particular Code section in court] is, or is not, 'inconsistent' with the notice of deficiency irrelevant, if the basis on which respondent relies was *not described in the notice of deficiency and requires different evidence.*" *Id.* at 195–196 (emphasis added).

The *Shea* reasoning suggests the possibility that broadly worded notices of deficiency are not only more likely to be found not to contain new matter but also to be found in compliance with section 7522. For example, subsequent to *Shea*, in *Sellers v. Commissioner*, T.C. Memo. 2000-235, the Tax Court stated:

> The purpose of section 7522 is to give the taxpayer notice of the Commissioner's basis for determining a deficiency. *See* Shea v. Commissioner, 112 T.C. 183, 196 (1999). Here the notice of deficiency sufficiently apprised petitioners of the basis for respondent's deficiency determination and identified the amount of tax due. At trial, respondent has taken no position that would require petitioners to present evidence different from that necessary to resolve the determinations that were described in the notice of deficiency, so as to justify placing the burden of proof on respondent. *Cf. Shea v. Commissioner, supra* at 197. The burden of proof remains with petitioners.

Id. In AOD, 2000-08 (Oct. 30, 2000), the IRS nonacquiesced in the *Shea* decision. The IRS's position in the AOD is that the Tax Court could have found that its issue raised on brief was "new matter," but, by contrast, compliance or noncompliance with section 7522 has no bearing on the burden of proof in a Tax Court case. *See* Leandra Lederman, "Deficient Statutory Notices and the Burden of Proof: A Reply to Mr. Newton," 92 Tax Notes 117, 123 n.86 (2001).

In *Estate of Mitchell v. Commissioner*, 250 F.3d 696 (9th Cir. 2001), the Estate of hairdresser Paul Mitchell argued that the burden of proof in the Tax Court proceeding should have been shifted to the IRS because of post-notice events in the Tax Court trial. Consider the opinion of the Court of Appeals for the Ninth Circuit:[10]

ESTATE OF MITCHELL v. COMMISSIONER
United States Court of Appeals, Ninth Circuit
250 F.3d 696 (2001)

OPINION: WARDLAW, Circuit Judge:

The Estate of Paul Mitchell (the "Estate") petitions for review of the United States Tax Court's decision allowing the Commissioner of the Internal Revenue Service (the "Commissioner") to assess an additional $2,404,571 in

---

[10] *Estate of Mitchell* also raised other issues that are discussed in Chapters 5 and 8.

federal estate taxes. * * * Although we find that the Commissioner's notice was timely, we nevertheless vacate the Tax Court's judgment and remand because the Tax Court failed to shift the burden of proving the accuracy of the additional estate tax to the Commissioner and failed to provide an adequate explanation for its valuation of the JPMS stock at the time of Paul Mitchell's death.

I. BACKGROUND

Paul Mitchell, co-founder of the highly successful hair-care products company of the same name, died on April 21, 1989. * * * The IRS received the Estate's return on Monday, July 23, 1990.

On July 21, 1993, the IRS mailed to the Estate a notice of deficiency (the "Notice"), determining a deficiency in the federal estate tax in the amount of $45,117,089, and a total of $8,543,643 in penalties. The IRS asserted that the Estate had undervalued its 1,226 shares of [John Paul Mitchell Systems (JPMS)] stock. The Estate had reported the stock was worth $28.5 million based on a valuation conducted by a private accounting firm. The IRS, however, calculated the stock's value at $105 million and assessed additional taxes based on the $76.5 million discrepancy.

* * *

On June 11, 1996, the Estate filed a motion with the Tax Court disputing that it bore the burden of persuasion to show the Commissioner's assessment was inaccurate. The Estate argued that the evidence established that it owned 49.04 percent of the outstanding stock in JPMS on the valuation date and thus its interest in JPMS was a minority interest, not a controlling interest. Therefore, the Commissioner's appraisal, determining that the Estate's 49.04 percent interest was a controlling interest, was erroneous, and any additional estate taxes were excessive. The Estate contended that pursuant to *Herbert v. Commissioner*, 377 F.2d 65 (9th Cir. 1966), the burden should be placed on the Commissioner to justify the government's original assessment or to submit a more accurate figure. On July 8, 1996, the Tax Court denied the Estate's motion to shift the burden of persuasion without explanation.

The dispute over the value of the stock proceeded to trial. In addition to a substantial amount of documentary evidence, both the Estate and the Commissioner offered the testimony of expert witnesses as to the value of the 1,226 shares of stock JPMS stock. The experts' testimony offered a wide variety of estimates and methods for calculating the stock's value. As may be expected, the experts for the Estate minimized the stock's value, testifying that its value on the date of Paul Mitchell's death ranged from approximately $20 to $29 million, while the experts for the Commissioner maximized the stock's value in a range from $57 to $165 million. The methodology each expert used was equally varied, with some producing estimates based on the stock prices of similar companies and others using elaborate economic formulae. * * *

In 1997, the Tax Court issued its opinion as to the stock's value. Estate of Mitchell v. Commissioner, 1997 Tax Ct. Memo LEXIS 546, 74 T.C.M. (CCH)

872, 1997 T.C. Memo 461 (1997). The Tax Court found that the stock's fair market value was $41,532,600. * * *

II. DISCUSSION

* * *

B. Shifting the Burden of Proof

The Estate argues that the Tax Court erred by denying its motion to shift the burden of persuasion, leaving the burden of proof on the Estate. *See* Herbert v. Comm'r, 377 F.2d 65, 69 (9th Cir. 1967). The Tax Court denied the Estate's motion without explanation, and we will refrain from speculating as to the reasons for its decision. We nevertheless review *de novo* the Tax Court's decision to deny the Estate's motion to shift the burden. *See* Moss v. Comm'r, 831 F.2d 833, 837 (9th Cir. 1987).

In *Cohen v. Commissioner*, 266 F.2d 5 (9th Cir. 1959), we stated:

> At the outset of a Tax Court proceeding to redetermine a tax deficiency, the Commissioner's determination is presumed to be correct. The burden of proof is thus placed upon the taxpayer to show that the Commissioner's determination is invalid.

> When the Commissioner's determination has been shown to be invalid, the Tax Court must redetermine the deficiency. The presumption as to the correctness of the Commissioner's determination is then out of the case. The Commissioner and not the taxpayer then has the burden of proving whether any deficiency exists and if so the amount. It is not incumbent upon the taxpayer under these circumstances to prove that he owed no tax or the amount of the tax which he did owe.

Id. at 11 (citations omitted).

According to the Notice, the Commissioner concluded the value of the JPMS stock at the time of Paul Mitchell's death was $105 million. The Estate had reported the value at $28.5 million in its tax return. Due to the $76.5 million difference in value, the Commissioner asserted that the Estate owed an additional $45,117,089 in estate taxes, not including a total of $8,543,643 in penalties. At trial, Martin Hanan, a witness for the Commissioner, valued the stock at $81 million — $34 million less than the Commissioner's original valuation. Furthermore, a letter written by the Commissioner's appraiser, AIBE Valuation, dated March 18, 1993, indicates that AIBE Valuation originally appraised Mitchell's interest at $85 million as a minority interest, but increased it to $105 million, at the request of the IRS, to reflect the Estate's interest as a controlling interest. We find that Hanan's testimony and the AIBE letter support the conclusion that the Commissioner's assessment was arbitrary and excessive. United States v. Stonehill, 702 F.2d 1288, 1294 (9th Cir. 1983) (holding that "where the assessment has separable items, . . . error which demonstrates a pattern of arbitrariness or carelessness will destroy the presumption for the entire assessment"); *Cohen*, 266 F.2d at 11 (holding that when the taxpayer has shown the determination to be arbitrary and excessive, the burden of persuasion shifts to the Commissioner to prove the correct amount of tax owed and the presumption as to the correctness of the Commissioner's determination is out of the case); *see also* Helvering v. Taylor, 293 U.S. 507, 513–15, 79 L. Ed. 623, 55 S. Ct. 287 (1935).

We conclude that the Tax Court erred in denying the Estate's Motion to Shift the Burden of Persuasion. Consistent with *Cohen*, because the Commissioner's determination was demonstrated, by its own experts, to be invalid, the Commissioner — and not the Estate — had the "burden of proving whether any deficiency exists and if so the amount." *Cohen*, 266 F.2d at 11. The Tax Court treated the case as one where the burden of proof made no difference; it did not find that one party failed to carry its burden, but proceeded with its own valuation, "weighing the evidence and choosing from among conflicting inferences and conclusions those which it considers most reasonable." Tax Court Order, Docket No. 21805-93 (July 8, 1998) (*citing* Comm'r v. Scottish Am. Inv. Co., 323 U.S. 119, 123–24 (1944)). However, in responding to the petitioner's second motion for reconsideration, the Tax Court erroneously stated that valuation was a matter of approximation and judgment "on which *the petitioner* has the burden of proof." (emphasis added). Because the burden of proving the evaluation of the Estate and the commensurate deficiency shifted to the Commissioner, it was error not to put the Commissioner to its proof.

* * *

CONCLUSION

* * * We grant the Estate's petition in part, vacate, and remand for the Tax Court to shift the burden of proof to the Commissioner regarding the determination of additional taxes and explain its valuation of the stock consistent with Leonard Pipeline [Contractors v. Commissioner, 142 F.3d 1133 (9th Cir. 1998)]. In light of the foregoing, we do not reach the question whether the Tax Court correctly valued the Estate, as we are unable to conduct a meaningful review.

AFFIRMED IN PART, VACATED AND REMANDED IN PART.

Is the Court of Appeals for the Ninth Circuit saying in *Mitchell* that the IRS bears the burden of proof on deficiencies *decreased* after the notice of deficiency was mailed? As stated above, the IRS bears the burden of proof on increased deficiencies under Tax Court Rule 142(a). Is there a reason why the IRS should bear the burden of proof on decreased deficiencies as well, or are decreased deficiencies more in the nature of concessions that should be encouraged?

[D] Invalid Notices of Deficiency

Thus far, this chapter has considered only "valid" notices of deficiency. Even notices that are "arbitrary and erroneous" are "valid" because those notices still have legal effect. As the above discussion reveals, the technical requirements for a valid notice of deficiency are relatively minimal.[11] However, the requirements that do exist are key. What are the consequences of violating section 6212's requirements? This portion of the chapter considers two major aspects of section 6212, the "last known address" aspect and the "determination" aspect.

[1] The "Last Known Address" Rule

The Code sets forth specific procedures the IRS must follow when providing the taxpayer with notice of a deficiency. It states:

> In the absence of notice to the Secretary . . . of the existence of a fiduciary relationship, *notice of a deficiency* in respect of a tax imposed by subtitle A, chapter 12, chapter 41, chapter 42, chapter 43, or chapter 44 *if mailed to the taxpayer at his last known address, shall be sufficient* for purposes of subtitle A, chapter 12, chapter 41, chapter 42, chapter 43, chapter 44, and this chapter even if such taxpayer is deceased, or is under a legal disability, or, in the case of a corporation, has terminated its existence.

I.R.C. § 6212(b)(1) (emphasis added). Notices are particularly susceptible to invalidation for failure to meet the "last known address" criterion of section 6212(b). *See, e.g., King v. Commissioner*, 857 F.2d 676 (9th Cir. 1988); *Monge v. Commissioner*, 93 T.C. 22 (1989); *Abeles v. Commissioner*, 91 T.C. 1019 (1988), *acq.*, 1989-2 C.B. 1.

Section 6212(b) is phrased in a noncompulsory way because mailing to the taxpayer's last known address is a safe harbor, a substitute for actual notice to the taxpayer. "If mailing results in actual notice without prejudicial delay . . . it meets the conditions of § 6212(a) no matter to what address the notice successfully was sent." *Clodfelter v. Commissioner*, 527 F.2d 754, 757 (9th Cir. 1975), *cert. denied*, 425 U.S. 979 (1976). What kind of delay do you think would constitute "prejudicial" delay?

The following case illuminates the "last known address" problem:

---

[11] Section 6212(a)(1) provides, in part: "If the Secretary determines that there is deficiency in respect of any tax imposed by subtitle A or B or chapter 41, 42, 43 or 44, he is authorized to send notice of such deficiency to the taxpayer by certified mail or registered mail." However, failure to send the notice by certified or registered mail also does not invalidate the notice. *See, e.g.,* Balkissoon v. Commissioner, 995 F.2d 525, 528 (4th Cir.), *cert. denied*, 510 U.S. 978 (1993) ("Commissioner's failure to comply with the authorization in section 6212(a) inviting the use of registered or certified mail proves to be a technical, but harmless violation"); Berger v. Commissioner, 404 F.2d 668, 673 (3d Cir.), *cert. denied*, 395 U.S. 905 (1969) ("Subsection (a) [of section 6212] authorizes a notice of deficiency to be sent by registered or certified mail. In authorizing such method of notice it does not forbid any other method. If a revenue agent personally delivers by hand a notice of deficiency to the taxpayer it could not rationally be suggested that the notice was invalid because it violated a requirement of subsection (a).").

WILLIAMS v. COMMISSIONER
United States Court of Appeals, Ninth Circuit
935 F.2d 1066 (1991)

HUG, CIRCUIT JUDGE:

Appellant Diane Williams ("Williams") appeals the Tax Court's dismissal of her petition for redetermination of a deficiency in income tax. The dismissal was based upon a finding by the Tax Court that the petition was untimely and, therefore, the Tax Court had no jurisdiction. We have jurisdiction pursuant to 26 U.S.C. § 7482. There is no question but that the petition was not filed within the prescribed period from the date the notice of deficiency was sent. Williams contends, however, that the time for filing the petition for redetermination did not commence to run because the notice of deficiency was not received by her and was not sent to her last known address. A notice of deficiency is valid if it is mailed to the taxpayer's last known address even if it is not received by the taxpayer. United States v. Zolla, 724 F.2d 808, 810 (9th Cir.), *cert. denied*, 469 U.S. 830, 83 L. Ed. 2d 59, 105 S. Ct. 116 (1984). "A taxpayer's last known address is that on his most recent return, unless the taxpayer communicates to the IRS 'clear and concise' notice of change of address." *Id.* (citations omitted).

Prior to the mailing of the notice of deficiency, Williams had filed a tax return showing a new address. The tax return was filed on or before April 15, 1987,[n.1] however, it had not yet been processed by the IRS so as to be available through a computer inquiry to the agent who sent the notice of deficiency at the time that notice was sent on June 17, 1987.

Williams contends that the mere filing of the 1986 tax return with the new address indicated thereon constitutes adequate notice of the change of address, relying upon our decision in *King v. Commissioner*, 857 F.2d 676 (9th Cir. 1988). In *King*, we reiterated this circuit's rule that a subsequently filed tax return with a new address gives the IRS notice of a change of address. *Id.* at 680. However, we did not specify when, after the filing of a return, the IRS is deemed to have notice of the change of address. In *Cool Fuel, Inc. v. Connett*, 685 F.2d 309, 312 (9th Cir. 1982), we acknowledged that "it is a question of fact as to what knowledge the IRS acquires concerning the taxpayer's address."

In applying the law of this circuit, the Tax Court, in *Abeles v. Commissioner*, 91 T.C. 1019 (1988), set forth a general rule in determining the "last known address" in these cases. The court stated:

> [A] taxpayer's last known address is that address which appears on the taxpayer's most recently filed return, unless [the Commissioner] has been given clear and concise notification of a different address . . . . [A] taxpayer's "most recently filed return" is that return which has been properly processed by an IRS service center such that the address appearing on such return was available to [the Commissioner's] agent when that agent prepared to send a notice of deficiency

---

[n.1] A tax return filed prior to the last day provided for filing is considered to be filed on such last day. 26 U.S.C. § 6501(b)(1).

> in connection with an examination of a previously filed return . . . .
> [T]he address from the more recently filed return is *available* to the
> agent issuing a notice of deficiency with respect to a previously filed
> return, if such address could be obtained by a computer generation
> of an IRS computer transcript using the taxpayer's TIN in the case
> of a separately filed return . . . .

Id. at 1035 (emphasis in original) (footnote references omitted).

In this case, the Tax Court determined that the reasonable business requirements of the IRS necessitated time for processing the filed return through its computer facilities in order for the new address to be "available" to agents sending notices of deficiency. Thus, before the change of address is considered "available" to the agent sending the notice of deficiency, a reasonable amount of time must be allowed to process and transfer the information to the IRS's central computer system. The Tax Court found that the lapse of time between the date of the filing of the return and the date the notice of deficiency was sent did not exceed a reasonable time for processing the information. Thus, it held that the change of address was not "available" to the agent.

This ruling does involve a hiatus in which a taxpayer has notified the IRS of a change in address by the filing of a tax return, yet the IRS is deemed not to have knowledge of the change while it is being placed in an accessible computer data base. This is a practical operational necessity. Appropriate notification to the post office by the taxpayer to forward mail to the taxpayer's new address would avoid notification problems during this period.

We review the determination by the Tax Court of the taxpayer's "last known address" for clear error. *See King*, 857 F.2d at 678–79. Under the circumstances of this case, we conclude that the Tax Court's determination that the change of address was not reasonably available to the agent sending the notice of deficiency was not clearly erroneous; and, therefore, that the notice of deficiency was sent to the last known address. Consequently, the filing of the petition for review was untimely and the judgment of the Tax Court must be affirmed.

In January 2001, the Treasury promulgated regulations regarding the "last known address" rules of Code section 6212. *See* Treas. Reg. § 301.6212-2. Under the regulations, the general rule remains that a taxpayer's last known address is the one shown on his most recently filed tax return, unless the taxpayer has provided the IRS with "clear and concise notification of a different address." Treas. Reg. § 301.6212-2(a). Revenue Procedure 2001-18, 2001-8 I.R.B. 708, provides that the notification may be provided on a properly completed Form 8822. The Revenue Procedure also provides that a return showing a new address normally will be "properly processed" after a 45-day processing period.[12] *See id.* at § 5.02(1).

---

[12] Note that this processing period corresponds to the 45-day period that the IRS may process, interest-free, a taxpayer's return claiming a refund. *See* I.R.C. § 6611(e)(1). The interest rules are discussed in detail in Chapter 11.

The regulations also provide an important exception to this general rule. The IRS has begun updating its database of addresses by using the United States Postal Service National Change of Address database, which retains address changes for 36 months. Treas. Reg. § 301.6212-2(b)(2). Under the regulations, if the taxpayer's name and last known address in the IRS's records match the taxpayer's name and prior mailing address in the Postal Service database, the new address in the postal database is deemed to be the taxpayer's last known address absent "clear and concise notification" to the IRS of a new address.

The Court of Appeals in *Williams* points out that if the taxpayer receives timely actual notice despite lack of mailing to the last known address, that is also sufficient. In that light, consider the following case:

MULVANIA v. COMMISSIONER
United States Court of Appeals, Ninth Circuit
769 F.2d 1376 (1985)

GOODWIN, CIRCUIT JUDGE:

The Commissioner of the Internal Revenue Service appeals a decision of the Tax Court that it lacked jurisdiction to assess a deficiency against taxpayer, Richard L. Mulvania, because he did not receive a valid notice of deficiency within the three-year statute of limitations on assessments. We affirm.

Mulvania timely filed an income tax return for 1977 showing his address as 57 Linda Isle Drive, Newport Beach, California. The return was prepared by Gerald F. Simonis Accountants, Inc. On June 13, 1979, the IRS sent a letter to Mulvania setting forth proposed adjustments to his 1974 and 1977 income tax. A copy of that letter was also forwarded to Simonis, who held a power of attorney requesting that copies of all documents sent to Mulvania also be sent to him. Mulvania received the letter.

On December 31, 1980, the IRS sent a letter to Mulvania requesting an extension of the limitations period for assessing Mulvania's 1977 tax liability, which was never executed. On April 15, 1981, the last day of the three-year statutory period in which the IRS could assess a tax deficiency, the IRS sent Mulvania a notice of deficiency with respect to the tax year 1977. The notice was sent by certified mail, addressed as "St. Linda Isle Drive," rather than "57 Linda Isle Drive," Mulvania's correct address. The postal service returned the notice to the IRS on April 21, 1984, marked "Not deliverable as addressed." The IRS placed the returned notice in Mulvania's file and, because the statutory period had expired, did not attempt to remail it.

On the same date that the misaddressed notice of deficiency was mailed to Mulvania, the IRS sent a copy of the notice by ordinary mail to Simonis, who received it on or about April 17, 1981. Expecting that Mulvania would soon call him about the notice, Simonis filed the notice and made a note to follow up. About June 1, 1981, when Simonis called Mulvania to discuss the notice of deficiency, he found out that Mulvania had never received the notice. There is no evidence in the record that Simonis discussed the contents of the notice with Mulvania.

On or about June 15, 1981, after Simonis (who is not a lawyer) advised Mulvania that Simonis' notice was not a valid notice of deficiency for 1977, Mulvania decided not to file a petition in the Tax Court for a redetermination of assessment of deficiency. Mulvania changed his mind, however, and, on April 1, 1983, filed a petition in the Tax Court requesting a redetermination of the deficiency for 1977.

Both parties then filed cross-motions to dismiss for lack of jurisdiction. The Commissioner argued that Mulvania's petition, which was filed almost two years after the notice of deficiency was mailed, was untimely pursuant to 26 U.S.C. § 6123(a). Mulvania claimed the Tax Court lacked jurisdiction to assess a deficiency for 1977 because the three-year statute of limitations had run, and Mulvania had never received a valid notice of deficiency which would have tolled the statute of limitations as provided in 26 U.S.C. § 6503(a).

The Tax Court granted Mulvania's motion to dismiss for lack of jurisdiction and denied the Commissioner's motion to dismiss. This appeal followed. * * *

Cases interpreting the interplay of * * * sections [6501(a), 6503(a), and 6212] have fallen into three broad categories.

First, a notice of deficiency actually, physically received by a taxpayer is valid under § 6212(a) if it is received in sufficient time to permit the taxpayer, without prejudice, to file a petition in the Tax Court even though the notice is erroneously addressed. Clodfelter v. Commissioner, 527 F.2d 754, 757 (9th Cir. 1975), *cert. denied*, 425 U.S. 979, 48 L. Ed. 2d 805, 96 S. Ct. 2184 (1976); Mulvania v. Commissioner, 81 T.C. 65 (1983).

Second, a notice of deficiency mailed to a taxpayer's last known address is valid under § 6212(b)(1) regardless of when the taxpayer eventually receives it. De Welles v. United States, 378 F.2d 37, 39–40 (9th Cir.), *cert. denied,* 389 U.S. 996, 88 S. Ct. 501, 19 L. Ed. 2d 494 (1967).

Third, an erroneously addressed and undelivered registered notice of deficiency is not valid under either § 6212(a) or 6212(b)(1) even if the Commissioner also sends a copy of the notice by regular mail to the taxpayer's attorney. D'Andrea v. Commissioner, 105 U.S. App. D.C. 67, 263 F.2d 904, 907 (D.C. Cir. 1959); *see* Reddock v. Commissioner, 72 T.C. 21 (1979).

In this case the actual notice of deficiency which was mailed to Mulvania became null and void when it was returned to the IRS; at that time, the IRS then knew that the notice had been misaddressed and had not been received. This is not a case in which the notice was improperly addressed, but the postal authorities nonetheless delivered the letter to the taxpayer. *Clodfelter*, 527 F.2d at 756. Mulvania has never physically received a notice of deficiency.

The Commissioner argues that because Mulvania's accountant received a courtesy copy of the notice and called Mulvania before the 90 days had expired, Mulvania therefore received valid notice and now lacks a basis for a petition in the Tax Court. Mulvania argues that a courtesy copy of a notice of deficiency cannot be transformed into a valid notice of deficiency simply because the accountant called and told the taxpayer about the notice.

With a broad power of attorney, registered notice to the attorney or accountant may also serve as notice to the taxpayer under the law of principal and agent if the taxpayer himself received some notification in time to file a petition before the tax court. Commissioner v. Stewart, 186 F.2d 239, 242 (6th Cir. 1951). *But see D'Andrea*, 263 F.2d at 907–08 (copy sent by ordinary mail insufficient where there was no evidence that taxpayer reasonably received the information contained in the notice to his attorney). A taxpayer may also designate the address of his representative as that to which any deficiency notice should be sent. Expanding Envelope and Folder Corp. v. Shotz, 385 F.2d 402, 404 (3rd Cir. 1967); *see D'Andrea*, 263 F.2d at 907.

Because Simonis did not have a broad power of attorney, however, the law of principal and agent does not apply. Mulvania had only granted him a power of attorney which requests that courtesy copies of all communication be sent to his representative. The IRS clearly knew that Simonis was not to be the addressee of the official notice of deficiency; it sent him only a copy and only by ordinary, unregistered, uncertified mail. *See D'Andrea*, 263 F.2d at 905. *See also* Keeton v. Commissioner, 74 T.C. 377 (1980); Houghton v. Commissioner, 48 T.C. 656 (1967).

The Commissioner relies on two Tax Court cases for the proposition that the copy of the notice sent to Simonis sufficed to toll the three-year statute of limitations. In *Lifter v. Commissioner*, 59 T.C. 818 (1973), the notice of deficiency was sent to the taxpayers' last known address but was returned undelivered. The Commissioner then sent a copy of the notice to the taxpayers' attorney who had been appointed to handle their federal income tax matters. The taxpayers learned of the notice before the running of the statute of limitations and timely filed a petition with the Tax Court. The notice of deficiency was held valid.

Lifter may be distinguished from this case in three respects. First, the IRS sent the notice to what was reasonably believed to be petitioners' last known address, and a notice of deficiency mailed to a taxpayer's last known address is valid even if the taxpayer does not receive it. *DeWelles*, 378 F.2d at 39. Second, taxpayers invoked the jurisdiction of the Tax Court by filing a timely petition. By timely invoking Tax Court jurisdiction, taxpayers effectively waived any objection to the notice of deficiency. Finally, the attorney to whom a copy of the notice was sent apparently had a broad power of attorney, beyond mere receipt of copies of notices sent to taxpayers. The Commissioner in *Lifter* could have sent the original notice to the attorney alone. *See D'Andrea*, 263 F.2d at 905.

In *Whiting v. Commissioner*, T.C. Memo 1984–142 (1984), the notice was sent to taxpayers' previous address although the IRS had been informed of the change of address. The notice was returned undelivered. A copy of the notice was also sent to their attorney who eventually informed them of the notice. The taxpayers filed a timely petition with the Tax Court. They challenged the validity of the notice, but the Tax Court held it was valid because the petitioners became aware that the notice had been issued and timely filed a petition.

Whiting and this case differ in two critical respects. First, in *Whiting* the notice was sent to the wrong address, even after the IRS had been informed of the change of address. Here the notice was misaddressed because of a typographical error. Second, in *Whiting*, petitioners chose to invoke jurisdiction of the Tax Court after learning of the notice from their attorney. As in *Lifter*, by timely invoking Tax Court jurisdiction, taxpayers essentially acknowledged notice; the purpose of § 6212 had been satisfied. Here Mulvania has never acknowledged notice by invoking Tax Court jurisdiction in a timely manner.

In *Whiting*, the Tax Court engaged in a cursory analysis of the validity of the notice, concluding that an error in the address to which the notice of deficiency is mailed does not render the notice invalid when the petition is timely filed, citing *Mulvania*, 81 T.C. at 68. In *Mulvania*, however, the taxpayer received the actual, physical notice of deficiency although it had been mailed to his former address and had later been hand delivered by his child.

The resolution of this issue is a "least-worse" result. Mulvania argues that he never received the actual written notice of deficiency because it was misaddressed. The IRS sent the notice on the last day of the statutory period, making it impossible for the Commissioner to remail the notice within the prescribed time once the error was discovered. To decide for the Commissioner would relieve the IRS of its cumulative errors, and create uncertainty in the law. The IRS argues, however, that this is a mobile society, clerical mistakes do happen, and the taxpayer had actual knowledge of the notice even if not its contents.

The Tax Court was understandably concerned that a decision in the Commissioner's favor would result in an uncertain rule depending on whether the tax adviser happened to be a lawyer. As a lawyer, a tax adviser's call to Mulvania regarding the notice would have been privileged. The Tax Court correctly believed that a decision for the Commissioner would result in an uncertain rule, subject to manipulation by taxpayers who authorize copies to be sent to their accountant or lawyer, or by taxpayers with the most sophisticated tax advisers.

It is better for the government to lose some revenue as the result of its clerical error than to create uncertainty. If Simonis, either intentionally or unintentionally, had not informed Mulvania of the receipt of the copy of the notice of deficiency, then Mulvania would not have received any notification of the deficiency. Tax law requires more solid footings than the happenstance of a tax adviser telephoning a client to tell him of a letter from the IRS.

We conclude that, where a notice of deficiency has been misaddressed to the taxpayer or sent only to an adviser who is merely authorized to receive a copy of such a notice, actual notice is necessary but not sufficient to make the notice valid. The IRS is not forgiven for its clerical errors or for mailing notice to the wrong party unless the taxpayer, through his own actions, renders the Commissioner's errors harmless. In this case, the notice of deficiency became null and void when it was returned to the IRS undelivered. Regardless of the coincidence by which Mulvania later came to know of its existence, the taxpayer's actual knowledge did not transform the void notice into a valid one.

Had Mulvania timely petitioned the Tax Court for a redetermination of deficiency, the IRS error might have fallen into the line of harmless error cases where the taxpayer suffered no ill effects for the Commissioner's inadvertence. Such is not the case here.

Affirmed.

Was the court correct in holding that verbal notice to Mr. Mulvania by his accountant, Mr. Simonis, of receipt by Simonis of a copy of a notice directed to Mulvania did not constitute *actual notice* to Mulvania of the notice of deficiency? Simonis was an accountant but not a lawyer, so his communication to Mulvania was not privileged under then-existing law. Recall the discussion in Chapter 1 of Code section 7525, the federally authorized tax practitioner (FATP) privilege, which extends the attorney-client privilege to non-attorneys providing tax advice in civil proceedings. Would the existence of the FATP privilege affect the outcome of a case similar to *Mulvania* arising today?

In this regard, consider *St. Joseph Lease Capital Corp. v. Commissioner*, 235 F.3d 886 (4th Cir. 2000). In that case, the IRS mailed a notice of deficiency on October 6, 1994 with respect to federal income tax returns filed on October 15, 1991. However, the notice was not mailed to the taxpayer's last known address, and it was returned to the IRS. On November 2, 1994, the taxpayer's new attorney, Mr. Levin, discovered that a notice had been issued, and requested a copy. The IRS faxed him a copy on November 10. On January 3, 1995, the taxpayer filed a Tax Court petition, and argued that the three-year statute of limitations on assessment had expired. The Tax Court found that the October 6 mailing tolled the statute of limitations under Code section 6503(a) because the taxpayer received actual notice of the deficiency in time to file a petition with the Tax Court.

In *St. Joseph Lease Capital Corp.*, the taxpayer argued that the misaddressed notice was a nullity, ineffective for all purposes. However, the Court of Appeals for the Fourth Circuit affirmed the Tax Court under the same rationale it had used. Do you agree with that decision? Does it mean that an "invalid" notice of deficiency may toll the statute of limitations on assessment? Is that consistent with *D'Andrea* and *Reddock*, discussed above in the *Mulvania* case? What does the *St. Joseph Lease Capital Corp.* decision imply about what action the taxpayer's new lawyer, Mr. Levin, should have taken with respect to the notice of deficiency?

[2] Invalidating a Notice of Deficiency for IRS Failure to Make a "Determination"

Failure to send a notice to the taxpayer's last known address or provide actual notice without prejudicial delay is not the only ground on which a taxpayer has succeeded in obtaining a court decision invalidating a notice of deficiency. Section 6212(a) reads, "If the Secretary *determines* that there is a deficiency . . . ." (emphasis added). One area of dispute is whether the statute requires a substantive "determination" of the taxpayer's liability by the IRS or whether the notice itself conclusively evidences a determination of a deficiency. Recall the *Greenberg's Express* case, which reflects the general proposition that courts will not "look behind" the notice of deficiency to examine the motives or methods of the IRS in determining the deficiency. *Scar v. Commissioner*, the next case, is the leading case invalidating a notice of deficiency for failure of the IRS to make a "determination." How does the court address the question of whether it is "looking behind" the notice of deficiency?

SCAR v. COMMISSIONER
United States Court of Appeals, Ninth Circuit
814 F.2d 1363 (1987)

FLETCHER, CIRCUIT JUDGE:

Taxpayers Howard and Ethel Scar petition for review of the Tax Court's denial of their motion to dismiss for lack of jurisdiction and denial of their two summary judgment motions. Taxpayers argue that the Tax Court lacked jurisdiction because the Commissioner of the Internal Revenue Service (IRS) issued an invalid notice of deficiency. Alternatively, they argue that the Tax Court incorrectly denied their motions for summary judgment and should not have granted the Commissioner's request to amend his answer. We reverse.

BACKGROUND

On September 3, 1979, petitioners Howard and Ethel Scar filed a joint return for tax year 1978.[n.1] The Scars claimed business deductions totaling $26,966 in connection with a video-tape tax shelter,[n.2] and reported total taxes due of $3,269.

On June 14, 1982, the Commissioner mailed to the Scars a letter (Form 892); it listed taxpayers' names and address, the taxable year at issue (the year ending December 31, 1978), and specified a deficiency amount ($96,600). The body of the letter stated in part:

> We have determined that there is a deficiency (increase) in your income tax as shown above. This letter is a NOTICE OF DEFICIENCY sent to you as required by the law.

It informed the taxpayers that if they wished to contest the deficiency they must file a petition with the United States Tax Court within 90 days.

Attached to the letter was a Form 5278 ("Statement — Income Tax Changes") purporting to explain how the deficiency had been determined. It showed an adjustment to income in the amount of $138,000 designated as "Partnership — Nevada Mining Project." The Form 5278 had no information in the space on the form for taxable income as shown on petitioners' return as filed. It showed as the "total corrected income tax liability" the sum of $96,600 and indicated that this sum was arrived at by multiplying 70 percent times $138,000.

[n.1] The return was timely, the Scars having received an extension of time to file.

[n.2] The Scars also claimed deductions and credits with regard to this tax shelter on their 1977 returns. They received a notice of deficiency in April of 1981 and petitioned the Tax Court for a redetermination in June of 1981. In February of 1985 the Tax Court made a deficiency determination of $10,410 for the tax year 1977.

Another attached document, designated as "Statement Schedule 2," with the heading "Nevada Mining Project, Explanation of Adjustments," stated as follows:

> In order to protect the government's interest and since your original income tax return is unavailable at this time, the income tax is being assessed at the maximum tax rate of 70%.
>
> The tax assessment will be corrected when we receive the original return or when you send a copy of the return to us.
>
> The increase in tax may also reflect investment credit or new jobs credit which has been disallowed.

Also attached to the letter was a document, designated as "Statement Schedule 3," with the heading "Nevada Mining Project, Explanation of Adjustments." This document explained why the Nevada Mining Project deductions were being disallowed.

On July 7, 1982, the taxpayers filed a timely petition with the Tax Court to redetermine the deficiency asserted. In their petition, they alleged that they had never been associated with the "Nevada Mining Project Partnership" and had not claimed on their 1978 return any expenses or losses related to that venture. The Commissioner, on August 30, 1982, filed an answer denying the substantive allegations of the petition.

Sometime in September 1982, the Commissioner conceded in a telephone conversation with the taxpayers that the June 14 notice of deficiency was incorrect because it overstated the amount of disallowed deductions and wrongly connected taxpayers with a mining partnership. Nevertheless, the Commissioner maintained that the notice of deficiency was valid. The Commissioner confirmed his position in a letter dated November 29, 1982, stating "the taxpayers should not be surprised by the fact that the Commissioner means to disallow the deductions claimed in 1978 for Executive Productions, Inc." because similar objections had been made to the deductions claimed for the same tax shelter on taxpayers' 1977 return. The Commissioner enclosed with this letter a revised Form 5278, which contained the appropriate shelter explanation and decreased the amount of tax due to $10,374, and notified the taxpayers that he intended to request leave from the Tax Court to amend his answer.

On December 6, 1982 the taxpayers filed a motion to dismiss for lack of jurisdiction, claiming that the June 14 notice of deficiency was invalid because the Commissioner failed to make a "determination" of additional tax owed before issuing the notice of deficiency. The Commissioner filed a response which conceded the inaccuracy of the notice of deficiency but maintained that it was sufficient to give the Tax Court jurisdiction. On March 21, 1983, the Tax Court held a hearing on the taxpayers' motion to dismiss. At the hearing, counsel for the Commissioner attempted to explain why the Form 5278 sent to the taxpayers contained a description of the wrong tax shelter. He stated that an IRS employee transposed a code number which caused the IRS to assert the deficiency on the basis of the Nevada mining project instead of the videotape tax shelter. No witness, however, testified to this fact at the hearing,[n.3] and no explanation was ever offered for the discrepancy of over $80,000 between the deficiency notice assessment and that later conceded to be the correct amount.

Following the March 21 hearing, the taxpayers filed a motion for summary judgment based on the Commissioner's concession that they had not been involved in any mining partnerships. The Commissioner shortly thereafter filed his motion to amend his answer to correct the error made in the notice of deficiency and accompanying documents. On November 17, 1983 the Tax Court, in an opinion reviewed by the full court, ruled on these various motions. The Tax Court majority upheld the validity of the June 14 notice of deficiency, finding that it satisfied section 6212(a), which states the formal requirements for a deficiency notice. The Tax Court further ruled that the Commissioner could amend his answer as requested, and denied taxpayers' motion for summary judgment. The reviewed opinion contained several concurring and dissenting opinions. Five dissenting judges would have denied jurisdiction on the basis that the deficiency notice was invalid and four dissenting judges would not have permitted the Commissioner to amend his answer.

The Commissioner amended his answer and asserted in it, despite the patent incorrectness of the notice of deficiency and the acknowledgment of error by the Service, that the taxpayer had the burden of disproving the correctness of the Commissioner's revised determinations. The taxpayers renewed their motion for summary judgment. The Tax Court denied this second motion for summary judgment on the ground that triable issues of fact remained concerning whether the taxpayers' primary motivation for entering the videotape venture was the prospect of earning a profit or avoiding tax. On February 22, 1985, the Tax Court entered a decision, pursuant to a stipulation, that taxpayers owed $10,377 in additional tax. The stipulation afforded the taxpayers the right to file a petition for review of the Tax Court's adverse rulings.

DISCUSSION

In order to decide whether the Tax Court had jurisdiction we review *de novo* the Tax Court's interpretation of section 6212(a). Orvis v. Commissioner, 788 F.2d 1406, 1407 (9th Cir. 1986); Ebben v. Commissioner, 783 F.2d 906, 909 (9th Cir. 1986).

Section 6212(a) states in part: "If the Secretary determines that there is a deficiency in respect of any tax imposed . . . he is authorized to send notice of such deficiency to the taxpayer by certified mail or registered mail." Section 6213(a) provides in part: "Within 90 days . . . after the notice of deficiency authorized in section 6212 is mailed . . . taxpayer may file a petition with the Tax Court for a redetermination of the deficiency." The Tax Court has jurisdiction only when the Commissioner issues a valid deficiency notice, and the taxpayer files a timely petition for redetermination. "A valid petition is the basis of the Tax Court's jurisdiction. To be valid, a petition must be filed from a valid statutory notice." Stamm International Corp. v. Commissioner,

---

[n.3] The Commissioner argues that a witness was present at the hearing, but since taxpayers failed to object to counsel's explanation of the IRS's mistake, the witness was never called.

84 T.C. 248, 252 (1985). *See* Midland Mortgage Co. v. Commissioner, 73 T.C. 902, 907 (1980).

The taxpayers correctly note that section 6212(a) authorizes the Commissioner to send a notice of deficiency only if he first "determines that there is a deficiency." Because the deficiency notice mailed to the taxpayers contained an explanation of a tax shelter completely unrelated to their return, contained no adjustments to tax based on their return as filed, and stated affirmatively that the taxpayers's return is "unavailable at this time," taxpayers maintain that the Commissioner could not have "determined" a deficiency with respect to them. The taxpayers assert that, in the absence of a determination, the deficiency notice was invalid and therefore the Tax Court lacked jurisdiction.

The Tax Court rejected this argument, finding that "[t]he requirements of section 6212(a) are met if the notice of deficiency sets forth the amount of the deficiency and the taxable year involved." Scar v. Commissioner, 81 T.C. 855, 860-61 (1983).

We agree with the Tax Court that no particular form is required for a valid notice of deficiency, Abrams v. Commissioner, 787 F.2d 939, 941 (4th Cir.), *cert. denied*, 479 U.S. 882, 107 S. Ct. 271, 93 L. Ed. 2d 248 (1986); Benzvi v. Commissioner, 787 F.2d 1541, 1542 (11th Cir.), *cert. denied,* 479 U.S. 883, 107 S. Ct. 273, 93 L. Ed. 2d 250 (1986), and the Commissioner need not explain how the deficiencies were determined. Barnes v. Commissioner, 408 F.2d 65, 68 (7th Cir.) (*citing* Commissioner v. Stewart, 186 F.2d 239, 242 (6th Cir. 1951)), *cert. denied*, 396 U.S. 836, 90 S. Ct. 94, 24 L. Ed. 2d 86 (1969). The notice must, however, "meet certain substantial requirements." *Abrams*, 787 F.2d at 941. "The notice must at a minimum indicate that the IRS has determined the amount of the deficiency." *Benzvi*, 787 F.2d at 1542. The question confronting us is whether a form letter that asserts that a deficiency has been determined, which letter and its attachments make it patently obvious that no determination has in fact been made, satisfies the statutory mandate.

In none of the cases on which the Tax Court relied was the notice challenged on the basis that there was no determination. *See* Abatti v. Commissioner, 644 F.2d 1385, 1389 (9th Cir. 1981) (notice valid although it did not advise the taxpayer under which code section the IRS would proceed because fair warning was given before trial); *Barnes*, 408 F.2d at 68 (notice need not state the basis for the deficiency determination nor contain particulars of explanations concerning how alleged deficiencies were determined); Foster v. Commissioner, 80 T.C. 34, 229–30 (1983) (notice must advise taxpayer that Commissioner has, in fact, determined a deficiency, and must specify the year and amount), *aff'd in part and vacated in part,* 756 F.2d 1430 (9th Cir. 1985), *cert. denied,* 474 U.S. 1055, 106 S. Ct. 793, 88 L. Ed. 2d 770 (1986); Hannan v. Commissioner, 52 T.C. 787 (1969) (deficiency notice valid where record did not show that Commissioner had not assessed a deficiency even though Commissioner asserted that no deficiency existed and that the notice had been issued in error). The cases assume that the deficiency determination was made. With the exception of *Hannan*, they deal instead with the question of whether the notice imparted enough information to provide the taxpayer with fair notice.

The Tax Court asserts that it is following long-established policy not to look behind a deficiency notice to question the Commissioner's motives and procedures leading to a determination. * * *

We agree that courts should avoid oversight of the Commissioner's internal operations and the adequacy of procedures employed. This does not mean, however, that the courts cannot or should not decide the validity of a notice that can be determined solely by references to applicable statutes and review of the notice itself.

In this case, we need not look behind the notice sent to the taxpayers to determine its invalidity. The Commissioner acknowledges in the notice that the deficiency is not based on a determination of deficiency of tax reported on the taxpayers' return and that it refers to a tax shelter the Commissioner concedes has no connection to the taxpayers or their return.

Section 6212(a) "authorize[s]" the sending of a deficiency notice "if the Secretary *determines* that there is a deficiency." (emphasis added). We agree with Judge Goffe's statement in this case that "even a cursory review of this provision [section 6212(a)] discloses that Congress did not grant the Secretary unlimited and unfettered authority to issue notices of deficiency." *Scar*, 81 T.C. at 872 (Goffe, J., dissenting). In *Appeal of Terminal Wine Co.,* 1 B.T.A. 697, 701 (1925), the Board of Tax Appeals construed the meaning of the term "determine" as applied to deficiency determinations: "By its very definition and etymology the word 'determination' irresistibly connotes consideration, resolution, conclusion, and judgment."

* * * A literal reading of relevant code sections, and the absence of evidence of contrary legislative intent, leads us to conclude that the Commissioner must consider information that relates to a particular taxpayer before it can be said that the Commissioner has "determined" a "deficiency" in respect to that taxpayer. To hold otherwise would entail ignoring or judicially rewriting the plain language of the Internal Revenue Code.[n.9]

This reading of the Code is not a new one. Almost sixty years ago, the Board of Tax Appeals, while refusing to examine the intent, motive or reasoning of the Commissioner, emphasized that

> the statute clearly contemplates that before notifying a taxpayer of a deficiency and hence before the Board can be concerned, a determination must be made by the Commissioner. This must mean a thoughtful and considered determination that the United States is

---

[n.9] The dissent, characterizing the deficiency notice as a " 'ticket' to the tax court" suggests that the majority fails "to grasp the function of the deficiency notice." Dissent at 1372. What the dissent fails to grasp, however, is that processes that may "serve their intended purposes" nonetheless may be legally insufficient. For example, notice by telephone would not suffice if written notice were required. Here, the statute requires that the Commissioner make a determination. None was made. The fact that the taxpayers received a deficiency notice does not cure the failure to make a determination.

The dissent in looking only to the fact that notice was sent skips over the Commissioner's failure to make the statutorily required determination. We readily agree with the dissent that in the usual case the sending of the notice of deficiency presumes a determination. * * * Where, however, the notice belies that presumption, it is both reasonable and necessary that the Commissioner demonstrate his compliance with the statute.

entitled to an amount not yet paid. If the notice of deficiency were other than the expression of a *bona fide* official determination, and were, say, a mere formal demand for an arbitrary amount as to which there were substantial doubt, the Board might easily become merely an expensive tribunal to determine moot questions and a burden might be imposed on taxpayers of litigating issues and disproving allegations for which there had never been any substantial foundation.

Couzens v. Commissioner, 11 B.T.A. 1040, 1159–60 (1928).

These cases inform our judgment here. They support the view that the "determination" requirement of section 6212(a) has substantive content. The Commissioner's and the dissent's contention that the issuance of a formally proper notice of deficiency[11] of itself establishes that the Commissioner has determined a deficiency must be rejected. To hold otherwise, would read the determination requirement out of section 6212(a).[12]

Finally, the Commissioner asserts that the proper remedy in this case is to eliminate the presumption of correctness that normally attaches to deficiency determinations, *see, e.g.,* Dix v. Commissioner, 392 F.2d 313 (4th Cir. 1968), not to dismiss for lack of jurisdiction. He relies, however, on cases that challenge the correctness of the determination, and not its existence. The Commissioner's belated willingness to assume the burden of proof before the Tax Court cannot cure his failure to determine a deficiency before imposing on taxpayers the obligation to defend themselves in potentially costly litigation in Tax Court. Jurisdiction is at issue here. Failure to comply with statutory requirements renders the deficiency notice null and void and leaves nothing on which Tax Court jurisdiction can rest. *See* Sanderling Inc. v.

---

[11] In the case before us the Commissioner argues that, because the notice contained the Taxpayers' names, social security number, the tax year in question, and "the" amount of deficiency, it was "clearly sufficient." It is quite clear, however, that the notice did not contain the amount of deficiency, but rather contained *an* amount unrelated to any deficiency for which the Scars were responsible.

[12] Judge Sterrett, in dissenting, offered a sample of a valid deficiency letter under the statutory construction urged by the IRS and accepted by the Tax Court:

Dear Taxpayer:

There is a rumor afoot that you were a participant in the Amalgamated Hairpin Partnership during the year 1980. Due to the press of work we have been unable to investigate the accuracy of the rumor or to determine whether you filed a tax return for that year. However, we are concerned that the statute of limitations may be about to expire with respect to your tax liability for 1980.

Our experience has shown that, as a general matter, taxpayers tend to take, on the average, excessive (unallowable) deductions, arising out of investments in partnerships comparable to Amalgamated that aggregate some $10,000. Our experience has further shown that the average investor in such partnerships has substantial taxable income and consequently has attained the top marginal tax rate.

Accordingly, you are hereby notified that there is a deficiency in tax in the amount of $7,000 due from you for the year 1980 in addition to whatever amount, if any, you may have previously paid.

Sincerely yours,

Commissioner of Internal Revenue

Scar, 81 T.C. at 869 (Sterrett, J., dissenting).

Commissioner, 571 F.2d 174, 176 (3d Cir. 1978) ("The Tax Court has held that it has no jurisdiction where the deficiency notice does not cover a proper taxable period.") (citing Columbia River Orchards, Inc. v. Commissioner, 15 T.C. 253 (1950)); McConkey v. Commissioner, 199 F.2d 892 (4th Cir. 1952), *cert. denied,* 345 U.S. 924, 73 S. Ct. 782, 97 L. Ed. 1355 (1953) (where taxpayer paid alleged deficiency before notice of deficiency was mailed, Tax Court lacked jurisdiction as there was no deficiency on which the court's jurisdiction could operate); United States v. Lehigh, 201 F. Supp. 224 (W.D. Ark. 1961) (statement of "Income Tax Due" was invalid deficiency notice where it was not labeled as a deficiency notice, incorrectly stated the tax year involved, and was confusing in that it did not provide certain figures that the terms of the statement said were provided). *Cf.* Mall v. Kelly, 564 F. Supp. 371 (D. Wyo. 1983) (deficiency assessments void where IRS had failed to meet requirement of reasonably and diligently determining and mailing sufficient notice to taxpayers' last known address).

Section 6212(a) of the Internal Revenue Code requires the Commissioner to determine that a deficiency exists before issuing a notice of deficiency. Because the Commissioner's purported notice of deficiency revealed on its face that no determination of tax deficiency had been made in respect to the Scars for the 1978 tax year, it did not meet the requirements of section 6212(a). Accordingly, the Tax Court should have dismissed the action for want of jurisdiction.[n.13]

Petition for review granted.

Cynthia Holcomb Hall, Circuit Judge, dissenting:

Today, the majority fortifies the impediments to tax collection on behalf of errant taxpayers seeking "no taxation without litigation." R. Jackson, Struggle for Judicial Supremacy 141 (1941). I believe the majority undermines the jurisdiction of the Tax Court by constructing a superfluous yet substantial hurdle to its jurisdiction. In reaching the conclusion that section 6212(a) of the Internal Revenue Code, 26 U.S.C. § 6212(a), imposes a substantive requirement on the Commissioner of the Internal Revenue Service to prove that he has reviewed specific data before making a determination, the majority eagerly expands jurisdictional requirements while discarding the carefully-honed and expedient jurisdictional rules that exist.

I.

The majority first turns a blind eye to reality when it finds that the incorrect explanation for the deficiency "[makes] it patently obvious that no determination has in fact been made." *See ante* at 1367. The 1978 tax return of taxpayers Howard and Ethel Scar was hardly an unlikely object of the Commissioner's suspicion. In 1977 the taxpayers participated in a videotape tax shelter, investing $6,500 in cash, signing a promissory note for $93,500, and then deducting over $15,000 in depreciation and other expenses from their 1977

[n.13] *Cf.* United States v. Lehigh, 201 F. Supp. 224, 234 (W.D. Ark. 1961) ("The procedures set forth in the Internal Revenue Code were prescribed for the protection of both Government and taxpayer. Neglect to comply with those procedures may entail consequences which the neglecting party must be prepared to face, whether such party be the taxpayer or the Government.").

tax return based on their "investment." The Commissioner audited this 1977 return and determined a deficiency of $15,875, finding that the taxpayers' "purchase of the film was lacking in profit motive and economic substance other than the avoidance of tax." The Commissioner mailed a notice of deficiency to the taxpayers, who responded by filing a petition for redetermination of the deficiency with the Tax Court on June 30, 1981.

The taxpayers' 1978 return included additional deductions totaling $27,040 based upon the now suspect videotape shelter. In all likelihood, the Commissioner's decision to issue a second deficiency notice regarding this 1978 return resulted from the continuation of the audit process which began with the previous year's tax return. This second deficiency notice, however, incorrectly explained the deficiency in terms of a Nevada mining venture in which the taxpayers had never participated. At the Tax Court hearing on March 21, 1983, counsel for the Commissioner explained that this misdescription resulted from a technical error: an IRS employee had transposed a code number, resulting in the incorrect identification of the basis of the deficiency as being the Nevada mining project instead of the videotape tax shelter. The Commissioner argues that a witness able to testify to this numerical error was present at the hearing, but was not called since the taxpayers did not object to this explanation of the IRS's mistake.

The procedural history of the taxpayers' efforts to challenge the 1978 deficiency consists largely of motions attempting to exploit this apparent mishap. These motions evince the tactics of delay employed by "every litigious man or every embarrassed man, to whom delay [is] more important than the payment of costs." Tennessee v. Sneed, 96 U.S. (6 Otto) 69, 75, 24 L. Ed. 610 (1877).

II.

The majority correctly recognizes that section 6212(a) authorizes the Commissioner to send a notice of deficiency only if he first determines that there is a deficiency. The taxpayers themselves concede that the notice of deficiency in this case satisfied section 6212(a)'s formal requirements of stating the amount of the deficiency and the taxable year involved. *See* Stamm International Corp. v. Commissioner, 84 T.C. 248, 253 (1985); Foster v. Commissioner, 80 T.C. 34, 229–30 (1983), *aff'd in part and vacated in part,* 756 F.2d 1430 (9th Cir. 1985), *cert. denied,* 474 U.S. 1055, 106 S. Ct. 793, 88 L. Ed. 2d 770 (1986); Ziegler v. Commissioner, T.C. Memo 1984-620, 49 T.C.M. (CCH) 182, 189 (1984); Stevenson v. Commissioner, T.C. Memo 1982-16, 43 T.C.M. (CCH) 289, 290–91 (1982) (citing Commissioner v. Stewart, 186 F.2d 239,242 (6th Cir. 1951)). *See also* Andrews, *The Use of the Injunction as a Remedy for an Invalid Federal Tax Assessment,* 40 Tax L. Rev. 653, 661 n.39 (1985).

The majority then proceeds to overload the statutory requirement of a "determination" of a deficiency with burdensome substantive content. First, the majority ignores the rule that a deficiency notice need not contain any explanation whatsoever. Abatti v. Commissioner, 644 F.2d 1385, 1389 (9th Cir. 1981); Barnes v. Commissioner, 408 F.2d 65, 69 (7th Cir.), *cert. denied,*

396 U.S. 836, 90 S. Ct. 94, 24 L. Ed. 2d 86 (1969); *Stevenson,* 43 T.C.M.(CCH) at 290. *See also B. Bittker,* Federal Taxation of Income, Estates and Gifts ¶ 115.2.2 at 115–14 (1981) ("Federal Taxation").

Second, the majority fails to grasp the function of the deficiency notice. It is nothing more than "a jurisdictional prerequisite to a taxpayer's suit seeking the Tax Court's redetermination of [the Commissioner's] determination of the tax liability." *Stamm,* 84 T.C. at 252. "The notice is only to advise the person who is to pay the deficiency that the Commissioner means to assess him; anything that does this unequivocally is good enough." Olsen v. Helvering, 88 F.2d 650, 651 (2nd Cir. 1937).[n.1] Nothing more is required as a predicate to Tax Court jurisdiction.[n.2] In fact, this Circuit has recognized that " 'it is not the *existence* of a deficiency that provides a predicate for Tax Court jurisdiction.' " Stevens v. Commissioner, 709 F.2d 12, 13 (5th Cir. 1983) (quoting Hannan v. Commissioner, 52 T.C. 787, 791 (1969) (emphasis in original)). The *Stevens* court lucidly commented:

> That seems obvious: the very purpose of the Tax Court is to adjudicate contests to deficiency notices. If the existence of an error in the determination giving rise to the notice deprived the Court of jurisdiction, the Court would lack power to perform its function.

709 F.2d at 13.

Therefore, the deficiency notice is effectively the taxpayer's "ticket" to the Tax Court. This "ticket" gives the taxpayer access to the only forum where he can litigate the relevant tax issue without first paying the tax assessed. If a properly-addressed deficiency notice states the amount of the deficiency, the taxable year involved, and notifies the taxpayer that he has 90 days from the date of mailing in which to file a petition for redetermination, then the notice is valid. The merits of the Commissioner's deficiency should not be litigated in the form of a motion to dismiss for lack of jurisdiction; once jurisdiction has been established, both sides will have the opportunity to press their views before the Tax Court.

[n.1] The notice of deficiency mailed to the taxpayers included two forms: Form 892 and Form 5278. Form 892 is the basic deficiency notice. It includes the taxpayer's name, social security number, amount of the deficiency for the taxable year, and a short explanation of the taxpayer's options. Here, the Commissioner properly completed the Form 892. If the Commissioner had mailed only the Form 892, and nothing else, it is clear that this would have been a valid deficiency notice. *Abatti,* 644 F.2d at 1389; *Barnes,* 408 F.2d at 69; *Stevenson,* 43 T.C.M. (CCH) at 290. The Tax Court's jurisdiction would have been established, even though the Commissioner relied on the wrong tax shelter in making the determination.

[n.2] "It may well be true that the [Commissioner] erred in his determination that a deficiency existed for this period. But when he once determined that there was a deficiency, that fact gives us jurisdiction to determine whether or not it was correctly arrived at." H. Milgrim & Bros. v. Commissioner, 24 B.T.A. 853, 854 (1931).

The key question is whether the inclusion of an erroneous Form 5278, which purports to explain the deficiency in terms of an unrelated tax shelter, invalidates the deficiency notice. I believe the inclusion of the wrong Form 5278 constitutes a preparation error which does not invalidate the deficiency notice. "An error in a notice of deficiency, which otherwise fulfills its purpose, will be ignored where the taxpayer is not misled thereby and is provided by it with information sufficient for the preparation of his case for trial." Meyers v. Commissioner, 81 T.C.M. (P-H) 276, 278 (1981). Here, the taxpayers were not misled by the stray Form 5278 because they had notice from the IRS that a mistake had been made before the Tax Court had set a trial date for either the 1977 or 1978 disputes concerning the videotape tax shelter.

The majority escapes from under the undesirable weight of authority requiring that the validity of a deficiency notice be determined primarily by its form by distinguishing these cases as not addressing the challenge that no determination was made by the Commissioner. In light of the emphasis of this authority on the form of the deficiency notice, I cannot agree with such a strained interpretation of these cases. *See* B. Bittker, FEDERAL TAXATION ¶ 115.2.2 at 115-12 ("the requirement of an IRS *determination* coalesces with the requirement of a *notice* of deficiency, since the usual evidence that a deficiency has been 'determined' is the notice") (emphasis in original)

For example, in *Hannan v. Commissioner*, 52 T.C. 787 (1969), the Tax Court concluded that there was a valid notice of deficiency, despite the Commissioner's contentions that he neither determined a deficiency nor sought to collect one. The Tax Court rejected the Commissioner's position and found it had jurisdiction:

> Here petitioners were sent a letter which admittedly meets all the formal requirements of a statutory notice of deficiency, notifying them that "We [respondent] have determined the income tax deficiencies shown above" and listing tax deficiencies and additions to tax under section 6651(a). This was a determination of a deficiency in tax, even though, as respondent argues, on trial it may develop that there is in fact no deficiency.

Id. at 791 (footnotes omitted).

The majority misreads *Hannan* in denying that *Hannan* stands for the proposition that deficiency notices are to be judged on their face, rather than on the substance of the Commissioner's determination. * * * It is true that the Tax Court partly explained its decision by stating that there was no proof that the Commissioner was not in fact asserting a deficiency and that the taxpayers could only protect their interests by filing a petition. Although one might read this statement as implying that the Tax Court based its decision on more than a facial examination of the deficiency notice, I understand the Tax Court to mean that because the notice was ambiguous, the taxpayers had no alternative but to file a petition. This concern does not detract from the court's emphasis on the *form* of the deficiency notice.

Judging the deficiency notice in this case by the standards discussed above, I believe that the notice warned the taxpayers that the Commissioner had, rightly or wrongly, determined a deficiency and that the notice complied with the formal requirements of section 6212(a). The Commissioner clearly determined that the taxpayers had invested in a tax shelter without economic substance in order to avoid taxes. The inclusion of an erroneous explanation of the basis of the deficiency should not in itself deprive the Tax Court of jurisdiction to decide the question of whether the Commissioner can sustain the asserted deficiency.

The majority contends that here, it "need not look beyond the notice sent to the taxpayers to determine its invalidity." * * * This, however, is exactly what the majority requires when it concludes that the "determination" requirement is only satisfied where the Commissioner shows he has determined a deficiency with respect to a particular taxpayer beyond the notice itself.[n.4]

As a matter of tax policy, the rule against looking behind the deficiency notice appears to be well-grounded in the administrative necessities of the Commissioner's job. The Commissioner must administer tens of thousands of deficiency notices per year. A requirement that he prove the basis of his determination before the Tax Court can assert jurisdiction would unduly burden both the Commissioner and the Tax Court.

In addition, the majority's ruling that the inclusion of an erroneous explanation invalidates a deficiency notice creates an incentive for the Commissioner not to disclose his theory for asserting a deficiency when he sends the deficiency notice. If the Commissioner discloses his theory at this stage, the majority's rule invites every taxpayer to litigate whether the Commissioner has made a determination before litigating the merits.[n.5] Because it is to the

---

[n.4] The majority * * * makes much of the government's statement that, "In order to protect the government's interest and since your original income tax return is unavailable at this time, the income tax is being assessed at the maximum rate of 70%." The majority points to this statement as evidence supporting their conclusion that the Commissioner did not make a determination. I disagree.

Although the "unavailability" of the Scars' return may indicate that the Scars' original paper return was not before the Commissioner, it does not show that specific data on that return or relating to the video-tape tax shelter was not considered. Due to the computerization of the IRS, the Commissioner no longer operates from original paper returns. See, e.g., Murphy, *Glitches and Crashes at the IRS,* TIME, Apr. 29, 1985, at 71; *New Machines Helping IRS,* Dun's Business Month, Jan. 1984, at 24; IRS, *1980 Annual Report,* 9, 14, 42–43 (1981). With well over 100 million income tax returns plus an even larger number of information returns, such as Forms W-2's and 1099's, being filed annually, it is no wonder the Commissioner has turned to the computer. See Klott, *Fewer IRS Workers to Process Tax Returns,* N.Y. Times, Dec. 24, 1986, at 30, col. 3; IRS, *1981 Annual Report* 5, 42–43 (Table 6) (1982). When a return is filed in a Service Center, pertinent summary data is entered into the computer system. *1980 Report* at 14; Quaglietta, *How IRS Service Centers Process Returns,* 16 Prac. Acct. 63 (1983). Such summary data includes the fact that a return was filed, whether the tax was paid or a refund check was mailed, and other data needed to match information returns with the taxpayer's return. See *1980 Report* at 4, 14; Cloonan, *Compliance Programs,* 16 Prac. Acct. 67 (1983). This matching is done by computer. *1980 Report* at 4, 14; Walbert, *A Net Too Wide,* FORBES, Mar. 12, 1984, at 154. It is conceivable that the Commissioner had enough information on the computer to match information regarding both the tax shelter promoted by Executive Productions, Inc. and the Scars' suspect 1977 return to their 1978 income tax taxpayer's return, but not enough to determine the exact amount of a deficiency without calling up from storage the actual return. Thus, the Commissioner assessed the Scars at the 70% rate.

As of 1980, the Commissioner had identified approximately 27,000 abusive tax shelters. *1980 Report* at 3. In light of this number, the punching of the wrong computer key during an audit at the partnership level is a viable explanation for the unfortunate error of one of the 26,999 inapplicable tax shelters popping up and then being entered on the Scars' Form 5278.

So, as a result of the need to computerize information regarding the millions of filed returns and the huge number of tax shelters, we have a reasonable explanation for the two errors on the gratuitously prepared Form 5278 (the wrong shelter and the wrong tax rate of 70%). The taxpayer could have contested these errors and probably would have settled the amount of the tax due promptly. The importance of these errors is further undermined by the fact that they are found in Form 5278, which the Commissioner is not required to send with the basic deficiency notice, Form 892. *See ante* n.1.

[n.5] This "invitation to litigation" represents a major step backward for those of us who believe that litigation should be streamlined, attorneys' fees should be kept within reasonable bounds, and courts should not be further over-burdened.

taxpayer's advantage that the Commissioner disclose his theory when the notice is sent, I believe it is undesirable to establish a rule which would discourage him from doing so. *See* Stewart v. Commissioner, 714 F.2d 977, 986 (9th Cir. 1983).

I view this case as presenting two related policy goals. One goal is to ensure that early in the assessment procedure each individual taxpayer receives fair notice as to the theory on which the Commissioner based his deficiency. The other goal is to encourage the Commissioner to disclose the theory on which he intends to rely in the deficiency notice whenever possible. However, because the Commissioner is not required to disclose his theory in the notice, the majority's rule that invalidates a deficiency notice accompanied with an erroneous description encourages the Commissioner to issue deficiency notices without *any* explanation. Such a rule detracts from the goal of early notice and taxpayers, on the whole, will suffer because the Commissioner is likely to use the deficiency notice solely for jurisdictional purposes and only thereafter reveal his reasons for issuing the notice. I believe that preserving the Tax Court tradition of not looking behind the deficiency notice promotes the goal of ensuring early notice to the taxpayer.

Finally, alternative remedies exist to protect the taxpayer's interests besides dismissal of the case for lack of jurisdiction. If the taxpayers are confused by the Commissioner's theory or explanation supporting the deficiency, they may seek clarification prior to trial. The Tax Court Rules "contemplate that after the case is at issue the parties will informally confer in order to exchange necessary facts, documents, and other data with a view towards defining and narrowing the areas of dispute. Rules 38, 70(a)(1), 91(a)." *Foster*, 80 T.C. at 230. *See also Stevenson*, 43 T.C.M. (CCH) at 291. Here, the informal contacts between the parties resulted in the Commissioner's disclosure of his mistake within two months of when the taxpayers filed their petition for redetermination in the Tax Court.

Furthermore, the presumed correctness of the Commissioner's deficiency notice disappears if the deficiency is arbitrary or capricious, since the burden of proof then shifts to the Commissioner. Helvering v. Taylor, 293 U.S. 507, 513–16, 79 L. Ed. 623, 55 S. Ct. 287 (1935); Weimerskirch v. Commissioner, 596 F.2d 358, 362 & n.8 (9th Cir. 1979); Jackson v. Commissioner, 73 T.C. 394, 401(1979). *See also* Rule 142(a).[13]

These measures are more than adequate to prevent the Commissioner from littering the country with baseless deficiency notices. *Scar*, 81 T.C. at 869 (Sterrett, J., dissenting). The precedent holding that the validity of the deficiency notice is to be determined on its face was effective in furthering

---

[13] [Now Interim Rule 142(a)(1). Eds.]

policy goals which benefit the taxpayer and the public. The majority's opinion sabotages the machinery of tax collection, thereby portending injury to the taxpayer and to the public. I therefore dissent.

Do you agree with the court's holding in *Scar* that failure to make a thoughtful "determination" invalidates a notice of deficiency? Is the dissent's approach better? Is there some other remedy the *Scar* majority could have applied to correct the errors in the notice of deficiency and/or to encourage the IRS to be more careful when sending out future notices?

In the following case, the taxpayer raised the *Scar* issue. Note how his case differs from *Scar*.

PORTILLO v. COMMISSIONER
United States Court of Appeals, Fifth Circuit
932 F.2d 1128 (1991)

GOLDBERG, CIRCUIT JUDGE:

Ramon Portillo appeals from the Tax Court's rejection of his challenge to a notice of deficiency from the Internal Revenue Service (the "I.R.S."). Portillo initially argues that the simple computerized matching of Portillo's employer's Form 1099 with Portillo's Form 1040 was not a "determination" as required by section 6212(a) of the Internal Revenue Code (the "Code"). We reject this argument, finding that the I.R.S. adequately linked Portillo to the alleged deficiency. We do agree with Portillo, however, that the notice of deficiency was arbitrary and erroneous because the I.R.S. failed to substantiate in any way its claim that Portillo received unreported income.

We readily affirm, however, the Tax Court's refusal to reconstruct Portillo's expenses for eighteen weeks in which Portillo was not able to document his expenditures. The Tax Court correctly determined that Portillo failed to meet his burden of proof that he actually incurred these expenses.

FACTS AND PROCEEDINGS BELOW

Ramon Portillo is a self-employed painting subcontractor who lived and worked in El Paso, Texas during 1984, the tax year in question. In 1984, Portillo bid for contracts to paint both residential and commercial property. According to Portillo, the general contractor he subcontracted for would pay him weekly, usually by check, for the work his crew performed. Portillo would then record his total receipts in the gross receipt portion of a ledger book he kept for his business. Since Portillo did not have a bank account, he would cash the contractor's check and then pay his workers in cash. Portillo kept a separate ledger to record his payroll expenses.

Typically, Portillo purchased all of his own supplies for his work. Portillo purchased most of these supplies from the Hanley Paint Store. Each Friday he would pay the supply store for the week's supplies and record these payments into the ledger as costs of goods sold. As a favor to Portillo, Hanley

Paint Store kept copies of their invoices for these supplies, apparently with the intention that they would return them to Portillo each year end.

At the end of the year, Portillo would meet with Mrs. Rosales, a bookkeeper with Independent Businessman Bookkeeping and Tax Services, Inc., so that she could prepare his taxes. Portillo would total the gross receipts from his ledger and give them to Rosales as a basis for his Form 1040 gross income. Portillo used the Form 1099's from his various employers to confirm the gross receipts amounts. In 1984, however, Portillo had not received a 1099 from one of the contractors, Mr. Navarro, when Rosales was preparing his Form 1040. Therefore, Portillo determined his gross receipts from Navarro solely from his ledger.

On his 1984 federal income tax return, Portillo reported gross receipts in the amount of $ 142,108.93 and deductions of $ 30,917 for costs of goods sold. Included in the amount of gross receipts was $ 10,800 reported as the amount Navarro paid to Portillo. Sometime in mid-1985, Navarro filed a Form 1099 reporting payments to Portillo in the amount of $ 35,305, which was significantly more than Portillo had reported receiving from him.

In January 1987, the I.R.S. audited Portillo's 1984 tax return. At the time of the audit, Portillo could not produce any records or receipts concerning his gross receipts for 1984 because his ledger was stolen from his truck in 1985. In addition, Portillo was unable to produce invoices for materials and supplies purchased during eighteen weeks in 1984 because he had relied on Hanley Paint Store to save these for him and they apparently lost a portion of these invoices. Portillo claimed he had worked continuously during these eighteen weeks, except for holidays and during inclement weather.

Based on the discrepancy between Navarro's 1099 and Portillo's 1040 forms, I.R.S. Agent Shumate determined that Portillo had not reported $ 24,505 in income from Navarro. Although Portillo acknowledged that he inadvertently neglected to report $ 3,125 in income from Navarro, Portillo denied receiving any more than $ 13,925 from Navarro. Shumate contacted Navarro who could produce copies of checks paid to Portillo in the amount of $ 13,925, but could not produce records justifying the remaining $ 21,380 he claims he paid Portillo in cash.

Shumate used an indirect method of reconstructing Portillo's income and made an adjustment to incorporate the increased amount into Portillo's income for the year. An I.R.S. reviewer, Glenda Jackson, analyzed Shumate's report. She did not believe the indirect method of confirming the income supported Shumate's adjustment. Jackson stated that there appeared to be several ways to follow up to check if the taxpayer could have received the cash, and she recommended that Shumate check Navarro's tax return.

Shumate replied to this review by stating that it was Portillo's burden to prove that he did not get the payments. The I.R.S. took the position that Navarro's Form 1099 was presumed correct. Therefore the I.R.S. issued a statutory notice of deficiency for federal income taxes of $ 8,473 for the taxable year 1984, plus penalties assessed under Code sections 6653(a)(1), (a)(2), and 6661(a).

The Portillos filed a petition for redetermination of this alleged tax deficiency in Tax Court. The Tax Court held for the government, finding that

Portillo had not met his burden of proving that he had not received the additional income from Navarro. * * *

DISCUSSION

A. Unreported Income

The Tax Court's interpretation of section 6212(a) of the Code is reviewable *de novo. See* Rutter v. Commissioner, 853 F.2d 1267 (5th Cir. 1988); Scar v. Commissioner, 814 F.2d 1363 (9th Cir. 1987). Section 6212(a) states in part: "If the Secretary determines that there is a deficiency in respect of any tax imposed . . . he is authorized to send notice of such deficiency to the taxpayer by certified mail or registered mail." Section 6213(a) provides in part: "Within 90 days . . . after the notice of deficiency authorized in section 6212 is mailed . . . taxpayer may file a petition with the Tax Court for a redetermination of the deficiency." Therefore, the Tax Court only has jurisdiction when the Commissioner issues a valid deficiency notice and the taxpayer files a timely petition for redetermination. Stamm Int'l Corp. v. Commissioner, 84 T.C. 248, 252 (1985).

Although there is no prescribed form for a deficiency notice, the notice must at a minimum (1) advise the taxpayer that the I.R.S. has determined that a deficiency exists for a particular year, and (2) specify the amount of the deficiency or provide the information necessary to compute the deficiency. Donley v. Commissioner, 791 F.2d 383 (5th Cir. 1986). As Portillo correctly points out, in order for a notice of deficiency to be valid, the I.R.S. must have made a "determination" of a tax deficiency. *See* 26 U.S.C. § 6212(a). Portillo argues that in this case the I.R.S. failed to make such a "determination" and therefore the notice was invalid and the tax court consequently lacked jurisdiction.

Remarkably few cases have considered what requirements must be met before the I.R.S. can say that it has made a "determination." The courts which have dealt with this issue have held that a determination as contemplated by section 6212(a) means "a thoughtful and considered determination that the United States is entitled to an amount not yet paid." *Scar,* 814 F.2d at 1369 (quoting Couzens v. Commissioner, 11 B.T.A. 1040, 1159–60 (1928)). In Terminal Wine Co. v. Commissioner, 1 B.T.A. 697, 701 (1925), the Board of Tax Appeals construed the meaning of the term "determine" as applied to deficiency determinations as follows: "By its very definition and etymology the word 'determination' irresistibly connotes consideration, resolution, conclusion, and judgment."

Portillo argues that in this case the I.R.S. failed to make a "determination" because the I.R.S. merely matched Navarro's Form 1099 with Portillo's Form 1040 without ever attempting to establish the reliability of Navarro's 1099 filing. According to Portillo, this lacked any indicia of a "thoughtful and considered determination" and therefore was insufficient under section 6212(a). The I.R.S. maintains, however, that all that is required for a determination is that the Commissioner consider information relating to the particular taxpayer. *See Scar,* 814 F.2d at 1368; *see also* Abrams v. Commissioner, 787 F.2d 939, 940–41 (4th Cir.), *cert. denied,* 479 U.S. 882, 107 S. Ct. 271, 93 L.

Ed. 2d 248 (1986); Benzvi v. Commissioner, 787 F.2d 1541, 1543 (11th Cir.), *cert. denied,* 479 U.S. 883, 107 S. Ct. 273, 93 L. Ed. 2d 250 (1986).

In *Scar,* one of the few cases finding that the I.R.S. failed to make a determination, the Ninth Circuit held that the tax court should have dismissed the action for want of jurisdiction because the purported notice of deficiency revealed on its face that no determination of tax deficiency had been made. *Scar,* 814 F.2d at 1370. In *Scar* the Commissioner acknowledged that the notice of deficiency referred to a tax shelter that had no connection with the taxpayer's return. *Id.* at 1368. Consequently, it was apparent that the notice of deficiency was not the result of a determination based on the taxpayers' return. Therefore the court held that the Commissioner had failed to make a "determination."

In contrast to *Scar,* in this case the I.R.S. did consider information directly relating to Portillo's income tax return. The I.R.S. also investigated somewhat whether a deficiency indeed existed. Therefore, this is not a case where the I.R.S. had no basis for sending the notice of deficiency; the I.R.S. did adequately link the deficiency to Portillo.

Portillo argues that if this court should find that the Commissioner did in fact make a substantive determination, the ensuing notice of deficiency was nevertheless arbitrary and erroneous. In addressing this argument, we begin with the well settled principle that the government's deficiency assessment is generally afforded a presumption of correctness. *See* United States v. Janis, 428 U.S. 433, 441, 96 S. Ct. 3021, 3025, 49 L. Ed. 2d 1046 (1976); Helvering v. Taylor, 293 U.S. 507, 515, 55 S. Ct. 287, 290, 79 L. Ed. 623 (1935). This presumption is a procedural device that places the burden of producing evidence to rebut the presumption on the taxpayer. *See Janis,* 428 U.S. at 441, 96 S. Ct. at 3025; Anastasato v. Commissioner, 794 F.2d 884, 886 (3d Cir. 1986). In essence, the taxpayer's burden of proof and the presumption of correctness are for the most part merely opposite sides of a single coin; they combine to require the taxpayer to prove by a preponderance of the evidence that the Commissioner's determination was erroneous. Carson v. United States, 560 F.2d 693, 695–96 (5th Cir. 1977); *see also Janis,* 428 U.S. at 440, 96 S. Ct. at 3025; Bar L Ranch, Inc. v. Phinney, 426 F.2d 995, 998 (5th Cir. 1970).

In a Tax Court deficiency proceeding, like this one, once the taxpayer has established that the assessment is arbitrary and erroneous, the burden shifts to the government to prove the correct amount of any taxes owed. In a refund suit, on the other hand, the taxpayer bears the burden of proving both the excessiveness of the assessment and the correct amount of any refund to which he is entitled. *Carson,* 560 F.2d at 696; *see also Janis,* 428 U.S. at 440, 96 S. Ct. at 3025.

The presumption of correctness generally prohibits a court from looking behind the Commissioner's determination even though it may be based on hearsay or other evidence inadmissible at trial. *See* Clapp v. Commissioner, 875 F.2d 1396, 1402–03 (9th Cir. 1989); Zuhone v. Commissioner, 883 F.2d 1317, 1326 (7th Cir. 1989); Dellacroce v. Commissioner, 83 T.C. 269, 280 (1984). Justification for the presumption of correctness lies in the government's strong need to accomplish swift collection of revenues and in the need to encourage taxpayer recordkeeping. *Carson*, 560 F.2d at 696. The need for tax collection does not serve to excuse the government, however, from providing some factual foundation for its assessments. *Id*. "The tax collector's presumption of correctness has a Herculean muscularity of Goliathlike reach, but we strike an Achilles' heel when we find no muscles, no tendons, no ligaments of fact." *Id*.

In this case we find that the notice of deficiency lacks any "ligaments of fact." As the Supreme Court has held, the presumption of correctness does not apply when the government's assessment falls within a narrow but important category of a " 'naked' assessment without any foundation whatsoever . . . ." *Janis*, 428 U.S. at 442, 96 S. Ct. at 3026. Several courts, including this one, have noted that a court need not give effect to the presumption of correctness in a case involving unreported income if the Commissioner cannot present some predicate evidence supporting its determination. *Carson*, 560 F.2d at 696; *Anastasato*, 794 F.2d at 887; Weimerskirch v. Commissioner, 596 F.2d 358, 360 (9th Cir. 1979); Pizzarello v. United States, 408 F.2d 579 (2d Cir.), *cert. denied,* 396 U.S. 986, 90 S. Ct. 481, 24 L. Ed. 2d 450 (1969). Although a number of these cases involved unreported illegal income, given the obvious difficulties in proving the nonreceipt of income,[n.2] we agree with the Third Circuit that this principle should apply whether the unreported income was allegedly obtained legally or illegally. *See Anastasato,* 794 F.2d at 887.

Therefore, before we will give the Commissioner the benefit of the presumption of correctness, he must engage in one final foray for truth in order to provide the court with some indicia that the taxpayer received unreported income. The Commissioner would merely need to attempt to substantiate the charge of unreported income by some other means, such as by showing the taxpayer's net worth, bank deposits, cash expenditures, or source and application of funds. *See Weimerskirch,* 596 F.2d at 362. In these types of unreported income cases, the Commissioner would not be able to choose to rely solely upon the naked assertion that the taxpayer received a certain amount of unreported income for the tax period in question.

In this case the Commissioner's determination that Portillo had received unreported income of $ 24,505 from Navarro was arbitrary. The Commissioner's determination was based solely on a Form 1099 Navarro sent to the I.R.S. indicating that he paid Portillo $ 24,505 more than Portillo had reported on his return. The Commissioner merely matched Navarro's Form 1099 with Portillo's Form 1040 and arbitrarily decided to attribute veracity to Navarro and assume that Portillo's Form 1040 was false. Navarro, however, was not able to document $ 21,380 of cash payments he allegedly made to Portillo. In a situation like this, the Commissioner had some duty to investigate Navarro's bald assertion of payment and determine if Navarro's position was supported by his books, receipts, or other records.

In addition, the Commissioner failed to substantiate by any other means, such as analyzing Portillo's cash expenditures or his source and application

---

[n.2] The Supreme Court has specifically noted that "as a practical matter it is never easy to prove a negative." Elkins v. United States, 364 U.S. 206, 218, 80 S. Ct. 1437, 1444, 4 L. Ed. 2d 1669 (1960); *see also Weimerskirch,* 596 F.2d at 361.

of funds, his charge that Portillo received unreported income. Instead, the Commissioner merely chose to rely upon the presumption of correctness. We hold in situations like this involving unreported income, the presumption of correctness does not apply to the notice of deficiency.

In summary, we find that the Tax Court had jurisdiction to consider this case because the Commissioner did issue a valid deficiency notice. However, since the Commissioner failed to substantiate his charge that Portillo received cash payments from Navarro, the deficiency determination is clearly arbitrary and erroneous. Therefore, the judgment below regarding unreported income must be reversed.

* * *

CONCLUSION

The portion of the Tax Court's judgment regarding the unreported income is reversed. The portion of the Tax Court's judgment regarding the cost of goods sold deduction is affirmed. The judgment is remanded for the limited purpose of recalculating the net tax, interest and penalties due from Portillo in accordance with this opinion.

What doctrine does *Portillo* draw upon in deciding how to handle the discrepancy between Navarro's 1099 Form and Portillo's Form 1040? If instead of relying on a Form 1099 to determine a deficiency, the IRS relied on the taxpayers' consent with a state government for increased state income taxes for the years in question, would that raise the same concerns? In *Sunik v. Commissioner*, T.C. Memo. 2001-195, the Tax Court distinguished *Portillo* on the ground that the IRS relied not on the statement of a third party, but on the taxpayers' agreement to an increase in their income.

After reading both *Scar* and *Portillo*, do you think a court would or should invalidate a notice of deficiency for failure to notify the taxpayer of his right to contact the local office of the taxpayer advocate, as is now required by section 6212? Consider also *Smith* and *Rochelle*, discussed above in Section 7.02[B], which held valid notices that omitted the deadline date to file a Tax Court petition.

Morgan v. Commissioner, T.C. Memo. 2000-231, *aff'd*, 2001 U.S. App. LEXIS 27105 (9th Cir. 2001) (unpublished op.), involved notices of deficiency that allegedly did not contain the taxpayer advocate information required by section 6212. In that case, the Tax Court stated, "[w]e conclude and hold that the notices of deficiency mailed to petitioners' last known address were valid. In so concluding, we reject without further discussion petitioners' assertion that all information required by section 6212(a) must be included on the face of the notice of deficiency in order to comply with that section." In *Morgan*, each notice of deficiency was mailed with a separate notice of taxpayer rights that included a toll-free number to obtain taxpayer advocate assistance, as well as the local phone numbers of taxpayer advocate offices. What might the result be if a notice of deficiency informs the taxpayer of the right to contact the taxpayer advocate, does not include "the location and phone number of the appropriate office," but instead includes the location and phone number of a taxpayer advocate's office in another part of the country?

PROBLEMS

1. On March 4, 2002, the IRS mailed to Peter at his home in San Diego, California a notice of deficiency dated the same day. Peter received the notice on March 8, 2002. When is the last day on which Peter can file a timely Tax Court petition?

2. Kyle recently received a notice of deficiency from the IRS. The asserted deficiency amount was $25,000, and the only explanation was "unreported income." Kyle claims that all of his income was from wages, interest, and dividends, which he duly reported on his return. Kyle timely petitioned the Tax Court in response to the notice. Under current law, who will bear the burden of going forward? Who will bear the burden of persuasion?

3. George received a notice of deficiency on February 20, 1999 with respect to his 1995 return. The notice of deficiency is based on unreported income. George timely petitioned the Tax Court on April 9, 1999. Several months before trial, on June 1, 2000, the IRS raised an additional issue (the disallowance of certain deductions on his 1995 return), and moved to amend its answer to the petition. What procedural defenses or arguments can George raise with respect to the new issue?

4. On April 20, 2000, Sheila received a notice of deficiency from the IRS with respect to her 1996 taxable year. The notice was dated December 1, 1999. It had been mailed to her prior address, where her former roommate still resides. Sheila filed her 1997 and 1998 returns after moving to her current address, and that address was on those returns. Sheila also has a forwarding order in with the Post Office, but they delivered the notice to her old address anyway. Her former roommate apparently received the envelope but did not open it. She finally put it in the mail to Sheila with some other documents; Sheila received it yesterday and brought it to you to ask what to do. She is concerned because the notice reflects an asserted deficiency of $50,000, which she cannot afford to pay in full. What do you advise?

5. Sabrina Brown, who is single, has just received a notice of deficiency from the IRS, and she is not sure how to respond to it. Sabrina would like to know the deadline, if any, for petitioning the United States Tax Court, and the likelihood that she will be able to convince the court to dismiss the case on procedural grounds. Please respond accordingly, for each of the following *alternative* scenarios:

A. The notice of deficiency was erroneously mailed to Sabina's mother's house in another state. Sabrina has not lived there for several years, and has used her own address on her tax returns since she moved out of her mother's house. Her mother received the notice, which was dated and postmarked January 3 of this year, on January 7. On February 1, her mother put the notice in the mail, and Sabrina received it on February 4.

B. The notice was mailed to Sabrina where she currently resides, but instead of reflecting her correct apartment number, 304, the address listed apartment number 403. The error resulted in a delivery delay of several days, so that although the notice was dated January 3, Sabrina received it on January 12.

C. The notice was mailed to Sabrina's current residence, and her address and Social Security number were completely correct. She received the notice, which was mailed on January 3, on January 6. However, the notice was addressed to "Mr. and Mrs. Sabrina and Gerald Brown," although Sabrina has never been married, and does not even know a Gerald Brown. The notice reflects a deficiency of $20,000, based on unreported income from a job as a financial consultant. Sabrina informs you that she is an electrical engineer, with no background or skill in finance. She worked full-time for a single employer during the year in question, as reflected in the sole W-2 she attached to her tax return, and did no consulting work.

6. On May 31, 1999, the IRS mailed Gloria a notice of deficiency with respect to her 1996 tax year. Gloria had filed her 1996 return on April 1, 1997. The IRS erroneously did not send the notice of deficiency to Gloria's last known address. It was ultimately forwarded to Gloria, and she received it on August 15, 1999. Subsequently, an IRS employee who was working on Gloria's case realized that the notice had not been sent to Gloria's last known address. On April 20, 2000, the IRS mailed a duplicate copy of the notice to Gloria's last known address. She received it on April 25, 2000. On June 1, 2000, Gloria petitioned the Tax Court. In her petition, Gloria moved to dismiss the case for lack of jurisdiction on the ground that no notice of deficiency was mailed to her within the time period required by the statute of limitations on assessment.

A. Is the 1999 notice of deficiency invalid?

B. Would your answer to A. differ if Gloria had petitioned the Tax Court on August 20, 1999 instead of June 1, 2000?

C. Assume that the 1999 notice of deficiency was invalid.

    i. Is the notice of deficiency that the IRS mailed in 2000 invalid as a "second notice" under Code section 6212(c)?

ii.   Assume that the notice of deficiency mailed to Gloria
      in the year 2000 is not a prohibited second notice and
      does not suffer from any other infirmities. Under what
      circumstances, if any, would the notice be timely?

Chapter 8

OVERPAYMENTS, REFUND CLAIMS, AND REFUND LITIGATION

Reading Assignment: Code §§ 1311, 1312(1), 6213, 6401(a)–(c), 6402(a), 6404(a), 6511(a)–(c), (h), 6512(a), (b), 6513(a), (b), (d), 6514, 6532(a), (b), 7405, 7422(a), (e); Treas. Reg. § 301.6402-2.

§ 8.01 Introduction: Overview of Refund Claims and Refund Suits

If a taxpayer realizes that he has overpaid his taxes, whether through withholding or otherwise, how does he go about obtaining a refund of the overpayment? If the taxpayer is filing his initial income tax return for the year, the taxpayer can simply claim the refund on that return. If the taxpayer seeks an income tax refund after having already filed a return, but without having received a notice of deficiency from the IRS, the taxpayer must file an amended return claiming the refund. *See* I.R.C. § 7422(a).

Refund claims also arise routinely out of audits. If, in the course of an audit, the taxpayer realizes that he made an overpayment, he may file a refund claim at that point. In fact, even if the IRS has already sent the taxpayer a notice of deficiency, the taxpayer can both contest the deficiency and pursue a refund of an overpayment. The notice of deficiency provides the taxpayer with a choice of responses. As you know from Chapter 7, the notice of deficiency affords the taxpayer the right to petition the Tax Court and request a review of the asserted deficiency. As explained in this chapter, the Tax Court also has jurisdiction with respect to overpayment claims arising out of the same tax year for which the taxpayer receives a notice of deficiency and files a petition. I.R.C. § 6512(b)(1). The taxpayer simply must allege in the petition that he made an overpayment of taxes. The taxpayer's alternative to petitioning the Tax Court is to pay the asserted deficiency and file a refund claim for both the amount paid in response to the notice and the prior overpayment. Upon disallowance of the claim, waiver of disallowance, or after waiting six months, I.R.C. § 6532(a)(1), the taxpayer can sue the IRS in either District Court or the Court of Federal Claims, I.R.C. § 7422(a); 28 U.S.C. § 1346(a)(1). The taxpayer may not file suit once two years have passed from the date of the notice of disallowance was mailed or the taxpayer's waiver was filed.

> *Example*: Sara filed her 1999 return on April 17, 2000. Her return showed a tax liability of $10,000, $9,000 of which was covered through withholding, and the remaining $1,000 of which was sent in with her return. The IRS mailed Sara a notice of deficiency on

March 1, 2002, alleging that she has a deficiency of $2,000 attributable to unreported income. Sara disagrees, and upon examining her records, discovers that she failed to take an allowable deduction that would have saved her $500 in taxes. Sara has a choice. She can petition the Tax Court, contesting the $2,000 deficiency and pursuing the $500 overpayment as well. Alternatively, Sara can pay the $2,000 deficiency and claim a refund of $2,500 from the IRS, with an eye toward eventual refund litigation if the IRS denies her claim. [1]

Refund claims can also arise in other circumstances. For example, in *United States v. Williams*, 514 U.S. 527 (1995), Lori Williams paid under protest a tax for which she was not liable, and then claimed a refund of the amount paid. The tax had been assessed against her ex-husband, and a tax lien placed on the home Ms. Williams owned jointly with him, which she had received in a divorce without notice of the lien. *Id.* at 529–530. In *Williams*, the United States Supreme Court held that Ms. Williams had standing to sue for the refund after the denial of her claim, although the tax had not been assessed against her. *See id.* at 530–531.

§ 8.02 Refund Claims

[A] Overpayments of Tax

In general, to obtain a refund from the IRS, a taxpayer must have made an "overpayment" of tax. What is an "overpayment"? The Code does not specifically define the term. However, Code section 6401(a) provides that an overpayment "includes" payment of any internal revenue tax that is assessed or collected after the applicable statute of limitations has expired. In addition, refundable credits that exceed the amount of income tax imposed for the year are "considered" overpayments of tax. I.R.C. § 6401(b). Excessive withholding tax and estimated tax payments are therefore treated as overpayments. Furthermore, Code section 6401(c) provides that an amount paid as tax may constitute an overpayment even if there is no tax liability for which the tax was paid.

In *Jones v. Liberty Glass Co.*, 332 U.S. 524, 531–32 (1947), the United States Supreme Court considered what constitutes an overpayment, stating:

> In the absence of some contrary indication, we must assume that the framers of these statutory provisions intended to convey the ordinary meaning which is attached to the language they used. *See* Rosenman v. United States, 323 U.S. 658, 661. Hence we read the word "overpayment" in its usual sense, as meaning any payment in excess of that which is properly due. Such an excess payment may be traced to an error in mathematics or in judgment or in interpretation of facts or law. And the error may be committed by the taxpayer

---

[1] As indicated above, the statutes of limitations on refund suits restrict Sara to acting within certain time periods. The statutes of limitations on refund claims do too. These statutes are discussed in detail later in the chapter.

or by the revenue agents. Whatever the reason, the payment of more than is rightfully due is what characterizes an overpayment.

That this ordinary meaning is the one intended by the authors of § 322(b)(1) [currently I.R.C. § 6511. Eds.] is quite evident from the legislative history which we have detailed. The word "overpayment" first appeared in § 281 of the 1924 Revenue Act, one of the direct ancestors of § 322(b)(1). The word was there used as a substitute for the previous reference to payments "in excess of that properly due," a phrase that is a perfect definition of an overpayment and that is not necessarily confined to overpayments occasioned by errors made by taxpayers. The immediate predecessor of § 281 had employed that phrase and had been enacted in 1923 with the expressed intention of including claims growing out of illegal assessments. There was not the slightest indication that the substitution of the word "overpayment" was designed to narrow the scope of § 281. It apparently was a mere simplification in phraseology. But it does make clear the sense in which the word was first used in this context. The generic character of the word was emphasized from the start. And we see no basis for making it over into a word of art at this late date.

Under the Supreme Court's approach to overpayments, what two pieces of information do you need to compute an overpayment? In what circumstances might a taxpayer have made an overpayment of tax?

[B] Which Remittances are "Payments"?

An overpayment requires that the taxpayer have made a "payment" of tax. Superficially, it might seem that any remittance by the taxpayer to the IRS is a tax payment. But, in fact, some remittances are mere "deposits" that do not become payments until some time later, if ever. A deposit is refundable to the taxpayer at any time, but a payment is not. As discussed later in this chapter, a taxpayer must follow specific procedures, including filing a timely refund claim, to obtain a refund of a payment.

Generally, the reason a taxpayer may make an early remittance is to stop the running of interest, as discussed in Chapter 11. Because both "payments" and "deposits" suspend further interest accruals, the taxpayer may not initially make clear to the IRS which he intended his remittance to be. For statute of limitations purposes, however, the date of "payment" is key. As a result, many cases distinguishing between payments and deposits arise in the context of the statute of limitations on refund claims. The following case is no exception:

ROSENMAN v. UNITED STATES
United States Supreme Court
323 U.S. 658 (1945)

MR. JUSTICE FRANKFURTER delivered the opinion of the Court.

* * *

Petitioners are executors of the will of Louis Rosenman, who died on December 25, 1933. Under appropriate statutory authority, the Commissioner of Internal Revenue extended the time for filing the estate tax return to February 25, 1935. But there was no extension of the time for payment of the tax which became due one year after the decedent's death, on December 25, 1934. The day before, petitioners delivered to the Collector of Internal Revenue a check for $120,000, the purpose of which was thus defined in a letter of transmittal: "We are delivering to you herewith, by messenger, an Estate check payable to your order, for $120,000, as a payment on account of the Federal Estate tax . . . . This payment is made under protest and duress, and solely for the purpose of avoiding penalties and interest, since it is contended by the executors that not all of this sum is legally or lawfully due." This amount was placed by the Collector in a suspense account to the credit of the estate. In the books of the Collector the suspense account concerns moneys received in connection with federal estate taxes and other miscellaneous taxes if, as here, no assessment for taxes is outstanding at the time. On February 25, 1935, petitioners filed their estate tax return according to which there was due from the estate $80,224.24. On March 28, 1935, the Collector advised petitioners that $80,224.24 of the $120,000 to their credit in the suspense account had been applied in satisfaction of the amount of the tax assessed under their return. On the basis of this notice, petitioners, on March 26, 1938, filed a claim for $39,775.76, the balance between the $120,000 paid by them under protest and the assessed tax of $80,224.24.

Upon completion, after nearly three years, of the audit of the return, the Commissioner determined that the total net tax due was $128,759.08. No appeal to the Board of Tax Appeals having been taken, a deficiency of $48,534.84 was assessed. The Collector thereupon applied the balance of $39,775.76 standing to the credit of petitioners in the suspense account in partial satisfaction of this deficiency, and on April 22, 1938, petitioners paid to the Collector the additional amount of $10,497.34, which covered the remainder of the deficiency plus interest. The Commissioner then rejected the petitioners' claim for refund filed in March of that year. On May 20, 1940, petitioners filed with the Collector a claim, based on additional deductions, for refund of $24,717.12. The claim was rejected on the ground, so far as now relevant, that the tax claimed to have been illegally exacted had been paid more than three years prior to the filing of the claim, except as to the amount of $10,497.34 paid by petitioners in 1938. Petitioners brought this suit in the Court of Claims which held that recovery for the amount here in dispute was barred by statute, 53 F. Supp. 722. To resolve an asserted conflict of decisions in the lower courts we brought the case here.

Claims for tax refunds must conform strictly to the requirements of Congress. A claim for refund of an estate tax "alleged to have been erroneously or illegally assessed or collected must be presented to the Commissioner within three years next after the payment of such tax." On the face of it, this requirement is couched in ordinary English, and, since no extraneous relevant aids to construction have been called to our attention, Congress has evidently meant what these words ordinarily convey. The claim is for refund of a tax "alleged to have been erroneously or illegally assessed or collected," and the claim must have been filed "after the payment of such tax," that is, within three years after payment of a tax which according to the claim was erroneously or illegally collected. The crux of the matter is the alleged illegal assessment or collection, and "payment of such tax" plainly presupposes challenged action by the taxing officials.

The action here complained of was the assessment of a deficiency by the Commissioner in April 1938. Before that time there were no taxes "erroneously or illegally assessed or collected" for the collection of which petitioners could have filed a claim for refund. The amount then demanded as a deficiency by the Commissioner was, so the petitioners claimed, erroneously assessed. It is this erroneous assessment that gave rise to a claim for refund. Not until then was there such a claim as could start the time running for presenting the claim. In any responsible sense payment was then made by the application of the balance credited to the petitioners in the suspense account and by the additional payment of $10,497.34 on April 22, 1938. Both these events occurred within three years of May 20, 1940, when the petitioners' present claim was filed.

But the Government contends "payment of such tax" was made on December 24, 1934, when petitioners transferred to the Collector a check for $120,000. This stopped the running of penalties and interest, says the Government, and therefore is to be treated as a payment by the parties. But on December 24, 1934, the taxpayer did not discharge what he deemed a liability nor pay one that was asserted. There was merely an interim arrangement to cover whatever contingencies the future might define. The tax obligation did not become defined until April 1938. And this is the practical construction which the Government has placed upon such arrangements. The Government does not consider such advances of estimated taxes as tax payments. They are, as it were, payments in escrow. They are set aside, as we have noted, in special suspense accounts established for depositing money received when no assessment is then outstanding against the taxpayer. The receipt by the Government of moneys under such an arrangement carries no more significance than would the giving of a surety bond. Money in these accounts is held not as taxes duly collected are held but as a deposit made in the nature of a cash bond for the payment of taxes thereafter found to be due. *See* Ruling of the Comptroller General, A-48307, April 14, 1933, 1 (1935) Prentice-Hall Tax Service, Special Reports, paragraph 45. Accordingly, where taxpayers have sued for interest on the "overpayment" of moneys received under similar conditions, the Government has insisted that the arrangement was merely a "deposit" and not a "payment" interest on which is due from the Government if there is an excess beyond the amount of the tax eventually assessed. *See* Busser v. United States, 130 F.2d 537, 538; Atlantic Oil Producing Co. v. United States, 35 F. Supp. 766; Moses v. United States, 28 F. Supp. 817; Chicago Title & Trust Co. v. United States, 45 F. Supp. 323; Estate of Rogers v. Commissioner, 1942

Prentice-Hall B.T.A. Memorandum Decisions, paragraph 42,275. If it is not payment in order to relieve the Government from paying interest on a subsequently determined excess, it cannot be payment to bar suit by the taxpayer for its illegal retention. It will not do to treat the same transaction as payment and not as payment, whichever favors the Government. *See United States v. Wurts*, 303 U.S. 414. * * * [B]y allowing such a deposit arrangement, the Government safeguards collection of the assessment of whatever amount tax officials may eventually find owing from a taxpayer, while the taxpayer in turn is saved the danger of penalties on an assessment made, as in this case, years after a fairly estimated return has been filed. The construction which in our view the statute compels safeguards the interests of the Government, interprets a business transaction according to its tenor, and avoids gratuitous resentment in the relations between Treasury and taxpayer.

Reversed.

In response to the *Rosenman* decision, courts have manifested confusion over the test for distinguishing a "payment" from a "deposit." Two circuits initially followed a *"per se"* test that treated a remittance as a payment only when made after the tax due had been determined by an IRS assessment or the filing of a return. *See United States v. Dubuque Packing Co.*, 233 F.2d 453, 460 (8th Cir. 1956); *Thomas v. Mercantile Nat'l Bank*, 204 F.2d 943, 944 (5th Cir. 1953). However, subsequent decisions of these courts have criticized this *"per se"* test or have simply failed to apply it. *See Ford v. United States*, 618 F.2d 357, 359–61 (5th Cir. 1980); *Essex v. Vinal*, 499 F.2d 226, 229–30 (8th Cir. 1974), *cert. denied,* 419 U.S. 1107 (1975). Several other circuits have also rejected the *per se* test in favor of a balancing test that looks at the facts and circumstances surrounding the remittance, so that some remittances made prior to assessment are payments, and some are deposits. *See Malachinski v. Commissioner*, 268 F.3d 497, 507 (7th Cir. 2001); *New York Life Ins. Co. v. United States*, 118 F.3d 1553, 1556–57 (Fed. Cir. 1997), *cert. denied,* 523 U.S. 1094 (1998); *Ewing v. United States*, 914 F.2d 499, 503 (4th Cir. 1990), *cert. denied,* 500 U.S. 905 (1991); *Fortugno v. Commissioner*, 353 F.2d 429, 435–36 (3d Cir. 1965).

Some circuits apply the facts and circumstances approach by focusing on the statutory scheme surrounding the type of remittance involved. These courts have held that a remittance made with an application for automatic extension of time to file constitutes a payment as a matter of law. *See, e.g., Ertman v. United States*, 165 F.3d 204 (2d Cir. 1999); *Ott v. United States*, 141 F.3d 1306, 1309–10 (9th Cir. 1998); *Gabelman v. Commissioner*, 86 F.3d 609, 611 (6th Cir. 1996); *Weigand v. United States*, 760 F.2d 1072, 1074 (10th Cir. 1985). However, the Tax Court has held that an undesignated remittance made at a time when no tax liability has been "ascertained or even proposed" will generally be assumed to be a deposit. *See Risman v. Commissioner*, 100 T.C. 191, 197 (1993). *Risman* also involved a remittance with an application for automatic extension of time to file. *See id.* at 193. This case has been criticized by several courts. *See Gabelman*, 86 F.3d at 612; *David v. United States*, 964

F. Supp. 31, 37 (D. Mass. 1997) (adopting magistrate's judgment); *Holtvogt v. United States*, 887 F. Supp. 994, 999 (S.D. Ohio 1995).

In Revenue Procedure 84-58, 1984-2 C.B. 501, the IRS cleared up some of the confusion by issuing guidance concerning whether a remittance would be treated as a payment or a deposit and how the IRS treats undesignated remittances. The primary purpose of the Revenue Procedure is to inform taxpayers how to make remittances that stop the running of interest on deficiencies. The Revenue Procedure is therefore discussed in more detail in Chapter 11. It is worth noting at this point the IRS's distinction between deposits and payments, as relevant to refund claims:

> Rev. Proc. 82-51 distinguished between payments made in satisfaction of a tax liability and "deposits in the nature of a cash bond" made merely to stop the running of interest. A deposit in the nature of a cash bond is not a payment of tax, is not subject to a claim for credit or refund, and, if returned to the taxpayer, does not bear interest. * * *

> Subject to the provisions of subparagraph 3, a remittance made after the mailing of a notice of deficiency in complete or partial satisfaction of the deficiency will, absent any instructions from the taxpayer, be considered a payment of tax and will be posted to the taxpayer's account as such as soon as possible. Such a remittance will not deprive the Tax Court of jurisdiction over the deficiency.

> A remittance made after the mailing of a notice of deficiency but before the expiration of the 90-day or 150-day period, or, if a petition is filed, before the decision of the Tax Court is final, and is specifically designated by the taxpayer in writing as a "deposit in the nature of a cash bond," will be treated as such by the Service. * * *

> A remittance made before the mailing of a notice of deficiency that is designated by the taxpayer in writing as a deposit in the nature of a cash bond will be treated as such by the Service. Such a deposit is not subject to a claim for credit or refund as an overpayment. The taxpayer may request the return of all or part of the deposit at any time before the Service is entitled to assess the tax. That amount will be returned to the taxpayer, without interest, unless the Service determines that assessment or collection of the tax determined to be due would be in jeopardy, or that the amount should be applied against any other liability. * * *

> A remittance not specifically designated as a deposit in the nature of a cash bond will be treated as a payment of tax if it is made in response to a proposed liability, for example, as proposed in a revenue agent's or examiner's report, and remittance in full of the proposed liability is made. A partial remittance will not be treated as a partial payment of tax unless the taxpayer specifically designates what portion of the proposed liability the taxpayer intends to satisfy. If the remittance is treated as a partial payment of tax, it will be posted to the taxpayer's account as a payment as of the date it is received. That amount may be taken into account by the Service

in determining the amount for which a notice of deficiency must be mailed. If the Service is unable to determine whether a partial remittance is intended to be a payment of tax or a deposit in the nature of a cash bond, the Service will treat the remittance as a deposit in the nature of a cash bond. * * *

Any undesignated remittance not described in section 4.03 made before the liability is proposed to the taxpayer in writing (e.g., before the issuance of a revenue agent's or examiner's report), will be treated by the Service as a deposit in the nature of a cash bond. Such a deposit is not subject to a claim for credit or refund and the excess of the deposit over the liability ultimately determined to be due will not bear interest under section 6611 of the Code. The taxpayer will be notified concerning the status of the remittance, and may elect to have the deposit returned, without interest, at any time before the issuance of a revenue agent's or examiner's report, subject to the provisions of subparagraph 1 of section 4.02.

* * *

In *VanCanagan v. United States*, 231 F.3d 1349 (Fed. Cir. 2000), the Court of Appeals for the Federal Circuit held that a remittance made by the taxpayers with their application for an automatic four-month extension of time to file was a payment rather than a deposit. In *Baral v. United States*, 528 U.S. 431 (2000), the United States Supreme Court considered whether estimated taxes and withholding taxes are "paid" on the due date of the return under Code section 6513(b), or are instead mere "deposits" under *Rosenman* until the return is filed. In a short opinion, the Court held that section 6513(b) applies.

What if a taxpayer remits an amount with the intent to pay a deficiency and the IRS fails to formally assess the tax before the statute of limitations on assessment expires—is the remittance refundable? If the remittance is considered a payment, it is not refundable after the statute of limitations on refund claims expires. If it is considered a deposit, it is returnable by the IRS, and the subsequent assessment will not convert the deposit into a payment because assessment is barred by the statute of limitations. *See* I.R.C. § 6401(a). Prior to *Rosenman*, several courts had held that the taxpayer was not entitled to a refund of a remittance described above. *See, e.g., Crompton & Knowles Loom Works v. White*, 65 F.2d 132, 133 (1st Cir.), *cert. denied,* 290 U.S. 669 (1933); *Meyersdale Fuel Co. v. United States*, 70 Ct. Cl. 765, 44 F.2d 437, 446 (Ct. Cl. 1930), *cert. denied,* 283 U.S. 860 (1931). However, post-*Rosenman* case law considering whether assessment is a prerequisite for payment is more relevant to the resolution of this issue.

In Revenue Ruling 85-67, 1985-1 C.B. 364, the IRS stated that although it cannot assess an amount sent in after the statute of limitations on assessment has expired, *see* I.R.C. § 6401(a), the IRS does not have to return to the taxpayer a remittance made while the statute of limitations was still open. The IRS reasoned that a remittance made before the statute of limitations on assessment has expired does not constitute an overpayment, even though the statute subsequently expires without assessment being made. Various courts have applied this principle. *See, e.g., Moran v. United States*, 63 F.3d 663 (7th Cir. 1995) (overruled on other grounds); *Ewing v. United States*, 914 F.2d 499 (4th Cir. 1990), *cert. denied,* 500 U.S. 905 (1991); *Fisher v. United States*, 28 Fed. Cl. 88 (1993); *cf. Cohen v. United States*, 995 F.2d 205 (Fed. Cir. 1993).

[C] Submission and Timing of the Refund Claim

A refund claim invites the IRS to examine the return that is the subject of the claim. As discussed in Chapter 2, the IRS does turn some refund claims over to an examining agent for audit. Thus, it is wise to review the underlying return before filing the claim and, if the statute of limitations on assessment remains open, consider carefully the risks and relative merits of possible claims before deciding whether to seek a refund. Note also that income, estate, gift, and certain excise tax refunds that exceed a certain dollar amount are subject to review by the Joint Committee on Taxation. *See* I.R.C. § 6405(a). Until recently, the threshold dollar amount was $1 million, but the Community Tax Relief Act of 2000 increased it to $2 million. *See* I.R.C. § 6405.

Of course, the risk that the IRS will make a deficiency adjustment in response to a refund claim is smaller where the IRS has already examined the underlying return. To reduce the risk of adjustment by the IRS even further, a claim for refund can be filed after the statute of limitations on assessment has run, assuming that the statute of limitations on refund claims has not also run. Even when the assessment limitations period has already expired, the IRS can still make an adjustment to a carryover or continuing item that affects other years' returns. Also consider the possibility raised by the following case:

LEWIS v. REYNOLDS
United States Supreme Court
284 U.S. 281 (1932)[2]

Mr. Justice McReynolds delivered the opinion of the Court.

Petitioners sued the respondent Collector in the United States District Court for Wyoming, September 20, 1929, to recover $7,297.16 alleged to have been wrongfully exacted as income tax upon the estate of Cooper.

February 18, 1921, the administrator filed a return for the period January 1 to December 12, 1920, the day of final settlement. Among others, he reported deductions for attorney's fees, $20,750, and inheritance taxes paid to the State, $16,870. The amount of tax as indicated by the return was paid.

November 24, 1925, the Commissioner, having audited the return, disallowed all deductions except the one for attorney's fees and assessed a

---

[2] *Modified*, 284 U.S. 599 (1932).

deficiency of $7,297.16. This sum was paid March 21, 1926; and on July 27, 1926, petitioners asked that it be refunded.

A letter from the Commissioner to petitioners, dated May 18, 1929, and introduced in evidence by them, stated that the deduction of $20,750 for attorney's fees had been improperly allowed. He also set out a revised computation wherein he deducted the state inheritance taxes. This showed liability greater than the total sums theretofore exacted. The Commissioner further said: "Since the correct computation results in an additional tax as indicated above which is barred from assessment by the statute of limitations your claim will be rejected on the next schedule to be approved by the commissioner."

The trial court upheld the Commissioner's action and its judgment was affirmed by the Circuit Court of Appeals.

Counsel for petitioners relies upon the five year statute of limitations (Rev. Act. 1926, § 277).[n.1] He maintains that the Commissioner lacked authority to redetermine and reassess the tax after the statute had run.

After referring to § 284, Revenue Act of 1926, 44 Stat. 66, and § 322, Revenue Act of 1928, 45 Stat. 861, the Circuit Court of Appeals said [48 F.2d 515, 516] —

> "The above quoted provisions clearly limit refunds to overpayments. It follows that the ultimate question presented for decision, upon a claim for refund, is whether the taxpayer has overpaid his tax. This involves a redetermination of the entire tax liability. While no new assessment can be made, after the bar of the statute has fallen, the taxpayer, nevertheless, is not entitled to a refund unless he has overpaid his tax. The action to recover on a claim for refund is in the nature of an action for money had and received, and it is incumbent upon the claimant to show that the United States has money which belongs to him."

We agree with the conclusion reached by the courts below.

While the statutes authorizing refunds do not specifically empower the Commissioner to reaudit a return whenever repayment is claimed, authority therefor is necessarily implied. An overpayment must appear before refund is authorized. Although the statute of limitations may have barred the assessment and collection of any additional sum, it does not obliterate the right of the United States to retain payments already received when they do not exceed the amount which might have been properly assessed and demanded.

Bonwit Teller & Co. v. United States, 283 U.S. 258, says nothing in conflict with the view which we now approve.

[n.1] "Sec. 277. (a) Except as provided in § 278 [not here important] —. . .(3) The amount of income, excess-profits, and war profits taxes imposed by. . . the Revenue Act of 1918, and by any such Act as amended, shall be assessed within five years after the return was filed, and no proceeding in court without assessment for the collection of such taxes shall be begun after the expiration of such period." [The current statute of limitations on assessment in section 6501(a) is three years. Eds.]

Affirmed.

The *Lewis* Court applied what is known as "setoff." Specifically, what did that allow the IRS to do?

[D] Content of the Refund Claim

As a general matter, a refund claim must set forth in detail each ground on which the taxpayer claims a credit or refund and include sufficient facts to inform the IRS of the basis of the claim. A claim for refund of an overpayment may be made on the initial return for the year, an amended return, or a special form provided by the IRS, depending on the circumstances and the type of tax involved. If an income tax return has already been filed, the claim must be submitted on the amended return appropriate for the particular type of taxpayer (for example, for individuals, the form is Form 1040X, Amended U.S. Individual Income Tax Return, and for corporations it is Form 1120X, Amended U.S. Corporation Income Tax Return). Claims for refund of taxes, penalties, and other additions relating to taxes other than income taxes must be made on Form 843, Claim for Refund and Request for Abatement. The claim must also be filed by or on behalf of the person who made the overpayment, and it must be verified. For all income, gift, estate and federal unemployment tax refund claims, a separate claim must be prepared and filed for each type of tax for each taxable period.

Forms 1040X and 1120X have the following key parts:

(1)   the year involved;

(2)   information relating to the identity of the taxpayer;

(3)   the filing status on the original return and whether it has been audited (Form 1040X); the place of filing of the original return (Form 1120X);

(4)   the revised amount of income, deductions, and payment credits for the taxable year;

(5)   computation of the overpayment to be refunded;

(6)   an explanation of the changes in computation;

(7)   schedules; and

(8)   the signature of the taxpayer and that of the paid preparer, if any.[3]

---

[3] A federal district court found invalid a return and its accompanying refund claim because the return had an attachment and language added between the jurat and the taxpayer's signature. *See* Letscher v. United States, 2000-2 U.S.T.C. 50,723 (S.D.N.Y. 2000). The added language stated, "Without prejudice, See attachment dated 4/13/96." The attachment was a one-page document entitled "First Amendment Right for a Redress of Grievances: Attachment to 1995 Federal Tax Return." The court held that the altered jurat called into question the veracity and accuracy of the return, and violated the requirement that a return be signed under penalty of perjury. The court therefore dismissed the refund suit for lack of subject matter jurisdiction.

The refund claim should also indicate whether the taxpayer wishes to have the overpayment refunded or applied against estimated tax for the following year. Form 843 calls for essentially the same information, in a somewhat reduced format. In addition, because Form 843 is used for several types of taxes, the type of tax and the kind of return filed must be indicated.

A refund claim must include both the grounds for the claim and the supporting facts, but it need not contain any legal argument. The statement of facts need not be exhaustive, but should include the principal factual elements on which the taxpayer relies. The grounds supporting the refund claim are set forth in the explanation section of the claim. Each ground supporting the credit or refund should be set forth in detail. Treas. Reg. § 301.6402-2(b)(1). The IRS has the power to waive this requirement and consider a general claim on its merits, but it is safer not to rely on the possibility of such a waiver. As with court pleadings, claims for refund may set forth alternative grounds for relief that are not internally consistent. However, a claim for refund may not be based on equitable grounds, although it can be advisable to add such grounds as a protective measure. After a refund claim is filed, it may be amended to add new grounds, but not after the statute of limitations on refund claims has expired.

Careful phrasing of the grounds is critical because a subsequent refund suit is limited to the assertions raised in the claim. *See, e.g., United States v. Felt & Tarrant Mfg. Co.*, 283 U.S. 269 (1931); *Hempt Bros. v. United States*, 354 F. Supp. 1172, 1182 (M.D. Pa. 1973) ("a court lacks jurisdiction of an action to recover taxes except upon grounds reasonably encompassed by the claim for refund as originally filed or properly amended"). Consider the following case:

DECKER v. UNITED STATES
United States District Court, District of Connecticut
93-2 U.S.T.C. ¶ 50,408

CABRANES, CHIEF JUDGE:

* * *

BACKGROUND

The plaintiff is the former wife of Malcolm B. Decker ("Decker"). They were married in 1951. On November 29, 1969, Decker and the plaintiff were divorced in a unilateral divorce action in Juarez, Mexico where only Decker was present.

Prior to the entry of the Mexican divorce decree, the plaintiff and Decker entered into a separation agreement dated November 10, 1969, the terms of which are undisputed ("Separation Agreement"). Pursuant to the terms of the Separation Agreement, Decker was obligated to pay the plaintiff $8,000 per year plus cost-of-living escalations until the death of either party or the plaintiff's remarriage. As of September, 1976, Decker was in arrears in alimony payments due under the Separation Agreement. At that time, the plaintiff obtained a judgment against Decker in the State of New York for arrearages in the amount of $13,567. Decker did not pay that judgment and thereafter continued to fall behind in his alimony obligations.

On January 11, 1983, the plaintiff commenced three separate proceedings in state court in Connecticut. The three separate actions sought the following relief: (1) to set aside the Mexican divorce decree; (2) to enforce the New York judgment and for arrearages following the date of that judgment; and (3) a judgment of divorce premised on the invalidity of the Mexican divorce decree. These three actions were consolidated and subsequently settled on July 8, 1985 ("Settlement").

The Settlement provided that (a) the Mexican decree is a valid and binding decree of dissolution or divorce; (b) there existed an arrearage of alimony of $126,000; (c) in exchange for a satisfaction of judgment in all three cases, Decker would pay to the plaintiff at least $100,000 in full and final satisfaction of all past debts due for alimony and/or support and all future obligations pertaining to alimony and/or support; and (d) the payment was to be made by a transfer of real property located in the Town of Fairfield, Connecticut worth approximately $100,000. Decker guaranteed that the plaintiff would receive at least $100,000 net proceeds from the sale of the property. To the extent she received proceeds in excess thereof, she was entitled to keep them.

The transfer of the property did not occur at the time provided for in the Settlement. However, on December 31, 1985 at approximately 2:30 p.m., Decker recorded a deed in the Town of Fairfield land records purporting to transfer the property to the plaintiff. In the deed of conveyance, Decker assigned the property a value of $110,000. On January 7, 1986, a court-appointed appraiser valued the property at $105,000. Thereafter, on February 27, 1986, the plaintiff sold the property to an unrelated third party for $125,000. The plaintiff's net proceeds from the sale were $113,000.

On his federal income tax return for 1985, Decker claimed an alimony deduction in the amount of $113,000. The plaintiff, though, did not include any amount of the sale proceeds as alimony income on her 1985 return. Subsequently, the Internal Revenue Service ("Service") determined that the value of the property ($113,000) should have been included in the plaintiff's gross income for the 1985 tax year. This resulted in additional tax liability of $41,117, which amount was remitted by the plaintiff in 1989. In 1990, the Service assessed $19,365.03 against the plaintiff for interest on the additional tax liability; this amount was also remitted by the plaintiff. The plaintiff filed a timely claim for a refund and, receiving no response from the Service, filed this action seeking a total refund of $60,082.03.[n.3]

[n.3] The Service also proposed to assess a tax deficiency against Decker in order to avoid the so-called "whipsaw" effect of Decker's deduction and the plaintiff's failure to include the proceeds as income. Decker petitioned the Tax Court and, on October 30, 1990, the Tax Court entered a decision finding no income tax deficiency with respect to Decker.

DISCUSSION

* * *

In its motion, the Government contends that IRC Section 71, as in effect prior to the amendments of the Tax Reform Act of 1984 ("Old Section 71"), applies in this case and that, under that Code section, the proceeds received by the plaintiff from the sale of the property were properly included in her gross income (the so-called "taxability issue"). Moreover, the Government claims that the proceeds were appropriately applied to the 1985 tax year (the so-called "timing issue"). The plaintiff, however, contends that Old Section 71 does not apply to the transaction in question and that, under Section 71, as amended in 1984 ("New Section 71"), the proceeds in question are not properly included in her gross income. The plaintiff argues also that, even if Old Section 71 applies, she still should not be taxed because the property transfer does not constitute "alimony" under that statute. * * *

A.

We turn first to the issue of the taxability of the proceeds received by the plaintiff from the sale of the property. A threshold question which must be resolved in addressing this issue is, of course, which version of IRC Section 71 applies in this case: Old Section 71 or New Section 71? If, as the plaintiff maintains, New Section 71 governs, the Government's motion must be denied. If, however, Old Section 71 applies, the plaintiff may be entitled to a refund.

(1)

In her opposition papers to the Government's motion, the plaintiff raises for the first time the issue of the applicability of New Section 71: it appears neither in her claim for a refund filed with the Service nor in her Complaint. Relying upon the so-called "variance doctrine," the Government argues that the plaintiff is barred from introducing this issue at this late juncture. The "variance doctrine" holds that "in an action for a refund . . . the law is clear that the district court is limited to those grounds which were raised in the claim for refund presented to the Commissioner." Campagna v. United States, 290 F.2d 682, 685 (2d Cir. 1961).

Before a taxpayer may sue to recover federal income taxes she must file a claim for a refund or credit with the Service setting out the material facts on which the claim is based. 26 U.S.C. § 7422(a). Moreover, "a claimant in a refund suit may not raise a wholly new factual basis for [her] claim at the later trial . . . also [she] may not shift the legal theory of [her] claim." Scovill Manufacturing Company v. Fitzpatrick, 215 F.2d 567, 569 (2d Cir. 1954) (citations omitted) (collecting cases). However, "not every minor variation between the original claim and the complaint in a civil suit thereon is fatal to recovery," Gada v. United States, 460 F. Supp. 859, 869 n.5 (D. Conn. 1978); Cities Service Company v. United States, 316 F. Supp. 61, 73 (S.D.N.Y. 1970). As our Court of Appeals stated of the predecessor statute to Section 7422 in Scovill: "We think that [§ 7422] goes no further than to require the taxpayer to set forth facts sufficient to enable the Commissioner of Internal Revenue to make an intelligent administrative review of the claim." *Scovill,* 215 F.2d at 569.

A review of the cases drawn to the court's attention by the Government indicates that the court may properly consider the plaintiff's claim that New Section 71 applies. In most of those cases cited by the Government, the claimants attempted to shift the fundamental nature of their cause of action or to raise significant new factual issues in their civil suits.[n.6] In other cases cited, the taxpayer's initial refund claim was so deficient that it failed to apprise the Service of any clear basis for a refund. None of these decisions is similar to the instant case. Although the plaintiff's initial claim for a refund may not have specified that, in her view, New Section 71 governs, the plaintiff has consistently maintained that she is entitled to a refund on the ground that the property transfer did not give rise to alimony income and that the characterization of the transaction as producing either income or property is to be determined by applying Section 71. In other words, in arguing that the then-recently-amended version of Section 71 applies, the plaintiff has not altered her basic contention that the transaction is not taxable as alimony under the applicable Code section. Rather, she has simply raised the issue of which version of that Code section applies. Clearly, the Service was reasonably on notice that this issue might be raised by the plaintiff inasmuch as New Section 71 went into effect at the beginning of the very year that the Service claims the plaintiff received income from the transaction. Indeed, it is arguable that it was the Government rather than the plaintiff who first introduced this issue in this litigation. The possible applicability of New Section 71 was first formally suggested in this action in the Government's memorandum in support of its motion for summary judgment. While the record does not suggest a waiver by the Government of its right to invoke the variance doctrine in this case (as the plaintiff argues), it certainly buttresses the conclusion that the issue cannot have escaped the notice of the Service when it examined the plaintiff's claim for a refund. In sum, the court is not persuaded that the plaintiff is barred from arguing that New Section 71 applies because she did not make that specific argument in her claim for a refund.

[n.6] *See, e.g.,* Goelet v. United States, 266 F.2d 881 (2d Cir. 1959) (court refused to consider new ground for taxpayer's claim where neither that ground nor the necessary facts to support it were presented to the Commissioner); Young v. United States, 203 F.2d 686 (8th Cir. 1953) (where original claim was rejected by Commissioner, taxpayer could not "amend" claim to seek a refund for a different year); Nemours Corp. v. United States, 188 F.2d 745 (3d Cir. 1951) (taxpayer could not rely in its civil case upon a code section not stated as a basis for his claim for refund presented to Commissioner); Ronald Press Company v. Shea, 114 F.2d 453 (2d Cir. 1940) (taxpayer barred from switching basis of his claim after Commissioner had rejected the initial grounds for refund based upon a different set of facts). *See also* Mallette Brothers Construction Co. v. United States, 695 F.2d 145 (5th Cir. 1983) (taxpayer barred from raising new factual allegation that contradicted grounds set forth in claim for refund); *Campagna, supra* (court refuses to consider new issue raised involving new factual basis); Samara v. United States, 129 F.2d 594 (2d Cir. 1942) (taxpayer barred from raising facts not previously presented to the Commissioner).

* * *

What is the "variance doctrine" discussed in the case? As noted in *Decker*, the IRS can waive application of the variance doctrine. *See Tucker v. Alexander*, 275 U.S. 228, 231 (1927).

[E] Informal Claims for Refund

In some circumstances, the taxpayer need not file a formal refund claim. Following an audit, for example, if the IRS determines that the taxpayer made an overpayment, Form 870 — which is used by the IRS to reflect a mutually agreed upon settlement — will serve as the refund claim. Form 870-AD — the second type of settlement agreement — provides that "no claim for refund shall be filed or prosecuted" for the years covered by the agreement. As discussed in Chapter 4, although Form 870-AD is not a formal settlement or closing agreement that would be binding on the IRS under the Code, some courts have held Form 870-AD to be binding on the parties by estoppel. *See, e.g., Elbo Coals, Inc. v. United States*, 763 F.2d 818 (6th Cir. 1985); *Stair v. United States*, 516 F.2d 560 (2d Cir. 1975); *Kretchmar v. United States*, 9 Cl. Ct. 191 (1985).

Although it is wise for a taxpayer who wishes to pursue a refund to file a formal refund claim (unless he has signed a Form 870 that will serve as his claim), at times taxpayers have submitted documents that purported to claim a refund but failed to comply with the necessary requirements. Case law provides that a document can be treated as an *informal* refund claim if, as a factual matter, the following are true: (1) the court determines that an informal claim was filed; (2) the claim is in writing or has a written component; and (3) the matters set forth in writing are sufficient to apprise the IRS that a refund is sought and to focus the IRS's attention on the merits of the dispute so that the IRS may commence an examination of the claim if it so desires. *See, e.g., Arch Engineering Co., Inc. v. United States*, 783 F.2d 190, 192 (Fed. Cir. 1986); *American Radiator & Standard Sanitary Corp. v. United States*, 318 F.2d 915, 920 (Ct. Cl. 1963). The written component of the informal claim need not be in a single document, but notification is vital; the claim must be actually communicated to the IRS. Mere availability of the information is not the equivalent of notice. Moreover, it must appear from the surrounding facts, including the written element, that the taxpayer is actually requesting a refund. The mere filing of an erroneous return does not constitute a refund claim. Consider this case:

NIGHT HAWK LEASING COMPANY v. UNITED STATES
United States Court of Claims
84 Ct. Cl. 596 (1937)

Littleton, Judge, delivered the opinion of the court.

The only question in this case is whether the formal refund claim for 1928 and 1929 filed by plaintiff October 31, 1932, can be held to have been a perfection of informal claims filed by plaintiff with the collector shortly after June 26, 1930. The informal claims were written on the backs of the two checks executed on that date, payable to and delivered to the Collector of Internal Revenue, as follows: "This check is accepted as paid under protest pending final decision of the higher courts."

We are of opinion that when these informal claims are considered in the light of the facts and the circumstances existing at the time, the formal refund claim filed October 31, 1932, was but a perfection of the informal claims written by plaintiff on the backs of the checks delivered to the collector in June 1930. The collector accepted these checks on the conditions specified and endorsed his name immediately under the written claim of plaintiff that the tax therein specified was being accepted pending final decision of the higher courts. * * * The fact that the collector may have been negligent in preserving the same in his records, or forwarding the same to the Commissioner or advising the Commissioner of the contents thereof, does not render the claim void or ineffectual. A written document constituting a demand for the return on a proper ground of the money paid, when accepted as such by the collector, is sufficient to constitute an informal claim for refund subject to completion and perfection at a later date if not previously acted upon by the Commissioner. The fact that the Commissioner did not receive from the collector the taxpayer's demand for the return of the amount paid upon the condition specified and accepted by the collector should not prejudice the taxpayer's right later to perfect such demand by formal claim. The collector knew when he received and accepted the checks and cashed them that the taxpayer was thereby filing claims for refund of such tax based upon its claim then pending in the court that the taxes for 1928 and 1929 were not due. Prior to the payment of the additional tax here involved for 1928 and 1929 the Commissioner had determined deficiencies for the years 1923 to 1927, inclusive, by the denial of deductions which gave rise to the additional taxes paid for 1928 and 1929 and had notified the taxpayer thereof by letter. In reply thereto the plaintiff advised the Commissioner that it was taking the questions before the United States Board of Tax Appeals and called his attention to the fact that the same dispute was involved in the tax liability for 1928 and 1929.

* * *

On March 13, 1930, the Board of Tax Appeals decided against the plaintiff, 19 B.T.A. 258, with respect to its tax liability for the years 1923 to 1927, inclusive, which years involved the same questions upon which the informal demands for the return of the tax paid for 1928 and 1929 were based. Immediately thereafter plaintiff took an appeal from the decision of the Board to the Court of Appeals of the District of Columbia and that court, in March 1932, reversed the decision of the Board and held that plaintiff was entitled to the deductions claimed. That decision became final and on October 19, 1932, the Commissioner mailed plaintiff refund checks for the overpayments for 1923 to 1927, inclusive. Thereupon, plaintiff called the Commissioner's attention to a formal claim for refund for 1928 and 1929 perfecting its timely informal claims made to the collector shortly after June 26, 1930. The Commissioner refused to refund the overpayments for 1928 and 1929 and rejected plaintiff's claim.

We are of opinion, under the facts and circumstances of this case, that the claims filed were sufficient for allowance of the refunds of the overpayments for 1928 and 1929 and, having been rejected by the Commissioner, that plaintiff is entitled in this proceeding to recover the overpayments with interest. Judgment will be entered in favor of plaintiff for $6,787.66 with interest as provided by law. It is so ordered.

WHALEY, JUDGE; WILLIAMS, JUDGE; GREEN, JUDGE; and BOOTH, CHIEF JUSTICE, concur.

Why did the judge in *Night Hawk Leasing* rule in favor of the plaintiff? Did the informal claims written on the back of the two checks suffice as a refund claim?

§ 8.03   Refund Suits and Overpayment Suits

[A]   Refund Suits

The United States Code provides the statutory basis for federal tax refund jurisdiction:

> The district courts shall have original jurisdiction, concurrent with the United States Claims Court [United States Court of Federal Claims], of: * * * Any civil action against the United States for the recovery of any internal-revenue tax alleged to have been erroneously or illegally assessed or collected, or any penalty claimed to have been collected without authority or any sum alleged to have been excessive or in any manner wrongfully collected under the internal-revenue laws . . . .

28 U.S.C. § 1346(a)(1).

As discussed above, a refund suit must be based on the same "grounds" as those stated in the refund claim. I.R.C. § 7422(a); Treas. Reg. § 301.6402-2(b)(1). Refund suits have another jurisdictional prerequisite: "full payment" of the tax. This United States Supreme Court case established the "full payment" requirement:

FLORA v. UNITED STATES
United States Supreme Court
362 U.S. 145 (1960)[4]

MR. CHIEF JUSTICE WARREN delivered the opinion of the Court.

The question presented is whether a Federal District Court has jurisdiction under 28 U.S.C. § 1346(a)(1) of a suit by a taxpayer for the refund of income tax payments which did not discharge the entire amount of his assessment.

---

[4] *Reh'g denied*, 362 U.S. 972 (1960).

This is our second consideration of the case. In the 1957 Term, we decided that full payment of the assessment is a jurisdictional prerequisite to suit, 357 U.S. 63. Subsequently the Court granted a petition for rehearing. 360 U.S. 922. The case has been exhaustively briefed and ably argued. After giving the problem our most careful attention, we have concluded that our original disposition of the case was correct.

* * *

THE FACTS

The relevant facts are undisputed and uncomplicated. This litigation had its source in a dispute between petitioner and the Commissioner of Internal Revenue concerning the proper characterization of certain losses which petitioner suffered during 1950. Petitioner reported them as ordinary losses, but the Commissioner treated them as capital losses and levied a deficiency assessment in the amount of $28,908.60, including interest. Petitioner paid $5,058.54 and then filed with the Commissioner a claim for refund of that amount. After the claim was disallowed, petitioner sued for refund in a District Court. The Government moved to dismiss, and the judge decided that the petitioner "should not maintain" the action because he had not paid the full amount of the assessment. But since there was a conflict among the Courts of Appeals on this jurisdictional question, and since the Tenth Circuit had not yet passed upon it, the judge believed it desirable to determine the merits of the claim. He thereupon concluded that the losses were capital in nature and entered judgment in favor of the Government. 142 F. Supp. 602. The Court of Appeals for the Tenth Circuit agreed with the district judge upon the jurisdictional issue, and consequently remanded with directions to vacate the judgment and dismiss the complaint. 246 F.2d 929. We granted certiorari because the Courts of Appeals were in conflict with respect to a question which is of considerable importance in the administration of the tax laws.

THE STATUTE

The question raised in this case has not only raised a conflict in the federal decisions, but has also in recent years provoked controversy among legal commentators. In view of this divergence of expert opinion, it would be surprising if the words of the statute inexorably dictated but a single reasonable conclusion. Nevertheless, one of the arguments which has been most strenuously urged is that the plain language of the statute precludes, or at the very least strongly militates against, a decision that full payment of the income tax assessment is a jurisdictional condition precedent to maintenance of a refund suit in a District Court. If this were true, presumably we could but recite the statute and enter judgment for petitioner — though we might be pardoned some perplexity as to how such a simple matter could have caused so much confusion. Regrettably, this facile an approach will not serve.

Section 1346(a)(1) provides that the District Courts shall have jurisdiction, concurrent with the Court of Claims, of

"(1) Any civil action against the United States for the recovery of *any internal-revenue tax* alleged to have been erroneously or illegally assessed or collected, or *any penalty* claimed to have been collected without authority or *any sum* alleged to have been excessive or in any manner wrongfully collected under the internal-revenue laws . . . ." (Emphasis added.)

It is clear enough that the phrase "any internal-revenue tax" can readily be construed to refer to payment of the entire amount of an assessment. Such an interpretation is suggested by the nature of the income tax, which is "A tax . . . imposed for each taxable year," with the "amount of *the* tax" determined in accordance with prescribed schedules. (Emphasis added.) But it is argued that this reading of the statute is foreclosed by the presence in § 1346(a)(1) of the phrase "any sum." This contention appears to be based upon the notion that "any sum" is a catchall which confers jurisdiction to adjudicate suits for refund of part of a tax. A catchall the phrase surely is; but to say this is not to define what it catches. The sweeping role which petitioner assigns these words is based upon a conjunctive reading of "any internal-revenue tax," "any penalty," and "any sum." But we believe that the statute more readily lends itself to the disjunctive reading which is suggested by the connective "or." That is, "any sum," instead of being related to "any internal-revenue tax" and "any penalty," may refer to amounts which are neither taxes nor penalties. Under this interpretation, the function of the phrase is to permit suit for recovery of items which might not be designated as either "taxes" or "penalties" by Congress or the courts. One obvious example of such a "sum" is interest. And it is significant that many old tax statutes described the amount which was to be assessed under certain circumstances as a "sum" to be added to the tax, simply as a "sum," as a "percentum," or as "costs." Such a rendition of the statute, which is supported by precedent, frees the phrase "any internal-revenue tax" from the qualifications imposed upon it by petitioner and permits it to be given what we regard as its more natural reading — the full tax. Moreover, this construction, under which each phrase is assigned a distinct meaning, imputes to Congress a surer grammatical touch than does the alternative interpretation, under which the "any sum" phrase completely assimilates the other two. Surely a much clearer statute could have been written to authorize suits for refund of any part of a tax merely by use of the phrase "a tax or any portion thereof," or simply "any sum paid under the internal revenue laws." This Court naturally does not review congressional enactments as a panel of grammarians; but neither do we regard ordinary principles of English prose as irrelevant to a construction of those enactments. *Cf.* Commissioner v. Acker, 361 U.S. 87.

We conclude that the language of § 1346(a)(1) can be more readily construed to require payment of the full tax before suit than to permit suit for recovery of a part payment. But, as we recognized in the prior opinion, the statutory language is not absolutely controlling, and consequently resort must be had to whatever other materials might be relevant.

LEGISLATIVE HISTORY AND HISTORICAL BACKGROUND

Although frequently the legislative history of a statute is the most fruitful source of instruction as to its proper interpretation, in this case that history is barren of any clue to congressional intent.

* * *

We are not here concerned with a single sentence in an isolated statute, but rather with a jurisdictional provision which is a keystone in a carefully articulated and quite complicated structure of tax laws. From * * * related statutes, all of which were passed after 1921, it is apparent that Congress has several times acted upon the assumption that § 1346(a)(1) requires full payment before suit. Of course, if the clear purpose of Congress at any time had been to permit suit to recover a part payment, this subsequent legislation would have to be disregarded. But, as we have stated, the evidence pertaining to this intent is extremely weak, and we are convinced that it is entirely too insubstantial to justify destroying the existing harmony of the tax statutes. The laws which we consider especially pertinent are the statute establishing the Board of Tax Appeals (now the Tax Court), the Declaratory Judgment Act, and § 7422 (e) of the Internal Revenue Code of 1954.

THE BOARD OF TAX APPEALS

The Board of Tax Appeals was established by Congress in 1924 to permit taxpayers to secure a determination of tax liability before payment of the deficiency. The Government argues that the Congress which passed this 1924 legislation thought full payment of the tax assessed was a condition for bringing suit in a District Court; that Congress believed this sometimes caused hardship; and that Congress set up the Board to alleviate that hardship. Petitioner denies this, and contends that Congress's sole purpose was to enable taxpayers to prevent the Government from collecting taxes by exercise of its power of distraint.

We believe that the legislative history surrounding both the creation of the Board and the subsequent revisions of the basic statute supports the Government. The House Committee Report, for example, explained the purpose of the bill as follows:

> "The committee recommends the establishment of a Board of Tax Appeals to which a taxpayer may appeal *prior to the payment* of an additional assessment of income, excess-profits, war-profits, or estate taxes. *Although a taxpayer may, after payment of his tax, bring suit for the recovery thereof* and thus secure a judicial determination on the questions involved, he can not, in view of section 3224 of the Revised Statutes, which prohibits suits to enjoin the collection of taxes, secure such a determination prior to the payment of the tax. The right of appeal after payment of the tax is an incomplete remedy, and does little to remove the hardship occasioned by an incorrect assessment. The payment of a large additional tax on income received several years previous and which may have, since

its receipt, been either wiped out by subsequent losses, invested in nonliquid assets, or spent, sometimes forces taxpayers into bankruptcy, and often causes great financial hardship and sacrifice. These results are not remedied by permitting the taxpayer *to sue for the recovery of the tax after this payment.* He is entitled to an appeal and to a determination of his liability for the tax prior to its payment." (Emphasis added.)

Moreover, throughout the congressional debates are to be found frequent expressions of the principle that payment of the full tax was a precondition to suit: "pay his tax . . . then . . . file a claim for refund"; "pay the tax and then sue"; "a review in the courts after payment of the tax"; "he may still seek court review, but he must first pay the tax assessed"; "in order to go to court he must pay his assessment"; "he must pay it [his assessment] before he can have a trial in court"; "pay the taxes adjudicated against him, and then commence a suit in a court"; "pay the tax . . . then . . . sue to get it back"; "paying his tax and bringing his suit"; "first pay his tax and then sue to get it back"; "take his case to the district court — conditioned, of course, upon his paying the assessment."

Petitioner's argument falls under the weight of this evidence. It is true, of course, that the Board of Tax Appeals procedure has the effect of staying collection, and it may well be that Congress so provided in order to alleviate hardships caused by the long-standing bar against suits to enjoin the collection of taxes. But it is a considerable leap to the further conclusion that amelioration of the hardship of prelitigation payment as a jurisdictional requirement was not another important motivation for Congress's action. * * *

In sum, even assuming that one purpose of Congress in establishing the Board was to permit taxpayers to avoid distraint, it seems evident that another purpose was to furnish a forum where full payment of the assessment would not be a condition precedent to suit. The result is a system in which there is one tribunal for prepayment litigation and another for post-payment litigation, with no room contemplated for a hybrid of the type proposed by petitioner.

* * *

SECTION 7422(e) OF THE 1954 CODE

One distinct possibility which would emerge from a decision in favor of petitioner would be that a taxpayer might be able to split his cause of action, bringing suit for refund of part of the tax in a Federal District Court and litigating in the Tax Court with respect to the remainder. In such a situation the first decision would, of course, control. Thus if for any reason a litigant would prefer a District Court adjudication, he might sue for a small portion of the tax in that tribunal while at the same time protecting the balance from distraint by invoking the protection of the Tax Court procedure. On the other hand, different questions would arise if this device were not employed. For example, would the Government be required to file a compulsory counterclaim for the unpaid balance in District Court under Rule 13 of the Federal Rules of Civil Procedure? If so, which party would have the burden of proof?

Section 7422(e) of the 1954 Internal Revenue Code makes it apparent that Congress has assumed these problems are nonexistent except in the rare case where the taxpayer brings suit in a District Court and the Commissioner then notifies him of an additional deficiency. Under § 7422(e) such a claimant is given the option of pursuing his suit in the District Court or in the Tax Court, but he cannot litigate in both. Moreover, if he decides to remain in the District Court, the Government may — but seemingly is not required to — bring a counterclaim; and if it does, the taxpayer has the burden of proof. If we were to overturn the assumption upon which Congress has acted, we would generate upon a broad scale the very problems Congress believed it had solved.

These, then, are the basic reasons for our decision, and our views would be unaffected by the constancy or inconstancy of administrative practice. However, because the petition for rehearing in this case focused almost exclusively upon a single clause in the prior opinion — "there does not appear to be a single case before 1940 in which a taxpayer attempted a suit for refund of income taxes without paying the full amount the Government alleged to be due," 357 U.S., at 69 — we feel obliged to comment upon the material introduced upon reargument. The reargument has, if anything, strengthened, rather than weakened, the substance of this statement, which was directed to the question whether there has been a consistent understanding of the "pay first and litigate later" principle by the interested government agencies and by the bar.

* * *

There is strong circumstantial evidence that this view of the jurisdiction of the courts was shared by the bar at least until 1940, when the Second Circuit Court of Appeals rejected the Government's position in *Coates v. United States*, 111 F.2d 609. Out of the many thousands of refund cases litigated in the pre-1940 period — the Government reports that there have been approximately 40,000 such suits in the past 40 years — exhaustive research has uncovered only nine suits in which the issue was present, in six of which the Government contested jurisdiction on part-payment grounds.[37] The Government's failure to raise the issue in the other three is obviously entirely without significance. Considerations of litigation strategy may have been thought to militate against resting upon such a defense in those cases. Moreover, where only nine lawsuits involving a particular issue arise over a period of many decades, the policy of the Executive Department on that issue can hardly be expected to become familiar to every government attorney. But most important, the number of cases before 1940 in which the issue was

---

[37] Petitioner cites a number of cases in support of his argument that neither the bar nor the Government has ever assumed that full payment of the tax is a jurisdictional prerequisite to suit for recovery. The following factors rob these cases of the significance attributed to them by the petitioner:

* * *

(b) A number of the cited cases involved excise taxes. The Government suggests — and we agree — that excise tax deficiencies may be divisible into a tax on each transaction or event, and therefore present an entirely different problem with respect to the full-payment rule.

* * *

present is simply so inconsequential that it reinforces the conclusion of the prior opinion with respect to the uniformity of the pre-1940 belief that full payment had to precede suit.

A word should also be said about the argument that requiring taxpayers to pay the full assessments before bringing suits will subject some of them to great hardship. This contention seems to ignore entirely the right of the taxpayer to appeal the deficiency to the Tax Court without paying a cent.[n.38] If he permits his time for filing such an appeal to expire, he can hardly complain that he has been unjustly treated, for he is in precisely the same position as any other person who is barred by a statute of limitations. On the other hand, the Government has a substantial interest in protecting the public purse, an interest which would be substantially impaired if a taxpayer could sue in a District Court without paying his tax in full. * * *

In sum, if we were to accept petitioner's argument, we would sacrifice the harmony of our carefully structured twentieth century system of tax litigation, and all that would be achieved would be a supposed harmony of § 1346(a)(1) with what might have been the nineteenth century law had the issue ever been raised. Reargument has but fortified our view that § 1346(a)(1), correctly construed, requires full payment of the assessment before an income tax refund suit can be maintained in a Federal District Court.

Affirmed.

––––––––––––––

If the amount sought to be refunded includes interest and penalties, does *Flora* require the taxpayer to pay those amounts before jurisdiction will be granted? The answer is unclear. Courts have held that whether "full payment" requires the payment of interest and penalties depends on whether those amounts were part of the assessment and whether they are at issue in the litigation. *Compare Shore v. United States*, 9 F.3d 1524, 1527–1528 (Fed. Cir. 1993) ("Only if the taxpayers assert a claim over assessed interest or penalties on grounds not fully determined by the claim for recovery of principal must they prepay such interest and penalties as well as the assessed tax principal."), *with Magnone v. United States*, 902 F.2d 192, 193; (2d Cir.), *cert. denied*, 498 U.S. 853 (1990) ("full payment" required payment of the entire assessment, including penalties and interest); *Greenhouse v. United States*, 738 F. Supp. 709, 713 (S.D.N.Y. 1990) ("It is well settled that, under the full payment rule, a federal court has jurisdiction over a tax refund suit only after the taxpayer has made full payment of the assessment, including penalties and interest."). Does federal income tax withheld from a taxpayer's wages constitute tax "paid" within the meaning of *Flora*? What if the taxes were withheld on behalf of an employee but (illegally) were not turned over by the employer to the IRS?

There is no "hardship" exception to *Flora*. *See, e.g., Curry v. United States*, 774 F.2d 852 (7th Cir. 1985). Thus, in responding to a notice of deficiency,

---

[n.38] Petitioner points out that the Tax Court has no jurisdiction over excise tax cases. *See* 9 Mertens, Law of Federal Income Taxation (Zimet Rev. 1958), § 50.08. But this fact provides no policy support for his position, since, as we have noted, excise tax assessments may be divisible into a tax on each transaction or event, so that the full-payment rule would probably require no more than payment of a small amount. *See* note 37, *supra*.

the "full payment" rule is an important consideration in deciding whether to pursue the matter as a deficiency case in the Tax Court or as a refund action.

With respect to disputes involving certain types of taxes, such as excise taxes, the Tax Court has no jurisdiction whatsoever. In those cases, the "divisible tax" rule mitigates the hardship that might accompany the full payment rule by providing that payment of a single "divisible" tax, such as excise or employment tax, constitutes full payment. *See Steele v. United States*, 280 F.2d 89, 90–91 (8th Cir. 1960) (full payment rule is not applicable to employment taxes because they are divisible into separate taxes for each employee); *see also Flora v. United States*, 362 U.S. 145, 174 n.37 (1960) ("The Government suggests — and we agree — that excise tax deficiencies may be divisible into a tax on each transaction or event, and therefore present an entirely different problem with respect to the full-payment rule.").

As with much of tax procedure, refund suits are subject to strict time limits. As you now know, a condition precedent to filing a refund suit is that the taxpayer file a refund claim. I.R.C. § 7422(a). Once the taxpayer files the refund claim, the taxpayer must wait until the IRS denies the claim or six months go by, whichever comes first, before the taxpayer can file suit. I.R.C. § 6532(a). The taxpayer also has the option of requesting an immediate notice of disallowance of the claim (a "waiver.") *Id.* Why might the taxpayer do that?

As an outside limit, the taxpayer has two years to file suit from the date the notice of disallowance is mailed or from the date the taxpayer's waiver is "filed." I.R.C. § 6532(a)(1). The Fourth Circuit has held that a waiver of notice is "filed" when received by the IRS. *Hull v. United States*, 146 F.3d 235 (4th Cir. 1998). Note that the two-year period does not begin to run until the IRS mails the notice of disallowance or the taxpayer waives notice.

[B] Overpayment Litigation in Tax Court

As you learned in Chapter 7, Tax Court subject matter jurisdiction requires a notice of deficiency and timely responsive petition. Therefore, to pursue in Tax Court a refund of an overpayment, a taxpayer must have received a notice of deficiency and petitioned the court. When that occurs, the Tax Court has jurisdiction to find an overpayment, I.R.C. § 6512(b)(1), and jurisdiction to enforce payment by the IRS, I.R.C. § 6512(b)(2). Overpayment jurisdiction also includes jurisdiction over overpayments of interest. *See Winn-Dixie v. Commissioner*, 110 T.C. 291 (1998).

A claim for refund with the IRS is not required in order to pursue overpayment litigation in Tax Court. Because of the absence of a refund claim requirement, the statute of limitations for claiming a refund in Tax Court has an additional layer of complexity. The issues that arise are discussed below, in Section 8.04.

[C] Coordination of Fora

Given that overpayment issues may be heard by the Tax Court as well as the District Court and Court of Federal Claims, the Code resolves the otherwise duplicative litigation that could result. Take a look at section

7422(e), which was discussed in *Flora*. If the IRS mails the taxpayer a notice of deficiency after the taxpayer has filed a refund suit in court but before the court has heard the case, can the taxpayer petition the Tax Court? If the taxpayer does petition the Tax Court, which court, the Tax Court or the refund court, hears the taxpayer's overpayment claim? Each of these questions is answered by section 7422(e). Consider also the situation where the IRS mails the taxpayer a notice of deficiency after the refund court has heard the matter but before it has entered a decision. Can the taxpayer petition the Tax Court at that point? Is the IRS likely to issue a notice of deficiency in those circumstances?

§ 8.04 Statutes of Limitations on Refund Claims

[A] Overview

In general, a claim for refund or credit of an overpayment is timely if it is filed within three years from the date the return was filed or within two years of when the claimed tax was paid, whichever is later. I.R.C. § 6511(a). (Why isn't just the three-year rule sufficient? Without the two-year rule, could a taxpayer access a refund court after receiving a notice of deficiency?) If no return was filed, the statutory period is two years from when the tax was paid. I.R.C. § 6511(a). Recall that Code section 7502 establishes that a return timely mailed is timely filed. Because late-mailed returns or claims are not filed until actually received, it is important to determine, when filing a refund claim, if it was timely mailed.[5]

When calculating these time periods under section 6511, it is helpful to know that an early return is deemed filed on the due date of the return. I.R.C. § 6513(a). Similarly, any portion of tax paid before the last day prescribed for payment is considered paid on the last day. I.R.C. § 6513(a). The same is true for withholding taxes. I.R.C. § 6513(b).

Because of the two-years-from-payment rule, theoretically at least, a taxpayer could pay to the IRS $1 on a date more than three years after filing his return, and soon thereafter file a refund claim for not only the $1 but also for all taxes paid with the return. For that reason, section 6511 also contains a "limitation on amount." Where the claim is not timely within the three-year period, the refund amount is measured by and limited to the tax paid within two years before the taxpayer filed the claim. Therefore, in the hypothetical situation of the belated $1 payment, the statute of limitations would allow the taxpayer only to claim a refund of $1, not any additional amount paid with the return.

Similarly, in cases where the three-year period applies, the refund amount is measured by and limited to the tax paid within three years before the taxpayer filed the claim, plus any extension of time the taxpayer had for filing the return. I.R.C. § 6511(b)(2)(A). If the taxpayer has not filed a claim but the IRS allows a refund, the refund amount is measured by the amount that

---

[5] Does an initial return mailed after its due date benefit from section 7502 if it contains a refund claim that would be timely if measured by the date the document was mailed? *See* Treas. Reg. § 301.7502-1(f).

would be allowed or made if a claim had been filed on the date the credit or refund is allowed. I.R.C. § 6511(b)(2)(C).

> *Example*: Theresa timely filed her 1996 return on March 21, 1997. Her return accurately reflected a tax liability of $7,000, and with-holding of $6,000. She mailed a check for $1,000 to the IRS with the return. All $7,000 of tax is considered paid on April 15, 1997, and her return is deemed filed on April 15 as well. I.R.C. § 6513(a), (b). The latest date on which she can file a refund of any of the $7,000 is April 15, 2000. Assume that the IRS mails Theresa a notice of deficiency in the amount of $2,000 on March 1, 1999, and Theresa pays the $2,000 on April 1, 1999. Under section 6511, Theresa has until April 1, 2001 to claim a refund of up to $2,000 on any tax issue, but she only has until April 15, 2000 to claim a refund up to a maximum of $9,000 (the $7,000 she previously paid, plus the $2,000 paid in response to the notice of deficiency).

What happens if the last day to file a return falls on a non-business day? Code section 7503 provides that "when the last day . . . for performing any act falls on Saturday, Sunday, or a legal holiday, the performance of such act shall be considered timely if it is performed on the next succeeding day which is not a Saturday, Sunday, or a legal holiday." I.R.C. § 7503. In general, the application of this section is relatively clear. However, it is not as clear how this section applies if the act in question is not actually performed on the "next succeeding day."

For example, if a return is due on Monday, April 17 of Year 1 because April 15 was a Saturday, does a taxpayer have until April 17 of Year 4 (assuming a three-year period applies) to claim a refund on his first return for the year? In FSA 200021010, the IRS stated that section 7503 did not extend the deadline to file a refund claim until April 17, Year 4 from April 15, Year 4 because "I.R.C. section 7503 only applies if the act is *actually performed* on the next succeeding day which is not a Saturday, Sunday, or a legal holiday." FSA 200021010 (emphasis added). Subsequently, in Chief Counsel Notice 2001-019, the IRS stated "If a case involves the more complicated factual situation in which the due date (including an extended due date) for the return is a Saturday, Sunday, or legal holiday, and the taxpayer mails the late-filed return three years from the next succeeding day after the due date that is not a Saturday, Sunday, or legal holiday, guidance from the National Office should be requested."[6]

[B] Statutory Period Applicable When the Taxpayer Extended the Statute of Limitations on Assessment

If the taxpayer agrees to extend the statute of limitations on assessment of tax, special rules apply if the extension was made within the § 6511(a)

---

[6] The reason why the application of section 7503 in this context is more complicated will become more apparent after you read Section 8.04[D], below.

Section 7503 applies not only to taxpayer documents such as returns and refund claims, but also to IRS documents such as the notice of deficiency. Its application to a notice of deficiency is discussed in Chapter 5 in the context of *Estate of Mitchell v. Commissioner*, 250 F.3d 696 (9th Cir. 2001), a case that is reproduced in Chapter 7.

period for filing a refund claim, subject to certain exceptions explained below. If the special rules apply, the taxpayer is permitted to file a claim for credit or refund of an overpayment at any time within the extended period provided in the agreement plus an additional six months. I.R.C. § 6511(c)(1). If the taxpayer files a claim within that time (within six months after the extended assessment date), the amount of the credit or refund may include not only the portion of the tax paid after the agreement was executed, but the amount of tax that could have been refunded if a claim had been filed on the date the extension agreement was executed. I.R.C. § 6511(c)(2). If the taxpayer files the refund claim more than six months after the extended assessment period, his refund is subject to the general rule of section 6511(a) and therefore generally is limited to tax payments made within the prior two years. These special rules do not apply if the taxpayer filed a claim (or a refund was made) either before the extension agreement was executed or more than six months after the expiration of the extended assessment period.[7] I.R.C. § 6511(c).

[C]   Statutes of Limitations on Refund Claims Applicable in Tax Court Cases

Because taxpayers are authorized to assert in a Tax Court petition the refund of an overpayment, without ever filing a refund claim, a special statute of limitations applies in Tax Court cases. Read section 6512(b)(3) carefully. It has three parts. Section 6512(b)(3)(A) allows a refund of any amount paid after the notice of deficiency was mailed. Because the taxpayer could have claimed a refund of that amount and pursued the refund method at that time, the treatment in Tax Court is parallel to the treatment under the refund procedures. Section 6512(b)(3)(C) entitles the taxpayer to a refund for which the taxpayer already filed a timely refund claim before the notice of deficiency was mailed, and with respect to which the taxpayer had not already been time-barred under the refund method. Again, this makes the Tax Court treatment of overpayment claims parallel to the refund method.

The hardest provision to follow is section 6512(b)(3)(B). What it does, in a situation in which the taxpayer did *not* file a refund claim *before* the notice of deficiency was mailed, and the payment in question was made after the notice was mailed, is to *deem* the date the notice was mailed to be the date of a hypothetical refund claim for purposes of determining timeliness of that claim under section 6511. As a result, under section 6512(b)(3)(B), the taxpayer can obtain a refund in Tax Court only of amounts that would have been recoverable under the provisions of section 6511. The intent seems to be to make the Tax Court treatment parallel to the refund method, using the date of the notice of deficiency because it is required for Tax Court cases, whereas a refund claim is not. This complex provision is analyzed in depth in *Commissioner v. Lundy*, reproduced immediately below in connection with the statute of limitations on delinquent returns.

---

[7] Note that an agreement to extend the statute of limitations on collection, rather than the statute of limitations on assessment, does not extend the period for filing a refund claim.

[D]   Application of the Statutes of Limitations to Delinquent Returns

The application of the limitations periods in Code sections 6511 and 6512 become much more complicated in the case of late-filed returns. If a taxpayer files his return late, does that mean "no return was filed" so that a two-year statute of limitations applies? Prior to the United States Supreme Court's decision in *Lundy,* numerous cases had arisen in which the taxpayer did not file a return, received a notice of deficiency from the IRS, and petitioned the Tax Court, both contesting the deficiency and claiming a refund. In part, *Lundy* discusses that history. Why do you think this situation was relatively common? In answering this question, consider why a taxpayer entitled to a refund might not file a return. Is the IRS likely to send such a taxpayer a notice of deficiency?

Prior to *Lundy,* there were also a few *refund court* cases in which the taxpayer did not file a timely return, and subsequently filed a first return for the year claiming a refund. Upon denial of the claim, the taxpayer litigated the issue of timeliness of the claim in a refund court. *See, e.g., Miller v. United States,* 38 F.3d 473 (9th Cir. 1994); *Oropallo v. United States,* 994 F.2d 25 (1st Cir. 1993), *cert. denied,* 510 U.S. 1050 (1994); *Mills v. United States,* 805 F. Supp. 448 (E.D. Tex. 1992); *Arnzen v. IRS,* 1990 U.S. Dist. LEXIS 17236. Does *Lundy* resolve the limitations period applicable to delinquent return cases litigated in the refund fora?

COMMISSIONER v. LUNDY
United States Supreme Court
516 U.S. 235 (1996)

Justice O'Connor delivered the opinion of the Court.

In this case, we consider the "look-back" period for obtaining a refund of overpaid taxes in the United States Tax Court under 26 U.S.C. § 6512(b)(3)(B), and decide whether the Tax Court can award a refund of taxes paid more than two years prior to the date on which the Commissioner of Internal Revenue mailed the taxpayer a notice of deficiency, when, on the date the notice of deficiency was mailed, the taxpayer had not yet filed a return. We hold that in these circumstances the 2-year look-back period set forth in § 6512(b)(3)(B) applies, and the Tax Court lacks jurisdiction to award a refund.

I.

During 1987, respondent Robert F. Lundy and his wife had $10,131 in federal income taxes withheld from their wages. This amount was substantially more than the $6,594 the Lundys actually owed in taxes for that year, but the Lundys did not file their 1987 tax return when it was due, nor did they file a return or claim a refund of the overpaid taxes in the succeeding 2½ years. On September 26, 1990, the Commissioner of Internal Revenue mailed Lundy a notice of deficiency, informing him that he owed $7,672 in additional taxes and interest for 1987 and that he was liable for substantial penalties for delinquent filing and negligent underpayment of taxes. *See* 26 U.S.C. §§ 6651(a)(1) and 6653(1).

Lundy and his wife mailed their joint tax return for 1987 to the Internal Revenue Service (IRS) on December 22, 1990. This return indicated that the Lundys had overpaid their income taxes for 1987 by $3,537 and claimed a refund in that amount. Six days after the return was mailed, Lundy filed a timely petition in the Tax Court seeking a redetermination of the claimed deficiency and a refund of the couple's overpaid taxes. The Commissioner filed an answer generally denying the allegations in Lundy's petition. Thereafter, the parties negotiated towards a settlement of the claimed deficiency and refund claim. On March 17, 1992, the Commissioner filed an amended answer acknowledging that Lundy had filed a tax return and that Lundy claimed to have overpaid his 1987 taxes by $3,537.

The Commissioner contended in this amended pleading that the Tax Court lacked jurisdiction to award Lundy a refund. The Commissioner argued that if a taxpayer does not file a tax return before the IRS mails the taxpayer a notice of deficiency, the Tax Court can only award the taxpayer a refund of taxes paid within two years prior to the date the notice of deficiency was mailed. *See* 26 U.S.C. § 6512(b)(3)(B). Under the Commissioner's interpretation of § 6512(b)(3)(B), the Tax Court lacked jurisdiction to award Lundy a refund because Lundy's withheld taxes were deemed paid on the date that his 1987 tax return was due (April 15, 1988), *see* § 6513(b)(1), which is more than two years before the date the notice was mailed (September 26, 1990).

The Tax Court agreed with the position taken by the Commissioner and denied Lundy's refund claim. Citing an unbroken line of Tax Court cases adopting a similar interpretation of § 6512(b)(3)(B), *e.g.,* Allen v. Commissioner, 99 T.C. 475, 479–480 (1992); Galuska v. Commissioner, 98 T.C. 661, 665 (1992); Berry v. Commissioner, 97 T.C. 339, 344–345 (1991); White v. Commissioner, 72 T.C. 1126, 1131–1133 (1979) (renumbered statute); Hosking v. Commissioner, 62 T.C. 635, 642–643 (1974) (renumbered statute), the Tax Court held that if a taxpayer has not filed a tax return by the time the notice of deficiency is mailed, and the notice is mailed more than two years after the date on which the taxes are paid, the look-back period under § 6512(b)(3)(B) is two years and the Tax Court lacks jurisdiction to award a refund. 65 T.C.M. (CCH) 3011, 3014–3015 (1993), ¶ 93,278 RIA Memo TC.

The Court of Appeals for the Fourth Circuit reversed, finding that the applicable look-back period in these circumstances is three years and that the Tax Court had jurisdiction to award Lundy a refund. 45 F.3d 856, 861 (1995). Every other Court of Appeals to have addressed the question has affirmed the Tax Court's interpretation of § 6512(b)(3)(B). *See* Davison v. Commissioner, 9 F.3d 1538 (CA2 1993) (judgt. order); Allen v. Commissioner, 23 F.3d 406 (CA6 1994) (judgt. order); Galuska v. Commissioner, 5 F.3d 195, 196 (CA7 1993); Richards v. Commissioner, 37 F.3d 587, 589 (CA10 1994); *see also* Rossman v. Commissioner, 46 F.3d 1144 (CA9 1995) (judgt. order) (*aff'g on other grounds*). We granted certiorari to resolve the conflict, 515 U.S. 1102 (1995*)*, and now reverse.

II.

A taxpayer seeking a refund of overpaid taxes ordinarily must file a timely claim for a refund with the IRS under 26 U.S.C. § 6511. That section contains two separate provisions for determining the timeliness of a refund claim. It first establishes a *filing* deadline: The taxpayer must file a claim for a refund "within 3 years from the time the return was filed or 2 years from the time the tax was paid, whichever of such periods expires the later, or if no return was filed by the taxpayer, within 2 years from the time the tax was paid." § 6511(b)(1) (incorporating by reference § 6511(a)). It also defines two *"look-back" periods*: If the claim is filed "within 3 years from the time the return was filed," *ibid.*, then the taxpayer is entitled to a refund of "the portion of the tax paid within the 3 years immediately preceding the filing of the claim." § 6511(b)(2)(A) (incorporating by reference § 6511(a)). If the claim is not filed within that 3-year period, then the taxpayer is entitled to a refund of only that "portion of the tax paid during the 2 years immediately preceding the filing of the claim." § 6511(b)(2)(B) (incorporating by reference § 6511(a)).

Unlike the provisions governing refund suits in United States District Court or the United States Court of Federal Claims, which make timely filing of a refund claim a jurisdictional prerequisite to bringing suit, *see* 26 U.S.C. § 7422(a); Martin v. United States, 833 F.2d 655, 658–659 (CA7 1987), the restrictions governing the Tax Court's authority to award a refund of overpaid taxes incorporate only the look-back period and not the filing deadline from § 6511. *See* 26 U.S.C. § 6512(b)(3). Consequently, a taxpayer who seeks a refund in the Tax Court, like respondent, does not need to actually file a claim for refund with the IRS; the taxpayer need only show that the tax to be refunded was paid during the applicable look-back period.

In this case, the applicable look-back period is set forth in § 6512(b)(3)(B), which provides that the Tax Court cannot award a refund of any overpaid taxes unless it first determines that the taxes were paid:

> "within the period which would be applicable under section 6511(b)(2) . . . if on the date of the mailing of the notice of deficiency a claim had been filed (whether or not filed) stating the grounds upon which the Tax Court finds that there is an overpayment."

The analysis dictated by § 6512(b)(3)(B) is not elegant, but it is straightforward. Though some courts have adverted to the filing of a "deemed claim," *see Galuska,* 5 F.3d at 196; *Richards,* 37 F.3d at 589, all that matters for the proper application of § 6512(b)(3)(B) is that the "claim" contemplated in that section be treated as the only mechanism for determining whether a taxpayer can recover a refund. Section 6512(b)(3)(B) defines the look-back period that applies in Tax Court by incorporating the look-back provisions from § 6511(b)(2), and directs the Tax Court to determine the applicable period by inquiring into the timeliness of a hypothetical claim for refund filed "on the date of the mailing of the notice of deficiency."

To this end, § 6512(b)(3)(B) directs the Tax Court's attention to § 6511(b)(2), which in turn instructs the court to apply either a 3-year or a 2-year look-back period. *See* §§ 6511(b)(2)(A) and (B) (incorporating by reference § 6511(a)); *see supra,* 516 U.S. at 240. To decide which of these look-back periods to apply, the Tax Court must consult the filing provisions of § 6511(a) and ask whether the claim described by § 6512(b)(3)(B) — a claim filed "on the date of the mailing of the notice of deficiency" — would be filed "within 3 years from the time the return was filed." *See* § 6511(b)(2)(A) (incorporating by reference § 6511(a)). If a claim filed on the date of the mailing of the notice of deficiency would be filed within that 3-year period, then the look-back period is also three years and the Tax Court has jurisdiction to award a refund of any taxes paid within three years prior to the date of the mailing of the notice of deficiency. §§ 6511(b)(2)(A) and 6512(b)(3)(B). If the claim would not be filed within that 3-year period, then the period for awarding a refund is only two years. §§ 6511(b)(2)(B) and 6512(b)(3)(B).

In this case, we must determine which of these two look-back periods to apply when the taxpayer fails to file a tax return when it is due, and the Commissioner mails the taxpayer a notice of deficiency before the taxpayer gets around to filing a late return. The Fourth Circuit held that a taxpayer in this situation is entitled to a 3-year look-back period if the taxpayer actually files a timely claim at some point in the litigation, *see infra,* 516 U.S. at 246, and respondent offers additional reasons for applying a 3-year look-back period, *see infra,* 516 U.S. at 249–252. We think the proper application of § 6512(b)(3)(B) instead requires that a 2-year look-back period be applied.

We reach this conclusion by following the instructions set out in § 6512(b)(3)(B). The operative question is whether a claim filed "on the date of the mailing of the notice of deficiency" would be filed "within 3 years from the time the return was filed." *See* § 6512(b)(3)(B) (incorporating §§ 6511(b)(2) and 6511(a)). In the case of a taxpayer who does not file a return before the notice of deficiency is mailed, the claim described in § 6512(b)(3)(B) could not be filed "within 3 years from the time the return was filed." No return having been filed, there is no date from which to measure the 3-year filing period described in § 6511(a). Consequently, the claim contemplated in § 6512(b)(3)(B) would not be filed within the 3-year window described in § 6511(a), and the 3-year look-back period set out in § 6511(b)(2)(A) would not apply. The applicable look-back period is instead the default 2-year period described in § 6511(b)(2)(B), which is measured from the date of the mailing of the notice of deficiency, *see* § 6512(b)(3)(B). The taxpayer is entitled to a refund of any taxes paid within two years prior to the date of the mailing of the notice of deficiency.

*   *   *

Therefore, if the taxpayer has already filed a return (albeit perhaps a faulty one), any claim filed "on the date of the mailing of the notice of deficiency" would necessarily be filed within three years from the date the return is filed. In these circumstances, the applicable look-back period under § 6512(b)(3)(B) would be the 3-year period defined in § 6511(b)(2)(A), and the Tax Court would have jurisdiction to award a refund.

Therefore, in the case of a taxpayer who files a timely tax return, § 6512(b)(3)(B) usually operates to toll the filing period that might otherwise deprive the taxpayer of the opportunity to seek a refund. If a taxpayer contesting the accuracy of a previously filed tax return in Tax Court discovers for the first time during the course of litigation that he is entitled to a refund, the taxpayer can obtain a refund from the Tax Court without first filing a timely claim for refund with the IRS. It does not matter, as it would in district court, see § 7422 (incorporating § 6511), that the taxpayer has discovered the entitlement to a refund well after the period for filing a timely refund claim with the IRS has passed, because § 6512(b)(3)(B) applies "whether or not [a claim is] filed," and the look-back period is measured from the date of the mailing of the notice of deficiency. *Ibid.* Nor does it matter, as it might in a refund suit, see 26 CFR § 301.6402-2(b)(1) (1995), whether the taxpayer has previously apprised the IRS of the precise basis for the refund claim, because 26 U.S.C. § 6512(b)(3)(B) posits the filing of a hypothetical claim "stating the grounds upon which the Tax Court finds that there is an overpayment."

Section 6512(b)(3)(B) treats delinquent filers of income tax returns less charitably. Whereas timely filers are virtually assured the opportunity to seek a refund in the event they are drawn into Tax Court litigation, a delinquent filer's entitlement to a refund in Tax Court depends on the date of the mailing of the notice of deficiency. Section 6512(b)(3)(B) tolls the limitations period, in that it directs the Tax Court to measure the look-back period from the date on which the notice of deficiency is mailed and not the date on which the taxpayer actually files a claim for refund. But in the case of delinquent filers, § 6512(b)(3)(B) establishes only a 2-year look-back period, so the delinquent filer is not assured the opportunity to seek a refund in Tax Court: if the notice of deficiency is mailed more than two years after the taxes were paid, the Tax Court lacks jurisdiction to award the tax-payer a refund.

The Tax Court properly applied this 2-year look-back period to Lundy's case. As of September 26, 1990 (the date the notice was mailed), Lundy had not filed a tax return. Consequently, a claim filed on that date would not be filed within the 3-year period described in § 6511(a), and the 2-year period from § 6511(b)(2)(B) applies. Lundy's taxes were withheld from his wages, so they are deemed paid on the date his 1987 tax return was due (April 15, 1988), *see* § 6513(b)(1), which is more than two years prior to the date the notice of deficiency was mailed (September 26, 1990). Lundy is therefore seeking a refund of taxes paid outside the applicable look-back period, and the Tax Court lacks jurisdiction to award such a refund.

III.

In deciding Lundy's case, the Fourth Circuit adopted a different approach to interpreting § 6512(b)(3)(B) and applied a 3-year look-back period. Respondent supports the Fourth Circuit's rationale, but also offers an argument for applying a uniform 3-year look-back period under § 6512(b)(3)(B). We find neither position persuasive.

The Fourth Circuit held:

> "[T]he Tax Court, when applying the limitation provision of § 6511(b)(2) in light of § 6512(b)(3)(B), should substitute the date of the mailing of the notice of deficiency for the date on which the taxpayer filed the claim for refund, but only for the purpose of determining the benchmark date for measuring the limitation period and not for the purpose of determining whether the two-year or three-year limitation period applies." 45 F.3d at 861.

* * *

Contrary to the Fourth Circuit's interpretation, the fact that Lundy actually filed a claim for a refund after the date on which the Commissioner mailed the notice of deficiency has no bearing in determining whether the Tax Court has jurisdiction to award Lundy a refund. *See supra*, 516 U.S. at 240–241. Once a taxpayer files a petition with the Tax Court, the Tax Court has exclusive jurisdiction to determine the existence of a deficiency or to award a refund, *see* 26 U.S.C. § 6512(a), and the Tax Court's jurisdiction to award a refund is limited to those circumstances delineated in § 6512(b)(3). Section 6512(b)(3)(C) is the only provision that measures the look-back period based on a refund claim that is actually filed by the taxpayer, and that provision is inapplicable here because it only applies to refund claims filed "before the date of the mailing of the notice of deficiency." § 6512(b)(3)(C). Under § 6512(b)(3)(B), which is the provision that does apply, the Tax Court is instructed to consider only the timeliness of a claim filed "on the date of the mailing of the notice of deficiency," not the timeliness of any claim that the taxpayer might actually file.

The Fourth Circuit's rule also leads to a result that Congress could not have intended, in that it subjects the timely, not the delinquent, filer to a shorter limitations period in Tax Court. Under the Fourth Circuit's rule, the availability of a refund turns entirely on whether the taxpayer has in fact filed a claim for refund with the IRS, because it is the date of *actual filing* that determines the applicable look-back period under § 6511(b)(2) (and, by incorporation, § 6512(b)(3)(B)). *See* 45 F.3d at 861; *supra,* 516 U.S. at 246. This rule might "eliminate the inequities resulting" from adhering to the 2-year look-back period, 45 F.3d at 863, but it creates an even greater inequity in the case of a taxpayer who dutifully files a tax return when it is due, but does not initially claim a refund. We think our interpretation of the statute achieves an appropriate and reasonable result in this case: The taxpayer who files a timely income tax return could obtain a refund in the Tax Court under § 6512(b)(3)(B), without regard to whether the taxpayer has actually filed a timely claim for refund. *See supra,* 516 U.S. at 244–245.

* * * It is unlikely that Congress intended for a taxpayer in Tax Court to be worse off for having filed a timely return, but that result would be compelled under the Fourth Circuit's approach.

Lundy offers an alternative reading of the statute that avoids this unreasonable result, but Lundy's approach is similarly defective. The main thrust of Lundy's argument is that the "claim" contemplated in § 6512(b)(3)(B) could be filed "within 3 years from the time the return was filed," such that the applicable look-back period under § 6512(b)(3)(B) would be three years, if the claim were itself filed on a tax return. Lundy in fact argues that Congress must have intended the claim described in § 6512(b)(3)(B) to be a claim filed on a return, because there is no other way to file a claim for refund with the IRS. Brief for Respondent 28, 30 (citing 26 CFR § 301.6402-3(a)(1) (1995)). Lundy therefore argues that § 6512(b)(3)(B) incorporates a uniform 3-year look-back period for Tax Court cases: If the taxpayer files a timely return, the notice of deficiency (and the "claim" under § 6512(b)(3)(B)) will necessarily be filed within three years of the return and the look-back period is three years; if the taxpayer does not file a return, then the claim contemplated in § 6512(b)(3)(B) is deemed to be a claim filed with, and thus within three years of, a return and the look-back period is again three years.

Like the Fourth Circuit's approach, Lundy's reading of the statute has the convenient effect of ensuring that taxpayers in Lundy's position can almost always obtain a refund if they file in Tax Court, but we are bound by the terms Congress chose to use when it drafted the statute, and we do not think that the term "claim" as it is used in § 6512(b)(3)(B) is susceptible of the interpretation Lundy has given it. The Internal Revenue Code does not define the term "claim for refund" as it is used in § 6512(b)(3)(B), *cf.* 26 U.S.C. § 6696(e)(2) ("For purposes of sections 6694 and 6695 . . . the term 'claim for refund' means a claim for refund of, or credit against, any tax imposed by subtitle A"), but it is apparent from the language of § 6512(b)(3)(B) and the statute as a whole that a claim for refund can be filed separately from a return. Section 6512(b)(3)(B) provides that the Tax Court has jurisdiction to award a refund to the extent the taxpayer would be entitled to a refund "if on the date of the mailing of the notice of deficiency *a claim* had been filed." (Emphasis added.) It does not state, as Lundy would have it, that a taxpayer is entitled to a refund if on that date "a claim and a return had been filed."

Perhaps the most compelling evidence that Congress did not intend the term "claim" in § 6512 to mean a "claim filed on a return" is the parallel use of the term "claim" in § 6511(a). Section 6511(a) indicates that a claim for refund is timely if it is "filed by the taxpayer within 3 years from the time the return was filed," and it plainly contemplates that a claim can be filed even "if no return was filed." If a claim could *only* be filed with a return, as Lundy contends, these provisions of the statute would be senseless, *cf.* 26 U.S.C. § 6696 (separately defining "claim for refund" and "return"), and we have been given no reason to believe that Congress meant the term "claim" to mean one thing in § 6511 but to mean something else altogether in the very next section of the statute. The interrelationship and close proximity of these provisions of the statute "presents a classic case for application of the 'normal rule of statutory construction that identical words used in different parts of the same act are intended to have the same meaning.'" Sullivan v. Stroop, 496 U.S. 478, 484, 110 L. Ed. 2d 438, 110 S. Ct. 2499 (1990) (quoting Sorenson v. Secretary of Treasury, 475 U.S. 851, 860, 89 L. Ed. 2d 855, 106 S. Ct. 1600 (1986) (internal quotation marks omitted)).

The regulation Lundy cites in support of his interpretation, 26 CFR § 301.6402-3(a)(1) (1995), is consistent with our interpretation of the statute. That regulation states only that a claim must "in general" be filed on a return, *ibid.*, inviting the obvious conclusion that there are some circumstances in which a claim and a return can be filed separately.

We have previously recognized that even a claim that does not comply with federal regulations might suffice to toll the limitations periods under the Tax Code, *see, e. g.,* United States v. Kales, 314 U.S. 186, 194, 86 L. Ed. 132, 62 S. Ct. 214 (1941) ("notice fairly advising the Commissioner of the nature of the taxpayer's claim" tolls the limitations period, even if "it does not comply with formal requirements of the statute and regulations"), and we must assume that if Congress had intended to require that the "claim" described in § 6512(b)(3)(B) be a "claim filed on a return," it would have said so explicitly.

IV.

* * *

Lundy also suggests that our interpretation of the statute creates a disparity between the limitations period that applies in Tax Court and the periods that apply in refund suits filed in district court or the Court of Federal Claims. In this regard, Lundy argues that the claim for refund he filed with his tax return on December 28 would have been timely for purposes of district court litigation because it was filed "within 3 years from the time the return was filed," § 6511(b)(1) (incorporating by reference § 6511(a)); *see also* Rev. Rul. 76-511, 1976-2 Cum. Bull. 428, and within the 3-year look-back period that would apply under § 6511(b)(2)(A). Petitioner disagrees that there is any disparity, arguing that Lundy's interpretation of the statute is wrong and that Lundy's claim for refund would not have been considered timely in district court. *See* Brief for Petitioner 12, 29–30, and n.11 (*citing* Miller v. United States, 38 F.3d 473, 475 (CA9 1994)).

We assume without deciding that Lundy is correct, and that a different limitations period would apply in district court, but nonetheless find in this disparity no excuse to change the limitations scheme that Congress has crafted. The rules governing litigation in Tax Court differ in many ways from the rules governing litigation in the district court and the Court of Federal Claims. Some of these differences might make the Tax Court a more favorable forum, while others may not. *Compare* 26 U.S.C. § 6213(a) (taxpayer can seek relief in Tax Court without first paying an assessment of taxes) *with* Flora v. United States, 362 U.S. 145, 177, 4 L. Ed. 2d 623, 80 S. Ct. 630 (1960) (28 U.S.C. § 1346(a)(1) requires full payment of the tax assessment before taxpayer can file a refund suit in district court); and *compare* 26 U.S.C. § 6512(b)(3)(B) (Tax Court must assume that the taxpayer has filed a claim "stating the grounds upon which the Tax Court" intends to award a refund) *with* 26 CFR § 301.6402-2(b)(1) (1995) (claim for refund in district court must state grounds for refund with specificity). To the extent our interpretation of § 6512(b)(3)(B) reveals a further distinction between the rules that apply in these forums, it is a distinction compelled by the statutory language, and it is a distinction Congress could rationally make. As our discussion of § 6512(b)(3)(B) demonstrates, *see supra*, at 244–245, all a taxpayer need do to preserve the ability to seek a refund in the Tax Court is comply with the law and file a timely return.

We are bound by the language of the statute as it is written, and even if the rule Lundy advocates might "accord with good policy," we are not at liberty "to rewrite [the] statute because [we] might deem its effects susceptible of improvement." Badaracco [v. Commissioner, 464 U.S. 386 (1984)] at 398. Applying § 6512(b)(3)(B) as Congress drafted it, we find that the applicable look-back period in this case is two years, measured from the date of the mailing of the notice of deficiency. Accordingly, we find that the Tax Court lacked jurisdiction to award Lundy a refund of his overwithheld taxes. The judgment is reversed.

It is so ordered.

JUSTICE STEVENS, dissenting.

Justice Thomas has cogently explained why the judgment of the Court of Appeals should be affirmed. I therefore join his opinion. Because one point warrants further emphasis, I add this additional comment. In my view the Commissioner's position, and that of the majority, misses the forest by focusing on the trees. The predecessor to 26 U.S.C. § 6512(b) was amended to protect the interests of a taxpayer who receives a notice of deficiency from the IRS and later determines that the asserted underpayment was in fact an overpayment. *Post,* 516 U.S. at 261–262. Congress expressly intended to guard against the possibility that the time for claiming a refund might lapse before the taxpayer in these circumstances realizes that he is entitled to claim a refund. As Justice Thomas has demonstrated, there is no need to read § 6512(b)(3)(B) — a provision designed to benefit the taxpayer who receives an unexpected deficiency notice — as giving the IRS an arbitrary right to shorten the taxpayer's period for claiming a refund if that taxpayer has not yet filed a return. The Court's reading of the statute converts an intended benefit into a handicap.

JUSTICE THOMAS, with whom JUSTICE STEVENS joins, dissenting.

Under the Internal Revenue Service's longstanding interpretation of 26 U.S.C. §§ 6511(a) and (b), Lundy would have collected a refund if he had filed suit in district court. The majority assumes, and I am prepared to hold, that that interpretation of § 6511 is correct. Section 6512(b)(3)(B) incorporates the look-back periods of § 6511 for proceedings to recover a refund in Tax Court. Section 6512(b)(3)(B) also contains some language that permits a taxpayer in certain circumstances to collect a refund although he has not actually filed an administrative claim (or has not filed one in what would be a timely fashion under § 6511(a)). Because in my opinion nothing in § 6512(b)(3)(B) suggests that Congress intended to shorten the look-back period in a proceeding in Tax Court, I would hold that Lundy is entitled to his refund.

I.

Since 1976, the Service has taken the position that if a taxpayer files a delinquent return containing an accurate claim for a refund within three years after the date on which the tax is deemed to have been over-withheld from his pay, then he can obtain a refund of that tax. *See* Rev. Rul. 76-511, 1976-2 Cum. Bull. 428 (construing 26 U.S.C. § 6511(a)). This is because "[a] return shall be a claim for refund if it contains a statement setting forth the amount determined as an overpayment and advising that such amount shall be refunded to the taxpayer," Rev. Rul. 76-511, 1976-2 Cum. Bull. 428, and because a claim filed simultaneously with a return is filed "within 3 years from the time the return was filed" under 26 U.S.C. § 6511(a). The net effect of the interpretation of §§ 6511(a) and (b) adopted in Revenue Ruling 76-511 is that "if (i) a return is filed more than two but less than three years after it is due and (ii) a refund claim is filed contemporaneously or subsequently, 'the refund would [be] allowable since the overpayment would have been made within the 3-year period immediately preceding the filing of the claim.' " Brief for Petitioner 29, n.11 (*quoting* Rev. Rul. 76-511, 1976-2 Cum. Bull., at 429). The majority assumes that this interpretation of § 6511 is correct. * * * Under this reading of § 6511, Lundy would have received a 3-year look-back period and a refund if he had filed a suit in a district court or the Court of Federal Claims, rather than filing a petition in the Tax Court.

The harder step is determining whether the Service's interpretation of § 6511 itself is correct. Arguably, § 6511(a) is ambiguous as to what point in time is relevant in determining whether "no return was filed." The Ninth Circuit has held in *Miller v. United States*, 38 F.3d 473, 475 (1994), that "the point at which one must determine whether a return has or has not been filed [for purposes of § 6511(a)] must be two years after payment" of the taxes.

Congress' intent on this issue is difficult to discern. There is reason to think that Congress simply did not consider how being delinquent in filing a return would affect a taxpayer's right to recover a refund — in *any* forum. It appears that Congress chose the 3-year limitation period in § 6511(a) to correspond with the amount of time the Government has to make an assessment. *See* S. Rep. No. 1983, 85th Cong., 2d Sess., 98–99 (1958). As construed by the Service in Revenue Ruling 76-511, subsection (a) of § 6511 *does* create a limitation period for any taxpayer that will correspond with the period for assessment: the taxpayer has three years from the time he files his return to file a claim, and the Government usually has three years from the time the taxpayer files a return, for assessment. However, in cases where the taxpayer does not timely file his return, subsection (b) takes back the symmetry that subsection (a) bestows. In those cases, the taxpayer may only recover a refund of tax that was paid within the three years prior to his claim, yet the 3-year statute of limitation on assessments is triggered by the filing of the *return*. These facts suggest that in enacting § 6511, Congress quite likely was simply not thinking about the effects on delinquent filers. Or, to put it another way, Congress may have had *no* intent regarding whether §§ 6511(a) and (b) would permit a taxpayer to take advantage of a 3-year look-back period where the taxpayer's return is not filed on time, and where the 3-year period thus cannot correlate with the Government's assessment period.

Nevertheless, in light of the language of § 6511(a), the absence of any reason to think that Congress affirmatively intended to prevent taxpayers who file their returns more than two years late (but less than three years late) from collecting refunds, and the Service's 20-year interpretation of § 6511 in its Revenue Ruling, I would interpret § 6511 in conformity with the Revenue Ruling.

II.

Section 6512(b), rather than § 6511, directly governs the amount of a tax refund that may be awarded in the Tax Court. The most striking aspect of § 6512(b)(3)(B), however, is that it incorporates the look-back provisions of § 6511 — it directs the Tax Court to determine what portion of tax was paid "within the period which would be applicable under section 6511(b)(2)." To my mind, then, the question is whether the additional language in § 6512(b)(3)(B) (that directing the Tax Court to pretend that "on the date of the mailing of the notice of deficiency a claim had been filed"), the statute's legislative history, or other related statutory provisions indicate that Congress meant to prevent a taxpayer from receiving his refund from the Tax Court, even though the other courts could have ordered the refund.

*   *   *

Congress likely failed to state specifically in § 6512(b) whether a subsequently filed claim should be considered in Tax Court because it simply did not consider how that statute would be applied to the taxpayer who failed to file a timely return — just as it likely did not consider how § 6511 itself would be applied to the delinquent filer.

*   *   *

Because § 6512(b)(3)(B) incorporates the look-back periods of § 6511(b) and because it appears that the variance in the Tax Court statute was meant to be *more* protective of the taxpayer litigating in the Tax Court in certain circumstances, I would hold that Lundy may recover his refund.

*   *   *

The statutes discussed in *Lundy* are technical and complicated. The crux of the case involves an interpretation of section 6512(b)(3)(B), which does not seem to contemplate a delinquent return. Yet *Lundy* raises several important issues that transcend its specific holding. First, what is a "refund claim"? Can a return also constitute a refund claim? Second, if section 6512 is ambiguous, should the Court interpret it in such a manner that the same statutory period will apply to a taxpayer who litigates a claimed overpayment in Tax Court as would apply to that taxpayer in a refund court? Third, the 1976 Revenue Ruling, discussed by the dissent, arguably supported Lundy's position. Should the IRS be bound by the Revenue Ruling if it believes it is incorrect?

After the *Lundy* decision, Congress amended section 6512(b)(3) to add the following sentence:

> In a case described in subparagraph (B) where the date of the mailing of the notice of deficiency is during the third year after the due date (with extensions) for filing the return of tax and no return was filed before such date, the applicable period under subsections (a) and (b)(2) of section 6511 shall be 3 years.

Does this amendment overrule *Lundy*? Does it put a nonfiler who is "caught" by the IRS in a better position with respect to a refund claim than one who is not? Are those situations distinguishable?

As discussed above, prior to *Lundy,* there were several cases in which the taxpayer did not file a timely return, subsequently filed a first return for the year claiming a refund, and, upon denial of the claim, litigated the issue of timeliness of the claim in a refund court. Does *Lundy,* coupled with the above amendment to section 6512, provide the limitations period applicable in those cases? What *should* the statutory period be in those cases?

If a return is filed late but the refund claim on it is arguably timely (because its deadline is so much later), can section 7502 apply to only the claim? During 2000, the Second and Eighth Circuits split on this issue. *Compare Weisbart v. U.S. Dept. of Treasury*, 222 F.3d 93 (2d Cir. 2000), *acq.*, AOD CC-2000-09 (applying section 7502), *with Anastasoff v. United States*, 223 F.3d 898 (8th Cir. 2000) (refusing to apply section 7502). *Anastasoff* was vacated as moot because the IRS conceded the issue. *See Anastasoff v. United States*, 235 F.3d 1054 (8th Cir. 2000). Subsequently, the IRS issued new, final regulations under section 7502 that treat a claim for refund made on a late-filed income tax return as timely made if the postmark date is timely. An example provides:

> (i) Taxpayer A, an individual, mailed his 2001 Form 1040, "U.S. Individual Income Tax Return," on April 15, 2005, claiming a refund of amounts paid through withholding during 2001. The date of the postmark on the envelope containing the return and claim for refund is April 15, 2005. The return and claim for refund are received by the Internal Revenue Service (IRS) on April 18, 2005. Amounts withheld in 2001 exceeded A's tax liability for 2001 and are treated as paid on April 15, 2002, pursuant to section 6513.

> (ii) Even though the date of the postmark on the envelope is after the due date of the return, the claim for refund and the late filed return are treated as filed on the postmark date for purposes of this paragraph (f). Accordingly, the return will be treated as filed on April 15, 2005. In addition, the claim for refund will be treated as timely filed on April 15, 2005. *Further, the entire amount of the refund attributable to withholding is allowable as a refund under section 6511(b)(2)(A).*

Treas. Reg. § 301.7502-1(f)(3) (emphasis added).

The italicized language implied that the IRS might no longer argue that a two-year limitations period applies to refund claims made on delinquent returns under *Miller v. United States*, 38 F.3d 473 (9th Cir. 1994). In March of 2001, the IRS cleared up this issue, issuing a Chief Counsel Notice stating that it disagreed with *Miller* and would no longer rely on it to deny refund claims. *See* Chief Counsel Notice 2001-19.

[E] Tolling of Statutes of Limitations on Refund Claims

The refund statutes of limitations are applied fairly strictly to cut off untimely claims. *United States v. Brockamp* discusses the possibility of tolling the statute for equitable reasons where the taxpayer had a disability that prevented him from filing a timely refund claim. What are the policy reasons for the Court's decision? Do you agree with them?

UNITED STATES v. BROCKAMP
United States Supreme Court
519 U.S. 347 (1997)*

[The basic facts of *Brockamp* are as follows: "In April 1984, Mr. McGill, who was 93 years old at the time, mailed a check to the Internal Revenue Service ('IRS') for $ 7,000, along with an application for an automatic extension of time to file his 1983 income tax return. He made no indication of his reason for sending the $ 7,000. Despite his extension request, Mr. McGill never filed an income tax return for 1983. * * * Mr. McGill died intestate on November 7, 1988 at the age of 98. During the administration of his estate, Mrs. Brockamp discovered the $ 7,000 payment and requested a refund. In a letter to the IRS, Mrs. Brockamp characterized her father as 'senile' and stated that he had mistakenly sent the check for $7,000 rather than $ 700." Brockamp v. United States, 67 F.3d 260 (9th Cir. 1995).

The basic facts of *Scott*, the companion case, are these: "In the early 1980s, Nicholas Scott began to experience severe difficulties resulting from his alcohol abuse, including multiple citations for driving under the influence of alcohol and the loss of his job. He turned over power of attorney for his financial affairs to his father. In 1984, pursuant to the power of attorney, Mr. Scott's father made a number of federal tax deposits on Mr. Scott's behalf. Then, after Mr. Scott revoked the power of attorney, he himself made a final estimated tax payment in January 1985. Altogether, the payments made toward Mr. Scott's 1984 taxes totalled $ 30,096. In actuality, Mr. Scott had no tax liability that year. Mr. Scott filed tax returns for the 1984–88 tax years on November 29, 1989 and claimed a refund of $ 30,096 plus interest." Scott v. United States, 95-2 U.S.T.C. (CCH) (9th Cir. 1995). Eds.]

BREYER, J., delivered the opinion for a unanimous Court.

The two cases before us raise a single question. Can courts toll, for nonstatutory equitable reasons, the statutory time (and related amount) limitations for filing tax refund claims set forth in § 6511 of the Internal Revenue Code of 1986? We hold that they cannot.

These two cases present similar circumstances. In each case a taxpayer initially paid the Internal Revenue Service (IRS) several thousand dollars that he did not owe. In each case the taxpayer (or his representative) filed an administrative claim for refund several years after the relevant statutory time period for doing so had ended. In each case the taxpayer suffered a disability (senility or alcoholism), which, he said, explained why the delay was not his fault. And in each case he asked the court to extend the relevant statutory time period for an "equitable" reason, namely, the existence of a mental disability—a reason not mentioned in § 6511, but which, we assume, would permit a court to toll the statutory limitations period *if, but only if*, § 6511 contains an implied "equitable tolling" exception. *See* 4 C. Wright & A. Miller, Federal Practice and Procedure § 1056 (2d ed. 1987 and Supp. 1996); *see also* Wolin v. Smith Barney, Inc., 83 F.3d 847, 852 (CA7 1996) (defining equitable tolling).

---

* Together with *United States v. Scott*, also on certiorari to the same court.

In both cases, the Ninth Circuit read § 6511 as if it did contain an implied exception that would permit "equitable tolling." It then applied principles of equity to each case. It found those principles justified tolling the statutory time period. And it permitted the actions to proceed. 67 F.3d 260 (1995); judgt. order reported at 70 F.3d 120 (1995). All other Circuits that have considered the matter, however, have taken the opposite view. They have held that § 6511 does not authorize equitable tolling. *See* Amoco Production Co. v. Newton Sheep Co., 85 F.3d 1464 (CA10 1996); Lovett v. United States, 81 F.3d 143 (CA Fed. 1996); Webb v. United States, 66 F.3d 691 (CA4 1995); Oropallo v. United States, 994 F.2d 25 (CA1 1993) (per curiam); and Vintilla v. United States, 931 F.2d 1444 (CA11 1991). We granted certiorari to resolve this conflict. And we conclude that the latter Circuits are correct.

The taxpayers rest their claim for equitable tolling upon *Irwin v. Department of Veterans Affairs*, 498 U.S. 89, 111 S. Ct. 453, 112 L. Ed. 2d 435 (1990), a case in which this Court considered the timeliness of an employee's lawsuit charging his Government employer with discrimination, in violation of Title VII of the Civil Rights Act of 1964, 42 U.S.C. § 2000e *et seq.* The Court found the lawsuit untimely, but nevertheless tolled the limitations period. It held that the "rule of equitable tolling" applies "to suits against the Government, in the same way that it is applicable" to Title VII suits against private employers. 498 U.S. at 94–95. The Court went on to say that the "same rebuttable presumption of equitable tolling applicable to suits against private defendants should also apply to suits against the United States." *Id.* at 95–96.

The taxpayers, pointing to *Irwin,* argue that principles of equitable tolling would have applied had they sued private defendants, *e.g.,* had they sought restitution from private defendants for "Money Had and Received." *See* C. Keigwin, CASES IN COMMON LAW PLEADING 220 (2d ed. 1934). They add that given *Irwin*'s language, there must be a "presumption" that limitations periods in tax refund suits against the Government can be equitably tolled. And, they say, that "presumption," while "rebuttable," has not been rebutted. They conclude that, given *Irwin,* the Ninth Circuit correctly tolled the statutory period for "equitable" reasons.

In evaluating this argument, we are willing to assume, favorably to the taxpayers but only for argument's sake, that a tax refund suit and a private suit for restitution are sufficiently similar to warrant asking *Irwin*'s negatively phrased question: Is there good reason to believe that Congress did not want the equitable tolling doctrine to apply? *But see* Flora v. United States, 362 U.S. 145, 153–154, 4 L. Ed. 2d 623, 80 S. Ct. 630 (1960) (*citing* Curtis's Administratrix v. Fiedler, 67 U.S. 461, 2 Black 461, 479, 17 L. Ed. 273 (1863)) (distinguishing common-law suit against the tax collector from action of assumpsit for money had and received); George Moore Ice Cream Co. v. Rose, 289 U.S. 373, 382–383, 77 L. Ed. 1265, 53 S. Ct. 620 (1933); *see also* Plumb, Tax Refund Suits Against Collectors of Internal Revenue, 60 Harv. L. Rev. 685, 687 (1947) (describing collector suit as a fiction solely designed to bring the Government into court). We can travel no further, however, along *Irwin*'s road, for there are strong reasons for answering *Irwin*'s question in the Government's favor.

Section 6511 sets forth its time limitations in unusually emphatic form. Ordinarily limitations statutes use fairly simple language, which one can often plausibly read as containing an implied "equitable tolling" exception. *See, e.g.,* 42 U.S.C. § 2000e-16(c) (requiring suit for employment discrimination to be filed "within 90 days of receipt of notice of final [EEOC] action . . . "). But § 6511 uses language that is not simple. It sets forth its limitations in a highly detailed technical manner, that, linguistically speaking, cannot easily be read as containing implicit exceptions. Moreover, § 6511 reiterates its limitations several times in several different ways. * * *

The Tax Code reemphasizes the point when it says that refunds that do not comply with these limitations "shall be considered erroneous," § 6514, and specifies procedures for the Government's recovery of any such "erroneous" refund payment. §§ 6532(b), 7405. In addition, § 6511 sets forth explicit exceptions to its basic time limits, and those very specific exceptions do not include "equitable tolling." *See* § 6511(d) (establishing special time limit rules for refunds related to operating losses, credit carrybacks, foreign taxes, self-employment taxes, worthless securities, and bad debts); *see also* United States v. Dalm, 494 U.S. 596, 610, 108 L. Ed. 2d 548, 110 S. Ct. 1361 (1990) (discussing mitigation provisions set forth in 26 U.S.C. §§ 1311–1314); § 507 of the Revenue Act of 1942, 56 Stat. 961 (temporarily tolling limitations period during wartime).

To read an "equitable tolling" provision into these provisions, one would have to assume an implied exception for tolling virtually every time a number appears. To do so would work a kind of linguistic havoc. Moreover, such an interpretation would require tolling, not only procedural limitations, but also substantive limitations on the amount of recovery—a kind of tolling for which we have found no direct precedent. Section 6511's detail, its technical language, the iteration of the limitations in both procedural and substantive forms, and the explicit listing of exceptions, taken together, indicate to us that Congress did not intend courts to read other unmentioned, open-ended, "equitable" exceptions into the statute that it wrote. There are no counterindications. Tax law, after all, is not normally characterized by case-specific exceptions reflecting individualized equities.

The nature of the underlying subject matter—tax collection—underscores the linguistic point. The IRS processes more than 200 million tax returns each year. It issues more than 90 million refunds. *See* Dept. of Treasury, Internal Revenue Service, 1995 Data Book 8–9. To read an "equitable tolling" exception into § 6511 could create serious administrative problems by forcing the IRS to respond to, and perhaps litigate, large numbers of late claims, accompanied by requests for "equitable tolling" which, upon close inspection, might turn out to lack sufficient equitable justification. *See* H. R. Conf. Rep. No. 356, 69th Cong., 1st Sess., 41 (1926) (deleting provision excusing tax deficiencies in the estates of insane or deceased individuals because of difficulties involved in defining incompetence). The nature and potential magnitude of the administrative problem suggest that Congress decided to pay the price of occasional unfairness in individual cases (penalizing a taxpayer whose claim is unavoidably delayed) in order to maintain a more workable tax enforcement system. At the least it tells us that Congress would likely have wanted to decide explicitly whether, or just where and when, to expand the statute's limitations periods, rather than delegate to the courts a generalized power to do so wherever a court concludes that equity so requires.

The taxpayers' counterrebuttal consists primarily of an interesting historical analysis of the Internal Revenue Code's tax refund provisions. They try to show that § 6511's specific, detailed language reflects congressional concern about matters not related to equitable tolling. They explain some language, for example, in terms of a congressional effort to stop taxpayers from keeping the refund period open indefinitely through the device of making a series of small tax payments. *See* S. Rep. No. 398, 68th Cong., 1st Sess., 33 (1924). They explain other language as an effort to make the refund time period and the tax assessment period coextensive. *See* H.R. Rep. No. 2333, 77th Cong., 2d Sess., 52 (1942). Assuming all that is so, however, such congressional efforts still seem but a smaller part of a larger congressional objective: providing the Government with strong statutory "protection against stale demands." *Cf.* United States v. Garbutt Oil Co., 302 U.S. 528, 533, 82 L. Ed. 405, 58 S. Ct. 320 (1938) (statute of limitations bars untimely amendment of claim for additional refund). Moreover, the history to which the taxpayers point reveals that § 6511's predecessor tax refund provisions, like § 6511, contained highly detailed language with clear time limits. * * * And that history lacks any instance (but for the present cases) of equitable tolling. On balance, these historical considerations help the Government's argument.

For these reasons, we conclude that Congress did not intend the "equitable tolling" doctrine to apply to § 6511's time limitations. The Ninth Circuit's decisions are

Reversed.

After *Brockamp* was decided, Congress enacted Code section 6511(h) as part of the IRS Reform Act. What is the policy behind the new provision? What effects might it have on refund litigation?

In Revenue Procedure 99-21, 1999-1 C.B. 786, the IRS explained how a taxpayer may obtain "equitable tolling" of the statute of limitations on refund claims based on a financial disability. It provides, in part:

> Unless otherwise provided in IRS forms and instructions, the following statements are to be submitted with a claim for credit or refund of tax to claim financial disability for purposes of § 6511(h).
>
> (1)   a written statement by a physician (as defined in § 1861(r)(1) of the Social Security Act, 42 U.S.C. § 1395x(r)), qualified to make the determination, that sets forth:
>
>> (a)   the name and a description of the taxpayer's physical or mental impairment;
>>
>> (b)   the physician's medical opinion that the physical or mental impairment prevented the taxpayer from managing the taxpayer's financial affairs;
>>
>> (c)   the physician's medical opinion that the physical or mental impairment was or can be expected to result in death, or that it has lasted (or can be expected to

last) for a continuous period of not less than 12 months;

(d)   to the best of the physician's knowledge, the specific time period during which the taxpayer was prevented by such physical or mental impairment from managing the taxpayer's financial affairs; and

(e)   the following certification, signed by the physician:

I hereby certify that, to the best of my knowledge and belief, the above representations are true, correct, and complete.

(2)   A written statement by the person signing the claim for credit or refund that no person, including the taxpayer's spouse, was authorized to act on behalf of the taxpayer in financial matters during the period described in paragraph (1)(d) of this section. Alternatively, if a person was authorized to act on behalf of the taxpayer in financial matters during any part of the period described in paragraph (1)(d), the beginning and ending dates of the period of time the person was so authorized.

In *LaBerge v. United States*, 2000-1 U.S.T.C. 50,233 (E.D. Mich. 2000), a District Court refused to allow equitable relief from the statute of limitations on refund claims based on the taxpayer-wife's obsessive-compulsive disorder. The taxpayers had consistently filed their returns late. The IRS assessed penalties and interest. The taxpayers filed a complaint, alleging that they were entitled to a tax refund or credit for the filing penalties because taxpayer-wife's illness "caused her to hoard every piece of paper and object with which she came in contact," resulting in their late filing. The court held that because the taxpayers had not filed a timely refund claim, it lacked jurisdiction over the case.

[F]   The Statutory Mitigation Provisions and Equitable Recoupment

Under limited circumstances, the expiration of the statute of limitations on refund claims may not bar the claim. For example, what if, in 2003, the taxpayer loses a court case and is required by the court to include in income for his 1997 tax year an amount that the taxpayer had already included in 1998: can the taxpayer claim a refund of the amount paid with respect to the 1998 year if the statute of limitations on refund claims for that year has already expired? Recall the statutory mitigation provisions, which were discussed in Chapter 5. In Chapter 5, the discussion focused on the *IRS's* reliance on these provisions to reopen a barred year to *make an assessment*. Look again at sections 1311 and 1312(1). Notice that the mitigation provisions also apply to allow the *taxpayer* to reopen a barred year to *claim a refund* in order to avoid, for example, inclusion of the same income amount in two different tax years.

In situations in which the statutory mitigation provisions do not afford the taxpayer relief, a doctrine known as "equitable recoupment" might help the taxpayer. As indicated in Chapter 5, "equitable recoupment" has been utilized in tax cases to allow one party to recover a time-barred claim by offsetting it against an amount owed to the other party. It is based upon the concept that "one taxable event should not be taxed twice, once on a correct theory and once on an incorrect theory . . . and that to avoid this happening the statute of limitations will be waived."

Mann v. United States, 552 F. Supp. 1132, 1135 (N.D. Tex. 1982) (*quoting Minskoff v. United States*, 490 F.2d 1283, 1285 (6th Cir. 1974)).

In a refund action, it would generally be the IRS that would assert the defense of equitable recoupment to reduce or eliminate the taxpayer's refund.[8] The IRS would argue that a time-barred deficiency arose out of the same transaction. For example, the amount recoverable by an estate in a suit for refund of income taxes might be subject to offset by an amount of additional estate tax, otherwise barred by the statute of limitations on assessment, based on the theory adopted in the income tax suit.

The following excerpt from *Wilmington Trust Co. v. United States*, 221 Ct. Cl. 686, 701 (1979) reviews the United States Supreme Court's application of equitable recoupment:

The Supreme Court three times has considered the doctrine of equitable recoupment in tax cases. It has allowed recoupment twice and denied it once. The three decisions together explain the doctrine and its parameters.

The first case was *Bull v. United States*, 295 U.S. 247 (1935). Under the partnership agreement of the decedent's firm, his estate received the equivalent of the decedent's share of the partnership income for the year following his death. The Commissioner initially treated this amount as part of the estate and subject to the estate tax. He subsequently assessed an income tax deficiency against the estate, which the estate paid.

The executor filed suit in this court, seeking alternatively (1) refund of the income tax on the ground that the partnership's payment to the estate was corpus and not income, or (2) if the amount were income, a credit by the government for the overpayment of the estate tax resulting from the treatment of the payment as part of the estate. By that time the statute of limitations barred any direct claim by the executor for refund of the estate tax he had paid. This court denied the offset as barred by limitations, after first holding that the payment was income to the estate.

The Supreme Court reversed the denial of the offset. It ruled that because the government "through a palpable mistake" collected a larger estate tax "than it was entitled to," its "[r]etention of the money was against morality and conscience." *Id.* at 260. It held that when the government "brought a new proceeding [to collect the income tax]

---

[8] Many refund suits that discuss equitable recoupment claims involve the plaintiff invoking the doctrine as an independent basis for a refund suit, sometimes because the statute of limitations has expired. However, equitable recoupment cannot serve that purpose. United States v. Dalm, 494 U.S. 596, 598 (1990).

arising out of the same transaction involved in the earlier proceeding [the payment by the partnership to the estate]," the money belonging to the estate that the government "unjust[ly] re[tained] . . . may be used by way of recoupment and credit in an action by the United States arising out of the same transaction." *Id.* at 261. It stated (*id.* at 262, footnote omitted) that "recoupment is in the nature of a defense arising out of some feature of the transaction upon which the plaintiff's action is grounded" and that "[s]uch a defense is never barred by the statute of limitations so long as the main action itself is timely."

* * *

In the third case, *Rothensies v. Electric Storage Battery Co.*, 329 U.S. 296 (1946), however, the Court denied equitable recoupment. In so doing, it significantly limited what appeared to be the broad implications of the language in *Bull* * * * .

In *Rothensies* the taxpayer, between 1919 and 1926, had paid excise taxes on sales that it and the government believed were subject to tax. In 1926 the company changed its mind and sued for a refund of the taxes it had paid between 1922 and 1926, claiming that the tax was not payable on those sales. At that time the statute of limitations had already run on the taxes paid for the earlier years. In 1935, pursuant to a judgment in its favor, the taxpayer received a refund of the taxes it had paid for 1922 to 1926.

The Commissioner treated the refund as income to the taxpayer in 1935 and assessed additional income and excess profits taxes for that year. In a suit by the taxpayer for the refund of those additional taxes, the taxpayer contended that if the refund were income, it should be permitted to apply against the additional tax the barred excise taxes it had erroneously paid between 1919 and 1922. The lower court permitted recoupment.

The Supreme Court reversed. It stated (*id.* at 299) that recoupment

> has never been thought to allow one transaction to be offset against another, but only to permit a transaction which is made the subject of suit by a plaintiff to be examined in all its aspects, and judgment to be rendered that does justice in view of the one transaction as a whole.

> It added that "recoupment in tax litigation" is given only "limited scope." *Id.* It pointed out (*id.* at 299–300) that in [*Bull*] "a single transaction constituted the taxable event claimed upon and the one considered in recoupment," and that "the single transaction or taxable event had been subjected to two taxes on inconsistent legal theories, and what was mistakenly paid was recouped against what was correctly due." The Court rejected the view of the Court of Appeals that the recoupment doctrine applied in *Bull* * * * "was 'based on concepts of fairness' " * * *.

The Court explained that statutes of limitations also rest upon concepts of fairness, since they protect litigants against stale claims they may have difficulty in meeting. * * *

Following *Rothensies* this court and other courts have considered the application of equitable recoupment in tax cases in a variety of situations. The cases have gone both ways, as the courts dealt with varying facts.[9] In all of them, however, the inquiry was whether the tax for which recoupment was sought arose out of the same transaction as that involved in the main action.

How does the doctrine of equitable recoupment differ from the doctrine of setoff, which was applied by the Supreme Court in *Lewis v. Reynolds*, reproduced above in Section 8.02[C]?

§ 8.05   Erroneous Refunds and Abatements of Tax

Code section 7405 allows an action for recovery of refunds erroneously made by the IRS.[9] Code section 6532(b) grants the IRS a two-year statute of limitations for suing for recovery of an erroneous refund, unless the refund, or any part of it, was induced by fraud or the taxpayer's misrepresentation of a material fact. In either case, the period starts to run from issuance of the refund. What section 7405 does not reflect is the fact that there are two types of erroneous refunds, "rebate refunds" and "non-rebate refunds." Although the law is not entirely clear on this point, the better argument seems to be that section 7405 applies only to non-rebate refunds. *See O'Bryant v. United States*, 49 F.3d 340 7th Cir. (1995); *see also* Chief Counsel Advice 200137051.

---

[9] Recoupment denied: Kramer v. United States, 186 Ct. Cl. 684, 406 F.2d 1363 (1969) (government sought recoupment of taxes owed by one beneficiary of a multibeneficiary estate); Ford v. United States, 149 Ct. Cl. 558, 276 F.2d 17 (1960) (assets valued twice, once for estate tax purposes and once for income tax purposes at the time of subsequent sale, resulting in higher estate tax assessment under first valuation and higher income tax assessment under second valuation); Minskoff v. United States, 490 F.2d 1283 (2d Cir. 1974), *aff'g* 349 F. Supp. 1146 (S.D.N.Y. 1972) (estate tax paid on estate including cash representing full sale price of recently disposed asset; capital gains tax deficiency for that sale subsequently assessed against the estate); Missouri Public Service Co. v. United States, 245 F. Supp. 954 (W.D. Mo. 1965), *aff'd*, 370 F.2d 971 (8th Cir. 1967) (adjustments to correct repeated IRS mistreatments of depreciation of assets increased one year's taxes and decreased another's); Kojes v. United States, 241 F. Supp. 762 (E.D.N.Y. 1965) (essentially the same facts as in *Minskoff, supra*).

Recoupment allowed: National Biscuit Co. v. United States, 140 Ct. Cl. 443, 156 F. Supp. 916 (1957) (incorrect excess profits credit led to overpayment of some taxes and underpayment of others); E. I. DuPont DeNemours & Co. v. United States, 137 Ct. Cl. 191, 147 F. Supp. 486 (1957) (incorrect treatment of rescission of excess profits tax deferral led to unnecessary payment of interest on one tax deficiency and nonpayment of interest on another deficiency); Pond's Extract Co. v. United States, 133 Ct. Cl. 43, 134 F. Supp. 476 (1955) (incorrect treatment of payment of income tax settlement decreased subsequent excess profits taxes and increased a subsequent income tax); Boyle v. United States, 355 F.2d 233 (3d Cir. 1965) (estate tax paid on arrearage of cumulative preferred stock dividends extant at decedent's death; income tax assessed on subsequent payments against the arrearage); United States v. Bowcut, 287 F.2d 654 (9th Cir. 1961) (underpayment of income taxes by decedent taxpayer led to overpayment of estate taxes); United States v. Herring, 240 F.2d 225 (4th Cir. 1957) (same as *Bowcut, supra;* government did not assert deficiency claim against the estate until after the estate tax limitations period expired).

[9] Section 7405 does not create the right to recover erroneous refunds, but merely declares it; the government's right to sue exists independent of the statute. United States v. Wurts, 303 U.S. 414, 415 (1938); *see also* Marshall v. United States, 158 F. Supp. 793, 795 (E.D. Tex. 1958).

Recall that the definition of a deficiency in Code section 6211(a) refers to "rebates." In general, ignoring prior rebates, a rebate is any portion of a repayment made by the IRS to a taxpayer on the ground that the tax imposed was less than the amounts admitted by the taxpayer on his return plus assessments previously made. Payment of the rebate through a refund of taxes constitutes a rebate refund. If the IRS later reevaluates the merits of the tax and determines that the rebate was in error, the payment of the rebate will have created a deficiency within the meaning of section 6211. That is because, in this context, the determination will be based on a substantive redetermination of tax liability. Accordingly, the deficiency procedures of section 6212 and 6213 should apply.

A refund made for some other reason is a non-rebate refund. This type of refund may be made erroneously for such reasons as a mathematical, clerical, or computer error. Such a refund does not create a deficiency within the meaning of section 6211(a) because it is not a "rebate" within the meaning of Code section 6211(b)(2). *See Groetzinger v. Commissioner*, 69 T.C. 309, 314 (1977). Instead, the refund creates an underpayment of tax that is based on the original assessment, which the taxpayer already had the opportunity to contest on the merits. This type of refund may be recovered under section 7405, within the limitations period specified by section 6532(b).

The discussion above focuses on erroneous tax refunds. If a tax liability has not yet been paid when the IRS determines that it is too high, the IRS will not make a refund, but rather will abate the tax. *See* I.R.C. § 6404(a). If the abatement is in error, it will constitute an erroneous abatement. As above, if the error was on the merits, then the IRS must reassess the tax liability within the limitations period under section 6501 in order to reverse the abatement. *See* Notice CC-2001-014, 2001 TNT 40-22. However, if the abatement was based on a mathematical or clerical error, the IRS may simply reverse the abatement and reinstate the original assessment, regardless of whether the limitations period for assessments has run, so long as the limitations period for collection is still open. *See id.*

PROBLEMS

1. Joanne filed her 1998 return on April 1, 1999. She owed $500, which she mailed with her return. The rest of her tax liability, $7,000, was covered by withholding. After examining her return a few months later, she realized that she made an error that may entitle her to a refund of $1,000.

    A. How can Joanne claim a refund of the $1,000?

    B. When is the last day she can claim a refund?

    C. How, if at all, would your answer to B. change if Joanne had filed her return on April 15, 1999 instead?

    D. How, if at all, would your answer to B. change if Joanne had granted the IRS a one-year extension of the statute of limitations on assessment with respect to her 1998 tax year?

E.   Assume that Joanne filed a timely refund claim on July 8, 1999.

    i.   If the IRS does not ever respond to her claim, when is the first day she can file a refund suit? When is the last day?

    ii.   Assume the IRS denied Joanne's refund claim on January 3, 2000. When is the first day she can file a refund suit? When is the last day?

2.   Adrian has received a notice of deficiency from the IRS in the amount of $5,000 with respect to his 2002 tax year. After receiving the notice, and within 45 days of the date on the notice, Adrian mailed the IRS a $5,000 check with only the notation "2002 tax year" on the memo line of the check.

A.   Is Adrian still entitled to petition the Tax Court in response to the notice of deficiency?

B.   How would it affect Adrian's rights if instead he had printed "deposit—2002 taxes" on the memo line of his check?

C.   Would your answer to A. differ if Adrian had mailed in $5,000 after receiving a 30-day letter but before receiving the notice of deficiency?

D.   Assume that Adrian does not petition the Tax Court. If the statute of limitations on assessment expires after Adrian's remittance of the $5,000 without an assessment by the IRS of the $5,000, is the IRS obligated to refund the $5,000 to Adrian?

3.   Mary filed her 1996 tax return on May 1, 1997, without having obtained an extension of time to file. A total of $10,000 of tax had been withheld from her wages. She computed a tax liability of $11,000, so she mailed a check for $1,000 with the 1996 return. On April 20, 2000, the IRS mailed Mary a notice of deficiency, which she received on April 25, 2000, reflecting the Commissioner's determination of a deficiency of $500. The $500 deficiency is attributable to income allegedly received by Mary and not reported on the return. Mary believes that she does not owe the $500 and that she is in fact entitled to a refund of $700 of the amounts already paid.

A.   Assume that Mary filed a Tax Court petition on May 1, 2000, contesting the notice of deficiency and claiming that she made an overpayment of $700. Can the Tax Court order the IRS to refund $700 to Mary if the court agrees with her on the merits?

B.   Assume Mary paid the $500 deficiency on May 1, 2000.

    i.   If Mary wishes to pursue a refund in federal district court of the $1,200 (the $500 paid in response to the notice plus the $700 alleged overpayment), when is the last day on which she can file a timely refund claim with the IRS to be entitled to pursue a refund of at least some of the $1,200?

    ii.   Assume that Mary filed a timely claim for refund only of the $500, and, after receiving a notice of disallowance of her claim, filed a timely suit for refund of the $500 on June 1, 2001. The IRS has not only contested Mary's entitlement to a refund of the $500, but also has counterclaimed for $800 based on the disallowance of certain deductions. If the court enters a decision on May 5, 2002 in Mary's favor on the $500 issue and in the IRS's favor on the $800 issue, what amount, if any, may each side collect from the other?

4.   Dan negligently failed to mail his 1993 return until May 10, 1996. When filed, the return reflected a tax liability of $3,000 for the 1993 year, and wage withholding credits of $2,500 (consistent with the Form W-2 included with the return). Accordingly, he mailed a $500 payment in with the return, which the IRS received with the return on May 13, 1996. On April 1, 1999, the IRS mailed Dan a notice of deficiency in the amount of $1,000 based on income Dan allegedly received but did not report.

    A.   Assume that Dan failed to respond in any way to the notice of deficiency, and the IRS assesses the $1,000 deficiency on July 15, 1999. Is the assessment timely?

    B.   Alternatively, assume instead that Dan responded to the notice by filing a petition in the United States Tax Court on April 30, 1999. He alleges never having received the income referenced in the notice of deficiency. In addition, he alleges that he is entitled to additional deductions entitling him to a refund of $700. Assuming that the Tax Court agrees with Dan on the merits, does the Tax Court have jurisdiction to order the IRS to award Dan a $700 refund?

    C.   Do both the statute of limitations on assessment of a $1,000 deficiency for Dan's 1993 tax year and the statute of limitations for Dan to claim a refund of $700 with respect to his 1993 tax year expire on the same day? Is your answer affected by whether or not Dan petitions the Tax Court?

5.   June is a recovering addict who, over the past few years, has been through several outpatient treatment programs designed to help those with substance abuse problems. She has refrained from using illegal drugs since January 1 of this year. June recently realized that she had neglected to file her tax returns for 1994 through last year, although she was employed for portions of each year and is owed a refund for each year. She explains that she was unable to timely file those returns

because she was incapacitated by her drug addiction. No one was authorized to act on her behalf with respect to her financial matters. June has never been contacted by the IRS. Can she claim a refund for any of those years, or has the statute of limitations expired on all of them?

6. Bob filed his 1999 return on April 3, 2000. On March 1, 2002, Bob filed a refund claim for $1,000, specifying that the reason for the claim is that he erroneously included excludable damages from an age discrimination lawsuit in gross income. On November 1, 2002, the IRS denied the claim, and Bob plans to bring suit in the local U.S. District Court. However, Bob has since realized that the damages were includible in gross income because they were not received on account of physical injury. However, he believes that he is nonetheless entitled to a $700 refund as a result of medical expenses relating to psychiatric treatment. Assuming that Bob's suit would be timely, is there any procedural barrier to Bob's litigation of this issue in order to prove his entitlement to a refund?

7. Tara Green asks your assistance in claiming a refund from the IRS. After timely filing her 1998 Form 1040 by mail in March 1999, she realized that she had forgotten to deduct $6,000 in home mortgage interest, real property taxes of $2,000, and state income taxes of $4,000 she had paid in 1998. (She had not itemized her deductions on her original return, but instead took the standard deduction of $4,250. She also took her personal exemption in the correct amount of $2,700). She has no other deductions or income items. Tara is single, has no dependents, and had adjusted gross income of $60,000 in 1998, consisting entirely of salary. $10,000 had been withheld from Tara's wages for federal income tax purposes, and she had paid the remainder of her tax liability ($1,566) with her return. She still resides at 125 Main St., Wayne, NJ 07470, where she lived when she filed the return in question. Her Social Security number is 222-33-4444 and her telephone number is (973) 264-9872. She did not and does not wish to make a Presidential Election Campaign Fund designation. Assume that Tara's refund claim will be timely; draft the claim for her.

Chapter 9

RELIANCE ON TREASURY REGULATIONS AND IRS POSITIONS

Reading Assignment: Code §§ 6110, 7805(a), (b), (e), (f).

§ 9.01 Introduction

As you know from your prior tax courses, substantive tax law can be a highly technical and complicated subject. The fact that so many tax questions remain unanswered speaks to the complexity of the Internal Revenue Code and to the ingenuity of tax advisors seeking to minimize their clients' tax liabilities. To interpret the Code, tax practitioners turn not only to court cases, but also to Treasury regulations and to other guidance released by the IRS, including Revenue Rulings and Revenue Procedures. Section 9.02 of this Chapter considers the taxpayer's ability to rely on these types of sources and the amount of deference a court will accord these items.

In some cases, tax practitioners may find it necessary to seek the views of the IRS in order to confirm how the Code should apply to a given set of facts. Section 9.03 discusses taxpayer-specific guidance issued in the form of letter rulings (commonly referred to as private letter rulings or PLRs) and determination letters. As discussed in Chapter 3, the IRS must release PLRs and determination letters under the mandate in section 6110, with identifying details redacted. Section 9.03 also examines sources of guidance prepared primarily for the internal use of the IRS, such as Technical Advice Memoranda, Chief Counsel Advice, and Action on Decision memoranda. These internal sources, which are also required to be released either under section 6110 or the Freedom of Information Act (FOIA), may help the taxpayer and his representative ascertain the IRS's current or expected position on a particular issue.

Finally, Section 9.04 explains how to obtain taxpayer-specific guidance from the IRS. The chapter considers the letter ruling request process in general, focusing specifically on situations in which the IRS will and will not issue guidance, and on the type of information the requesting party must include in the letter ruling application. In addition, Section 9.04 highlights some advantages and pitfalls associated with the taxpayer's decision to seek a letter ruling from the IRS.

As you read this chapter, consider the extent to which each of these sources of published authority, whether precedential or not, contributes to the uniform application and interpretation of the tax laws. What effect does this goal of uniform treatment by the IRS have on a taxpayer's incentive to comply with the law?

§ 9.02   Reliance on Published Authority

[A]   Treasury Regulations

[1]   Procedures for Enacting Treasury Regulations

The Secretary of the Treasury is authorized by the Code to "prescribe all needful rules and regulations for the enforcement of [the Code]." I.R.C. § 7805(a). Although the Secretary has delegated much of this rule-making authority to the IRS Chief Counsel's Office, which drafts most regulations, the Treasury Department actually issues those regulations. Treasury regulations represent official interpretations of the Code. In addition to explaining the statutory language to which they relate, regulations also may contain helpful examples of how and when a Code provision should apply.

There are two types of final regulations, interpretative regulations and legislative regulations. Interpretative regulations are released pursuant to the general grant of Congressional authority in section 7805(a). Legislative regulations are those released under an express delegation of Congressional authority in the particular Code section they address. *See, e.g.*, I.R.C. §§ 263A(i), 385(a).

Legislative regulations must be issued under the procedural requirements of the Administrative Procedure Act (APA), 5 U.S.C. § 553, which requires notice to the public and an opportunity to comment on the regulations before they are finalized. Once comments are received, the regulations must be published in their final form in the Federal Register at least 30 days prior to their effective date. The notice and comment procedures, however, need not be followed when revision of a regulation serves only to benefit taxpayers. 5 U.S.C. § 553(b)(3)(B). Interpretative regulations, issued under the broad authority of section 7805, are not subject to the 30-day notice and comment period, but the Treasury tends to follow that procedure anyway.[1]

In order to fulfill its obligations under the APA, the Treasury normally issues regulations initially in proposed form. The Treasury may also issue Temporary regulations when an immediate interpretation of a new statute is required. Temporary regulations are effective until superseded by final regulations, but in no event may they remain effective for more than three years after enactment. I.R.C. § 7805(e). Temporary regulations need not follow the usual APA notice and comment procedures. 5 U.S.C. § 553(b)(3)(B).

Until relatively recently, Code section 7805(b) allowed the Secretary of the Treasury to prescribe the extent to which, if any, a regulation would be applied *without* retroactive effect. However, the Taxpayer Bill of Rights 2, Pub. L. No. 104-168, § 1101, 110 Stat. 1452, 1468 (1996), removed this presumption of retroactivity. Under § 7805(b)(1)(B), final regulations generally do not take effect before the date on which related Proposed or Temporary regulations were filed with the Federal Register.

---

[1] Regulations are issued in sets, with the prefix designating the type of tax involved. Income tax regulations, for example, carry the prefix "1," estate tax regulations the prefix "20," and gift tax regulations the prefix "25." The "301" prefix designates Treasury regulations that are procedural in nature.

[2] Courts' Deference to Treasury Regulations

While courts generally give deference to Treasury regulations, they do have the power to invalidate them. The leading case on courts' deference to government agency pronouncements is *Chevron U.S.A., Inc. v. Natural Resources Defense Council, Inc.*, 467 U.S. 837 (1984), which is not a tax case. In that case, the Supreme Court stated:

> When a court reviews an agency's construction of the statute which it administers, it is confronted with two questions. First, always, is the question whether Congress has directly spoken to the precise question at issue. If the intent of Congress is clear, that is the end of the matter; for the court, as well as the agency, must give effect to the unambiguously expressed intent of Congress. If, however, the court determines Congress has not directly addressed the precise question at issue, the court does not simply impose its own construction on the statute, as would be necessary in the absence of an administrative interpretation. Rather, if the statute is silent or ambiguous with respect to the specific issue, the question for the court is whether the agency's answer is based on a permissible construction of the statute.

Id. at 843. The Court added in a footnote:

> The court need not conclude that the agency construction was the only one it permissibly could have adopted to uphold the construction, or even the reading the court would have reached if the question initially had arisen in a judicial proceeding.

Id. at 843 n.11 (citations omitted).

There is considerable debate over the extent to which "*Chevron* deference" applies in tax cases. *Bankers Casualty Co,* provides the following discussion both of *Chevron* deference to Treasury regulations (which the court refers to as "general tax regulations") and of the difference between legislative and interpretative regulations:

BANKERS LIFE AND CASUALTY CO. v. UNITED STATES
United States Court of Appeals, Seventh Circuit
142 F.3d 973 (1998)[2]

TERENCE T. EVANS, CIRCUIT JUDGE.

* * *

Before explaining Bankers Life's substantive arguments or the government's responses, we need to cover the basic structure of a challenge to a tax regulation. Essentially, we must determine the degree of deference owed to a Treasury Regulation issued under I.R.C. § 7805(a) with notice and comment procedures. This seemingly simple inquiry leads us into a free-fire zone of judicial debate over the proper level of judicial deference to various IRS

---

[2] *Cert. denied*, 525 U.S. 961 (1998).

interpretations of the revenue laws. The basic question is whether *Chevron* deference (from *Chevron U.S.A., Inc. v. Natural Resources Defense Council, Inc.,* 467 U.S. 837, 81 L. Ed. 2d 694, 104 S. Ct. 2778 (1984), and its progeny) applies to tax regulations. *See, e.g.,* Central Pa. Sav. Ass'n v. Commissioner, 104 T.C. 384, 390–91 (1995) (discussing the "checkered career" of *Chevron* deference in the tax arena), *supplemented by,* 71 T.C.M. (CCH) 2724, 1996 WL 165489 (1996). In addition to the debate in the case law, the topic has generated heated scholarly commentary. *See* Ellen P. Aprill, Muffled Chevron: Judicial Review of Tax Regulations, 3 Fl. Tax Rev. 51 (1996) (describing and advocating a fusion of *Chevron* and *National Muffler,* 440 U.S. 472, 59 L. Ed. 2d 519, 99 S. Ct. 1304 (1979)); * * * John F. Coverdale, Court Review of Tax Regulations and Revenue Rulings in the Chevron Era, 34 Geo. Wash. L. Rev. 35 (1995) (arguing for distinct levels of non-*Chevron* deference for each type of tax interpretation); * * *.

The IRS interprets the tax code in four significantly different ways: (1) regulations issued pursuant to a specific directive from Congress, (2) regulations issued under the IRS's general authority to interpret the tax laws, (3) revenue rulings, and (4) private letter rulings. Each of these categories often receives different deference from the courts. While the first three categories constitute interpretations of general applicability, letter rulings apply only to the parties who specifically request them. Neither the courts nor the IRS may rely on letter rulings as precedent. *See* I.R.C. § 6110(j)(3) (1988) [currently I.R.C. § 6110(k)(3). Eds.];* * *. At the other end of the spectrum from letter rulings are regulations issued under specific grants from Congress. The tax code contains a myriad of specific congressional instructions regarding rule-making. *See* Coverdale, *supra,* at 52 (estimating the number of specific grants at over 1000 and providing examples). Pursuant to the Administrative Procedures Act ("APA"), the IRS issues these rules with full notice and comment. *See* 5 U.S.C. § 553 (1994). In the middle, between letter rulings and specific authority regulations, are general authority regulations and revenue rulings. The IRS issues general authority regulations under its power to "prescribe all needful rules and regulations." *See* I.R.C. § 7805(a) (1994). While the IRS takes the position that regulations issued solely under this general authority do not require notice and comment, the agency nevertheless usually follows full notice and comment procedures. *See* First Chicago NBD Corp. v. Commissioner, 135 F.3d 457, 1998 WL 28113, *2 (7th Cir. 1998). In contrast, the IRS does not follow notice and comment procedures for revenue rulings. Revenue rulings typically contain the IRS's interpretation of how the law applies to a set of hypothetical facts. Revenue rulings do not have broad application like regulations, but the IRS does consider them authoritative and binding. *See* Rev. Proc. 95-1, § 2.05 (codified at Treas. Reg. § 601.201 (West 1998)); Rev. Proc. 89-14, § 7.01 (codified at Treas. Reg. § 601.601 (West 1998)).

Revenue rulings receive the lowest degree of deference—at least in this circuit. In *First Chicago,* we held that revenue rulings deserve "some weight," 135 F.3d at 459, and are "entitled to respectful consideration, but not to the deference that the *Chevron* doctrine requires in its domain," *id.* at 458 (citations omitted). In other circuits this question has generated inconsistent rulings ranging from *Chevron* deference to no deference. * * *

Determining the level of deference accorded to regulations is more difficult. Initially it may appear that we can resolve the problem by resorting to the APA's distinction between legislative and interpretive regulations. *See* 5 U.S.C. § 553(b)(3)(A) (1994). Administrative law scholars usually treat legislative regulations as rules of full legal effect—they create new legal duties binding on the parties and the courts and, therefore, require full notice and comment procedures. Interpretive rules, on the other hand, only clarify existing duties and do not bind; thus, they do not require notice and comment. In the tax world, however, these terms and classifications seem to provide more confusion than clarity. Tax experts refer to specific authority regulations as "legislative" and to general authority regulations as "interpretive." The confusion arises because the "interpretive" designation does not mesh with the characteristics of the IRS's general authority regulations. While the IRS calls its general authority regulations interpretive, the agency promulgates them according to the same formal procedures it employs for its specific regulations. Moreover, both the specific authority and general authority regulations, create duties and have binding effect. *See* Aprill, *supra,* at 55–56; Coverdale, *supra,* 48–50.

If this legislative versus interpretive distinction held up for tax regulations, we could apply the simple rule described in *Hanson v. Espy*, 8 F.3d 469 (7th Cir. 1993). In that case, we explained the distinction between nontax legislative and interpretive regulations and said that *Chevron* applied to legislative regulations only. *See id.* 472 n.3. General tax regulations seem to carry the force of law, they are developed according to notice and comment, and they have the imprimatur of a congressional delegation of authority. In substance, general tax regulations fall short of being full legislative regulations only because the congressional delegation is general rather than specific. This distinction, however, may not have any effect at all on the standard of deference because *Chevron* itself dealt with a regulation promulgated under an arguably general grant of authority to the EPA under the Clean Air Act. Furthermore, *Chevron* stated that its framework applied to implicit congressional delegations as well as to specific and explicit directives. *See Chevron,* 467 U.S. at 844.[n.4]

In any event, courts uniformly give tremendous deference to regulations issued under a specific directive from Congress. In fact, some courts give these regulations the same force as statutes, focusing only on whether the agency promulgated the regulation properly within its scope of authority. *See* Coverdale, *supra,* at 53 (citing cases). We basically follow the same approach. In *Gehl Co. v. Commissioner*, 795 F.2d 1324 (7th Cir. 1986), we explained that "a court's main focus in examining a legislative regulation issued under a specific statutory authority 'is whether the interpretation or method is within the delegation of authority.' " *Id.* at 1329 (*quoting* Rowan Co. v. United States,

---

[n.4] *Chevron* arguably, therefore, altered the understanding of a line of Supreme Court cases often applied to "interpretive" tax regulations. *See* National Muffler Dealers Ass'n v. United States, 440 U.S. 472, 59 L. Ed. 2d 519, 99 S. Ct. 1304 (1979); Rowan Co. v. United States, 452 U.S. 247, 68 L. Ed. 2d 814, 101 S. Ct. 2288 (1981); United States v. Vogel, 455 U.S. 16, 70 L. Ed. 2d 792, 102 S. Ct. 821 (1982). These cases all distinguished between regulations issued under specific grants of authority (full deference) and regulations issued under general grants of authority (less deference).

452 U.S. 247, 253, 68 L. Ed. 2d 814, 101 S. Ct. 2288 (1981)). One commentator suggests that this level of deference accords even greater respect to the IRS's views than *Chevron*. *See* Coverdale, *supra,* at 55. We leave that hypothesis for another day.

Where then does all of this leave tax regulations promulgated under general authority? The question would be easier if the IRS did not employ notice and comment rulemaking procedures—in other words, if general authority tax regulations more truly resembled interpretive regulations. In *Atchison, Topeka and Santa Fe Railway v. Pena*, 44 F.3d 437 (7th Cir. 1994) (*en banc*), *aff'd without discussion, Brotherhood of Locomotive Engineers v. Atchison, Topeka and Santa Fe Railway*, 516 U.S. 152, 133 L. Ed. 2d 535, 116 S. Ct. 595 (1996), we held that courts should accord only moderate deference to interpretive regulations issued without notice and comment by an agency without general rulemaking powers. *See id* at 442; *see also* Central Midwest Interstate Low-Level Radioactive Waste Comm'n v. Pena, 113 F.3d 1468, 1473 (7th Cir. 1997) ("we do not apply *Chevron's* 'rubber stamp' to interpretive rules"). As the *Atchison* court explained:

> Whatever degree of deference due these interpretive rules is dictated by the circumstances surrounding the agency's adoption of its statutory interpretation. "The weight given to an agency interpretation depends on many factors, including the validity of its reasoning, its consistency with earlier and later agency pronouncements and whether the administrative document was issued contemporaneously with the passage of the statute being interpreted." Doe v. Reivitz, [830 F.2d 1441, 1447 (7th Cir. 1987), *amended*, 842 F.2d 194 (7th Cir. 1988)]. In short, we look to "the thoroughness, validity, and consistency of the agency's reasoning." Orrego v. 833 West Buena Joint Venture, 943 F.2d 730, 736 (7th Cir. 1991) (*citing* United States v. Markgraf, 736 F.2d 1179, 1184 (7th Cir. 1984)).

Atchison, 44 F.3d at 442.

In accord with its emphasis on the "circumstances surrounding the agency's adoption" of the regulation, the *Atchison* court understood *Chevron* either to apply or not to apply based on the extent to which an agency follows full notice and comment rulemaking procedures. The court explained that the notice and comment process provides a critical component in our decision to grant *Chevron* deference:

> The principal rationale underlying [*Chevron*] deference is that in this context the agency acts as a congressional proxy; Congress develops the statutory framework and directs the agency to flesh out the operational details. But Congress typically does not permit the agency to run free in this endeavor; the Administrative Procedures Act establishes certain procedures that the agency must follow. Chief among them is the notice-and-comment provision of the APA. 5 U.S.C. § 553. This rulemaking process bears some resemblance to the legislative process and serves to temper the resultant rules such that they are likely to withstand vigorous scrutiny. It is this process that entitles the administrative rules to judicial deference.

Id. at 441–42.

In this regard *Atchison* is not unique. For instance, in *Pennington v. Didrickson*, 22 F.3d 1376 (7th Cir. 1994), we explained "[w]e are mindful of our obligation to defer to the interpretation of the agency whenever that interpretation can be said to embody a deliberate and considered interpretation of the legislative intent." *Id.* at 1383. When an agency undertakes notice and comment procedures it elevates the status of a regulation above mere interpretation. Similarly, in *Doe v. Reivitz*, 830 F.2d 1441, 1446–47 (7th Cir. 1987), *amended,* 842 F.2d 194 (7th Cir. 1988), we characterized regulations promulgated with the full panoply of procedures as "high powered" rules meriting *Chevron* deference. Thus, in this circuit it appears that rules developed pursuant to notice and comment procedures constitute full legislative regulations.

So, is there an answer to the question of whether we give *Chevron* deference to general authority tax regulations promulgated with notice and comment? At first it might appear that we shut the door on that question in *Bell Federal Savings & Loan Ass'n v. Commissioner*, 40 F.3d 224, 226 (7th Cir. 1994). Unfortunately, that case does not provide definitive closure.

In *Bell Federal* we considered an IRS regulation promulgated under the general authorization statute, I.R.C. § 7805(a), just like the regulation in this case. We weighed whether to apply *Chevron* deference (as the Sixth Circuit did in *Peoples Federal Savings & Loan Ass'n v. Commissioner*, 948 F.2d 289, 304–05 (6th Cir. 1991)) or whether to apply a more narrow traditional rule of deference to tax regulations (as the Ninth Circuit did in *Pacific First Federal Savings Bank v. Commissioner*, 961 F.2d 800, 805–08 (9th Cir. 1992)). The *Bell Federal* court opted for the traditional rule apparently because it was more narrowly tailored to tax regulations:

> The proper test for the validation of a challenged regulation thus requires only that the regulation issued by the Commissioner constitute a reasonable implementation of Congress's mandate. The Commissioner's interpretation need not be the only, or even the most, reasonable interpretation possible as "the choice among reasonable interpretations is for the Commissioner, not the courts."

40 F.3d at 227 (*quoting* National Muffler Dealers Ass'n v. United States, 440 U.S. 472, 488, 59 L. Ed. 2d 519, 99 S. Ct. 1304 (1979)). *Bell Federal* continued by explaining that courts should inquire into whether the regulation " 'harmonizes with the plain language of the statute, its origin, and its purpose.' " *Id.* (*quoting National Muffler,* 440 U.S. at 477).

Bell Federal's choice of the traditional rule appeared eminently reasonable at the time. In *Cottage Savings Ass'n v. Commissioner*, 499 U.S. 554, 560–61, 113 L. Ed. 2d 589, 111 S. Ct. 1503 (1991), the Supreme Court conspicuously did not cite *Chevron* and appeared to apply the traditional rule of tax deference: "Because Congress had delegated to the Commissioner the power to promulgate 'all needful rules and regulations for the enforcement of [the Internal Revenue Code],' 26 U.S.C. § 7805(a), we must defer to his regulatory interpretations of the Code so long as they are reasonable." *Id.* at 560–61 (*citing National Muffler*).

The *Bell Federal* court equivocated, however, on whether there was any real difference between *Chevron* and the traditional rule. *Chevron* upholds a regulation if the agency based its interpretation on a permissible construction of a statute, *see* 467 U.S. at 843, while the traditional rule validates the regulation if the agency reasonably implemented Congress's mandate. Noting that "both approaches apply essentially the same test," the *Bell Federal* court stated that "the difference between these two approaches is negligible at best—any regulation which is 'based upon a permissible construction' of an ambiguous statute will almost always 'implement the congressional mandate in some reasonable manner' and vice versa . . . ." 40 F.3d at 227.

While *Bell Federal's* hedging about the difference between *Chevron* and the traditional rule gives us pause, we hesitate to apply the traditional rule for another reason. We think that the *en banc* decision in *Atchison* reopened the door that *Bell Federal* seemed to have shut. As Chief Judge Posner stated in *First Chicago,* "we consider [*Chevron's*] application to interpretive rules issued by the Treasury to be open in this circuit, since the Treasury has decided to use the notice and comment procedure for interpretive rules, though not required to do so by statute." 135 F.3d at 459 (citation omitted).

Atchison explained that the notice and comment procedure was the sine qua non for *Chevron* deference. Because the IRS promulgates general authority regulations through a notice and comment process, *Atchison* militates forcefully in favor of according *Chevron* deference to those regulations. Thus, after *Bell Federal, Atchison* altered the balance and tipped the scales in favor of *Chevron.*

Furthermore, we think *Bell Federal's* description of a "negligible" difference between the approaches might overstate the true extent of the divergence. *Chevron* held that "a court may not substitute its own construction of a statutory provision for a reasonable interpretation made by the administrator of an agency." 467 U.S. at 844. While the two approaches articulate the level of deference differently, they both come down to one operative concept—reasonableness. Thus, *Chevron* and the traditional rule constitute two different formulations of a reasonableness test. There may be some subtle difference in the phrasing of each framework, but we should be wary of attempts to discern too many gradations of reasonableness. As we explained in *Boyce v. Fernandes,* 77 F.3d 946 (7th Cir. 1996), "human ability to make fine distinctions is limited." *Id.* at 948 (describing the difficulty in distinguishing between the inquiries into a police officer's probable cause for an arrest and whether that officer receives qualified immunity). Viewed from this perspective at least, the supposed gap between *Chevron* and the traditional rule is a distinction without a difference.

The Tax Court shares our suspicion that *Chevron* merely repackages the traditional rule: "[W]e are inclined to the view that the impact of the traditional, *i.e., National Muffler* standard, has not been changed by Chevron but has merely been restated in a practical two-part test with subtle distinctions as to the role of legislative history and the degree of deference to be accorded to a regulation." Central Pa. Sav. Ass'n v. Commissioner, 104 T.C. 384 (1995), *supplemented by* 71 T.C.M. (CCH) 2724, 1996 WL 165489 (1996). Thus, as one might expect, other circuits and the Tax Court apply *Chevron* to general authority tax regulations. *See, e.g.,* Western Nat'l Mut. Ins. Co. v. Commissioner, 65 F.3d 90, 93 (8th Cir. 1995); Redlark v. Commissioner, 106 T.C. 31, 38–39, 1996 WL 10243 (1996).

This all leads us to the $64,000 question: If the deference test walks like *Chevron* and talks like *Chevron,* why shouldn't we just call it *Chevron*? Or, phrased differently, if the two standards are the same, does our denomination make any difference? Our answer lies with consistency. While we do not doubt that "foolish consistency is the hobgoblin of little minds, adored by little statesmen and philosophers and divines," Ralph Waldo Emerson, SELF RELIANCE, ESSAYS: FIRST SERIES (1841), we hope that our emphasis on consistency does not qualify as foolishness. On the contrary, consistency in the law forms the backbone of effective jurisprudence. *See, e.g.,* Piper Aircraft Corp. v. Wag-Aero, Inc., 741 F.2d 925, 937 (7th Cir. 1984) (Posner, J., concurring) ("The most important function of appellate review is to maintain the consistency of the law; if consistency is not a desideratum, the argument for appellate review is weakened."). Because the APA imposes uniform procedures on agencies that formulate rules, there is some incentive for courts to apply a uniform framework for challenges to regulations developed with notice and comment. A consistent approach might help alleviate the tensions evident in the now-resolved conflict between the Sixth Circuit and the Tax Court over *Chevron. See* Peoples Fed. Sav. & Loan Ass'n v. Commissioner, 948 F.2d 289, 304–05 (6th Cir. 1991) ("[W]e conclude that the Tax Court used the wrong standard to decide this case. Entirely ignoring *Chevron* . . . the Tax Court employed the standard in *National Muffler Dealers* which seemed to allow a plenary review of the legislative history without the deference requirements found in *Chevron* . . . ."). More practically, our decision signals an effort to move toward a resolution of the current circuit split on the issue. Currently the Sixth Circuit accords *Chevron* deference to all tax regulations. *See Peoples Federal.* Meanwhile, the Third and Fifth Circuits have rejected *Chevron* for general authority tax regulations. *See* E.I. du Pont de Nemours & Co. v. Commissioner, 41 F.3d 130, 135–36 & n.23 (3d Cir. 1994); Nalle v. Commissioner, 997 F.2d 1134, 1138–39 (5th Cir. 1993). Furthermore, we wish to avoid the situation in the Third Circuit—divergent treatment for notice and comment regulations depending on whether they are tax or nontax rules. *See* Elizabeth Blackwell Health Ctr. for Women v. Knoll, 61 F.3d 170, 182 (3d Cir. 1995) (applying *Chevron* to a nontax interpretive regulation), *cert. denied,* 516 U.S. 1093, 133 L. Ed. 2d 760, 116 S. Ct. 816 (1996). We see no reason that nontax regulations issued with notice and comment should receive *Chevron* deference while tax regulations promulgated with the same procedures receive something different.

More importantly, in contrast to our foregoing analysis of the similarities between the traditional rule and *Chevron,* there are some important differences. These considerations also argue in favor of *Chevron. Chevron* is the focus of ongoing development by the Supreme Court, especially regarding the scope of the initial inquiry into statutory meaning. *See, e.g.,* National R.R. Passenger Corp. v. Boston & Marine Corp., 503 U.S. 407, 417–18, 118 L. Ed. 2d 52, 112 S. Ct. 1394 (1992) (reformulating the first step of *Chevron* analysis by focusing on the plain language of the statute rather than the intent of Congress). We do not labor under the illusion that *Chevron* will provide monolithic certainty for all courts reviewing administrative rules—we recognize the Court's own inconsistency regarding *Chevron*. * * * We do hope, however, that by employing a uniform framework for challenges to administrative regulations we can better stay abreast of the Court's dictates.

We also favor *Chevron* because many courts contend that the traditional rule accords less than *Chevron* deference to tax regulations. The Sixth Circuit, for instance, characterizes *National Muffler* as allowing "plenary review" contrasted with *Chevron* deference. *See Peoples Federal,* 948 F.2d at 305. The Third and Fifth Circuits believe that the traditional rule entitles a regulation to "less deference" than under *Chevron. See E.I. du Pont,* 41 F.3d 130 at 135 n. 23; *Nalle,* 997 F.2d at 1139. As *Atchison* explains, we owe full *Chevron* deference to a regulation issued with the full deliberative procedures. Although we acknowledge the gulf between the idealized *Chevron* and the realized one, we do believe that the structure of *Chevron* encourages a court to defer rather than to interpret. We, therefore, prefer it.

Under *Chevron* deference we apply a two-step analysis: (1) We examine the text of the statute — in this case, the relevant section of the tax code. If the plain meaning of the text either supports or opposes the regulation, then we stop our analysis and either strike or validate the regulation. But if we conclude the statute is either ambiguous or silent on the issue, we continue to the second step: (2) We examine the reasonableness of the regulation. If the regulation is a reasonable reading of the statute, we give deference to the agency's interpretation. *See National R.R. Passenger Corp.,* 503 U.S. at 417–18; *Chevron,* 467 U.S. at 842–43, 81 L. Ed. 2d 694, 104 S. Ct. 2781–82.

While this circuit has examined legislative history during the first step of *Chevron, see* Illinois EPA v. United States EPA, 947 F.2d 283, 289 (7th Cir. 1991) ("To ascertain the intent of the law, we must examine the plain meaning of the statute at issue, the language and design of the statute as a whole, and, where necessary, less satisfactory indicia of congressional intent such as legislative history." (citations omitted)), we now seem to lean toward reserving consideration of legislative history and other appropriate factors until the second *Chevron* step, *cf.* Alex v. City of Chicago, 29 F.3d 1235, 1239 (7th Cir. 1994) ("when statutory meaning is clear with respect to the issue at bar judicial inquiry normally should end without heed to the embellishments of secondary materials like legislative history"). In the second step, the court determines whether the regulation harmonizes with the language, origins, and purpose of the statute. While not dispositive, a court may find various considerations informative—these considerations might include the consistency of the agency's interpretation, the contemporaneousness of the interpretation, and the robustness of the regulation following congressional reenactment of the underlying statute. Although we sometimes describe *Chevron* as a "rubber stamp," *see Atchison,* 44 F.3d at 442, we know that agencies occasionally act unreasonably. Given the scope of the permissible inquiry under *Chevron's* second step, we believe that courts can rein in the excesses of unreasonable administrative rulemaking. With that said, however, we reiterate *Chevron's* fundamental dictate that a court must not "substitute its own construction of a statutory provision for a reasonable interpretation" by the agency in question. 467 U.S. at 84, 104 S.Ct. at 2782.

* * *

Bankers Casualty Co. provides a valuable, albeit long-winded, exposition of the "traditional" rule relating to tax regulations and the *Chevron* rule. Based on the court's analysis were you able to discern in the end which rule gives more deference to regulations? Does it matter whether the regulation is interpretative or legislative?

Although the Supreme Court recently had the opportunity to do so, the Court did not give a definitive indication of whether, in tax cases, the *Chevron* or the traditional (*National Muffler*) rule applies to Treasury regulations. *See United States v. Cleveland Indians Baseball Co.*, 532 U.S. 200 (2001) (citing *National Muffler*, but not citing *Chevron*). What is clear is that deference under *Skidmore v. Swift & Co.*, 323 U.S. 134 (1944), does not apply to tax regulations. *Skidmore* is discussed below in Section 9.02[B][2].

The Supreme Court's more recent decision in *United States v. Mead Corp.*, 533 U.S. 218 (2001), discussed in more detail in Section 9.02[B], sets forth a test for when *Chevron* deference should apply to an agency interpretation. According to the Court, *Chevron* deference applies "when it appears that Congress delegated authority to the agency generally to make rules carrying the force of law, and that the agency interpretation claiming deference was promulgated in the exercise of that authority. Delegation of such authority may be shown in a variety of ways, as by an agency's power to engage in adjudication or notice-and-comment rulemaking, or by some other indication of a comparable congressional intent." *Id.* at 2166. Would both legislative and interpretive tax regulations fall within those parameters?

Assuming that the *Chevron* standard controls, how should the two-part test be applied? In the final paragraph of *Bankers Casualty Co.*, notice that the Seventh Circuit would reserve an inquiry into the legislative history of the statute until the second step of the *Chevron* analysis. A recent Supreme Court decision involving the issue of whether the Food and Drug Administration has the authority to regulate tobacco as a "drug" (it does not), *FDA v. Brown & Williamson*, 529 U.S. 120, 132 (2000), indicates that a court should consider the legislative history of the underlying statute as part of its initial inquiry into whether Congress has already spoken to the specific question at issue. Does an examination of legislative history in step one of the *Chevron* analysis lead to greater or lesser deference to the agency's interpretation? *See* Irving Salem and Richard Bress, "Agency Deference Under the Judicial Microscope of the Supreme Court," 88 Tax Notes 1257 (2000).

One of the factors the Seventh Circuit will consider when deciding whether the regulation harmonizes with the origin and purpose of the underlying statute is the "robustness of the regulation following congressional re-enactment of the underlying statute." What does the Seventh Circuit mean by this? The Supreme Court has explained the legislative re-enactment doctrine in a slightly different manner. "Treasury regulations and interpretations long continued without substantial change, applying to unamended or substantially reenacted statutes, are deemed to have received congressional approval and have the effect of law." *Helvering v. Winmill*, 305 U.S. 79, 82 (1938). Is it possible that when re-enacting a statute, Congress rubber stamps, or may even be unaware of, the accompanying regulations? Should that matter?

What if the Treasury releases regulations, but those regulations do not specifically address the question raised? In other words, the issue is not the validity of the regulation, but how the regulation should be interpreted. The Supreme Court commented on this issue in two recent cases. In *United States v. Cleveland Indians Baseball Co.*, 532 U.S. 200 (2001), the Court had to decide whether back pay awards were subject to employment tax based upon the year in which the awards were paid or the year to which the back pay awards related. Noting that the Treasury regulations did not specifically address the issue, the Court upheld the IRS's interpretation that back pay awards are taxed based upon the year in which they are actually paid. According to the Court, the IRS's longstanding interpretation of its own regulation is entitled to "substantial judicial deference" if that interpretation is reasonable. *Id.* at 1444. How close is this formulation to the *Chevron* deference standard? Note that the Court did not cite the *Chevron* case in its opinion.

Compare *Cleveland Indians Baseball* with the Court's decision in *United Dominion Indus., Inc. v. United States*, 532 U.S. 822 (2001). *United Dominion* involved the appropriate method for calculating net operating losses of an affiliated group of corporations electing to file a consolidated return. Responding to a specific grant of regulatory authority in Code section 1504(a)(5), the Treasury released voluminous regulations defining an affiliated group. These regulations, however, did not deal with the precise question of how the taxpayer should calculate net operating losses involving product liability claims. The majority ruled that the taxpayer's approach was correct, and rejected the Government's argument that its method of calculation, although not mandated by the regulations, was at least consistent with existing section 1504 regulations and therefore should be upheld. Justice Stevens dissented:

> When a provision of the Internal Revenue Code presents a patent ambiguity, Congress, the courts, and the IRS share a preference for resolving the ambiguity via executive action. *See, e.g.,* National Muffler Dealers Assn., Inc. v. United States, 440 U.S. 472, 477, 59 L. Ed. 2d 519, 99 S. Ct. 1304 (1979). This is best achieved by the issuing of a Treasury Regulation resolving the ambiguity. *Ibid.* In this instance, however, the Secretary of the Treasury issued no such regulation. In the absence of such a regulation, the majority has scoured tangentially related regulations, looking for clues to what the Secretary might intend. For want of a more precise basis for resolving this case, that approach is sound.

*   *   *

In short, I find no answer to this case in the text of the statute or in any Treasury Regulation. However, the government does forward a valid policy concern that militates against petitioner's construction of the statute: the fear of tax abuse. *See* Brief for United States 40–42. Put simply, the Government fears that currently unprofitable but previously profitable corporations might receive a substantial windfall simply by acquiring a corporation with significant product liability expenses but no product liability losses. *See id.* at 40. On a subjective level, I find these concerns troubling. *Cf. Woolford Realty Co.*, 286 U.S. at 330 (rejecting "the notion that Congress in permitting a consolidated return was willing to foster an opportunity for juggling so facile and so obvious"). More importantly, however, I credit the Secretary of the Treasury's concerns about the potential scope of abuse. Perhaps the Court is correct in suggesting that these concerns can be alleviated through applications of other anti-abuse provisions of the Tax Code, *see ante*, at 15, but I am not persuaded of my own ability to make that judgment. When we deal "with a subject that is highly specialized and so complex as to be the despair of judges," Dobson v. Commissioner, 320 U.S. 489, 498, 88 L. Ed. 248, 64 S. Ct. 239 (1943), an ounce of deference is appropriate.

United Dominion Indus., 532 U.S. at 840-842 (Stevens, J., dissenting) (footnote omitted).

Justice Thomas filed a concurring opinion in which he took issue with Justice Stevens' approach:

I agree with the Court that the Internal Revenue Code provision and the corresponding Treasury Regulations that control consolidated filings are best interpreted as requiring a single-entity approach in calculating product liability loss. I write separately, however, because I respectfully disagree with the dissent's suggestion that, when a provision of the Code and the corresponding regulations are ambiguous, this Court should defer to the Government's interpretation. *See post*, at 1–2. At a bare minimum, in cases such as this one, in which the complex statutory and regulatory scheme lends itself to any number of interpretations, we should be inclined to rely on the traditional canon that construes revenue-raising laws against their drafter. *See* Leavell v. Blades, 237 Mo. 695, 700–701, 141 S.W. 893, 894 (1911) ("When the tax gatherer puts his finger on the citizen, he must also put his finger on the law permitting it"); United States v. Merriam, 263 U.S. 179, 188, 68 L. Ed. 240, 44 S. Ct. 69 (1923) ("If the words are doubtful, the doubt must be resolved against the Government and in favor of the taxpayer"); Bowers v. New York & Albany Literage Co., 273 U.S. 346, 350, 71 L. Ed. 676, 47 S. Ct. 389 (1927) ("The provision is part of a taxing statute; and such laws are to be interpreted liberally in favor of the taxpayers"). *Accord* American Net & Twine Co. v. Worthington, 141 U.S. 468, 474, 35 L. Ed. 821, 12 S. Ct. 55 (1891); Benziger v. United States, 192 U.S. 38, 55, 48 L. Ed. 331, 24 S. Ct. 189 (1904).

Id. at 838-839 (Thomas, J., concurring).

Justice Stevens responded:

> JUSTICE THOMAS accurately points to a tradition of cases constru-
> ing "revenue-raising laws" against their drafter. *See ante*, at 1
> (THOMAS, J., concurring). However, when the ambiguous provision
> in question is not one that imposes tax liability but rather one that
> crafts an exception from a general revenue duty for the benefit of some
> taxpayers, a countervailing tradition suggests that the ambiguity
> should be resolved in the government's favor. *See, e.g.,* INDOPCO, Inc.
> v. Commissioner, 503 U.S. 79, 84, 117 L. Ed. 2d 226, 112 S. Ct. 1039
> (1992); Interstate Transit Lines v. Commissioner, 319 U.S. 590, 593,
> 87 L. Ed. 1607, 63 S. Ct. 1279 (1943); Deputy v. Du Pont, 308 U.S.
> 488, 493, 84 L. Ed. 416, 60 S. Ct. 363 (1940); New Colonial Ice Co.
> v. Helvering, 292 U.S. 435, 440, 78 L. Ed. 1348, 54 S. Ct. 788 (1934);
> Woolford Realty Co. v. Rose, 286 U.S. 319, 326, 76 L. Ed. 1128, 52
> S. Ct. 568 (1932).

Id. at 839 n.1 (Stevens, J., dissenting).

In response to the decision in *United Dominion*, would the Treasury be
permitted to amend its section 1504 regulations to provide that its calculation
approach, which was rejected by the majority, was the only permissible
method of calculating net operating losses? In this regard, consider *Bankers
Trust N.Y. Corp. v. United States*, 225 F.3d 1368 (Fed. Cir. 2000). In that case,
the Federal Circuit held that an executive agency regulation cannot effectively
construe a statute in a manner different from a prior definitive ruling of the
court. The regulation at issue, Treasury Regulation section 4.901-2(f), adopted
an interpretation that was in direct conflict with an earlier decision of the
Court of Federal Claims. The Court of Appeals for the Federal Circuit held
that the Court of Federal Claims erred in finding that the subsequently
enacted regulation was a valid exercise of authority delegated to the IRS. The
Federal Circuit concluded that permitting the IRS, or any executive agency
branch, to overrule an established statutory construction of the court by
issuing regulations that are contrary to the court's prior decision would violate
the "separation of powers" doctrine. *See Bankers Trust*, 225 F.3d at 1376. ("The
Chevron doctrine, which requires us to defer to reasonable agency 'gap filling'
interpretations of a statute as expressed in agency regulations, is not in conflict with stare decisis as it applies to this case, which requires adherence to
precedential decisions of this court and of our predecessor courts.").

[B]   IRS Authorities

The IRS issues several forms of guidance to the public. For use by all
taxpayers, the IRS publishes procedural regulations, Revenue Rulings, and
Revenue Procedures. Those forms of guidance are discussed in this section.
The IRS also provides private guidance to taxpayers in the form of letter
rulings and determination letters. Furthermore, it issues internal guidance,
ostensibly for use only within the agency, which is nonetheless made available
to the public. Private and internal forms of IRS guidance are discussed in
Section 9.03.

[1] Procedural Regulations

The regulations in the IRS Statement of Procedural Rules, 26 CFR Part 601, are promulgated by the IRS, not the Treasury, and are not subject to the APA. These regulations generally address internal IRS "housekeeping" matters, yet may provide a valuable source of information on matters relating to IRS organization and procedure. *See, e.g.*, Proc. Reg. § 601.204, instructing a taxpayer how to gain consent from the IRS to change a method of accounting.

[2] Revenue Ruling Procedures and the Debate over Courts' Deference to Revenue Rulings

Revenue Rulings, also issued by the national office of the IRS, represent the IRS's official interpretation of the Code as it applies to a particular set of facts. *See* Rev. Proc. 2000-1, 2000-1 I.R.B. 4. Public release of Revenue Rulings began in 1953, in response to criticism from Congress and private practitioners that the IRS's failure to release private letter rulings permitted favoritism, protected the use of influence, and put taxpayers at an unfair disadvantage in disputes with revenue agents. The IRS describes the objectives of the Revenue Rulings program as promoting uniform application of the tax laws and assisting taxpayers in attaining maximum voluntary compliance. Proc. Reg. § 601.601(d)(2)(iii). Although the extent of their precedential authority is unclear, *see Estate of McLendon*, which is reproduced below, Revenue Rulings do serve as important sources of guidance that a taxpayer might use when planning a transaction and determining the tax results that flow from that transaction.

Given the purposes of the Revenue Rulings program, the rulings that are chosen to be published represent those that, in the opinion of the national office, contain information and guidance that are likely to be important to a wide class of taxpayers.[3] Topics for Revenue Rulings are often drawn from the IRS's annual business plan and, in some cases, the Treasury Department will suggest a topic for a Revenue Ruling to the IRS. Revenue Rulings are drafted and reviewed by attorneys in the Office of the Chief Counsel. After approval by the Chief Counsel, the Commissioner and the Treasury's Assistant Secretary (Tax Policy) review the proposed rulings. Because Revenue Rulings are not subject to APA procedures, the IRS does not generally afford the public an opportunity to comment on proposed rulings.[4] They are initially published in the Internal Revenue Bulletin, and then compiled as part of the semi-annual Cumulative Bulletin.

As a general rule, Revenue Rulings may be applied on a retroactive basis. Section 7805(b), unlike in the case of Treasury regulations, also permits the IRS the discretionary authority to *revoke* a Revenue Ruling retroactively.

---

[3] In some cases, a Revenue Ruling is simply an edited or slightly modified version of a previously issued private letter ruling. Because Revenue Rulings tend to be fact-specific, the IRS cautions that such rulings are applicable to other cases only when the facts involved are substantially similar. Proc. Reg. § 601.601(e).

[4] Occasionally the IRS does request comments on proposed Revenue Rulings. *See* John F. Coverdale, "Court Review of Tax Regulations and Revenue Rulings in the *Chevron* Era," 34 Geo. Wash. L. Rev. 35, 79 & n.300 (1995) (pointing out that Announcement 95-25, 1995-14 I.R.B. 11, requested comments on a proposed Revenue Ruling).

I.R.C. § 7805(b)(8); *see also Dixon v. United States*, 381 U.S. 68 (1965). The IRS has stated, however, that if a newly issued Revenue Ruling modifies or revokes a previously published ruling, the new ruling will not be applied retroactively to the extent that the revocation would have adverse tax consequences to the taxpayer. *See* Rev. Proc. 89-14 § 7, 1989-1 C.B. 814; *see also Estate of McLendon v. Commissioner*, 135 F.3d 1017 (1998) (reproduced below).

In many cases, Revenue Rulings are revoked or modified because subsequent legislation, court decisions, and Treasury regulations affect the underlying basis of the ruling's conclusion. When this happens the IRS publishes this fact in the "Finding List of Current Action," which appears at the beginning of each Cumulative Bulletin volume. Even when a Revenue Ruling is not officially modified or made obsolete by the IRS as a result of a change in the law underlying the ruling, taxpayers must be careful to take into account the impact of the change on the ruling's continued validity.

The debate over *Chevron* deference to IRS interpretations of the Code is also present with respect to Revenue Rulings. In the case of Revenue Rulings that do not favor the taxpayer, courts' views on the deference question vary widely. The last time the Supreme Court directly addressed the weight of a Revenue Ruling, *Davis v. United States*, 495 U.S. 472 (1990), the Court stated: "Although the Service's interpretive rulings do not have the force and effect of regulations, . . . we give an agency's interpretations and practices considerable weight where they involve the contemporaneous construction of a statute and where they have been in long use." *Id.* at 484.[5] In a subsequent case, the Court again commented on the precedential weight of a Revenue Ruling, stating, "Though this Revenue Ruling is not before us, we note that 'the service's interpretive rulings do not have the force and effect of regulations,' and they may not be used to overturn the plain language of a statute." *Commissioner v. Schleier*, 515 U.S. 323, 336 n.8 (1995) (dictum). In dissent, Justice O'Connor argued that under *Davis*, IRS interpretations are entitled to considerable weight. *See id.* at 345. She also wrote:

> The Court states that it does not accord the Commissioner's reply brief any special deference in light of the "differing interpretations of her own regulation," *ante*, at 334, n.7. But ignoring the Commissioner's off-hand assertion in this case does not wipe the slate clean. There still remain 35 years of formal interpretations upon which taxpayers have relied and of agency positions upon which courts, including this one, have based their decisions. Unless the Court is willing to declare these positions to be unreasonable, they cannot be ignored.

Id. Neither *Davis* nor *Schleier* considers the possible applicability of *Chevron*.

Given the lack of guidance from the Supreme Court, lower courts have reached conflicting opinions. At one extreme is the Sixth Circuit, which applied *Chevron* deference to a Revenue Ruling in *Johnson City Med. Ctr. v. United States*, 999 F.2d 973, 976 (6th Cir. 1993). The Tax Court, at the other

---

[5] The Court also applied the legislative reenactment doctrine in support of its holding. *Davis*, 495 U.S. at 482; *see also* Linda Galler, "Emerging Standards for Judicial Review of IRS Revenue Rulings," 72 B.U. L. Rev. 841, 857–58 (1992).

extreme, maintains that "[a]bsent exceptional circumstances, revenue rulings are viewed as 'merely an opinion of a lawyer in the agency', they are not considered to have the effect of law, and they are not binding on the Commissioner or the courts." *Estate of McLendon v. Commissioner*, T.C. Memo. 1997-307 (*citing* I.R.C. § 6110 and *Foil v. Commissioner*, 920 F.2d 1196, 1201 (5th Cir. 1990), *aff'g* 92 T.C. 376 (1989)).

Other courts have adopted intermediate positions. The Seventh Circuit in *Bankers Life & Casualty Co.*, *supra*, stated that Revenue Rulings deserve "respectful consideration, but not [ ] the deference that the *Chevron* doctrine requires in its domain." 142 F.3d at 975 (citing *First Chicago NBD Corp. v. Commissioner*, 135 F.3d 457, 458 (7th Cir. 1998)). In yet another variation, the D.C. Circuit Court would apply *Skidmore* deference to a Revenue Ruling, a standard that affords the ruling some deference, but not the same degree that *Chevron* would. *Del Commercial Properties, Inc. v. Commissioner*, 251 F.3d 210 (D.C. Cir. 2001), *citing Christensen v. Harris County*, 529 U.S. 576, 587 (2000), *quoting Skidmore v. Swift & Co.*, 323 U.S. 134 (1944). Under *Skidmore*, the government agency's interpretation is owed respect in accordance with "the thoroughness evident in its consideration, the validity of its reasoning, its consistency with earlier and later pronouncements, and all those facts which give it the power to persuade, if lacking power to control." *Skidmore*, 323 U.S. at 140.

A recent decision of the Supreme Court indicates that *Skidmore* deference might be the appropriate standard for Revenue Rulings. *United States v. Mead Corp.*, 533 U.S. 218 (2001), discussed above, involved the appropriate level of deference to be afforded a tariff ruling letter issued by the United States Customs Service. Regulations issued by the Treasury Department grant the Customs Service the authority to issue tariff ruling letters. These regulations provide that "no other person should rely on the ruling letter or assume that the principles of that ruling will be applied in connection with any transaction other than one described in the letter." The Supreme Court ruled that because Congress did not expressly delegate to the Customs Service the authority to issue tariff rulings carrying the force of law, and the Customs Service did not follow notice and comment procedures before issuing the rulings, the tariff ruling letters were not entitled to *Chevron* deference. The Court further held, however, that the tariff ruling letters were entitled to respect in accordance with *Skidmore*. According to the Court, "where the regulatory scheme is highly detailed" and the administrative agency "can bring the benefit of specialized experience to bear on the subtle questions" in a case, the agency's interpretation should be afforded *Skidmore* deference. This level of deference, as discussed above, recognizes the ruling's power to persuade but not the power to control.

The *McLendon* decision, reproduced below, considers a slightly different issue: To what extent should Revenue Rulings be binding on the IRS?

ESTATE OF McLENDON v. COMMISSIONER
United States Court of Appeals, Fifth Circuit
135 F.3d 1017 (1998)

E. GRADY JOLLY, CIRCUIT JUDGE:

The only question remaining in this appeal is whether Gordon B. McLendon was sufficiently close to death on March 5, 1986, to require him to depart from the actuarial tables published by the Commissioner of Internal Revenue (the "Commissioner") in valuing a remainder interest and related annuity. The Tax Court determined that he was, from which final decision McLendon's Estate appeals. We reverse.

I.

Although this case raises several contentious legal questions, the underlying facts are not in serious dispute. Through various partnership interests, McLendon was the principal owner and director of a vast broadcasting and entertainment empire. His interests ranged from the 458-station Liberty Broadcasting System to numerous individual radio stations, television stations, and movie theaters. Over his life time, McLendon became a very wealthy man.

Mortality hovers over the castle as well as the cottage, however, and in May 1985 McLendon was diagnosed with esophageal cancer. Although his condition initially improved following radiation therapy, the cancer recurred in September. At this point, McLendon's cancer was categorized as "systemic"—the most severe of three types of cancer growth. There is no dispute that the cancer was very likely terminal from this point forward, with a 2–3% overall survival rate. In particular, any remissions achieved after this point were generally expected by McLendon's doctors to be temporary.

Nonetheless, from October 1985 through March 1986, McLendon received six courses of chemotherapy at M.D. Anderson's world-renowned cancer treatment facility in Houston, Texas. On December 3, 1985, after three courses of chemotherapy, McLendon's doctor wrote on his discharge summary:

> The patient had an esophagogastroduodenoscopy on November 26, 1985, and it showed complete endoscopic remission confirmed by multiple biopsies of the affected area.

Despite this upbeat news, on December 5, 1985, McLendon attempted suicide by shooting himself in the head with a handgun. A suicide note reflected his belief that he would eventually succumb to the cancer and his desire not to prolong the suffering of his family. After being hospitalized for over a month for treatment of injuries from the failed suicide, McLendon began a fourth course of chemotherapy. He returned home in late January 1986 and began to receive periodic in-home examinations and treatment from a Dr. Gruebel. Her impression at the time was that he was doing well.

* * *

At the end of February, McLendon returned home under twenty-four hour care from a staff of private duty nurses. Notes taken by these nurses show that during the period from March 2 through March 5, McLendon was able to take short walks and perform minor tasks, but was at times sick to his stomach, was in constant need of pain medication, and was receiving artificial sustenance to ensure proper caloric intake. McLendon was examined at home on March 5 by the optimistic Dr. Gruebel. It was her impression at that time that McLendon was "markedly improved" and in the best condition since he had come into her care in January. The Commissioner subsequently presented undisputed expert testimony, however, that McLendon's chances of surviving for more than one year from this date were approximately 10 percent. This estimate was based principally on the likelihood of recurrence in a case like McLendon's.

On March 5, McLendon entered into a private annuity transaction with his son and the newly minted McLendon Family Trust. This transaction involved the transfer of remainder interests in McLendon's partnership holdings to his son and the Trust in exchange for $250,000 and an annuity to be paid to McLendon for life. The amount of the annuity was set such that its aggregate present value would equal the present value of the remainder interests. In valuing the remainder interests and the annuity, the parties referred to the Commissioner's actuarial tables for life expectancy then contained in Treas. Reg. § 25.2512-5(f). McLendon was sixty-five years old on March 5, 1986, resulting in an actuarial life expectancy of fifteen years from that date. Based on this figure, the parties ultimately determined that the remainder interests had a value of $5,881,695, and that the annuity would need to be $865,332 in order to match.

In late March, McLendon completed his final course of chemotherapy. In May, tests revealed a major recurrence of the cancer. Treatments were discontinued within a few weeks, and McLendon died at home on September 14. From the time that he was first admitted to M.D. Anderson in October 1985 until his death, McLendon survived longer than 75% of patients diagnosed with esophageal cancer.

II.

McLendon's estate tax return relied on a presumption that he had received an adequate and full consideration for the assets transferred in the private annuity transaction. The Commissioner disagreed with this presumption, taking issue with both the use of the actuarial tables and certain substantive aspects of the valuation of the partnership interests.

With regard to the actuarial tables, the Commissioner took the position that McLendon's life expectancy was sufficiently predictable on March 5, 1986, to make their use unnecessary and erroneous. Based on the medical evidence, the Commissioner further found that McLendon's actual life expectancy on this date was less than one year. Because this was significantly less than the fifteen-year figure used by the parties, the Commissioner concluded that the remainder interests had been so undervalued, and the annuity so overvalued, that the March 5 transfer had not been for an adequate and full consideration. As such, the Commissioner declared several million dollars in gift and estate tax deficiencies based on McLendon's erroneous use of the actuarial tables.

Additional deficiencies were declared based on the substantive valuation issues.

McLendon's Estate took this dispute to the Tax Court, where the issues were reduced by joint stipulation to six discrete questions. One of these questions was whether it was proper for McLendon to apply the actuarial tables to determine his life expectancy in valuing the remainder interests and annuity. The rest of the questions concerned the substantive aspects of the valuation of the partnership interests. On September 30, 1993, the Tax Court issued its first opinion in this case, generally agreeing with the Commissioner and imposing $12.5 million in additional gift and estate taxes. Of significance to the instant appeal, the Tax Court held that use of the actuarial tables was improper because McLendon's life expectancy was reasonably predictable at the time the private annuity transaction occurred, being approximately one year.

McLendon's Estate appealed the Tax Court's ruling to this court. Estate of McLendon v. Commissioner of Internal Revenue, 77 F.3d 477 (5th. Cir. 1995). In an unpublished opinion, the panel reversed the Tax Court on the substantive valuation questions, but remanded as to use of the actuarial tables. Writing for the court, Judge Jones stated that:

> [W]e are unable to discern whether the Tax Court followed Revenue Ruling 80-80 or found reason to depart from it [in resolving the actuarial table question]. The Tax Court's opinion is both ambiguous and ambivalent regarding the revenue ruling, as it holds that Gordon had a life expectancy of one year, a finding that would suggest to us under the express language of the revenue ruling that death was not clearly imminent. We must remand for the court to clarify its position with regard to the applicability of Revenue Ruling 80-80 so that we will have a sounder basis for appellate review.

On July 8, 1996, the Tax Court issued its second opinion. It held that, although neither party had argued a position inconsistent with Rev. Rul. 80-80, the court had not felt obliged to follow that ruling, and had instead applied a standard gleaned from prior case law. It noted, however, that the result would have been the same under the ruling anyway. In the light of this clarification, McLendon's Estate now continues its appeal of the Tax Court's determination that use of the actuarial tables was improper.

* * *

IV.

As the prior panel foresaw, the remainder of this case turns on the applicability of Rev. Rul. 80-80. Because we hold that the ruling provides the legal test applicable to McLendon's situation, we find that his use of the actuarial tables was proper.

A.

The controversy in this case ultimately stems from 26 U.S.C. §§ 2036(a) and 2512(b). Under § 2036(a), a decedent's gross estate for estate tax purposes is defined to include any property transferred by him in which he retained a life estate, "except in case of a bona fide sale for an adequate and full consideration in money or money's worth." Similarly, under § 2512(b), a taxable gift is defined as a transfer of property "for less than an adequate and full consideration." Here, the transfer in question was the March 5 exchange of the partnership remainder interests for the cash and annuity. As the parties concede, the question whether that transfer was for "an adequate and full consideration" turns on the proper valuation of the remainder interests and the annuity.

At the time of the events in this case, Treas. Reg. § 25.2512-5 provided that "the fair market value of annuities, life estates, terms for years, remainders, and reversions transferred after November 30, 1983, is their present value determined in this section." Because the economic present value of these assets is dependent upon the predicted length of a measuring life, the regulation goes on to provide actuarial tables for life expectancy and instructions for using them to arrive at valuations of the assets in question. There is no dispute in this case over the valuation formulas contained in the regulation. The parties concede that the only question is whether the circumstances of McLendon's case allowed him to use a life expectancy figure derived from the tables of § 25.2512-5, or instead required him to use some other method to determine his "actual" life expectancy. * * *

B.

This question is less straightforward than it might seem. Despite their apparently clear command, Treas. Reg. § 25.2512-5 and its predecessors have not always been vigorously enforced by the courts. In particular, in *Miami Beach First National Bank v. United States*, 443 F.2d 116, 119–20 (5th Cir. 1971), this court held that "where there is sufficient evidence regarding the actual life expectancy of a life tenant, the presumptive correctness of the Treasury tables will be overcome."

At the time of the events in this case, the effective ruling was Rev. Rul. 80-80. It provides, in relevant part:

> The actuarial tables in the regulations are provided as an administrative necessity, and their general use has been readily approved by the courts.

> The actuarial tables are not based on data that exclusively involve persons of "good" or "normal" health. They reflect the incidence of death by disease and illness as well as by accident. The actuarial tables are properly applicable to the vast majority of individual life interests, even though the health of a particular individual is obviously better or worse than that of the "average" person of the same age and sex. Occasionally, however, the actual facts of an individual's condition are so exceptional as to justify departure from the actuarial tables.

* * *

In view of recent case law, the resulting principle is as follows: the current actuarial tables in the regulations shall be applied if valuation of an individual's life interest is required for purposes of the federal estate or gift taxes unless the individual is known to have been afflicted, at the time of the transfer, with an incurable physical condition that is in such an advanced stage that death is clearly imminent. Death is not clearly imminent if there is a reasonable possibility of survival for more than a very brief period. *For example, death is not clearly imminent if the individual may survive for a year or more and if such a possibility is not so remote as to be negligible.*

Rev. Rul. 80-80, 1980-1 C.B. 194 (emphasis added, citations omitted).

McLendon's Estate argues that Rev. Rul. 80-80 clearly allows his use of the tables. In this regard, the Estate notes that the undisputed testimony of the Commissioner's own expert was that McLendon had a 10 percent chance of surviving for a year or more on March 5, 1986. As such, the Estate concludes that McLendon's possibility of surviving for a year or more from that date was not so remote as to be negligible, and that he therefore was permitted and required to use the tables under the clear terms of the ruling.

Although the Commissioner maintains that this court is not bound to follow Rev. Rul. 80-80, he also purports to take the position that the ruling does not mandate the result indicated by the Estate. The Commissioner argues that, although the ruling is a correct statement of the law, it cannot be taken at face value, and must be interpreted in the light of *Miami Beach First National Bank.* The Commissioner contends that under this reading McLendon's use of the tables was inappropriate since there was "sufficient evidence" of his actual life expectancy on March 5, 1986.

If Rev. Rul. 80-80 does govern this case, we, like the earlier panel of this court, find it undeniable that it supports the Estate's position. The ruling states a clear standard, expressed in language and example unneedful of further interpretation, and we are convinced that the 10 percent figure is sufficient to satisfy it. Whatever "negligible" might mean in a closer case, we are certain that it does not refer to a one-in-ten chance. As such, McLendon's use of the tables was clearly proper under the ruling.

The question, then, is whether Rev. Rul. 80-80 states the legal test applicable to McLendon's situation. If it does, then it is clear that McLendon's use of the actuarial tables was proper. The Tax Court ultimately chose not to apply Rev. Rul. 80-80 to this case. This choice was a purely legal decision, and is thus reviewed *de novo.*

C.

We note at the outset that the Tax Court has long been fighting a losing battle with the various courts of appeals over the proper deference to which revenue rulings are due. Whereas virtually every circuit recognizes some form of deference,[n.10] the Tax Court stands firm in its own position that revenue rulings are nothing more than the legal contentions of a frequent litigant, undeserving of any more or less consideration than the conclusory statements in a party's brief. Although the Supreme Court has not spoken definitively on the subject, its recent jurisprudence tends to support the view that the courts owe revenue rulings a bit more deference than the Tax Court would have us believe. Still, revenue rulings are odd creatures unconducive to precise categorization in the hierarchy of legal authorities. They are clearly less binding on the courts than treasury regulations or Code provisions, but probably (and in this circuit certainly) more so than the mere legal conclusions of the parties. Apart from that, little can be said with any certainty, and in the absence of a definitive statement from on high, the Tax Court continues its crusade to ignore them in toto.

This bit of background explains a great deal with regard to the posture of this case. In support of its general position on deference, the Tax Court went to great lengths to avoid applying Rev. Rul. 80-80 to McLendon's situation. The earlier panel of this court noticed this slight, and asked the Tax Court if it really wanted an open confrontation on the issue. Sticking to its guns, the Tax Court replied that it did. The result was the instant appeal.

As it turns out, however, this case does not require us to step squarely into the fray. Most questions of deference to a revenue ruling involve an argument by the taxpayer that a particular ruling is contrary to law. Here, however, the argument to ignore or minimize the effect of Rev. Rul. 80-80 comes from the Commissioner, the very party who issued the ruling in the first place.[n.13] In such a situation, this circuit has a well established rule that is sufficient to resolve this case without probing the penumbrae of the general deference question.

In *Silco, Inc. v. United States*, 779 F.2d 282, 286 (5th Cir. 1986), we held that a taxpayer was entitled to rely on the legal standard implied by two revenue rulings extant at the time of his transaction, even though they had been subsequently abrogated. In reaching this conclusion, we noted that:

> Treas. Reg. § 601.601(e) provides that taxpayers may generally rely on published revenue rulings in determining the tax treatment of their own transactions, if the facts and circumstances of their transactions are substantially the same as those that prompted the ruling.

Id. at 286.[n.14] Because the statute, regulations, and case law were less than clear at the time of the taxpayer's transaction, we found that the rulings

---

[n.10] * * * In this circuit, revenue rulings are generally "given weight as expressing the studied view of the agency whose duty it is to carry out the statute." Foil [v. Commissioner, 920 F.2d 1196, (5th Cir. 1990)].

[n.13] The Commissioner's position is not entirely clear in this case. He purports to maintain that Rev. Rul. 80-80 is an accurate statement of the law, yet would prefer the court decide the case based on the rule of *Miami Beach First National Bank*. This rule, he implies, is the same as that of Rev. Rul. 80-80. The Commissioner cannot eat his cake and have it too. As we explained above, Rev. Rul. 80-80 is unambiguous in its support for the Estate's position. To the extent that he argues for a rule inconsistent with the ruling's clear language, we construe the Commissioner's position to be that the ruling should not apply.

[n.14] Treas. Reg. § 601.601(e) states: "Taxpayers generally may rely upon Revenue Rulings pub-

"provided the only insight available to [the] taxpayer at the time of [his] transaction as to the conceptual approach the [Commissioner] would use," and that the Commissioner acted improperly in subsequently applying a different test to that taxpayer. *Id.* at 287.

Silco stands for the proposition that the Commissioner will be held to his published rulings in areas where the law is unclear, and may not depart from them in individual cases. Furthermore, under *Silco* the Commissioner may not retroactively abrogate a ruling in an unclear area with respect to any taxpayer who has relied on it.[n.15]

Applying *Silco* to this case, it quickly becomes clear that Rev. Rul. 80-80 must govern our decision. McLendon went to great lengths to structure his transaction to comply with applicable law, and the Commissioner does not dispute that in so doing McLendon expressly relied on Rev. Rul. 80-80's clarification of the admittedly murky area of future and dependent interest valuation. The Commissioner ignored the clear language of his own ruling in declaring deficiencies, and it is precisely this kind of tactic that *Silco* declares to be intolerable. Because McLendon was entitled to rely on Rev. Rul. 80-80, the Tax Court was not at liberty to disregard it. Its decision to do so was error, and we reverse on that basis. Furthermore, because the application of Rev. Rul. 80-80 clearly sustains the Estate's position, we need not remand yet again for further proceedings. Consistent with our discussion of the application of the ruling above, we render for McLendon's Estate.

V.

Where the Commissioner has specifically approved a valuation methodology, like the actuarial tables, in his own revenue ruling, he will not be heard to fault a taxpayer for taking advantage of the tax minimization opportunities

---

lished in the Bulletin in determining the tax treatment of their own transactions . . . ." Although not cited therein, *Silco* also finds support in Treas. Reg. § 601.601(d), which provides that revenue rulings "are published to provide precedents to be used in the disposition of other cases."

[n.15] This latter portion of *Silco* might be read to be in conflict with the Supreme Court's well established rule that the Commissioner may retroactively revoke certain revenue rulings, even where taxpayers may have relied on them to their detriment. *See* Automobile Club of Michigan v. Commissioner of Internal Revenue, 353 U.S. 180, 183–84, 1 L. Ed. 2d 746, 77 S. Ct. 707 (1957) (Brennan, J.); Dixon v. United States, 381 U.S. 68, 72–73, 14 L. Ed. 2d 223, 85 S. Ct. 1301 (1965) (Brennan, J.). For a number of reasons, however, we perceive no conflict.

First, the *Automobile Club* rule applies only where the Commissioner revokes a prior ruling that is contrary to the Internal Revenue Code. This was not the case in *Silco*, nor is it the case here. The *Silco* rule is expressly limited to areas where the Code does not provide a clear answer. Second, *Silco* is grounded on the Commissioner's invitation to taxpayers to rely on his revenue rulings as set out in Treas. Reg. § 601.601(e), a factor not present in the *Automobile Club* or *Dixon* cases. The essence of the *Silco* rule is that traditional notions of equity and fair play prevent the Commissioner from changing his position after inviting reliance with his own regulations. Finally, even if there were some tension between *Silco* and *Automobile Club*, we would be bound in this case by our past circuit precedent. "One panel of this Court may not overrule another (absent an intervening decision to the contrary by the Supreme Court or the en banc court . . .)." Hogue v. Johnson, 131 F.3d 466, 491 (5th Cir. 1997) (Garwood, J.) (emphasis added). *See also* United States v. McPhail, 119 F.3d 326, 327 (5th Cir. 1997) (Smith, J., dissenting), and cases cited therein. Supposed conflicts with *prior* Supreme Court precedent are grist for the en banc mill, but not for ad hoc panel revision. *See* 5th Cir. IOP to Fed. R. App. P. 35. For all of these reasons, we are content that *Silco* continues to be good law.

inherent therein. Here, the Commissioner had no right to ignore Rev. Rul. 80-80 and the Tax Court was bound to apply it consistent with McLendon's right of reliance. The Tax Court's manifest failure to apply the ruling was clearly wrong, and, accordingly, we reverse its judgment and render for the Estate.

---

[3] Revenue Procedures

Revenue Procedures are like Revenue Rulings except that they cover procedural processes. The IRS describes a Revenue Procedure as "an official statement of a procedure . . . that either affects the rights or duties of taxpayers or other members of the public under the Internal Revenue Code . . . or, although not necessarily affecting the rights and duties of the public, should be a matter of public knowledge." Rev. Proc. 89-14, 1989-1 C.B. 814. The first Revenue Procedure issued each year describes the processes necessary to request a letter ruling or determination letter. *See, e.g.,* Rev. Proc. 2002-1, 2002-1 I.R.B. 1, a portion of which is reproduced below. Revenue Procedures, like Revenue Rulings, are first published in the Internal Revenue Bulletin, and then compiled as part of the Cumulative Bulletin. Revenue Procedures are rarely contested in court.

§ 9.03   Private and Internal IRS Authorities

[A] Reliance on the Various Private and Internal IRS Authorities

Private guidance provided by the IRS to a particular taxpayer (in the form of a letter ruling or determination letter) has no precedential value, and may be relied upon only by the taxpayer to whom the letter ruling or determination letter relates. I.R.C. § 6110(k)(3). Nonetheless, these items are made available to the public pursuant to section 6110, after any identifying details have been redacted. I.R.C. § 6110(c). Although letter rulings and determination letters may not be used or cited as precedent by a third party, these sources can prove helpful to other taxpayers seeking to obtain general guidance on the IRS's position with respect to a particular issue.

A "letter ruling" is a written statement issued to a taxpayer by the National Headquarters of the IRS that interprets and applies the tax laws to a specific set of facts described in the letter ruling request. Rev. Proc. 2002-1, 2002-1 I.R.B. 1. As mentioned above, letter rulings are often referred to as "private letter rulings," and are abbreviated "PLR." PLRs are numbered for the year in which they are released, the week, and the number of the PLR within that week. For example, PLR 9722011 is the eleventh PLR that was released in the 22nd week of 1997. Beginning in 1999, PLRs are numbered with four-digit year numbers, so that, for example, PLR 199937040 is the fortieth ruling released during the 37th week of 1999.

A "determination letter" applies the principles and precedents previously announced by the National Headquarters to a specific set of facts. While similar to a PLR, a determination letter is issued by a local IRS official, rather than the national office, and normally covers a completed transaction, rather than a proposed transaction.

Determination letters most often relate to the qualification of an employee benefit plan as an exempt entity under Code section 401 or the tax-exempt status of an organization under Code section 501. The IRS has announced that it will issue a determination letter only when a determination can be made on the basis of clearly established rules in the statute, the regulations, or a published court decision. *See* Rev. Proc. 2002-1, 2002-1 I.R.B. 1. As a result, if the requested determination involves a novel issue or doubt exists concerning the application of precedent, no letter will be given.

In addition to these types of taxpayer-specific pronouncements, the IRS also publishes guidance prepared by various IRS divisions primarily for the use of its own personnel. Such internal guidance includes Technical Advice Memoranda, Chief Counsel Advice, and Action on Decision memoranda. Each type is briefly described below.[6]

The national office will furnish advice during the examination stage of a tax controversy in response to requests from IRS field personnel and at the prompting of taxpayers. Technical Advice Memoranda (TAMs) are the written statements encompassing this advice. As with a letter ruling, TAMs contain the national office's views on how the Code, regulations and judicial precedent should be applied to a specific fact pattern. Also like letter rulings, TAMs are made available under section 6110, and may not be used or cited as precedent by taxpayers other than the taxpayer to which the TAM directly relates. TAMs are also numbered like PLRs. The procedures for requesting technical advice and the circumstances under which it will be issued are described in an annual revenue procedure. *See* Rev. Proc. 2002-2, 2002-1 I.R.B. 82.

Chief Counsel Advice, as explained in Chapter 3, is broadly defined in section 6110(i) to include any advice issued by the Office of Chief Counsel concerning a legal or policy interpretation. Encompassed within the definition of Chief Counsel Advice is Field Service Advice (FSA). FSAs are issued in response to requests from IRS field personnel regarding legal and technical issues. FSAs state the facts, the issues, analyze the law, and reach legal conclusions. FSAs also state any limitations to which the conclusions may be subject. *See Tax Analysts v. IRS*, 117 F.3d 607, 609 (D.C. Cir. 1997). These types of pronouncements may also contain helpful discussions of cases and other precedent, and may reveal the Chief Counsel's litigation strategy with respect to a particular transaction. FSAs are numbered like PLRs, and, because they are subject to section 6110, are required to be disclosed to the public. FSAs also generally may not be relied upon as precedent.[7]

In the past, the Chief Counsel's Office also prepared General Counsel Memoranda (GCMs) in response to requests for legal advice from within the

---

[6] A more complete discussion of the various types of IRS pronouncements is included in Chapter 16.

[7] Chief Counsel Advice also includes a host of other memoranda and pronouncements prepared by the Office of Chief Counsel for the benefit of IRS personnel, including Litigation Guideline Memoranda, Litigation Bulletins and Criminal Tax Bulletins.

IRS. Much like FSAs, GCMs normally contain lengthy legal analysis of substantive legal questions, along with opinions and recommendations. Most commonly, GCMs were drafted to accompany proposed Revenue Rulings, PLRs, and TAMs and explain the analysis used by the drafter to reach his conclusions. *See Taxation with Representation Fund v. IRS*, 646 F.2d 666, 669 (D.C. Cir. 1989). While many GCMs remain current, the IRS has stopped the practice of drafting GCMs, in favor of FSAs.

When the IRS loses a case in the Tax Court, a Federal District Court, the Court of Federal Claims, or a United States Court of Appeals, the attorney in the Tax Litigation Division responsible for review of the case prepares for the Chief Counsel a memorandum called an Action on Decision (AOD), which sets forth the issue that was decided against the IRS, briefly discusses the facts, and recommends that the IRS Commissioner either "acquiesce" or "non-acquiesce" in the court decision. *See Taxation Without Representation Fund*, 646 F.2d at 672. AODs are published in the Internal Revenue Bulletin and again in the Cumulative Bulletin. An acquiescence on the part of the Commissioner indicates that the Commissioner accepts the conclusions reached by the court, but not necessarily the reasoning used by the court to reach that decision. It also indicates that the Commissioner does not intend to challenge in the future the tax consequences that were upheld on the facts of the acquiesced case. A non-acquiescence on the part of the Commissioner indicates that he does not accept the conclusions reached in the case, and may seek to have the conclusions rejected in future litigation. While intended primarily for IRS personnel, AODs provide the taxpayer a means of predicting the IRS's reaction to similar cases. In addition, the drafter's reasoning behind his recommendation to acquiesce or not, which forms a part of the AOD, can provide an in-depth analysis of legal and interpretive issues. AODs may not, however, be cited as precedent.

[B]   The "Duty of Consistency"

One of the policies underlying the IRS's letter ruling program is to help ensure that the agency determines and applies the tax law on a uniform and consistent basis. If that is the case, why does the Code prevent a third party taxpayer from relying on the IRS's conclusions reached in a PLR or other form of taxpayer-specific guidance? Despite the non-precedential nature of many forms of IRS guidance, *should* the IRS have a duty to treat similarly situated taxpayers similarly? In other words, should the IRS have a duty to be consistent in its interpretation of the Code? Consider this excerpt from an article by Professor Zelenak:

SHOULD COURTS REQUIRE THE INTERNAL REVENUE SERVICE TO BE CONSISTENT?*
40 Tax L. Rev. 411 (1985)
By Lawrence Zelenak

An administrative agency must follow its precedents or offer a reasoned explanation for departing from them; a court, faced with a departure from

---

* Copyright 1985, Deborah H. Schenk, Editor-in-Chief. Used with permission.

agency precedents which the agency does not satisfactorily explain and justify, will usually require the agency to adhere to its own precedents. What applies to other agencies, however, does not necessarily apply to the Internal Revenue Service. The Service takes the position that it need not treat similarly situated taxpayers consistently, and the courts have generally accepted the Service's contention.

The Service's claim for exemption from the requirement of administrative consistency is not as outrageous as it may seem. Two considerations peculiar to the Service support its position. First, the cases which impose a duty of consistency on other agencies are overwhelmingly concerned with situations where an agency's statutory mandate gives it broad discretion, and the agency could take any of several different positions without violating its governing statute. By contrast, most of the positions taken by the Service are interpretations of detailed statutes which vest the Service with little discretion in implementation. The question of whether a court should impose a duty of consistency on the Service arises when the Service asserts a position against one taxpayer which is justified under the court's interpretation of the relevant provisions of the Internal Revenue Code, but which the Service has not asserted and does not intend to assert against other similarly situated taxpayers. To impose a duty of consistency in those situations is to give taxpayers lenient treatment that is not justified under the substantive law. This is not a problem with the cases involving agencies given broad discretion by statute, since in those cases courts can require agencies to adhere to their precedents without violating the governing law. This distinction could explain and justify the Service's refusal to recognize a duty of consistency to taxpayers.

* * *

Professor Davis remarks: "Of all the agencies of the government, the worst offender against sound principles of administrative consistency may be the Internal Revenue Service." He argues that the same duty of consistency that applies to other agencies should apply to the Service. He harshly characterizes, almost ridicules, the Service's position: "Its basic attitude is that because consistency is impossible, an effort to be consistent is unnecessary; therefore it need not consider precedents, and it may depart from precedents without explaining why."

There is a crucial difference, however, between the cases noted by Professor Davis as establishing the duty of administrative consistency and the Service's situation. Virtually all of the cited cases involve statutory grants of authority giving broad discretion to the agencies; in these situations, a court can require agency adherence to precedent (if the agency fails to distinguish and declines to disavow its precedent) without countermanding the statutory command of Congress. But the vast majority of the cases involving the Service is different. Congress, in the Internal Revenue Code, has defined what is and what is not includable in or deductible from income. The Service views its task as determining and applying the one true meaning of that statute, not as exercising discretion in deciding what federal income tax policy should be.

* * *

The cases do not foreclose the possibility of imposing a duty of consistency on the Service. Both Justice Frankfurter, in *United States v. Kaiser*, [363 U.S. 299 (1960)] and Judge Friendly, in the first *Sirbo Holdings* [476 F.2d 981 (2nd Cir. 1973)] opinion, took the idea seriously; and the Tax Court was careful to leave the possibility open in its *Davis* [65 T.C. 1014 (1976), and 69 T.C. 716 (1978)] opinions and actually imposed such a duty in *Vesco* [39 T.C.M. (CCH) 101 (1979)]. Since the cases neither establish nor reject a duty of consistency on the Service, the question remains whether that duty should be imposed. It is not dispositive that cases have imposed a duty of consistency on other agencies because those cases do not involve the problem of whether a court should require consistency at the cost of failing to apply the court's interpretation of the substantive law.

I believe that there are circumstances in which it is appropriate for courts to require the Service to afford one taxpayer the same favorable treatment it has given all other similarly situated taxpayers, even if the treatment is inconsistent with that mandated by Congress. The facts of *Vesco* are an example of an appropriate situation for elevating consistency over the substantive law. If the Service has not taxed, and has no intention of taxing, any other taxpayers on the value of relatives' trips on business flights of company jets, then it seems fundamentally unfair to allow the Service to tax Mr. Vesco, regardless of whether the trips fall within the broad sweep of the section 61 definition of gross income. I find equally compelling Professor Davis' hypothetical in which a college faculty member has his child's tuition at another college paid by his employer. Even if a court interprets section 61 to include such a fringe benefit in gross income, it should hold for the taxpayer if the Service has issued and continues to issue private letter rulings to other taxpayers, stating that those tuition payments are not taxable. I admit that my response is a visceral reaction; other people's viscera may react differently. Still, I think there are good reasons to seek equal justice over strict adherence to the substantive law.

* * *

Does the taxpayer have a duty of consistency? For example, does the taxpayer have a duty, if applying a nonrecognition provision, to apply the basis rule in that provision even if it results in a lower basis than Code section 1012 (cost basis) would? If the taxpayer has a duty of consistency, does that mean that the IRS should necessarily also have a duty of consistency? Taken to its logical extreme, would a duty of consistency require the IRS to audit all taxpayers (or all taxpayers of a particular type) if it audits one taxpayer?

Duty of consistency issues sometimes arise in the context of retroactive revocation of a letter ruling, as in the *IBM* case, which is discussed in the following excerpt.

STICHTING PENSIOENFONDS VOOR DE GEZONDHEID v. UNITED STATES[8]
United States Court of Appeals, District Of Columbia Circuit
129 F.3d 195 (1997)

TATEL, CIRCUIT JUDGE:

A Dutch pension fund jointly controlled by employers and unions and claiming to be a "labor organization" as described in section 501(c)(5) of the Internal Revenue Code challenges the Internal Revenue Service's denial of its application for exemption from federal income taxation. Because tax exemptions require unambiguous proof and because we can find no authority directly entitling the pension fund to an exemption, we affirm the district court's grant of summary judgment for the United States.

I.

Appellant Stichting Pensioenfonds Voor de Gezondheid, Geestelijke en Maatschappelijke Belangen (the "Fund") is a Dutch pension plan formed in 1969 following negotiations between labor unions representing hospital workers and the Dutch national hospital employers' association. Soon after the Fund's formation, the Dutch government granted it "compulsory treatment," thus requiring all private hospitals and their employees to participate. The Fund has since expanded to include fourteen health and social welfare sectors in the Netherlands. The Fund has no principal place of business in the United States, nor does it engage in any trade or business here.

* * *

The Fund invests in U.S. stocks and mutual funds. In 1993, its U.S. security custodians withheld and paid to the U.S. Treasury over eight million dollars in income tax. Claiming tax-exempt status as a labor organization under section 501(c)(5) of the Internal Revenue Code, *see* 26 U.S.C. § 501(c)(5) (1994), the Fund filed a claim for this amount. Receiving no response from the Service, the Fund filed suit in the U.S. District Court for the District of Columbia.

Noting that taxpayers must prove exemptions "unambiguously," and finding that the Fund lacked "a sufficient nexus with a more traditional labor organization to qualify as a tax-exempt labor organization itself," the district court granted summary judgment for the United States. Stichting Pensioenfonds Voor De Gezondheid, Geestelijke En Maatschappelijke Belangen v. United States, 950 F. Supp. 373, 374, 379 (D.D.C. 1996). In doing so, the district court rejected the Fund's alternative argument that, even if not entitled to tax-exempt status, it should have received a refund pursuant to section 7805(b) of the Code, 26 U.S.C. § 7805(b) (1994) (superceded by 28 U.S.C.A. § 7805(b)(8) (West Supp. 1997)). *Stichting Pensioenfonds*, 950 F. Supp. at 381. We review the district court's grant of summary judgment *de novo*. Tao v. Freeh, 307 U.S. App. D.C. 185, 27 F.3d 635, 638 (D.C. Cir. 1994).

---

[8] *Cert. denied,* 525 U.S. 811 (1998).

II.

* * *

We begin, of course, with the Internal Revenue Code. Section 501(c)(5) exempts labor, agricultural, and horticultural organizations from taxation. 26 U.S.C. § 501(c)(5). The Code neither defines the term "labor organization" nor elaborates on its meaning. The legislative history, moreover, provides no unambiguous guidance. The early twentieth-century congressional debates on whether to include the term "labor organization" in section 501(c)'s precursor had nothing to do with whether jointly controlled entities providing pension benefits should be exempt from federal taxation. Instead, the debates focused on whether the Code's exemption for "fraternal beneficiary socie- ties. . . providing for the payment of life, sick, accident, or other benefits to members" would be understood as covering all labor organizations, a question that Congress answered negatively when it explicitly exempted labor organi- zations. *See* 44 Cong. Rec. 4154–55 (1909). We agree with the district court that this legislative history provides "little help" in understanding the scope of the term "labor organization." *See Stichting Pensioenfonds,* 950 F. Supp. at 375.

* * *

III.

We turn finally to the Fund's argument that even if not entitled to an exemption under section 501(c)(5), it should have received a refund pursuant to section 7805(b) of the Code, which gives the Service discretion to apply its rulings retroactively. *See* 26 U.S.C. § 7805(b). The Fund cites *IBM v. United States*, 170 Ct. Cl. 357, 343 F.2d 914 (Ct. Cl. 1965). After the Service granted Remington Rand, a direct IBM competitor, an excise tax exemption for its Univac computers, IBM applied for a similar ruling for its competing com- puter. Several years later, the Service denied IBM's request, at the same time revoking Remington's exemption. Invoking section 7805(b), the court held that the Service had abused its discretion by taxing IBM but not Remington in the years prior to the revocation of Remington's exemption. *Id.* Relying on this decision, the Fund argues that because the Service has exempted two similarly situated British pension funds in private determination letters, it likewise abused its discretion by failing to give the Fund a refund for the period in question, *i.e.*, 1993. We disagree.

To begin with, *IBM* applies only to direct competitors. In its very first sentence, the court stressed the competitive relationship between IBM and Remington Rand: "International Business Machines Corporation . . . and Remington Rand were, in the years 1951-1958, the two competitors in the manufacture, sale, and leasing of larger electronic computing systems." *Id.* at 915–16. Treating direct competitors similarly for tax purposes, the court emphasized, "is peculiarly essential to free and fair competition," *id.* at 923; *see also id.* at 921 n.8 (noting that IBM and Remington "were the only two competitors as to the type of devices involved in the Service's rulings"); *id.*

at 923 (indicating that the Service's treatment "favor[ed] the other competitor so sharply that fairness called upon the Commissioner . . . to establish a greater measure of equality"). In view of this language, courts interpreting *IBM* have limited it to cases involving direct competitors. *See, e.g.,* Wilson v. United States, 588 F.2d 1168, 1172 (6th Cir. 1978) (characterizing *IBM* as applying to Service regulations or rulings that "would lead to inequality of treatment between competitor taxpayers"); Anderson, Clayton & Co. v. United States, 562 F.2d 972, 981 (5th Cir. 1977) (same). Because the Fund does not allege—as of course it could not—that it competes with the two exempt British funds, *IBM* has no applicability to this case.

We also doubt that section 7805 even applies here. By its terms, section 7805 only applies to a decision by the Service to limit the retroactive effect of a ruling. Here, the Service has simply denied a refund, taking no action whatsoever with respect to retroactivity. Moreover, neither the plain language of section 7805 nor any of the cases that the Fund cites stands for the proposition that once the Service has treated one taxpayer a certain way, it must thereafter treat every similarly situated taxpayer exactly the same way. In fact, to the extent that Treasury's new regulation denying section 501(c)(5) tax-exempt status to pension funds, * * *, represents a repudiation of the Service's previous decision to exempt the British funds, nothing requires the Service to perpetuate its original error by granting the same mistaken exemption to other taxpayers. *See* Sirbo Holdings, Inc. v. Commissioner of Internal Revenue, 509 F.2d 1220, 1222 (2d Cir. 1975) ("While even-handed treatment should be the Commissioner's goal . . . the making of an error in one case, if error it was, gives other taxpayers no right to its perpetuation.").

We affirm the district court's grant of summary judgment for the United States.

So ordered.

IBM v. United States, 170 Ct. Cl. 357 (1965), which is discussed briefly in the case reprinted above, is an unusual case, both on its facts, and in the holding for the taxpayer. In *IBM,* the IRS had issued IBM's sole competitor, Remington Rand, a favorable ruling exempting it from excise tax. The IRS waited more than two years on IBM's similar ruling request, and then denied its request. IBM and Remington Rand each applied for refunds of the excise taxes paid, and only Remington Rand was issued a refund. When the IRS subsequently revoked Remington Rand's ruling prospectively, this still left unequal treatment for roughly six years, at a cost of approximately $13 million to IBM. The Court of Claims held that the IRS had abused its discretion under section 7805(b) based on an equality of treatment rationale. Thus, the court ordered the IRS to refund to IBM the excise tax paid for the period during which Remington Rand was exempt from the tax under the ruling. As illustrated by the discussion in *Stichting Pensioenfonds Voor De Gezondheid,* taxpayers have found little solace in citing *IBM* because it has been limited to its narrow facts.

§ 9.04   Obtaining Private Guidance for a Taxpayer

[A]   Reporting Requirements

If the taxpayer obtains a letter ruling from the National Office, he must attach the letter ruling to his tax return for the year in question. A return submitted with an attached letter ruling may cause the IRS to take a closer than normal look at the return in order to confirm whether (1) the return properly reflects the conclusions stated in the ruling; (2) the representations upon which the letter ruling was based reflected an accurate statement of the material facts; (3) the transaction was carried out substantially as proposed; and (4) there has been no change in the law that applies to the period during which the transaction or continuing series of transactions were consummated. Rev. Proc. 2002-1, 2002-1 I.R.B. 1. If, for example, the actual facts surrounding the completed transaction are at variance with those represented in the letter ruling request, or if the taxpayer carries out the transaction in a manner different from that represented in the request, the ruling is effectively nullified. *Id.*

Although the IRS is not legally bound by a letter ruling, its long standing policy has been to honor a ruling issued directly to a taxpayer. Unless it is accompanied by a closing agreement, however, the IRS may revoke or modify a letter ruling following (1) the enactment of legislation or ratification of a tax treaty; (2) a decision of the United States Supreme Court; (3) the issuance of temporary or final regulations; or (4) the issuance of a revenue ruling, revenue procedure, notice, or other statement published in the Internal Revenue Bulletin. *Id.* If, on examination of the taxpayer's return, the IRS finds that a letter ruling should be revoked or modified, the findings and recommendations of the agent in charge will be forwarded to the National Headquarters for consideration before further action is taken. Such a referral to the national office is treated as a request for technical advice. *Id.* In most circumstances, the revocation will operate only prospectively, not retroactively.[9]

[B]   Areas in Which the IRS Will Not Issue Letter Rulings

The IRS's authority to decline a letter ruling request is, for the most part, discretionary. The stated policy of the IRS is to issue letter rulings only with respect to completed transactions for a year in which the taxpayer has yet to file a return and for prospective transactions that have not been consummated. Probably the most important fields in which the IRS will issue prospective rulings relate to the tax effects of corporate reorganizations and liquidations. There are certain topics on which the IRS has made it clear that it will not issue letter rulings. Generally the third Revenue Ruling of each year lists the "no rule" areas for domestic taxation. Revenue Procedure 2002-3, 2002-1 I.R.B. 117, provides, in part, that the IRS will not rule on the following *general* areas:

---

[9] If the taxpayer desires absolute certainty regarding the tax effects of a transaction, he must request that the IRS enter into a closing agreement. Closing agreements conclusively determine the tax treatment that should be accorded a particular transaction and can be revoked by the IRS only in the case of fraud or misrepresentation of a material fact. *See* I.R.C. § 7121. Closing agreements are discussed in more detail in Chapter 4.

(1) The results of transactions that lack a *bona fide* business purpose or have as their principal purpose the reduction of federal taxes.

(2) A matter upon which a court decision adverse to the Government has been handed down and the question of following the decision or litigating further has not yet been resolved.

(3) A matter involving alternate plans of proposed transactions or involving hypothetical situations.

(4) Whether under Subtitle F (Procedure and Administration) reasonable cause, due diligence, good faith, clear and convincing evidence, or other similar terms that require a factual determination exist.

(5) Whether a proposed transaction would subject the taxpayer to a criminal penalty.

(6) A request that does not comply with the provisions of Rev. Proc. 2002-1.

Rev. Proc. 2002-3, § 3.02, 2002-1 I.R.B. 117, 121.

The Rev. Proc. also lists *specific* "no rule" areas and areas on which the IRS "ordinarily" will not rule. A few of the specific "no rule" areas are the following:

*   *   *

(12) Section 119.—Meals or Lodging Furnished for the Convenience of the Employer.—Whether the value of meals or lodging is excludible from gross income by an employee who is a controlling shareholder of the employer.

(13) Section 121 and former § 1034.—Exclusion of Gain from Sale of Principal Residence; Rollover of Gain on Sale of Principal Residence.—Whether property qualifies as the taxpayer's principal residence.

*   *   *

(15) Section 162.—Trade or Business Expenses.—Whether compensation is reasonable in amount.

*   *   *

(18) Section 213.—Medical, Dental, Etc., Expenses.—Whether a capital expenditure for an item that is ordinarily used for personal, living, or family purposes, such as a swimming pool, has as its primary purpose the medical care of the taxpayer or the taxpayer's spouse or dependent, or is related directly to such medical care.

* * *

(21)   Section 269.—Acquisitions Made to Evade or Avoid Income Tax.—Whether an acquisition is within the meaning of § 269.

(22)   Section 274.—Disallowance of Certain Entertainment, Etc., Expenses.—Whether a taxpayer who is traveling away from home on business may, in lieu of substantiating the actual cost of meals, deduct a fixed per-day amount for meal expenses that differs from the amount prescribed in the revenue procedure providing optional rules for substantiating the amount of travel expenses for the period in which the expense was paid or incurred, such as Rev. Proc. 97-59, 1997-2 C.B. 594, or its successor, Rev. Proc. 98-64, 1998-2 C.B. 825.

* * *

(28)   Section 312.—Effect on Earnings and Profits.—The determination of the amount of earnings and profits of a corporation.

* * *

(30)   Sections 332, 351 and 368(a)(1)(A), (B), (C), (E) and (F) and 1036. Complete Liquidations of Subsidiaries; Transfer to Corporation Controlled by Transferor; Definitions Relating to Corporate Transfers and Reorganizations; and Stock for Stock of Same Corporation.—Whether a transaction qualifies under § 332, § 351, or § 1036 for nonrecognition treatment, or whether it constitutes a corporate reorganization within the meaning of § 368(a)(1)(A) (including a transaction that qualifies under § 368(a)(1)(A) by reason of § 368(a)(2)(D) or § 368(a)(2)(E)), § 368(a)(1)(B), § 368(a)(1)(C), § 368(a)(1)(E) (or a transaction that also qualifies under § 1036) or § 368(a)(1)(F), and whether various consequences (such as nonrecognition and basis) result from the application of that section, unless the Service determines that there is a significant issue that must be resolved in order to decide those matters. * * *

SIGNIFICANT ISSUE: A significant issue is an issue of law that meets the three following tests: (1) the issue is not clearly and adequately addressed by a statute, regulation, decision of a court, tax treaty, revenue ruling, revenue procedure, notice, or other authority published in the Internal Revenue Bulletin; (2) the resolution of the issue is not essentially free from doubt; and (3) the issue is legally significant and germane to determining the major tax consequences of the transaction.

* * *

Id. § 3.01. The final category enumerated above prevents taxpayers from getting "comfort" rulings when the tax consequences of a reorganization transaction are relatively clear.

Situations in which the IRS "ordinarily" will not issue a letter ruling include the following general areas:

(1) Any matter in which the determination requested is primarily one of fact, *e.g.*, market value of property, or whether an interest in a corporation is to be treated as stock or indebtedness.

(2) Situations where the requested ruling deals with only part of an integrated transaction. Generally, a letter ruling will not be issued on only part of an integrated transaction. If, however, a part of a transaction falls under a no-rule area, a letter ruling on other parts of the transaction may be issued. Before preparing the letter ruling request, a taxpayer should call the Office of the Associate Chief Counsel with jurisdiction over the matters on which the taxpayer is seeking a letter ruling to discuss whether a letter ruling will be issued on part of the transaction.

* * *

(4) The tax effect of any transaction to be consummated at some indefinite future time.

(5) Any matter dealing with the question of whether property is held primarily for sale to customers in the ordinary course of a trade or business.

(6) The tax effect of a transaction if any part of the transaction is involved in litigation among the parties affected by the transaction, except for transactions involving bankruptcy reorganizations.

* * *

Id. § 4.02.

[C]   How to Request a Letter Ruling or Determination Letter

To request a letter ruling or determination letter, the taxpayer or his authorized representative must submit to the IRS a request containing specific information. The first Revenue Procedure of each year describes the letter ruling request process, including what information must be included in the request and further guidance on when the IRS will or will not issue a ruling.[10] Because Revenue Procedure 2002-1 is long and detailed, only portions of it are reproduced below. Notice in particular that the requesting party must furnish as part of the letter ruling request a complete statement of facts, a statement of supporting authorities and copies of all relevant documents related to the transaction.

---

[10] The Revenue Procedure "may be modified or amplified during the year." Rev. Proc. 2002-1, 2002-1 I.R.B 1.

REVENUE PROCEDURE 2002-1
2002-1 I.R.B. 1

* * *

SECTION 8. WHAT ARE THE GENERAL INSTRUCTIONS FOR REQUESTING LETTER RULINGS AND DETERMINATION LETTERS?

This section explains the general instructions for requesting letter rulings and determination letters on all matters. Requests for letter rulings and determination letters require the payment of the applicable user fee listed in Appendix A of this revenue procedure. For additional user fee requirements, see section 15 of this revenue procedure.

Specific and additional instructions also apply to requests for letter rulings and determination letters on certain matters. Those matters are listed in section 9 of this revenue procedure followed by a reference (usually to another revenue procedure) where more information can be obtained.

.01   Certain information required in all requests

Facts

(1) Complete statement of facts and other information. Each request for a letter ruling or a determination letter must contain a complete statement of all facts relating to the transaction. These facts include—

(a) names, addresses, telephone numbers, and taxpayer identification numbers of all interested parties. (The term "all interested parties" does not mean all shareholders of a widely held corporation requesting a letter ruling relating to a reorganization or all employees where a large number may be involved.);

(b) the annual accounting period, and the overall method of accounting (cash or accrual) for maintaining the accounting books and filing the federal income tax return, of all interested parties;

(c) a description of the taxpayer's business operations;

(d) a complete statement of the business reasons for the transaction; and

(e) a detailed description of the transaction.

The Service will usually not rule on only one step of a larger integrated transaction. See section 7.03 of this revenue procedure. However, if such a letter ruling is requested, the facts, circumstances, true copies of relevant documents, etc., relating to the entire transaction must be submitted.

Documents and foreign laws

(2) Copies of all contracts, wills, deeds, agreements, instruments, other documents, and foreign laws.

(a) Documents. True copies of all contracts, wills, deeds, agreements, instruments, trust documents, proposed disclaimers, and other documents pertinent to the transaction must be submitted with the request.

If the request concerns a corporate distribution, reorganization, or similar transaction, the corporate balance sheet and profit and loss statement should also be submitted. If the request relates to a prospective transaction, the most recent balance sheet and profit and loss statement should be submitted.

If any document, including any balance sheet and profit and loss statement, is in a language other than English, the taxpayer must also submit a certified English translation of the document, along with a true copy of the document. For guidelines on the acceptability of such documents, see paragraph (c) of this section 8.01(2).

Each document, other than the request, should be labeled and attached to the request in alphabetical sequence. Original documents, such as contracts, wills, etc., should not be submitted because they become part of the Service's file and will not be returned.

* * *

Analysis of material facts

(3) **Analysis of material facts.** All material facts in documents must be included, rather than merely incorporated by reference, in the taxpayer's initial request or in supplemental letters. These facts must be accompanied by an analysis of their bearing on the issue or issues, specifying the provisions that apply.

Same issue in an earlier return

(4) **Statement regarding whether same issue is in an earlier return.** The request must state whether, to the best of the knowledge of both the taxpayer and the taxpayer's representatives, the same issue is in an earlier return of the taxpayer (or in a return for any year of a related taxpayer within the meaning of § 267 or of a member of an affiliated group of which the taxpayer is also a member within the meaning of § 1504).

* * *

Statement of authorities supporting taxpayer's views

(8) **Statement of supporting authorities.** If the taxpayer advocates a particular conclusion, an explanation of the grounds for that conclusion and the relevant authorities to support it must be included. Even if not advocating a particular tax treatment of a proposed transaction, the taxpayer must still furnish views on the tax results of the proposed transaction and a statement of relevant authorities to support those views.

In all events, the request must include a statement of whether the law in connection with the request is uncertain and whether the issue is adequately addressed by relevant authorities.

Statement of authorities contrary to taxpayer's views

(9) **Statement of contrary authorities.** The taxpayer is also encouraged to inform the Service about, and discuss the implications of, any authority believed to be contrary to the position advanced, such as legislation (or

pending legislation), tax treaties, court decisions, regulations, notices, revenue rulings, revenue procedures, or announcements. If the taxpayer determines that there are no contrary authorities, a statement in the request to this effect would be helpful. If the taxpayer does not furnish either contrary authorities or a statement that none exists, the Service in complex cases or those presenting difficult or novel issues may request submission of contrary authorities or a statement that none exists. Failure to comply with this request may result in the Service's refusal to issue a letter ruling or determination letter.

Identifying and discussing contrary authorities will generally enable Service personnel to understand the issue and relevant authorities more quickly. When Service personnel receive the request, they will have before them the taxpayer's thinking on the effect and applicability of contrary authorities. This information should make research easier and lead to earlier action by the Service. If the taxpayer does not disclose and distinguish significant contrary authorities, the Service may need to request additional information, which will delay action on the request.

Statement identifying pending legislation

(10) Statement identifying pending legislation. At the time of filing the request, the taxpayer must identify any pending legislation that may affect the proposed transaction. In addition, if legislation is introduced after the request is filed but before a letter ruling or determination letter is issued, the taxpayer must notify the Service.

Deletions statement required by § 6110

(11) Statement identifying information to be deleted from copy of letter ruling or determination letter for public inspection. The text of letter rulings and determination letters is open to public inspection under § 6110. The Service makes deletions from the text before it is made available for inspection. To help the Service make the deletions required by § 6110(c), a request for a letter ruling or determination letter must be accompanied by a statement indicating the deletions desired ("deletions statement"). If the deletions statement is not submitted with the request, a Service representative will tell the taxpayer that the request will be closed if the Service does not receive the deletions statement within 21 calendar days. See section 10.06 of this revenue procedure.

(a) Format of deletions statement. A taxpayer who wants only names, addresses, and identifying numbers to be deleted should state this in the deletions statement. If the taxpayer wants more information deleted, the deletions statement must be accompanied by a copy of the request and supporting documents on which the taxpayer should bracket the material to be deleted. The deletions statement must indicate the statutory basis under § 6110(c) for each proposed deletion.

If the taxpayer decides to ask for additional deletions before the letter ruling or determination letter is issued, additional deletions statements may be submitted.

(b) Location of deletions statement. The deletions statement must not appear in the request, but instead must be made in a separate document and placed on top of the request for a letter ruling or determination letter.

(c) Signature. The deletions statement must be signed and dated by the taxpayer or the taxpayer's authorized representative. A stamped signature is not permitted.

(d) Additional information. The taxpayer should follow the same procedures above to propose deletions from any additional information submitted after the initial request. An additional deletions statement, however, is not required with each submission of additional information if the taxpayer's initial deletions statement requests that only names, addresses, and identifying numbers are to be deleted and the taxpayer wants only the same information deleted from the additional information.

(e) Taxpayer may protest deletions not made. After receiving from the Service the notice under § 6110(f)(1) of intention to disclose the letter ruling or determination letter (including a copy of the version proposed to be open to public inspection and notation of third-party communications under § 6110(d)), the taxpayer may protest the disclosure of certain information in the letter ruling or determination letter. The taxpayer must send a written statement within 20 calendar days to the Service office indicated on the notice of intention to disclose. The statement must identify those deletions that the Service has not made and that the taxpayer believes should have been made. The taxpayer must also submit a copy of the version of the letter ruling or determination letter and bracket the deletions proposed that have not been made by the Service. Generally, the Service will not consider deleting any material that the taxpayer did not propose to be deleted before the letter ruling or determination letter was issued.

Within 20 calendar days after the Service receives the response to the notice under § 6110(f)(1), the Service will mail to the taxpayer its final administrative conclusion regarding the deletions to be made. The taxpayer does not have the right to a conference to resolve any disagreements concerning material to be deleted from the text of the letter ruling or determination letter. However, these matters may be taken up at any conference that is otherwise scheduled regarding the request.

*   *   *

Signature on request

(12) Signature by taxpayer or authorized representative. The request for a letter ruling or determination letter must be signed and dated by the taxpayer or the taxpayer's authorized representative. A stamped signature is not permitted.

*   *   *

Power of attorney and declaration of representative

(14) Power of attorney and declaration of representative. Any authorized representative, whether or not enrolled to practice, must also comply with the conference and practice requirements of the Statement of Procedural Rules (26 C.F.R. § 601.501-601.509 (2001)), which provide the rules for representing a taxpayer before the Service. It is preferred that Form 2848,

Power of Attorney and Declaration of Representative, be used to provide the representative's authorization (Part I of Form 2848, Power of Attorney) and the representative's qualification (Part II of Form 2848, Declaration of Representative). The name of the person signing Part I of Form 2848 should also be typed or printed on this form. A stamped signature is not permitted. An original, a copy, or a facsimile transmission (fax) of the power of attorney is acceptable as long as its authenticity is not reasonably disputed. For additional information regarding the power of attorney form, see section 8.02(2) of this revenue procedure.

For the requirement regarding compliance with Treasury Department Circular No. 230, see section 8.08 of this revenue procedure.

Penalties of perjury statement

(15) Penalties of perjury statement.

(a) Format of penalties of perjury statement. A request for a letter ruling or determination letter and any change in the request submitted at a later time must be accompanied by the following declaration: **"Under penalties of perjury, I declare that I have examined [Insert, as appropriate: this request or this modification to the request], including accompanying documents, and, to the best of my knowledge and belief, [Insert, as appropriate: the request or the modification] contains all the relevant facts relating to the request, and such facts are true, correct, and complete."**

* * *

(b) Signature by taxpayer. The declaration must be signed and dated by the taxpayer, not the taxpayer's representative. A stamped signature is not permitted.

The person who signs for a corporate taxpayer must be an officer of the corporate taxpayer who has personal knowledge of the facts and whose duties are not limited to obtaining a letter ruling or determination letter from the Service. If the corporate taxpayer is a member of an affiliated group filing consolidated returns, a penalties of perjury statement must also be signed and submitted by an officer of the common parent of the group.

The person signing for a trust, a state law partnership, or a limited liability company must be, respectively, a trustee, general partner, or member-manager who has personal knowledge of the facts.

* * *

Appendix A of Revenue Procedure 2002-1 contains a schedule of user fees, Appendix B contains a sample format for a letter ruling request, and Appendix C contains a detailed checklist entitled "Is Your Letter Ruling Request Complete?" The purpose of the checklist is to ensure that all the necessary information and documents are furnished with the request. In addition, "If the checklist in Appendix C is not received, a branch representative will ask the taxpayer or the taxpayer's representative to submit the checklist, which may delay action on the letter ruling request." *Id.* Anyone making a letter ruling request would be well advised to follow the guidelines in Appendix B.

A sample letter ruling request might look something like this:[11]

SAMPLE LETTER RULING REQUEST

November 1, 2002

Internal Revenue Service
Associate Chief Counsel Domestic
Attn: CC: PA: T
P.O. Box 7604
Ben Franklin Station
Washington, D.C. 20044

Dear Sir or Madam:

The taxpayer, United Cancer Research Institute (the Institute) requests a ruling on whether certain research stipends it awards constitute payment for services within the meaning of section 117(c) of the Internal Revenue Code (the Code), whether the Institute will be required to withhold any taxes from the stipends, and whether the Institute will have reporting obligations with respect to the stipends.

A. STATEMENT OF FACTS

1. Taxpayer Information

The Institute is a Pennsylvania corporation that is exempt from Federal income taxation under Code section 501(c)(3). The complete address and telephone number of the Institute are:

United Cancer Research Institute
555 Main Line Drive
Philadelphia, PA 19010
(215) 526-9898

The Institute's employer identification number is 333-44-2222. The Institute keeps its books on a calendar year basis, and uses the accrual method of accounting.

2. Description of Taxpayer's Business Operations

The Institute conducts clinical and theoretical research, training, and educational programs on the development, progress, and treatment of cancer.

3. Facts Relating to Transaction

As part of its core research mission, the Institute conducts a nationally known training program designed to train postdoctoral fellows to become research scientists. The focus of the training program is the development and

---

[11] This letter ruling request is loosely based on PLR 199933021.

improvement of research skills. The training programs generally last from two to four years. To help defray the fellows' living expenses during their training, the Institute pays modest stipends. Each year, the Institute pays stipends to approximately 75 fellows. Research fellows are not required to have performed services or to agree to perform services for the Institute (such as working as a laboratory technician) as a condition to receiving a stipend.

B. RULING REQUESTED

The Institute requests a ruling that the research stipends awarded do not represent compensation for services within the meaning of section 117(c) of the Code, and that they do not constitute "wages" for purposes of section 3401(a). The Institute also requests a ruling that the stipends are not subject to section 3402 (withholding for income taxes at source), section 3102 (withholding under the Federal Insurance Contribution Act (FICA)), or section 3301 (Federal Unemployment Tax Act (FUTA)), and that the Institute is not required to file Forms W-2, or any information returns under section 6041, with respect to the stipends.

C. STATEMENT OF LAW

Code section 117 governs the federal income tax treatment of qualified scholarships and fellowship grants. Section 117(a) provides that gross income does not include any amount received as a "qualified scholarship" by an individual who is a candidate for a degree at an educational organization described in section 170(b)(1)(A)(ii). A qualified scholarship is defined as an amount expended for "qualified tuition and related expenses."

Section 117(c) of the Code provides that the exclusion for qualified scholarships shall not apply to that portion of any amount received which represents payment for teaching, research, or other services by the student required as a condition for receiving the qualified scholarship or fellowship. A scholarship or fellowship grant represents payment for services when the grantor requires the recipient to perform services in return for the granting of the scholarship or fellowship. A requirement that the recipient pursue studies, research, or other activities primarily for the benefit of the grantor is treated as a requirement to perform services. A scholarship or fellowship grant conditioned upon either past, present, or future services by the recipient, or upon services that are subject to the direction or supervision of the grantor, represents payment for services. *See* Bingler v. Johnson, 394 U.S. 741 (1969).

Although payments for research services are not excludable under section 117, not all payments for research activities represent payment for services. Under Code section 117 and the regulations thereunder, a qualified scholarship includes any amount paid or allowed to aid an individual in the pursuit of study or research. Accordingly, research activities by a student may qualify for exclusion from gross income. It is only where the research required by the grantor falls within section 117(c) that a payment must be included in gross income.

A scholarship or fellowship grant that is includible in gross income under section 117(c) of the Code is considered "wages" for purposes of section 3401(a).

The grantor of such an amount is subject to certain withholding and reporting requirements respecting wages, including withholding for income taxes and the filing of Forms W-2. The application of Federal Insurance Contributions Act (FICA) and Federal Unemployment Tax Act (FUTA) taxes depends on the nature of the employment and the status of the grantor. *See* Notice 87-31, 1987-1 C.B. 475.

D. ANALYSIS

The Institute does not compensate research fellows for services, but rather subsidizes fellows' expenses as they learn to become research scientists. The stipends are disinterested grants to fellows to enable them to pursue research training independent of any benefit to the Institute. Therefore, the stipends do not represent compensation for services within the meaning of section 117(c) of the Code. *Cf.* Rev. Rul. 83-93, 1983-1 C.B. 364.

Because the stipends do not constitute payments for services under Code section 117(c), they are not "wages" for purposes of section 3401(a). In addition, they are not subject to section 3402 (relating to withholding for income taxes at source), section 3102 (relating to withholding under the Federal Insurance Contribution Act (FICA)), or section 3301 (relating to the Federal Unemployment Tax Act (FUTA)). Therefore, the Institute is not required to file Forms W-2 or any information returns under section 6041 with respect to the stipends.

E. CONCLUSION

The Institute's research stipends awarded do not represent compensation for services within the meaning of section 117(c) of the Code. The stipends also do not constitute "wages" for purposes of section 3401(a), and they are not subject to section 3402 (relating to withholding for income taxes at source), section 3102 (relating to withholding under the Federal Insurance Contribution Act (FICA)), or section 3301 (relating to the Federal Unemployment Tax Act (FUTA)). In addition, the Institute is not required to file Forms W-2, or any information returns under section 6041, with respect to the stipends.

F. PROCEDURAL MATTERS

1. Revenue Procedure 2002-1 Statements

a. The issue that is the subject of this letter ruling request is not reflected in any earlier return of the taxpayer or a predecessor, or in a return for any year of a related taxpayer.

b. The IRS has not previously ruled on the same or similar issue for the taxpayer, a related taxpayer, or a predecessor taxpayer.

c. No one, including the taxpayer, a related taxpayer, a predecessor, or any representatives previously submitted a request involving the same or similar issue but withdrew the request before a letter ruling was issued.

d. No one, including the taxpayer, a related taxpayer, or any predecessor taxpayer, has submitted a letter ruling request involving the same or a similar issue that is currently pending with the IRS.

e. Neither the taxpayer nor any related taxpayer is submitting another request to the IRS involving the same or a similar issue.

f. The law on the issues raised in this letter ruling request is uncertain, and is not adequately addressed by existing authorities.

g. The Institute has been unable to find any contrary authorities.

h. The Institute requests a conference on the issues involved in the letter ruling request.

2. Administrative

a. The deletions statement and checklist required by Revenue Procedure 2002-1 are enclosed.

b. The required user fee of $6,000 is enclosed.

c. A completed Power of Attorney form is enclosed.

Very truly yours,

Frances Farnwell
Attorney for United Cancer Research Institute
November 1, 2002

Under penalties of perjury, I declare that I have examined this request, including accompanying documents, and, to the best of my knowledge and belief, the request contains all the relevant facts relating to the request, and such facts are true, correct, and complete.

United Cancer Research Institute

By: Daniel D. Doe
November 1, 2002

Although Revenue Procedure 2002-1 governs most letter rulings requests, the IRS has issued additional Revenue Procedures that cover ruling requests that relate to a particular type of transaction. Revenue Procedure 96-30, 1996-1 C.B. 696, for example, contains a checklist of additional information and representations that a taxpayer must submit in order to receive a ruling confirming that a distribution of a subsidiary's stock qualifies under section 355. Before submitting a ruling request, the taxpayer should carefully determine whether an additional pronouncement applies to the taxpayer's request. Section 9 of Revenue Procedure 2002-1 (not included in the text) lists these additional Revenue Procedures and the transactions to which they relate.

[D] Requesting a Conference with the IRS

When pursuing a letter ruling request, a taxpayer is normally entitled to a conference at the national office, as a matter of right. If the taxpayer requests a conference, the IRS will notify the taxpayer of the time and place of the conference, which must then be held within 21 calendar days. The conference of right affords both the IRS representative and the taxpayer an opportunity to clarify the issues involved, and to request and respond to additional factual information or representations. *See generally* Rev. Proc. 2002-1 § 11.

A taxpayer may request that his conference of right be held by telephone. A taxpayer might make this request if, for example, he believes that the issue involved does not warrant incurring the expense of travelling to Washington, D.C. If a taxpayer makes such a request, the IRS will decide if it is appropriate in the particular case to hold the conference by telephone. If the request is approved, the taxpayer will be advised when to call the IRS representatives. *Id.* at § 11.08.

In addition to the conference of right, the IRS may offer the taxpayer additional conferences if the IRS feels they will be helpful. In general, the IRS will offer the taxpayer an additional conference if an adverse holding is proposed. During the conference, the taxpayer should furnish to the National Office any additional documentation that was proposed by the taxpayer and discussed at the initial conference but not previously or adequately presented in writing. These conferences with IRS representatives prior to issuance of a ruling can, when conducted appropriately, significantly increase the taxpayer's chances of receiving a favorable ruling. The taxpayer's representative should come to the conference well prepared, having thoroughly researched the legal issues involved and with a full understanding of the relevant facts. *See id.* at § 11.05.

Occasionally the IRS will hold a conference before the taxpayer submits the letter ruling request in order to discuss substantive or procedural issues relating to a proposed transaction. Such conferences are held only if the taxpayer actually intends to make a request, only if the request involves a matter on which a letter ruling is ordinarily issued, and only on a time-available basis. Generally, the taxpayer will be asked to provide before the pre-submission conference a draft of the letter ruling request or other detailed written statements of the proposed transaction and the issues involved. As discussed more fully below, the taxpayer can use the pre-submission conference to gauge the likelihood that an adverse ruling may be issued, at which point the taxpayer may wish to either forego the ruling process or restructure the transaction. Any discussion of substantive issues at a pre-submission conference is advisory only, is not binding on the IRS, and cannot be relied upon as a basis for obtaining retroactive relief under the provisions of Code section 7805(b). *See id.* at § 11.07.

[E] Whether to Request a Letter Ruling and Whether to Withdraw a Ruling Request

The letter ruling process essentially allows a taxpayer to ask the IRS to confirm the appropriate tax treatment of an item or proposed transaction. Such confirmation may be desirable where uncertainties exist in the law, and in cases where severe adverse tax consequences might result. If a ruling is requested and a favorable result is received, the taxpayer can proceed with the transaction with reasonable certainty of its tax consequences. Although a letter ruling may sound like a convenient method of resolving a potential dispute, a taxpayer should carefully consider the anticipated benefits and the potential drawbacks associated with initiating the ruling process.

One of the most important factors bearing upon whether the taxpayer should request a letter ruling is the likelihood of obtaining a favorable result. Once the taxpayer submits the formal request, the national office is made aware of a transaction, the tax consequences of which are, more likely than not, uncertain and important enough to the taxpayer to require special consideration. Experts will then scrutinize the transaction carefully in an effort to confirm the underlying facts and determine the appropriate tax consequences. Any flaws in the taxpayer's position, whether factual or legal, are much more likely to be discovered as part of the ruling application process as compared to a routine examination of the taxpayer's return.

While the taxpayer will normally be offered the opportunity to withdraw the letter ruling request if the IRS intends on ruling adversely, the taxpayer's withdrawal will not prevent the national office from retaining the related files and transmitting that information to the office that will have audit jurisdiction over the taxpayer's return. As a practical matter, therefore, if the taxpayer is informed of or issued an adverse ruling, he must be prepared to restructure the transaction, forego it, or litigate the matter. Particularly when the taxpayer wishes to proceed with a transaction regardless of whether or not the tax consequences are favorable, a letter ruling request can present a serious risk.

In addition to the risks associated with an adverse determination, the taxpayer should also be advised of the costs related to the ruling process. These costs include not only the user fees imposed by the IRS, but also the representative's billable time necessary to prepare and negotiate the request. Especially when the issues involved are complex and the risk of an adverse ruling is relatively great, preparation costs can mount quickly. The amount the taxpayer should be willing to spend on a letter ruling will vary, of course, with the potential tax liability in issue. In making this cost/benefit analysis, the taxpayer must also take into account the expense associated with an IRS examination should the transaction be selected for audit.

A final consideration relates to the time involved in obtaining a letter ruling. In some cases, the transaction cannot wait for a favorable ruling and must be consummated even though a ruling might lend the parties important peace of mind. Although no general rule exists, the estimated waiting period for a letter ruling in the income tax area is eight to twelve weeks. As the complexity of the issue and the potential tax liability involved increase, so generally does the waiting period.

Taxpayers can minimize the wait for a letter ruling by ensuring that the ruling request is submitted properly, with all required documentation. Revenue Procedure 2002-1 also permits a taxpayer to file a ruling request on an expedited basis. Expedited consideration will only be given when the parties will suffer undue hardship or be irreparably prejudiced from taking certain actions if a prompt response to the ruling request is not issued. Self-imposed deadlines and other time limitations created by the parties are not sufficient justifications for requesting expedited consideration. To obtain priority, the taxpayer must submit with the ruling request a separate letter that explains why expedited consideration is appropriate under the circumstances. Rev. Proc. 2002-1 § 8.02(4).

Although the IRS may issue a letter ruling with respect to a completed transaction that has not yet been reported on the taxpayer's return, these types of rulings should be requested sparingly. What risks does the taxpayer incur with respect to this type of ruling?

[F] Pre-Filing Agreements

As a result of a new IRS initiative, a taxpayer may also obtain resolution of an issue before filing a return by requesting a pre-filing agreement (PFA). The goal of the PFA program, similar to that of the letter ruling program, is to allow taxpayers and the IRS to resolve, before a taxpayer files a return, issues that would otherwise be disputed in a post-filing audit. The resulting PFA, which specifies how the transaction will be reported on returns filed after the agreement date, is treated as a closing agreement and, unlike a letter ruling, is not subject to public disclosure under FOIA or section 6110. Although the scope and details of the program are still being worked out, it appears that the PFA program is designed primarily to resolve specific factual issues involving established legal principles, as compared to the letter ruling program, which is broader in scope and capable of resolving interrelated factual and legal issues that may arise in a multi-step transaction. Valuation questions, for example, might be resolved through the use of a PFA, while determining the tax treatment of a like-kind exchange or corporate reorganization would be more suitable for a letter ruling. For details relating to the program, *see* Rev. Proc. 2001-22, 2001-9 I.R.B. 745; *see also* Section 4.02[6]. At the current time the PFA program is open only to those taxpayers in the Large and Mid-Size Business Operating Division.

PROBLEMS

1.   In recent audits, IRS personnel have observed that a number of taxpayers have engaged in what the IRS believes were tax-motivated sham transactions. These transactions relied on what the IRS considers a distorted interpretation of a Code section that was repealed in 2001. The IRS would like to put a stop to the revenue loss caused by these shelter transactions. Its concern is not prospective revenue loss, but rather lost revenue from the 1996-2000 tax years.

    A.   Following notice and comment procedures, can a Treasury regulation enacted today, but with an effective date of January 1, 1996, close the loophole?

    B.   Can the IRS instead issue today a Revenue Ruling that closes the loophole, and apply it to all transactions with respect to the pre-2001 provision that are now or will subsequently be under examination or in litigation?

2.   In several cases cited or reprinted in this chapter, courts applied the legislative reenactment doctrine. Under what

circumstances should nonaction on the part of Congress carry precedential significance?

3.   Marvin is the majority shareholder of a small corporation. He is interested in entering into a complicated merger transaction that will result in diversification of his business and the acquisition of several subsidiaries. One of his former competitors, Dale, who retired last year, engaged in a very similar transaction two years ago. Dale told Marvin that she obtained a favorable letter ruling from the IRS before consummating the transaction. She is willing to send Marvin a copy of the ruling. Marvin asks you the following questions:

   A.   If he engages in exactly the transaction described in Dale's ruling, can Marvin rely on Dale's ruling, and simply carry out his transaction assured of favorable tax treatment?

   B.   Would he be better off, after engaging in the transaction described in Dale's ruling, to attach a copy of the ruling to his return with a statement that he expects the IRS to accord him the same treatment? Marvin is curious about whether that will create an enforceable obligation on the part of the IRS to treat his transaction in accordance with Dale's ruling.

4.   Katrina has been breeding pedigreed hairless Sphynx cats for several years. The food and veterinary bills for the cats are costly, and Katrina has not been able to sell enough kittens to recoup her expenses. She has been content to run the cattery at a small loss because she makes a good income from her full-time job as a professor, from which she has been deducting her losses. Recently, a colleague who teaches tax courses mentioned to her that the cattery sounded more like a "hobby" than a true business, and that perhaps Katrina should not be deducting the cattery's losses. Katrina has come to you to ask whether she can and should obtain a ruling from the IRS on her cattery so that she will know how to treat it for tax purposes next year. What do you advise?

5.   At the request of a client of his firm, Kenny has incorporated an entity that the client intends to run as a charitable organization that promotes friendly soccer and softball games between co-ed teams composed of children of divorced parents. The client would like to be assured that the intended activities of the corporation will not preclude tax exemption under Code section 501(c)(3). How can Kenny request such assurance from the IRS?

6.   In 2001, Helen Miller, an individual calendar-year, cash-method taxpayer, purchased land and a building with the intention of converting the site into an international food emporium offering fresh produce and prepared ethnic cuisine. The building, located in Hopewell, Georgia, a suburb of Atlanta, was originally constructed in 1925 for use as a cotton warehouse. Constructed

of brick with many lovely architectural details, the building had remained a warehouse facility until 1980. During the period from 1980 to the date of Helen's purchase, the warehouse building sat vacant. The purchase price for the property was $2.7 million, with $1 million being allocated to the land and $1.7 million allocated to the building. Helen purchased the property with cash.

At the time she acquired the property, Helen owned a chain of grocery stores located throughout Atlanta. Although the food emporium would be a separate venture, Helen believed her extensive experience in the grocery business would prove valuable. She first had the idea for the venture while visiting The Old Mill, a nineteenth century factory building in Chattanooga, Tennessee that had been successfully converted into high-end retail space for clothing and related retailers.

Shortly after acquiring the site in 2001, Helen hired a marketing consultant to draft a business plan for the venture. While the consultant believed the idea of an international food emporium was a potentially profitable one in the Atlanta market, he informed Helen that the location of her recently purchased site was not ideal from the standpoint of attracting customers. No major roadways led to the parcel, and commercial and residential development in Hopewell had become stagnant in the mid-1990s. He also anticipated that few Atlantans would make the drive to Hopewell in order to shop at the market.

Helen's architectural and design consultant, hired in 2002, also had discouraging news. Having remained vacant for more than 15 years, the warehouse building had fallen into a state of disrepair. Although not immediately apparent, many of the supporting beams were rotted and the paint covering the building's interior was lead-based. Even more distressing was the news that most of the pipes in the building were covered with asbestos insulation. A local contractor estimated that the cost to safely remove the paint and asbestos would run as high as $800,000. While Helen knew initially that renovation costs for the site would be significant, she did not anticipate this additional expense. She decided, at the end of 2002, to temporarily postpone any repairs or renovations.

Since the date of her purchase, Helen has paid both real estate taxes and property insurance on the site. Helen's 2002 property tax assessment for the land and building was $3 million, an increase of $300,000 over the prior year. Helen decided to contest the value of the site with the local tax assessor; fortunately, she received a reduction in the valuation to $2.5 million. Helen also decided in 2002 to reduce her insurance coverage on the building to reflect the new lower valuation. To prevent vandals from doing further damage to the warehouse building, Helen constructed a chain link fence around the property and posted signs warning intruders of the building's unsafe condition.

By early 2003, Helen's grocery store chain began showing financial problems. To generate cash Helen removed and auctioned off architectural details from the warehouse building. Helen also canceled her property insurance for the site, retaining only hazard insurance in case an intruder injured himself on the property. Helen's last visit to the site, in February of 2003, was to padlock the chain link fence and lament her failed venture. Assume that Helen's adjusted basis in the land and building remains $2.7 million.

Because of the expense of owning the property, Helen is considering abandoning it immediately and notifying the local tax authorities that she will no longer claim any ownership of it. However, Helen will only abandon the property if, for federal income tax purposes, she will be able to claim an abandonment loss deduction under section 165 of the Code.

A.   What factors should Helen consider in deciding whether to request a letter ruling from the IRS confirming the deductibility of the loss?

B.   Assume that Helen decides that she will submit a letter ruling request to the IRS, and she asks you, her attorney, to draft it for her. Based on the foregoing facts, draft a request for a letter ruling on the issue of whether if Helen abandons the land and building as described above, she will sustain a deductible abandonment loss in 2003. Helen's social security number is 555-44-9999. She currently resides at 2101 Miami Beach Drive, Ft. Lauderdale, FL 33322, and her telephone number is (305) 498-2692. The letter ruling request must comply with the requirements of this year's Revenue Procedure on letter ruling requests (the first Revenue Procedure of the year).

Chapter 10

CIVIL TAX PENALTIES

Reading Assignment: Code §§ 6651, 6662, 6663, 6664, 6694, 6721, 6722, 6724, 7701(a)(36); Treas. Reg. §§ 301.6651-1; 1.6662-3, -4; 1.6694-1, -2, -3; 301.6721-1; 301.6724-1; 301.7701-15.

§ 10.01 Introduction: The Role of Penalties

As discussed in previous chapters, a primary goal of the IRS is to encourage voluntary taxpayer compliance. Noncompliance results not only from a failure to file a return but also from a failure by the taxpayer to determine and report on the return the correct amount of tax. The tax penalty system, along with the IRS's audit function and its efforts (post-1998) to assist taxpayers in meeting their obligations under the Code, significantly enhances the IRS's ability to deter this type of noncompliant behavior. The following policy statement reflects the IRS's philosophy on the imposition of penalties:

INTERNAL REVENUE MANUAL
PART XX
Penalty Policy Statement P-1-18

Penalties constitute one important tool of the Internal Revenue Service in pursuing its mission of collecting the proper amount of tax revenue at the least cost. Penalties support the Service's mission only if penalties enhance voluntary compliance. Even though other results, such as raising of revenue, punishment, or reimbursement of the costs of enforcement, may also arise when penalties are asserted, the Service will design, administer, and evaluate penalty programs solely on the basis of whether they do the best possible job of encouraging compliant conduct.

In the interest of an effective tax system, the Service uses penalties to encourage voluntary compliance by: (1) helping taxpayers understand that compliant conduct is appropriate and non-compliant conduct is not; (2) deterring noncompliance by imposing costs on it; and (3) establishing the fairness of the tax system by justly penalizing the non-compliant taxpayer.

To this end, the IRS administers a penalty system that is designed to:

— ensure consistency;

— ensure accuracy of results in light of the facts and the law;

— provide methods for the taxpayer to have his or her interests heard and considered;

— require impartiality and a commitment to achieve the correct decision;

- allow for prompt reversal of initial determinations when sufficient information has been presented to indicate that the penalty is not appropriate;

- ensure that penalties are used for their proper purpose and not as bargaining points in the development or processing of cases.

I.R.M. Part XX Exhibit 120.1.1-1 — Penalties (commonly called the "Consolidated Penalty Handbook").

In an attempt to address many of the concerns expressed in the current Policy Statement, Congress substantially revised the Code's penalty provisions in 1989. *See* Improved Penalty Administration and Compliance Act of 1989 ("IMPACT"), Pub. L. No. 101-239, 103 Stat. 2395, applicable generally to returns filed after December 31, 1989. The tax penalty structure that existed prior to IMPACT developed primarily as a response to the tax shelter industry and reflected the piecemeal way in which the rules evolved. In particular, the pre-IMPACT regime was characterized by extreme complexity, inconsistent application by the IRS, and a lack of precise standards for imposing penalties. Moreover, the prior rules allowed the IRS to "stack" penalties, that is, impose more than one penalty with respect to the same understatement of tax liability. A taxpayer who filed his return after the prescribed due date, for example, might have been subject to a delinquency penalty, a negligence penalty, and a substantial understatement penalty, all with respect to the same underpayment of tax.

The IMPACT legislation did away with penalty stacking (for the most part) and established a more coordinated effort at imposing penalties. Even today, however, the Code contains over 100 civil tax penalties. As you read through the chapter, reflect upon the IRS's Policy Statement and judge for yourself whether the current structure achieves its goals. This chapter focuses on taxpayer-related penalties — those imposed upon taxpayers for understatements of tax and delinquent filing or payment. These taxpayer-related penalties represent the type most frequently assessed by the IRS and most frequently litigated by taxpayers. Although Code section 6751 requires that notices asserting a penalty contain an explanation and a computation of the penalty being asserted, a practitioner's understanding of when these additions to tax can apply remains important for purposes of advising clients of their obligations under the Code, formulating return positions, and planning transactions.[1]

---

[1] The Community Renewal Tax Relief Act of 2000, Pub. L. No. 106-554, extended until June 30, 2001 the original December 31, 2000 deadline by which the IRS must comply with section 6751. Moreover, for any notice of penalty issued before June 30, 2003, the IRS need only include a telephone number at which the taxpayer may obtain a copy of the assessment and payment history relating to the asserted penalty. By including the telephone number, the IRS is deemed to satisfy the notice provisions in section 6751, which would otherwise require the IRS to include the name of the penalty, the Code section under which it is imposed, and the computation of the penalty.

§ 10.02   Specific Civil Penalties and Defenses to Those Penalties

[A]   The Delinquency Penalty — Code Section 6651

The delinquency penalty in section 6651 seeks to encourage timely reporting and timely payment of tax. Both the late filing and late payment portions of the penalty apply to all types of taxes for which a taxpayer is required to file a return, including individual and corporate income taxes, gift and estate taxes, and most excise taxes. A separate failure to file penalty applies to information returns, and is discussed below. Establishing the timeliness of filing and payment implicates many of the issues addressed in Chapter 2, particularly those relating to due dates, filing extensions, and the sufficiency of a return.

[1]   The Failure to File Penalty

The penalty under Code section 6651(a)(1) for failure to timely file a return applies on a graduated basis. The late filing penalty equals five percent of the amount of tax required to be shown on the return for each month (or fraction of a month) during which the failure to file continues, up to a maximum of 25 percent. If the taxpayer's failure to file is fraudulent, the penalty rate increases to 15 percent per month, up to a maximum of 75 percent. I.R.C. § 6651(f). The penalty period commences the first day after the return is due (taking into account extensions of time to file) and ends once the IRS actually receives the delinquent return, rather than the date the taxpayer mails the return. Rev. Rul. 73-133, 1973-1 C.B. 605. The late filing penalty is computed based on the *net* amount of tax required to be shown on the return. For this purpose, the liability shown on the return is reduced by tax pre-payments, estimated tax payments, and allowable credits (including the wage withholding credit under Code section 31). I.R.C. § 6651(b)(1).

Section 6651 contains a minimum penalty provision that applies specifically to income tax returns. If the return is filed more than 60 days late, the late filing penalty cannot be less than the lesser of $100 or the net amount required to be shown on the return. Under this formulation, would a delinquent return showing no net tax due still incur a $100 penalty? The Tax Court takes the position, supported by legislative history, that unless the delinquent return reflects some tax due, no late filing penalty, not even the $100 penalty, applies. *See Patronik-Holder v. Commissioner*, 100 T.C. 374 (1993) (*citing* H.R. Conf. Rep. No. 97-760, at 571 (1982)), *acq.* 1993-2 C.B. 1.

[2]   The Failure to Pay Penalty

As you learned in Chapter 2, the due date for a tax payment is normally the date on which the tax return is required to be filed. I.R.C. § 6151(a). Failure to timely pay the tax shown on the return triggers the late payment portion of the delinquency penalty in section 6651(a)(2). The late payment penalty also applies on a graduated basis, starting at .5 percent for the first month during which the tax remains unpaid and increasing an addition- al .5 percent for each month (or fraction thereof) during which the tax remains outstanding, up to a maximum of 25 percent. The penalty stops accruing on the date the IRS receives payment.[2]

The late payment penalty may also be triggered by the taxpayer's failure to timely pay an assessed deficiency. I.R.C. § 6651(a)(3). For deficiencies of less than $100,000, the taxpayer is given 21 calendar days after notice and demand is made to pay. If the amount demanded is $100,000 or more, the allotted time period drops to ten business days after the date of the notice and demand. *See* Treas. Reg. § 301.6651-1(a)(3). As with the late filing addition, the late payment penalty is calculated based on the net amount due. Moreover, if the amount of tax required to be shown on the return is less than the amount actually shown on the return, the lesser amount is used to calculate the penalty. I.R.C. § 6651(c)(2).

Under section 6651(c)(1), if both the late filing and late payment penalties apply, the taxpayer may offset the late payment portion of the penalty against the late filing portion. As a result, during the period of time in which both additions apply, the combined penalty amount may not exceed 5 percent per month (composed of a 4.5 percent penalty for filing late and a .5 percent penalty for paying late). Consider the following example.

> *Example:* Mary, an individual calendar-year taxpayer, mails her 2001 income tax return on August 14, 2002, without having obtained an extension of time to file. The return is received by the IRS on August 19. Mary's 2001 return reflects $33,000 of tax liability, of which $28,000 has been paid through wage withholding. Mary pays the balance due as shown on the return ($5,000) on August 31, 2002. The late payment penalty under section 6651(a)(2) totals $125 ($5,000 multiplied by 2.5 percent: .5 percent per month for the 4 full months from April 16 through August 15, and .5 percent for the fractional part of the month from August 16 through August 31). In addition, Mary is subject to a late filing penalty under section 6651(a)(1) totaling $1,125 ($5,000 multiplied by 25 percent: 5 percent per month for the 4 full months from April 16 through August 15 and an additional 5 percent for the fractional part of the month from August 16 through August 18, reduced by $125, the late filing penalty that accrued during that same time period).

Notice that the 25 percent maximum rate applicable to each of the late filing and late payment additions applies separately. As a result, the late payment penalty may continue to accrue beyond the 5-month period after which the late filing penalty reaches its maximum. The combined delinquency penalty, therefore, can reach as high as 47.5 percent. Note also that the late payment portion of the delinquency penalty applies only if the taxpayer files a return. Would a taxpayer be well advised to avoid the late payment penalty by not filing a return for the year?

The number of months during which the late payment penalty accrues is determined by taking into account extensions of time to pay. Recall from

---

[2] The failure to pay penalty is reduced for individuals who timely file their returns and enter into installment agreements with the IRS to pay their tax liability over time. *See* I.R.C. § 6651(h). The penalty is reduced from .5 percent per month to .25 percent per month during the period of the installment agreement. Installment agreements are discussed in Chapter 12.

Chapter 2 that an extension of time to file a return does *not* extend the date prescribed for payment. Under the section 6651 regulations, however, obtaining an automatic extension of time to file an individual income tax return is treated as an extension of time to pay the tax if (1) at least 90 percent of the tax shown on the return is paid on or before the regular due date for the return and (2) the balance of the tax due is paid with the return. Treas. Reg. § 301.6651-1(c)(3). A similar rule applies to an automatic extension of time to file a corporate income tax return obtained by filing Form 7004. Treas. Reg. § 301.6651-1(c)(4).

[3] The Reasonable Cause Defense

Neither the late filing nor late payment addition applies if the delinquency is due to reasonable cause and not willful neglect. The section 6651 regulations describe in some detail the circumstances under which the delinquency penalty may be abated. *See* Treas. Reg. § 301.6651-1(c). The following case raises the question of when a taxpayer's reliance upon professional advice will constitute reasonable cause.

UNITED STATES v. BOYLE
Supreme Court of the United States
469 U.S. 241 (1985)

CHIEF JUSTICE BURGER delivered the opinion of the Court.

We granted certiorari to resolve a conflict among the Circuits on whether a taxpayer's reliance on an attorney to prepare and file a tax return constitutes "reasonable cause" under § 6651(a)(1) of the Internal Revenue Code, so as to defeat a statutory penalty incurred because of a late filing.

I.

A.

Respondent, Robert W. Boyle, was appointed executor of the will of his mother, Myra Boyle, who died on September 14, 1978; respondent retained Ronald Keyser to serve as attorney for the estate. Keyser informed respondent that the estate must file a federal estate tax return, but he did not mention the deadline for filing this return. Under § 6075(a), the return was due within nine months of the decedent's death, *i.e.*, not later than June 14, 1979.

Although a businessman, respondent was not experienced in the field of federal estate taxation, other than having been executor of his father's will 20 years earlier. It is undisputed that he relied on Keyser for instruction and guidance. He cooperated fully with his attorney and provided Keyser with all relevant information and records. Respondent and his wife contacted Keyser a number of times during the spring and summer of 1979 to inquire about the progress of the proceedings and the preparation of the tax return; they were assured that they would be notified when the return was due and that the return would be filed "in plenty of time." App. 39. When respondent called Keyser on September 6, 1979, he learned for the first time that the return was by then overdue. Apparently, Keyser had overlooked the matter because of a clerical oversight in omitting the filing date from Keyser's master calendar. Respondent met with Keyser on September 11, and the return was filed on September 13, three months late.

B.

Acting pursuant to 26 U.S.C. § 6651(a)(1), the Internal Revenue Service assessed against the estate an additional tax of $17,124.45 as a penalty for the late filing, with $1,326.56 in interest. Section 6651(a)(1) reads in pertinent part:

> "In case of failure . . . to file any return . . . on the date prescribed therefor . . . , *unless it is shown that such failure is due to reasonable cause and not due to willful neglect,* there shall be added to the amount required to be shown as tax on such return 5 percent of the amount of such tax if the failure is for not more than 1 month, with an additional 5 percent for each additional month or fraction thereof during which such failure continues, not exceeding 25 percent in the aggregate . . . ." (Emphasis added.)

A Treasury Regulation provides that, to demonstrate "reasonable cause," a taxpayer filing a late return must show that he "exercised ordinary business care and prudence and was nevertheless unable to file the return within the prescribed time." 26 CFR § 301.6651-1(c)(1) (1984).[n.1]

Respondent paid the penalty and filed a claim for a refund. He conceded that the assessment for interest was proper, but contended that the penalty was unjustified because his failure to file the return on time was "due to reasonable cause," *i.e.*, reliance on his attorney. Respondent brought suit in the United States District Court, which concluded that the claim was controlled by the Court of Appeals' holding in *Rohrabaugh v. United States*, 611 F.2d 211 (CA7 1979). In *Rohrabaugh,* the United States Court of Appeals for the Seventh Circuit held that reliance upon counsel constitutes "reasonable cause" under § 6651(a)(1) when: (1) the taxpayer is unfamiliar with the tax law; (2) the taxpayer makes full disclosure of all relevant facts to the attorney that he relies upon, and maintains contact with the attorney from time to time during the administration of the estate; and (3) the taxpayer has otherwise exercised ordinary business care and prudence. 611 F.2d at 215, 219. The

---

[n.1] The Internal Revenue Service has articulated eight reasons for a late filing that it considers to constitute "reasonable cause." These reasons include unavoidable postal delays, the taxpayer's timely filing of a return with the wrong IRS office, the taxpayer's reliance on the erroneous advice of an IRS officer or employee, the death or serious illness of the taxpayer or a member of his immediate family, the taxpayer's unavoidable absence, destruction by casualty of the taxpayer's records or place of business, failure of the IRS to furnish the taxpayer with the necessary forms in a timely fashion, and the inability of an IRS representative to meet with the taxpayer when the taxpayer makes a timely visit to an IRS office in an attempt to secure information or aid in the preparation of a return. Internal Revenue Manual (CCH) § 4350, (24) ¶ 22.2(2) (Mar. 20, 1980) (Audit Technique Manual for Estate Tax Examiners). If the cause asserted by the taxpayer does not implicate any of these eight reasons, the district director determines whether the asserted cause is reasonable. "A cause for delinquency which appears to a person of ordinary prudence and intelligence as a reasonable cause for delay in filing a return and which clearly negatives willful neglect will be accepted as reasonable." *Id.,* ¶ 22.2(3).

District Court held that, under *Rohrabaugh,* respondent had established "reasonable cause" for the late filing of his tax return; accordingly, it granted summary judgment for respondent and ordered refund of the penalty. A divided panel of the Seventh Circuit, with three opinions, affirmed. 710 F.2d 1251 (1983).

We granted certiorari, 466 U.S. 903 (1984), and we reverse.

II.

A.

Congress' purpose in the prescribed civil penalty was to ensure timely filing of tax returns to the end that tax liability will be ascertained and paid promptly. The relevant statutory deadline provision is clear; it mandates that all federal estate tax returns be filed within nine months from the decedent's death, 26 U.S.C. 6075(a). Failure to comply incurs a penalty of 5 percent of the ultimately determined tax for each month the return is late, with a maximum of 25 percent of the base tax. To escape the penalty, the taxpayer bears the heavy burden of proving both (1) that the failure did not result from "willful neglect," and (2) that the failure was "due to reasonable cause." 26 U.S.C. § 6651(a)(1).

The meaning of these two standards has become clear over the near-70 years of their presence in the statutes. As used here, the term "willful neglect" may be read as meaning a conscious, intentional failure or reckless indifference. *See* Orient Investment & Finance Co. v. Commissioner, 83 U.S. App. D.C. 74, 75, 166 F.2d 601, 602 (1948) * * * . Like "willful neglect," the term "reasonable cause" is not defined in the Code, but the relevant Treasury Regulation calls on the taxpayer to demonstrate that he exercised "ordinary business care and prudence" but nevertheless was "unable to file the return within the prescribed time." 26 CFR § 301.6651(c)(1) (1984); *accord, e.g.,* Fleming v. United States, 648 F.2d 1122, 1124 (CA7 1981) * * * . The Commissioner does not contend that respondent's failure to file the estate tax return on time was willful or reckless. The question to be resolved is whether, under the statute, reliance on an attorney in the instant circumstances is a "reasonable cause" for failure to meet the deadline.

B.

In affirming the District Court, the Court of Appeals recognized the difficulties presented by its formulation but concluded that it was bound by *Rohrabaugh v. United States,* 611 F.2d 211 (CA7 1979). The Court of Appeals placed great importance on the fact that respondent engaged the services of an experienced attorney specializing in probate matters and that he duly inquired from time to time as to the progress of the proceedings. As in *Rohrabaugh, see id.,* at 219, the Court of Appeals in this case emphasized that its holding was narrowly drawn and closely tailored to the facts before it. The court stressed that the question of "reasonable cause" was an issue to be determined on a case-by-case basis. *See* 710 F.2d at 1253-1254; *id.,* at 1254 (Coffey, J., concurring).

Other Courts of Appeals have dealt with the issue of "reasonable cause" for a late filing and reached contrary conclusions. In *Ferrando v. United States*, 245 F.2d 582 (CA9 1957), the court held that taxpayers have a personal and nondelegable duty to file a return on time, and that reliance on an attorney to fulfill this obligation does not constitute "reasonable cause" for a tardy filing. *Id.*, at 589. The Fifth Circuit has similarly held that the responsibility for ensuring a timely filing is the taxpayer's alone, and that the taxpayer's reliance on his tax advisers — accountants or attorneys — is not a "reasonable cause." Millette & Associates v. Commissioner, 594 F.2d 121, 124–125 (per curiam), *cert. denied*, 444 U.S. 899 (1979); Logan Lumber Co. v. Commissioner, 365 F.2d 846, 854 (1966). The Eighth Circuit also has concluded that reliance on counsel does not constitute "reasonable cause." Smith v. United States, 702 F.2d 741, 743 (1983) *(per curiam)* * * * .

III.

We need not dwell on the similarities or differences in the facts presented by the conflicting holdings. The time has come for a rule with as "bright" a line as can be drawn consistent with the statute and implementing regulations. Deadlines are inherently arbitrary; fixed dates, however, are often essential to accomplish necessary results. The Government has millions of taxpayers to monitor, and our system of self-assessment in the initial calculation of a tax simply cannot work on any basis other than one of strict filing standards. Any less rigid standard would risk encouraging a lax attitude toward filing dates. Prompt payment of taxes is imperative to the Government, which should not have to assume the burden of unnecessary ad hoc determinations.

Congress has placed the burden of prompt filing on the executor, not on some agent or employee of the executor. The duty is fixed and clear; Congress intended to place upon the taxpayer an obligation to ascertain the statutory deadline and then to meet that deadline, except in a very narrow range of situations. Engaging an attorney to assist in the probate proceedings is plainly an exercise of the "ordinary business care and prudence" prescribed by the regulations, 26 CFR § 301.6651-1(c)(1) (1984), but that does not provide an answer to the question we face here. To say that it was "reasonable" for the executor to *assume* that the attorney would comply with the statute may resolve the matter as between them, but not with respect to the executor's obligations under the statute. Congress has charged the executor with an unambiguous, precisely defined duty to file the return within nine months; extensions are granted fairly routinely. That the attorney, as the executor's agent, was expected to attend to the matter does not relieve the principal of his duty to comply with the statute.

This case is not one in which a taxpayer has relied on the erroneous advice of counsel concerning a question of law. Courts have frequently held that "reasonable cause" is established when a taxpayer shows that he reasonably relied on the advice of an accountant or attorney that it was unnecessary to file a return, even when such advice turned out to have been mistaken. *See, e.g.,* United States v. Kroll, 547 F.2d 393, 395-396 (CA7 1977) * * * . This Court also has implied that, in such a situation, reliance on the opinion of a tax adviser may constitute reasonable cause for failure to file a return. *See* Commissioner v. Lane-Wells Co., 321 U.S. 219, 88 L. Ed. 684, 64 S. Ct. 511 (1944) (remanding for determination whether failure to file return was due to reasonable cause, when taxpayer was advised that filing was not required).

When an accountant or attorney *advises* a taxpayer on a matter of tax law, such as whether a liability exists, it is reasonable for the taxpayer to rely on that advice. Most taxpayers are not competent to discern error in the substantive advice of an accountant or attorney. To require the taxpayer to challenge the attorney, to seek a "second opinion," or to try to monitor counsel on the provisions of the Code himself would nullify the very purpose of seeking the advice of a presumed expert in the first place. *See Haywood Lumber, supra,* at 771. "Ordinary business care and prudence" do not demand such actions.

By contrast, one does not have to be a tax expert to know that tax returns have fixed filing dates and that taxes must be paid when they are due. In short, tax returns imply deadlines. Reliance by a lay person on a lawyer is of course common; but that reliance cannot function as a substitute for compliance with an unambiguous statute. Among the first duties of the representative of a decedent's estate is to identify and assemble the assets of the decedent and to ascertain tax obligations. Although it is common practice for an executor to engage a professional to prepare and file an estate tax return, a person experienced in business matters can perform that task personally. It is not unknown for an executor to prepare tax returns, take inventories, and carry out other significant steps in the probate of an estate. It is even not uncommon for an executor to conduct probate proceedings without counsel.

It requires no special training or effort to ascertain a deadline and make sure that it is met. The failure to make a timely filing of a tax return is not excused by the taxpayer's reliance on an agent, and such reliance is not "reasonable cause" for a late filing under § 6651(a)(1). The judgment of the Court of Appeals is reversed.

It is so ordered.

Following *Boyle,* what do you think the outcome should be in a case in which a taxpayer has a return prepared, signed, and delivered to the company comptroller with instructions to "file" it, and the comptroller files it in the company's files (rather than with the IRS), believing it is a copy? In *Henry v. United States*, 73 F. Supp. 1303 (N.D. Fla. 1999), the court held that under *Boyle,* as a matter of law, this mistake could not constitute "reasonable cause" so as to avoid the late-filing penalty.

In applying the reasonable cause standard, the Supreme Court in *Boyle* drew a distinction between reliance on an expert's advice relating to a substantive matter of law and reliance on an expert's advice relating to a procedural matter.[3] Would the reasonable cause exception apply to a taxpayer

---

[3] However, subsequent to *Boyle,* in *Brown v. Revenue Agent*, 630 F. Supp. 57 (M.D. Tenn. 1985), a federal district court found reasonable cause for late filing of an estate tax return by the

who relied on an attorney's advice that, on the facts presented to the attorney, no tax return was required to be filed?

[B] The Estimated Tax Penalty — Code Section 6654

Because the tax payment system entitles the government to collect taxes throughout the year, section 6654 provides a penalty that applies when a taxpayer owes too much with the return, which can happen when the taxpayer's tax liability is not sufficiently covered by withholding and the taxpayer has failed to make quarterly estimated tax payments. For purposes of section 6654, withholding payments are deemed estimated tax payments, and are deemed paid equally through the year, I.R.C. § 6654(g), so that most taxpayers with wage income are not required to make estimated tax payments. Estimated taxes are discussed in more detail in Chapter 2.

Under section 6654, if the taxpayer owes $1,000 or more with the return, after taking into account withholding tax, *see* I.R.C. § 6654(e)(1), the taxpayer is liable for a penalty unless he has already paid either 90 percent of the tax due for the year or 100 percent of his tax liability for the prior year,[4] I.R.C. § 6654(d)(1)(B), or, under certain circumstances, had no tax liability for the preceding year, I.R.C. § 6654(e)(2). The penalty is computed by applying the interest rate applied to underpayments to the amount of the underpayment for the period of the underpayment. I.R.C. § 6654(a). For amounts due with the return, the period runs from January 15 of the year the return is due until April 15 of that year or until the amount is paid, whichever is earlier. I.R.C. § 6654(b)(2), (c)(2).

[C] Accuracy-Related Penalties — Code Section 6662

The delinquency penalty in section 6651 addresses only one aspect of taxpayer noncompliance. As important as timely filing and payment may be, ensuring that taxpayers accurately report their tax liabilities on their returns is essential and, from a compliance standpoint, presents a greater challenge for the IRS. Prior to the IMPACT legislation in 1989, the Code contained separate penalty provisions relating to negligence, substantial understatements of tax liability, and inaccuracies resulting from valuation overstatements and understatements. Current section 6662, applicable to tax returns due after December 31, 1989, imposes a single accuracy-related penalty, accompanied by uniform definitions. The amount of the penalty equals 20 percent of the portion of the underpayment of tax attributable to one or more of the following types of misconduct: (1) negligence or disregard of rules and regulations; (2) any substantial understatement of tax; (3) any substantial valuation misstatement; (4) any substantial overstatement of pension liabilities; and (5) any substantial estate or gift tax valuation understatement.

---

administrator of the estate where he was elderly, high-school educated, had no experience with tax matters, was in poor health, had not been told the deadline for filing, and the accountant who was supposed to file the return became ill and was hospitalized. Is *Brown* consistent with *Boyle*?

[4] Higher percentages apply to taxpayers with adjusted gross income above $150,000. These percentages vary depending on the tax year.

Notice that the maximum accuracy-related penalty that may be imposed on any portion of a tax underpayment is 20 percent, even if the underpayment is attributable to more than one type of misconduct. Thus, if a portion of the tax underpayment results from both negligence and a substantial valuation misstatement, the maximum accuracy-related penalty that may be applied to that portion is 20 percent. Although section 6662(a) does not permit penalty "stacking," if the taxpayer files the return after the prescribed due date, both the accuracy-related penalty and the late filing penalty in section 6651 may apply to the same portion of a tax underpayment. However, the accuracy-related penalty does not apply to any portion of an underpayment subject to the civil fraud penalty, discussed below.[5] I.R.C. § 6662(b).

The base to which the accuracy-related penalty applies is the "portion of an underpayment of tax required to be shown" on the return. The term underpayment is defined in section 6664 as the amount by which the "correct tax" exceeds the amount of tax shown on the return (plus amounts not shown on the return but which have been previously assessed or collected without assessment), reduced by the amount of any rebates. Amounts collected without assessment include both withholding credits and estimated tax payments. As a general rule, the amount of the underpayment will normally equal the balance due as shown in the revenue agent's report issued at the conclusion of the audit.

[1] Negligence or Disregard of Rules or Regulations

Section 6662(b)(1) imposes the 20 percent accuracy-related penalty for negligence or disregard of rules or regulations. The statute defines negligence "as any failure to make a reasonable attempt to comply with" the Code, while a taxpayer's "disregard" of rules or regulations must be careless, reckless, or intentional. The regulations expand upon these basic definitions and provide more concrete examples — some more helpful than others — of the type of conduct prohibited. Read carefully Regulation section 1.6662-3. Are the standards set forth in the regulations objective or subjective? What role does a tax advisor play in determining whether the penalty applies? Also consider the following case, dealing with an investor's reliance on a tax shelter opinion letter.

COLEMAN v. COMMISSIONER
United States Tax Court
T.C. Memo. 1990-511

WELLS, JUDGE:

[The basic facts of *Coleman* are as follows: Petitioners Edward and Margaret Maher invested in a limited partnership formed for the purpose of funding research and development activities relating to a silver recovery system. The

---

[5] Does this mean that fraud is a defense to application of the negligence portion of the accuracy-related penalty? In *Ames v. Commissioner*, 112 T.C. 304 (1999), the Tax Court found Aldrich Ames liable for the negligence penalty with respect to unreported income from espionage, although he argued that his conduct had been fraudulent, not negligent. The court stated, "It is rather obvious that fraudulent concealment goes far beyond and is inclusive of 'negligence or disregard of rules or regulations.'" *Id.* at 315.

partnership deducted close to $600,000 of fees during taxable years 1981 and 1982 relating to the research and development activities, which deductions were disallowed by the Commissioner for failure to establish that the fees were incurred in connection with a trade or business, as required by Code section 174. A private placement memorandum, accompanied by a 62-page tax opinion — both of which the petitioners claimed they relied upon when making their investment in the partnership — warned investors that the partnership's tax treatment of its activities might not be sustained. The Tax Court, in an earlier opinion, sustained the Commissioner's determination that the partnership's activities were not "in connection with a trade or business," and sustained the application of the negligence penalty against the petitioners. *Coleman v. Commissioner*, T.C. Memo 1990-357. Eds.]

The instant case is before us on petitioners' motion for reconsideration of our opinion in *Coleman v. Commissioner*, T.C. Memo. 1990-357, filed on July 16, 1990 (prior opinion).

Petitioners contend, among other things, that the addition to tax for negligence was imposed erroneously against petitioners Edward and Margaret Maher. Upon reconsideration, however, after reviewing petitioners' contentions, we adhere to our conclusion in our prior opinion that the negligence addition was appropriately determined.

In our prior opinion, we found petitioner Edward Maher's reliance on the tax opinion prepared by his law firm, the K-1 he received from the Partnership, and Mr. Beningson's business reputation insufficient to satisfy the Maher's burden of proof with respect to the negligence addition. Petitioners argue that, in refusing to accept Mr. Maher's reliance on the tax opinion as sufficient to defeat a finding of negligence, we have "created a conflict" with three of our prior decisions; namely, *Ewing v. Commissioner*, 91 T.C. 396 (1998) (on appeal, 9th Cir., June 7, 1990; on appeal, 5th Cir., June 12, 1990); *Gralnek v. Commissioner*, T.C. Memo. 1989-433; and *Davis v. Commissioner*, T.C. Memo. 1989-607, and have disregarded the Supreme Court's decision in *United States v. Boyle*, 469 U.S. 241 (1985). We disagree.

While the *Ewing* and *Gralnek* cases cited by petitioners do attach significance to the taxpayers' reliance on tax opinions included in promotional materials, the cases do not establish a blanket rule that such reliance defeats imposition of the negligence addition. As we stated in *Freytag v. Commissioner*, 89 T.C. 849, 888 (1987), *aff'd*, 904 F.2d 1011 (5th Cir. 1990), "Reliance on professional advice, standing alone, is not an absolute defense to negligence, but rather a factor to be considered. First, it must be established that the reliance was reasonable." Negligence is defined as a "lack of due care or failure to do what a reasonable and ordinarily prudent person would do *under the circumstances*." Neely v. Commissioner, 85 T.C. 934, 947 (1985) (*quoting* Marcello v. Commissioner, 380 F.2d 499, 506 (5th Cir. 1967)) (emphasis supplied).

In *Ewing v. Commissioner, supra,* we found that the taxpayers' "good faith" reliance on a law firm to formulate the straddle program in issue (including reliance on the firm's tax opinion included in promotional materials) was not unreasonable "under the circumstances of this record." 91 T.C. at 423. We specifically noted in *Ewing* that the tax opinion "described in detail, with citations to case law and statutes, the tax consequences which, in the opinion of the author, could be expected by investors from different methods of closing positions in straddles." 91 T.C. at 406. Unlike *Ewing,* we found in our prior opinion that "The content of the tax opinion allegedly relied upon by Mr. Maher should * * * have alerted him as to the necessity of seeking independent advice on the availability of the promised tax benefits." Coleman v. Commissioner, 60 T.C.M. 123, 135, 59 P-H Memo. T.C. ¶ 90,357 at 1704. Our reference to "the content of the tax opinion," was meant to encompass not only its warning to investors not to construe the opinion as advice but also its lack of reasoning in the section of the opinion dealing with profit objective.

* * *

At the time that Mr. Maher decided to invest in the Partnership, he had been an attorney at Townley & Updike, the firm that prepared the tax opinion, for 37 years; he specialized in corporate and commercial work, including security offerings. (Mr. Maher's name appeared fourth on the Townley & Updike letterhead used for the first page of the tax opinion.) A person of Mr. Maher's experience should have heard "warning bells" in view of the tax opinion's reliance on a profit objective representation from the general partner and lack of meaningful analyses of the profit objective issue. *See Freytag v. Commissioner*, 89 T.C. at 889. * * *

The *Davis* case cited by petitioners is also distinguishable in that it focuses primarily on the taxpayer's reliance on their *own* attorney, who recommended the investment at issue. We believe that there is a distinction between relying on a "trusted and long-term adviser," as in *Davis*; and relying on a tax opinion that specifically warns the investor not to regard it as advice but to consult independent tax counsel. While petitioners criticize our reference to such disclaimers on the grounds that they are well known as "Boiler Plate provisions," petitioners characterize such provisions as "included to protect the attorneys from being in privity with the reader and thereby shield the attorneys from any claims of malpractice," a characterization that reinforces our reasoning. It also should be noted that our prior opinion is not unique in referring to such disclaimers in support of a finding of negligence. *See* Owen v. Commissioner, T.C. Memo. 1990-172; Foerstel v. Commissioner, T.C. Memo. 1987-546; Bowman v. Commissioner, T.C. Memo. 1987-545. None of these cases cited in petitioners' motion mention such disclaimers.

For similar reasons, petitioners' reference to the Supreme Court's decision in *United States v. Boyle*, 469 U.S. 241 (1985), is unpersuasive. In *Boyle,* the Supreme Court held that an executor was not excused from the late filing addition under section 6651(a)(1) although such late filing resulted from an oversight by the attorney he retained to handle the estate. In reaching that conclusion, the Court distinguished a taxpayer's failure to meet a statutory filing deadline — which cannot be excused by reason of reliance on an attorney — from a situation in which "an accountant or attorney *advises* a taxpayer on a matter of tax law," 469 U.S. at 251 (emphasis in original). In the latter situation, the Supreme Court stated that:

> When an accountant or attorney *advises* a taxpayer on a matter
> of tax law, such as whether a liability exists, it is reasonable for

the taxpayer to rely on that advice. Most taxpayers are not competent to discern error in the substantive advice of an accountant or attorney. To require the taxpayer to challenge the attorney, to seek a "second opinion," or try to monitor counsel on the provisions of the Code himself would nullify the very purpose of seeking the advice of a presumed expert in the first place. "Ordinary business care and prudence" do not demand such actions. [469 U.S. at 251; emphasis in original and citation omitted.]

The foregoing language in no way suggests that a taxpayer may be excused from the negligence addition based on his reliance on a tax opinion and prospectus that specifically disavow such reliance. Requiring the taxpayer to seek independent advice in circumstances such as those present herein is not equivalent to requiring him to seek "advice" for the first time. *Cf.* Heasley v. Commissioner, 902 F.2d 380 (5th Cir. 1990) (unsophisticated investors not liable for negligence addition where they relied on the expertise of their financial advisor and accountant and monitored their investment).

* * *

We have considered all of petitioners' other arguments and find them without merit.

To reflect the foregoing, an appropriate order will be issued.

As *Coleman* illustrates, an opinion letter from a tax advisor is not a complete defense against imposition of a negligence penalty. *See also West v. Commissioner*, T.C. Memo. 2000-389 ("For reliance on professional advice to excuse a taxpayer from the negligence additions to tax, the taxpayer must show that the professional had the expertise and knowledge of the pertinent facts to provide informed advice on the subject matter."). Would the tax shelter opinion in *Coleman*, which did not address the primary legal issue surrounding the tax consequences of the transaction and which warned potential investors not to rely on the opinion letter as legal advice, pass muster under A.B.A. Formal Opinion 346, included in Section 1.06[A] of Chapter 1?

The "disregard of rules or regulations" component of the accuracy-related penalty (as distinguished from the negligence component) may be avoided if the taxpayer adequately discloses to the IRS the relevant facts affecting the items' tax treatment. Treas. Reg. § 1.6662-3(c)(1). The disclosure exception applies if the position has a "reasonable basis" and the taxpayer maintains adequate books and records to substantiate the items properly. Review Regulation section 1.6662-3(b)(3), which explains the reasonable basis standard. Is the standard likely to encourage or discourage disclosure?

For tax returns due before January 1, 1994, the minimum standard a disclosed position had to satisfy to qualify for the adequate disclosure exception was that the position be "not frivolous." Prior regulations defined a frivolous position as one that was "patently improper." Legislative history described the not frivolous standard as one that was "merely arguable." H.R.

Rep. No. 103-213 (1993). Does the current minimum standard improve upon the old? Which is the higher standard? Disclosure is discussed further in the next Section, in connection with the substantial understatement penalty.

[2] Substantial Understatement of Tax and Its Defenses

[a] Substantial Understatement of Tax

As any student of tax law knows, the complexity surrounding the Code's substantive rules leads to "gray areas" — arguable positions with varying degrees of uncertainty. Within these gray areas of the law, the negligence standard may prove to be an insufficient check on noncompliant behavior. The second prong of the accuracy-related penalty imposes a cost on taxpayers who take aggressive return positions (although not necessarily negligent) that do not have substantial legal support.

Section 6662(b)(2) imposes the 20 percent accuracy-related penalty on any portion of an underpayment attributable to a "substantial understatement" of income tax. An understatement of tax is considered substantial if the understatement exceeds the greater of 10 percent of the tax required to be shown on the return, or $5,000 ($10,000 for corporations other than S corporations and personal holding companies).

> *Example*: Miranda filed her 2002 income tax return showing taxable income of $35,000 and a corresponding tax liability of $12,150. An audit reveals that Miranda failed to report on the return additional gross income of $25,000. Miranda's total tax liability for 2002, including the tax on the unreported income, equals $20,000. Because the resulting $7,850 understatement of tax ($20,000 − $12,150 = $7,850) is greater than $5,000 and greater than 10 percent of the correct tax ($20,000 × .10 = $2,000), the substantial understatement penalty applies.

In this example, is the correct amount of the penalty 20 percent of $25,000 or 20 percent of $7,850?

[b] Defenses to the Penalty

[i] Substantial Authority

For purposes of determining whether the difference between the tax liability reported on the return and the correct liability is "substantial," the amount of the tax understatement is reduced by items supported by substantial authority. The regulations at section 1.6662-4(d) define in some detail the substantial authority standard and the process for determining whether substantial authority exists. The types of sources that are considered for purposes of establishing whether a position is or is not supported by substantial authority are intended to reflect the types of authorities used by practitioners and courts. These sources include the Code, Treasury Regulations, court decisions, Revenue Rulings and Procedures, certain legislative history sources, and private letter rulings. Treatises, legal periodicals and tax opinions, however, are specifically excluded from the list of sources that may be considered. Although the Code mandates that the Secretary publish a list of positions the IRS believes are not supported by substantial authority, *see* I.R.C. § 6662(d)(2)(D), to date the Secretary has not done so.

Substantial authority exists for the tax treatment of a particular item only if "the weight of authorities supporting the treatment is substantial in relation to the weight of authorities supporting contrary treatment." Treas. Reg. § 1.6662-4(d)(3)(i). Balancing the weight of authorities requires a careful consideration of the relevance and persuasiveness of the cited authority and an understanding of the precedential value of a particular source. Does the substantiality standard require that the taxpayer actually "prevail" on the underlying substantive issue in order to avoid a substantial understatement penalty? Consider *Osteen*:

OSTEEN v. COMMISSIONER
United States Court of Appeals, Eleventh Circuit
62 F.3d 356 (1995)

RONEY, SENIOR CIRCUIT JUDGE:

Harry and Gail Osteen (taxpayers) appeal the United States Tax Court's decision disallowing certain tax deductions attributable to their farming and horse breeding operation on the grounds that this activity was not engaged in for profit and assessing tax deficiencies and penalties for a substantial tax understatement.

We hold that the Tax Court's factual findings that the Osteens lacked a profit objective are not clearly erroneous and affirm its decision on that issue. We reverse the Tax Court, however, on its assessment of the understatement penalty because there was substantial authority for the taxpayers' position.

The facts of this case are discussed in detail in the Tax Court's memorandum opinion, T.C. Memo. 1993-519, 66 T.C.M. (CCH) 1237, and will not be repeated here. During the years at issue, Harry Osteen was employed full-time as a bank executive. His wife, Gail Osteen, was a full-time registered nurse. The Osteens became interested in breeding and raising Percheron horses in Florida. Percherons are a breed of large draft horses that originally were bred for moving or towing heavy objects before the advent of tractors. There were no Percheron horse breeders nor was there an established market for Percherons in Florida at the time. The Osteens' intent was to breed the horses, train them by showing them and using them to operate a horse-powered farm, and then to sell the horses. For several consecutive years, the Osteens generated losses from the horse breeding activity.

PROFIT OBJECTIVE

A taxpayer who is carrying on a trade or business may deduct ordinary and necessary expenses incurred in connection with the operation of the business. I.R.C. § 162. An activity constitutes a "trade or business" within the meaning of section 162 if the taxpayer's actual and honest objective is to realize a profit. Dreicer v. Commissioner, 78 T.C. 642, 645, *aff'd*, 702 F.2d 1205 (D.C. Cir.1983). The courts have relied on factors set forth in section 183 in making the requisite profit motive analysis under section 162. Brannen v. Commissioner, 722 F.2d 695, 704 (11th Cir.1984).

Section 183 specifically precludes deductions for activities "not engaged in for profit," such as pursuing hobbies or generating losses to shelter unrelated income. I.R.C. § 183(a); S. Rep. No. 552, 91st Cong., 1st Sess. (1969), reprinted in 1969 U.S.C.C.A.N. 1645, 2133 (legislative history of § 183). Although the taxpayer's expectation of profit does not have to be reasonable, objective facts and circumstances must indicate that the taxpayer's intent was to make a profit. A taxpayer's subjective statements of intent to make a profit are not sufficient. Treas. Reg. § 1.183-2(a) (1972). The regulations list nine factors to guide courts in determining whether an activity is engaged in for profit. These are not exclusive considerations, however, and no single factor or mathematical preponderance of factors is determinative. Treas. Reg. § 1.183-2(b) (1972).

* * *

A review of the record reveals that the Tax Court properly followed the nine factors listed in the regulations, viewed all facts and circumstances of the case, and was not clearly erroneous in determining that the Osteens engaged in the Percheron breeding business without a bona fide profit motive. The Tax Court relied on facts such as the taxpayers' inexperience in breeding Percheron horses and their failure to hire experienced assistants or bring in experienced partners, the lack of any profitability assessment of breeding Percherons in Florida, the limited time spent managing the operation, the string of consistent losses, and the significant income Osteen earned as a bank executive which allowed him to tolerate such losses.

SUBSTANTIAL UNDERSTATEMENT PENALTY

The Osteens appeal the Tax Court's assessment of section 6661 [currently I.R.C. § 6662. Eds.] understatement penalties. The Osteens do not dispute that their tax understatements for the two years in question met the definition of "substantial understatements" under this provision. The Osteens contend, however, that they had substantial authority to believe they could claim the farming and horse breeding losses, an exception to the imposition of understatement penalties.

* * *

For our purposes, section 6661(b)(2)(A) defines the "understatement" as the excess of:

(i) the amount of the tax required to be shown on the return for the taxable year, over

(ii) the amount of the tax imposed which is shown on the return
. . . .

The understatement, for the purposes of imposing the addition, *shall* be reduced "by that portion of the understatement which is attributable to the tax treatment of any item by the taxpayer if there is or was *substantial authority* for such treatment . . . ." * * *

The application of a substantial authority test is confusing in a case of this kind. If the horse breeding enterprise was carried on for profit, all of the deductions claimed by the Osteens would be allowed. There is no authority to the contrary. If the enterprise was not for profit, none of the deductions would be allowed. There is no authority to the contrary. Nobody argues, however, not even the Government, that because the taxpayers lose on the factual issue, they also must lose on what would seem to be a legal issue.

The Tax Court in this case, as it seems to do in most of the cases, gives little explanation as to why there is substantial authority in one case, but not in another: "Based on the discussion above, we are convinced that there was not substantial authority for petitioners' position." Order at 15. *Cf.* Harston v. Commissioner, T.C. Memo. 1990-538, 60 T.C.M. (CCH) 1008 (1990) ("Although [the taxpayers] were not successful enough to show that they were entitled to the [§ 183] losses claimed, petitioners have convinced us that they had substantial authority for their position.").

There are no court decisions that give us guidance, and the regulations themselves, although speaking in terms of a test, are unsatisfactory in application to an all or nothing case of this kind.

If the Tax Court was deciding that there was no substantial authority because of the weakness of the taxpayers' *evidence* to establish a profit motive, we reverse because a review of the record reveals there was evidence both ways. In our judgment, under the clearly erroneous standard of review, the Tax Court would be due to be affirmed even if it had decided this case for the taxpayers. With that state of the record, there is substantial authority from a factual standpoint for the taxpayer's position. Only if there was a record upon which the Government could obtain a reversal under the clearly erroneous standard could it be argued that from an evidentiary standpoint, there was not substantial authority for the taxpayer's position.

If the Tax Court was deciding there was not substantial *legal* authority for the deductions, we reverse because of the plethora of cases in which the Tax Court has found a profit motive in the horse breeding activities of taxpayers that were similar to those at hand. *E.g.,* Engdahl v. Commissioner, 72 T.C. 659, 1979 WL 3705 (1979) (profit motive found; taxpayer had businesslike operation, consulted experts, kept quarterly records, showed horses, and did physical labor and menial chores); Holbrook v. Commissioner, T.C. Memo. 1993-383, 66 T.C.M. (CCH) 484, 1993 WL 325083 (1993) (husband and wife engaged in horse breeding for profit; activities conducted in businesslike manner; wife kept detailed records while husband developed expertise in horse breeding); * * * .

Although it can be properly argued that those cases are distinguishable from the case at hand, as well they are because the ultimate facts were found for the taxpayer rather than against the taxpayer as in this case, they are not so dissimilar that they must be discarded as providing no substantial authority for the tax returns filed in this case.

As a bottom line, we find little distinction between this case and the Tax Court case of *Harston*. The imposition of additions to the tax under § 6661 must turn on some analysis other than the conclusory decision of the Tax Court. The Tax Court should articulate some consistent and workable test to justify the imposition of additions in all or nothing situations of this kind, otherwise the imposition of the addition is left to the educated reaction of the particular Tax Court judge hearing the case.

We affirm the Tax Court's finding of tax deficiencies for lack of a profit motive, but we reverse the Tax Court's imposition of a penalty for substantial understatement.

Affirmed in part, reversed in part.

The substantial authority exception to the substantial understatement penalty applies in more limited circumstances for any item attributable to a "tax shelter." For a taxpayer other than a corporation, the substantial authority standard does not apply to any tax shelter item unless "the taxpayer reasonably believed that the tax treatment of such item by the taxpayer was *more likely than not* the proper treatment." I.R.C. § 6662(d)(2)(C)(i)(II) (emphasis added). For a corporate taxpayer, the substantial authority exception does not apply to tax shelter items at all. I.R.C. § 6662(d)(2)(C)(ii). A "tax shelter" is broadly defined in section 6662(d)(2)(C)(iii) to refer to any plan or entity, a significant purpose of which is "the avoidance or evasion of Federal income tax." Why do you think the Code imposes an additional restriction on the substantial authority rules for tax shelter items?

[ii]   Disclosure

For purposes of determining whether an understatement of tax is substantial, the amount of the understatement is also reduced by amounts attributable to an item if the relevant facts relating to the tax treatment of the item are "adequately disclosed" on the return or in a statement attached to the return and there is a "reasonable basis" for the taxpayer's tax treatment of the item. A taxpayer may use Form 8275, Disclosure Statement, to disclose a return position. The disclosure exception does not apply at all to tax shelter items. *See* I.R.C. § 6662(d)(2)(C).

Revenue Procedure 2001-11 sets forth in more detail the circumstances under which disclosure *on the return itself* is considered adequate.

REVENUE PROCEDURE 2001-11
2001-2 I.R.B. 275

SECTION 1. PURPOSE

.01 This revenue procedure updates Rev. Proc. 99-41, 1999-46 I.R.B. 566, and identifies circumstances under which the disclosure on a taxpayer's return of a position with respect to an item is adequate for the purpose of reducing the understatement of income tax under § 6662(d) of the Internal Revenue Code (relating to the substantial understatement aspect of the accuracy-related penalty), and for the purpose of avoiding the preparer penalty under § 6694(a) (relating to understatements due to unrealistic positions). This revenue procedure does not apply with respect to any other penalty provision (including the negligence or disregard provisions of the § 6662 accuracy-related penalty).

* * *

SECTION 4. PROCEDURE

.01 Additional disclosure of facts relevant to, or positions taken with respect to, issues involving any of the items set forth below is unnecessary for purposes of reducing any understatement of income tax under § 6662(d) provided that the forms and attachments are completed in a clear manner and in accordance with their instructions. The money amounts entered on the forms must be verifiable, and the information on the return must be disclosed in the manner described below. For purposes of this revenue procedure, a number is verifiable if, on audit, the taxpayer can demonstrate the origin of the number (even if that number is not ultimately accepted by the Internal Revenue Service) and the taxpayer can show good faith in entering that number on the applicable form.

(1) Form 1040, Schedule A, Itemized Deductions:

    (a) Medical and Dental Expenses: Complete lines 1 through 4, supplying all required information.

    (b) Taxes: Complete lines 5 through 9, supplying all required information. Line 8 must list each type of tax and the amount paid.

    (c) Interest Expense: Complete lines 10 through 14, supplying all required information. This section 4.01(1)(c) does not apply to (i) amounts disallowed under § 163(d) unless Form 4952, Investment Interest Expense Deduction, is completed, or (ii) amounts disallowed under § 265.

    (d) Contributions: Complete lines 15 through 18, supplying all required information. Merely entering the amount of the donation on Schedule A, however, will not constitute adequate disclosure if the taxpayer receives a substantial benefit from the donation shown. If a contribution of property other than cash is made and the amount claimed as a deduction exceeds $500, a properly completed Form 8283, Noncash Charitable Contributions, must be attached to the return. This section 4.01(1)(d) will not apply to any contribution of $250 or more unless the contemporaneous written acknowledgment requirement of § 170(f)(8) is satisfied.

    (e) Casualty and Theft Losses: Complete Form 4684, Casualties and Thefts, and attach to the return. Each item or article for which a casualty or theft loss is claimed must be listed on Form 4684.

(2) Certain Trade or Business Expenses (including, for purposes of this section 4.01(2), the following six expenses as they relate to the rental of property):

(a) Casualty and Theft Losses: The procedure outlined in section 4.01(1)(e) above must be followed.

(b) Legal Expenses: The amount claimed must be stated. This section 4.01(2)(b) does not apply, however, to amounts properly characterized as capital expenditures, personal expenses, or nondeductible lobbying or political expenditures, including amounts that are required to be (or that are) amortized over a period of years.

(c) Specific Bad Debt Charge-off: The amount written off must be stated.

(d) Reasonableness of Officers' Compensation: Form 1120, Schedule E, Compensation of Officers, must be completed when required by its instructions. The time devoted to business must be expressed as a percentage as opposed to "part" or "as needed." * * *

(e) Repair Expenses: The amount claimed must be stated. This section 4.01(2)(e) does not apply, however, to any repair expenses properly characterized as capital expenditures or personal expenses.

(f) Taxes (other than foreign taxes): The amount claimed must be stated.

* * *

(5) Other:

(a) Moving Expenses: Complete Form 3903, Moving Expenses, and attach to the return.

(b) Employee Business Expenses: Complete Form 2106, Employee Business Expenses, or Form 2106-EZ, Unreimbursed Employee Business Expenses, and attach to the return. This section 4.01(5)(b) does not apply to club dues, or to travel expenses for any non-employee accompanying the taxpayer on the trip.

* * *

As mentioned above, the adequate disclosure exception to the substantial understatement penalty will not apply if the taxpayer's treatment of the item giving rise to the understatement has no reasonable basis. *See* I.R.C. § 6662(d)(2)(B)(ii)(II); Treas Reg. § 1.6662-4(e)(2)(iii). The "reasonable basis" standard is tied to Treasury Regulation § 1.6662-3(b)(3), which also applies to the disregard of rules or regulations portion of the accuracy-related penalty. How useful do you think the disclosure exception is to the taxpayer?[6]

---

[6] In general, a penalty can apply to an amended return, just as it can to an original return. *See, e.g.,* Colton v. Gibbs, 902 F.2d 1462, 1463 (9th Cir. 1990) (frivolous return penalty can apply

[3] Valuation Misstatements

The remaining prongs of the accuracy-related penalty single out specific types of taxpayer misconduct relating to valuation misstatements. Under section 6662(b)(3), the 20 percent addition applies to an underpayment of tax attributable to a "substantial valuation misstatement." The substantial valuation misstatement penalty applies most commonly to a taxpayer who, in an attempt to inflate a charitable contribution deduction, overstates the value of property, or to a taxpayer who, in an attempt to increase cost recovery deductions or reduce the amount of realized gain, overstates the adjusted basis of property reported on the return. In order to trigger the penalty, the overstatement of value or basis must be at least 200 percent greater than the correct value or the correct adjusted basis, as the case may be, and the tax underpayment attributable to the valuation misstatement must exceed $5,000 ($10,000 in the case of a corporation other than an S corporation or a personal holding company). If the value or adjusted basis of any property claimed on a return is 400 percent or more of the amount determined to be the correct valuation or adjusted basis, the penalty rate increases to 40 percent of the resulting underpayment. I.R.C. § 6662(h). Does the valuation misstatement penalty apply to valuation *under*statements? In what circumstances would a valuation understatement occur?

If the IRS denies a deduction resulting from a valuation misstatement, is the underpayment of tax attributable to the valuation misstatement or to the improper deduction? Consider the following case.

HEASLEY v. COMMISSIONER
United States Court of Appeals, Fifth Circuit
902 F.2d 380 (1990)

GOLDBERG, CIRCUIT JUDGE:

STATEMENT OF FACTS

Between 1981 and 1983, Gaylen Danner, a self-styled economic and financial consultant and securities dealer, introduced Kathleen and Dennis Heasley to numerous investment plans. Before meeting Danner, the Heasleys invested in a mutual fund plan and held $3,000 in stocks as part of Mr. Heasley's job benefit plan. They had no other investment experience. Both held blue collar jobs. Neither Heasley graduated from high school, although Ms. Heasley earned a G.E.D. and 18 college credits, one course at a time. Worried about their future and that of their four children, but not knowledgeable enough to invest on their own, the Heasleys accepted Danner's investment advice.

---

to amended return); Mattingly v. United States, 90-1 U.S.T.C. ¶ 50,012 (E.D. Mo. 1989) (penalty for aiding and abetting understatement of tax liability can apply to amended return). Also, a correct amended return does not preclude the application of a penalty to an incorrect original return. *See, e.g.,* Evans Cooperage Co., Inc. v. United States, 712 F.2d 199, 201 (5th Cir. 1983); (estimated tax penalty); *cf.* Toronto v. Commissioner, 99-2 U.S.T.C. ¶ 50,604 (3d Cir. 1999) (filing of amended return does not prove absence of fraud in original return; amended return was filed after taxpayer pled guilty to a criminal charge); Shah v. Commissioner, T.C. Memo. 1999-71 (fraud penalty applied to original returns; amended returns were admissions of underpayment).

In December, 1983, Danner introduced the Heasleys to the investment that generated this lawsuit. Danner told the Heasleys that the O.E.C. Leasing Corporation ("O.E.C.") had an energy conservation program ("the plan") that would generate the future income they sought. The plan required the Heasleys to lease energy savings units ("units") from O.E.C. at $5,000 per unit per year. O.E.C. valued the units at $100,000 each. A service company then installed the units in businesses ("end users"). The units reduce energy consumption, thus reducing end users' energy bills. The end users would pay a percentage of their utility savings to investors such as the Heasleys. The higher the price of energy, the more money saved, and the greater the return on the investment.

Danner reviewed the O.E.C. prospectus with the Heasleys. They focused on the cash flow charts, which showed a positive cash flow of $2,000 in 1984 increasing to $11,876 in 1992. Danner also discussed the investment's tax advantages. Already somewhat familiar with the home version of the energy savings unit, the Heasleys believed the O.E.C. investment would generate future income.

The Heasleys invested $10,000 to buy two units and $4,161 for start-up costs, including installation, telephone hook-ups, and insurance. In a late December closing, they signed documents Danner prepared, including service agreements for the two units. The manufacturer of the units later sent the Heasleys warranty cards, unit serial numbers, and photographs of the units. The servicing agent sent them photographs and addresses of the businesses where the servicing agent installed the two units.

In the past, the Heasleys always prepared their own tax returns. However, they did not know how to report the O.E.C. investment. At Danner's suggestion, the Heasleys employed Gene Smith, a C.P.A., to prepare their 1983 tax return. Smith reviewed the O.E.C. prospectus and the accompanying tax and legal opinions and found everything in order. He then deducted the $10,000 advance rents for the two units and claimed a $20,000 investment tax credit. Because the investment generated a larger investment tax credit than the Heasleys could use in 1983, Smith carried the investment tax credit back to 1980 and 1981. As a result of the O.E.C.-generated deduction and investment tax credit, the Heasleys received more than $23,000 in refunds for the three years from the Internal Revenue Service ("I.R.S."). The Heasleys used the refunds to recoup the money they invested in the plan. They also invested $3,000 of the refunds in a time share plan recommended by Danner. They put $10,000 of the money into a certificate of deposit as collateral for one of Danner's business loans.

Despite Danner's rosy predictions and the Heasleys' high hopes, the Heasleys earned not one penny off of the units or any other of Danner's suggested investments. Even worse, they lost every penny they invested with Danner (more than $25,000). Their loss exceeded the tax refund generated by the plan.

In 1986, the I.R.S. sent the Heasleys a prefiling notification letter. The Heasleys contacted Danner. He assured them that their investment would pass muster with the I.R.S. Danner was wrong. In September, 1986, the I.R.S. totally disallowed the $10,000 advance rental payments and the $20,000 investment tax credit. As a result, the Heasleys' income tax liability increased by approximately $23,000 plus interest. The I.R.S. also assessed penalties totaling $7,419.75: a $1,153.05 negligence penalty * * * ; a $5,940.90 valuation overstatement penalty * * * ; and a $325.80 substantial understatement penalty * * * . The I.R.S. also increased the interest due on the disallowed investment tax credit under 26 U.S.C. Section 6621(c).

After exhausting their administrative remedies, the Heasleys sued the I.R.S. They do not dispute the tax deficiency but instead challenge the I.R.S.'s assessment of penalties. The tax court found for the I.R.S. The Heasleys appealed. We must decide whether the tax court erred in upholding the I.R.S.'s assessment of the penalties and interest. We need not decide, nor did the tax court decide, the Heasleys' tax liability.

* * *

THE VALUATION OVERSTATEMENT PENALTY

The I.R.S. may impose a valuation overstatement penalty for any underpayment of tax "attributable to a valuation overstatement." The Heasleys overvalued each unit by $95,000. Because the Heasleys overvalued the units, the I.R.S. imposed the valuation overstatement penalty. The tax court upheld the penalty. The court reasoned that the Heasleys's $10,000 investment tax credit depended upon the value of the units. "Thus," the court concluded, "to the extent the underpayment is due to the disallowed credits, the underpayment is attributable to a valuation overstatement." Mem. Op. at 21.

After the Tax Court issued its opinion in this case, we interpreted the meaning of "attributable to a valuation overstatement" in *Todd v. I.R.S.*, 862 F.2d 540 (5th Cir. 1988). In *Todd,* as in this case, the I.R.S. completely disallowed the taxpayer's deductions and credits. On appeal, we compared Todd's actual tax liability (without the improperly claimed deductions and credits) with his actual tax liability including the valuation overstatement. *Todd,* 862 F.2d at 542-543. We arrived at the same figure for both calculations because the I.R.S. completely disallowed the deductions and credits containing the valuation overstatement. Because we arrived at the same figure, we concluded that Todd's valuation overstatement did not attribute to the underpayment. Therefore, the I.R.S. could not assess a valuation overstatement penalty.

We see no reason to treat this case any differently than *Todd.* Whenever the I.R.S. totally disallows a deduction or credit, the I.R.S. may not penalize the taxpayer for a valuation overstatement included in that deduction or credit. In such a case, the underpayment is not attributable to a valuation overstatement. Instead, it is attributable to claiming an improper deduction or credit. In this case, the Heasleys' actual tax liability does not differ one cent from their tax liability with the valuation overstatement included. In other words, the Heasleys' valuation overstatement does not change the amount of tax actually owed. Therefore, the I.R.S. erred when it assessed the valuation overstatement penalty and the Tax Court erred as a matter of law by upholding that assessment.

* * *

CONCLUSION

The I.R.S. should not exact every penalty possible in every case where taxpayers pay less than the full amount of tax due. Here, on rather questionable facts, the I.R.S. did just that. This case simply does not support such draconian efforts. Therefore, we REVERSE the decision of the Tax Court and the I.R.S.'s assessment of penalties and interest.

Do you find the reasoning in *Heasley* persuasive? There is currently a split in the circuits on the issue of whether the valuation overstatement penalty applies in the context of a deduction disallowed as a result of an erroneous valuation. *Heasley* reflects the minority view. *Compare Heasley v. Commissioner*, 902 F.2d 380 (5th Cir. 1990) (penalty does not apply); *Gainer v. Commissioner*, 893 F.2d 225, 226-228 (9th Cir. 1990) (same); *with Merino v. Commissioner*, 196 F.3d 147, 158 (3d Cir. 1999) (penalty applied; *Heasley* is distinguishable); *Zfass v. Commissioner*, 118 F.3d 184, 190-191 (4th Cir. 1997) (penalty does apply); *Massengill v. Commissioner*, 876 F.2d 616, 619-20 (8th Cir. 1989) (same); *Illes v. Commissioner*, 982 F.2d 163, 167 & n.2 (6th Cir. 1992) (penalty applied; *Heasley* is distinguishable), *cert. denied*, 507 U.S. 984 (1993); *Gilman v. Commissioner*, 933 F.2d 143, 151 (2d Cir. 1991) (penalty does apply), *cert. denied*, 502 U.S. 1031 (1992).

How would you explain the weight of authority contrary to *Heasley*? Does the exceptional holding in *Heasley* hinge on the fact that the court found that the Heasleys' valuation overstatement did not affect the amount of their underpayment because their deduction would have been disallowed regardless of any overstatement? *Cf. McCrary v. Commissioner*, 92 T.C. 827, 859-860 (1989) (distinguishing, in determining whether a transaction was tax-motivated, valuation overstatements that are inseparable from the ground for disallowing a deduction from those that are separable); *but see, e.g., Massengill,* 876 F.2d at 619-20 ("when an underpayment stems from disallowed depreciation deductions or investment credits due to lack of economic substance, the deficiency is attributable to overstatement of value, and subject to the [overstatement] penalty."). Is *Heasley* distinguishable from many other cases involving valuation misstatements because the Heasleys had a genuine (though uninformed) profit motive? *See, e.g., Donahue v. Commissioner of Internal Revenue*, 1992 U.S. App. LEXIS 7139 (6th Cir. 1992) ("[in *Heasley,*] the taxpayers, unlike Donahue, were found to have operated with a profit motive."). Was the Court of Appeals for the Fifth Circuit simply overly sympathetic to the Heasleys because of their victimization by Gaylen Danner? *See, e.g., Merino,* 196 F.3d at 158 ("we do not find the *Heasley* rationale persuasive here because the court's decision appears to have been driven by understandable sympathy for the Heasleys rather than by a technical analysis of the statute."); *Zfass,* 118 F.3d at 190 n.8 ("the Heasleys were indeed scammed out of a considerable sum of money."). Or do different courts reasonably differ on the interpretation of the applicable Code section? *See*

Gainer, 893 F.2d at 226-228 (agreeing with *Todd v. Internal Revenue Service,* 862 F.2d 540 (5th Cir. 1988), followed in *Heasley,* on the interpretation of the language of the valuation overstatement penalty, based in part on legislative history).

The substantial valuation misstatement penalty applies to a section 482 valuation misstatement as well, a topic best discussed as part of an international tax course. Separate prongs of the accuracy-related penalty may also apply to an employer who attempts to inflate pension contribution deductions, I.R.C. § 6662(b)(4), or to a taxpayer who understates the value of property reported on a gift or estate tax return, I.R.C. § 6662(b)(5).

[D] Reasonable Cause Exception

As part of its effort to consolidate the Code's penalty regime, Congress created a single reasonable cause exception applicable to the accuracy-related penalty in section 6662, the delinquency penalty in section 6651, and the civil fraud penalty in section 6663, among others. I.R.C. § 6664(c).[7] To qualify for the exception, the taxpayer must establish that there was reasonable cause for the tax underpayment and that the taxpayer acted in good faith. The regulations under section 6664(c) focus almost exclusively on the conditions necessary to establish reasonable cause within the context of the accuracy-related penalty. *See* Treas. Reg. § 1.6664-3. In addition, the Consolidated Penalty Handbook includes a summary of the pertinent facts and circumstances that the IRS will consider when deciding whether reasonable cause exists:

INTERNAL REVENUE MANUAL
PART XX — Penalties

Reasonable Cause

1.3.1

General

(1) Reasonable cause is based on all facts and circumstances in each situation and allows the Service to provide relief from a penalty that would otherwise be assessed. Reasonable cause relief is generally granted when the taxpayer exercises ordinary business care and prudence in determining their tax obligations but is unable to comply with those regulations.

---

[7] Notice the overlap between the uniform reasonable cause exception in section 6664(c) and the reasonable cause condition inherent in section 6651, discussed above. Although the two standards differ somewhat (the 6664(c) exception requires a showing of good faith while the 6651 condition requires that the taxpayer establish that the failure to file or pay was not due to willful neglect), the same facts and circumstances are taken into account in both situations. Significantly, most of the case law dealing with the question of whether reasonable cause exists has developed with respect to the delinquency penalty. *See United States v. Boyle, supra.*

* * *

(5)   Taxpayers have reasonable cause when their conduct justifies the nonassertion or abatement of a penalty. Each case must be judged individually based on the facts and circumstances at hand. Consider the following in conjunction with specific criteria identified in the remainder of IRM 1.3.

- What happened and when did it happen?

- During the period of time the taxpayer was non-compliant, what facts and circumstances prevented the taxpayer from filing a return, paying a tax, or otherwise complying with the tax law?

- How did the facts and circumstances prevent the taxpayer from complying?

- How did the taxpayer handle the remainder of their affairs during this time?

- Once the facts and circumstances changed, what attempt did the taxpayer make to comply?

(6)   Reasonable cause **does not exist** if, after the facts and circumstances that explain the taxpayer's noncompliant behavior cease to exist, the taxpayer fails to comply with the tax obligation within a reasonable period of time.

Ordinary Business Care and Prudence

1.3.1.2

(1)   Ordinary business care and prudence includes making provision for business obligations to be met when reasonably foreseeable events occur. A taxpayer may establish reasonable cause by providing facts and circumstances showing the taxpayer executed ordinary business care and prudence (taking that degree of care that a reasonably prudent person would exercise), but nevertheless was unable to comply with the law.

(2)   In determining if the taxpayer exercised ordinary business care and prudence, review available information including the following:

    a.   **Taxpayer's Reason.** The taxpayer's reason should address the penalty imposed. To show reasonable cause, the dates and explanations should clearly correspond with events on which the penalties are based. If the dates and explanations do not correspond to the events on which the penalties are based, request additional information from the taxpayer that may clarify the explanation (*See* IRM 120.1.1.3.1.).

    b.   **Compliance History.** Check the preceding tax years (at least 2) for payment patterns and the taxpayer's overall compliance history. The same penalty, previously assessed or abated, may indicate that the taxpayer is not exercising ordinary business care. If this is the taxpayer's first incident of noncompliant behavior, weigh this factor with other reasons the taxpayer gives for reasonable cause, since a first time failure to comply does not by itself establish reasonable cause.

c. **Length of Time.** Consider the length of time between the event cited as a reason for noncompliance and subsequent compliance. *See* IRM 120.1.1.3.1. Consider when the act was required by law, the period of time during which the taxpayer was unable to comply with the law due to circumstances beyond the taxpayer's control, and when the taxpayer complied with the law.

d. **Circumstances Beyond the Taxpayer's Control.** Consider whether or not the taxpayer could have anticipated the event that caused the noncompliance. Reasonable cause is **generally** established when the taxpayer exercises ordinary business care and prudence but, due to circumstances beyond the taxpayer's control, the taxpayer was unable to timely meet the tax obligation. The taxpayer's obligation to meet the tax law requirements is ongoing. Ordinary business care and prudence requires that the taxpayer continue to attempt to meet the requirements, even though late.

* * *

Ignorance of the Law

1.3.1.2.1

(1) In some instances taxpayers may not be aware of specific obligations to file and/or pay taxes. The **ordinary business care and prudence standard** requires that taxpayers make reasonable efforts to determine their tax obligations. Reasonable cause may be established if the taxpayer shows ignorance of the law in conjunction with other facts and circumstances.

(2) For example, consider:

a. The taxpayer's education,

b. If the taxpayer has been subject to the tax,

c. If the taxpayer has been penalized, or

d. If there were recent changes in the tax forms or law which a taxpayer could not reasonably be expected to know.

(3) The level of complexity of a tax or compliance issue is another factor that should be considered in evaluating reasonable cause because of ignorance of the law.

(4)   Reasonable cause should never be presumed, even in cases where ignorance of the law is claimed.

(5)   The taxpayer may have reasonable cause for noncompliance if:

    a.   a reasonable and good faith effort was made to comply with the law, or

    b.   the taxpayer was unaware of a requirement and could not reasonably be expected to know of the requirement.

Mistake Was Made

1.3.1.2.2

(1)   The taxpayer may try to establish reasonable cause by claiming that a mistake was made.

    a.   Generally, this is not in keeping with the **ordinary business care and prudence standard** and does not provide a basis for reasonable cause.

    b.   However, the reason for the mistake may be a supporting factor if additional facts and circumstances support the determination that the taxpayer exercised **ordinary business care and prudence.**

Forgetfulness

1.3.1.2.3

(1)   The taxpayer may try to establish reasonable cause by claiming forgetfulness or an oversight by the taxpayer or another party caused the noncompliance. Generally, this is not in keeping with **ordinary business care and prudence standard** and does not provide a basis for reasonable cause.

    a.   Relying on another person to perform a required act is generally sufficient for establishing reasonable cause.

    b.   It is the taxpayer's responsibility to file a timely and accurate return and to make timely deposits or payments. This responsibility cannot be delegated.

(2)   Information to consider when evaluating a request for an abatement or nonassertion of a penalty based on a mistake or a claim of ignorance of the law includes, but is not limited to:

- When and how the taxpayer became aware of the mistake,

- The extent to which the taxpayer corrected the mistake,

- The relationship between the taxpayer and the subordinate;

- If the taxpayer took timely steps to correct the failure after it was discovered; and

- The supporting documentation.

Death, Serious Illness, or Unavoidable Absence

1.3.1.2.4

(1) Death, serious illness, or unavoidable absence of the taxpayer may establish reasonable cause for late filing, payment, or deposit, for the following:

   a. An **individual**: If there was a death, serious illness, or unavoidable absence of the taxpayer or a death or serious illness in that taxpayer's immediate family (i.e., spouse, sibling, parents, grandparents, children).

*   *   *

(2) If someone, other than the taxpayer or the person responsible, is authorized to meet the obligation, consider the reasons why that person did not meet the obligation when evaluating the request for relief. In the case of a business, if only one person was authorized, determine whether this was in keeping with ordinary business care and prudence.

(3) Information to consider when evaluating a request for penalty relief based on reasonable cause due to death, serious illness or unavoidable absence includes, but is not limited to, the following:

   Step   1: The relationship of the taxpayer to the other parties involved.

   Step   2: The date of death.

   Step   3: The dates, duration, and severity of illness.

   Step   4: The dates and reasons for absence.

   Step   5: How the event prevented compliance.

   Step   6: If other business obligations were impaired.

   Step   7: If tax duties were attended to promptly when the illness passed, or within a reasonable period of time after a death or absence.

Unable to Obtain Records

1.3.1.2.5

(1) Explanations relating to the inability to obtain the necessary records may constitute reasonable cause in some instances, but may not in others.

(2) Consider the facts and circumstances relevant to each case and evaluate the request for penalty relief.

(3)   If the taxpayer was unable to obtain records necessary to comply with a tax obligation, the taxpayer may or may not be able to establish reasonable cause. Reasonable cause may be established if **the taxpayer exercised ordinary business care and prudence, but due to circumstances beyond the taxpayer's control they were unable to comply**.

(4)   Information to consider when evaluating such a request includes, but is not limited to, an explanation as to:

- Why the records were needed to comply;

- Why the records were unavailable and what steps were taken to secure the records;

- When and how the taxpayer became aware that they did not have the necessary records;

- If other means were explored to secure needed information;

- Why the taxpayer did not estimate the information;

- If the taxpayer contacted the Service for instructions on what to do about the missing information;

- If the taxpayer promptly complied once the missing information was received; and

- Supporting documentation such as copies of letters written and responses received in an effort to get the needed information.

* * *

[E]   The Civil Fraud Penalty — Code Section 6663

The civil fraud penalty in section 6663 applies when the taxpayer's behavior extends substantially beyond a failure to exercise reasonable care, and evidences an intentional effort to underpay his taxes. The increased penalty rate, 75 percent of the portion of an underpayment attributable to fraud, reflects the higher level of culpability that must exist in order to trigger the addition. The civil fraud penalty applies only if a tax return has been filed. If the taxpayer's failure to file a return is fraudulent, this triggers a 75 percent delinquency penalty under section 6651(f) instead. While under prior law, the accuracy-related penalties and the civil fraud penalty could be asserted simultaneously with respect to the same underpayment, current law confirms that the accuracy-related penalties apply only to that portion of an underpayment not attributable to fraud. I.R.C. § 6662(b).

The initial burden of proving fraud on the part of the taxpayer rests with the IRS. *See* I.R.C. § 7454(a). If the IRS can establish by clear and convincing evidence that any portion of an underpayment is attributable to fraud, the statute presumes the entire underpayment is attributable to fraud. The burden of proof then shifts to the taxpayer to establish, by a preponderance of the evidence, the portion of the underpayment *not* attributable to fraud. I.R.C. § 6663(b). Proof of fraud requires a showing that the taxpayer engaged in intentional wrongdoing with the specific intent to avoid a tax known or believed to be owning. *Stoltzfus v. United States*, 398 F.2d 1002 (3d Cir. 1968), *cert. denied,* 393 U.S. 1020. Fraud is normally proven by the IRS based on circumstantial evidence. The *Meier* case, which is reproduced below, lists some of the badges of fraud. Notice also the IRS's use of the prior accounting proceeding involving Meier to meet its burden of proof under section 6663.

MEIER v. COMMISSIONER
United States Tax Court
91 T.C. 273 (1988)

[The basic facts of *Meier* are as follows:

In his capacity as an employee of Hughes Tool Co. (Hughes), John Meier (Petitioner) was directed to acquire silver mining claims. In derogation of his duty to his employer, Petitioner, through agents or co-conspirators, purchased the mining claims for nominal amounts, and then sold them to Hughes at inflated prices. The sales proceeds were then channeled overseas, at Petitioner's direction and for his benefit, to avoid detection by his employer and to avoid United States income tax.

Hughes filed an accounting proceeding against Petitioner in the Federal District Court for the District of Utah seeking recoupment of the wrongfully acquired proceeds. Hughes Tool Co. v. Meier, 489 F. Supp. 354 (D. Utah 1977), *aff'd per curiam* No. 78-1565 (10th Cir. 1980). Hughes was successful in seeking an accounting, and the District Court found that Meier had "secretly divert[ed] funds . . . for his own use and benefit." *Id.* at 356.

In the instant case, the Tax Court ruled that the IRS, although not a party to the accounting proceedings, could offensively utilize collateral estoppel to preclude Petitioner from denying diversion of the funds in connection with his failure to report such amounts as income on his income tax returns. The IRS also asserted the civil fraud penalty against Petitioner with respect to his underpayment of tax. Eds.]

GERBER, JUDGE:

* * *

FRAUD/SECTION 6653(b)[8] ADDITION

Respondent argues that petitioner's failure to report diverted funds and other income on his tax returns for 1968, 1969, and 1970 is fraudulent. If any part of any underpayment for the taxable years is due to fraud, the addition under section 6653(b) will apply, * * * . Fraud must be proved by clear and convincing evidence. Sec. 7454; Rule 142(b). The existence of fraud is a question of fact to be resolved upon consideration of the entire record. Gajewski v. Commissioner, 67 T.C. 181 (1976), *affd. without published opinion* 578 F.2d 1383 (8th Cir. 1978); Mensik v. Commissioner, 328 F.2d 147 (7th

---

[8] [Currently I.R.C. § 6663. Eds.]

Cir. 1964), *affg.* 37 T.C. 703 (1962), *cert. denied* 379 U.S. 827 (1964). Fraud is never presumed, but rather must be established by some independent evidence. Beaver v. Commissioner, 55 T.C. 85 (1970). Fraud may be proven by circumstantial evidence and reasonable inferences drawn from the facts because direct proof of the taxpayer's intent is rarely available. Spies v. United States, 317 U.S. 492 (1943); Rowlee v. Commissioner, 80 T.C. 1111 (1983); Stephenson v. Commissioner, 79 T.C. 995 (1982), *affd.* 748 F.2d 331 (6th Cir. 1984). The taxpayer's entire course of conduct may establish the requisite fraudulent intent. *Rowlee v. Commissioner, supra;* Stone v. Commissioner, 56 T.C. 213 (1971).

In a recently decided case, *Bradford v. Commissioner*, 796 F.2d 303 (9th Cir. 1986), *affg.* T.C. Memo. 1984-601 (*Bradford*), the Court of Appeals for the Ninth Circuit reaffirmed that it is appropriate to infer fraudulent intent from various kinds of circumstantial evidence and set forth a nonexclusive list of the "badges of fraud" that demonstrate fraudulent intent. These include: (1) The understatement of income; (2) inadequate records; (3) failure to file tax returns; (4) implausible or inconsistent explanations of behavior; (5) concealment of assets; and (6) failure to cooperate with tax authorities. The following are additional indicia of fraud: (1) Engaging in illegal activities; (2) attempting to conceal these activities; (3) dealing in cash; and (4) failing to make estimated tax payments. *Bradford v. Commissioner, supra* at 307-308.

Respondent has established that Meier's returns for the years involving the mining transactions were fraudulent. The first indicia of fraud in *Bradford* is understating income. We have already found that petitioner diverted funds of Hughes to his own use and control and that said funds constituted substantial income from the mining transactions during the 1969 and 1970 taxable years. Through introducing petitioners' returns into evidence, respondent has shown the failure to report any of this income. The failure to report said income resulted in large understatements of income on petitioners' 1969 and 1970 joint returns.

Part of the evidence relied upon by respondent to carry his burden of establishing fraud has been established through the offensive use of collateral estoppel. Accordingly, we must consider the burden of proof required in both proceedings. Civil tax fraud must be proven by clear and convincing evidence. Sec. 7454; Rule 142(b). Section 27, Restatement, Judgments 2d (1982), and the holding in *Synanon Church v. United States*, 820 F.2d 421 (D.C. Cir. 1987), state the general rule that a fact found in a first case may be established by means of collateral estoppel either as an evidentiary or ultimate fact in the second case. Subsection (4) of section 28, Restatement, Judgments 2d (1982), recommends an exception in the following circumstances where "The party against whom preclusion is sought had a significantly heavier burden of persuasion with respect to the issue in the initial action than in the subsequent action; the burden has shifted to his adversary; or the adversary has a significantly heavier burden than he had in the first action." Accordingly, we consider the standard of proof for an accounting action brought in a Federal District Court in Utah.

* * *

The District Court in *Hughes Tool Co.* used language in its opinion indicating that the quantum of proof would have, at a minimum, met a clear and convincing standard. The Court held as follows: "In view of the foregoing findings, the court concludes as a *matter of law* defendant Meier must * * * render an accounting." *Hughes Tool Co. v. Meier, supra* at 369 (emphasis supplied).

> Defendant Meier appears to misapprehend the quantity and quality of the evidence which has been presented in this case to date * * * . As the court rehearsed in great detail * * * there is substantial evidence in the record upon which to base a ruling fixing liability on defendant * * * . That is, plaintiff established [the sales transactions and that the funds were the responsibility of Meier]. [*Hughes Tool Co. v. Meier, supra* at 373.]

"The court is of the opinion that *all* of the evidence in this matter shows that the sum of * * * is due the plaintiff." *Hughes Tool Co. v. Meier, supra* at 374. Although not entirely clear, we conclude that the standard of proof required in this type proceeding in Utah is "clear and convincing." Based upon our review of Judge Anderson's opinion and the record in the District Court proceeding, we believe that Hughes Tool was held to a "clear and convincing" standard of proof in establishing that Meier, through a breach of his fiduciary duty, secretly diverted Hughes' funds for his own use and control.

Another indicia of fraud in *Bradford* is the failure to keep records or keeping inadequate records. In this case, many of the documents were back-dated or dated "as of" a certain date, to retroactively reflect the transactions in the light petitioner wanted them to appear, *i.e.*, making the foreign corporations the owners of the claims. Additionally, Meier's role on both sides of these transactions is not reflected in the records (of necessity, to conceal his involvement). In the context of this case, the records of the transactions are inadequate and were intended, at the very least, to conceal information from petitioner's employer and likely from the taxing authorities, including respondent.

Another indicia noted in *Bradford* is the concealment of assets. This is a highly probative factor here. The sales proceeds were almost immediately transferred overseas after the execution of the transactions. In addition, the documentation makes it appear that the foreign corporations were the owners of the funds, while the funds were under the control of and for the benefit of petitioner. We find it highly indicative of fraudulent intent that the funds, after being channeled through two different foreign corporations, ended up in a trust for the benefit of petitioner. This conduct, calculated to mislead and conceal, is indicative of fraud. Spies v. United States, 317 U.S. 492 (1943). Gajewski v. Commissioner, 67 T.C. 181 (1976), *affd. without published opinion* 578 F.2d 1383 (8th Cir. 1978).

Petitioner contends that his so-called "fraudulent intent," because of the transfer of funds, was merely "tax planning" by a group of knowledgeable advisers. We find that the use of the foreign entities, in the context of this case, was a sham or subterfuge to disguise the real owner, avoid identification of petitioner, and to evade Federal income taxes.

A final factor relevant here is whether the activity was illegal. While we know of no State criminal charges filed in connection with this case, petitioner rather egregiously breached his fiduciary duty to his employer, to the extent of benefitting by several million dollars. We find that this situation is not significantly different than a case involving embezzlement or other kind of theft. The lack of potential for criminal punishment or penalty seems to be a distinction without a difference in this setting; petitioner's activities are no less illegal or improper.

Respondent need not prove the precise amount of the underpayment resulting from fraud. Otsuki v. Commissioner, 53 T.C. 96, 105 (1969). In any event, some amount of underpayment has been established for the years 1969 and 1970. We conclude, therefore, based on the facts in the record, that petitioner intended not only to conceal his activities from his employer, Hughes, but also fraudulently intended to evade Federal income tax.

*   *   *

[F] Information Reporting Penalties — Code Sections 6721 and 6722

One of the most important tools the IRS has to combat under reporting and non-reporting of income is its Information Returns Program (IRP). The IRP verifies whether a taxpayer's income has been fully reported by digitally matching data on information returns filed by employers and other payors with the recipient's income tax return. Failure by the taxpayer to include income reported on an information return normally results in the IRS sending the taxpayer a notice explaining the discrepancy and requesting payment of any resulting tax adjustment. Under current law, information returns are required for numerous types of payments, including wages (Form W-2), interest (Form 1099-INT), dividends (Form 1099-DIV), and broker transactions (Form 1099-B). In addition to reporting these amounts to the IRS, the payor must also send a copy of the return to the income recipient (a "payee statement") so that the recipient can accurately and timely complete his own return. I.R.C. §§ 6041–6053.

The effectiveness of the IRP hinges upon information returns and payee statements being timely filed and correctly completed. To ensure that this occurs, the Code applies a series of information reporting penalties against those who fail to meet their reporting obligations. A payor who fails to timely file an information return or to properly include all the required information on the return is subject to a penalty of $50 per return, up to a maximum of $250,000 per calendar year. I.R.C. § 6721. Although a single return may contain more than one reporting error, only one penalty is imposed with respect to a single information return. Treas. Reg. § 301.6721-1. To encourage payors to correct errors as soon as possible, the per-return and maximum yearly penalty amounts decrease based upon when the filer rectifies the errors. If the reporting failures are corrected within 30 days after the due date of the return (normally March 30), the penalty amount is reduced to $15 per return, with a maximum yearly penalty of $75,000. Reporting failures corrected after March 30 but before August 1 carry a $30 per return penalty, not to exceed $150,000 per year. I.R.C. § 6721(c). Errors or omissions that are "inconsequential" and do not prevent the IRS from matching the information return to the corresponding payee statement are ignored. Treas. Reg. § 301.6721-1(c)(1).

A similar set of penalties applies to a payor's failure to timely furnish a required payee statement or to include in the payee statement all the correct information. I.R.C. § 6722. The penalty equals $50 for each statement with respect to which the failure occurs, up to a maximum penalty amount of $100,000 per year. The exception for inconsequential errors also applies to payee statements but, unlike the information reporting penalty in section 6721, the 6722 penalty amount is not reduced for prompt corrections. This reflects Congress' concern that payee statements be provided early enough in the process (normally by February 28) so that taxpayers can carry out their own filing requirements on time. *See* H.R. Rep. No. 101-386, at 1385 (1989).

The reporting penalties in sections 6721 and 6722 may both be waived if the filer shows that the failure was due to reasonable cause and that the filer acted in a responsible manner. I.R.C. § 6724. In this context, reasonable cause may be established by a showing that (1) there are significant mitigating factors for the failure (for example, the filer has an established history of complying with the reporting requirements with respect to which the failure occurred), or (2) the failure arose from events beyond the filer's control. Treas. Reg. § 301.6724-1(a), (b). Events beyond the filer's control include the unavailability of relevant business records caused by unforseen circumstances; reasonable and good faith reliance on erroneous information supplied by the IRS; failure by the payee to furnish correct information; or reasonable reliance on a third party agent to file the returns. Treas. Reg. § 301.6724-1(c).

[G] Preparer Penalties — Code Section 6694

The income tax return preparer penalties are designed to buttress the penalty structure applicable to taxpayers. In particular, the rules seek to discourage practitioners from cooperating with taxpayers who seek to underreport their liabilities and to prevent practitioners from encouraging inaccurate reporting. If an income tax return preparer knows (or reasonably should know) that an understatement on the taxpayer's return is due to an "unrealistic position," the preparer is subject to a $250 penalty. I.R.C. § 6694(a). An unrealistic position is one that has no realistic possibility of being sustained on the merits:

> A position is considered to have a realistic possibility of being sustained on its merits if a reasonable and well-informed analysis by a person knowledgeable in the tax law would lead such a person to conclude that the position has approximately a one in three, or greater, likelihood of being sustained on its merits (realistic possibility standard). In making this determination, the possibility that the

position will not be challenged by the Internal Revenue Service (e.g., because the taxpayer's return may not be audited or because the issue may not be raised on audit) is not to be taken into account.

Treas. Reg. § 1.6694-2(b).[9]

For purposes of applying the realistic possibility of success standard, the preparer employs the same type of analysis (and may consider the same type of authorities) as that used to determine whether there is substantial authority for purposes of the substantial understatement penalty in section 6653(b)(3). Note that the pre-IMPACT standard of conduct for the return preparer penalty was based on negligence. How does the currently applied standard differ from a negligence-based standard? The penalty under section 6694 increases to $1,000 if the understatement of tax reflected on the return results from willful, reckless, or intentional conduct. The regulations in section 1.6694-3 define these standards with a similar degree of specificity.

In assessing exposure to these penalties, to what extent must the return preparer verify the information provided to him by the taxpayer? As a general rule, a preparer may rely in good faith on information furnished by the taxpayer, and need not review the taxpayer's books and records for accuracy and completeness. Although a return preparer is not required to independently verify information provided by the taxpayer, the $250 penalty may apply where the preparer fails to inquire as to furnished information that appears, based upon facts actually known to him, to be incomplete or incorrect. Treas. Reg. § 1.6694-1(e). Moreover, if the preparer reports an expense on the taxpayer's return for which the Code requires substantiation, the preparer must inquire of the taxpayer whether the supporting documents exist. Failure to request such information, resulting in an understatement of tax, triggers the penalty. The regulations include the following example:

> *Example*: A taxpayer, during an interview conducted by the preparer, stated that he had paid $6,500 in doctor bills and $5,000 in deductible travel and entertainment expenses during the tax year, when in fact he had paid smaller amounts. On the basis of this information, the preparer properly calculated deductions for medical expenses and for travel and entertainment expenses which resulted in an understatement of liability for tax. The preparer had no reason to believe that the medical expense and travel and entertainment expense information presented was incorrect or incomplete. The preparer did not ask for underlying documentation of the medical expenses but inquired about the existence of travel and entertainment expense records. The preparer was reasonably satisfied by the taxpayer's representations that the taxpayer had adequate records (or other sufficient corroborative evidence) for the deduction of $5,000 for travel and entertainment expenses. The preparer is not subject to a penalty under section 6694.

Treas. Reg. § 1.6694-1(e)(2) Ex. What if the preparer knew that the taxpayer had been denied a travel and entertainment expense deduction in an earlier

---

[9] An individual who consistently engages in the type of conduct giving rise to the § 6694 penalty may be enjoined by the IRS from acting as an income tax return preparer. I.R.C. § 7407.

year because the taxpayer failed to properly document the deduction? How might the preparer protect himself against liability?

The penalties in section 6694, along with the reporting and disclosure penalties in section 6695, apply to an "income tax return preparer." What type of involvement causes a person to be considered a return preparer? *See* I.R.C. § 7701(a)(36); Treas. Reg. § 301.7701-15. In Revenue Ruling 86-55, 1986-1 C.B. 373, reproduced in Chapter 1, the IRS ruled that a used car dealership that offered to prepare returns free of charge to customers who purchased an automobile from the dealership with the resulting refund was an income tax return preparer.

Given the rapidly expanding electronic filing program and the charges of widespread fraud and abuse surrounding the system, the IRS has announced that, when appropriate, it will apply the return preparer penalties against electronic filers. Rev. Proc. 97-60, 1997-2 C.B. 602. In response to practitioner concerns that the preparer penalties would be used as a bargaining chip against their clients whose returns were being audited, the IRS announced that it will not automatically assess return preparer penalties based solely on a deficiency proposed against the taxpayer. I.R.M. Policy Statement P-1-18.

Should the person who prepared a taxpayer's return also represent the taxpayer during the examination of that return? Why or why not?

§ 10.03 Assessment, Abatement, and Suspension of Penalties

The procedural rules surrounding when and how the IRS may assess penalty additions are somewhat confusing. While relatively few penalties are explicitly subject to the deficiency assessment procedures described in Chapter 5, if a penalty is based on liability determined under those procedures, the penalty itself will be assessed in the same manner. *See* I.R.C. § 6665. As a practical matter, therefore, because the accuracy-related and civil fraud penalties hinge upon an underpayment of tax (which must be assessed as a deficiency), the penalties themselves must also be included in the notice of deficiency, and may be reviewed by the Tax Court, before they can be formally assessed. Moreover, the Appeals Division will consider the penalty addition at the same time it considers the underlying tax liability. However, with respect to the delinquency penalty in section 6651, in most cases, the IRS need only notify the taxpayer of a penalty assessment resulting from a failure to file or pay and make a demand for payment. After notice and demand, the IRS may collect the resulting amount. Subject to the abatement procedures described below, the taxpayer's only recourse at that point is to file a refund claim and, if the claim is rejected, file a suit in a District Court or the Court of Federal Claims for a refund of the penalty amount.

Neither the information reporting nor the preparer penalties are subject to the deficiency assessment procedures. I.R.C. § 6671(a). Nevertheless, the IRS has created a pre-assessment appeals procedure for preparer penalty cases that is similar to that followed in deficiency cases. Under this procedure, the IRS issues the preparer a 30-day letter and provides an opportunity for the preparer to protest the penalty before it is assessed. Treas. Reg. § 1.6694-4(a). Once the section 6694 penalty is assessed, the preparer can delay collection of the full amount by paying 15 percent of the assessed penalty and filing a claim for refund. If the refund claim is denied, the preparer can maintain a refund suit in District Court to recover the previously paid amount. I.R.C. § 6694(c).

The IRS has authority to waive or abate an asserted penalty under specified circumstances. The Code itself, for example, allows the return preparer penalty to be abated if it is later established as part of a final administrative determination or judicial proceeding that the return on which the penalty was based contained no understatement of tax. I.R.C. § 6694(d). The IRS has also established an administrative appeals procedures under which a taxpayer may request waiver of the penalty after it has already been assessed. I.R.M. 120.1.1.4. The post-assessment appeals procedure applies to most penalties that may be waived based on a reasonable cause, due diligence, good conscience or other similar exception. Taxpayers most commonly utilize these appeals procedures to protest delinquency penalties. If the abatement request is denied, the taxpayer can protest that denial with the Appeals Division. If the Appeals Division refuses to abate the penalty, the taxpayer is left to file a claim for refund and then a refund suit. I.R.M. 120.1.1.4.1.2.

Prior to the IRS Reform Act, the IRS generally did not abate a penalty simply because it had delayed contacting the taxpayer about an asserted deficiency. Code section 6404(g) now requires the IRS to suspend the imposition of a penalty in cases where the IRS does not properly notify the taxpayer of additional liability within an 18-month period after the taxpayer files his return. In such a case, penalties are suspended beginning on the day after the close of the 18-month period. (This period decreases to one year for 2004 and later tax years.) The suspension rule applies to any penalty "which is computed by reference to the period of time the failure continues to exist." This provision specifically excludes the delinquency penalty under section 6651 and the fraud penalty under 6663 from qualifying for relief. What types of penalties discussed in this chapter would qualify for suspension under this rule? Note that section 6404(g) also applies to interest accruals. The application of section 6404(g) is discussed in more detail in Chapter 11 in the context of underpayment interest.

§ 10.04   Burden of Proof with Respect to Penalties

Code section 7491, which is discussed in Chapter 6, provides a special rule for penalties, placing an initial burden of production on the IRS in any court proceeding relating to an individual's liability for penalties. In the first reported case to apply the section 7491(c) burden of production rule for penalties, *Higbee v. Commissioner*, 116 T.C. 438 (2001), the initial portion of which is included in Chapter 6, the Tax Court held that the Commissioner had carried the burden of production with regard to the late filing penalty in section 6651 and the accuracy-related penalty in section 6662:

> Although the statute does not provide a definition of the phrase "burden of production", we conclude that Congress' intent as to the meaning of the burden of production is evident from the legislative history. The legislative history of section 7491(c) sets forth:

[I]n any court proceeding, the Secretary must initially come forward with evidence that it is appropriate to apply a particular penalty to the taxpayer before the court can impose the penalty. This provision is not intended to require the Secretary to introduce evidence of elements such as reasonable cause or substantial authority. Rather, the Secretary must come forward initially with evidence regarding the appropriateness of applying a particular penalty to the taxpayer; if the taxpayer believes that, because of reasonable cause, substantial authority, or a similar provision, it is inappropriate to impose the penalty, it is the taxpayer's responsibility (and not the Secretary's obligation) to raise those issues. [H. Conf. Rept. 105-599, 1998-3 C.B. at 995.]

Therefore, with regard to section 7491(c), we conclude that for the Commissioner to meet his burden of production, the Commissioner must come forward with sufficient evidence indicating that it is appropriate to impose the relevant penalty.

The legislative history to section 7491(c), however, also discloses that the Commissioner need not introduce evidence regarding reasonable cause, substantial authority, or similar provisions. In addition, the legislative history indicates that it is the taxpayer's responsibility to raise those issues. We therefore conclude that the taxpayer bears the burden of proof with regard to those issues.

Finally, we note that Congress placed only the burden of production on the Commissioner pursuant to section 7491(c). Congress' use of the phrase "burden of production" and not the more general phrase "burden of proof" as used in section 7491(a) indicates to us that Congress did not desire that the burden of proof be placed on the Commissioner with regard to penalties.[n.6] See sec. 7491(c). Therefore, once the Commissioner meets his burden of production, the taxpayer must come forward with evidence sufficient to persuade a Court that the Commissioner's determination is incorrect.

Having described the framework of section 7491(c), we evaluate whether respondent has met his burden of production with regard to the section 6651(a)(1) addition to tax and the section 6662 accuracy-related penalty. We also discuss whether petitioners have presented any evidence which would cause us not to sustain respondent's determinations with regard to the addition to tax and the accuracy-related penalty.

Section 6651(a)(1) imposes an addition to tax for a taxpayer's failure to file a required return on or before the specified filing date, including extensions. The amount of the liability is based upon a percentage of

---

[n.6] We note that sec. 6665(a)(2) provides that any reference to tax shall be deemed also to refer to penalties. However, the application of sec. 6665(a)(2) is limited by the language "Except as otherwise provided in this title". Considering that limiting language of sec. 6665(a)(2), the reference in sec. 7491(a) to tax liabilities imposed by subtitle A or B (whereas penalties are imposed by subtitle F), and the structure of sec. 7491 as a whole, we believe that Congress intended for sec. 7491(c) (and not sec. 7491(a)) to apply to penalties.

the tax required to be shown on the return. *See* sec. 6651(a)(1). The addition to tax is inapplicable, however, if the taxpayer's failure to file the return was due to reasonable cause and not to willful neglect. *See* sec. 6651(a)(1). Under section 7491(c), . . . the Commissioner bears the burden of production with regard to whether the section 6651(a)(1) addition to tax is appropriate, but he does not bear the burden of proof with regard to the "reasonable cause" exception of section 6651(a).

Respondent determined that petitioners are liable for a section 6651(a)(1) addition to tax with regard to their 1996 tax return. The parties have stipulated that petitioners filed their 1996 return on April 18, 1998, approximately 1 year after it was due. Accordingly, we conclude that respondent has produced sufficient evidence to show that the section 6651(a)(1) addition to tax is appropriate, unless petitioners prove that their failure to file was due to reasonable cause.

Petitioners have not provided any evidence indicating that their failure to file was due to reasonable cause. Therefore, an addition to tax of 25 percent of the amount required to be shown as tax on the return is sustained in the instant case. * * *.

Pursuant to section 6662(a), a taxpayer may be liable for a penalty of 20 percent on the portion of an underpayment of tax (1) attributable to a substantial understatement of tax or (2) due to negligence or disregard of rules or regulations. *See* sec. 6662(b). A substantial understatement of tax is defined as an understatement of tax that exceeds the greater of 10 percent of the tax required to be shown on the tax return or $5,000. *See* sec. 6662(d)(1)(A). The understatement is reduced to the extent that the taxpayer has (1) adequately disclosed his or her position and has a reasonable basis for such position or (2) has substantial authority for the tax treatment of the item. *See* sec. 6662(d)(2)(B). In addition, section 6662(c) defines "negligence" as any failure to make a reasonable attempt to comply with the provisions of the Internal Revenue Code, and "disregard" means any careless, reckless, or intentional disregard.

Whether applied because of a substantial understatement of tax or negligence or disregard of the rules or regulations, the accuracy-related penalty is not imposed with respect to any portion of the understatement as to which the taxpayer acted with reasonable cause and in good faith. *See* sec. 6664(c)(1). The decision as to whether the taxpayer acted with reasonable cause and in good faith depends upon all the pertinent facts and circumstances. *See* sec. 1.6664-4(b)(1), Income Tax Regs. Relevant factors include the taxpayer's efforts to assess his proper tax liability, including the taxpayer's reasonable and good faith reliance on the advice of a professional such as an accountant. *See id.* Further, an honest misunderstanding of fact or law that is reasonable in light of the experience, knowledge, and education of the taxpayer may indicate reasonable cause and good faith. *See* Remy v. Commissioner, T.C. Memo 1997-72.

For the 1997 tax year, respondent determined that petitioners are liable for an accuracy-related penalty attributable to a substantial understatement of tax or, in the alternative, due to negligence or disregard of rules or regulations. Petitioners have conceded that they are not entitled to $30,245 in itemized deductions relating to NOL carryovers ($28,036) and certain taxes ($2,209) claimed on Schedule A of their 1997 tax return. With regard to respondent's determination that petitioners were negligent and disregarded rules and regulations, respondent argues that he has met his burden of production under section 7491(c) through petitioners' above concessions, along with evidence in the record indicating that petitioners were experienced in business affairs. Further, respondent contends that because petitioners have failed to introduce any evidence to indicate that they were not negligent, petitioners have failed to meet their burden of proof, which they retain despite the application of section 7491(c).

Respondent has shown that petitioners have failed to keep adequate books and records or to substantiate properly the items in question. Such a failure in the instant case is evidence of negligence. *See* sec. 1.6662-3(b), Income Tax Regs. Consequently, we conclude that respondent has met his burden of production for his determination of the accuracy-related penalty based on negligence or disregard of rules or regulations. Additionally, with regard to that determination, petitioners have failed to meet their burden of proving that they acted with reasonable cause and in good faith. We therefore sustain respondent's determination that petitioners are liable for the accuracy-related penalty on the underpayment associated with the disallowed itemized deductions conceded by petitioners.

In *Higbee*, the Commissioner relied largely on the taxpayers' own stipulations and concessions to carry the burden of production. If the taxpayers had not made these concessions, what sort of evidence might the IRS have introduced to sustain its burden? The taxpayers also helped the government's case by not introducing any evidence to support a penalty defense. Given the fact that the taxpayer still must bear the burden of proving any penalty defenses, such as reasonable cause or adequate disclosure, will the new rule likely affect the IRS's willingness to assert a penalty?

PROBLEMS

1. Elaine mailed in her 2002 individual income tax return on May 9, 2003, and it was received by the IRS on May 12. Elaine's employer had withheld from her wages during the year a total of $15,000 in tax, as compared to Elaine's liability reflected on the 2002 return of $25,000. Elaine paid the entire balance due ($10,000) at the time she filed her return.

    A. Assume that the reason Elaine mailed her return on May 9 is because, on April 14, she gave the return to her friend Newman, who works at the Post Office, and asked him to mail it for her. He left the envelope in his jacket and did not remember or discover it until May 9, when he promptly mailed it (with an attached note explaining that the delay was entirely his fault). Is Elaine liable for a delinquency penalty under section 6651 and, if so, in what amount?

B.   Assume instead that Elaine had obtained an automatic extension of time to file her return by timely filing Form 4868.

   i.   Is Elaine liable for a delinquency penalty under section 6651 and, if so, in what amount?

   ii.   Upon audit, the IRS determined, much to Elaine's satisfaction, that her total correct tax liability for 2002 was only $23,000. What, if anything, is the amount of the delinquency penalty she will owe?

2.   At his employer's annual 2002 picnic, Carlos won as part of a grand prize drawing a vintage 1967 Chevrolet Camaro. Although it was announced at the picnic that the car had a value of $15,000, the 1099-MISC information return that Carlos received from his employer showed the value of the Camaro at $1,000. Prior to filing his 2002 return, Carlos was advised by his son, a CPA, that the fair market value of the car (which amount the son did not specify) had to be reported as gross income. Following his son's advice, Carlos timely filed his 2002 tax return including an additional $1,000 of gross income, reflecting the receipt of the car.

A.   Assuming the IRS can establish that the Camaro's actual fair market value on the date of the drawing was $15,000, on what basis might the IRS impose an accuracy-related penalty with respect to Carlos's 2002 return? Describe how the potential penalty amount would be calculated.

B.   What defenses might Carlos assert to avoid the penalty amount?

C.   Describe the potential penalty applicable to Carlos's employer based upon the Form 1099-MISC.

3.   Mary owns and leases out an office building in downtown Kansas City. As the result of a hail storm in 2003, Mary was forced to replace one-half of the building's roof at a total cost of $250,000. Mary was advised by the accountant who prepared her 2003 return that the roofing costs had to be capitalized and depreciated rather than deducted in full in 2003. In response to Mary's objections, the accountant drafted a memorandum to her that cited relevant case and administrative law dealing with the issue. Although the proper treatment of the roofing costs was not 100 percent clear, the accountant concluded in the memorandum that the costs should be capitalized. Understanding the risk involved, Mary insisted that the costs be deducted in full and threatened to fire the accountant if he did

not comply. Reluctantly, the accountant deducted the roofing costs in full and signed the return as preparer.

A. Can Mary be liable for the substantial understatement portion of the accuracy-related penalty in this case?

B. Is there any potential penalty liability for the accountant?

4. Meghan is planning a transaction that will lower her total tax liability for the year if her tax position is respected by the IRS. Her primary concern is that, if she is audited and the IRS does not respect her characterization of the transaction, the IRS will add penalties to the tax deficiency. What type of sources may Meghan consult to try to determine the IRS's tax treatment of similar transactions?

5. Lucinda filed her 2001 return on June 17, 2002. The IRS has sent Lucinda a notice of deficiency that includes a fraud penalty, and Lucinda has timely petitioned the Tax Court.

A. Which party bears the burden of proving fraud on Lucinda's part?

B. Can the IRS assert for the first time in its answer that Lucinda's return was not timely filed?

     i. Assuming that the IRS can raise the late-filing issue in its answer, can the IRS assert a delinquency penalty in addition to the fraud penalty?

     ii. Assuming that the IRS can raise the late-filing issue in its answer, and that if Lucinda's return was late, it will affect the amount of the penalties that Lucinda may owe, who will bear the burden of proof on this issue?

C. Can a negligence penalty automatically apply in either of the following circumstances?

     i. Lucinda prevails on the issue of fraud.

     ii. Lucinda loses on the issue of fraud.

D. If the IRS loses on the fraud issue, does that outcome affect the deadline for assessing any tax that may be due for Lucinda's 2001 tax year?

6. Dylan is representing a client who recently received a 30-day letter from the IRS. The client is eager to settle the case. Dylan has explained to the client the IRS Appeals process, and the advantages and disadvantages of a nondocketed IRS Appeal, which Dylan is inclined to pursue. The client fears that if Dylan tries to negotiate a settlement with the Appeals Division, the IRS will assert additional civil penalties. How realistic is that fear?

Chapter 11

INTEREST ON DEFICIENCIES
AND OVERPAYMENTS

Reading Assignment: Code §§ 6404(e), (g), (i), 6601(a), (c), (e), (f), (g), 6611, 6621(a)-(d), 6622, 6631; Treas. Reg. §§ 1.163-9T, 301.6601-1, 301.6611-1, 301.6621-3.

§ 11.01 Introduction

A taxpayer who fails to report his tax liability correctly and on time is subject to another addition to that liability in the form of interest. Conversely, a taxpayer is entitled to receive interest from the government when he overpays his taxes either by mistake or as a result of an erroneous IRS determination. Consider the role that interest charges play to encourage taxpayer compliance:

> Interest is not a penalty, although it may be perceived by some taxpayers as tantamount to a penalty. Interest is a charge or compensation for the use or forbearance of money. Compensation for the use of money has been the principal, and at times the only, rationale for charging interest with respect to tax deficiencies or overpayments. . . . [T]he broad principle of interest as a charge for the use of money subsumes a number of different, related theories that individually may justify charging interest—that interest reflects the time value of money, that it provides incentives for prompt satisfaction of debts, or that it is compensation for the credit risk of lending money and collecting unpaid debt.

> With respect to the time value of money rationale, a fundamental premise underlying financial markets is that a dollar receivable in the future is worth less than a dollar received today. The discount may be attributable to the opportunity cost of alternative investments (*e.g.,* prevailing rates of return, including interest rates) as well as inflation and the lenders' expectation concerning risk and the creditworthiness of the borrower. In the commercial context, therefore, interest must be charged to render the lender whole (apart from any profit derived from the service of lending). The failure to charge interest on a tax debt (underpayment or overpayment) for which payment is long-delayed would leave the creditor (either the government or the taxpayer) worse off for having the right to be paid than if that party had been paid immediately.

> Interest provides an incentive for prompt payment of debts. Relative interest rates on different borrowings can affect which creditors a taxpayer with limited resources will prefer to pay. If taxpayers were

not charged interest on a tax debt, they would have an incentive to defer payment of their tax debt and to utilize the funds either for other investment purposes on which a positive rate of return would be earned or to pay other creditors who charged interest. The government would have a similar incentive if it were not charged interest on its tax refunds. . . . Providing that a tax debt bears a market-related interest charge neutralizes (or at least reduces) the advantages that otherwise could be obtained by avoiding payment and investing elsewhere or paying off other creditors. Consequently, interest charges are necessary in both directions to prevent either taxpayers or the government from receiving perverse incentives to fail to settle their tax accounts.

Department of the Treasury, *Report to The Congress on Penalty and Interest Provisions of the Internal Revenue Code, October 1999* (footnotes omitted).

Understanding the theoretical role of interest on overpayments and underpayments is only one piece of the interest puzzle. It is also important to understand the computation of interest on overpayments and underpayments of tax, including applicable rates and accrual periods. The chapter discusses those mechanics, and also examines how interest charges may be minimized through proper planning and the use of administrative remedies. Finally, the chapter discusses the technical rules for netting interest on underpayments and overpayments.

§ 11.02 Interest on Underpayments

As explained above, without an interest charge on unpaid taxes, taxpayers might have an incentive to defer payment of their tax liabilities, in effect obtaining from the government interest-free loans. Under current law, interest charges can amount to a significant portion of the total figure assessed against the taxpayer. Beginning in 2003, the IRS must include with each notice to an individual taxpayer that contains an interest charge (1) the Code section under which the interest is imposed and (2) a detailed computation of the interest charged. I.R.C. § 6631.[1] Notwithstanding this requirement, a practitioner should verify the rate of interest applied and the period during which it is due in order to confirm the IRS's calculations. Specialized software is available to facilitate this calculation.

Contesting the IRS's calculation of interest owed by the taxpayer on an underpayment raises some fairly complicated procedural issues. Section 7481(c) grants the Tax Court jurisdiction to determine interest in a deficiency case, but only after the decision has been entered by the court. Prior to the entry of a decision, the Tax Court has no jurisdiction to consider the question of interest in a deficiency case. To carry out its jurisdictional grant under section 7481, the Tax Court adopted Tax Court Rule 261, which provides for

---

[1] The deadline by which the IRS must comply with the notice requirements in section 6631 was extended from December 31, 2000 until June 30, 2001. Community Renewal Tax Relief Act of 2000, Pub. L. No. 106-554, § 302. Moreover, for any notice issued before June 30, 2003, the IRS, in lieu of providing a detailed computation of the interest charge, need only include a telephone number at which the taxpayer may obtain a copy of the assessment and payment history relating to the interest charge.

a post-decision supplemental proceeding during which disputes concerning interest on deficiencies can be raised. Before the Tax Court will consider the issue, however, the taxpayer must pay the deficiency redetermined by the Tax Court and the interest determined by the IRS.[2]

[A] Applicable Interest Rates

Historically, the interest rate applicable to tax underpayments (deficiencies) was significantly higher than prevailing market interest rates, thereby helping to ensure that taxpayers would pay their tax liabilities promptly. During the 1970s, due to high levels of inflation, the underpayment rate, which was a flat six percent, fell below commercial rates. Concerned that taxpayers would find it more profitable to "borrow" tax funds at the relatively lower underpayment rate rather than pay their correct tax liabilities when due, Congress introduced a regime under which the underpayment (and overpayment) rates were tied directly to the prime rate of interest charged by commercial banks. S. Rep. No. 1357, 93d Cong., 2d Sess. 12-18 (1974). This regime was further refined by the Tax Reform Act of 1986, which based the applicable rate on a fluctuating federal short-term rate. *See* Pub. L. No. 99-514, § 1511(a), 100 Stat. 2085.

Currently, the interest rate on tax deficiencies is computed based on the federal short-term rate specified in section 1274(d), increased by three percentage points. I.R.C. § 6621(a). Most penalties also bear interest at the same rates as tax underpayments. Underpayment interest compounds on a daily basis. I.R.C. § 6622. The federal short-term rate itself is based on the average yield on marketable United States obligations with remaining maturity dates of three years or less. *See* I.R.C. § 6621(b). The IRS publishes the applicable underpayment rate in a quarterly Revenue Ruling, *see, e.g.,* Rev. Rul. 2001-47, 2001-39 I.R.B. 293, which keys the prevailing rate to a series of factor tables in Revenue Procedure 95-17, 1995-1 C.B. 556. The tables permit the taxpayer to calculate the specific dollar amount of interest owed.

The underpayment rate increases to five percentage points above the federal short-term rate for large corporate underpayments owed by a Subchapter C corporation (commonly referred to as "hot interest"). A large corporate underpayment is defined as "any underpayment of a tax by a C corporation for any taxable period if the amount of such underpayment for such period exceeds $100,000." I.R.C. § 6621(c)(3)(A). Although the increased interest rate may also apply to penalties, interest, and additions to the underlying tax, the $100,000 underpayment threshold is computed without regard to these additional amounts. Treas. Reg. § 301.6621-3(b)(2). Assuming a large corporate underpayment exists for a particular year, the increased interest rate applies from the "applicable date," generally the earlier of 30 days after the date of a 30-day letter or notice of deficiency that proposes a deficiency greater than $100,000. I.R.C. § 6621(c)(2). If the corporation pays the tax within 30 days after the date of the letter or notice that triggers the accrual period, the increased interest rate will not apply. I.R.C. § 6621(c)(2)(B)(ii).

---

[2] In addition, the Tax Court has jurisdiction to review a taxpayer's request for interest abatement, a topic discussed in Section 11.02[D][2], and jurisdiction to determine overpayment interest, in certain cases. *See* Section 11.03.

Example: Zylar, Inc., a C corporation, timely filed its 1998 return on March 15, 1999 and included payment of the entire amount of tax shown to be due. On June 1, 2000, the IRS mails to Zylar a 30-day letter proposing a $110,000 tax deficiency, along with penalty and interest additions totaling $60,000. Zylar's threshold underpayment for 1998 is $110,000, thereby triggering the section 6621(c) rate. The "applicable date" is July 1, the 30th day after the IRS sent to Zylar the 30-day letter containing the greater than $100,000 asserted deficiency. During the period March 16, 1999 through July 1, 2000, the interest rate applicable to the $110,000 underpayment, as well as any penalty and interest accruals, is three percentage points above the federal short-term rate. The underpayment rate for the period after July 1, 2000 is five percentage points above the short-term rate.

If underpayment interest is imposed in order to compensate the government for periods during which tax liability is deferred, why apply a higher interest rate to large corporate underpayments? Is the section 6621(c) rate more in the nature of a penalty rather than a remedial measure?

[B] Accrual and Suspension Periods

Interest on a tax deficiency normally begins to run from the last date prescribed for payment of the tax (generally the same date that the underlying return is due). I.R.C. §§ 6601(a), 6151. Even when the taxpayer obtains a valid extension of time either to file the return or to pay the tax, underpayment interest accrues from the original due date of the return. Underpayment interest ceases to accumulate in favor of the government on the date the tax is paid, which is normally considered the date on which the IRS receives the payment, rather than the date the payment is mailed. I.R.C. § 6601(a); Treas. Reg. § 301.6601-1(a)(1).[3]

A rule of administrative convenience allows interest to stop accruing on the date the IRS issues a notice and demand for the underpayment if the taxpayer submits payment within 21 calendar days of the notice and demand (10 business days if the amount demanded exceeds $100,000). I.R.C. § 6601(e)(3). Without this statutory grace period, a taxpayer would otherwise have to estimate when payment would be received by the IRS and then calculate interest appropriately.

As in the case of a tax deficiency, interest accrues on the failure to file penalty in section 6651(a)(1) and the accuracy-related and civil fraud penalties (imposed under "Part I of Subchapter A of Chapter 68") from the due date for the underlying return (including extensions) to the date the penalty is paid. I.R.C. § 6601(e)(2)(B). In addition, prompt payment of these three penalties within the 21 or 10-day window after notice and demand for their payment prevents any further accrual of interest during the period after the date of

---

[3] The IRS must assess and collect underpayment interest within the period that the underlying tax may be collected. I.R.C. § 6601(g). The deadline, therefore, is measured with reference to the last day for collecting the tax under section 6502, rather than the last day for assessing the related tax under section 6501. Underpayment interest is assessed and collected in the same manner as taxes. I.R.C. § 6601(e).

the notice and demand. Treas. Reg. § 301.6601-1(f)(4). For most other penalties and additions to tax, a special rule in Code section 6601(e)(2) affords the taxpayer an opportunity to *prevent* any interest from accruing if those amounts are paid within 21 days after notice and demand for their payment (10 days if the amount in issue equals or exceeds $100,000). Even if the taxpayer does not promptly pay the penalty within these specified time periods, interest accrues only from the date the IRS issues the notice and demand. I.R.C. § 6601(e)(2).

A taxpayer who decides not to contest the results of an IRS examination can also suspend interest on a tax deficiency by executing a Waiver of Restrictions on Assessment (Form 870). If the IRS does not make notice and demand for payment within 30 days after the taxpayer files the waiver, underpayment interest is suspended for the period starting after the 30-day period following the filing of the waiver. Interest starts to accrue again on the date the IRS issues a notice and demand. I.R.C. § 6601(c).

As noted in Chapter 10, the IRS Reform Act introduced a new suspension period that applies to both interest and penalties when the IRS delays in notifying the taxpayer that additional tax may be due. *See* I.R.C. § 6404(g). Set forth below is an excerpt from the legislative history of section 6404(g), explaining how the new provision operates and its underlying purpose.

CONFERENCE COMMITTEE REPORT ON INTERNAL REVENUE SERVICE RESTRUCTURING AND REFORM ACT OF 1998
H.R. Conf. Rep. No. 105-599 (1998)

Suspension of interest and certain penalties where Secretary fails to contact individual taxpayer. (Sec. 3305 of the bill and Sec. 6404 of the Code)

[Senate Report]

Present Law

In general, interest and penalties accrue during periods for which taxes are unpaid without regard to whether the taxpayer is aware that there is tax due.

Reasons for Change

The Committee believes that the IRS should promptly inform taxpayers of their obligations with respect to tax deficiencies and amounts due. In addition, the Committee is concerned that accrual of interest and penalties absent prompt resolution of tax deficiencies may lead to the perception that the IRS is more concerned about collecting revenue than in resolving taxpayer's problems.

Explanation of Provision

The provision suspends the accrual of penalties and interest after 1 year if the IRS has not sent the taxpayer a notice of deficiency within 1 year following the date which is the later of (1) the original due date of the return or (2) the date on which the taxpayer timely filed the return. The suspension only applies to taxpayers who file a timely tax return. The provision applies only to individuals and does not apply to the failure to pay penalty, in the case of fraud, or with respect to criminal penalties. Interest and penalties resume 21 days after the IRS sends a notice and demand for payment to the taxpayer.

Effective Date

The provision is effective for taxable years ending after the date of enactment.

House Bill

No provision.

Conference Agreement

The conference agreement follows the Senate amendment, with the following modifications. With respect to taxable years beginning before January 1, 2004, the 1-year period is increased to 18 months. Interest and penalties are suspended if the IRS fails to send a notice specifically stating the taxpayer's liability and the basis for the liability within the specific period. Interest and penalties resume 21 days after the IRS sends the notice to the taxpayer. The provision is applied separately with respect to each item or adjustment. The provision does not apply when a taxpayer has self-assessed the tax.

The notice required by Code section 6404(g) must "specifically stat[e] the taxpayer's liability and the basis for the liability. . . ." I.R.C. § 6404(g)(1)(A). The Office of Chief Counsel released guidance in 2000 explaining what information the notice must contain to satisfy section 6404(g). Notice N(35)000-172 (March 22, 2000). The following is an excerpt:

> For purposes of section 6404(g), the Service provides notice of the tax liability to the taxpayer if it sends a writing to the taxpayer at his or her last known address and that writing includes the amount of the liability, the basis for that liability, and sufficient information or explanation regarding the adjustment to enable the taxpayer to challenge the adjustment. Math error notices, Underreporter Program (URP) notices, revenue agent reports (RARs), 30-day letters with accompanying RARs, and statutory notices of deficiency with accompanying Form 886A, Explanation of Items, generally will be sufficient notices for purposes of section 6404(g). This list is not exclusive, and notice may be provided by letter or other writing that satisfies the statutory requirements. Audit letters that only state which items are under examination, however, are not sufficient to constitute notice for purposes of section 6404(g).

In the case of an adjustment resulting in an increased deficiency in a Tax Court proceeding, service of the pleading affirmatively alleging the increased deficiency will constitute notice of the liability. If the increased deficiency is not raised in the pleadings, but is agreed to by the parties in a stipulated decision, the stipulated decision and a letter transmitting such decision to the petitioner for signature will constitute notice of the liability. Therefore, if the increased deficiency was not affirmatively raised in the pleadings, the letter transmitting the proposed decision document to the petitioner must include the information needed to constitute a notice under section 6404(g), i.e., the amount of the liability, the basis for that liability, and sufficient information or explanation regarding the adjustment to enable the taxpayer to challenge the adjustment.

* * *

EXAMPLE 2. T, an individual taxpayer, filed his 1998 individual income tax return on April 15, 1999. The IRS informed T that an examination of his return would be conducted. The audit was completed on January 8, 2001, when, at a closing conference, the IRS presented to T an RAR which explained in detail various adjustments to T's return, resulting in a proposed deficiency of $5,250. The section 6651(a)(3) penalty was imposed on T for failure to pay an amount required to be shown on a return, and the section 6662(b) penalty was imposed on T for the substantial understatement of income tax.

The RAR constitutes a notice under section 6404(g) because it states the amount of the liability and provides sufficient information and explanation regarding the adjustments to T's return to enable him to challenge the adjustments. Because the RAR was provided after the close of the 18-month period prescribed under section 6404(g)(1)(A), interest on the deficiency is suspended beginning on October 17, 2000. (The 18-month period ends on Monday, October 16, 2000, because section 7503 provides that, when the last day prescribed under authority of the internal revenue laws for performing any act falls on Saturday, Sunday, or a legal holiday, the performance of the act shall be considered timely if performed on the next succeeding day which is not a Saturday, Sunday, or a legal holiday.) Interest that accrued on the deficiency during the preceding 18-month period is not abated. The last day for the suspension of interest is January 29, 2001, which is the 21st day after the day on which the RAR was provided (January 8, 2001).

Under section 6404(g), the section 6651(a)(3) penalty is not suspended for T even though the IRS failed to provide a notice within the time period prescribed in section 6404(g)(1)(A). Interest on the section 6651(a)(3) penalty is not suspended because, under section 6601(e)(2)(A), interest is imposed on the penalty from the date of notice and demand. Thus, any interest that may accrue on the section 6651(a)(3) penalty will do so only after the suspension period because the suspension period ends prior to notice and demand. In addition, section 6404(g) does not apply to the section 6662(b) penalty because the penalty is, in general, 20% of the taxpayer's underpayment and is not computed by reference to the period of time a failure relating to the return continues to exist. Therefore, the section 6662(b) penalty is not suspended for T. Under section 6601(e)(2)(B), interest is imposed on the section 6662(b) penalty from the date on which the return is required to be filed (including extensions) until the date the penalty is paid. Therefore, interest on the section 6662(b) penalty is suspended for T during the suspension period (October 17, 2000, to January 29, 2001).

EXAMPLE 3. T, an individual taxpayer, filed his 1998 individual income tax return on April 15, 1999. On December 4, 1999, the IRS mailed to T's last known address an Underreporter Program (URP) notice proposing that T had a deficiency of $150 resulting from the underreporting of interest income, which was detected through the computerized matching of Forms 1099 INT. Penalties were found not to apply with respect to this adjustment. The URP notice included a list of the Forms 1099 submitted to the IRS for T by a particular payor and revealed that the interest income reported by the payor was greater than the interest income shown on T's return. T's return was also selected for examination, and on October 19, 2000, the IRS mailed to T's last known address a 30-day letter with an RAR proposing that T had an additional deficiency of $350 resulting from the disallowance of deductions for travel and entertainment, professional fees, and subscriptions to trade publications due to a lack of substantiation. Penalties were found not to apply with respect to these adjustments.

The URP notice is a notice under section 6404(g) because it states the amount of the liability and provides sufficient information and explanation regarding the underreporting to enable T to challenge the adjustment. Inasmuch as the notice was provided before the close of the 18-month period prescribed in section 6404(g)(1)(A), interest on the deficiency resulting from the underreporting of interest income is not suspended under this section. The 30-day letter is also a notice under section 6404(g) because it provides sufficient information and explanation regarding the disallowance of the deductions to enable T to challenge the adjustment. The 30-day letter, however, was provided after the close of the 18-month period prescribed in section 6404(g)(1)(A). The URP notice, which was issued prior to the close of the 18-month period prescribed in section 6404(g)(1)(A), pertained only to the underreporting of interest income and does not prevent the suspension of interest for other items not in the URP notice. Thus, interest on the deficiency resulting from the disallowance of deductions, as set forth in the 30-day letter, is suspended beginning on October 17, 2000. Interest that accrued on the deficiency during the preceding 18-month period is not abated. The last day for the suspension of interest is November 9, 2000, which is the 21st day after the day on which the notice was provided (October 19, 2000).

Is the interest suspension provision in section 6404(g) consistent with the use of money principles underlying the interest rules? *See* Section 11.01. Is it fair?

[C] Deductibility of Interest on Underpayments

In considering the actual cost of a deficiency, taxpayers should consider not the pre-tax interest cost, but its after-tax cost. This raises the question of whether interest on underpayments is deductible. As you may recall from your income tax class, Code section 163(a) permits an above-the-line deduction for interest on indebtedness properly allocable to a trade or business activity. In contrast, personal interest (defined by exclusion in section 163(h)), is not deductible. If an individual taxpayer incurs interest on an underpayment of tax liability, is that underpayment interest properly characterized as nondeductible personal interest? What if the interest is attributable to a tax underpayment arising from the taxpayer's trade or business activities?

Temporary Treasury Regulation 1.163-9T specifically provides that personal interest includes interest "[p]aid on underpayments of individual Federal, State or local income taxes and on indebtedness used to pay such taxes . . . regardless of the source of the income generating the tax liability." The validly of this regulatory interpretation of section 163 has lead to a considerable amount of litigation. Consider the following case.

REDLARK v. COMMISSIONER
United States Court of Appeals, Ninth Circuit
141 F.3d 936 (1998)

FLETCHER, CIRCUIT JUDGE:

The Commissioner of Internal Revenue appeals the decision of the tax court striking down Temporary Treasury Regulation § 1.163-9T(b)(2)(i)(A). That regulation disallows the deduction of interest paid on overdue individual income taxes, even when the source of the personal income that gives rise to the tax deficiency is a business or trade. Plaintiffs James and Cheryl Redlark claim that the regulation is in conflict with the relevant provision of the tax code, 26 U.S.C. ("I.R.C.") § 163(h)(2)(A). A sharply divided tax court accepted the Redlarks' position. *See* Redlark v. C.I.R., 106 T.C. 31, 106 T.C. No. 2 (1996). The only other circuit to address this question, however, has concluded that the regulation constitutes a permissible construction of a facially ambiguous statutory provision. *See* Miller v. U.S., 65 F.3d 687 (8th Cir. 1995). We agree with the Eighth Circuit and reverse the decision of the tax court.

I.

The facts in this case are not in dispute, so we summarize them only briefly. Between 1979 and 1985, James and Cheryl Redlark operated an unincorporated business, Carrier Communications, that installed telephone equipment. The Redlarks kept the books and records of the business using the accrual method of accounting. They reported the income and expenses on their joint federal income tax returns, however, using the cash-basis method of accounting. When the Internal Revenue Service examined the Redlarks' returns for these years, it determined that extensive adjustments were necessary. After the parties settled several tax shelter issues and corrected various accounting errors, the adjustments resulted in additional assessments for tax, penalties, and interest for the years 1982-84.

The interest on these assessments amounted to $361,345 for 1982, $42,279 for 1984, and $42,126 for 1985. The Redlarks made the interest payments in installments from 1987 to 1990. They then claimed deductions on their personal income tax returns for portions of the interest payments: On their 1989 return, they claimed a business expense of $195,463 based on the interest paid in that year on their 1982, 1984 and 1985 tax deficiencies; and in 1990, they claimed $23,323 as a business expense for the interest paid on their 1985 deficiency. These deductions represented the interest payments on the portions of the deficiencies that the Redlarks determined to have resulted from accounting errors and that were thus (they asserted) allocable to Carrier Communications. During an audit of the Redlarks' 1989 and 1990 returns, however, the Commissioner determined that none of the interest on tax deficiencies was properly deductible. The controlling regulation, Temporary Treasury Regulation § 1.163-9T(b)(2)(i)(A), specifies that interest on income tax deficiencies is not attributable to a taxpayer's conduct of trade or business, regardless of the source of the income, but rather is "personal interest" within the meaning of I.R.C. § 163(h).

The issue before us is whether § 1.163-9T(b)(2)(i)(A) is a permissible interpretation of I.R.C. § 163(h). On its face, I.R.C. § 163(h) does not address the deductibility of interest payments on business-related personal income tax deficiencies. The statute simply disallows deductions for all "personal interest," unless the interest in question is "paid or accrued on indebtedness *properly allocable* to a trade or business (other than the trade or business of performing services as an employee)." I.R.C. § 163(h)(2)(A) (emphasis added). In promulgating Temporary Treasury Regulation § 1.163-9T(b)(2)(i)(A), the Commissioner took the position that interest on personal income tax deficiencies always constitutes a personal obligation and so is never "properly allocable to a trade or business." The parties agree that the disputed interest amounts are not deductible under the regulation. The parties disagree vigorously as to whether the regulation constitutes a valid interpretation of the Internal Revenue Code.

II.

This dispute centers on the meaning of the words, "properly allocable," in I.R.C. § 163(h)(2)(A). The Redlarks argue that those words refer narrowly and unambiguously to questions of accounting practice. Prior to the addition of § 163(h)(2)(A) to the tax code in the Tax Reform Act of 1986, they explain, there was a consistent body of case law holding that interest on business-related personal income tax deficiencies was deductible, provided that the deficiencies constituted an ordinary and necessary expense in the conduct of the business. *See* I.R.C. § 162(a) ("There shall be allowed as a deduction all the ordinary and necessary expenses paid or incurred during the taxable year in carrying on any trade or business . . . ."); *see also* Miller v. U.S., 65 F.3d 687, 690 (8th Cir. 1995) ("Prior to the 1986 Tax Reform Act, courts consistently held that tax deficiency interest arising from business income was deductible as an ordinary and necessary business expense under I.R.C. §§ 62(a)(1) and 162."). It is the Redlarks' position that Congress incorporated this body of case law into I.R.C. § 163(h)(2)(A) when it used the words, "properly allocable." Under their reading, those words refer only to the "propriety," from an accounting standpoint, of "allocating" personal income tax deficiencies to the conduct of a trade or business. The statute must be read, the Redlarks argue, to incorporate the pre-1986 case law and thus to provide unambiguously that interest from income tax deficiencies is deductible when the deficiencies in question constitute an ordinary and necessary expense in the relevant trade or business.

According to the Commissioner, however, the Redlarks' reading of I.R.C. § 163(h)(2)(A) is far too narrow. It is the Commissioner's position that the words, "properly allocable," are deliberately ambiguous and constitute a delegation of authority to the Commissioner to determine when an expense may "properly" be "allocated" to a trade or business and when it may not. That determination, the Commissioner argues, may legitimately involve questions of accounting policy, provided that the policies that the Commissioner promotes are consistent with other provisions of the statute and the purpose of the Code as a whole. Thus, while the Redlarks may have provided a reasonable argument for the proposition that their personal income tax deficiencies should "properly" be considered "allocable" to their business as an accounting matter, theirs is not the only reasonable construction of the phrase "properly allocable," its pedigree from earlier tax court decisions notwithstanding. Rather, the Commissioner argues, the I.R.S. has determined, as a matter of general policy, that personal income tax always constitutes a personal obligation so that deficiencies in meeting that obligation are never "properly allocable" to the taxpayer's trade or business. It is the Commissioner's position that such a determination constitutes an appropriate exercise of the authority that Congress delegated to the Commissioner by using a deliberately ambiguous term in the statute.

We agree with the Commissioner. It is not our function to determine what would be the best or most advisable method for the Commissioner to employ in implementing the tax code. "Congress has delegated to the Commissioner, not to the courts, the task of prescribing all needful rules and regulations for the enforcement of the Internal Revenue Code." United States v. Correll, 389 U.S. 299, 307, 19 L. Ed. 2d 537, 88 S. Ct. 445 (1967). So long as the Commissioner issues regulations that "implement the congressional mandate in some reasonable manner," Rowan Cos. v. United States, 452 U.S. 247, 252, 68 L. Ed. 2d 814, 101 S. Ct. 2288 (1981), we must defer to the Commissioner's interpretation. Only if the code has a meaning that is clear, unambiguous, and in conflict with a regulation does a court have the authority to reject the Commissioner's reasoned interpretation and invalidate the regulation. *See* Chevron U.S.A. v. Natural Resources Defense Council, 467 U.S. 837, 841-44,

81 L. Ed. 2d 694, 104 S. Ct. 2778 (1984). "If Congress has explicitly left a gap for the agency to fill, there is an express delegation of authority to the agency to elucidate a specific provision of the statute by regulation." *Id.* at 843-44. Where this is so, prior decisions of reviewing courts that seem to have favored a different interpretation of the statute will not override the agency's reasonable construction. *See id.* at 841-42. Rather, "legislative regulations are given controlling weight unless they are arbitrary, capricious, or manifestly contrary to the statute." *Id.* at 844. *See also* NationsBank of North Carolina, N.A. v. Annuity Life Ins., 513 U.S. 251, 256-57, 130 L. Ed. 2d 740, 115 S. Ct. 810 (1995).

As an initial matter, we find untenable the Redlarks' assertion that the words, "properly allocable," unambiguously specify that interest on business-related personal income tax deficiencies should be deductible. The Eighth Circuit has stated the matter succinctly.

> I.R.C. § 163(h)(2)(A) generally disallows any deduction for personal interest paid or accrued by a noncorporate taxpayer. Personal interest is defined as any interest with specified exceptions including interest on debt allocable to a trade or business. The provision, however, does not define what constitutes business interest. Therefore, there is an implicit legislative delegation of authority to the Commissioner to clarify whether income tax deficiency interest is "properly allocable to a trade or business."

Miller, 65 F.3d at 690. When Congress uses such broad, generalized language in defining an important term in a statute, a claimant must make a compelling argument, based on the language and history of the statute itself, that Congress can only have intended one meaning to attach to that language before we will find that the administering agency has no authority to employ a different construction. The Redlarks have offered no such compelling arguments.[n.1]

[n.1] We note that the "properly allocable" language was not a part of the Tax Reform Act as originally drafted, but entered the Code by amendment in 1988. Originally, I.R.C. § 163(h)(2) provided:

> For purposes of this subsection, the term "personal interest" means any interest allowable as a deduction under this chapter other than—

> (A) interest paid or accrued on indebtedness incurred or continued in connection with the conduct of a trade or business (other than the trade or business of performing services as an employee).

I.R.C. § 163(h)(2) (1986). Congress amended this definition in the Technical and Miscellaneous Revenue Act of 1988, Pub. L. No. 100-647, 102 Stat. 3342, 3390. That Act replaced the words, "incurred or continued in connection with the conduct of a trade or business," with the "properly allocable" language that is now before us. Clearly, the original language of the statute would have strengthened, at least to some extent, the Redlark's position that Congress intended for interest incurred on business-related expenses, perhaps including ordinary tax deficiencies on personal income derived from a trade or business, to be deductible.

As is so frequently the case, one could use this amendment of the statutory language to craft arguments militating either in favor of a finding of ambiguity, or against it. One could argue, for example, that Congress intended to change the import of § 163 by replacing the original, specific language with the more general "properly allocable;" or, alternatively, that a change effected in a "Technical and Miscellaneous Revenue Act" is merely ministerial, such that "properly allocable" should be read in harmony with the more specific language that preceded it. While we find the former argument to be the more persuasive, we expressly do not depend upon it in reaching our decision today. We simply rely on the statutory language in its current form.

Contrary to the Redlarks' assertions, the fact that courts consistently allowed the type of deduction they are now seeking before the enactment of the Tax Reform Act of 1986 and its implementing regulations does not lend support to the argument that such a deduction must continue to be allowable under the new statute. Congress regularly affords administrative agencies leeway in which to change or modify their regulations in response to changing economic conditions and policy concerns. That is the entire point of a delegation of limited policy-making authority under an ambiguously worded statute. "An initial agency interpretation is not instantly carved in stone. On the contrary, the agency, to engage in informed rulemaking, must consider varying interpretations and the wisdom of its policy on a continuing basis." *Chevron,* 467 U.S. at 863-64. Thus, an agency may "from time to time change[ ] its interpretation" of a statutory term without calling into question its authority to interpret that term. *Id.* at 863. If an agency's own previous gloss on an ambiguous statute does not render the statute any the less a proper object of interpretation, neither does the previous gloss of a reviewing court do so. *See also id.* at 841-42.

Having determined that the term, "properly allocable," is subject to interpretation by the Commissioner, we now must decide whether Temporary Treasury Regulation § 1.163-9T(b)(2)(i)(A) represents a reasonable interpretation of the term. We have little trouble in doing so. As the Eighth Circuit noted, the legislative history that attended the enactment of I.R.C. § 163(h) is entirely consonant with the Commissioner's conclusion that personal income tax obligations are always essentially personal in nature. *See Miller,* 65 F.3d at 690-91. In explaining the import of I.R.C. § 163(h), the report of the Conference Committee says that "personal interest also generally includes interest on tax deficiencies." H.R. Conf. Rep. No. 841, 99th Cong., 2d Sec. II-154. There is no suggestion in the report that Congress intended to preserve an exception for interest on income tax deficiencies that arise in the ordinary course of a business.

The General Explanation of the Tax Reform Act of 1986 likewise supports the Commissioner's interpretation of the Code. *See* Staff of the Joint Committee on Taxation, 100th Cong., 1st Sess., *General Explanation of the Tax Reform Act of 1986* 266 (Comm. Print 1987). While such post-enactment explanations cannot properly be described as "legislative history," they are at least instructive as to the reasonableness of an agency's interpretation of a facially ambiguous statute. *See Miller,* 65 F.3d at 690; Estate of Wallace v. Commissioner, 965 F.2d 1038, 1050-51 n.15 (11th Cir. 1992); McDonald v. Commissioner, 764 F.2d 322, 336 n.25 (5th Cir. 1985). In this case, the general explanation clearly supports the Commissioner's interpretation, providing that "personal interest also includes interest on underpayments of individual Federal, State or local income taxes notwithstanding that all or a portion of the income may have arisen in a trade or business, because such taxes are not considered derived from the conduct of a trade or business." *General Explanation, supra,* at 266; *see also id.* at 266 n.60 ("Personal interest does not include interest on taxes, *other than income taxes,* that are incurred in connection with a trade or business.") (emphasis added); *Miller,* 65 F.3d at 690-91.

All that the Redlarks have done to support their argument that the Commissioner's interpretation of the Code is an unreasonable one is to point once again to the consistent practice, prior to 1986, of allowing deductions on income tax deficiency interest of the kind that they seek here. But, as we have explained, the fact that the reasonable construction that an agency adopts in interpreting an ambiguous statute is inconsistent with past interpretations or the past practice of the agency does not, without more, call into question the propriety or the reasonableness of the new construction. *See Chevron,* 467 U.S. at 863-64; *see also* National Muffler Dealers Assoc. v. United States, 440 U.S. 472, 485-86, 59 L. Ed. 2d 519, 99 S. Ct. 1304 (1979).

Temporary Treasury Regulation § 1.163-9T(b)(2)(i)(A) represents a reasonable interpretation of a facially ambiguous statute. It is neither arbitrary, capricious, nor in conflict with any other statutory provision or the purposes of the Code as a whole. That being so, our inquiry is at an end.

We reverse the decision of the tax court and remand for further proceedings consistent with this opinion. Reversed and remanded.[4]

Notwithstanding the legislative history relied upon by both the Tax Court and Ninth Circuit in *Redlark,* is there any reason from a policy standpoint to treat underpayment interest allocable to a trade or business activity any differently from any other trade or business expense? Would it make a difference if the interest expense the taxpayer seeks to deduct arises not from the taxpayer's activities as a sole proprietor, but instead relates to deficiencies assessed against a partnership or S corporation in which the taxpayer was a partner or shareholder? *See Fitzmaurice v. United States*, 87 A.F.T.R. 2d 1254 (S.D. Tex. 2001) (deficiency interest similarly not deductible under section 163); *Davis v. United States*, 71 F. Supp. 2d 622 (W.D. Tex. 1999) (same).

If we accept the majority's position that underpayment interest is nondeductible under Code section 163, could the interest be deducted under section 212(3) as an ordinary and necessary expense "in connection with the determination, collection, or refund of any tax"? *See* Keith E. Engel, "Deducting Interest on Federal Income Tax Underpayments: A Roadmap Through a 50-Year Quagmire," 16 Va. Tax Rev. 237 (1996); *see also McDonnell v. United States*, 180 F.3d 721 (6th Cir. 1999).

---

4 [There remains a split of authority over whether Temporary Treasury regulation 1.163-9T is valid, but the tide of support seems to favor the regulation. The Fourth, Sixth, Seventh, Eighth and Ninth Circuits, as well as some District Courts, have upheld the validity of the regulation. *See, e.g.,* Kikalos v. Commissioner, 109 F.3d 791 (7th Cir. 1999) (citing cases); Allen v. United States, 173 F.3d 533 (4th Cir. 1999) (same); *see also* Stecher v. United States, 1998 U.S. Dist. LEXIS 10173, 82 A.F.T.R.2d (RIA) 5110 (D. Colo. 1998); In re Vale, 204 B.R. 716 (Bankr. N.D. Ind. 1996). The Tax Court and other District Courts have found it invalid, but have been reversed on appeal. *See, e.g.,* Redlark v. Commissioner, 106 T.C. 31 (1996), *rev'd*, 141 F.3d 936 (9th Cir. 1998); *Kikalos, supra.* Eds.]

[D] Limiting the Accrual of Deficiency Interest

[1] Advance Remittances

A taxpayer who is under examination faces the prospect of interest accruing on the subsequently determined tax deficiency from the date the underlying tax return was due. Having received from the IRS a 30-day letter, what steps might the taxpayer take to prevent any further interest accumulation? Revenue Procedure 84-58, discussed in Section 8.02[B] of Chapter 8 in connection with tax refunds, provides one alternative. That is, to avoid the accumulation of interest on underpayments during the audit and appeals process, a taxpayer may remit an amount to the IRS prior to formal assessment of the deficiency. Revenue Procedure 84-58 clarifies the rules for characterizing advance remittances as either tax payments or deposits in the nature of cash bonds. Treatment of the remittance as a payment or deposit depends in part upon whether the remittance is made before or after the IRS formally proposes liability against the taxpayer. Unless designated by the taxpayer as a payment, a remittance made prior to the issuance of a written proposed liability (for example, a 30-day letter) will be treated as a deposit in the nature of a cash bond. Rev. Proc. 84-58 § 4.04(1). Absent a designation to the contrary, an advance remittance made *in response to* a proposed liability will generally be treated as a payment. *Id.* at § 4.03(1).

Whether characterized as a deposit or payment, the remittance stops the accrual of interest from the date the amount is received by the IRS. *Id.* at § 5.01. Designating the remittance as a deposit, however, affords the taxpayer the opportunity to stop the running of interest, while retaining the right, in most cases, to request a return of the remittance prior to the time the IRS assesses the tax. *Id.* at § 4.03(1). A remittance designated as a payment is returnable to the taxpayer only as an overpayment. If the taxpayer requests a return of the deposited amount prior to assessment (or the deposited amount exceeds any assessment), the amount returned will not include interest paid for the time the remittance was in the IRS's possession. *Id.* at § 5.04. A payment, on the other hand, accrues interest in the taxpayer's favor from the date the payment is made on the amount that is ultimately returned to the taxpayer. *Id.* at § 5.01.

A taxpayer who makes a remittance to the IRS in order to suspend interest accruals must be careful to ensure that the remittance does not deprive the Tax Court of jurisdiction over the deficiency. As discussed in Chapter 7, as a general rule, a remittance properly characterized as a deposit does not impair a taxpayer's right to petition and contest the proposed deficiency determination in Tax Court. If an amount characterized as a payment is remitted *prior to* the receipt of a statutory notice of deficiency, the taxpayer may be denied access to Tax Court unless the IRS subsequently determines a deficiency in excess of the amount paid. If the taxpayer pays an asserted deficiency *in response to* a validly issued notice of deficiency, that payment will not deprive the Tax Court of jurisdiction over the proposed deficiency. I.R.C. § 6213(b)(4); *see also* Rev. Proc. 84-58 at § 4.01.

[2] Interest Abatement

Under most circumstances, the IRS views the application of interest as nothing more than a mathematical computation based on the rate of interest and the appropriate accrual period. Consequently, the interest portion of an amount owed the government normally may not be reduced except where the underlying tax liability is reduced as well. Over the years, however, Congress has identified situations where, in the interests of fairness, the IRS should consider abating a taxpayer's interest charge on an otherwise unchanged liability.

Under Code section 6404(e), the IRS has discretionary authority to abate interest accruing on tax deficiencies where an IRS official fails to perform a ministerial or managerial act in a timely manner or makes an error in the performance of such an act. The authority to abate interest applies to interest that accrued during the period attributable to the unreasonable error or delay and only if no significant aspect of the delay or error is attributable to the actions of the taxpayer.[5] According to Treasury Regulation § 301.6404-2(b)(2), a ministerial act is a procedural or mechanical act occurring during the processing of a taxpayer's case that does not involve the exercise of judgment or discretion on the part of the IRS representative. Examples include: (1) a failure to timely transfer a case to another IRS office after the taxpayer's transfer request has been approved, and (2) an untimely issuance of a notice of deficiency after the examination of a taxpayer's return has been completed and the notice prepared. *See* Treas. Reg. § 301.6404-2(c).

The IRS's abatement discretion was expanded in 1996 to take into account unreasonable errors or delays by the IRS while performing a managerial act, defined as "an administrative act that occurs during the processing of a taxpayer's case involving a temporary or permanent loss of records or the exercise of judgment or discretion relating to management of personnel." Treas. Reg. § 301.6404-2(b)(1). Managerial acts also include delays that might occur when an IRS employee is transferred or the employee suffers an extended absence due to illness, leave or retraining. *See* Treas. Reg. § 301.6404-2(c). Exs. 3-5. An IRS representative's interpretation of substantive federal tax law does not constitute either a ministerial or managerial act.

The Tax Court is afforded jurisdiction to review the IRS's failure to exercise its abatement authority. I.R.C. § 6404(h)(1). The statutorily prescribed standard of review is abuse of discretion. Consider this case.

---

[5] *See also* I.R.C. § 6404(d) (authorizing IRS to abate interest on a deficiency attributable to a mathematical error made by an IRS employee while assisting a taxpayer in preparing a return), (e)(2) (authorizing IRS to abate underpayment interest on an erroneous refund until such time as the IRS demands repayment of the erroneous refund).

KRUGMAN v. COMMISSIONER
United States Tax Court
112 T.C. 230 (1999)

COLVIN, JUDGE:

On April 10, 1997, respondent issued a final determination partially disallowing petitioner's claim to abate interest. Petitioner timely filed a petition under section 6404(g)[6] and Rule 280.

* * *

FINDINGS OF FACT

Some of the facts have been stipulated and are so found.

A. Petitioner

Petitioner lived in Grand Junction, Colorado, when he filed the petition to abate interest. He graduated from the University of Nebraska with degrees in architecture and construction management. He worked in energy conservation before 1995 and in home construction after 1995.

B. Petitioner's Returns For 1985–91

On July 21, 1992, petitioner read an article in the Rocky Mountain News which said that respondent had designed a program to encourage nonfilers to file late returns without being subject to criminal penalties. The program required nonfilers to pay back taxes and penalties. The program offered a payment plan for payment of taxes and penalties. The article did not mention interest payments. On October 27, 1992, in response to the article, petitioner filed Federal income tax returns for 1985 to 1991.

Petitioner reported on his 1985 return that he owed $3,199 in tax and that he had not paid any of that amount. He did not make any payment with his 1985 return.

C. Respondent's Notices in 1993

On April 12, 1993, respondent sent petitioner a notice stating that petitioner owed tax of $3,416.31 and a penalty of $854.08 for filing late, for a total of $4,270.39. The notice said:

> We changed your 1985 return because: an error was made on your return when the amount of your social security self employment was transferred from Schedule SE (Form 1040).

> As a result of these changes, you owe $4,270.39. Please pay the amount you owe by April 22, 1993, to avoid more interest and penalties. * * *

---

[6] [This was redesignated as section 6404(i) by the IRS Reform Act, Pub. L. 105-206, secs. 3305(a), 3309(a), 112 Stat. 685, 743, 745, and redesignated again as section 6404(h)(1) by the Victims of Terrorism Tax Relief Act of 2001, Pub. L. 107-134. Eds.]

On June 21, 1993, respondent notified petitioner that he had an unpaid tax balance of $3,695.34. Respondent calculated this amount by subtracting from $4,270.39 (balance shown on the April 12, 1993, notice), overpayments from petitioner's returns of $238 for 1989 and $337.05 for 1990. This notice stated that petitioner did not owe a late payment penalty or interest. The notice said: "To avoid additional penalties and interest, send your payment for the amount you owe by 07-01-93."

D. The Installment Agreement Form and Petitioner's Payments

In July 1993, petitioner signed a preprinted installment agreement (Form 433-D), which had no dollar amounts written on it, and sent it to respondent. The Form 433-D that respondent used in 1993 states in part:

I/We agree that the Federal taxes shown above, *PLUS ALL PENALTIES AND INTEREST PROVIDED BY LAW,* will be paid as follows: [Emphasis in original.]

$_____ will be paid on _____ and $_____ will be paid no later than the _____ of each month thereafter until the total liability is paid in full. I/we also agree that the above installment payment will be increased or decreased as follows:

Date of increase (or decrease)	/ /	/ /
Amount of increase (or decrease)	$	
New installment amount	$	

In July 1993, petitioner paid respondent $1,000 to be applied to his 1985 tax liability. On August 16, 1993, respondent sent petitioner a letter stating in pertinent part the following:

We have set up an installment agreement to help you pay the amount you owe for the tax period(s) shown above. Your payments are $74.87, due on the 15th of each month, beginning on Sep. 15, 1993.

* * *

In about six weeks, we will send you a notice showing the amount of tax, penalty, and interest you owe. You do not have to answer that notice.

Petitioner did not receive any other correspondence relating to his 1985 tax liability until around September 1, 1993, when he received a payment notice which said that he had a monthly payment of $74.87 due by September 15, 1993. It said: "Total balance owed including penalties and interest: $2,695.34."

Respondent sent petitioner a statement each month for 19 months which stated the amount of the payment due ($74.87), the due date of the next installment, and erroneously stated the "Total balance owed including penalties and interest", with an amount that declined with each payment. None of the notices included interest.

Petitioner timely paid at least $100 per month, which was more than respondent's notices said was due. Respondent's notice dated March 1, 1995, said that "total balance owed including penalties and interest" was $180.24. On March 9, 1995, petitioner paid $180.24 to respondent.

E. Respondent's August 9, 1995, Notice of Interest Due and Events Thereafter

On August 7, 1995, respondent assessed interest of $5,284.44 that had accrued for petitioner's 1985 tax year from April 15, 1986, to August 7, 1995.

Respondent sent petitioner a notice on August 9, 1995, which stated in part as follows:

YOUR NEXT PAYMENT IS DUE SOON

Your next payment of $74.87 is due on 08-15-95.

The current status of your account is shown below. We apply installment payments to tax periods in the order they are assessed.

| | | TAX PERIOD | |
FORM NUMBER	CAF	ENDED	AMOUNT
1040	0	12-31-85	$ 6,019.10
Payment due	—	—	$ 74.87

The amount shown doesn't include accumulated penalty and interest. Please contact us for the total amount due.

On September 14, 1995, petitioner wrote a letter to respondent in which he stated that he had made his final payment of $180.24 for his 1985 tax liability and asked respondent to abate the $6,019.10 claim. On April 21, 1996, petitioner filed a Claim for Refund and Request for Abatement (Form 843) for his 1985 tax year, in which he asked respondent to abate interest that had accrued because of respondent's errors and delays and additional but unspecified, penalties. Petitioner contacted respondent's Problem Resolution Office in August 1996. The case was assigned to the Problem Resolution Office by August 29, 1996.

On September 12, 1996, respondent abated $352.11 of interest that had accrued from March 1, 1995, to August 7, 1995, but otherwise rejected petitioner's request without providing any helpful explanation. In that letter, respondent's Problem Resolution Program[7] staff said:

We are sorry, but we cannot allow your request to remove all of the interest charged for the tax period shown above [ending December 31, 1985]. This letter is your notice that your request is partially disallowed. We allowed only $352.11 of the request for the following reasons:

Interest waiver applies from March 1, 1995, through August 7, 1995. A notice was issued on March 1, 1995, giving you an erroneous

---

[7] [The IRS Reform Act replaced the Problem Resolution Program with local Taxpayer Advocates who coordinate with the National Taxpayer Advocate to resolve taxpayer-specific problems. *See* Section 1.03 of Chapter 1. Eds.]

payoff amount which you paid. The prior notices issued cannot be considered because the total payoff amounts were not paid. On August 7, 1995 a notice was issued giving you a correct payoff amount. For your information, enclosed is a detailed interest computation of your tax account for 1985.

The current balance due for the tax period ended December 31, 1985, is $5,159.23, which includes interest computed to October 7, 1996. Interest will continue to accrue until the balance due is paid in full.

On October 10, 1996, petitioner wrote to ask respondent's Appeals Office to consider his case. On March 4, 1997, an Appeals officer for respondent wrote to petitioner to acknowledge that respondent's 19 erroneous notices were "misleading", and explained that, despite those notices, petitioner was liable for interest for 1985:

I received your claim for abatement of interest for 1985 in Appeals. The installment agreement states the balance owed as of a certain date. The installment agreement also states *plus all penalties and interest provided by law*. Thus, interest continues to accrue on the unpaid balance during the installment period until paid in full. However, the additional interest which accrues on the unpaid balance during the installment period is not recalculated until the end of the installment period. I will agree that the statement on your monthly bills "including penalties and interest" is misleading and I will attempt to get this language revised. However, since you did not pay off the stated balance due until March, 1995, I cannot recommend abatement of interest in excess of what Examination Division has already recommended.

On April 10, 1997, one of respondent's Appeals officers issued a final determination of petitioner's claim to abate interest under section 6404(e).

On August 17, 1997, respondent issued a levy to petitioner's bank which stated that he had an unpaid assessment for 1985 of $5,426.38 and statutory additions of $147.21, for a total of $5,573.59. On September 18, 1997, respondent collected $127.96 from the levy.

Interest accrued on petitioner's tax liability for 1985 as follows:

Period	Interest
Apr. 15, 1986–Apr. 11, 1993	$ 4,022.76
Apr. 12, 1993–Aug. 8, 1995	1,106.81
Aug. 9, 1995–date of trial	1,354.30

Petitioner meets the net worth requirements under 28 U.S.C. section 2412(d)(2)(B) (1994).

Petitioner petitioned this Court to review respondent's refusal to abate interest in the amount of $5,426.38. Petitioner also alleged in the petition that he is not liable for additions to tax (other than that which he already paid in installments), that respondent improperly levied his bank account, and that he may offset his 1985 income tax liability with a refund from 1995. Respondent filed an answer generally denying the contentions in the petition.

At trial, respondent filed a motion to dismiss for lack of jurisdiction over the part of the case with respect to petitioner's claim for abatement of penalties and wrongful levy.

OPINION

[Note: The Tax Court concluded that it did not have jurisdiction to decide the Petitioner's contentions about a wrongful levy, refund offset, and liabilities for additions to tax or penalties. Eds.]

* * *

B. Abatement of Interest

1. Contentions of the Parties

The parties agree that respondent's monthly payment notices had incorrect payoff figures, but they disagree about the effect of respondent's error.

Petitioner contends that he is not liable for interest for 1985 because he fully complied with respondent's payment notices, in which respondent repeatedly said the payments included interest. He contends that respondent should not charge interest after establishing payment terms which he fully met. Petitioner contends that respondent's failure to abate interest that accrued from April 15, 1986, to April 11, 1993, is an abuse of discretion.

Respondent concedes that petitioner is entitled to an abatement of interest which accrued on his deficiency and addition to tax from April 12, 1993 (the date that respondent first told petitioner that he owed tax and an addition to tax, but incorrectly failed to notify him that he owed interest), to August 9, 1995 (the day respondent corrected the error and first told petitioner how much interest he owed for 1985). Respondent contends that petitioner is not entitled to further abatement of interest under section 6404(e).

2. The Commissioner's Authority to Abate Interest

Under section 6404(e)(1), the Commissioner may abate part or all of an assessment of interest on any deficiency or payment of income, gift, estate, and certain excise tax to the extent that any error or delay in payment is attributable to erroneous or dilatory performance of a ministerial act by an officer or employee of the Commissioner if (a) the Commissioner notified the taxpayer in writing about the deficiency or payment, and (b) the taxpayer did not contribute significantly to the error or delay. Congress intended for the Commissioner to abate interest under section 6404(e) "where failure to abate interest would be widely perceived as grossly unfair" but not that it "be used routinely to avoid payment of interest". H. Rept. 99-426, at 844 (1985), 1986-3 C.B. (Vol. 2) 1, 844; S. Rept. 99-313, at 208 (1986), 1986-3 C.B. (Vol. 3) 1, 208.

3. Jurisdiction of the Tax Court

We have jurisdiction to decide whether respondent's failure to abate interest under section 6404(e)(1)(B) is an abuse of discretion because (a) petitioner made a claim under section 6404(e) to abate interest on unpaid tax, (b) after July 30, 1996, respondent issued a final determination which disallowed a part of petitioner's claim to abate interest, and (c) petitioner timely filed a petition to review the failure to abate interest. Sec. 6404(g)(1).

4. Whether Respondent's Refusal to Abate Interest from April 15, 1986, to April 11, 1993, was an Abuse of Discretion

a. April 15, 1986, to April 11, 1993

Petitioner's 1985 return was due on April 15, 1986. He filed that return on October 27, 1992. Respondent issued a notice on April 12, 1993. Petitioner contends that respondent's refusal to abate interest from April 15, 1986, to April 11, 1993, was an abuse of discretion under section 6404(e).

We disagree with petitioner. Section 6404(e) applies only after respondent has contacted the taxpayer in writing about the deficiency or payment of tax. Sec. 6404(e)(1) (flush language); H. Rept. 99-426, *supra,* 1986-3 C.B. (Vol. 2) at 844 ("This provision does not therefore permit the abatement of interest for the period of time between the date the taxpayer files a return and the date the IRS commences an audit, regardless of the length of that time period."). Thus, petitioner is not entitled to relief under section 6404 for the period from April 15, 1986, to April 11, 1993.

b. April 12, 1993, to August 9, 1995

Respondent concedes that the failure to include interest on the notice dated April 12, 1993, was an error, that petitioner is not liable for interest from April 12, 1993, to August 9, 1995, and that interest for that period should be abated.

To reflect the foregoing and concessions, an appropriate order will be issued.

Procedurally, a taxpayer requests interest abatement by filing Form 843, Claim for Refund and Request for Abatement.

For an example of a case in which the IRS did abuse its discretion by failing to abate interest, *see Douponce v. Commissioner*, T.C. Memo 1999-398. In *Douponce*, the taxpayer asked an IRS employee for his "total amount due" for three previous years. The employee responded with specific figures, and the taxpayer promptly paid those amounts. The taxpayer understood that the figures given him included all the tax due, plus interest and penalties. In fact, the IRS employee did not include all of the accrued but unassessed interest in the amounts reported to the taxpayer. Given that the taxpayer promptly paid his liability when he was notified, the court assumed that "the only reasons for the delay [in payment of the full amount] was caused by respondent's failure to tell petitioner the correct amounts due when the petitioner requested the information." *Id*. Under the circumstances, the IRS's failure to abate interest that accrued from the date the taxpayer paid the total amount he was told was due constituted an abuse of discretion.

§ 11.03   Interest on Overpayments

Just as a taxpayer must reimburse the government for using its money to fund an underpayment, the government must reimburse a taxpayer for the period of time it held a payment in excess of the taxpayer's correct liability. For an analysis of when an overpayment exists, see Chapter 8. In most cases, the IRS pays overpayment interest in connection with the allowance of a refund or credit. If the IRS grants the taxpayer's administrative refund claim but does not include overpayment interest, the taxpayer can simply request that the IRS pay the interest owed. The request for overpayment interest need not be accompanied by a formal claim for refund because the taxpayer is not seeking a refund of an amount previously paid.

If the taxpayer files suit in order to recover a refund, the District Court or Court of Federal Claims will also consider whether the taxpayer is entitled to overpayment interest. The taxpayer may also file suit in either of these courts to recover overpayment interest alone. *See* 28 U.S.C. §§ 1346(a)(2) (District Court action limited to a $10,000 recovery), 1491(a)(1) (no dollar limitation on recovery in Court of Federal Claims action). The statute of limitations on a suit for overpayment interest is six years from the date the right of action first accrues, 28 U.S.C. §§ 2401 (District Court), 2501 (Court of Federal Claims). The right of action first accrues on the date the refund is allowed.

The Tax Court also has jurisdiction, in certain cases, to determine overpayment interest. If the Tax Court otherwise acquires supplemental jurisdiction relating to an overpayment under section 6512, it may determine interest attributable to the overpayment, and has authority to order the IRS to pay the overpayment interest. I.R.C. § 6512(b)(1), (2). The Tax Court's jurisdiction under section 7481(c), which permits it to determine underpayment interest after the decision of the Tax Court is entered, also permits it to determine overpayment interest on a post-decisional basis. *See* Tax Court Rule 261.

[A]   Applicable Interest Rates

Prior to the IRS Reform Act, the rate of interest on overpayments equaled the federal short-term rate plus two percentage points — one percentage point below the then-existing underpayment rate. The one percent differential applied to refunds owing to both corporate and noncorporate taxpayers. The IRS Reform Act increased the overpayment rate payable to noncorporate taxpayers to three percentage points above the federal short-term rate, thereby equalizing the before-tax overpayment and underpayment rates.[8] For corporate taxpayers, however, the overpayment rate remains at its prior level of two percentage points above the federal rate, and drops to one-half

---

[8] Given that overpayment interest is fully includible in the individual taxpayer's gross income, while underpayment interest is not deductible, the *effective* interest rate on underpayments payable by a noncorporate taxpayer remains above the overpayment rate, despite the elimination in 1998 of the difference in the *nominal* rates applied to noncorporate taxpayers' underpayments and overpayments. Assuming a federal short-term rate of 6 percent and a 35 percent marginal tax rate, the after-tax rate of interest on deficiencies is 9 percent, while the after-tax rate applicable to refunds is only 5.85 percent. *See* Marvin J. Garbis & Miriam L. Fischer, "The Tilted Table: Penalties and Interest on Federal Tax Deficiencies," 7 Va. Tax Rev. 485 (1988).

percentage point above the federal short-term rate for corporate overpayments exceeding $10,000. *See* I.R.C. § 6621(a)(1). As in the case of tax underpayments, interest on overpayments compounds on a daily basis. I.R.C. § 6622.[9]

[B] Accrual and Suspension Periods

As noted in Chapter 8, an overpayment may be refunded directly to the taxpayer or credited by the IRS against any unpaid assessment of other tax liability. *See* I.R.C. § 6402. In either case, overpayment interest begins to accrue from the "date of the overpayment." I.R.C. § 6611(b)(1), (2). According to the regulations, the date of overpayment of any tax is the date of payment of the first amount which (when added to previous payments) is in excess of the taxpayer's correct liability (including any interest, addition to the tax, or additional amount). Treas. Reg. § 301.6601-1(b). When applying this formulation, payments made before the return's due date, estimated tax payments, and income taxes withheld from wages are all deemed to be paid on the due date of the return. I.R.C. § 6611(d); Treas. Reg. § 301.6601-1(d). Moreover, the section 7502 "mailbox rule" may cause the date the taxpayer mails the payment to be deemed the payment date.

> *Example*: Ken timely files, by certified mail, his income tax return for calendar year 1999 on April 15, 2000. The return reflects a tax liability of $40,000, $35,000 of which was prepaid by Ken through wage withholding, and the remaining $5,000 of which was submitted by him with the return. On October 5, 2002, the IRS assesses an additional $10,000 tax deficiency, which Ken pays on November 1st of the same year. It is ultimately determined, in February of 2003, that Ken's correct liability for taxable year 1999 is only $38,000. The amounts withheld from Ken's wages during 1999 and the $5,000 payment submitted with the return are deemed paid by him on April 15, 2000. As a result, the entire tax liability of $38,000 was satisfied on that date. The balance of the payment deemed to have been made on April 15, 2000 ($2,000) and the amount paid on November 1, 2002 in response to the assessment ($10,000) constitute the amount of the overpayment. The date of the $2,000 overpayment is April 15, 2000, while the date of the $10,000 overpayment is November 1, 2002.

See Prop. Reg. § 301.6611-1(c) Ex. 2. If a taxpayer files his return after the required due date (taking into account extensions), overpayment interest does not accrue during the period before the return is filed. I.R.C. § 6611(b)(3).

When an overpayment is refunded, interest ceases to accrue in favor of the taxpayer on a date (determined within the IRS's discretion) not more than 30 days preceding the date of the refund check. I.R.C. § 6611(b)(2). Like the 10 or 21-day grace period allowed the taxpayer for paying underpayment interest, the 30-day interval permits the IRS an interest-free time period in which to process and deliver the refund check to the taxpayer. This general rule is subject to an exception in section 6611(e), which grants the IRS a

---

[9] Revenue Procedure 95-17, 1995-1 C.B. 556, also includes tables allowing interest computations for overpayments.

specified time period in which to refund an overpayment without having to pay the taxpayer any interest at all. *See* I.R.C. § 6611(e). If the IRS issues a refund within 45 days after the due date of the return reflecting the overpayment (without regard to extensions of time to file the return), no interest accrues in favor of the taxpayer. If the return is filed late, the 45-day interest-free period runs from the date the return was actually filed. This provision explains why most taxpayers who file a return that reflects an overpayment due to excessive withholding credits receive no interest on the resulting refund. *See* I.R.C. § 6611(e)(1).

The 45-day period also applies when the taxpayer files an amended return in order to claim a refund of the overpayment. If the IRS refunds an overpayment within 45 days after the claim for refund is filed, no interest accrues from the date the claim is filed to the date the refund is made. I.R.C. § 6611(e)(2). Under those circumstances, however, interest would accrue from the date of overpayment to the date the refund claim was filed.

If instead of refunding the overpayment to the taxpayer, the IRS credits the amount against an outstanding liability, overpayment interest runs from the date of the overpayment to the original due date of the return against which the overpayment is credited. I.R.C. § 6611(b)(1). Thus, for example, if the overpayment is credited against an underpayment in a subsequent taxable year, interest accrues from the date of the overpayment in the earlier year to the due date of the subsequent year's return.

> *Example*: Julie timely files her 1999 and 2000 income tax returns. A subsequent examination reveals that the 1999 return reflects a $1,000 overpayment while the 2000 return reflects a $600 underpayment. The IRS credits the $1,000 overpayment against the $600 underpayment on April 15, 2002. Interest accrues on the $1,000 overpayment from April 15, 2000 (the date of the overpayment) to April 15, 2001 (the due date of the amount against which the overpayment is credited). Overpayment interest accrues on the $400 balance ($1,000 overpayment less $600 underpayment) from April 15, 2001 to a date not more than 30 days prior to the date of the refund check.

Treas. Reg. § 301.6601-1(b) Ex. 2. *See Marsh & McLennan Co. Inc. v. United States*, 50 Fed. Cl. 140 (2001) (ending date for the calculation of overpayment interest credited against a later-arising liability is the original due date of the return for the period to which the overpayment amount was credited, not the date the IRS actually applied the overpayment against the later-arising liability). If the IRS credits an overpayment against an underpayment from an earlier taxable year, no overpayment interest accrues. What explains this result?

Crediting an overpayment against an underpayment affects also the period during which underpayment interest accrues in favor of the government. According to Code section 6601(f), if any part of an underpayment for one taxable year is satisfied by credit of any overpayment for another year, underpayment interest does not accrue on the portion of the underpayment so satisfied for any period during which interest would have been allowed on the overpayment if it had been refunded to the taxpayer instead of credited.

Although the formulation in 6601(f) may sound complicated, it merely serves to offset overpayment and underpayment interest against one another during any period for which both amounts are outstanding. In the example above, for instance, because a refund of the $600 portion of the 1999 overpayment credited against the subsequent year's underpayment would have resulted in interest accruing on such amount from April 15, 2000, no interest is imposed on the underpayment. Revenue Ruling 88-97 further clarifies the application of § 6601(f) and provides some helpful examples.

REVENUE RULING 88-97
1988-2 C.B. 355

ISSUE

If a liability for one tax year is satisfied by the credit of an overpayment for a subsequent year, to what date does interest run on the underpayment?

FACTS

Situation 1. A, an individual who files income tax returns on a calendar year basis, timely filed Form 1040, U.S. Individual Income Tax Return, for 1984 showing tax due of 10x dollars. A did not pay the amount due. On February 15, 1986, A filed Form 1040 for 1985 showing tax of 20x dollars and income tax withholding of 40x dollars.

Situation 2. The facts are the same as in *Situation 1*, except that A filed Form 1040 for 1985 on August 15, 1986, after having filed a timely application for an automatic four-month extension of time to file.

Situation 3. The facts are the same as in *Situation 1,* except that A filed Form 1040 for 1985 on December 15, 1986.

LAW AND ANALYSIS

Section 6601(a) of the Internal Revenue Code provides that if any amount of tax is not paid on or before the last date prescribed for payment, interest is payable for the period running from that date to the date paid.

Section 6601(f) of the Code provides that if any portion of a tax is satisfied by credit of an overpayment, then no interest shall be imposed under section 6601 on the portion of the tax so satisfied for any period during which, if the credit had not been made, interest would have been allowable with respect to the overpayment.

Section 6611 of the Code sets forth rules for determining the period for which interest is allowed on overpayments. Section 6611(b)(1) provides that, in the case of a credit, interest is allowable from the date of overpayment. In the case of a refund, section 6611(b)(2) provides that interest is allowable from the date of the overpayment.

Section 301.6611-1(d) of the Regulations on Procedure and Administration provides that in the case of advance payment of tax, payment of estimated tax, or credit for income tax withholding, the provisions of section 6513 (except for section 6513(c)) of the Code are applicable in determining the date of overpayment for purposes of computing interest.

Under section 6513(b) of the Code, taxes withheld at the source or paid as estimated taxes are deemed paid on the due date of the return (determined without regard to any extension of time for filing).

For returns filed after October 3, 1982, section 6611(b)(3) of the Code, as enacted by the Tax Equity and Fiscal Responsibility Act of 1982 (TEFRA), section 346(a), 1982-2 C.B. 462, 579, provides that, notwithstanding section 6611(b)(1) or (2), in the case of a return of tax that is filed after the last date prescribed for filing (determined with regard to extensions), no interest shall be allowed or paid for any day before the date the return is filed.

Section 6601(f) of the Code is intended to prevent the imposition of interest on any portion of an underpayment relating to one taxable year that is satisfied by credit of an overpayment relating to a subsequent taxable year for the period during which interest would run on the overpayment so credited if the credit had not been made (e.g., if the overpayment had instead been refunded). *See* S. Rep. No. 1983, 85th Cong., 2d Sess. 99 (1958), 1958-3 C.B. 922, 1155.

In *Situation 1* and *Situation 2*, if there had been no outstanding liability for 1984 and A's 1985 overpayment had therefore been refunded, interest would not have been allowable for any period before the due date for filing the 1985 return (determined without regard to extensions) because section 301.6611-1(d) of the regulations and section 6513(b) of the Code establish the due date as the date of overpayment. Under section 6601(f), therefore, the due date for the 1985 return is the date to which interest on the 1984 underpayment is imposed in both situations. *See* sections 3.02(3) and 3.02(5)c. of Rev. Proc. 60-17, 1960-2 C.B. 942.

In *Situation 3*, if the overpayment had been refunded, interest would only have been allowable from the date the return was filed, because section 6611(b)(3) of the Code does not allow interest for any period prior to the filing date. The date the return was filed is therefore the date to which interest on the 1984 underpayment is imposed under section 6601(f).

HOLDINGS

Situation 1. Interest on a liability for one year that is satisfied by the credit of an overpayment from a return for a subsequent year filed on or before the original due date runs from the due date of the return for the earlier year to the due date of the subsequent year's return. A owes interest for the period from April 15, 1985, to April 15, 1986.

Situation 2. Interest on a liability for one year that is satisfied by the credit of an overpayment from a subsequent year's return filed after the original due date but within a valid extension period also runs to the due date of the subsequent year's return (determined without regard to extensions). A owes interest for the period from April 15, 1985, to April 15, 1986.

Situation 3. Interest on a liability for one year that is satisfied by the credit of an overpayment claimed on a delinquent return for a subsequent year runs from the due date of the return for the earlier year to the date the return for the subsequent year is filed. A owes interest for the period from April 15, 1985, to December 15, 1986, the date on which the late return was filed.

———————————

Rules for determining when the IRS will credit a claimed overpayment against a succeeding year's estimated taxes (which also serve to determine when interest begins to run on a subsequently determined deficiency) are found in Revenue Ruling 99-40, 1999-40 I.R.B. 441. *See also* I.R.C. § 6402(b) (authorizing IRS to credit overpayments against estimated taxes).

§ 11.04 Netting Underpayment and Overpayment Interest

Calculating the correct amount of interest owed by and to the government when a taxpayer has outstanding both an underpayment and an overpayment has long been a source of controversy. If a taxpayer simultaneously owes tax liability for one year and is due a refund for a separate year, should the taxpayer be able to net the overlapping overpayment and underpayment before calculating the appropriate amount of interest due or payable?[10] During periods when the underpayment rate payable by the taxpayer exceeded the overpayment rate payable by the government, a failure to net the underlying amounts allowed the IRS to collect a net interest charge on the underpayment even though an offsetting overpayment existed. Congress responded to this perceived inequity initially by enacting Code section 6402(a), which authorizes the IRS to credit an overpayment for one taxable year against an assessed liability arising in a different taxable year. As noted above, if the IRS credits an underpayment against an overpayment, this has the ultimate effect of applying a zero rate of interest during the period of time that the taxpayer's overpayments and underpayments overlap. *See* I.R.C. § 6601(f).

Prior to 1998, the IRS interpreted its grant of authority under section 6402(a) as permitting credit of an overpayment only against an "outstanding" or unpaid underpayment liability. *See Northern States Power Co. v. United States*, 73 F.3d 764 (8th Cir.), *cert. denied*, 519 U.S. 862 (1996). If the taxpayer had already paid an asserted liability, no netting computation took place.

Example: Xena, Inc. is a calendar year corporation. As a result of an audit of Xena, Inc.'s 2000 income tax return, the IRS determined that Xena, Inc. underpaid its income tax by $500,000. Xena, Inc. paid the $500,000 underpayment, along with interest calculated under section 6601, on June 1, 2001. During the same year, Xena, Inc. filed an amended return for its 1999 taxable year showing a tax overpayment of $500,000. The IRS paid the refund on August 1, 2001, with overpayment interest calculated under section 6611 for the period from March 15, 2000, to July 8, 2001.

———————————

[10] The IRS will net all increases or decreases in a taxpayer's liability arising in the *same* taxable year. *See* Rev. Proc. 94-60, 1994-2 C.B. 774. For any one taxable year, therefore, the taxpayer will have either a net underpayment or a net overpayment.

From March 15, 2001, the due date of the 2000 return, until June 1, 2001, the date the underpayment was paid, there is a period of mutual indebtedness. In other words, during this time period Xena, Inc. owed the government $500,000 and the government owed Xena, Inc. an equal amount. Under prior law, the IRS resisted netting the underpayment and overpayment during this period of mutual indebtedness because Xena, Inc. had already satisfied the $500,000 underpayment. If no netting took place, Xena, Inc. would owe the government interest on that portion of the underpayment in excess of $100,000 calculated at a rate that is 4.5 percentage points higher than the interest rate that the government would have to use when calculating underpayment interest payable to Xena, Inc.

The failure of the IRS to credit an overpayment against an underpayment when the underpayment was no longer outstanding produced an incentive, at least according to some practitioners, for taxpayers to postpone paying outstanding tax deficiencies in the hopes of using those amounts in the netting computation. *Cf. Mecom v. Commissioner*, 101 T.C. 374, 392 (1993) ("petitioner contributed to the delay by asking respondent to close his 1976 year contemporaneously with other years to offset his refunds and deficiencies."), *aff'd without op.*, 40 F.3d 385 (5th Cir. 1994). As part of the IRS Reform Act, Congress mandated a zero rate of interest to the extent overpayments and underpayments exist for any period, regardless of whether the overpayment or underpayment is currently outstanding. *See* I.R.C. § 6621(d); H.R. Conf. Rep. No. 105-599 (1998). In other words, in determining the applicable interest rate, the IRS must take into account previously determined overpayments and underpayments, even if interest on these amounts has already been paid. This concept is referred to as "global" interest netting.

Revenue Procedure 2000-26, 2000-1 C.B. 1257, provides guidance on the application of the zero net interest rate under section 6621(d) for interest accruing on or after October 1, 1998. Admitting that it does not currently have the technology necessary to automatically apply the netting computation under Revenue Procedure 2000-26, the IRS advises taxpayers to request the net zero rate. Taxpayers are asked to file Form 843, Claim for Refund and Request for Abatement, and label the top of the form, "Request for Net Interest Rate of Zero Under Rev. Proc. 2000-26." As part of the request, the taxpayer must identify the periods for which the taxpayer overpaid and underpaid taxes and, if applicable, when the underpayment was paid or the refund received. The taxpayer is also requested to calculate the amount of interest the taxpayer believes should be refunded or abated in order to generate a net interest rate of zero.

Revenue Procedure 2000-26 also details how the IRS will apply the zero net rate. If the statute of limitations for refunding underpayment (deficiency) interest (generally, three years from the time the return was filed or two years from the time the interest was paid, whichever expires later, I.R.C. § 6511(a)) is open at the time a claim is filed, the IRS will apply the net rate of zero by *decreasing* underpayment interest owed *by* the taxpayer. (Note that if the taxpayer has already paid the underpayment interest, the decrease in interest owed by the taxpayer may be reflected as a refund to the taxpayer of the interest differential for the overlapping period.)[11] If, however, the period of limitations for refunding underpayment interest has expired at the time the claim is filed, but the period for paying additional overpayment interest remains open (generally, the six year period beginning on the date the refund is allowed and within which a suit must be filed against the government, *see* 28 U.S.C. §§ 2401 and 2501), the IRS will apply the net rate of zero by *increasing* overpayment interest owed *to* the taxpayer. If both periods of limitation have expired, no interest netting takes place.

> *Example*: Assume the same basic facts as in the previous Example involving Xena, Inc. That is, in 2001, Xena, Inc. files an amended return for 1999 and also paid underpayment interest with respect to its 2000 taxable year. Assume also that the 6-year period of limitation for claiming additional overpayment interest on Xena's 1999 refund and the 2-year period of limitation for claiming a refund of underpayment interest paid in 2001 are open. Notwithstanding the fact that the underpayment has already been paid by Xena, Inc., the zero net rate for the period during which the underpayment and overpayment overlap (March 15, 2001, the due date of the 2000 return, until June 1, 2001, the date the deficiency was paid) is applied by having the IRS refund to Xena, Inc. a portion of the previously paid underpayment interest in an amount equal to the difference between the underpayment interest paid on $500,000 for that period and the overpayment interest computed and paid on $500,000 for the same period.

Global interest netting under Code section 6621(d) applies to all types of taxes imposed by the Code, meaning that income taxes may be offset against estate taxes, estate taxes may be offset against excise taxes, and the like. The equalization of interest rates applicable to overpayments and underpayments renders the expanded interest netting rules somewhat less important for individual taxpayers.[12] Corporate taxpayers, on the other hand, particularly benefit from interest netting, not only because of the continued rate differential applicable to corporate taxpayers, but also because the net zero rate can apply even when the underpayment would otherwise be subject to the increased interest rate on large corporate underpayments or when the overpayment would otherwise be subject to a reduced interest rate because it was in excess of $10,000. This benefit is illustrated in the Example above.

PROBLEMS

1.   Scott, an individual, timely filed his 1998 income tax return on April 15, 1999. On August 1, 2000, the IRS mailed to Scott a 30-day letter (arising from an audit commenced early in 2000), reflecting the revenue agent's disallowance of $15,000

---

[11] If the netting computation requires a decrease in underpayment interest owed by the taxpayer, but the taxpayer has not yet paid the interest previously assessed, the taxpayer can request an interest abatement, rather than a refund, to reflect the decrease.

[12] The IRS takes the position that it will not apply global netting computations for individual taxpayers with respect to interest accruing on or after January 1, 1999 (the period after which the interest rates on underpayments and overpayments are equal). *See* Rev. Proc. 2000-26, 2000-24 I.R.B. 1257. For guidance regarding interest accruing before October 1, 1998, *see* Revenue Procedure 99-43, 1999-2 C.B. 579.

of claimed deductions. The proposed adjustment resulted in a $4,200 asserted tax deficiency, along with a negligence penalty equal to $840 (20 percent of $4,200). On August 10, 2001, Scott filed a Form 870. Two weeks later, on August 28th, the IRS issued a notice and demand for payment. Scott mailed a check to the IRS on September 10, and it was received on September 15. Assuming that the federal short-term rate in effect throughout the time periods involved is 6 percent, specify the applicable underpayment rate and the inclusive time periods during which interest accrues.

A. Assume the same facts as in Problem 1 except that the 30-day letter (the first official notice that Scott received in connection with his 1998 return) was not issued by the IRS until December 15, 2000. What is the applicable underpayment rate and the time period during which interest accrues?

B. Assume the same facts as in Problem 1 except that, in response to Scott's Form 870, the IRS issued the notice and demand for payment on October 1, 2001. Scott mailed payment to the IRS on October 5, 2001 and it was received by the IRS on October 10. What is the applicable underpayment rate and the time period during which interest accrues?

C. Assume the same facts as in Problem 1 except that instead of filing a Form 870, Scott appealed the proposed assessment set forth in the 30-day letter. Unable to reach a settlement with the Appeals Division, and having received a notice of deficiency asserting a $4,200 tax deficiency and an $840 negligence penalty, Scott timely filed a petition in Tax Court to challenge these amounts. When will interest stop accruing?

D. Assume the same facts as in Problem 1 except (1) Scott is Scott, Inc., a corporation taxable under Subchapter C of the Code; (2) Scott, Inc. timely filed its 1998 return on March 15, 1999; and (3) the deficiency proposed in the 30-day letter amounts to $125,000 (not including interest and penalties). What is the applicable underpayment rate and the time period during which interest accrues?

2. Ruth is the sole proprietor of a local grocery store. Accordingly, she reports all of the income and expenses of the store on her Form 1040, Schedule C. As a result of a recent audit by the IRS, Ruth has been assessed a deficiency resulting from the recharacterization of certain renovation costs as capital expenditures rather than currently deductible repair expenses. The interest on the tax deficiency amounts to $2,000. Is the interest paid by Ruth on the deficiency deductible for federal income tax purposes?

3. Marie filed her 1999 return on Monday, April 17, 2000. She was entitled to a refund of $200, representing amounts previously withheld by her employer during 1999. The IRS mailed the refund check on June 28, 2000 and Marie received the check on July 1, 2000. Is Marie entitled to interest on her refund?

4. In June of 2001, Darma, Inc. (D Corporation) filed an amended return for its 1999 taxable year, showing an overpayment of $10,000. Later in 2001, the IRS audited D Corporation's 2000 income tax return and determined that it had made a $30,000 underpayment for its taxable year 2000. On December 1, 2001, D Corporation paid the $30,000 underpayment along with interest determined at the underpayment rate. Assume that both the statute of limitations for claiming additional overpayment interest with respect to the $10,000 overpayment made during 1999 and the statute of limitations for claiming a refund of underpayment interest paid during 2001 are open.

    A. Is the IRS obligated to apply a zero rate of interest to D Corporation's tax underpayment for any period of time on these facts?

    B. If the IRS is obligated to pay interest, on what dollar amount does it apply, and for what period of time?

5. On March 5, 2002, No Dice, Inc., a manufacturer of children's board games, received a 30-day letter from the IRS asserting a $150,000 deficiency with respect to its 1999 tax year.

    A. If No Dice wishes to suspend the accrual of underpayment interest on the potential tax deficiency by remitting $150,000 to the IRS, should No Dice designate the remittance as a payment or a deposit in the nature of a cash bond?

    B. Assume that No Dice does not designate the remittance as either a payment or deposit.

        i. How will the remittance be treated by the IRS? *See* Revenue Procedure 84-58, § 4.03, 1984-2 C.B. 501.

        ii. What affect will the undesignated payment have on No Dice's ability to ultimately contest the $150,000 asserted deficiency arising from taxable year 1999 in Tax Court?

    C. Assume that, instead of receiving a 30-day letter, on April 1, 2002, No Dice received a notice of deficiency from the IRS in the amount of $150,000 with respect to its 1999 taxable year. In response, No Dice mailed to the IRS a check for $150,000 with no further designation. The check was received by the IRS on July 1, 2002. Shortly thereafter, No Dice timely filed a Tax Court petition in response to the notice. The Tax Court conducted a trial in the case, and entered a decision that became final on August 5, 2004. The decision found that No Dice was liable for a tax deficiency of $60,000. The IRS assessed the $60,000 on September 1, 2004.

    i.   Does the IRS owe No Dice, Inc. interest for the period of time it held the $150,000 prior to assessment?

    ii.   If the IRS does owe No Dice, Inc. interest, on what amount does it owe interest? *See* Revenue Procedure 84-58, § 5, 1984-2 C.B. 501.

Chapter 12

TAX COLLECTION

Reading Assignment: Code §§ 6159, 6303, 6311, 6321–6322, 6323(a)–(c), (f), (h), 6325(a)–(b), 6326, 6330(a)–(e), 6331(a)–(e), (h), (j)–(k), 6332(a), (d), 6334(a), (d)–(e), 6335, 6337, 6342, 6502, 6503(a)–(c), 7122, 7403; Treas. Reg. §§ 301.6320-1, 301.6323(a)-1, (b)-1, (h)-1, 301.6326-1, 301.6330-1, 301.6335-1, 301.6343-1(a)–(c), 301.7122-1T. Skim Code §§ 6304, 6343, 6651, 7123.

§ 12.01 Introduction

Having explained how the IRS properly assesses taxes, penalties, and interest, the text now considers the final step in the administrative process — collection of these amounts. As you may recall from Chapter 5, a valid assessment of the underlying tax liability is a prerequisite to administrative collection efforts on the part of the IRS.[1] This chapter considers the procedures the IRS uses to collect assessed amounts, restrictions on collection activity, and options a representative should consider in order to preserve a taxpayer's assets and otherwise minimize the effects of an enforced collection proceeding.

There are two different procedures generally utilized by the IRS to collect an unpaid assessment: administrative collection procedures and judicial collection procedures. The more important, and more often utilized, are the administrative collection procedures, which allow the IRS to collect tax without judicial intervention. These procedures are the primary focus of this chapter. The federal tax lien forms the foundation of the IRS's administrative collection activities, and is discussed in detail below.

The IRS does not use judicial collection procedures as frequently as administrative collection procedures. The reluctance on the part of the government to use the judicial process as a collection mechanism reflects the expensive and time-consuming nature of litigation. However, if the IRS is unable to levy on the taxpayer's property, or to do so is not administratively feasible, the government can protect its lien rights by filing suit. The two most common types of collection-related lawsuits instituted by the government are suits to foreclose a federal tax lien and suits to reduce a tax lien to a personal judgment. *See* I.R.C. §§ 7401, 7403. A foreclosure action normally is used to subject the delinquent taxpayer's property to the payment of tax and to work out any priority conflicts among the government and other third party creditors also claiming an interest in the taxpayer's property. A suit to reduce

---

[1] As discussed in Chapter 5, the types of assessments include summary assessments, deficiency assessment, jeopardy assessments, and termination assessments. Assessment occurs once the IRS records the taxpayer's name and liability on a list of debts owed to the IRS.

an assessment to personal judgment generally is utilized to extend the statute of limitations on collection, as noted below. Although this chapter does not focus specifically on judicial collection procedures, their operation is reflected in several of the cases included in the chapter.

Whether the IRS carries out collection through administrative or judicial procedures, does the prospect of enforced collection action by the IRS substantially impact voluntary compliance? In an effort to increase taxpayers' due process rights during collection proceedings, the IRS Reform Act placed limitations on the use of many of the IRS's enforcement tools and added additional procedures to the collection process. For example, section 6304 now requires the IRS to comply with certain provisions of the Fair Debt Collection Practices Act, 15 U.S.C. 1692. Among other restrictions, the IRS is prohibited from communicating with taxpayers at a time or place inconvenient to the taxpayer, and from attempting to contact the taxpayer at his place of employment if the IRS has reason to know that the taxpayer's employer prohibits such communications. I.R.C. § 6304(a). The IRS may not engage in any conduct intended to harass or abuse the taxpayer, including threats of violence or use of obscene language. I.R.C. § 6304(b). If the IRS violates any of these provisions, the taxpayer may bring a civil action against the United States in District Court under section 7433 to recover damages. I.R.C. § 6304(c).

The IRS also recently announced a new "risk-based" approach to collections in general. The following is an excerpt from the IRS's Organization Blueprint:

> The Service thus positions itself to move from a "one size fits all" approach to a philosophy of "the right treatment, for the right taxpayer, at the right time." For example, the current [collection] system is based on a series of notices that are sent to each and every delinquent taxpayer. The same number of delinquent notices are sent at the same time intervals regardless of the taxpayer's circumstances or prior payment history with the IRS. In the future, the IRS will have a model that assesses the payment/filing histories and other characteristics to determine the appropriate treatment for that taxpayer. If it is determined that this taxpayer is low-risk, the IRS may try to quickly reach that person through correspondence and attempt to set up flexible arrangements. If, however, that taxpayer has a long history of noncompliance, the IRS may decide to immediately telephone the taxpayer or send the case directly to a collection officer. In addition to tailoring the approach to match the level of risk, this approach will enable the IRS to intervene much earlier for those taxpayers representing the greatest risk, resulting in a greater likelihood of resolution and prevention of additional liability.

Internal Revenue Service, ORGANIZATION BLUEPRINT: 1999 PHASE IIA: MODERNIZATION PLANS. Because the approach described above has not yet been fully implemented, it remains to be seen how delinquent taxpayers will respond.

What has been confirmed is that the number of enforced collection cases (liens, levies and seizures) has declined dramatically in recent years. According to one government report based on the IRS's own data, 1999 collections from delinquent taxpayers were down about $2 billion when compared to 1996 levels. Similarly, lien filings were down 69 percent, levies were down about 86 percent, and seizures were down almost 98 percent. *See* Statement of James White, "IRS Modernization: Long-term Effort Under Way, But Significant Challenges Remain," May 3, 2000, GAO/T-GGD/AIMD-00-154; *see also* Statement of David C. Williams, Treasury Inspector General for Tax Administration, May 3, 2000 ("During the first five months of Fiscal Year 2000, the IRS had only conducted 28 seizures, as compared with 10,000 in Fiscal Year 1997."); George Guttman, "The Interplay of Enforcement and Voluntary Compliance," 83 Tax Notes 1683 (1999). To what do you attribute this decline? How might the drop in enforcement cases (or the publicity surrounding such a drop) affect voluntary compliance in the future? Attempting to answer these questions might be premature at this point, but consider these issues as you read the remainder of this chapter.

§ 12.02   IRS Collection Procedures

[A]   Structure of the IRS's Collection Operation

Under the prior IRS organizational structure, primary responsibility for collecting unpaid liabilities rested with a separate IRS Collection Division. The Collection Division, as a stand-alone unit, is in the process of being dismantled as part of the IRS's ongoing reorganization efforts. Under the new organizational structure, each of the four operating divisions will screen its own collection cases and attempt to process delinquent accounts first through correspondence and telephone contacts. The initial screening and processing functions are handled largely through the use of IRS computers. Once an unpaid account is identified, the taxpayer will receive a series of computer-generated bills notifying the taxpayer of a delinquent account. The first, in the form of a "Request for Payment," advises the taxpayer of the amount owed and requests the taxpayer to submit the amount within 10 days. If the amount remains unpaid after the Request for Payment is sent, the taxpayer receives, normally at five-week intervals, subsequent notices that become increasingly more insistent in their demands for payment. If these notices prove unsuccessful, the account is then assigned to an Automated Collection System ("ACS"). ACS is a computerized collection system that prompts IRS personnel to contact taxpayers by phone in an effort to collect unpaid amounts.

If ACS efforts are unsuccessful, the account normally is transferred to a revenue officer for a field investigation. Under the reorganization plan, the Wage and Investment, Large and Small Business and Tax Exempt Divisions of the IRS will "subcontract" this collection activity out to revenue officers in the Small Business/Self-Employed Division. Revenue officers have front-line responsibility for the investigation and enforced collection of delinquent accounts. Once assigned to a case, a revenue officer will contact the taxpayer to determine the current status of the taxpayer's account and will again demand immediate and full payment of all delinquent accounts. If the taxpayer fails to appear at the interview or otherwise refuses to cooperate, the revenue officer can issue a summons requiring the taxpayer to appear and provide financial information. If the outstanding liability cannot be collected by the revenue officer at the initial meeting, he will attempt to ascertain information about the taxpayer's assets and will eventually decide whether enforced collection activity, discussed below, is necessary and how is should proceed.

[B] The Notice and Demand for Payment

Once the IRS makes a valid assessment, the billing process described above begins. The IRS must, as soon as possible and no later than 60 days after tax is assessed, send to each person liable for the unpaid amount a written notice setting forth the amount of the liability and demanding payment (the "notice and demand"). I.R.C. § 6303. A taxpayer's failure to pay the amount owed within 21 days after notice and demand (10 days in the case of liabilities of $100,000 or more) triggers the failure to pay penalties under section 6651(a)(3), discussed in Chapter 10.

The notice and demand may be left at the taxpayer's dwelling or usual place of business, or mailed to his last known address. If an agency relationship exists among two or more taxpayers, a single notice to one taxpayer is generally considered notice to all. Section 6303 incorporates no other formal requirements for the notice and demand, and unlike the treatment afforded a notice of deficiency, courts have been lenient towards the IRS in accepting evidence that a valid notice and demand has been made.[2] In the usual case, the first computer-generated bill issued to the taxpayer, the Request for Payment, satisfies this statutory requirement.[3]

Because the administrative collection procedures are expressly conditioned upon notice and demand, the IRS's failure to provide a valid notice and demand to the delinquent taxpayer precludes it from using the lien and levy procedures to collect the unpaid amount. I.R.C. §§ 6321; 6311. Failure by the IRS to issue a notice and demand does not, however, invalidate the underlying tax assessment, *see Blackston v. United States*, 91-2 U.S.T.C. ¶ 50,507 (D. Md. 1991), nor does it prevent the IRS from suing the taxpayer to collect the amount owed under the judicial collection procedures. *See United States v. Berman*, 825 F.2d 1053 (6th Cir. 1987).

§ 12.03 Statutes of Limitations on Collection

Once the IRS assesses a tax or other liability, it generally has ten years from the date of the assessment to collect the tax by levy or through a judicial proceeding. I.R.C. § 6502. Prior to the IRS Reform Act, section 6502 permitted the IRS to request that the taxpayer agree to extend the limitations period on collection. Believing that the IRS should collect all taxes within ten years, Congress amended section 6502 to prohibit the IRS from requesting an extension, except in limited circumstances.[4] *Cf.* I.R.C. § 6501 (relating to

---

[2] Code section 7522(a) requires that IRS notices, such as a notice and demand, describe the basis for and identify the amount of the tax due, along with interest and any assessable penalties. An inadequate description of the amount due, however, will not invalidate a notice and demand. I.R.C. § 7522(a).

[3] The same "last known address" issues surrounding a notice of deficiency, discussed in Chapter 7, arise in this context as well.

[4] Section 6502(a), permitting the IRS to request an extension of the statute of limitations only in *limited* circumstances, applies to requests made after December 31, 1999.

assessments). If, for example, the taxpayer enters into an installment agreement to pay the outstanding liability over a period of time, the IRS is permitted to request an extension of the statute of limitations to cover the period during which payment is to take place. In that case, the limitations period expires after the agreed-upon date, plus 90 days. I.R.C. § 6502(a)(2)(A). [5]

Section 6503 specifies circumstances under which the limitations period may be suspended or tolled. As in the case of the statute of limitations on assessment, the limitations period in section 6502 is tolled during the prohibited period set forth in section 6213(a) (that is, 90 or 150 days after the mailing of the notice of deficiency or, if the taxpayer files a Tax Court petition, until the decision of the Tax Court becomes final) plus an additional 60 days. I.R.C. § 6503(a)(1). The period may also be suspended during the time the taxpayer is out of the country, I.R.C. § 6503(c), or during any period in which the taxpayer's property is in the custody or control of a federal or state court. In addition, if the taxpayer requests a collection due process hearing (discussed below) in response to a lien or levy notice, the statute of limitations on collection of tax is tolled during the period in which the hearing, and any appeal from the hearing, are pending. I.R.C. § 6330(e). Furthermore, commencement by the IRS of a personal judgment suit against the taxpayer tolls the limitations period and, should the government prevail in the suit, creates a judgment lien. The judgment lien remains enforceable for the life of the judgment as determined by state law, which can run far beyond the statute of limitations period in the Code.

§ 12.04   Administrative Collection Proceedings

As noted above, administrative collection cases normally begin with a written demand for payment by the IRS. Unless the taxpayer or his representative intervenes to negotiate a compromise or deferred payment, or the IRS determines that the unpaid liability is uncollectible, the process may lead to seizure and sale of the taxpayer's assets to satisfy the amounts owed. The IRS can collect an outstanding liability pursuant to these administrative collection procedures without the need for any judicial intervention because of the statutory federal tax lien. Each step in the administrative collection process is discussed below, with particular emphasis on the role of the federal tax lien. Those special procedures that apply to amounts immediately assessed under the jeopardy assessment procedures are also discussed.

[A]   The Statutory Federal Tax Lien

If a taxpayer neglects or refuses to pay the entire assessed amount after notice and demand, a lien in favor of the IRS automatically attaches to all of the taxpayer's property. I.R.C. § 6321. The federal tax lien is retroactive to the date of assessment. [6] In the case of a jeopardy assessment, the federal

---

[5] Another exception extends the limitations period if there has been a levy on any part of the taxpayer's property before the 10-year period expired, and the extension is agreed upon in writing before a release of levy under section 6343.

[6] While the Code provides for no express time delay before the lien arises, the initial notice

tax lien arises automatically upon assessment, with no notice and demand required. Although a federal tax lien represents nothing more than a claim or encumbrance against the taxpayer's property, the lien is important because it allows the IRS to levy and seize the taxpayer's property, which may then be sold to generate funds to pay the tax.

[1] Attachment of the Federal Tax Lien

The federal tax lien arises at the time the underlying tax liability is assessed and continues until the amount assessed is paid or becomes unenforceable because of a lapse of time. The tax lien attaches (encumbers) "all property and rights to property, whether real or personal, tangible or intangible, belonging to" the delinquent taxpayer. Treas. Reg. § 301.6321-1. The tax lien also attaches to assets that the delinquent taxpayer acquires after the lien arises, provided that the lien is still in effect. *Id*. The ultimate question of whether the section 6321 lien applies to the delinquent taxpayer's interest in property requires a consideration of both state and federal law. The following case distinguishes between these separate determinations.

DRYE v. UNITED STATES
United States Supreme Court
528 U.S. 49 (1999)

JUSTICE GINSBURG delivered the opinion of the Court.

This case concerns the respective provinces of state and federal law in determining what is property for purposes of federal tax lien legislation. At the time of his mother's death, petitioner Rohn F. Drye, Jr., was insolvent and owed the Federal Government some $325,000 on unpaid tax assessments for which notices of federal tax liens had been filed. His mother died intestate, leaving an estate with a total value of approximately $233,000 to which he was sole heir. After the passage of several months, Drye disclaimed his interest in his mother's estate, which then passed by operation of state law to his daughter. This case presents the question whether Drye's interest as heir to his mother's estate constituted "property" or a "right to property" to which the federal tax liens attached under 26 U.S.C. § 6321, despite Drye's exercise of the prerogative state law accorded him to disclaim the interest retroactively.

We hold that the disclaimer did not defeat the federal tax liens. The Internal Revenue Code's prescriptions are most sensibly read to look to state law for delineation of the taxpayer's rights or interests, but to leave to federal law the determination whether those rights or interests constitute "property" or "rights to property" within the meaning of § 6321. "Once it has been determined that state law creates sufficient interests in the [taxpayer] to satisfy the requirements of [the federal tax lien provision], state law is inoperative to prevent the attachment of liens created by federal statutes in favor of the

---

and demand allows the taxpayer ten days in which to pay. Moreover, section 6331(d) requires the IRS to wait 30 days after providing the taxpayer with a Notice of Intent to Levy before the taxpayer's property may be levied upon. This time delay affords the taxpayer an opportunity to pay the tax before levy proceedings may be instituted.

United States." *United States v. Bess*, 357 U.S. 51, 56-57, 2 L. Ed. 2d 1135, 78 S. Ct. 1054 (1958).

I.

A.

The relevant facts are not in dispute. On August 3, 1994, Irma Deliah Drye died intestate, leaving an estate worth approximately $233,000, of which $158,000 was personalty and $75,000 was realty located in Pulaski County, Arkansas. Petitioner Rohn F. Drye, Jr., her son, was sole heir to the estate under Arkansas law. *See* Ark. Code Ann. § 28-9-214 (1987) (intestate interest passes "first, to the children of the intestate"). On the date of his mother's death, Drye was insolvent and owed the Government approximately $325,000, representing assessments for tax deficiencies in years 1988, 1989, and 1990. The Internal Revenue Service (IRS or Service) had made assessments against Drye in November 1990 and May 1991 and had valid tax liens against all of Drye's "property and rights to property" pursuant to 26 U.S.C. § 6321.

Drye petitioned the Pulaski County Probate Court for appointment as administrator of his mother's estate and was so appointed on August 17, 1994. Almost six months later, on February 4, 1995, Drye filed in the Probate Court and land records of Pulaski County a written disclaimer of all interests in his mother's estate. Two days later, Drye resigned as administrator of the estate.

Under Arkansas law, an heir may disavow his inheritance by filing a written disclaimer no later than nine months after the death of the decedent. Ark. Code Ann. §§ 28-2-101, 28-2-107 (1987). The disclaimer creates the legal fiction that the disclaimant predeceased the decedent; consequently, the disclaimant's share of the estate passes to the person next in line to receive that share. The disavowing heir's creditors, Arkansas law provides, may not reach property thus disclaimed. § 28-2-108. In the case at hand, Drye's disclaimer caused the estate to pass to his daughter, Theresa Drye, who succeeded her father as administrator and promptly established the Drye Family 1995 Trust (Trust).

On March 10, 1995, the Probate Court declared valid Drye's disclaimer of all interest in his mother's estate and accordingly ordered final distribution of the estate to Theresa Drye. Theresa Drye then used the estate's proceeds to fund the Trust, of which she and, during their lifetimes, her parents are the beneficiaries. Under the Trust's terms, distributions are at the discretion of the trustee, Drye's counsel Daniel M. Traylor, and may be made only for the health, maintenance, and support of the beneficiaries. The Trust is spendthrift, and under state law, its assets are therefore shielded from creditors seeking to satisfy the debts of the Trust's beneficiaries.

Also in 1995, the IRS and Drye began negotiations regarding Drye's tax liabilities. During the course of the negotiations, Drye revealed to the Service his beneficial interest in the Trust. Thereafter, on April 11, 1996, the IRS filed with the Pulaski County Circuit Clerk and Recorder a notice of federal tax lien against the Trust as Drye's nominee. The Service also served a notice of levy on accounts held in the Trust's name by an investment bank and notified the Trust of the levy.

B.

On May 1, 1996, invoking 26 U.S.C. § 7426(a)(1), the Trust filed a wrongful levy action against the United States in the United States District Court for the Eastern District of Arkansas. The Government counterclaimed against the Trust, the trustee, and the trust beneficiaries, seeking to reduce to judgment the tax assessments against Drye, confirm its right to seize the Trust's assets in collection of those debts, foreclose on its liens, and sell the Trust property. On cross-motions for summary judgment, the District Court ruled in the Government's favor.

The United States Court of Appeals for the Eighth Circuit affirmed the District Court's judgment. Drye Family 1995 Trust v. United States, 152 F.3d 892 (1998). The Court of Appeals understood our precedents to convey that "state law determines whether a given set of circumstances creates a right or interest; federal law then dictates whether that right or interest constitutes 'property' or the 'right to property' under § 6321." 152 F.3d at 898.

We granted certiorari, 526 U.S. 1063 (1999), to resolve a conflict between the Eighth Circuit's holding and decisions of the Fifth and Ninth Circuits.[n.1] We now affirm.

II.

Under the relevant provisions of the Internal Revenue Code, to satisfy a tax deficiency, the Government may impose a lien on any "property" or "rights to property" belonging to the taxpayer. Section 6321 provides: "If any person liable to pay any tax neglects or refuses to pay the same after demand, the amount . . . shall be a lien in favor of the United States upon all property and rights to property, whether real or personal, belonging to such person." 26 U.S.C. § 6321. A complementary provision, § 6331(a), states:

> "If any person liable to pay any tax neglects or refuses to pay the same within 10 days after notice and demand, it shall be lawful for the Secretary to collect such tax . . . by levy upon all property and rights to property (except such property as is exempt under section 6334) belonging to such person or on which there is a lien provided in this chapter for the payment of such tax."

The language in §§ 6321 and 6331(a), this Court has observed, "is broad and reveals on its face that Congress meant to reach every interest in property

---

[n.1] In the view of those courts, state law holds sway. Under their approach, in a State adhering to an acceptance-rejection theory, under which a property interest vests only when the beneficiary accepts the inheritance or devise, the disclaiming taxpayer prevails and the federal liens do not attach. If, instead, the State holds to a transfer theory, under which the property is deemed to vest in the beneficiary immediately upon the death of the testator or intestate, the taxpayer loses and the federal lien runs with the property. See Leggett v. United States, 120 F.3d 592, 594 (CA5 1997); Mapes v. United States, 15 F.3d 138, 140 (CA9 1994); accord, United States v. Davidson, 55 F. Supp. 2d 1152, 1155 (Colo. 1999). Drye maintains that Arkansas adheres to the acceptance-rejection theory.

that a taxpayer might have." United States v. National Bank of Commerce, 472 U.S. 713, 719-720, 86 L. Ed. 2d 565, 105 S. Ct. 2919 (1985) (*citing* 4 B. Bittker, FEDERAL TAXATION OF INCOME, ESTATES AND GIFTS ¶ 111.5.4, p. 111-100 (1981)); *see also* Glass City Bank v. United States, 326 U.S. 265, 267, 90 L. Ed. 56, 66 S. Ct. 108 (1945) ("Stronger language could hardly have been selected to reveal a purpose to assure the collection of taxes."). When Congress so broadly uses the term "property," we recognize, as we did in the context of the gift tax, that the Legislature aims to reach " 'every species of right or interest protected by law and having an exchangeable value.' " Jewett v. Commissioner, 455 U.S. 305, 309, 71 L. Ed. 2d 170, 102 S. Ct. 1082 (1982) (*quoting* S. Rep. No. 665, 72d Cong., 1st Sess., 39 (1932); H. R. Rep. No. 708, 72d Cong., 1st Sess., 27 (1932)).

Section 6334(a) of the Code is corroborative. That provision lists property exempt from levy. The list includes 13 categories of items; among the enumerated exemptions are certain items necessary to clothe and care for one's family, unemployment compensation, and workers' compensation benefits. §§ 6334(a)(1), (2), (4), (7). The enumeration contained in § 6334(a), Congress directed, is exclusive: "Notwithstanding any other law of the United States . . . , no property or rights to property shall be exempt from levy other than the property specifically made exempt by subsection (a)." § 6334(c). Inheritances or devises disclaimed under state law are not included in § 6334(a)'s catalog of property exempt from levy. *See Bess*, 357 U.S. at 57 ("The fact that . . . Congress provided specific exemptions from distraint is evidence that Congress did not intend to recognize further exemptions which would prevent attachment of [federal tax] liens[.]"); United States v. Mitchell, 403 U.S. 190, 205, 29 L. Ed. 2d 406, 91 S. Ct. 1763 (1971) ("The language [of § 6334] is specific and it is clear and there is no room in it for automatic exemption of property that happens to be exempt from state levy under state law."). The absence of any recognition of disclaimers in §§ 6321, 6322, 6331(a), and 6334(a) and (c), the relevant tax collection provisions, contrasts with § 2518(a) of the Code, which renders qualifying state-law disclaimers "with respect to any interest in property" effective for federal wealth-transfer tax purposes and for those purposes only.

Drye nevertheless refers to cases indicating that state law is the proper guide to the critical determination whether his interest in his mother's estate constituted "property" or "rights to property" under § 6321. His position draws support from two recent appellate opinions: Leggett v. United States, 120 F.3d 592, 597 (CA5 1997) ("Section 6321 adopts the state's definition of property interest."); and Mapes v. United States, 15 F.3d 138, 140 (CA9 1994) ("For the answer to the question [whether taxpayer had the requisite interest in property], we must look to state law, not federal law."). Although our decisions in point have not been phrased so meticulously as to preclude Drye's argument,[4] we are satisfied that the Code and interpretive case law place under federal, not state, control the ultimate issue whether a taxpayer has a beneficial interest in any property subject to levy for unpaid federal taxes.

---

[4] *See, e.g.,* United States v. National Bank of Commerce, 472 U.S. 713, 722, 86 L. Ed. 2d 565, 105 S. Ct. 2919 (1985) ("The federal statute 'creates no property rights but merely attaches consequences, federally defined, to rights created under state law.' ") (*quoting* United States v. Bess, 357 U.S. 51, 55, 2 L. Ed. 2d 1135, 78 S. Ct. 1054 (1958)).

III.

As restated in *National Bank of Commerce*: "The question whether a state-law right constitutes 'property' or 'rights to property' is a matter of federal law." 472 U.S. at 727. We look initially to state law to determine what rights the taxpayer has in the property the Government seeks to reach, then to federal law to determine whether the taxpayer's state-delineated rights qualify as "property" or "rights to property" within the compass of the federal tax lien legislation. *Cf.* Morgan v. Commissioner, 309 U.S. 78, 80, 84 L. Ed. 585, 60 S. Ct. 424 (1940) ("State law creates legal interests and rights. The federal revenue acts designate what interests or rights, so created, shall be taxed.").

In line with this division of competence, we held that a taxpayer's right under state law to withdraw the whole of the proceeds from a joint bank account constitutes "property" or the "right to property" subject to levy for unpaid federal taxes, although state law would not allow ordinary creditors similarly to deplete the account. *National Bank of Commerce*, 472 U.S. at 723-727. And we earlier held that a taxpayer's right under a life insurance policy to compel his insurer to pay him the cash surrender value qualifies as "property" or a "right to property" subject to attachment for unpaid federal taxes, although state law shielded the cash surrender value from creditors' liens. *Bess*, 357 U.S. at 56-57. By contrast, we also concluded, again as a matter of federal law, that no federal tax lien could attach to policy proceeds unavailable to the insured in his lifetime. 357 U.S. at 55-56 ("It would be anomalous to view as 'property' subject to lien proceeds never within the insured's reach to enjoy.").

Just as "exempt status under state law does not bind the federal collector," *Mitchell*, 403 U.S. at 204, so federal tax law "is not struck blind by a disclaimer," United States v. Irvine, 511 U.S. 224, 240, 128 L. Ed. 2d 168, 114 S. Ct. 1473 (1994). Thus, in *Mitchell*, the Court held that, although a wife's renunciation of a marital interest was treated as retroactive under state law, that state-law disclaimer did not determine the wife's liability for federal tax on her share of the community income realized before the renunciation. *See* 403 U.S. at 204 (right to renounce does not indicate that taxpayer never had a right to property).

IV.

The Eighth Circuit, with fidelity to the relevant Code provisions and our case law, determined first what rights state law accorded Drye in his mother's estate. It is beyond debate, the Court of Appeals observed, that under Arkansas law Drye had, at his mother's death, a valuable, transferable, legally protected right to the property at issue. *See* 152 F.3d at 895 (although Code does not define "property" or "rights to property," appellate courts read those terms to encompass "state-law rights or interests that have pecuniary value and are transferable"). The court noted, for example, that a prospective heir may effectively assign his expectancy in an estate under Arkansas law, and the assignment will be enforced when the expectancy ripens into a present estate. *See* 152 F.3d at 895-896 (citing several Arkansas Supreme Court decisions, including: Clark v. Rutherford, 227 Ark. 270, 270-271, 298 S.W.2d 327, 330 (1957); Bradley Lumber Co. of Ark. v. Burbridge, 213 Ark. 165, 172, 210 S.W.2d 284, 288 (1948); Leggett v. Martin, 203 Ark. 88, 94, 156 S.W.2d 71, 74-75 (1941)).[n.7]

Drye emphasizes his undoubted right under Arkansas law to disclaim the inheritance, *see* Ark. Code Ann. § 28-2-101 (1987), a right that is indeed personal and not marketable. *See* Brief for Petitioners 13 (right to disclaim is not transferable and has no pecuniary value). But Arkansas law primarily gave Drye a right of considerable value — the right either to inherit or to channel the inheritance to a close family member (the next lineal descendant). That right simply cannot be written off as a mere "personal right . . . to accept or reject [a] gift." Brief for Petitioners 13.

In pressing the analogy to a rejected gift, Drye overlooks this crucial distinction. A donee who declines an inter vivos gift generally restores the status quo ante, leaving the donor to do with the gift what she will. The disclaiming heir or devisee, in contrast, does not restore the status quo, for the decedent cannot be revived. Thus the heir inevitably exercises dominion over the property. He determines who will receive the property — himself if he does not disclaim, a known other if he does. *See* Hirsch, "The Problem of the Insolvent Heir," 74 Cornell L. Rev. 587, 607-608 (1989). This power to channel the estate's assets warrants the conclusion that Drye held "property" or a "right to property" subject to the Government's liens.

* * *

In sum, in determining whether a federal taxpayer's state-law rights constitute "property" or "rights to property," "the important consideration is the breadth of the control the [taxpayer] could exercise over the property." *Morgan*, 309 U.S. at 83, 84 L. Ed. 2d 585, 60 S. Ct. 424. Drye had the unqualified right to receive the entire value of his mother's estate (less administrative expenses), *see National Bank of Commerce*, 472 U.S. at 725 (confirming that unqualified "right to receive property is itself a property right" subject to the tax collector's levy), or to channel that value to his daughter. The control rein he held under state law, we hold, rendered the inheritance "property" or "rights to property" belonging to him within the meaning of § 6321, and hence subject to the federal tax liens that sparked this controversy.

[n.7] In recognizing that state-law rights that have pecuniary value and are transferable fall within § 6321, we do not mean to suggest that transferability is essential to the existence of "property" or "rights to property" under that section. For example, although we do not here decide the matter, we note that an interest in a spendthrift trust has been held to constitute " 'property' for purposes of § 6321" even though the beneficiary may not transfer that interest to third parties. *See Bank One*, 80 F.3d at 176. Nor do we mean to suggest that an expectancy that has pecuniary value and is transferable under state law would fall within § 6321 prior to the time it ripens into a present estate.

For the reasons stated, the judgment of the Court of Appeals for the Eighth Circuit is

Affirmed.

The Court does not specifically identify what type of property interest under state law (fee simple, remainder, leasehold) Drye held in the assets comprising his mother's estate. The closest the Court comes to characterizing Drye's state law right to the assets is his "control rein" over them. What measure of control must the taxpayer possess over an asset in order for it to be subject to the federal tax lien?

Separate from the issue of how state property rights are characterized for federal tax purposes is the issue of how much deference a federal court must afford a state court's determination of local property law. The United States Supreme Court's ruling in *Commissioner v. Estate of Bosch*, 387 U.S. 456 (1967), a case you may have read in your federal income tax course, considered the effect of a state court ruling on the federal court's determination of state law.

> These * * * cases present a common issue for our determination: Whether a federal court or agency in a federal * * * tax controversy is conclusively bound by a state trial court adjudication of property rights or characterization of property interests when the United States is not made a party to such proceeding. * * *
>
> [W]hen the application of a federal statute is involved, the decision of a state trial court as to an underlying issue of state law should a fortiori not be controlling. This is but an application of the rule of *Erie R. Co. v. Tompkins*, 304 U.S. 64 (1938), where state law as announced by the highest court of the State is to be followed. This is not a diversity case but the same principle may be applied for the same reasons, viz., the underlying substantive rule involved is based on state law and the State's highest court is the best authority on its own law. If there be no decision by that court then federal authorities must apply what they find to be the state law after giving "proper regard" to relevant rulings of other courts of the State. * * *

Id. at 465.

Because of the importance of state law principles to the application of Code section 6321, drawing broad conclusions as to which property interests are subject to attachment can be difficult. In virtually all cases, however, the delinquent taxpayer's separate interest in property held as tenants in common is subject to the federal tax lien, *see, e.g., United States v. Kocher*, 468 F.2d 503 (2d Cir. 1972), *cert. denied*, 411 U.S. 931 (1973), as are partial interests in property such as life estates, *see, e.g., United States v. United Banks of Denver*, 542 F.2d 819 (10th Cir. 1976), and future interests such as contingent remainders, *see, e.g., Dominion Trust v. United States*, 7 F.3d 233 (6th Cir. 1993). While it also seems clear that the federal tax lien attaches to the delinquent taxpayer's interest in property held with another as joint tenants with rights of survivorship, *see, e.g.*, *Shaw v. United States*, 331 F.2d 493 (9th Cir. 1964), whether the tax lien survives the delinquent taxpayer's death depends upon state law. *Compare Fecarotta v. United States*, 154 F. Supp. 592 (D. Ariz. 1956) (applying Arizona law, death of delinquent taxpayer terminates delinquent taxpayer's interest in joint tenancy, thus lien expires), *with United States v. Librizzi*, 108 F.3d 136 (7th Cir. 1997) (applying Wisconsin law, surviving joint tenant takes property subject to lien arising from liability of deceased joint tenant).

A tenancy by the entireties interest, a type of unitary property interest limited to married individuals, also carries with it rights of survivorship and shared rights of use and possession, much like a joint tenancy interest. In those states that recognize tenancies by the entireties, neither spouse is considered to hold a separate interest in the property; instead, the property is held by the marital unit. As a result, most courts have ruled that a federal tax lien arising from the separate liability of one spouse cannot attach to property held as tenants by the entireties. *See, e.g.*, *Craft v. United States*, 233 F.3d 358 (6th Cir. 2000) (confirming its earlier opinion that, under Michigan law, individual spouse possesses no present or future interest in entireties property, thus there is no property interest to which the federal tax lien can attach), *cert. granted*, 122 S. Ct. 23 (2001); *see also* Steve R. Johnson, "The Good, the Bad, and the Ugly in Post-Drye Tax Lien Analysis," 5 Fla. Tax Rev. 415 (2002). For the lien attachment rules relating to community property interests, *see* David A. Schmudde, FEDERAL TAX LIENS (4th ed. 2001).

As an illustration of the breadth of the federal tax lien, the lien may attach to property interests that are conditioned upon future action of the taxpayer, *see United States v. Kogan*, 257 B.R. 1 (C.D. Cal. 2000) (under California law, attorney's work in progress, even with respect to cases covered by contingent fee arrangements, constitutes property to which federal tax lien can attach); *In re Jeffrey*, 261 B.R. 396 (W.D. Pa. 2001) (under Pennsylvania law, taxpayer/debtor's medical malpractice cause of action against third party is property in which taxpayer/debtor has an interest; as a result, tax lien attaches to cause of action and will attach to damage award should taxpayer prevail on the malpractice claim), as well as those conditioned upon the future action of some third party, *see United States v. Murray*, 217 F.3d 59 (1st Cir. 2000) (federal tax lien attaches to taxpayer's interest in a trust holding marital home in which taxpayer had a one-half interest, even though trustees could divest taxpayer's interest under a separation agreement). State-created exemptions generally do not affect a federal tax lien that has attached to the subject property. For example, the tax lien can attach to a delinquent taxpayer's property despite another party's homestead interest in the same property. *See United States v. Rodgers*, 461 U.S. 677 (1983), which is reproduced below.

[2] Lien Priorities

Once a federal tax lien attaches, no additional action on the part of the IRS or judicial intervention is required to establish the government's interest in the taxpayer's property. For this reason, the federal tax lien is often referred to as a "secret lien." Although the existence of the tax lien may be known only to the taxpayer and the IRS, the government may still have priority against third-party creditors asserting an interest in the taxpayer's property.

Priority conflicts between a federal tax lien and the interests of competing creditors are common. Under prior law, in order for a competing creditor to retain priority over a federal tax lien, the creditor's lien must have arisen prior to assessment of the underlying tax liability, and must have been "choate" prior to the time the tax was assessed. *See, e.g., United States v. City of New Britain*, 347 U.S. 81 (1954).[7] In order to satisfy this choateness standard, the competing creditor had to establish the specific identity of the lienor, the amount of the lien, and the identity of the property to which the lien attached. *Id.* Although the choateness standard still exists, lien priorities are now determined primarily under section 6323. Section 6323 sets forth a series of rules that provide protection for classes of creditors who might otherwise acquire property subject to the federal tax lien without knowledge of the lien's existence. Congress amended section 6323 in 1966 to further clarify its application and to better conform the treatment of priority rights relating to federal tax liens to those that exist under the Uniform Commercial Code. *See* S. Rep. No. 89-1708, at 2 (1966).

Section 6323(a) provides that the federal tax lien is not valid against any purchaser, holder of a security interest, mechanic's lienor, or judgment lien creditor until the Secretary files (records) a Notice of Federal Tax Lien, Form 668, in accordance with the Code. Once the Secretary properly records the notice, the lien normally takes priority over *subsequent* purchasers, security interest holders, mechanic's lienors, and judgment creditors. Section 6323(a) is intended, therefore, to provide protection for interests transferred or created between the time the federal tax lien arose and the time the IRS files notice of the lien.

> *Example*: On May 1, 2001, the IRS assessed against Sally a $1,000 deficiency arising from her failure to pay income taxes for taxable year 1999. Sally owns $10,000 worth of stock in XAnte Corporation. On May 20, 2001, Sally obtains a loan from her bank for $5,000, transferring the XAnte Corporation stock to the bank as collateral. On June 30, 2001, the IRS properly files a Notice of Federal Tax Lien with respect to Sally's delinquent tax liability. Because Sally's bank acquired and perfected a security interest in the stock before the IRS recorded the tax lien, the tax lien is not valid against the bank to the extent of the bank's security interest. Had the bank loaned funds to Sally and acquired its security interest in the XAnte Corporation stock after June 30, 2001, the security interest held by the bank would not be entitled to priority over the government's tax lien.

The Code and regulations detail who may fall within the protection of the four categories listed in section 6323(a). In each of the four cases, the Code and regulations not only define the nature of the creditor interest, but also attach prerequisites that must be satisfied before the creditor is protected.

---

[7] Whether this choateness doctrine continues to apply as an independent requirement after the amendment of section 6323 by the Federal Tax Lien Act of 1966, Pub. L. No. 89-719, 80 Stat. 1125, remains unresolved. *Compare* United States v. Central Bank of Denver, 843 F.2d 1300 (10th Cir. 1988), *with* Aetna Ins. Co. v. Texas Thermal Industries Inc., 591 F.2d 1035 (5th Cir. 1979). *See also United States v. McDermott*, reproduced below.

As a general rule, the creditor must "perfect" his interest under state law before the IRS files a Notice of Federal Tax Lien in order to obtain priority over the tax lien. Read section 6323(h)(1), which defines a security interest in much the same manner as the Uniform Commercial Code. A security interest is considered to exist for purposes of section 6323 only if (1) the property subject to the security interest is in existence and the security interest has become protected under local law against a subsequent judgment lien arising out of an unsecured obligation (another way of saying that the security interest must be perfected under local law) and (2) the security holder parts with money or money's worth. *See* Treas. Reg. § 301.6323(h)-1(a)(2). Only if the security holder satisfies these requirements before the IRS files its Notice of Federal Tax Lien does his interest become protected against a subsequently filed lien.[8] Similarly, a judgment lien does not arise for purposes of section 6323(a) until the judgment lien creditor perfects the lien on the property that it affects. If, under local law, the judgment lien is not perfected until the judgment creditor dockets the judgment in the county where the debtor is located, the creditor must do so in order to retain priority. Treas. Reg. § 301.6323(h)-1(g).

Even timely filing a Notice of Federal Tax Lien does not assure the IRS's priority. Section 6323(b) describes classes of purchasers and lien holders who are afforded a "superpriority," protecting the party's interest *despite the fact* that the IRS may have previously filed a Notice of Federal Tax Lien. As a general matter, section 6323(b) establishes priority for these third parties in cases where it may be unreasonable to assume that the third party purchaser would check for federal tax liens and in situations where a third party lender or service provider increases the value of the taxpayer's property and thereby increases the likelihood that the IRS will collect against the property by levy. This preferred status is granted with respect to ten separate interests, including (1) securities purchased without actual notice or knowledge of the tax lien; (2) motor vehicles purchased without prior knowledge of the federal tax lien; (3) tangible personal property purchased at retail in the ordinary course of the seller's business; and (4) personal property, such as household furnishings and personal effects, purchased in a casual sale. Liens covering real property taxes, payments for repairs and improvements of the taxpayer's personal residence, and attorney's fees are also accorded superpriority status if the specific requirements of the statute are met. *See also* Treas. Reg. § 301.6323(b)-1.

> *Example*: Marshall, a delinquent taxpayer against whom a Notice of Federal Tax Lien has been filed, sells his automobile to Fred, an automobile dealer. Subsequent to his purchase, Fred learns of the existence of the tax lien against Marshall. Even though notice of the lien was filed prior to Fred's purchase, the lien is not valid against Fred because he did not know of the existence of the lien before the purchase and before acquiring actual possession of the car.

---

[8] Because of these prerequisites, a security interest for section 6323 purposes is more limited in scope than a security interest under the Uniform Commercial Code.

Treas. Reg. § 301.6323(b)-1(b)(2) Ex. (2). To facilitate the use of common financing techniques, section 6323(c) also confers superpriority status on certain security interests resulting from commercial transaction financing agreements. *See* I.R.C. § 6323(c)(2); Treas. Reg. § 301.6323(c)-1.

Although the Code and regulations provide detailed descriptions and examples of how section 6323 is intended to operate, it leaves some priority questions unanswered. Recall that a federal tax lien also attaches to *after-acquired* property of the taxpayer. The issue presented in the *McDermott* case, reproduced below, is how priority should be determined when a judgment creditor first dockets his judgment, the government subsequently files its Notice of Federal Tax Lien, and later still, the debtor/taxpayer acquires the property in question. Notice the Court's reliance on the choateness principles mentioned above.

UNITED STATES v. McDERMOTT
United States Supreme Court
507 U.S. 447 (1993)

JUSTICE SCALIA delivered the opinion of the Court.

We granted certiorari to resolve the competing priorities of a federal tax lien and a private creditor's judgment lien as to a delinquent taxpayer's after-acquired real property.

I.

On December 9, 1986, the United States assessed Mr. and Mrs. McDermott for unpaid federal taxes due for the tax years 1977 through 1981. Upon that assessment, the law created a lien in favor of the United States on all real and personal property belonging to the McDermotts, 26 U.S.C. §§ 6321 and 6322, including after-acquired property, Glass City Bank v. United States, 326 U.S. 265, 90 L. Ed. 56, 66 S. Ct. 108 (1945). Pursuant to 26 U.S.C. § 6323(a), however, that lien could "not be valid as against any purchaser, holder of a security interest, mechanic's lienor, or *judgment lien creditor* until notice thereof . . . has been filed." (Emphasis added.) The United States did not file this lien in the Salt Lake County Recorder's Office until September 9, 1987. Before that occurred, however — specifically, on July 6, 1987 — Zions First National Bank, N. A. (Bank), docketed with the Salt Lake County Clerk a state-court judgment it had won against the McDermotts. Under Utah law, that created a judgment lien on all of the McDermotts' real property in Salt Lake County, "owned . . . at the time or . . . thereafter acquired during the existence of said lien." Utah Code Ann. § 78-22-1 (1953).

On September 23, 1987, the McDermotts acquired title to certain real property in Salt Lake County. To facilitate later sale of that property, the parties entered into an escrow agreement whereby the United States and the Bank released their claims to the real property itself but reserved their rights to the cash proceeds of the sale, based on their priorities in the property as of September 23, 1987. Pursuant to the escrow agreement, the McDermotts brought this interpleader action in state court to establish which lien was entitled to priority; the United States removed to the United States District Court for the District of Utah.

On cross-motions for partial summary judgment, the District Court awarded priority to the Bank's judgment lien. The United States Court of Appeals for the Tenth Circuit affirmed. McDermott v. Zions First Nat. Bank, N. A., 945 F.2d 1475 (1991). We granted certiorari. 504 U.S. 939 (1992).

II.

Federal tax liens do not automatically have priority over all other liens. Absent provision to the contrary, priority for purposes of federal law is governed by the common-law principle that " 'the first in time is the first in right.' " United States v. New Britain, 347 U.S. 81, 85, 98 L. Ed. 520, 74 S. Ct. 367 (1954); *cf.* Rankin v. Scott, 25 U.S. 177, 12 Wheat. 177, 179, 6 L. Ed. 592 (1827) (Marshall, C. J.). For purposes of applying that doctrine in the present case — in which the competing state lien (that of a judgment creditor) benefits from the provision of § 6323(a) that the federal lien shall "not be valid . . . until notice thereof . . . has been filed" — we must deem the United States' lien to have commenced no sooner than the filing of notice. As for the Bank's lien: Our cases deem a competing state lien to be in existence for "first in time" purposes only when it has been "perfected" in the sense that "the identity of the lienor, *the property subject to the lien,* and the amount of the lien are established." *United States v. New Britain*, 347 U.S. at 84 (emphasis added); *see also id.,* at 86; United States v. Pioneer American Ins. Co., 374 U.S. 84, 10 L. Ed. 2d 770, 83 S. Ct. 1651 (1963).

The first question we must answer, then, is whether the Bank's judgment lien was perfected in this sense before the United States filed its tax lien on September 9, 1987. If so, that is the end of the matter; the Bank's lien prevails. The Court of Appeals was of the view that this question was answered (or rendered irrelevant) by our decision in *United States v. Vermont*, 377 U.S. 351, 12 L. Ed. 2d 370, 84 S. Ct. 1267 (1964), which it took to "stand for the proposition that a non-contingent . . . lien on all of a person's real property, perfected prior to the federal tax lien, will take priority over the federal lien, regardless of whether after-acquired property is involved."[n.1] 945 F.2d at 1480. That is too expansive a reading. Our opinion in *Vermont* gives no indication that the property at issue had become subject to the state lien only by application of an after-acquired-property clause to property that the debtor acquired after the federal lien arose. To the contrary, the opinion says that the state lien met (presumably at the critical time when the federal lien arose) "the test laid down in *New Britain* that . . . 'the property subject to the lien . . . [be] established.' " 377 U.S. at 358 (citation omitted). The argument of the United States that we rejected in *Vermont* was the contention that a state lien is not perfected within the meaning of *New Britain* if it "attach[es] to *all* of the taxpayer's property," rather than "to specifically identified portions of

---

[n.1] As our later discussion will show, we think it contradictory to say that the state lien was "perfected" before the federal lien was filed, insofar as it applies to after-acquired property not acquired by the debtor until after the federal lien was filed. The Court of Appeals was evidently using the term "perfected" (as the Bank would) in a sense not requiring attachment of the lien to the property in question; our discussion of the Court of Appeals' opinion assumes that usage.

that property." 377 U.S. at 355 (emphasis added). We did not consider, and the facts as recited did not implicate, the quite different argument made by the United States in the present case: that a lien in after-acquired property is not "perfected" as to property yet to be acquired.

The Bank argues that, as of July 6, 1987, the date it docketed its judgment lien, the lien was "perfected as to all real property then and thereafter owned by" the McDermotts, since "nothing further was required of [the Bank] to attach the non-contingent lien on after-acquired property." Brief for Respondent 21. That reflects an unusual notion of what it takes to "perfect" a lien.[n.4] Under the Uniform Commercial Code, for example, a security interest in after-acquired property is generally not considered perfected when the financing statement is filed, but only when the security interest has attached to particular property upon the debtor's acquisition of that property. §§ 9-203(1) and (2), 3 U.L.A. 363 (1992); § 9-303(1), 3A U.L.A. 117 (1992). And attachment to particular property was also an element of what we meant by "perfection" in *New Britain*. *See* 347 U.S. at 84 ("when . . . the property subject to the lien . . . [is] established"); *id.*, at 86 ("The priority of each statutory lien contested here must depend on the time it attached to the property in question and became [no longer inchoate]").[n.5] The Bank concedes that its lien did not actually attach to the property at issue here until the McDermotts acquired rights in that property. Brief for Respondent 16, 21. Since that occurred *after* filing of the federal tax lien, the state lien was not first in time.

But that does not complete our inquiry: Though the state lien was not first in time, the federal tax lien was not necessarily first in time either. Like the state lien, it applied to the property at issue here by virtue of a (judicially inferred) after-acquired-property provision, which means that it did not attach until the same instant the state lien attached, viz., when the McDermotts acquired the property; and, like the state lien, it did not become "perfected" until that time. We think, however, that under the language of § 6323(a)

[n.4] The dissent accepts the Bank's central argument that perfection occurred when "there was 'nothing more to be done' by the Bank 'to have a choate lien'" on any real property the McDermotts might acquire." (*quoting United States v. New Britain, supra*). This unusual definition of perfection has been achieved by making a small but substantively important addition to the language of *New Britain*. "'Nothing more to be done . . . to have a choate lien'" (the language of *New Britain*) becomes "nothing more to be done *by the Bank* to have a choate lien." Once one recognizes that the dissent's concept of a lien's "becoming certain as to the property subject thereto," is meaningless, it becomes apparent that the dissent, like the Bank, would simply have us substitute the concept of "best efforts" for the concept of perfection.

[n.5] The dissent refuses to acknowledge the unavoidable realities that the property subject to a lien is not "established" until one knows what specific property that is, and that a lien cannot be anything other than "inchoate" with respect to property that is not yet subject to the lien. Hence the dissent says that, upon its filing, the lien at issue here "was perfected, even as to the real property later acquired by the McDermotts, in the sense that it was definite as to the property in question, noncontingent, and summarily enforceable." * * * But how could it have been, at that time, "definite" as to this property, when the identity of this property (established by the McDermotts' later acquisition) was yet unknown? Or "noncontingent" as to this property, when the property would have remained entirely free of the judgment lien had the McDermotts not later decided to buy it? Or "summarily enforceable" against this property when the McDermotts did not own, and had never owned, it? The dissent also says that "the lien was *immediately enforceable* through levy and execution against all the debtors' property, *whenever acquired*." *Ibid.* (emphasis added.) But of course it was *not* "immediately enforceable" (as of its filing date, which is the relevant time) against property that the McDermotts had not yet acquired.

("shall not be valid as against any . . . judgment lien creditor until notice . . . has been filed"), the filing of notice renders the federal tax lien extant for "first in time" priority purposes regardless of whether it has yet attached to identifiable property. That result is also indicated by the provision, two subsections later, which accords priority, even against *filed* federal tax liens, to security interests arising out of certain agreements, including "commercial transactions financing agreement[s]," entered into before filing of the tax lien. 26 U.S.C. § 6323(c)(1). That provision protects certain security interests that, like the after-acquired-property judgment lien here, will have been recorded before the filing of the tax lien, and will attach to the encumbered property after the filing of the tax lien, and simultaneously with the attachment of the tax lien (*i.e.,* upon the debtor's acquisition of the subject property). According *special* priority to certain state security interests in these circumstances obviously presumes that otherwise the federal tax lien would prevail — *i.e.,* that the federal tax lien is ordinarily dated, for purposes of "first in time" priority against § 6323(a) competing interests, from the time of its filing, regardless of when it attaches to the subject property.[n.7]

The Bank argues that "by common law, the first lien of record against a debtor's property has priority over those subsequently filed unless a lien-creating statute clearly shows or declares an intention to cause the statutory lien to override." Brief for Respondent Zions First National Bank, N. A., 11. Such a strong "first-to-record" presumption may be appropriate for simultaneously perfected liens under ordinary statutes creating private liens, which ordinarily arise out of voluntary transactions. When two private lenders both exact from the same debtor security agreements with after-acquired-property clauses, the second lender knows, by reason of the earlier recording, that that category of property will be subject to another claim, and if the remaining security is inadequate he may avoid the difficulty by declining to extend credit. The Government, by contrast, cannot indulge the luxury of declining to hold the taxpayer liable for his taxes; notice of a previously filed security agreement covering after-acquired property does *not* enable the Government to protect itself. A strong "first-to-record" presumption is particularly out of place under the present tax-lien statute, whose *general rule* is that the tax collector prevails even if he has not recorded *at all.* 26 U.S.C. §§ 6321 and 6322; United States v. Snyder, 149 U.S. 210, 37 L. Ed. 705, 13 S. Ct. 846 (1893). Thus, while we would hardly proclaim the statutory meaning we have discerned in this opinion to be "clear," it is evident enough for the purpose at hand. The federal tax lien must be given priority.

[n.7] The dissent contends that "there is no persuasive reason for not adopting as a matter of federal law the well-recognized common-law rule of parity and giving the Bank an equal interest in the property." As we have explained, the persuasive reason is the existence of § 6323(c), which displays the assumption that all perfected security interests are defeated by the federal tax lien. There is no reason why this assumption should not extend to judgment liens as well. A "security interest," as defined in § 6323, is not an insignificant creditor's preference. The term includes only interests protected against subsequent judgment liens. *See* 26 U.S.C. §§ 6323(h)(1) and 6323(c)(1)(B). Moreover, the text of § 6323(a) ("The lien . . . shall not be valid as against any purchaser, holder of a security interest, mechanic's lienor, or judgment lien creditor") treats security interests and judgment liens alike. Parity may be, as the dissent says, a "well-recognized common-law rule," * * * but we have not hitherto adopted it as the federal law of tax liens in 127 years of tax lien enforcement.

The judgment of the Court of Appeals is reversed, and the case is remanded for further proceedings consistent with this opinion.

So ordered.

JUSTICE THOMAS, with whom JUSTICE STEVENS and JUSTICE O'CONNOR join, dissenting.

I agree with the Court that under 26 U.S.C. § 6323(a) we generally look to the filing of notice of the federal tax lien to determine the federal lien's priority as against a competing state-law judgment lien. I cannot agree, however, that a federal tax lien trumps a judgment creditor's claim to after-acquired property whenever notice of the federal lien is filed before the judgment lien has "attached" to the property. In my view, the Bank's ante-cedent judgment lien "had [already] acquired sufficient substance and had become so perfected," with respect to the McDermotts' after-acquired real property, "as to defeat [the] later-filed federal tax lien." United States v. Pioneer American Ins. Co., 374 U.S. 84, 88, 10 L. Ed. 2d 770, 83 S. Ct. 1651 (1963).

Applying the governing "first in time" rule, the Court recognizes — as it must — that if the Bank's interest in the property was "perfected in the sense that there [was] nothing more to be done to have a choate lien" before September 9, 1987 (the date the federal notice was filed), United States v. New Britain, 347 U.S. 81, 84, 98 L. Ed. 520, 74 S. Ct. 367 (1954), "that is the end of the matter; the Bank's lien prevails." * * * Because the Bank's identity as lienor and the amount of its judgment lien are undisputed, the choateness question here reduces to whether "the property subject to the lien" was sufficiently "established" as of that date. New Britain, supra, at 84. Accord, Pioneer American, supra, at 89. See 26 CFR § 301.6323(h)-1(g) (1992). The majority is quick to conclude that "establish[ment]" cannot precede at-tachment, and that a lien in after-acquired property therefore cannot be sufficiently perfected until the debtor has acquired rights in the proper-ty. * * * That holding does not follow from, and I believe it is inconsistent with, our precedents.

We have not (before today) prescribed any rigid criteria for "establishing" the property subject to a competing lien; we have required only that the lien "become certain as to . . . the property subject thereto." New Britain, supra, at 86 (emphasis added). Our cases indicate that "certain" means nothing more than "determined and definite," Pioneer American, supra, at 90, and that the proper focus is on whether the lien is free from "contingencies" that stand in the way of its execution, United States v. Security Trust & Savings Bank, 340 U.S. 47, 50, 95 L. Ed. 53, 71 S. Ct. 111 (1950). In Security Trust, for example, we refused to accord priority to a mere attachment lien that "had not ripened into a judgment," New Britain, supra, at 86, and was therefore "contingent upon taking subsequent steps for enforcing it," 340 U.S. at 51. And in United States v. Vermont, 377 U.S. 351, 12 L. Ed. 2d 370, 84 S. Ct. 1267 (1964), we recognized the complete superiority of a general tax lien held by the State of Vermont upon all property rights belonging to the debtor, even though the lien had not "attached to [the] specifically identified portions of that property" in which the Federal Government claimed a competing tax lien. Id., at 355. With or without specific attachment, Vermont's general lien was "sufficiently choate to obtain priority over the later federal lien," because it was "summarily enforceable" upon assessment and demand. *Id.,* at 359, and n.12.

Although the choateness of a state-law lien under § 6323(a) is a federal question, that question is answered in part by reference to state law, and we therefore give due weight to the State's " 'classification of [its] lien as specific and perfected.' " *Pioneer American, supra,* at 88, n.7 (quoting *Security Trust, supra,* at 49). Here, state law establishes that upon filing, the Bank's judgment lien was perfected, even as to the real property later acquired by the McDermotts, in the sense that it was definite as to the property in question, noncontingent, and summarily enforceable. Pursuant to Utah statute, from the moment the Bank had docketed and filed its judgment with the Clerk of the state court on July 6, 1987, it held an enforceable lien upon all nonexempt real property owned by the McDermotts or thereafter acquired by them during the existence of the lien. *See* Utah Code Ann. § 78-22-1 (1953). The lien was immediately enforceable through levy and execution against all the debtors' property, whenever acquired. *See* Belnap v. Blain, 575 P.2d 696, 700 (Utah 1978). *See also* Utah Rule Civ. Proc. 69. And it was "unconditional and not subject to alteration by a court on equitable grounds." Taylor National, Inc. v. Jensen Brothers Constr. Co., 641 P.2d 150, 155 (Utah 1982). Thus, the Bank's lien had become certain as to the property subject thereto, whether then existing or thereafter acquired, and all competing creditors were on notice that there was "nothing more to be done" by the Bank "to have a choate lien" on any real property the McDermotts might acquire. *New Britain, supra,* at 84. *See Vermont, supra,* at 355.

The Court brushes aside the relevance of our *Vermont* opinion with the simple observation that that case did not involve a lien in after-acquired property. * * * This is a wooden distinction. In truth, the Government's "specificity" claim rejected in *Vermont* is analytically indistinguishable from the "attachment" argument the Court accepts today. Vermont's general lien applied to all of the debtor's rights in property, with no limitation on when those rights were acquired, and remained valid until the debt was satisfied or became unenforceable. *See* 377 U.S. at 352. The United States claimed that its later-filed tax lien took priority over Vermont's as to the debtor's interest in a particular bank account, because the State had not taken "steps to perfect its lien by attaching the bank account in question" until after the federal lien had been recorded. Brief for United States in United States v. Vermont, O. T. 1963, No. 509, p. 12. "Thus," the Government asserted, "when the federal lien arose, the State lien did not meet one of the three essential elements of a choate lien: that it attach to specific property." *Ibid.* In rejecting the federal claim of priority, we found no need even to mention whether the debtor had acquired its property interest in the deposited funds before or after notice of the federal lien. If specific attachment is not required for the state lien to be "sufficiently choate," 377 U.S. at 359, then neither is specific acquisition.

* * *

I acknowledge that our precedents do not provide the clearest answer to the question of after-acquired property. * * * But the Court's parsimonious reading of *Vermont* undercuts the congressional purpose — expressed through repeated amendments to the tax lien provisions in the century since *United States v. Snyder*, 149 U.S. 210, 37 L. Ed. 705, 13 S. Ct. 846 (1893) — of "protecting third persons against harsh application of the federal tax lien," Kennedy, *The Relative Priority of the Federal Government: The Pernicious Career of the Inchoate and General Lien*, 63 Yale L. J. 905, 922 (1954). The attachment requirement erodes the "preferred status" granted to judgment creditors by § 6323(a), and renders a choate judgment lien in after-acquired property subordinate to a "secret lien for assessed taxes." *Pioneer American,* 374 U.S. at 89. I would adhere to a more flexible choateness principle, which would protect the priority of validly docketed judgment liens.

Accordingly, I respectfully dissent.

Is the majority's holding that priority questions should be determined with reference to the date the federal tax lien was filed by the IRS consistent with its holding that the federal tax lien was not perfected until the taxpayer obtained an interest in the after-acquired property? Is the holding consistent with the purpose of section 6323(a) to provide protection to pre-existing creditors against a non-filed (secret) federal tax lien? *See generally* William H. Baker, "The *McDermott* Tax Lien Case: And the First Shall Be Last," 55 La. L. Rev. 879 (1995).

[3] Notice of Federal Tax Lien

[a] Filing

The formalities the IRS must follow when filing a Notice of Federal Tax Lien are contained in section 6323(f), which generally refers to state law procedures.[9] The IRS Reform Act also requires the IRS to notify the delinquent taxpayer in writing of the existence of the lien within five days after it files the notice. I.R.C. § 6320(a). The taxpayer is then afforded an opportunity to request a hearing with an IRS Appeals officer (the "Collection Due Process" or "CDP Hearing") within a 30-day period beginning on the date after the five-day period expires. I.R.C. § 6320(b). The CDP Hearing and the issues that may be discussed at the hearing are explained below.

Because a Notice of Federal Tax Lien filed against a taxpayer's property may result in a significant hardship for the taxpayer and may prevent him from borrowing funds to pay the assessed liability, revenue officers do not automatically file the notice immediately upon the taxpayer's failure to pay in response to the notice and demand. The Internal Revenue Manual instructs revenue officers to provide the taxpayer with an opportunity to pay the assessment or to work out a security or deferred payment arrangement before filing the Notice of Federal Tax Lien. Officers must also explain to the taxpayer the negative effects a Notice of Federal Tax Lien may have on the

[9] For example, in Kansas, the Notice of Federal Tax Lien is required to be filed with the Secretary of State's office in the case of most personal property and, in the case of real property, in the register of deeds office in the county in which the real property is located. *See* Kan. Stat. Ann. § 79-2614 (1997).

taxpayer's normal business operations and credit rating. I.R.M. 5.12.1.4. In cases in which the outstanding unpaid balance is $5,000 or more, or the taxpayer indicates that he is intending to file a bankruptcy proceeding, the revenue officer *must* file notice of the lien. *Id.* 5.12.1.13(2). The IRS will typically not file a Notice of Federal Tax Lien in cases in which the unpaid balance is less than $5,000, the taxpayer is deceased and no estate assets exist, or when there are indications that the taxpayer's liability has already been paid, is incorrect, or will be offset with existing tax credits. *See id.*

[b] Release and Discharge

Section 6325 specifies the circumstances under which the IRS will release a federal tax lien or discharge property from the lien. A lien must be released no later than 30 days after the day on which the lien has been satisfied in full or becomes legally unenforceable. The lien must also be released if the taxpayer posts an acceptable bond that is conditioned upon payment of the assessed amount plus interest. I.R.C. § 6325(a). In addition, the IRS has stated its willingness to release a lien once an offer in compromise, discussed below, is accepted, provided the taxpayer pays the offered amount and otherwise complies with the offer agreement. I.R.M. 5.12.2.2.4. A release occurs when the IRS files a Certificate of Release of Federal Tax Lien. Although the statute specifies the time period in which the release must take place, as a practical matter taxpayers usually must request a release from the IRS to ensure prompt action. *See* Treas. Reg. § 301.6325-1(f) (procedures for requesting release).

Unlike a release, which frees up all the taxpayer's property from the tax lien, a discharge applies only to a specific item of property. The IRS has discretionary authority to discharge property from a tax lien, without the necessity of payment or bond, if the remaining property covered by the tax lien has a fair market value at least twice the amount of the tax lien plus the amount of any other liens that have priority over the tax lien. *See* I.R.C. § 6325(b)(1). For example, if the taxpayer owes $2,000 in unpaid taxes and also owns a parcel of real property with a fair market value of $20,000, the IRS may discharge the taxpayer's other property from the lien as long as any other prior liens on the real property do not exceed $8,000. *See* Treas. Reg. § 301.6325-1(b)(1)(ii) Ex. Form 669-A, Certificate of Discharge of Property from Federal Tax Lien, is used for this purpose. The IRS may also issue a Certificate of Discharge with respect to a specific item of property if the taxpayer pays the government an amount equal to its equity interest in that property. Form 669-B is used for these purposes.[10]

Finally, the tax lien encumbering property may be discharged in order to permit the delinquent taxpayer to sell the subject property. In that case, the IRS substitutes its lien on the property for one on the proceeds derived from the sale. I.R.C. § 6325(b)(3); Treas. Reg. § 301-6325-1(b)(3). Such a procedure is common when a dispute arises among competing claimants and the property

---

[10] If the IRS determines that the government's interest in certain property has no value (because, for example, the value of prior encumbrances exceed the total value of the property), the IRS may issue a certificate releasing the property from the tax lien. I.R.C. § 6325(b)(2)(B). A request for release may be made by the taxpayer on Form 669-C.

is sold to facilitate a resolution. Instructions relating to an application for a lien discharge, including a list of all supporting documents required, are contained in Publication 783, How to Apply for Certificate of Discharge of Property from Federal Tax Lien.[11]

[4] Erroneously Filed Liens

A taxpayer who believes that the IRS has erroneously filed a Notice of Federal Tax Lien against his property may file an administrative appeal with the IRS under section 6326 to release the lien. A lien notice is considered to have been erroneously filed where the liability was already satisfied at the time of filing; the liability was assessed in violation of the section 6213 deficiency procedures; or the statute of limitations on collection had expired prior to filing the notice of lien. Treas. Reg. § 301.6326-1(b). This appeal procedure does not permit the taxpayer to contest the merits of the underlying assessment. *Id.* The regulations accompanying section 6326 specify the applicable procedures and methods of proof required to establish that the lien was erroneously filed. If the taxpayer prevails, the IRS will provide a copy of the release and a letter of apology to the taxpayer's creditors. I.R.M. 5.12.2.5.

In the situation where the IRS mistakenly files a Notice of Federal Tax Lien with respect to property not owned by the delinquent taxpayer, the actual owner may suffer serious damage from having the property encumbered by the lien. The Code provides a third party a number of avenues of relief in the case of an erroneously filed lien. Section 6325(b)(4), for example, permits a third-party owner of property against which a federal tax lien has been filed to obtain a certificate discharging the property from the tax lien if the third party deposits with the IRS funds equal to the value of the government's interest in the property or provides a bond in a like amount. After receiving the certificate of discharge, the third party may file a civil action in federal district court in order to determine whether and to what extent the property was encumbered by the tax lien. I.R.C. § 7426(g)(3). If the IRS does not have a valid interest in the property, or the IRS interest turns out to be valued at an amount less than the deposited or bonded amount, the district court can order a refund of the deposited amount, with interest, and a release of the bond. Relief may also be afforded third parties under section 6325(e), which authorizes the IRS to issue a certificate specifying that the tax lien does not attach to the property of the third party. Nonattachment usually occurs when, because of similarities in names, the IRS files the tax lien with respect to the wrong taxpayer's property.

---

[11] In addition to these procedures relating to release and discharge, section 6323(j) and Treas. Reg. § 301.6323(j)-1(b) set forth circumstances under which the IRS may be willing to withdraw a Notice of Federal Tax Lien, including (1) the filing of the notice was premature or otherwise not in accordance with administrative procedures; (2) the taxpayer has entered into an installment agreement to satisfy the liability for which the lien was imposed; (3) the withdrawal notice will facilitate collection of the tax liability; or (4) the withdrawal notice would be in the best interests of both the taxpayer and the government.

[B] Levy and Sale

A federal tax lien is merely an encumbrance against the taxpayer's property. The primary method used by the IRS to enforce the tax lien is the administrative procedure of levy and sale. Section 6331 permits the IRS to levy upon the taxpayer's property and sell the property at public auction in order to generate proceeds to satisfy the unpaid liability.[12] I.R.C. § 6331(b). No judicial intervention is required. In cases not involving a jeopardy assessment, the IRS must wait to levy against the taxpayer's property until after the expiration of a ten-day period following the issuance of a Notice and Demand for Payment, discussed above. In the usual case, the IRS will issue one or two additional demands for payment before resorting to levy. If the taxpayer can convince the IRS that he is making a sincere effort to pay the liability, the levy may be postponed. In such a case, the revenue officer will likely require the taxpayer to enter into an agreement providing for full payment of the assessed liability within a reasonable period of time. The procedures relating to installment agreements are discussed below.

[1] Notification of Intent to Levy and the Collection Due Process Notice

Before seizing the taxpayer's property, the IRS must mail or deliver a written statement notifying the taxpayer of its intent to levy and describing the statutory and administrative procedures relating to levy and sale and the alternatives that may be available to the taxpayer to prevent a levy (the Notice of Intent to Levy, Form 668-A). I.R.C. § 6331(d). The IRS must provide the Notice of Intent to Levy at least 30 days prior to levying on the taxpayer's property.[13] *Id.* Effective for collection activities after December 31, 2000, the IRS Reform Act requires supervisor approval before the IRS can issue a levy notice and before it can levy on or seize the taxpayer's property. IRS Reform Act § 3421. In the case of a jeopardy assessment, the Code permits the IRS to levy and seize a delinquent taxpayer's property immediately after making notice and demand with no prior notice required. I.R.C. § 6331(a).

The IRS Reform Act created a new, separate pre-levy notice procedure, described in Code section 6330, which is similar to the procedure in section 6320 relating to notification after a Notice of Federal Tax Lien has been filed. The required contents of the notice are virtually the same as those for a Notice of Intent to Levy and must be provided within the same 30-day period before a levy takes place. I.R.C. § 6330(a). In addition, the section 6330 notice must inform the taxpayer of his right to protest the proposed levy with the Appeals Division, also referred to as a CDP Hearing. The issues that may be raised in the CDP Hearing are discussed in Section 12.05[A]. A delinquent taxpayer in a jeopardy case is not entitled to a CDP notice prior to levy, but still has

---

[12] A levy transfers an interest in property to the government. Levy normally is followed by seizure of the property. However, for intangible property not represented by a document or other physical asset, the levy itself generally suffices. *See* United States v. Donahue Indus., 905 F.2d 1325, 1329 (9th Cir. 1990).

[13] Code section 6213 also prohibits the IRS from making a levy until 90 days after mailing a notice of deficiency or, if a petition is filed in the Tax Court, until the Tax Court's decision becomes final.

a right to request a due process hearing within a reasonable amount of time after the levy occurs. I.R.C. § 6330(f)(1). Similarly, section 6330 does not require that the taxpayer be granted a pre-levy CDP Hearing before issuing a levy to collect a state tax refund owed the taxpayer. As in a jeopardy case, a post-levy hearing is all that is required. Treas. Reg. § 301.6330-1(a)(2).

[2]   Property Subject to Levy

A levy may be made on all of the delinquent taxpayer's property or rights to property, real or personal, tangible or intangible, unless specifically exempted. In addition, property that is encumbered by the federal tax lien is subject to levy whether the property is in the taxpayer's or someone else's possession. I.R.C. § 6331(a). Unlike the federal tax lien, a levy does not operate prospectively to subject after-acquired property to seizure. In other words, the IRS may impose a levy only on the taxpayer's property or rights to property (including future interests and obligations owed the taxpayer) existing at the time of levy. *See, e.g., Tull v. United States*, 69 F.3d 394 (9th Cir. 1995). An exception is made in the case of wages, salaries and certain other periodic payments. In these specific cases, the levy is deemed to be continuous, thereby permitting the IRS to collect amounts accruing after the date of levy so long as the liability remains unpaid. I.R.C. § 6331(e), (h). Outside these special cases, if the value of the taxpayer's property levied upon is insufficient to cover the entire outstanding debt, the IRS can reach additional or after-acquired property only by making an additional levy. I.R.C. § 6331(c). These successive levies must satisfy the notice requirements applicable to all levies.

Section 6334(a) enumerates classes of property that are exempt from levy. Among other items, property exempt from levy includes ordinary clothing and schoolbooks necessary for the taxpayer or members of his family; certain household and personal effects with a value not in excess of $6,250; up to $3,125 worth of books and tools necessary for a trade or business; salary and wages that must be paid under a child support order; and minimum amounts of wages and other income, which are determined in part based on the number of the taxpayer's dependents. I.R.C. § 6334(d).[14]

Exemptions from levy are specifically limited to those types of property listed in section 6334. As a result, *state* laws that may exempt property from levy do not protect against federal collection efforts. The following case, which involves a judicially enforced levy under section 7403, illustrates the hardship that may be caused to an individual who owns an interest in property also owned by the delinquent taxpayer. The case also contrasts the section 7403 judicial collection procedures with administrative collection procedures.

---

[14] Although property exempt from levy may still be subject to the federal tax lien, the IRS normally will not file a Notice of Federal Tax Lien against such property. The IRS need not, however, file a Notice of Federal Tax Lien before levying on the taxpayer's non-exempt property.

UNITED STATES v. RODGERS
United States Supreme Court
461 U.S. 677 (1983)

JUSTICE BRENNAN delivered the opinion of the Court.

These consolidated cases involve the relationship between the imperatives of federal tax collection and rights accorded by state property laws. Section 7403 of the Internal Revenue Code of 1954, 26 U. S. C. § 7403 (1976 ed. and Supp. V), authorizes the judicial sale of certain properties to satisfy the tax indebtedness of delinquent taxpayers. The issue in both cases is whether § 7403 empowers a federal district court to order the sale of a family home in which a delinquent taxpayer had an interest at the time he incurred his indebtedness, but in which the taxpayer's spouse, who does not owe any of that indebtedness, also has a separate "homestead" right as defined by Texas law. We hold that the statute does grant power to order the sale, but that its exercise is limited to some degree by equitable discretion. We also hold that, if the home is sold, the nondelinquent spouse is entitled, as part of the distribution of proceeds required under § 7403, to so much of the proceeds as represents complete compensation for the loss of the homestead estate.

* * *

B.

The substance of Texas law related to the homestead right may usefully be divided into two categories. *Cf.* Woods v. Alvarado State Bank, 118 Tex. 586, 590, 19 S.W. 2d 35, 35 (1929). First, in common with a large number of States, Texas establishes the family home or place of business as an enclave exempted from the reach of most creditors. Thus, under Tex. Const., Art. 16, § 50:

> "The homestead of a family, or of a single adult person, shall be, and is hereby protected from forced sale, for the payment of all debts except for [certain exceptions not relevant here] . . . . No mortgage, trust deed, or other lien on the homestead shall ever be valid, except for [certain exceptions not relevant here]."

Second, in common with a somewhat smaller number of States, Texas gives members of the family unit additional rights in the homestead property itself. Thus, in a clause not included in the above quotation, Tex. Const., Art 16, § 50, also provides that "the owner or claimant of the property claimed as homestead [may not], if married, sell or abandon the homestead without the consent of the other spouse, given in such manner as may be prescribed by law." Equally important, Art. 16, § 52, provides:

> "On the death of the husband or wife, or both, the homestead shall descend and vest in like manner as other real property of the deceased, and shall be governed by the same laws of descent and distribution, but it shall not be partitioned among the heirs of the deceased during the lifetime of the surviving husband or wife, or so long as the survivor may elect to use or occupy the same as a

homestead, or so long as the guardian of the minor children of the deceased may be permitted, under the order of the proper court having the jurisdiction, to use and occupy the same."

The effect of these provisions in the Texas Constitution is to give each spouse in a marriage a separate and undivided possessory interest in the homestead, which is only lost by death or abandonment, and which may not be compromised either by the other spouse or by his or her heirs.[n.10] It bears emphasis that the rights accorded by the homestead laws vest independently in each spouse regardless of whether one spouse, or both, actually owns the fee interest in the homestead. Thus, although analogy is somewhat hazardous in this area, it may be said that the homestead laws have the effect of reducing the underlying ownership rights in a homestead property to something akin to remainder interests and vesting in each spouse an interest akin to an undivided life estate in the property. *See* Williams v. Williams, 569 S.W. 2d 867, 869 (Tex. 1978), and cases cited; Paddock v. Siemoneit, 147 Tex. 571, 585, 218 S.W. 2d 428, 436 (1949), and cases cited; Hill v. Hill, 623 S.W. 2d 779, 780 (Tex. App. 1981), and cases cited. This analogy, although it does some injustice to the nuances present in the Texas homestead statute, also serves to bring to the fore something that has been repeatedly emphasized by the Texas courts, and that was reaffirmed by the Court of Appeals in these cases: that the Texas homestead right is not a mere statutory entitlement, but a vested property right. * * * As the Supreme Court of Texas put it, a spouse "has a vested estate in the land of which she cannot be divested during her life except by abandonment or a voluntary conveyance in the manner prescribed by law." * * * .

II.

The two cases before us were consolidated for oral argument before the United States Court of Appeals for the Fifth Circuit, and resulted in opinions issued on the same day. *United States v. Rogers, supra*; Ingram v. Dallas Dept. of Housing & Urban Rehabilitation, 649 F.2d 1128 (1981). They arise out of legally comparable, but quite distinct, sets of facts.

A.

Lucille Mitzi Bosco Rodgers is the widow of Philip S. Bosco, whom she married in 1937. She and Mr. Bosco acquired, as community property, a residence in Dallas, Texas, and occupied it as their homestead. Subsequently, in 1971 and 1972, the Internal Revenue Service issued assessments totaling more than $900,000 for federal wagering taxes, penalties, and interest, against Philip for the taxable years 1966 through 1971. These taxes remained unpaid at the time of Philip's death in 1974. Since Philip's death, Lucille has

---

[n.10] The homestead character of property is not destroyed even by divorce, if one of the parties to the divorce continues to maintain the property as a proper homestead. *See* Renaldo v. Bank of San Antonio, 630 S.W. 2d 638, 639 (Tex. 1982); Wierzchula v. Wierzchula, 623 S.W. 2d 730, 732 (Tex. Civ. App. 1981). The courts may, however, partition the property, award it to one or the other spouse, or require one spouse to compensate the other, as part of the disposition of marital property attendant to the divorce proceedings. *See* Hedtke v. Hedtke, 112 Tex. 404, 248 S.W. 21 (1923); Brunell v. Brunell, 494 S.W. 2d 621, 622–623 (Tex. Civ. App. 1973).

continued to occupy the property as her homestead, and now lives there with her present husband.

On September 23, 1977, the Government filed suit under 26 U. S. C. §§ 7402 and 7403 in the United States District Court for the Northern District of Texas against Mrs. Rodgers and Philip's son, daughter, and executor. The suit sought to reduce to judgment the assessments against Philip, to enforce the Government's tax liens, including the one that had attached to Philip's interest in the residence, and to obtain a deficiency judgment in the amount of any unsatisfied part of the liability. On cross-motions for summary judgment, the District Court granted partial summary judgment on, among other things, the defendants' claim that the federal tax liens could not defeat Mrs. Rodgers' state-created right not to have her homestead subjected to a forced sale. Fed. Rule Civ. Proc. 54(b).

The Court of Appeals affirmed on the homestead issue, holding that if "a homestead interest is, under state law, a property right, possessed by the nontaxpayer spouse at the time the lien attaches to the taxpayer spouse's interest, then the federal tax lien may not be foreclosed against the homestead property for as long as the nontaxpayer spouse maintains his or her homestead interest under state law." 649 F.2d, at 1125 (footnotes omitted). The court implied that the Government had the choice of either waiting until Mrs. Rodgers' homestead interest lapsed, or satisfying itself with a forced sale of only Philip Bosco's interest in the property.

B.

Joerene Ingram is the divorced wife of Donald Ingram. During their marriage, Joerene and Donald acquired, as community property, a residence in Dallas, Texas, and occupied it as their homestead. Subsequently, in 1972 and 1973, the Internal Revenue Service issued assessments against Donald Ingram relating to unpaid taxes withheld from wages of employees of a company of which he was president. Deducting payments made on account of these liabilities, there remains unpaid approximately $9,000, plus interest. In addition, in 1973, the Service made an assessment against both Donald and Joerene in the amount of $283.33, plus interest, relating to their joint income tax liability for 1971. These amounts also remain unpaid.

In March 1975, at about the time the Ingrams were seeking a divorce, their residence was destroyed by fire. In September 1975, the Ingrams obtained a divorce. In connection with the divorce, they entered into a property settlement agreement, one provision of which was that Donald would convey to Joerene his interest in the real property involved in this case in exchange for $1,500, to be paid from the proceeds of the sale of the property. Joerene tried to sell the property, through a trustee, but was unsuccessful in those efforts, apparently because of the federal tax liens encumbering the property. To make matters worse, she then received notice from the City of Dallas Department of Housing and Urban Rehabilitation (Department) that unless she complied with local ordinances, the remains of the fire-damaged residence would be demolished. Following a hearing, the Department issued a final notice and a work order to demolish. Joerene Ingram and the trustee then filed suit in

Texas state court to quiet title to the property, to remove the federal tax liens, and to enjoin demolition. The defendants were the United States, the Department, and several creditors claiming an interest in the property.

The United States removed the suit to the District Court for the Northern District of Texas. It then filed a counterclaim against Joerene Ingram and Donald Ingram (who was added as a defendant on the counterclaim) for both the unpaid withholding taxes and the joint liability for unpaid income taxes. In its prayer for relief, the Government sought, among other things, judicial sale of the property under § 7403. Pursuant to a stipulation of the parties, the property was sold unencumbered and the proceeds (approximately $16,250) were deposited into the registry of the District Court pending the outcome of the suit. The parties agreed that their rights, claims, and priorities would be determined as if the sale had not taken place, and that the proceeds would be divided according to their respective interests. On cross-motions for summary judgment, the District Court granted summary judgment on the Government's counterclaims.

The Court of Appeals affirmed in part, and reversed and remanded in part. It agreed that the Government could foreclose its lien on the proceeds from the sale of the property to collect the $283.33, plus interest, for the unpaid income tax owed by Joerene and Donald Ingram jointly. Applying its decision in *Rodgers,* however, it also held that the Government could not reach the proceeds of the sale of the property to collect the individual liability of Donald Ingram, assuming Joerene Ingram had maintained her homestead interest in the property. The court remanded, however, for a factual determination of whether Joerene had "abandoned" the homestead by dividing the insurance proceeds with Donald and by attempting — even before the stipulation entered into with the Government — to sell the property and divide the proceeds of that sale with Donald.[n.15]

C.

The Government filed a single petition for certiorari in both these cases. See this Court's Rule 19.4. We granted certiorari, 456 U.S. 904 (1982), in order to resolve a conflict among the Courts of Appeals as to the proper interpretation of § 7403.

III.

A.

The basic holding underlying the Court of Appeals' view that the Government was not authorized to seek a sale of the homes in which respondents held a homestead interest is that "when a delinquent taxpayer shares his ownership interest in property jointly with other persons rather than being the sole owner, his 'property' and 'rights to property' to which the federal tax

---

[n.15] The Court of Appeals did suggest that neither the fire nor the intention to sell the house would, in and of themselves, necessarily indicate an abandonment of the homestead. 649 F.2d, at 1132, and n.6. * * *

lien attaches under 26 U.S.C. § 6321, and on which federal levy may be had under 26 U.S.C. § 7403(a), involve only his *interest* in the property, and not the entire property." 649 F.2d, at 1125 (emphasis in original). According to the Court of Appeals, this principle applies, not only in the homestead context, but in any cotenancy in which unindebted third parties share an ownership interest with a delinquent taxpayer. *See* Folsom v. United States, 306 F.2d 361 (CA5 1962).

We agree with the Court of Appeals that the Government's lien under § 6321 cannot extend beyond the property interests held by the delinquent taxpayer. We also agree that the Government may not ultimately collect, as satisfaction for the indebtedness owed to it, more than the value of the property interests that are actually liable for that debt. But, in this context at least, the right to collect and the right to seek a forced sale are two quite different things.

The Court of Appeals for the Fifth Circuit recognized that it was the only Court of Appeals that had adopted the view that the Government could seek the sale, under § 7403, of only the delinquent taxpayer's "*interest* in the property, and not the entire property." 649 F.2d, at 1125, and n.12. We agree with the prevailing view that such a restrictive reading of § 7403 flies in the face of the plain meaning of the statute. *See, e.g.,* United States v. Trilling, 328 F.2d 699, 702–703 (CA7 1964); Washington v. United States, 402 F.2d 3, 6–7 (CA4 1968); United States v. Overman, 424 F.2d 1142, 1146 (CA9 1970); United States v. Kocher, 468 F.2d 503, 506–507 (CA2 1972); *see also* Mansfield v. Excelsior Refining Co., 135 U.S. 326, 339–341 (1890).

Section 7403(a) provides not only that the Government may "enforce [its] lien," but also that it may seek to "subject *any property,* of whatever nature, of the delinquent, or *in which he has any right, title, or interest,* to the payment of such tax or liability" (emphasis added). This clause in and of itself defeats the reading proposed by the Court of Appeals. Section 7403(b) then provides that "[all] persons having liens upon *or claiming any interest in the property involved in such action* shall be made parties thereto" (emphasis added). Obviously, no joinder of persons claiming independent interests in the property would be necessary if the Government were only authorized to seek the sale of the delinquent taxpayer's own interests. Finally, § 7403(c) provides that the district court should "determine the merits of all claims to and liens upon the property, and, in all cases where a claim or interest of the United States therein is established, may decree a sale *of such property . . . and a distribution of the proceeds of such sale according to the findings of the court in respect to the interests of the parties and of the United States*" (emphasis added). Again, we must read the statute to contemplate, not merely the sale of the delinquent taxpayer's own interest, but the sale of the entire property (as long as the United States has any "claim or interest" in it), and the recognition of third-party interests through the mechanism of judicial valuation and distribution. * * *

Our reading of § 7403 is consistent with the policy inherent in the tax statutes in favor of the prompt and certain collection of delinquent taxes. * * * It requires no citation to point out that interests in property, when sold separately, may be worth either significantly more or significantly less than the sum of their parts. When the latter is the case, it makes considerable sense to allow the Government to seek the sale of the whole, and obtain its fair share of the proceeds, rather than satisfy itself with a mere sale of the part.

* * *

Finally, our reading of the statute is significantly bolstered by a comparison with the statutory language setting out the administrative levy remedy also available to the Government. Under 26 U.S.C. § 6331(a), the Government may sell for the collection of unpaid taxes all nonexempt "property and rights to property . . . *belonging to such person* [*i.e.,* the delinquent taxpayer] or on which there is a lien provided in this chapter for the payment of such tax" (emphasis added). This language clearly embodies the limitation that the Court of Appeals thought was present in § 7403, and it has been so interpreted by the courts. Section 6331, unlike § 7403, does not require notice and hearing for third parties, because no rights of third parties are intended to be implicated by § 6331. Indeed, third parties whose property or interests in property have been seized inadvertently are entitled to claim that the property has been "wrongfully levied upon," and may apply for its return either through administrative channels, 26 U.S.C. § 6343(b), or through a civil action filed in a federal district court, § 7426(a)(1); *see* §§ 7426(b)(1), 7426(b)(2)(A). In the absence of such "wrongful levy," the entire proceeds of a sale conducted pursuant to administrative levy may be applied, without any prior distribution of the sort required by § 7403, to the expenses of the levy and sale, the specific tax liability on the seized property, and the general tax liability of the delinquent taxpayer. 26 U.S.C. § 6342.

We are not entirely unmoved by the force of the basic intuition underlying the Court of Appeals' view of § 7403 — that the Government, though it has the "right to pursue the property of the [delinquent] taxpayer with all the force and fury at its command," should not have any right, superior to that of other creditors, to disturb the settled expectations of innocent third parties. *Folsom v. United States*, 306 F.2d, at 367–368. In fact, however, the Government's right to seek a forced sale of the entire property in which a delinquent taxpayer had an interest does not arise out of its privileges as an ordinary creditor, but out of the express terms of § 7403. Moreover, the use of the power granted by § 7403 is not the act of an ordinary creditor, but the exercise of a sovereign prerogative, incident to the power to enforce the obligations of the delinquent taxpayer himself, and ultimately grounded in the constitutional mandate to "lay and collect taxes." *Cf. Bull v. United States*, 295 U.S., at 259–260; Phillips v. Commissioner, 283 U.S. 589, 595–597 (1931); United States v. Snyder, 149 U.S. 210, 214–215 (1893).

Admittedly, if § 7403 allowed for the gratuitous confiscation of one person's property interests in order to satisfy another person's tax indebtedness, such a provision might pose significant difficulties under the Due Process Clause of the Fifth Amendment. But, as we have already indicated, § 7403 makes no further use of third-party property interests than to facilitate the extraction of value from those concurrent property interests that *are* properly liable for the taxpayer's debt. To the extent that third-party property interests are "taken" in the process, § 7403 provides compensation for that "taking" by requiring that the court distribute the proceeds of the sale "according to the findings of the court in respect to the interests of the parties and of the United States." *Cf. United States v. Overman,* 424 F.2d, at 1146. Moreover, we hold, on the basis of what we are informed about the nature of the homestead estate in Texas, that it is the sort of property interest for whose loss an innocent third party must be compensated under § 7403. *Cf.* United States v. General Motors Corp., 323 U.S. 373, 377–378 (1945). We therefore see no contradiction, at least at the level of basic principle, between the enforcement powers granted to the Government under § 7403 and the recognition of vested property interests granted to innocent third parties under state law.

The exact method for the distribution required by § 7403 is not before us at this time. But we can get a rough idea of the practical consequences of the principles we have just set out. For example, if we assume, *only for the sake of illustration,* that a homestead estate is the exact economic equivalent of a life estate, and that the use of a standard statutory or commercial table and an 8% discount rate is appropriate in calculating the value of that estate, then three nondelinquent surviving or remaining spouses, aged 30, 50, and 70 years, each holding a homestead estate, would be entitled to approximately 97%, 89%, and 64%, respectively, of the proceeds of the sale of their homes as compensation for that estate. In addition, if we assume that each of these hypothetical nondelinquent spouses also has a protected half-interest in the underlying ownership rights to the property being sold, then their total compensation would be approximately 99%, 95%, and 82%, respectively, of the proceeds from such sale.

In sum, the Internal Revenue Code, seen as a whole, contains a number of cumulative collection devices, each with its own advantages and disadvantages for the tax collector. Among the advantages of administrative levy is that it is quick and relatively inexpensive. Among the advantages of a § 7403 proceeding is that it gives the Federal Government the opportunity to seek the highest return possible on the forced sale of property interests liable for the payment of federal taxes. The provisions of § 7403 are broad and profound. Nevertheless, § 7403 is punctilious in protecting the vested rights of third parties caught in the Government's collection effort, and in ensuring that the Government not receive out of the proceeds of the sale any more than that to which it is properly entitled. Of course, the exercise in any particular case of the power granted under § 7403 to seek the forced sale of property interests other than those of the delinquent taxpayer is left in the first instance to the good sense and common decency of the collecting authorities. 26 U.S.C. § 7403(a). We also explore in Part IV of this opinion the nature of the limited discretion left to the courts in proceedings brought under § 7403. But that the power exists, and that it is necessary to the prompt and certain enforcement of the tax laws, we have no doubt.

B.

There is another, intermeshed but analytically distinguishable, ground advanced by the Court of Appeals and the respondents — and reiterated by the dissent — for denying the Government the right to seek the forced sale of property held as a homestead by a nondelinquent third party. Taken in itself, this view would hold that, even if § 7403 normally allows for the forced sale of property interests other than those directly liable for the indebtedness of the delinquent taxpayer, the special protections accorded by the exemption aspect of Texas homestead law, *see supra,* should immunize it from the reach of § 7403.

The Court of Appeals conceded that "the homestead interest of a *taxpayer* spouse, *i.e.*, that of one who himself has tax liability, clearly cannot by itself defeat [the enforcement under § 7403 of] a federal tax lien." 649 F.2d, at 1121 (emphasis in original); *see also* 649 F.2d, at 1132 (authorizing levy on proceeds in *Ingram* case to the extent of the $283.33 liability jointly owed by Mr. and Mrs. Ingram). This proposition, although not explicit in the Code, is clearly implicit in 26 U.S.C. § 6334(c) (relating to exemptions from levy), and in our decisions in *United States v. Mitchell*, 403 U.S., at 204–205; *Aquilino v. United States*, 363 U.S., at 513–514; and *United States v. Bess*, 357 U.S., at 56–57, * * * . The Court of Appeals also held that, if the homestead interest under Texas law were "merely an exemption" without accompanying vested property rights, it would not be effective against the Federal Government in a § 7403 proceeding, even in the case of a nondelinquent spouse. 649 F.2d, at 1125. Nevertheless, the court concluded that, if the homestead estate both was claimed by a nondelinquent spouse and constituted a property right under state law, then it would bar the Federal Government from pursuing a forced sale of the entire property.

We disagree. If § 7403 is intended, as we believe it is, to reach the entire property in which a delinquent taxpayer has or had any "right, title, or interest," then state-created exemptions against forced sale should be no more effective with regard to the entire property than with regard to the "right, title, or interest" itself. *Accord, United States v. Overman*, 424 F.2d, at 1145–1147; Herndon v. United States, 501 F.2d 1219, 1223–1224 (CA8 1974) (Ross, J., concurring). No exception of the sort carved out by the Court of Appeals appears on the face of the statute, and we decline to frustrate the policy of the statute by reading such an exception into it. *Cf.* Hisquierdo v. Hisquierdo, 439 U.S. 572, 586–587 (1979); *United States v. Mitchell, supra,* at 205–206. Moreover, the Supremacy Clause which provides the underpinning for the Federal Government's right to sweep aside state-created exemptions in the first place — is as potent in its application to innocent bystanders as in its application to delinquent debtors. *See United States v. Union Central Life Insurance Co.*, 368 U.S., at 293–295 (federal tax lien good against bona fide purchaser, even though lien not filed in accordance with provisions of state law); *cf. Hisquierdo v. Hisquierdo, supra,* at 585–586; United States v. Carmack, 329 U.S. 230, 236–240 (1946). Whatever property rights attach to a homestead under Texas law are adequately discharged by the payment of compensation, and no further deference to state law is required, either by § 7403 or by the Constitution.

The dissent urges us to carve out an exception from the plain language of § 7403 in that "small number of joint-ownership situations . . . [in which] the delinquent taxpayer has no right to force partition or otherwise to alienate the entire property without the consent of the co-owner." * * * Its primary argument in favor of such an exception is that it would be consistent with traditional limitations on the rights of a lienholder. * * * If § 7403 truly embodied traditional limitations on the rights of lienholders, however, then we would have to conclude that *Folsom v. United States*, 306 F.2d 361 (CA5 1962), discussed *supra,* was correctly decided, a proposition that even the dissent is not willing to advance. * * * More importantly, we believe that the better analogy in this case is not to the traditional rights of lienholders, but to the traditional powers of a taxing authority in an *in rem* enforcement proceeding. * * *

IV.

A.

Although we have held that the Supremacy Clause allows the federal tax collector to convert a nondelinquent spouse's homestead estate into its fair cash value, and that such a conversion satisfies the requirements of due process, we are not blind to the fact that in practical terms financial compensation may not always be a completely adequate substitute for a roof over one's head. *Cf.* United States v. 564.54 Acres of Land, 441 U.S. 506, 510-513 (1979). This problem seems particularly acute in the case of a homestead interest. First, the nature of the market for life estates or the market for rental property may be such that the value of a homestead interest, calculated as some fraction of the total value of a home, would be less than the price demanded by the market for a lifetime's interest in an equivalent home. Second, any calculation of the cash value of a homestead interest must of necessity be based on actuarial statistics, and will unavoidably undercompensate persons who end up living longer than the average. Indeed, it is precisely because of problems such as these that a number of courts, in eminent domain cases involving property divided between a homestead interest and underlying ownership rights or between a life estate and a remainder interest, have refused to distribute the proceeds according to an actuarial formula, and have instead placed the entire award in trust (or reinvested it in a new parcel of property) with the income (or use) going to the life-estate holder during his or her lifetime, and the corpus vesting in the holder of the remainder interest upon the death of the life-estate holder.

If the sale and distribution provided for in § 7403 were mandatory, the practical problems we have just described would be of little legal consequence. The statute provides, however, that the court in a § 7403 proceeding *"shall . . . proceed to adjudicate all matters involved therein and finally determine the merits of all claims to and liens upon the property, and, in all cases where a claim or interest of the United States therein is established, may decree a sale of such property . . ."* (emphasis added), and respondents argue that this language allows a district court hearing a § 7403 proceeding to exercise a degree of equitable discretion and refuse to authorize a forced sale in a particular case. *See* Tillery v. Parks, 630 F.2d 775 (CA10 1980); United States v. Eaves, 499 F.2d 869, 870–871 (CA10 1974); *United States v. Hershberger*, 475 F.2d, at 679–680; *United States v. Overman*, 424 F.2d, at 1146; United States v. Morrison, 247 F.2d 285, 289–291 (CA5 1957). The Court of Appeals agreed with this interpretation of the statute, although it does not appear to have relied on it, 649 F.2d, at 1125, and in any event neither it nor the District Court undertook any particularized equitable assessment of the cases now before us. We find the question to be close, but on balance, we too conclude that § 7403 does not require a district court to authorize a forced sale under absolutely all circumstances, and that some limited room is left in the statute for the exercise of reasoned discretion.

B.

* * *

Finally, we are convinced that recognizing that district courts may exercise a degree of equitable discretion in § 7403 proceedings is consistent with the policies of the statute: unlike an absolute exception, which we rejected above, the exercise of limited equitable discretion in individual cases can take into account both the Government's interest in prompt and certain collection of delinquent taxes and the possibility that innocent third parties will be unduly harmed by that effort.

C.

To say that district courts need not always go ahead with a forced sale authorized by § 7403 is not to say that they have unbridled discretion. We can think of virtually no circumstances, for example, in which it would be permissible to refuse to authorize a sale simply to protect the interests of the delinquent taxpayer himself or herself. And even when the interests of third parties are involved, we think that a certain fairly limited set of considerations will almost always be paramount.

First, a court should consider the extent to which the Government's financial interests would be prejudiced if it were relegated to a forced sale of the partial interest actually liable for the delinquent taxes. Even the Government seems to concede that, if such a partial sale would not prejudice it at all (because the separate market value of the partial interest is likely to be equal to or greater than its value as a fraction of the total value of the entire property) then there would be no reason at all to authorize a sale of the entire property. Tr. of Oral Arg. 7, 13; Reply Brief for United States 8, n.5. We think that a natural extension of this principle, however, is that, even when the partial interest would be worth *less* sold separately than sold as part of the entire property, the possibility of prejudice to the Government can still be measured as a matter of degree. Simply put, the higher the expected market price, the less the prejudice, and the less weighty the Government's interest in going ahead with a sale of the entire property.

Second, a court should consider whether the third party with a nonliable separate interest in the property would, in the normal course of events (leaving aside § 7403 and eminent domain proceedings, of course), have a legally recognized expectation that that separate property would not be subject to forced sale by the delinquent taxpayer or his or her creditors. If there is no such expectation, then there would seem to be little reason not to authorize the sale. Again, however, this factor is amenable to considerations of degree. The Texas homestead laws are almost absolute in their protections against forced sale. The usual cotenancy arrangement, which allows any cotenant to seek a judicial sale of the property and distribution of the proceeds, but which also allows the other cotenants to resist the sale and apply instead for a partition in kind, is further along the continuum. And a host of other types of property interests are arrayed between and beyond.

Third, a court should consider the likely prejudice to the third party, both in personal dislocation costs and in the sort of practical undercompensation described *supra* [in Part IV. A. of the Opinion, Eds.].

Fourth, a court should consider the relative character and value of the nonliable and liable interests held in the property: if, for example, in the case of real property, the third party has no present possessory interest or fee interest in the property, there may be little reason not to allow the sale; if, on the other hand, the third party not only has a possessory interest or fee interest, but that interest is worth 99% of the value of the property, then there might well be virtually no reason to allow the sale to proceed.

We do not pretend that the factors we have just outlined constitute an exhaustive list; we certainly do not contemplate that they be used as a "mechanical checklist" to the exclusion of common sense and consideration of special circumstances. *Cf.* Moses H. Cone Hospital v. Mercury Construction Corp., 460 U.S. 1, 16 (1983). We do emphasize, however, that the limited discretion accorded by § 7403 should be exercised rigorously and sparingly, keeping in mind the Government's paramount interest in prompt and certain collection of delinquent taxes.

V.

In these cases, no individualized equitable balance of the sort we have just outlined has yet been attempted. In the *Rodgers* case, the record before us, although it is quite clear as to the legal issues relevant to the second consideration noted above, affords us little guidance otherwise. In any event, we think that the task of exercising equitable discretion should be left to the District Court in the first instance.

The *Ingram* case is a bit more complicated, even leaving aside the fact of the stipulated sale by which we are constrained to treat the escrow fund now sitting in the registry of the District Court as if it were a house. First, as the Court of Appeals pointed out, there remains a question under Texas law as to whether Joerene Ingram abandoned the homestead by the time of the stipulated sale. Second, the Government, in addition to its lien for the individual debt of Donald Ingram, has a further lien for $283.33, plus interest, on the house, representing the joint liability of Donald and Joerene Ingram. Because Joerene Ingram is not a "third party" as to that joint liability, we can see no reason, as long as that amount remains unpaid, not to allow a "sale" of the "house" (*i.e.,* a levy on the proceeds of the stipulated sale) for satisfaction of the debt. Moreover, once the dam is broken, there is no reason, under our interpretation of § 7403, not to allow the Government also to collect on the individual debt of Donald Ingram *out of that portion of the proceeds of the sale representing property interests properly liable for the debt.* On the other hand, it would certainly be to Mrs. Ingram's advantage to discharge her personal liability before the Government can proceed with its "sale," in which event, assuming that she has not abandoned the homestead, the District Court will be obliged to strike an equitable balance on the same general principles as those that govern the *Rodgers* case.

The judgment of the Court of Appeals in *Rodgers* is reversed, its judgment in *Ingram* is vacated, and both cases are remanded with directions that they be remanded to the District Court for further proceedings consistent with this opinion.

So ordered.

JUSTICE BLACKMUN, with whom JUSTICE REHNQUIST, JUSTICE STEVENS, and JUSTICE O'CONNOR join, concurring in the result in part and dissenting in part.

The Court today properly rejects the broad legal principle concerning 26 U.S.C. § 7403 that was announced by the Court of Appeals. * * * I agree that, in some situations, § 7403 gives the Government the power to sell property *not* belonging to the taxpayer. Our task, however, is to ascertain how far Congress intended that power to extend. In my view, § 7403 confers on the Government the power to sell or force the sale of jointly owned property only insofar as the *tax debtor's* interest in that property would permit *him* to do so; it does not confer on the Government the power to sell jointly owned property if an unindebted co-owner enjoys an *indestructible* right to bar a sale and to continue in possession. Because Mrs. Rodgers had such a right, and because she is not herself indebted to the Government, I dissent from the Court's disposition of her case.

I.

It is basic in the common law that a lienholder enjoys rights in property no greater than those of the debtor himself; that is, the lienholder does no more than step into the debtor's shoes. 1 L. Jones, LAW OF LIENS § 9, pp. 9-10 (1914). * * *

In most situations in which a delinquent taxpayer shares property with an unindebted third party, it does no violence to this principle to order a sale of the entire property so long as the third party is fully compensated. A joint owner usually has at his disposal the power to convey the property or force its conveyance. Thus, for example, a joint tenant or tenant in common may seek partition. *See generally* W. Plumb, FEDERAL TAX LIENS 35 (3d ed. 1972). If a joint tenant is delinquent in his taxes, the United States does no more than step into the delinquent taxpayer's shoes when it compels a sale.

In a small number of joint-ownership situations, however, the delinquent taxpayer has no right to force partition or otherwise to alienate the entire property without the consent of the co-owner. These include tenancies by the entirety and certain homestead estates. *See* Plumb, "Federal Liens and Priorities — Agenda for the Next Decade II," 77 Yale L. J. 605, 634 (1968). In this case, the homestead estate owned by the delinquent taxpayer — Mrs. Rodgers' deceased husband — did not include the right to sell or force the sale of the homestead during Mrs. Rodgers' lifetime without her consent. Mrs.

Rodgers had, and still has, an indefeasible right to possession, an interest, as the Court recognizes, "akin to an undivided life estate." * * * A lienholder stepping into the shoes of the delinquent taxpayer would not be able to force a sale.

II.

By holding that the District Court has the discretion to order a sale of Mrs. Rodgers' property, the Court necessarily finds in the general language of § 7403 a congressional intent to abrogate the rule that the tax collector's lien does not afford him rights in property in excess of the rights of the delinquent taxpayer. I do not dispute that the general language of § 7403, standing alone, is subject to the interpretation the Court gives it. From its enactment in 1868 to the present day, the language of this statute has been sweeping; read literally, it admits of no exceptions. But when broadly worded statutes, particularly those of some antiquity, are in derogation of common-law principles, this Court has hesitated to heed arguments that they should be applied literally. *See* Imbler v. Pachtman, 424 U.S. 409, 417 (1976). In such cases, the Court has presumed in the absence of a clear indication to the contrary that Congress did not mean by its use of general language to contravene fundamental precepts of the common law.

A.

Apart from the general language of the statute, the Court points to nothing indicating a congressional intent to abrogate the traditional rule. It seems to me, indeed, that the evidence definitely points the other way. Scholarly comment on § 7403, and on § 6321, the tax lien provision, consistently has maintained that, in States such as Texas that confer on each spouse absolute rights to full use and possession of the homestead for life, the homestead property rights of an unindebted spouse may not be sold by the tax collector to satisfy the other spouse's tax debt. Court decisions addressing this point have been to the same effect. * * *

* * *

III.

Without direct evidence of congressional intent to contravene the traditional — and sensible — common-law rule, the Court advances three arguments purporting to lend indirect support for its construction of § 7403.

A.

First, the Court claims that its construction is consistent with the policy favoring "the prompt and certain collection of delinquent taxes." * * * This rationale would support any exercise of governmental power to secure tax payments. Were there two equally plausible suppositions of congressional intent, this policy might counsel in favor of choosing the construction more favorable to the Government. But when one interpretation contravenes both traditional rules of law and the common sense and common values on which they are built, the fact that it favors the Government's interests cannot be dispositive.

Moreover, the Government's interest would not be compromised substantially by a rule permitting it to sell property only when the delinquent taxpayer could have done so. In this case, the delinquent taxpayer's homestead interest, it is assumed, gave him a "half-interest in the underlying ownership rights to the property being sold." * * * An immediate forced sale of the entire property would yield for the Government no more than half the present value of the remainder interest, the residue left after the present values of the nondelinquent spouse's life estate and half-interest in the remainder are subtracted. As the Court notes, the Government can expect to receive only a small fraction of the proceeds. * * * An immediate sale of the delinquent taxpayer's future interest in the property might well command a commensurate price.

Alternatively, the Government could maintain its lien on the property until Mrs. Rodgers dies and then could force a sale. Because the delinquent taxpayer's estate retains a half-interest in the remainder, the Government would be entitled to half of the proceeds at that time. The Government's yield from this future sale, discounted to its present value, should not differ significantly from its yield under the Court's approach. The principal difference is that, following the common-law rule, Mrs. Rodgers' entitlement to live out her life on her homestead would be respected.

* * *

B.

The Court also would support its construction by contrasting § 7403 with the more restrictive language of § 6331, the administrative tax levy provision. * * * It is true that § 6331 permits the sale only of "property and rights to property . . . belonging to" the taxpayer, while § 7403 generally authorizes the sale of property in which the taxpayer has an interest. But the greater power conferred by § 7403 is needed to enable the Government to seek the sale of jointly owned property whenever the tax debtor's rights in the property would have permitted *him* to seek a forced sale. Section 7403 certainly permits the Government, in such circumstances, to seek partition of the property in federal, rather than state, court, to seek authority to sell the tax debtor's part or the whole, and, in the same proceeding, to have determined the entitlements of the various claimants, including competing lienholders, to the proceeds of the property sold. *See generally* Plumb, 77 Yale L. J., at 628–629. Absent the more expansive language of § 7403, this would not be possible. That language, however, does not manifest congressional intent to produce the extraordinary consequences yielded by the Court's interpretation.

C.

The Court also asserts that its construction of § 7403 is consistent with "the traditional powers of a taxing authority in an *in rem* enforcement proceeding," even if it is not consistent with the traditional rights of lienholders. * * * This, with all respect, is not so. *In rem* tax enforcement proceedings never have been used to sell property belonging to unindebted third parties in order to satisfy a tax delinquency unrelated to the property sold. As the Court recognizes, * * * such proceedings are brought to sell land in order to satisfy delinquent ad valorem taxes assessed on the land itself. 2 T. Cooley, Law of Taxation 866, 910 (3d ed. 1903). It is said that the land itself is liable for such taxes, and that conflicting ownership rights thus do not bar its sale. *See id.,* at 866-868; H. Black, Law of Tax Titles 296 (1888); W. Burroughs, Law of Taxation 346–349 (1877). The cases relied upon by the Court for the proposition that *in rem* tax proceedings extinguish the homestead rights of an unindebted spouse merely applied this rule. Lucas v. Purdy, 142 Iowa 359, 120 N.W. 1063 (1909); Robbins v. Barron, 32 Mich. 36 (1875); Jones v. Devore, 8 Ohio St. 430 (1858).

* * *

IV.

The Court recognizes that Mrs. Rodgers has an indestructible property right under Texas law to use, possess, and enjoy her homestead during her lifetime, and that the delinquent taxpayer's property interests would not have enabled him to disturb that right against her will. The Court recognizes that Mrs. Rodgers has no outstanding tax liability and that the Government has no lien on Mrs. Rodgers' property or property rights. Because I conclude that Congress did not intend § 7403 to permit federal courts to grant property rights to the Government greater than those enjoyed by the tax debtor, I would hold that the Government may not sell Mrs. Rodgers' homestead without her consent. To the extent the Court holds to the contrary, I respectfully dissent.

V.

Mrs. Ingram's case, however, is materially different. Like her husband, Mrs. Ingram was liable for back taxes, and consequently the Government had a lien on her interests in property as well as on her husband's interests. Exercising both spouses' rights in the homestead, the Government is entitled to force a sale, Plumb, 13 Tax L. Rev., at 263; *see* Shambaugh v. Scofield, 132 F.2d 345 (CA5 1942), subject only to the discretion of the District Court. * * * Second, when Mrs. Ingram and her former husband were divorced, the homestead became subject to partition under Texas law. * * * In Mrs. Ingram's case, therefore, I concur in the result.

Do you think the result in *Rodgers* would have differed if applicable state law provided instead that a joint tenant could not convey his homestead interest without the other tenant's consent?

[3] Seizure of Property Subject to Levy

Once a valid levy is made, the IRS will seek to obtain possession of the levied property. In most cases, the IRS will first seek to levy upon the delinquent taxpayer's bank deposits, if any, and wages owing from an employer. In the case of a wage levy, the employer must withhold the nonexempt portion of the taxpayer's wages and remit the amount directly to the IRS. Because a levy on wages and salaries is continuous, the employer must continue to remit portions of the taxpayer's salary to the IRS until the liability is satisfied in full. In the case of a bank levy, the financial institution is required to hold the taxpayer's accounts for 21 days after receiving notice of the levy in order to permit the taxpayer time to seek a release of the levy. After the 21-day period, the bank must remit the entire account balance to the IRS. I.R.C. § 6332(c). The IRS uses Form 668-W in the case of wage levies and Form 668-A in the case of bank or other third party levies.

> *Example*: Acme Bank is served with a Notice of Levy, Form 668-A, for an unpaid tax liability due from Jim Smith in the amount of $2,000. Acme Bank holds $1,000 in a checking account in Jim's name at the time the notice is issued. Acme Bank must hold the funds for a period of 21 days, at which time it must remit the entire $1,000 to the IRS if the levy has not been released. If Jim deposits an additional amount in the checking account after the initial Notice of Levy is issued, Acme Bank is not required to remit that additional deposit to the IRS. The IRS, however, may issue a successive bank levy in order to obtain possession of the later deposit.

If the property sought to be levied upon is in the hands of the taxpayer, the IRS uses Form 668-B, Levy, to demand possession. Beginning in 2002, the IRS will also impose a continuous levy on the taxpayer's social security benefits in an effort to collect unpaid tax accounts. *See* IR-2001-89.

The IRS Reform Act imposed significant restrictions on the IRS's ability to seize the taxpayer's personal residence and business-related assets in an effort to ensure that these assets are seized only as a last resort. If the IRS wishes to seize the taxpayer's principal residence, the IRS must obtain prior written approval of a United States District Court. I.R.C. § 6334(e)(1). Moreover, the IRS may not seize any residence used by the taxpayer, or any nonrental real property of the taxpayer that is used as a residence by someone else, for a deficiency (including taxes, interest and penalties) of $5,000 or less. I.R.C. § 6334(a)(13). Would this new requirement affect the outcome in a case like *Rodgers*?

Congress was also concerned that a seizure of property used by the taxpayer to carry out his trade or business could adversely affect the taxpayer's ability to pay his tax liability. As a result, the Code now requires prior written approval from an IRS official before such assets may be seized. Levy approval may be granted only if the IRS official determines that the taxpayer's other assets are insufficient to cover the unpaid assessment. I.R.C. § 6334(a)(13)(B). As a practical matter, therefore, the IRS must exhaust all other payment options before seizing the taxpayer's business assets.

The taxpayer or third party in possession of the property subject to levy normally must surrender the property to the IRS on demand. I.R.C. § 6332(a).

Once a third party surrenders an asset or payment to the IRS in response to a levy notice, that party is discharged from any liability to the delinquent taxpayer regarding the surrendered amount. I.R.C. § 6332(e). If the party in possession does not surrender the levied property upon demand, he becomes personally liable to the United States in an amount equal to the value of the property not surrendered. I.R.C. § 6332(d). In addition, if the person who is required to surrender the levied property fails to do so without reasonable cause, he becomes liable for a penalty equal to 50 percent of the amount of the liability.

In cases where the property is not voluntarily turned over, the IRS may forcibly seize the property from the taxpayer or the party in possession. Depending upon the type of property involved, the revenue officer will remove the property to a storage area or padlock it to prevent the taxpayer from retaking possession. As soon as practical after the property is seized, the IRS must provide the owner or possessor of the seized property with a notice describing the property and the amount demanded by the IRS for its release. Treas. Reg. § 301.6335-1(a). The IRS uses Form 2433, Notice of Seizure, for this purpose. Other restrictions relating to the seizure of property are described in section 6335.

Before the IRS attempts to sell a seized asset, the taxpayer is normally given a last opportunity to come to some payment arrangement with the IRS. If the taxpayer and the IRS agree upon a final payment and such payment is made, the IRS will release the levy and, if necessary, return the seized property to the owner. *See* I.R.C. § 6337(a). The IRS is also required to release a levy if (1) the underlying liability for which the levy was made becomes unenforceable due to a lapse of time; (2) the release will facilitate collection of the tax liability; (3) the levy causes an economic hardship for the taxpayer (by, for example, preventing him from meeting basic living expenses); or (4) the taxpayer enters into an agreement for paying the tax in installments. I.R.C. § 6343; Treas. Reg. § 301.6343-1(b). The IRS may find that a release facilitates collection if the taxpayer is willing to place the property in escrow to secure payment or to provide an acceptable bond conditioned upon payment. Treas. Reg. § 301.6343-1(b)(2). Procedures for requesting a levy release are contained in Treas. Reg. § 301.6343-1(c).

If the property owner can prove that the property has been wrongfully levied upon (because the IRS failed to satisfy the procedural requirements before seizure, for instance), the owner can seek a return of the levied property or payment of an amount of money equal to the amount realized on the sale of the property. I.R.C. § 6343(b). In addition, an owner other than the delinquent taxpayer may bring a wrongful levy action in district court seeking similar relief, as well as an injunction prohibiting the IRS from levying upon or selling the subject property. *See* I.R.C. § 7426; *Sessler v. United States*, 7 F.3d 1449 (9th Cir. 1993).

[4]   Sale Following Seizure

If, following the Notice of Seizure, the taxpayer is unable to obtain a release of the levy, the IRS can sell the seized property. Before doing so, however, the IRS must provide the delinquent taxpayer with a Notice of Sale, which specifies the property to be sold and the time, place, and manner of the sale. The Notice of Sale must also be published locally in a newspaper of general circulation. I.R.C. § 6335(b). As an additional prerequisite before sale, the IRS must conduct a pre-sale investigation that confirms the taxpayer's liability, assures that the levy will yield a meaningful sum for the IRS (beyond levy expenses), and considers (or reconsiders) the possibility of alterative means of collection. I.R.C. § 6331(j). If the IRS proceeds with the sale, the property will be sold to the highest bidder at a public auction not less than ten days or more than 40 days following the Notice of Sale. I.R.C. § 6335(d). Only the delinquent taxpayer's right, title, and interest is offered for sale, and such interest is sold subject to all encumbrances and liens that are superior to the government's tax lien.[15] Treas. Reg. § 301.6335-1(c)(5)(iii); *see generally* I.R.C. § 6335(e) for procedures relating to the sale of seized property.[16]

Proceeds from the sale are first applied to reimburse the IRS for levy and sale expenses, then to the delinquent taxpayer's liability. I.R.C. § 6342(a). Any surplus is paid to the person or persons (including the taxpayer) who make an application and provide satisfactory proof that they are entitled to the remaining amounts. I.R.C. § 6342(b); Treas. Reg. § 301.6342-1(b). If competing claimants exist, the government may institute an interpleader action to determine who is legally entitled to the surplus sales proceeds. In the case of real estate, even though the property has been sold, the taxpayer is given a final opportunity to redeem (buy back) the real property within 180 days of the sale. The taxpayer must pay the purchaser the amount paid at auction plus interest calculated at a rate of 20 percent. I.R.C. § 6337(b). This post-sale right of redemption does not apply to personal property.

§ 12.05 Minimizing Collection Activities

As a general proposition, a taxpayer's ability to pay an asserted deficiency is not taken into account in determining the extent of the taxpayer's liability, nor is it taken into account during compromise negotiations with the IRS. Even if the taxpayer or his representative is successful in negotiating a settlement totaling only a fraction of the originally asserted deficiency, this may be a hollow victory if the taxpayer cannot come up with the funds to pay the settled amount. Because the IRS's enforced collection procedures can seriously disrupt the taxpayer's business and employment relationships and jeopardize his credit rating, it is crucial for the taxpayer and his representative to attempt to negotiate the method of payment before the IRS files a Notice of Federal Tax Lien. This part of the negotiation can be just as important as settling the underlying tax liability.

All too often, however, an attorney may be called in to assist the taxpayer in a collection matter at the "last minute," after a Notice of Federal Tax Lien is filed. Even at this late date, the representative should confirm that the

[15] Sale of the levied property extinguishes the government's tax lien, as well as all liens inferior to the tax lien. The sale does not extinguish liens that are superior to or have priority over the federal tax lien.

[16] To reduce the appearance of impropriety, the IRS Reform Act revised the sale procedures to provide that sales of seized assets can no longer be conducted by a revenue officer. *See* Act § 3443.

underlying liability has been properly assessed and determine whether the statute of limitations on collection remains open. Both these matters can be established by requesting from the IRS a copy of the taxpayer's transcript of account, obtained by filing Form 4506, Request for Copy or Transcript of Tax Form. If the IRS does not provide the transcript voluntarily, the representative may have to make a FOIA request for the item.[17] Identifying the assessment date is important not only for purposes of confirming whether the statute of limitations on collection has expired, but also because the date of assessment fixes the date on which the federal tax lien arose. This latter determination may be important should priority conflicts arise. The representative should also consider the possibility of innocent spouse relief, discussed in Chapter 2, and the possibility of penalty abatement, discussed in Chapter 10. *See generally* Richard A. Carpenter, "Get the Best Deal for Clients from the IRS Collection Division," Taxation for Lawyers (Sept./Oct. 1998).

The following discussion identifies other procedures a taxpayer or his representative should consider once the IRS threatens adverse collection proceedings. In many cases, the revenue officer can be persuaded that some alternative to levy and seizure of the taxpayer's assets is in the best interest of the government.

[A]   Further Administrative Remedies: Taxpayer Assistance Orders and the Collection Due Process Hearing

The Code contains a number of administrative remedies available to a taxpayer who is being threatened with enforced collection action. Pursuant to Congressional mandate, the IRS recently expanded the procedures permitting an early referral of a collection issue to the Appeals Division (before a lien is filed) (the "Collection Appeals Program" or CAP). I.R.C. § 7123. Issues that may be considered by Appeals as part of this CAP process include Notices of Federal Tax Lien, Notices of Intent to Levy, Notices of Seizure, and denials of installment agreements. Revenue Procedure 99-28, 1999 I.R.B. 109; *see also* Publication 1660, "Collection Appeal Rights." Code section 7811 also permits the Office of Taxpayer Advocate to stop IRS collection activity as part of a Taxpayer Assistance Order ("TAO"), if to do otherwise would result in significant hardship for the taxpayer. A taxpayer might utilize a TAO to prevent or stop a wage garnishment or to prevent seizure of a particular asset. *See* Treas. Reg. § 301.7811-1(c); *see generally* Treas. Reg. § 301.7811-1 for procedures relating to a request for a TAO.

Effective for collection activities initiated on or after January 19, 1999, the taxpayer is afforded an additional opportunity to suspend collection activities in order to request a hearing with the Appeals Division. The Code requires the taxpayer to be notified of his right to request a CDP (Collection Due Process) Hearing in two separate instances: after the IRS files a Notice of

[17] The exact date of assessment is determined based on the record of assessment signed by the assessment officer. *See* Treas. Reg. § 301.6203-1. The assessment date appearing in the taxpayer's transcript of account normally reflects the record date. A copy of the taxpayer's record of assessment may also be obtained through a FOIA request. *See Powers v. Gibbs*, reproduced below. The procedures for making a FOIA request are discussed in Chapter 3.

Federal Tax Lien with respect to his property, I.R.C. § 6320, and before the IRS levies on the property. I.R.C. § 6330(a). To conserve resources, the two hearings may be consolidated. I.R.C. § 6320(b)(4). A taxpayer requests a CDP Hearing by filing Form 12153, Request for a Collection Due Process Hearing.

Although the types of issues that may be considered as part of a CDP Hearing are somewhat more limited as compared to those that may be raised in a CAP Hearing, the scope of the CDP Hearing is still significant.[18] At the hearing, an Appeals Officer who has not previously been involved in the taxpayer's case must first verify that the Code procedures relating to the creation of the federal tax lien or proposed levy have been satisfied (for example, that the IRS properly issued the Notice and Demand for Payment or the Notice of Intent to Levy). In addition, the taxpayer may raise any issue relevant to the lien or levy action, including innocent spouse claims, collection alternatives such as offers in compromise and installment agreements, and suggestions as to which of the taxpayer's assets should be levied upon to satisfy the outstanding liability. I.R.C. § 6330(c); *see also* Treas. Reg. §§ 301.6320-1 and 301.6330-1 for details relating to the notice requirement and conduct of the CDP Hearing. As a general matter, however, the taxpayer cannot use the CDP Hearing to challenge the existence or amount of the underlying tax liability, except in a case where the taxpayer did not receive a statutory notice of deficiency or has not otherwise been given the opportunity to contest the existence of the liability. *See* Treas. Reg. §§ 301.6320-1(e) and 301.6330-1(e). If the taxpayer raises an issue during the post-lien CDP Hearing under section 6320, he is not permitted to raise the same issue during the pre-levy CDP Hearing under section 6330. *Id.*

The results of the CDP Hearing appear in a Notice of Determination prepared by the Appeals Officer, which is sent to the taxpayer. Treas. Reg. §§ 301.6320-1(e)(3) A-E8 and 301.6330-1(e)(3) A-E8. The Notice of Determination must confirm that all procedural requirements were met in the taxpayer's case and decide the merits of any issues raised by the taxpayer during the hearing. If the parties reach an agreement concerning any relief or other action to be taken, the Notice of Determination will set forth the terms of that agreement. *Id.* A taxpayer who receives an adverse ruling has 30 days to appeal the findings in the Notice of Determination to the Tax Court. I.R.C. § 6330(d). If the Tax Court does not have jurisdiction over the type of liability contested, then an appeal lies to the United States District Court. The court will review the Appeals Officer's determination using an abuse of discretion standard. *Goza v. Commissioner*, 114 T.C. 176 (2000) (*de novo* review of Appeals' administrative determination applies when underlying liability is at issue). Both the Tax Court and District Courts have the authority to enjoin collection activity during the resolution of a CDP dispute. I.R.C. § 6330(e), as amended by the Community Renewal Tax Relief Act of 2000, § 313, Pub. L. No. 106-554.

The CDP Hearing procedure holds the prospect of a meaningful opportunity for the taxpayer to resolve most of his concerns relating to the lien and levy process, and to further negotiate with the IRS over the how collection efforts

---

[18] Morever, only the CDP procedure permits direct judicial review of the Appeals Office's determination.

will proceed. Save for the fact that the statute of limitations on collection is tolled during the hearing period, there appear to be no strategic drawbacks associated with the process. *See* I.R.C. § 6330(e).

Taxpayer response to the CDP process has been so overwhelming that the Appeals Division has had to devote a significant portion of its resources to these types of hearings. Daniel L. Black, "Appeals Collection Developments," Tax Adviser 487 (July, 2001). An IRS official estimated that the Appeals Division received 8,000 requests for such hearings in fiscal year 2000, and anticipates as many as 23,000 requests in 2001.

From a jurisdictional standpoint, the Tax Court has analogized the Notice of Determination issued at the conclusion of a CDP Hearing to the statutory Notice of Deficiency that must be issued prior to a deficiency assessment. Recall from Chapter 7 that a valid Notice of Deficiency is a prerequisite for Tax Court jurisdiction and that, as a general rule, the Tax Court will not "look behind" the Notice of Deficiency to question how or why the IRS asserted a deficiency. *See Greenberg's Express, Inc. v. Commissioner*, 62 T.C. 324 (1974), excerpted in Section 7.02[C] of Chapter 7. How far should the analogy between Notices of Determination and Notices of Deficiency extend? Consider the following case:

LUNSFORD v. COMMISSIONER
United States Tax Court
117 T.C. 159 (2001)

RUWE, Judge.

This case arises from a petition for judicial review filed under section 6330(d)(1)(A). The issue for decision is whether this Court has jurisdiction to review respondent's determination to proceed with collection by way of levy. At the time petitioners filed their petition, they resided in Asheville, North Carolina. When this case was called for trial, the parties submitted the case fully stipulated. For convenience, we combine the facts, which are not in dispute, with our opinion.

Section 6331(a) authorizes the Commissioner to levy against property and property rights where a taxpayer fails to pay taxes within 10 days after notice and demand for payment is made. Section 6331(d) requires the Secretary to send notice of an intent to levy to the taxpayer, and section 6330(a) requires the Secretary to send a written notice to the taxpayer of his right to a hearing. Section 6330(b) affords taxpayers the right to a "fair hearing" before an "impartial" IRS Appeals officer. Section 6330(c)(1) requires the Appeals officer to obtain verification that the requirements of any applicable law or administrative procedure have been met. Section 6330(c)(2)(A) specifies issues that the taxpayer may raise at the Appeals hearing. The taxpayer is allowed to raise "any relevant issue relating to the unpaid tax or the proposed levy" including spousal defenses, challenges to the appropriateness of collection action, and alternatives to collection. Sec. 6330(c)(2)(A). The taxpayer cannot raise issues relating to the underlying tax liability if the taxpayer received a notice of deficiency or the taxpayer otherwise had an opportunity to dispute the tax liability. Sec. 6330(c)(2)(B).

Section 6330(c)(3), provides that a determination of the Appeals officer shall take into consideration the verification under section 6330(c)(1), the issues raised by the taxpayer, and whether the proposed collection action balances the need for the efficient collection of taxes with the legitimate concern of the person that any collection action be no more intrusive than necessary. Section 6330(d)(1) then provides:

> (1) Judicial review of determination. — The person may, within 30 days of a determination under this section, appeal such determination —
>
> > (A) to the Tax Court (and the Tax Court shall have jurisdiction with respect to such matter); or
> >
> > (B) if the Tax Court does not have jurisdiction of the underlying tax liability, to a district court of the United States.

Thus, if we have general jurisdiction over the type of tax involved, a "determination" by Appeals and a timely petition are the only requirements for the exercise of our jurisdiction under section 6330. Temporary regulations promulgated under section 6330 [now permanent, Eds.] require that the "determination" by Appeals be issued in the form of a "written" notice. Sec. 301.6330-1T(e)(3), Q&A-E7, Temporary Proced. & Admin. Regs, 64 Fed. Reg. 3411-3412 (Jan. 22, 1999). Thus, we have held that our jurisdiction under section 6330(d)(1) depends upon the issuance of a valid notice of determination and a timely petition for review. Sarrell v. Commissioner, 2001 U.S. Tax Ct. LEXIS 42, 117 T.C. 11 (2001); Offiler v. Commissioner, 114 T.C. 492, 498 (2000); Goza v. Commissioner, 114 T.C. 176, 182 (2000).

On April 30, 1999, respondent issued a notice of intent to levy to petitioners. The proposed levy was to collect unpaid income taxes of $83,087.85 for the taxable years 1993, 1994, and 1995. On May 24, 1999, petitioners filed a Form 12153, Request for a Collection Due Process Hearing, in which they raised the following issue regarding the validity of the assessments made by respondent:

> I do not agree with the collection action of levy and notice of intent to levy 4-30-99. The basis of my complaint is what I believe to be the lack of a valid summary record of assessment pursuant to 26 CFR 301.6203-1. Without a valid assessment there is no liability. Without a liability there can be no levy, no notice of intent to levy, nor any other collection actions.

On September 2, 1999, the Appeals officer wrote a letter to petitioners indicating that the validity of the assessments had been verified and attached a Form 4340, Certificate of Assessments and Payments, which clearly shows that the assessments in question were made and remained unpaid. The Appeals officer concluded the letter stating: "If you wish to discuss other matters, such as resolution of the liability please contact me by September 16, 1999. Otherwise, we will issue a determination." Petitioners made no response to this letter. No further proceedings or exchange of correspondence occurred prior to the Appeals officer's determination.

On November 3, 1999, a notice of determination was sent to petitioners by the IRS Appeals Office which sustained the proposed levy. The notice of determination included findings that: (1) All procedural, administrative, and statutory requirements were met; (2) the Form 4340 satisfied the requirements of section 6203;[n.4] (3) petitioners failed to present any collection alternatives; and (4) the proposed levy was justified. On December 2, 1999, petitioners filed a timely petition to the Tax Court.

Neither petitioners nor respondent has moved or argued that we lack jurisdiction in this case. However, questions regarding jurisdiction were raised by the trial judge at the time the case was called for trial. The specific jurisdictional question concerned whether petitioners were offered an opportunity for a hearing with an IRS Appeals officer. The trial judge's inquiry was based on our opinion in *Meyer v. Commissioner*, 115 T.C. 417, 422-423 (2000), which held that we lacked jurisdiction under section 6330(d) if the taxpayer was not given an opportunity for an Appeals hearing.

In *Meyer v. Commissioner, supra* at 422-423, we looked behind the notice of determination to find that the taxpayer was not offered an Appeals hearing. We then found that the notice of determination was invalid and that the Tax Court was without jurisdiction to review the Appeals officer's determination. *Id.* For the reasons discussed below, we now conclude that our opinion in Meyer was incorrect.

As a preliminary matter, we point out that this Court should not have decided whether the notice of determination was valid in *Meyer v. Commissioner, supra*, because we did not have subject matter jurisdiction. We have held that we lack jurisdiction under section 6330(d) when the tax in issue is one over which we normally do not have jurisdiction. *See Johnson v. Commissioner*, 2001 U.S. Tax Ct. LEXIS 47, 117 T.C. ___ (2001); *Moore v. Commissioner*, 114 T.C. 171 (2000). The tax in *Meyer v. Commissioner, supra*, was a frivolous return penalty over which we normally have no jurisdiction. We therefore had no subject matter jurisdiction under section 6330(d). *Van Es v. Commissioner*, 115 T.C. 324 (2000). In that situation, section 6330(d) provides that "If a court determines that the appeal was to an incorrect court, a person shall have 30 days after the court determination to file such appeal with the correct court." Thus, in *Meyer v. Commissioner, supra*, we decided an issue regarding the adequacy of the hearing opportunity and its ramifications which should have been considered in the first instance by a district court with subject matter jurisdiction.

Secondly, in *Meyer v. Commissioner, supra*, our holding that the notice of determination was invalid was improperly predicated on facts regarding procedures that were followed prior to the issuance of the notice of determination rather than on the notice of determination itself. 115 T.C. at 422-423. Our analysis in *Meyer* improperly required us to look behind the notice of determination.

[n.4] Sec. 6203 requires the Secretary to record the liability of the taxpayer and to furnish a copy of the record of assessment to the taxpayer on request. Sec. 301.6203-1, Proced. & Admin. Regs., provides that an assessment officer shall make the assessment and sign the "summary record of assessment. The summary record, through supporting records, shall provide identification of the taxpayer, the character of the liability assessed, the taxable period, if applicable, and the amount of the assessment."

In *Offiler v. Commissioner*, 114 T.C. at 498, we analogized a notice of determination issued pursuant to section 6330(c)(3) to a notice of deficiency issued pursuant to section 6212, and said that the notice of determination is the jurisdictional "equivalent of a notice of deficiency."[n.6] In the context of a notice of deficiency, we have consistently held that as a general rule we do not look behind the notice to determine its validity. Pietanza v. Commissioner, 92 T.C. 729, 735 (1989), *affd. without published opinion* 935 F.2d 1282 (3d Cir. 1991); Riland v. Commissioner, 79 T.C. 185, 201 (1982); Estate of Brimm v. Commissioner, 70 T.C. 15, 22 (1978); Greenberg's Express, Inc. v. Commissioner, 62 T.C. 324, 327 (1974). It is well established that the Tax Court will generally examine only the notice of deficiency to determine whether the notice was valid for jurisdictional purposes. *See* Sealy Power, Ltd. v. Commissioner, 46 F.3d 382, 388 n.25 (5th Cir. 1995), *affg. in part and revg. in part* T.C. Memo. 1992-168; Clapp v. Commissioner, 875 F.2d 1396, 1402 (9th Cir. 1989).

We believe the same principles are applicable to a section 6330 determination. Our jurisdiction under section 6330(d)(1)(A) is established when there is a written notice that embodies a determination to proceed with the collection of the taxes in issue, and a timely filed petition. To the extent that *Meyer v. Commissioner*, 115 T.C. 417 (2000), holds that we must first look behind the determination to see whether a proper hearing was offered in order to have jurisdiction, *Meyer* is overruled.

We are, of course, cognizant of the role *stare decisis* plays in this Court and in other Federal courts, especially in the context of statutory construction. *See, e.g.,* Sec. State Bank v. Commissioner, 111 T.C. 210, 213-214 (1998), *affd.* 214 F.3d 1254 (10th Cir. 2000). Nevertheless, when this Court decided *Meyer v. Commissioner, supra,* lien and levy cases under section 6330 were just starting to reach this Court. In the nascent stages of our section 6330 jurisprudence, we made a decision limiting our jurisdiction. After almost a year of experience in dealing with lien and levy cases, we have come to the conclusion that the jurisdictional analysis in *Meyer* was incorrect and has resulted in unjustified delay in the resolution of cases. Whether there was an appropriate hearing opportunity, or whether the hearing was conducted properly, or whether the hearing was fair, or whether it was held by an impartial Appeals officer, or whether any of the other nonjurisdictional provisions of section 6330 were properly followed, will all be factors that we must take into consideration under section 6330 in deciding such cases. But none of these factors should

---

[n.6] In *Meyer v. Commissioner*, 115 T.C. 417, 421 (2000), we correctly stated the role that a notice of determination and timely petition play in our jurisdiction as follows:

> Section 6330(d) imposes certain procedural prerequisites on judicial review of collection matters. Much like the Court's deficiency jurisdiction, the Court's jurisdiction under section 6330(d) is dependent upon a valid determination letter and a timely filed petition for review. *See* Rule 330(b). Like a notice of deficiency under section 6213(a), an Appeals Office determination letter is a taxpayer's "ticket" to the Tax Court. *See* Offiler v. Commissioner, 114 T.C. 492, 498 (2000); *see also* Mulvania v. Commissioner, 81 T.C. 65, 67 (1983); Gati v. Commissioner, 113 T.C. 132, 134 (1999). Moreover, a petition for review under section 6330 must be filed with the appropriate court within 30 days of the mailing of the determination letter. *See* McCune v. Commissioner, 115 T.C. 114 (2000).

preclude us from exercising our jurisdiction under section 6330(d), in order to resolve the underlying dispute in a fair and expeditious manner.

In the instant case, there is nothing in the notice of determination which leads us to conclude that the determination was invalid. The notice of determination clearly embodies the Appeals officer's determination that collection by way of levy may proceed. Thus, regardless of whether petitioners were given an appropriate hearing opportunity, there was a valid determination and a timely petition. Those are the only statutory requirements for jurisdiction in section 6330(d)(1)(A). Accordingly, we hold that we have jurisdiction to review the determination in this case.

An appropriate order will be issued.

Reviewed by the Court.

* * *

WELLS, COHEN, SWIFT, GERBER, COLVIN, GALE, and THORNTON, JJ., agree with this majority opinion.

Read section 6330(b) through (d) carefully. As a matter of statutory construction, can the IRS issue a valid Notice of Determination if there has been no hearing? If the Notice of Determination is invalid, can the Tax Court take jurisdiction over the case? *See Lunsford v. Commissioner*, 117 T.C. 159 (2001) (reviewed by the court) (Foley, J., dissenting). The Tax Court has not always shown such a willingness to accept jurisdiction to review a CDP case. *See Offiler v. Commissioner*, 114 T.C. 492 (2000) (no jurisdiction to hear CDP claim when the taxpayer fails to timely request an appeals hearing under section 6330 within 30 days of the IRS's Notice of Intent to Levy); *McCune v. Commissioner*, 115 T.C. 114 (2000) (no jurisdiction to review CDP hearing because taxpayer's petition for review to the Tax Court was untimely).[19]

The petitioners in *Lunsford* did not receive a face-to-face hearing with an IRS Appeals Officer before receiving the Notice of Determination, although the petitioners did receive a letter from the Appeals Officer denying the petitioners' underlying claim and offering an opportunity to schedule a hearing. Is this sufficient for purposes of section 6330(b)? In an earlier decision, *Katz v. Commissioner*, 115 T.C. 329 (2000), the Tax Court granted the IRS's motion for summary judgment over the taxpayer's numerous challenges, one of which was that he never received (or had the opportunity for) an adequate CDP Hearing. Having been notified of the time for the hearing and the location, the taxpayer refused to appear on the ground that the scheduled location, about 100 miles from the taxpayer's home, was inconvenient to him and his witnesses. The Appeals Officer called the taxpayer to explain that

---

[19] Interim Tax Court Rules 330 through 334 provide procedural guidance to taxpayers appealing the Appeals Officer's findings in the Notice of Determination. As part of the Community Renewal Tax Relief Act of 2000, § 313(f), Pub. L. No. 106-554 (effective December 21, 2000), Congress added Code section 7463(f), which permits a taxpayer to appeal the results of a CDP hearing to the Tax Court using its small tax case procedures.

Appeals hearings were not available in the taxpayer's hometown, but rather were conducted at the Appeals Office. During the same call, the Appeals Officer discussed the substantive issues in the taxpayer's case. Two days later, the Appeals Officer issued to the taxpayer a written Notice of Determination under 6330, denying all relief. The taxpayer subsequently petitioned the Tax Court for review of the determination.

Noting that neither the statute nor legislative history addressed the appropriate location for a CDP Hearing or whether it can occur over the telephone, the Tax Court relied on procedural regulations relating to the time and place of an IRS examination to guide its decision. Because the taxpayer could not explain why commuting 100 miles would constitute an undue burden, the Tax Court rejected his complaint. The court went on to note:

> Because of petitioner's insistence of an Appeals hearing in West Palm Beach, Florida, the Appeals officer attempted to accommodate petitioner by offering to discuss his case over the telephone. From the record, we conclude that petitioner and the Appeals officer did in fact discuss his case over the telephone and that the Appeals officer heard and considered petitioner's arguments. We thus further conclude that, through the communications between petitioner and the Appeals officer in the instant case, petitioner received an Appeals hearing as provided for in section 6320(b).

Id. at 332. The Tax Court has also held that a taxpayer does not have the right to examine witnesses under oath during the CDP Hearing or to subpoena documents. *Davis v. Commissioner*, 115 T.C. 35 (2000) (noting that hearings "at the Appeals level have historically been conducted in an informal settling" and that neither the language of section 6330 nor the legislative history indicated that Congress intended to change this format).[20]

Having taken jurisdiction over the Lunsfords' appeal, the Tax Court, in a second court-reviewed opinion, was then left to review the Appeals Officer's Notice of Determination for abuse of discretion. *See Lunsford v. Commissioner*, 117 T.C. 183 (2001) (reviewed by the court). Instead of remanding the matter for an in-person CDP hearing, the majority resolved the case in favor of the Commissioner based on the record before it. According to the majority, the petitioners did not contest their failure to receive a CDP Hearing, but instead raised only the issue of whether the Appeals Officer properly verified the underlying assessment. The majority rejected the petitioners' argument, finding it neither "necessary or productive" to remand the case for a hearing. *See id.* The three dissenting opinions (by Judges Colvin, Laro, and Foley) took issue with the majority's narrow reading of the case and the majority's failure to speak to the issue of whether the petitioners were entitled to a CDP Hearing.

In his concurring opinions in the two Lunsford proceedings, Judge Halpern discussed the issue of what constitutes an adequate section 6330(b) hearing, approaching it from a different standpoint. Relying on *Chevron U.S.A., Inc. v. Natural Resources Defense Council, Inc.*, 467 U.S. 837 (1984), discussed in

---

[20] The IRS updated its Internal Revenue Manual in August of 2000 to provide instructions to Appeals Officers concerning CDP Hearings. *See* I.R.M. 5.11.1 *et seq.*

Section 9.02, Judge Halpern argued that the decision not to afford every taxpayer an in-person CDP Hearing is one for the IRS to make:

> In *Chevron, U.S.A., Inc. v. Natural Res. Def. Council, Inc.*, [467 U.S. 837 (1984)], the Supreme Court established the framework for judicial review of an agency's interpretation of a statute under its administration. At the outset, a court must ask whether "Congress has directly spoken to the precise question at issue," *id.* at 842; if so, then the court "must give effect to the unambiguously expressed intent of Congress" and may not defer to a contrary agency interpretation, *id.* at 842-843. If the statute is "silent or ambiguous with respect to the specific issue," however, the court proceeds to ask "whether the agency's answer is based on a permissible construction of the statute," *id.* at 843; if so, then the court must defer to the agency's construction. The *Chevron* framework has been applied in determining that an agency can interpret the term "hearing" to mean a written exchange of views. *See, e.g.*, Chem. Waste Mgmt., Inc. v. U.S. Envtl. Prot. Agency, 873 F.2d 1477 (D.C. Cir. 1989).

*   *   *

Nothing in the language of section 6330 can be interpreted as Congress's having "directly spoken" to whether a section 6330 hearing must include an oral interview. Moreover, in *Davis v. Commissioner*, 115 T.C. 35 (2000), we found that Congress intended an informal administrative hearing, of the type that, traditionally, had been conducted by appeals and was prescribed by section 601.106(c), Statement of Procedural Rules. Those procedural rules contemplate that Appeals may grant a conference, but do not require an oral interview. Sec. 601.106(c), Statement of Procedural Rules ("At any conference granted by the Appeals"). Moreover, respondent's Publication 1660 (Rev. 05-2000), Collection Appeal Rights, specifically addresses procedures applicable to a section 6330(b) hearing. The publication states that, at the time a taxpayer requests a section 6330(b) hearing, she must address all of her reasons for disagreeing with the proposed collection action. The publication further states: "The Office of Appeals will contact you to schedule a hearing. Your hearing may be held either in person, by telephone, or by correspondence."[n.6] In the instant case, the exchange of correspondence between the Appeals officer and petitioners, ending with the Appeals officer's offer to

---

[n.6] Chief Counsel Advisory 200123060 (June 8, 2001), referred to by some of the dissenters, states: "Appeals would strive to grant, at a minimum, face-to-face conferences to all requesting taxpayers." The advisory states a goal, not a mandate. The record in *Watson v. Commissioner*, T.C. Memo. 2001-213, contains a memorandum from respondent's counsel emphasizing that the advisory expresses an aspiration. Moreover, the usual view of this Court is that even revenue rulings, an official publication of respondent's (which the advisory is not), get no deference, since they are merely opinions of a lawyer in the agency. *See, e.g.*, N. Ind. Pub. Serv. Co. v. Commissioner, 105 T.C. 341, 350 (1995), *affd.* 115 F.3d, 506 (7th Cir. 1997). But see *United States v. Mead Corp.*, 533 U.S. 218 (2001), for a discussion of the deference, less than *Chevron* deference, owed to certain agency interpretations of a statute.

discuss other matters constitutes a hearing as contemplated in Publication 1660.

Lunsford, 117 T.C. 159 at ____.

Code section 6330(b)(3) specifies that the CDP Hearing must be conducted by an impartial Appeals Officer. The following case illustrates this point, along with a number of other important issues concerning the CDP process. The case was heard in District Court because the tax liability in issue (payroll taxes) was of a type over which the Tax Court does not have jurisdiction. *See* I.R.C. § 6330(d)(1)(B). Compare the District Court's approach to that of the Tax Court in *Lunsford*.

MESA OIL, INC. v. UNITED STATES
United States District Court, District of Colorado
86 A.F.T.R. 2d 7312 (D. Colo. 2000)*

Babcock, C. J.

Plaintiff, Mesa Oil ("Mesa"), appeals the administrative decision of the Defendant, the Internal Revenue Service Appeals Office. The issues are fully briefed and argued. Jurisdiction is proper pursuant to 26 U.S.C. § 6330(d)(1)(B). For the reasons set forth below, I remand the case for further consideration.

I. Statement of Facts

Mesa Oil is an oil recycling company. In business since 1981, it is headquartered in Colorado and employs about sixty people. Mesa buys used oil, primarily from automobile oil change services, recycles it, and sells it to asphalt manufacturers. Prior to 1998, Mesa was current on all taxes.

In 1998 the price of crude oil began to fall. By February of 1999 it reached a twenty-year low. These market fluctuations had a negative impact on Mesa's cash flow, and it fell behind on its payroll tax deposits. From the second quarter of 1998 through the third quarter of 1999, Mesa accumulated approximately $425,000 in past due taxes.

As a result, on August 12, 1999 the Internal Revenue Service ("IRS") issued a Notice of Intent to Levy and Notice of Your Right to a Hearing, pursuant to I.R.C. § 6330. Four days later the IRS filed a Notice of Federal Tax Lien with the Colorado Secretary of State, and issued Mesa Oil a Notice of Federal Tax Lien Filing and Your Right to a Hearing, pursuant to I.R.C. § 6320. Mesa, through its President and co-founder Larry Meers, requested a collection due process hearing. At the same time Mr. Meers wrote to the IRS and proposed that the lien be released, and Mesa be allowed to make payments of $40,000 per month for 12 months. Mesa asserts that any levy would result in the sale of all assets required for day-to-day operations and, thus, sound the death-knell for the company.

The IRS responded to these requests via letter. Lavada Harmon, Appeals Settlement Officer ("AO"), wrote Mr. Meers on November 5, 1999. She

---

* *Remanded*, 87 A.F.T.R. 2d 486 (D. Colo. 2000), *dismissed*, 2001 U.S. Dist. LEXIS 22650 (D. Colo. 2001).

informed him that a hearing had been scheduled and his proposed installment plan reviewed. The AO then recited the terms of I.R.C. § 6323(j), which sets out the circumstances under which a tax lien may be withdrawn. The AO determined that none of the provisions were met, but invited Mesa to suggest additional collection options.

The due process hearing was held on December 8, 1999. On March 27, 2000 the Rocky Mountain Appeals Office issued a "Notice of Determination Concerning Collection Action(s) Under Section 6320 and/or 6330." The Determination found that the Notice of Federal Tax Lien was appropriate and the Appeal should not restrict the proposed collection action. The Determination states that this conclusion was reached because: (1) the Secretary provided sufficient verification that applicable law and administrative procedure had been met; (2) No evidence had been provided to show that withdrawal was appropriate under 26 U.S.C. § 6323(j); (3) installment privileges were not appropriate because sufficient assets exist from which full payment can be secured as provided under Internal Revenue Manual Section 105.2.4.2.1; (4) installment privileges were further not appropriate because the taxpayer refused to provide a bond or letter of credit; and finally (5) the lien filed "and the proposed collection action balances the need for efficient collection of taxes with the taxpayer's legitimate concern that any collection action be no more intrusive than necessary." Plaintiff's Exhibit 6. There is no administrative or appeal record beyond these letters. Mesa appealed the AO's decision to this Court.

*   *   *

B. The Balancing Analysis

Mesa first argues that the AO abused her discretion in concluding that the proposed collection action balances the need for the efficient collection of taxes with the legitimate concern of the person that any collection action be no more intrusive than necessary. *See* Plaintiff's Exhibit 6. Mesa specifically asserts that the AO's Determination was incorrect because a levy would put Mesa out of business. I agree, to the extent that a proper balancing analysis did not occur.

As discussed above, I.R.C. § 6330(c)(3) requires that the AO balance the IRS's concerns regarding collection with the taxpayer's concerns regarding intrusion. Both the statute and the courts are silent on what factors must be considered in this analysis.

In cases where a statute is unclear as to its exact requirements, the court may engage in statutory construction. The purpose of statutory construction is to ascertain the intent of Congress. *See* Richardson v. Sullivan, 1993 U.S. App. LEXIS 16840, No. 92-4209, 1993 WL 214569 (10th Cir. June 18, 1993). "To determine the intent of Congress, the court must look first to the language of the statute, and then to the legislative history of the Act." United States v. Hollis, 971 F.2d 1441, 1450 (10th Cir. 1992); United States v. Lovett, 964 F.2d 1029, 1041 (10th Cir. 1992); United States v. LaBonte, 70 F.3d 1396, 1405 (1st Cir. 1995) ("When the plain meaning of a law is not readily apparent on its face, the next resort is to the traditional tools of statutory construction

— reviewing legislative history and scrutinizing statutory structure and design — in an effort to shed light on Congress's intent."), *rev'd on other grounds*, 520 U.S. 751, 137 L. Ed. 2d 1001, 117 S. Ct. 1673 (1997) (concluding statute unambiguous).

Here, the legislative history addressed I.R.C. § 6330(c)(3). The Senate Committee Report for the RRA indicates that the legislature saw the hearings as a three-part process. First,

> "during the hearing, the IRS is required to verify that all statutory, regulatory, and administrative requirements for the proposed collection action have been met. IRS verifications are expected to include (but not be limited to) showings that: . . . (4) with respect to the seizure of the assets of a going business, the revenue officer recommending the collection action has thoroughly considered the facts of the case, including the availability of alternative collection methods, before recommending the collection action." *Id.*

Next, the taxpayer may raise any relevant issue. Finally, the AO must make a Determination.

> "The determination of the appeals officer is to address whether the proposed collection action balances the need for the efficient collection of taxes with the legitimate concern of the taxpayer that the collection action be no more intrusive than necessary. A proposed collection action should not be approved solely because the IRS shows that it has followed appropriate procedures." *Id.*

In her Determination, the AO recites that applicable law and procedure have been followed, but does not address whether the collection officer considered appropriate factors given that Mesa Oil is an on-going business. The AO next states that "the proposed collection action balances the need for the efficient collection of taxes with the legitimate concern of the taxpayer that the collection action be no more intrusive than necessary." *See* Plaintiff's Exhibit 7. The AO gives no statement of facts, no legal analysis, and no explanation of how or why the proposed levy balanced the need for collection with Mesa's interests. The AO's declaration, written nine months after the hearing in this case, sheds no further light on the topic. *See* Declaration of Lavada Harmon. The Determination's blank recitation of the statute gives no indication that the statutory goal of a "meaningful hearing" was accomplished, or that actual balancing occurred. Instead, the sparse Determination gives every indication that the "proposed collection action [was] approved solely because the IRS showed that it had followed appropriate procedures." S. Rep. No. 105-174.

The IRS makes a number of arguments for the propriety of the Determination, including that withdrawal of the lien was not required under I.R.C. § 6323(j); an installment agreement was not appropriate because sufficient assets existed to satisfy the lien and Mesa was not then current on employment taxes, and the AO considered less intrusive measures. It is unnecessary for me to consider each of theses contentions individually. There is no indication that the AO actually engaged in the required analysis prior to making her Determination. I therefore remand for consideration of the appropriate factors and a fully elucidated Determination that explains the reasons for the conclusion.

C. Other Statutory Violations

Even if I were to find that a proper analysis had been made, further statutory violations require remand. Mesa argues that the AO prejudged the case, and that the lack of an appeals record makes judicial review meaningless. Although Mesa raises these issues under the rubric of due process, I find they may be decided on narrower statutory grounds.

1. Appeals Officer Impartiality

Mesa first argues that the letter written by the AO indicates she prejudged the case, a violation of her statutory mandate. I agree. Under both I.R.C. §§ 6320 and 6330, the appeal must be heard by a neutral officer. "The hearing . . . shall be conducted by an officer or employee who has had no prior involvement with respect to the unpaid tax . . . before the first hearing . . . A taxpayer may waive the requirement of this paragraph." I.R.C. § 6320(b)(3), § 6330(b)(3).

Mesa requested a hearing and attached a letter setting out the company's financial problems and suggesting an installment payment plan. There is no indication that the right to an impartial AO was waived. In return, Mesa received a letter from the AO stating that the letter had been received and reviewed. The AO indicated that I.R.C. § 6323(j) set out the circumstances under which a lien may be withdrawn. That section states,

> "The Secretary may withdraw a notice of a lien filed under this section and this chapter shall be applied as if the withdrawn notice had not been filed, if the Secretary determines that— (A) the filing of such notice was premature or otherwise not in accordance with administrative procedures of the Secretary, (B) the taxpayer has entered into an agreement under section 6159 to satisfy the tax liability for which the lien was imposed by means of installment payments, unless such agreement provides otherwise, (C) the withdrawal of such notice will facilitate the collection of the tax liability, or (D) with the consent of the taxpayer or the National Taxpayer Advocate, the withdrawal of such notice would be in the best interests of the taxpayer (as determined by the National Taxpayer Advocate) and the United States."

The AO went on to state that,

> "My review of the facts of the case reflect that the filing of the NFTL was not premature. . . . The facts of the case indicate withdrawal of the NFTL would not facilitate collection because withdrawal would jeopardize the government's position in relation to other creditors. . . .Installment agreement privileges have been denied because Mesa Oil, Inc. has assets which can be levied and/ or liquidated to satisfy the tax obligations, and because Mesa Oil, Inc., is not in compliance with the tax laws. . . . If you have other evidence or

arguments, or have other alternative collection proposals, please be prepared to discuss them during your hearing."

Plaintiff's Exhibit 5.

The AO declares that, "In addition to scheduling the collection due process hearing, the purpose of the letter was to provide Mesa Oil with an opportunity to present facts and arguments to show why the decision reached by the Internal Revenue Service was incorrect. Additionally, I invited Mesa Oil to make other collection proposals." *See* Declaration of Lavada Harmon at P 4.

The government argues that the AO did not prejudge the issues, and that the letter by the AO only set forth the conclusions reached by the Collection Function of the IRS, and informed Mesa of its burden at the Appeals Hearing. This contention is not supported by either the AO's declaration or the language of the letter. The AO's declaration does not indicate that the letter was nothing more than a restatement of the revenue officer's conclusions, and the letter itself states that its conclusions are based on "My [the AO's] review of the facts." *See* Plaintiff's Exhibit 5. The facts indicate that the AO conducted a thorough review of the file and the IRS's arguments prior to the first hearing. The statute requires the AO be impartial and have no involvement with the case prior to the hearing. I conclude that the letter from the AO was a violation of these statutory mandates. I therefore remand for a due process hearing before an impartial appeals officer.

2. Judicial Review

Mesa next argues that the IRS's failure to make an adequate record of the administrative proceedings has damaged Mesa's statutory right to judicial review. I agree. Congress has indicated its intent that the taxpayer have a "meaningful hearing." S. Rep. No. 105-174, followed by judicial review. *See* I.R.C. § 6330(d)(1)(B). Congress presumed that this review would be aided by a record of some sort. *See* H. Conf. Rept. 105-599 (1998) ("Judicial review. The conferees expect the appeals officer will prepare a written determination addressing the issues presented by the taxpayer and considered at the hearing. . . .").

Although Congress envisioned a review of the AO's Determination, "hearings at the Appeals level have historically been conducted in an informal setting." Davis v. Commissioner, 115 T.C. 35, 115 T.C. No. 4 (2000). "Proceedings before the Appeals are informal. Testimony under oath is not taken, although matters alleged as facts may be required to be submitted in the form of affidavits, or declared to be true under the penalties of perjury." C.F.R. § 601.106(c). "No stenographer is present to record the discussions of the facts and the law relating to the issue involved." Saltzman, IRS PRACTICE AND PROCEDURE, ¶ 9.05[3], at 9–37 (2d ed. 1991). Congress did not specifically vary that standard with the passage of I.R.C. §§ 6320 and 6330, and no new IRS regulations have been passed in this regard. Thus, the United States Tax Court has held that a taxpayer has no right to subpoena witnesses, despite the due process protections of §§ 6320 and 6330. *See* Davis v. Commissioner, 115 T.C. 35, 115 T.C. No. 4 (2000).

Here, no record of the hearing was kept, no record of the evidence or arguments presented at that hearing was made, and no analysis of the evidence or arguments was presented in the Determination.

The IRS argues that under the current appeals framework no record is required. It points to both the holding in *Davis* and C.F.R. § 601.106(c) for support. The government is correct that these rulings and provisions support the informal nature of the hearing. Yet informality does not completely obviate the need for a record of some sort. While a full stenographic record is not required, there must be enough information contained in the documentation created by the IRS for a court to draw conclusions about statutory compliance and whether the AO abused his or her discretion. Here, the scant letters and Notice of Determination make those tasks difficult if not impossible. The government's own arguments illustrate this problem. It asserts, for example, that Mesa points to no evidence or argument offered at the due process hearing which was ignored by the AO. Yet the lack of a record makes it impossible to tell what was discussed at the hearing, and what factors were considered by the AO in making her Determination. Thus, the lack of a record erodes Mesa's statutory right to judicial review, in violation of I.R.C. § 6330(d)(1)(B).

Accordingly, I ORDER that:

(1) The March 27, 2000 administrative decision is REMANDED to the Commissioner with directions to remand to a new Appeals Officer;

(2) A collection due process hearing be held upon adequate record which conforms to the statutory requirements of officer impartiality;

(3) An adequate record be created of proceedings at the administrative level sufficient to record the evidence or arguments presented at the hearing, as well as the analysis used by the Appeals Officer in making a Determination. This record may be made either through audio tape recording, video tape recording, or stenographer; along with all paper documents presented by the parties; and

(4) The Appeals Officer enter findings of fact and conclusions of law in her Notice of Determination, including a review those arguments raised by each side at the appeals hearing, those factors taken into consideration in the final conclusion, and citations to supporting statutes and regulations.

(5) Costs are awarded to the Plaintiff.

The IRS issued a nonacquiescence in response to *Mesa Oil. See* 2001 AOD LEXIS 5 ("To the extent the district court in this case intended to hold that CDP hearings must be recorded by videotape, audiotape or stenographic transcription, we disagree. CDP hearings should be carefully documented by appeals officers in determination letters and case memoranda which, with any documents provided by the taxpayers or otherwise obtained by the appeals officers, will constitute the record for review by the court.").

Unless the taxpayer protests the appropriateness of the lien or levy, the CDP Hearing will likely focus on whether alternative collection methods are appropriate under the circumstances. The two most common types of alternative methods, an installment agreement and an offer in compromise, are discussed below.

[B] Installment Agreements

Although revenue officers are instructed to request immediate payment of an outstanding liability, it will be obvious to the revenue agent in many cases that the taxpayer is unable to comply with such a request. As an alternative to enforced collection action, the IRS may be willing to defer payment in return for the taxpayer's commitment to pay the full liability. If the taxpayer simply needs additional time to access funds to pay the amount owed, the revenue officer can grant an extension of up to 60 days without any formalities. I.R.M. 5.14.3.2. If a taxpayer has a more serious liquidity problem, the IRS will require the taxpayer to enter into a formal installment agreement. I.R.C. § 6159. Payments under the installment agreement will include an interest charge computed on the unpaid balance subject to the agreement, using the underpayment rate in Code section 6621. *See* I.R.C. § 6601(b)(1).

Except as noted below, a taxpayer's ability to enter into an installment agreement is largely subject to the discretion of the IRS.[21] The IRS normally will not consider an installment agreement unless the taxpayer is otherwise in compliance with his filing and payment obligations for the current year. Furthermore, to ensure that the taxpayer is truly unable to make an immediate payment in full, the IRS requires the taxpayer to furnish a financial statement detailing the taxpayer's assets and liabilities, bank accounts, employment information, and future income prospects (Form 433-A, Collection Statement for Individuals, reproduced below, and/or Form 433-B, Collection Statement for Businesses). Based on this Collection Statement, the IRS will attempt to determine the taxpayer's equity in assets (and his ability to borrow against these assets from third parties in order to pay the liability); whether the taxpayer has any extravagant property (such as airplanes or yachts) that could be sold to satisfy the liability; and the taxpayer's cash flow. A determination of the taxpayer's cash flow, which will be used by the revenue officer to calculate the amount of the payments, is based on monthly income and expense information reported in Section V of the Collection Statement. The Collection Statement also provides the IRS levy source information (such as an employer's name and address and the existence of bank accounts and other asset information), which permits the IRS to more easily collect by levy should the taxpayer default on the installment agreement.

If the taxpayer's assets do not provide a readily available source for payment (for example, the taxpayer has no equity in the assets or they are not readily disposable), the IRS will collect the tax through payments based on the taxpayer's disposable income, determined based on the Collection Statement. When evaluating the amount to be paid, the revenue officer is instructed to make an objective economic judgment as to how much the IRS can collect without jeopardizing the taxpayer's ability to support his family, pay current

[21] The aggrieved taxpayer need not wait until contacted by a revenue officer before proposing an installment agreement. Such an agreement may be proposed after receiving the Notice and Demand.

taxes, and earn income from which to pay future installments.[22] *See* I.R.M. 5.14.1.2. The revenue officer will generally insist on an immediate payment of part of the outstanding liability, followed by equal month payments. Equal payments amounts permit the IRS to monitor collection through its computer system and remind taxpayers of when an installment payment is due. If necessary, the taxpayer will also be asked to extend the statute of limitations on collection for the duration of the installment agreement. I.R.M. 5.14.1.7. Moreover, if the installment payments are to continue for more than 12 months, the IRS may insist that the taxpayer provide follow-up financial information, which can be used to modify or terminate the installment agreement if there has been a significant change in the taxpayer's financial condition. I.R.C. § 6159(b)(3).

Under prior law, the IRS utilized a "streamlined procedure" that allowed for a quick approval of installment arrangements for taxpayers with a liability of $10,000 or less, without requiring any financial information. Following the IRS Reform Act, the Code now *requires* the IRS to accept an installment agreement from an individual taxpayer if certain conditions are met. I.R.C. § 6159(c). Among others, the taxpayer must show that during the preceding five years, he has filed all required income tax returns and paid any tax shown on those returns. He must also agree to pay the outstanding liability in full within three years, and agree to comply with all provisions of the Code while the agreement is in effect. *Id.* Not to be outdone (or be accused of hard-heartedness), the IRS expanded its streamlined process to go beyond those conditions set forth in section 6159(c). The IRS is now willing to accept installment agreements if the taxpayer agrees to pay a balance due of $25,000 or less within a five-year period. Memorandums for Regional Chief Compliance Officers (March 29, 1999). Consider the type of taxpayer (financially) that is most likely to qualify for an installment agreement.

---

[22] To help ensure consistency, the IRS has established a set of uniform financial standards (based on local and national estimates for necessary and conditional expenses) to be used to determine the taxpayer's ability to pay. *See* I.R.M. 5.5. The IRS website, www.irs.gov, now contains an interactive calculator that assists taxpayers who wish to file for an installment agreement to compute their expected monthly payments. The site then prints out an installment agreement request, Form 9465, that taxpayers can file with the IRS. IRS News Release IR-1999-69.

Collection Information Statement for Wage Earners and Self-Employed Individuals

Department of the Treasury
Internal Revenue Service

www.irs.gov

Form 433-A (Rev. 5-2001)
Catalog Number 20312N

Complete all entry spaces with the most current data available.

Important! Write "N/A" (not applicable) in spaces that do not apply. We may require additional information to support "N/A" entries.

Failure to complete all entry spaces may result in rejection or significant delay in the resolution of your account.

Section 1

Personal Information

1. Full Name(s) _____

Street Address _____
City_____ State_____ Zip _____
County of Residence _____
How long at this address?_____

1a. Home Telephone (____) _____

Best Time To Call:
____ am ____ pm
(Enter Hour)

2. Marital Status:
☐ Married   ☐ Separated
☐ Unmarried (single, divorced, widowed)

3. Your Social Security No.(SSN) _____
4. Spouse's Social Security No. _____

3a. Your Date of Birth (mm/dd/yyyy) _____
4a. Spouse's Date of Birth (mm/dd/yyyy) _____

5. ☐ Own Home   ☐ Rent   ☐ Other (specify, i.e. share rent, live with relative) _____

6. List the dependents you can claim on your tax return: (Attach sheet if more space is needed.)

First Name	Relationship	Age	Does this person live with you?	First Name	Relationship	Age	Does this person live with you?
_____	_____	___	☐ No ☐ Yes	_____	_____	___	☐ No ☐ Yes
_____	_____	___	☐ No ☐ Yes	_____	_____	___	☐ No ☐ Yes

☐ Check this box when all spaces in Sect. 1 are filled in.

Section 2

Your Business Information

☐ Check this box when all spaces in Sect. 2 are filled in and attachments provided.

7. Are you or your spouse self-employed or operate a business? (Check "Yes" if either applies)

☐ No   ☐ Yes   If yes, provide the following information:

7a. Name of Business _____
7b. Street Address _____
City _____ State _____ Zip _____

7c. Employer Identification No., if available : _____
7d. Do you have employees?   ☐ No ☐ Yes
7e. Do you have accounts/notes receivable? ☐ No ☐ Yes
If yes, please complete Section 8 on page 5.

ATTACHMENTS REQUIRED: Please include proof of self-employment income for the **prior 3 months** (e.g., invoices, commissions, sales records, income statement).

Section 3

Employment Information

☐ Check this box when all spaces in Sect. 3 are filled in and attachments provided.

8. Your Employer _____
Street Address _____
City_____ State_____ Zip _____
Work telephone no. (_____) _____
May we contact you at work? ☐ No ☐ Yes
8a. How long with this employer? _____
8b. Occupation _____

9. Spouse's Employer _____
Street Address _____
City_____ State_____ Zip _____
Work telephone no. (_____) _____
May we contact you at work? ☐ No ☐ Yes
9a. How long with this employer? _____
9b. Occupation _____

ATTACHMENTS REQUIRED: Please provide proof of gross earnings and deductions for the past 3 months from each employer (e.g., pay stubs, earnings statements). If year-to-date information is available, send only 1 such statement as long as a **minimum of 3 months** is represented.

Section 4

Other Income Information

☐ Check this box when all spaces in Sect. 4 are filled in and attachments provided.

10. Do you receive income from sources other than your own business or your employer? (Check all that apply.)

☐ Pension   ☐ Social Security   ☐ Other (specify, i.e. child support, alimony, rental) _____

ATTACHMENTS REQUIRED: Please provide proof of pension/social security/other income for the past 3 months from each payor, including any statements showing deductions. If year-to-date information is available, send only 1 such statement as long as a **minimum of 3 months** is represented.

Section 5 begins on page 2 →
(Rev. 5-2001)

Collection Information Statement for Wage Earners and Self-Employed Individuals   Form 433-A

Name _____   SSN _____

Section 5	11. CHECKING ACCOUNTS. List all checking accounts. (If you need additional space, attach a separate sheet.)				

Section 5

Banking, Investment, Cash, Credit, and Life Insurance Information

Complete all entry spaces with the most current data available.

11. CHECKING ACCOUNTS. List all checking accounts. (If you need additional space, attach a separate sheet.)

	Type of Account	Full Name of Bank, Savings & Loan, Credit Union or Financial Institution	Bank Routing No.	Bank Account No.	Current Account Balance
11a. Checking		Name			$
		Street Address _____			
		City/State/Zip _____			
11b. Checking		Name _____			$
		Street Address _____			
		City/State/Zip _____	11c. Total Checking Account Balances		$

12. OTHER ACCOUNTS. List all accounts, including brokerage, savings, and money market, not listed on line 11.

	Type of Account	Full Name of Bank, Savings & Loan, Credit Union or Financial Institution	Bank Routing No.	Bank Account No.	Current Account Balance
12a. ____		Name _____			$
		Street Address _____			
		City/State/Zip _____			
12b. ____		Name _____			$
		Street Address _____			
		City/State/Zip _____	12c. Total Other Account Balances		$

ATTACHMENTS REQUIRED: Please include your current bank statements (checking, savings, money market, and brokerage accounts) for the past three months for all accounts.

13. INVESTMENTS. List all investment assets below. Include stocks, bonds, mutual funds, stock options, certificates of deposits, and retirement assets such as IRAs, Keogh, and 401(k) plans. (If you need additional space, attach a separate sheet.)

¤ **Current Value:** indicate the amount you could sell the asset for today.

	Name of Company	Number of Shares / Units	¤ Current Value	Loan Amount	Used as collateral on loan?
13a.	_____	_____	$	$	☐ No ☐ Yes
13b.	_____	_____			☐ No ☐ Yes
13c.	_____	_____			☐ No ☐ Yes
	13d. Total Investments		$		

14. CASH ON HAND. Include any money that you have that is not in the bank.

			14a. Total Cash on Hand	$

15. AVAILABLE CREDIT. List all lines of credit, including credit cards.

	Full Name of Credit Institution	Credit Limit	Amount Owed	Available Credit
15a. Name	_____	_____	_____	$
	Street Address _____			
	City/State/Zip _____			
15b. Name	_____	_____	_____	$
	Street Address _____			
	City/State/Zip _____	15c. Total Credit Available		$

Page 2 of 6

Section 5 continued on page 3 →
(Rev. 5-2001)

Collection Information Statement for Wage Earners and Self-Employed Individuals   Form 433-A

Name_____   SSN_____

Section 5 continued	**16. LIFE INSURANCE.** Do you have life insurance with a cash value? ☐ No ☐ Yes

(Term Life insurance does not have a cash value.)

If yes:

16a. Name of Insurance Company _____

16b. Policy Number(s) _____

16c. Owner of Policy _____

16d. Current Cash Value $ _____   **16e.** Outstanding Loan Balance $_____

Subtract "Outstanding Loan Balance" line 16e from "Current Cash Value" line 16d = 16f $_____

☐ Check this box when all spaces in Sect. 5 are filled in and attachments provided.

ATTACHMENTS REQUIRED: Please include a statement from the life insurance companies that includes type and cash/loan value amounts. If currently borrowed against, include loan amount and date of loan.

Section 6
Other Information

17. OTHER INFORMATION. Respond to the following questions related to your financial condition: (Attach sheet if you need more space.)

17a. Are there any garnishments against your wages? ☐ No ☐ Yes
If yes, who is the creditor?_____   Date creditor obtained judgement _____   Amount of debt $_____

17b. Are there any judgments against you? ☐ No ☐ Yes
If yes, who is the creditor?_____   Date creditor obtained judgement _____   Amount of debt $_____

17c. Are you a party in a lawsuit? ☐ No ☐ Yes
If yes, amount of suit $_____   Possible completion date _____   Subject matter of suit _____

17d. Did you ever file bankruptcy? ☐ No ☐ Yes
If yes, date filed _____   Date discharged _____

17e. In the past 10 years did you transfer any assets out of your name for less than their actual value? ☐ No ☐ Yes
If yes, what asset? _____   Value of asset at time of transfer $_____
When was it transferred?_____   To whom was it transferred? _____

17f. Do you anticipate any increase in household income in the next two years? ☐ No ☐ Yes
If yes, why will the income increase? _____   (Attach sheet if you need more space.)
How much will it increase? $_____

17g. Are you a beneficiary of a trust or an estate? ☐ No ☐ Yes
If yes, name of the trust or estate_____   Anticipated amount to be received $_____
When will the amount be received? _____

☐ Check this box when all spaces in Sect. 6 are filled in.

17h. Are you a participant in a profit sharing plan? ☐ No ☐ Yes
If yes, name of plan _____   Value in plan $_____

Section 7
Assets and Liabilities

18. PURCHASED AUTOMOBILES, TRUCKS AND OTHER LICENSED ASSETS. Include boats, RV's, motorcycles, trailers, etc.
(If you need additional space, attach a separate sheet.)

⊠ **Current Value:** Indicate the amount you could sell the asset for today.

Description (Year, Make, Model, Mileage)	⊠ Current Value	Current Loan Balance	Name of Lender	Purchase Date	Amount of Monthly Payment
18a. Year ____ Make/Model ____ Mileage ____	$_____	$_____	_____	_____	$_____
18b. Year ____ Make/Model ____ Mileage ____	$_____	$_____	_____	_____	$_____
18c. Year ____ Make/Model ____ Mileage ____	$_____	$_____	_____	_____	$_____

Collection Information Statement for Wage Earners and Self-Employed Individuals   Form 433-A

Name_____   SSN_____

Section 7 continued	19.	**LEASED AUTOMOBILES, TRUCKS AND OTHER LICENSED ASSETS.** Include boats, RV's, motorcycles, trailers, etc. (If you need additional space, attach a separate sheet.)

	Description (Year, Make, Model)	Lease Balance	Name and Address of Lessor	Lease Date	Amount of Monthly Payment
19a.	Year _____ Make/Model _____	$			$
19b.	Year _____ Make/Model _____	$			$

ATTACHMENTS REQUIRED: Please include your current statement from lender with monthly car payment amount and current balance of the loan for each vehicle purchased or leased.

20. **REAL ESTATE.** List all real estate you own. (If you need additional space, attach a separate sheet.)

	Street Address, City, State, Zip, and County	Date Purchased	Purchase Price	¤ Current Value	Loan Balance	Name of Lender or Lien Holder	Amount of Monthly Payment	*Date of Final Payment
20a.	_____		$	$	$		$	
20b.	_____		$	$	$		$	

¤ **Current Value:** Indicate the amount you could sell the asset for today.

* **Date of Final Payment:** Enter the date the loan or lease will be fully paid.

ATTACHMENTS REQUIRED: Please include your current statement from lender with monthly payment amount and current balance for each piece of real estate owned.

21. **PERSONAL ASSETS.** List all Personal assets below. (If you need additional space, attach separate sheet.) *Furniture/Personal Effects* includes the total current market value of your household such as furniture and appliances. *Other Personal Assets* includes all artwork, jewelry, collections (coin/gun, etc.), antiques or other assets.

	Description	¤ Current Value	Loan Balance	Name of Lender	Amount of Monthly Payment	*Date of Final Payment
21a.	Furniture/Personal Effects	$	$		$	
	Other: (List below)					
21b.	Artwork	$	$		$	
21c.	Jewelry					
21d.						
21e.						

22. **BUSINESS ASSETS.** List all business assets and encumbrances below, include Uniform Commercial Code (UCC) filings. (If you need additional space, attach a separate sheet.) *Tools used in Trade or Business* includes the basic tools or books used to conduct your business, excluding automobiles. *Other Business Assets* includes any other machinery, equipment, inventory or other assets.

	Description	¤ Current Value	Loan Balance	Name of Lender	Amount of Monthly Payment	*Date of Final Payment
22a.	Tools used in Trade/Business	$	$		$	
	Other: (List below)					
22b.	Machinery	$	$		$	
22c.	Equipment					
22d.						
22e.						

☐ Check this box when all spaces in Sect. 7 are filled in and attachments provided.

Collection Information Statement for Wage Earners and Self-Employed Individuals   Form 433-A

Name_____   SSN_____

Section 8
Accounts/
Notes
Receivable

Use only if needed.

☐ *Check this box if Section 8 not needed.*

23. ACCOUNTS/NOTES RECEIVABLE. List all accounts separately, including contracts awarded, but not started. (If you need additional space, attach a separate sheet.)

Description	Amount Due	Date Due	Age of Account
23a. Name _____ Street Address _____ City/State/Zip _____	$ ____	____	☐ 0 - 30 days ☐ 30 - 60 days ☐ 60 - 90 days ☐ 90+ days
23b. Name _____ Street Address _____ City/State/Zip _____	$ ____	____	☐ 0 - 30 days ☐ 30 - 60 days ☐ 60 - 90 days ☐ 90+ days
23c. Name _____ Street Address _____ City/State/Zip _____	$ ____	____	☐ 0 - 30 days ☐ 30 - 60 days ☐ 60 - 90 days ☐ 90+ days
23d. Name _____ Street Address _____ City/State/Zip _____	$ ____	____	☐ 0 - 30 days ☐ 30 - 60 days ☐ 60 - 90 days ☐ 90+ days
23e. Name _____ Street Address _____ City/State/Zip _____	$ ____	____	☐ 0 - 30 days ☐ 30 - 60 days ☐ 60 - 90 days ☐ 90+ days
23f. Name _____ Street Address _____ City/State/Zip _____	$ ____	____	☐ 0 - 30 days ☐ 30 - 60 days ☐ 60 - 90 days ☐ 90+ days
23g. Name _____ Street Address _____ City/State/Zip _____	$ ____	____	☐ 0 - 30 days ☐ 30 - 60 days ☐ 60 - 90 days ☐ 90+ days
23h. Name _____ Street Address _____ City/State/Zip _____	$ ____	____	☐ 0 - 30 days ☐ 30 - 60 days ☐ 60 - 90 days ☐ 90+ days
23i. Name _____ Street Address _____ City/State/Zip _____	$ ____	____	☐ 0 - 30 days ☐ 30 - 60 days ☐ 60 - 90 days ☐ 90+ days
23j. Name _____ Street Address _____ City/State/Zip _____	$ ____	____	☐ 0 - 30 days ☐ 30 - 60 days ☐ 60 - 90 days ☐ 90+ days
23k. Name _____ Street Address _____ City/State/Zip _____	$ ____	____	☐ 0 - 30 days ☐ 30 - 60 days ☐ 60 - 90 days ☐ 90+ days
23l. Name _____ Street Address _____ City/State/Zip _____	$ ____	____	☐ 0 - 30 days ☐ 30 - 60 days ☐ 60 - 90 days ☐ 90+ days

☐ *Check this box when all spaces in Sect. 8 are filled in.*

Add "Amount Due" from lines 23a through 23i = 23m $ _____

Collection Information Statement for Wage Earners and Self-Employed Individuals   Form 433-A

Name_____   SSN_____

Section 9	Total Income			Total Living Expenses		
Monthly Income and Expense Analysis	Source	Gross Monthly		Expense Items [4]	Actual Monthly	
	24. Wages (Yourself)[1]	$		35. Food, Clothing and Misc.[5]	$	
If only one spouse has a tax liability, but both have income, list the total household income and expenses.	25. Wages (Spouse)[1]			36. Housing and Utilities[6]		
	26. Interest - Dividends			37. Transportation[7]		
	27. Net Income from Business[2]			38. Health Care		
	28. Net Rental Income[3]			39. Taxes (Income and FICA)		
	29. Pension/Social Security (Yourself)			40. Court ordered payments		
	30. Pension/Social Security (Spouse)			41. Child/dependent care		
	31. Child Support			42. Life insurance		
	32. Alimony			43. Other secured debt		
	33. Other			44. Other expenses		
	34. Total Income	$		45. Total Living Expenses	$	

[1] **Wages, salaries, pensions, and social security:** Enter your gross monthly wages and/or salaries. Do not deduct withholding or allotments you elect to take out of your pay, such as insurance payments, credit union deductions, car payments etc.
To calculate your gross monthly wages and/or salaries:
    If paid weekly - multiply weekly gross wages by 4.3. Example: $425.89 x 4.3 = $1,831.33
    If paid bi-weekly (every 2 weeks) - multiply bi-weekly gross wages by 2.17. Example: $972.45 x 2.17 = $2,110.22
    If paid semi-monthly (twice each month) - multiply semi-monthly gross wages by 2. Example: $856.23 x 2 = $1,712.46

[2] **Net Income from Business:** Enter your monthly net business income. This is the amount you earn after you pay ordinary and necessary monthly business expenses. This figure should relate to the yearly net profit from your Form 1040 Schedule C. If it is more or less than the previous year, you should attach an explanation. If your net business income is a loss, enter "0". Do not enter a negative number.

[3] **Net Rental Income:** Enter your monthly net rental income. This is the amount you earn after you pay ordinary and necessary monthly rental expenses. If your net rental income is a loss, enter "0". Do not enter a negative number.

[4] **Expenses not generally allowed:** We generally do not allow you to claim tuition for private schools, public or private college expenses, charitable contributions, voluntary retirement contributions, payments on unsecured debts such as credit card bills, cable television and other similar expenses. However, we may allow these expenses, if you can prove that they are necessary for the health and welfare of you or your family or for the production of income.

[5] **Food, Clothing and Misc.:** Total of clothing, food, housekeeping supplies and personal care products for one month.

[6] **Housing and Utilities:** For your principal residence: Total of rent or mortgage payment. Add the average monthly expenses for the following: property taxes, home owner's or renter's insurance, maintenance, dues, fees, and utilities. Utilities include gas, electricity, water, fuel, oil, other fuels, trash collection and telephone.

[7] **Transportation:** Total of lease or purchase payments, vehicle insurance, registration fees, normal maintenance, fuel, public transportation, parking and tolls for one month.

ATTACHMENTS REQUIRED: Please include:

*   A copy of your last Form 1040 with all Schedules.
*   Proof of all current expenses that you paid for the past 3 months, including utilities, rent, insurance, property taxes, etc.
*   Proof of all non-business transportation expenses (e.g., car payments, lease payments, fuel, oil, insurance, parking, registration).
*   Proof of payments for health care, including health insurance premiums, co-payments, and other out-of-pocket expenses, for the past 3 months.
*   Copies of any court order requiring payment and proof of such payments (e.g., cancelled checks, money orders, earning statements showing such deductions) for the past 3 months.

☐ Check this box when all spaces in Sect. 9 are filled in and attachments provided.

☐ Check this box when all spaces in all sections are filled in and all attachments provided.

Failure to complete all entry spaces may result in rejection or significant delay in the resolution of your account.

Certification: Under penalties of perjury, I declare that to the best of my knowledge and belief this statement of assets, liabilities, and other information is true, correct and complete.

_____   _____   _____
Your Signature   Spouse's Signature   Date

Page 6 of 6

(Rev. 5-2001)

[C]   Offers in Compromise

As discussed above, the IRS's willingness to enter into an installment agreement is conditioned upon the taxpayer's agreement to pay the entire liability owed. If, however, the taxpayer has few assets and little prospect of generating sufficient income to pay the liability in full, the taxpayer may be allowed to strike a settlement for less than 100 cents on the dollar. The statutory authority for making an "offer in compromise" is section 7122.[23] An offer in compromise accepted by the IRS permits the taxpayer a fresh start by eliminating the excess liability over the amount offered. *See* I.R.M. 5.8.1 (the "Offer in Compromise" Handbook). A taxpayer submits the offer by filing Form 656, reproduced below.

The conditions under which the IRS will accept a settlement offer are circumscribed. Historically, the IRS would compromise tax liability on only two grounds: doubt as to the existence of the liability and doubt as to its collectibility. The IRS Reform Act authorized the IRS to compromise tax liabilities based on additional criteria, including considerations of effective tax administration, discussed below. *See* I.R.C. § 7122(c); H.R. Conf. Rep. No. 105-599, at 289 (1998). Moreover, the 1998 legislation required the IRS to publish schedules of estimated national and local living costs that are used to ensure that taxpayers entering into compromise agreements will be left with sufficient resources to provide for basic living expenses. These financial standards are also used to determine whether the taxpayer is entitled to enter into a compromise agreement in the first instance. The IRS has posted these standards on its website. Section 7122 also prohibits the IRS from rejecting an offer from a low-income taxpayer based solely on the amount of the offer. I.R.C. § 7122(c).

Given that a taxpayer has other avenues available to negotiate with the IRS over the extent of his tax liability, compromises on the basis of doubt as to liability are far rarer than those for doubt as to collectibility. Particularly when the taxpayer has exhausted the pre-assessment administrative appeals procedure, the taxpayer's ability to obtain a compromise on the basis of doubt as to liability is slim. In a case where a deficiency assessment was made with little or no action by the taxpayer to defend against it, however, a representative may be able to compromise a previously assessed liability by raising the possibility that the taxpayer might prevail in a refund action following payment.[24]

---

[23] An Offer in Compromise is not solely a tax-collection tool. An offer can be made at virtually any stage of an IRS proceeding, including during audit, at Appeals, or even in Tax Court. However, Offers in Compromise based on doubt as to collectibility — the offers most commonly accepted — are usually negotiated in response to a Notice and Demand for Payment.

[24] As discussed above, the offer in compromise procedure can be used to raise any issue of liability that has not previously been determined in a settlement or a final decision of the Tax Court. An offer based on doubt as to liability might also relate to innocent spouse relief or the assertion of penalties.

Form 656

Offer in Compromise

Department of the Treasury
Internal Revenue Service
www.irs.gov
Form 656 (Rev. 5-2001)
Catalog Number 16728N

IRS RECEIVED DATE

Item 1 — Taxpayer's Name and Home or Business Address

Name

Name

Street Address

City   State   ZIP Code

Mailing Address *(if different from above)*

Street Address

City   State   ZIP Code

DATE RETURNED

Item 2 — Social Security Numbers

(a) Primary _____

(b) Secondary _____

Item 3 — Employer Identification Number *(included in offer)*

_____

Item 4 — Other Employer Identification Numbers *(not included in offer)*

_____

_____

Item 5 — To: Commissioner of Internal Revenue Service

I/We (includes all types of taxpayers) submit this offer to compromise the tax liabilities plus any interest, penalties, additions to tax, and additional amounts required by law (tax liability) for the tax type and period marked below: (Please mark an "X" in the box for the correct description and fill-in the correct tax period(s), adding additional periods if needed).

❏ 1040/1120 Income Tax — Year(s) _____

❏ 941 Employer's Quarterly Federal Tax Return — Quarterly period(s) _____

❏ 940 Employer's Annual Federal Unemployment (FUTA) Tax Return — Year(s) _____

❏ Trust Fund Recovery Penalty as a responsible person of (enter corporation name) _____

for failure to pay withholding and Federal Insurance Contributions Act Taxes (Social Security taxes), for period(s) ending _____

❏ Other Federal Tax(es) [specify type(s) and period(s)] _____

Note: If you need more space, use another sheet titled "Attachment to Form 656 Dated _____ ." Sign and date the attachment following the listing of the tax periods.

Item 6 — I/We submit this offer for the reason(s) checked below:

❏ **Doubt as to Liability** — "I do not believe I owe this amount." You must include a detailed explanation of the reason(s) why you believe you do not owe the tax in Item 9.

❏ **Doubt as to Collectibility** — "I have insufficient assets and income to pay the full amount." You must include a complete Collection Information Statement, Form 433-A and/or Form 433-B.

❏ **Effective Tax Administration** — "I owe this amount and have sufficient assets to pay the full amount, but due to my exceptional circumstances, requiring full payment would cause an economic hardship or would be unfair and inequitable." You must include a complete Collection Information Statement, Form 433-A and/or Form 433B **and** complete Item 9.

Item 7

I/We offer to pay $ _____ (must be more than zero). Complete item 10 to explain where you will obtain the funds to make this offer.

Check one of the following:

❏ **Cash Offer (Offered amount will be paid in 90 days or less.)**

Balance to be paid in: ❏ 10; ❏ 30; ❏ 60; or ❏ 90 days from written notice of acceptance of the offer.

❏ **Short-Term Deferred Payment Offer (Offered amount will be paid in MORE than 90 days but within 24 months from written notice of acceptance of the offer.)**

$_____ within_____ days (not more than 90 — See Instructions Section, **Determine Your Payment Terms**) from written notice of acceptance of the offer; and

beginning in the _____ month after written notice of acceptance of the offer, $_____ on the _____ day of each month for a total of _____ months. (Cannot extend more than 24 months from written notice of acceptance of the offer.)

❏ **Deferred Payment Offer (Offered amount will be paid over the life of the collection statute.)**

$_____ within_____ days (not more than 90 — See Instructions Section, **Determine Your Payment Terms**) from written notice of acceptance of the offer; and

beginning in the first month after written notice of acceptance of the offer, $_____ on the _____ day of each month for a total of _____ months.

NOTE: Signature(s) of taxpayer required on last page of Form 656

Item 8 — By submitting this offer, I/we understand and agree to the following conditions:

(a) I/We voluntarily submit all payments made on this offer.

(b) The IRS will apply payments made under the terms of this offer in the best interest of the government.

(c) If the IRS rejects or returns the offer or I/we withdraw the offer, the IRS will return any amount paid with the offer. If I/we agree in writing, IRS will apply the amount paid with the offer to the amount owed. If I/we agree to apply the payment, the date the IRS received the offer remittance will be considered the date of payment. I/We understand that the IRS will not pay interest on any amount I/we submit with the offer.

(d) **I/We will comply with all provisions of the Internal Revenue Code relating to filing my/our returns and paying my/our required taxes for 5 years or until the offered amount is paid in full, whichever is longer. In the case of a jointly submitted offer to compromise joint tax liabilities, I/we understand that default with respect to the compliance provisions described in this paragraph by one party to this agreement will not result in the default of the entire agreement. The default provisions described in Item 8(n) of this agreement will be applied only to the party failing to comply with the requirements of this paragraph. This provision does not apply to offers based on Doubt as to Liability.**

(e) I/We waive and agree to the suspension of any statutory periods of limitation (time limits provided for by law) for the IRS assessment of the tax liability for the periods identified in Item 5. I/We understand that I/we have the right not to waive these statutory periods or to limit the waiver to a certain length or to certain issues. I/We understand, however, that the IRS may not consider this offer if I/we refuse to waive the statutory periods for assessment or if we provide only a limited waiver. The amount of any Federal tax due for the periods described in Item 5 may be assessed at any time prior to the acceptance of this offer or within one year of the rejection of this offer.

(f) The IRS will keep all payments and credits made, received or applied to the total original tax liability before submission of this offer. The IRS may keep any proceeds from a levy served prior to submission of the offer, but not received at the time the offer is submitted. If I/we have an installment agreement prior to submitting the offer, I/we must continue to make the payments as agreed while this offer is pending. Installment agreement payments will not be applied against the amount offered.

(g) **As additional consideration beyond the amount of my/our offer, the IRS will keep any refund, including interest, due to me/us because of overpayment of any tax or other liability, for tax periods extending through the calendar year that the IRS accepts the offer. I/We may not designate an overpayment ordinarily subject to refund, to which the IRS is entitled, to be applied to estimated tax payments for the following year. This condition does not apply if the offer is based on Doubt as to Liability.**

(h) I/We will return to the IRS any refund identified in (g) received after submission of this offer. This condition does not apply to offers based on Doubt as to Liability.

(i) The IRS cannot collect more than the full amount of the tax liability under this offer.

(j) I/We understand that I/we remain responsible for the full amount of the tax liability, unless and until the IRS accepts the offer in writing and I/we have met all the terms and conditions of the offer. The IRS will not remove the original amount of the tax liability from its records until I/we have met all the terms of the offer.

NOTE: Signature(s) of taxpayer required on last page of Form 656

(k) I/We understand that the tax I/we offer to compromise is and will remain a tax liability until I/we meet all the terms and conditions of this offer. If I/we file bankruptcy before the terms and conditions of this offer are completed, any claim the IRS files in the bankruptcy proceedings will be a tax claim.

(l) Once the IRS accepts the offer in writing, I/we have no right to contest, in court or otherwise, the amount of the tax liability.

(m) The offer is pending starting with the date an authorized IRS official signs this form. The offer remains pending until an authorized IRS official accepts, rejects, returns or acknowledges withdrawal of the offer in writing. If I/we appeal an IRS rejection decision on the offer, the IRS will continue to treat the offer as pending until the Appeals Office accepts or rejects the offer in writing. If I/we don't file a protest within 30 days of the date the IRS notifies me/us of the right to protest the decision, I/we waive the right to a hearing before the Appeals Office about the offer in compromise.

(n) If I/We fail to meet any of the terms and conditions of the offer and the offer defaults, then the IRS may:

- immediately file suit to collect the entire unpaid balance of the offer

- immediately file suit to collect an amount equal to the original amount of the tax liability as liquidating damages, minus any payment already received under the terms of this offer

- disregard the amount of the offer and apply all amounts already paid under the offer against the original amount of the tax liability

- file suit or levy to collect the original amount of the tax liability, without further notice of any kind.

The IRS will continue to add interest, as Section 6601 of the Internal Revenue Code requires, on the amount the IRS determines is due after default. The IRS will add interest from the date the offer is defaulted until I/we completely satisfy the amount owed.

(o) The IRS generally files a Notice of Federal Tax Lien to protect the Government's interest on deferred payment offers. This tax lien will be released when the payment terms of the offer agreement have been satisfied.

(p) **I/We understand that the IRS employees may contact third parties in order to respond to this request and I authorize the IRS to make such contacts. Further, by authorizing the Internal Revenue Service to contact third parties, I understand that I will not receive notice, pursuant to section 7602(c) of the Internal Revenue Code, of third parties contacted in connection with this request.**

NOTE: Signature(s) of taxpayer required on last page of Form 656

Item 9 — Explanation of Circumstances

I am requesting an offer in compromise for the reason(s) listed below:

Note: If you are requesting compromise based on doubt as to liability, explain why you don't believe you owe the tax.
If you believe you have special circumstances affecting your ability to fully pay the amount due, explain your situation.
You may attach additional sheets if necessary.

Item 10 — Source of Funds

I/we shall obtain the funds to make this offer from the following source(s):

Item 11

If I/we submit this offer on a substitute form, I/we affirm that this form is a verbatim duplicate of the official Form 656, and I/we agree to be bound by all the terms and conditions set forth in the official Form 656.

Under penalties of perjury, I declare that I have examined this offer, including accompanying schedules and statements, and to the best of my knowledge and belief, it is true, correct and complete.

_____
11(a) Signature of Taxpayer

_____
Date

_____
11(b) Signature of Taxpayer

_____
Date

For Official Use Only

I accept the waiver of the statutory period of limitations for the Internal Revenue Service.

_____
Signature of Authorized Internal Revenue Service Official

_____
Title

_____
Date

NOTE: Signature(s) of taxpayer required on last page of Form 656

Most often, the IRS accepts an offer in compromise when doubt exists as to the taxpayer's ability to pay the assessed tax. In evaluating offers on this basis, the IRS conducts a thorough examination of the taxpayer's assets, liabilities, and earnings potential. As with an installment agreement, the taxpayer must submit financial statements on Form 433-A or B, setting forth a full and complete description of the taxpayer's financial condition. I.R.M. 5.8.1.3. To determine whether the amount offered by the taxpayer should be accepted, the revenue officer looks primarily at two factors: (1) The taxpayer's future ability to pay, determined based on the difference between expected monthly income and necessary expenses; and (2) the net value of all assets owned by the taxpayer. Although other factors may be considered, the IRS normally requires the taxpayer to offer an amount equal to the present value of the taxpayer's ability to pay over a four-year period[25] plus the net realizable value of the taxpayer's assets. The net realizable value of the taxpayer's assets is normally their "quick sale" value, generally defined as 80% of the current fair market value of the assets. I.R.M. 5.8.5.3.1. Using a quick sale value takes into account the hardship caused when the taxpayer must sell an asset in a short period of time. Because of the unique nature of certain assets (such as going concern value and retirement plans) the IRS has established guidelines to be used in determining whether these types of assets should be considered when calculating the minimum offer required. *See generally* I.R.M. 5.8.4 and 5.8.5. As noted above, the IRS uses national and local estimates of living expenses to determine the taxpayer's future ability to pay.

Taking Congress up on its invitation/mandate to expand the offer in compromise program to include equity and hardship cases, the IRS has issued temporary regulations that spell out in more detail the circumstances that would justify an offer based on "effective tax administration." *See* Temp. Treas. Reg. § 301.7122-1T(b)(4). Under these temporary regulations, taxpayers may be eligible for a compromise if collection of the entire tax liability would create economic hardship, or exceptional circumstances exist that would cause collection of the entire tax liability to be detrimental to voluntary compliance. *Id.*

The temporary section 7122 regulations include several examples applying these new standards.[26] Temp. Treas. Reg. § 301.7122-1T(b)(4)(iv)(D). Economic hardship might exist, for instance, if a taxpayer (or his dependent) faces a long-term illness, medical condition, or disability and it is foreseeable that the taxpayer's financial resources would be exhausted as a result. Economic hardship can also cover cases where the sale or liquidation of assets to pay a tax bill would prevent the taxpayer from meeting basic living expenses. An example might include a retiree with a retirement fund large enough to pay the tax bill, but use of the funds for this purpose might deprive the retiree of basic support and maintenance in the future. The IRS's willingness to grant a compromise based on exceptional circumstances requires an extraordinary event beyond the taxpayer's control. An example might include a taxpayer who was hospitalized for several years, during which time the taxpayer could not manage his financial affairs and was unable to file tax returns. Temp. Treas. Reg. § 301.7122-1T(b)(4)(iv)(E). Whether based on hardship or extraordinary circumstances, the taxpayer seeking the offer must have a history of

---

[25] As a result of the IRS Reform Act, taxpayers are directed to use a four-year value test for cash offers and a five-year value test for offers to be paid over time. I.R.M. 5.8.5.4. The IRS allows the taxpayer three different payment options: (1) a cash offer, payable within 90 days; (2) a short-term deferred payment offer, payable over a two-year period; and (3) a deferred payment offer, payable over the number of years remaining in the statute of limitations on collection. I.R.M. 5.8.1.3.5(3).

[26] The IRS has updated the Internal Revenue Manual to include a separate chapter on the new offer category relating to effective tax administration. *See* I.R.M. 5.8.11. A taxpayer seeking relief on the basis of economic hardship must submit Form 656-A in addition to Offer in Compromise Form 656.

timely paying his taxes and filing his returns. Moreover, the IRS warns that the expanded offer in compromise program is tailored for taxpayers involved in very severe circumstances, not those with temporary financial problems.[27]

Once a taxpayer submits an offer in compromise, collection action is normally postponed while the IRS processes the offer.[28] I.R.M. 5.8.3.7.; *see also* I.R.C. § 6331(k); Policy Statement P-5-100. The taxpayer's offer generally is processed by an IRS revenue officer who will initially review the offer for completeness and may contact the taxpayer's representative for the purpose of soliciting additional information or explanations required to evaluate the offer. *See* I.R.M. 5.8.3.3. Once an offer in compromise is accepted, the settlement will not be reopened unless the IRS discovers that the taxpayer falsified information, concealed assets, or there was a mutual mistake of fact between the parties.[29] Temp. Treas. Reg. § 301.7122-1T(d)(5). If the taxpayer fails to carry out his obligations under the compromise agreement, the IRS can rescind the agreement and proceed to reassess and collect the originally determined liability, reduced by any payments previously made.[30]

If the revenue officer rejects the taxpayer's offer, an internal review procedure takes place, after which the taxpayer is granted the right to appeal the rejection with the IRS Appeals Division. *See* I.R.M. 5.8.7; Temp. Treas. Reg. § 301.7122-1T(e). If the liability sought to be compromised is $2,500 or less, an oral or short written appeal is sufficient to trigger the appeal rights. For liabilities in excess of $2,500, the taxpayer must file a written protest. *Id.*. The Appeals Office may also be asked to consider the availability of an Offer in Compromise as part of a CDP Hearing. If the taxpayer's offer is rejected, the decision is subject to judicial review by the Tax Court. I.R.C. § 6330(d).

If an accepted offer is payable in installments, the taxpayer will be required to agree to extend the statute of limitations on collection for the period the offer remains in force. Temp. Treas. Reg. § 301.7122-1T(h). During the taxable year the offer is accepted, the IRS will also retain any refund to which the taxpayer would otherwise be entitled and apply that refund against the taxpayer's outstanding tax liability. *See* I.R.M. 5.8.1.8.

---

[27] The expanded offer in compromise program has led to a backlog in the IRS's ability to process offers in a timely manner. To reduce this backlog, the IRS has established an on-line offer in compromise procedure, which permits taxpayers to request a compromise electronically in cases where the total amount in issue is $50,000 or less. The taxpayer makes the request by using special on-line forms (656-P Offer in Compromise; 433-OIC Financial Statement). The on-line program may be accessed through the IRS's website at www.irs.gov/ind_info/index/html.

[28] The IRS Reform Act added a rule prohibiting the IRS from levying against the taxpayer's property during the period that any offer in compromise is pending, during the 30-day period following rejection of the offer, or during the period any appeal of a rejected offer is pending. *See* I.R.C. § 6331(k). This prohibition does not apply if the IRS believes that the taxpayer is engaging in compromise negotiations primarily for delay, and that collection of the liability is in jeopardy. I.R.C. § 6331(k)(3), (i)(3)(A)(ii).

[29] When preparing the financial statement, taxpayers should consider section 7206, which makes it a felony to conceal property or falsify evidence on the Form 656.

[30] The IRS is planning to require that taxpayers submit a $100 fee before the IRS will process the taxpayer's offer. If the offer is ultimately accepted, the taxpayer would then pay an additional fee equal to 10% of the taxes owed, up to a maximum of $371. Taxpayers with incomes below a specified level and those whose offers are accepted based upon effective tax administration would have their fees waived.

[D] The Bankruptcy Option

Another alternative available to a delinquent taxpayer facing the threat of enforced IRS collection proceedings is to file a petition in bankruptcy. The Bankruptcy Code, 11 U.S.C. § 101 *et seq.*, provides that certain tax liabilities are dischargeable in bankruptcy, and also contains rules affecting the priority of competing claimants, including the IRS. Although a broad treatment of the bankruptcy rules relating to tax liabilities is beyond the scope of this text, some understanding of the IRS's status as a creditor in a bankruptcy proceeding is necessary to advise the taxpayer of his options.

The taxpayer's filing of a bankruptcy petition automatically stays most collection proceedings, including attempts by the IRS to levy against the debtor/taxpayer's assets. The petition in bankruptcy also creates a bankruptcy estate, into which flows all assets (if not otherwise exempt) in which the debtor has a legal or equitable interest. If the IRS has already seized the debtor's assets in order to satisfy a tax liability but has not yet sold the assets, the IRS may be required to turn the seized assets back over to the bankruptcy estate in exchange for adequate protection. *See United States v. Whiting Pools, Inc.*, 462 U.S. 198 (1983). Like most other creditors, the IRS generally must file a claim with the bankruptcy court in order to collect any unpaid liability, notwithstanding the fact that either (1) the IRS may have already assessed the liability or (2) the liability is the subject of a continuing Tax Court proceeding.

Once the bankruptcy estate is created and the debtor's assets are retrieved, the bankruptcy court determines which of the IRS's tax claims are allowed, as well as the order and amount of payment. Tax claims arising out of a taxable year ending before the taxpayer/debtor files a bankruptcy petition (a pre-petition claim) are initially divided into secured and unsecured claims. As a general rule, the IRS has a secured claim if it filed a Notice of Federal Tax Lien prior to the commencement of the bankruptcy proceeding. 11 U.S.C. § 506. Tax claims not supported by a timely filed notice are considered unsecured claims, which are further categorized into general and priority claims. Priority unsecured tax claims include those relating to income taxes for which a return was due within three years before the petition was filed, income taxes assessed not more than 240 days before the petition was filed (even if the due date for the underlying return was beyond the three year period), and withholding and other employment taxes paid by an employer on behalf of an employee (commonly called "trust fund" taxes). 11 U.S.C. § 507. Post-petition tax claims relating to the operation of the debtor/taxpayer's business during the bankruptcy proceeding are treated as administrative expenses and also afforded priority. *Id.* § 507(a)(1). Tax claims not qualifying for priority are treated as general unsecured claims.

The order in which creditor's claims are satisfied out of the bankruptcy estate and the manner in which they may be paid (lump sum versus deferred payment) differs based on the type of proceeding involved — Chapter 7, Chapter 11, or Chapter 13. In a Chapter 7 liquidation proceeding, for example, the IRS's secured tax claims are subordinated to non-tax claims that were filed prior to the Notice of Federal Tax Lien as well as certain other unsecured non-tax priority claims (up to the value of the IRS's secured tax claims). After paying off other general secured claims, the IRS's unsecured priority claims are satisfied, with the remainder of the bankruptcy estate distributed to satisfy general unsecured claims. *See* 11 U.S.C. § 724. In both Chapter 11 and Chapter 13 bankruptcies, the amount recoverable by the IRS for its tax claims depends upon whether the claims are secured or unsecured, and the priority of those unsecured claims.

The Bankruptcy Code also lists those tax debts for which personal liability can be discharged. Once the debtor's tax liabilities are discharged in bankruptcy, the IRS is enjoined from seeking to collect any further amounts not recovered through the bankruptcy proceeding. 11 U.S.C. § 524. As a general rule, all tax claims except priority claims are dischargeable in bankruptcy. Thus, income taxes may be discharged if they were (1) due more than three years before the bankruptcy petition is filed and (2) assessed more than 240 days before such date. The employer's share of employment taxes (not trust fund taxes) that were due more than three years prior to filing the petition are also dischargeable. In addition to priority claims, tax underpayments attributable to fraudulent returns or willful tax evasion, regardless of when the fraud or evasion occurred, and claims relating to taxes for which a required return was not filed or was filed late (but within two years before the petition date) are not discharged. *Id.* § 523. Furthermore, the taxpayer's transfer of nonexempt assets in an attempt to delay or defraud creditors (including the IRS) will prevent his debts from being discharged in bankruptcy. *Id.* § 727(a). These non-dischargeable tax claims survive the bankruptcy proceeding and are recoverable from the debtor after the automatic stay is lifted.

For a taxpayer whose total liabilities substantially exceed his assets and whose tax liability is presently dischargeable, a bankruptcy petition may present a viable option. However, because a bankruptcy action implicates important non-tax considerations, a delinquent taxpayer should consider this alternative carefully before deciding it is best. Faced with the possibility of seeking an Offer in Compromise or filing a bankruptcy petition, for instance, the taxpayer must weigh the discharged tax liabilities against the negative effect the bankruptcy filing may have on his credit rating. If the taxpayer's net worth is positive, bankruptcy relief may not be available, and the possibility that the IRS will accept an Offer in Compromise is slim. In such a case, an installment agreement may be the only option.

§ 12.06 Judicial Action Against the Government for Improper Collection Activity

Because of its sovereign immunity, the United States cannot be sued in court without its specific consent. Although Code section 7421, referred to as the "Anti-Injunction Act," contains a specific prohibition against suits to restrain assessment or collection of any tax, it does not operate as an absolute bar. The Code itself lists a series of statutory exceptions, while the Supreme Court has created a judicial exception to the general rule prohibiting injunctions. How broad is this judicially created exception?

POWERS v. GIBBS
United States District Court, District of Columbia
1989 U.S. Dist. LEXIS 12302 (1989)

THOMAS F. HOGAN, UNITED STATES DISTRICT JUDGE:

This action is before the Court on defendants' motion to dismiss. Because the Court has considered matters outside of the pleadings, the motion shall be treated as one for summary judgment. Rule 12(b) Fed. R. Civ. P.

On July 14, 1988, plaintiff, a citizen of Ohio, filed this suit to enjoin the Internal Revenue Service (the "IRS") from seizing his property and from continuing to levy on his wages. In 1987, the IRS assessed a deficiency against the plaintiff to recover taxes owed in 1982 and 1983. Plaintiff alleges that the collection activities are void and violate his constitutional due process rights because the IRS failed to assess his deficiency or provide him with the required notice of assessment and demand for payment. In addition to the equitable relief, plaintiff requests $500,000 in compensatory damages and $500,000,000 in punitive damages. Defendants argue that the Court lacks subject matter jurisdiction to entertain plaintiff's claim for equitable relief and that defendants are immune from suit for damages. For the reasons stated below, the Court shall grant summary judgment to defendants and shall dismiss this case.

Plaintiff's suit is essentially one to enjoin the federal government from collecting revenue. Such suits are generally barred by 26 U.S.C. § 7421 (the "Anti-Injunction Act"). The Anti-Injunction Act states that "except as provided in sections 6212(a) and (c), 6672(b), 6694(c), 7426(a) and (b)(1), and 7429(b), no suit for the purposes of restraining the assessment or collection of any tax shall be maintained in any court by any person, whether or not such person is the person against whom such tax was assessed." The purpose of the Act is to permit the United States to assess and collect taxes without judicial interference and to require that disputes be determined in a suit for refund. The United States is thus assured of prompt collection of its lawful revenue. Enochs v. Williams Packing & Navigation Co., 370 U.S. 1 (1962).

The Anti-Injunction Act, however, does not bar suit in equity if the taxpayer establishes facts that bring him under one of the statutory exceptions. In addition, a judicially-created exception permits a federal court to entertain a suit to enjoin the IRS's tax collection activities, but only if the taxpayer can show: (1) that under the most liberal view of the law and facts available to the government at the time of the suit, it is apparent that the government cannot prevail on the merits; and (2) that irreparable injury will occur for which there is no adequate remedy at law. *Enochs v. Williams Packing & Navigation Co.*, 370 U.S. at 6–7.

Plaintiff does not allege any facts that bring him within any of the Act's exceptions. He contends merely that the levy and seizure are illegal because the IRS did not properly "assess" his deficiency. The plaintiff also contends that the IRS failed to notify him formally of the assessment and demand payment of the deficiency. Before these claim can be considered, a brief summary of the relevant IRS administrative procedures is necessary.

The IRS may not collect a tax deficiency until it sends, by certified or registered mail, a notice of deficiency to the taxpayer. 26 U.S.C. §§ 6212(a), 6213. The taxpayer has 90 days from the date the notice is mailed to petition the Tax Court for redetermination of the deficiency. Failure to file within the 90 day period deprives the Tax Court of jurisdiction to consider the deficiency. Keado v. United States, 853 F.2d 1209, 1212 (5th Cir. 1988). If the taxpayer does not file a petition with the Tax Court within 90 days, the IRS may assess the deficiency. Thereafter, the IRS must within sixty days notify the taxpayer of the assessment and demand payment of the unpaid tax. 26 U.S.C. § 6303. If the taxpayer neglects or refuses to pay within ten days after notice and demand, the IRS may commence collection action. 26 U.S.C. § 6331.[n.2] Once a notice of deficiency has been properly mailed to the taxpayer and the deficiency properly assessed, the taxpayer's only recourse to challenge the IRS's determination is to pay the deficiency and commence a refund suit in the district court. 26 U.S.C. § 7421–22; *Enochs v. Williams Packing and Navigation Co.*, 370 U.S. at 8.

The record shows that plaintiff did not petition the Tax Court for redetermination of his deficiency for either 1982 or 1983. Plaintiff does not contend that the IRS failed to properly mail the deficiency notices. However, he claims that the deficiency was not properly assessed because the defendants have not produced a document known a Form 23-C, which must be executed if a deficiency is to be properly assessed. The relevant code provision requires "[t]hat assessment shall be made by recording the liability of the taxpayer in the office of the Secretary in accordance with rules and regulations prescribed by the Secretary." 26 U.S.C. § 6203. In addition, 26 C.F.R. 301.6203-1 provides that "[t]he assessment shall be made by an assessment officer signing the summary record of assessment. The summary record through supporting records, shall provide identification of the taxpayer, the character of the liability assessed, the taxable period, if applicable, and the amount of the assessment . . . The date of the assessment is the date the summary record is signed by an assessment officer . . . ." The document described in the above regulation is known as "Form 23-C." *United States v. Dixon*, 672 F. Supp. at 503, 504. Defendants have produced a "Certificate of Assessment and Payments" for each year's deficiency which plaintiff has not rebutted. The Certificate is signed by an IRS officer certifying that it is a true transcript of all the assessments, penalties, interests, and payments on record for the plaintiff. Specifically, the Certificate reflects that deficiencies were assessed on October 12, 1987, and October 26, 1989 (the "23-C" dates) for 1982 and 1983. The Certificate is presumptive proof of a valid assessment in this case, notwithstanding the fact that the IRS has failed to produce the "23-C" form. *See* United States v. Miller, 318 F.2d 637, 639 (7th Cir. 1983); United States v. Dixon, 672 F. Supp. 503, 505–506 (M.D. Ala. 1987). Furthermore, the Court takes judicial notice that the "23-C" date in the Certificate refers to the dates on which the proper records were signed by the assessment officer. United States v. Posner, 405 F. Supp. 934, 937 (D. Md. 1975). The Court therefore

---

n.2 The Court finds no merit to the plaintiff's argument that the IRS's prejudicial levy activities violate his Fifth Amendment due process rights. The constitutionality of the statutory levy procedures is well-established. Commissioner of Internal Revenue v. Shapiro, 424 U.S. 614, 630–32 n.12 (1976); Baddour, Inc. v. United States, 802 F.2d 801, 807 (5th Cir. 1986).

finds that there is no genuine issue regarding whether or not a valid assessment was performed.

In addition to his claim of an invalid assessment, plaintiff contends that the levy and seizure must be enjoined because he was not provided a post-assessment notice and demand for payment as required by 26 U.S.C. § 6303. This claim also lacks merit. The Court notes that the Certificate of Records and Assessments, which is a record of the transactions and correspondence following the assessment, reflects that the plaintiff received "first notices" for both the 1982 and 1983 assessments. The IRS's Notice of Levy on plaintiff's wages recites that notice and demand were made on the defendant pursuant to the Internal Revenue Code. Plaintiff made four payments following assessment of the 1982 deficiency. *See* Defendants' Motion to Dismiss, Exhibit B. The Court therefore also finds no genuine issue of fact on the present record that defendants fully complied with section 6303. *See* United States v. Lorson Electric Co., 480 F.2d 554 (2d Cir. 1973) (IRS complied with § 6303 requirements when its tax lien notice stated that there had been a demand for payment and the Certificate of Assessments and Payments stated that the taxpayer had received a first notice).

As the prior discussion makes clear, plaintiff's case does not fall within the *Enochs* exception to the Anti-Injunction Act because plaintiff has failed to satisfy the first prong of the *Enochs* test, as it is likely that the IRS will prevail on the merits. Notwithstanding that finding, however, the Court additionally finds that plaintiff has failed to satisfy the second prong of the *Enochs* test, as plaintiff has not shown that he will suffer irreparable injury.[n.3]

With respect to the second prong of the *Enochs* test, plaintiff has alleged that he is unable to provide for his family's basic needs as a result of the IRS's continuing to levy on his assets. Even if these unsupported claims were true, the Court finds that the plaintiff has an adequate remedy at law — namely, paying the delinquent taxes and filing a refund suit. Moreover, it is well established that financial hardship alone is insufficient to justify injunctive relief against IRS collection activities. Laino v. United States, 633 F.2d 626, 630 (2d Cir. 1980) ("[I]t is decisive that [plaintiff] failed to exhaust [his] legal remedies by neglecting to petition the Tax Court for redetermination of the deficiency . . . [Plaintiff] here [has] utterly failed to explain why [he] chose not to follow this generous avenue of relief. Under the circumstances, [plaintiff] cannot be heard to complain [he] now lack[s] an adequate remedy at law"); Lucia v. United States, 474 F.2d 565, 577 (5th Cir. 1973) (hardship alone is insufficient to justify injunctive relief).

The Court therefore lacks subject matter jurisdiction to entertain plaintiff's claim for equitable relief pursuant to the Anti-Injunction Act.

Plaintiff's remaining damages claims must also fail for the reasons stated above. The Court has found no genuine issue of material fact regarding whether or not defendants acted lawfully. Defendants are therefore entitled

---

[n.3] Both prongs of the *Enochs* test must be satisfied before the clear command of the Anti-Injunction Act can be overcome. Bob Jones University v. Simon, 416 U.S. 725, 745 (1974); Kemlon Products and Development Co. v. United States, 638 F.2d 1315 (5th Cir.), *modified on other grounds*, 646 F.2d 223 (1981).

to immunity from such damages claims for acts taken in their official capacities. *See* Harlow v. Fitzgerald, 457 U.S. 800, 818 (1981).

Accordingly, the Court shall grant summary judgment for defendants and shall dismiss this action. An Order in accordance with this Memorandum Opinion shall be issued herewith.

* * *

Ordered that defendants' motion to dismiss, which the Court has treated as one for summary judgment, is hereby granted and this case is hereby dismissed.

Is the right to file a refund suit an adequate remedy at law for a taxpayer who does not have the funds to gain jurisdiction to a refund forum?

Another type of proceeding that may involve the government, despite the Anti-Injunction Act prohibition, is a suit filed under 28 U.S.C. § 2410. This provision permits the United States to be joined as a party to a quiet title proceeding relating to property against which the United States holds a lien. Normally the suit is filed by a third party lienholder claiming priority over the government's lien in an attempt to obtain an adjudication confirming their superior status. The following case, brought by the taxpayers themselves, raises the question of whether the parties may litigate the validity of the government's tax lien as part of a quiet title suit.

ROBINSON v. UNITED STATES
United States Court of Appeals, Third Circuit
920 F.2d 1157 (1990)

WEIS, CIRCUIT JUDGE.

Asserting a procedural defect, taxpayers challenged an Internal Revenue Service lien via a suit under 28 U.S.C. § 2410(a). The district court dismissed for lack of jurisdiction concluding that the taxpayers' attack necessarily struck at the underlying assessment, a result it believed was barred by this Court's precedent. We reverse. Our prohibition against assaults on the "merits of an assessment" applies to the amount of tax due and does not prevent scrutiny of procedural lapses by the IRS.

In 1971 the Internal Revenue Service assessed plaintiffs for unpaid income taxes for the years 1968 and 1969. Because of taxes assertedly due for those years, the IRS filed liens in Montgomery County, Pennsylvania against the home that plaintiffs own.

Plaintiffs filed this action to quiet title under 28 U.S.C. § 2410(a). The complaint alleged that the government failed to comply with the statutory procedures for creating a lien, specifically that the IRS never issued a notice of deficiency to plaintiffs before assessing the tax due. For the purposes of its motion to dismiss, the IRS conceded that a notice of deficiency was not sent, but asserted that jurisdiction was lacking because sovereign immunity barred plaintiffs from attacking the merits of the assessment under section 2410(a). The district court agreed that the suit was essentially a challenge to the assessments, and dismissed for lack of jurisdiction.

I.

In the Internal Revenue Code Congress has specified steps for the creation of a lien arising out of unpaid taxes. After preliminary steps, when the IRS believes that the taxpayers have not paid all or any part of their income tax due, the following procedures apply.

1. The IRS mails a notice of deficiency to the taxpayers by certified or registered mail. 26 U.S.C. § 6212(a). Once this notice has been mailed, the taxpayers have ninety days in which to file a petition for redetermination in the Tax Court. 26 U.S.C. § 6213.

The notice of deficiency, sometimes called a "ninety day" letter, is the taxpayers' "ticket to the Tax Court" to litigate the merits of the deficiency determination, Delman v. Commissioner, 384 F.2d 929, 934 (3d Cir. 1967), cert. denied, 390 U.S. 952, 88 S. Ct. 1044, 19 L. Ed. 2d 1144 (1968), and is a jurisdictional prerequisite to a suit in that forum. Laing v. United States, 423 U.S. 161, 165 n.4, 46 L. Ed. 2d 416, 96 S. Ct. 473 (1976). Until ninety days have passed, the IRS can neither make an assessment nor utilize Court procedures for collection. Holof v. Commissioner, 872 F.2d 50, 53 (3d Cir. 1989). If the taxpayers file in the Tax Court within that period, the restraint on the IRS continues until the decision of the Court becomes final. 26 U.S.C. § 6213(a).

2. If the taxpayers do not file a petition in the Tax Court within the specified time, the IRS makes an assessment. 26 U.S.C. § 6213(c). A duly designated official for the district or regional tax center signs the summary record of the assessment, which identifies the taxpayers, the type of tax owed, the taxable period and the amount of the assessment. 26 U.S.C. § 6203; Treas. Reg. § 301.6203-1.

3. As soon as practicable and within sixty days after making the assessment, the IRS must issue a "notice and demand letter" to the taxpayers, specifying the amount due and demanding payment. 26 U.S.C. § 6303.

4. If the taxpayers do not pay after demand, the IRS may file a lien against their property. 26 U.S.C. § 6321. *See generally* Wilkens & Matthews, "A Survey of Federal Tax Collection Procedure: Rights and Remedies of Taxpayers and the Internal Revenue Service," 3 Alaska L. Rev. 269 (1986).

The first of these procedures — the provision requiring the IRS to issue a notice of deficiency — is the focal point of this case.

The notice is a "pivotal feature of the Code's assessment procedures," *Holof,* 872 F.2d at 53, because it serves as a prerequisite to a valid assessment by the IRS. The Internal Revenue Code is clear that "no assessment of a deficiency . . . and no levy or proceeding in court for its collection shall be made, begun, or prosecuted until such notice [of deficiency] has been mailed to the taxpayer, nor until the expiration of such 90-day . . . period." 26 U.S.C. § 6213(a). By providing an opportunity to litigate the merits of the deficiency in the Tax Court without requiring payment of the full amount allegedly owed, the statute provides substantial benefits to taxpayers.

Because this is an appeal from an order granting a motion to dismiss, we accept the plaintiffs' allegations that the IRS did not send a notice of deficiency but did file a lien in the county courthouse. *See* Matthews v. Freedman, 882 F.2d 83, 84 (3d Cir. 1989). Although these facts present a seemingly straightforward case of the IRS's failure to comply with the Code, the jurisdictional aspect of the suit in the district court must be resolved.

II.

In this appeal the IRS maintains that taxpayers' remedies are restricted to injunctive relief, refund actions or petitions to the Tax Court. Having "provided for situations such as this, and dictated the manner in which taxpayers should proceed," IRS Brief at 23, Congress did not intend to waive sovereign immunity in such cases brought under 2410(a). Plaintiffs point out that the absence of a notice of deficiency barred their right to proceed in the Tax Court, and that injunctive relief is not available.

III.

28 U.S.C. § 2410(a) provides that "the United States may be named a party in any civil action or suit in any district court . . . (1) to quiet title to . . . real or personal property on which the United States has or claims a mortgage or other lien."

Despite the broad wording of section 2410(a), courts have been cautious in permitting its use in tax cases. Recognizing that Congress has provided an elaborate system for litigating tax claims in the Tax Court before payment and in District Court and the Court of Claims for refunds, courts have hesitated to add to the remedies provided by the Internal Revenue Code. Section 2410(a) is a statute of general applicability, applying to all liens and not limited to those created by tax delinquencies, and therefore the courts have favored the specific procedures of the Code. *See e.g.,* Flora v. United States, 362 U.S. 145, 157, 4 L. Ed. 2d 623, 80 S. Ct. 630 (1960).

This attitude is reflected in the oft-cited opinion of *Falik v. United States*, 343 F.2d 38 (2d Cir. 1965). There, the IRS placed a lien on the taxpayer's home after determining that, as a responsible corporate officer, she was liable for social security and withholding taxes. The taxpayer attempted to use section 2410(a) to contest the validity of the lien on the ground that the IRS erred in holding her liable. The Court of Appeals concluded that Congress did not intend section 2410(a) to overturn the long-standing principle that except as to matters within the jurisdiction of the Tax Court, "a person whose sole claim is that a federal tax assessment was not well grounded in fact and law must 'pay first and litigate later.'" *Id.* at 42. Significantly, however, access to the Tax Court was not available to the taxpayer in that case.

The principle that a taxpayer cannot use section 2410(a) to challenge the extent of, or existence of, substantive tax liability is well-settled. In *Yannicelli v. Nash*, 354 F. Supp. 143, 151 (D. N.J. 1972), the district court noted that our Court has interpreted section 2410(a) to confer subject matter jurisdiction "provided that the plaintiff refrains from collaterally attacking the merits of the Government's tax assessment itself." In ruling on a motion for reconsideration, the district judge emphasized that "the 'merits' which the district court may not review in such an action include any issue touching upon the actual extent of the taxpayer's federal tax liability." *Id.* at 157 n.4.

The most significant case addressing the issue before us is *Aqua Bar & Lounge, Inc. v. United States*, 539 F.2d 935 (3d Cir. 1976). There, we confronted a challenge to the legality of the IRS's seizure and sale of a taxpayer's property because of non-payment of taxes. The taxpayer admitted that the tax was due, but asserted that the IRS had failed to comply with the statutory requirements for a sale. We concluded that section 2410(a) waived sovereign immunity to a suit "which challenges the validity of a federal tax lien and sale so long as the taxpayer refrains from contesting the merits of the underlying tax assessment itself." *Id.* at 939–40.

In several instances in the *Aqua Bar* opinion the Court referred to disputes over the "merits of the underlying tax assessment" and determined that so long as no such attack was made, a suit under section 2410(a) did not "undermine the established administrative and judicial framework for resolving an individual's tax liability." *Id.* at 939. Significantly, the panel said "in the absence of a Congressional directive to the contrary, we refuse to place such a narrowing construction on § 2410 and thus deprive a taxpayer of any remedy against arbitrary administrative action." *Id.*

Other Courts of Appeals have cited *Aqua Bar* with approval. *See* Estate of Johnson, 836 F.2d 940, 944 (5th Cir. 1988) ("Several circuits have held that a taxpayer may use section 2410(a) to contest the procedural regularity of a lien."); Pollack v. United States, 819 F.2d 144, 145 (6th Cir. 1987) ("A suit under 28 U.S.C. § 2410 is proper only to contest the procedural regularity of a lien; it may not be used to challenge the underlying tax liability.").

IV.

Against this background we consider the issue raised by the parties. Any suit against the federal government must of course clear the hurdle of sovereign immunity and, in many tax cases, the Anti-Injunction Act, 26 U.S.C. § 7421(a). That statute provides that "except as provided in section[] . . . 6213(a), . . . no suit for the purpose of restraining the assessment or collection of any tax shall be maintained in any court by any person." Section 6213(a) states, "Notwithstanding the provisions of section 7421(a) [the Anti-Injunction Act], the making of such assessment or the beginning of such proceeding or levy during the time such prohibition is in force may be enjoined by a proceeding in the proper court."

Because section 6213(a), requiring a notice of assessment, provides an exception to the Anti-Injunction Act, at first glance it would appear that plaintiffs could have sought an injunction. However, "Congress, in enacting Section 6213(a), did not repudiate the principle that injunctive relief is an extraordinary remedy which is unavailable absent a showing of irreparable injury and no adequate remedy at law." Flynn v. United States, 786 F.2d 586,

590 (3d Cir. 1986). *See also* Commissioner v. Shapiro, 424 U.S. 614, 633, 47 L. Ed. 2d 278, 96 S. Ct. 1062 (1976).

Plaintiffs assert that it is unlikely that they could show the absence of a remedy at law, particularly because the option to file a refund action is available. The IRS seems to agree and, in addition, asserts that another remedy is available — a petition in the Tax Court. The IRS, however, has directed us to no authority on the latter point. We have found no instance in which the Tax Court has been granted jurisdiction over an income tax claim when a notice of deficiency was not sent. Indeed, the statutory language and case law are to the contrary. *Laing,* 423 U.S. at 165 n.4; *Delman,* 384 F.2d at 934 (3d Cir. 1967) ("It is true that unless a notice of deficiency is mailed to the taxpayer the Tax Court may not acquire jurisdiction.").

In the absence of a remedy in the Tax Court, the IRS argument seems to be reduced to the proposition that the possibility of filing a refund suit indicates that Congress did not intend to waive sovereign immunity in tax cases filed under section 2410(a). Because there is no evidence of such a Congressional intent and the IRS position is not supported by case law or logic, we reject that argument as not persuasive.

In addition, the IRS asserts that *Aqua Bar* does not apply because failure to send out a notice of deficiency inevitably undermines the procedures required to establish a valid assessment and, therefore, the challenge to the procedural integrity of the lien is in reality an attack on the substantive tax assessment. For the purpose of this suit, however, plaintiffs admit that the taxes are due and, consequently, they maintain there is no attack on the assessment. According to the district court, plaintiffs attacked the assessments: "If it were true that [plaintiffs] are challenging the tax liens on any basis which does not also amount to a challenge of the underlying assessment, their argument might be acceptable. But I am not persuaded that is the case."

Relying on *Aqua Bar,* plaintiffs maintain that a challenge to the procedural irregularity of the tax lien creates jurisdiction, particularly because they concede the amount owed. Certainly the plaintiffs' request for relief is based solely on the lien's procedural infirmity resulting from the failure to send the notice of deficiency. But, as the district court recognized, the theoretical prospect of remedying that procedural defect without altering the assessment itself presents some difficulties in practice. Although we think the distinction could be made in some highly sophisticated and rather unrealistic fashion, in the end we believe it is unnecessary to do so.

We reach that conclusion because the IRS has misconstrued the "merits of the underlying tax assessment" as articulated in *Aqua Bar.* A proper reading is that for jurisdictional purposes under section 2410(a), "merits" refers to the liability for the amount, if any, of tax due. *See Yannicelli,* 354 F. Supp. 143. *Aqua Bar* does not prohibit inquiry into procedural defects, and indeed the Court refused to adopt a narrow construction of section 2410(a) that would deprive taxpayers of a remedy against arbitrary administrative action.

Critical to our resolution of this issue is that the IRS's failure to send a notice of deficiency denied plaintiffs an opportunity to litigate the merits of the alleged deficiency in the Tax Court. This factor was not present either in *Aqua Bar* or in *Falik*. In both cases the Courts were concerned with preserving the expeditious methods of tax collection which Congress had created. Consequently, the taxpayers were not allowed to use section 2410(a) to evade "the pay first and sue later" refund suits — the only remedy authorized in the factual circumstances of those cases.

In the income tax case here, however, Congress has authorized an additional remedy, suit in the Tax Court before payment, and has clearly spelled out the prerequisites. Had the notice of deficiency been sent, plaintiffs would have had the right to file a petition in the Tax Court and under section 6213(a) no assessment could have been made before a decision by that Court. Opening the procedural deficiencies of the assessment to question under section 2410(a) in these circumstances, therefore, does not do violence to the collection system created in the Internal Revenue Code. Indeed, to read section 2410(a) in this manner preserves the options granted to the taxpayers and grants them the means, perhaps not otherwise available, to correct an arbitrary administrative action.

For these reasons we hold that in an income tax dispute cognizable in the Tax Court, jurisdiction under section 2410(a) is proper when the procedural error blocking access to the Tax Court may also impugn the procedural validity of the assessment. Consistent with the weight of authority we neither permit attacks on the amount of the assessment nor entertain assertions that no tax is owed.

We recognize that our decision on this point may seem to be at odds with those of the Courts of Appeals for the Ninth and Tenth Circuits in *Elias v. Connett*, 908 F.2d 521 (9th Cir. 1990) and *Schmidt v. King*, 913 F.2d 837 (10th Cir. 1990), respectively. We are uncertain about the position of those Courts in those two cases because the opinions are unclear in discussing the governmental errors which are encompassed within section 2410(a) jurisdiction. To the extent, however, that those opinions may be understood to hold that the "merits of the underlying assessment" include procedural defects and prevents examination of such errors under section 2410(a), they are inconsistent with *Aqua Bar* and we find them nonpersuasive.

Congress has created an elaborate system for the collection and dispute of tax matters. Adherence to these procedures is required by both citizens and the IRS alike. As one commentator remarked, "The procedural provisions of the Code appear to be the creation of a scholastic, but whimsical, mind. In general, however, the courts take them literally: the game must be played according to the rules." Johnson, "An Inquiry Into the Assessment Process," 35 Tax L. Rev. 285, 286 (1980). In the factual situation assumed here, the IRS broke the rules.

Accordingly, the order of the district court will be reversed. The case will be remanded for further proceedings consistent with this Opinion, including a resolution of contested factual matters.

Also consider *Koff v. United States*, 3 F.3d 1297 (9th Cir. 1993) (O'Scannlain, Circuit Judge, concurring), *cert. denied,* 511 U.S. 1030 (1994), which highlights the "split of authority" in the Ninth Circuit concerning whether a notice of deficiency represents a procedural or substantive question of law for purposes of 28 U.S.C. § 2410. Procedurally, how might the plaintiffs in *Robinson* have litigated the issue of the validity of the tax lien in Tax Court?

PROBLEMS

1. On May 1, 1999, the IRS mailed to Molly's last known address a notice and demand for payment of a $10,000 income tax liability. Molly consented to the assessment of the liability by signing a Form 870. Accordingly, on February 1, 2000, the IRS assessed the liability.

   A. Assuming the IRS does not file a Notice of Federal Tax Lien against Molly's assets, on what date does the federal tax lien covering the $10,000 arise and to what property interests does it attach? What items of property that Molly may own would be exempt from the lien?

   B. Prior to her grandfather's death eight months ago, Molly provided him with substantial personal and financial support. Molly claims that she provided this care in exchange for her grandfather's promise to leave her in his will a one-half interest in his home. Molly's grandfather died intestate. After a protracted battle with her relatives, a local probate court rejected Molly's claim for a one-half interest in her deceased grandfather's home.

      i. Does the probate court's ruling preclude the IRS from filing a Notice of Federal Tax Lien against Molly's alleged one-half interest in the home?

      ii. Assuming the IRS files a valid lien against Molly's one-half interest in the home, and assuming that the IRS follows all other applicable procedural requirements, can the IRS levy against the home and sell it to satisfy Molly's tax liability? Does it matter whether the home is occupied by another family member?

2. Bill operates a local appliance store as a sole proprietorship. On June 1, 2000, the IRS validly assessed a $25,000 liability arising from Bill's failure to pay income taxes during 1998. On March 1, 2001, after Bill repeatedly ignored IRS notices and demands for payment, the IRS properly recorded a Notice of Federal Tax Lien against all of Bill's assets.

   A. Six months prior to the recording of the federal tax lien, on September 1, 2000, Bill borrowed $50,000 from the Third National Bank. To secure payment of the $50,000 advanced to Bill, the bank took a security interest in the inventory of Bill's appliance store. The bank made no effort to perfect its security interest until April 1, 2001.

      i. Does the bank's security interest take priority over the government's federal tax lien?

      ii.   Would the answer in (i) change if the bank had perfected its security interest under state law on September 15, 2000?

3.   Marge, who is 70 years old, is retired and living off her social security payments. Her only other means of support consists of $6,000 worth of dividend income from a minority stock interest she holds in Exx Corporation. Her Exx Corporation stock has an estimated value of $70,000. Her only other asset with any significant value is her home, which she owns free of debt, and which has a fair market value of $75,000. The IRS has validly assessed an unpaid tax liability of $4,000.

    A.   Assuming that no doubt exists as to Marge's liability for the $4,000 assessment, what relief might be available to Marge either to defer payment of the $4,000 or to settle the debt for less than the entire $4,000?

       i.   What procedures would Marge need to follow in order to qualify for relief?

      ii.   Would the IRS be likely to accept deferred payment from Marge, settle for less than the full amount, or neither option?

    B.   How, if at all, would your answer to A. change if Marge's liability were $120,000 instead of $4,000?

    C.   Marge recently learned from her doctor that she needs to begin a course of treatment for a liver ailment. Marge anticipates that the treatment will involve an expenditure of several thousand dollars that will not be covered by insurance. Would an IRS agent be willing to consider this future expense in determining whether compromise of the tax liability is appropriate?

4.   After Joel was audited by the IRS in early 1999, the IRS determined a $15,000 income tax liability arising from Joel's 1997 tax year. At the conclusion of the audit, in March 1999, Joel moved from New York to California, and timely submitted his 1998 return in April 1999 using his new California address. In August 1999, the IRS mailed to Joel's prior address in New York a notice of deficiency setting forth the $15,000 liability. Months later, when Joel did not respond to the notice of deficiency, the IRS sent a notice and demand for payment to the New York address. Because Joel did not respond to either notice, the IRS has sought to levy against an undeveloped tract of land Joel owns in California. What judicial remedies are available to Joel to prevent the IRS from collecting the tax liability by seizing and selling the California property?

5.   Angie was married to Gary from June 1998 until August 1999. Angie divorced Gary because she discovered that his primary source of income was selling stolen motorcycles. Angie and Gary filed a joint return for 1998. According to Angie, Gary prepared

the return, did not let her read it, and insisted that she sign it. Angie does not know what was on the return, but, because a refund check arrived in 1999 for nearly all of the federal withholding from Angie's salary as a nurse's aide, Angie suspects that Gary did not report any of his illegal income. In March 2001, Angie received a notice of deficiency in the amount of $20,000 with respect to the 1998 tax year. The notice was based on unreported income. Angie ignored the notice because she thought Gary would take care of the deficiency. He did not, and the IRS assessed the deficiency and placed a lien on Angie's bank account. She has received notice of her right to a "collection due process" hearing.

A.   How can Angie obtain a collection due process hearing, and who will hear her case?

B.   Assume that you have mention the "innocent spouse" concept to Angie, and that she is interested in asserting innocent spouse status as a defense to liability for the deficiency.

       i.   Is it too late for Angie to assert an innocent spouse defense?

      ii.   What are the procedures for Angie to assert the defense? Can she assert the defense in the collection due process hearing?

    iii.   Assuming Angie properly and timely asserts the innocent spouse defense but the IRS denies her claim, can she obtain Tax Court review of her claim?

6.   In 1995 and 1996, Candice, who is single, worked as an independent contractor providing management consulting services. Diamond, Inc. was her biggest client in both years. In 1995, Candice earned a $200,000 fee from Diamond, Inc., which was paid to her in December of 1995. When she had not received a 1099 form for 1995 from Diamond, Inc. by late March of 1996, she questioned her contact there who assured her that they were "working on it" and that she would receive the Form 1099 in time to file her income tax return by April 15. Candice followed up several times, but Diamond, Inc. never mailed her a copy of a 1099 form. When Candice prepared her 1995 taxes in April of 1996, she included only those amounts for which she had received Forms 1099, which totaled $40,000. Candice continued to work for Diamond, Inc. until May 1996, at which point, she billed them $150,000. They paid her the $150,000 in July 1996. In February of 1997, Candice received a Form 1099 from Diamond, Inc., reflecting payments to her of $350,000 for 1996. Candice asked her contact to have the form corrected. After several phone calls, he told her that the company had decided it was too much trouble to correct the form and that it really should not matter to Candice because at some

time or another she had been paid everything that was reflected in the Form 1099. Candice was frustrated because she had anticipated that only $150,000, plus about $80,000 from other jobs would be reported to the IRS, and she therefore had not set aside enough money to pay the full tax liability. She received an automatic extension of time to file her 1996 return, but her additional extension request was denied. After procrastinating filing her return for several more months, Candice rationalized in December of 1997 that there would be no harm to the IRS if she did not file a return for the 1996 year and made it up to the IRS by not taking as many deductions as she legally could the following year.

In early 1999, Candice received a notice of deficiency from the IRS with respect to her 1996 tax year. The deficiency was for $115,000, which included unpaid taxes on the income that was reported to the IRS for 1996, a negligence penalty, a failure to file penalty, an estimated tax penalty, and interest. Candice felt responsible for her lack of payment because it resulted from her failure to file, so she signed the included Form 870, reflecting her agreement to the amount stated, and wrote the IRS a note saying that she did not have the money to pay the tax liability. After sending the signed Form 870 and note back to the IRS, she realized that she might benefit from some legal advice, and consulted you about what she should do to resolve the matter with the IRS. She still has not filed a return for 1996, though she did timely file for both 1997 and 1998. She also cannot afford to pay more than $15,000 of the $115,000 at this time. How would you advise Candice to proceed?

Chapter 13

TAX CRIMES

_____

Reading Assignment: Code §§ 6012, 6531, 7201–7203, 7205–7207, 7212; 18 U.S.C. §§ 2, 287, 371, 1001.

§ 13.01   Introduction

Although the IRS seeks to encourage voluntary compliance with the tax laws, enforcement action is sometimes necessary. Chapter 10 discussed civil penalties that may serve to deter negligent and fraudulent activity. In some cases, the government pursues criminal prosecution in order to punish tax evaders and deter similar activity in others. This chapter discusses tax crimes targeting taxpayers and tax professionals, the statute of limitations on tax crimes, and the application of the federal sentencing guidelines to tax offenses.[1] Chapter 14 covers tax prosecution procedures, strategies, and defenses.

Tax crimes include attempts to evade or defeat tax; willful failure to file a return, supply information or pay tax; willful failure to collect or pay over tax; providing a fraudulent withholding exemption certificate; making certain false statements; and attempting to interfere with the administration of the Internal Revenue laws. *See* I.R.C. §§ 7201–7203; 7205–7206; 7212. Tax evaders may also be guilty of currency offenses, *see* I.R.C. § 6050I, and crimes under Title 18 of the U.S. Code, such as conspiracy to defraud the United States, *see* 18 U.S.C. § 371, mail fraud, *see* 18 U.S.C. § 1341, or even influencing or injuring an officer, juror or witness, *see* 18 U.S.C. § 1503. As discussed below, some crimes can apply to both taxpayers and tax professionals.

§ 13.02   Criminal Conduct Under the Internal Revenue Code

[A]   Willful Failure to File a Return, Supply Information, or Pay Tax

Under Code section 7203, any person required to pay tax, or required to make a return, keep any records, or supply any information, who willfully fails to do so is guilty of a misdemeanor. The elements of the offense are (1) an omission of one of the four required acts listed above, and (2) willfullness. Section 7203 surfaces in the *Spies* case, reproduced below in connection with tax evasion. Note also that section 7203 can be a lesser included offense to

_____

[1] This chapter and Chapter 14 are intended as an introduction to tax crimes and criminal tax procedure. An exhaustive discussion or analysis of the many issues that may arise in criminal tax cases is beyond the scope of this text.

a charge of tax evasion under section 7201. Unlike section 7201, section 7203 does not require proof of a deficiency. Can section 7203 apply to a tax professional?

[B] Tax Evasion

Review Code section 7201. Under that section, it is a felony to "willfully attempt[ ] in any manner to evade or defeat any tax imposed by this title or the payment thereof . . . ." The three elements of a *prima facie* tax evasion case are (1) a tax deficiency, (2) an affirmative act of tax evasion or attempted evasion, and (3) willfullness. A taxpayer's conviction under section 7201 collaterally estops him from denying fraud in an ensuing civil fraud case. *See, e.g., Rodney v. Commissioner*, 53 T.C. 287, 306 (1969); *Fagan v. Commissioner*, T.C. Memo. 2001-222.

"[Section] 7201 includes the offense of willfully attempting to evade or defeat the assessment of a tax as well as the offense of willfully attempting to evade or defeat the payment of a tax." *Sansone v. United States*, 380 U.S. 343, 354 (1965). Notice that section 7201 involves an element of intent. What behavior constitutes "willfullness"? Does *knowingly* failing to file a return and pay tax amount to a willful attempt to evade tax? Or does the statute require an evil purpose? Consider the *Spies* case:

SPIES v. UNITED STATES
United States Supreme Court
317 U.S. 492 (1943)

MR. JUSTICE JACKSON delivered the opinion of the Court.

Petitioner has been convicted of attempting to defeat and evade income tax, in violation of * * * § 145 (b) of the Internal Revenue Code [currently I.R.C. § 7201. Eds.]. * * *

Petitioner admitted at the opening of the trial that he had sufficient income during the year in question to place him under a statutory duty to file a return and to pay a tax, and that he failed to do either. The evidence during nearly two weeks of trial was directed principally toward establishing the exact amount of the tax and the manner of receiving and handling income and accounting, which the Government contends shows an intent to evade or defeat the tax. Petitioner's testimony related to his good character, his physical illness at the time the return became due, and lack of willfullness in his defaults, chiefly because of a psychological disturbance, amounting to something more than worry but something less than insanity.

Section 145 (a) [currently I.R.C. § 7203. Eds.] makes, among other things, willful failure to pay a tax or make a return by one having petitioner's income at the time or times required by law a misdemeanor. Section 145 (b) makes a willful attempt in any manner to evade or defeat any tax such as his a felony. Petitioner was not indicted for either misdemeanor. The indictment contained a single count setting forth the felony charge of willfully attempting to defeat and evade the tax, and recited willful failure to file a return and willful failure to pay the tax as the means to the felonious end.

The petitioner requested an instruction that "You may not find the defendant guilty of a willful attempt to defeat and evade the income tax, if you find only that he had willfully failed to make a return of taxable income and has willfully failed to pay the tax on that income." This was refused, and the Court charged that "If you find that the defendant had a net income for 1936 upon which some income tax was due, and I believe that is conceded, if you find that the defendant willfully failed to file an income tax return for that year, if you find that the defendant willfully failed to pay the tax due on his income for that year, you may, if you find that the facts and circumstances warrant it find that the defendant willfully attempted to evade or defeat the tax." The Court refused a request to instruct that an affirmative act was necessary to constitute a willful attempt, and charged that "Attempt means to try to do or accomplish. In order to find an attempt it is not necessary to find affirmative steps to accomplish the prohibited purpose. An attempt may be found on the basis of inactivity or on refraining to act, as well."

It is the Government's contention that a willful failure to file a return, together with a willful failure to pay the tax, may, without more, constitute an attempt to defeat or evade a tax within § 145 (b). Petitioner claims that such proof establishes only two misdemeanors under § 145 (a), and that it takes more than the sum of two such misdemeanors to make the felony under § 145 (b). The legislative history of the section contains nothing helpful on the question here at issue, and we must find the answer from the section itself and its context in the revenue laws.

The United States has relied for the collection of its income tax largely upon the taxpayer's own disclosures rather than upon a system of withholding the tax from him by those from whom income may be received. This system can function successfully only if those within and near taxable income keep and render true accounts. In many ways, taxpayers' neglect or deceit may prejudice the orderly and punctual administration of the system as well as the revenues themselves. Congress has imposed a variety of sanctions for the protection of the system and the revenues. The relation of the offense of which this petitioner has been convicted to other and lesser revenue offenses appears more clearly from its position in this structure of sanctions. The penalties imposed by Congress to enforce the tax laws embrace both civil and criminal sanctions. The former consist of additions to the tax upon determinations of fact made by an administrative agency and with no burden on the Government to prove its case beyond a reasonable doubt. The latter consist of penal offenses enforced by the criminal process in the familiar manner. Invocation of one does not exclude resort to the other. Helvering v. Mitchell, 303 U.S. 391.

The failure in a duty to make a timely return, unless it is shown that such failure is due to reasonable cause and not due to willful neglect, is punishable by an addition to the tax of 5 to 25 per cent thereof, depending on the duration of the default. § 291 of the Revenue Act of 1936 and of the Internal Revenue Code [currently I.R.C. § 6651. Eds.]. But a duty may exist even when there is no tax liability to serve as a base for application of a percentage delinquency penalty; the default may relate to matters not identifiable with tax for a particular period; and the offense may be more grievous than a case for civil penalty. Hence the willful failure to make a return, keep records, or supply information when required, is made a misdemeanor, without regard to existence of a tax liability. § 145 (a). Punctuality is important to the fiscal system, and these are sanctions to assure punctual as well as faithful performance of these duties.

Sanctions to insure payment of the tax are even more varied to meet the variety of causes of default. It is the right as well as the interest of the taxpayer to limit his admission of liability to the amount he actually owes. But the law is complicated, accounting treatment of various items raises problems of great complexity, and innocent errors are numerous, as appears from the number who make overpayments. It is not the purpose of the law to penalize frank difference of opinion or innocent errors made despite the exercise of reasonable care. Such errors are corrected by the assessment of the deficiency of tax and its collection with interest for the delay. §§ 292 and 294 of the Revenue Act of 1936 and of the Internal Revenue Code. [*See* I.R.C. §§ 6201, 6601. Eds.] If any part of the deficiency is due to negligence or intentional disregard of rules and regulations, but without intent to defraud, five per cent of such deficiency is added thereto; and if any part of any deficiency is due to fraud with intent to evade tax, the addition is 50 per cent thereof. § 293 of the Revenue Act of 1936 and of the Internal Revenue Code. [*See* I.R.C. §§ 6622, 6623. Eds.] Willful failure to pay the tax when due is punishable as a misdemeanor. § 145 (a). The climax of this variety of sanctions is the serious and inclusive felony defined to consist of willful attempt in any manner to evade or defeat the tax. § 145 (b). The question here is whether there is a distinction between the acts necessary to make out the felony and those which may make out the misdemeanor.

A felony may, and frequently does, include lesser offenses in combination either with each other or with other elements. We think it clear that this felony may include one or several of the other offenses against the revenue laws. But it would be unusual and we would not readily assume that Congress by the felony defined in § 145 (b) meant no more than the same derelictions it had just defined in § 145 (a) as a misdemeanor. Such an interpretation becomes even more difficult to accept when we consider this felony as the capstone of a system of sanctions which singly or in combination were calculated to induce prompt and forthright fulfillment of every duty under the income tax law and to provide a penalty suitable to every degree of delinquency. The difference between willful failure to pay a tax when due, which is made a misdemeanor, and willful attempt to defeat and evade one, which is made a felony, is not easy to detect or define. Both must be willful, and willful, as we have said, is a word of many meanings, its construction often being influenced by its context. United States v. Murdock, 290 U.S. 389. It may well mean something more as applied to nonpayment of a tax than when applied to failure to make a return. Mere voluntary and purposeful, as distinguished from accidental, omission to make a timely return might meet the test of willfulness. But in view of our traditional aversion to imprisonment for debt, we would not without the clearest manifestation of Congressional intent assume that mere knowing and intentional default in payment of a tax, where there had been no willful failure to disclose the liability, is intended to constitute a criminal offense of any degree. We would expect willfulness in such a case to include some element of evil motive and want of justification in view of all the financial circumstances of the taxpayer.

Had § 145 (a) not included willful failure to pay a tax, it would have defined as misdemeanors generally a failure to observe statutory duties to make timely returns, keep records, or supply information — duties imposed to facilitate administration of the Act even if, because of insufficient net income, there were no duty to pay a tax. It would then be a permissible and perhaps an appropriate construction of § 145 (b) that it made felonies of the same willful omissions when there was the added element of duty to pay a tax. The definition of such nonpayment as a misdemeanor, we think, argues strongly against such an interpretation.

The difference between the two offenses, it seems to us, is found in the affirmative action implied from the term "attempt," as used in the felony subsection. It is not necessary to involve this subject with the complexities of the common-law "attempt." The attempt made criminal by this statute does not consist of conduct that would culminate in a more serious crime but for some impossibility of completion or interruption or frustration. This is an independent crime, complete in its most serious form when the attempt is complete, and nothing is added to its criminality by success or consummation, as would be the case, say, of attempted murder. Although the attempt succeed in evading tax, there is no criminal offense of that kind, and the prosecution can be only for the attempt. We think that in employing the terminology of attempt to embrace the gravest of offenses against the revenues, Congress intended some willful commission in addition to the willful omissions that make up the list of misdemeanors. Willful but passive neglect of the statutory duty may constitute the lesser offense, but to combine with it a willful and positive attempt to evade tax in any manner or to defeat it by any means lifts the offense to the degree of felony.

Congress did not define or limit the methods by which a willful attempt to defeat and evade might be accomplished and perhaps did not define lest its effort to do so result in some unexpected limitation. Nor would we by definition constrict the scope of the Congressional provision that it may be accomplished "in any manner." By way of illustration, and not by way of limitation, we would think affirmative willful attempt may be inferred from conduct such as keeping a double set of books, making false entries or alterations, or false invoices or documents, destruction of books or records, concealment of assets or covering up sources of income, handling of one's affairs to avoid making the records usual in transactions of the kind, and any conduct, the likely effect of which would be to mislead or to conceal. If the tax-evasion motive plays any part in such conduct the offense may be made out even though the conduct may also serve other purposes such as concealment of other crime.

In this case there are several items of evidence apart from the default in filing the return and paying the tax which the Government claims will support an inference of willful attempt to evade or defeat the tax. These go to establish that petitioner insisted that certain income be paid to him in cash, transferred it to his own bank by armored car, deposited it, not in his own name but in the names of others of his family, and kept inadequate and misleading records.

Petitioner claims other motives animated him in these matters. We intimate no opinion. Such inferences are for the jury. If on proper submission the jury found these acts, taken together with willful failure to file a return and willful failure to pay the tax, to constitute a willful attempt to evade or defeat the tax, we would consider conviction of a felony sustainable. But we think a defendant is entitled to a charge which will point out the necessity for such an inference of willful attempt to defeat or evade the tax from some proof in the case other than that necessary to make out the misdemeanors; and if the evidence fails to afford such an inference, the defendant should be acquitted.

The Government argues against this construction, contending that the milder punishment of a misdemeanor and the benefits of a short statute of limitation should not be extended to violators of the income tax laws such as political grafters, gamblers, racketeers, and gangsters. We doubt that this construction will handicap prosecution for felony of such flagrant violators. Few of them, we think, in their efforts to escape tax, stop with mere omission of the duties put upon them by the statute, but if such there be, they are entitled to be convicted only of the offense which they have committed.

Reversed.

After reading Code sections 7201 and 7203, do you believe Spies should have been convicted of a misdemeanor, a felony, or nothing at all? What if Spies had merely made a mistake of law, but an objectively unreasonable mistake, would that constitute willfullness? The Supreme Court answered that question in the negative in *Cheek v. United States*, 498 U.S. 192 (1991).

As discussed above, another element of section 7201 is an affirmative act of evasion. What were the affirmative acts in *Spies*? Following *Spies*, courts have set a low threshold for finding an affirmative act. *See, e.g., United States v. Winfield*, 960 F.2d 970, 973 (11th Cir. 1992) ("An affirmative act constituting an evasion or attempted evasion of the tax occurs when false statements are made to the IRS after the tax was due . . . ."); *United States v. Williams*, 928 F.2d 145 (5th Cir. 1991) (previous year's filing of false W-4 form reflecting 50 exemptions was affirmative act where uncorrected W-4 was still in effect in tax years at issue); *United States v. Copeland*, 786 F.2d 768 (7th Cir. 1985) ("filing a false and fraudulent tax withholding certificate, although a misdemeanor offense, constitutes valid and sufficient evidence of willful commission.").

[C] Willful Failure to Collect or Pay Over Tax

Review Code section 7202. Under that section, it is a felony for any person "required under this title to collect, account for, and pay over any tax imposed by this title [to] . . . willfully fail[ ] to collect or truthfully account for and pay over such tax . . . ." The elements of this offense are (1) a duty to collect, account for, and pay over tax; (2) failure to fulfill that duty; and (3) willfullness. In what kinds of situations are people required to collect and pay over tax? Like section 7201 (the statute governing tax evasion), section 7202 penalizes only "willful" activity. Section 7202 phrases the duties of collecting, accounting for, and paying over tax in the conjunctive. Has a person who collects the tax and truthfully accounts for it but willfully fails to pay it over violated section 7202? The Court of Appeals for the Third Circuit considered that question in *United States v. Thayer*, 201 F.3d 214, 220-221 (3d Cir. 1999), *cert. denied*, 530 U.S. 1244 (2000).

> Thayer contends the statute imposes criminal liability only on one who neither accounts for nor pays over withholding taxes. Since he did account for the withheld funds, Thayer argues the evidence was insufficient to convict him under § 7202.

> As noted, § 7202 applies to one who "willfully fails to collect or truthfully account for and pay over" employees' income taxes. Thayer and the government both interpret this language to criminalize either of two acts: (1) willful failure to collect employees' income taxes or (2) willful failure to truthfully account for and pay over withheld taxes. Because Thayer accounted for the withheld taxes by reporting the withholdings on the corporations' quarterly tax returns, he can be convicted only under the second prong. Therefore, the question is whether a person who collects and accounts for but does not pay over taxes has failed to account for and pay over those taxes. Because this is a question of statutory interpretation, we will exercise plenary review. *See Parise*, 159 F.3d at 794; *Hayden*, 64 F.3d at 128.

> The Court of Appeals for the Second Circuit faced the identical question and, relying on the reasoning in *United States v. Brennick*, 908 F. Supp. 1004 (D. Mass. 1995), ruled that § 7202 requires employers to both account for and pay over the taxes. The court held the plain language of the statute supported this reading: " 'The phrase "truthfully account for and pay over" is . . . unambiguously conjunctive. A person who was required to "truthfully account for and pay over" a tax would be required to do both things to satisfy the requirement.' " United States v. Evangelista, 122 F.3d 112, 121 (2d Cir. 1997) (*quoting Brennick*, 908 F. Supp. at 1016) (omission in original). The court also noted that a contrary interpretation " 'would result in a greater penalty for one who simply failed to collect trust fund taxes than for one who collected them and, as is charged here, used them for his own selfish purposes . . ., so long as he notified the IRS that he had collected the tax. That Congress intended to make such a distinction is simply inconceivable.' " 122 F.3d at 121 (*quoting Brennick*, 908 F. Supp. at 1017) (omission in original). We agree.

> Thayer points out that, as the Second Circuit interpreted § 7202, the phrase "willfully fails to . . . truthfully account for and pay over" has the same meaning as "willfully fails to . . . truthfully account for or pay over," arguing that Congress might have exempted those who account for but do not pay over withholding taxes to encourage reporting, thereby facilitating collections. Conceding ambiguity, Thayer seeks to rely on the rule of lenity. *See, e.g.,* United States v. Turcks, 41 F.3d 893, 901 (3d Cir. 1994). But "the simple existence of some statutory ambiguity . . . is not sufficient to warrant application of the rule [of lenity], for most statutes are ambiguous to some

degree. . . . The rule of lenity applies only if, after seizing everything from which aid can be derived, we can make no more than a guess as to what Congress intended." *Muscarello v. United States*, 524 U.S. 125, 138, 141 L. Ed. 2d 111, 118 S. Ct. 1911 (1998) (internal quotation marks and ellipses omitted).

Thayer suggests a rationale why Congress might have penalized more severely those who neither report nor pay over withholding taxes than those who report but fail to pay over the taxes, but does not convincingly answer the Second Circuit's telling analysis: that on Thayer's reading, those who collect the taxes and spend them on personal expenses, effectively stealing the tax moneys, will receive no criminal penalties, whereas those who never collect the taxes at all face criminal sanctions. We agree with the Court of Appeals for the Second Circuit that Congress could not plausibly have intended Thayer's reading of the statute.

We also note the title of a section can assist in resolving ambiguities. *See* I.N.S. v. National Ctr. for Immigrants' Rights, Inc., 502 U.S. 183, 189, 116 L. Ed. 2d 546, 112 S. Ct. 551 (1991). Section 7202 is entitled, "Willful failure to collect or pay over tax," suggesting the section covers willful failure either to collect or to pay over the taxes. For the reasons stated, we hold Thayer was properly convicted under § 7202 for accounting for but failing to pay over withheld income taxes.

[D] Submitting False Returns or Documents

Code section 7207 provides in part that "[a]ny person who willfully delivers or discloses to the Secretary any list, return, account, statement, or other document, known by him to be fraudulent or to be false as to any material matter," is guilty of a misdemeanor. Conviction under section 7207 requires proof of (1) willfullness, (2) an affirmative act of delivery or disclosure of a document known to be false or fraudulent, and (3) materiality. Recognize that there is no requirement that the act be done with the intention of evading taxes. Could Spies have been indicted and convicted under this section?

Code section 7206(1) provides that it is a felony to "Willfully make[ ] and subscribe[ ] any return, statement, or other document, which contains or is verified by a written declaration that it is made under the penalties of perjury, and which [the signer] does not believe to be true and correct as to every material matter . . ." I.R.C. § 7206(1). The five elements necessary to establish this offense are (1) making and subscribing a return, statement or other document, (2) a written declaration under the penalties of perjury, (3) a lack of belief by the signer that the document is true and correct, (4) willfullness, and (5) materiality. Even if the taxpayer's accountant prepared the return, the taxpayer can be liable under section 7206(1) if the accountant prepared the return solely on the basis of information provided by the taxpayer. *United States v. Badwan*, 624 F.2d 1228, 1232 (4th Cir. 1980), *cert. denied*, 449 U.S. 1124 (1981).

Like Code section 7203, discussed at the beginning of this Chapter, section 7206(1) does not require a tax deficiency as an element of the offense. *See United States v. Scholl*, 166 F.3d 964, 980 (9th Cir.), *cert. denied*, 528 U.S. 873 (1999). This means that the government can prosecute a taxpayer under section 7206(1) even if, for example, the taxpayer's false return did not result in any underpayment of tax. What policy might support such a prosecution?

Code sections 7206 and 7207 both contain the willfullness element considered in *Spies*. Should "willfully" be interpreted the same in misdemeanor and felony statutes? This issue is discussed in *Pomponio*.

UNITED STATES v. POMPONIO
United States Supreme Court
429 U.S. 10 (1976)[2]

PER CURIAM.

After a jury trial, respondents were convicted of willfully filing false income tax returns in violation of 26 U.S.C. § 7206(1). Based on its reading of *United States v. Bishop*, 412 U.S. 346 (1973), the Court of Appeals held that the jury was incorrectly instructed concerning willfulness, and remanded for a new trial. 528 F.2d 247 (1975). The United States petitioned for certiorari. We reverse.

The respondents were charged with falsifying tax returns in two principal ways: (1) they allegedly caused corporations they controlled to report payments to them as loans, when they knew the payments were really taxable dividends; and (2) they allegedly claimed partnership losses as deductions knowing that the losses were properly attributable to a corporation. Their defense was that these transactions were correctly reported, or at least that they thought so at the time. The jury was instructed that respondents were not guilty of violating § 7206(1) unless they had signed the tax returns knowing them to be false,[n.2] and had done so willfully. A willful act was defined in the instructions as one done "voluntarily and intentionally and with the specific intent to do something which the law forbids, that is to say with [the] bad purpose either to disobey or to disregard the law." Finally, the jury was instructed that "[g]ood motive alone is never a defense where the act done or omitted is a crime," and that consequently motive was irrelevant except as it bore on intent. The Court of Appeals held this final instruction improper because "the statute at hand requires a finding of a bad purpose or evil

---

[2] *Reh'g denied*, 429 U.S. 987 (1976).

[n.2] We agree with the Court of Appeals that the instructions on this point were "full and complete." 528 F.2d 247, 249–250 (1975). The jury was told that the Government contended that respondents "couldn't claim this [the partnership losses] as a deduction. . . because by so doing they would know that they were filing a false report of their total gross income." Later the jury was instructed that, if they found the loans were incorrectly reported, they must also find that the return was "made willfully and with the specific intent and knowledge at the time they made it that it was in fact a false return." In explaining intent, the trial judge said that "[t]o establish the specific intent the Government must prove that these defendants knowingly did the acts, that is, filing these returns, knowing that they were false, purposely intending to violate the law." The jury was told to "bear in mind the sole charge that you have here, and that is the violation of 7206, the willful making of the false return, and subscribing to it under perjury, knowing it not to be true and [sic] to all material respects, and that and that alone."

motive." 528 F.2d, at 249. In so holding, the Court of Appeals incorrectly assumed that the reference to an "evil motive" in *United States v. Bishop*, *supra*, and prior cases meant something more than the specific intent to violate the law described in the trial judge's instruction.

In *Bishop* we held that the term "willfully" has the same meaning in the misdemeanor and felony sections of the Revenue Code, and that it requires more than a showing of careless disregard for the truth.[n.3] We did not, however, hold that the term requires proof of any motive other than an intentional violation of a known legal duty. We explained the meaning of willfulness in § 7206 and related statutes:

> "The Court, in fact, has recognized that the word 'willfully' in these statutes generally connotes a voluntary, intentional violation of a known legal duty. It has formulated the requirement of willfulness as 'bad faith or evil intent,' [*United States v.*] *Murdock*, 290 U.S. [389,] 398, or 'evil motive and want of justification in view of all the financial circumstances of the taxpayer,' *Spies* [*v. United States*], 317 U.S. [492,] 498, or knowledge that the taxpayer 'should have reported more income than he did.' *Sansone* [*v. United States*], 380 U.S. [343,] 353. *See* James v. United States, 366 U.S. 213, 221 (1961); McCarthy v. United States, 394 U.S. 459, 471 (1969)."

412 U.S. at 360.

Our references to other formulations of the standard did not modify the standard set forth in the first sentence of the quoted paragraph. On the contrary, as the other Courts of Appeals that have considered the question have recognized, willfulness in this context simply means a voluntary, intentional violation of a known legal duty. United States v. Pohlman, 522 F.2d 974, 977 (CA8 1975) (en banc), *cert. denied*, 423 U.S. 1049 (1976); United States v. McCorkle, 511 F.2d 482, 484–485 (CA7) (en banc), *cert. denied*, 423 U.S. 826 (1975); United States v. Greenlee, 517 F.2d 899, 904 (CA3), *cert. denied*, 423 U.S. 985 (1975); United States v. Hawk, 497 F.2d 365, 366–369 (CA9), *cert. denied*, 419 U.S. 838 (1974). The trial judge in the instant case adequately instructed the jury on willfulness. An additional instruction on good faith was unnecessary. As an alternative ground for ordering a new trial, the Court of Appeals held that respondents were entitled to instructions exonerating them if they believed that the payments to them were loans and that the losses belonged to the partnership, 528 F.2d, at 250. Our inspection of the record indicates that such instructions were given and that they were adequate.

The respondents' other allegations of error which the Court of Appeals found it unnecessary to reach should be considered by that court in the first instance.

[n.3] The Court of Appeals in *Bishop* held that the evidence under the misdemeanor statute "need only show unreasonable, capricious, or careless disregard for the truth or falsity of income tax returns filed." 455 F.2d 612, 615 (CA9 1972). This Court rejected the view that this lesser degree of culpability was required for a violation of the misdemeanor statute, and held on the contrary that "Congress used the word 'willfully' to describe a constant rather than a variable in the tax penalty formula." 412 U.S., at 359–360.

The petition for certiorari is granted, the judgment of the Court of Appeals is reversed, and the case is remanded for further proceedings consistent with this opinion.

It is so ordered.

Did the Supreme Court interpret "willfully" the same way in *Pomponio* as it did in *Spies*?

[E] Attempts to Interfere with the Administration of the Internal Revenue Laws

Review Code section 7212, governing "attempts to interfere with administration of internal revenue laws." What kind of conduct does section 7212 criminalize? Would intentionally filing a false tax return be violative of this section? Consider the 7212 activity in the following case:

UNITED STATES v. BAILEY
United States Court of Appeals, Tenth Circuit
1995 U.S. App. LEXIS 32692; 79 A.F.T.R.2d (RIA) 1045

ORDER AND JUDGMENT[*]

* * *

Ralph E. Bailey appeals his jury conviction of two counts of attempting to interfere with the administration of internal revenue laws under 26 U.S.C. Section 7212(a). We affirm.

BACKGROUND

Mr. Bailey was originally indicted, along with his wife, for two counts of "Obstruction of Justice by Interfering with the Administration of the Internal Revenue Laws" under 26 U.S.C. Section 7212(a), and for two counts of aiding and abetting in the commission of these crimes under 18 U.S.C. Section 2. The indictment alleged that Mr. Bailey had delayed the collection of his unpaid taxes by filing fraudulent liens against Internal Revenue Service employees involved in tax collection. Although the indictment against Mr. Bailey's wife was ultimately dismissed, his case went to trial, and he was found guilty by a jury of the two counts under Section 7212(a). Mr. Bailey now makes several arguments as to why his conviction should not stand. We discuss each separately below.

---

[*] This order and judgment is not binding precedent, except under the doctrines of law of the case, res judicata, and collateral estoppel. The court generally disfavors the citation of orders and judgments; nevertheless, an order and judgment may be cited under the terms and conditions of the court's General Order. 151 F.R.D. 470 (10th Cir. 1993).

DISCUSSION

* * *

Sufficiency of the Indictment

Mr. Bailey also argues that the indictment was not sufficiently specific so as to give him proper notice of the charges against him. 26 U.S.C. Section 7212(a) makes it a crime to "corruptly . . . endeavor[ ] to intimidate or impede any officer or employee of the United States acting in an official capacity under this title, or [to] in any other way corruptly . . . obstruct[ ] or impede[ ], or endeavor[ ] to obstruct or impede, the due administration of this title . . ." The indictment returned against Mr. Bailey read, in pertinent part:

> On or about the 30th day of September, 1992, at Tulsa, Oklahoma, in the Northern District of Oklahoma, [the defendants] . . . did corruptly endeavor to obstruct or impede the due administration of the Internal Revenue Laws of the United States, by the following means and methods:
>
> . . .
>
> 3. On or about September 30, 1992, in order to divert the time and attention of the [Internal Revenue] Employees from pursuing the collection of taxes as noted herein, the defendants illegally and unlawfully attempted to place liens in the amount of $350,000.00 on the property of each of the Employees, by filing or causing to be filed in the records of the Clerk of Tulsa County, Oklahoma, a document entitled "A SECURITY (15 USC) Claim of Commercial Lien and Affidavit." Said document falsely and fraudulently purported to seize the real and personal property of each of the Employees for payment of false and fictitious bond.

Rec. vol. I, doc. 1.

Mr. Bailey argues that the indictment was insufficient for two reasons: First, he argues that because the style of the indictment referred to the charged crime as "Obstruction of Justice by Interfering with the Administration of Internal Revenue Laws," Rec. vol. I, doc. 1, he was misled and was not sufficiently put on notice of the nature of the charged crime. In this regard, he points out that obstruction of justice is a separate crime under 18 U.S.C. Section 1501 *et seq.* We do not, however, agree that the use of this language in the style of the indictment was misleading. The indictment set forth the elements necessary to constitute an offense under 26 U.S.C. Section 7212(a) and stated Mr. Bailey's alleged acts with particularity. Mr. Bailey has also failed to allege how this purported error served to prejudice him. He therefore has failed to allege a ground for reversal of his conviction. *See* Fed. R. Crim. P. 7(c)(3) ("Error in the citation [of the charged crime] or its omission shall not be ground for dismissal of the indictment or information or for reversal of a conviction if the error or omission did not mislead the defendant to the defendant's prejudice.").

Mr. Bailey also argues that the indictment was insufficient because the word "corrupt" was not contained in the indictment and it is an element of the offense. However, it is clear from a review of the indictment that Mr. Bailey is in error. The indictment clearly alleged that Mr. Bailey "did corruptly endeavor to obstruct or impede the due administration of the Internal Revenue Laws." Rec. vol. I, doc. 1 (emphasis added).

Constitutionality of 26 U.S.C. Section 7212(a)

26 U.S.C. Section 7212(a) makes it an offense to "corruptly" obstruct or impede the administration of internal revenue laws. Mr. Bailey argues that this statute is unconstitutionally vague because it leaves the definition of "corruptly" open to conflicting interpretations.

"A penal statute is void for vagueness if it: (1) fails to 'define the criminal offense with sufficient definitiveness [so] that ordinary people can understand what conduct is prohibited,' or it (2) fails to 'establish minimal guidelines to govern law enforcement' so as to invite arbitrary and discriminatory enforcement." United States v. Easter, 981 F.2d 1549, 1557 (10th Cir. 1992) (quoting Kolender v. Lawson, 461 U.S. 352, 357, 358, 75 L. Ed. 2d 903, 103 S. Ct. 1855 (1983)) (citation omitted) (alteration in original), cert. denied, 113 S. Ct. 2448 (1993).

This court has previously considered the meaning of the word "corruptly" in the context of the obstruction of justice statute, 18 U.S.C. Section 1503, which makes it illegal to "corruptly . . . endeavor[ ] to influence, intimidate, or impede" a juror or an officer of the court. In United States v. Ogle, 613 F.2d 233, 238 (10th Cir. 1979), cert. denied, 449 U.S. 825, 66 L. Ed. 2d 28, 101 S. Ct. 87 (1980), we stated that "corruptly" "really means unlawful." Thus, in the context of the obstruction of justice statute, "an endeavor to influence a juror in the performance of his or her duty or to influence, obstruct or impede the due administration of justice is per se unlawful and is tantamount to doing the act corruptly." Id. Black's Law Dictionary defines "corruptly" as follows: "When used in a statute, this term, generally imports a wrongful design to acquire some pecuniary or other advantage." Black's Law Dictionary 345 (6th ed. 1990). Additionally, the district court in this case instructed the jury that "[a] person acts 'corruptly' within the meaning of the law when he acts with the intention to secure an unlawful benefit for himself or for another person." Aplee. Supp. App. at 67.

The evidence at Mr. Bailey's trial was that he filed liens against IRS agents in response to a wage levy filed by the IRS. Mr. Bailey admitted that his purpose was to cause the IRS to cease its lawful tax collection duties. See Aplee. Supp. App. at 45. We believe an ordinary person would know that attempting to avoid payment of taxes is unlawful. Unlawful activities clearly fall within the meaning of "corrupt" acts under any plain construction of the term. The statute is therefore not unconstitutionally vague as applied in this case.

* * *

CONCLUSION

The judgment of the district court is accordingly Affirmed.

---

§ 13.03 Selected Criminal Code Provisions Applicable in Tax Cases

In addition to tax crimes under the Internal Revenue Code, taxpayers and tax professionals may commit offenses punishable under the criminal code. A few of those crimes are considered here.

[A] Conspiracy

> If two or more persons conspire either to commit any offense against the United States, or to defraud the United States, or any agency thereof in any manner or for any purpose, and one or more of such persons do any act to effect the object of the conspiracy, each shall be fined under this title or imprisoned not more than five years, or both. If, however, the offense, the commission of which is the object of the conspiracy, is a misdemeanor only, the punishment for such conspiracy shall not exceed the maximum punishment provided for such misdemeanor.

18 U.S.C. § 371. This section contains two separate offenses, conspiracy to commit any offense against the United States and conspiracy to defraud the United States. The latter type of offense is generally known as a *"Klein conspiracy." See United States v. Klein*, 247 F.2d 908 (2d Cir. 1957), *cert. denied,* 355 U.S. 924 (1958). The elements of each section 371 offense are (1) an agreement between two or more persons to commit a crime against the United States, (2) the defendant's knowing and voluntary participation in the conspiracy, and (3) an overt act by a participant in furtherance of the conspiracy. Note that the overt act can be almost anything that moves the conspiracy closer to its goal. In addition, in *United States v. Gambone*, 125 F. Supp. 2d 128, 137 (E.D. Pa. 2000), the court held that the government properly alleged a *Klein* conspiracy under the "defraud" clause of 18 U.S.C. § 371 although the allegations did not include the word "defraud."

How much knowledge of the goal of the conspiracy and its details is required in order to be a co-conspirator? This question is considered in *Krasovich*.

UNITED STATES v. KRASOVICH
United States Court of Appeals, Ninth Circuit
819 F.2d 253 (1987)

SCHROEDER, CIRCUIT JUDGE:

The dispositive issue in this appeal is the sufficiency of the evidence underlying the appellant's conviction of conspiracy to defraud the United States in violation of 18 U.S.C. § 371. Appellant Krasovich was convicted on one count (Count Eight) of a multi-count, multi-defendant indictment. That count charged Krasovich with conspiracy to defraud the Internal Revenue Service "in the ascertainment, computation, assessment, and collection of . . . the personal income taxes of John Thomas Drummond."

The underlying facts are not now disputed. John Drummond and his wife Andrea Drummond were in the cocaine business. Krasovich was their mechanic, servicing and repairing various vehicles for them. In December of 1984, the government arrested the Drummonds and instituted civil forfeiture proceedings against vehicles and earth moving equipment they allegedly owned. The vehicle that was the subject of Count Eight of the indictment was a used pickup truck purchased several months later, in April, 1985. Krasovich paid for the truck with money provided by Andrea Drummond. Krasovich registered the truck in his name and later confessed to a drug enforcement agent that he did this so that the truck would not be registered in Andrea's name.

The evidence at trial showed that Krasovich knew that the Drummonds were involved in the drug trade. It also showed that Krasovich had filed false statements with the government claiming ownership of other vehicles and equipment belonging to the Drummonds. There was evidence showing that an Internal Revenue Service agent had previously told Krasovich in connection with those false claims, but not in connection with the pickup truck, that it could be illegal to claim another's property as his own.

As explained more fully below, there was no evidence, direct or circumstantial, to indicate that when Krasovich purchased the truck in April of 1985, he intended or agreed with anyone else to impede the Internal Revenue Service in its collection of taxes, as charged in the indictment. The appellant therefore argues, and we hold, that the evidence was insufficient to permit a jury reasonably to find Krasovich guilty of the crime charged in the indictment. The conviction must be reversed.

The principal purpose of an indictment is to "provide the defendant with a description of the charges against him in sufficient detail to enable him to prepare his defense and plead double jeopardy at a later prosecution." United States v. Lane, 765 F.2d 1376, 1380 (9th Cir. 1985). The indictment must contain the elements of the offense charged and apprise the defendant of what he must be prepared to meet. See Russell v. United States, 369 U.S. 749, 763–64, 82 S. Ct. 1038, 1047, 8 L. Ed. 2d 240 (1962). "An indictment charging a conspiracy under 18 U.S.C. § 371 should allege an agreement, the unlawful object toward which the agreement is directed, and an overt act in furtherance of the conspiracy." Lane, 765 F.2d at 1380; see also United States v. Giese, 597 F.2d 1170, 1177 (9th Cir.), cert. denied, 444 U.S. 979, 100 S. Ct. 480, 62

L. Ed. 2d 405 (1979); United States v. Charnay, 537 F.2d 341, 350 (9th Cir.), *cert. denied,* 429 U.S. 1000, 97 S. Ct. 527, 50 L. Ed. 2d 610 (1976). The indictment in this case charged an agreement with Andrea Drummond, the object of which was to impede the collection of federal income taxes owed by Andrea's husband John.

The existence of a conspiratorial agreement or common purpose may be inferred from the evidence. * * * "We view the evidence and all inferences reasonably drawn from the evidence in the light most favorable to the government." United States v. Ramirez, 710 F.2d 535, 548 (9th Cir. 1983). Knowledge of the objective of the conspiracy is an essential element of any conspiracy conviction. * * *

It therefore follows that where, as here, the objective is alleged to be interference with "the ascertainment, computation, assessment, and collection of . . . the personal income taxes of John Thomas Drummond," the government must prove knowledge of that objective. Thus, in *Ingram* [*v. United States,* 360 U.S. 672 (1959)], the defendants were charged with a conspiracy to evade federal wagering tax. The Supreme Court reversed the convictions of two lower-level functionaries because of the absence of any proof that they were aware of the tax liability. Cautioning that the crime of conspiracy must not become a dragnet for every substantive offense, the Court found the proof insufficient, even though the defendants were involved in concealing a gambling operation. 360 U.S. at 679–80, 79 S. Ct. at 1320. This case is similar in all material respects. The government did not show that the defendant knew the alleged objective of the conspiracy.

Not only must the government prove knowledge of the illegal objective, it must also prove an agreement with a co-conspirator to pursue that objective as a common one. Thus, a conviction has been held improper where one alleged conspirator, in enlisting another, told him the operation's objective was tax evasion when in fact it was cashing fraudulent checks. *See* United States v. Rosenblatt, 554 F.2d 36 (2d Cir. 1977). There the court held that although both alleged co-conspirators agreed to commit offenses against the United States, they had not agreed on the same offense. *Id.* at 38–40. Thus, in the absence of any proof that the defendant knew of the tax objective of an alleged co-conspirator there can be no adequate proof of an agreement to pursue that objective.

An extensive discussion of the requirements for proof involving an indictment under § 371 for revenue fraud is found in recent decisions of the Eleventh and Fifth Circuits in *United States v. Browning,* 723 F.2d 1544 (11th Cir. 1984), and *United States v. Enstam,* 622 F.2d 857 (5th Cir. 1980), *cert. denied,* 450 U.S. 912, 101 S. Ct. 1351, 67 L. Ed. 2d 336 (1984). In *Enstam,* the court said that the government's burden is not met if it shows only that the object of a conspiracy was to hide the source of money rather than specifically to impede the collection or assessment of income taxes. *See Enstam,* 622 F.2d at 861. The court emphasized later in *Browning,* where the indictment charged impairing the IRS in its function of identifying revenue and collecting taxes, that the evidence must demonstrate that the conspirators knew of that objective. *Browning,* 723 F.2d at 1546–47. This ruling comports with the general principle that although a defendant may be found guilty of conspiracy even if he did not know all of the details of the scheme, the evidence must demonstrate that he knew the conspiracy's essential objectives. *See* Blumenthal v. United States, 332 U.S. 539, 554–57, 68 S. Ct. 248, 255–56, 92 L. Ed. 154 (1947).

In this case, there may well have been ample evidence that Andrea Drummond intended to use Krasovich to hide true ownership of property in order to evade income taxes. There is, however, no basis on which a reasonable jury could conclude that the defendant Krasovich had the same objective with respect to the transaction alleged in Count Eight. Nothing in the circumstances of the transaction suggests that Krasovich knew that the purpose of the concealment was to evade taxes.

Andrea Drummond may have wished to conceal ownership of the truck because she wanted to use it in illegal activities, or because she wanted to avoid drawing attention to herself or her finances, or because she feared seizure of the truck under the forfeiture statute if her ownership became known. "This is not a case where efforts at concealment would be reasonably explainable only in terms of motivation to evade taxation." *Ingram*, 360 U.S. at 679, 79 S. Ct. at 1320; *see also id.* at 678–80, 79 S. Ct at 1319–20. Indeed, the only link between the defendant and the tax laws on the evidence before the jury was a conversation between Krasovich and the IRS agent approximately a month before Krasovich claimed ownership of the pickup truck. In sum, the evidence is not sufficient to show that Krasovich conspired with Andrea Drummond with the objective of interfering with the Internal Revenue Service's collection of John Drummond's taxes, Andrea Drummond's taxes, or any other taxes.

The judgment is reversed.

Do you agree with the court that Krasovich should not have been convicted of conspiring with Andrea Drummond to defraud the IRS? What additional evidence might have helped the government establish its case?

[B] Aiding and Abetting

"Whoever commits an offense against the United States or aids, abets, counsels, commands, induces or procures its commission, is punishable as a principal." 18 U.S.C. § 2(a). This offense may be applied to taxpayers, or, as in the following case, to tax professionals. In the following case, concentrate on Lloyd's attempts to present evidence undermining the government's "aiding and abetting" case.

UNITED STATES v. LLOYD
United States Court of Appeals, District of Columbia Circuit
71 F.3d 408 (1995)

SENTELLE, CIRCUIT JUDGE:

Charles N. Lloyd, Jr., a tax preparer, was convicted on three counts of aiding and abetting in the preparation of false federal income tax returns and one count of first degree fraud in causing a false District of Columbia income tax return to be filed. On a previous appeal, we remanded the case for reconsideration of Lloyd's claim that he was unfairly prejudiced by the trial court's refusal to order the government to disclose the returns of the government's taxpayer witnesses for the years immediately preceding the years of the returns upon which the indictment was based. United States v. Lloyd, 301 U.S. App. D.C. 186, 992 F.2d 348 (D.C. Cir. 1993). On remand, the District Court concluded that the undisclosed tax returns probably would not have produced an acquittal on any of the four counts. It accordingly denied Lloyd's motion for a new trial, and Lloyd appeals that denial to this court. Because we conclude that the District Court applied the wrong legal standard to the new trial motion and erroneously determined that a new trial was not required, we reverse the convictions in Counts 7 and 11 and remand for new trial. We uphold the convictions in Counts 3 and 5.

I. FACTUAL BACKGROUND

In 1991, Charles N. Lloyd, Jr., was convicted under 26 U.S.C. § 7206(2) (1988) and 18 U.S.C. § 2 (1988) on three counts of aiding and abetting in the preparation of false federal income tax returns and under 22 D.C. Code Ann. §§ 3821(a), 3822(a)(1) and 105 (Repl. 1989) on one count of first degree fraud in helping to file a false District of Columbia income tax return. Since the early 1980s, Lloyd had owned and operated a tax preparation business in Southeast Washington, D.C., called Delta Tax Service. Many of Lloyd's clients were unable to pay him at the time he prepared their returns, so he arranged for their tax refund checks to be sent to his post office box. The client would pay Lloyd out of the refund proceeds. Following a lengthy investigation, Lloyd was indicted on numerous tax fraud counts stemming from tax returns he had prepared for some of his clients.

Lloyd sought pre-trial discovery of tax returns for his clients named in the indictment for the three years preceding the years of the returns which Lloyd had prepared. The government obtained some of the requested prior returns, but determined that 26 U.S.C. § 6103 (1988) prohibited disclosing the tax returns without a court order. Lloyd requested such an order, arguing that if the earlier tax returns revealed that the clients had filed fraudulent returns in the past, it would support his defense that the clients themselves, and not Lloyd, supplied the false information in the indictment returns. The court refused to issue the order, concluding that Lloyd had failed to meet his burden of showing that the returns would be useful in his defense. After trial, the jury convicted Lloyd on four counts: Count 3, aiding and abetting in the preparation of a false federal income tax return for Phyllis Burton for the tax year 1984; Count 5, the same charge involving Juanita Pressley's 1985 return;

Count 7, the same charge involving Diane Caldwell's 1985 return; and Count 11, first degree fraud in causing D.C. to be deprived of tax revenues. Count 11 involved the D.C. tax returns of Calvin Toler, Diane Caldwell, Michael Worthy, Thelma Davis and Donald Cooper.

On appeal, we examined Lloyd's claim that the District Court had erred by inflating the materiality standard in Fed. R. Crim. P. 16 because of the statutory prohibitions on disclosing the tax returns without a court order. We concluded that a materiality standard more demanding than Rule 16 might be appropriate in some cases involving the disclosure of tax returns for discovery purposes, but that Lloyd's case was not one of them. We then remanded the case for consideration of a new trial motion, instructing the District Court to appraise the returns' materiality under the normal standard of Rule 16. United States v. Lloyd, 301 U.S. App. D.C. 186, 992 F.2d 348, 352 (D.C. Cir. 1993). On remand, the parties agreed to stipulate to the materiality of the returns for discovery purposes and allow the court to proceed directly to the merits of the new trial motion. The District Court applied *Thompson v. United States*, 88 U.S. App. D.C. 235, 188 F.2d 652 (D.C. Cir. 1951), which set forth the test for whether newly discovered evidence requires a new trial. The court denied the new trial motion, concluding that the undisclosed returns (1) were irrelevant to the convictions in Counts 3 and 5, (2) were of only slight impeachment value as to the conviction in Count 7 and were unlikely to produce an acquittal, and (3) were either cumulative or useless for impeachment as to the conviction in Count 11.

II. LEGAL ANALYSIS

A. History and Standards

In denying Lloyd's motion for a new trial, the District Court applied the rule of *Thompson v. United States*, 88 U.S. App. D.C. 235, 188 F.2d 6752 (D.C. Dir. 1951):

> To obtain a new trial because of newly discovered evidence (1) the evidence must have been discovered since the trial; (2) the party seeking the new trial must show diligence in the attempt to procure the newly discovered evidence; (3) the evidence relied on must not be merely cumulative or impeaching; (4) it must be material to the issues involved; and (5) of such nature that in a new trial it would probably produce an acquittal.

188 F.2d at 653. The District Court based its denial squarely on the grounds that the undisclosed returns would probably not have produced an acquittal. However, we have already made it clear that the *Thompson* test does not apply where the evidence in question was not newly discovered, but was available to the prosecution at the time of trial, at least when the prosecution withheld that evidence in violation of due process standards under *Brady v. Maryland*, 373 U.S. 83, 86–88, 10 L. Ed. 2d 215, 83 S. Ct. 1194 (1963). United States v. Kelly, 252 U.S. App. D.C. 308, 790 F.2d 130, 133 (D.C. Cir. 1986). "The fact that such evidence was available to the prosecutor and not submitted to the defense places it in a different category than if it had simply been discovered

from a neutral source after trial." United States v. Agurs, 427 U.S. 97, 111, 49 L. Ed. 2d 342, 96 S. Ct. 2392 (1976).

The present facts present the distinct question of whether the *Thompson* standard applicable to newly discovered evidence or the *Brady* standard applicable to evidence which existed and was known to the prosecution at the time of trial applies in a case in which the prosecution withheld the disputed evidence but without wrongdoing on the part of the government and with full disclosure to the court. We hold that it is the *Brady* analysis which must govern. The purpose in *Brady* is not to punish a wrongdoing prosecutor, but rather to assure that the defendant was not convicted without due process of law. As the Supreme Court stated in *Brady,* "suppression by the prosecution of evidence favorable to an accused . . . violates due process where the evidence is material either to guilt or to punishment, irrespective of the good faith or bad faith of the prosecution." *Brady,* 373 U.S. at 87 (emphasis added). Thus, the District Court should have analyzed the effect of the erroneous withholding of the tax returns under the analysis applicable to *Brady* evidence rather than the *Thompson* standard applicable to newly discovered evidence.

That leads us to the questions: What standard applies to *Brady* evidence, and was that standard met in the present case? In *Kelly,* we applied the Supreme Court's test of whether the defendant's lack of access to undisclosed evidence justifies a new trial:

> The District Court must determine whether the undisclosed evidence was "material" to Kelly's conviction. . . . The Supreme Court has recently held that undisclosed information is material if "there is a reasonable probability that, had the evidence been disclosed to the defense, the result of the proceeding would have been different. A 'reasonable probability' is a probability sufficient to undermine confidence in the outcome." United States v. Bagley, 473 U.S. 667, 105 S. Ct. 3375, 3384, 87 L. Ed. 2d 481 (1985).

Kelly, 790 F.2d at 135–36. If the undisclosed evidence is "material" in the *Bagley/Kelly* sense, then the defendant is entitled to a new trial. The Supreme Court recently elaborated on the meaning of materiality under *Bagley,* stressing that the relevant inquiry focuses on the fairness of the trial the defendant actually received rather than on whether a different result would probably have occurred had the undisclosed evidence been revealed:

> [A] showing of materiality does not require demonstration by a preponderance that disclosure of the suppressed evidence would have resulted ultimately in the defendant's acquittal. . . *Bagley's* touchstone of materiality is a "reasonable probability" of a different result, and the adjective is important. The question is not whether the defendant would more likely than not have received a different verdict with the evidence, but whether in its absence he received a fair trial, understood as a trial resulting in a verdict worthy of confidence. A "reasonable probability" of a different result is accordingly shown when the Government's evidentiary suppression "undermines confidence in the outcome of the trial." *Bagley,* 473 U.S. at 678, 105 S. Ct. at 3381.

Kyles v. Whitley, 131 L. Ed. 2d 490, 115 S. Ct. 1555, 1566 (1995). * * *

The government argues in a footnote in its brief that the proper remedy for a District Court's use of the wrong legal standard in ruling on a new trial motion is "to remand the case back to the district court . . . where the appropriate fact-based determination can best be made" under the proper standard. Brief for Appellee at 21 n.18. While it is true that the determination of materiality for *Brady* purposes "is inevitably fact-bound and so is committed to the trial judge in the first instance," *Kelly*, 790 F.2d at 136, it is also true that the facts necessary to the determination of this motion are clear and undisputed. The undisclosed returns are part of the record, and no further facts need be determined for resolution of the new trial motion. The remaining question is one of law, not fact—did the nondisclosure of the returns violate Lloyd's *Brady* rights as a matter of law? Such a determination was impossible the first time this case was before us, for the returns were not part of the record at that time. *See* United States v. Lloyd, 301 U.S. App. D.C. 186, 992 F.2d 348, 351–52 (D.C. Cir. 1993) (remanding for reconsideration of the Rule 16 materiality of the undisclosed returns). But now that the returns are a part of the record, we can determine the proper resolution of Lloyd's new trial motion without overstepping the bounds of appropriate appellate jurisprudence.

When we last considered this case, we discussed different ways in which the undisclosed returns might be materially exculpatory. First, if a taxpayer who claimed that Lloyd was the source of the fabrication in the indictment return could be shown to have made similar claims in prior returns which Lloyd did not prepare, that evidence would help Lloyd demonstrate that the taxpayer, not Lloyd, was the source of the fabrication. Second, if a taxpayer took the stand and claimed that Lloyd was the source of the false information in the indictment returns, these prior returns not prepared by Lloyd would "have the makings of a promising tool for impeachment." *Lloyd*, 992 F.2d at 351. In this context, we note that the Supreme Court has specifically held that there is not "any difference between exculpatory and impeachment evidence for *Brady* purposes." *Kyles*, 115 S. Ct. at 1565. With that background, we will proceed to examine each conviction and determine whether the returns are materially exculpatory under *Bagley* and *Kyles*.

B. Application

1. Count 7

Count 7 alleged that Lloyd aided and abetted in the preparation and presentation of a false federal income tax return for the year 1985 for the taxpayer Diane Caldwell. The District Court did not order prosecution disclosure of any prior returns for Caldwell at trial, but the record now contains Caldwell's 1984 federal return, which is under seal. (The government placed the 1984 return into the sealed record in the proceedings on the new trial motion in the court below after stipulating to the materiality of the return for discovery purposes.) Having reviewed this sealed 1984 return, we conclude that it contains materially exculpatory evidence of just the sort contemplated in our previous opinion in this case. This undisclosed evidence raises a reasonable probability of a different result had it been disclosed at trial. We therefore hold that the District Court erred in denying Lloyd's new trial motion as to Count 7.

2. Counts 3 and 5

Count 3 mirrored Count 7 except it involved the tax return of Phyllis Burton for the tax year 1984. The record, however, contains no prior-year return for Burton. Apparently, the government was unable to produce any prior returns for Burton. *Lloyd*, 992 F.2d at 350. When this case was previously before this court, Lloyd claimed that the government's search was inadequate, but we held at that time that he had failed to raise that claim below and was therefore barred from raising it on appeal. *Id.* Count 5 also mirrored Count 7 except it involved the tax return of Juanita Pressley for the tax year 1985. The record also contains no prior returns for Pressley.

Lloyd challenges his convictions in both Counts 3 and 5 on the grounds that the nondisclosure of all the prior returns that were retrieved corrupts all four convictions, not just those based on later returns of the individuals for whom prior returns were retrieved. To support this argument, he points to the statement in *Kyles* that *Bagley* materiality is defined "in terms of suppressed evidence considered collectively, not item by item." *Kyles*, 115 S. Ct. at 1567. More specifically, "the effect of each nondisclosure must not only be considered alone, for the cumulative effect of the nondisclosures might require reversal even though, standing alone, each bit of omitted evidence may not be sufficiently 'material' to justify a new trial." United States ex rel. Marzeno v. Gengler, 574 F.2d 730, 736–37 (3d Cir. 1978). Having considered the nondisclosed returns as a whole, however, we are not convinced that they would have provided any assistance to Lloyd in impeaching either Burton or Pressley or in buttressing his version of events as to their returns. We accordingly reject this "corruption" argument.

As to Count 5 alone, Lloyd points to a comparison the prosecution made between Lloyd's testimony regarding the Caldwell indictment return and his testimony regarding the Juanita Pressley return, the basis of Count 5. According to Lloyd, this "linking" of the two returns shows that the nondisclosed Caldwell return could have helped him to boost his credibility on Count 7, thereby having a parallel effect as to Count 5. But examination of the trial transcript shows the weakness of this argument. *See* Trial Transcript at 81–82. The prosecutor was attempting to show that Lloyd had falsified "original worksheets" for those returns which were being investigated by the IRS, including the Caldwell and Pressley returns. All that Lloyd could have shown with the undisclosed Caldwell return now in the sealed record was that he was not the source of the false information in the Caldwell indictment return itself. The prior Caldwell return offers no evidence to counter the prosecutor's suggestion that Lloyd falsified "original worksheets" for all the returns under investigation. Even if Lloyd had not falsified the Caldwell indictment return, he had plenty of incentive to falsify the "original worksheets" for the returns being investigated by the IRS—he had failed to preserve adequate records of the sources of the information in those returns. We therefore reject Lloyd's invitation to grant a new trial as to Count 5.

* * *

4. Other uses of the earlier returns

Lloyd suggests other theories under which the earlier returns now part of the sealed record could have been used at trial to impeach the government's witnesses as to all four counts on which convictions were obtained. We have already held that the undisclosed returns contain materially exculpatory evidence as to Counts 7 and 11, so it is unnecessary to consider Lloyd's other theories for those counts. Lloyd is free, of course, to make use of these additional impeachment strategies against government witnesses in a new trial on these two counts. None of the undisclosed returns in the sealed record are related to Counts 3 or 5, however, so Lloyd's theorized impeachment strategies could have had no effect on them. Lloyd's theories give us no reason to order a new trial as to these two counts.

III. CONCLUSION

For the foregoing reasons, we hold that the relevant undisclosed returns constitute materially exculpatory evidence under *Bagley, Kyles* and *Kelly* as to the convictions in Counts 7 and 11. The District Court erred in denying Lloyd's new trial motion as to these two counts. We affirm the District Court's denial of the new trial motion as to the convictions in Counts 3 and 5, but we reverse the District Court's denial of the motion as to Counts 7 and 11 and remand with instructions to grant the motion as to the latter two counts.

In *Sandefer v. United States*, 447 U.S. 10 (1980), the Supreme Court held that a conviction for aiding and abetting could stand even if the principal was not convicted of the underlying offense. Subsequently, lower courts have held that the principal need not even be identified, so long as the prosecution establishes that the underlying offense was committed by someone. *See, e.g., United States v. Campa*, 679 F.2d 1006 (1st Cir. 1982); *United States v. Harper*, 579 F.2d 1235, 1239 (10th Cir.), *cert. denied*, 439 U.S. 968 (1978).

[C] False Statements

Under 18 U.S.C. § 1001, with various statutory exceptions,

> whoever, in any matter within the jurisdiction of the executive, legislative, or judicial branch of the Government of the United States, knowingly and willfully— (1) falsifies, conceals, or covers up by any trick, scheme, or device a material fact; (2) makes any materially false, fictitious, or fraudulent statement or representation; or (3) makes or uses any false writing or document knowing the same to contain any materially false, fictitious, or fraudulent statement or entry; shall be fined under this title or imprisoned not more than 5 years, or both. . . .

The elements of this offense are (1) jurisdiction, (2) a false, fictitious or fraudulent statement, (3) knowledge, (4) willfullness, and (5) materiality. In *United States v. Gaudin*, 515 U.S. 506 (1995), which involved a prosecution under 18 U.S.C. § 1001 for alleged false statements on documents used to obtain loans from the Federal Housing Administration, the United States Supreme Court held that materiality was a jury question. With respect to the materiality element, also consider *Meuli*, reproduced below. Consider Meuli's "multiplicity" argument as well. Why does the *Meuli* court find that the multiple counts under 18 U.S.C. § 1001 were not duplicative?

UNITED STATES v. MEULI
United States Court of Appeals, Tenth Circuit
8 F.3d 1481 (1993)[3]

BALDOCK, CIRCUIT JUDGE.

Defendant Gene E. Meuli was convicted of eight counts of making a false statement, 18 U.S.C. § 1001, and one count of filing a false income tax return, 26 U.S.C. § 7206(1). Defendant appeals his convictions on all counts, and the district court's imposition of a $1,000.00 fine, U.S.S.G. 5E1.2. We have jurisdiction under 28 U.S.C. § 1291 and 18 U.S.C. § 3742.

Defendant obtained a series of loans from the Federal Land Bank, Kansas, and the Farmers Home Administration, a federal agency. These loans were secured by mortgages on Defendant's farm property in Kansas. Upon Defendant's defaults on these loans, the Federal Land Bank and the Farmers Home Administration obtained judgments foreclosing the mortgages. The two judgments obtained by the Federal Land Bank were in the amounts of $160,355.69 and $39,275.17. The subsequent sale of Defendant's property by the Farmers Home Administration was in the amount of $83,200.00.

In December 1989, Defendant mailed notices of bills due and payable and requests for taxpayer identification numbers to several bank officers of the Federal Land Bank at their home addresses. The worksheets attached to the statements reflected that Defendant based the bills on the earlier judgments obtained by the bank against Defendant. In January 1990, Defendant sent these same officers Internal Revenue Service Forms 1099s. In these forms, Defendant alleged that he had paid $287,123.32 in non-employee compensation to each bank officer. Like the amounts on the earlier bills, the amounts listed on the 1099 forms reflected judgments obtained by the bank against Defendant. On the face of the 1099 forms was the following notice:

> This is important tax information and is being furnished to the Internal Revenue Service. If you are required to file a return, a negligence penalty or other sanction may be imposed on you if this income is taxable and the IRS determines that it has not been reported.

Upon receiving the 1099 forms from Defendant, the bank office contacted the bank attorney, who in turn notified the United States Postal Inspection

---
[3] *Cert. denied*, 511 U.S. 1020 (1994).

Service and the Internal Revenue Service ("IRS"). In February 1990, Defendant sent 1096 forms to the IRS claiming that he had paid non-employee compensation to the bank officers. To the 1096 forms, Defendant attached copies of the 1099 forms that he had previously mailed to the individual officers.

On his 1989 tax return, Defendant claimed entitlement to a $1,000,000.00 refund. The return, signed by Defendant, inaccurately indicated that he had received income of $1,600,000.00 in 1989 through default judgments.

Upon receiving the complaint concerning the 1099 forms from the Federal Land Bank attorney, the IRS initiated an investigation of Defendant in March 1990. On July 6, 1990, pursuant to a separate investigation, IRS Inspector Dwight Boesee met with Dwayne Mellies, who was involved in a similar scheme, and informed Mr. Mellies that he was serving grand jury subpoenas on various individuals involved in the scheme. The evidence at trial indicated that Defendant and Mellies were acquainted with each other, had been seen together, and Defendant's signature appeared on sworn affidavits obtained by the IRS in the investigation of Mr. Mellies. On July 30, 1990, Inspector Boesee served Defendant with a subpoena for handwriting and fingerprint exemplars. Fifteen days prior to that, on July 16, 1990, Defendant completed and sent a corrected 1989 tax return to the IRS. On this amended return, Defendant stated that errors on his previous return were due to misinformed error. Defendant attached corrected 1096 and 1099 forms to this amended return.

Defendant's trial began on December 7, 1992. The case was submitted to the jury late in the afternoon on December 8. * * * The jury returned the next day, and after obtaining responses to three notes it sent to the court, the jury returned a verdict of guilty on all counts.

The district court sentenced Defendant to concurrent six-month terms of imprisonment on each count, to be followed by two years supervised release. The court also imposed a fine of $1,000.00. U.S.S.G. 5E1.2.

Defendant raises six issues on appeal. Defendant claims (1) the evidence was insufficient to sustain his convictions on counts five through eight, (2) the indictment was multiplicious in charging the same offenses in counts one through four as in counts five through eight, (3) Defendant was subjected to double jeopardy by multiple convictions on counts one through four and five through eight, (4) Defendant's convictions on all counts should be reversed because Defendant filed amended forms with the IRS * * *.

Defendant's first claim is that the evidence was insufficient to sustain his convictions on counts five through eight. The 1099 forms mailed to the bank officers formed the bases of these counts. Defendant argues that any false statements contained in the 1099 forms were not material in that they were incapable of influencing IRS action. Materiality is a question of law we review *de novo*. United States v. Brittain, 931 F.2d 1413, 1415 (10th Cir. 1991).

To prove a violation of 18 U.S.C. § 1001, the government must show that the defendant knowingly and willfully made a false statement regarding a material fact that is within the jurisdiction of a federal agency or department. *Id.* The false statement need not be made directly to the agency or department,

United States v. Wolf, 645 F.2d 23, 25 (10th Cir. 1981), and the government need not prove that the Defendant had actual knowledge of the federal agency jurisdiction. United States v. Yermian, 468 U.S. 63, 69, 104 S. Ct. 2936, 2939, 82 L. Ed. 2d 53 (1984). Section 1001 "does not limit its prohibition of falsification to matters which another statute or regulation requires be provided." United States v. Olson, 751 F.2d 1126, 1127 (9th Cir. 1985). Finally, "[a] false statement is material if it has a natural tendency to influence, or is capable of influencing, the decision of the tribunal in making a determination required to be made." *Brittain*, 931 F.2d at 1415 (citation omitted).

Defendant first argues that the false statements he made on the 1099 forms were not capable of influencing the IRS because the bank officers were under no obligation to forward that information because it was false. We reject this argument because § 1001 prohibits false statements whether or not another law requires the information be provided. We further note that to simply accept Defendant's argument would turn § 1001 on its head—*i.e.*, Defendant would be ultimately relieved from liability for making a false statement because of the falsity itself.

Defendant also argues that the false 1099 forms mailed to the bank officers were not capable of influencing IRS action on their own without the subsequent filing of the 1096 forms and 1099 forms with the IRS. We disagree.

Defendant made the false statements on official IRS 1099 forms. The forms themselves contained a warning to the recipient that the information would be forwarded separately to the IRS, and if the recipient did not reflect this information in his income tax return, he did so at his peril. Given the importance of this information to the recipient, it is not only reasonably foreseeable, but inevitable, that the recipient would contact the IRS concerning these false statements. The bank officers in this case did, in fact, do so. It further follows that once put on notice, the IRS would initiate an investigation. Because the circumstances surrounding the false information that Defendant furnished the bank officers made it likely that they would contact the IRS, and because the false statements influenced the possibility that an IRS investigation would ensue, the false 1099 forms had the natural tendency or were capable of influencing the IRS, and were therefore material. *See, e.g.*, United States v. Hansen, 249 U.S. App. D.C. 22, 772 F.2d 940, 949 (D.C. Cir. 1985) (false statement was material under 1001 when it increased the possibility that investigation might commence), *cert. denied*, 475 U.S. 1045, 89 L. Ed. 2d 571, 106 S. Ct. 1262 (1986); United States v. Dick, 744 F.2d 546, 554 (7th Cir. 1984) (false statements made to sureties were material where SBA would rely on statements sureties would in turn make to the SBA).

Defendant next contends that the indictment was multiplicious in charging the same offenses in counts one through four as in counts five through eight. The 1096 forms sent to the IRS formed the bases of counts one through four, and the 1099 forms mailed to the bank officers formed the bases of counts five through eight. Defendant argues that the mailings to the bank officers were not separate crimes from the mailings to the IRS; rather, they were part of the same continued conduct.

"Multiplicity refers to multiple counts of an indictment which cover the same criminal behavior." United States v. Dashney, 937 F.2d 532, 540 n.7 (10th

Cir.), *cert. denied*, 116 L. Ed. 2d 351, 112 S. Ct. 402 (1991). The same act or transaction may constitute separate offenses if each offense requires some fact not required to establish the other. United States v. Larsen, 596 F.2d 410, 411 (10th Cir. 1979). In reviewing multiplicity claims we look to the language of the statute to determine whether Congress intended multiple convictions and sentences under the statute. United States v. Morehead, 959 F.2d 1489, 1506, *aff'd on reh'g en banc*, 971 F.2d 1461 (10th Cir. 1992).

In *United States v. Bettenhausen*, 499 F.2d 1223, 1234 (10th Cir. 1974), we examined the language of § 1001. In that case, the defendants were convicted of four counts of making a false statement where they submitted four different documents in support of a single tax return. *Id.* at 1234. The defendants argued that there was only one offense under the statute because they had submitted all the documents at one time. *Id.* Looking to the language of § 1001, we rejected that argument, stating:

> in the clause [of § 1001] we are concerned with the statute turned to the singular terms—"any false writing or document. . . ." We feel the statute aims at the making or using of each "false writing or document" and intends the wrong connected with each to be a separate offense.

Id. (quoting 18 U.S.C. § 1001).

Under our reasoning in *Bettenhausen*, we hold that Defendant was not subjected to a multiplicious indictment; rather, the false statements on the 1099 forms were separate and distinct criminal acts apart from the false statements Defendant made on the 1096 forms. Defendant made the false statements on entirely different forms. He sent the forms to different parties — the 1099 forms to the bank officers and the 1096 forms to the IRS. Defendant sent the 1099 forms to the bank officers on January 23, 1990, and he did not send the 1096 forms to the IRS until February 27, 1990. The proof required to support counts one through four was entirely different from the evidence that supported counts five through eight. In other words, "each offense required some fact not required to establish the other." *See Larson*, 596 F.2d at 411. As in *Bettenhausen*, each of Defendant's false statements was a separate offense under § 1001.[n.3]

Defendant contends that his convictions on all counts should be reversed because, he alleges, he filed amended forms with the IRS prior to being put on notice that he was the subject of an IRS investigation. Defendant sent the amended 1989 tax return along with corrected 1096 and 1099 forms to the IRS on July 16, 1990. On July 30, 1990, Defendant was first served with a subpoena pursuant to the ongoing investigation against him. Defendant failed to raise this argument below; therefore we only review for plain error. United States v. Jefferson, 925 F.2d 1242, 1254 (10th Cir.), *cert. denied*, 116 L. Ed. 2d 194, 112 S. Ct. 238, 112 S. Ct. 239 (1991).

[n.3] Because we have concluded that counts one through four were separate offenses requiring different proof from counts five through eight, we also reject Defendant's double jeopardy claim. *See* Miranda v. Cooper, 967 F.2d 392, 403 (10th Cir.) (double jeopardy clause not offended so long as separate counts based upon different facts), *cert. denied*, 121 L. Ed. 2d 262, 113 S. Ct. 347 (1992).

Defendant relies on an Eighth Circuit case, *United States v. Cowden*, 677 F.2d 417, 420 (8th Cir. 1982). In *Cowden*, the court overturned a conviction under § 1001 because the defendant had corrected a prior false statement—wherein he falsely denied having more than $5,000.00 in currency—before the Customs officials discovered the currency. *Id.* at 420. The court explained that the conviction could not stand because Customs regulations permitted a traveller to amend his declaration up to the time an undeclared article is found, and the defendant had amended his prior false statement and declared the currency before Customs officials discovered it. The government argues that the instant case is more closely related to *United States v. Fern*, 696 F.2d 1269 (11th Cir. 1983). In *Fern,* the court found *Cowden* inapposite and upheld the defendant's conviction because he "changed his story only after the [IRS] became suspicious." *Id.* at 1275.

We conclude that it was not plain error for the jury to have convicted Defendant on all counts despite the subsequent amendment of his 1989 tax return, 1096 forms, and 1099 forms he sent to the IRS. At the outset, we uphold Defendant's convictions on counts five through eight because Defendant never sent amended 1099 forms to the bank officers. As to counts one through four, we hold that there was sufficient evidence from which the jury could have concluded that Defendant knew, prior to July 16, 1990, that the IRS had become suspicious of his activities. In fact, the IRS had not only become suspicious of Defendant, it had begun a formal investigation of Defendant in March 1990. The government presented evidence that Mr. Mellies was involved in a similar scheme and was the subject of an IRS investigation, Defendant knew Mr. Mellies, and Defendant's signature was on certain documents discovered in the IRS's investigation of Mr. Mellies. Furthermore, Inspector Boesee testified that he informed Mr. Mellies on July 6, 1990 that the IRS would be serving grand jury subpoenas to various individuals involved in this scheme. From this evidence, together with Inspector Boesee's testimony that it was common practice for those under investigation to file amended returns, the jury could conclude that Defendant knew, prior to July 16, 1990, of the IRS's investigation of Mr. Mellies, and also was put on notice, through Mr. Mellies, that the IRS was suspicious of him. In such case, Defendant's amended return, 1096 forms, and 1099 forms came too late. *See Fern*, 696 F.2d at 1275 (§ 1001 conviction upheld where defendant does not correct statement until he knew IRS was suspicious).

* * *

Affirmed.

[D]   False Claims

Whoever makes or presents to any person or officer in the civil, military, or naval service of the United States, or to any department or agency thereof, any claim upon or against the United States, or any department or agency thereof, knowing such claim to be false, fictitious, or fraudulent, shall be imprisoned not more than five years and shall be subject to a fine in the amount provided in this title.

18 U.S.C. § 287. Note that the statute requires the intent element of "knowingly" presenting the false claim. Tax prosecutions under this section generally involve false refund claims. For example, in *United States v. Dunigan*,[4] 163 F.3d 979 (6th Cir. 1999):

> Dunigan solicited individuals living in public housing projects in Chattanooga to file false 1991 and 1992 income tax returns. The individuals used their true names and social security numbers; however, Dunigan, or an individual working for Dunigan, supplied false W-2 forms that set forth fabricated employment and salary information for the individuals filing the returns. Additionally, Dunigan encouraged the individuals to list nonexistent dependent children on the returns so that they could file as a head-of-the-household and obtain earned income tax credit.

> Dunigan instructed the individuals to file the false returns electronically in order to request refund anticipation loans, or "rapid refunds." When a recruited individual received a check for the fraudulent refund, Dunigan, or someone at his direction, would escort the individual to a check-cashing business. To facilitate the cashing of the checks, Dunigan would assist the individuals who filed the false returns to obtain photographic identity cards. Typically, the individual who filed the return received approximately $500. If another person recruited the individual to file the false tax return, that person received $100 to $200. Dunigan kept the balance of the refund.

> As a result of Dunigan's scheme, fifty-four false claims for refunds were filed for the 1991 tax year and sixty-four false claims for refunds were filed for the 1992 tax year. Dunigan netted $319,171, of which the IRS was able to recover $7,566.

Id. at 980. Dunigan was prosecuted not only under 18 U.S.C. §§ 2 and 287 for making and presenting to the IRS false claims for payment, but also under 18 U.S.C. § 286 for conspiring to defraud the United States.[5] *Id.*

§ 13.04   Offenses Committed by Tax Professionals

In addition to the tax crimes discussed above, many of which can be applied to tax professionals, and in addition to the applicable civil penalties discussed

---

[4] *See also* United States v. Mockus, 1996 U.S. App. LEXIS 16449 (7th Cir. 1996) (unpublished); United States v. Levy, 1996 U.S. App. LEXIS 14385 (6th Cir. 1996) (unpublished); Mathis v. United States, 376 F.2d 595 (5th Cir. 1967), *rev'd*, 391 U.S. 1 (1968); United States v. Madoch, 935 F. Supp. 965 (N.D. Ill. 1996), *appeal dismissed in part*, 149 F.3d 596 (7th Cir. 1998).

[5] Dunigan entered into a plea agreement under which he plead guilty only to the conspiracy count. *Dunigan,* 163 F.3d at 979. "The district court sentenced Dunigan to 31 months' imprisonment, three years of supervised release, an assessment of $50 and full restitution in the amount of $311,605." *Id.* at 981. The litigation involved in the case cited above related to the amount of the restitution Dunigan was required to pay.

in Chapter 10, the Code contains a criminal provision targeting tax professionals, although it can apply to others as well. Code section 7206(2) provides:

> Any person who— . . . Willfully aids or assists in, or procures, counsels, or advises the preparation or presentation under, or in connection with any matter arising under, the internal revenue laws, of a return, affidavit, claim, or other document, which is fraudulent or is false as to any material matter, whether or not such falsity or fraud is with the knowledge or consent of the person authorized or required to present such return, affidavit, claim, or document . . . shall be guilty of a felony and, upon conviction thereof, shall be fined not more than $ 100,000 ($ 500,000 in the case of a corporation), or imprisoned not more than 3 years, or both, together with the costs of prosecution.

What are the elements of this offense? Consider *Dixon*, reproduced immediately below. Observe also that *Dixon* discusses the possibility of enhancing the defendant's sentence. The sentencing guidelines are discussed in more detail in section 13.06, below.

UNITED STATES v. DIXON
United States Court of Appeals, Ninth Circuit
79 A.F.T.R. 2d 2854

CONTI, DISTRICT JUDGE:

MEMORANDUM *

Gail Dixon (Dixon) appeals her conviction and sentence on 14 counts of aiding and abetting the preparation of false or fraudulent tax returns, 26 U.S.C. § 7206(2). We affirm.

FACTS AND PROCEEDINGS

Dixon operated a tax preparation service in East Palo Alto, California. For the years involved here, Dixon's employees generally met with clients to obtain the information necessary to complete the tax returns. Either the employees or Dixon input the information into a computer that then generated the tax return. According to office policy, Dixon was to review, stamp, and sign all tax returns.

In 1992, the Internal Revenue Service conducted an undercover investigation involving Dixon and then raided her business. After a jury trial, Dixon was convicted on 14 counts involving overstated itemized deductions for four taxpayers, but acquitted of 5 counts involving false child care credits, earned income credits, and overstated itemized deductions for two other taxpayers.

The district court enhanced Dixon's sentence by two points for being the leader of a criminal activity. Dixon was sentenced to 27 months imprisonment,

---

* This disposition is not appropriate for publication and may not be cited to or by the courts of this circuit except as provided by Ninth Cir. R. 36-3.

fined $5,000, and ordered to pay a special assessment of $700. Dixon appeals the sufficiency of the evidence supporting her conviction and her sentence.

ANALYSIS

I. Sufficiency of the Evidence to Convict

The elements of the offense of aiding and abetting the preparation of a false tax return under 26 U.S.C. § 7206(2) are: "(1) the defendant aided, assisted, or otherwise caused the preparation and presentation of a return; (2) that the return was fraudulent or false as to a material matter; and (3) the act of the defendant was willful." United States v. Salerno, 902 F.2d 1429, 1432 (9th Cir. 1990). Willfullness can be established by showing that defendant either: (1) acted with bad purpose or evil motive, or (2) voluntarily and intentionally violated a known legal duty. United States v. Kellogg, 955 F.2d 1244, 1248 (9th Cir. 1992). Proof that defendant had actual knowledge of the legal duty is sufficient to prove willfulness if the government negates any claim of ignorance or misunderstanding of the law. *Id.* Willfulness may be proved by circumstantial evidence. United States v. Conforte, 624 F.2d 869, 875 (9th Cir. 1980). Construing the evidence in the light most favorable verdict, we hold that a rational juror could have found beyond a reasonable doubt that Dixon was guilty. *See* Jackson v. Virginia, 443 U.S. 307, 319, 61 L. Ed. 2d 560, 99 S. Ct. 2781 (1979).

As to the first element, the signature on nine of the returns was identified as Dixon's. On the other five returns, Dixon's signature was added either by stamp or by another employee. According to office policy, however, Dixon reviewed and finalized those five returns and authorized an employee to sign or stamp her name. The second element was proved by the testimony of Dixon's clients that the actual amounts of several itemized deductions were lower than the amounts shown on the returns underlying the counts of conviction and that they did not give the incorrect amounts to Dixon.

Circumstantial evidence proved the third element, Dixon's willfulness. One of Dixon's former employees and a witness for the defense testified that Dixon was "fairly knowledgeable" on tax matters. Other former employees testified about Dixon's policy of falsifying exemptions or earned income or child care credits on short-form returns (returns with no itemized deductions) to generate a refund. *See* United States v. Conlin, 551 F.2d 534, 536 (2nd Cir. 1977) (pattern of overstated deductions and unusually high tax return preparation fees based on excessive tax refunds that followed sufficiently demonstrated willfulness). The receptionist at Dixon's office told the IRS agent who conducted the undercover operation that "the lady" could provide him with a letter if there were any problems with the IRS concerning the inflated deductions shown on the return Dixon prepared for him. *See* United States v. Miller, 529 F.2d 1125, 1127 (9th Cir. 1976) (pattern of overstated deductions coupled with false documentation to verify false deductions proves intent); Amos v. United States, 496 F.2d 1269, 1273–74 (8th Cir. 1974) (same).

II. Sentencing Enhancement

The district court enhanced Dixon's sentence by two points for being "an organizer, leader, manager, or supervisor" in the criminal activity. U.S.S.G. § 3B1.1(c). This enhancement applies only where the defendant was the organizer, leader, manager, or supervisor of one or more other persons who are criminally responsible. United States v. Anderson, 942 F.2d 606, 617 (9th Cir. 1991) (en banc); U.S.S.G. § 3B1.1 appl. n.1 & 2. The other criminally responsible person need not be convicted. United States v. Helmy, 951 F.2d 988, 997 n.7 (9th Cir. 1991); U.S.S.G. § 3B1.1, appl. n.1. Relevant conduct to be considered in determining the scope of the criminal activity and whether the defendant was a leader includes not only the actions underlying the counts of conviction but also actions involving the same course of conduct or common scheme or plan as the counts of conviction. United States v. Lillard, 929 F.2d 500, 502–03 (9th Cir. 1991); U.S.S.G. § 1B1.3; U.S.S.G. Ch. 3, Pt.B, intro. comment.

Dixon argues the enhancement is improper because the inquiry for sentencing of an aiding and abetting conviction should focus on the taxpayers, whom Dixon argues she did not direct and supervise and who could not have been criminally liable for aiding and abetting themselves. We see no reason to limit the application of § 3B1.1 in this way. Dixon argues alternatively that even if the focus is on employees, there is no evidence that she directed her employees to falsify entries on the false tax returns for which she was convicted. We disagree. Dixon instructed several employees to falsify dependent exemptions on short-form returns and told one employee that she could falsify charitable deductions on the client information sheets. Although none of the employees were indicted, they were aware at some point that their conduct, undertaken at Dixon's direction, was illegal. The sentencing enhancement was proper.

The convictions and sentence are affirmed.

---

§ 13.05   Statutes of Limitations on Tax Crimes

Under Code section 6531, the general statute of limitations on tax crimes is three years, subject to eight exceptions that nearly swallow the rule. The statutory period is six years for cases falling within the exceptions. The limitations period starts running on the date the offense was committed, generally the date the return was filed. The statute is tolled for any period during which the taxpayer is outside the United States or a fugitive from justice. In addition, a taxpayer's action to quash a summons issued to a third party tolls both the statute of limitations on tax crimes and the statute of limitations on assessment during the pendency of the action. *See* I.R.C. § 7609(e). The summons power is discussed in Chapter 14.

Study section 6531 carefully. Should a three-year or six-year period apply to a violation of Code section 7202 for failure to pay over withholding taxes? Consider the following case:

UNITED STATES v. GOLLAPUDI
United States Court of Appeals, Third Circuit
130 F.3d 66 (1997)[6]

ROTH, CIRCUIT JUDGE.

I. INTRODUCTION

* * * Gollapudi was charged with failing to account for and pay over to the Internal Revenue Service federal income taxes, deducted and collected from the total taxable wages of his employees, between 1989 and 1991, in violation of 26 U.S.C. § 7202. * * * Gollapudi now appeals on the grounds (1) that his prosecution for violating 26 U.S.C. § 7202 is barred by the three-year statute of limitations of § 6531, and (2) that because the responses on the 1040 he filed were truthful he cannot be found guilty of filing a false statement under § 7206(1). For reasons set forth below, we affirm the decision of the District Court.

II. FACTS

From the company's inception in 1984, the appellant, Rao Gollapudi, has been the president and sole shareholder of Softstar Computer Consultants, Incorporated ("Softstar"), a Michigan corporation involved in the business of analyzing and improving computer systems for Fortune 500 companies. Following the departure of his partner from the company in 1986, Gollapudi became solely responsible for preparing and filing the company's tax returns and paying the wages of its employees. Shortly after assuming this responsibility, Gollapudi failed to make any payment of employment taxes and stopped filing Employer's Quarterly Tax Returns ("941's") with the IRS.

* * *

After an IRS tax examiner discovered that Softstar had failed to file the required 941's and remit any tax refunds to the federal government, Gollapudi admitted that although he collected the appropriate taxes from his employees, he did not turn over the withholdings to the IRS. Instead, he kept the money in the company. Gollapudi further admitted that, although he was aware of his obligations, he did not file the required 941's, W-2's, or corporate tax forms with the IRS. Subsequently, Gollapudi contacted an accountant, David Karpel, who on behalf of Gollapudi filed the delinquent 941's and corporate tax returns and paid $591,000 in back taxes.

* * *

On April 19, 1996, Gollapudi was indicted on nine counts of failing to account for and pay over to the IRS federal income taxes and FICA taxes, deducted and collected from the total taxable wages of his employees, for the final quarter of 1989 and for all four quarters of the years 1990 and 1991,

---

[6] *Cert. denied,* 523 U.S. 1006 (1998).

in violation of 26 U.S.C. § 7202. In addition, Gollapudi was charged with three counts of filing false personal income tax returns for the calendar years 1989 through 1991 in violation of 26 U.S.C. § 7206(1). Prior to trial, Gollapudi moved to dismiss the first nine counts of the indictment as barred by the three year statute of limitations. This motion was denied. Gollapudi was found guilty on all counts and now appeals.

* * *

IV. DISCUSSION

A. Statute of Limitations

The first issue before the court is whether a violation of 26 U.S.C. § 7202, which prohibits the willful failure "to collect or truthfully account for and pay over" any tax, is subject to a three-or six-year statute of limitations. For the following reasons, we hold that the violation is subject to a six-year statute of limitations and thus will affirm the decision of the District Court on this issue.

The statute of limitations governing 26 U.S.C. § 7202, as well as other criminal tax violations, is set forth in 26 U.S.C. § 6531. This section generally provides that criminal tax proceedings must be initiated within three years of the offense, unless the offense falls into one of eight exceptions providing for a six-year period of limitations. Specifically, the relevant section, § 6531(4), provides that:

* * *

No person shall be prosecuted, tried, or punished for any of the various offenses arising under the internal revenue laws unless the indictment is found or the information instituted within 3 years next after the commission of the offense, except that the period of limitations shall be 6 years —

(4) for the offense of willfully failing to pay any tax, or make any return (other than a return required under authority of part III of subchapter A of chapter 61) at the time or times required by law or regulations;

26 U.S.C. § 6531(4). The question here is whether a failure to "pay over" any tax under § 7202 constitutes a failure to "pay any tax, or make any return," under § 6531(4), and thus is subject to a six rather than three-year statute of limitations.

While the Third Circuit has not yet addressed the issue of whether § 6531(4) applies to criminal offenses under § 7202, the District Court followed the decisions of the Second and Tenth Circuits in holding that prosecutions for violations of § 7202 must be commenced within six years under § 6531(4). Conversely, two district courts that have addressed the issue have held that section 6531(4) does not apply to § 7202 offenses and that the applicable statute of limitations is three years. Gollapudi contends that the two district court cases are more persuasive in their analysis than the opinions of the circuit courts and the District Court in this case.

Relying on *United States v. Block*, 497 F. Supp. 629 (N.D. Ga. 1980), and *United States v. Brennick*, 908 F. Supp. 1004 (D. Mass. 1995), Gollapudi maintains that the plain language of the statute dictates that failure "to pay any tax, or make any return" under § 6531(4) does not encompass "the offense of failing to collect, account for or pay *over* any tax" under § 7202 (emphasis added). Gollapudi contends that because Congress explicitly distinguished between the failure to "pay" a tax and the failure to "pay over" a tax collected from another in other sections of the Internal Revenue Code and did not include such "pay over" language in § 6531, it did not intend to include the failure to "pay over" any tax in § 6531(4).

In support of his first argument, Gollapudi notes that in designing the criminal tax offense set forth in 26 U.S.C. § 7202 *et seq.*, Congress explicitly distinguished between the failure to pay a tax and the failure to pay over a tax collected from another, as is evident in the comparison between §§ 7202 and 7203. Furthermore, Gollapudi maintains that the phrase "pay over" or "paid over" was used by Congress sixteen times in the Internal Revenue Code and, thus, constitutes a statutory term of art, referring to (1) third-party taxes as in §§ 3505(b), 6672(a) and 7501; (2) other amounts collected from third parties as in §§ 3304(a)(3) and 7652(b)(3); and (3) non-tax amounts as in §§ 143(g)(3)(D) and 6096(a). Gollapudi argues that because the phrase is a term of art, "pay over" has a specific meaning which is not included in nor interchangeable with "pay".

Next, Gollapudi argues that because § 6531(4) applies to "the offense" (singular) of willfully failing to pay any tax or make any return, as opposed to any other offense, and because § 7203 is "the offense" which criminalized such acts, Congress intended that § 6532(4) apply only to the offense identified in § 7203, and not to other criminal tax violations. *See Block*, 497 F. Supp. at 632 (finding persuasive fact that § 6531(4) is directed at "the offense" of wilfully failing to pay tax, as opposed to class of offenses); *Brennick*, 908 F. Supp. at 1019 (finding that Congress had expressed its will "in reasonably plain terms" that § 6531(4) applies only to single offense described in § 7203).

In interpreting a statute, the starting point is the language of the statute itself. National Union Fire Ins. Co. of Pittsburgh v. City Sav., F.S.B., 28 F.3d 376, 384 (3d Cir. 1994); United States v. Cicco, 10 F.3d 980, 984 (3d Cir. 1993). "In most situations, the plain language rule is the preferred method of statutory interpretation." United States v. Zheng, 768 F.2d 518, 523 (3d Cir. 1985), *cert. denied*, 474 U.S. 1060, 88 L. Ed. 2d 781, 106 S. Ct. 806 (1986). "Only the most extraordinary showing of contrary intentions" in the legislative history will justify a departure from that language. Garcia v. United States, 469 U.S. 70, 75, 83 L. Ed. 2d 472, 105 S. Ct. 479 (1984).

Under a plain reading of this statute, we find it clear that violations of § 7202 are subject to a six-year statute of limitations under § 6531(4). Specifically, 26 U.S.C. § 7202 makes it an offense for an employer to willfully fail to "account for and pay over" to the IRS taxes withheld from employees. Given that § 6531 pertains to "failing to pay any tax," the District Court correctly found that the failure to pay third-party taxes as covered by § 7202 constitutes failure to pay "any tax," and thus, is subject to the six-year statute of limitations under § 6531(4). * * *

Although we could conclude our analysis here as the statutory language in § 6531(4) is plain and unambiguous, *United States v. Cicco*, 10 F.3d 980, 984 (3d Cir. 1993) (unambiguous language deemed "conclusive"), we will address why we find the Georgia and Massachusetts cases relied upon by Gollapudi to be unpersuasive.

In *United States v. Block*, the court found that Congress had the statutory scheme of 26 U.S.C. § 7201 *et seq.* in mind when fashioning § 6531. 497 F. Supp. at 632. This was inferred from the facts that there are specific references to § 7201 *et seq.* provisions in § 6531, and that the language of § 6531 borrows extensively from various § 7201 *et seq.* sections. The *Block* court reasoned "it seems unlikely . . . that Congress would have used the language of so many of the § 7202 *et seq.* code sections when drafting the subsections of § 6531 but omit use of the key words of § 7202 if it had intended to make failure to 'pay over' third-party taxes subject to the six-year statute of limitations." *Id.*

We find this line of reasoning in *Block* unpersuasive. The statute of limitations for all criminal tax violations is set forth in 26 U.S.C. § 6531. The offenses which fall under the eight exceptions to § 6531 are included either by general description of the proscribed conduct or by a reference to a specific section of the code. It is clear to us that where Congress intended to limit the applicability of the § 6531 exceptions, it unambiguously did so. Thus, whereas subsections five, six, seven and eight of § 6531 are expressly limited to offenses arising under §§ 7206(1) and 7202, 7212(a), 7214(a), and 18 U.S.C. § 371 respectively, the District Court correctly held that subsection four contains a general description of offenses, not limited to violations of § 7203 or to any other specific offense. [United States v.] Gollapudi, 947 F. Supp. [763 (D. N.J. 1996)] at 766. [United States v.] Musacchia, 900 F.2d [493, (2d Cir. 1990)] at 500. As the District Court stated, "the focus must be on the duty imposed by these specific sections of the Code, not on the particular words present or absent in an attempt to reconstruct congressional intent. An employer's duty to pay taxes withheld from his employees is at least as great as the duty to pay personal income taxes." *Gollapudi*, 947 F. Supp. at 767.

Furthermore, the fact that § 6531(4) uses the word "offense" rather than "offenses" does not convince us that Congress intended § 6531(4) to be limited to violations of § 7203. Conversely, we agree with the rationale of the Second Circuit in *United States v. Musacchia* that "the language of section 6531(4) — applying the six-year statute of limitations to 'the offense of willfully failing to pay any tax, or make any return . . . at the time or times required by law or regulations' — suggests that it applied to any of several sections of the Code that define such an offense." 900 F.2d at 500 (citing 26 U.S.C. § 6531(4)).

Moreover, we find the District Court's reliance on the Second Circuit's decision that it would be inconsistent for Congress to have prescribed a six-year limitation period for the misdemeanor offense defined in 26 U.S.C. § 7203 (failure to file a return or pay a tax) while providing only a three-year limitation period for the felony offense defined in § 7202, to be well-founded. *Gollapudi*, 947 F. Supp. at 766 (citing *Musacchia*, 900 F.2d at 500). As the court in *Musacchia* concluded, it would make little sense if the period in which an offense could be prosecuted for the misdemeanor of failing to file a tax return was twice as long as the period in which an offender could be prosecuted for the felony of failure to pay taxes over to the IRS collected on behalf of employees. As the District Court stated, "the focus must be on the duty imposed by these specific sections of the Code, not on the particular words present or absent in an attempt to reconstruct congressional intent. An employer's duty to pay taxes withheld from his employees is at least as great as the duty to pay personal income taxes." *Gollapudi*, 947 F. Supp. at 767.

* * *

V. CONCLUSION

For the above reasons, we will affirm the decision of the District Court.

COWEN, CIRCUIT JUDGE, dissenting.

The majority errs in concluding that the criminal conduct of an employer in failing to pay over taxes withheld from the wages of employees, in violation of 26 U.S.C. § 7202, falls within the fourth exception to the three-year statute of limitations for violations of the Internal Revenue Code (I.R.C.), 26 U.S.C. § 6531(4). I respectfully dissent from section IV-A of the majority's opinion that the statute of limitations for violations of § 7202 is six years rather than the normal three years. The conviction of the defendant, Rao Gollapudi, should be vacated due to the expiration of the three-year statute of limitations.

* * *

[T]he Tenth Circuit's decision, holding that § 6531(4) covers § 7202, is conclusory and furnishes no analytical assistance or weighty precedential authority. The decision offers a string of citations, but none deals with the relationship between § 7202 and § 6531(4). *See* [United States v.] Porth, 426 F.2d 519 [(10th Cir. 1970)], at 521; *see also Block*, 497 F. Supp. at 631 (the cases mentioned in *Porth* do not support Porth's conclusion); *Brennick*, 908 F. Supp. at 1018 n.6 (none of the cases cited by *Porth* supports Porth's conclusion). In addition to the lack of analysis, the Tenth Circuit in *Porth* also argued in the alternative, stating immediately after its § 6531(4) pronouncement that the first indictment in the case, which occurred within three years of the offenses, should be looked to for statute of limitations purposes despite the fact that the first indictment was dismissed for technical reasons. *See Porth*, 426 F.2d at 521. The Tenth Circuit itself appears uncertain of the strength of its own § 6531(4) conclusion, undermining the authority of its decision.

IV.

I respectfully disagree with the arguments raised by the majority and by the Second Circuit in *Musacchia*. The majority claims that the plain meaning of § 6531(4) clearly encompasses § 7202, vitiating any need for other techniques of statutory interpretation. However, the meaning of § 6531(4) is anything but plain and unambiguous. While the majority claims that § 6531(4) is clear by stressing the importance of the word "any[,]" the majority ignores the fact that applying § 6531(4) effectively swallows the general rule of a three-year statute of limitations for tax offenses. Nearly every violation of the I.R.C. translates into an attempt not to pay taxes. Seizing on "any" to broaden the reach of § 6531(4) in order to include § 7202 has the net effect of vastly expanding § 6531(4), shrinking the applicability of the three-year statute of limitations to near oblivion and rendering the other seven exceptions to the three-year statute of limitations nugatory. The majority provides no principled rationale for delineating the contours of its expanded § 6531(4). As I argue below, the term "any" could properly refer only to tax obligations encompassed by the word "pay" but not obligations to "pay over" taxes. Accordingly, the meaning of § 6531(4) is far from plain and unambiguous. It calls for judicial interpretation.

Resolving § 6531(4)'s ambiguity activates two venerated members of the canon of statutory interpretation which the majority ignored. First, 'excepting' clauses are to be interpreted narrowly. *See* United States v. McElvain, 272 U.S. 633, 639, 47 S. Ct. 219, 220, 71 L. Ed. 451 (1926); *see also* United States v. Scharton, 285 U.S. 518, 521–2, 52 S. Ct. 416, 417, 76 L. Ed. 917 (1932). Second, criminal statutes are to be interpreted in favor of repose. *See* United States v. Marion, 404 U.S. 307, 322 n.14, 92 S. Ct. 455, 464 n.14, 30 L. Ed. 2d 468 (1971). These principles provide the framework for determining the meaning and scope of § 6531(4). As a result, the excepting clause of § 6531(4) must be interpreted narrowly, especially given that the instant statute deals with criminal liability.

Moving to the text at issue here, the majority dismisses the difference between the terms "pay" and "pay over" too handily. Both § 7202 and its civil analogue, 26 U.S.C. § 6672, use the term "pay over" in the context of transferring employees' withheld funds to the government, strongly implying that "pay over" is a statutory term of art referring to transferring a third-party's taxes to the government. While the use of the term "pay over" by the United States Code does not rise to the level of a statutory term of art, the term "pay over" does have a strong tendency to refer to transferring a third-party's taxes to the government. Accordingly, the majority misses the point by stressing the importance of "any" in § 6531(4). Even if "any" is to be interpreted expansively as referring to all taxes owed, the expansiveness is only within the category of taxes that are "paid," not the category of funds "paid over."

*   *   *

For the above reasons, I respectfully dissent from the majority's conclusion that violations of § 7202 receive a six-year rather than a three-year statute of limitations. The district court's decision should be reversed and the conviction of Gollapudi vacated due to the expiration of the three-year statute of limitations prior to the commencement of prosecution.

———————

Whose analysis in *Gollapudi* better reflects the language and intent of Code section 6531(4), the majority's or the dissent's?

§ 13.06 Application of the Federal Sentencing Guidelines in Tax Cases

The Sentencing Reform Act of 1984, Pub. L. No. 98-473, 98 Stat. 1987, provided for the development of guidelines to further the purposes of sentencing under 18 U.S.C. § 3553, which include deterrence, incapacitation, just punishment, and rehabilitation. To this end, it established the United States Sentencing Commission (Sentencing Commission) as an independent agency within the judicial branch. The United States Supreme Court upheld the constitutionality of the sentencing guidelines in *Mistretta v. United States*, 488 U.S. 361 (1989).

Under the Sentencing Reform Act, each of 43 "base offense levels," listed down the side of a sentencing matrix, intersects with six "criminal history categories" along the horizontal axis of the matrix, to provide ranges of permissible sentences (provided in number of months of imprisonment). The criminal history category refers to the criminal history of the defendant who is being sentenced. The base offense level is determined as described below.

The Sentencing Commission has prescribed a "base offense level" for each type of offense. *Koff*, reproduced immediately below, considers the proper base offense level for violation of Code section 7212, attempts to interfere with the administration of Internal Revenue laws. For many tax crimes, the base offense level is based on the amount of tax loss. The *Bryant* case, reproduced after *Koff*, demonstrates this principle.

Once the court determines the initial base offense level, it will depart from that offense level if the case has features requiring adjustments under the sentencing guidelines or if it "finds an aggravating or mitigating circumstance of a kind, or to a degree, not adequately taken into consideration by the Sentencing Commission in formulating the guidelines." 18 U.S.C. § 3553(b). *Dixon*, which was reproduced above, reflects that principle: Dixon's offense level was enhanced "by two points for being an organizer, leader, manager, or supervisor in the criminal activity." *United States v. Dixon*, 79 A.F.T.R. 2d 2854 (9th Cir. 1997). The *Jeffries* case, below, focuses on the role of aggravating or mitigating circumstances in setting the base offense level.

In general, the party seeking an upward or downward departure from the initial base offense level bears the burden of proving the facts justifying that departure by a preponderance of the evidence. *See, e.g., United States v. Rice*, 52 F.3d 843, 848 (10th Cir. 1995), *cert. denied*, 518 U.S. 1011 (1996); *United States v. Restrepo*, 946 F.2d 654, 655–57 (9th Cir. 1991) (*en banc*), *cert. denied*, 503 U.S. 961 (1992). However, the Ninth Circuit has stated, "When a sentencing factor has an extremely disproportionate effect on the sentence relative to the offense of conviction," the clear and convincing evidence standard may apply to the government. *Restrepo,* 946 F.2d at 659. *See also United States v. Kikumura,* 918 F.2d 1084, 1101–02 (3d Cir. 1990) (factor that greatly increased defendant's sentence had to be proven by clear and convincing evidence).

Once the applicable guideline range has been determined by finding the intersection of the base offense level and the criminal history category, the sentencing court must select a sentence from within that range, unless the sentence under the guidelines would fall below the mandatory minimum sentence for the crime, in which case the mandatory minimum must be imposed. Similarly, if the guideline range exceeds the maximum sentence established by statute for the offense, the statutory maximum sentence for the offense (including applicable sentence enhancements, as discussed below) is imposed.

Note that, for some crimes, the maximum sentence may in fact be more than it appears from the relevant statute because the statutory scheme may provide for certain sentencing enhancements. In *Apprendi v. New Jersey,* 530 U.S. 466 (2000), the United States Supreme Court held that, for a sentence to be increased beyond the stated statutory maximum to reflect relevant statutory sentencing enhancements provided by statute, the fact-finder, a jury in that case, must apply a "beyond a reasonable doubt" standard of proof. The Court stated that it was not overruling *McMillan v. Pennsylvania,* 477 U.S. 79 (1986), but was limiting its applicability to only those cases that "do not involve the imposition of a sentence more severe than the statutory maximum for the offense established by the jury's verdict." *Id.* at 487 n.13. *McMillan* had upheld as constitutional a Pennsylvania statute that subjected a criminal defendant to a mandatory minimum sentence of five years imprisonment if the judge found, by a preponderance of the evidence, that the defendant had "visibly possessed a firearm" in the course of committing a specified felony. *Id.* at 485–486.

Apprendi was a state case, but its holding is applicable in Sentencing Guidelines cases as well. Following *Apprendi,* several cases have held that the "preponderance of the evidence" standard applies to factors that would not increase a sentence beyond the statutory maximum. *See, e.g., United States v. Simonelli,* 237 F.3d 19, 30 (1st Cir. 2001), *cert. denied,* 122 S. Ct. 54 (2001); *United States v. Doggett,* 230 F.3d 160, 164–65 (5th Cir. 2000), *cert. denied,* 531 U.S. 1177 (2001); *United States v. Corrado,* 227 F.3d 528, 542 (6th Cir. 2000).

In May 2001, the Sentencing Commission sent to Congress the 2001 Guideline Amendments. *See* 66 F.R. 30512. The amendments took effect on November 1, 2001. With respect to tax offenses, the changes include (1) summing corporate and individual tax losses where the same action causes both, without reduction for the corporate-level tax, as was done in *United States v. Cseplo,* 42 F.3d 360 (6th Cir. 1994); (2) renaming "sophisticated concealment" of an offense "sophisticated means" and mandating a minimum offense level of 12; and (3) including interest and penalties in the tax loss calculation in payment evasion cases. The new guidelines would also significantly change the treatment of money laundering offenses.

[A] Base Offense Levels Applicable in Tax Cases

As discussed above, the Sentencing Guidelines require a judge to determine the base offense level of the crime committed by the defendant. The base offense level is determined by first arriving at an initial offense level and then adjusting it up or down as discussed above. Consider the courts' analysis in determining the appropriate base offense level in *Koff* and *Bryant*. Note that neither *Koff* nor *Bryant* involves upward or downward departures from the initial base offense level.

UNITED STATES v. KOFF
United States Court of Appeals, Ninth Circuit
43 F.3d 417 (1994)[7]

CYNTHIA HOLCOMB HALL, CIRCUIT JUDGE:

Irwin and Darline Koff were each indicted by a grand jury and charged with making false claims against the United States in violation of 18 U.S.C. § 287, and with making and subscribing false tax returns in violation of 26 U.S.C. § 7206(1). Together, they were indicted for and charged with corruptly obstructing and impeding the due administration of the tax laws in violation of 26 U.S.C. § 7212(a), and aiding and abetting such offense, in violation of 18 U.S.C. § 2. After a bench trial, the Koffs were convicted on all counts. We have jurisdiction over this timely appeal.

* * *

I. FACTS

In 1989, the Internal Revenue Service ("IRS") assessed deficiencies for unpaid taxes against the Koffs, based on their failure to file returns for the years 1982–85. The IRS began collection proceedings.

The Koffs employed a scheme to avoid paying the taxes that the IRS claimed they owed. Each of them sent a series of "conduct assessments" to various IRS officials whom the Koffs believed were associated with their cases, including the acting Commissioner of the IRS, the Sacramento District Director, the Assistant Regional Commissioner, an auditor, and a case worker. The "conduct assessment" letters stated that the IRS employees' conduct had been "arbitrary, unreasonable, capricious, misleading, and unwarranted," and purported to "assess" money owed to the Koffs.

The Koffs also sent the IRS officials past due notices for the amounts claimed in the conduct assessments; IRS forms 1099 reflecting income to the officials in the same amount as in the assessments, plus interest; documents entitled "Notice of Placement for Collection and Default Statement," claiming that the conduct assessments had been placed with the IRS for collection; and Uniform Commercial Code Financing Statements claiming that liens in the amount of the conduct assessments plus interest had been placed upon the officials' assets. Several of the IRS officials testified that they had been

---

[7] *Cert. denied*, 514 U.S. 1008 (1995).

concerned that the false 1099s could lead to IRS audits and possible disciplinary action against them, and that the false U.C.C. liens would adversely affect their financial situations.

In January 1990, both Darline and Irwin Koff signed and filed, under penalty of perjury, forms 1096, which are used to transmit to the IRS 1099 forms issued by payors of income during a tax year. They attached the 1099s issued to the various IRS officials and other targets of the scheme. Irwin Koff represented on his 1096 that he had paid a total of $738,327 to the "recipients" in 1989; Darline Koff claimed to have paid $560,510.28.

Next, both Koffs signed and filed, under penalty of perjury, forms 1040. Each defendant reported the total 1099 "payments" as "other income from accounts receivable" and claimed that the IRS had withheld the same amount as taxes. As a result, Darline Koff claimed that the IRS owed her a refund of $404,435, and Irwin Koff claimed a refund of $532,463. The defendants attempted to use these false refund claims as set-offs against the deficiency assessed by the IRS for earlier years.

The Koffs were convicted of all charges and now appeal.

II. PROPER SENTENCING GUIDELINE FOR 26 U.S.C. § 7212(a)

The Koffs were convicted of violating 26 U.S.C. § 7212(a), which prohibits corrupt activity designed to obstruct or impede the due administration of the federal tax laws. The Statutory Index to the 1989 Sentencing Guidelines Manual, which the district court applied in sentencing the Koffs, designated U.S.S.G. § 2A2.2, Aggravated Assault, and § 2A2.3, Minor Assault, as the appropriate guidelines for violations of 26 U.S.C. § 7212(a). Because the Koffs' crimes did not involve actual violence against I.R.S. agents or property, the district court properly determined that these guidelines were not appropriate, and that it should look to the most analogous guideline to the Koffs' conduct to determine their sentence. *See, e.g.*, United States v. Hanson, 2 F.3d 942, 947 (9th Cir. 1993).

Relying on *United States v. Dykstra*, 991 F.2d 450 (8th Cir.), *cert denied*, 126 L. Ed. 2d 177, 114 S. Ct. 222 (1993), the district court found § 2J1.2, Obstruction of Justice, with a base offense level of 12, to be most analogous. *Hanson*, a Ninth Circuit case decided several weeks before the Koffs were sentenced, found instead that § 2T1.5, Fraudulent Returns, Statements, or Other Documents, with a base offense level of 6, was the most analogous guideline in another § 7212(a) case. 2 F.3d at 947. After receiving briefs on this question, we now conclude that the district court properly applied § 2J1.2.

Whether a particular guideline applies to a specific set of facts is a question of law reviewed *de novo*. *Hanson*, 2 F.3d at 947. Because the Koffs did not object to the district court's determination of their sentences, however, we review only for plain error. United States v. Martinez, 956 F.2d 891, 893 (9th Cir. 1992).

Hanson involved a scheme similar to the one employed by the Koffs. *Hanson* filed false forms 1099 and 1096, claiming to have made payments of over

$78,000,000; he then filed a form 1040, falsely claiming a refund of almost $34,000,000. *Hanson*, 2 F.3d at 944–45. Hanson was convicted of violating § 7212(a), among other laws, and the district court sentenced him under guideline § 2T1.9, Conspiracy to Impair, Impede, or Defeat Tax. This court reversed, finding the conspiracy guideline inappropriate because Hanson acted alone, and concluding without argument that § 2T1.5 applied to Hanson's conduct. *Id.* at 947. We find that under the facts of the present case, however, the district court correctly applied the general obstruction of justice guideline, § 2J1.2.

In *Hanson*, the targets of the false documents scheme were not IRS officials and were apparently not involved in any sort of legal proceeding against Hanson. The only effect on the IRS in that case was the administrative burden of detecting, investigating and prosecuting the offender.

By contrast, the Koffs began their scheme shortly after receiving a deficiency notice from the IRS for the tax years 1982–85, and after the agency began collection proceedings. They specifically targeted and attempted to intimidate IRS officials whom they believed were involved in the proceedings against them, from the acting Commissioner all the way down to the caseworker working on the Koffs' cases. In addition, they attempted to use the fake "refunds" they claimed the IRS owed them directly to offset the tax liability the IRS had assessed for 1982–85.

Such conduct goes beyond the misdemeanor offense contemplated by guideline § 2T1.5, Fraudulent Returns, Statements, or Other Documents. *See* U.S.S.G. § 2T1.5, comment. (backg'd) (1989). Instead, the Koffs engaged in obstruction of justice, and we agree with the conclusion of the Eighth Circuit in *Dykstra*, 991 F.2d at 454, on virtually identical facts, that § 2J1.2 was the appropriate guideline. The district court therefore did not err in sentencing the Koffs.

* * *

Accordingly, the convictions and sentences of both Irwin and Darline Koff are affirmed.

The determination of base offense level in *Bryant*, which follows, focuses on the amount of lost revenue. Why did the *Koff* court not consider that factor?

UNITED STATES v. BRYANT
United States Court of Appeals, Second Circuit
128 F.3d 74 (1997)

PER CURIAM:

Defendant Anthony Bryant appeals from a judgment entered in the United States District Court for the Southern District of New York following a jury trial before John F. Keenan, Judge, convicting him on 22 counts of assisting in the preparation of false federal income tax returns, in violation of 26 U.S.C.

§ 7206(2) (1994), and sentencing him principally to 60 months' imprisonment, to be followed by a one-year term of supervised release. In computing Bryant's sentence under the Sentencing Guidelines ("Guidelines"), the district court set his base offense level at 22 pursuant to §§ 2T1.4(a)(1) and 2T4.1 on the ground that the loss caused by his frauds totaled "at least" $5,115,203. That figure was the sum of (a) $53,570 in tax losses attributable to the 22 returns that Bryant was convicted of falsifying, (b) $4,461,633 in losses suffered by the government on other tax returns prepared by Bryant that had been audited by the Internal Revenue Service ("IRS"), and (c) "at least" $600,000 in losses that the presentence report ("PSR") estimated the government to have suffered on returns prepared by Bryant that were not audited. On appeal, Bryant contends that the attribution to him of $600,000 in losses with respect to unaudited returns was speculative and unfair. In his pro se brief, Bryant also contends that he was unfairly denied access to the tax documents from which the $4,461,633 loss was calculated. Finding no merit in any of these contentions, we affirm.

In establishing sentencing tables that tie a defendant's offense level to the amount of loss caused by his offense, *see, e.g.*, Guidelines § 2T4.1 (loss caused by tax offenses); *id.* § 2B1.1(b)(1) (loss caused by theft offenses); *id.* § 2F1.1(b)(1) (loss caused by fraud offenses), the Guidelines do not require that the sentencing court calculate the amount of loss with certainty or precision. The § 2T1.1 commentary, which is applicable to a violation of § 7206(2), states that "the amount of the tax loss may be uncertain," and it envisions that "indirect methods of proof [may be] used . . ." Guidelines § 2T1.1 Application Note 1. It states expressly that "the guidelines contemplate that the court will simply make a reasonable estimate based on the available facts." *Id.*

Similarly, the commentaries to § 2B1.1 and § 2F1.1 state that, for purposes of calculating the offense level for theft and fraud offenses, respectively, "the loss need not be determined with precision. The court need only make a reasonable estimate of the loss, given the available information." Guidelines § 2B1.1 Application Note 3; *id.* § 2F1.1 Application Note 8. A § 2F1.1 "estimate, for example, may be based upon the approximate number of victims and an estimate of the average loss to each victim . . ." *Id.* In keeping with this philosophy, it is permissible for the sentencing court, in calculating a defendant's offense level, to estimate the loss resulting from his offenses by extrapolating the average amount of loss from known data and applying that average to transactions where the exact amount of loss is unknown. Thus, in *United States v. Sutton*, 13 F.3d 595, 596–97 (2d Cir. 1994) (per curiam), where the defendant had received payments of $80-$1,500, usually in the $750–$1,200 range, for fraudulently issued driver's licenses, we found it not unreasonable for the sentencing court to compute the loss attributable to her scheme by estimating a payment of $250 per license and multiplying that sum by the total number of applications. *See id.* at 599–600.

We see no reason why the same methodology may not be used in a § 7206(2) case in which, as here, the defendant has been convicted of assisting in the preparation of numerous fraudulent tax returns, and government records show many more such instances. Although extrapolation might not be reasonable if, for example, there were few instances of fraud, or if the returns audited constituted a minuscule percentage of the total that the defendant prepared or in whose preparation he assisted, we see no unreasonableness here. The evidence at trial showed that in 1991–1993, Bryant ran an income-tax-refund "mill," preparing some tax returns in as little as three minutes, and routinely recording arbitrary deductions for his clients with no regard for actual expenditures. A review of IRS files revealed that in that period, Bryant assisted in preparing a total of 8,521 individual federal income tax returns for his clients, more than 99% of which resulted in refunds. More than 20% of these returns were audited. The 22 fraudulent returns whose preparation Bryant was convicted of assisting averaged $2,435 in underreported taxes. Similarly, the court found substantially accurate the PSR's report that 1,683 other returns prepared by Bryant and audited by the IRS revealed tax under-reporting totaling $4,461,633, for an average tax loss to the government of $2,651 per return. The sentencing court could well have estimated the tax loss caused by Bryant on the remaining nearly 7,000 unaudited returns based on the average loss caused by the returns that had been audited. The court's acceptance of the PSR's recommendation to use an estimated total loss of $600,000—an average of less than $100 per unaudited return, instead of the more than $2,400-per-return average revealed in audits—far from being unfair to Bryant, was highly generous to him. We see no error.

Nor do we find merit in Bryant's *pro se* contention that he was denied an adequate opportunity to review the tax returns and other documents used in the audits. He was given access to all of the papers he requested at an IRS office and was informed that the government would accommodate any reasonable request for duplication. He in fact examined the papers for parts of 19 days. His contention that the government was required to copy the entire set of documents for him, or to give him possession of the originals while he was incarcerated, is meritless.

We have considered all of Bryant's contentions on this appeal and have found them to be without merit. The judgment of the district court is affirmed.

[B]   Upward and Downward Departures

[1]   Departures Reflected in the Sentencing Guidelines

As indicated above, determining the base offense under the Sentencing Guidelines involves considering Guidelines factors that require upward or downward adjustments from the initial base offense level. *Jeffries*, reproduced below, considers two adjustments contemplated in the Sentencing Guidelines: an increase in the base offense level for obstruction of justice, and a decrease in the base offense level for acceptance of responsibility.

UNITED STATES v. JEFFRIES
United States Court of Appeals, Ninth Circuit
1993 U.S. App. LEXIS 13320

MEMORANDUM

Alan Hardy Jeffries appeals his 10-month sentence following entry of a guilty plea to filing false income tax returns and aiding and abetting in violation of 18 U.S.C. §§ 2, 287. Jeffries contends that the district court erred by (1) admitting expert testimony regarding his handwriting, (2) increasing his offense level for obstruction of justice under U.S.S.G. § 3C1.1, and (3) failing to decrease his offense level for acceptance of responsibility under U.S.S.G. § 3E1.1. We have jurisdiction under 28 U.S.C. § 1291 and affirm.

* * *

We review for abuse of discretion the district court's decision to admit expert testimony. *See* United States v. Rahm, No. 92-10429, slip op. 4727, 4734 (9th Cir. May 11, 1993). We review for clear error the district court's determinations that Jeffries obstructed justice and that he did not accept responsibility for his criminal conduct. *See* United States v. Morales, 977 F.2d 1330, 1331 (9th Cir. 1992) (U.S.S.G. § 3C1.1); United States v. Ramos, 923 F.2d 1346, 1360 (9th Cir. 1991) (U.S.S.G. § 3E1.1).

At sentencing, the district court admitted expert testimony by William DeVries, an Internal Revenue Service ("IRS") document examiner. DeVries testified that his analysis of two handwriting exemplars, which were provided by Jeffries to the IRS pursuant to grand jury subpoenas, indicated that Jeffries deliberately disguised his handwriting by speeding it up in one exemplar and slowing it down in the other. The district court found that Jeffries obstructed justice by disguising his handwriting in the exemplars, and that there were no unusual circumstances warranting a reduction of his offense level for acceptance of responsibility.

I. EXPERT TESTIMONY

Jeffries contends that the district court erred by admitting expert handwriting testimony because it has not been established that handwriting analysis is a science. This contention is foreclosed by our decision in *United States v. Fleishman*, 684 F.2d 1329, 1337 (9th Cir.) ("It is undisputed that handwriting analysis is a science in which expert testimony assists a jury."), *cert. denied*, 459 U.S. 1044 (1982).

* * *

II. SENTENCE ADJUSTMENTS

Jeffries contends that the district court erred by increasing his offense level for obstruction of justice and failing to decrease his offense level for acceptance of responsibility. These contentions are without merit.

The Guidelines provide that "if the defendant willfully obstructed or impeded, or attempted to obstruct or impede, the administration of justice during the investigation, prosecution, or sentencing of the instant offense, increase the offense level by 2 levels." U.S.S.G. § 3C1.1; United States v. Marks, 977 F.2d 1330, 1331 (9th Cir. 1992), *cert. denied*, 113 S. Ct. 1399 (1993). Obstructive conduct includes "concealing . . . evidence that is material to an official investigation or judicial proceeding . . . or attempting to do so." U.S.S.G. § 3C1.1 comment. (3(d)).

The Guidelines further provide that a district court may reduce a defendant's offense level by two points if he has accepted responsibility for his criminal conduct. U.S.S.G. § 3E1.1. Ordinarily, a determination that the defendant has obstructed justice indicates that he has not accepted responsibility. U.S.S.G. § 3E1.1, comment. (4); United States v. Lato, 934 F.2d 1080, 1083 (9th Cir.), *cert. denied*, 112 S. Ct. 271 (1991).

Here, evidence of Jeffries's handwriting was material to the investigation of the instant offenses. *See* United States v. Blackwood, 878 F.2d 1200, 1202 (9th Cir. 1989) (evidence of defendant's handwriting was material in prosecution for filing false income tax returns). Jeffries attempted to conceal this evidence by deliberately disguising his handwriting in the exemplars he provided to the IRS. Accordingly, the district court did not err by determining that Jeffries obstructed justice under the Guidelines. *See* U.S.S.G. § 3C1.1 comment. (3(d)); *Marks*, 977 F.2d at 1331; *see also* United States v. Reyes, 908 F.2d 281, 290 (8th Cir. 1990) (defendant obstructed justice by refusing to comply with court order requiring him to provide a handwriting exemplar), *cert. denied*, 111 S. Ct. 1111 (1991).

Jeffries also contends that the district court incorrectly determined that its finding of obstruction of justice precluded a finding of acceptance of responsibility. Our examination of the record indicates that the district court recognized its authority to decrease Jeffries's offense level for acceptance of responsibility but determined that there were no unusual circumstances warranting such an adjustment. Jeffries does not challenge this determination. Accordingly, there is no error. *See* U.S.S.G. § 3E1.1 comment. (4); *Lato*, 934 F.2d at 1083.

Affirmed.

---

[2]   Departures Not Reflected in the Sentencing Guidelines

As discussed above, upon motion of a party, the judge sentencing a convicted criminal defendant may depart from the base offense level (up or down) for factors that were "not adequately taken into consideration by the Sentencing Commission in formulating the guidelines." 18 U.S.C. § 3553(b). Under the Sentencing Guidelines, the grant or denial of the motion is appealable by the losing party. *United States v. Bala*, reproduced below, explains in more detail the legal limitations on this type of upward and downward departures from the base offense level.

UNITED STATES v. BALA
United States Court of Appeals, Second Circuit
236 F.3d 87 (2000)

OPINION:

POOLER, Circuit Judge:

Kantilal Patel appeals from the October 4, 1999, judgment of the United States District Court for the Northern District of New York (Thomas J. McAvoy, then-Chief Judge) sentencing him principally to 51 months imprisonment after a trial jury convicted him of conspiracy to launder money and substantive money laundering, in violation of 18 U.S.C. § 1956(h) and (a)(3). Although Patel raises several arguments on appeal relating to his trial, our primary focus is his contention that Judge McAvoy erred in refusing to grant a downward departure at the time of sentencing for "imperfect entrapment." We affirm Patel's conviction and sentence in all respects.

BACKGROUND

The government filed a sealed five-count indictment on October 29, 1998, charging Patel with three counts and Abdul Majid Bala with two counts of money laundering and both with one count of conspiracy to launder money. The indictment flowed from a government investigation using undercover agents from the Criminal Investigation Division of the Internal Revenue Service ("IRS") and a cooperating defendant. The investigation began in September 1996, when IRS agents arranged several meetings with Bharat Vakharia to negotiate money laundering transactions. Authorities arrested Vakharia in December 1996, and he agreed to cooperate with the government. Vakharia's cooperation led authorities to Patel. Vakharia told the government that Patel had invited him to a party in the summer of 1996 and that the two men discussed money laundering. Based on this background information, Vakharia made several telephone calls to Patel in January, February and May 1997, and the government monitored the calls. In their May conversation, the men discussed money laundering transactions.

On May 15, 1997, Patel met with Vakharia and an undercover agent in Endicott, New York and arranged to launder $25,000 in alleged heroin trafficking proceeds for a fee. Patel completed the transaction in a June 4, 1997, meeting. At the June 4 meeting, Patel introduced the agent to Bala, whom Patel had recruited. Patel had met Bala, who was Canadian, only the day before. A Canadian businessman whom Patel knew referred Patel's money laundering inquiries to Bala. On November 20, 1997, Bala met with an undercover agent in Buffalo to launder $50,000 in alleged heroin trafficking proceeds for a fee. The agent had first contacted Patel in order to reach Bala. On March 6, 1998, Patel and Bala met an undercover agent in Manhattan to launder $140,000 in alleged heroin trafficking proceeds. The agent had arranged the meeting directly with Bala, but Bala brought Patel along and gave Patel a portion of his fee. Finally, on November 9, 1998, Bala met with an undercover agent in Buffalo to launder $231,250. Police arrested Bala during the November 1998 meeting. Police arrested Patel on December 3, 1998.

Bala pleaded guilty to a charge of conspiracy to launder money on January 25, 1999. In a superseding indictment filed on March 11, 1999, the government charged Patel with conspiracy to engage in money laundering and five substantive money laundering counts based on the four transactions outlined above. Although he initially cooperated with authorities, Patel went to trial on April 19, 1999. The jury returned a guilty verdict against him on all counts on April 23, 1999. In the course of post-verdict motion practice, Judge McAvoy granted defendant's motion to dismiss counts 2 and 3 of the indictment, which concerned the $25,000 transaction in Endicott, because the government failed to prove that the deal had a nexus to interstate or foreign commerce as Section 1956(a)(3) required. The district court denied defendant's motion in all other respects. Judge McAvoy sentenced Patel on September 24, 1999, to 51 months imprisonment, two years supervised release, $16,000 fine, and $400 special assessment. Patel appeals his conviction and sentence.

DISCUSSION

I. Downward Departure for Imperfect Entrapment

Patel claims that Judge McAvoy misapprehended his authority to make a downward departure at Patel's sentencing for "imperfect entrapment." The government responds that the imperfect entrapment doctrine is questionable in this circuit and does not apply to the facts of this case in any event. The government also contends that the district court rejected on the merits Patel's contentions related to entrapment when it denied defendant's post-verdict challenges to the jury's findings of guilt.

A defendant may not appeal a district court's decision not to make a discretionary downward departure unless the court relied "on the mistaken belief that it lacked authority to depart." United States v. Martin, 78 F.3d 808, 814 (2d Cir. 1996) (quoting United States v. Ekhator, 17 F.3d 53, 55 (2d Cir. 1994)). We review a district court's decision to make a sentencing departure for abuse of discretion, which includes making an error of law. See United States v. Bryson, 163 F.3d 742, 746 (2d Cir. 1998). In the case of the district court's refusal to grant a downward departure, we review the decision only if the sentencing judge imposed a sentence in violation of law or incorrectly applied the Sentencing Guidelines. See United States v. Campo, 140 F.3d 415, 418 (2d Cir. 1998) (per curiam). Some circuits have determined that "imperfect entrapment," described as "aggressive encouragement of wrongdoing, although not amounting to a complete defense," is a proper ground for downward departure at sentencing pursuant to U.S.S.G. § 5K2.12. * * *

Patel's imperfect entrapment argument is that a departure was warranted because he led a law-abiding life until encountering the government's sting operation and he was so inept at his crime that no real criminal would have done business with him. The sentencing transcript shows that Judge McAvoy refused to consider imperfect entrapment as a ground for a downward departure motion because he believed that Second Circuit law did not authorize it.

The Supreme Court has established a two-part test to determine whether a particular factor is a permissible basis for a downward departure. *See* Koon v. United States, 518 U.S. 81, 109, 135 L. Ed. 2d 392, 116 S. Ct. 2035 (1996). The court must first determine whether reliance on the factor is "proscribed, as a categorical matter," by the guidelines, and if it is not, the court must then determine whether the factor "takes the case outside the heartland of the applicable Guideline." *Id.* The first question — "whether a factor is a permissible basis for departure under any circumstances" — is a matter of law, and therefore "the court of appeals need not defer to the district court's resolution of the point." *Id.* at 100.

While to date we have not decided whether imperfect entrapment is proscribed by the guidelines as a ground for downward departure, we can find nothing in the guidelines to prohibit a district court from considering conduct by the government that does not give rise to an entrapment defense but that is nonetheless "aggressive encouragement of wrongdoing." *Garza-Juarez*, 992 F.2d at 912; *see also* United States v. Giles, 768 F. Supp. 101, 103–04 (S.D.N.Y.), *aff'd without op.*, 953 F.2d 636 (2d Cir. 1991). Moreover, the policy statement in Section 5K2.12 can reasonably be read to authorize such a departure in appropriate cases. Nevertheless, it is for the district courts to decide for themselves whether, in a particular case, a downward departure based on imperfect entrapment would remove that case from the "heartland of the applicable Guideline." *See* United States v. Bonnet-Grullon, 212 F.3d 692, 700 (2d Cir. 2000) ("The determination of whether a case is within the heartland of the applicable guideline cannot be a matter of generalization."). We recognize the district courts' "institutional advantage over appellate courts in making these sorts of determinations." *Koon*, 518 U.S. at 98.

Although the district court here apparently believed that, as a matter of law, it was unable to consider imperfect entrapment, its misapprehension was harmless. In imposing sentence in the present case, Judge McAvoy noted that after looking at all of the evidence before him, he had concluded that Patel became involved in the money-laundering scheme solely out of greed. Although there might be cases whose circumstances would warrant a downward departure on the basis of imperfect entrapment, the record here does not suffice to take Patel out of the heartland of the relevant guideline, U.S.S.G. § 2S1.1. Accordingly, the district court would have abused its discretion had it applied imperfect entrapment to justify a downward departure in this case. *Cf.* United States v. Rivera, 192 F.3d 81, 86 (2d Cir. 1999) (refusing to remand notwithstanding that district court incorrectly believed that it could not, as a matter of law, depart downward, because to have departed on the facts presented would have been abuse of discretion).

Patel also contends that he was subjected to sentencing entrapment or sentencing manipulation, in that his punishment, which is directly related to the value of the funds at issue, increased because IRS agents arranged the $231,250 transaction with Bala in November 1998, after a grand jury already indicted Patel and Bala. This court has not determined whether either sentencing entrapment or sentencing manipulation is a valid departure ground. *See* United States v. Caban, 173 F.3d 89, 93 n.1 (2d Cir.), *cert. denied*, 120 S. Ct. 174 (1999); United States v. Gomez, 103 F.3d 249, 256 (2d Cir.

1997); United States v. Knecht, 55 F.3d 54, 57 (2d Cir. 1995). We have held that there was no basis to find sentencing entrapment where a defendant's principal contention concerned the timing of his arrest after entering a sting transaction. *See* United States v. Rosa, 17 F.3d 1531, 1551 (2d Cir. 1994) (holding that "even if we were prepared to suggest that the courts should inject their views into the government's exercise of discretion as to whether and when its investigation was sufficiently complete that it should have been terminated, we surely would not second-guess the government in the present case"). We also have suggested that, if a departure on the ground of sentencing entrapment or sentencing manipulation is valid, it would likely require a showing of "outrageous" government conduct. *Knecht*, 55 F.3d at 57 (sentencing entrapment); *Gomez*, 103 F.3d at 256 (sentencing manipulation). Although the status of either concept as a departure ground remains unclear, it is plain that these concepts were unavailable to Patel, for the present record provides no basis for finding the government's conduct outrageous.

*   *   *

CONCLUSION

We have considered defendant's remaining arguments and find them to be without merit. For the forgoing reasons, we affirm Patel's conviction and sentence in all respects.

How does Patel's "imperfect entrapment" argument differ from his "sentencing entrapment" argument? Is either one more convincing than the other? As indicated above, under the Sentencing Guidelines, the grant or denial of a motion for an upward or downward departure not provided in the Guidelines is appealable by the losing party. Given that fact, how frequently do you think judges provide for upward or downward departures not reflected in the Guidelines?

Based on the cases reproduced above, do you think that the sentencing guidelines better serve the purposes of punishment and deterrence than if the sentencing judge had complete discretion over sentences?

PROBLEMS

1. Marcus believes that the Internal Revenue Code is unconstitutional. He therefore does not file tax returns or pay any federal income tax on his substantial self-employment income (ranging from $200,000 to $300,000 per year). Which tax crimes, if any, has Marcus committed?

2. Sherry sold some investment property for a substantial gain in late 2002. When working on her 2002 tax return, she was dismayed to discover that she would owe approximately $20,000 in federal income tax. Her friend Violet, who was

taking some accounting courses at the local Community College, told Sherry that if she created some large imaginary deductions, she could eliminate her tax liability, and that the IRS would never catch her. Sherry took the advice and prepared and filed the 2002 return accordingly.

   A.   What tax crimes, if any, has Sherry committed?

   B.   What tax crimes, if any, has Violet committed?

3.   Julius accidentally omitted from his 2001 return certain dividend income that had been reported by the payor to the IRS. In 2002, Julius discovered his error but failed to correct it. What tax crimes, if any, has Julius committed?

4.   Cornelia is the leader of a large narcotics ring. She also prepares the tax returns for herself and the various narcotics dealers who work for her. In order to disguise the nature of the income reported on the returns, Cornelia knowingly falsifies the returns and W-2s. If Cornelia is convicted of tax fraud, can her sentence be enhanced as the leader of a criminal activity?

5.   Darren received a notice of deficiency from the IRS with respect to his 2002 tax return. Irate, Darren sent letters to various IRS employees whom he believed were working on his case. The letters threatened to bomb IRS offices and the employees' homes if they pursued the matter further. What tax crimes, if any, has Darren committed?

6.   Bill is a self-described "compulsive gambler" who intentionally did not report any of his gambling winnings on his tax returns, which he prepared himself. He also did not keep records of his gambling wins and losses each year. On audit, the IRS discovered that Bill intentionally omitted his winnings from the returns, but because of Bill's lack of records, the government is not sure it can prove that any tax deficiency resulted.

   A.   Can the government prosecute Bill criminally without introducing evidence of a deficiency, and if so, under what statute or statutes?

   B.   How might the government reconstuct Bill's income to establish the existence and amount of a deficiency?

7.   Dana intentionally filed a fraudulent (but timely) tax return for 2002, omitting from the return cash tips she received as a taxi driver.

   A.   What is the statutory period of limitations on this offense?

   B.   Assume that Dana has been convicted of criminal conduct based on her intentional filing of a fraudulent tax return.

      i.   Can the IRS also pursue Dana civilly, sending her a notice of deficiency that includes a fraud penalty?

      ii.   If the IRS is entitled to pursue a civil fraud penalty, how, if at all, can it use Dana's criminal conviction in its favor?

iii.   What is the statutory period of limitations on assessment with respect to Dana's 2002 return?

Chapter 14

CRIMINAL TAX PROCEDURE

Reading Assignment: U.S. Const. Amend. IV, V; Code §§ 7402(b), 7602, 7604, 7605(b), 7608, 7609, 7622; Fed. R. Crim. P. 6(e), 41; Fed. R. Evid. 408.

§ 14.01 Introduction

Chapter 13 discussed various tax crimes arising under the Internal Revenue Code and the Criminal Code. This chapter focuses on the procedural aspects of investigation and prosecution of tax crimes, including taxpayer defenses and strategies. In particular, Section 14.02 discusses investigation of tax crimes, Section 14.03 analyzes strategies in representing a taxpayer during a criminal investigation, Section 14.04 focuses on the IRS's tools used in a criminal investigation, Section 14.05 discusses methods of proof, Section 14.06 considers defense techniques, and Section 14.07 discusses grand jury proceedings in criminal tax cases.

Code section 7608(b) provides general authority to the Intelligence Division of the IRS to investigate tax crimes. In addition, under sections 7602 and 7622 of the Code, the IRS is authorized to examine books, papers, records, or memoranda relating to the matters required to be included in tax returns, to require and take testimony relative thereto, and to administer oaths. The IRS Criminal Investigation Division (CID) carries out that role. "The mission of [the CID] is to enforce the criminal statutes relative to tax administration and related financial crimes, in order to encourage and achieve, directly or indirectly, voluntary compliance with the Internal Revenue laws." I.R.M. 9.1.1.2. CID field agents are known as Special Agents.

The criminal sections of the Department of Justice's (DOJ) Tax Division supervise the prosecution of tax cases by United States attorneys, sometimes trying cases or assisting at trial.[1] The Tax Division of the DOJ is directed by an Assistant Attorney General. Investigation and prosecution of tax cases by CID and DOJ are discussed further below.

§ 14.02 Investigation of Tax Crimes

The IRS may begin a criminal investigation if a routine audit reveals indications of fraud. Information reported in a newspaper suggesting fraudulent activity or unreported income may also trigger an investigation, as might currency transaction reports or an informant's tip, as in *Lefkowitz,* reproduced below. If a revenue agent suspects fraudulent activity, he will try to gather more information, in order to establish a "firm indication of fraud." I.R.M.

---

[1] There are three regional criminal trial sections in the Tax Division.

25.1.2.1. Once that is established, the civil tax audit will be suspended without disclosing the reason to the taxpayer or his representative. Once the audit is suspended, the case is referred to CID. However, there is a risk that statements made to the revenue agent by the taxpayer may be used against him in any ensuing criminal proceeding. In *United States v. Kontny*, 238 F.3d 815 (7th Cir.), *cert. denied*, 532 U.S. 1022 (2001), the Court of Appeals for the Seventh Circuit stated:

> It is true that the Internal Revenue Service by regulation requires that a civil investigation cease when the investigator develops firm indications of fraud, Internal Revenue Manual sec. sec. 4565.21(1), 9311.83(1), which the Kontnys argued happened before the fatal interview and the check-shredding phone conversation. But the federal exclusionary rule, which forbids the use of evidence obtained in violation of the Fourth or Fifth Amendments, does not extend to violations of statutes and regulations. The Supreme Court so held in *United States v. Caceres*, 440 U.S. 741, 755 (1979),[2] with specific reference to a regulation of the IRS. * * * The Kontnys do not claim to have relied, reasonably or unreasonably, on the existence of the regulation that required [IRS Revenue Agent] Furnas to back off as soon as he obtained firm indications of fraud. *United States v. Caceres*, *supra*, 440 U.S. at 752–53; United States v. Ani, 138 F.3d 390, 392 (9th Cir. 1998); United States v. Pipes, 87 F.3d 840, 842 (6th Cir. 1996). But this means, as *Pipes* makes clear, that there was no causal relation between Furnas's alleged violation of the regulation and the Kontnys' decision to make incriminating statements. "The defendant obviously did not know that the officers were violating [the statute]. Thus, the officers' failure to comply with [it] had no impact on defendant's decision to commit the offense." *Id.* * * *

Once a case is referred to CID, if the CID Chief agrees that the case exhibits possible fraud, CID will assign a Special Agent to the case. If the Special Agent determines that the case warrants a full-scale investigation, the Special Agent will contact the taxpayer without prior notice, often early in the morning or late at night, accompanied by another agent who can serve as a corroborating witness to events. The agent must identify himself as a Special Agent and must also give the taxpayer a *Miranda*—type warning, as discussed in *Wohler,* reproduced below. The taxpayer is best advised to remain silent and retain counsel.

The Special Agent may use the summons power under section 7602, and in some circumstances, may obtain a search warrant. These techniques are discussed further below. After completing the investigation, the Special Agent prepares a report summarizing his findings and making a recommendation about prosecution. "In order to recommend criminal prosecution, the evidence must be sufficient to establish guilt beyond a reasonable doubt; and a reasonable probability of conviction must exist." Chief Counsel Directives Manual (CCDM) § (31)310. In addition,

> All the facts and circumstances surrounding a criminal tax case must be considered when deciding whether to recommend

---

[2] [*Caceres* is reproduced later in this chapter. Eds.]

prosecution. Consideration must be given to various factors, including but not limited to whether a voluntary disclosure was made, whether dual or successive prosecution exists, the health, age and mental condition of the taxpayer and whether solicitation of returns has occurred. The presence of any of the foregoing may impact on willfulness and significantly impair or eliminate the probability of conviction. * * *

CCDM § (31)320.

If the Special Agent recommends prosecution, CID forwards the case to IRS counsel, and CID normally sends a letter to the taxpayer notifying him of the transfer. The taxpayer is normally invited to a conference with an attorney from the Chief Counsel's Office or the IRS Criminal Tax Division. The objectives of the conference are to notify the taxpayer of the CID's recommendation, explain criminal tax procedures, and to afford the taxpayer an opportunity to present defenses and supply information that may be relevant to Counsel's ultimate determination of whether to refer the case to the Tax Division of the DOJ. Because these "docket attorneys" are not normally very experienced in criminal matters, they are predisposed to recommend that the matter be referred to DOJ. The taxpayer may present additional evidence and defenses of a technical or policy nature to the attorney at the conference. That attorney can also observe the taxpayer's demeanor, clarify admissions made by the taxpayer, and develop additional evidence regarding potential weaknesses in the case. Because Federal Rule of Evidence 408 makes evidence of settlement or attempted settlement of a disputed claim inadmissible when offered as admission of liability or the amount of liability, the IRS will not consider or discuss at the conference plea bargains, civil settlements, and/or compromise of tax liabilities.

If IRS counsel agrees with CID's recommendation of prosecution, it transfers the case to the Tax Division of the DOJ. There, an attorney experienced in criminal cases makes a final review of the case. If the taxpayer desires a conference, he or his attorney must request one in writing. Such conferences are held in Washington, D.C., and plea bargains may be considered. The DOJ attorney may decline prosecution, may refer the matter to the U.S. Attorney with or without discretion to prosecute, or may refer the matter to the U.S. Attorney with an authorization for a grand jury investigation.[3] If a case is referred for grand jury investigation, the U.S. Attorney may appoint the Special Agents who assist the investigation. The grand jury has special powers, discussed further below.

Before referral to DOJ, a taxpayer represented by counsel may enter a guilty plea, unless the taxpayer is accused of a tax crime arising out of income from illegal sources. The taxpayer is warned that a plea agreement will have no effect on his civil tax liability. If a represented taxpayer indicates an interest in plea discussions, the case is referred simultaneously to the DOJ and the U.S. Attorney. IRS counsel is contacted to determine whether the charges are accurate and whether there is sufficient evidence to support a guilty plea. If IRS counsel responds affirmatively, a modified Special Agent's Report is

---

[3] The U.S. Attorney, CID, and the Tax Division of DOJ are all empowered to initiate a grand jury investigation of a tax crime.

prepared and given to the U.S. Attorney. The U.S. Attorney conducts the plea discussions, but IRS counsel must also sign off on any agreement.

§ 14.03 Representing a Taxpayer During a Criminal Investigation

A taxpayer who is being investigated by CID should not speak to a Special Agent without the presence of counsel. The taxpayer generally should remain silent and let counsel do the talking. If the taxpayer consults counsel soon after the initial meeting, the attorney should contact the Special Agent to determine the scope of the investigation and to try to narrow it, if possible. The attorney should also review all the evidence, including the taxpayer's returns, to begin preparing the defense. In addition, the taxpayer is often best served by letting his attorney meet with the Special Agent outside his presence. Therefore, the attorney should submit to the investigating agents an executed power-of-attorney form as quickly as possible.

In general, counsel should advise the taxpayer not to cooperate with the Special Agent. Although a cooperative attitude may sometimes be a helpful strategy, cooperating with a Special Agent may simply provide more leads and evidence for the government. If the taxpayer volunteers information to the Special Agent, the agent may still contact others to corroborate that information, so the taxpayer may not save himself the embarrassment of having his affairs communicated to third parties. In addition, it is generally unwise to make an offer to a Special Agent to pay more tax, or to file an amended return. If, during the criminal investigation, the taxpayer admits an understatement of tax and files an amended return, the amended return probably will be used as evidence against the taxpayer in any criminal trial.

Communications between the taxpayer and counsel generally are protected by the attorney-client privilege, but communications shared with third parties lose their privileged status. Therefore, counsel should warn the taxpayer not to discuss the matter with anyone, including his accountant, relatives, friends, and coworkers.[4] The taxpayer should retrieve any business records being held by a third party, such as an accountant, because, if those records are in the taxpayer's possession, they may be protected by the privilege against self-incrimination. In addition, in order to obtain the benefit of the attorney-client privilege, if an accountant is needed, the attorney, not the taxpayer, should hire one. That accountant should be a different accountant than the one who prepared the return, in order to avoid arguments over which communications are privileged and which are not.

The study of the confidentiality and disclosure provisions required by the IRS Reform Act and performed by the Joint Committee on Taxation (released on January 28, 2000) included a section on disclosure of criminal investigation. That section recommends that IRS Special Agents identify themselves as Special Agents of the Criminal Investigation Division of the IRS to all third parties they contact during an investigation, and that agents inform those

---

[4] *See* Lee A. Sheppard, "What Tax Advice Privilege?", 80 Tax Notes 9 (1998) (discussing the new "federally authorized tax practitioner" privilege), reproduced in Chapter 1. Does the federally authorized tax practitioner privilege apply to criminal cases? *See* I.R.C. § 7525.

third parties as to the nature of the investigation (identifying by name the taxpayer who is the target of the investigation). This recommendation differs from that of the Treasury Department in its October 2000 report to Congress on confidentiality and disclosure. The Treasury recommended permitting but not requiring Special Agents to identify their affiliation and the criminal nature of their investigation. Notification to third parties of the criminal nature of the investigation of the taxpayer may help third parties take appropriate action to protect themselves. However, the disclosures may damage the reputation of the taxpayer under investigation regardless of whether he is ever indicted.

The strategy discussion above assumes that it is clear that the taxpayer is under criminal investigation. As discussed above, an audit should be suspended as soon as a revenue agent establishes a firm indication of fraud. The Internal Revenue Manual prohibits revenue agents from using a civil investigation to develop a criminal tax case against a taxpayer. *See* I.R.M. 104.6.8.5.3; *United States v. Powell*, 835 F.2d 1095, 1100 & n.12 (5th Cir. 1988). However, at times it can be difficult to ascertain when a civil investigation has ended and a criminal investigation has begun. The Court of Appeals for the Sixth Circuit recently commented:

> This case illustrates that the substantive distinction between an IRS civil audit and a criminal tax investigation is not always clear. As the district court put it in a manner reminiscent of the Watergate Hearings, the issues in this case are essentially: "(1) What did the IRS know about the McKees' individual and corporate tax affairs?; and (2) when did the IRS know it?"

United States v. McKee, 192 F.3d 535, 537 (6th Cir. 1999). In that case, the court upheld the IRS's use in a criminal prosecution of information obtained in a civil audit, although referral to CID arguably could have occurred earlier than it did. However, the court stated:

> It is particularly troubling that almost all of the government's evidence against the McKees was practically handed to the CID on a silver platter as a result of the civil investigation. Cases involving similar factual scenarios as the one *sub judice* are not in short supply. * * * We recognize that revenue agents are not charged with criminal law enforcement. Nevertheless, as this case exemplifies, the reality is that revenue agents sometimes perform the same functions of evidence gathering as their CID counterparts, and such evidence is often admissible at a criminal trial. Our nation's tax collection system is based on voluntary compliance. * * * If the IRS's internal operating procedures afford anything less than faithful adherence to constitutional guarantees, then public confidence in the IRS will necessarily be undermined. While we agree that the IRS's "firm indication of fraud" rule comports with the requirements of the Constitution, we do encourage revenue agents to err on the side of protecting taxpayers' constitutional rights when they conduct their investigations.

Id. at 544.

§ 14.04   IRS Investigatory Tools

[A]   Summons Authority

As you may recall from the discussion of the summons power in Chapter 2, Code section 7602 grants broad summons authority to the IRS. This summons power applies to both civil and criminal tax cases.[5] Code section 7609 provides authority for the IRS to summon third parties is order to obtain testimony concerning documents in the hands of the third party. In general, the taxpayer is entitled to receive notice of the third-party summons. *See* I.R.C. § 7609(a)(1), (c)(2). Note, however, that Code section 7605(b) prohibits "unnecessary" examinations and investigations. According to the Supreme Court, this subsection prohibits examinations conducted for an improper purpose. *See United States v. Powell*, 379 U.S. 48 (1964). Under this principle, a valid ground for objecting to a summons is that the IRS already has the information summoned. *Id.*

The application of sections 7602 and 7609 is considered in *Cermak*:

CERMAK v. UNITED STATES
United States Court of Appeals, Seventh Circuit
1997 U.S. App. LEXIS 13706; 79 A.F.T.R.2d (RIA) 3127

GILBERT, JUDGE:

Raymond and Judith Cermak failed to file federal income tax returns for the years 1992, 1993 and 1994. The IRS assigned Revenue Agent Ted Knapp to investigate their tax liabilities for those years. Knapp issued an administrative summons pursuant to 26 U.S.C. §§ 7602, 7609 to Boatmen's Bank of Mt. Vernon, the Cermaks' bank, to produce various financial records relating to the Cermaks. The Cermaks filed a petition to quash the summons, *see* 26 U.S.C. § 7609(b), which the district court denied. This appeal followed.

On appeal, the Cermaks first argue that the summons Knapp issued to Boatmen's Bank stated only that it was "issued under the authority of the Internal Revenue Code," but failed to specify under which section of the code it was issued. Accordingly, the Cermaks argue, the summons was invalid. This argument is meritless. Section 7602 gives the IRS the authority to summon witnesses and documents to verify the correctness of any tax return; section 7609 specifies the procedures to be followed in cases in which the documents summoned are in the possession of a third-party record keeper, such as a bank. Neither section requires the summons to specify the exact section of the Internal Revenue Code pursuant to which it was issued, and thus, we will not read into the statute such a requirement. *See* United States v. Euge, 444 U.S. 707, 711, 63 L. Ed. 2d 141, 100 S. Ct. 874 (1980) (the IRS's authority to issue summonses "should be upheld absent express statutory prohibition or substantial countervailing policies"); *see also* United States v. Arthur Young & Co., 465 U.S. 805, 816, 79 L. Ed. 2d 826, 104 S. Ct. 1495 (1984) ("The very language of § 7602 reflects . . . a congressional policy choice in favor of

---

[5] Chapter 2 discussed the summons power in the context of civil examinations. That material is not repeated here, although much of it applies in the criminal context as well.

disclosure of all information relevant to a legitimate IRS inquiry. In light of this explicit statement by the Legislative Branch, courts should be chary in recognizing exceptions to the broad summons authority of the IRS.").[n.1]

The Cermaks next contend that Agent Knapp has not been delegated the authority to issue summonses under section 7602. They argue that section 7602 authorizes the Secretary of the Treasury to issues summonses, and that the Secretary has delegated that authority to the Commissioner of the Internal Revenue Service pursuant to 26 C.F.R. section 301.7602-1(b). According to the Cermaks, the delegation of authority under section 7602 stops there, and hence, Agent Knapp had no authority to issue the summons. Not so: the Commissioner has, in turn, delegated the authority to issue summonses to revenue agents, such as Agent Knapp. *See* IRS Delegation Order No. 4 (Rev. 20), 55 Fed. Reg. 7626 (1990). United States v. Derr, 968 F.2d 943, 947 (9th Cir. 1992); *see also* Codner v. United States, 17 F.3d 1331, 1333 (10th Cir. 1994).

*   *   *

The Cermaks' third argument is that the summons Knapp issued was invalid because it was not signed under the penalties of perjury, as required by 26 U.S.C. section 6065. Section 6065 states:

> Any return, declaration, statement or other document required to be made under any provision of the internal revenue laws . . . shall contain or be verified by a written declaration that it is made under the penalties of perjury.

26 U.S.C. section 6065. The Cermaks would have us read out of section 6065 the phrase "required to be made" and thereby apply that section to any document made under any provision of the internal revenue laws. This we cannot do. Congress limited the applicability of section 6065 to only those documents "required to be made" under the internal revenue laws, and we must give effect to Congress's intent. The phrase "required to be made" limits the applicability of section 6065 to documents that must be filed with the IRS, and not documents issued by the IRS. Morelli v. Alexander, 920 F. Supp. 556, 558 (S.D.N.Y. 1996). The Internal Revenue Code does not require the IRS to issue any summonses at all; it merely authorizes the IRS to do so. Accordingly, a summons under section 7602 is not a document "required to be made" under

---

[n.1] The Cermaks state in their reply brief that they are not arguing that the summons must identify the section of the Internal Revenue Code under which it was issued in order to be valid; rather, they claim that "there was no summons issued under section 7602." Moreover, they maintain that Knapp issued the summons pursuant to 26 U.S.C. section 7608. They then submit that because Knapp is not an investigator in the Intelligence Division or the Internal Security Division of the IRS, he lacked the authority to issue a summons under section 7608. *See* 26 U.S.C. § 7608(b).

The Cermaks provide no explanation for their conclusion that the summons was issued pursuant to section 7608. They state only that the phrase " 'issued under [the] authority of the Internal Revenue Code' . . . would include Internal Revenue Code section 7608(a) . . . ." This argument makes no sense. The Cermaks may not choose under which section of the Internal Revenue Code Knapp issued the summons simply because the summons does not explicitly state that it was issued pursuant to section 7602. Agent Knapp lawfully could—and did—issue the summons in this case pursuant to section 7602.

the Internal Revenue Code, and hence, section 6065 is not applicable to this case.

The Cermaks next submit that under the Right to Financial Privacy Act, 12 U.S.C. section 3401–22, the IRS was not entitled to summon their financial records. But 12 U.S.C. section 3413(c) clearly states that "nothing in this chapter prohibits the disclosure of financial records in accordance with procedures authorized by Title 26." The Cermaks submit that section 3413(c) requires the IRS to comply with the requirements of section 7602 and section 7609 before a bank may disclose their financial records. But we have already rejected all of the Cermaks' challenges to the propriety of the summons issued to Boatmen's Bank, and thus, under section 3413(c), the IRS was entitled to access to the Cermaks' financial data.

Finally, the Cermaks argue that a summons issued under section 7602 and section 7609 is not self-enforcing, and that Boatmen's Bank was therefore not obligated to comply with the summons. Presumably, they mean that Boatmen's Bank could not comply with the summons absent a court order: The bank has already complied with the IRS's summons, and thus, if the Cermaks are contending only that compliance with a third-party summons is optional absent a court order, their argument would be irrelevant because the bank has chosen to comply with the summons. In any case, the Cermaks are incorrect. Section 7602 states:

> [T]he Secretary is authorized . . . to summon . . . any person having possession, custody, or care of books of account containing entries relating to the business of the person liable for tax . . . to appear before the Secretary . . . to produce such books, papers, records, or other data . . . .

26 U.S.C. section 7602(a)(2). By its own terms, section 7602 is self-enforcing. In the case of a third-party summons, section 7609 entitles persons identified in the summons (in this case, the Cermaks) to notice of the summons and the right to petition a district court to quash the summons. In such a proceeding to quash the summons, the Secretary may, in response, seek to compel compliance with the summons. 26 U.S.C. section 7609(b)(2)(A). But absent a proceeding to quash the summons under section 7609(b), the summons is self–enforcing, and the Secretary did not need to petition the court to compel compliance with the summons.

* * *

Is the *Cermak* court correct that a summons issued under section 7602 is self-enforcing? That is, does section 7602 allow the IRS to compel compliance or punish noncompliance? How may the IRS seek enforcement of a summons? *See* I.R.C. § 7402(b).

In *United States v. Arthur Young & Co.*, 465 U.S. 805 (1984), the United States Supreme Court considered whether summons of accountants' tax accrual workpapers was proper, or whether a privilege protected them from disclosure. First, the Court explained the importance of tax accrual workpapers:

> The independent auditor draws upon many sources in evaluating the sufficiency of the corporation's tax accrual account. Initially, the corporation's books, records, and tax returns must be analyzed in light of the relevant Code provisions, Treasury Regulations, Revenue Rulings, and case law. The auditor will also obtain and assess the opinions, speculations, and projections of management with regard to unclear, aggressive, or questionable tax positions that may have been taken on prior tax returns. In exploring the tax consequences of certain transactions, the auditor often engages in a "worst-case" analysis in order to ensure that the tax accrual account accurately reflects the full extent of the corporation's exposure to additional tax liability. From this conglomeration of data, the auditor is able to estimate the potential cost of each particular contingency, as well as the probability that the additional liability may arise.

> The auditor's tax accrual workpapers record this process of examination and analysis. Such workpapers may document the auditor's interviews with corporate personnel, judgments on questions of potential tax liability, and suggestions for alternative treatments of certain transactions for tax purposes. Tax accrual workpapers also contain an overall evaluation of the sufficiency of the corporation's reserve for contingent tax liabilities, including an item-by-item analysis of the corporation's potential exposure to additional liability. In short, tax accrual workpapers pinpoint the "soft spots" on a corporation's tax return by highlighting those areas in which the corporate taxpayer has taken a position that may, at some later date, require the payment of additional taxes.

Id. at 812–813.

The Court then considered whether a privilege should override the IRS's authority under section 7602:

> The Court of Appeals * * * concluded that "substantial countervailing policies," * * * required the fashioning of a work-product immunity for an independent auditor's tax accrual workpapers. To the extent that the Court of Appeals, in its concern for the "chilling effect" of the disclosure of tax accrual workpapers, sought to facilitate communication between independent auditors and their clients, its remedy more closely resembles a testimonial accountant-client privilege than a work-product immunity for accountants' workpapers. But as this Court stated in *Couch v. United States*, 409 U.S. 322, 335 (1973), "no confidential accountant-client privilege exists under federal law, and no state-created privilege has been recognized in federal cases." In light of *Couch*, the Court of Appeals' effort to foster candid communication between accountant and client by creating a self-styled work-product privilege was misplaced, and conflicts with what we see as the clear intent of Congress.

Nor do we find persuasive the argument that a work-product immunity for accountants' tax accrual workpapers is a fitting analogue to the attorney work-product doctrine established in *Hickman v. Taylor*, 329 U.S. 495 (1947). The *Hickman* work-product doctrine was founded upon the private attorney's role as the client's confidential adviser and advocate, a loyal representative whose duty it is to present the client's case in the most favorable possible light. An independent certified public accountant performs a different role. By certifying the public reports that collectively depict a corporation's financial status, the independent auditor assumes a public responsibility transcending any employment relationship with the client. The independent public accountant performing this special function owes ultimate allegiance to the corporation's creditors and stockholders, as well as to the investing public. This "public watchdog" function demands that the accountant maintain total independence from the client at all times and requires complete fidelity to the public trust. To insulate from disclosure a certified public accountant's interpretations of the client's financial statements would be to ignore the significance of the accountant's role as a disinterested analyst charged with public obligations.

Id. at 817–818. Does the statutory adoption in Code section 7525 of a "Federally Authorized Tax Practitioner" privilege (discussed in Chapter 1) overrule *Arthur Young & Co.*? If an identical case were to arise now, how should the Supreme Court decide it?

[B] Search Warrants

A Special Agent may request a search warrant in "significant" tax cases. Significance of the case depends on the amount of tax due, the nature of the fraud involved in the case, and the importance of the case for voluntary compliance. IRS Counsel must approve the agent's request for a warrant, and some requests must be approved by others as well. To obtain the warrant, the Special Agent must establish to a federal judge or magistrate that there is probable cause that the taxpayer has committed a tax crime and that evidence of the crime will be found on the premises to be searched. U.S. Const. Amend. IV; Fed. R. Crim. P. 41(e). The warrant must describe with particularity the place to be searched and the items to be seized. The following case considers the validity of a search warrant obtained on the basis of an informant's tip:

UNITED STATES v. LEFKOWITZ
United States Court of Appeals, Ninth Circuit[6]
618 F.2d 1313 (1980)

CHOY, CIRCUIT JUDGE:

Lefkowitz appeals from his convictions for various tax fraud offenses. He challenges the validity of the search warrants issued to search his home and his corporate offices, focusing on the failure of the supporting affidavit to

[6] *Cert. denied*, 449 U.S. 824 (1980).

disclose the identity of the IRS's secret informant: his estranged wife Helen. This failure, he says, prevented the magistrate from exercising an informed, independent judgment in issuing the warrants and renders the affidavit insufficient to support a finding of probable cause. He further argues that the privilege against adverse spousal testimony or the confidential marital communications privilege prohibits the use of his wife as an informant. We affirm.

I. STATEMENT OF THE CASE

Lefkowitz was convicted after a bench trial on stipulated facts of violating 18 U.S.C. §§ 371 and 1001 and 26 U.S.C. §§ 7201, 7203 and 7206(1). He was sentenced to four years imprisonment and placed on three years probation to begin after his prison term.

Lefkowitz was the president of several related small corporations, most of them in the car rental/leasing business. On June 12, 1975, IRS agents went to the Lefkowitz corporate offices, told Lefkowitz that he and his corporations were under investigation for possible violations of the tax laws and served him with a summons calling for the 1971–74 books and records of the Lefkowitz corporations to be produced at the IRS offices on June 23, 1975.

Sometime during the next week Lefkowitz, his lawyer Babic and his accountant Fisher met in Lefkowitz's private office to discuss the impending IRS document inspection. In response to Lefkowitz's concern over large cash shortages evidenced by the 1973 books for N/U Rent-A-Car, one of the Lefkowitz entities, Fisher jokingly suggested burning the books. The less drastic solution of rewriting the books was chosen, and a secret, separate office was rented in which Fisher could perform his cosmetic accounting.

On June 23, the three conspirators met with agents at the IRS offices and Babic represented that the records called for in the summons did not exist or had been lost or destroyed. The date of July 14, 1975 was set for the production of whatever records could be found by then.

The next week Lefkowitz, with the help of his secretary Patricia Sullivan, Fisher, Mark Nestico (an employee) and Helen Lefkowitz, moved boxes of corporate records to Sullivan's apartment. On July 14, the IRS agents were given the then-completed spurious 1973 N/U Rent-A-Car records.

On November 7 and 10, 1975, IRS agents received information from a confidential source (later revealed to be Helen Lefkowitz). She told the agents about the falsified books and about the removal of the original records to Sullivan's apartment, and added that some of the original records had been moved back into the corporate offices after July 14, when the false N/U Rent-A-Car documents had been produced. She had seen these records in the corporate offices as late as mid-October.

On November 17, an IRS agent interviewed Nestico, who admitted that on Lefkowitz's instructions he had helped move some boxes of records from the Sullivan apartment to Lefkowitz's residence, where he had seen them as late as the end of October. Nestico also saw records in the corporate offices at the end of October.

On the basis of an affidavit by IRS agent Laffer reciting this and other information, search warrants were issued on November 17 for the Lefkowitz corporate offices and Lefkowitz's residence. The affidavit did not reveal that the secret informant was Helen Lefkowitz. Much of the evidence used to convict Lefkowitz was obtained through the execution of these warrants.

II. THE NONDISCLOSURE THAT THE SECRET INFORMANT WAS HELEN LEFKOWITZ

* * *

The affidavit is clearly sufficient on its face to support a finding of probable cause. The information from the two hearsay sources satisfied both prongs of the *Aguilar* [*v. Texas*, 378 U.S. 108, 111 (1964)] test.

B. The Challenge to the Affidavit

Lefkowitz argues, however, that this court should look beyond the four corners of the affidavit and consider its sufficiency given Helen's identity and the accompanying credibility problems.

In *Franks v. Delaware*, 438 U.S. 154, 98 S. Ct. 2674, 57 L. Ed. 2d 667 (1978), the Supreme Court held that in order to challenge an affidavit valid on its face, a defendant must show (1) the affidavit contains intentionally or recklessly false statements, and (2) the affidavit purged of its falsities would not be sufficient to support a finding of probable cause.

Lefkowitz satisfies neither of these requirements. He asserts no intent or recklessness in the omission of Helen's identity (in fact, Laffer swore that he offered the identity to the magistrate, who declined it). Moreover, even if the affiant had revealed Helen's identity, the affidavit still would have sufficed to support a finding of probable cause to issue search warrants.

True, Helen Lefkowitz was the estranged wife of the appellant and as such may have had motivation to contact the IRS other than a sense of civic duty. After being married for 23 years, appellant and Helen Lefkowitz separated in August 1975. Appellant began living with Sullivan, his secretary, in September 1975. Helen Lefkowitz contacted the IRS in November 1975. The Lefkowitzes were eventually divorced in 1977. Inferences of spite, vengeance, and perhaps a desire to obtain advantageous property settlement information via an IRS investigation might spring from this scenario. However, the district court expressly found that the magistrate could have found Helen credible even considering her identity, and thus the affidavit would support a finding of probable cause even if the omission was cured. This is not, therefore, a case like *United States v. Esparza*, 546 F.2d 841 (9th Cir. 1976), where the misinformation was crucial to the finding of probable cause; rather, it is more like *United States v. Taxe*, 540 F.2d 961, 967 (9th Cir. 1976), *cert. denied,* 429 U.S. 1040, 97 S. Ct. 737, 50 L. Ed. 2d 751 (1977), where omissions from an affidavit were deemed immaterial. The district court's determination here was not clearly erroneous.

The nondisclosure of Helen Lefkowitz's identity does not require us to look beyond the four corners of the facially valid affidavit under the *Franks v. Delaware* test. Even considering her identity, she could still be found a credible informant.[n.4]

III. THE PRIVILEGE AGAINST ADVERSE SPOUSAL TESTIMONY AND THE CONFIDENTIAL MARITAL COMMUNICATIONS PRIVILEGE

Although Lefkowitz confuses these privileges, they are distinct. *See* United States v. Bolzer, 556 F.2d 948, 951 (9th Cir. 1977). The first can be invoked to prevent one spouse from testifying against the other.[n.6] * * * The second can be invoked to prevent the disclosure of confidential communications arising out of the marital relationship. * * *

The privilege against adverse spousal testimony is of no use to Lefkowitz here because his wife did not "testify" against him, but provided information used to support the issuance of a search warrant. * * * Moreover, this privilege does not preclude the use of a wife's statements against a defendant husband at trial when they are testified to by a third person. United States v. Tsinnijinnie, 601 F.2d 1035 (9th Cir. 1979). Here, Helen Lefkowitz did not personally appear before the magistrate; her information was recited in the affidavit of a third person. Therefore, the privilege did not bar this use of her statements.

The confidential marital communications privilege is also unavailable to Lefkowitz. It applies only to utterances or expressions intended to be communicative (i.e., to convey a message from one spouse to the other) *and* confidential. * * *

The information Helen Lefkowitz provided to the IRS concerned the following facts: (1) the records turned over to the IRS were fraudulent; (2) the original records were removed from the corporate offices; (3) some of these records were moved to Sullivan's apartment; and (4) some of the original records were later moved back into the corporate offices (where they eventually were seized).[n.7]

Her information that the records given to the IRS were false and that some of the original records were moved back into the corporate offices and remained there was based on her personal observations. There was no communicative utterance or expression by her husband and therefore her divulgence of this information did not violate the confidential marital communications privilege. *See* United States v. Bolzer, 556 F.2d at 951.

[n.4] Lefkowitz's argument that the affidavit fails to support a finding of probable cause that a federal offense had been committed is frivolous. Even if Helen's information were to be disregarded, the affidavit was replete with information from the IRS's own files and investigations which showed that tax offenses had been committed.

[n.6] This privilege is sometimes called the "antimarital facts" privilege. *E.g.,* United States v. Bolzer, 556 F.2d 948, 951 (9th Cir. 1977). This term is descriptively inaccurate and perhaps contributes to the confusion of the two privileges. We shall therefore refer to the first privilege as the privilege against adverse spousal testimony.

[n.7] Nestico, not Mrs. Lefkowitz, asserted that some of the records were to be found in the Lefkowitz residence. His information suffers from no infirmity. * * *

The original records were removed from the corporate offices in the presence, and with the assistance, of Sullivan, Fisher and Nestico. Even assuming such actions were communicative, *see generally* United States v. Lewis, 140 U.S. App. D.C. 40, 44–45, 433 F.2d 1146, 1150–51 (D.C. Cir. 1970), the presence of others destroys confidentiality and renders the privilege inapplicable. *See* Pereira v. United States, 347 U.S. 1, 6, 74 S. Ct. 358, 98 L. Ed. 435 (1954); United States v. Lustig, [555 F.2d 737, 748 (9th Cir. 1977), *cert. denied*, 434 U.S. 1045 (1978)].

The only information based on a communication by Lefkowitz and arguably intended as confidential was that some records were moved to Sullivan's apartment. This piece of information can easily be disregarded without impairing the sufficiency of the affidavit. Nestico, the other informant relied on in the affidavit, provided essentially the same information, stating that he personally moved boxes of records, of a description strikingly similar to Mrs. Lefkowitz's description of the boxes of records she helped move, from Sullivan's apartment to the Lefkowitz residence. The fact that these records were ever in the Sullivan apartment, moreover, was not essential, because that apartment was never searched. The nature of these records was sufficiently demonstrated to the magistrate by the fact that Lefkowitz had warned Nestico not to tell anyone about them. The affidavit was therefore sufficient even disregarding Helen Lefkowitz's and Nestico's information about the Sullivan apartment.

Thus, neither the privilege against adverse spousal testimony nor the confidential marital communications privilege precluded the use of any facts obtained from Helen Lefkowitz which were essential to the sufficiency of the affidavit.

Lefkowitz finally contends that these marital privileges are somehow grounded in various constitutional amendments and implement a constitutionally-protected right of marital privacy. These privileges, however, do not have constitutional underpinnings. United States v. Doe, 478 F.2d 194 (1st Cir. 1973).

IV. CONCLUSION

The nondisclosure of Helen Lefkowitz's identity as the IRS's secret informant was not fatal to the affidavit. The privileges against adverse spousal testimony and of confidential marital communications do not preclude the use of any information essential to the sufficiency of the affidavit. Therefore, the search warrants were properly issued.

Affirmed.

---

§ 14.05 Methods of Proof

Chapter 2 considered, in the civil context, various methods, such as the "net worth method," that the IRS uses to reconstruct a taxpayer's income where the taxpayer's records are false or inadequate. The IRS also uses those techniques in criminal tax cases. In fact, *Holland v. United States*, 348 U.S.

121 (1954), the leading United States Supreme Court case on the net worth method, was a criminal case. *Holland* is discussed both in *Schwarzkopf,* reproduced in Chapter 2, and in the *Smith* case reproduced below. Consider Smith's arguments about the IRS's use of the net worth method and the specific items method, as well as the court's discussion of the rule that the IRS must show a "likely source" of taxable but unreported income.

UNITED STATES v. SMITH
United States Court of Appeals, Fifth Circuit
890 F.2d 711 (1989)

LITTLE, DISTRICT JUDGE:

The conviction of Bobby M. Smith on one of four counts of tax evasion prompts this appeal. We affirm the conviction.

BACKGROUND

Smith was convicted of the willful attempt to evade the payment of income tax for calendar year 1983. Specifically, the count of the indictment upon which Smith was convicted provides in part:

> That on or about July 16, 1989, . . . Bobby M. Smith . . . did willfully attempt to evade and defeat a large part of the income tax due and owing by him and his spouse to the United States of America for the calendar year 1983 by preparing and causing to be prepared, and by signing and causing to be signed, a false and fraudulent joint U.S. Individual Income Tax Return Form 1040, on behalf of himself and his spouse, which was filed with the Internal Revenue Service, wherein it was stated that there was a negative taxable income for said calendar year of $10,507.20, and that the amount due and owing thereon was zero, whereas, as he then and there well knew and believed, their joint taxable income for the said calendar year was the sum of $81,361.30, upon which said joint taxable income there was owing to the United States of America an income tax of $29,570.64. In violation of Title 26, United States Code, Section 7201.

Smith asserts that the jury verdict requires reversal as it was contrary to the law and the weight of the evidence in six specific areas. Alternatively, Smith seeks a new trial claiming that he was prejudiced by the trial tactics of the government representatives. We will address each of appellant's concerns. We will measure those concerns by this circuit's standard of review which requires us to uphold a jury's verdict unless that verdict is based upon record evidence which no rational trier of fact could have found guilt beyond a reasonable doubt. United States v. Montalvo, 820 F.2d 686, 688 (5th Cir. 1987).

APPELLANT'S OPENING NET WORTH

Before discussing the error asserted by appellant, it is best for us to describe generally the mechanics of a net worth case. An income tax return reflects the taxpayer's statement to the government that the taxpayer received money (or items of value) and that the receipts, after appropriate deduction, were subject to the applicable tax. The government may question a taxpayer's voluntary disclosure and certification of correctness by employing one or both of two generally accepted analytical methods. The government can present evidence that a specific item of income was not disclosed on the return, i.e., taxpayer did not include wages from his employment with XYZ Corporation or his interest income from a savings account with ABC Homestead. The government may also demonstrate that specific deductions were not experienced by the taxpayer, or were inflated. This procedure is known as the specific items theory. Another method which may be employed is the net worth analysis. Simply stated, an increase in a taxpayer's patrimony must be traced to acquisitions with after tax income, donations or non-taxable transactions. If these sources fail to explain the increase and the increase can reasonably be attributed to sources which should have been reported, but were not, the taxpayer may well be convicted of tax fraud.

The government utilized both the specific items method and the net worth method in prosecuting its case against the taxpayer. For the return year of the taxpayer's defeat, 1983, only the net worth method was invoked. The net worth method has long been approved as a tool to prove a willful violation as required by 26 U.S.C. § 7201. *See* Holland [v. United States], 348 U.S. 121, 75 S. Ct. 127, 99 L. Ed. 150 (1954); *Tax Management Criminal Tax Procedure,* 162-Second A10–13. Essential to this methodology is the taxpayer's opening net worth. The government must prove the taxpayer's opening net worth for calendar year 1983 with reasonable certainty. *Holland,* 348 U.S. at 132; United States v. Terrell, 754 F.2d 1139, 1146 (5th Cir.), *cert. denied,* 472 U.S. 1029, 105 S. Ct. 3505, 87 L. Ed. 2d 635 (1985); United States v. Sorrentino, 726 F.2d 876 (1st Cir. 1984). We join the Seventh Circuit in observing that sloppy or mediocre financial and accounting evaluation upon which a conviction is obtained can be the genesis for reversal. United States v. Achilli, 234 F.2d 797 (7th Cir. 1956), *aff'd on other grounds,* 353 U.S. 373, 1 L. Ed. 2d 918, 77 S. Ct. 995 (1957).

But evidence of irresponsible accounting and financial analysis is lacking in the instant case. The contrary is revealed by the record. Agent Lindsay's testimony as to the taxpayer's cash on hand of $31,234 was supported by evidence that the taxpayer possessed three cashier's checks and cash totalling that sum. While we recognize that slipshod methods of financial analysis will not be tolerated, one need not be letter perfect. Reasonable certainty is required but not mathematical exactitude. *Terrell,* 754 F.2d at 1146. At no time during the investigation did the defendant or his spouse disclose evidence of a cash hoard. At trial the defendant's spouse claimed to have cash in a vase in the sum of $23,000, that she had paid $23,000 cash for an automobile and that she saved a large sum of money from cash gifts from her parents. The existence and source of these cash transactions were never disclosed to the investigating agent. The defendant's spouse merely told the agent about a small amount of cash on hand and didn't believe the agent's questions were applicable to other funds and transactions. To the same extent, the taxpayer concludes that a corporation was a receptacle of his funds and that the value of the corporation should be included in the opening net worth. There is no evidence that funds were diverted by the taxpayer to his corporation or that the corporation had assets actually belonging to the taxpayer or that the taxpayer parked assets in the corporate name. The government's opening net worth conclusions had firm support in fact and were prepared with reasonable certainty. The return subject to scrutiny was that filed for calendar year 1983. Loan repayments to the taxpayer in other years were too remote to enter into an opening inventory figure.

The defendant's argument as to the appreciated value of the family home not having been accounted for by the agent is also without merit. The house was built in 1975 at a cost unknown to the taxpayer. The house was owned by the taxpayer at the beginning and end of the year in question. The unaccounted for appreciation, if any, plays no part in this controversy. It's absence does not distort the opening or closing inventory. United States v. Schafer, 580 F.2d 774, 778 (5th Cir.), *cert. denied,* 439 U.S. 970, 99 S. Ct. 463, 58 L. Ed. 2d 430 (1978).

The complaint that the opening net worth figure for 1983 does not include bearer bonds owned by the taxpayer is without effect. The agent was unable to establish the year of acquisition or the cost of the investment. The agent did remove from net worth calculations all interest paid on the bonds as well as money received by the taxpayer for bond redemption. Again, distortion is absent.

FAMILY NET WORTH

Another area of alleged defective analysis is the failure of the government to exclude assets of the defendant's spouse and child. The agent testified, and her schedules reveal, that the income of the defendant's daughter and gifts to defendant's wife and daughter were excluded before arriving at a final net worth determination. The agent did not present a family net worth calculation. Only the financial condition of defendant and spouse appears. No confusion or adulteration is present. The fabric of the financial blanket is so closely woven that a computation of net worth on the joint income of the spouses is clearly permissible. *See* United States v. Brown, 667 F.2d 566 (6th Cir. 1982); United States v. Giacalone, 574 F.2d 328 (6th Cir.), *cert. denied*, 439 U.S. 834, 99 S. Ct. 114, 58 L. Ed. 2d 129 (1978).

A LIKELY SOURCE OF TAXABLE, BUT UNREPORTED INCOME

The government is required to prove likely sources of unreported income or negate nontaxable sources of income. *Holland,* 348 U.S. at 137; United States v. Massei, 355 U.S. 595, 78 S. Ct. 495, 2 L. Ed. 2d 517 (1958). A likely source of income, according to the government, was proved when evidence was presented showing that defendant actively participated in the operations of businesses which he owned including furniture stores, a jewelry store, a cemetery monument company, a pawn shop and a recreational center. Further, the defendant's investments included producing mineral interests, real estate and stock, bonds and commodities. The record reflects that all of those endeavors provided liquid funds. Evidence was also presented that defendant engaged in gambling activities involving significant sums. Thus, a likely source of non-reported but taxable income was clearly indicated. "Proof of a likely source from which the jury could reasonably find that the net worth increases sprang is sufficient." *Holland,* 348 U.S. at 138.

FAILURE TO NEGATE THE EXISTENCE OF NON-TAXABLE SOURCES OF MONEY

The defendant also asserts that the government failed to negate the presence of non-taxable funds. The government counters that the only lead given it by defendant was family gifts from defendant's in-laws. The record reflects that the agent did make deductions for gifts and inheritances. Gift deductions were allowed to the maximum authorized by law. No evidence exists that taxpayer received gifts in excess of the statutory non-taxable amount. In fact, gift tax records for defendant's in-laws were examined for the years 1975 through 1983. No returns were unearthed supporting gifts in excess of the amounts deducted by the government. The examination conducted by the government was thorough within the meaning of *Massei* and *United States v. Hiett,* 581 F.2d 1199, 1202 (5th Cir. 1978). The government did what was required. It made a reasonable investigation into the only lead supplied by the taxpayer, and the taxpayer received the maximum benefit from that lead.

* * *

PREJUDICIAL TRIAL TACTICS

* * *

Over the defendant's objection, evidence of the defendant's proclivity to gamble was introduced. The evidence was relevant to prove a likely source of unexpected income. The defendant's complaint is based on the government's pretrial denial that it would introduce the defendant's gambling escapades and that the probative evidence of social misconduct is outweighed by its prejudicial effect. The defendant's concerns are misplaced as the trial court did not abuse its discretion. [United States v.] Reed, [715 F.2d 870 (5th Cir. 1983)] 715 F.2d at 875. When confronted with knowledge that evidence of gambling would be introduced, counsel for the defendant complained but refused the court's offer to request a continuance of the trial. The trial judge afforded the defendant's counsel time to interview the government's witnesses on the issue of gambling. No prejudice to the defendant resulted. * * *

As we have stated, the government is required, under *Holland,* 348 U.S. at 137, to demonstrate a likely source of unreported income. If that likely source is gambling winnings, then the evidence of gambling is relevant and admissible. Suppression of that evidence cannot be denied when the government is required to disclose that very evidence. [United States v.] Tunnell, [481 F.2d 149, 151 (5th Cir. 1973), *cert. denied,* 415 U.S. 948 (1974)].

Refusal to give five jury instructions is the final trial error on the defendant's schedule. We must review the court's charge in its entirety and in the light of the trial and closing argument. * * *

The trial judge refused defendant's instruction # 39. The desired instruction, as submitted, reads:

> The government has utilized the net worth method of proof in this case. Any proof as to any specific items of omitted income may be considered by you only as corroborative evidence of the net worth proof.

> The trial court properly refused to give charge # 39. The government used a two prong approach to demonstrate taxable income omissions by the defendant on four annual tax returns. One was circumstantial proof of a net worth increase from other than reported income. The other was direct proof of specific items of income which the taxpayer had failed to report. *Holland* supports the government's methodology. Taxpayer's reliance in this circuit's decision in United States v. Horton, 526 F.2d 884 (5th Cir.), *cert. denied,* 429 U.S. 820, 97 S. Ct. 67, 50 L. Ed. 2d 81 (1976), is misplaced. The *Horton* case involved bank deposits to corroborate specific items of income (receipt of attorney fees from clients) which the taxpayer neglected to report on his returns. But, as we have said, the government used the bank deposits as circumstantial evidence of unreported income *in addition* to specific items of unreported income. In sum, the instructions given and those refused present no reversible error.

Affirmed.

––––––––––––––––

Note that if the government uses an indirect method of proving income, such as the net worth method, it may review not only the tax years in question, but also prior or subsequent tax years. Therefore, it is important for the attorney to obtain that information from the taxpayer, in order to prepare the defense.

§ 14.06   Defense Techniques

The defense has a variety of available strategies, some of which are discussed above. For example, the defense should be prepared to make privilege claims for anything protected by the attorney-client or work product privilege. This section focuses on the possibility of claiming the protections of the Fifth Amendment or Fourth Amendment in a tax prosecution.

[A] Pleading the Fifth Amendment with Respect to Tax Return Information

The Fifth Amendment to the Constitution protects a witness from testifying against himself. Should the privilege against self-incrimination protect against the requirement of filing a tax return or answering specific questions, if the return information or answers might be incriminating? What if the taxpayer's occupation is "narcotics dealer," a patently illegal occupation? What if the taxpayer's occupation is "gambler," which may include legal and illegal activities? Consider how the Supreme Court handled this in *Garner*.

GARNER v. UNITED STATES
United States Supreme Court
424 U.S. 648 (1976)

MR. JUSTICE POWELL delivered the opinion of the Court.

This case involves a nontax criminal prosecution in which the Government introduced petitioner's income tax returns to prove the offense against him. The question is whether the introduction of this evidence, over petitioner's Fifth Amendment objection, violated the privilege against compulsory self-incrimination when petitioner made the incriminating disclosures on his returns instead of then claiming the privilege.

I.

Petitioner, Roy Garner, was indicted for a conspiracy involving the use of interstate transportation and communication facilities to "fix" sporting contests, to transmit bets and information assisting in the placing of bets, and to distribute the resultant illegal proceeds. 18 U.S.C. §§ 371, 224, 1084, 1952. The Government's case was that conspirators bet on horse races either having fixed them or while in possession of other information unavailable to the general public. Garner's role in this scheme was the furnishing of inside information. The case against him included the testimony of other conspirators and telephone toll records that showed calls from Garner to other conspirators before various bets were placed.

The Government also introduced, over Garner's Fifth Amendment objection, the Form 1040 income tax returns that Garner had filed for 1965, 1966, and 1967. In the 1965 return Garner had reported his occupation as "professional gambler," and in each return he reported substantial income from "gambling" or "wagering." The prosecution relied on Garner's familiarity with "the business of wagering and gambling," as reflected in his returns, to help rebut his claim that his relationships with other conspirators were innocent ones.

The jury returned a guilty verdict. Garner appealed to the Court of Appeals for the Ninth Circuit, contending that the privilege against compulsory self-incrimination entitled him to exclude the tax returns despite his failure to claim the privilege on the returns instead of making disclosures. Sitting en banc the Court of Appeals held that Garner's failure to assert the privilege on his returns defeated his Fifth Amendment claim. 501 F. 2d 236. We agree.

II.

In *United States v. Sullivan*, 274 U.S. 259 (1927), the Court held that the privilege against compulsory self-incrimination is not a defense to prosecution for failing to file a return at all. But the Court indicated that the privilege could be claimed against specific disclosures sought on a return, saying:

> "If the form of return provided called for answers that the defendant was privileged from making he could have raised the objection in the return, but could not on that account refuse to make any return at all." *Id.,* at 263.[n.3]

Had Garner invoked the privilege against compulsory self-incrimination on his tax returns in lieu of supplying the information used against him, the Internal Revenue Service could have proceeded in either or both of two ways. First, the Service could have sought to have Garner criminally prosecuted under § 7203 of the Internal Revenue Code of 1954 (Code), 26 U.S.C. § 7203, which proscribes, among other things, the willful failure to make a return. Second, the Service could have sought to complete Garner's returns administratively "from [its] own knowledge and from such information as [it could] obtain through testimony or otherwise." 26 U.S.C. § 6020 (b)(1). Section 7602(2) of the Code authorizes the Service in such circumstances to summon the taxpayer to appear and to produce records or give testimony. 26 U.S.C. § 7602(2). If Garner had persisted in his claim when summoned, the Service could have sued for enforcement in district court, subjecting Garner to the threat of the court's contempt power. 26 U.S.C. § 7604.

Given *Sullivan,* it cannot fairly be said that taxpayers are "volunteers" when they file their tax returns. The Government compels the filing of a return much as it compels, for example, the appearance of a "witness" before a grand jury. The availability to the Service of § 7203 prosecutions and the summons procedure also induces taxpayers to disclose unprivileged information on their returns. The question, however, is whether the Government can be said to have compelled Garner to incriminate himself with regard to specific disclosures made on his return when he could have claimed the Fifth Amendment privilege instead.

III.

We start from the fundamental proposition:

> "[A] witness protected by the privilege may rightfully refuse to answer unless and until he is protected at least against the use of his compelled answers and evidence derived therefrom in any subsequent criminal case in which he is a defendant. Kastigar v. United States, 406 U.S. 441 (1972). Absent such protection, if he is nevertheless compelled to answer, his answers are inadmissible against him in a later criminal prosecution. Bram v. United States, [168 U.S. 532 (1897)]; Boyd v. United States, [116 U.S. 616 (1886)]." Lefkowitz v. Turley, 414 U.S. 70, 78 (1973).

[n.3] In *Sullivan,* Mr. Justice Holmes, writing for the Court, said: "It would be an extreme if not an extravagant application of the Fifth Amendment to say that it authorized a man to refuse to state the amount of his income because it had been made in crime. But if the defendant desired to test that or any other point he should have tested it in the return so that it could be passed upon." 274 U.S., at 263–264. We have no occasion in this case to decide what types of information are so neutral that the privilege could rarely, if ever, be asserted to prevent their disclosure. *See also* California v. Byers, 402 U.S. 424 (1971). Further, the claims of privilege we consider here are only those justified by a fear of self-incrimination other than under the tax laws. Finally, nothing we say here questions the continuing validity of *Sullivan's* holding that returns must be filed.

See Murphy v. Waterfront Comm'n, 378 U.S. 52, 57 n.6 (1964).

Because the privilege protects against the use of compelled statements as well as guarantees the right to remain silent absent immunity, the inquiry in a Fifth Amendment case is not ended when an incriminating statement is made in lieu of a claim of privilege. Nor, however, is failure to claim the privilege irrelevant.

The Court has held that an individual under compulsion to make disclosures as a witness who revealed information instead of claiming the privilege lost the benefit of the privilege. United States v. Kordel, 397 U.S. 1, 7–10 (1970). Although *Kordel* appears to be the only square holding to this effect, the Court frequently has recognized the principle in dictum. Maness v. Meyers, 419 U.S. 449, 466 (1975); Rogers v. United States, 340 U.S. 367, 370–371 (1951); Smith v. United States, 337 U.S. 137, 150 (1949); United States v. Monia, 317 U.S. 424, 427 (1943); Vajtauer v. Commissioner of Immigration, 273 U.S. 103, 112–113 (1927). These decisions stand for the proposition that, in the ordinary case, if a witness under compulsion to testify makes disclosures instead of claiming the privilege, the Government has not "compelled" him to incriminate himself.[n.9]

> "The Amendment speaks of compulsion. It does not preclude a witness from testifying voluntarily in matters which may incriminate him. If, therefore, he desires the protection of the privilege, he must claim it or he will not be considered to have been 'compelled' within the meaning of the Amendment."

United States v. Monia, supra, at 427 (footnote omitted).

In their insistence upon a claim of privilege, *Kordel* and the older witness cases reflect an appropriate accommodation of the Fifth Amendment privilege and the generally applicable principle that governments have the right to everyone's testimony. * * * Despite its cherished position, the Fifth Amendment addresses only a relatively narrow scope of inquiries. Unless the Government seeks testimony that will subject its giver to criminal liability, the constitutional right to remain silent absent immunity does not arise. An individual therefore properly may be compelled to give testimony, for example, in a noncriminal investigation of himself. *See, e.g.,* Gardner v. Broderick, 392 U.S. 273, 278 (1968). Unless a witness objects, a government ordinarily may assume that its compulsory processes are not eliciting testimony that he

---

[n.9] This conclusion has not always been couched in the language used here. Some cases have indicated that a nonclaiming witness has "waived" the privilege, *see, e.g.,* Vajtauer v. Commissioner of Immigration, 273 U.S. 103, 113 (1927). Others have indicated that such a witness testifies "voluntarily," *see, e.g.,* Rogers v. United States, *supra,* at 371. Neither usage seems analytically sound. The cases do not apply a "waiver" standard as that term was used in *Johnson v. Zerbst,* 304 U.S. 458 (1938), and we recently have made clear that an individual may lose the benefit of the privilege without making a knowing and intelligent waiver. *See* Schneckloth v. Bustamonte, 412 U.S. 218, 222–227, 235–240, 246–247 (1973). Moreover, it seems desirable to reserve the term "waiver" in these cases for the process by which one affirmatively renounces the protection of the privilege, *see, e.g.,* Smith v. United States, 337 U.S. 137, 150 (1949). The concept of "voluntariness" is related to the concept of "compulsion." But it may promote clarity to use the latter term in cases where disclosures are required in the face of a claim of privilege, while reserving "voluntariness" for the concerns discussed in Part IV, *infra,* * * *, where we consider whether some factor prevents a taxpayer desiring to claim the privilege from doing so.

deems to be incriminating. Only the witness knows whether the apparently innocent disclosure sought may incriminate him, and the burden appropriately lies with him to make a timely assertion of the privilege. If, instead, he discloses the information sought, any incriminations properly are viewed as not compelled. In addition, the rule that a witness must claim the privilege is consistent with the fundamental purpose of the Fifth Amendment — the preservation of an adversary system of criminal justice. *See* Tehan v. United States ex rel. Shott, 382 U.S. 406, 415 (1966). That system is undermined when a government deliberately seeks to avoid the burdens of independent investigation by compelling self-incriminating disclosures. In areas where a government cannot be said to be compelling such information, however, there is no such circumvention of the constitutionally mandated policy of adversary criminal proceedings. * * *

IV.

The information revealed in the preparation and filing of an income tax return is, for purposes of Fifth Amendment analysis, the testimony of a "witness," as that term is used herein. Since Garner disclosed information on his returns instead of objecting, his Fifth Amendment claim would be defeated by an application of the general requirement that witnesses must claim the privilege. Garner, however, resists the application of that requirement, arguing that incriminating disclosures made in lieu of objection are "compelled" in the tax-return context. He relies specifically on three situations in which incriminatory disclosures have been considered compelled despite a failure to claim the privilege. But in each of these narrowly defined situations, some factor not present here made inappropriate the general rule that the privilege must be claimed. In each situation the relevant factor was held to deny the individual a "free choice to admit, to deny, or to refuse to answer." Lisenba v. California, 314 U.S. 219, 241 (1941). For the reasons stated below, we conclude that no such factor deprived Garner of that free choice.

A.

Garner relies first on cases dealing with coerced confessions, *e.g., Miranda v. Arizona*, 384 U.S. 436 (1966), where the Court has required the exclusion of incriminating statements unless there has been a knowing and intelligent waiver of the privilege regardless of whether the privilege has been claimed. *Id.,* at 467–469, 475–477. Garner notes that it has not been shown that his failure to claim the privilege was such a waiver. It is evident that these cases have little to do with disclosures on a tax return. The coerced-confession cases present the entirely different situation of custodial interrogation. *See id.,* at 467. It is presumed that without proper safeguards the circumstances of custodial interrogation deny an individual the ability freely to choose to remain silent. *See ibid.* At the same time, the inquiring government is acutely aware of the potentially incriminatory nature of the disclosures sought. Thus, any pressures inherent in custodial interrogation are compulsions to incriminate, not merely compulsions to make unprivileged disclosures. Because of the danger that custodial interrogation posed to the adversary system favored by the privilege, the Court in *Miranda* was impelled to adopt the extraordinary safeguard of excluding statements made without a knowing and intelligent waiver of the privilege. * * * Nothing in this case suggests the need for a similar presumption that a taxpayer makes disclosures on his return rather than claims the privilege because his will is overborne. In fact, a taxpayer, who can complete his return at leisure and with legal assistance, is even less subject to the psychological pressures at issue in *Miranda* than a witness who has been called to testify in judicial proceedings. *Cf. United States v. Kordel*, 397 U.S., at 9–10; *Miranda, supra,* at 461.

B.

Garner relies next on *Mackey v. United States*, 401 U.S. 667 (1971), the relevance of which can be understood only in light of *Marchetti v. United States*, 390 U.S. 39 (1968), and *Grosso v. United States*, 390 U.S. 62 (1968). In the latter cases the Court considered whether the Fifth Amendment was a defense in prosecutions for failure to file the returns required of gamblers in connection with the federal occupational and excise taxes on gambling. The Court found that any disclosures made in connection with the payment of those taxes tended to incriminate because of the pervasive criminal regulation of gambling activities. *Marchetti, supra,* at 48–49; *Grosso, supra*, at 66–67. Since submitting a claim of privilege in lieu of the returns also would incriminate, the Court held that the privilege could be exercised by simply failing to file.[n.11]

In *Mackey,* the disclosures required in connection with the gambling excise tax had been made before *Marchetti* and *Grosso* were decided. Mackey's returns were introduced in a criminal prosecution for income tax evasion. Although a majority of the Court considered the disclosure on the returns to have been compelled incriminations, 401 U.S., at 672 (plurality opinion); *id.,* at 704–705 (Brennan, J., concurring in judgment); *id.,* at 713 (Douglas, J., dissenting), Mackey was not immunized against their use because *Marchetti* and *Grosso* were held nonretroactive. 401 U.S., at 674–675 (plurality opinion); *id.,* at 700–701 (Harlan, J., concurring in judgment). Garner assumes that if Mackey had made his disclosures after *Marchetti* and *Grosso,* they could not have been used against him. He then concludes that since Mackey would have been privileged to file no returns at all, *Mackey* stands for the proposition that

---

[n.11] As we have noted, the privilege is an exception to the general principle that the Government has the right to everyone's testimony. A corollary to that principle is that the claim of privilege ordinarily must be presented to a "tribunal" for evaluation at the time disclosures are initially sought. *See* Albertson v. SACB, 382 U.S. 70, 78–79 (1965); Vajtauer v. Commissioner of Immigration, 273 U.S., at 113; Mason v. United States, 244 U.S. 362, 364–365 (1917). This early evaluation of claims allows the Government to compel evidence if the claim is invalid or if immunity is granted and therefore assures that the Government obtains all the information to which it is entitled. In the gambling tax cases, however, making a claim of privilege when the disclosures were requested, i.e., when the returns were due, would have identified the claimant as a gambler. The Court therefore forgave the usual requirement that the claim of privilege be presented for evaluation in favor of a "claim" by silence. *See Marchetti, supra,* 390 U.S., at 50. Nonetheless, it was recognized that one who "claimed" the privilege by refusing to file could be required subsequently to justify his claim of privilege. *See id.,* at 61. If a particular gambler would not have incriminated himself by filing the tax returns, the privilege would not justify a failure to file.

an objection at trial always suffices to preserve the privilege even if disclosures have been made previously.

Assuming that Garner otherwise reads *Mackey* correctly, we do not think that case should be applied in this context. The basis for the holdings in *Marchetti* and *Grosso* was that the occupational and excise taxes on gambling required disclosures only of gamblers, the great majority of whom were likely to incriminate themselves by responding. *Marchetti, supra,* 390 U.S., at 48–49, 57; *Grosso, supra,* 390 U.S., at 66–68. Therefore, as in the coerced-confession cases, any compulsion to disclose was likely to compel self-incrimination. Garner is differently situated. Although he disclosed himself to be a gambler, federal income tax returns are not directed at those " 'inherently suspect of criminal activities.' " *Marchetti, supra,* at 52, *supra.* As noted in *Albertson v. SACB,* 382 U.S. 70, 79 (1965), "the questions in [an] income tax return [are] neutral on their face and directed at the public at large." The great majority of persons who file income tax returns do not incriminate themselves by disclosing their occupation. The requirement that such returns be completed and filed simply does not involve the compulsion to incriminate considered in *Mackey.* [n.15]

* * *

V.

In summary, we conclude that since Garner made disclosures instead of claiming the privilege on his tax returns, his disclosures were not compelled incriminations. [n.21] He therefore was foreclosed from invoking the privilege when such information was later introduced as evidence against him in a criminal prosecution.

The judgment is affirmed.

MR. JUSTICE STEVENS took no part in the consideration or decision of this case.

MR. JUSTICE MARSHALL, with whom MR. JUSTICE BRENNAN joins, concurring in the judgment.

I agree with the Court that petitioner, having made incriminating disclosures on his income tax returns rather than having claimed the privilege

---

[n.15] Garner contends that whatever the case may be with regard to taxpayers in general, a gambler who might be incriminated by revealing his occupation cannot claim the privilege on the return effectively. This contention stems from the fact that certain specialized tax calculations are required only of gamblers. *See* § 165(d) of the Code, 26 U.S.C. § 165(d); Recent Cases, 86 Harv. L. Rev. 914, 916 n.13 (1973). Garner argues that the process of claiming the privilege with respect to these calculations will reveal a gambler's occupation. We need not address this contention, since Garner found it unnecessary to make any such special calculations. 501 F.2d, at 237 n.3.

[n.21] No language in this opinion is to be read as allowing a taxpayer desiring the protection of the privilege to make disclosures concurrently with a claim of privilege and thereby to immunize himself against the use of such disclosures. If a taxpayer desires the protection of the privilege, he must claim it instead of making disclosures. Any other rule would deprive the Government of its choice between compelling the evidence from the claimant in exchange for immunity and avoiding the burdens of immunization by obtaining the evidence elsewhere. *See Mackey v. United States,* 401 U.S., at 711–713 (Brennan, J., concurring in judgment).

against self-incrimination, cannot thereafter assert the privilege to bar the introduction of his returns in a criminal prosecution. I disagree, however, with the Court's rationale, which is far broader than is either necessary or appropriate to dispose of this case.

This case ultimately turns on a simple question — whether the possibility of being prosecuted under 26 U.S.C. § 7203 for failure to make a return compels a taxpayer to make an incriminating disclosure rather than claim the privilege against self-incrimination on his return. In discussing this question, the Court notes that only a "willful" failure to make a return is punishable under § 7203, and that "a defendant could not properly be convicted for an erroneous claim of privilege asserted in good faith." * * * Since a good-faith erroneous assertion of the privilege does not expose a taxpayer to criminal liability, I would hold that the threat of prosecution does not compel incriminating disclosures in violation of the Fifth Amendment. The protection accorded a good-faith assertion of the privilege effectively preserves the taxpayer's freedom to choose between making incriminating disclosures and claiming his Fifth Amendment privilege, and I would affirm the judgment of the Court of Appeals for that reason.

* * *

Do you agree with the *Garner* majority? At what point is it too late to raise the Fifth Amendment privilege with respect to a tax return?

[B]   Application of the Exclusionary Rule in Tax Prosecutions

The Fourth Amendment of the Constitution protects individuals from unreasonable searches and seizures. As *Payner, Wohler,* and *Caceres,* all reproduced below, make clear, the remedy generally applied when evidence is obtained in violation of the Fourth Amendment is suppression of the evidence. All three cases are suppression cases. Are they all Fourth Amendment cases?

UNITED STATES v. PAYNER
United States Supreme Court
447 U.S. 727 (1980)[7]

MR. JUSTICE POWELL delivered the opinion of the Court.

The question is whether the District Court properly suppressed the fruits of an unlawful search that did not invade the respondent's Fourth Amendment rights.

---

[7] *Reh'g denied,* 448 U.S. 911 (1980).

I.

Respondent Jack Payner was indicted in September 1976 on a charge of falsifying his 1972 federal income tax return in violation of 18 U.S.C. § 1001. The indictment alleged that respondent denied maintaining a foreign bank account at a time when he knew that he had such an account at the Castle Bank and Trust Company of Nassau, Bahama Islands.[8] The Government's case rested heavily on a loan guarantee agreement dated April 28, 1972, in which respondent pledged the funds in his Castle Bank account as security for a $100,000 loan.

Respondent waived his right to jury trial and moved to suppress the guarantee agreement. With the consent of the parties, the United States District Court for the Northern District of Ohio took evidence on the motion at a hearing consolidated with the trial on the merits. The court found respondent guilty as charged on the basis of all the evidence. The court also found, however, that the Government discovered the guarantee agreement by exploiting a flagrantly illegal search that occurred on January 15, 1973. The court therefore suppressed "all evidence introduced in the case by the Government with the exception of Jack Payner's 1972 tax return . . . and the related testimony." 434 F. Supp. 113, 136 (1977). As the tax return alone was insufficient to demonstrate knowing falsification, the District Court set aside respondent's conviction.

The events leading up to the 1973 search are not in dispute. In 1965, the Internal Revenue Service launched an investigation into the financial activities of American citizens in the Bahamas. The project, known as "Operation Trade Winds," was headquartered in Jacksonville, Fla. Suspicion focused on the Castle Bank in 1972, when investigators learned that a suspected narcotics trafficker had an account there. Special Agent Richard Jaffe of the Jacksonville office asked Norman Casper, a private investigator and occasional informant, to learn what he could about the Castle Bank and its depositors. To that end, Casper cultivated his friendship with Castle Bank vice president Michael Wolstencroft. Casper introduced Wolstencroft to Sybol Kennedy, a private investigator and former employee. When Casper discovered that the banker intended to spend a few days in Miami in January 1973, he devised a scheme to gain access to the bank records he knew Wolstencroft would be carrying in his briefcase. Agent Jaffe approved the basic outline of the plan.

Wolstencroft arrived in Miami on January 15 and went directly to Kennedy's apartment. At about 7:30 p.m., the two left for dinner at a Key Biscayne restaurant. Shortly thereafter, Casper entered the apartment using a key supplied by Kennedy. He removed the briefcase and delivered it to Jaffe. While the agent supervised the copying of approximately 400 documents taken from the briefcase, a "lookout" observed Kennedy and Wolstencroft at dinner. The observer notified Casper when the pair left the restaurant, and the briefcase was replaced. The documents photographed that evening included papers evidencing a close working relationship between the Castle Bank and the Bank

---

[8] [In addition to 18 U.S.C. § 1001, under current law, the Bank Secrecy Act and its accompanying Treasury Regulations criminalize the failure to report the ownership of a foreign bank account. *See* 31 U.S.C. §§ 5314, 5322. Eds.]

of Perrine, Fla. Subpoenas issued to the Bank of Perrine ultimately uncovered the loan guarantee agreement at issue in this case.

The District Court found that the United States, acting through Jaffe, "knowingly and willfully participated in the unlawful seizure of Michael Wolstencroft's briefcase . . . ." *Id.,* at 120. According to that court, "the Government affirmatively counsels its agents that the Fourth Amendment standing limitation permits them to purposefully conduct an unconstitutional search and seizure of one individual in order to obtain evidence against third parties . . . ." *Id.,* at 132–133. The District Court also found that the documents seized from Wolstencroft provided the leads that ultimately led to the discovery of the critical loan guarantee agreement. *Id.,* at 123. Although the search did not impinge upon the respondent's Fourth Amendment rights, the District Court believed that the Due Process Clause of the Fifth Amendment and the inherent supervisory power of the federal courts required it to exclude evidence tainted by the Government's "knowing and purposeful *bad faith hostility* to any person's fundamental constitutional rights." *Id.,* at 129; *see id.,* at 133, 134–135.

The Court of Appeals for the Sixth Circuit affirmed in a brief order endorsing the District Court's use of its supervisory power. 590 F.2d 206 (1979) (*per curiam*). The Court of Appeals did not decide the due process question. We granted certiorari, 444 U.S. 822 (1979), and we now reverse.

II.

This Court discussed the doctrine of "standing to invoke the [Fourth Amendment] exclusionary rule" in some detail last term. Rakas v. Illinois, 439 U.S. 128, 138 (1978). We reaffirmed the established rule that a court may not exclude evidence under the Fourth Amendment unless it finds that an unlawful search or seizure violated the defendant's own constitutional rights. *Id.,* at 133–140. *See, e.g.,* Brown v. United States, 411 U.S. 223, 229–230 (1973); Alderman v. United States, 394 U.S. 165, 171–172 (1969); Simmons v. United States, 390 U.S. 377, 389 (1968). And the defendant's Fourth Amendment rights are violated only when the challenged conduct invaded his legitimate expectation of privacy rather than that of a third party. *Rakas v. Illinois,* 439 U.S., at 143; *id.,* at 149–152 (Powell, J., concurring); Combs v. United States, 408 U.S. 224, 227 (1972); Mancusi v. DeForte, 392 U.S. 364, 368 (1968).

The foregoing authorities establish, as the District Court recognized, that respondent lacks standing under the Fourth Amendment to suppress the documents illegally seized from Wolstencroft. 434 F. Supp., at 126. The Court of Appeals did not disturb the District Court's conclusion that "Jack Payner possessed no privacy interest in the Castle Bank documents that were seized from Wolstencroft." *Ibid.*; *see* 590 F.2d, at 207. Nor do we. *United States v. Miller,* 425 U.S. 435 (1976), established that a depositor has no expectation of privacy and thus no "protectable Fourth Amendment interest" in copies of checks and deposit slips retained by his bank. *Id.,* at 437; *see id.,* at 442. Nothing in the record supports a contrary conclusion in this case.

The District Court and the Court of Appeals believed, however, that a federal court should use its supervisory power to suppress evidence tainted by gross illegalities that did not infringe the defendant's constitutional rights. The United States contends that this approach — as applied in this case — upsets the careful balance of interests embodied in the Fourth Amendment decisions of this Court. In the Government's view, such an extension of the supervisory power would enable federal courts to exercise a standardless discretion in their application of the exclusionary rule to enforce the Fourth Amendment. We agree with the Government.

III.

We certainly can understand the District Court's commendable desire to deter deliberate intrusions into the privacy of persons who are unlikely to become defendants in a criminal prosecution. *See* 434 F. Supp., at 135. No court should condone the unconstitutional and possibly criminal behavior of those who planned and executed this "briefcase caper."[5] Indeed, the decisions of this Court are replete with denunciations of willfully lawless activities undertaken in the name of law enforcement. * * * But our cases also show that these unexceptional principles do not command the exclusion of evidence in every case of illegality. Instead, they must be weighed against the considerable harm that would flow from indiscriminate application of an exclusionary rule.

Thus, the exclusionary rule "has been restricted to those areas where its remedial objectives are most efficaciously served." United States v. Calandra, 414 U.S. 338, 348 (1974). The Court has acknowledged that the suppression of probative but tainted evidence exacts a costly toll upon the ability of courts to ascertain the truth in a criminal case. *E.g., Rakas v. Illinois,* 439 U.S., at 137–138; United States v. Ceccolini, 435 U.S. 268, 275–279 (1978); Stone v. Powell, 428 U.S. 465, 489–491 (1976); *see* Michigan v. Tucker, 417 U.S. 433, 450–451 (1974). Our cases have consistently recognized that unbending application of the exclusionary sanction to enforce ideals of governmental rectitude would impede unacceptably the truth-finding functions of judge and jury. *E.g., Stone v. Powell, supra,* at 485–489; *United States v. Calandra, supra,* at 348. After all, it is the defendant, and not the constable, who stands trial.

---

[5] "The security of persons and property remains a fundamental value which law enforcement officers must respect. Nor should those who flout the rules escape unscathed." Alderman v. United States, 394 U.S. 165, 175 (1969). We note that in 1976 Congress investigated the improprieties revealed in this record. *See* Oversight Hearings into the Operations of the IRS before a Subcommittee of the House Committee on Government Operations (Operation Tradewinds, Project Haven, and Narcotics Traffickers Tax Program), 94th Cong., 1st Sess. (1975). As a result, the Commissioner of Internal Revenue "called off" Operation Trade Winds. Tr. of Oral Arg. 35. The Commissioner also adopted guidelines that require agents to instruct informants on the requirements of the law and to report known illegalities to a supervisory officer, who is in turn directed to notify appropriate state authorities. IR Manual §§ 9373.3 (3), 9373.4 (Manual Transmittal 9–21, Dec. 27, 1977). Although these measures appear on their face to be less positive than one might expect from an agency charged with upholding the law, they do indicate disapproval of the practices found to have been implemented in this case. We cannot assume that similar lawless conduct, if brought to the attention of responsible officials, would not be dealt with appropriately. To require in addition the suppression of highly probative evidence in a trial against a third party would penalize society unnecessarily.

The same societal interests are at risk when a criminal defendant invokes the supervisory power to suppress evidence seized in violation of a third party's constitutional rights. The supervisory power is applied with some caution even when the defendant asserts a violation of his own rights. In *United States v. Caceres*, 440 U.S. 741, 754–757 (1979), we refused to exclude all evidence tainted by violations of an executive department's rules. And in *Elkins v. United States*, 364 U.S. 206, 216 (1960), the Court called for a restrained application of the supervisory power.

> "[A]ny apparent limitation upon the process of discovering truth in a federal trial ought to be imposed only upon the basis of considerations which outweigh the general need for untrammeled disclosure of competent and relevant evidence in a court of justice." *Ibid.*

See also Nardone v. United States, 308 U.S. 338, 340 (1939).

We conclude that the supervisory power does not authorize a federal court to suppress otherwise admissible evidence on the ground that it was seized unlawfully from a third party not before the court. Our Fourth Amendment decisions have established beyond any doubt that the interest in deterring illegal searches does not justify the exclusion of tainted evidence at the instance of a party who was not the victim of the challenged practices. *Rakas v. Illinois, supra,* at 137; *Alderman v. United States*, 394 U.S., at 174–175. The values assigned to the competing interests do not change because a court has elected to analyze the question under the supervisory power instead of the Fourth Amendment. In either case, the need to deter the underlying conduct and the detrimental impact of excluding the evidence remain precisely the same.

The District Court erred, therefore, when it concluded that "society's interest in deterring [bad faith] conduct by exclusion outweigh[s] society's interest in furnishing the trier of fact with all relevant evidence." 434 F. Supp., at 135. This reasoning, which the Court of Appeals affirmed, amounts to a substitution of individual judgment for the controlling decisions of this Court. Were we to accept this use of the supervisory power, we would confer on the judiciary discretionary power to disregard the considered limitations of the law it is charged with enforcing. We hold that the supervisory power does not extend so far.

The judgment of the Court of Appeals is reversed.

MR. CHIEF JUSTICE BURGER, concurring.

I join the Court's opinion because Payner — whose guilt is not in doubt — cannot take advantage of the Government's violation of the constitutional rights of Wolstencroft, for he is not a party to this case. The Court's opinion makes clear the reason for that sound rule.

Orderly government under our system of separate powers calls for internal self-restraint and discipline in each Branch; this Court has no general supervisory authority over operations of the Executive Branch, as it has with respect to the federal courts. I agree fully with the Court that the exclusionary rule is inapplicable to a case of this kind, but the Court's holding should not be read as condoning the conduct of the IRS "private investigators" disclosed by this record, or as approval of their evidence-gathering methods.

MR. JUSTICE MARSHALL, with whom MR. JUSTICE BRENNAN and MR. JUS-
TICE BLACKMUN join, dissenting.

The Court today holds that a federal court is unable to exercise its supervisory powers to prevent the use of evidence in a criminal prosecution in that
court, even though that evidence was obtained through intentional illegal and
unconstitutional conduct by agents of the United States, because the defendant does not satisfy the standing requirement of the Fourth Amendment.
That holding effectively turns the standing rules created by this Court for
assertions of Fourth Amendment violations into a sword to be used by the
Government to permit it deliberately to invade one person's Fourth Amendment rights in order to obtain evidence against another person. Unlike the
Court, I do not believe that the federal courts are unable to protect the
integrity of the judicial system from such gross Government misconduct.

I.

The facts as found by the District Court need to be more fully stated in order
to establish the level of purposeful misconduct to which agents of the United
States have sunk in this case. Operation Trade Winds was initiated by the
Internal Revenue Service (IRS) in 1965 to gather information about the
financial activities of American citizens in the Bahamas. The investigation
was supervised by Special Agent Richard Jaffe in the Jacksonville, Fla., office.
It was not until June 1972 that the investigation focused on the Castle Bank
and Trust Company of the Bahamas. In late October 1972 Jaffe asked one
of his informants, Norman Casper, to obtain the names and addresses of the
individuals holding accounts with the Castle Bank. Casper set to work soon
thereafter. He was already an acquaintance of Michael Wolstencroft, vice
president and trust officer of the Castle Bank. Casper knew that Wolstencroft
frequently visited the United States carrying a briefcase with documents from
the Castle Bank. Casper therefore introduced Wolstencroft to Sybol Kennedy,
a private detective who worked for Casper. In early January 1973, Casper
learned that Wolstencroft planned a business trip to the United States on
January 15, 1973, and that he would have Castle Bank records with him on
that trip. Plans for the "briefcase caper," as Casper called it, began in earnest.

As found by the District Court, Casper discussed the details of the plan with
Jaffe on several occasions during the week before Wolstencroft's trip.[n.1] Casper told Jaffe that he could get the needed documents from Wolstencroft, but
that Jaffe would have to supply photographic services. On January 11, Casper
specifically informed Jaffe that he planned to enter an apartment and take
Wolstencroft's briefcase. Jaffe then stated that he would have to clear the
operation with his superior, Troy Register, Jr., Chief of the IRS Intelligence
Division in Jacksonville. Clearance was obtained, and Jaffe told Casper to
proceed with the plan. Casper called Jaffe the following day and asked if the

---

[n.1] The Court rather blandly states that "Agent Jaffe approved the basic outline of the
plan," * * * . Such a characterization is misleading in light of the findings of the District Court.
As is noted in the text *infra*, Jaffe knew explicit details of the operation in advance and helped
to make the arrangements by recommending a locksmith who could be "trusted," by providing
a safe and convenient location for the photographing of the documents, and by providing a
photographer from the IRS.

IRS could refer him to a locksmith who could be "trusted." Jaffe gave him such a referral.

The plans were finalized by the time of Wolstencroft's arrival on January 15. Wolstencroft went directly to Sybol Kennedy's apartment. The couple eventually went to a restaurant for dinner. Using a key provided by Kennedy, Casper entered the apartment and *stole* Wolstencroft's briefcase. Casper then rendezvoused with the IRS-recommended locksmith in a parking lot five blocks from the apartment; the locksmith made a key to fit the lock on the case. Casper took the briefcase and newly made key to the home of an IRS agent. Jaffe had selected that location for the photographing because it was only eight blocks from the parking lot where Casper met the locksmith and Jaffe knew there was a need to act with haste. The briefcase was opened in Jaffe's presence. Jaffe, Casper, and an IRS photography expert then photographed over 400 documents.[n.7] Casper had arranged for Kennedy and Wolstencroft to be watched on their date, and this lookout called Casper at the IRS agent's home when the couple finished their dinner. After all the documents had been copied, Casper relocked the briefcase and returned it to Kennedy's apartment. The entire "caper" lasted approximately one and one-half hours.

The illegalities of agents of the United States did not stop even at that point, however. During the following two weeks, Jaffe told Casper that the IRS needed additional information. Casper therefore sent Kennedy to visit Wolstencroft in the Bahamas. While there, acting pursuant to Casper's instructions, Kennedy stole a rolodex file from Wolstencroft's office. This file was turned over to Jaffe, who testified in the District Court that he had not cared how the rolodex file had been obtained.

The IRS paid Casper $8,000 in cash for the services he rendered in obtaining the information about Castle Bank. Casper in turn paid approximately $1,000 of this money to Kennedy for her role in the "briefcase caper" and the theft of the rolodex file.

The "briefcase caper" revealed papers which showed a close relationship between the Castle Bank and a Florida bank. Subpoenas issued to that Florida bank resulted in the uncovering of the loan guarantee agreement which was the principal piece of evidence against respondent at trial. It is that loan agreement and the evidence discovered as a result of it that the District Court reluctantly suppressed under the Due Process Clause of the Fifth Amendment and under its supervisory powers.

The District Court made several key findings concerning the level of misconduct of agents of the United States in these activities. The District Court found that "the United States, through its agents, Richard Jaffe, and others, knowingly and willfully participated in the unlawful seizure of Michael Wolstencroft's briefcase, and encouraged its informant, Norman Casper, to

---

[n.7] As noted previously, Casper had told Jaffe to provide the photographic equipment. Jaffe testified that one of the cameras used was a "microfilmer" which was "much quicker" than a regular camera. This camera had been brought by the IRS because "Casper had to get the documents and the briefcase back to the apartment prior to the return of the owner." *Id.*, at 493–495. This testimony again shows that Jaffe was fully aware in advance that the activities of the evening were improper.

arrange the theft of a rolodex from the offices of Castle Bank." 434 F. Supp. 113, 120–121 (ND Ohio 1977) (footnotes omitted). The District Court concluded that "the United States was an active participant in the admittedly criminal conduct in which Casper engaged. . . ." *Id.,* at 121. The District Court found that "the illegal conduct of the government officials involved in this case compels the conclusion that they knowingly and purposefully obtained the briefcase materials with *bad faith hostility* toward the strictures imposed on their activities by the Constitution." *Id.,* at 130 (footnote omitted) (emphasis in original). The District Court considered the actions of Jaffe and Casper "outrageous," *ibid.,* because they "plotted, schemed and ultimately acted in contravention of the United States Constitution and laws of Florida, knowing that their conduct was illegal." *Ibid.*

The most disturbing finding by the District Court, however, related to the intentional manipulation of the standing requirements of the Fourth Amendment by agents of the United States, who are, of course, supposed to uphold and enforce the Constitution and laws of this country. The District Court found:

> "It is evident that the Government and its agents, including Richard Jaffe, were, and are, well aware that under the standing requirement of the Fourth Amendment, evidence obtained from a party pursuant to an unconstitutional search is admissible against third parties who's [*sic*] own privacy expectations are not subject to the search, even though the cause for the unconstitutional search was to obtain evidence incriminating those third parties. This Court finds that, in its desire to apprehend tax evaders, a desire the Court fully shares, the Government affirmatively counsels its agents that the Fourth Amendment standing limitation permits them to purposefully conduct an unconstitutional search and seizure of one individual in order to obtain evidence against third parties, who are the real targets of the governmental intrusion, and that the IRS agents in this case acted, and will act in the future, according to that counsel. Such governmental conduct compels the conclusion that Jaffe and Casper transacted the 'briefcase caper' with a purposeful, bad faith hostility toward the Fourth Amendment rights of Wolstencroft in order to obtain evidence against persons like Payner."

Id., at 131–133 (footnotes omitted).

The Court of Appeals did not disturb any of these findings. 590 F.2d 206 (CA6 1979) (per curiam). Nor does the Court today purport to set them aside. * * * It is in the context of these findings — intentional illegal actions by Government agents taken in bad-faith hostility toward the constitutional rights of Wolstencroft for the purpose of obtaining evidence against persons such as the respondent through manipulation of the standing requirements of the Fourth Amendment — that the suppression issue must be considered.

II.

This Court has on several occasions exercised its supervisory powers over the federal judicial system in order to suppress evidence that the Government obtained through misconduct. * * * The rationale for such suppression of evidence is twofold: to deter illegal conduct by Government officials, and to protect the integrity of the federal courts. * * * The Court has particularly stressed the need to use supervisory powers to prevent the federal courts from becoming accomplices to such misconduct. *See, e.g.,* McNabb v. United States, [318 U.S. 332 (1943)] at 345 ("Plainly, a conviction resting on evidence secured through such a flagrant disregard of the procedure which Congress has commanded cannot be allowed to stand without making the courts themselves accomplices in willful disobedience of law"); Mesarosh v. United States, [352 U.S. 1 (1956)] at 14 (the Court should use its supervisory powers in federal criminal cases "to see that the waters of justice are not polluted"); Elkins v. United States, [364 U.S. 206 (1960)] at 223 (federal courts should not be "accomplices in the willful disobedience of a Constitution they are sworn to uphold").

The need to use the Court's supervisory powers to suppress evidence obtained through governmental misconduct was perhaps best expressed by Mr. Justice Brandeis in his famous dissenting opinion in *Olmstead v. United States*, 277 U.S. 438, 471–485 (1928):

> "Decency, security and liberty alike demand that government officials shall be subjected to the same rules of conduct that are commands to the citizen. In a government of laws, existence of the government will be imperiled if it fails to observe the law scrupulously. Our Government is the potent, the omnipresent teacher. For good or for ill, it teaches the whole people by its example. Crime is contagious. If the Government becomes a lawbreaker, it breeds contempt for law; it invites every man to become a law unto himself; it invites anarchy. To declare that in the administration of the criminal law the end justifies the means — to declare that the Government may commit crimes in order to secure the conviction of a private criminal — would bring terrible retribution. Against that pernicious doctrine this Court should resolutely set its face."
> *Id.,* at 485. * * *

Mr. Justice Brandeis noted that "a court will not redress a wrong when he who invokes its aid has unclean hands," *id.*, at 483, and that in keeping with that principle the court should not lend its aid in the enforcement of the criminal law when the government itself was guilty of misconduct. "Then aid is denied despite the defendant's wrong. It is denied in order to maintain respect for law; in order to promote confidence in the administration of justice; in order to preserve the judicial process from contamination." *Id.*, at 484. *See also id.*, at 469–471 (Holmes, J., dissenting); *id.*, at 488 (Stone, J., dissenting); Lopez v. United States, 373 U.S. 427, 453, n.3 (1963) (Brennan, J., dissenting).

The reason for this emphasis on the need to protect the integrity of the federal courts through the use of supervisory powers can be derived from the factual contexts in which supervisory powers have been exercised. In large part when supervisory powers have been invoked the Court has been faced with intentional illegal conduct. It has not been the case that "[t]he criminal is to go free because the constable has blundered," People v. Defore, 242 N.Y. 13, 21, 150 N.E. 585, 587 (1926). In these cases there has been no "blunder" by the Government agent at all; rather, the agent has intentionally violated the law for the explicit purpose of obtaining the evidence in question. *Cf. Lopez v. United States, supra,* at 440 (supervisory powers should be exercised only if there has been "manifestly improper conduct by federal officials"). If the federal court permits such evidence, the intended product of deliberately illegal Government action, to be used to obtain a conviction, it places its imprimatur upon such lawlessness and thereby taints its own integrity.

The present case falls within that category. The District Court found, and the record establishes, a deliberate decision by Government agents to violate the constitutional rights of Wolstencroft for the explicit purpose of obtaining evidence against persons such as Payner. The actions of the Government agents — stealing the briefcase, opening it, and photographing all the documents inside — were both patently in violation of the Fourth Amendment rights of Wolstencroft and plainly in violation of the criminal law.[n.12] The Government knew exactly what information it wanted, and it was that information which was stolen from Wolstencroft. Similarly, the Government knew that it wanted to prosecute persons such as Payner, and it made a conscious decision to forgo any opportunity to prosecute Wolstencroft in order to obtain illegally the evidence against Payner and others.

Since the supervisory powers are exercised to protect the integrity of the *court*, rather than to vindicate the constitutional rights of the defendant, it is hard to see why the Court today bases its analysis entirely on Fourth Amendment standing rules. The point is that the federal judiciary should not be made accomplices to the crimes of Casper, Jaffe, and others. The only way the IRS can benefit from the evidence it chose to obtain illegally is if the evidence is admitted at trial against persons such as Payner; that was the very point of the criminal exercise in the first place. If the IRS is permitted to obtain a conviction in federal court based almost entirely on that illegally obtained evidence and its fruits, then the judiciary has given full effect to the deliberate wrongdoings of the Government. The federal court does indeed become the accomplice of the Government lawbreaker, an accessory after the fact, for without judicial use of the evidence the "caper" would have been for nought. Such a pollution of the federal courts should not be permitted.[n.14]

It is particularly disturbing that the Court today chooses to allow the IRS deliberately to manipulate the standing rules of the Fourth Amendment to achieve its ends. As previously noted, the District Court found that "the Government affirmatively counsels its agents that the Fourth Amendment standing limitation permits them to purposefully conduct an unconstitutional

---

[n.12] The Court characterizes the actions of Jaffe and Casper in the briefcase incident as "possibly criminal behavior," *ibid.* The District Court concluded that the actions of the IRS appeared to constitute a prima facie case of criminal larceny under Florida law, and possibly violated other criminal laws of that State as well. 434 F. Supp., at 130, n.66. Casper admitted in the District Court that he knew he was committing an illegal act. Tr. 452–453. The stealing of the rolodex file from Wolstencroft's office was also both unconstitutional and criminal. That theft, however, produced no additional evidence against Payner. *See* 434 F. Supp., at 123, n. 56.

[n.14] It is simply not a sufficient cure for the Court to denounce the actions of the IRS * * * , while at the same time rewarding the Government for this conduct by permitting the IRS to use the evidence in the very manner which was the purpose of the illegal and unconstitutional activities.

search and seizure of one individual in order to obtain evidence against third parties, who are the real targets of the governmental intrusion, and that the IRS agents in this case acted, *and will act in the future,* according to that counsel." 434 F. Supp., at 132–133 (emphasis supplied). Whatever role those standing limitations may play, it is clear that they were never intended to be a sword to be used by the Government in its deliberate choice to sacrifice the constitutional rights of one person in order to prosecute another.

*   *   *

I would affirm the judgment of the Court of Appeals and suppress the fruits of the Government's illegal action under the Court's supervisory powers. Accordingly, I dissent.

Do you agree with the majority or with the dissent? Why did the *Payner* majority not simply apply the Fourth Amendment to suppress the illegally seized evidence?

UNITED STATES v. WOHLER
United States District Court, Northern District Of Utah
382 F. Supp. 229 (1973)

MEMORANDUM AND ORDER

Aldon J. Anderson, District Judge.

The defendant has been charged with several counts of income tax evasion in violation of 26 U.S.C. § 7201 and several counts of making and subscribing false returns in violation of 26 U.S.C. § 7206(1). He has filed a motion to suppress certain evidence and to dismiss the indictment.

On May 5, 1970, Special Agent Harrington of the Intelligence Division of the Internal Revenue Service began an investigation into the defendant's potential tax liability with a view towards possible criminal prosecution. At the time Special Agent Harrington first contacted and interviewed the defendant he had been assigned to the case as a representative of the Intelligence Division which is charged with responsibility for investigating criminal violations of the tax laws. IRS procedures require the special agent to give the taxpayer a warning concerning his constitutional rights at the "initial meeting" with the taxpayer after such an assignment is made.

On May 6, 1970, pursuant to an earlier phone conversation with Special Agent Harrington and at his behest, the defendant brought certain of his tax records to the agent's office for a conference. At the beginning of the interview Special Agent Harrington endeavored to give the defendant a "*Miranda*-type" warning in accordance with IRS procedures as published for the benefit of the public in IRS news releases IR-897, and IR-949.[n.1]

[n.1] IR-949 provides:

     Changes in the procedure for advising taxpayers of their rights during an investigation

* * *

This warning satisfied the requirements of the previously-mentioned news release except that the defendant was not informed of his right to refuse to produce his documents for agency perusal.[n.2] At the conclusion of the initial conference the following conversation took place:

> Special Agent Harrington: What I would like to do now, and of course this is up to you and as I told you before you don't have to submit anything to me, but I would like to give you a receipt for the items you have there (referring to Mr. Wohler's records) and I would like to keep it for a few days and look at it. Is that all right?
>
> Mr. Wohler: I would assume so.
>
> Special Agent Harrington: Now of course this is up to you. It's not up to me. In other word [sic], I cannot force you to do it.
>
> Mr. Wohler: Yes.

Some six months later the records were returned to the defendant who then retained Mr. Bill Bayes, a Certified Public Accountant, to assist him in this matter. During the defendant's subsequent discussion with the IRS, Mr. Bayes played an active role. As a result of a conference held between the accountant, the special agent, and the defendant, Mr. Bayes was directed to reconcile the defendant's financial statements with his tax returns. At the special agent's request, he was given the accountant's worksheets. Additional exchanges took place and a revenue agent was called in. According to the affidavits of Mr. Bayes and the defendant, IRS agents created the impression that this was

---

conducted by a Special Agent of the IRS Intelligence Division were announced today by the Internal Revenue Service.

The new procedure goes beyond most legal requirements that are designed to advise persons of their rights.

One function of a Special Agent is to investigate possible criminal violations of Internal Revenue laws. At the initial meeting with a taxpayer, a Special Agent is now required to identify himself, describe his function, and advise the taxpayer that anything he says may be used against him. The Special Agent will also tell the taxpayer that he cannot be compelled to incriminate himself by answering any questions or producing any documents, and that he has the right to seek the assistance of an attorney before responding.

Previously, the Special Agent identified himself and described his function at the first meeting with the taxpayer but was not required to give further advice unless the taxpayer was in custody or the investigation proceeded beyond the preliminary stage.

IRS has made no change in its existing instructions that if it becomes necessary to interview a person who is in custody, an Agent must give a comprehensive statement of rights before any interrogation.

[n.2] A troublesome point, however, concerns the lack of time that the defendant was given to weigh the implications of the warning. An examination of the record indicates that the questioning appears to have commenced immediately upon the conclusion of the giving of the warning. While the record would not disclose the time allowed for reflection, it would be most helpful to the trier of fact if an inquiry were directed to the person being examined as to whether or not he understood his rights and whether he desired to proceed further. If this were done then one reviewing the record could more easily ascertain whether or not these were knowingly waived. Otherwise, as in this case, one must depend upon an assessment of the overall context to determine whether an intelligent waiver has taken place.

a civil matter. Mr. Bayes stated that he formulated the opinion that this was a civil controversy on the basis of three factors: (1) that a revenue agent was called in to compute the tax owing on the basis of the "evidence" he had submitted; (2) he was informed that "all my future dealings" would be with a revenue agent rather than a special agent; and (3) Mr. Bayes asked Special Agent Harrington if his client should consult an attorney, and was informed that it was not necessary "at this time."[n.3] Subsequently, the defendant was indicted.

The defendant contends that the warning given him concerning his constitutional rights was defective in three respects. First, because the warning given the taxpayer was not given at the "initial meeting" as required by IRS procedure. Second, the defendant contends that the warning was not as complete as that required by IRS news release IR-949, issued November 26, 1968. Third, and finally, because the warning given did not conform to the standards of *Miranda v. Arizona*, 384 U.S. 436, 86 S. Ct. 1602, 16 L. Ed. 2d 694 (1966), and *Escobedo v. Illinois*, 378 U.S. 478, 84 S. Ct. 1758, 12 L. Ed. 2d 977 (1964) as required by *United States v. Lockyer*, 448 F.2d 417 (10th Cir. 1971), and *United States v. Wainwright*, 284 F. Supp. 129 (D. Colo. 1968). The defendant also maintains that the United States obtained evidence said to be incriminating through misrepresentation, fraud, deceit, or other misconduct in violation of his rights under the Fourth and Fifth Amendments.

I.

INITIAL MEETING

The special agent and the taxpayer held a telephone conversation on May 5, 1970, which resulted in the May 6, 1970, conference. According to the defendant, the "initial meeting" was thus the telephone conversation, and the failure at that time of the special agent to inform the defendant of his constitutional rights was a violation of the before-mentioned news release IR-949. No allegation has been made, however, that potentially incriminating information was elicited from the defendant during this telephone call. There are perhaps situations where a telephone conversation should properly be considered the initial meeting for purposes of delivering the required warning. Here, however, there is no indication that the taxpayer's right to remain silent was jeopardized. A warning was given before any pertinent information was disclosed by the taxpayer, and this is all that is required.

II.

COMPLIANCE WITH IRS PROCEDURES

Public concern and inquiry regarding the "hybrid civil-criminal" nature of tax investigation prompted the Internal Revenue Service to issue news

[n.3] Although as the defendant's agent, it was not necessary for the IRS to inform the accountant of the nature of the proceeding, representations made to him should be considered as having been made to the defendant.

releases IR-897 and IR-949. Because the procedures announced in these releases are for the benefit of the taxpayer and designed to encourage his reliance, assuring agency compliance with these procedures is a matter of judicial concern. This court is in agreement with previous decisions from other jurisdictions holding that the IRS agents are obligated to comply with the terms of these releases. United States v. Leahey, 434 F.2d 7 (1st Cir. 1970); United States v. Heffner, 420 F.2d 809 (4th Cir. 1969). Cases in this circuit also suggest agreement with this position. *See* Rosenberg v. Commissioner of Internal Revenue, 450 F.2d 529 (10th Cir. 1971); United States v. Lockyer, 448 F.2d 417 (10th Cir. 1971).

The warning given taxpayers by special agents should be carefully scrutinized to assure that the taxpayer's rights are protected, and to ensure full compliance with administrative procedures. Such examination, however, should not be permitted to form the basis for objection to agency investigations, where a complete warning has in fact been given, although not in a memorized fashion. United States v. Bembridge, 458 F.2d 1262 (1st Cir. 1972).

In the present case, a warning satisfying the requirements of stated IRS procedures was given. At the outset of the interview, the warning Special Agent Harrington gave the defendant covered each specific point of procedure except informing him that he could not be required to produce his documents for inspection. However, as is evident from the recitation of the facts of this matter, the defendant was informed of this right prior to the time that he relinquished his records to the special agent. Thus, although the warning was a little disjointed in point of time, it was sufficient to satisfy the requirements of IRS procedure in apprising the defendant of his rights. It should be noted, however, that although exactitude in wording is not required, any deviance, discrepancy, or omission prejudicing the taxpayer is adequate justification for imposing restrictions upon the use of information obtained in such circumstances.

III.

THE NATURE OF THE WARNING REQUIRED IN TAX PROCEEDINGS

Because of the dual civil-criminal nature of most tax investigations, the question of when a taxpayer should be warned concerning his constitutional rights is perplexing. The terms "custody" and "deprived of his freedom of action in any significant way" often appear to be an incongruity in tax proceedings concerning when the *Miranda* warning should be given. This question has not been resolved by the United States Supreme Court, and there is a difference of opinion among the courts which have considered the matter.

The majority view is that despite the unique nature of a tax investigation it is not necessary to give the taxpayer the *Miranda* warning unless he is in custody or otherwise deprived of his freedom in a significant manner. United States v. Miriani, 422 F.2d 150 (6th Cir. 1970) and cases cited therein. The majority viewpoint is that it is the inherently compulsive nature of the setting which requires a warning to be given, not the "strength or extent of the government's suspicion" at the time of interrogation. *United States v. Squeri,* 398 F.2d 785, 790 (2nd Cir. 1968).

The minority view is that a taxpayer becomes an "accused" when his case is referred to the Intelligence Division of the Internal Revenue Service, and that a warning concerning the taxpayer's constitutional rights is then required. As was noted in *United States v. Turzynski,* 268 F. Supp. 847 (N.D. Ill. 1967), at 850:

> To hold otherwise would lead to the anomalous conclusion that a person suspected of bank robbery, sale of narcotics, murder, rape or other serious crime is entitled to greater protection of his constitutional rights than a person suspected of violating the internal revenue laws. For when the silent transition from civil to criminal investigation takes place in a tax case, the taxpayer being interrogated and asked to furnish his books and records is just as surely a prime suspect and candidate for criminal prosecution as the individual under interrogation as a suspect for other crimes. * * *

In some respects the tax investigation is more insidious and dishonest than the custodial interrogation, for the suspect in custody well knows his interrogators are seeking evidence to convict him of a crime while a tax suspect is permitted and even encouraged to believe that no criminal prosecution is in contemplation.

Courts approving this position restrict the use of information obtained without first warning the taxpayer because it is "procured in violation of fundamental standards of fairness." *United States v. Wainwright, supra,* 284 F. Supp. at 132.

This circuit has not ruled on this question although it has been discussed in several cases. In *Hensley v. United States,* 406 F.2d 481 (10th Cir. 1968), the Tenth Circuit Court of Appeals noted that *Mathis v. United States,* 391 U.S. 1, 88 S. Ct. 1503, 20 L. Ed. 2d 381 (1968) made it clear that *Miranda* applied to tax investigations, but did not appear to broaden the application beyond custodial interrogations. It was, however, not necessary to resolve the issue because the information obtained was in the form of corporate records not protected by the Fifth Amendment. *Hensley, supra,* 406 F.2d at 484–485. In *United States v. Lockyer, supra,* the court reversed a district court decision ordering the suppression of certain evidence because of a failure of IRS agents to comply with internal agency procedures. At this time, however, it was noted that the "better reasoned cases" required that the taxpayer be given a warning concerning his constitutional rights "at the inception of the first contact" after the case is assigned to the Intelligence Division. *Lockyer, supra,* 448 F.2d at 422. * * * Thus, although this court is not constrained by judicial precedent, it is in agreement with Judge Doyle's observation in *Lockyer, supra,* that the better reasoned result is to require that the taxpayer be given a warning concerning his constitutional rights.

The seeming disagreement between the majority and minority viewpoints is not as pronounced as it appears. In *United States v. Dickerson,* 413 F.2d 1111 (7th Cir. 1969), a case holding that a warning is required, it was pointed out that in almost every case cited in support of the majority rule, some warning was in fact given. In *Wainwright, supra*, 284 F. Supp. at 131–132, other of these cases were also distinguished. Thus it can be fairly said that many courts have determined that some form of warning is necessary, but for the most part are unwilling to require that the requirements of *Miranda* must be satisfied because of the burden this would impose upon routine tax and administrative inquiries.

Although agreeing in principle with the court in *Morgan* that reasonable latitude should be permitted in governmental investigations, it does not follow that requiring the government to inform the taxpayer of his Sixth Amendment right to counsel invariably requires the government to inform the taxpayer in a non-custodial situation. As a minimum, fundamental fairness requires that the *Miranda* warning be given in the custodial situation and that the assistance of counsel be provided. This does not mean that the standard in non-custodial proceedings is necessarily the same or that no warning can be required in such circumstances. Of necessity, the standard must be flexible.

The setting where a taxpayer is interrogated concerning his tax history often, because of the nature of the proceeding, is pervaded with a compulsive aura. Although the taxpayer may be free to go or to refuse to answer any questions, he may not know this. Where the taxpayer is suspected of criminal misconduct, to allow the government to interrogate him or examine his records without somewhat informing the taxpayer of his rights would seem to violate basic notions of fairness.

Commendably, the Internal Revenue Service has recognized the inherent unfairness of this situation and, via the before-mentioned news releases, has endeavored to protect the constitutional rights of the taxpayer. Nothing less than the procedures required by the news releases will suffice in protecting the rights of the individual taxpayer.

Thus in this case the defendant's contention that the warning given him was inadequate because it did not completely comport with *Miranda* is not well taken. In the non-custodial tax investigation where the matter has been assigned to the Intelligence Division of the Internal Revenue Service, the warning required by published IRS news releases is sufficient to meet the standard of fundamental fairness required in such matters.

<h1 style="text-align:center">IV.</h1>

<h1 style="text-align:center">ALLEGATION OF MISREPRESENTATIONS</h1>

It does not appear from the facts that IRS agents fraudulently misled the defendant. Nevertheless, it is clear that as a result of the procedures followed by the agents the defendant was given the impression at some point that the controversy was now only civil in nature. This is evidenced by Special Agent Harrington's negative reply to the accountant's query concerning whether the defendant should obtain legal assistance.

If subsequent to the warning an agency is permitted via unsound procedures to mislead the taxpayer with impunity, the purpose for giving the warning is thwarted. Consequently, neither the good faith of the agent nor the intent of the agency justify misleading the taxpayer. Although the defendant initially cooperated with IRS agents, he maintains that he subsequently provided certain information because he was misled into believing that the probe was now only civil in nature. The facts indicate that he was misled and that the agency was responsible for his misapprehension.

The exact point in the investigation where agency representations were sufficient to justify the defendant's conclusion is not clear. Certainly the defendant's assumption was justified when Special Agent Harrington assured the defendant's agent that the defendant did not need an attorney. It is not clear at what point in the investigation prior to this assurance that the defendant was justified in assuming that the criminal inquiry had been dropped. It is clear, however, that the stage of the investigation when such an impression was proper was earlier than the time of Special Agent Harrington's representation to the accountant. Thus, in the interest of justice and to assure essential fairness, the court considers it necessary to order that the worksheets obtained from Mr. Bayes, and all other information subsequently obtained from the defendant and his accountant, be suppressed. Otherwise, the salutary purpose of the warning will not serve to protect constitutional rights as was intended.

Wherefore, it is hereby ordered that the before-mentioned evidence be suppressed and that in all other respects the defendant's motion is denied.

Caceres, which was cited in *Payner,* with respect to suppression as a remedy for the IRS's violation of its rules, is reproduced below. It is also a suppression case, but it reflects a different type of violation by the IRS. Consider *Caceres* in light of *Wohler.* How would you decide *Caceres?*

UNITED STATES v. CACERES
United States Supreme Court
440 U.S. 741 (1979)

MR. JUSTICE STEVENS delivered the opinion of the Court. The question we granted certiorari to decide is whether evidence obtained in violation of Internal Revenue Service (IRS) regulations may be admitted at the criminal trial of a taxpayer accused of bribing an IRS agent. 436 U.S. 943 (1978).

Unbeknown to respondent, three of his face-to-face conversations with IRS Agent Yee were monitored by means of a radio transmitter concealed on Yee's person. Respondent moved to suppress tape recordings of the three conversations on the ground that the authorizations required by IRS regulations had not been secured. The District Court granted the motion. The Court of Appeals for the Ninth Circuit reversed as to the third tape; it concluded that adequate authorization had been obtained. As to the first two tapes, however, the Court of Appeals agreed with the District Court both that the IRS regulations had not been followed and that exclusion of the recordings was therefore required. It is the latter conclusion that is at issue here.

The Government argues that exclusion of probative evidence in a criminal trial is an inappropriate sanction for violation of an executive department's regulations. In this case, moreover, it argues that suppression is especially inappropriate because the violation of the regulation was neither deliberate nor prejudicial, and did not affect any constitutional or statutory rights. We agree that suppression should not have been ordered in this case, and therefore reverse the judgment of the Court of Appeals.

I.

Neither the Constitution nor any Act of Congress requires that official approval be secured before conversations are overheard or recorded by Government agents with the consent of one of the conversants. Such "consensual electronic surveillance" between taxpayers and IRS agents is, however, prohibited by IRS regulations unless appropriate prior authorization is obtained.

The IRS Manual sets forth in detail the procedures to be followed in obtaining such approvals. For all types of requests the regulations require an explanation of the reasons for the proposal, the type of equipment to be used, the names of the persons involved, and the duration of the proposed monitoring.

* * *

II.

On March 14, 1974, Agent Yee met with respondent and his wife in connection with an audit of their 1971 income tax returns. After Mrs. Caceres left the meeting, respondent offered Yee a "personal settlement" of $500 in exchange for a favorable resolution of the audit. When he returned to the IRS office, Yee reported the offer to his superiors and prepared an affidavit describing it.

The record reflects no further discussion of the offer until January 1975. It does indicate, however, that one telephone conversation between Yee and respondent, on March 21, 1974, was recorded with authorization, and that authority was also obtained to monitor face-to-face conversations with respondent from time to time during the period between March and September 1974.[n.7] Yee continued to work on the audit of respondent's records throughout this period, but his meetings, until January 1975, were with Mrs. Caceres and the Cacereses' accountant.

[n.7] Requests for authorization to use electronic equipment to monitor nontelephone conversations are made on a form (No. 5177) that requires disclosure of the dates of previous authorizations. The form dated January 31, 1975, App. 63, is termed an extension, and reports prior authorizations dated March 25, April 24, May 24, June 27, July 23, and August 29, 1974. Under the regulations, a single authorization may cover a period of up to 30 days; the intervals between the dates of prior authorizations in this case are consistent with successive 30-day authorizations, although this has not been established by any evidence called to our attention.

* * *

In subsequent conversations initiated by Agent Yee, all of which were monitored,[n.10] respondent indicated that he was not prepared for another meeting with Yee. Finally, in a conversation on January 30 at 5:15 p.m., respondent agreed to a meeting the following day at 2 p.m. At 8:15 a.m. on the 31st, the Regional Inspector in San Francisco telephoned the Director of Internal Security in Washington and obtained emergency approval for the use of electronic equipment to monitor the meeting that afternoon. On the same day, a written request for authority to monitor face-to-face conversations for a period of 30 days was initiated and, in due course, forwarded to Washington for submission to the Department of Justice.

At the meeting on the 31st, respondent gave Yee $500 and promised to give him an additional $500 when he received a notice from IRS showing his deficiency at an amount upon which he and Yee had agreed. As in all his future meetings with respondent, Yee wore a concealed radio transmitter which allowed other agents to monitor and record their conversation.

Yee next called respondent on February 5 and arranged a meeting for the next day to review the audit agreement. Because the Department of Justice had not yet acted on, or perhaps even received, the request for a 30-day authorization, the Regional Inspector again requested and obtained emergency approval to monitor the meeting with respondent. At the February 6 meeting, respondent renewed his promise to pay an additional $500 in connection with the 1971 return, and also offered Yee another $2,000 for help in settling his 1973 and 1974 returns.

On February 11, a Deputy Assistant Attorney General approved the request for authority to monitor Yee's conversations with respondent for 30 days. The approval was received in time to cover a meeting held that day at which Yee was paid the additional $500. Because the 30-day period did not commence until February 11, however, no approval from the Department of Justice was ever obtained for the earlier monitorings of January 31 and February 6.

The District Court and the Court of Appeals both held that the two earlier meetings had not been monitored in accordance with IRS regulations, since Justice Department approval had not been secured. The courts recognized that such approval is not required, by the terms of the regulations, in "emergency situations" when less than 48 hours is available to secure authorization. They recognized, too, that in each instance, less than 48 hours did exist between the time the IRS initiated its request for monitoring approval and the time of the scheduled meeting with Yee. But the courts concluded that neither meeting fell within the emergency provision of the regulations because the exigencies were the product of "government-created scheduling problems."

The Government does not challenge that conclusion. We are therefore presented with the question whether the tape recordings, and the testimony

[n.10] In the District Court, respondent moved to suppress evidence relating to these telephone conversations on the grounds that the monitoring had not been properly authorized. The District Court rejected that challenge, concluding that the applicable IRS regulations had been followed with respect to these conversations. App. to Pet. for Cert. 16a-17a. That ruling is not at issue here.

of the agents who monitored the January 31 and February 6 conversations, should be excluded because of the violation of the IRS regulations.

III.

A court's duty to enforce an agency regulation is most evident when compliance with the regulation is mandated by the Constitution or federal law. In *Bridges v. Wixon*, 326 U.S. 135, 152–153, for example, this Court held invalid a deportation ordered on the basis of statements which did not comply with the Immigration Service's rules requiring signatures and oaths, finding that the rules were designed "to afford [the alien] due process of law" by providing "safeguards against essentially unfair procedures."

In this case, however, unlike *Bridges v. Wixon*, the agency was not required by the Constitution or by statute to adopt any particular procedures or rules before engaging in consensual monitoring and recording. While Title III of the Omnibus Crime Control and Safe Streets Act of 1968, 18 U.S.C. § 2510 et seq., regulates electronic surveillance conducted without the consent of either party to a conversation, federal statutes impose no restrictions on recording a conversation with the consent of one of the conversants.

Nor does the Constitution protect the privacy of individuals in respondent's position. In *Lopez v. United States*, 373 U.S. 427, 439, we held that the Fourth Amendment provided no protection to an individual against the recording of his statements by the IRS agent to whom he was speaking. In doing so, we repudiated any suggestion that the defendant had a "constitutional right to rely on possible flaws in the agent's memory, or to challenge the agent's credibility without being beset by corroborating evidence that is not susceptible of impeachment," concluding instead that "the risk that petitioner took in offering a bribe to [the IRS agent] fairly included the risk that the offer would be accurately reproduced in court, whether by faultless memory or mechanical recording." The same analysis was applied in *United States v. White*, 401 U.S. 745, to consensual monitoring and recording by means of a transmitter concealed on an informant's person, even though the defendant did not know that he was speaking with a Government agent[.]

* * *

Our decisions in *Lopez* and *White* demonstrate that the IRS was not required by the Constitution to adopt these regulations.[n.14] It is equally clear that the

---

[n.14] It does not necessarily follow, however, as a matter of either logic or law, that the agency had no duty to obey them. "Where the rights of individuals are affected, it is incumbent upon agencies to follow their own procedures. This is so even where the internal procedures are possibly more rigorous than otherwise would be required." Morton v. Ruiz, 415 U.S. 199, 235. *See, e.g.,* United States ex rel. Accardi v. Shaughnessy, 347 U.S. 260 (holding habeas corpus relief proper where Government regulations "with the force and effect of law" governing the procedure to be followed in processing and passing upon an alien's application for suspension of deportation were not followed); Service v. Dulles, 354 U.S. 363 (invalidating Secretary of State's dismissal of an employee where regulations requiring approval of the Deputy Undersecretary and consultation of full record were not satisfied); Vitarelli v. Seaton, 359 U.S. 535 (invalidating dismissal of Interior Department employee where regulations governing hearing procedures for national security dismissals were not followed). *See also* Yellin v. United States, 374 U.S. 109 (reversing contempt conviction where congressional committee had not complied with its rules requiring it to consider a witness' request to be heard in executive session).

violations of agency regulations disclosed by this record do not raise any constitutional questions.

It is true, of course, that respondent's conversations were monitored without the approval of the Department of Justice, whereas the conversations of others in a similar position would, assuming the IRS generally follows its regulations, be recorded only with Justice Department approval. But this difference does not even arguably amount to a denial of equal protection. No claim is, or reasonably could be, made that if the IRS had more promptly addressed this request to the Department of Justice, it would have been denied. As a result, any inconsistency of which respondent might complain is purely one of form, with no discernible effect in this case on the action taken by the agency and its treatment of respondent.

Moreover, the failure to secure Justice Department authorization, while conceded here to be a violation of the IRS regulations, was attributable to the fact that the IRS officials responsible for administration of the relevant regulations, both in San Francisco and Washington, construed the situation as an emergency within the meaning of those regulations. Their construction of their own regulations, even if erroneous, was not obviously so. That kind of error by an executive agency in interpreting its own regulations surely does not raise any constitutional questions.

Nor is this a case in which the Due Process Clause is implicated because an individual has reasonably relied on agency regulations promulgated for his guidance or benefit and has suffered substantially because of their violation by the agency. Respondent cannot reasonably contend that he relied on the regulation, or that its breach had any effect on his conduct. He did not know that his conversations with Yee were being recorded without proper authority. He was, of course, prejudiced in the sense that he would be better off if all monitoring had been postponed until after the Deputy Assistant Attorney General's approval was obtained on February 11, 1975, but precisely the same prejudice would have ensued if the approval had been issued more promptly. For the record makes it perfectly clear that a delay in processing the request, rather than any doubt about its propriety or sufficiency, was the sole reason why advance authorization was not obtained before February 11.

* * *

IV.

Respondent argues that the regulations concerning electronic eavesdropping, even though not required by the Constitution or by statute, are of such importance in safeguarding the privacy of the citizenry that a rigid exclusionary rule should be applied to all evidence obtained in violation of any of their provisions. We do not doubt the importance of these rules. Nevertheless, without pausing to evaluate the Government's challenge to our power to do so, we decline to adopt any rigid rule requiring federal courts to exclude any evidence obtained as a result of a violation of these rules.

* * * Although we do not suggest that a suppression order in this case would cause the IRS to abandon or modify its electronic surveillance regulations, we cannot ignore the possibility that a rigid application of an exclusionary rule to every regulatory violation could have a serious deterrent impact on the formulation of additional standards to govern prosecutorial and police procedures. Here, the Executive itself has provided for internal sanctions in cases of knowing violations of the electronic-surveillance regulations. To go beyond that, and require exclusion in every case, would take away from the Executive Department the primary responsibility for fashioning the appropriate remedy for the violation of its regulations. But since the content, and indeed the existence, of the regulations would remain within the Executive's sole authority, the result might well be fewer and less protective regulations. In the long run, it is far better to have rules like those contained in the IRS Manual, and to tolerate occasional erroneous administration of the kind displayed by this record, than either to have no rules except those mandated by statute, or to have them framed in a mere precatory form.

Nor can we accept respondent's further argument that even without a rigid rule of exclusion, his is a case in which evidence secured in violation of the agency regulation should be excluded on the basis of a more limited, individualized approach. Quite the contrary, this case exemplifies those situations in which evidence would not be excluded if a case-by-case approach were applied. The two conversations at issue here were recorded with the approval of the IRS officials in San Francisco and Washington. In an emergency situation, which the agents thought was present, this approval would have been sufficient. The agency action, while later found to be in violation of the regulations, nonetheless reflected a reasonable, good-faith attempt to comply in a situation in which no one questions that monitoring was appropriate and would have certainly received Justice Department authorization, had the request been received more promptly. In these circumstances, there is simply no reason why a court should exercise whatever discretion it may have to exclude evidence obtained in violation of the regulations.

The judgment of the Court of Appeals is Reversed.

MR. JUSTICE MARSHALL, with whom MR. JUSTICE BRENNAN joins, dissenting.

The Court today holds that evidence obtained in patent violation of agency procedures is admissible in a criminal prosecution. In so ruling, the majority determines both that the Internal Revenue Service's failure to comply with its own mandatory regulations implicates no due process interest, and that the exclusionary rule is an inappropriate sanction for such noncompliance. Because I can subscribe to neither proposition, and because the Court's decision must inevitably erode respect for law among those charged with its administration, I respectfully dissent.

*   *   *

This Court has consistently demanded governmental compliance with regulations designed to safeguard individual interests even when the rules were not mandated by the Constitution or federal statute. * * * Thus, where internal regulations do not merely facilitate internal agency housekeeping, *cf.* American Farm Lines v. Black Ball Freight Service, 397 U.S. 532, 538

(1970), but rather afford significant procedural protections, we have insisted on compliance.

That the IRS regulations at issue here extend such protections is beyond dispute. As this Court recognized in *Berger v. New York*, 388 U.S. 41, 63 (1967), "[few] threats to liberty exist which are greater than that posed by the use of eavesdropping devices." An agency's self-imposed constraints on the use of these devices, no less than limitations mandated by statute or by the Fourth Amendment, operate to preserve a "measure of privacy and a sense of personal security" for individuals potentially subject to surveillance. *See* United States v. White, 401 U.S. 745, 790 (1971) (Harlan, J., dissenting).

* * *

Implicit in these decisions, and in the Due Process Clause itself, is the premise that regulations bind with equal force whether or not they are outcome determinative. As its very terms make manifest, the Due Process Clause is first and foremost a guarantor of process. It embodies a commitment to procedural regularity independent of result. To focus on the conduct of individual defendants rather than on that of the government necessarily qualifies this commitment. If prejudice becomes critical in measuring due process obligations, individual officials may simply dispense with whatever procedures are unlikely to prove dispositive in a given case. Thus, the majority's analysis invites the very kind of capricious and unfettered decision making that the Due Process Clause in general and these regulations in particular were designed to prevent.

* * *

II.

Having found a due process violation, I would require that the fruits of that illegality be suppressed in respondent's criminal prosecution. Mapp v. Ohio, 367 U.S. 643 (1961). Accordingly, under my analysis, it would be unnecessary to consider the scope of our supervisory powers, discussed in Part IV of the Court's opinion. Because, however, the Court addresses that issue, I must register my profound disagreement with both its reasoning and ultimate conclusion.

* * *

In my judgment, the Court has utterly failed to demonstrate why the exclusionary rule is inappropriate under the circumstances presented here. Equally disturbing is the majority's refusal even to acknowledge countervailing considerations. Quite apart from specific deterrence, there are significant values served by a rule that excludes evidence secured by lawless enforcement of the law. Denying an agency the fruits of noncompliance gives credibility to the due process and privacy interests implicated by its conduct. Also, and perhaps more significantly, exclusion reaffirms the Judiciary's commitment to those values.

* * *

I would affirm the judgment of the court below.

Why is there no Fourth Amendment issue in *Caceres*? Why do you think the outcome in *Caceres* differs from the outcome in *Wohler,* the *Miranda–*warning case reproduced above? Finally, think about how the IRS policy violated in *Wohler* differs from the IRS policy violated in *Caceres*.

The Fourth Amendment applies in civil cases as well as criminal ones. In tax controversies, a Fourth Amendment claim may arise when property subject to a lien is seized. In *Rogers v. Vicuna*, 264 F.3d 1 (1st Cir. 2001), for example, the IRS seized cars from the taxpayer's driveway. They showed him a Notice of Seizure and Notice of Levy, but did not have a warrant. The court upheld the seizure as constitutional under the Fourth Amendment because the vehicles on the driveway were visible from the road; the taxpayer had no expectation of privacy in his driveway.

§ 14.07   Grand Jury Proceedings

A federal grand jury may be involved in the investigation of a tax case, and performs its accusatory role via an indictment. The grand jury has subpoena power to compel testimony and production of records. Although counsel may not be present during a witness' grand jury testimony, witnesses may step outside to consult with counsel. A witness may attempt to avoid testifying by filing a motion to quash a subpoena, but its denial is not appealable. A witness' only other option is to refuse to testify; the Fifth Amendment applies in grand jury proceedings.

Because of the grand jury's expansive subpoena power, the government may obtain evidence in a criminal tax case that it could not obtain in a civil investigation of the same taxpayer. The issue then arises whether the IRS may use the evidence in a civil proceeding. Look at Fed. R. Crim. P. 6(e), and consider *DiLeo*:

DILEO v. COMMISSIONER
United States Court of Appeals, Second Circuit
959 F.2d 16 (1992)[9]

FEINBERG, CIRCUIT JUDGE:

Joseph R. DiLeo, Mary A. DiLeo, Walter E. Mycek, Jr., Michele A. Mycek and Arcelo Reproduction Company, Inc. (the taxpayers) appeal from judgments of the United States Tax Court, Arthur L. Nims, C.J., dated September 5, 1991, determining that they were liable for deficiencies in their federal income taxes. This appeal also raises issues preserved for appeal following a proceeding in the United States District Court for the Southern District of New York, Vincent L. Broderick, J., involving the same parties. The principal

---

[9] *Cert. denied*, 506 U.S. 868 (1992).

issue before us is whether certain documents, which had previously been the subject of a grand jury subpoena, were properly admitted into evidence against the taxpayers in the Tax Court. The taxpayers claim that the evidence should have been suppressed under Rule 6(e) of the Federal Rules of Criminal Procedure and that absent that evidence, most of their alleged tax deficiencies would have been barred by the statute of limitations. For the reasons given below, we affirm.

I. BACKGROUND

In March 1986, the Commissioner of Internal Revenue issued statutory notices of deficiency to the DiLeos and the Myceks for the tax years 1978 through 1981 and 1978 through 1982, respectively. In March 1987, the Commissioner issued a statutory notice of deficiency for the tax years 1978 through 1982 to Arcelo, a company in which Joseph DiLeo and Walter Mycek, Jr., were sole shareholders and corporate officers. In June 1986, the DiLeos and the Myceks filed petitions in the Tax Court for redeterminations of these deficiencies and in June 1987, Arcelo also sought such redetermination. The Tax Court subsequently consolidated the three cases for trial commencing in January 1988.

In early December 1987, the Commissioner served trial subpoenas duces tecum upon three banks—Chase Manhattan, Citibank and State National Bank of Connecticut, now Connecticut Bank and Trust Co. (CBT)—seeking production of "all books, records or other documents pertaining to [Arcelo's account] during the years 1977 through 1983." These records had originally been provided to a grand jury in the Southern District during a criminal investigation of the taxpayers that resulted in the indictments of Joseph R. DiLeo and Walter E. Mycek, Jr. for various tax and tax-related criminal violations. Philip B. Kirschen was the special agent of the Criminal Investigation Division (CID) of the Internal Revenue Service (IRS) assigned to assist the United States Attorney's office and the grand jury. Pursuant to plea agreements, Mycek and DiLeo pled guilty in May 1984 and March 1985, respectively, to various counts in the indictments and each received a sentence of one year and a day in prison.

After the Mycek and DiLeo criminal cases were closed in 1985, the records obtained from the banks were not returned to them. Instead, Agent Kirschen took all of the records that had accumulated during the grand jury's investigation to his CID office in Newburgh, New York, sealed them in boxes and labelled the boxes. The boxes were then transported to the IRS facility management area located in the basement of a federal building in Albany, New York. The boxes were kept inside a cage, the key to which was maintained by the CID in Albany. These boxes included the records subsequently sought by the December 1987 trial subpoenas. In response to these subpoenas, each bank separately authorized the Commissioner to obtain the records requested. Agent Kirschen obtained these records from the CID storage cage in which the grand jury documents were stored. All remaining records not requested were returned to the boxes, which were then resealed.

The consolidated Tax Court cases proceeded to trial early in 1988. The taxpayers moved to suppress the bank records on the principal ground that they were obtained in violation of Fed. R. Crim. P. 6(e), which deals with disclosure of "matters occurring before the grand jury," and that disclosure of the documents at trial would violate the law. In September 1989, after holding an evidentiary hearing and receiving briefs on the issue, the Tax Court denied the taxpayers' motion, holding that the bank records at issue were not "matters occurring before the grand jury" and were therefore not encompassed by Rule 6(e). The Tax Court also ruled that the IRS was not estopped from making this argument after withholding under Rule 6(e) other documents that had been requested by the taxpayers.

In November 1989, after this ruling of the Tax Court, Mycek and DiLeo commenced a proceeding in the Southern District to enjoin the Commissioner from using the bank records in the Tax Court trial. In September 1990, Judge Broderick issued an order (followed by an opinion in January 1991) authorizing the use of the documents in the Tax Court because the documents did not constitute "matters occurring before the grand jury," under *United States v. Interstate Dress Carriers, Inc.*, 280 F.2d 52 (2d Cir. 1960). However, Judge Broderick sharply criticized the manner in which the government handled the records after the Mycek and DiLeo criminal cases had ended. The judge also held that the Tax Court did not have the power to authorize disclosure of the grand jury material.

In November 1990, the taxpayers appealed from Judge Broderick's order to this court. In January 1991, the appeal was dismissed under a stipulation allowing the taxpayers to preserve their right to raise any issues they might have presented in that appeal on a subsequent appeal from a decision in the Tax Court case. Thereafter, the Tax Court issued an opinion in June 1991, upholding the deficiencies found by the Commissioner.

* * *

II. DISCUSSION

Matters Occurring Before the Grand Jury

Rule 6(e) of the Federal Rules of Criminal Procedure prohibits, with certain specified exceptions, the disclosure of "matters occurring before the grand jury."[n.1] A knowing disclosure, except as otherwise provided in the rules, may

---

[n.1] The rule provides in pertinent part:

(e) Recording and Disclosure of Proceedings.

* * *

(2) General Rule of Secrecy. A grand juror, an interpreter, a stenographer, an operator of a recording device, a typist who transcribes recorded testimony, an attorney for the government, or any person to whom disclosure is made under paragraph 3(A)(ii) of this subdivision shall not disclose matters occurring before the grand jury, except as otherwise provided for in these rules. No obligation of secrecy may be imposed on any person except in accordance with this rule. A knowing violation of Rule 6 may be punished as a contempt of court.

(3) Exceptions.

(A) Disclosure otherwise prohibited by this rule of matters occurring before the grand jury, other than its deliberations and the vote of any grand juror, may be made to

be punished as a contempt of court. This rule of nondisclosure serves to effectuate several important policies. The rule protects the safety of witnesses who testify before the grand jury. It thereby also helps to ensure that witnesses will be willing to come forward and that they will be able to testify fully and frankly, without fear of retribution. The secrecy also prevents suspects who might otherwise learn of investigations from fleeing their jurisdictions and from attempting to influence grand jurors prior to indictment. Finally, nondisclosure protects the reputations of suspects who are ultimately exonerated by the grand jury. United States v. Sells Engineering, Inc., 463 U.S. 418, 424 (1983).

The bank records at issue here were first obtained by a grand jury in the Southern District. They were turned over to the Commissioner several years later in response to the December 1987 trial subpoenas. The same records were ultimately used against the taxpayers at trial. Appellant taxpayers claim that this procedure improperly disclosed "matters occurring before the grand jury." The Commissioner disputes this view, relying heavily on our decision in *Interstate Dress*. The taxpayers claim, however, that *Interstate Dress* no longer represents the state of the law after the Supreme Court's decision in *John Doe Agency v. John Doe Corp.*, 493 U.S. 146 (1989). In *John Doe Agency,* the Supreme Court held that certain records were exempt from production under the Freedom of Information Act (FOIA), thereby reversing a decision of this circuit holding that the records were not exempt under that Act. In our decision, we had also rejected a claim that the information involved could not be disclosed under Rule 6(e), apparently applying the *Interstate Dress* standard, although we did not cite that case by name. *See* John Doe Corp. v. John Doe Agency, 850 F.2d 105, 109 (2d Cir. 1988). The taxpayers argue that by reversing this circuit, the Supreme Court implicitly overruled the standard of *Interstate Dress*.

The taxpayers' argument is flawed. Although we did say in *John Doe Corp.* that Rule 6(e) permitted disclosure, 850 F.2d at 109, the Supreme Court did not address that issue but ruled only that the requested documents were exempt from disclosure under § 7 of the FOIA, 5 U.S.C. § 522(b)(7). The holding revolved around an analysis of the statutory language of the FOIA. *See* 493 U.S. at 153. Having found that the documents could not be disclosed, the Court did not reach the Rule 6(e) issue and made absolutely no reference to Rule 6(e) in its entire opinion. *Interstate Dress* therefore remains the law in this circuit regarding the proper interpretation of Rule 6(e).

Under *Interstate Dress,* "when testimony or data is sought for its own sake—for its intrinsic value in the furtherance of a lawful investigation—rather than to learn what took place before the grand jury, it is not a valid defense to disclosure that the same information was revealed to a grand jury or that the same documents had been, or were presently being, examined by a grand

---

(i) an attorney for the government for use in the performance of such attorney's duty; and

(ii) such government personnel (including personnel of a state or subdivision of a state) as are deemed necessary by an attorney for the government to assist an attorney for the government in the performance of such attorney's duty to enforce federal criminal law.

jury." 280 F.2d at 54. Presumably, this rule rested upon the implicit assumption that in such instances disclosure would not "seriously compromise the secrecy of the grand jury's deliberations." In re Special March 1981 Grand Jury, 753 F.2d 575, 578 (7th Cir. 1985). * * *

In this case, the taxpayers concede that the revenue agent originally assigned to the Tax Court matter by the Commissioner did not use either the Chase, Citibank or CBT records in his preparation of the report providing the basis for the statutory notices of deficiency. The IRS had an independent public source for its knowledge that the grand jury had possession of the bank records. This is clear because the account numbers, bank names and locations, and annual information concerning deposits and withdrawals were specifically set forth in the publicly-filed indictments of Mycek and DiLeo. In response to the December 1987 trial subpoenas, the three banks also indicated to the IRS that the records had been previously provided to the Southern District grand jury in response to grand jury subpoenas served years earlier. Before the IRS received the records, all references to the grand jury were removed. The IRS was therefore not learning anything about the grand jury proceedings from the bank records that it did not already know prior to obtaining them. The records admitted into evidence in the Tax Court were sought for their own sake and not to learn what took place before the grand jury and clearly did not compromise the secrecy of the grand jury's deliberations. Under *Interstate Dress,* the records were not "matters occurring before the grand jury" within the meaning of Rule 6(e).

Disclosure Order

The taxpayers contend, and Judge Broderick held, that even if the bank records were not "matters occurring before the grand jury," Rule 6(e) still prohibited their disclosure absent a prior order from the district court. The taxpayers go on to argue that the records had been turned over to the IRS long before Judge Broderick's order and that the order could not "retroactively" cure the illegal disclosure. We do not accept this argument.

We share Judge Broderick's concern over the government's unduly informal manner in handling the bank records. It is certainly advisable for a government official to seek a judicial declaration that particular documents are not "matters occurring before the grand jury" rather than simply disclosing them and risking contempt and perhaps other sanctions because of an incorrect assumption. Nevertheless, the express terms of Rule 6(e) require a court order only to permit disclosure of material that falls within that category. Thus, the disclosure did not violate Rule 6(e) and no order, retroactive or otherwise, was absolutely necessary to validate it. In *Interstate Dress,* moreover, this court specifically addressed the requirements for disclosure of matters not occurring before the grand jury and noted that "documents produced pursuant to a grand jury subpoena remain the property of the person producing them . . . and their inspection by persons other than the grand jury and the prosecuting attorneys is therefore dependent upon the consent of the owner *or* upon a court order." 280 F.2d at 54 (citations omitted) (emphasis added). *Cf. In re Special March 1981 Grand Jury,* 753 F.2d at 579. Here, the owners of the relevant records—Chase, Citibank and CBT—gave their consent prior to the disclosure of the documents to any revenue agent involved in the civil case.

The taxpayers argue that the consents obtained from the banks were illusory and therefore failed to satisfy the requirements of *Interstate Dress.* In this case, the government retained custody of the documents at issue under claim of right from July 1985, when the grand jury investigation concluded, until December 1987, when the subpoenas were served. Since the IRS attorneys knew this fact when they solicited the consent of the banks, the taxpayers contend that the consents were irrelevant to disclosure. We reject this argument.

It is undisputed that the banks were asked for their consent to disclosure of the records. It is also undisputed that prior to this request for consent, there had been no disclosure to IRS agents, even though the relevant documents had been in the government's possession "under claim of right" for several years. After consent was obtained, the documents were disclosed. The banks have not voiced any objections to this disclosure nor have the taxpayers made a plausible argument that the banks had any interest in withholding their consent to the disclosure. Because no court order was required and because the government obtained consent as required under *Interstate Dress,* the bank records were properly disclosed and the Tax Court properly admitted them into evidence.

Allegedly Wrongful Conduct by the IRS

The taxpayers argue that the proceedings in the Tax Court were so defective that, at the very least, the burden of proof with respect to the alleged deficiencies should have been shifted to the IRS. First, the taxpayers contend that the Commissioner possessed all the grand jury records and used those that assisted the IRS while refusing production of those that would have assisted the taxpayers. Therefore, the taxpayers assert, the Commissioner had an unfair discovery advantage and the Tax Court should have shifted the burden of proof to the Commissioner. We should accordingly vacate the deficiency judgments. As the Commissioner argues, however, the assertions upon which this argument is based are unsupported by the record.

At the conclusion of the grand jury proceedings, Agent Kirschen, with the authorization of the Assistant United States Attorney, removed the specific bank records in question. Kirschen was authorized to possess these records as a government employee "deemed necessary" to assist the prosecutor under Fed. R. Crim. P. 6(e)(3)(A)(ii). *See supra* note 1. In December 1987, the Commissioner's trial subpoena requested only the bank records, the existence of which was evident from public documents. Kirschen provided only those specific documents, after removing all references to the grand jury, after consents were obtained from the owners of the records. Thus, the Commissioner did not have open access to the grand jury records.

Moreover, with regard to the information and records sought by the taxpayers, they in fact sought neither a court order nor the consent of the owners of the records prior to disclosure, as required by *Interstate Dress.* The taxpayers have therefore failed to demonstrate that they were denied access to grand jury materials to which they were entitled, an important qualification that distinguishes the bank records introduced by the Commissioner.

The taxpayers also claim that Agent Kirschen should not have been present in the courtroom during the civil trial. The Commissioner requested that Kirschen be allowed to remain for the limited purpose of providing certified documents and hearing testimony to determine whether there was any reason to believe that perjury had been committed. The taxpayers assert that the presence of the special agent was improper because he had had access to grand jury material under Rule 6(e)(3)(A)(ii). This assertion is inconsistent with the principle that a government employee who has participated in a criminal prosecution may participate in the civil phase of the dispute without obtaining a court order to do so under Rule 6(e). * * * As the Supreme Court stated in *United States v. John Doe, Inc. I* [, 481 U.S. 102, 107–111 (1987)], the prohibition in Rule 6(e) is against disclosing grand jury matters to another. 481 U.S. at 109. There is no evidence that Kirschen disclosed any Rule 6(e) information to counsel for the Commissioner. There was therefore nothing improper about his presence as a representative of the Commissioner at the trial.

Since we find nothing improper about Kirschen's conduct, we have no occasion to consider whether or not shifting the burden of proof would have been an appropriate remedy for the sort of impropriety alleged by the taxpayers. Because we find that the admission of the bank records into evidence was neither improper nor unfair, it is also unnecessary for us to reach the questions whether the proper remedy for a Rule 6(e) violation is suppression rather than a contempt of court charge and whether, if the bank records were suppressed, there would have been sufficient evidence of fraud to support the extension of the statute of limitations for the tax deficiencies.

We have considered all of the taxpayers' remaining arguments and none justify reversal of the Tax Court. We therefore affirm.

What is the policy behind Federal Rule of Criminal Procedure 6(e)? Was that policy served in *DiLeo*?

In *United States v. Hubbell*, 530 U.S. 27 (2000), the United States Supreme Court considered the federal indictment of former United States Associate Attorney General Webster Hubbell for various tax-related crimes:

UNITED STATES v. HUBBELL
Supreme Court of the United States
530 U.S. 27 (2000)

OPINION:

JUSTICE STEVENS delivered the opinion of the Court.

The two questions presented concern the scope of a witness' protection against compelled self-incrimination: (1) whether the Fifth Amendment privilege protects a witness from being compelled to disclose the existence of incriminating documents that the Government is unable to describe with reasonable particularity; and (2) if the witness produces such documents pursuant to a grant of immunity, whether 18 U.S.C. § 6002 prevents the Government from using them to prepare criminal charges against him.

I

This proceeding arises out of the second prosecution of respondent, Webster Hubbell, commenced by the Independent Counsel appointed in August 1994 to investigate possible violations of federal law relating to the Whitewater Development Corporation. The first prosecution was terminated pursuant to a plea bargain. In December 1994, respondent pleaded guilty to charges of mail fraud and tax evasion arising out of his billing practices as a member of an Arkansas law firm from 1989 to 1992, and was sentenced to 21 months in prison. In the plea agreement, respondent promised to provide the Independent Counsel with "full, complete, accurate, and truthful information" about matters relating to the Whitewater investigation.

The second prosecution resulted from the Independent Counsel's attempt to determine whether respondent had violated that promise. In October 1996, while respondent was incarcerated, the Independent Counsel served him with a *subpoena duces tecum* calling for the production of 11 categories of documents before a grand jury sitting in Little Rock, Arkansas. * * * On November 19, he appeared before the grand jury and invoked his Fifth Amendment privilege against self-incrimination. In response to questioning by the prosecutor, respondent initially refused "to state whether there are documents within my possession, custody, or control responsive to the Subpoena." * * * Thereafter, the prosecutor produced an order, which had previously been obtained from the District Court pursuant to 18 U.S.C. § 6003(a), directing him to respond to the subpoena and granting him immunity "to the extent allowed by law." Respondent then produced 13,120 pages of documents and records and responded to a series of questions that established that those were all of the documents in his custody or control that were responsive to the commands in the subpoena, with the exception of a few documents he claimed were shielded by the attorney-client and attorney work-product privileges.

The contents of the documents produced by respondent provided the Independent Counsel with the information that led to this second prosecution. On April 30, 1998, a grand jury in the District of Columbia returned a 10-count indictment charging respondent with various tax-related crimes and mail and wire fraud. The District Court dismissed the indictment relying, in part, on the ground that the Independent Counsel's use of the subpoenaed documents violated § 6002 because all of the evidence he would offer against respondent at trial derived either directly or indirectly from the testimonial aspects of respondent's immunized act of producing those documents. 11 F. Supp. 2d 25, 33–37 (DDC 1998). Noting that the Independent Counsel had admitted that he was not investigating tax-related issues when he issued the subpoena, and that he had " 'learned about the unreported income and other crimes from studying the records' contents,' " the District Court characterized the subpoena as "the quintessential fishing expedition." 11 F. Supp. 2d at 37.

The Court of Appeals vacated the judgment and remanded for further proceedings. 167 F.3d 552 (CADC 1999). The majority concluded that the District Court had incorrectly relied on the fact that the Independent Counsel did not have prior knowledge of the contents of the subpoenaed documents. The question the District Court should have addressed was the extent of the Government's independent knowledge of the documents' existence and authenticity, and of respondent's possession or control of them. It explained:

> "On remand, the district court should hold a hearing in which it seeks to establish the extent and detail of the Government's knowledge of Hubbell's financial affairs (or of the paperwork documenting it) on the day the subpoena issued. It is only then that the court will be in a position to assess the testimonial value of Hubbell's response to the subpoena. Should the Independent Counsel prove capable of demonstrating with reasonable particularity a prior awareness that the exhaustive litany of documents sought in the subpoena existed and were in Hubbell's possession, then the wide distance evidently traveled from the subpoena to the substantive allegations contained in the indictment would be based upon legitimate intermediate steps. To the extent that the information conveyed through Hubbell's compelled act of production provides the necessary linkage, however, the indictment deriving therefrom is tainted." 167 F.3d at 581.

In the opinion of the dissenting judge, the majority failed to give full effect to the distinction between the contents of the documents and the limited testimonial significance of the act of producing them. In his view, as long as the prosecutor could make use of information contained in the documents or derived therefrom without any reference to the fact that respondent had produced them in response to a subpoena, there would be no improper use of the testimonial aspect of the immunized act of production. In other words, the constitutional privilege and the statute conferring use immunity would only shield the witness from the use of any information resulting from his subpoena response "beyond what the prosecutor would receive if the documents appeared in the grand jury room or in his office unsolicited and unmarked, like manna from heaven." 166 F.3d at 602.

On remand, the Independent Counsel acknowledged that he could not satisfy the "reasonable particularity" standard prescribed by the Court of Appeals and entered into a conditional plea agreement with respondent. In essence, the agreement provides for the dismissal of the charges unless this Court's disposition of the case makes it reasonably likely that respondent's "act of production immunity" would not pose a significant bar to his prosecution. * * * The case is not moot, however, because the agreement also provides for the entry of a guilty plea and a sentence that will not include incarceration if we should reverse and issue an opinion that is sufficiently favorable to the Government to satisfy that condition. * * * Despite that agreement, we granted the Independent Counsel's petition for a writ of certiorari in order to determine the precise scope of a grant of immunity with respect to the production of documents in response to a subpoena. 528 U.S. (1999). We now affirm.

* * *

III

Acting pursuant to 18 U.S.C. § 6002, the District Court entered an order compelling respondent to produce "any and all documents" described in the grand jury subpoena and granting him "immunity to the extent allowed by law." App. 60–61. In *Kastigar v. United States*, 406 U.S. 441, 32 L. Ed. 2d 212, 92 S. Ct. 1653 (1972), we upheld the constitutionality of § 6002 because the scope of the "use and derivative-use" immunity that it provides is coextensive with the scope of the constitutional privilege against self-incrimination.

* * *

IV

The Government correctly emphasizes that the testimonial aspect of a response to a *subpoena duces tecum* does nothing more than establish the existence, authenticity, and custody of items that are produced. We assume that the Government is also entirely correct in its submission that it would not have to advert to respondent's act of production in order to prove the existence, authenticity, or custody of any documents that it might offer in evidence at a criminal trial; indeed, the Government disclaims any need to introduce any of the documents produced by respondent into evidence in order to prove the charges against him. It follows, according to the Government, that it has no intention of making improper "use" of respondent's compelled testimony.

The question, however, is not whether the response to the subpoena may be introduced into evidence at his criminal trial. That would surely be a prohibited "use" of the immunized act of production. *See* In re Sealed Case, 253 U.S. App. D.C. 8, 791 F.2d 179, 182 (CADC 1986) (Scalia, J.). But the fact that the Government intends no such use of the act of production leaves open the separate question whether it has already made "derivative use" of the testimonial aspect of that act in obtaining the indictment against respondent and in preparing its case for trial. It clearly has.

It is apparent from the text of the subpoena itself that the prosecutor needed respondent's assistance both to identify potential sources of information and to produce those sources. * * * Given the breadth of the description of the 11 categories of documents called for by the subpoena, the collection and production of the materials demanded was tantamount to answering a series of interrogatories asking a witness to disclose the existence and location of particular documents fitting certain broad descriptions. The assembly of literally hundreds of pages of material in response to a request for "any and all documents reflecting, referring, or relating to any direct or indirect sources of money or other things of value received by or provided to" an individual or members of his family during a 3-year period * * * is the functional equivalent of the preparation of an answer to either a detailed written interrogatory or a series of oral questions at a discovery deposition. Entirely apart from the contents of the 13,120 pages of materials that respondent produced in this case, it is undeniable that providing a catalog of existing documents fitting within any of the 11 broadly worded subpoena categories could provide a prosecutor with a "lead to incriminating evidence," or "a link in the chain of evidence needed to prosecute."

Indeed, the record makes it clear that that is what happened in this case. The documents were produced before a grand jury sitting in the Eastern District of Arkansas in aid of the Independent Counsel's attempt to determine whether respondent had violated a commitment in his first plea agreement. The use of those sources of information eventually led to the return of an indictment by a grand jury sitting in the District of Columbia for offenses that apparently are unrelated to that plea agreement. What the District Court characterized as a "fishing expedition" did produce a fish, but not the one that the Independent Counsel expected to hook. It is abundantly clear that the testimonial aspect of respondent's act of producing subpoenaed documents was the first step in a chain of evidence that led to this prosecution. The documents did not magically appear in the prosecutor's office like "manna from heaven." They arrived there only after respondent asserted his constitutional privilege, received a grant of immunity, and — under the compulsion of the District Court's order — took the mental and physical steps necessary to provide the prosecutor with an accurate inventory of the many sources of potentially incriminating evidence sought by the subpoena. It was only through respondent's truthful reply to the subpoena that the Government received the incriminating documents of which it made "substantial use . . . in the investigation that led to the indictment." * * *

For these reasons, we cannot accept the Government's submission that respondent's immunity did not preclude its derivative use of the produced documents because its "possession of the documents [was] the fruit only of a simple physical act — the act of producing the documents." * * * It was unquestionably necessary for respondent to make extensive use of "the contents of his own mind" in identifying the hundreds of documents responsive to the requests in the subpoena. *See* Curcio v. United States, 354 U.S. 118, 128, 1 L. Ed. 2d 1225, 77 S. Ct. 1145 (1957); *Doe v. United States*, 487 U.S. at 210. The assembly of those documents was like telling an inquisitor the combination to a wall safe, not like being forced to surrender the key to a strongbox. 487 U.S. at 210, n. 9. The Government's anemic view of respondent's act of production as a mere physical act that is principally non-testimonial in character and can be entirely divorced from its "implicit" testimonial aspect so as to constitute a "legitimate, wholly independent source" (as required by *Kastigar*) for the documents produced simply fails to account for these realities.

In sum, we have no doubt that the constitutional privilege against self-incrimination protects the target of a grand jury investigation from being compelled to answer questions designed to elicit information about the existence of sources of potentially incriminating evidence. That constitutional privilege has the same application to the testimonial aspect of a response to a subpoena seeking discovery of those sources. Before the District Court, the Government arguably conceded that respondent's act of production in this case had a testimonial aspect that entitled him to respond to the subpoena by asserting his privilege against self-incrimination. *See* 167 F.3d at 580 (noting District Court's finding that "Hubbell's compelled act of production required him to make communications as to the existence, possession, and authenticity of the subpoenaed documents"). On appeal and again before this Court, however, the Government has argued that the communicative aspect of respondent's act of producing ordinary business records is insufficiently "testimonial" to support a claim of privilege because the existence and possession of such records by any businessman is a "foregone conclusion" under our decision in *Fisher v. United States*, 425 U.S. at 411. This argument both misreads Fisher and ignores our subsequent decision in *United States v. Doe*, 465 U.S. 605, 79 L. Ed. 2d 552, 104 S. Ct. 1237 (1984).

As noted in Part II, *supra*, *Fisher* involved summonses seeking production of working papers prepared by the taxpayers' accountants that the IRS knew were in the possession of the taxpayers' attorneys. 425 U.S. at 394. In rejecting the taxpayers' claim that these documents were protected by the Fifth Amendment privilege, we stated:

> "It is doubtful that implicitly admitting the existence and possession of the papers rises to the level of testimony within the protection of the Fifth Amendment. The papers belong to the *accountant*, were prepared by him, and are the kind usually prepared by an accountant working on the tax returns of his client. Surely the Government is in no way relying on the 'truthtelling' of the *taxpayer* to prove the existence of or his access to the documents. . . . The existence and location of the papers are a foregone conclusion and the taxpayer adds little or nothing to the sum total of the Government's information by conceding that he in fact has the papers." 425 U.S. at 411 (emphases added).

Whatever the scope of this "foregone conclusion" rationale, the facts of this case plainly fall outside of it. While in *Fisher* the Government already knew that the documents were in the attorneys' possession and could independently confirm their existence and authenticity through the accountants who created them, here the Government has not shown that it had any prior knowledge of either the existence or the whereabouts of the 13,120 pages of documents ultimately produced by respondent. The Government cannot cure this deficiency through the overbroad argument that a businessman such as respondent will always possess general business and tax records that fall within the broad categories described in this subpoena. The *Doe* subpoenas also sought several broad categories of general business records, yet we upheld the District Court's finding that the act of producing those records would involve testimonial self-incrimination. 465 U.S. at 612–614, and n.13.

Given our conclusion that respondent's act of production had a testimonial aspect, at least with respect to the existence and location of the documents sought by the Government's subpoena, respondent could not be compelled to produce those documents without first receiving a grant of immunity under § 6003. As we construed § 6002 in *Kastigar*, such immunity is co-extensive with the constitutional privilege. *Kastigar* requires that respondent's motion to dismiss the indictment on immunity grounds be granted unless the

Government proves that the evidence it used in obtaining the indictment and proposed to use at trial was derived from legitimate sources "wholly independent" of the testimonial aspect of respondent's immunized conduct in assembling and producing the documents described in the subpoena. The Government, however, does not claim that it could make such a showing. Rather, it contends that its prosecution of respondent must be considered proper unless someone — presumably respondent — shows that "there is some substantial relation between the compelled testimonial communications implicit in the act of production (as opposed to the act of production standing alone) and some aspect of the information used in the investigation or the evidence presented at trial." * * * We could not accept this submission without repudiating the basis for our conclusion in *Kastigar* that the statutory guarantee of use and derivative-use immunity is as broad as the constitutional privilege itself. This we are not prepared to do.

Accordingly, the indictment against respondent must be dismissed. The judgment of the Court of Appeals is affirmed.

It is so ordered.

* * *

Why did the Court dismiss the indictment? How did a document production raise Fifth Amendment concerns?

Note that evidence that the IRS obtained *prior* to the grand jury investigation, which was later presented to the grand jury, is admissible in a subsequent civil trial without violation of Rule 6(e). *See Sisk v. Commissioner*, 791 F.2d 58 (6th Cir. 1986).

PROBLEMS

1. Your client Matthew has called to tell you that he has just been interviewed by an IRS employee who identified himself as a "Special Agent" and that he was given some sort of *Miranda*-type warning. He is eager to terminate the investigation and to resolve the matter as quickly as possible. What should you advise your client, and what should you do next?

2. The Local Times has reported a statement by the owner of the Dancerama Night Club that "the Club makes so much money I don't know what to do with it all. But I better not say any more, because I don't want to get in trouble with the IRS!" Is this the kind of information that CID might use to begin a criminal investigation?

3. Dara has significant income from illegal sources. Should she (1) not file a tax return; (2) file a return but fail to disclose the income; (3) file a return reporting the income, with a fictitious legal source for the income; (4) file the return with an explicit

Fifth Amendment claim on the return; or (5) follow some other course of action?

4.   Charlene operates an unincorporated landscaping business. An IRS Special Agent has been investigating Charlene's 1999 and 2000 tax years for some time. Recently, the IRS issued a summons to Charlene's accountant to appear and produce certain documents.

   A.   Assume that the accountant did not appear or otherwise respond to the summons. How might the IRS seek enforcement of the summons?

   B.   Assume instead that the accountant did appear, but refused to turn over the documents on the ground that they are subject to the privilege created by section 7525 of the Code. Does that privilege prevent the IRS from obtaining the documents?

   C.   Assume that the accountant did appear in response to the summons, but refused to turn over the documents on the ground that he no longer had them because he had turned them over to Charlene, who had given them to her lawyer, so that they were now protected by the attorney-client privilege. Would this prevent the IRS from obtaining the documents?

5.   Is the application of indirect methods of proving income different in the criminal context from the civil context?

6.   In what kinds of situations must a Special Agent give an actual *Miranda* warning, as opposed to the particularized IRS *Miranda*-type warning?

7.   CID referred your client Tim's case for investigation by a grand jury. The grand jury dismissed the case without an indictment. Can the IRS use the evidence obtained by the grand jury in a civil case against Tim?

Chapter 15

REPRESENTING CLIENTS IN TAX CASES

§ 15.01 Introduction

Low-income taxpayer clinics (LITCs) have proliferated since Congress authorized matching grants as part of the IRS Reform Act. *See* I.R.C. § 7526. Many of these clinics are located in academic settings, while others are run by not-for-profit organizations. This chapter explains the basic skills an attorney will need to represent clients involved in tax controversies. The chapter focuses on representation in a tax clinic setting, but the skills involved are equally relevant to private tax clients; a clinic is much like a small law firm. However, low-income clients may present special challenges that other clients do not. In general, clinic clients may have financial, educational, cultural and/or linguistic barriers to resolving their tax problems. These special concerns are discussed further below.

Because effective representation requires a careful determination of the relevant facts, Chapter 15 begins, in Section 15.02, with a discussion of this fact-finding process, the initial client interview. Only after the relevant facts have been reviewed will the legal issues involved begin to appear. Researching these legal issues is the subject of Chapter 16, which describes the sources of federal income tax law and the process for locating those sources, in order to conduct productive tax research. Section 15.03 focuses on counseling the client at each stage of the controversy following analysis of the facts and applicable law. Finally, in Section 15.04, the chapter addresses the fundamentals of negotiation, a skill that is extremely important in tax controversy work.

§ 15.02 Client Interviewing

[A] Goals and Structure of the Client Interview

The lawyer-client relationship begins with the initial client interview.[1] Therefore, the attorney should try to establish an initial level of trust and rapport by making his client as comfortable as possible. Naturally, the attorney should introduce himself to the client using his first and last names, and should shake hands. Robert F. Cochran, Jr. et al., THE COUNSELOR-AT-LAW: A COLLABORATIVE APPROACH TO CLIENT INTERVIEWING AND COUNSELING 59, 64 (1999). "Small talk" about a topic other than the client's case is a good way to begin the interview both because it helps put the client at ease, and also because it may actually elicit background information relevant to

---

[1] For convenience, the chapter uses the terms "attorney" and "lawyer" to refer to the representative, even though the representative may be a student working under the supervision of a licensed attorney.

resolving the client's tax problems.[2] *See id.* at 65–69. For example, asking the client if he had any trouble finding the clinic might elicit a response that he used to work nearby. As this hypothetical response indicates, this "chit chat" may establish commonalities that help bridge any cultural gap between client and attorney.

The client may have been screened over the telephone before he was invited to an in-person interview. The screening may have included a brief discussion of the tax problem that prompted the client to call the clinic. However, the attorney should not assume that he already knows the nature of the problem. Instead, he should use the initial interview to find out the facts of the client's tax problem and what result he or she is looking for. Both goals are served by listening well to the client's story. Questions should therefore focus on developing that story. The attorney should also take detailed notes throughout the interview.

A number of routine matters should be addressed in the initial client interview. The attorney should ascertain or confirm that the client meets the income and amount-in-controversy guidelines of the clinic. *See* Christian A. Johnson & Mary Grossman, "The Tax Law Clinic: Loyola Chicago's Decade of Experience," 50 J. L. Educ. 376, 380 (2000). The attorney should also confirm or ascertain the client's legal name, address, telephone number, social security number, employer's name and address, and the name and social security numbers of the client's spouse and any dependents he may have. *Id.* It is worth double-checking that all names are spelled correctly, and that social security numbers have been accurately recorded. Nina Olson with Michael A. Lormand, "Client Intake Interviewing and Preliminary Procedures" in Jerome Borison, EFFECTIVELY REPRESENTING YOUR CLIENT BEFORE THE "NEW" IRS (ABA 2000) at B-4. If a client interview will be videotaped, the attorney should make sure to receive the client's consent to the taping, after explaining how the videotape will be used by the clinic.

The client is likely to be unfamiliar with legal rules and doctrines. Therefore, the attorney should explain early in the interview the extent of the confidentiality of the initial interview, subsequent meetings, and any videotapes of the meetings. *See* Cochran et al., *supra*, at 61. In addition, he should notify the client of any time constraints on the interview. *Id.* at 69. Cochran et al. provide the following sample statement to begin a client interview (the discussion of fees has been deleted):

> Before we get started, let me tell you about those papers you received in the waiting room. One paper describes what lawyers call the rules on confidentiality. That generally means that I cannot tell anyone what we talk about unless you give me permission, but that paper explains some of the exceptions to the rule. . . . Do you have any questions about . . . confidentiality?
>
> Ok, I've set aside 45 minutes for this conference. If we need more time we can schedule another appointment at your convenience.

---

[2] For an excellent discussion of this phenomenon, with examples, *see* Gay Gellhorn, "Law and Language: An Empirically-Based Model for the Opening Moments of Client Interviews," 4 Clinical L. Rev. 321 (1998).

Id. at 73. The attorney should also discuss any fees or court costs that the case may involve. He should also ascertain whether the client has consulted with another lawyer or accountant about the problem, primarily to ascertain whether proceedings are already ongoing.

Throughout the interview, the lawyer should try to put the client at ease by listening, smiling, looking at the client, leaning forward, keeping his arms unfolded, speaking clearly, remaining genuine, and demonstrating that he is focused on and engaged by the interview. *See id.* at 59, 63. It may help to use the client's own terminology or phrasing when asking questions. *See id.* In addition, the attorney should avoid being distracted by ringing telephones or other people who may be walking nearby or chatting in adjacent rooms.

To begin the fact-gathering portion of the interview, the lawyer should ask the client what has prompted him to come to the clinic. This question should generally be broad and open-ended so that the client feels free to answer in the way he feels comfortable. *See id.* at 79. The tax problems of tax clinic clients frequently involve the earned income credit, filing status issues, dependency exemptions, and substantiation of deductions. Janet Spragens & Nina E. Olson, "Tax Clinics: The New Face of Legal Services," 88 Tax Notes 1525, 1526 (2000).

> The LITCs are now seeing all of these issues and more: a steady stream of denied child care credits, home office deductions, start-up business expenses, unreported tip income, car expenses, substantiation (of cost of goods sold, interest payments, charitable contributions, etc.), worker classification issues, disability income, pensions, hobby losses, and self employment tax — to name just a few. The taxpayers are taxi drivers, maintenance workers, nurses, restaurant workers, bus drivers, artists, auto mechanics, hairdressers, retirees, agricultural workers, police officers, gas station attendants, teachers — even prisoners.

Id. In addition, tax clinic clients may have tax collection issues.

If the client received a letter from the IRS, it may help the attorney determine the stage of the controversy (is it a 30-day letter, 90-day letter, notice and demand for payment, or something else?) and whether immediate, emergency action must be taken. The letter may also indicate the type of tax, tax years involved, and what the issue is. However, the attorney should make sure not to focus on letters and other documents to the detriment of listening to the client and developing rapport with him.

After identifying the basic nature of the tax problem, the attorney should elicit a narrative of it. Open-ended questions will advance the narrative while also providing the attorney with a sense of some of the causes of the client's problems. The attorney should be nonjudgmental, conveying acceptance of the problem so that the client feels comfortable making further confidences. A tax client is likely to be anxious about the tax matter and its implications for his financial wherewithal, and perhaps frustrated by ineffective attempts to resolve the problem with the IRS on his own. Supportive feedback can facilitate communication of all of the facts.

Therefore, during the narrative, the lawyer should avoid cutting off the client, limiting his responses, or "cross-examining" him. Many people have a natural tendency to interrupt others in conversation. Lawyers, in particular, tend to interrupt clients to elicit information in a particular order or to ascertain details they view as important. *See* Cochran et al., *supra*, at 88. By doing so, they may make clients uncomfortable in revealing relevant information, thereby actually lengthening the interviewing process. *See id.* at 101–104. However, supportive "interruptions" such as expressions of understanding or agreement should facilitate communication.[3]

After the client tells his "story," the attorney may need to follow up with more specific, targeted questions to ascertain details the client may have omitted. *See id.* at 76. Drawing on the traditional reporters' questions of "who, what, when, where, why, and how" should help in covering all of the details. Make sure that the client is focused on the taxable year in question, which will likely be several years prior to the time the interview takes place. This may require prodding the client's recollection on issues as to the members of his household in that year, his employers, and the like. If the client cannot remember, the attorney should ask him to consult with others who might have the information, such as family members or former employers.

For a collections matter, one source, which does not focus specifically on low-income clients, recommends the following course of action:

> Whenever an IRS Collection Division matter arises, a client meeting needs to be arranged immediately to obtain the following key information:
>
> **What happened and why.** Ask the client what happened; why is the tax liability outstanding? . . . [K]nowing this information is critical when dealing with the Collection Division on the client's behalf. The most likely scenarios are:
>
>> (1) The client filed his or her last income tax return showing a balance due and did not send in a check with the return. Possibly the client was self-employed and did not make sufficient estimated tax payments.
>>
>> (2) The client went through an IRS audit that resulted in a tax deficiency, which was never paid.
>>
>> (3) The client operates a small business with several employees and then fell behind in remitting payroll taxes.
>
> Knowing why it happened is equally as important:
>
>> (1) Did the client have a significant reduction in income?
>>
>> (2) Did a new competitor take most of the customers away?
>>
>> (3) Was the client out of work for part of the year (perhaps due to sickness)?
>>
>> (4) Did the client expand too rapidly?

---

[3] This technique is termed "active listening." *See* Stefan H. Krieger et al., ESSENTIAL LAWYERING SKILLS 66–67 (1999).

(5) Was the client simply living a more luxurious lifestyle than the client's income allowed?

Tax years involved. Determine whether the client owes money to the IRS for only one tax period, or whether a consistent pattern of not paying the IRS exists year after year.[4] Obviously, it is easier for the tax professional to deal with the IRS if the client is behind for only one income tax year (or one payroll tax quarter) and has always paid other past taxes on time.

If, on the other hand, the client consistently falls behind in paying taxes each and every year, then what is to prevent it from happening again? Corrective action by the client will need to be taken.

Review all notices. Review all IRS notices the client has already received to determine what stage the Collection Division process is at. For instance, the tax professional needs to determine whether the client has received only the initial Notice and Demand for Payment from the IRS Service Center, or whether the client has already received a more serious bank levy and possibly a Notice of Federal Tax Lien.[5]

Were all returns filed? Some taxpayers who owe the IRS money are also behind a year or two in filing their tax returns. Negotiating with the IRS on behalf of a client who is still behind in filing tax returns is difficult. Thus, immediate steps should be taken to prepare all late tax returns.

Review tax liability. A thorough review of the client's tax liability should be made. Possibly the underlying tax shown on the IRS notice is wrong — e.g., the IRS filed a substitute tax return (under Section 6020(b)(1)) that was inaccurate. Perhaps the IRS assessed payroll taxes for a business that actually closed months earlier without notifying the IRS. Also, check to determine whether all IRS penalties added on were proper. The IRS makes mistakes every day.

Review limitations period. A common misconception is that once a taxpayer owes the IRS money, the government can continue to collect on it forever. . . .[6]

Richard A. Carpenter, "Get the Best Deal for Clients from the IRS Collection Division," 27 Tax'n for Lawyers 77, 81 (1998).

Once the attorney has what seems to be the complete story, he should summarize it for the client in order to be certain it is clear. This will also provide an opportunity for the client to mention additional facts that he may have forgotten to relate earlier. The attorney should be clear in the summary that these are the facts, as he understands them, for the taxable year in question, not the current year. After determining what the tax problem is, allowing the client to tell the full story, and summarizing it for the client, the

---

[4] [If the client has consistently underpaid taxes in the past, the attorney should be prepared to stress to the IRS the client's forward-looking compliance with the tax laws. Eds.]

[5] [These documents, as well as the CDP notice, are discussed in Chapter 12. Eds.]

[6] [The statute of limitations on collections is discussed in Chapter 12. Eds.]

lawyer should ask the client what his goals are. Some clinics may prefer that this step, and those following it, take place in a second interview, after the lawyer has had time to research the legal issues and discuss the case with others, such as a supervising attorney.

It is very important that the attorney ascertain the client's goals before focusing on courses of action because the client may have goals other than simply resolving the tax case. Those goals may include such things as demonstrating that he is not a "tax cheat," or keeping others, such as an employer or ex-spouse, unaware of his tax problem. If the lawyer does not find out the client's goals, what the lawyer might consider a "win" may actually disappoint or anger the client. *See* Clark D. Cunningham, "The Lawyer as Translator, Representation as Text: Towards an Ethnography of Legal Discourse," 77 Cornell L. Rev. 1298, 1304 (1992).

For example, the client may have sought the clinic's help with filing tax returns for prior years.[7] The normal process is to mail the completed returns to the IRS, retaining a photocopy. However, if the client's reason for coming to the clinic is that he needs to prove in an upcoming immigration hearing that he has filed his tax returns, photocopies of completed returns will not be sufficient for the client's purposes. Instead, the client will need to have duplicate originals brought to the IRS in person, so that one original may be stamped "received" by the IRS and retained by the client.

As another example, the client's reason for enlisting the help of the clinic to obtain a tax refund retained by the IRS may be that he is facing eviction and urgently needs the money to pay his rent. The facts of the case may be such that obtaining a refund may require a request to the IRS for audit reconsideration or another slow process. If the attorney does not explain the reality that, even if he is successful in obtaining a refund, the process may take much longer than the client assumed, the client may be furious even if he eventually receives the money. Thus, it is key that the attorney ascertain the client's goals, rather than assuming that the client's only goal is to pay the least amount of tax possible or obtain a refund.

Occasionally, clients may have goals that are not realistic, such as the desire to receive, in addition to a full concession by the IRS, a letter of apology. In those cases, the attorney should try to diffuse the client's anger at the IRS. He may sympathize with the client and explain that IRS personnel are simply doing their jobs. It may also help to explain to the client that the audit rate on certain issues, such as the earned income credit, is very high; the IRS has not singled out the client.

In this regard, it may help to ascertain during the initial interview to what extent the client has already dealt with the IRS and the nature of those experiences. That is, if the client is extremely frustrated with the IRS, it is better to ascertain that early and try to diffuse the client's anger so that it does not pose a problem during the resolution of the controversy. The attorney may need to explain that the IRS does not write the tax law and that the IRS

---

[7] "LITCs have been permitted to prepare tax returns because the IRS has taken the position that preparing tax returns for ESL [English-as-second-language] taxpayers constitutes a program to inform ESL taxpayers about their rights and responsibilities." *See* Leslie Book, "Tax Clinics: Past the Tipping Point and to the Turning Point," 92 Tax Notes 1089 (2001).

is not trying to harass the client, but simply making sure that the client has complied with the law.

Some clients may push to take a case to trial in order to be able to tell their stories to a judge. The attorney should explain to the client that most tax cases settle, and that even the Tax Court discourages trials through its requirement of stipulations of the facts and techniques such as encouraging counsel to discuss settlement. The attorney may need to explain that it will only hurt the client's case if he insists on going to trial in spite of a reasonable settlement offer by the IRS. Moreover, if a client insists on making "tax protestor" arguments — for example, that the entire income tax is unconstitutional — the attorney must tell him that courts do not permit those arguments and very likely will impose monetary sanctions on the client if those arguments are made. *See* I.R.C. § 6673(a) (discussed in Chapter 6); *see also Philips v. Commissioner*, T.C. Memo. 1995-540 (reproduced in Chapter 6). Similarly, an attorney cannot ethically make such arguments on a client's behalf.

On the other hand, some clients may wish to avoid making certain arguments, or may prefer to concede certain issues. For example, the facts of a client's case may suggest a compelling claim for innocent spouse relief. However, the client may be reluctant to portray his or her spouse or ex-spouse in a bad light. A victim of domestic violence may be extremely reluctant to testify to it in Tax Court, a public forum, even though the testimony would support the claim for innocent spouse relief. An attorney needs to be sensitive to this issue, and not simply assume that the client will be willing to tell his or her story to anyone. As another example, the client may be unwilling or unable to gather the documentation necessary to prove an issue such as "head of household" filing status, and prefer to move forward only on another issue, such as the earned income credit.

Once the client's goals have been identified, attorney and client can focus on possible ways to obtain that outcome. This will require a familiarity with tax procedure in general and specific options relevant to the client's situation in particular. For example, in a collections matter, options include making an audit reconsideration request; submitting an offer-in-compromise; entering into an installment agreement with the IRS; convincing the IRS that the account is uncollectible; paying the tax and conceding the case, perhaps by borrowing the money or selling assets; or, depending on the taxes involved, seeking bankruptcy protection. *See* Carpenter, *supra*, at 82–83 (footnotes omitted).

If Tax Court litigation is a possibility, the attorney should explain the basics of the court and its procedures, including those of the small tax case division. Very few tax cases go to trial, but Tax Court petitions are filed in many cases. The attorney should make the client aware that the taxpayer generally bears the burden of proving the facts in a litigated tax case. He should also explain to the client the importance of substantiating the relevant facts of the tax year in question. Records relating to the current year will not establish to the IRS where the client lived or the amount of his income or expenses from the tax year in issue. The client will need to understand that, without records, the resolution of factual questions will likely rest on the credibility of the client and his witnesses.

The discussion of possible ways of resolving the case should help the lawyer ascertain what resolution the client is seeking and what resolution, short of that, the client would be willing to accept. The lawyer should couch the available options in terms of those that occur to him off the "top of his head" in case there are others as well. Note that, under legal ethics rules, the client is entitled to make most of the decisions in his case. *See* Model Rule of Professional Conduct 1.2(a). If the client is unsure of what resolution he wants, the attorney can ask the client to reflect both on the client's goals and on the desired outcome. *See* Cochran, et al., *supra*, at 107. He can also ask the client to think about possible ways to accomplish that outcome, which may help the client remain personally invested in the case. *Id.*

An experienced attorney may be able to assess the likely outcome of particular options. Inexperienced attorneys probably will be unable to evaluate the likely outcome, and should not make an uneducated guess. Instead, the attorney should tell the client that he will need to review the facts, perform research, and get back to him. Similarly, if the attorney does not know the length of time a particular course of action will take, he should not give one. Moreover, the attorney should avoid the temptation to promise a client a favorable outcome. Instead, he should make clear that he cannot guarantee any particular result.

If the attorney is experienced, and he knows the likely outcome of a particular option (such as an innocent spouse claim or a Tax Court trial), he should explain that to the client. If the likely outcome of a particular option is unfavorable, the attorney should communicate that and should not back off of the negative evaluation even if pressured by the client. *See id.* at 159 (*quoting* Linda F. Smith, "Medical Paradigms for Counseling: Giving Clients Bad News," 4 Clinical L. Rev. 391–393, 417–427, 430–431 (1998)). If the outcome of a particular course of action is uncertain, the attorney should convey that.

If the attorney, even an experienced one, does not perceive any way to obtain a desirable outcome in the client's case, it may be best to wait until after the interview to convey that. *See* Krieger et al., *supra* note 3, at 217. First, reflection on the problem and consultation with others may suggest additional options.[8] In addition, as discussed below, people generally handle bad news better if they are given a complete explanation of why the news is what it is. Waiting before delivering the news provides time to prepare for likely client questions in that regard. *See id.*

---

[8] Janet Spragens and Nina Olson provide an example of the creativity that may be necessary to resolve clients' tax problems:

> [T]his year the AU tax clinic successfully challenged the asserted tax on $10,000 of unreported lottery income won by one of its clients–by showing a pattern of regular gambling activity that produced offsetting losses. Even though the taxpayer, a construction worker, had thrown away his losing lottery tickets for the year in question, the student-attorney assigned to the case interviewed and obtained affidavits from the liquor store employees where the client had established a regular pattern of buying five tickets per day, six days per week (not Sundays), over several years. Indeed, in the initial client interview with the clinic, the taxpayer took out his wallet and pulled out the five tickets he had bought for that day, which the students immediately photocopied and later showed to the IRS.

Spragens & Olson, *supra*, at 1527.

At the close of the interview, the attorney should make sure that the client understands what will happen next. If additional information or documentation is needed from the client, the lawyer should explain what is needed, preferably providing the client with a written list.[9] If there are deadlines, including statutes of limitations, the attorney should inform the client about them and follow up with a letter that also provides the information. For example, if a client chooses not to pursue Tax Court litigation after receiving a notice of deficiency, the attorney should tell him the last day a petition may be filed so that the client knows the timetable under which he may change the decision not to petition the court. *See* Cochran et al., *supra*, at 108.

At the conclusion of the interview, the attorney should also tell the client how he may contact the attorney or the clinic as the case goes forward. This will assure the client of the clinic's continuing availability for follow-up interviews and counseling. *Id.* at 106–107. Once the clinic decides to take the case, the lawyer may need to ask the client to sign a representation agreement. That agreement should require clients to agree to maintain contact with the clinic and to update their contact information as it changes. Tax clinic clients may have financial problems that result in interruption of their telephone service and frequent moves. Regardless of whether a formal agreement is signed, the attorney should stress to the client how important it is that the clinic be able to contact him. In addition, once the clinic takes the case, the attorney should obtain a signed power of attorney from the client if the clinic will be representing the client before the IRS. This may be done by mail if the clinic's practice is to decide whether to take the case after the initial client interview.

As the discussion above indicates, a client interview is composed of several parts. Some of these parts may be carried out in an interview subsequent to the initial one. The attorney will likely do a better job of obtaining the facts and establishing an initial level of trust if he has organized the interview in advance. *See* Krieger et al., *supra* note 3, at 69. The seven main components of the interview are (1) the introductions and "small talk"; (2) routine collection of basic client information; (3) the information-gathering phase during which the client tells his story; (4) a goal-identification stage; (5) an informative stage in which the attorney conveys relevant tax law and tax procedure; (6) a discussion of strategy or possible courses of action; and (7) a closing stage in which attorney and client agree on the steps that will follow the interview. *See id.*; Cochran et al., *supra*, at 59–61.

[B] Special Challenges

[1] Generally

As indicated above, low-income clients may present special challenges caused by economic, educational, cultural and/or linguistic barriers.

---

[9] If the client did not keep a copy of his tax return, the attorney will need to request it from the IRS. If the client did not keep other documents, creativity may be necessary to find alternatives, as in the example regarding documenting lottery losses. *See* note 8, *supra*.

Many LITC clients are those often least able to help themselves, including relative newcomers to the country who may speak English as a second language (ESL). These ESL taxpayers, while diverse in their backgrounds, often share significant language barriers, a fear of government, and fear of financial institutions. They also often have little understanding of our nation's voluntary system of tax self-assessment. Other clients include those who have reentered or just entered the workforce from the welfare rolls, and recently separated or divorced taxpayers. A significant number of LITC clients lack access to computers and to the Internet that many of us now take for granted in our lives, and have limited literacy skills and educational backgrounds. A large percentage of LITC clients has limited means of transportation, and are overextended, balancing the demands of both work and family in single-parent households.

Leslie Book, *supra* note 7, at 1089, 1090 (2001) (footnote omitted). Thus, for example, even arranging a time for an interview may be difficult for a low-income client because the client may have an inflexible work schedule or transportation may be a problem. Olson with Lormand, *supra*, at B-1. At times, the client may have no choice but to bring a child to the interview. *Id.*

Some clients may be illiterate. For those clients, it is important to explain everything orally. A complicating factor is that the client may be embarrassed about his illiteracy and reluctant to confide it. Therefore, the attorney should wait until he has developed an initial rapport with the client before asking questions related to literacy. He might start out by asking the client about his education level. He can then comment that the tax law is very complicated and many people have trouble understanding notices from the IRS. He can ask if the client has trouble with that as well. This may not establish for the attorney whether the client has basic literacy and therefore can read letters from the clinic, but it may help. In addition, if the client admits to trouble reading or understanding IRS notices, the attorney should ask him to send or bring a copy of any such notices to the clinic immediately after receiving them.

Because the literacy issue may not be resolved in the first interview, it is important that the attorney follow up an interview with a new client not only with a representation letter but also with a telephone call that conveys the information. The attorney should document in the file when he called the client and what information he relayed.

[2] Language Barriers

Identifying the problem, ascertaining the facts, and developing rapport may be more challenging if the client and attorney have different cultural backgrounds, and even more difficult if they can communicate only through an interpreter. *See* Kevin R. Johnson & Amagda Perez, "Clinical Legal Education and the U.C. Davis Immigration Law Clinic: Putting Theory into Practice and Practice into Theory," 51 SMU L. Rev. 1423, 1439 (1998). Inevitably, some tax clinic clients will not speak English well enough to communicate with an English-speaking attorney without an interpreter. When using an interpreter, the lawyer should face the client and speak to him rather than to the interpreter. Questions should be addressed to the client directly (e.g., "Where did you live in 1999?") rather than to the interpreter (*e.g.*, "Ask him where he lived in 1999.").

Interpretation problems can hinder the fact-gathering portion of the client interview. For example, a Spanish-speaking client who is asked his marital status may say that he is "soltero" (which may be translated as "single") even if he is in fact divorced.[10] The distinction between being single and divorced may matter to the tax case because it may be important whether the client was married during the tax year in question. In such a case, the attorney may need to follow up a statement that a client is "single" with a question about whether he has ever been married. The following example from a law school clinic raises a similar issue.

> In . . . [one case] our client was charged with the misdemeanor of Operating a Vehicle While Under the Influence of Liquor . . . and a companion per se violation of operating a vehicle with a blood-alcohol level in excess of 0.10%. When the students presented the case to me after the intake interview, they reported that the client admitted that he was guilty. . . .
>
> The representation had an unusual complicating factor: the client's native language was Spanish and his ability to speak English was limited. Accordingly, we had arranged for a law student fluent in Spanish to attend the intake interview as a translator. As we reviewed the video tape, I noted that when the students asked the client, "What happened?" his first response was "Yo soy culpable." The translator paused for a moment and then said, for the client, "I'm guilty." . . . The students confirmed that this exchange was the basis for their report that the client "admitted" he was guilty.
>
> I was curious to find out why the client's words were translated as "I'm guilty," and so I sought out the translating law student. The translator confirmed my suspicion that the Spanish word used by our client, "culpable," was a close cognate of the English word bearing the same form. As a result, the client's statement could have also been translated: "I am culpable" or "I am blameworthy." Thus the client could have been saying something more like, "I feel bad about what I did," or "I accept personal responsibility for the consequences of my action." If the client's words had been given these latter possible translations, the students might well have reached a different conclusion about his admission of "guilt."

Clark D. Cunningham, "A Tale of Two Clients: Thinking about Law as Language," 87 Mich. L. Rev. 2459, 2464 (1989) (footnote omitted).

This example also reveals the importance of using a trained interpreter whenever possible. Interpretation is a skill that goes beyond the ability to speak two languages fluently. In part, it may require translating concepts rather than translating individual words. It may also require sensitivity to the fact that the meaning of words is influenced by cultural context. In

---

[10] In fact, this may reflect a cultural difference in the concept of marital status that could occur even if the client speaks English.

addition, tax cases present terms of art that may pose a challenge to an interpreter who is not familiar with them. For example, it may be particularly difficult to explain the difference between an IRS Appeals Conference and an appeal from a court decision if the interpreter is not familiar with tax procedure.

Of course, it may not always be possible to use a professional interpreter. If that is the case, the attorney should consider who might serve as an interpreter. Sometimes the client will bring a family member to interpret, but that can pose additional problems. A client may bring a grade-school aged child to interpret for him, for example. A child is unlikely to be able to translate the legal and tax vocabulary necessary for attorney and client to communicate. Even an adult family member who serves as an interpreter may pose problems not present if an unrelated party interprets, because the family dynamic may hinder representation. For example, in an innocent spouse case, the client may be reluctant to talk about the details of his or her marriage in the presence of a family member.

If a non-professional interpreter is used, he should be instructed to tell the attorney if he is unsure of the meaning of a question or answer, rather than guessing at the translation. In addition, the interpreter should limit his interaction with the client to interpretation, so that the interpreter does not attempt to give legal advice to the client or inadvertently hamper the attorney's development of rapport with the client. It may also be worth recording the interview if the client is comfortable with that and the clinic has appropriate safeguards to keep the recording confidential. That way, the lawyer can refer back to the recording and seek additional translation, if needed.

A client who cannot speak English likely cannot read it, either. It is therefore important to stress to a client who is not fluent in English that if he receives any mail from the government, or any other mail that may relate to his tax case, he should immediately send or bring a copy of it to the clinic. The IRS is not infallible, so filing a power of attorney under which the IRS sends copies to the clinic does not guarantee that the clinic will receive copies of everything.

[C] Following Up: Representation Letters and Retainer Agreements

After the initial interview, the attorney or the clinic should follow up with a letter to the client. The letter may include a retainer agreement, if that is the clinic's practice. Retainer agreements are discussed briefly below. The letter should be cordial, with an opening pleasantry and a closing expressing the attorney's interest in working with the client on the tax matter. In addition, the letter should avoid the use of legal jargon that the client might not understand. Furthermore, as indicated above, because of the possibility that the client is illiterate, it is worth telephoning him to convey the same information orally. The attorney should document the call in the client's file.

A representation letter should detail the facts of the case and ask the client to inform the attorney of any inaccuracies as soon as possible. It should also list any options summarized at the initial interview and any others that the attorney has thought of subsequently. In addition, it should reiterate that the attorney cannot guarantee any particular result. If the attorney needs particular documents from the client, the letter should list them. If a deadline, such as the deadline to file a Tax Court petition, has already passed, the letter should include that information. If there are deadlines that have not expired, the letter should specify them clearly. In addition, the letter should notify the client about the timing of the next contact between attorney and client, such as a statement that the attorney will contact the client if he has not heard from him by a certain date. The letter should also ask the client to inform the attorney as soon as possible if anything new happens with respect to the case.

A retainer agreement is a contract between the clinic and the client. It should specify the terms of the agreement, including (1) the clinic's fees, if any; (2) the extent to which the client is responsible for any costs incurred by the clinic on the client's behalf; (3) the client's obligation to notify the clinic of changes in his financial circumstances that may affect his eligibility for representation; (4) the clinic's right to retain any attorney's fees awarded in the case; (5) a confidentiality statement; (6) the clinic's right to withdraw from representation; and (7) the client's agreement to cooperate with the clinic. *See* Olson with Lormand, *supra*, Appendix H.

[D] Declining Representation

After the initial interview of the client, the clinic may decide to decline representation of the client for such reasons as (1) the client or his case do not meet the income level or other guidelines of the clinic, (2) the client seems uncooperative, unreliable, or untrustworthy, (3) the client's only case may consist of illegal "tax protestor" arguments, (4) the matter does not present a legal problem, (5) the situation may be simple enough that the client can handle it himself after some direction, (6) the clinic does not have the resources to provide quality representation of the client, (7) the client contacted the clinic too late for it to be able to help him, or (8) the matter presents a conflict of interest for the clinic. *See* Johnson & Grossman, *supra*, at 379–380; Olson with Lormand, *supra*, at B-2–B-3.

If the clinic declines representation, the clinic or the attorney who interviewed the client should inform the client both orally and in writing. This should forestall problems that could arise if the client were to believe or allege that the clinic had taken his case, and statutes of limitations were therefore allowed to run. Accordingly, the attorney should document in the file the oral communication with the client.

The letter declining representation should be as cordial as a representation letter, and similarly should avoid the use of legalese, even if it is a form letter. It should specify the reason that representation was declined. The letter should also inform the client that he may wish to seek other counsel promptly, to avoid allowing any legal deadlines to lapse. However, the letter should be clear that its author has not researched what those deadlines might be.

§ 15.03   Client Counseling

[A]   Overview

The ultimate goal of client counseling by the attorney is to facilitate the client's process of deciding among various options as they present themselves throughout the pendency of the case. This will require the attorney (1) to ascertain the key facts and the client's goals, (2) to inform the client about applicable tax law and procedure, and (3) to advise the client on how to reach his goals given the facts and applicable law. *See* Cochran et al., *supra*, at 132. These steps involve building rapport between the attorney and the client and negotiating the terms of the attorney-client relationship. Hurder, *supra*, at 91. The attorney may have already completed part or all of one or more of the three steps during the initial client interview. However, it is likely that the client and attorney will need to talk additional times before the case is resolved.

A tax controversy may comprise several stages, each of which may warrant meeting with the client. Those stages may include an Appeals conference, negotiating with IRS counsel, Tax Court or other litigation, and resolution of collections issues. It is important that the attorney prepare for each meeting. Staying up-to-date on the case demonstrates a minimum level of professional competence and shows respect for the client by avoiding the need for him to repeat information previously conveyed. Thus, the attorney should review the facts of the client's case, the client's goals, and applicable substantive and procedural law. *See* Krieger et al., *supra*, at 187. He should also consider how to explain legal terms and concepts to a lay person. *Id.* at 208. In addition, the attorney should analyze the available options and their costs and benefits. *Id.* at 187. This will prepare him to assist client decisionmaking, as discussed below.

During each meeting with the client, the attorney should discuss the options presented, taking the lead on explaining the legal risks and benefits of each option, so as to inform the client fully. Some clients may benefit from seeing this information in writing. If the options are tentative because the next set of negotiations has not yet commenced, the attorney should make that clear to the client. Donald G. Gifford, "The Synthesis of Legal Counseling and Negotiation Models: Preserving Client-Centered Advocacy in the Negotiation Context," 34 UCLA L. Rev. 811, 845 (1987).

As in the initial interview, during each encounter with the client, the attorney should avoid interrupting the client, and try to put the client at ease by demonstrating that he is focused on and engaged by the interview. Sitting together at a conference table or other table may make the client more comfortable than sitting with a desk between client and attorney. *See* Krieger et al., *supra*, at 209. In addition, the attorney should block out enough time for the meeting that the client is not rushed into a decision. Cochran et al., *supra*, at 153.

A lawyer effective at counseling clarifies his clients' goals, provides emotional support for his clients during the decisionmaking process, informs clients about available options, and encourages clients to organize the information in a way that facilitates decisionmaking. *Id.* at 113. Cochran et al.

suggest beginning follow-up discussions with a client with the open-ended question such as "Has anything happened that I should know about?" *Id.* at 135. In addition, specific, directed questions may be appropriate when the attorney knows that a particular event may have happened during the intervening time. *See id.* at 135–136.

As indicated above, legal ethics rules generally provide that the client, not the lawyer, is the decisionmaker. The lawyer is merely the client's agent in making those decisions. A client may choose to concede or settle a case that has a good chance at winning in court or press to litigate a case with little chance of success. The client may want the lawsuit to go away as soon as possible, or may want a day in court. In general, those decisions are the client's, subject to the prohibitions against frivolous litigation. More typically, the client may be basing his decisions on how to proceed on the advice of his attorney. In this regard, preparation by the attorney, as discussed above, is key.

Following the initial question about whether anything has transpired since the last meeting, the attorney should propose an agenda for the conference. Alex J. Hurder, "Negotiating the Lawyer-Client Relationship: A Search for Equality and Collaboration," 44 Buffalo L. Rev. 71, 92 (1996). Once client and attorney agree on the agenda, the attorney should summarize the material to be discussed. This will help with efficient use of time. The summary should cover the key facts of the case, relevant tax law and procedure, and the options presented. *See* Cochran et al., *supra*, at 134. Note that these three parts of the summary correspond to the three points discussed at the beginning of this section. In addition, in order to advise the client, the attorney should ascertain whether the client's goals have changed since the last discussion. *Id.* at 135.

In presenting the available options, the attorney should list *all* options, even those he might dismiss if he were the client. *See id*. at 136, 138. Depending on the stage of the tax controversy, as discussed in Chapters 4, 6 and 12, these options may include requesting a settlement conference with the IRS Appeals Division, requesting mediation from the IRS, seeking to arbitrate with the IRS, petitioning the United States Tax Court, filing a refund claim, suing the government in a federal District Court or the Court of Federal Claims, negotiating a collection dispute with the IRS, or requesting a Collection Due Process hearing. The attorney may suggest that some options are more feasible or appealing than others and explain why, but he should not eliminate options without at least mentioning them. Recall that the client, not the attorney, must make any decisions about his case. Without complete information, the client will not be able to make an informed decision.

Once all of the options are on the table, the client and attorney should discuss the pros and cons of each option, in light of the client's goals. *See id.* at 141. In establishing the criteria to be used to evaluate each option, the attorney should ask the client what criteria matter to him. The attorney can also assist the client in establishing the criteria by suggesting additional or different criteria that seem to reflect the client's goals and concerns. *Id.* at 144. If criteria emerge that seem inconsistent with the client's stated goals, the attorney should explore whether the client has additional, unarticulated goals. *Id.* at 145.

Once the criteria are established, they need to be applied to each available course of action. In order to apply the criteria systematically to each option, the attorney and the client should identify all of the consequences of each option, including consequences to third parties; assess both the positive and negative aspects of those consequences and the importance of each of these "pros" and "cons"; and evaluate the likelihood that each consequence will come to pass. *Id.* at 146–147. If the client states that he needs more information to evaluate the options, the attorney should provide it or arrange to get it to him. *Id.* at 155.

The attorney should also be prepared for the possibility that the client will try to avoid making a decision. If the client is unclear that the decision is his, not his attorney's, the attorney should reiterate that the decision in the client's case belongs to the client. *See* Krieger et al., *supra*, at 210. However, it is human nature to avoid difficult decisions by procrastinating. The attorney can facilitate appropriate decisionmaking by establishing with the client the criteria to be used to evaluate each option under discussion and applying the criteria systematically to each option. *See* Cochran et al., *supra*, at 143. In addition, it may help to inform the client that, until the case is resolved, interest will continue to accrue on any amounts ultimately due to the IRS, as discussed in Chapter 11.

It is also possible that the client will disclaim responsibility for the decision, perhaps telling the attorney that he will do whatever the lawyer advises him to do or asking the attorney what he would do if he were the client. The attorney should try to assist the client in making the decision for himself. He can tell the client that it is the client's decision because it is the client who will suffer the consequences; it is not the attorney who will have to pay the taxes. The attorney can enumerate the options and ask the client which one looks best. If the client absolutely refuses to choose an option, and insists that the lawyer make the decision, the lawyer can specify which option he thinks best meets the client's goals and ask if the client agrees with that decision. In specifying the option that seems best, the attorney should be sure to specify the drawbacks and risks of that option. Most importantly, he should prepare the client for the worst case scenario that could result from the choice. If the client agrees with the choice, the lawyer should record the decision in the client's file and follow up with a letter confirming that the client agreed to that choice during the meeting.

During the decisionmaking process, particularly if the client resists making a decision, the attorney should ascertain whether the client would like to discuss the options with someone else (such as a family member) before making a choice. Once the client has made a decision, the attorney may follow up with questions about whether the option satisfies the client's goals. *Id.* at 155. This will help ensure that the client does not simply "settle" for a suboptimal choice. *See id.* at 152. Finally, once the client has reached a decision, the attorney should discuss contingency plans in case the choice proves ineffective. *Id.* at 156.

If the client makes a decision that the attorney feels is extremely unwise given the facts, the client's stated goals, and the law, the attorney should question the client to ascertain the reasons for the client's decision. He should also warn the client of the likely negative consequences of that decision. *See* Krieger et al., *supra* at 219. The warning should be couched as concern for the client, rather than as a lecture. *Id.* It is not appropriate to argue with the client. Also, the attorney should make clear that he will follow through on the client's decision although he may disagree with it. *Id.*

[B] Delivering Bad News

Sometimes it will be necessary to give a client bad news. Before doing so, the attorney should gather all of the relevant information, so that he is prepared for any questions the client may ask. Cochran et al., *supra*, at 157 (*quoting* Linda F. Smith, "Medical Paradigms for Counseling: Giving Clients Bad News," 4 Clinical L. Rev. 391–393, 417–427, 430–431 (1998)). In general, bad news should be conveyed in person, not by telephone, and with adequate time for the client to process it. *Id.* at 158 (*quoting* Smith, *supra*). The attorney should not hide the information but should avoid "dropping a bombshell" on the client by conveying it as soon as the counseling session begins. *Id.* Instead, the attorney should indicate that he has bad news to share and empathize with the client after relaying the bad news. *See* Krieger et al., *supra*, at 218; Cochran et al., *supra*, at 159 (*quoting* Smith, *supra*).

Depending on the type of bad news, the attorney may be able to continue to provide assistance to the client. For example, a client may come to a tax clinic with a legal issue on which the IRS is clearly right.

> In those cases, and there are many of them, the clinics perform an important "second opinion" service by helping the client evaluate the merits of the case and understand in fact that they do owe the money and that further litigation is just an exercise in building up interest charges. Often, the government attorneys have already told them this, but the clients are distrustful of the source of the information and tend not to believe it. Clinic attorneys can explain the law and the adjustments to the client in a way that often results in the taxpayer settling the case. In many instances, clients are not protesting the underlying liability but are simply unable to pay the tax. Clinics can then counsel and represent the client in the collection matter. . . .

Spragens & Olson, *supra*, at 1528.

The lawyer should also be able to help the client with bad news that arises later in the tax controversy process. For example, if a particular strategic choice did not resolve itself as attorney and client had hoped, they can turn to the contingency plan developed at the time the strategic decision was made. On the other hand, if the situation is such that there is nothing more that the attorney can do, he should consider whether there are other resources available to the client, and make an appropriate referral. He may also be able to advise the client how to handle the tax issue in the future so that the same problem does not arise again.

§ 15.04 Negotiating a Tax Controversy

Given that more than 90 percent of all tax disputes settle prior to actual litigation, tax practitioners must constantly strive to improve their negotiation skills. Settlement-oriented negotiations may take place at various stages of the tax controversy process: at the conclusion of the audit, during the administrative appeal of an asserted deficiency or refund denial, during litigation, and during administrative collection proceedings. The goal in each case is to persuade the IRS representative that a settlement offer makes sense for both the client and the government.

While actual experience may be the best method for developing and improving one's negotiation techniques, there are aspects of the bargaining process in general, and the tax settlement process in particular, that a tax clinic student can learn through reading and study. This Section is divided into two parts: first, a presentation of some basic considerations relating to negotiation and bargaining; and second, an examination of tactical issues tailored to each stage of the tax controversy process. The discussion assumes that the negotiation process can be broken down into identifiable steps. In reality, the steps commonly overlap and there can be movement back and forth from one step to another. Moreover, only parts of the negotiation process may be applicable to any given situation. As a result, the discussion serves primarily as a guideline for narrowing options, rather than an attempt to provide precise answers to all questions.

This section builds upon material discussed in other chapters. First and foremost, the chapter assumes an understanding of the various stages of tax controversies, explained in Chapter 1, Section 1.05. In addition, knowledge of the examination process, discussed in Chapter 2, is helpful background information for this section. Finally, Chapter 4 raises some fundamental considerations concerning negotiations with the IRS Appeals Division, including how to draft a protest letter and whether to approach settlement negotiations at the Appeals level before or after filing a Tax Court petition.

[A] Negotiation Styles: Competitive and Cooperative

There are two basic negotiation styles: competitive and cooperative. A negotiator's style refers to his attitudinal approach or demeanor when interacting with the opposing party. Negotiation *style* is distinguishable from negotiation *strategy*. While style focuses on interpersonal behavior, strategy refers to the methods or tactics that the negotiator employs to reach the most favorable settlement possible. The distinction between style and strategy is often blurry, however. A negotiator may adopt a particular bargaining style in order to advance or camouflage his bargaining strategy.

As the name suggests, a cooperative negotiating style is characterized by courteous and tactful behavior, with a view toward an open and free flow of information between the parties. A cooperative negotiator perceives the bargaining process as a joint effort in which both sides can succeed, or at least feel that they have succeeded. To achieve a joint solution, such an attorney tries to create a positive atmosphere of trust, conducive to finding common ground, shared interests, and compromise. Expressing a willingness to compromise does not mean that the cooperative negotiator should appear weak or uncommitted. He must still clearly identify the relevant issues and options and guard against sending conflicting signals to the other side.

A competitive negotiator, on the other hand, does not view the bargaining process as a joint effort, but instead as an adversarial proceeding in which the interests of his own client must prevail. The competitive style is characterized by firmness, aggressiveness, and a dominating attitude. By seeking to control the negotiations, the competitive negotiator hopes to put his opponent on the defensive and force the opponent to make mistakes and unintentional concessions. A negotiator adopting the competitive style also is less likely to share information or ideas with the opposing side and more likely to use threats and arguments to attempt to force the other side to accept his bottom line position.

Each negotiation style, when carried out effectively, can lead to a successful result. In all cases, the negotiator should try to maintain a respectful and courteous attitude toward the IRS representative and avoid making personal attacks. As between the two types of behavior, competitive behavior may ultimately lead to a more favorable settlement, yet it also carries a higher risk that settlement talks will fail. A competitive negotiator who uses threats and intimidation may quickly lose his objectivity, causing the process to degenerate into an ego contest between the participants. This tendency seems particularly strong among less experienced negotiators. Moreover, short-term successes using highly aggressive tactics may result in long-term damage to the negotiator's credibility, which may adversely affect the negotiator's ability to reach agreement with the IRS in future cases.

A purely cooperative style, however, carries its own risks. As noted above, an opponent may misinterpret a cooperative style as weakness or as a signal that the representative is willing to settle on any terms. A cooperative negotiator must also guard against making too many concessions and committing to an agreement that is, upon reflection, not in the client's bests interests. Cooperative behavior is also less effective when the opponent adopts a non-cooperative attitude. A tax clinic student with little experience must be wary of IRS employees, especially those at lower levels, who feel no compulsion to achieve a result that is acceptable to both sides. Using a purely cooperative stance in these instances may be counter-productive. *See* Paul M. Lisnek, Effective Negotiation and Mediation: A Lawyer's Guide Ch. 4 (1992); ALI-ABA, Skills and Ethics in the Practice of Law Ch. 6 (1993).

It may be that adopting one style — purely competitive or purely cooperative — in any given case is a mistake. If it appears that the style initially chosen is not advancing the process, the negotiator should consider shifting to a different style in order to maintain control of the discussions. A shift in styles might be planned from the outset. A negotiator could decide to maintain a firm, competitive stance until such time as he is ready to make his final offer. To reach a final agreement, the negotiator might be willing to make a few last-minute concessions specifically contingent on the final agreement. Conversely, the negotiator might choose to make incremental concessions early in the negotiation process in a spirit of cooperation and good faith, and then rely on the resulting goodwill to justify holding firm on those issues that, unknown to the other party, are the most important to his client. This ability to adjust from one negotiating style to another is effective, but may not be possible for all negotiators. One's own personality and traits may dictate the approach. Attempting to use a competitive style when you are not comfortable with threats and conflict likely will lead to a disappointing result.

[B] Negotiation Process

[1] Preparation and Planning

Whether the negotiator plans to adopt a cooperative or competitive style, planning and preparation are the keys to success. At the earliest stages, preparation involves thoroughly investigating the facts and carefully researching the underlying legal issues. Without an accurate and complete view of the facts and the law, a negotiator cannot properly evaluate the costs and benefits of a given settlement position.

Gathering all of the relevant facts requires good client interviewing skills, which are discussed in Section 15.02, above. The lawyer should encourage the client to be candid and to reveal to him any information that might be useful. The lawyer should also request that the client provide verification of those facts that he thinks the IRS will challenge. Even at this early stage of the process, the lawyer should start thinking about a bargaining range (maximum and minimum extremes) and how points along that range might be justified. One of the best sources for information that can be used to justify a bargaining position is the client himself. The lawyer might explore with the client such matters as industry-wide standards and the client's business and financial history. Information relating to the client's finances is particularly important when the lawyer is negotiating an installment agreement or offer in compromise in a collection case.

A lawyer who can adequately justify his own position can more easily change the opponent's perceptions about the dispute. Research in advance of settlement discussions should start with an exploration of arguments and legal theories supporting the client's positions. While developing justifications for a particular bargaining stance is important, an effective negotiator must also anticipate responses of the opponent and the legal theories the opponent will likely rely upon to support his own bargaining range. A lawyer who fails to delve into his opponent's expected bargaining stance may end up finding that his own position is unrealistically optimistic or, even worse, the lawyer's own settlement offer is much less favorable to his client than what the opposing party might otherwise have accepted. The process of researching tax law is discussed in Chapter 16.

Related to the idea of anticipating the opponent's response is identifying the client's external exposure. Through the same process of factual and legal research, the attorney should try to detect any liability exposure beyond amounts that are currently in issue. While a client with external exposure is at a disadvantage in the bargaining process, it is better to know and prepare for this potential liability than to be surprised by it during the actual negotiation. The best way to identify probable issues is to review the client's tax returns for the taxable year in issue, as well as those from prior years open under the statute of limitations. Common examples of external liability exposure include new issues, increased deficiencies, and fraud liability. The

IRS may also bear some external exposure in the forms of recoverable administrative costs, unexpected refunds, and new issues or theories supporting the taxpayer's position. These, too, should be identified and researched.

Preparation also involves learning as much as possible about the person with whom you will be negotiating and any limitations under which the opposing party will be bargaining. Without insights from prior interactions, determining the individual characteristics of the opponent (experience, skill, and honesty) can be difficult. As a general matter, auditors and agents at the examination level tend to have a firmer grasp of the facts (they performed the audit), but less understanding of detailed legal issues. Appeals Officers, on the other hand, have more experience with technical legal arguments, but normally must rely on the examining agent's report to provide them with the facts.

The perspectives of the examining agent and the Appeals Officer may also differ. The examining agent may be more interested in defending the conclusions and arguments he plans to record in his report and, therefore, may be less willing to negotiate in the traditional sense. Furthermore, the examining agent and his supervisor are limited in their settlement authority: They may not strike a compromise that is contrary to a published IRS legal interpretation. Appeals Officers (and IRS Counsel) tend to adopt more of a "give-and-take" view of the negotiation process and, at least at the outset, want the case settled. As explained in Chapter 4, Appeals Officers have relatively broad settlement authority and must take the hazards of litigation into account when settling a case. The same is generally true of IRS Counsel.

The best source of information about the specific procedures and processes of the IRS at any stage of the controversy is the IRS's own Internal Revenue Manual. The manual is divided into major parts dealing with, among other topics, audits, appeals, refunds, and collection matters, and is further divided into separate handbooks dealing with more specific topics.

As indicated above, although it is helpful conceptually to separate the preparation and planning phase of the negotiation process from later phases, it also may be a bit misleading. The planning processes discussed above must continue even after negotiation sessions begin. Every strategic and tactical move the negotiator employs should be carefully planned in advance and reassessed when conditions change.

[2] Information Exchange

The strengths and weaknesses of the client's case, which will ultimately guide the attorney's offer and concession strategy, should have been revealed during the research and investigation process. Once negotiations actually begin, the attorney typically wants to reveal to the opposing party the client's strengths and withhold any weaknesses.

The negotiator's ability to withhold information during the audit phase of the controversy (prior to actual settlement talks) is limited by the IRS's broad summons authority in Code section 7602. As discussed in Chapter 2, during this pre-negotiation stage, the flow of information is one-sided — from the taxpayer to the IRS.[11] Once the audit concludes and the examining agent issues a revenue agent's report, the attorney can begin pursuing information held and created by the IRS. The attorney gains access to such information by requesting the client's administrative file or, if necessary, by making a Freedom of Information Act request, a topic discussed in Chapter 3.

An attorney's willingness to share information with the opposing party during the negotiation depends in part on whether he adopts a competitive or cooperative style. In almost all cases, however, the lawyer eventually wants to "share" the strengths of the client's position, usually at the beginning of the proceedings. Keep in mind that statements made on behalf of the client by a representative who acts under a power of attorney are not protected and may be used as admissions. As a result, the attorney must be extremely careful before making *any* representation, favorable or unfavorable, to the IRS. An experienced attorney double checks to ensure that the statements and information provided are accurate and do not unintentionally raise issues that are not already under consideration.

Protecting sensitive, damaging aspects of the client's case from being revealed to the opposing party raises a more difficult issue. As a general matter, the lawyer has no obligation to correct an IRS employee's misunderstanding of the law or the facts, but he must be careful not to misrepresent the law or the facts. Misrepresenting material facts constitutes unethical behavior under the Model Rules of Professional Conduct. DR 7–102(a)(5). Misrepresentations also threaten the lawyer's credibility with the opposing party. Once that credibility is lost, the negotiator may have difficulty persuading the opposing party that the client's position or settlement offer is valid.

A lawyer who is asked a direct question about a weakness in the client's case has another option that falls somewhere between answering truthfully and misrepresenting the client's position. The negotiator may try to "block" the opponent's inquiry. Listed below are some common blocking techniques:

Answer a Question with a Question. Responding to a question by posing another is the natural tendency of most lawyers anyway. The technique is effective because it is not merely a form of evasion, but is also a way to clarify or elaborate a position. The negotiator should formulate his follow-up questions in advance should the opposing party inquire about sensitive information.

Provide an Incomplete or Overly Broad Answer. The goal in this case is to respond with more information than has been asked for, or to respond to only the nonsensitive part of the topic contained in the question. In other words, respond to general questions with specific answers, and to specific questions with general answers.

Answer Another Question. If the opponent seems distracted, the negotiator can respond by answering a question that has already been asked, but with a slightly different response; or by reframing the question. The question might

---

[11] *See* Chapter 2 for a discussion of IDRs (Information Document Requests) and other techniques for controlling the flow of information during the audit phase. After the taxpayer files a petition in the Tax Court or a complaint in one of the refund fora, the flow of information back and forth is largely controlled by that court's discovery rules.

be reframed by using introductory phrases such as "I assume you're asking about . . ." or "If I understand your question correctly, you're looking for . . . ."

Claim that the Question is Out of Bounds. The negotiator can claim that the question delves into information protected by the attorney-client privilege or is irrelevant to the proceedings.

Change the Topic. The goal of this technique is to avoid the question asked by delving into a related topic in which the opponent has some interest. As with all these blocking techniques, the negotiator should plan this move in advance so that its execution is barely noticeable. Robert M. Bastress & Joseph D. Harbaugh, INTERVIEWING, COUNSELING, AND NEGOTIATING: SKILLS FOR EFFECTIVE REPRESENTATION 422–425 (1990).

Overuse of these blocking techniques can backfire. If a lawyer consistently evades a particular question, it might eventually reveal to the opponent a weakness in the client's case. Before applying a blocking technique, the negotiator should carefully consider whether the information being protected is truly damaging to the client's case and whether it might be more advantageous to develop a truthful answer supported by a persuasive explanation.

[3] Offers and Concessions

In the opening moments of any face-to-face bargaining session, the parties typically try to establish some rapport with one another, and at the same time feel one another out for signs of bargaining style and strategy. Some negotiators suggest talking first about issues that are completely unrelated to the case, such as the weather or recent events. From there the lawyer can ease into a vague description of the client's case. Eventually, though, the parties must confront the specific issues involved. In almost all negotiations there will be controversial and noncontroversial issues. The lawyer's prior research should help him predict which issues will be controversial and which noncontroversial. During the actual negotiations, however, it is the opposing party's view of the issues that is important. In a surprisingly high percentage of cases, the IRS representative is willing to concede without a fight those issues that the lawyer initially believed would be the most contentious. Detecting agreement before launching any offer and concession strategy can save time and leave the lawyer in a stronger bargaining position. With respect to those issues upon which the opponent's initial view is at odds with the client's position, the negotiator should encourage the opposing party to acknowledge the strengths of the client's case and solicit the opposing party's perceptions about the weaknesses of his own case. Any resulting points of agreement can prove to be valuable bargaining chips if concessions eventually have to be made.

To the negotiator, the controversial issues — whether they be strengths or weaknesses — will typically be of greater importance than the noncontroversial issues. There is no clear answer as to whether noncontroversial or controversial issues should be discussed first. On the one hand, seeking agreement on minor issues at the outset establishes a climate of cooperation and builds trust between the participants. Early agreement also helps create momentum and allows a party to defer using competitive techniques, if they become necessary, until later in the process. There are, however, risks associated with putting controversial issues off until the end. Attorneys who isolate controversial issues for separate treatment later in the process may be left with no arguments or positions left to bargain with once those topics are eventually discussed. Despite any early agreements, the negotiations could end in deadlock. Taking up big, controversial issues early may also cause the parties to become more committed to the overall process. Once the larger issues are resolved, the lawyers may find that smaller points and details more easily fall into place. Whichever tact the negotiator decides to use, he should map out his agenda in advance.

Planning an agenda also involves creating an offer and concession strategy. At both the audit and appeals levels, the attorney is usually expected to make the first settlement offer. *See* IRS Reg. § 601.106(f). He should have developed, in consultation with the client, the client's minimum and maximum exposure. This information is crucial when deciding upon the opening offer. The attorney's initial offer will likely be rejected by the opponent and it should, in some ways, reflect that eventuality. Proposing *too* outrageous an opening offer, however, could alienate the opposing party and stall the negotiations. The lawyer can also help decide upon an opening offer by predicting what his opponent might be willing to accept. Looking at the matter from the opponent's viewpoint will also allow the lawyer to recognize a favorable counteroffer from the opponent and be ready to act on it quickly before it is withdrawn.[12]

In addition to creating an offer strategy, the lawyer must also be prepared to make concessions. Concessions can play an important strategic role in reaching a final agreement. If movement toward a final agreement has begun to wane, a concession can jump start the negotiations or help reclaim some goodwill that may have been lost during prior adversarial bargaining. Deciding when and how much to concede must be considered in tandem with the offer strategy. One common tactic is to start with a relatively high opening offer, then make a series of small concessions until an agreement is reached. The attorney must employ this tactic carefully. Once the opposing party detects that the negotiator is readily making concessions, he may be inclined to raise his expectations and look for more concessions to follow. To avoid this, the attorney might make any concession on his part contingent upon a concession from the other side. Another tactic is to maintain a high unyielding position with a jump to an agreement at the very last minute. In this case the lawyer might make the concession specifically contingent upon a final agreement. Like any other competitive technique, this tactic may increase tensions between the parties, cause delay, and eventually lead to breakdown of the negotiations. *See* I. William Zartman & Maureen R. Berman, THE PRACTICAL NEGOTIATOR 166–175 (1982). In all cases, the concession strategy must be planned ahead. Once a concession has been made, it can be difficult to withdraw later in the process.

---

[12] The attorney's final settlement offer on behalf of the client, whether made during the Appeals process or just prior to litigation, should take into account Code section 7430, under which the taxpayer can make a "qualified offer" to settle the dispute. If the qualified offer is not accepted by the IRS and the taxpayer subsequently obtains a judgment that is as favorable as the taxpayer's offer, the taxpayer is deemed to be the prevailing party and therefore may be eligible to recover litigations costs from the IRS. Section 4.02[A] of Chapter 4 explains the requirements for making a qualified offer. *See also* Section 6.06 of Chapter 6.

[4] Responding to Deadlock

Even after the parties have made concessions, there may remain some areas of disagreement that prevent a final settlement. The lawyer must eventually decide, in consultation with the client, whether to agree to a proposed, but somewhat unfavorable, settlement, or to simply walk away from the negotiations with no agreement. Before doing either, he should consider the following techniques that can help break an impasse and move the proceedings along toward a final settlement.

Creating an Internal Deadline. Deadlines tend to encourage agreement. There are some timing deadlines, of course, over which the negotiating parties have little control — an approaching trial date, for instance. Alternatively, the parties might decide to create their own "internal" deadline, after which voluntary bargaining sessions cease. The internal deadline must be both reasonable and serious. An unreasonably short deadline might cause the parties to begin preparing for failure prematurely, rather than focusing on areas of agreement. If the deadline chosen is not taken seriously, it may also cause the parties to harden their positions in the hope that the other side concedes. *Id.* at 191–199.

Bluffing. When a lawyer bluffs, he concedes a position that he ostensibly values in order to achieve a position he actually wants to attain. Bluffing can relate not only to the importance that the negotiator places on a given settlement position, but also to the extent of the negotiator's commitment to seeing a final outcome. Bluffing raises ethical concerns, and also carries the risk that the opponent will call the bluff and expect the negotiator to follow through with his threat. When cooperative efforts have not resulted in an agreement, bluffing can be used to alter the opponent's perceptions in such a way that the opponent begins to believe that he has gained a bargaining position when, in fact, he has not. Lisnek, *supra*, Ch. 6.

Warnings and Threats. Highlighting the adverse consequences that will result from the opponent's failure to accept a final agreement (a warning) can help shape that party's perceptions. A threat is similar to a warning except that the negotiator vows to take some affirmative action against the opposing side if his demands are not met. Both techniques should be used sparingly and each must be credible if it is to be effective. In the case of a threat, the negotiator must be willing to back it up and show at least some willingness to do so. *Id.*

Predictions and Promises. A prediction is sort of the inverse of a warning. Instead of accentuating the negative ramifications, a prediction focuses on the positive outcomes that will flow from agreement. A promise, unlike a threat, carries the prospect of a reward rather than a punishment if the opponent takes certain action. It is often effective to combine a promise with a threat: A promise of a satisfactory outcome if agreement is reached accompanied by a warning of an unsatisfactory outcome if agreement is not reached. *Id.*

[C] Tactical Issues at Each Stage of the Tax Controversy

The discussions above concerning negotiation styles and techniques impact on almost any bargaining situation, whether during audit, appeal, or as part of a collection matter. The material that follows examines tactical issues that are more specific to each stage of the tax controversy process. However, at whatever stage the attorney is first brought in, he must not overlook the importance of planning and preparation.

[1] Audit

When it comes to adopting a negotiation style at the examination level, most practitioners seem to agree that the attorney should, at the outset at least, assume a cooperative attitude. Later in the process, if the risks associated with the competitive style (primarily, the prospect of deadlock) appear to be inevitable, then a more adversarial attitude may be appropriate. When choosing a negotiation style, the attorney must also be mindful early on of the potential for a burden of proof shift under Code section 7491. To cause the burden of proof to shift to the IRS during an eventual court proceeding, the taxpayer must establish, among other conditions, that he "cooperated" with reasonable requests for information and other documents. I.R.C. § 7492(a)(2)(B). Cooperation, for these purposes, focuses on the taxpayer's granting the IRS access to available information and exhausting administrative remedies. While establishing the cooperation element of section 7491 and maintaining a competitive negotiation style do not seem to be mutually exclusive, the attorney should bear section 7491 in mind if he plans eventually to make a case for the burden of proof to shift.

The most common issues that arise during the examination phase relate to the taxpayer's ability to substantiate a return position, usually a deduction, through adequate documentation. These issues are also typical in tax clinic settings. If the revenue agent raises the issue, the lawyer should review the Code, Treasury Regulations, and Internal Revenue Manual for acceptable methods of substantiation,[13] and work with the client to gather the necessary receipts and supporting information. At this juncture, negotiations with the revenue agent will likely focus on the scope and quantity of information the agent seeks. Before submitting any information to the IRS, the attorney should review it carefully to ensure that it does not raise additional issues that are not currently under consideration. Thomas C. Pearson & Dennis R. Schmidt, "Successful Preparation and Negotiation May Reduce the Time and Breadth of an IRS Audit," 40 Tax'n for Acct. 234, 236 (1988). If the client cannot locate the supporting documents, the lawyer should consider other sources of corroborating evidence, such as statements (and possibly affidavits) from third parties. If the client can generate no supporting evidence at all, conceding the issue and paying the resulting deficiency may be the best course of action.

Substantiating a return position primarily involves a question of fact. Factual questions, in a technical sense, are not subject to negotiation. Facts can, however, be perceived by the parties in different ways. The lawyer may find himself "negotiating" the importance of certain facts and their meaning in the broader context of the client's case. As noted above, an examining agent's prior experience and level of training make him better equipped to

---

[13] For example, Code section 274(d) and the accompanying Treasury regulations set forth the specific substantiation requirements applicable to travel and entertainment expenses.

understand factual arguments as opposed to complex legal theories. Even if questions of law hinder a satisfactory settlement, however, the attorney should ensure that the facts that are recorded in the revenue agent's report are accurate and, if at all possible, consistent with the client's position. A poor or inaccurate factual record will only make it more difficult for the attorney later in the process. If it appears that no progress is being made toward a final resolution, the attorney's best course of action is to begin preparing for the Appeals process.

[2]   Administrative Appeal

The important strategic decision of whether to approach settlement negotiations with the Appeals Division on a docketed or nondocketed basis is discussed in Chapter 4. In short, negotiating with the Appeals Officer on a nondocketed basis avoids the time pressures associated with a looming trial date — which may or may not be advantageous to the taxpayer depending upon the issues involved — and preserves the possibility for the taxpayer to recover litigation costs from the IRS under Code section 7430. However, the nondocketed route is generally more time-consuming than the docketed route. Furthermore, negotiating with Appeals before a statutory notice of deficiency has been issued raises the prospect that the Appeals Officer will include newly discovered issues in the deficiency notice sent to the taxpayer. If the same issues had been raised by the IRS after the notice of deficiency had been sent, the IRS would have borne the burden of proof in an ensuing Tax Court trial with respect to those "new matters." *See generally* Section 4.02 of Chapter 4. The attorney should discuss with the client how these considerations bear upon the client's specific case and help the client decide upon the appropriate route.

Settlement negotiations with the Appeals Officer will proceed in much the same manner whether the client chooses the docketed or nondocketed route. In both cases, the Appeals Officer, unlike the examining agent, must take account of the "hazards of litigation" when deciding whether to accept a settlement offer. The risk that the Government will not prevail in litigation becomes the attorney's most important bargaining chip during the negotiations, and all effort should be made to highlight this risk to the Appeals Officer.[14] The Appeals conferences themselves, as explained in the excerpt in Chapter 4, are conducted in an informal manner, yet this does not mean that the attorney should come to the table unprepared. The attorney's offer and concession strategy should be meticulously planned before any meeting takes place.

Most Appeals Officers do not have the time or the resources to prepare for the Appeals conference as well as they would like. They are heavily reliant on the examining agent for factual development and on the taxpayer's protest letter, if one was submitted, to guide their legal research. As a result, they appreciate whatever cooperation they receive from the attorney, and most are willing to respond in kind when it comes to finding a satisfactory settlement.

---

[14] If the negotiations take place on a nondocketed basis, the hazards of litigation should be explored in the protest letter. *See* Section 4.02[c][2] of Chapter 4 for suggestions on drafting protest letters.

An existing, favorable relationship between the attorney and the Appeals Officer, built on credibility and fair play, might encourage the Appeals Officer to give the client the benefit of the doubt. Barbara T. Kaplan, "Leveling the Playing Field in Federal Income Tax Controversies," 56 N.Y.U. Ann. Inst. Fed. Tax'n § 32.10 (1997). When choosing a style and strategy, the attorney should also consider the fact that the Appeals Officer normally must seek the approval of a superior before any settlement can be finalized. The Appeals Officer may have an easier time convincing the reviewer to accept the agreement if he can explain that the attorney for the taxpayer bargained in good faith and was willing to make concessions in order to reach an agreement.

[3] During Litigation

What has been said about negotiations with the Appeals Division applies just as well to negotiations with IRS Counsel and attorneys from the Department of Justice. Some experienced negotiators maintain that it is easier to strike a settlement at this late stage because the government attorney is keenly aware of the costs and time commitment associated with a trial. While the Appeals Officer must take litigation risks into account, the Officer's knowledge of the subtle issues that can affect the outcome of a trial is limited. The government attorney will be more attuned to litigation-related issues such as burden of proof, admissibility of evidence, and discovery procedures. However, there are some issues for which the government will seek a judicial interpretation and therefore will not settle prior to trial. If, for example, courts have issued conflicting decisions with regard to the same issue, the government might seek further judicial review in an effort to achieve a uniformly accepted interpretation. *See* Peter R. Steenland, Jr. & Peter A. Appel, "The Ongoing Role of Alternative Dispute Resolution in Federal Government Litigation," 27 U. Tol. L. Rev. 805, 809 (1996).

[4] Collection Process

Negotiations with the IRS after it has assessed a deficiency typically involve efforts by the attorney to suspend or otherwise lessen the impact of enforced collection action such as levy or seizure. Most often, the attorney will attempt to settle the client's unpaid account for less than the balance due (an offer in compromise) or spread payment of the accrued liability over a period of months or years (an installment agreement). Before the IRS will consider either form of collection relief, the taxpayer must be in current compliance, having filed all past and current tax returns. If this is not the case, the attorney should assist the client in rectifying the situation.

As noted in Chapter 12, the IRS may compromise a tax liability for one of three reasons: doubt as to liability; doubt as to collectibility; and for effective tax administration. I.R.C. § 7122. The attorney's approach will differ slightly in each case. If the compromise offer is based on doubt as to liability, the request will end up in the hands of a revenue agent who will essentially "audit" the request. As in the case of a typical audit, preparation and information control are of key importance.

To obtain a compromise based on doubt as to collectibility, the taxpayer must establish that his existing assets and expected income do not permit him to pay the full assessed liability. To successfully negotiate an offer on this basis, the attorney must work with the client to meticulously prepare financial disclosure statements (Form 433-A, Collection Information Statement for Individuals or Form 433-B, Collection Information Statement for Businesses). On the disclosure forms, the client values his assets and liabilities (net worth) and lists his monthly income and expense figures. The financial information becomes the basis of the offer, which is made by submitting Form 656, Offer in Compromise. The attorney should carefully review the current offer in compromise regulations, Temporary Regulations 301.7122-1T, and the Internal Revenue Manual's Offer in Compromise Handbook, Section 5.8, to determine an acceptable offer range.

Although the minimum acceptable offer will depend primarily upon a mechanical application of national and local personal expense standards, there is still room for negotiation.[15] In addition, with respect to an offer from a low-income taxpayer, the IRS cannot reject it "solely on the basis of the amount of the offer." I.R.C. § 7122(c)(3)(A). In general, much of the attorney's time will be spent negotiating the adequacy and correctness of the financial statements. Two experienced practitioners suggest the following:

> The opportunity to provide the greatest benefit to the taxpayer in the [offer in compromise] process is in the valuation of assets for purposes of determining an acceptable offer amount. The lower the net realizable value of a taxpayer's assets, the smaller the offer needed to meet acceptance standards. On the other hand, grossly undervaluing an asset or assets will not be viewed favorably by the IRS. The IRS can and will perform its own valuations in complex cases and those involving substantial dollars.

> Taxpayers should use realistic valuations, and their practitioners should encourage this. In addition, seek the advice of knowledgeable valuation specialists where possible.

* * *

> While unrealistically low valuations should be avoided, the submission of an [offer in compromise] requires the practitioner to be a strong advocate for the taxpayer and taking an aggressive stance on valuation matters should be both expected and respected by knowledgeable IRS personnel.

> Income-producing real estate, intangibles, and small closely held business or professional practices are all candidates for zealous valuation "advocacy" by taxpayer representatives. The practitioner should make sure to have good facts and sound arguments to support the valuations presented.

Kip Dellinger & Royal Dellinger, OFFER IN COMPROMISE PROCESS: INSIGHTS AND STRATEGIES 66–67 (1999). Even when the client has few assets to report, careful completion of the financial disclosure statement can mean the difference between acceptance or rejection of the compromise offer. In the case of

---

[15] A more detailed discussion of settlement ranges and the role of personal expense standards can be found in Section 12.05[C] of Chapter 12.

low-income clients, the attorney should question the client about outstanding loans from family members, overdue mortgage and credit card payments, and any other outstanding liabilities that impact on the client's ability to pay.

To obtain a compromise based on effective tax administration, the taxpayer must prove that, in light of all the surrounding facts and circumstances, collecting the full amount owed would result in economic hardship or, regardless of the taxpayer's financial condition, would be detrimental to voluntary taxpayer compliance. The offer should explain the taxpayer's position in detail. The attorney must understand, however, that the IRS has been hesitant to grant this relief. Accordingly, creativity and factual investigation will be necessary if the taxpayer is to have a strong case.

Negotiating an installment agreement with the IRS is similar to negotiating a compromise offer based on doubt as to collectibility. *See* I.R.C. § 6159. The same financial disclosure statements required when submitting an offer in compromise are also used to determine whether an installment agreement will be accepted by the IRS, as well as to set the payments terms under that agreement. The attorney must also be familiar with the Internal Revenue Manual's standardized expenditure allowances, set out in Section 5.3 of the Manual, which the revenue agent will use to determine the client's ability to pay, and ultimately the minimum acceptable monthly installment amount. These standardized allowances are divided into "necessary expenses" and "conditional expenses." The attorney must negotiate with the IRS not only that the client will incur a particular necessary or conditional expense, but also the anticipated amount of the expense.[16] *See* Mark H. Ely, "Negotiating Installment Agreements with the IRS Collection Division," Tax Advisor, Oct. 2000, at 742.

The attorney can raise the possibility of entering into an offer in compromise or installment agreement at any time, even before the IRS assesses the underlying tax liability. More often, though, requests are made after the IRS begins collection enforcement action. If the attorney has not previously been involved in the client's case, he should first review all notices sent to the client to determine where the case stands in the collection process. Of particular importance is the notice granting the client the right to request a Collection Due Process (CDP) Hearing. The CDP notice must be sent once the IRS files a notice of federal tax lien or proposes to levy on the client's property, after which he has only 30 days to request a hearing. I.R.C. §§ 6320, 6330. As explained in more detail in Chapter 12, a CDP Hearing is conducted before a neutral Appeals Officer who must first confirm whether the IRS satisfied all Code procedures relating to the validity of the lien, including whether the IRS properly issued all the required notices and demands. This is an opportunity for the attorney to raise any procedural discrepancies. The Appeals Officer is not required to discuss the client's underlying tax liability, however, unless the client did not receive a notice of deficiency or has not otherwise had an opportunity to dispute the liability. The latter may be true of a tax clinic client who has allowed the case to proceed from audit to collection without making any efforts to question the IRS's asserted deficiency. If

---

[16] The installment agreement procedure is explained in more detail in Section 12.05[B].

substantive liability is in issue, the negotiations will proceed much like any other Appeals hearing.

Even if the question of liability has already been determined, the attorney can raise any issue during the CDP Hearing relating to the lien or proposed levy, including the appropriateness of an installment agreement or offer in compromise. If these issues have not been raised before, the Appeals Officer may refer the case to a revenue agent who will investigate whether such relief is warranted. If so, the negotiation will proceed as described above. If the prospect of an installment agreement or compromise has already been considered and rejected by a revenue agent earlier in the process, the Appeals Officer must judge whether the revenue agent's conclusion was correct. The attorney should point out any misinterpretations the revenue agent may have made when analyzing the taxpayer's financial statements, and if necessary update those statements to reflect the most current information available. If the Appeals Officer denies the taxpayer's request at the CDP phase, the taxpayer can seek review of the Appeals Officer's determination in either the Tax Court or a District Court, depending on the type of tax in dispute. The Appeals Officer's decision is reviewed using, in most cases, an abuse of discretion standard. Overturning the Appeals Officer's adverse determination will, therefore, be difficult.

PROBLEMS

Problems 1 through 3 and 4B are role-playing problems.

1. You have been assigned to interview José Rodriguez, a new client of the tax clinic. Ascertain his tax problem and inform him of the next steps you plan to take in his case.

2. You were assigned to interview Ingrid Alfiori, a young woman who has an appointment with the clinic. Ascertain her tax problem and inform her of the next steps you plan to take on her case.

3. Sidney Smith has owned a small family restaurant as a sole proprietorship for many years. All of Sidney's assets are invested in the restaurant, which is slightly profitable; Sidney has an income from it of about $25,000 per year, and has no income from other sources. Sidney was recently audited for the first time. The IRS agent concluded that Sidney was not reporting most cash receipts, and asserted a proposed deficiency of $22,000. Sidney came to the clinic with a 30-day letter from the agent to seek help resolving the dispute.

    A. Conduct an initial interview with Sidney.

    B. Assume that in the initial interview, you and Sidney decided to request an Appeals conference. You did not write a Tax Protest. Conduct the Appeals conference on Sidney's behalf.

    C. Assume that you were not able to reach a satisfactory settlement with Appeals, so you have scheduled a conference with Sidney to decide how to proceed with the case. Conduct that conference.

4. Jamie White, a teacher's aide, recently received a letter from the IRS denying her $2,328 earned income credit for her two children, Mary, age 5, and Donald, age 7. Apparently, her ex-husband, Daniel White, who does not live with them, also claimed the credit. Jamie receives $300 per month of child support from her ex-husband, a carpenter who earns approximately $15,000 to $18,000 per year. Jamie earns $12,000 per year from the school district, and has no other source of income. She told you in the initial interview that she spends most of that money on her children.

    A. Assume that the amount of the credit (if allowable) is correct and the only issue is whether Jamie may claim it. Draft a representation letter to Jamie. She resides at 100 April St., Apt. 3C, Aberdeen, New Jersey 07747.

    B. Assume that, after interviewing Jamie the first time, you checked the law and ascertained that it is Jamie, not her ex-husband, who is entitled to take the credit. Jamie was unsure of how far she wanted to pursue the matter, for fear of angering her ex-husband and thus jeopardizing the $300 per month of child support. You had agreed that you would call the IRS and try to resolve the matter by phone. The telephone calls proved unsuccessful, so you have scheduled a conference with Jamie to discuss how to proceed with the case.

5. Jack Pope owns a small hardware store in Lancaster, Pennsylvania through a closely-held C corporation, Pope Inc. Assume that Pope Inc. files its income tax returns on a cash method, calendar year basis. During 2001, Pope Inc. paid $150,000 in salary to Jack and deducted that amount under Code section 162 as compensation. The $150,000 payment represented almost 90 percent of Pope Inc.'s total net earnings for the year. Pope Inc. also contributed some of its unsold inventory to a local church and claimed a charitable contribution on the corporation's return equal to $15,000. The tax-exempt charitable organization that received the gift failed to send Pope Inc. a notice reflecting the contribution as required by the section 170 regulations. The corporation also paid $50,000 for a new warehouse space constructed as an addition to the existing hardware store, and deducted the entire amount as a current business expense rather than capitalizing the expense.

    The IRS audited Pope Inc.'s 2001 income tax returns. Jack decided to handle the audit himself and not seek the advice of an accountant or attorney. At the conclusion of the audit, the corporation received a 30-day letter with the following proposed adjustments: (1) denial of the salary deduction in full on the basis that the payment represented an unreasonable compensation payment, resulting in a $30,000 asserted deficiency; and (2) denial of the charitable contribution deduction in full for failure to substantiate the amount, resulting in a $3,000 asserted deficiency. The 30-day letter made no mention of the warehouse addition.

Jack has hired you, on behalf of Pope Inc., to meet with the examining agent and attempt to work out a settlement. Assume for these purposes that, based upon the law and the facts, the corporation has a 40 percent chance of establishing to the IRS that the salary payment was fully deductible under section 162, and only a 10 percent chance that a court would deny the compensation deduction in full. (There is a 50 percent likelihood that a court would allow only a portion of the deduction — assume, for purposes of this problem, that if only a portion is allowed, that portion will be $80,000 and the resulting deficiency will be $ 14,000.) Assume also that the charitable organization that received the inventory is unable to locate any documentation reflecting the gift, but that the organization's president is willing to draft a letter to the IRS, with the current date, stating that based upon his best recollection, Pope Inc. made the gift reflected on the corporation's return. Given this state of affairs, you predict that Pope Inc. has a 25 percent chance of prevailing on this issue and a 75 percent chance that a court would deny the deduction.

A. How would you approach the negotiations with the examining agent?

B. Assume that the settlement negotiations in Part A end in deadlock. Jack, on behalf of the corporation, asks you to appeal the deficiencies asserted in the 30-day letter to the IRS Appeals Division. The case has been assigned to Doris Morgan, an Appeals Officer with whom you have had extensive and generally favorable dealings with in the past. Having drafted a protest letter setting out the corporation's position on the compensation and charitable deductions, how would you approach the settlement negotiations with Ms. Morgan and what would be your opening settlement offer? How does the warehouse expenditure issue impact your approach to the negotiation?

6. Your client Stacy Gurnsey suffers from a lifelong neurological condition that has rendered her mentally challenged. For most of her life, Stacy, an only child whose father passed away when she was young, lived with her mother in their family home. Following the death of her mother, Stacy, then age 55, was left the family home, a run down mobile home (on a lot under a 99-year ground lease), and an annuity that her mother had hoped would provide for Stacy's care for the rest of her life.

Shortly after her mother's death, a local contractor talked Stacy into making numerous, but unnecessary, repairs to the home. To fund the repairs, Stacy withdrew large amounts from her annuity in 2001. When she filed her 2001 income tax return, Stacy failed to report the annuity withdrawals as income. She was not aware that the withdrawals would give rise to gross income. Two years after filing the return, the IRS mailed to Stacy a notice of deficiency asserting a deficiency in the amount of $3,000, including interest but no penalties. Stacy, unsure what to do, did not respond to the notice of deficiency and the IRS assessed the tax and related charges.

After filing a notice of federal tax lien against Stacy's home, the IRS sent her a Collection Due Process Notice under Code section 6320. Assume, that as of the current date, Stacy's house is valued at $90,000 and that the annuity generates $12,000 per year, which is just enough to cover Stacy's annual living expenses. Assume also that the mobile home has been condemned as unfit for habitation and that the mobile home park where it is located has filed a $1,000 lien against the mobile home for Stacy's failure to pay park association dues.

At the CDP Hearing, you intend to make an offer in compromise on behalf of your client based on effective tax administration. How would you go about preparing the offer? How would you prepare for the CDP hearing?

Chapter 16

TAX RESEARCH

§ 16.01 Introduction

By the conclusion of the client interview, the attorney is likely to have some general idea of the nature of the client's tax problem. Even experienced tax attorneys, however, are unable (and unwilling) to provide detailed answers to substantive or procedural tax questions off the top of their heads. Before the attorney can accurately describe to the client his available options, including the potential for a negotiated settlement, the attorney must carefully research the specific legal issues involved in light of the facts the client has conveyed. Because of the complex and ever-changing nature of federal tax law, tax research must be performed with a high degree of technical accuracy. And while the general research method is the same as in other areas of the law, some knowledge of specialized tax sources and research techniques is necessary. [1]

The discussion in this Chapter focuses on how to research a civil, federal income tax question. [2] The section describes the primary and secondary sources of tax law, with special emphasis placed on identifying and locating those sources that are likely to be found in a typical law firm or law school library. While some mention is made of the precedential weight carried by each of the primary legal sources, reference should be made to Chapter 9 for a more in-depth discussion of that issue. The remainder of this Chapter suggests a methodology that a student unfamiliar with tax research might use when researching a tax problem.

§ 16.02 Primary Sources

There are three primary sources of federal tax law: (1) legislative; (2) administrative; and (3) judicial.

[A] Legislative Sources

[1] Internal Revenue Code

Federal tax law may well be the purest form of statutory law. [3] The answer to almost any tax question will depend upon an interpretation of the statutory

---

[1] For a more detailed description of tax sources, see Gail Levin Richmond, FEDERAL TAX RESEARCH: GUIDE TO MATERIALS AND TECHNIQUES (5th ed. 1997); Robert L. Gardner et al., TAX RESEARCH TECHNIQUES (5th ed. 2000).

[2] The discussion assumes that the student is already familiar with traditional legal research methods, including the Westlaw Reporter System and the Shepard's and Key Cite citator services. The student is also assumed to have basic proficiency in computer-based research.

[3] In federal civil tax controversies, the United States Constitution plays a limited role and is,

language. The primary source of federal tax statutes is the Internal Revenue Code, which is Title 26 of the United States Code. The current version is officially titled the Internal Revenue Code of 1986 (the "Code"). The current Code was preceded by the Internal Revenue Code of 1954, and prior to that by the Internal Revenue Code of 1939. Before 1939, Congress enacted revenue acts, each constituting a complete body of federal tax law, every two to three years.

The Code is divided into eleven subtitles (designated by letter), each of which is further divided into chapters (designated by number), which in turn are divided into variously designated subchapters, parts, subparts, sections, subsections, paragraphs, subparagraphs, sentences and clauses. The attorney must be alert to these divisions, as some Code provisions apply throughout the entire Code, while others govern only a specific title, subtitle, or chapter. The scope of a particular provision, if meaningful, is usually indicated by introductory language, such as "For purposes of this subtitle." Most of the income tax provisions are contained in Chapter 1 of Subtitle A. The procedural provisions that apply to all types of tax issues are located in Subtitle F.

[a] Current Version

While the Internal Revenue Code is included in the official United States Code set, it is most commonly accessed by tax practitioners through one of the commercially published looseleaf reporter services. The two most widely used services are published by the Research Institute of America (RIA) and Commerce Clearing House (CCH). Each of them publishes the complete Code, updated on a regular basis, in a two-volume set. Both also publish an expanded multi-volume looseleaf reporter series organized by Code section. Following the official text of a Code section are the following: excerpts from selected legislative history; final, temporary, and proposed regulations; editorial explanations of the Code and regulation language; and digests of cases, revenue rulings and letter rulings. The RIA income tax series, *United States Tax Reporter*, spans sixteen volumes while the CCH equivalent, *Standard Federal Tax Reporter*, runs to nineteen volumes.

[b] Prior Code Versions

As explained in Chapters 5 and 8, respectively, the IRS normally has three years from the time a tax return is filed to assess a tax deficiency, and the taxpayer normally has three years after filing a return to claim a refund. In either case, the attorney often finds himself arguing over a Code provision that, at the time the controversy is joined by the IRS, has already been amended or repealed. Prior versions of the Code can also be important when doing substantive tax research, as interpretations of an amended Code section may inform the application of its current counterpart.

The attorney can find the full text of the Internal Revenue Code for any year after 1953 by looking in *U.S. Code Congressional & Administrative*

---

therefore, rarely consulted as part of the tax research process. In criminal tax proceedings, constitutional objections relating to such issues as self-incrimination, searches and seizures, and due process sometimes arise. *See generally* Chapter 14.

News—Internal Revenue Code, published by West Group. Pre-1954 Internal Revenue Code versions may be located in *Seidman's Legislative History of Federal Income and Excess Profits Tax Laws*. Non-current versions of the Code can also be found using an on-line service, LEXIS (from 1978 forward) or Westlaw (from 1984 forward).

Tracking additions, deletions, and other amendments to the Code over a period of years presents more of a challenge. Although many of the old sections of the 1954 Code retained their same numbering in the 1986 version, all but one of the 1939 Code section numbers were changed in the 1954 version. Both the CCH and RIA looseleaf reporter series contain tables cross-referencing provisions of the 1939 and 1954 Codes, as well as amendment notes that describe prior changes to a particular Code section, but the coverage is limited. To help researchers identify specific amendments and changes in statutory language, RIA publishes a multi-volume looseleaf series titled *Cumulative Changes*. A separate set of volumes exists for the 1939, 1954, and 1986 Codes. *Cumulative Changes* volumes consist of a series of charts, one for each Code section. Each chart contains public law numbers for the original Act and any amendments, effective and enactment dates, as well as the full text of any amended or repealed provision. The charts also include internal changes within Code sections, such as redesignated subsections, added or repealed subsections, and rewritten subsections.

[2] Legislative History

Although the Code is highly detailed, many provisions may seem ambiguous when applied to a given set of facts. The meaning of an ambiguous Code section may be gleaned by resorting to legislative history to determine Congressional intent. The three primary sources of legislative history in the tax area are (1) hearings before Congressional committees, (2) debates on the floor of the House of Representatives and Senate, and (3) Congressional committee reports.

These three sources of legislative history are the byproducts of the tax legislative process.[4] The legislative process usually originates with one or more proposals from the President delivered to Congress as part of the State of the Union Address in January. Written proposals from the President are issued in the form of general and technical explanations of proposed amendments, rather than in the form of a proposed bill. These explanations are prepared by the Assistant Secretary for Tax Policy in the Treasury Department.

The United States Constitution requires that bills for raising revenue originate in the House of Representatives. U.S. Const. Art. 1, § 7. Legislative counsel in the House, assisted by Treasury and IRS staff members, draft the initial language of a tax bill, which is then assigned a bill (H.R.) number. Once the bill is submitted in the House it is referred to the House Ways and Means Committee. The Ways and Means Committee holds public hearings at which

---

[4] The material in this section describes the typical route of a tax bill from introduction to final passage. Numerous exceptions exist. *See generally* Bradford L. Ferguson et al., "Reexamining the Nature and Role of Tax Legislative History in Light of the Changing Realities of the Process," 67 Taxes 804 (1989).

Treasury Department officials and representatives from private interest groups comment on the likely effect of the proposed legislation. The Ways and Means Committee eventually prepares a detailed House Report explaining the proposed legislation, and the bill is debated on the House floor. A similar process takes place in the Senate under the authority of the Senate Finance Committee. The Finance Committee holds its own set of hearings on the legislation (referred to as an Act at that point), publishes its own Senate Report, and makes whatever changes to the House version it deems appropriate. After the Senate debates and passes its version of the legislation, the matter goes to a Conference Committee made up of House and Senate members who seek to iron out any differences and craft compromise legislation. The Conference Committee prepares its own Report and sends the compromise version back to both houses. If passed by both, it is sent to the President for signature. Once the Act becomes law, it receives a public law (P.L.) number, which has no relation to the Act's earlier bill number.

Hearings before the House Ways and Means Committee and the Senate Finance Committee may help illuminate technical issues and offer insight into the meaning of the newly enacted legislation. Transcripts of selected hearings are published by the Government Printing Office (GPO) and are mostly easily obtained through the Library of Congress' website, thomas.loc.gov. Thomas also provides access to Committee Reports and the *Congressional Record* from the 104th Congress to the present.

Hearings transcripts are also available on microfiche from the *Congressional Information Service* (C.I.S.), a commercial publisher that also prepares a helpful finding index (*C.I.S. Index*) for these sources. Text of the House and Senate floor debates are published in the *Congressional Record*. Debate transcripts might be consulted to ascertain the policy behind a last minute amendment that occurs on the floor of the House or Senate. Of these three basic sources of tax legislative history, Committee Reports tend to be the most important.

Committee Reports typically include a general explanation section that describes present law, the need for the legislation, and the expected impact the bill will have on various taxpayers. The report may also have a technical explanation of each section of the bill. Committee Reports have become increasingly more detailed, many incorporating examples and instructions to the Treasury for drafting regulations. Courts frequently rely on Committee Reports to aid construction of the statute and they can be valuable sources of guidance for taxpayers, particularly with respect to Code sections for which regulations have not been issued. Among the House, Senate, and Conference Committee Reports, the Conference Report (which is assigned a House Report number) is usually the most helpful as it highlights areas of disagreement between the House and Senate versions and describes the legislation that may eventually become law.

Selected Committee Reports are reprinted in the *U.S. Code Congressional and Administrative News* (U.S.C.C.A.N.), published by West Group, as well as the *Cumulative Bulletin*. Reprints in the *Cumulative Bulletin* are generally more complete and, if available, should be consulted first. A compilation of Committee Reports for all revenue acts from 1913 to 1938 is contained in a separate edition of the *Cumulative Bulletin*, 1939-1 C.B. Part 2. Selected Committee Reports for revenue legislation from 1939 until 1953 are scattered throughout the *Cumulative Bulletin* for the relevant years. The *Cumulative Bulletin* did not reprint legislative history surrounding the enactment of the 1954 Code. This material is found in Volume 3 of the *U.S.C.C.A.N.* for 1954. Most Committee Reports relating to revenue legislation after 1954 can be found in the *Cumulative Bulletin*, including the House, Senate, and Conference Committee Reports surrounding the Tax Reform Act of 1986, which are contained in 1986-3 C.B. Volumes 2-4.

Several commercial publishers have issued special compilations of tax legislative history. These include: *Seidman's Legislative History of Federal Income Tax and Excess Profits Tax Laws* (through 1953); Reams & McDermott, *Legislative History of the Internal Revenue Acts of the U.S.* (1950 to present); and BNA Tax Management, *Primary Sources* (1969 to present). These resources can be extremely helpful tools for locating relevant legislative history.

[3]   Joint Committee Explanation ("Bluebook")

Following enactment of major tax legislation, the staff of the Joint Committee on Taxation (composed of representatives of the House Ways and Means Committee and the Senate Finance Committee) may issue a single-volume "general explanation" of newly enacted or amended Code sections. These post-enactment explanations are organized in much the same way as Committee Reports: Prior Law; Reasons for Change; Explanation of Provision. Typically bound in a blue cover, these sources are known, colloquially, as "Bluebooks" and are published by several commercial publishers.

Because Bluebook explanations are written after the bill is made law, they are not technically legislative history. Nonetheless, courts routinely cite Bluebook explanations just as they would other Committee Reports. When the Bluebook explanation is consistent with the other legislative history, this may be appropriate. However, when the Joint Committee Staff expresses an opinion on an issue left unresolved by the Committee Reports, the precedential weight of these comments is debatable. *Compare Redlark v. Commissioner*, 106 T.C. 31 (1996), *rev'd by* 141 F.3d 936 (9th Cir. 1998) ("[The Bluebook] is not part of the legislative history although it is entitled to respect. Where there is no corroboration in the actual legislative history, we shall not hesitate to disregard the General Explanation as far as congressional intent is concerned. Given the clear thrust of the conference committee report, the General Explanation is without foundation and must fall by the wayside. To conclude otherwise would elevate it to a status and accord it a deference to which it is simply not entitled." (citations omitted)) *with Redlark v. Commissioner*, 141 F.3d 936, 941 (9th Cir. 1998) ("While such post-enactment explanations cannot properly be described as 'legislative history,' they are at least instructive as to the reasonableness of an agency's interpretation of a facially ambiguous statute."). *See also* Treas. Reg. § 1.6662-4(d)(iii) (including the Bluebook in the list of authorities that may be relied upon by taxpayers to avoid the substantial understatement penalty in Code section 6662(b)(2)).[5]

---

[5] The substantial understatement penalty is discussed in Section 10.02[C][2] of Chapter 10.

[B]   Administrative Sources

The IRS, alone or in conjunction with other Treasury Department divisions, issues a wide variety of pronouncements pursuant to its administrative rule-making authority. These pronouncements are discussed below.

[1]   Treasury Regulations

Treasury Regulations represent formal and authoritative interpretations of the Code. The Treasury Department officially releases all final regulations, although responsibility for initially drafting the regulations rests with the IRS Office of Chief Counsel. As explained in more detail in Chapter 9, most courts accord regulations a significant degree of deference, although a regulation may be declared invalid if the agency's interpretation is inconsistent with Congressional intent or is otherwise unreasonable. *See* Section 9.02[A] of Chapter 9 (discussing the differences between legislative and interpretive regulations and the amount of deference accorded to each). Regulations help explain complex statutory provisions, resolve doubtful questions of interpretation, and often include specific examples of how Congress intended a Code section to operate. Of all the administrative sources of tax law, regulations are the most important and should be consulted whenever available. Not all Code sections, however, have corresponding regulations.

Regulations issued under both the 1986 and 1954 versions of the Internal Revenue Code are numbered by a prefix designation and then by the Code section number that the regulation interprets. A regulation's prefix indicates its basic subject matter: Income tax regulations have the prefix "1," estate tax have the prefix "20", gift tax have the prefix "25," and procedural and administrative regulations have the prefix "301." Regulations relating to income tax provisions of the 1939 Internal Revenue Code were issued in sets, with the prefix designation being determined by the location of that regulation in the official Code of Federal Regulations. Income tax regulations under the 1939 Code carried the prefix "29."

The Administrative Procedure Act, 5 U.S.C. § 553, obligates government agencies to issue most regulations first in proposed form and to solicit comments from the general public before the regulations are finalized. Proposed regulations, along with the invitation to make comments, are published in the *Federal Register* as Notices of Proposed Rulemaking. Before being finalized, proposed regulations do not technically carry the force and effect of law. Nonetheless, they cannot be ignored because if they are eventually made final, they are usually made effective retroactively to the date on which they where originally proposed. *See* I.R.C. § 7805(b)(1). If proposed regulations are not finalized, courts need not accord them any deference, but may do so if the regulation represents a reasonable interpretation of the statute. *See Vanscoter v. Sullivan*, 920 F.2d 1441 (9th Cir. 1990).

When Congress enacts a new Code provision and taxpayers need immediate guidance in order to comply with the newly enacted law, regulations may be issued in temporary form. Unlike proposed regulations, temporary regulations have the same force and effect as final regulations from the date of original issuance. The Code now requires temporary regulations to be issued simultaneously with proposed regulations in order to comply with notice and comment procedures in the Administrative Procedure Act. Temporary regulations retain their legal effect for a period of three years from the date of issuance, or until superceded by final regulations, whichever first occurs. I.R.C § 7805(e)(2).

Final and Temporary Regulations, and any amendments thereto, are officially issued in the form of Treasury Decisions (T.D.s), which are eventually codified into Title 26 of the *Code of Federal Regulations (26 C.F.R.)*. T.D.s are reprinted in the *Cumulative Bulletin*, an official publication of the IRS released at least twice a year.[6] Instead of looking in the *C.F.R.* or *Cumulative Bulletin* for the text of a regulation, practitioners usually rely on one of the looseleaf tax services, which include proposed, temporary, and final regulations in the material following the Code section to which the regulation relates.

When reading regulations, be aware that many have not been updated to reflect subsequent amendments to the underlying Code section. *See, e.g.*, 1.351-1(a) (still referring to stock *or securities* as permissible consideration when determining the 80 percent control requirement, even though securities have been eliminated from the statute). To the extent that the regulation is still consistent with the Code, it retains its value. Both looseleaf tax services make an effort to warn readers of regulations that have not been updated to reflect Code changes, but the warnings are in very general terms. Proper analysis of a regulation provision also requires the attorney to determine whether the regulation has been upheld, invalidated, or otherwise commented upon by a court. To do so, the attorney can consult one of a number of tax citator volumes: RIA, *United States Tax Reporter — Citator*; CCH, *Standard Federal Tax Reporter — Citator*; *Shepard's Federal Tax Citator*. These volumes list cases (and in the case of the RIA and CCH services, rulings and other pronouncements) that have cited the regulations, and whether the citing authority's analysis follows, invalidates, or criticizes the regulation.

If the attorney needs to obtain the text of a prior version of a regulatory provision, he can do so by using RIA's *Cumulative Changes* series, discussed above in the context of prior versions of the Code. The *Cumulative Changes* Regulation volumes include charts tracing amendments to the regulatory language, along with T.D. cites, enactment dates, and cross-references to the *Cumulative Bulletin*.

[2] IRS Pronouncements

[a] Procedural Regulations

An attorney can better represent a client if the attorney knows, before the fact, how the IRS will approach a particular issue or controversy. One source of information about the IRS's internal operations is the Statement of Procedural Rules. The regulations included in the Statement of Procedural Rules are issued by the IRS, without the need for Treasury Department approval, and are codified in Title 26 of the *Code of Federal Regulations*. IRS

---

[6] Most Treasury Decisions begin with a Preamble, which can be an important source of regulatory intent. The Preamble summarizes the regulation and often explains why the proposed version of the regulation may have been changed before being finalized.

procedural regulations carry the prefix "601." Some procedural regulations describe general IRS processes that may affect the rights and duties of taxpayers, *see, e.g.,* Proc. Reg. § 601.105 (examination of returns and claims for refund), while others instruct taxpayers as to how to gain the consent of the IRS to make changes in reporting methods, *see, e.g.,* Proc. Reg. § 601.204 (changes in accounting periods and in methods of accounting). The full text of the IRS Statement of Procedural Rules may also be located in either of the looseleaf reporter series (RIA Volume 28; CCH Volume 18).

[b]   Internal Revenue Manual

Another important source of information about how the IRS implements the law is the *Internal Revenue Manual* (I.R.M.). The I.R.M. includes detailed instructions for IRS personnel on such topics as corporate and individual audits, the Appeals process, and collection procedures, just to name a few. While the I.R.M. is written specifically for the IRS's own employees, the material is equally valuable to practitioners because it alerts the practitioner to issues of IRS concern. Once the client receives notice of an impending audit, for example, the attorney would be well advised to review the audit guidelines for the issues that are, or likely will be, under examination. These guidelines catalog audit procedures, along with exhibits and instructions to the examining agent for gathering information from the taxpayer. By reviewing these guidelines in advance, the attorney can better prepare the client for questioning and can begin compiling the documentation that the IRS will likely request. The material in the I.R.M. can also assist the attorney when advising the client during the planning phase of transaction, before it is reported on the client's return. In this instance, the attorney can use the information in the I.R.M. to assess the risk that the IRS will challenge the tax consequences of a reporting position. In light of this information, the attorney might suggest that the client alter the transaction to conform to the IRS's views expressed in the I.R.M. or, alternatively, counsel the client to compile documentary evidence supporting the client's tax treatment, which can be used should the IRS eventually question the taxpayer's reporting position.

Commerce Clearing House issues the entire I.R.M. in a two-part looseleaf series, along with a cumbersome index system. The three Audit volumes contain guidelines relating to the IRS's examination function. The six Administrative volumes include I.R.M. parts relating to Appeals, Exempt Organization, Collection, Criminal Investigation, and Penalties. The I.R.M. can also be accessed and searched using LEXIS or Westlaw.

[c]   Revenue Rulings and Revenue Procedures

Revenue Rulings (Rev. Ruls.) represent the IRS's official interpretation of the Code as it applies to a given set of facts. IRS examining agents and Appeals Officers will normally follow the IRS's own Revenue Rulings and, as a result, taxpayers may rely upon them to support a reporting position if the taxpayer's facts are substantially identical to those in the ruling. *See Estate of McLendon v. Commissioner*, 135 F.3d 1017 (5th Cir. 1998) (IRS will not be permitted to depart from a Revenue Ruling in an individual case where the law is unclear). Beyond that, the precedential weight accorded Revenue Rulings is somewhat uncertain. *See id.* at 1023-24 ("[R]evenue Rulings are odd creatures unconducive to precise categorization in the hierarchy of legal authorities. They are clearly less binding on the courts than treasury regulations or Code provisions, but probably . . . more so than the mere legal conclusions of the parties."). *See also* Section 9.02[B][2] of Chapter 9.

Revenue Procedures (Rev. Procs.) describe IRS practices in relation to specific issues and provide taxpayers with instructions for requesting information from the IRS. As noted in Chapter 9, the first Revenue Procedure of each year lists the general guidelines for requesting a letter ruling or determination letter. *See* Section 9.04 of Chapter 9. While many Revenue Procedures are merely directive, others necessarily affect the application of substantive tax law. For example, Revenue Procedure 89-30, 1989-1 C.B. 895, outlines the detailed information that must be submitted by the taxpayer in order to obtain a letter ruling confirming the status of a transaction as a corporate reorganization. The detailed representations required by the Revenue Procedure incorporate the IRS's views on substantive matters such as business purpose, continuity of interest, and continuity of business enterprise.

Both Revenue Rulings and Revenue Procedures are issued bi-weekly in the *Internal Revenue Bulletin* (I.R.B.) and are reprinted in a consolidated, a semi-annual *Cumulative Bulletin* (C.B.) volume. Revenue Rulings and Procedures are numbered based upon the year of issuance and order of issuance within that year. A typical cite, Rev. Rul. 99-19, 1999-1 C.B. 204, refers to the 19th Revenue Ruling issued in 1999, published in the first volume of the 1999 Cumulative Bulletin, on page 204. Within any given C.B. volume, Rulings and Procedures are organized by Code section, rather than numerical order. The C.B. includes a numerical finding index at the beginning of each volume, which allows the attorney to find the specific page number for a given ruling or procedure. The spine of each volume includes the inclusive numbers for Rulings and Procedures, which allows the attorney to quickly choose the correct volume from the shelf.

Before relying on a Revenue Ruling to support the client's position, the attorney must ensure that the Ruling has not been modified or otherwise declared invalid by the IRS. Changes in the Code, regulations, or a subsequent court decision may cause all or a portion of the Revenue Ruling or Procedure to be affected. Each volume of the C.B. contains a *List of Current Action* that catalogs Revenue Rulings and Procedures that have been superseded by announcements within that particular C.B. volume. Using the *List of Current Action* to update a Ruling or Procedure, therefore, would require that the attorney review the *List* in every C.B. volume subsequent to the one in which the instant ruling or procedure was initially published. This would be unnecessarily time-consuming.

If the attorney is only concerned with the current administrative status of the Revenue Ruling or Procedure, he can check that status using either of the looseleaf reporter services, both of which include tables of obsolete, revoked, and superceded Rulings and Procedures. A better method, however, would be to use the one of the tax citators noted above. Not only does the citator specify whether the Ruling or Procedure has been superseded, it also lists cases and other pronouncements that cite the Ruling or Procedure, along with an analysis of whether the citing material approves or criticizes the Ruling or Procedure being researched. The Shepard's citation service can also be accessed on-line through LEXIS.

[d]   Letter Rulings

Letter Rulings (often called "private letter rulings" or "PLRs") are written responses from the Office of Chief Counsel to a taxpayer who formally requests advice concerning the tax consequences of a specific transaction. As explained in more detail in Section 9.04 of Chapter 9, a taxpayer often requests a letter ruling to assure himself of the tax results of a transaction before consummating or reporting the transaction on his return.[7] During the research process, the attorney may discover a series of letter rulings all dealing with a single point of law. Although a letter ruling may be cited as precedent only by the taxpayer to whom the ruling was issued, I.R.C. § 6110(k)(3), a series of similar letter rulings might help the attorney predict for the client the IRS's probable approach in a given situation. Letter rulings also constitute authority for avoiding the substantial understatement penalty in Code section 6662. *See* Treas. Reg. § 301.6662-4(d)(iii).

Letter Rulings are numbered according to the year of issuance, the week of issuance, and the order within that week. PLR 200139025, for instance, was the 25th letter ruling issued during the 39th week of 2001. Code section 6110 requires that the IRS release letter rulings to the public after identifying details have been redacted. While letter rulings are not officially reported, several commercial publishers obtain copies from the IRS and print the full text of letter rulings in looseleaf and microfiche form. These include RIA, *Private Letter Rulings,* and CCH, *IRS Letter Rulings Reports*. To locate a ruling that involves the application of a specific Code section, the attorney should consult a tax citator volume. Both the *Shepard's Federal Tax Citator* and *RIA's United State Tax Reporter—Citator* include letter rulings within the scope of their coverage. Given the sheer number of these rulings, probably the best way to access and search for letter rulings is through LEXIS.

[e]   Other IRS Pronouncements

The IRS National Office releases a host of other pronouncements that address both substantive and procedural issues. Some represent formal legal opinions that could affect an entire category of taxpayers, while others provide individualized guidance.[8] None constitutes precedent for anyone other than the taxpayer in issue, if any, yet they often reveal to the attorney the IRS's position and litigation strategy with respect to important issues or transactions.

Listed below is a description of some of these pronouncements and how they may be accessed.

Technical Advice Memoranda (TAM) — TAMs are similar to letter rulings, described above, except that the request for guidance from the Office of Chief Counsel is made during the examination or appeals process, rather

---

[7] Section 9.04 also discusses the administrative process for requesting private guidance.

[8] *See generally* "Inventory of IRS Guidance Documents–A Draft," 88 Tax Notes 305 (2000).

than prior to filing the return. In most cases, it is the IRS representative who initiates the request for advice, in which case the taxpayer is given the opportunity to submit information in support of the taxpayer's interpretation of the issues involved. *See* Rev. Proc. 2002-2, 2002-1 I.R.B. 82. TAMs are numbered like letter rulings and can be accessed and researched just like letter rulings.

General Counsel Memoranda (GCM) — GCMs are a historical form of guidance. There were released by the Office of Chief Counsel and set forth the reasoning underlying a Revenue Ruling, letter ruling, or TAM. A taxpayer can rely on the analysis and conclusions in a GCM only as authority to avoid the substantial understatement penalty. Treas. Reg. § 301.6662-4(d)(3)(iii). GCMs were numbered sequentially, with no reference in the title to the year of issuance. CCH's *IRS Positions* contains full text versions of GCMs, along with a Code section finding list and a table that cross-references a ruling with its underlying GCM. They are also available on LEXIS or Westlaw.

Actions on Decisions (AODs) — AODs are issued by the Office of Chief Counsel and explain the IRS's decision to acquiesce (Acq.) or nonacquiesce (Nonacq.) in a judicial determination adverse to the Government. An acquiescence does not necessarily mean that the IRS agrees with the court's reasoning, but only that, in the future, the IRS will treat similar disputes in a manner consistent with the conclusions reached in the acquiesced case. A nonacquiescence reflects the possibility that the IRS will pursue the issue in other cases, notwithstanding the adverse determination by a court. While AODs are intended for internal IRS guidance and may not cited as precedent by the taxpayer, the AOD conveys to the public the IRS's current litigating position on many important issues. They can also be used as authority for avoiding the substantial understatement penalty in Code section 6662. *See id.* AODs are numbered based the order of issuance within a given year. AOD 2002-032 would be the 32nd AOD issued in 2002. Full text versions of AODs are available in CCH's *IRS Positions*, as well as from the on-line services.

Chief Counsel Advice (CCA) — Chief Counsel Advice encompasses a wide variety of documents that must be released by the IRS under Code section 6110(i), including Field Service Advice, Litigation Guideline Memorandums, Service Center Advice, and Litigation Bulletins, discussed below. The term also describes a separate type of written advice (CCA) from the Office of Chief Counsel containing the analysis and legal conclusions of the Chief Counsel with respect to the resolution of a specific taxpayer's case. *See, e.g.*, CCA 200043006 (interpreting the 7122 regulations relating to the economic hardship basis for an offer in compromise). Individual CCAs are numbered like letter rulings and are available through LEXIS or Westlaw.

Field Service Advice (FSA) — Field Service Advice is similar to technical advice except that the IRS representative can request the advice from the Office of Chief Counsel without the knowledge or involvement of the taxpayer. *See, e.g.*, FSA 200122002 (concluding that cost of tires having a useful life of greater than one year must be capitalized). FSAs are numbered like letter rulings and are published in CCH's *IRS Positions*. They may also be accessed through LEXIS or Westlaw.

Litigation Guideline Memorandum (LGM) — LGMs are prepared by the Office of Chief Counsel and provide information and instructions to IRS Counsel outside the National Office relating to litigation methods and procedures. LGMs often include discussions of cases and precedents the attorney should follow. *See, e.g.*, LGM 1994 TL-100 (explaining the IRS's litigation position with respect to whether the IRS may rely on an information return when determining whether the taxpayer failed to report income). The best source for locating and researching LGMs is an on-line service.

Service Center Advice (SCA) — The National Office drafts SCAs to disseminate legal advice relating to the tax administration responsibilities of the Service Centers. SCAs that are released to the public under Code section 6110(i) provide advice on a legal issues that may be material to a wide number of taxpayers and filing situations. *See, e.g.*, SCA 199929036 (advising Service Center that a submission by the taxpayer on an incorrect form, signed under penalties of perjury and containing sufficient data to permit the Service Center to calculate the taxpayer's liability, constitutes a return). SCAs are numbered like letter rulings and may be accessed through LEXIS.

Bulletins (General Litigation; Criminal Tax; Disclosure Litigation) — These bulletins are published monthly by the IRS National Office and summarize for IRS attorneys recent developments in their respective areas. The Bulletins may include matters of substantive importance or matters of more general interest, such as recent court decisions, law review articles, and advisory opinions. The IRS considers Bulletins to be informational only, and instructs its attorneys not to cite the pronouncements as authority for any proposition of law. I.R.M. 34.11.2.1. Both LEXIS and Westlaw have files for the various types of Bulletins.

[f] IRS Forms and Publications

The IRS issues a variety of tax forms to help taxpayers comply with the law. The forms and accompanying instructions explain the requirements of the Code and regulations and guide taxpayers as to how to report items of income, deduction, and the like. In addition, the IRS drafts Publications to help taxpayers meet their reporting obligations. IRS Publications explain the reporting requirements applicable to different groups of taxpayers and provide more specific guidelines concerning important areas of the law. *See, e.g.*, IRS Pub. No. 594, The IRS Collection Process; IRS Pub. No. 596, Earned Income Credit. The IRS website (www.irs.gov) includes forms and publications that can be downloaded and printed. Both CCH and RIA also reprint forms and publications as part of a bound, hard copy service.

IRS Publications provide the attorney with an easy-to-use source of information about commonly encountered questions and filing issues. The attorney must be careful, however, when relying on discussions of substantive law in IRS Publications. The Publications rarely include citations to authority, nor do they indicate whether the position asserted in the Publication has been disputed. Moreover, while the IRS anticipates that taxpayers and their representatives will make use of these Publications when preparing tax returns, the IRS is not bound by statements made in the Publications.

[C] Judicial Sources

The Tax Court, the Federal District Courts, and the Court of Federal Claims all handle the trial of tax cases, all of which may be appealed to the appropriate Federal Circuit Court of Appeals and then, upon grant of certiorari, to the United States Supreme Court. In addition, as discussed in Chapter 6, the Bankruptcy Courts may also consider tax issues in bankruptcy cases.

Opinions in federal tax cases generally interpret and apply the Internal Revenue Code, and in the process consider Treasury Regulations, Revenue Rulings, and many of the other administrative authorities discussed above. Judicial decisions in the tax area have also generated a number of common law doctrines, including the "assignment of income doctrine," *see Lucas v. Earl*, 281 U.S. 111 (1930), and the "step transaction doctrine," *see American Bantam Car Co. v. Commissioner*, 11 T.C. 397 (1948), *aff'd* 177 F.2d 513 (3rd Cir. 1949), *cert. denied*, 339 U.S. 1920 (1950), which now pervade many areas of tax law. *See generally* Martin D. Ginsburg, "Making Tax Law Through the Judicial Process," 70 A.B.A. J. 74 (1984).

Tax opinions are published in a variety of different places. As discussed below, the reporter in which a court case will be published generally depends on which court issued the opinion. However, both CCH and RIA (formerly known as Prentice-Hall) publish annual compilations of tax decisions issued by federal district courts, the Court of Federal Claims, the Courts of Appeals, and the Supreme Court, all within a single set of volumes. These compilations may also contain "unpublished" decisions of the Court of Appeals. RIA's service is titled *American Federal Tax Reports* (A.F.T.R.), while CCH's service is *U.S. Tax Cases* (U.S.T.C.). These commercial publishers created the compilations to work in conjunction with their respective looseleaf reporter services, discussed above. CCH's looseleaf service, *Standard Federal Tax Reporter*, contains citations to the U.S.T.C., using paragraph numbers, while RIA cites cases in its looseleaf service, *United States Tax Reporter*, using the A.F.T.R. Thus, *Commissioner v. Glenshaw Glass Co.* may be cited as 348 U.S. 426 (1955), 75 S. Ct. 473 (1955), 99 L. Ed. 483 (1955), 55-1 U.S.T.C. (CCH) ¶ 9308, 47 A.F.T.R. (P-H) 162, and 1955-1 C.B. 207.

[1] The Principal Judicial Fora

[a] Tax Court

As indicated in Chapter 6, the United States Tax Court hears the overwhelming majority of litigated tax cases. Tax Court opinions fall into three principal categories, regular Tax Court opinions, Memorandum Opinions, and Summary Opinions.[9] The first two types of opinions apply to those decisions made outside the small tax case division of the court. Summary Opinions are those issued in small tax cases.[10] Tax Court opinions, regardless of type, are styled "[Taxpayer name] v. Commissioner."

---

[9] Pre-1942 decisions of the Tax Court's predecessor, the Board of Tax Appeals, are contained in the *Board of Tax Appeals Reports* (B.T.A.).

[10] The Tax Court's small tax case procedure is discussed in Section 6.02[E] of Chapter 6.

For each case other than a small tax case, the Chief Judge of the Tax Court decides whether the opinion will be issued as a regular Tax Court opinion or as a Memorandum Opinion. Theodore Tannenwald, Jr., "Tax Court Trials: A View from the Bench," 59 A.B.A. J. 295, 298 (1973). Only regular Tax Court opinions have unquestioned precedential value and are officially published. These regular opinions are sometimes called "division" opinions, *see* Meade Wittaker, "Some Thoughts on Current Tax Practice," 7 Va. Tax Rev. 421 (1988), because the Tax Court is divided into divisions. *See* I.R.C. § 7460 (referring to divisions of the Tax Court). In addition, they are also sometimes referred to as "T.C." opinions because, as noted below, the official reporter that publishes these opinions is abbreviated "T.C." for "Tax Court." Most regular opinions are authored by a single judge speaking for the entire Tax Court. However, a small percentage of these opinions is reviewed by all 19 judges of the Tax Court, in a court conference. Court-reviewed opinions state that they were "reviewed by the court." Because multiple judges review those opinions, there may be concurring and dissenting opinions.

The Chief Judge of the Tax Court generally designates as Memorandum Opinions those that apply well-settled law to the particular facts of the case.

> The memorandum opinions, that is, the ones that are not printed, are supposed to be limited to those having no value as a precedent. They include any case decided solely upon the authority of another, cases involving subjects already well covered by opinions appearing in the bound volumes of the reports, failure of proof cases, and some others. . . .

J. Edgar Murdock, "What Has the Tax Court of the United States Been Doing?," 31 A.B.A. J. 297 (1945). The memorandum designation, however, is sometimes misleading. There are Memorandum Opinions that appear to contain the Tax Court's first analysis of an issue, and some that become leading cases. *See* Mark F. Sommer & Anne D. Waters, "Tax Court Memorandum Decisions—What Are They Worth?," 80 Tax Notes 384, 384 n.10 (1998) (discussing *Bardahl Mfg. Corp. v. Commissioner*, T.C. Memo. 1965-200). The Tax Court's official policy is that it does not cite its Memorandum Opinions, *see McGah v. Commissioner*, 17 T.C. 1458, 1459 (1952), *rev'd on other grounds*, 210 F.2d 769 (9th Cir. 1954), and that it does not consider them to be "controlling precedent," *see Nico v. Commissioner*, 67 T.C. 647, 654 (1977), *aff'd in part and rev'd in part*, 565 F.2d 1234 (2d Cir. 1977). Nevertheless, the Tax Court has cited Memorandum Opinions, even in its regular opinions. *See, e.g.*, *Compaq Computer Corp. v. Commissioner*, 113 T.C. 214 (1999) (*citing UPS of Am. v. Commissioner*, T.C. Memo. 1999-268, as well as other Memorandum Opinions), *rev'd*, 277 F.3d 778 (5th Cir. 2001).

Attorneys can locate regular and Memorandum Opinions in a variety of sources. Only regular opinions are officially reported by the Tax Court. The official reporter service is the *United States Tax Court Reports*, which, as noted above, is cited as "T.C." Cites are to volume number, the reporter abbreviation, page number, and year. Regular opinions also appear in one of two commercially published compilations, RIA's *Tax Court Reports* and CCH's *Tax Court Reporter*. Memorandum Opinions, although not officially published by the Tax Court, are privately published by RIA and CCH, both of which use the name

Tax Court Memorandum Decisions for their reporter volumes. Memorandum Opinions are numbered by year, in the order of issuance. For example, the first memorandum opinion of 2001 is *Lawrence v. Commissioner*, T.C. Memo. 2001-1 (decided on January 3, 2001). In addition, the Tax Court releases all of its opinions, including Summary Opinions, on the court's website, located at www.ustaxcourt.gov.

Summary Opinions are the opinions issued in small tax cases. *See* I.R.C. § 7463(a) ("A decision, together with a brief summary of the reasons therefor, in any such case shall satisfy the requirements of sections 7459(b) and 7460."). They may cite regular Tax Court opinions and Memorandum Opinions, among other authorities. *See, e.g., Ramey v. Commissioner*, T.C. Summary Opinion 2001-156. Summary Opinions have no precedential value for other cases, and decisions in Summary Opinions may not be appealed. I.R.C. § 7463(b). However, they may illustrate how the Tax Court's small case division or particular Special Trial Judges tend to decide certain issues. As stated above, Summary Opinions are available on the Tax Court's web site. They are also published on line by Tax Analysts.

Tax Court cases, other than small tax cases which are not reviewable, generally are appealable to the Court of Appeals for the circuit in which the taxpayer resided at the time he filed his Tax Court petition. I.R.C. § 7482(b)(1). Under *Golsen v. Commissioner*, 54 T.C. 742, 756 (1970), *aff'd*, 445 F.2d 985 (10th Cir.), *cert. denied*, 404 U.S. 940 (1971), if that circuit has precedent "squarely in point," that precedent applies in Tax Court. Otherwise, the Tax Court will apply its own rule. Therefore, in reading Tax Court cases to determine the court's approach to an issue, it is important to determine whether the Tax Court reached a decision constrained by binding circuit precedent. If that is the case, the court will almost certainly cite *Golsen v. Commissioner*.

[b]   United States District Courts

As discussed in Chapter 8, the federal district courts have trial-level jurisdiction over federal tax refund cases. The opinions generally are styled "[Taxpayer name] v. United States." District court opinions in tax cases have no more precedential value than they do in other areas of the law, but they may be persuasive even to other courts. Some district court opinions are not officially published, though they may be reproduced on line. Those that are published are included in the *Federal Supplement*.

[c]   Court of Federal Claims

Just like the federal district courts, the Court of Federal Claims has trial-level jurisdiction over federal tax refund suits. The opinions are also styled "[Taxpayer name] v. United States." Decisions in these cases may be appealed to the Court of Appeals for the Federal Circuit. In addition to that Circuit precedent, the Court of Federal Claims is bound by decisions of its predecessor courts, the United States Court of Claims and the United States Court of Customs and Patent Appeals. *See Maniere v. United States*, 31 Fed. Cl. 410, 415 (1994). *Cf. South Corp. v. United States*, 690 F.2d 1368, 1370 (Fed. Cir.

1982) (*en banc*). Since 1992, decisions of the Court of Federal Claims have been reported in the *United States Court of Federal Claims Reporter* (Fed. Cl.).

[d] Courts of Appeals and United States Supreme Court

There are 13 Circuit Courts of Appeals, including the Court of Appeals for the D.C. Circuit and the Court of Appeals for the Federal Circuit. *See* 28 U.S.C. § 41. Cases decided by each Court of Appeals provide precedent for cases that fall within that circuit. They also provide persuasive authority for cases in other circuits.

There are special rules for two circuits. First, courts in the Eleventh Circuit follow Fifth Circuit precedents through September 30, 1981, when the Fifth Circuit was divided into two circuits. *Bonner v. City of Prichard*, 661 F.2d 1206, 1207 (11th Cir. 1981). Second, the decisions of the Court of Appeals for the Federal Circuit's "predecessor courts, the United States Court of Claims and the United States Court of Customs and Patent Appeals, announced by those courts before the close of business September 30, 1982," are binding precedent in the Court of Appeals for the Federal Circuit. *South Corp. v. United States*, 690 F.2d 1368, 1369 (Fed. Cir. 1982) (*en banc*).

Some Circuit Court opinions are not officially published, though they may nonetheless be reproduced on line. West has begun to publish all "unpublished" opinions in a new reporter entitled the *Federal Appendix*. Different circuits have different rules about citing their unpublished opinions. Recently, the Court of Appeals for the Eighth Circuit declared unconstitutional under Article III its rule permitting unpublished opinions. *Anastasoff v. United States*, 223 F.3d 898, 905 (8th Cir. 2000).[11]

The United States Supreme Court hears few tax cases each year. A Supreme Court opinion provides the highest form of case law authority. However, it is important to check whether the Code section or regulation analyzed by the Court has been amended or otherwise modified since the Supreme Court's decision. Sometimes Congress overrules a Supreme Court decision by statute. For example, *Commissioner v. Lundy*, 516 U.S. 235 (1996), which applied a two-year statute of limitations to an overpayment claim made in Tax Court when no return had been filed prior to the mailing of a notice of deficiency, was overruled by language added to Code section 6512(b)(3). *Lundy* and section 6512 are considered in Chapter 8.

Court of Appeals' decisions appear in the *Federal Reporter*, while Supreme Court decisions are officially reported in the *United States Reports* (U.S.), and unofficially reported in the *Supreme Court Reporter* (S. Ct.) and the *United States Supreme Court Reports, Lawyers' Edition* (L. Ed.). Supreme Court opinions are also published in the *Cumulative Bulletin*.

[2] Locating Relevant Case Law — Citators

There are several ways to locate relevant tax cases. One common way is to perform a key-word search (using relevant terms, phrases, or Code section

---

[11] This case is discussed in Section 6.09 of Chapter 6.

numbers) using LEXIS or Westlaw. Another way, which does not require on-line resources, is to consult secondary sources to identify the major cases on a particular topic. Helpful secondary sources are discussed below. Once the researcher has identified a case on a topic, he can use a "citator" to find additional cases. A citator service provides a list of cases and other legal documents, followed by a list of cases and other authorities that cite the main case or other document. If the attorney has the citation of even one relevant case, he can use a citator to find cases citing that case, cases citing those cases, and so on. The attorney can use this to locate a body of relevant cases, including those most on point.

The best known citator series is *Shepard's Citations*, which is available in hard copy or on-line through LEXIS. The Westlaw alternative, Key Cite, is only available on-line. In the field of federal tax law, the principal citators are *Shepard's Federal Tax Citator,* CCH's *Standard Federal Tax Reporter — Citator*, and RIA's *United States Tax Reporter — Citator*, all of which are mentioned above.

[3] Updating Case Research

A citator service not only lists cases and other documents that cite the principal case or document, it also indicates how the later source has treated the principal one. For example, a citator will indicate if a case has been affirmed, overruled, or questioned by a subsequent case. This is extremely valuable for ascertaining the state of the law and avoiding the potentially costly mistake of relying on cases that are no longer good law. LEXIS and Westlaw each provide a service that performs only the specific function of checking the validity of a citation, without listing all authorities citing the principal one, as Shepard's does. The LEXIS service is called Auto-Cite. The Westlaw service is part of Key Cite and is called Key Cite History.

§ 16.03 Secondary Sources

Because of the breadth of federal tax law, secondary (unofficial) sources play an important role in the research process. As discussed in more detail below, the attorney may find it helpful to begin with a general discussion of the law in a secondary source, and then move to primary sources to find a specific answer. The number and variety of secondary sources dealing with federal tax law is almost overwhelming and this Section makes no attempt to discuss every one available. Listed below, however, are the most widely used and, therefore, the ones most likely to be found in a law school or law firm library. Because the organization of each varies, many of these sources have their own set of instructions, which the attorney should consult in order to make efficient and effective use of the source.

[A] Tax Reporter Services

For many tax attorneys, a tax reporter service (commonly called a looseleaf service) is the most valuable and often-used research tool. Tax services allow the attorney to quickly access up-to-date versions of the Code and regulations, read expert commentary, and research cases and rulings interpreting a Code section, all within a single source.

As noted above, the two most popular reporter services are RIA's *United States Tax Reporter* and CCH's *Standard Federal Tax Reporter*, both of which issue their services in multi-volume, looseleaf binders. The services are organized, generally, in Code section order. With respect to each Code section, the reporter service includes (1) the Code text; (2) citations to, and in some cases, excerpts from selected legislative history; (3) texts of proposed, temporary and final regulations promulgated under the Code section (if any); (4) editorial commentary and planning tips; and (5) abstracts of cases, Revenue Rulings, Revenue Procedures, and letter rulings, organized by topic sub-headings. The editorial explanations scattered through the material following the Code language are well-written and extensive, yet the attorney should avoid relying on them as a substitute for reading the primary authority. The attorney should also avoid relying upon the case and ruling abstracts for guidance and should instead read the cited authority itself. *See* I. Richard Gershon, A STUDENT'S GUIDE TO THE INTERNAL REVENUE CODE § 8.02 (4th ed. 1999).

The looseleaf volumes can be accessed in one of two ways. If the attorney already knows the particular Code section he needs to research, he can choose the appropriate volume number by looking at the bindings, which indicate each volume's scope of coverage. If the attorney is unsure which Code section controls, he should consult the comprehensive, subject matter Index Volume. The indices refer to paragraph numbers within the Code volumes. Although the Code volumes also include consecutive page numbers, references and cross references are always made to paragraph numbers, a system that may take the attorney some time getting used to. In addition to the Index Volume, the reporter services incorporate a number of other devices that allow the attorney to locate the information he needs, including tables of cases, finding lists of rulings and other pronouncements, charts, and material on IRS organization.

The looseleaf services are kept current by weekly update pages. Once new legislation is enacted or new regulations issued, for example, the publisher quickly incorporates the new material (sometimes in a matter of days) into revised looseleaf pages that are forwarded to the subscriber. The old material is removed and the new pages inserted. Each service also publishes a separate binder that contains recent developments. (RIA Volume 16; CCH Volume 19). Included are full texts of recently released Revenue Rulings and Procedures, Treasury Decisions, Letter Rulings, and Tax Court decisions, accompanied by an index and finding list.

[B] Tax Management Portfolios

When researching a Code provision with which the attorney is unfamiliar, he may discover that a broader discussion of the purpose and application of the Code language is more helpful, at least initially, than merely reading the Code in isolation. In those cases, the attorney has his choice of a number of tax compilations organized by subject matter, rather than by Code section. Probably the most popular topic-based source is the *Tax Management Portfolios* series, published by the Bureau of National Affairs (BNA). The Portfolio series is divided into five major categories — U.S. Income; Estates, Gifts and Trusts; Compensation Planning; Real Estate; and Foreign Income. Within each category are a series of separate, spiral-bound Portfolio volumes (over 300 in total).

Each portfolio volume represents an individual treatise on a specific tax topic authored by a practitioner with recognized expertise in the area. Portfolios are organized in a standard pattern. The Detailed Analysis Section in Part A provides a narrative explanation and analysis of the topic in question, supplemented by extensive footnotes to statutory, administrative, and judicial sources. Many authors focus their discussion on tax planning opportunities and approaches the attorney might take to counter an expected IRS position. Part B of each Portfolio contains Worksheets which, depending upon the issues involved, might include procedural checklists, IRS forms and documents, sample letters and documents, and related IRS information. The Portfolio on Collection Procedures, for instance, reprints the national and local collection financial standards that the IRS will use in deciding whether to accept an offer in compromise. Each Portfolio concludes with a bibliography and reference list in Part C with citations to the Code, regulations, legislative history, and administrative sources, as well as cites to tax articles. A separate Index binder allows the attorney to access the Portfolios by topic, key word, or Code section. The Portfolios are updated on a regular basis with New Developments pages located at the beginning of each volume.

[C] Tax Treatises

A Tax Management Portfolio's depth of coverage is usually exceeded only by a tax treatise. One or more tax treatises exists for virtually every area of tax specialization. They, too, provide the attorney with in-depth, narrative discussion of specialized and general areas of the law. Most also provide extensive citations and references to primary source materials. The following is a list of frequently cited treatises, all of which are kept current with supplements.

- Boris I. Bittker & James S. Eustice, FEDERAL INCOME TAXATION OF CORPORATIONS AND SHAREHOLDERS (7th ed. 2001) (single volume treatise on corporate tax issues).

- Boris I. Bittker & Lawrence Lokken, FEDERAL TAXATION OF INCOME, ESTATES, AND GIFTS (3rd ed. 1999) (multi-volume treatise covering a wide range of tax areas, including individual, corporate, and partnership tax, as well as international tax and estate planning).

- Jack Crestol et al., THE CONSOLIDATED TAX RETURN: PRINCIPLES, PRACTICE, PLANNING (5th ed. 1993) (consolidated returns).

- Joel D. Kuntz & Robert J. Peroni, U.S. INTERNATIONAL TAXATION (1996) (three-volume treatise on international tax).

- William S. McKee et al., FEDERAL TAXATION OF PARTNERSHIPS AND PARTNERS (3rd ed. 1997) (two-volume treatise on partnership tax).

- Michael I. Saltzman, IRS PRACTICE AND PROCEDURE (2nd ed. 1991) (tax procedure).

- Deborah H. Schenk, FEDERAL TAXATION OF S CORPORATIONS (1985) (Subchapter S corporations).

[D] Tax—Related Periodicals

Journal articles devoted to tax issues range in scope from surveys of recent developments to analyses of sophisticated transactions. The attorney researching a given issue is likely to find one or more articles that bear upon the client's case

The following journals publish mostly practitioner-oriented articles: *Tax Lawyer; The Tax Adviser; Taxes — The Tax Magazine; Journal of Taxation; Journal of Corporate Taxation; Taxation for Lawyers;* and *Journal of Real Estate Taxation*. Other tax journals concentrate on tax policy-oriented articles. These include New York University's *Tax Law Review; Virginia Tax Review;* and *Florida Tax Review*. In addition, *Tax Notes*, mentioned below in connection with daily tax services, publishes articles on tax law and policy authored by tax professors as well as practitioners, as do related titles such as *State Tax Notes* and *Tax Notes International*.

Tax Institutes associated with various law schools, including New York University, the University of Southern California, Tulane University, and the University of Miami, conduct annual seminars addressing current tax topics. The proceedings of these tax institutes are published in separate volumes. *See, e.g., Annual New York University Institute on Federal Taxation*.

The attorney can locate relevant tax articles in a number of ways. Tax articles are commonly referenced in the footnotes of tax treatises and in the bibliography sections of Tax Management Portfolios. The attorney can also research articles addressing a particular topic by using one of the tax article indices. The *Index to Federal Tax Articles*, published by Warren Gorham & Lamont, allows the attorney to search for tax articles by subject matter or author. Cited articles are followed by a short description of the article's subject matter. A similar service published by CCH, *Federal Tax Articles*, also includes summaries of tax articles, but is organized in Code section order rather than by topic. Because the number of journals cited and the years of coverage differ between the two sources, to be thorough, the attorney may wish to consult both sources. Many tax publications, including all of those noted above, except *Taxes*, may also be found on-line, although historical coverage is limited.

[E] Daily/Weekly Tax Reports

The prior discussion has stressed the attorney's need to stay up-to-date on developments in the law. Given the speed with which changes take place in the tax area and the number of legal sources that must be monitored, this is not an easy task. In the area of tax planning in particular, the attorney not only must be aware of recent changes, he must also factor into his advice pending developments in the law that might impact the client's transaction in the future. Responding to this need to remain current, a number of publishers have developed daily and weekly tax services that report developments in statutory, administrative, and judicial authority.

Many tax attorneys begin their mornings by scanning the contents of a daily reporter service, typically Tax Analysts's *Tax Notes Today* series or BNA's *Daily Tax Report*. Both sources report on legislative and judicial developments in the law and reprint full text versions of selected cases, rulings, committee reports, proposed regulations and other matters. *Tax Notes*, a weekly magazine published by Tax Analysts, includes both that information and informative articles on substantive and procedural tax law. Many of these articles also appear in *Tax Notes Today*. *Tax Notes* and the *Daily Tax Report* are available in either print or on-line form, while *Tax Notes Today* is an on-line only publication.

§ 16.04   Developing a Research Methodology

Whether the attorney is rendering advice on the tax consequences of a proposed transaction, preparing a return, or preparing a case for trial, the first step in any research project is to obtain all the facts that might bear upon the ultimate solution to a tax problem. Section 15.02 of Chapter 15 describes the process by which the attorney gathers facts from the client during an initial interview. Once the attorney begins searching for authority, it may become clear that the attorney failed to obtain facts that are critical to the final outcome. In such cases, the attorney may have to conduct follow-up interviews with the client in order to collect additional facts or re-check facts in light of the substantive law that the attorney uncovered during the research process.

Once the attorney establishes the initial facts, he can begin researching the law that applies to those facts. Before delving into a particular source of law, however, he should have in mind a research strategy or methodology.[12] The attorney who does not consider in advance how he should approach a research question is likely to waste time and resources reviewing the same sources over again or, more seriously, risk reaching an incorrect conclusion because he failed to locate sources that bear directly upon his client's case. There are, of course, many different methods for conducting tax research. With practice and experience, the attorney will naturally begin to develop a method that works for him. For those who have not yet developed their own method, we offer the following two general strategies for approaching a tax question.

As noted initially in this Chapter, the answer to almost any tax question will derive from an interpretation of the Code. If the attorney is aware, or

---

[12] The research methodology the attorney chooses to employ may vary depending upon the goal of the project. An attorney may go about researching a question of tax policy differently than he would if he were researching the tax consequences of a specific transaction. The method may also vary depending upon whether the client expects only a general opinion relating to an area of the law, as opposed to a specific opinion relating to the client's own tax return. The discussion of the research process in this Section focuses on answering interpretive questions; that is, how the Code applies to a specific fact situation. The method used to answer interpretive questions is generally the same whether the question arises before the taxpayer reports the item on the return or after the IRS questions the return position during an audit.

believes he is aware, of the principal Code sections involved, then the Code language is the obvious place to start. The looseleaf reporter services provide the best source for Code language as they are updated more quickly than any other print source. Congress drafts most Code sections so that they have broad applicability, so it is not surprising that the client's facts may not fit neatly within the statutory language. After reading the statutory language, however, the attorney should have some understanding of the essential rules or elements applicable to the client's case. If the attorney determines that the answer to the client's tax question depends on the meaning of a particular word in the statute, he should review the legislative history following the Code language in the reporter service. Committee Reports and other sources can sometimes reveal why Congress chose to employ a specific term.

If the legislative history does not provide any helpful insight, the attorney should review the regulations accompanying the Code section. In many cases, the editors will have included editorial explanations of the regulatory language, which can help the attorney identify relevant material. Even after reviewing the regulations, a precise answer still may not have revealed itself. At this point, the attorney should consult the case and ruling annotations in the looseleaf service. The annotations are organized by topic and the editors have included, in most cases, short descriptions of the opinion's holding. Once a case or ruling that seems to fit the client's fact pattern is identified, the attorney should read the item in its entirety. As discussed above, the attorney can then use a citator service to locate additional cases and rulings.

Throughout this process, the attorney should keep a written record of what he has consulted so that he does not repeat himself should he return to the same research project at a later time. The attorney must also keep in mind the precedential weight of the source he is consulting and ensure that the source's effective date matches with his client's transaction. If the attorney discovers a case, ruling, or other pronouncement that he believes controls his client's case, he must update the item using the techniques described above to ensure that the item has not been overruled or otherwise declared invalid.

A second research approach applies when the attorney is unfamiliar with the area of tax law involved and therefore does not know the controlling Code section. One option would be to refer to the subject matter index of the reporter service, which will cross-reference paragraph cites within the reporter volumes. Once the relevant Code provision is found, the attorney can approach the research task as described above. In other cases, the attorney may find it helpful to familiarize himself with the broader subject matter area involved. Tax treatises and Tax Management Portfolios are each excellent sources for gaining an understanding of the underlying legal issues. They can also point the attorney towards Code references that apply to his case. Equally as important, these secondary sources highlight related issues that the attorney may not have considered and that may not have revealed themselves if the attorney had focused only on a single Code section. Because of the extensive use of detailed footnotes in these sources, in many cases the treatise or Portfolio will provide an quick answer to the client's specific question. If not, the attorney will at least have an idea of relevant Code sections, which he can access using the looseleaf reporter services.

Given the number of primary sources that may bear, directly or indirectly, on the client's case and the number of secondary sources that might provide helpful commentary, the attorney could spend several days compiling and reading all the relevant material. External time limitations and mounting fees that the client might not be willing to shoulder often require the attorney to formulate an answer or opinion based upon a limited amount of research. For the inexperienced attorney, knowing when he has adequately exhausted the available research sources can be difficult. Consider the following advice:

> Perhaps the hardest step in the research process is knowing when to stop searching. Although this can be relatively easy in some situations (*e.g.*, finding a regulation and accompanying example on point), too often it is not. Obviously, it is easier to know when to stop researching a straightforward and routine problem, as opposed to a complex and unusual one.

> One important rule is that the laws of probability apply to searches (*i.e.*, it is virtually impossible to find every *potentially* relevant document). . . . This usually occurs because one or more of the following:

> The difficulty of the research question.

> The depth and quality of the available electronic and hard-copy tax libraries.

> The adequacy of time and budget to devote to the research problem.

> The researcher's skill and experience.

> A second important rule is that there is always an answer, with varying degrees of certainty in its relevance to the research question. Tax practitioners reason by analogy, relying on precedent and making conclusions that are seldom absolutely certain. What does the researcher do when the question seems not to have been completely answered? At some point, a judgment has to be made. Sometimes the answer is arrived at simply by using the *best* reasoning and related available authority to generate an *acceptable* conclusion. Not every answer will be based on tax authority on point with the client's facts and research issue.

> If it is rare to find all documents relevant to the research question, how does one determine when the search is sufficient and should be concluded? Obviously, if there is certainty that the correct answer has been discovered, the research should stop. Certainty, however, is only relative, and what may appear complete to one researcher could seem incomplete to another. Therefore, in addition to the criteria discussed above, the following signs indicate that the research is complete (or at least adequate).

> What level of relevant tax authority was obtained during the research? Do the Code and underlying regulations provide the answer or has only a district court case in a circuit other than the client's been found?

Has the "loop been closed?" Do different tax services, treatises and/or primary authority keep pointing to the same tax authority in support of an answer?

* * *

Have all search possibilities been exhausted, or are there other factors that could prompt a different tactic?

While this list is not exhaustive, it does suggest the types of considerations involved in deciding the circumstances under which to stop searching.

Robert L. Black, "Tips, Tricks and Traps of CD-ROM Tax Research (Part II)," 27 Tax Adviser 23, 26 (1996).

§ 16.05 Computer-Assisted Research

The discussion so far has focused largely on print sources of tax law commonly found in public and private library collections. Most of the primary and secondary sources noted above are now available on-line through LEXIS or Westlaw, although the dates of coverage are limited. These sources can be researched using the key word search engines associated with each service. Whether the attorney chooses to approach initially the research project using on-line sources will depend upon a number of factors, not the least of which is the cost associated with on-line research.

Given the breadth of tax sources available on-line, one can easily become overwhelmed searching for background research. In many cases it is more cost-effective to use print sources first, and access on-line sources to update one's research or to retrieve specific items. It is particularly important when doing on-line research to organize the process. When searching for a specific answer, the tendency among many inexperienced researchers is to create a broad search query, combining many different files, with no consideration given to the relative precedential authority of each source. Even when using an on-line source, therefore, the attorney should formulate a research methodology and avoid the temptation to read only cases and rulings, rather than the Code and regulations.

The attorney can also use the Internet to research and access tax sources. In recent years, the availability of tax resources on the Internet has greatly expanded. The following websites provide access to tax-related materials:

- *CCH Access*: tax.cch.com (fee-based on-line tax library consisting of CCH Standard Federal Tax Reporter, along with free-text search capabilities).

- *IRS Website*: www.irs.gov (information concerning organization and operations of the IRS, as well as IRS Forms and Publications that can be downloaded and printed).

- *Tax Analysts* On-line: www.tax.org (news and information).

- *Tax Resources*: www.taxresources.com (index of tax forms, cases and professional articles).

Full text versions of the Code and Regulations, Revenue Rulings and Procedures, Letter Rulings, IRS publications, and other primary authorities are also available from tax service providers in a CD-ROM format. In addition, many of the secondary sources mentioned above, including the RIA and CCH looseleaf services, have been issued in CD-ROM form. Those just beginning tax research should first use the hard copy versions to familiarize themselves with what each contains and how the services are organized. Most CD-ROM products have "key word" search features, as well as "hyperlinks" that permit the researcher to instantly access the full text of Code sections, regulations, rulings, and cases by clicking on highlighted text. Some of the CD-ROM products, by publisher, are:

- CCH Incorporated, *Standard Federal Tax Reporter on CD-ROM* (full text)

- Matthew Bender & Co., *Tax and Estate Planning Law Library* (compilation of tax-related treatises, handbooks, and forms)

- RIA, *Tax Advisors Planning Systems (TAPS)* (tax planning ideas for closely-held businesses)

- Tax Analysts, *OneDisc* (full text of primary sources with commentary and analysis)

- Tax Management Inc., *Tax Management Tax Practice Series* (full text of Tax Practice Series, federal code and regulations, state codes and regulations, and IRS publications).

PROBLEMS

1. Elinor graduated from law school two years ago and immediately began working for Stickley & Brandt as an associate attorney in their general business division. Her duties at the firm included corporate transaction work as well as the occasional project dealing with the tax consequences of mergers and acquisitions. Elinor took a 6-month leave of absence from the firm in order to have her first child. Instead of returning to the law firm, she decided to enroll in New York University's Master's Degree in Taxation (LL.M.) program on a full-time basis. She completed the program in 9 months and immediately afterwards began working for a tax boutique firm in New York. Elinor incurred $35,000 in LL.M. tuition expenses and an additional $26,000 in living expenses (meals and lodging) during the 9-month term of the program. Locate relevant case law dealing with the issue of whether the educational expenses Elinor incurred to obtain the LL.M. are deductible under Code section 162.

   A. Begin your research using the CCH *Standard Federal Tax Reporter* looseleaf service. Keep a log of the sources you consulted.

   B. Begin your research using the *Tax Management Portfolios*. Which portfolios did you consult?

C.   Begin your research using one of the on-line services. Keep a log of the databases you consulted.

2.   Jerry Porter, a new client, contacts you regarding an audit of his calendar year 1992 return, which, because of numerous extensions of the statute of limitations, has been on-going since 1994. One of the issues raised in the audit concerns whether property sold by Jerry during the 1992 taxable year gave rise to capital gain or ordinary income. What tax rate(s) applied to capital gain income generated by an individual taxpayer as a result of sales of capital assets made during calendar year 1992? How did you ascertain that?

3.   Your first assignment as a new associate is to write a memorandum on Subpart F income. You did not take an international tax course in law school and, therefore, do not know the applicable Code section involved. How might you begin researching this issue?

4.   While preparing for a Collection Due Process (CDP) Hearing on behalf of a client, you come across a Field Service Advice memorandum (FSA) that contains an interpretation of Temporary Treasury Regulation 301.7122-1T(b)(4), which permits the IRS to compromise a tax liability if to do so would promote effective tax administration. The Office of Chief Counsel's interpretation in the FSA is favorable to your client's case. How might you use the FSA when negotiating with the Appeals Officer during the CDP Hearing?

5.   Jamie White, the teacher's aide discussed in problem 4 of Chapter 15, recently received a letter from the IRS denying her $2,328 earned income credit for her two children, Mary, age 5, and Donald, age 7. Apparently, her ex-husband, Daniel White, who does not live with them, also claimed the credit. Jamie receives $300 per month in child support from her ex-husband, a carpenter who earns approximately $15,000 to $18,000 per year. Jamie earns $12,000 per year from the school district, and has no other source of income. She told you in the initial interview that she spends most of that money on her children. Research the earned income credit to determine whether Jamie may be entitled to it. What facts would Jamie need to prove, and how could she prove them?

6.   * Acme, Inc. ("Acme"), a calendar-year, subchapter C corporation, engages in a variety of businesses, both domestically and overseas. As more fully described below, the IRS has filed a summons enforcement action in a local District Court (in the District in which Acme's document storage facility is located). Acme's outside counsel, Grungee & Bungee, a large Seattle—based firm, has appointed you as local counsel. The partner in charge of the case for Grungee & Bungee is Kirk Cobain, Esq.

---

* This problem is copyrighted by Bryan Camp and is used, as adapted, with permission.

One of Acme's wholly owned subsidiaries is the Giant Widget Investment Zone, Inc. ("GWIZ"), a Delaware company. Starting in 1998, GWIZ formed a joint venture with a British corporation, Widget Enterprise Technology, PLC ("WET"). The idea of the joint venture was first proposed in 1997 by Diana Rossi, the President and CEO of Acme. Rossi's idea was to form a joint venture to compete with the huge Japanese widget conglomerate, Hiabachi. Rossi approached WET and convinced its CEO to participate. In deciding what structure to use for the joint venture, Rossi asked her Vice President for Taxes, I.M. Heigh, to come up with the structure that would minimize the overall United States and British tax burden on the two companies. Heigh is a Certified Public Accountant and an attorney licensed to practice in California; she works out of Acme's Seattle Headquarters. Heigh wrote her counterpart at WET, U.R. Kute, Vice President of Inland Revenue, and proposed three possible structures: a joint venture, a Swiss partnership, and an Irish corporation. Kute is an attorney and a member in good standing of the British bar.

On September 2, 1997, Kute responded to Heigh's request in a letter ("Kute letter") entitled "Possible Structures for Widget Collaboration — U.S., U.K. Tax Treatment." It explained how each of the proposed structures would be treated under British law and analyzed the interplay of British and American tax law. The letter pointed out several possible problems with the joint venture model that, if either the British Inland Revenue or the IRS were to take certain positions about certain transactions, would make the joint venture model considerably less attractive. The letter also discussed certain proposed provisions that the IRS could use to greatly increase both Acme and WET's U.S. tax liabilities. Heigh used the Kute letter to help prepare a recommendation to Rossi.

During an audit of Acme's 1994-1997 tax years, before the joint venture started, Acme gave the IRS an index of files relating to various collaboration agreements it had entered into with other corporations, both domestic and foreign. On November 10, 1999, using that index, the IRS requested files that appeared relevant to the open examination. Acme and GWIZ attorneys and their paralegals then went through the files and, after removing documents they thought were protected by a privilege, provided the IRS with a list of withheld documents and allowed the IRS examination team access to the remainder. The examiners then reviewed the files, took notes, and selected certain documents to be copied. Under this process, files became available to the IRS piecemeal.

One file that the IRS asked to see was listed in the index as "File #70." The description of that file included a reference to a "Acme Tax Dept. memo — structures of Int'l collaborations."

As with other files, the IRS was allowed to review the documents in File #70 after a GWIZ paralegal had pre-reviewed the file for privileged documents. On January 9, 2000, GWIZ attorney Brittney Spares, Esq., signed a memorandum (the "Spares memo"), prepared by the paralegal, that notified Revenue Agent Ricardo Nunzio that files #69–89 were ready for examination but that 21 documents from those files were being withheld. Nunzio then reviewed the files.

One of the documents Nunzio selected for copying was a November 15, 1997 memo to I.M. Heigh prepared by M.T. Cann (the "Cann memo"), an accountant in the Acme Tax Department who worked under Heigh. The Cann memo provided an overview and history of various international agreements that Acme had been party to over the years. A number of documents were attached to the Cann memo, including a copy of the Kute letter. When Nunzio reviewed the Cann memo, he found the Kute letter. Based on that letter, he recommended that the IRS open audits for Acme and WET for 1998-2000.

Nunzio also asked about the disposition of several other files (#41-43) that he had wanted to review but had not been provided. He was told that those files had been moved from the GWIZ offices to the Acme's Tax Department for review. Acme's Tax Department decided to withhold documents in those files and listed 40 documents withheld in a February 15, 2000, memorandum from Paul Bouquet to Revenue Agent Nunzio (the "Bouquet memo"). Document #25 was described as "Letter dated September 2, 1997 from U.R. Kute to I.M. Heigh Re: Widget Collaboration — U.S. and U.K. Income Taxes."

On February 29, 2000, Nunzio told Heigh's secretary that he already had document #25. On March 13, 2000, Nunzio received a letter from Kirk Cobain, dated March 10, 2000, asserting that the Kute letter was not supposed to have been attached to the Cann memo and demanding the return of the Kute letter. Revenue Agent Nunzio made no response to the letter. Instead, Nunzio recommended to the Office of Chief Counsel that the IRS seek to enforce the summons as to the withheld documents. Accordingly, the IRS has filed a petition in District Court for enforcement of the summons requesting the documents withheld by Acme's Tax Department. Nunzio has filed a standard declaration that meets the requirements set forth in *United States v. Powell*, 379 U.S. 48 (1964).

A.   Is the Kute letter protected by the attorney-client privilege? Prepare a 5-7 page single-spaced research memo addressed to Kirk Cobain of the Grungee & Bungee law firm that gives your best legal analysis and advice. Confine your recitation of the facts to no more than one page, and focus your analysis on the law applicable in your Circuit. Do not consider the issue of whether the privilege, if applicable, has been waived.

B. Assuming that the Kute letter is protected by the attorney-client privilege, can Acme can get the letter back, or has the privilege been waived? Prepare a 5-7 page single-spaced research memo, addressed to Kirk Cobain of the Grungee & Bungee law firm, giving your best legal analysis and advice. Confine your recitation of the facts to no more than one page, and focus your analysis on the law applicable in your Circuit.

C. Assume that (1) Acme is legally entitled to return of the Kute letter because the letter was subject to the attorney-client privilege and (2) the privilege has not been waived by the inadvertent disclosure of the letter to the IRS. What procedure should Acme follow to obtain an order requiring the government to return the letter? What issues of law does the procedure raise? Confine your recitation of the facts to no more than one page, and focus your analysis on the law applicable in your Circuit.

TABLE OF CASES

[References are to page numbers; principal cases are in capital letters.]

[References are to page numbers; principal cases are in capital letters.]

[References are to page numbers; principal cases are in capital letters.]

[References are to page numbers; principal cases are in capital letters.]

[References are to page numbers; principal cases are in capital letters.]

[References are to page numbers; principal cases are in capital letters.]

H

[References are to page numbers; principal cases are in capital letters.]

[References are to page numbers; principal cases are in capital letters.]

[References are to page numbers; principal cases are in capital letters.]

[References are to page numbers; principal cases are in capital letters.]

[References are to page numbers; principal cases are in capital letters.]

[References are to page numbers; principal cases are in capital letters.]

[References are to page numbers; principal cases are in capital letters.]

[References are to page numbers; principal cases are in capital letters.]

TABLE OF STATUTES

[References are to page numbers]

[References are to page numbers]

Internal Revenue Code—Cont.

Internal Revenue Code—Cont.

[References are to page numbers]

Internal Revenue Code—Cont.

Internal Revenue Code—Cont.

[References are to page numbers]

Internal Revenue Code—Cont.

[References are to page numbers]

[References are to page numbers]

[References are to page numbers]

[References are to page numbers]

INDEX

[References are to pages.]

A

ACCESS TO IRS INFORMATION
Generally . . . 127
Confidentiality of taxpayer information, *versus* . . . 127
Freedom of information act (See FREEDOM OF INFORMATION ACT)
Privacy act of 1974 . . . 147
Written determinations under section 6110 . . . 148

ACCOUNTANTS
Privilege, tax advice . . . 49
Tax lawyers and, tension between . . . 45

AIDING AND ABETTING
Tax crimes . . . 667

ALTERNATIVE DISPUTE RESOLUTION
Settlement at IRS appeals division . . . 204

APPEALS
Administrative appeal, negotiation during . . . 793
Alternative dispute resolution; settlement at IRS appeals division . . . 204
IRS appeals division, settlement at (See SETTLEMENTS, subhead: Settlement at IRS appeals division)
Settlement with appeals . . . 200

ASSESSMENT OF TAX
Restrictions on (See RESTRICTIONS ON ASSESSMENT OF TAX)

ATTORNEYS
Accountants, tension between tax lawyers and . . . 45
Clients, representing (See REPRESENTING CLIENTS IN TAX CASES)
Declining representation . . . 779
Interviewing clients (See REPRESENTING CLIENTS IN TAX CASES)
Privilege, tax advice . . . 49

AUDITS
Generally . . . 93
Negotiation during . . . 792
Partnership audit procedures under tefra . . . 96
Strategy . . . 97

B

BANKRUPTCY
Avoiding tax collection . . . 635
Bankruptcy court's jurisdiction over federal tax claims . . . 319

BURDEN OF PROOF
Civil tax penalties . . . 521
Notice of deficiency (See NOTICE OF DEFICIENCY)
Tax litigation . . . 300

C

CHOICE OF FORUM
Tax litigation . . . 295

CIVIL TAX PENALTIES
Generally . . . 483
Abatement of penalties . . . 520
Assessment of penalties . . . 520
Burden of proof . . . 521
Defenses
    Delinquency penalty — code section 6651 . . . 487
    Substantial understatement of tax . . . 497
Specific civil penalties and defenses to those penalties
    Generally . . . 485
    Accuracy-related penalties — code section 6662
        Generally . . . 492
        Defenses; substantial understatement of tax . . . 497
        Disclosure . . . 501
        Negligence or disregard of rules or regulations . . . 493
        Substantial authority . . . 497
        Substantial understatement of tax and its defenses . . . 497
        Valuation misstatements . . . 504
    Civil fraud penalty — code section 6663 . . . 513
    Defenses
        Delinquency penalty — code section 6651 . . . 487
        Substantial understatement of tax . . . 497
    Delinquency penalty — code section 6651
        Failure to file penalty . . . 485
        Failure to pay penalty . . . 485
    Estimated tax penalty — code section 6654 . . . 492
    Information reporting penalties — code sections 6721 and 6722 . . . 517
    Preparer penalties — code section 6694 . . . 518
    Reasonable cause exception . . . 508
Suspension of penalties . . . 520

I–1

[References are to pages.]

[References are to pages.]

[References are to pages.]

RELIANCE ON TREASURY REGULATIONS AND IRS POSITIONS—Cont.
Obtaining private guidance for a taxpayer—Cont.

Determination letter, request for 466

Letter ruling, request for . . . 466

Pre-filing agreements . . . 478

Reporting requirements . . . 463

Requesting a conference with IRS . . . 475

Sample letter ruling request . . . 472

Private and internal IRS authorities

Generally . . . 455

"Duty of consistency" . . . 457

Reliance on . . . 455

Published authority, reliance on

Generally . . . 432

IRS authorities

Generally . . . 444

Courts' deference to revenue rulings . . . 445

Procedural regulations . . . 445

Revenue procedures . . . 455

Revenue ruling procedures . . 445

Treasury regulations

Generally . . . 432

Courts' deference to treasury regulations . . . 433

Enacting treasury regulations, procedures for . . . 432

REPRESENTING CLIENTS IN TAX CASES
Generally . . . 767

Bad news, delivering . . . 783

Counseling

Generally . . . 780

Delivering bad news . . . 783

Declining representation . . . 779

Interviewing clients

Generally . . . 767

Declining representation . . . 779

Following up: representation letters and retainer agreements . . . 778

Goals and structure of client interview . . . 767

Language barriers . . . 776

Special challenges

Generally . . . 775

Language barriers . . . 776

Language barriers . . . 776

Negotiation (See NEGOTIATION)

RESEARCH (See TAX RESEARCH)

RESTRICTIONS ON ASSESSMENT OF TAX
Generally . . . 227

Jeopardy and termination assessments . . . 229

RESTRICTIONS ON ASSESSMENT OF TAX—Cont.
Statutes of limitations on assessment of tax

Generally . . . 230

Exceptions to the statutes of limitations

Generally . . . 270

Equitable recoupment . . . 274

Statutory mitigation provisions . . 270

Exceptions to the three-year statutory period

Generally . . . 233

False or fraudulent return . . 239

Request for prompt assessment . . . 233

Substantial omission of items . . . 233

Extensions of time to assess tax . . 248

Tolling of statute of limitations on assessment . . . 248

Summary assessments . . . 228

Types of assessments

Generally . . . 227

General restrictions on deficiency assessments . . . 228

Jeopardy and termination assessments . . . 229

Summary assessments . . . 228

RETURNS (See TAX RETURNS AND EXAMINATION PROCESS)

S

SEARCH WARRANTS
IRS investigatory tools . . . 714

"SECRET LAW"
Access to IRS's . . . 143

SELF-ASSESSMENT SYSTEM
Generally . . . 1

SETTLEMENTS
Generally . . . 181

Alternative dispute resolution . . . 204

Closing agreements . . . 217

Court cases . . . 219

IRS appeals division, settlement at

Generally . . . 189

Alternative dispute resolution . . . 204

Background on IRS appeals division . . . 189

Disposing of a case at appeals . . . 205

Docketed *versus* nondocketed appeals . . . 196

Negotiating a settlement with appeals . . . 200

Protest letter . . . 191

[References are to pages.]

[References are to pages.]

TAX CRIMES—Cont.

Federal sentencing guidelines in tax cases—Cont.

    Base offense levels applicable in tax cases . . . 691

    Upward and downward departures

        Generally . . . 695

        Departures not reflected in the sentencing guidelines . . . 697

        Departures reflected in the sentencing guidelines . . . 695

Interference with administration of internal revenue laws . . . 661

Procedure (See CRIMINAL TAX PROCEDURE)

Statutes of limitations . . . 682

Tax evasion . . . 652

Tax professionals, offenses committed by . . . 679

TAX EVASION

Generally . . . 652

TAX LITIGATION

Generally . . . 279

Awards of administrative and litigation costs and fees to taxpayers . . . 308

Bankruptcy court jurisdiction over federal tax claims . . . 319

Burden of proof in tax cases . . . 300

Choice of forum . . . 295

Negotiation during . . . 794

Refund litigation

    Generally . . . 293

    Court of Federal Claims . . . 295

    Sample complaint . . . 293

    United States District Courts . . . 293

Sanctions . . . 310

United States Tax Court

    Generally . . . 280

    Discovery procedures . . . 285

    Equity in tax court . . . 290

    Pleading requirements . . . 281

    Precedent applicable to tax court cases . . . 287

    Sample tax court petition . . . 282

    Small tax case procedure . . . 290

Unpublished opinions . . . 320

TAX PROFESSIONALS

Accountants

    Privilege, tax advice . . . 49

    Tax lawyers and, tension between . . . 45

Attorneys (See ATTORNEYS)

Offenses committed by . . . 679

Tension between tax lawyers and accountants . . . 45

TAX RESEARCH

Generally . . . 801

Computer-assisted research . . . 824

Developing a research methodology . . . 821

IRS pronouncements

    Generally . . . 807

    Internal revenue manual . . . 808

    IRS forms and publications . . . 812

    Other IRS pronouncements . . . 810

    Procedural regulations . . . 807

    Revenue rulings and revenue procedures . . . 808

Judicial sources

    Generally . . . 813

    Court of Federal Claims . . . 815

    Courts of Appeals and United States Supreme Court . . . 816

    Locating relevant case law — citators . . . 816

    Principal judicial fora . . . 813

    Tax court . . . 813

    United States District Courts . . . 815

    Updating case research . . . 817

Legislative sources

    Generally . . . 801

    Internal revenue code . . . 801

    Joint committee explanation ("bluebook") . . . 805

    Legislative history . . . 803

Methodology, developing . . . 821

Primary sources

    Generally . . . 801

    Administrative sources

        Generally . . . 806

        IRS pronouncements (See subhead: IRS pronouncements)

    IRS pronouncements (See subhead: IRS pronouncements)

    Judicial sources (See subhead: Judicial sources)

    Legislative sources (See subhead: Legislative sources)

    Treasury regulations . . . 806

Secondary sources

    Generally . . . 817

    Daily/weekly tax reports . . . 820

    Tax management portfolios . . . 818

    Tax-related periodicals . . . 820

    Tax reporter services . . . 817

    Tax treatises . . . 819

TAX RETURNS AND EXAMINATION PROCESS

Generally . . . 59

Examinations

    Generally . . . 73

    Audits

        Generally . . . 93

[References are to pages.]